W9-DEE-666

Document 512 of U.S. Senate
23 rd. Congress, 1st Session

# THE INDIAN
# REMOVALS

## VOL. IV

Foreword by Brantley Blue

Introduction by John M. Carroll

Illustrations by Paul Rossi

## AMS PRESS
NEW YORK, 1974

Library of Congress Cataloging in Publication Data

United States. Subsistence Dept.
    The Indian removals.

    "Furnished in answer to a resolution of the Senate,
of 27th December, 1833, by the Commissary General of
Subsistence [G. Gibson]"
    Reprint of the 1834-35 ed. printed by D. Green,
Washington, as Document 512 of the U. S. Senate, 23d
Congress, 1st session, under title: Correspondence on
the subject of the emigration of Indians, between the
30th November, 1831, and 27th December, 1833.
    1. Indians of North America—Government relations—
1789-1869. I. Gibson, George, 1783-1861. II. United
States. 23d Congress, 1st session. Senate. III. Title.
IV. Series: United States. 23d Congress, 1st session.
Senate. Document 512.
E93.U979 1974    970.5    73-9797
ISBN 0-404-11210-2

Reprinted from the edition of 1835, Washington D.C.
First AMS edition published, 1974
Manufactured in the United States of America

International Standard Book Number:
Complete Set: 0-404-11210-2
Volume IV:  0-404-11214-5

AMS PRESS, INC.
New York, N.Y.  10003

# INDIAN REMOVALS

**CHICKASAW 1840**

© PAUL ROSSI 73

[ DOCUMENT 512. ]

# CORRESPONDENCE

ON THE SUBJECT OF THE

# EMIGRATION OF INDIANS,

BETWEEN

THE 30th NOVEMBER, 1831, AND 27th DECEMBER, 1833,

WITH ABSTRACTS OF EXPENDITURES BY DISBURSING AGENTS,

IN THE

Removal and Subsistence of Indians, &c. &c.

FURNISHED

IN ANSWER TO A RESOLUTION OF THE SENATE, OF 27th DECEMBER, 1833,

BY THE

COMMISSARY GENERAL OF SUBSISTENCE.

VOL. IV.

WASHINGTON:
PRINTED BY DUFF GREEN.
1835.

# LETTERS FROM AGENTS AND OTHERS.

---

ROCK RIVER, *January* 1, 1833.

MOST RESPECTED SIR: At the earnest request of the chiefs of the Winnebago Indians residing on this river, and lately assembled in council at my house, I venture to address you in their behalf, and attempt to make known to you their wishes.

The subject under consideration in council was the necessity of their immediate removal from this country. They profess to have acceded to and signed the late treaty at Rock Island under the influence of fear, but they do not the less regard it as binding on them to fulfil every article contained in it. It is, in part, in consideration of this, but more in consideration of their destitute situation, that they now, and through this means, humbly entreat you to grant them a respite of one year, to prepare for their migration. You may think it superfluous in me to attempt to describe the situation of an Indian tribe to one who has been so conversant with their customs and manners as yourself; but, sir, it requires that even I should be an eye-witness, to believe that human beings could endure the hardships and privations that have fallen to the lot of this poor and helpless people this season. You are aware that their country was overrun and occupied by the hostile Sacs and the troops of the United States during the whole of last summer; and while they were openly plundered by one party, they were suspected and threatened by the other. The result was, that they fled from both, and concealed themselves in the mazes of the forests and the marshes of the north until the end of the war. During this time they subsisted wholly upon roots, as they were afraid to leave their families unprotected while they should go in pursuit of game. When they were called upon to meet your commissioners in council at Rock Island, they came from their hiding places with a timid heart and trembling step, and proceeded to make any concessions that might be required of them; well knowing that a refusal on their part would be construed into an act of hostility. They, therefore, listened to what was said, and signed what was written, with little comment or reflection. The means that our Government have charitably supplied for their relief, I am sorry to say, is in a great measure ineffectual, owing to the distance of the stations at which provisions are issued from the hunting grounds of the Indians, and thereby obliging the Indian to abandon his hunting altogether, or deprive himself of the benefit of the charity intended him. In consideration of the foregoing, the said chiefs have determined to apply to you (whom they have so often met in council, and in whom they have every confidence) for permission to remain one year longer in their old villages, and provide corn and other necessaries to sustain their families, until they can provide means in the country to which they are to remove. They wish that their agent or some other suitable person be appointed to meet them, for the purpose of arranging the terms and taking such surety for their good conduct during the said year as you may think fit to impose on them, if you should condescend to grant their petition.

1‡

Circumstances have prevented this communication being made through an Indian agent, and the petitioners request that it should have the same effect and importance as though it had been made in a more formal manner. They furthermore desire that you would condescend to acquaint them with your decision on the subject as soon as convenient, either by dropping a line to me, or some one of their agents, on the subject.

I am, sir, respectfully,

Your humble servant,

STEPHEN MACK, Jr.

The Hon. Lewis Cass,
    *Secretary of War.*

---

Rock Island, *January* 2, 1833.

Sir: The time having elapsed which was given to the persons intruding on the west bank of the Mississippi, at Dubuque's mines, I have now the honor to inform you that they have all left the country.

In consequence of the resignation of the sub-agent heretofore stationed at Galena, I have necessarily been at considerable expense and trouble in obeying your orders, as many intruders have also gone over to the west side of the Mississippi at Flint hill. In order, therefore, to have your orders speedily and promptly executed, I found it advisable to appoint an individual to see that the intruders left the mining country within the time allotted them to remove their plunder, &c., whilst I should be engaged in ordering off the others.

The great distance (about two hundred and thirty miles) between the two points where intruders have gone over, rendered it wholly out of my power to superintend both in *propria personæ* until the object of the department could be effected. I must, therefore, particularly request that some allowance may be made for the attention bestowed by S. D. Carpenter, esq , of Galena, in seeing that the orders of the Government were obeyed, and reporting to me.

There being no regular mail route, Mr. C. came in person to make his report.

In consequence of the appointment of an agent by the claimants of Dubuque's mines, to superintend the same, some difficulty may hereafter occur, as he has already gone on for the purpose of taking possession, and letting out the ground to miners.

Mr. Carpenter will keep me advised on this subject.

I have the honor to be, &c.,

M. S. DAVENPORT,
    *Agent for Sacs and Foxes.*

The Hon. Lewis Cass,
    *Secretary of War.*

---

Choctaw Agency, West,
*January* 2, 1833.

Sir: Under the late treaty, I was entitled to one hundred and sixty acres of land by cultivation, as will appear by the books returned; I emigrated with my family with the first party that came by the Government, and left home in a great hurry, and without knowing the value of my land, or very little concerning it. There were standing in the field between two and three hundred bushels of corn, for which I received fifty dollars, at a time when corn was selling at fifty cents per bushel. I received for the land a wagon much used, and two yoke of oxen and a horse, which was all I ever received for my land.

To you, our great father, and the friend of the Choctaws, I look for protection, when the conduct of Grant and Clemmon is examined into, not only in my case, but in many other poor Choctaws who they have deluded.

My brother, Levi Pickins, who had the same quantity of land, and is since dead, sold his land for about one hundred dollars; he left a wife and children who are now here. I know our grievances will be redressed.

Your friend and brother,<br>
JOSEPH PICKINS.

Hon. LEWIS CASS.

---

CREEK AGENCY, January 3, 1833.

SIR: I have the honor to enclose herewith an account, abstracts, and vouchers of disbursements for the quarter ending 31st December, 1832, by which it will appear there is a balance due me of three thousand six hundred and forty-one dollars fifty-two cents, for the year commencing 1st of January, and ending 31st of December, 1832, for which I respectfully ask an early remittance. Three thousand five hundred dollars of this sum was for a part of the Creek annuity for 1831, detained by the accounting officer through a mistake at the time, which I subsequently explained to Mr. Kurtz, and he corrected the error, and I paid the amount to the chiefs, as will appear by the receipt forwarded with my accounts for the quarter; and two hundred and nineteen dollars for storage on rifles in Mobile. I also enclose the amount of presents to Indians in 1827 and 1828, when acting as commissioner to treat for the strip of land in Georgia, with a certificate of the clerk of the store where the articles were delivered. Also a certificate of the value of the agency buildings, and an office built previous to the agency buildings, all of which I hope will be satisfactory.

I have the honor to be,<br>
Your obedient servant,<br>
JOHN CROWELL.

The Hon. LEWIS CASS,
    *Secretary of War.*

---

ONEIDA, January 4, 1833.

DEAR SIR: We have not as yet received our goods from the Indian agent of the United States. The agent on the part of the General Government has heretofore furnished us goods, every year, in the early part of November. We have heard nothing from him this year. It is now about the middle of winter, and the naked children of our tribe feel sharply the inclemency of the season.   Please to let us know the cause of this delay.

Yours respectfully,

his

CHRISTIAN × BEACHTREE.

mark,

his

AUGUST × CORNELIUS.

mark,

his

ABRAHAM × SCHYLER.

mark,

*Chiefs of the Oneida tribe.*

Witness: JAMES THOMAS.

The above are chiefs of the Oneida Indians.

T. JULIUS,

*Attorney for the Oneida Indians.*

To the Hon. LEWIS CASS,
   *Secretary of War.*

---

*January 5*, 1833.

DEAR SIR: George S. Gaines, who was appointed to conduct an exploring party of Choctaws, to examine the country beyond the Mississippi; and directed at the same time to make, if practicable, an arrangement with the Chickasaws for the cession of their lands, has had a portion of his charge for performing those duties, particularly the last, suspended at the department. I am very desirous that his accounts may undergo an examination, and should the mode of settling such accounts forbid the allowance claimed by him, I wish a statement to be made that I may take measures to have Mr. Gaines compensated for services actually rendered.   Your attention to this subject will confer a particular favor on me.

Most respectfully,

Your obedient servant,

WILLIAM R. KING.

Hon. LEWIS CASS.

---

WASHINGTON, *January 5*, 1833.

SIR: I have the honor to report that, in conformity with your instructions of the third, I left this city on the fourth, and arrived at Urbanna, Ohio, on the eleventh of October.

Having ascertained that the emigrating expedition of Indians, from the State of Ohio, was then on its way to the west, and had been several days on its journey, and not upon a stage road, I had to change my mode of travelling; and, procuring a horse, I left Urbanna on the 13th October, in pursuit of them.

I moved with all the speed which such a mode of travelling admits, overtaking the rear detachment about five miles west of the Wabash, and the front detachment, with which I found Col. Gardiner, on the 25th of October, at Hickory Grove, within about forty miles of the Mississippi.

This detachment had halted here in order to give time to those in the rear to come up, and in order to make arrangements for that part of the emigration destined to the Neosho, and which would probably be separated from the main body at this place. Col. Gardiner had written to Gen. Clark, superintendent of Indian affairs at St. Louis, for information and advice on this subject.

As it is well known to you the great object of my mission was, to get this emigration to its destination this season; and, if possible, to reconcile the differences which were known to exist between the special agent and the disbursing officer; and which differences were considered as hazarding the emigration.

These differences I found had originated in different views, which each had given to his own instructions, and which, from that origin, had extended into such personalities, that no personal intercourse whatever, not even in relation to their duties, existed between them. It was soon evident to my judgment that reconciliation was impossible; and, without reconciliation and harmonious action, the emigration would, in all human probability, fail for that season.

In relation to the merit of these differences, and of the various accusations, official and personal, made by each against the other, I did not inquire. I saw clearly that any investigation on this subject would involve me in the most unpleasant labyrinth, waste that time which we had not to spare, and, in the end, produce results satisfactory to no one. I determined, therefore, at once, to leave any investigation which might be thought necessary, to other hands, and a more convenient season, and to give the whole of my efforts to the direction of the emigration.

Whatever may have been the difference between these agents, in relation to the authority of each, with that with which I was invested, there could be none. It was paramount to the authority of any other agent of the emigration, and adequate to the object with which I considered myself specially charged. But it was an authority which I could not delegate, and as its exercise was necessary to the well being of the emigration, it was equally necessary that I should remain with the emigration in order to exercise it.

Under all these considerations, I decided to take the direction of the emigration into my own hands; and, accordingly, on the morning of the 27th, being that of the second day after I had overtaken the special agent, I assumed the direction of the emigration, and thus became responsible for its successful termination.

The special agent, Col. Gardiner, was then immediately invited to accompany me as far at least as the Mississippi, and to aid me in the duties I had undertaken, by his information and advice: and it is no more than justice to him to acknowledge, that he accepted of this invitation with the greatest cheerfulness, rendering to me the most efficient and valuable services in the most polite and gentlemanlike manner. In fact, to the many valuable ideas which I acquired from him, during the few days of our association, in relation to the Indian character, generally, and to that of this emigration, in particular, as well as that of the several agents attached to it, may be attributed much of the success which afterwards attended my efforts.

On the 28th, all the rear detachments had arrived, and on the 29th of October, the party destined for the Neosho was started, under the direction of General Workman, who had been the principal conductor of the Neosho detachment to this place. I added an additional assistant conductor to this party, in the person of Mr. James Workman, a highly efficient and able man, and who had accompanied me from Urbanna, at my request. This party was made particularly strong in its agents, as it had to separate from me, intending myself to accompany the main body destined for the vicinity of the Kansas.

As a division of the emigration had now to take place, I applied to Gen. Atkinson for an officer to serve as an additional disbursing agent, in order to preserve to the department the usual military responsibility for expenditures. With the greatest promptness, he detached for the purpose that experienced and valuable officer, Capt. T. C. Palmer, who, as soon as he arrived, was placed upon duty with the large detachment which I accompanied, and Lieut. Lane was ordered to proceed, as the disbursing officer, to the smaller detachment, destined for the Neosho.

While at Hickory Grove, Mr. Robb, the principal conductor of the Shawnees, having been some time seriously indisposed, resigned his place, and Judge Shelby, assistant conductor to the same party, and highly deserving of the distinction, was immediately, and by the advice of Colonel Gardiner, promoted to fill the vacancy.

On the morning of the 30th, we moved with the main body towards the Mississippi, the vicinity of which we reached on the evening of the 31st, and passed over the river on the 1st and 2d days of November. This large detachment of the emigration being now west of the Mississippi, Colonel Gardiner, the special agent, who had hitherto remained with me, took his departure for his home under a leave of absence. Having myself no feelings in relation to this duty, but those emanating from an anxious desire that it should be successfully terminated during the present season, and having experienced great advantages from the advice and remarks of Col. Gardiner, I deemed it no more than justice to Government as well as to him, to invite him to continue with me, if consistent with his feelings, to the termination of the expedition. He, however, declined the invitation, stating his reasons in a letter, and returned home, as I before remarked, upon a leave of absence.

Major Pool, the assistant special agent, was then requested to take upon himself the direction of all details.

Without enumerating the many embarrassments which we experienced during the march. as well from the composition of the emigration, as from the cholera, which attacked the detachment of the Ottaways, I will briefly state that we commenced crossing the Mississippi, on the 1st of November, which occupied two days, arrived at the Missouri, at Arrow Rock, on the sixteenth, and were there detained five days in crossing the detachment, and by a violent storm of wind, rain, sleet, and snow; but in the end, were so fortunate as to reach the Shawnee village, twenty miles west of the town of Independence, during the afternoon of the 30th of November, which, after deducting the delays before stated, was completing the entire march of 320 miles in 23 days.

I cannot speak too highly of the conduct and exertions of Mr. Pool, the assistant special agent, and of all the conductors attached to the emigration. They were animated by the most ardent zeal, to get this emigration through as early as possible, and were gratified by seeing their efforts crowned with the most happy success before the inclemency of the winter came to oppress if not to defeat us.

It gives me pleasure also to state, that the party under General Workman, destined for the Neosho, was, when last heard from, within about one hundred and fifty miles of its home, which it has without doubt safely reached long before now.

Being fully aware that disquietudes, and many of them well grounded, existed with the main body which were conducted to the vicinity of the Kansas, I determined, before leaving them, if possible, by any reasonable arrangements, to appease these disquietudes, and to leave the Indians as sa- tisfied with the treatment extended towards them, as they evidently were with the appearance of their new lands. For this purpose, I had first all the Shawnee chiefs called together, and in the presence of the agents resident with them, as well as of those who had been employed in conducting them to their new homes, I expressed to them the great pleasure I felt at the for- tunate and early termination of the emigration. Then alluding to the losses which they had sustained during the route, and the desire I felt, from the known paternal feelings of their great father, the President, towards them, to fulfil in the most liberal spirit of the treaty, in relation to their emigration, I offered in lieu of and in full compensation of all these losses, to give to them the public horses yet remaining, and which had been used in the emi- gration of their tribe, and also the several sets of wagon gears and the pub- lic saddles which had been similarly used; these to be received by them in lieu of their losses during the march, and not as any part of the articles stipu- lated in the treaty.

I also stated to them that the feeding under the treaty would commence on the 1st of January, 1833, but, in the meantime, they would be fed as usual at the expense of the United States.

To prevent any misunderstanding on these subjects, I had the proposal twice explained and interpreted by that able interpreter, Mr. Shane, and as many of the chiefs spoke English well, there can be no doubt that the whole matter was correctly understood.

The chiefs, after a consultation with each other, expressed their satisfaction at the proposals I had made, and accepted them freely upon the conditions stated. A statement of the agreement was afterwards reduced to writing, having no means of writing at hand at that time, and herewith accompanies this report.

The chiefs then desired me to state to you, their great anxiety to have the special tract of 100,000 acres, intended for their use, surveyed as early as possible, and also that the farming utensils and the various tools provided for in the treaty might be delivered as early as possible. They wished to accompany the commissioners in this survey, and were particularly anxious that the mill sites should be selected, as their desire is to establish their per- manent residences as conveniently accessible to these as possible.

The chief, Perry, of the Shawnee village, and of the tribe removed thither some years since, desired me to assure you that he had rigidly followed the advice of his great father, in cultivating peace and harmony with all the ad- jacent tribes, between whom and the Shawnees, there existed the most cor- dial and friendly intercourse. That his people were generally separated upon distinct tracts, cultivating the soil, and were contented and comfort- able.

On the next day, I had a council for similar purposes with the small band of Ottawas, which formed a part of the emigration. This band is connected by intermarriages with the Shawnees of Waupaughkonetta, look up to them as an "elder brother," and accompanied them in the emigration.

Their particular selection of lands was selected about forty miles from the

Shawnee village, and amid strangers to them. The Shawnees had invited them to remain in the vicinity of the village until the spring, which they were extremely desirous of doing. contemplating the course of sending an exploring party upon their lands during the winter to select the spot upon which they were ultimately to settle. This was stated to me by the chiefs in council, with an expression of their strong desire to be indulged. So reasonable a desire was not opposed by me, and particularly as I was assured by the agent, Major Cummins, that they could be fed with much more certainty near the village, and could be much more carefully watched over, no special agent being yet appointed to attend to them, and they, on that account, being placed under his care.

I then, also, proposed to these chiefs the same remuneration for their losses which had been proposed to the Shawnees, adding, however, that, in consideration of permitting them to remain near the Shawnee village, they were to remove themselves to their new lands, about forty miles distant, at their own expense, as soon as the weather would admit.

The chiefs then complained of the disappointment in not yet receiving the $2,000 stipulated to be paid in the treaty, urged me to make some arrangements by which they should be paid at least a part of this sum, as it was absolutely necessary to meet their present wants. Fully aware of this and of the poverty of this tribe, I obtained three hundred dollars from the agent, and paid it to them as a part of the $2,000 stipulated for in the treaty.

The whole arrangement was then reduced to writing, and signed by the chiefs and myself; and I am happy to add, that it gave to them great satisfaction.

Having now completed all of the arrangements, which appeared to me necessary, in order to heal the disquietudes which had existed with these Indians—having seen them contented and preparing their lodges for winter, and the contractor on the ground and furnishing them with provisions, I considered myself as having fulfilled the duty which had been committed to me, and I took my departure from them, leaving them under the care of Major Cummins, the resident agent, and Major Campbell, his assistant, gentlemen whose intelligence, knowledge of their duties, and efficiency and benevolence of character could leave no doubt that the Government would be faithfully served, and the Indians kindly and correctly attended to.

On my return, I stopped at St. Louis, and duly informed General Clark, the superintendent of Indian affairs, of all the arrangements herein spoken of, and furnishing him with duplicates of such as had been reduced to writing, and then set out for this place, where I arrived on the 30th of December, and, on the 1st of January, 1833, again resumed the duties of my office.

With this report I have the honor to enclose:

First. The agreement alluded to between the Shawnees and myself, on behalf of the United States.

Second. A similar agreement with the Ottawas.

Third. A receipt from the Ottawas for three hundred dollars.

Fourth. A receipt from the Shawnees for twenty-three new rifles, delivered to them at Arrow Rock, on the Missouri. These are the rifles provided for in the treaty with the Shawnee, and which were received at Arrow Rock and delivered there.

Respectfully submitted by, sir,
Your most obedient servant,
J. J. ABERT, *Lt. Col. U. S. A.*,
*And special Commissioner of the Emigration.*

Hon. LEWIS CASS, *Secretary of War.*

*December* 2, 1832.

At a grand council held this day at Perry's village, being a council of the chiefs and head-men of the emigrating Shawnees from Ohio, it was mutually agreed, between the said chiefs and head-men on the one part, and Lieut. Col. John J. Abert, for and in behalf of the United States, on the other part:

That, in consideration of all losses of horses and other property, and of all expenses of every kind and nature whatsoever, incurred by the said Shawnees, during the emigration, they are willing, and do hereby receive, as a full and sufficient compensation, the public horses now with them, amounting to twenty-two, and the wagon gears, which have been in the use of the emigration, and the saddles and bridles. In testimony whereof, we, the undersigned, do state, that we were present at said council, and witnessed the agreement as above stated.

RICHARD W. CUMMINS.<br>
G. W. POOL.

Signed in duplicate.

A. Shane, Interpreter.

*Note.*—It was also expressly understood and agreed that the feeding, under the treaty, was to commence on the 1st of January, 1833; and that, in the mean time, that they were to be fed by the United States.

J. J. ABERT,<br>
Lt. Col. &c., in charge of the emigration.

------

The following agreement has been this day day entered into by the chiefs and head-men of the Ottoway tribe of emigrating Indians on the one part, and Lieut. Col. John J. Abert, in behalf of the United States, on the other part.

Article 1st. In consideration of the losses in horses and other property, and of the expenses incurred by the said tribe of emigrating Indians, of every nature whatsoever, during the emigration, it is mutually agreed, between the parties aforesaid, that all the public horses, saddles, and bridles, now in the use of the said Ottoway tribe, shall be delivered to the aforesaid chiefs and head-men, to be by them distributed to the said tribes, according to their several losses and necessities, as a full compensation of all said losses and expenses.

Article 2d. It is further agreed, between the parties aforesaid, that the said tribe of Ottoway Indians will remove upon their own lands as soon as the season will admit, from the vicinity of the Shawnee agency, where they now are, without any expense to the United States, for any means of transportation.

Article 3d. It is further agreed, between the parties aforesaid, that, in consideration of the necessity of wintering the said tribe near the Shawnee agency, and of its present wants, the above chiefs and head-men are to receive, and fairly to distribute to their tribe, the sum of three hundred dollars, which they are to receive as a part of the two thousand dollars, provided for in the fifth article of the treaty, with the said Ottaways, ratified and confirmed by the signature of the President of the United States, on the sixth day of April, one thousand eight hundred and thirty-two.

Article 4th. And it is further agreed, between the parties aforesaid, that, as in addition to the difficulties of moving the said Ottaways to their new lands at this inclement season, they have desired in council that they may remain near the Shawnee agency. They, the said head-men, will receive and consider the subsisting of them for one year, after they shall have arrived at their new lands, provided for in the treaty referred to in the third article of this agrement, as commencing on the first day of January, one thousand eight hundred and thirty-three, the United States, however, being bound to subsist them in the mean time.

| | | |
|---|---|---|
| OC-CO-NOX-CY, | his x mark. | [L. s.] |
| CHE-COAK, | his x mark. | [L. s.] |
| CORN-CHAW, | his x mark. | [L. s.] |
| EAU-BASS, | his x mark. | [L. s.] |
| PE-CHE-KEESE, | his x mark. | [L. s.] |
| OSHAW-WA-NON, | his x mark. | [L. s.] |
| NONDIA-WA, | his x mark. | [L. s.] |

JOHN J. ABERT,
*Lt. Col. U. S. A., in charge of the emigration.*

Signed, this third day of December, at the Shawnee agency, in our presence, and in the year of our Lord eighteen hundred and thirty two.

T. E. PHILIPS.
JOHN SHELBY.
DEWITT MERRITT.
G. W. POOL.

---

OFFICE OF COMMISSIONERS OF INDIAN AFFAIRS,
*Fort Gibson, January 6, 1833.*

SIR: The commissioners on Indian affairs had the honor of advising the department from Fort Smith, on the 22d of December, of the organization of the board, and the necessity existing for visiting the Seneca and Shawnee Indians, who had just emigrated to this country, under certain treaty stipulations.

The commissioners arrived at the Seneca agency on the 26th ultimo, and immediately entered upon the business which called them to that place. They have now the pleasure of transmitting to you a treaty concluded with the Senecas from Sandusky, who first emigrated, and the mixed band of Senecas and Shawnees who had refused to settle upon the land assigned them by treaty stipulations, requiring their removal from Ohio. You will perceive, by the talk had with the chiefs in council, that some change has been effected in both the locations of these people; the reasons for which will be found in the "journal of the proceedings of the council."

The commissioners were satisfied, not only from the representations of the chiefs and Lieutenant Lane, but from other concurring information, that the land assigned the mixed band of Senecas and Shawnees from Lewistown, Ohio, on the west side of Neosho or Grand river, was not fit for agricultural purposes, and entirely unadapted to the wants and comforts of the Indians.

You will perceive, by the treaty enclosed, that the former emigrants called the "Senaca tribe, from Sandusky," and the "mixed band of Senecas and Shawnees from Lewistown, Ohio," have united and become one nation.

This arrangement will accord with the views of the Government on that subject, and will doubtless be gratifying to you. They have ceded by this treaty all the lands claimed by them under former treaties lying on the west side of Grand river, for sixty thousand acres north of the present tract of the Senecas from Sandusky, and between the Grand river and the Missouri line. By this exchange the Senecas and Shawnees have received lands with which they are highly pleased; and which, from a personal examination made by the commissioners, are deemed amply sufficient for them, in conformity with the benevolent views of the Government, in the permanent location of the Indians; the present number of the united tribe not exceeding six hundred souls.

It is stipulated by this treaty that the United States will "immediately erect a grist and saw-mill, a blacksmith shop, and furnish the necessary materials and tools" for the same, as provided by the treaties made with these tribes on the 28th of February, and the 20th of July 1831. In the proceedings of the council the reasons for this stipulation are assigned, which we conceive will be satisfactory to the Government. The commissioners consider it a matter of little importance to the United States, whether these provisions made by former treaties with this people, be carried into immediate effect, or postponed until their lands in Ohio can be sold; as the whole expense eventually must be borne by the Indians as stipulated by the treaty. The sale of their lands in Ohio has been earnestly urged by the chiefs in council; and unless some good cause exists for deferring it, the commissioners would very respectfully recommend that they be sold with as little delay as possible, as the Indians interested might be much benefited by an immediate application of the funds under their treaty arrangements, in commencing their agricultural operations in their new country.

You will perceive, by the 4th article of the treaty, that one thousand dollars have been allowed for the losses sustained by these tribes in emigrating, and for forage purchased by the last emigrants before they reached the Mississippi river. The Indians manifested much anxiety about these losses, which were principally in horses. Upon an examination of their accounts, the commissioners stipulated for their settlement on terms which they believe equitable and just; and as these claims were intended by the Indians to be made a matter of future negotiation with the department, in which considerable expense would necessarily be incurred, the commissioners believe their adjustment now will meet your approbation. An appropriation by Congress to meet this allowance will be all that is necessary to carry the provisions of this treaty into effect, as no presents were delivered to the Indians, or any expenditures made in negotiating the treaty, beyond the ordinary expenses of the commission.

Upon reference to the several maps defining the boundaries of the country on file in the War Department, you will discover that the land relinquished by the present treaty to the Government, on the west side of Neosho river, adjoins the Cherokee country on the north, and can be very advantageously disposed of in the final adjustment of the pending difficulties between the Cherokee and Creek tribes; and should it not be wanted for that purpose, other Indians, to whom it may be hereafter assigned, must be greatly benefited by being bounded by so fine and important a river as the Neosho. Independent of these considerations, however, the change of location for the united tribe of Seneca and Shawnees, secures to these people plain natural boundaries, which is highly important to these Indians and to the Government.

The commissioners would respectfully solicit your attention to the wishes expressed by the head chief of the Senecas and Shawnees, on the subject of removing other remnants of their tribe, residing in New York and elsewhere, to this country. With the views of the Government upon this subject, and the expediency of the measure suggested, you are best acquainted, and your decision will doubtless be satisfactory to the parties concerned.

In traversing the country between Fort Smith and the Seneca agency, and thence to Fort Gibson, the commissioners had an opportunity of examining the country assigned to the Cherokees, over a distance of about three hundred miles; and from their own observation and information obtained from farmers on the road, they are enabled to pronounce it a highly desirable agricultural country. The soil is deep, rich, and uncommonly productive, abundantly supplied with wood and water, apparently from the purest springs, affords valuable hydraulic privileges.

The commissioners do not recollect any thing more necessary to communicate explanatory of the treaty enclosed. But they would beg leave, in closing this communication, to give it, as their opinion, formed upon safe data, that much trouble and expense would be saved to the Government, by making no *conditional* locations in negotiations for the removal of Indians hereafter. The country is much divided between extensive prairies, hills, and bottom lands, and great care should be taken in locating the various tribes to make the quantity of each proportionate to their wants. This can alone be done by a careful examination made by the commissioners appointed to treat with the Indians about to be removed, accompanied, when practicable, by a delegation of the Indians themselves. Their settlement afterwards, upon the lands assigned them, would depend upon no contingency.

With these views the treaty with the Senecas and Shawnees is respectfully submitted to you, for the consideration and confirmation of the President and Senate of the United States.

I have the honor to be,

S. C. STAMBAUGH,
*Secretary to Commissioners.*

To the SECRETARY OF WAR.

---

OFFICE OF COMMISSIONERS OF INDIAN AFFAIRS,
*Fort Gibson, January 7, 1833.*

SIR: I have the honor to acknowledge the receipt of a letter from the War Department, of the 24th November last, enclosing a copy of the report of Messrs. McCoy and Donelson, of their survey of the Indian country west of the Mississippi.

In reply to that part of your letter which refers to the Osages, the commissioners have the pleasure of informing you that they have made arrangements to hold a council with that tribe about the middle of next month, for the purpose of effecting a change of their present lands, for a more eligible location further north, and if possible, of improving their present condition. Col. A. P. Chouteau occupies the Osage reservation at the saline, a very central position for holding the treaty, and he has offered the commissioners comfortable accommodations for that purpose, and will furnish rations at the present contract price at Fort Gibson.

It is with equal pleasure that I inform the department that the commissioners have made arrangements to hold a general council with the Cherokee and Creek Indians, on the 29th of this month, for the purpose of adjusting the difficulties existing between those tribes. The commissioners entertain strong hopes of success in effecting a satisfactory settlement of the line between them, and, at the same time, securing a satisfactory location for the Seminoles, who are anxious to settle with the Creek nation.

There will not be time to communicate the result of these treaties before the end of the present session of Congress; and as it is expected to hold councils with the Pawnees, Delawares, and some other tribes, before the commencement of next session, the commissioners respectfully submit to the Secretary of War the above arrangements, in order to enable him to procure an appropriation at the present session sufficient to meet the expenditures necessary to effect the object contemplated; which, with the greatest regard to the most rigid enconomy, will necessarily be considerable.

I am very respectfully,
Your most humble servant,
S. C. STAMBAUGH,
*Secretary to Commissioners.*

Hon. LEWIS CASS, *Secretary of War.*

---

INDIAN QUEEN HOTEL, WASHINGTON CITY,
*January 8,* 1833.

The undersigned, principal chief of the Cherokee nation, east of the Mississippi, presents his respects to the honorable Secretary of War, and informs him of his arrival, together with the delegation of said nation, composed of Messrs. Richard Taylor, John F. Baldridge, and Joseph Vann, and who, with himself, would be happy to pay their respects to the President of the United States, and likewise to the honorable Secretary of War, whneever it shall be convenient to receive them.

Very respectfully, &c.,
I am, &c., &c.,
JOHN ROSS.

---

HOUSE OF REPRESENTATIVES.
*January 9,* 1833.

SIR: James Brown and John Brown, of the Cherokee nation, have each petitioned Congress for allowance, (under the treaty of 1819, between the United States and those Indians,) of the value of improvements made by them on lands ceded to the United States, by the provisions of the treaty of 1817, between the United States and those Indians, and confirmed by the treaty of 1819, aforesaid.

The sixth article of the treaty of 1817, provides that, " to those emigrants whose improvements add real value to their lands, the United States agree to pay a full valuation for the same, which is to be ascertained by a commissioner to be appointed by the President of the United States, for that purpose, and be paid for as soon after the ratification of this treaty, as practicable."

By the 2d article of the treaty of 1819, " the United States agree to pay according to the stipulations contained in the treaty of the eighth of July, 1817, for all improvements on land lying within the country ceded by the Cherokees, which add real value to the land."

The Committee on Indian Affairs have directed me to inquire of you whether these claims were presented to the commissioner appointed in conformity to the provisions of the before recited treaties, and if they were, to request you to inform the committee what disposition was made of them. If they were not so submitted, the committee request that you will favor them with any information within your power, which will aid in the investigation of the claims.

Very respectfully,
Your obedient servant,
WILEY THOMPSON.

Mr. ELBERT HERRING.

---

MARSHAL'S OFFICE, So. DIS. ALA.,
*Mobile, January* 12, 1833.

SIR: Your letter of the 27th ultimo is received, informing me that a requisition for five hundred dollars in my favor, had been made on the Treasury Department, on the 26th December, has been received by me; and also, that another for $712 67, on the 27th of same month, in my favor, had been made, and which has not been received; they were both within a day of each other, and should have been received by this time.

Very respectfully,
Your obedient servant,
ROBERT L. CRAWFORD.

ELBERT HERRING, Esq.,
*Office Indian Affairs.*

---

FORT MITCHELL, *January* 13, 1833.

SIR: Under the belief that it is important to you to possess all the information you can, of the affairs of the Creek Indians, before the appropriation bill shall have been passed by Congress, I make the following communication.

I have been here for some days, with Majors Abbott and Parsons, and have ascertained such facts and circumstances as come to their knowledge in passing through the nation, and as have come within my own observation.

The most of the head chiefs are, apparently, yet opposed to going west of the Mississippi; and the sway of the chiefs of the higher grade is so absolute, that the common Indians dare not express their desire to go. Yet I think I hazard nothing when I express the opinion, that if there were suitable agents, who were authorised to promise to each emigrant, entitled to a reservation, sixty-two and a half cents per acre, for his land, to be paid in part, at the time of enrolling and signing a deed of relinquishment to the United States, and the balance at the place of their final home, and to comply with the other stipulations of the treaty; and to afford the emigrants, after enrolled and assembled, support and protection, that, by May next, three thousand of the Indians might be started; and by October following, more than three thousand more. You know the effect the removing of considerable numbers would have upon those left behind.

For this service, the acquaintance with the country, language, and particular disposition of particular Indians, would enable Majors Abbot and Parsons to accomplish as much or more than other men; and, I am sure, both would be faithful to all concerned.

The plan of removing the Indians en masse, will not soon succeed; and I believe the sooner the locating agent can ascertain the particular lands of the Indians, the sooner they will emigrate. And if the agent shall have to ascertain that the persons claiming are the ones entitled by the census, and the particular tracts of land, which, according to the treaty, shall include improvements of Indians, one agent cannot do it for years; and if, for this, you wish more than one agent, for the reasons before stated, I think the persons before mentioned could best serve the Government. The investigation of claims here is a difficult task; and all I can promise is, that I will so act as to show, that the Government of the United States is, to the Indians, a just and paternal Government; and that I am faithful in the discharge of the trust in me reposed.

You must excuse me for frequently troubling you. It is with the view of discharging my duty; and you are not compelled to answer, only as far as you may deem necessary to a correct discharge of your duty.

Majors Abbott, Parsons, and myself, in explaining to the Indians their condition, moral and political, have pursued an open course, which I believe has acquired for us the confidence of the tribe; and we have, as far as we could, shielded them against every fraud; and, we hope, convinced many of their real situation, and of the necessity of removing.

I have, &c.,

Hon. Lewis Cass,　　　　　　　　　　ENOCH PARSONS.
　　*Secretary of War.*

———

Washington City, *January* 14, 1833.

Sir: In obedience to your wishes, expressed to us on Friday last, we have respectfully considered your suggestions in relation to depositing the proceeds of the twenty-five hundred sections, in the hands of the Government, for safe keeping. It is presumed no difficulty will arise in modeling both treaties to this effect, so as to leave all moneys in the hands of the Government, subject to the check of the nation, at pleasure.

This delegation feels it due to the President and themselves, to present for his consideration, their powers, and promptly say to him, that they act now, as they have constantly done, in perfect submission and good feeling; and are ready to open the negotiation, generously, in all things within their power. This delegation entertains for Gov. Cass, the most respectful impressions, as a great and good man; but as this matter commenced with Gen. Coffee, and as the treaty has gone to the world, and to the Senate, in his name, we have no wish to change the commissioner. Gen. Coffee has leisure, and Mr. Cass is pressed for time, and we want this question finished, and we are content to negotiate with Gen. Coffee alone. It is rumored that the treaty before the Senate, very probably, will be acted on to-day, and we most respectfully beg leave to remind you of your promise to have that treaty suspended—fearful, from the great press of business before you, it may have escaped your recollection.

We have the honor to be, with profound respect, your ob'dt. servants,

GEO. COLBERT, his x mark.
GREEN WOOD, his x mark.
PITMAN COLBERT,
JOHN L. ALLEN.

To the President of the United States.

BUFFALO CREEK AGENCY,

*January* 15, 1833,

Understanding that our agent, James Stryker, esq., is about visiting Washington, and will see our great father, the President, and Gov. Cass, the Secretary of War, we, the undersigned, chiefs of the Seneca nation, of New York Indians, desire to send by him our wishes in matters which very much concern our nation.

All our chiefs and our people have confidence in our agent. He has treated us well; has attended to our wants; paid us our annuities; and we thank the Secretary of War that he has sent us a man as our agent whom we can trust and go to for advice and assistance.

We have authorized him to express to the President and the Secretary of War, what we want in relation to ourselves—our situation, and our future prospects. He knows what arrangements are necessary, for the more convenient distribution of our annuities, and *we* have committed to his care some applications from some of our people, for allowance for military services, which they have rendered our white brethren, and to help them now that they are disabled by wounds.

On one subject we beg our father, the Secretary, to hear us. We have been informed that a treaty has been made with the Menominees, and lands provided for the New York Indians. We know that many of our people are desirous to secure those lands. They do not know how long they can be secure where they now are. The Government has been very good to us. Our father, the President, has been careful for us and our children. We shall be glad then to look at those lands, and to choose for our people, the Senecas, a share and an interest. Many of our nation already speak of going to the west, and we think it best for us not to lose the present opportunity. If the Government will provide us the means, some of our chiefs will go next spring, and choose land, and a place for the Seneca nation, on the land purchased from the Menominees.

Our agent, who carries this, knows our wishes. We will agree to whatever arrangements he may make in our name with the Government. We ask our father, the Secretary, to listen to his words, and to communicate through him, the intentions of the Government in regard to us and our nation.

YOUNG KING, his x mark.
POLLARD, his x mark.
DESTROY TOWN, his x mark.
LITTLE BILLY, his x mark.
JAMES STEVENSON, his x mark.
JOHN SNOW, his x mark.

On behalf of the Seneca chiefs and of the nation,
WILLIAM JONES, *Interpreter*, his x mark.

I certify that this paper was executed in my presence by the individuals whose names are hereto affixed, and whom I am acquainted with, and know to be principal chiefs of the Seneca nation of New York Indians.

GEO. BURT.

STATE OF NEW YORK,
    *City of Buffalo, ss:*

On this eighteenth day of January, in the year one thousand eight hundred and thirty-three, before me, Ebenezer Johnson, mayor of the city of Buffalo, came George Burt, of the said city, merchant, to me personally known, who, being sworn and examined, deposed that he saw the chiefs within named execute the within writing; that the same was first fully explained and interpreted to them; that he knows the said chiefs, and that they are principal chiefs of the Seneca nation, with full powers to act for that people; and that he subscribed his name as a witness, in their presence.

                               EBENEZER JOHNSON,
                                    *Mayor of the city of Buffalo.*

---

                               FORT GIBSON, *January* 17, 1833.

DEAR SIR: The commissioners of Indian affairs at this post, had the pleasure to transmit to the department a treaty with the Seneca Indians, and a report and talk accompanying the same, by Mr. West, sutler of this post, which, we trust, have been received.

I was not a little surprised to receive a line from the department, stating that my draft in favor of J. E. Herne, for $200, payable the 19th instant, had not been accepted.

I would ask whether there can be the shadow of a doubt whether I have this amount due for services? After travelling (3,000) three thousand miles since the acceptance of my commission, and which states that I shall be entitled to receive " eight dollars for every twenty miles travel," I shall extremely regret to hear, not on my own account merely, that this draft is not paid at maturity. I was apprized of the rule of the department, that no advances could be made to me, and, therefore, was careful to draw my draft payable at such a time as I supposed there could be no doubt that I had this amount and much more due *for services performed.*

By the treaty with the Senecas, I think a happy arrangement has been made for the Government, as we may want the lands west of the Neosho in our arrangements with the Cherokees and Creeks.

I think, from the terms of the Cherokee treaty, that Mr. McCoy has run the north line of the Cherokees about six miles further north than the treaty warrants, and which will give them on that line about 150,000 acres of land more than they are entitled to claim.

I hope we shall be able to settle the difficulties between the Creeks and Cherokees, at the council to be held on the 29th instant.

Make my respects to the President and Mr. Herring.
                               With great respect,
                                    Your humble servant,
                                         J. F. SCHERMERHORN.
To the Hon. LEWIS CASS,
    *Secretary of War.*

---

                                         *January* 18, 1833.

SIR: Your letter is received. At 10, to-morrow, we shall have an interview with the Indians.
    3‡

I think it advisable that we should have the late treaty, and the recent proposals, which the Chickasaws have submitted.

If Mr. Herring will send up the originals, time in copying will be saved, and we will be careful to send them over to him again.

Our place of meeting will be at the seven buildings, where Colonel Abert has his topographical corps. He will give us a place there, and there you can send any instructions or papers deemed material.

Very respectfully,

J. H. EATON.

SECRETARY OF WAR.

---

WASHINGTON CITY, *January* 21, 1833.

SIR: When I sent you the treaty which I made with the Chickasaw nation of Indians, in October last, I had no knowledge of any dissatisfaction on the part of the nation with the provisions of that treaty,—except of about fifty half-breeds, and white men with Indian families, who wanted reservations, and they were satisfied with the treaty in all respects,—except that the nation refused to allow them reservations of land in fee simple, to live on after the nation left their present country, or to sell them, as they preferred, and go along with the nation when they should remove to the west; they urged this right of reservation with much warmth and zeal for many days, debating the subject in full council, and smaller parties, among themselves, as I was informed; but, finally, seeing the nation was determined not to allow them reserves, they came to the conclusion, and so informed me, to yield all opposition to the treaty and let it be made. Thus the great obstacle to closing the treaty was removed. The treaty was then written out upon the principles agreed upon with the chiefs; the nation was called together in full council, when I read it to them, and had it interpreted by Benjamin Love, a half-breed of the nation, and now said to be the best interpreter in the nation; it was then delivered to the chief, Levi Colbert, with a request that he should carry it to the private national council, and have it interpreted and explained to all his people, until they were fully satisfied. The treaty was taken and kept several days, and, as I was informed, the chiefs were attentively engaged in explaining it to their people, to their entire satisfaction. I was informed that they were ready to sign the treaty. I then met them in full national council; they informed me that they were satisfied with the treaty, but they wished to add some additional articles, which they presented to me, and which was agreed to by me, but the closing article of the treaty had been written; it was agreed, that we would then sign the treaty as made out, and closed, and on the next day I would make a supplement to the treaty, to embrace the additional articles then agreed upon. The treaty was then signed in good faith by all the principal men of the nation, and, as I then believed, and yet believe, satisfactory to the whole nation. The supplement was made, and as agreed upon, and I believe satisfactory to all. For further particulars I refer you to the journal of the proceedings of the treaty, and particularly to that part where I had to remove John D. Terrill and others, white men, not of the nation, from the camp, on account of their secret interference, endeavoring to prevent the treaty being made at that time, alleging, as I understood to the Indians, that they could make better terms here provided they would then decline to treat with me, and ask permission of Government to send a delegation here to Washington.

This information was given me by such authority as I was bound to believe, and, therefore, I gave the order that he, Terrill, should leave the camp. John L. Allen, the sub-agent, was suspected to be concerned with Terrill at the time, but I was not willing to believe that an officer of the Government would act thus, until positive proof of the fact appeared. He was aware of his being suspected, and he mentioned the subject to me, denying the charge, which I received as satisfactory at the time, but subsequent circumstances, now known to you, satisfies my mind of his then guilt.

On or about the 10th of December last, I received information from the agent, Colonel Reynolds, saying that he had just received an intimation that the sub-agent, John L. Allen, with a few of the chiefs, were secretly preparing to set out for Washington City; their business was unknown to him, and to the nation at large, but supposed to be in opposition to the treaty which I had made. A few days thereafter, Colonel Reynolds came to see me, and informed me that he had learnt with more certainty, that Allen and his party were on the eve of starting, but was still trying to keep it a secret.

Soon after transmitting the treaty to you, I was advised by the President that it would be well for me to come on here, and, if required, explain the motives and principles of the treaty, as it was made on different principles from any treaty heretofore made with any of our Indian tribes. In consequence of this remark from the President, I had intended to come on here, but this movement of the sub-agent Allen and his party, induced me to start earlier than I had intended to set out. I was bound to believe that misrepresentations would be made here by Allen and his party, for otherwise their movements would not have been kept so secret, and having had no commissioner with me in making the treaty, I had called on the agent, and asked his co-operation with me in forming the treaty, which he agreed to, and was with me in all the principal transactions in making and signing the treaty; therefore, I thought it advisable that he should be here with me, to meet any misstatements which might be made on the subject of that whole business. With this impression, I prevailed on Colonel Reynolds to accompany me to this place, and he has brought with him, by my advice and consent, three other persons, to wit., Benjamin Love, the interpreter, who interpreted the treaty, and every public talk held with the nation, pending the making of the treaty, James A. Perry, a very intelligent and respectable half breed of the nation, and G. W. Long, connected with the nation by marriage; all of whom are here present, and will state such facts as came to their knowledge at and since the treaty was made, by which I think you will be convinced of corrupt motives by Allen and his party, as no doubt they believed they would deceive you and the President, and obtain their wishes before I could know any thing of it.

I will only remark further, that since my arrival here, I have seen a long document signed by the Indians, which, I am informed, was handed to the President by John D. Terrill, and is acknowledged by the Indians who are here present, to have been drawn up by him, Terrill, and John L. Allen. Let it be remembered that this Terrill is the same man whom I had to remove from the encampment at the treaty ground, on account of his improper interference with the Indians, and in endeavoring to prevent them from signing the treaty, as will be shown by reference to the journal of the treaty. This document purports to be a memorial to the President, making a sort of journal of the proceedings at the treaty, by which I am represented as the most odious and corrupt character. As I do not intend to descend to the level of this man Terrill, by finding and proving matters originating with him, I will only remark that the whole production, so far as regards myself, is a tissue of falsehood and misrepresentation, and which is shown by the statement of the agent, Colonel Reynolds, and the others with him, who were present and saw every part of the transactions during the pendency of the treaty.

I have thought it a duty to give you this statement, that you may be able to properly appreciate the motives of those men, Allen and Terrill.

I have the honor to be,

Sir, your obedient servant,

JNO. COFFEE.

To the Hon. Secretary of War.

---

Washington City, *January* 21, 1833.

Sir: I have carefully read, and now return to you, a long memorial, dated the 22d November, 1832, signed by Levi Colbert, and other chiefs and warriors of the Chickasaw nation, and which is acknowledged to have been written or dictated by John D. Terrill and J. L. Allen.

I confess that the statement set forth in the document has created with me much surprise. When you met at the treaty ground, Major Eaton, the associate commissioner not being present, you requested me to attend all the conferences which you had with the Indians, and throughout I did attend, and became intimately acquainted with every thing that took place. I can, therefore, speak with much confidence, and hesitate not to say, that the statements contained in the memorial, so far as they reflect upon any improper, illiberal, or unjust course pursued by you, is wholly incorrect. Your patience and forbearance were of a remarkable kind, and your whole course was frank and conciliatory towards the Indians.

After the treaty was concluded, I recollect that Tishomingo, the oldest chief in the nation, accompanied by the warriors and chiefs, (except Levi Colbert, who was sick,) visited you at your quarters, and manifested great satisfaction at the result of the negotiation.

I remained on the ground paying off the annuity, four days after you had left for your home, and during the time, I heard no murmurs or complaints on the part of any one; all appeared to be satisfied with what had taken place.

The first intimation I had that any dissatisfaction was entertained by the Indians, was the accidental discovery, that a delegation was on its way to Washington City. If the object was a proper one, I concluded that, being their agent, I should have been apprized of it, and not being apprized, I at once concluded that something wrong was in progress, and accordingly so communicated my opinion to you. They must have managed with great secrecy, and I am confident without the knowledge or consent of the great body of the nation.

Agreeably to the suggestions you made to me, before I left the agency, I have brought with me to this city, G. W. Long, one of the clerks, who assisted me during the pendency of the treaty and payment of the annuity, Joseph A. Perry, one of the chiefs of the nation, and Benjamin Love, the interpreter, whose statements are herewith enclosed; and I take pleasure in saying that those men stand unimpeached for veracity.

With great respect,

Your obedient servant,

BENJAMIN REYNOLDS,

*Indian Agent.*

General JOHN COFFEE.

————

WASHINGTON CITY, *January* 21, 1833.

SIR: Since my arrival in this city, a paper bearing the character of, a memorial, from Levi Colbert, principal chief of the Chickasaw nation, to the President and Senate of the United States, has been shown me. The professed object of this paper is, to induce a belief on the part of the President, that General Coffee, during the negotiations of the late treaty, had been actuated by impure motives. I have carefully perused the document, and unhesitatingly declare *of my own knowledge* that it is from beginning to end an elaborate falsehood. I deem it unnecessary here to particularize its different misrepresentations. I was frequently with General Coffee during the time above alluded to, and here solemnly aver, that I never heard the first syllable drop from him, that even envy could construe into a want of liberality to the Chickasaws. But, on the contrary, all his actions proved incontrovertibly, that his motives were governed by a strict regard to justice, and what he considered to be the true interest of the Chickasaws. Acquainted as I am with the Chickasaws, I might take the paper and give the true reasons for each assertion contained in it. But it is considered unnecessary. If, however, for the vindication of General Coffee, it should become important, I pledge myself to satisfy the most incredulous of the motives by which those concerned have been actuated.

Respectfully yours, &c.,

G. W. LONG.

Colonel BENJAMIN REYNOLDS,

*Agent for the Chickasaws.*

————

WASHINGTON CITY, *January* 21, 1833.

SIR: Since my arrival in Washington, a paper, purporting to be a memorial from Levi Colbert and other chiefs of the Chickasaw nation, has been shown me; many assertions that tend to impeach the character of General Coffee are contained in that document. I am a native of the Chickasaw nation, and at the late treaty acted as interpreter, and was present at every conference that took place between General Coffee and the nation.

General Coffee's course uniformly was frank and friendly; during the time, I heard no complaint against him from any of the Chickasaw people.

I and other half-breeds complained, not against General Coffee, but against those who would not concede to us a right to remain and possess our improvements if we wished to do so. My residence is within fifteen miles of the place at which the meeting is said to have taken place, for the purpose of objecting to General Coffee's treaty, and to present a new one.

I never heard of any such meeting; and feel satisfied that it was not known to the nation at large, and that it is really the acts and doings of a few persons.

I am, respectfully, &c.,
BENJAMIN LOVE.

To Col. Benj. Reynolds,
*Agent to the Chickasaws.*

———

Washington City, January 21, 1833.

Sir: Since my arrival in this place, a paper purporting to be a memorial from Levi Colbert and other chiefs of the Chickasaws has been shown me. From a careful examination of the document, I am warranted in the conviction that it is the offspring of disappointment. Its assertions I know to be incorrect. It is true there was some disaffection to the terms of the treaty, though not owing to any act of General Coffee's, but principally and chiefly to the obstinacy of the chiefs towards the half-breeds, in not allowing to those persons who wished to remain, a home. I am a native Chickasaw, and belong to that district governed by the king. I was at his house at the time that this meeting convened for the purpose of objecting to General Coffee's treaty from taking place, and the king was at home, and told me nothing of this meeting. If his signature is attached to any instrument of writing brought to this place, I am confident that it was attached without his knowledge. I further state, that not one present out of each hundred of my nation ever heard of this meeting.

Respectfully, &c.,
J. H. PERRY.

To Col. Benj. Reynolds,
*Agent to the Chickasaws.*

———

Washington City, January 21, 1833.

Sir: Agreeably to the authority contained in your note of the 14th instant, I have conferred with the Chickasaw delegation of Indians, on the subject of altering the provisions of a treaty recently concluded with them, and which is now before the Senate for consideration. In consequence of a memorial communicated from the War Department, signed by a number of the Chickasaws, which contained charges against General Coffee, and expressed their want of confidence in him, he early withdrew himself from the conference.

An essential alteration which the Indians wish to have made is, that the funds arising from a sale of their lands, instead of remaining in the hands and under the control of the Government, may be placed at their own disposal. This seems to be a questionable course of policy, the tendency of which may be, to throw the Indians upon the Government for support and protection, if the funds to be created for their use, may, before they obtain a home, be wasted through any improvident management.

I have forborne to enter into any thing with them in the shape of a treaty stipulation, inasmuch as it does not appear that they are clothed by their nation with powers to act. Even supposing their power of attorney to be genuine, and to be properly signed, and strong reasons exist to suppose the reverse, there is not adequate authority contained in it. It is not the act of the whole nation, being signed by the king and ten of the chiefs only. It delegates the right of making a new treaty to seven persons, and says, "the Chickasaw nation gives and establishes, in the above named persons, UNITED, all the necessary POWERS PLENIPOTENTIARY, to negotiate, conclude and sign, such new treaty as, in their UNDIVIDED discretion, will be satisfactory to the Government, and substantially within our treaty of this date."

You will perceive that it is a joint commission, and contains authority for the persons named to act for the nation; but that their acts shall be binding, in the event only, that they are the "UNITED, UNDIVIDED" doings of the whole. One of them, an old and highly esteemed chief (*Tish o-mingo*), not being present, it is obvious that no arrangement can take place within the letter of the authority under which they claim to act.

I have deemed it proper, therefore, to refer the matter back for your consideration, that further conferences with them may cease, or such other course be pursued, as the President and yourself may consider advisable and proper.

Very respectfully,

J. H. EATON.

LEWIS CASS, Esq.,
*Secretary of War.*

*Three o'clock, P.M.*

P. S. A letter just received from the delegation expresses a wish to proceed with the negotiation. I shall defer making any answer until I hear from you. General Coffee promises to make to you a separate communication.

J. H. E.

---

LEVI COLBERT'S, CHICKASAW NATION.

The Chickasaw nation sends to the President and Senate of the United States, Colonel George Colbert, Tish-o-mingo, Pitman Colbert, Ishtamelueta, John L. Allen, John D. Terrill, and John A. Bynum, and send by them two copies each of their treaty and memorial of this date, with full instructions, should it become necessary, to form a new treaty; and the Chickasaw nation hereby gives and establishes, in the above named persons united, all the necessary powers plenipotentiary to negotiate, conclude, and sign such new treaty as, in their undivided discretion, will be satisfactory to the Government, and substantially within our treaty of this date. All things necessary to be done in relation to this matter, by these persons, the whole Chickasaw nation hereby authorize and confirm for ever. In testimony of which, this nation, by the king, mingoes, and head-men thereof, have hereunto signed their names and affixed their seals, on the twenty-second day of November, eighteen hundred and thirty-two, in the presence of the following witnesses.

| | |
|---|---|
| HOTAPA, *King*, | [L. S.] |
| LEVI COLBERT, | his ✕ mark. |
| WILLIAM McGILVRAY, | his ✕ mark. |
| ISAAC ALBERTSON, | his ✕ mark. |
| PISH-TA-LA-TUBBE, | his ✕ mark. |
| IM-MA-LAO-LO-TUBBE, | his ✕ mark. |
| TOM CHICA, | his ✕ mark. |

AH-TO-KA-WOH,
CO-CHUBBE,                        his × mark.
JAMES COLBERT,            his × mark.
DOUGHERTY COLBERT,
    *Secretary of the Nation.*
ALEXANDER COLBERT,
WM. H. ALLEN, *of Mississippi.*

A true copy from the original.

                                    G. W. LONG.

---

FORT MITCHELL, *January* 21, 1833.

SIR: William McGilvery, one of the Creek chiefs who negotiated the treaty of March last with the Government, is one of the chiefs entitled to a section of land. Mr. McGilvery has two improvements upon tolerable land, and which cannot be included in his reserve, unless he can be allowed to take his in two half sections. He has two children, and wishes each to have a moiety of his reserve; and, therefore, submits to his father, the President, whether he will feel authorized, and the disposition to allow him the favor he solicits.

                We are, sir, yours &c.,
                        ENOCH PARSONS,
                        B. S. PARSONS.

Hon. LEWIS CASS,
    *Secretary of War.*

---

MARSHAL'S OFFICE, SOUTHERN DISTRICT ALA.,
                    *Mobile, January* 22, 1833.

SIR: I have been advised, from the Office of Indian Affairs, that you had directed the Second Auditor to settle my account for removing intruders from the Creek lands, and that a requisition in my favor for $712 67, was made and forwarded to the Treasury on the 27th December last, and, as yet, I have received nothing more from it. Your early attention to having me reimbursed, for money advanced by me, is very respectfully solicited, by
            Your obedient, humble servant,
                    ROBERT L. CRAWFORD.

Hon. LEWIS CASS,
    *Secretary of War.*

---

DETROIT, *January* 24, 1833.

SIR: In pursuance of the instructions contained in your letter of the 11th September, 1832, I proceeded to Green Bay, for the purpose of procuring, if practicable, the assent of the Menomonies to the change proposed by the Senate of the United States, at the last session, in their ratification of the treaty concluded with them, (the Menomonies,) at Washington, in February, 1831.

From the difficulty attending the navigation of our lakes, in the fall of the year, I did not reach Green Bay until the 20th of October. After per-

forming the duty assigned, it was found impossible to return to Detroit, otherwise than by land, through the Indian country. A report of my pro·ceedings could not, therefore, be made by the commencement of the present session of Congress.

To the full and minute journal kept by my secretary, which is enclosed, I must refer for all that occurred. The result of my labors will be found in the agreement entered into with the Menomonies; and also with the several tribes of New York Indians, which is herewith transmitted. By which, it will appear that an arrangement has been effected, satisfactory to them, and just to the Government.

On examining the resolution of the Senate of the United States contained in your instructions, and finding that the stipulation proposed therein contemplated the running of a new line to commence at a point on Fox river, one mile above the Grand Chute, (which is *along the shore* of Fox river, about twenty miles above the old mill-dam,) I anticipated an objection on the part of the Menomonies, and that they would not consent to the change proposed.

On meeting them in council, I found that my apprehensions were well founded. No consideration could induce them to assent to it. After asserting at every meeting that they would do nothing to please the New York Indians; that they had no right either to ask or expect any thing at their hands. The reasons particularly assigned for dissenting to this proposed change, were in substance these: That a part of the Menomonies lived above and part below the Grand Chute, and as far down as Menomonie river, they were constantly passing up and down Fox river in their boats; that a portage had to be made from the foot of the Grand Kakalin, near which is the house and confirmed claim of their trader, Augustus Grignon, to the Grand Chute; that this was their own trading ground, and they never would give it up; that they were urged, when at Washington, to cede to the United States the land between these two points, and would not; that, by the treaty, the United States are to erect a grist and saw-mill on Fox river for them; and the Grand Chute is the only place reserved to them, at which a mill can be erected on Fox river, and this is the spot at which it has been understood the mill would be put up; and that, as the New York Indians had, last winter, at Washington, only asked to extend their line from the old mill-dam up Fox river, as far as the lower line of Grignon's farm, (being upwards of nine miles along the margin of the river,) they should not now ask to come ten miles and a half further up, thereby depriving the Menominies of their portage and trading ground, of the advantages of a mill, and of ground peculiarly dear to them, which they always passed over in visiting the Little and Big Butte des Morts, and the upper trading post. All which will particularly appear, as expressed by themselves, on reference to the accompanying journal. (See pages 7 to 20 inclusive.)

Having thus failed in the first efforts which I was directed to make, viz: to procure, if possible, the unconditional assent of the Menominie chiefs to the treaty, as conditionally ratified by the Senate, without which it could not be binding on them, the next act, in compliance with your instructions, was, to endeavor to procure their assent to the best practicable terms short of those proposed by the Senate. After much pains and exertion, as will be seen by reference to the journal, (page 20 to 28 inclusive,) the Menominies consented to this proposition; viz: to cede the land along Fox river, from the old mill dam to the lower line of Grignon's farm, at the Grand Kakalin, and extending thence on a line parallel with the present south-west line of the tract of 500,000 acres, set apart by the treaty for the New York Indians, so far as to include 200,000 acres, in exchange for an equal quantity of land on the northeastern side of the tract.

It has been ascertained, by actual survey, that from the old mill dam, along the margin of the river, to the lower line of Grignon's farm, the distance is nine miles, twenty-four chains, and fifty links; the perpendicular breadth of the strip of land between parallel lines northwest and southeast, passing through these two points, would be equal to about eight and three-fourth miles. By running back forty miles, which is the extent of the southwest line of the 500,000 acres, this breadth of eight and three-fourth miles would include a tract of 224,000 acres.

It will be recollected, that, at Washington, in January, 1832, the tract thus described was that asked by Daniel Bread, the deputy representing the Six Nations of New York Indians; and because the Government could not grant it to him, as it belonged not to them, but to the Menominies, whose assent could not then be obtained, the compromise or adjustment of all existing difficulties was, on this account alone, defeated.

In pursuing my instructions, the next step was, to ascertain whether the New York Indians would signify their acceptance of the modifications required by the Menominies. All their chiefs and head men were accordingly assembled, and the proposition submitted to them. Owing, as is believed, to the conduct and misrepresentations of an interested individual, they were made to say, that they would not accept this just and liberal offer. The management taken of these Indians, the attempts to keep them from attending the council, and the means resorted to for accomplishing the rejection of the proposition submitted, are all set forth in the journal. (See pages 29 to 43 inclusive.) Very soon thereafter, many of these Indians were convinced of their folly, and voluntarily signed a paper, agreeing to accept of the modifications proposed by the Menominies. (See pages 44–5.)

This was followed by the suggestion, that if the whole of them could be brought together in council, a final arrangement might probably be made of the whole affair. They were, consequently, notified to attend at the council room, and assembled accordingly. A new proposition was now made *by them*. Mr. Williams, on their behalf, stated, that this was the last and final proposition of the New York Indians, and if it should be acceded to by the Menominies, they would agree to end all matters in dispute, and that the treaty should be ratified by the Senate of the United States. (See pages 49 to 52, inclusive, of the journal.) This proposition being repeated and explained to all of them, and assented to, as well understood, was then submitted to the Menominies, and they having signified their acceptance of it, an agreement for each was drawn up, signed, and executed, (see pages 52 to 54,) which are forwarded herewith to you.

After all the labor bestowed, the result is this, that the only modification of the proposition, contained in the resolution of the Senate of the United States, is this: that the Menominies are permitted, by the voluntary offer of the New York Indians, to retain the front on Fox river, and the land for three miles back, from the Little Rapid Croche up to and above the Grand Chute, being a distance of about eleven miles. I have since examined this land, in passing up Fox river; the soil is generally poor, the land considerably broken, and, for agricultural purposes, of but little value. As, on the land now secured to the New York Indians, they have a sufficiency of water power for mills, and hydraulic purposes generally, they do not need the fall at the Grand Chute; and, if secured to them, it is not probable that *they* would ever use it, being so far distant from the best lands, where their farms will be made.

Attached to the treaty is a draft, with the necessary explanations on its face, exhibiting the tract of 500,000 acres set apart by the treaty for these New York Indians; the change contemplated by the resolution of the Senate, and the modifications of the same now made by consent of the parties.

Hoping, therefore, that what has been done will meet your approbation, and be approved by the President and Senate of the United States,

I have the honor to be,<br>With great regard,<br>Your obedient servant,<br>G. B. PORTER.

To the Hon. LEWIS CASS, *Secretary of War.*

----

*Journal of George B. Porter, Governor of the Territory of Michigan, and superintendent of Indian affairs, on his visit to Green Bay, in pursuance of a letter of instructions from the honorable Lewis Cass, Secretary of War, dated 11th September, 1832.*

On the receipt of said letter of instructions, the necessary arrangements were made for proceeding to Green Bay by the first good vessel. Edmund A. Brush, esq., of the Indian department at this place, was requested to accompany me as secretary, under the belief that his services were really necessary. A knowledge of the subject and the experience of the past winter, left no room for doubting the propriety of having an assistant in the labors which would devolve upon me. He consented to serve.

Owing to contrary winds, the " Mariner," Captain Johnson, in which we had agreed to take passage, did not reach Detroit until the ninth of October. In consequence of ill health, Mr. Brush could not leave home; and thus I was deprived of all the advantages anticipated from his great experience, ability, and talents. I then employed Captain Joshua Boyer, as secretary; and the vessel having got ready for sailing on the subsequent day, we left Detroit for Green Bay.

I have examined the following journal of our proceedings, kept by him during our absence, and certify it to be correct.

G. B. PORTER.

DETROIT, *December* 10, 1832.

----

*Wednesday, October* 10, 1832, *M.*—Left Detroit in the " Mariner," Capt. Johnson, for Green Bay.

*Thursday morning, October* 11.—Run aground in the rapids of St. Clair, near Fort Gratiot, at 5 o'clock, A. M. After many hours spent in ineffectual attempts to get the vessel off, and the wind having changed, so as to render it impossible to get away, the Governor went on shore, and employed John Reily, a half-breed Indian, to proceed to Detroit, and bring any communications from the War Department which had reached there since his departure, being anxious to receive letters relative to the pay of the Menomonie warriors, the arms purchased for them, &c., which were daily expected; for which service he paid him twenty-five dollars.

In the evening of this day the vessel got afloat; but the wind being ahead, remained at anchor in the rapids.

*Friday, October* 12.—With a light breeze, overcame the rapids, and entered Lake Huron; lay at anchor until next morning.

*Saturday, October* 13.—At six o'clock, A. M., received from Detroit the papers sent for; wind ahead; remained at anchor. At five o'clock, P. M., wind more favorable, and weighed anchor; made Saginau bay during the night; but owing to a violent gale put back, and at daylight found ourselves in the St. Clair river, below Fort Gratiot.

*Sunday, October* 14.—Remained at anchor in the rapids of St. Clair.

*Monday, October* 15.—Weighed anchor; once more overcame the rapids, and went ahead.

*Tuesday, October* 16.—Made Michilimackinac; wind ahead; and remained at anchor during the night.

*Wednesday, October* 17.—Wind ahead; remained at Mackinac; visited the Indian agency in the charge of George Johnson, sub-agent; examined the state of the buildings, particularly as an appropriation had been asked for repairing them; visited the missionary school, fort, &c.

*Thursday, October* 18.—At one o'clock, A. M., weighed anchor, and set sail for Green Bay; during the night anchored in the mouth of the bay.

*Friday, October* 19.—Wind ahead, and made but little way.

*Saturday, October* 20.—About the middle of the day neared the fort, but for want of wind could not enter the mouth of Fox river; went ashore in a boat, and took lodgings at the public house of John P. Arndt, esq.

*Sunday, October* 21.—Went up in the afternoon to the house of the Indian agent, Colonel Boyd, about four miles distant; about which the Menomonie Indians had their encampment.

The chiefs and head-men, on learning that their father (the Governor) had arrived, insisted on seeing him, and were introduced to him by Colonel Boyd, in the council room. Those of them who had been at Washington in 1831, immediately recognized him, and all expressed much satisfaction. In answer to their various inquiries and complaints of the delay which had taken place, that they were tired of waiting, &c., the Governor informed them this was not the proper day for doing business; that this was the day set apart for worshipping the Great Spirit; but that, to-morrow, he would meet them in the council room, and explain every thing to them, and tell them all their great father, the President of the United States, wished them to do. He explained to them the cause of delay, and fixed on ten o'clock the next morning for meeting them in council. They requested that their father would bring an interpreter with him who understood the Menomonie language; that, heretofore, they had got into great trouble, in consequence of the interpreter not fully understanding *their* language; that the interpreter regularly employed at the agency (Mr. Prickett then present) was a good man, meant to do every thing rightly; that he understood the Chippewa language, well, and enough of the Menomonie to answer the common purpose of giving them their provisions, and otherwise attending to their wants; but they must have for this important business an interpreter who understood the Menomonie language well. To this, the Governor answered, tnat he had made himself acquainted with all that had been done about this business from the beginning; and, to guard against any mistake or misunderstanding in this council, he had employed Charles A. Grignon as interpreter, who understood their language very well, and whose character was unimpeachable. With this they were greatly pleased, and then retired.

*Monday, October 22.*—At the agency house at Green Bay. Present, his excellency G. B. Porter, Governor; Charles A. Grignon, interpreter; Col. George Boyd, Indian agent; Richard Pricket, interpreter; and a large concourse of citizens.

The chiefs and head-men of the Monomonies being introduced, the governor arose and addressed them at great length: explained to them the several provisions of the treaty which they had entered into with their great father, the President of the United States; expatiated upon the benefits secured to them by it; and stated the causes which had operated to prevent the ratification of it by the Senate of the United States. That the New York Indians had, last winter, sent on a deputation to Washington City to oppose the treaty. That knowing the great importance to all concerned of having an end put to the unfortunate controversy, which had so long been carried on, their great father sent for him, (the governor) and instructed him to meet the deputations from the different tribes, and endeavor to effect an arrangement which would be satisfactory to them and just to the Government. That he proceeded to Washington accordingly, and he would now explain to them, minutely and fully, all that had been done. He then referred to his report made to the Secretary of War, on the 3d day of February, 1832, and recapitulated the several propositions therein contained, and what the New York Indians had at last said they would agree to. That, after a satisfactory arrangement had been made with the Stockbridge, Munsee, and Brothertown tribes, by which they were to be located on the east side of Lake Winnebago, to be paid for their improvements, &c., &c.; the Six Nations and St. Regis tribe insisted upon an additional quantity of land, on the north side of Fox river, to the amount of at least 200,000 acres, to be laid off along the southwest line of the tract designated and set apart for the New York Indians in the late treaty, and *to extend up Fox river as far as the lower line of Grignon's farm.* That, in answer to this, he had informed them that the land thus described, between the old mill-dam and Grignon's line did not belong to the United States. That, by the treaty, it was reserved to the Menomonies; and hence he could not undertake to give it to them. That this did not satisfy them, and no arrangement was effected.

That he would here show them the final proposition drawn up by Samuel W. Beall, (who was now present listening to what he said,) and signed by Daniel Bread, at Washington, on the 14th January, 1832, in which it is stated, that " if the commissioners could guarantee an exchange of two hundred thousand acres, on the north side of this tract (five hundred thousand acres) for a like number to be added to the south side, the undersigned would agree to a settlement. But to effect this, the commissioners declare that they have no power." (The paper was exhibited to them.)

He wished that they might understand him perfectly. No final arrangement was made, because these New York Indians insisted upon having the land from the old mill-dam up to Grignon's lower line, and extending back along the southwest line of the 500,000 acres set apart for them by the treaty, so as to include 200,000 acres; in exchange for which they were willing to give up the like quantity on the northeast side of the tract. That as they, the Menomonies, were not present to give their assent to this, the Government of the United States would not undertake to grant it, as it belonged, not to them, but to the Menomonies.

That all attempts at negotiation having failed, the treaty, together with the objections made to its ratification, and all that had been done, were submitted to the Senate of the United States. That that honorable body had conditionally ratified the treaty, and he would here state to them the changes or alterations they had made. (The governor here read the resolution of the Senate, and on a large map placed before them, explained particularly the object and effect of it: Mr. Grignon, the interpreter, repeated it, until they all stated that they understood it perfectly well.) The governor then informed them that their great father, the President of the United States, had sent him here to obtain, if possible, their assent to these stipulations proposed by the Senate. That if they would consent the whole matter could be settled at once, and they would receive the benefits of the treaty; (upon which he again enlarged.) That until it was settled, they could get nothing. That he hoped they would take this into most serious consideration, and agree to give their unconditional assent to the treaty as ratified by the Senate. That he did not come here to advise them to do any thing that was wrong. That the advantages to accrue to them, if the treaty were ratified, would be so great, that he indulged the hope that they would consent to the proposed alteration. That they must not leave the council in ill humor, as some of them were about to do; but think well of all he had said, consult together, and give their answer to-morrow.

*Tuesday October 23d.*—At the agency house. Present his excellency G. B. Porter, Charles A. Grignon, interpreter; Colonel George Boyd, Indian agent; Richard Prickett, interpreter; and a great number of citizens.

The chiefs being introduced, the council was opened,

Grizzley Bear rose and said, that Osh-kosh, called the " Brave," or " The Claws," was their first chief, that he was not here; but his brother was here, fully authorized to act for him, and that he would speak; that all their other chiefs and principal men were here, and that if their father was ready to hear this young man he would speak. The young man thus referred to, was *Skee-o-ni-ni,* or *Little Brave.* He said, father, you say you are glad to see us; we also are pleased to see you; we have waited a great while to see you; and now, since you have come, we think we see in you, our great father, the President of the United States Many of our chiefs and principal men have seen our great father, and they believe he intends to do what is right for us and our people. We are a great way from him, and we hope you will say to him that we expect he will protect us and assist us; and we look to you, too, to protect us, and see that we are not wronged. When the first white man came to us, he said that we should not be wronged, and that they did not want to drive us away from our land; and as the white men who came with these New York Indians said, that they would not wrong us, if we would only let them sit down among us. It would be a long story to tell you all. Now, if we should go away, what would become of us? We hope, then, father, you will not let any one drive us away. No matter in what way it has been proposed to settle this old dispute, the New York Indians always opposed it. We ask you, therefore, father, to help us, so that we may get what we were to have by the treaty.

There is one thing that we would like to have done. There are some of these half-breeds who have been brought up among us, and live among us, and we wish them to have some of our land. We will let you know what we want for them hereafter. This man (Grizzley Bear) is our speaker; he will speak for us all. My grandfather was the first chief, and when he died, my father was the chief in his place; and, therefore, you see that I have a right to be considered a principal man. They had this man for their orator. He was born and brought up along side of them; and' he is our orator, as all our chiefs will inform you. He will now speak for us all. I have done.

Grizzley Bear prepared his pipe, and all smoked it. He remarked, father, this is our custom. We smoke to please the Great Spirit before we begin any important business like this. This is our war-chief's pipe. Now I will begin: Father, this man, who stands in the place of our first chief, has told you right; we are pleased to see you, and we think we see in you our great father, the President of the United States. We know all about this dispute, and what these New York Indians tried to do against us. But I need not go all over it. When Col. Stambaugh was here, and first talked to us about it, he said, your great father wants to see you. We thought we were going to settle, and agreed to go and see our great father. But we did not think that we were to give these New York Indians a right to make sugar on our land, and cut down our maple trees. When we were with our great father, the President, we told him that we would not allow these New York Indians any thing. But he said to us, my children, if you like me, you must let these New York Indians have a piece of your land, as much as will be necessary for them. We then began to make the bargain. We know what we agreed to. We sold (pointing to the map) all on this side of the river (the east side) and the lake, because the Pottawatamies had already sold a part of our land, on the same side, and got a heap of money and annuities, and we got none of it. We did not wish any more of our land sold by them, and we agreed to sell it ourselves, to our great father. Afterwards we gave away 500,000 acres for these New York Indians, and when they got us to agree to that, I told our great father, and every one about us heard it, that we would not give them a step more. First we offered to give a piece on the west side of Fox river, but not so big as it is now, (pointing to the 500,000 acres as laid down on the map.) But our great father then said, we should give more, and we agreed to do so. He said, my children, I ask you to grant a piece to the New York Indians, but I will pay you for it. We were then all satisfied, and we thought that the New York Indians there were all satisfied too. But they staid there to make objections. We don't know what they were. We don't like it, that they act so. Our great father said to us, now, my children, I am pleased that you have behaved so well. If these New York Indians will not accept of what you have agreed to give them, they shall not remain two days on your land. I will send them off. You have behaved very generously. You have given more than I expected you would have done.

Our father, Col. Boyd, tells us that he speaks to us with one mouth, that he has but one mouth and one heart. We say so too. We settle a matter in our hearts, and, as it is there, we all agree to it, and nothing else. Father, we have done as you have told us; we have all been together and consulted this morning; we all agree in what I tell you. It is bad enough that you have had to come so far; and bad enough that we have had to wait here, so that we cannot, for so long a time, get to our hunting ground. We are anxious to get away, and have, therefore, soon decided, and are all of one mind.

Father: You have Senators who think themselves great men. But they do not know one place from another, on this Fox river, or they never would ask us to do what is in the paper you read, and which was explained to us. They agree to make a thing such a way. We may be considered, by them, small. But we have our war chiefs; and we do, like your Senators, consult them all; and when we all agree on any thing, it cannot be made otherwise. Now I don't see why they refused what our war-chiefs offered. We were too generous—agreed to give them too much. But these New York Indians were not satisfied; and if we had given them half as much more, they would not have been satisfied. Our great father, the President, told us, when we sold to him all on the east side, you have all on the west side of Fox river. It is your own country and you can do with it as you please.

Now, father, I have told you what we agreed to give these New York Indians. We are not disposed to give them any more. I told our great father, the President, so. I cannot see their object in asking us to make this exchange. True it is, there is to be the like quantity given for it below. But if this land is good for them, it is good for us too.

Father: These New York Indians have behaved so badly, and opposed every thing that is right for so long a time, that we begin to hate them. They are dogs. They want to take our land from us without paying for it. They hunt on our land and kill our deer. Have they any right to do so? We are becoming angry, mad. Father, we have seen these New York Indians hunting on our land above the Grand Chute. They have killed a great many of our deer. They have been hunting all the way out to the Big river or river of the lake, (Wolf river.) Was this their agreement? No. They were to cultivate the land. This is what they wanted the land for, they said; not to hunt deer on.

Father: If they had fulfilled the first agreement as they ought to have done, complied with the provisions of it, we, perhaps, might have attempted to satisfy them. But they did not do so; and we dont know how to satisfy them.

Father: Our chief asked you to take care of us. In the name of all our people I tell you that we expect you will take care of us. We cannot do just whatever these New York Indians want. They are always wanting more.

Father: Here is this tract, we agreed to give them, on your map. I do not see why they should refuse it. Land is but land, nothing else. We are ignorant of the way you measure land. We do not know what you mean by the *acres* you speak of. What is it? Father, there is a house put up where they want this land, at the Grand Chute. So you see they made up their minds, before they went, to get the land by that house.

Father: You told us that these New York Indians said they bought a great deal of our land. I ask you, with what did they pay for it? We received nothing; nor did any of our people receive any thing of consequence. How then can they say they *bought* our land?

Father: You now understand me. We do not agree to the proposition made by the Senate. We cannot agree to it. And we ask you to tell all that we have said to our great father and the Senate, and to see that we are not wronged. We look to you to help us. Father, I am now done. If any of our chiefs wish to speak, they will do so.

*Ayahmatu:* Father, what this young man told you is true. My father was a chief. He was wise, and he had this man (Grizzley Bear) for his speaker. He was the orator. My father's name was Kahro. He was a chief. You see, therefore, father, that I am a principal man.

Father, all that our orator said is right. I approve of it all. These are my sentiments, and he spoke for all of us. The Great Spirit knows, and we call him to witness, that we all consulted together, and we came to the conclusion he has told you.

Father, we, your children, do not look well; we are ragged; and we have no good clothes. But we are all the principal men of the nation. Every one of us is here, but one; and this young man is here in his place.

Father, there is no use in talking the same thing over again; this is not our custom; we consult together, and when we have agreed, one of us speaks; that is sufficient. This is our custom; I have now done.

*Shawenogeshig:* Father, you see your children before you, all these here are our principal men of the nation. I have nothing to say more than our speaker told you; we all approve what he said. Father, we stand in need of clothes, and we have nothing to get them with; we have no money, and we have waited here so long to see you, that we have lost a great deal, which we would have had if we had gone out hunting, as we are accustomed to do.

Father, we have been expecting the annuity which was to be paid us for the land we ceded; we need it very much; we hoped it would come soon, but it did not come.

Father, I tell you this, we were looking anxiously; and every schooner we saw, we supposed brought our annuity money. Our children are in great want of clothes; they thought they would be supplied when a vessel would come here with our money; but all our thoughts are in vain.

Father, our families had nothing for a long time but potatoes to eat; we helped people to dig up potatoes, and got some of them. Now, father, we would like to grease our mouths with some meat.

*Chenomabeemee:* Father, I have something to say to you, and I did not know whether to say it now, or wait until you would be done speaking. But, as you say I may speak, I will tell you, father, I want to tell you something about the saw-mills on our land. The object of our great father in granting mill privileges, we understand is, that we might derive some benefit from it; that by having lumber sawed we could get some of it to have houses made for ourselves.

Father, Mr. Childs first spoke to my uncle, who died lately; he asked him for the privilege to build a mill on his river, (Goose river,) and said if he would grant him this privilege his great father would give him permission to do it. He afterwards built the mill, and while he had it he gave us a present every year, as he had promised he would do; but since he gave his right to another, or sold it to another, we never got any thing. This I wanted to tell you the first opportunity; and I thought I could not have a better chance. I went to Mr. Arndt, the present owner of the mill, and spoke to him about it, and he said that several of his cattle had been killed, and that the loss he had sustained thereby was more than would pay for these last four years. Now, father, is that a good answer? The pay is coming to me, in right of my uncle; and am I to be wronged out of it because others may have done wrong? Now, father, look at all these new

5‡

buildings you see in this country; all the lumber for them was made at Arndt's mill. He must make a great deal of money; will get rich; should not he give us something? He could very well afford to do it: he promised to do so; and he does not do it. I hope, father, you will see that justice is done to us. We do not complain of his having the mill; we only complain that he does not pay us as he promised.

This, father, is all I have to say, I wished to wait until all about the treaty was over. But as you asked if any of us had any thing more to say, I thought I would tell you of this matter.

*Pewaitenau, or the Rain:* Father, I come from the Menomonie river; I am glad to see you here, and I have something to say; I hope you will listen to me. I have a story like what this (last) young man told you. I am a chief: I sprung from the family, and am related to this young man, (alluding to the Little Brave.) I was brought up at Menomonie river; my grandfather's home was there, and so was my father's, and so is mine.

Father, I do not like to have the Menomonie river dammed up; is this what our great father gave them permission to do? Did he direct this? I ask you, father, is it the words of our great father that our river should be dammed up the whole way across? We used to catch plenty of fish; it was our principal means of subsistence. Father, I think these men should be satisfied with cutting down all our best timber and sawing it up, without stopping the fish. I have nothing to say against the grant. Our chiefs gave their permission—sent it to their great father. But have these men the right to dam the river, so that the fish cannot go up the river? Father, did we ever sell all the fish? I have no recollection of doing this. Father, this man says he owns all the fish in that river, and all the cranberries. We never sold all these; did we? [Here Governor Porter asked who it was he referred to, he replied it was the Otter, Farnsworth.]

Father, all I wish is that the channel of the river may be left open, so that the fish can go up and down, and that we may catch them as heretofore, to subsist on. [Here they were asked if they had any thing more to say; and having all answered, no; that they were done, Governor Porter informed them, that he wished to confer with their father, (Colonel Boyd,) and would return in a few minutes.]

On his return, Grizzley Bear said he had something more to say, and being told to proceed, he said: Father, I wish you to listen to me, as this young man (Little Brave) told you, there are several of these half-breeds— a great many of them half Menomonies—they have been brought up with us, and we have a good feeling for them; we are favorable to them; they are part of our blood. I mentioned this when we were at Washington, and a provision, in their behalf, was to have been inserted in the treaty. It was understood so; we intended it; but some how it was omitted; they forgot to put it in. Now, father, I want you to write down where these people are each to have a tract a piece. It is below the Grand Butte, and all along down the river on the west side. I told this to our great father when I saw him at Washington, and when we were making the treaty.

Father, I hope you will have pity on us; our great father has pity on his Menomonie children. He said he would give us farmers to live among us, and to raise for us corn and all kinds of vegetables. Now, father, about these farmers I have something to say. We do not like the idea of having them among us; we would rather have the money; the valuable consideration to be paid to them would do us good. Father, these farmers will eat up all the flour, and give the bran to their hogs; we will never get any thing of what they raise. You must tell our great father about all this. He also wished us to have mills; and to make these, it will require millwrights and carpenters. And we are told, that with these mills the boards will be sawed to make houses for us. Now, father, we do not want these mills, nor any mechanics among us; we can build our own houses. Do you tell our great father to give us the money—*the cash*—and it will do us more good; or, if he chooses to give us more money than all these things will cost, we will take it; our people know what to do with money. Our great father has pity on us; we know this. But, father, I wish to ask you—is *he* a a merchant? He sent us goods. Why did he do this? We want him to send us the *pewter*, and then we can buy our blankets, and every thing we need. We can do this ourselves. Our great father promised to send us money, too, but we have never seen it yet. Our people are poor, as you see, and they should have some.

I told our great father, the President, that my village was at the Butte des Morts, and that these half-breeds were with us there; and I wished them to have their land there, and from thence down the river. My father lived and died there. I live there; and the principal chief lives there too,—the brother of this young man—*(Little Wave.)*

Father, you know we always take the advice of our great father; and we do what he tells us to do; we, therefore, expect he will have pity on us, and protect us. You know, when the Sacs and Foxes killed some of our people, our great father said we must not raise the tomahawk and kill them; and, although it was very hard to restrain our war chiefs, and young warriors, we obeyed; and afterwards, when our great father sent us word to go after these Sacs and Foxes, we went at once, and had our satisfaction—our revenge.

Then, father, at the time that three Menomonies were killed, near Prairie du Chien, by the Chippewas, we did not go after them; when we were told we must not, we did not mind it; and so, father, you will find that we will do. If any more of our people should be killed, we will do just as our father here (Col. Boyd) may tell us to do.

Now, father, we are done; and we are anxious to go home, after we hear what you have further to say to us. We understood all you said; and we cannot agree to give to these New York Indians what is proposed by the Senate.

Gov. Porter here addressed them as follows:

My children, I am pleased to find that your orator has so good a recollection of all that passed when he and your chiefs were at Washington, to make the treaty. I had nothing to do with making this treaty; and cannot inform you why it was, that the reservations you wished to make for your friends, the half-breeds, were not inserted. But that cannot now be helped; I have not any authority to grant them.

The complaints you make concerning the mill privilege on Goose river, and the stoppage of the fish in Menomonie river, will be attended to by your father, Col. Boyd. Mr. Arndt is here, and states that he has paid the annual sum agreed on for the mill privilege, up to the last year, and that this has not been paid, because you will not agree to whom it shall be paid, the person who theretofore received it being dead. He is ready and willing to pay it when this shall be determined. But these are little matters, that I did not come here to talk about. Col. Boyd will attend to all such complaints.  I will caution the New York Indians, and tell them that they must not hunt on your lands, or injure your sugar camps.  But you must not entertain bad feeling against them.  You are all my children, and I wish to see you all living in peace and harmony.  I hope you will again consider what I stated to you yesterday, and consent that the treaty shall be ratified, with the alterations proposed by the Senate.

Here Grizzley Bear rose in haste, as though much enraged, and declared that they never would consent to any such thing; that no one who had any knowledge of the *ground*, could ask them to do it; that a part of their people lived above, and a part below, the Grand Chute; that, in passing up and down the river with their canoes, they had to make a portage at the Grand Chute, and at the Big Kakalin; and their people were in the constant habit of passing along the shore from the latter place, where one of these traders lived, to the Big Chute, and above it; and they never would consent to give up this ground; and that if these Wabenockies intended to rob them of it, they would defend themselves.  They had their guns; had gone, at the request of their great father, to fight the Sacs and Foxes, and ——

He was here interrupted by the Governor, who commanded him to stop; that he must not get out of humor, nor talk in this way; that he must listen patiently until he would hear all he had to say.

He then proceeded.

I am well aware of your conduct.  Your great father has heard with pleasure what his Menomonie warriors have done; and I have to tell you, that they will not go unrewarded.  Major Forsyth, the paymaster of the United States army, is now here, prepared to pay them in specie; and I have instructed your father, Col. Boyd, to give them the guns which they used during the campaign.  [This was received with great good feeling.]  But, remember, these guns are to *hunt* with, not to fight with, unless your great father so directs.  You see, then, how good your great father is to you.  You must not be obstinate.  When you tell me that you do not want farmers, nor mills, among you, and all this, I can very easily perceive that there have been " bad birds flying about your heads."  Your great father knows better than you do what will be for your good; and we will not send among you such millers and farmers as you describe; we will give you honest men. That you need money, as you state, I have no doubt; and I will tell you how you will get it.  You must listen to me.  I hope the words that I speak will go into your ears, and never come out again.  I have come a great distance to see you.  Your great father has sent me here to give you good advice; and you must give me your attention.  Until this treaty be ratified, you cannot expect to receive any benefit from the several provisions contained in it.  The Senate of the United States have refused to ratify it, as it was originally made.  All attempts at compromise or negotiation have hitherto failed.  If you will not assent to the several stipulations contained in this resolution of the Senate, which I understand you distinctly to say you will not, nor consent to any thing which will enable us to effect an arrangement, the whole treaty must fall to the ground; and what then will be your situation?  I beg you to reflect on this.

I wish you to consult together once more, and let me know what you will agree to do.  I do not ask you to do any thing to please these New York Indians: it is for your own good as well as theirs, that your great father is solicitous that this perplexing affair should be brought to a conclusion.  When at Washington, last winter, I stated to Daniel Bread and the other deputies there present, that I had no doubt but that you would agree to give up the land along Fox river, from the old mill-dam to the lower line of Grignon's tract, at the Big Kakalin, and extending thence on a line parallel with the present southwest line of the tract of 500,000 acres set apart by the treaty for these N. York Indians, so far as to include 200,000 acres, in exchange for an equal quantity of land on the northeastern side of the tract. (Here he explained it to them on the map.) But I could not undertake to guarantee this, as you were not present, and your decision for this reason could not be obtained. Your great father was of the same opinion; and at their request, he promised to recommend it to you to do so. This was all that these New York Indians finally asked, and because I could not, without your consent, grant it to them, the compromise was not effected. I now ask you whether you will agree to do this. I advise you to do it. Your father and friend, Colonel Boyd, is of opinion that you ought to do it. Should you consent to do it, I will transmit it as your proposition, for the consideration of the President and Senate of the United States. It will show that you are not obstinate, but willing to make a great sacrifice for the sake of peace. Besides this, it is reasonable to suppose that these New York Indians will assent to it. I will have them assembled, and should they signify their acceptance of your offer, an agreement can be entered into while I am here, which will insure the final ratification of the treaty at the next session of the Senate. You must be convinced that I would not advise you to do this, if I thought it was wrong. I will now give you time to consult together. Be cool and deliberate. Think well of all I have said to you, and come back with a good speech in your mouth.

As you are so very anxious to get away to your wigwams and your hunting grounds, I will stay here this day, and meet you at four o'clock this afternoon to hear your answer.

*Same day*, 4 *o'clock, P. M.*

The council again assembled, and Governor Porter having informed them that he was prepared to hear what they had to say, Grizzley Bear said:

Father, it seems to take you a long time to do business—you white men. It is many years that this matter has been unsettled; we have waited a long time to see you; you have given us good reasons why you could not come sooner. You could not control the winds and the sea. You see now all the principal men of our nation here; we ask you to take care of our nation, to protect us, and to be good to our children after we are dead.

Father, it does not take us so long to do our business. It would take us a long time to talk this matter all over. We do not talk much—we are so brought up. The forest is our life, and, as you perceive, we do not like to part with it, or any of our land, as we said to you before.

But, father, you are sent here; we take you to be a good man, and that you would not advise us to any thing that is not for our good. Your words have gone into our ears. We hold you fast by the hand. We never refuse good advise from our father. We hope you will tell us the truth. We expect that what we have agreed to do will satisfy the Senate. You must understand me, father—there must be no mistake—you have been very particular in making us understand all you have said; that is all right. Now understand what we agree to do. We agree to give the land from the old mill-dam, up along the river to the Big Kakalin, where one of our traders lives, (Augustus Grignon,) at the lower line; and then to extend back, as you have said, (on a line parallel with the southwest line of the tract of land described in the treaty,) so far as will include 200,000 acres; and we are to receive an equal quantity of land on the northeastern side of the tract, on the Oconto creek.

But we have one exception to make: Augustus Grignon has sugar camps, at which he makes sugar; we do not know exactly where they are, so as to describe them to you. They are back from the river, on this land which we agree to give up. He must have the privilege, as heretofore, to make sugar at his camps. And there are some others of our friends, the traders, who have sugar camps back here, and it is our wish that they may not be interfered with either.

Now, my father, I hope it will be as we have told you. And it must be understood that these New York Indians shall not hunt on our lands. We forbid them to do so—have told them so. And besides this, it must be understood that the communication shall not be stopped where we have let them have the land. The road is open to all, and we must have the right to pass along as other people will do.

Father, you should know, too, that we granted a tract of land to one man, and the Secretary of War gave him permission to hold it. He has the privilege. This is to be excepted in what we grant to the New York Indians. There is a mill seat on it. It is Apple creek. [Here Governor Porter enquired the name of the person to whom it was granted. The answer was, to Charles A. Grignon.] Father, I do not see why this was not included in the treaty, because I told our great father, before we signed the treaty, that he (Charles A. Grignon) was to have this section of land; and it appears it was not included in the treaty. You must also tell the New York Indians that they must not spoil these sugar camps.

We hope that what we have agreed to do, will be satisfactory to our great father, the President, and to the Senate of the United States, and to you. And after this, if the New York Indians hunt upon our lands, we will break their guns. This is our custom; and besides this, which is the practice of all your red children, the New York Indians will now have notice of what we will do, if we catch them hunting on our lands. Father, you must not be angry with us for this. We are determined to do so, and we rely on you to protect us and help us along. These New York Indians are hard to be satisfied. They are made like you are. They have education, and pride themselves upon it. But, father, they have no ears; they are like dogs; when we give them a piece, they want more. They have no hearts or souls, and I told you before they behave so badly that we hate them. What we agree to do now is for our great father's sake, and for your sake—you advise us to do, and we never refuse good advice coming from our father. They have no right to ask or expect any thing from us. I have told you all, except this which I now tell you, that you may let them know it; that we now agree to fix a line, and if we find a house of the New York Indians over this line, we will pull it down and put it back on their ground. Father, you must not be angry with us. You see we have, in pursuance of your advice, agreed to do so much for peace, and having done this, we are determined on what I last told you.

Father, we told you before about the half-breeds; that what we agreed to give them ought to have been included in the treaty, and that we told our great father, and all of them around us, this before we signed the treaty. I need not say any thing more.

I am done.

*Pe wait-e-naw:* Father, we are all of the same opinion. Our great speaker has told you what we have agreed to do. We are now all done.

Governor Porter here remarked to them that he did not wish to hear any thing about the privileges of these sugar camps. That although it might be just enough that they should be reserved for their friends, yet it would be very wrong to insist upon these trifling privileges, if they should be objected to by the New York Indians. And that it would be making a great deal out of a trifle, if this should be assigned as the cause, or furnish an excuse for preventing an adjustment and settlement.

Upon this a consultation was had among the chiefs, after which

Grizzley Bear replied: We do not agree to grant any thing to please the New York Indians; we do not care whether they like this or not; we have done so much to please you, under the hope that it will be satisfactory to our great father and the Senate, and these little privileges we insist on.

Governor Porter here informed them that he would communicate all that they had agreed to do to their great father, that it might be laid before the Senate. That they must understand it distinctly, that, in receiving their proposition, the Government is not to be considered as pledged to agree to the terms proposed by them, but that in receiving their proposition he did it with a view to transmit it for the consideration of the President and the Senate. That he was further instructed to see the New York Indians, and ascertain whether they would accept the modifications now required by them (the Menomonies). That if the New York Indians would signify their acceptance of the proposition now made, he would draw up a general agreement to that effect, have it signed, and the whole matter might then be considered as settled and determined. That he had invited these New York Indians to a council to-morrow; and, after he had heard what they would say, he would communicate the result to them the Menomonies. That as they were anxious to get away, he would try and do this to-morrow afternoon.

Having thus received the proposition of the Menomonies, the next step was, to assemble the chiefs of the different tribes of New York Indians, to submit it to them, and ascertain whether they would signify their acceptance of it. Several of the chiefs and head men were in the neighbourhood. Samuel W. Beall had called at the Governor's lodgings, and stated that all had been notified to attend, and he would undertake to have them assembled at twelve o'clock to-morrow.

### Wednesday, *October* 24.

The Governor, interpreters, and many citizens, met at the council room at the appointed hour, and remained there until two o'clock.

As none of the New York Indians attended, it was thought best to give them notice in writing; and the more especially so, as it was alleged that, notwithstanding what had been said by Mr. Beall, Daniel Bread and some others had not been notified to attend, and that some advantage would be taken of it. The following notice was then prepared, and copies of it served on all the chiefs and head-men of the tribes therein stated, viz:

"To the chiefs and head-men of the Six Nations of New York Indians, of the St. Regis tribe, and also of the Stockbridge, Munsee, and Brothertown tribes.

"Having been directed by the Secretary of War to come on to this place, for the purpose of procuring, if practicable, the assent of the Menomonies to the proviso or resolution of the Senate, in the ratification of the treaty made with the Menomonies at Washington, in February 1831, which assent is required before the treaty can be obligatory upon them; and having used my best efforts with them to effect this object, but without success; and having next proceeded according to my instructions, which were, that if I failed in obtaining their assent to the proposed alteration made in the treaty by the Senate, that I should endeavor to procure their assent to the best practicable terms, short of those proposed by the Senate; and having received from the Menomonies their last and final proposition; I am now, according to my instructions, to ascertain whether the New York Indians will signify their acceptance of the modifications required by the Menomonies."

"I have, therefore, to request you to meet me at the office of the Indian agent, Colonel Boyd, as soon after you receive this notice as practicable. I hope no delay will take place. The sooner you can come the better. This day, at twelve o'clock, was assigned as the hour of our first meeting. As none of you have attended, we shall meet again to-morrow, at ten o'clock, of which you will all take notice.

"G. B. PORTER.

"Green Bay, *October* 24, 1832."

Thursday, *October* 25.

The chiefs and head men of the Six Nations of New York Indians, of the St. Regis tribe, and also of the Stockbridge, Munsee, and Brothertown tribes, assembled at the agency house.

Present, his excellency the Governor, Colonel Boyd, Indian agent, Charles A. Grignon and Richard Prickett, interpreters, and a large concourse of citizens. [By request of Mr. Beall the Menomonies were not invited.]

Mr. John W. Quinney made a neat address in the English language, welcoming their father to this country, and hoped the Great Spirit would aid and assist him in putting an end to this perplexing affair. That from what he had seen during the last winter, at Washington, he was convinced their father would do every thing in his power to effect an adjustment of their differences on fair and just principles, and, being now assembled, they were anxious to hear what proposition he had to make to them.

The Governor, after returning the compliment, &c., addressed them at length; stated what his instructions were, what he had said to the Menomonies, and all that had passed or occurred in the various councils held with them; that they had absolutely refused to give their assent to the treaty, as ratified by the Senate; and that he had finally prevailed on them to agree to the proposition which he would now submit to them, and which he urged them strenuously to accept. [As the proposition and the substance of all that was said, are contained in the following writing, prepared by the Governor, agreeably to the request therein stated, it is needless here to repeat it.]

On concluding his remarks, they observed, that they were not prepared now to reply, but they would retire and consult together, and would return and give their answer at four o'clock this afternoon. After withdrawing from the council room, John W. Quinney returned, and requested to be furnished, in writing, with a copy of the proposition made by the Menomonies, together with their father's advice, what he had said, &c. It was accordingly prepared, and is in the following words:

"At a meeting of the head men of the Six Nations of New York Indians, of the St. Regis tribe, and also of the Stockbridge, Munsee, and Brothertown tribes, at the agency house at Green Bay, on the invitation of George B. Porter, commissioner, specially appointed, &c., on the 25th day of October, 1832, the said George B. Porter having explained to them what his instructions were, viz: to procure, if practicable, the assent of the Menomonies to the proviso expressed by the Senate of the United States, in their resolution of the 25th June, 1832, to the ratification of the treaty made with the Menomonies, at Washington, in February, 1831; which assent is requisite, before the treaty can be obligatory upon them, (the Menomonies;) and should he, (the said George B. Porter,) fail in this object, he would then endeavor to procure their assent to the best practicable terms short of those proposed by the Senate, with a view to transmit it for the consideration of the President and Senate; and, in case this course should become necessary, that it would be very desirable that the New York Indians would also signify their acceptance of the modifications required by the Menomonies.

"Having also read to them the said resolution of the Senate, and the conditional ratification of the said treaty, predicated thereon; and that his best efforts had been used to procure the unconditional assent of the Menomonies to the treaty, as ratified by the Senate, but without success; that he had, after failing in this object, endeavored to procure the assent of the said Menomonies to the best practicable terms, short of those proposed by the Senate, with a view to transmit it for the consideration of the President and Senate; and, having explained to the council present, what'the Menomonies had agreed to do, and that he had, therefore, assembled the New York Indians, to ascertain whether they would accept the modifications required by the Menomonies, by doing which, the perplexing dispute which had so long existed to the prejudice of all concerned, and the prosperity of this section of country, would be brought to a conclusion; and, having then explained to them what had been done during the last winter at Washington City, with a view to end this difficulty, and what prevented a final adjustment of the question then; and having advised them to consent and agree to the proposition now made by the Menomonies; and the said Indians being about to adjourn, to consult and confer together preparatory to giving their answer, a request is made, that the proposition of the Menomonies be given to them in writing.  In compliance with which, the following is given as the substance of what the Menomonies will agree to do, as stated by them in open council, viz:

"That, for the purpose of ending this dispute, and that they may then receive the benefits of the several stipulations in the treaty, and under the advice of their great father, and their father now present among them, and in the hope and expectation that what they have agreed to do, will be satisfactory to their great father, the President, and the Senate of the United States, they agree to give up and cede the land along Fox river, from the old mill-dam to the lower line of Augustin Grignon's tract, at the Big Kakalin, and extending thence on a northwest line, or a line parallel with the present southwestern line of thej tract of 500,000 acres, set apart by the treaty for the New York Indians, so far as to include a tract of 200,000 acres, without including any of the confirmed private land claims; and in lieu of this, the New York Indians to give in exchange an equal quantity (200,000 acres) of land, on the northeastern side of the tract on the Oconto creek, being a part

6‡

of the same tract of 500,000 acres, as aforesaid. The only exception to the said grant of the 200,000 acres as aforesaid, between the old mill-dam and the lower line of Grignon's farm as aforesaid, and extending back for quantity, being stated by the Menomonies as follows: that they had given a tract of land with a mill seat on it, and the privilege of erecting a mill, to Charles C. Grignon, being on Apple creek, and that the Secretary of War gave him permission to hold it, and that this was to be excepted in what they agree to grant to the New York Indians. Further, that Augustin Grignon has sugar camps, at which he makes sugar, somewhere on the land that they agree to give up, and that he must have the privilege to make sugar as heretofore at his camps; and that it is their wish, that such of their traders as are accustomed to make sugar, may not be interfered with; and that the sugar trees might not be cut down.

"And further, that the New York Indians shall be prevented from hunting or building houses on their (the Menomonies') land; and that it must be understood, that the communication must not be stopped, but the roads through the lands open to all, and that they shall have a right to pass along, as other people will do.

"G. B. PORTER."

*Same day, at 4 o'clock, P. M.*

Present, his excellency the Governor, Colonel Boyd, the interpreters, and many citizens.

The Indians did not appear, agreeably to appointment. Soon afterwards, the following note, signed by John Matoxin, but drawn up in the handwriting of Samuel W. Beall, was delivered by one of their runners:

"GREEN BAY, *October* 25.

"The undersigned, in behalf of the chiefs and head-men of the New York Indians, in council assembled, would respectfully inform his excellency that, in consequence of the late hour (4 o'clock) at which his communication arrived, they will be unable to meet the appointment as made for this afternoon.

"Any hour in the morning most convenient to his excellency to meet, will be equally agreeable to the New York Indians.

"JOHN MATOXIN.

"His Excellency, G. B. PORTER, Esq."

To which the Governor returned by the bearer this answer:

"*October* 25, 1832.

"At the request of the New York Indians, I will agree to wave the meeting this afternoon; and I assign 9 o'clock to-morrow morning as the hour of meeting to receive their answer.

"G. B. PORTER.

"To the CHIEFS and PRINCIPAL MEN
  "*of the several tribes of the N. Y. Indians.*"

FRIDAY, *October* 26.

At 9 o'clock, A. M., agreeable to appointment, the Governor, Col. Boyd, the interpreters, and many citizens, attended, but no Indians appeared.

About 10 o'clock, Sampson Marquis, a Stockbridge Indian, appeared, and addressing himself to the Governor, in the English language, remarked that the rest of the Indians, who had met us in council yesterday, were at Mr. Beall's office; that he was drawing up a paper for them to sign, by which they refused to accept of the proposition made by the Menomonies; and as soon as it should be completed a committee or deputation would bring it to the council room. That Mr. Beall had told them not to meet again in council; but to let him advise them, and draw up in writing an answer to any proposition which might be made to them; that he, Sampson Marquis, and many more of their people, were dissatisfied with this mode of doing business; that their chiefs and head-men did not understand what Mr. Beall would write down; that he would write it his own way, and not as they wanted it; and that it was hard when all the Stockbridges, Brothertowns, and Munsees were perfectly satisfied with the propositions made to them last winter at Washington, and which was still within their power, that Mr. Beall should prevent them from coming to a settlement; that he was astonished at their people for being so blind, not only to their own interest, but to the motives of Mr. Beall's conduct; that the contract entered into long ago with Mr. Beall, was, to pay him six hundred dollars per year, for his services *so long as the dispute remained unsettled;* that this sum was principally paid to him out of their money; that the six nations paid little or none of it; and now, when they (the Stockbridges, &c.,) had got all they wanted, it was asked that they should pay to keep up a dispute to their great prejudice, and seriously affecting their true interests; that he thought it his duty to come and state these facts, and to ask their father, whether something could not be done to prevent Mr. Beall from interfering in their concerns.

About one o'clock, P. M., John W. Quinney, accompanied by some others, appeared in the council room, and presented a paper, of which the following is a copy:

"GREEN BAY, *October* 26, 1832.

"We, the undersigned chiefs and principal men of the several tribes of New York Indians, now resident in the vicinity of Green Bay, having received and considered the propositions of the Menomonie tribes, (as contained in the letter of your excellency of October 25,) to amend the modification of the Senate to the treaty of February, 1831, and being advised by your excellency to accede to said amendment of the Menomonies, beg leave respectfully, but explicitly, to state that we have neither power nor inclination to close with any terms other than those expressed in the aforesaid modification of the Senate.

"We cannot express the surprise we feel, that an obstruction should be offered from any quarter to prevent a settlement of the matter, as it stood upon the final and impartial action of the Senate of the United States; and we are mortified to find that, after all our sacrifices, we should again be called on by the officers of the Government to make further concessions.

"We intreat your excellency, as the general father and head of all the tribes of the northwest, to review the past history of this long and distressing contest; and if you can then find it in your heart to term us obstinate and unyielding, we have erred in attributing to you feelings towards us you do not possess.

"If, in the course of the few remarks we shall make to your excellency at this time, an expression should escape us which may be wounding to your ear, or unbecoming the red man, when addressing his father, our apology will be found in the necessity of asserting our rights respectfully but firmly, and in the feelings we must possess in our present unparalleled condition.

" In the course of the various negotiations regarding our claims in this Territory, we have constantly retreated and yielded up our rights when called upon by the Government, until this spirit of concession seems to have rendered us contemptible in the eyes of the Menomonies.

" How else can they now ask more of us?

" If a desire of peace, and an attachment to the Government of the United States, has exposed us to privations and losses, we should otherwise have avoided, it cannot, therefore, be supposed that we will now, or at any time, yield any thing to the perfidy of our Menomonie brethren.

" No good reason exists why they should not cheerfully have yielded to the will of the Senate. 'We believe that, to the band residing on Oconto, the tract in that vicinity is more valuable than the land on the south, and that they would gladly have closed with the offer of exchange if left free to express an opinion.

" There is no weight in the remark, that the proviso of the Senate, by granting to the Six Nations the course of the river from the mill dam to the Grand Chute, worked an injury to the mills or farms of the Menomonies.

" The water power at the outlet of Winnebago lake is great—is included in their tract, and would be as useful and available for the Menomonies as that at the Grand Chute. Besides, from the report of Col. Stambaugh, we are to believe that the Oconto, and the streams in its vicinity, abound with excellent mill seats. Equally unfounded is the consideration, that if the Six Nations possess the river above Grignon's line, to the Grand Chute, the Menomonies will have no privilege of encampment and portage. With what nation of the world, and with what Indian tribe, is the permission of temporary rest from the peaceable traveller withheld? And why does not the objection, if good, hold the more strongly, for the difference in distance between the Rapides des Peres and Grignon's line, now proposed to be allowed to the New York Indians?

" But upon the assumption that the modification was of real injury to the milling operations of the Menomonies, as intended by the treaty to be centred at the Grand Chute, would it not be preferable that, by a subsequent arrangement, the Government should select the Winnebago rapids, or some other water power for that purpose, instead of jeopardizing the welfare of both parties in opening the door for another contest more bitter and obdurate from duration?

" It is manifestly so impossible that the exceptions in the proposition of the Menomonies, in favor of their traders, and some of the French inhabitants of the country, should be acceded to, that we would not refer to them, but that the attention of your excellency may be called to the quarter from whence all our difficulties have sprung; and that you may personally attest the influence which this part of the white population exercise upon the movements of the Menomonies.

" From our knowledge of the easy means, by which the Government effectuates its plans with Indians generally, and from all which has met our notice during the present negotiation with the Menomonies, justice to ourselves requires us to express the decided belief that, if the same persevering efforts which were exerted in obtaining the assent of the Menomonies to the proposition now submitted to us, had been employed in procuring their unconditional concurrence in the modification of the Senate, your excellency would have accomplished what we are informed has been the main object of your mission. As it is, we have the consoling reflection that, whatever may be result of the present violation, and of the will and expressed intention of the Senate by the non-acceptance of the Menomonies; however injurious to the interests of the country and the rights of individuals, no dispassionate tribunal will attribute to us any portion of folly or obloquy which may be attached to the transaction.

" *Oneidas.*

" HENRY PAWLES,     his x mark.

" JOHN ANTHONY,     x

" NATHANIEL NEDDY,     x

" CORNELIUS STEVENS,     x

" *Seneca.*

" GEORGE JAMIESON,     x

" *St. Regis and Tuscaroras.*

" E. WILLIAMS,

" *Brothertown.*

" RANDAL ABNER,

" *Stockbridge.*

" JOHN METOXIN,

" JACOB CHECKTHANCON,

" ROB'T. KANKAPOT,     x

" JOHN W. QUINNEY,

" *Munsee,*

" CAPT. PORTER,     x

" Attest: S. W. BEALL.

" To his Excellency GEORGE B. PORTER, Esq."

Upon reading it, the Governor remarked that he had expected something like this; that their friend Sampson Marquis had been here some time before, and gave him to understand what they were doing; and why it was that since the adjournment of the meeting yesterday morning, they had not attended at the council room, nor given any answer to the proposition submitted. He then repeated what Sampson had stated—explained to them the interest which Beall had in keeping up this dispute; that he was to receive of them yearly, and every year six hundred dollars; and that if a settlement or adjustment of their difficulties took place, he would lose what, according to the opinion of all the citizens of the place was the present means of affording him a livelihood; that he (the Governor,) had come here as their father, entertaining for them the best feelings of kindness and good will, to hold a council with them; that, instead of meeting him in the council room, according to their appointment, and stating to him candidly and honestly what their views and wishes were; they had suffered this interested man, Beall, to draw up a paper which they did not fully understand; that they had signed their names to it, and now presented it; that it contained insinuations and falsehoods, which even the author of it ought to be ashamed of; that Col. Boyd, the Indian agent at this place, and twenty other individuals, many of whom were now present, had attended the councils, and witnessed every thing which had passed since the first meeting with the Menomonies on Monday last; and could attest that the representations made to them (the N. Y. Indians) were false, and without even the semblance of truth.

The Governor then turned to several passages in the paper, and on reading each, inquired if this were true; to which they answered that they could not say it was; that they had no knowledge of it; and some remarked that they did not know that such a thing was in the paper.  He then told them that this showed how improper it was to do business in this way; that they should return and bring their friends with them; he wished to hear from themselves what they had to say, and what their answer was; that if they would only think and act for themselves, he did not despair of settling the whole matter before he went home; that they now had an opportunity which might not again occur, and they should embrace it; that no exertions should be spared to bring about a settlement of the differences which existed; that he would wait in the council room until they could return with such of their friends as chose to accompany them; that should they refuse to meet him in council, they must, on reflection, perceive that such conduct would not place them in a very enviable light before the President and Senate of the United States.

Soon afterwards the chiefs and head-men of the Stockbridge, Munsee, and Brothertown tribes, returned, and wished to hear, as they expressed it, their father's advice.

The Governor repeated to them what he had previously stated; the great evils which had been experienced by all concerned in this unprofitable controversy; the opportunity there now was of settling it; the liberal offer which he had prevailed on the Menomonies to make, with the view to the final adjustment of all their difficulties; and that the New York Indians should seriously reflect before they came to a decision refusing to accede to the proposition now made to them; that if they refused to accept now (when the assent of the Menomonies had been obtained) of what their deputation last winter asked, and were obstinate and unyielding in their demands, they might find, when it was too late, that such a course of conduct would not advance their interests; that, as the tribes or bands now present were satisfied with the propositions made in regard to them, it did not, in his opinion, become them to hold back, but that they should at once come forward and express their opinion (if such was their belief, and from what he had heard he had no doubt it was) that the offer now made by the Menomonies was such that all the New York Indians should signify their acceptance of it; that the expression of this opinion on their part might have the effect of inducing Daniel Bread and the other principal men of the Six Nation to come into the measure, and thus end all further trouble, and enable them to sit down in peace and harmony.

After consultation, it was remarked by some of them that they were perfectly satisfied; that the offer made by the Menomonies was reasonable and fair, and they were convinced that it ought to be accepted by all the New York Indians; but they had been told that they must all go together, and that if the others held back, they could not agree to any thing; and, situated as they were, they did not know whether it would be right for them to sign any agreement.

The Governor here informed them that he had said all he could say, and they should use their pleasure.

They then consulted together, spoke to their father, Col. Boyd, and then stated that they had determined to show their willingness to have the matter settled, and would sign an agreement.  Upon which, as it was late in the day, and they were anxious to get away, a short agreement was drawn upon the back of the proposition of the Menomonies, as drawn out in writing and furnished by Governor Porter to the New York Indians yesterday, (see it on pages of this journal,) and it was signed. It is in the following words:

" For the purpose of settling and adjusting this long, protracted dispute, we hereby acknowledge that we will accept the modifications required by the Menomonies.

"Done at the agency house at Green Bay, this 26th day of October, in the year of our Lord one thousand eight hundred and thirty two.

" JOHN METOXIN,
" JACOB CHICKS,
" ROBERT KONKAPOT, his x mark.
" THOS. J. HENDRICK,
" AUSTIN QUINNEY,
" SAMPSON MARQUIS,
" CAPT. PORTER, his x mark.
" WILLIAM DICK,
" DANIEL DICK,
" ELKANAH DICK, his x mark.

" Signed, sealed, and delivered in the presence of us,
"GEORGE BOYD,
" U. S. Indian Agent.
" SAMUEL ABBOTT,
" JOSHUA BOYER, Secretary.
" HENRY S. BAIRD,
" CHARLES A. GRIGNON,
" A. J. IRWIN,
" EBEN CHILDS."

John W. Quinney having objected to signing the agreement thus worded, an additional instrument was drawn up to meet his wishes, and was signed by him, of which the following is a copy:

"I hereby signify my acceptance of the modifications required by the Menomonies, as set forth in their proposition within stated, with this exception, that I am of opinion that the reservations which they wish to make of the privilege of Charles A. Grignon, and of the sugar camps, ought not to be made. My opinion is, that the Menomonies have agreed to grant a sufficient quantity of good land, and suitable in its location, for the New York Indians, but that the land should be clear of these incumbrances.

" Done at the agency house at Green Bay, this 26th day of October, A. D. one thousand eight hundred and thirty-two.

"JNO. W. QUINNEY.

" Signed, sealed, and delivered in presence of us,
"GEORGE BOYD,
" U. S. Indian Agent.
" SAMUEL ABBOTT.
" JOSHUA BOYER, Secretary.
" HENRY S. BAIRD,
" CHARLES A. GRIGNON,
" EBEN CHILDS."

On preparing to withdraw from the council, they were advised by the Governor to see Daniel Bread, and the other chiefs and head-men representing the Six Nations; tell them what they had done, and inform them that on the morrow the Governor intended closing the council, being anxious to set out on his return to Detroit, that if they had any thing further to say, he would attend at the council room to-morrow to hear it. They then left the room.

It having been stated that it was possible that the head-men of the Six Nations would yet assent to the proposition of the Menomonies, if it were varied in certain particulars, the Governor sent for the Menomonies, who soon after entered the council room.

The Governor stated to them that he was sorry that he had come here under the belief that all this dispute could be settled, but that the New York Indians would not agree to the offer made, and that they particularly objected to the reservation made by them of the sugar camps, Grignon's privilege, &c.; and that he wished, for the sake of peace, that his Menomonie children would agree to give up these exceptions or reservations; and also consent, if it could not be otherwise settled, that the line for the additional 200,000 acres should set out at some point higher up Fox river, to be agreed on by the parties; that in case the Menomonies would now agree to have this dispute compromised on these principles, he would give them corn, presents, provisions, &c., (mentioning the amount of each.)

Grizzley Bear rose and said:

Father: You do not seem to know us; we do not change our minds as soon as this; we have already told you that when we have any thing to do, we consult together and decide, and when done, so it must be. We have also told you that we do not care any thing for the New York Indians; whether they are pleased or not, we will not do any thing for *them*. We would not take all the money our great father has, nor all the good things you have offered, to give the *New York Indians* any more of our land. You tell us that if we do not agree to do something now by which a settlement will be effected, the treaty will fall to the ground, and we will lose all the advantages secured to us by it. We say no matter, let it fall to the ground; we will not do any more; we are willing to do what is right. We take you and our father, Col. Boyd, by the hand, believing that in so doing we take our great father by the hand; but we know that our great father would not ask us, *for his sake*, to do more. What you want us to do is *for the New York Indians*, and we say no! we will do nothing more.

He here appeared very much enraged, and all of them rose to go out.

After something said to soothe their feelings, they retired, being then late at night; it being understood that an agreement for them to sign would be prepared in the course of the next day, and that when it should be completed and signed, they might return home.

SATURDAY MORNING, *October 27th.*

At the suggestion of some of the New York Indians, a notice in writing, of which the following is a copy, was given to all the chiefs and head men, viz:

"To the chiefs and principal men of the New York Indians as well of the Stockbridge, Munsee and Brothertown tribes, as of the Six Nations and St. Regis tribe.

"Previously to closing with the Menomonies, by obtaining their signatures to the agreement which I have drawn up, I think it right to invite you to meet me at the agency house, that you may have an opportunity once more of saying whether you will all accept the proposition made by the Menomonies, or whether you have any thing further to say or propose to me when assembled in council. It is Saturday, and I must close my labors here to-day. The sooner you can come to the agency house to meet me the better. The Menomonies are very impatient, and threaten to go home immediately.

"G. B. PORTER.
"*Saturday Morning, Oct. 27th*, 1832."

---

Between twelve and one o'clock all the chiefs and head-men of the New York Indians, as well of the Stockbridge, Munsee, and Brothertown tribes, as of the Six Nations and St. Regis tribe, attended in the council room.

Present—His excellency Governor Porter, Colonel Boyd, the interpreters and a large concourse of citizens.

Eleazer Williams, rose and said,

Father, to show you that we are willing to make a sacrifice for the sake of having this dispute settled, we have attended agreeably to your notice of this morning, and I am instructed by the New York Indians to make this, as their last and final proposition, viz: The New York Indians will agree to settle this controversy, on condition that they have granted to them in exchange for 200,000 acres on the northeastern side of the tract of 500,000 acres, described in the treaty, an equal quantity on the southwest side to be laid off as follows:

Beginning at the old mill-dam, and thence extending up Fox river to the Little Rapide Croche, thence running back from the river three miles, thence in the direction of the course of Fox river, keeping back three miles from the same until it shall intersect the first stream which empties into Fox river above the Grand Chute, and thence running on a line parallel with the southwest boundary line of the tract of 500,000 acres, described in the treaty; the necessary distance to include 200,000 acres.

To this Governor Porter answered, that it was needless to confer longer about it if these boundaries were insisted on. That in no event could the line extend farther up Fox river than where it would intersect a line running N. W., commencing one mile above the Grand Chute, which was the point mentioned in the resolution of the Senate, and which had been pointed out again and again to the Menomonies. That, as in this proposition it was agreed not to ask the *front* on Fox river higher up than the Little Rapide Croche, and that above this point the claim of the New York Indians was not to approach nearer to the Fox river than three miles, he supposed one of the strongest objections which the Menomonies had heretofore made would thereby be removed. Their portage ground and trading post would remain free to them. And that if the proposition now made was varied so that the line should not run higher up than where it would intersect a northwest line, commencing one mile above the Grand Chute, it was possible that the Menomonies could be induced to accept of it; and that he would use every exertion to get them to agree to it; that they (the New York Indians) should confer together, and determine whether they would thus modify their proposition. After a few moments, they agreed so to vary their proposal.

Daniel Bread then said, that his only remaining objection to entering into an agreement to this effect was the reservation of the sugar camps and the privilege of Charles A. Grignon. That if these were removed he would willingly enter into the agreement; upon being informed that the privilege

7‡

of Charles A. Grignon was approved by the Secretary of War, and that the Governor had no power to destroy it, Daniel Bread said he would not object to this, but he hoped that the Secretary of War would grant him a privilege elsewhere, in lieu of this. (And Mr. Grignon, being present, said he would release this, if a privilege were given to him, in such other place as he should select, on the lands described in the treaty, as ceded to the United States or reserved to the Menomonies.)   Daniel Bread still objected to the reservation of the sugar camps; and as Augustin Grignon was not present, nor in the vicinity, no arrangement could be made with him concerning it.

The Governor then said, "Well, now let me understand you; you say you will consent to enter into an agreement, to end all matters in dispute, and that the treaty shall be ratified accordingly by the Senate of the United States, on condition that the Menomonies will agree to cede, for the benefit of the New York Indians, along the southwestern boundary line of the present 500,000 acres, described in the first article of the treaty as set apart for the New York Indians, a tract of land bounded as follows:

"Beginning on the said treaty line at the old mill-dam on the Fox river; and thence extending up along the Fox river to the Little *Rapide croche;* from thence running a northwest course three miles; thence on a line running parallel with the several courses of Fox river and three miles distant from the river, until it will intersect a line running on a northwest course commencing at a point one mile above the Grand Chute; thence on a line running northwest so far as will be necessary to include, between the said last line and the line described as the southwestern boundary line of the 500,000 acres in the treaty aforesaid, the quantity of 200,000 acres, and thence running northeast until it will intersect the line forming the southwestern boundary line aforesaid; and from thence along the said line to the old mill-dam or place of beginning, containing 200,000 acres.   Excepting and reserving therefrom, the *privilege* of Charles A. Grignon, for erecting a mill on Apple creek, &c., as approved by the Department of War on the twenty-second day of April, 1831; and all confirmed private land claims on Fox river.   The lines of said tract of land so granted to be run and laid off without delay by a commissioner, to be appointed by the President of the U. States. And that in exchange for the above quantity of land equal to that which is added to the southwestern side shall be taken off from the northeastern side of said tract, described in that article on the Oconto creek, to be run, marked, and determined by the commissioner to be appointed by the President of the United States as aforesaid, so that the whole number of acres to be granted to the Six Nations and St. Regis tribe of Indians, shall not exceed the quantity of 500,000 acres."

To this ALL GAVE THEIR ASSENT.

This done, the Governor informed them they might now retire, and he would have the Menomonies brought into the council room, and see whether they could be persuaded to accept of this proposition; and that he would expect them (the New York Indians) to return to the council room in the course of an hour, when he would communicate the answer which the Menomonies should give.

At three o'clock, P. M., the Menomonie chiefs and head-men came into the council room and the Governor explained to them the proposition now made by the New York Indians, and urged them most earnestly and strenuously to accept of it; pointed out the many benefits which would accrue to them if the treaty were confirmed; that this proposition was a new one; that it left free for their use all the land for three miles back, along Fox river, from the Little Rapide Croche to the Grand Chute and above it; and that he advised them as their father and their friend to agree to it; that they had been waiting here for a long time; their patience was exhausted, and they wanted to go home, &c., &c., &c.

Grizzley Bear inquired very particularly, so as to understand thoroughly the proposal made; and after having it fully explained to them all on the map, they conferred together for a considerable time. He then wished to be distinctly informed whether the Governor would give them what he said he would, viz: presents and clothing to the amount of $1000; five hundred bushels of corn, ten barrels of pork and ten barrels of flour, &c., &c. This being answered in the affirmative,

Grizzley Bear said,

Father, I shake hands with you all; I hold you fast by the hand; listen, I am now about to speak for all our nation; I am talking to you, but still I think I am talking to my great father, with whom I had the pleasure of shaking hands when we were at Washington. When I spoke with our great father he did not ask us to do this. But as it cannot be settled otherwise, and as you have been sent here by our great father, we must take your advice. You are strong, we are weak; I am not talking to those New York Indians, but to you; representing, as you do, our great father, and I am willing to do what is thought right by him and you; I am willing to leave the whole matter to him, and do as you say.

I hope our great father will have pity on us; when I shook hands with him I thought I would be happy. He told me we would be made comfortable; you have told us all, and how it is that we have been so long kept out of the money and every thing else. We leave it all to our great father; only put an end to it now, and let us go home.

I wish you would not intrude on our traders; they take care of us, and when they have a right, they should be permitted to hold it. (He here shook hands with all present.)

Now, father, I leave it altogether to my great father and you; if you think it right, we are perfectly willing to do so, as you explained it. We wish to get through it to-day; to-morrow is your Sunday, and if it is not finished to-night, we will be kept two days longer here.

We do not want to speak more about it to-day.

Father, I have a sore throat. Our father here, (Col. Boyd,) gave me something for it. I want you to do so too. You understand me. I am dry. And all our people here want to grease their mouths.

Governor Porter here remarked to them that it was now late in the day, and it would be impossible to draw up the writing for them to sign, before night came, and that they would not like to be called on in the night to sign it.

The reply was, no matter. Make it ready. We must sign it to night. We know all about it; and you will make it right. They then withdrew.

The New York Indians were then called in, and their part of the agreement being made ready, all present signed it. The Governor asked where Mr. Williams was, and why he was not present. The answer given by the others was, that, as to-morrow would be *Sunday*, he had to go home this afternoon; that he could not wait; that he had said, if the Menomonies agreed to the proposition made, he was perfectly satisfied that they should all sign it, and it was of no consequence whether he signed it or not. The

Governor then remarked, that if Mr. Williams came in again from his residence on Monday, he could call on him and put his name to the agreement;
and he wished them to tell him so.  When about to take leave, the Governor
stated to them all, that he was desirous of bringing them and the Menomonies together, and making peace among them; and for this purpose, he
invited them to dine with him on Monday.  This invitation being accepted,
they all withdrew.

Soon afterwards, the Menomonies were called into the council room, and
their agreement being fully explained to them, they all signed it, expressing
great satisfaction at the prospect now presented of soon getting away to their
homes and their hunting grounds.  They received and accepted the like
invitation for dinner on Monday, and then withdrew.

And thus closed the business of a busy week, after 10 o'clock on Saturday night.

*Monday, October* 29.—The chiefs and head-men of the Menomonie
nation, and of the several tribes of New York Indians dined with the Governor at the public house of John P. Arndt; much good feeling existed;
they shook hands and parted as friends, determining to forget and forgive
all that had passed, and to live hereafter in peace and harmony with each
other.

*Tuesday, October* 30.—This day was spent in delivering to the Menomonies the clothing, corn, pork, flour, &c., according to the agreement.

*Wednesday, October* 31.—The Governor settled his accounts, paid off
bills, and made arrangements for leaving Green Bay.

There being no vessel in port, nor any one expected, the hope of returning to Detroit by water had to be abandoned, and preparations were made
for a journey on horseback; visiting on the route the Indian agencies, at
Fort Winnebago, Chicago, and St. Joseph.

*Thursday, November* 1.—Left Green Bay for Fort Winnebago on
horseback, in company with John P. Arndt and Alexander J. Erwin, esqrs.;
crossed the Fox river, at Dickinson's ferry, about six miles above the fort:
passed up the west side, examining the country, and particularly the old
mill-dam, Little Kakalin, Rapide Croche, Big Kakalin, and as high up as
the Little Chute; returned to, and remained over night, at Augustin Grignon's.

*Friday, November* 2.—Crossed over Fox river to the east side, and viewed several of the improvements of the Stockbridge, Munsee, and Brothertown Indians; visited John W. Quinney, John Matoxin, and others; recrossed
the Fox river, and viewed the country from the Little Chute to the Big
Chute.  Thence up along Fox river to the Little Butte des Morts; and
from thence to the Big Butte des morts; stayed this night at Judge Por-
lier's, on the north side of the Upper Fox river.

*Saturday, November* 3.—Crossed the Upper Fox river, near the Big
Butte des Morts, and passing through the Winnebago country, arrived that
night at Paquette's farm, (within about fourteen miles distance of Fort Winnebago.)

*Sunday, November* 4.—Got to the house of the Indian sub-agent,
John H. Kinzie, esq., near Fort Winnebago in the forenoon.

*Monday, November* 5.—Remained at the agency examining the several matters connected therewith, especially the books and papers of the
agent; the manner of keeping his accounts and transacting his business;
the new house he had erected at the expense of the Government, the

blacksmiths shop, &c. The boat with the annuity money, not having yet reached there, by appointment, to-morrow is assigned for holding a council with the Indians at the agency house.

*Tuesday, November* 6.—After a stormy night, the ground in the morning being covered with snow, some inches deep, the boat arrived about the middle of the day. Owing to the severity of the weather, which prevented many of the Indians, who were bad off for clothing, from leaving their wigwams, and the advantages which the snow furnished for hunting, in consequence of which, many of the young men had left their encampments, they did not assemble in council, agreeably to the appointment. A postponement until to-morrow was asked by them, and acceded to by the Governor.

*Wednesday, November* 7.—The chiefs and head-men convened at the agency house. The speeches of the chiefs, and the reply of the Governor were carefully taken down by Mr. Kinzie. A copy will be forwarded to the Department of War. The arrangements for the payment of the annuity money being made, and the decisions had on the conduct of such of the Indians as had behaved improperly, agreeably to the instructions of the War Department, of 22d June, 1832, directing that no portion of the annuity should be paid to the families of such individuals as had been engaged in hostilities, to-morrow is assigned for the payment of the annuity to such as are entitled to it.

*Thursday, November* 8.—Annuity money paid by the sub-agent to all those entitled to receive it.

*Friday, November* 9.—Agreeably to the request of the chiefs, the Governor went over to the fort, and in the presence of the White Crow, Little Priest, and other chiefs, saw the seven individuals of their nation who had been surrendered, (as the murderers of United States citizens,) in compliance with the 9th article of the treaty of Fort Armstrong of the 15th September, 1832. Governor Porter having taken occasion to remark to these chiefs, that they now saw their complaints were groundless, the prisoners were comfortable and properly taken care of.

*Saturday, November* 10.—Set out for Chicago, through the Indian country, having employed Batte Grignon as guide, and he to receive $25 for the service of himself and horse. For this expedition the Governor purchased two riding horses, (for himself and secretary) and two pack horses, a saddle, bridle, halters, circingles, cruppers, corn, &c.; the pack-saddles and corn bags were obtained at the fort. The first night came to and remained at the deserted house on the Galena road.

*Sunday, November* 11.—Travelled forty odd miles, and that night encamped near Rock river, below the Four Lakes.

*Monday, November* 12.—Travelled forty odd miles, and that night encamped at Na-beck-kuck's village, at Lake Du Grandpied.

*Tuesday, November* 13.—The pack-horses being much fatigued, owing to the quantity of corn they were obliged to carry, the Governor purchased of John Latondre, an Indian trader, another horse, Indian saddle, &c.; came on this day to Fox river, the distance supposed to be fifty miles, and encamped on the west bank of the river.

*Wednesday, November* 14.—After a severe ride of about forty-five miles, reached Chicago, at a late hour in the evening, and put up with Mark Beaubien.

*Thursday, November* 15.—Visited the Indian agency; inspected the books, papers, &c., of Colonel Owen, the agent; saw the interpreters for the several Indians belonging to that agency, and was informed by them that some of the chiefs wished to call on the Governor and state their grievances. To-morrow was assigned for the purpose.

*Friday, November* 16.—Bad weather; the Governor considerably indisposed, having taken severe cold in his neck, while laying out at night; nothing done.

*Saturday, November* 17.—The Governor continued much indisposed, but, at the appointed hour, met the chiefs with their interpreters, Messrs. Calwell and Robinson, in the presence of Colonel Owen, the Indian agent, and other respectable citizens. The two chiefs who addressed the Governor observed, that they would not detain him as they saw he was unwell; that they came to complain of the manner in which the late treaties were made in Indiana; that they were dissatisfied with them; that they were made at night; and they knew no reason why all this should be done in the dark; that they had a memorial prepared and signed, which they wished to send to their great father, the President of the United States, and they begged that their father, (the Governor) would forward it to Washington. The memorial was then presented; after which the chiefs remarked that they had nothing more to say, except to entreat, that their situation, for want of provisions, as represented by their father, Colonel Owen, might be taken into serious consideration; that owing to the war they had raised no corn; and their people must die with hunger, if some assistance was not granted. They begged to be supplied with corn early in the spring.

*Sunday, November* 18.—The Governor much indisposed, unable to leave his bed.

*Monday, November* 19.—The Governor no better.

*Tuesday, November* 20.—Same as yesterday.

*Wednesday, November* 21.—Same as yesterday. Late in the evening Dr. Winslow, from Niles, (100 miles off) who had been sent for to take charge of the garrison, then without a United States surgeon, arrived, and commenced his attendance on the Governor.

*Thursday, November* 22 —The Governor still very unwell.

*Friday, November* 23.—The Governor was removed to Major Whistler's quarters, at the fort; still very unwell.

*Saturday, November* 24.—The Governor very unwell.

*Sunday, November* 25.—Same as yesterday.

*Monday, November* 26.—Same as yesterday.

*Tuesday, November* 27.—The Governor considerably relieved, but unable to travel.

*Wednesday, November* 28.—The Governor very unwell. In the afternoon set out for Detroit, and reached " Mann's," at the Little Calumet, that night.

*Thursday, November* 29.—Arrived at Baily's, on the Calumet, forty-five miles east of Chicago.

*Friday, November* 30.—Weather very bad: remained at Baily's all day, and until next morning.

*Saturday, December* 1.—Came on to Nichol's at the Kankapee.

*Sunday, December* 2.—Reached Niles, and remained there during the subsequent day.

*Monday, December* 3.—Visited the sub-agency of St. Joseph's, at the Carey mission; Colonel Stewart, sub-agent, viewed the agency buildings, farm, blacksmith shop, &c., &c.

*Tuesday, December* 4.—Left Niles, and came on this day to Mr. Savery's, at White Pigeon, (37 miles.)

*Wednesday, December* 5.—Came on to Mr. Morse's, on Cold Water Prairie, (44 miles.)

*Thursday, December* 6.—Came on to Mr. Blackemore's, (44½ miles.)

*Friday, December* 7.—Came on to Mr. Stackhouse's, in Ypsilanti, (38 miles.)

*Saturday, December* 8.—Arrived at Detroit, (30 miles.)

*Monday, December* 10.—Employed in completing this journal; copying treaty, &c.

JOSA. BOYER.

---

SUPERINTENDENCY OF INDIAN AFFAIRS,

*Detroit, January* 30, 1833.

SIR: I enclose the copy of a letter from Colonel John E. Hunt, of Maumee, dated 21st instant, stating the anxiety of the inhabitants of Upper Sandusky and the vicinity, that a treaty should be held with the Wyandots for the purchase of their lands. Should the department by this, or in any any other way, be satisfied that a council ought to be held with them, it could be attended to at any time that it might be thought most suitable.

Will you oblige me by having a duplicate of your answer directed to me at Maumee, Ohio, where it is probable I shall be, by the time it shall reach that place? Many of the individuals interested, will, I suppose, be at Maumee, while I am holding a treaty there, and on their account I ask this favor.

In a letter lately received from J. McCutchen, who writes on behalf of the band of Wyandot Indians, who sold their lands on the 19th January, 1832, he requests to know " when the amount of the valuation of their improvements will be paid to them, and through what source it will come." Will you please inform me how these inquiries shall be answered?

With much respect,

Your obedient servant,

G. B. PORTER.

The Hon. ELBERT HERRING,
*Commissioner of Indian Affairs.*

---

MAUMEE, *January* 21, 1833.

DEAR SIR: On my return from Columbus, a few days since, I stopped at Upper Sandusky, where Col. McElvain was paying the Wyandots, and from the information I received from Mr. McCutchen and others in the neighborhood, I am satisfied if you could make it convenient to visit that nation of Indians, that you would succeed in buying their lands. The Pagan party are anxious to sell, and some of the others have no objections.

I have made this communication at the particular request of the inhabitants of that neighborhood, who feel very anxious to get rid of those Indians, and I have understood the Pagan party have petitioned to have a commissioner appointed to treat with them.

I am very respectfully,

Your friend and obedient servant,

JOHN E. HUNT.

To GOV. G. B. PORTER.

WASHINGTON CITY, *January* 26, 1833.

SIR: I am just informed by Colonel Reynolds, agent for the Chickasaw nation, that it is now the intention of the Chickasaw chiefs, who came here under the guidance of Allen and Terrill, the two white men who accompanied them here for the purpose of having the late treaty so modified, as to allow them to use the money arising from the sale of the lands of the nation, in such way as they, the chiefs, should think proper, &c.. Having failed in that attempt, they now intend to present themselves before the Senate, or a committee of that body, and endeavor to prevent the ratification of the treaty; no doubt by the same foul misrepresentations which they presented to the President and yourself. I have thought it a duty to give you this information. that you may, if you think it advisable, inform the Senate of the designs of those men, and if it shall be desirable with that body to obtain further information, they can call on the agent, Colonel Reynolds, who is now here, and those Chickasaws who accompanied him to this place.

I have the honor to be, sir,
With great respect,
Your obedient servant,
JNO. COFFEE.

The SECRETARY OF WAR.

---

INDIAN AGENCY, INDIANA, *January* 26, 1833.

DEAR SIR: Agreeably to an order from the commissioners on the part of the United States, a proportion of the Pottawattamie Indians of this agency, were collected on the 12th instant, for the purpose of receiving a balance of goods due them under one of the provisions of the late treaty with them.

Not being able to attend to the delivery of the same myself, in consequence of extreme indisposition, I directed General N. D. Grover, sub-agent, to receive and deliver them. The goods were inspected by Mr. Dant, who was appointed inspector by the commissioners, and put in boxes in the presence of several individuals. One of the Messrs. Ewings being anxious to depart for the east on business, a draft was drawn in his favor before the delivery of his lot, for $10,801 12. The subsequent day, his goods, together with those of Messrs. Taber and Hamilton, were sent to the place assigned for their delivery to the Indians, and, upon examination, an error was discovered in the lot belonging to the Messrs. Ewings, which will be explained to you by General Grover, who is now on his way to the city. Both these gentlemen will meet at Washington, and I trust, adjust this matter satisfactorily.

I am, sir, very respectfully,
Your obedient servant,
WILLIAM MARSHALL,
*Indian Agent.*

Hon. LEWIS CASS,
*Secretary of War, Washington City, D. C.*

---

CREEK AGENCY, *January* 27, 1833.

SIR: The Board of Commissioners to investigate claims, according to your instructions, have been engaged in the business for three weeks, and had great difficulty in attempting to detect frauds; an account of which you will receive in our report, which it will take many days yet to prepare.

When we first met a great number of Indians attended, and after remaining some days, they (the Indians) appointed about twenty of their chiefs, half from the lower and half from the upper towns, who attended us during all the time of taking the testimony.

Benjamin Hawkins and Chilly McIntosh, from west of the Mississippi river, were present, and made many attempts to reconcile all matters of difference between the nation here, and that part of their people who have left this country. And, finally, both sides called upon the commissioners to aid in the adjusting of this matter, which we willingly did, and had the pleasure to see all matters amicably adjusted, and the Creek chiefs here, granted five sections, of the twenty-five at their disposal, to the people west of the Mississippi; and they signed a treaty of peace and friendship. This measure will materially aid the operations of the Government in removing the Indians.

The next difficulty is, the Indians wish to have their reservations allotted to them so that they may dispose of them, and then they will be quite ready to emigrate. If they do not soon have their reservations assigned to them, they will come to the conclusion, it is best for them to sell to the Government.

That one agent cannot soon locate them, I am sure, as I have before said. I am informed the Indians have written to you, requesting the appointment of additional agents to locate their lands. I am not acquainted with the men they wish appointed; but I have seen enough here to say, that they may be, and too frequently are, indeed, too designing men to request what ought not to be granted, and that there will often be reasons to reflect, before what they desire should be granted.

If the Government will place in the hands of a competent man a sum sufficient for the purchase of towns and parts of towns, and of individuals, their reservations, and to remove them, by May next, a considerable number of the Indians may be removed; and in the fall, a still larger number.

The Government have had such experience now, as to enable it to determine what sum it ought to cost to remove the Indians per head. And I will say, that if the Government feel disposed to make a specific contract of this kind to remove them, that I can have men who will use the Indians well, and remove as many as any other mode will, and who might purchase the reservations in the way before stated, (if the Government will so act) at any price specified.

In this way the Indians can be removed sooner than in any other.

You will excuse me for so frequently troubling you.

I have, &c.,

ENOCH PARSONS.

Hon. Lewis Cass,
  *Secretary of War.*

From information which I credit, if locating agents shall be selected who are connected with land companies, or engaged in purchasing Indian lands, or desirous to obtain particular tracts, the valuable lands will be acquired by such companies or persons. This is all I feel authorized to say at present. "A word to the wise is sufficient."

E. PARSONS.

8‡

CREEK AGENCY, *January* 28, 1833.

SIR: I have been here since September last, and engaged in persuading my red brothers of this part of the nation, and particularly my kin, to remove west of the Mississippi.

A considerable difficulty was in the way, to wit: The ill feelings occasioned by my father's death, and the transactions about this event had not subsided; and the breach could never be healed, until we, upon both sides, called in the mediation of the commissioners, which happily succeeded.

Now, I can take thirty or forty families of my connections with me, provided you will advance the fifteen dollars per head, and promise the other benefits allowed by the treaty; and pay to each head of a family the fair value of his reservation when he reaches his home.

To prevent fraud, you may appoint, if you please, an agent here to see the number I have upon my roll, and take a list of their names; and take deeds of relinquishment to the United States from those entitled to reservations, and their names and towns, and forward to you; and then let the number be taken, and names be taken, by our agent when I reach home; and by this means fraud cannot be committed.

If you will approve my plan, please to write to me at this place; and, as soon as I have arrived at home, I will return and gather more.

Your obedient servant,

CHILLY McINTOSH.

P. S. I will cheerfully render any assistance in my power in removing the Indians, if the Government will allow me a fair compensation.

CHILLY McINTOSH.

---

WASCISSA, *January* 28, 1833.

SIR: I have the honor to acknowledge the reception of your letter of the 19th ultimo, and to express my gratification, on the approval of the President and yourself, of the manner in which I have executed the duties entrusted to me. Blunt's party left the Appalachicola some weeks since, on their explorations west, and were accompanied by two or three of the younger chiefs of the Mulatto King, and Econchatimicco's town. On their return, I will seek an early opportunity of renewing my negotiations with those chiefs, for the removal of themselves and followers west; and, should they then decline, I will proceed to the enrolment of the younger chiefs and warriors who may be disposed to migrate on the terms suggested and approved in my previous communication to you. In the meantime, I would draw your attention to the additional article of the treaty of Camp Moultrie, with a view of ascertaining your opinion whether the terms of that article would recognize a division of the reservations of land between the old chiefs and those preferring to remain with them; and those younger chiefs and warriors who may be disposed to migrate on receiving payment for the proportional part allotted them. In the several communications held with them, I have rather encouraged the probability of such an arrangement, in addition to each chief and warrior enrolled, receiving, in advance, their proportion of the annuity under the treaty of Camp Moultrie, and a commutation in money for their expenses of removal, subsistence, &c., as was allowed in the agreement with Blunt. The division of land, if made, would have to be graduated, I suppose, according to the rank and consequence of the chiefs and warriors, as has been the practice in the distribution of the annuity. Indeed, that distribution may be the standard of the land apportionment, as it has been long recognized by the Indians. An idea, however, prevails among the younger chiefs and warriors disposed to migrate, and composing a decided majority of the towns, that they may in council depose the old chiefs, Mulatto King and Econchatimicco; and thus have the authority themselves of selling the reservations, and forcing their older chiefs, reduced to the station of subjects, to migrate with them. This movement has been agitated in their private meetings; but, in consultations with me, I have discountenanced it, believing it to be the wish of the Executive of the United States not to encourage divisions among his red men, but rather to convince,'by argument, that the policy of the General Government in removing them west, originated in the most humane feelings for their happiness and future preservation. No other language have I held, in all my negotiations, with the Florida Indians; and I have the satisfaction to state that the appeal, when properly interpreted and fairly comprehended, has never been without its effect. The difficulties encountered thus far with the Appalachicola bands, two of them at least, may be ascribed to the force of secret and interested influences; but these are in a fair way of being properly understood by the Indians themselves, who, in having the film removed from their eyes, will not be slow in understanding their real interests, and in recognizing their true friends.

Your obedient servant,
JAMES GADSDEN.

The Hon. L. Cass,
    Secretary of War.

----

United States Indian Agency at Prairie du Chien,
                                    January 28, 1833.

Sir: Domestic calamities and continued indisposition, has prevented an earlier communication from me on the subject of the Winnebago nation of Indians; and, even now, I am much debilitated and depressed.

A promising son, about eighteen or nineteen years of age, (who had spent two years in college,) on a visit at home, took sick in December, and died on the 1st day of January present. Mrs. Street's health is so much impaired, as to render me extremely uneasy lest she too may leave me; and my own ill health has incapacitated me for entering at large upon those views in relation to the Winnebago nation, which, having well considered and matured, I have been endeavoring to press upon the attention of the President since 1828. I mention these providences as an apology for my delay, and for the crude manner in which I shall hastily advert, at this time, to the most important things in relation to these Indians, now imperiously demanding to be considered by the treaty of 1832 with the Winnebagoes at Rock Island.

The proposition made to the honorable Secretary of War by my letter, in February, 1830, you will find to have been the purchase of the disputed territory lying between the Sioux and the Sacs and Foxes, from the Mississippi to the Missouri rivers; and the exchange of the country, so purchased with the Winnebagoes for the whole of their country south and east of the Wisconsin and Fox rivers, of Green bay; with an annuity to the Winnebagoes, to induce the sale and facilitate the removal. The commissioners effected one part of the plan, but made no attempt to carry into effect the other. They purchased the land very low, but made no effort to enter into a negotiation with the Winnebagoes for an exchange. It is true, white men were not backward in declaring that the Winnebagoes would not sell; that if they did, they could not live; but the same declarations were as freely made at the beginning of the council at Rock Island; yet the Winnebagoes have sold the very country first recommended by me, and have taken in exchange the same country I had proposed. The opinion expressed by the present honorable Secretary of War, in his first report, contains the correct ground upon which our Government must act, if they would do any service to the Indians. The Government should judge for them what will be best for to insure them happiness, and peace to us; and when we are convinced that their *removal* is necessary to their happiness and the security of the peace of our frontiers, we should take them by the hand and remove them to such place as we may deem best suited to their situation; giving them a liberal annuity for the country ceded to us and evacuated. Perceiving that attempts were making to influence the Indians inhabiting the ceded country not to remove to the west of the Mississippi, and believing that no movement short of the west of the Mississippi would effect the desired end, (which is the quiet and happiness of the Indians and security of the frontiers,) I early apprized the Government, through the regular channel, of all that I knew upon the subject, and respectfully submitted such views as I entertained of the probable effect. If measures are adopted by the exhibition of a competent force in this country, there will be no difficulty in the removal of the Indians *off the ceded country;* but other measures there recommended will be necessary, in order to induce them to go beyond the Mississippi; and I desire it may be borne in mind, that there will, in my opinion, *be little prospect of peace, so long as those Indians remain on the Wisconsin.* The maintenance of a considerable force, or a peculiar combination of circumstances, may maintain peace; but the first favorable moment will be seized to do mischief.

In the treaty of Rock Island, some measures intended to operate in ameliorating the situation of the Indians were wisely provided. These, or like measures, I have long desired might be engrafted into some treaty with the Winnebagoes, and that a full experiment should be given to measures calculated to save the fading remnant of a seemingly *fated* race.

Agricultural grants have heretofore been made to several nations, and the Government no doubt believes that due exertion has been made to induce the Indians to become agriculturists. I am not apprized of what is doing in any other quarter; but the grants and provisions that have come under my notice are so radically defective, that no benefit can possibly result to the Indians from the expenditure. I ardently hope, that, in the grant to the Winnebagoes, if the treaty of 1832 is ratified, the Government will take such measures as to insure the most ample and beneficial experiment with the agricultural reserve; that the money reserved be not divided into the cultivation of two or three little contemptible spots, under the management of men who can be hired *cheap*, but that the whole be employed on one *pattern farm*, to be conducted by a competent agriculturist, with selected hands, whose *morals shall instruct as well as their farm*. This farm should be established where it will be likely to remain the property of the Indians; and at a distance from, and not *liable to* contact with, our white settlements. To insure these last objects, it ought to be on the west of the Mississippi. If divided into several farming establishments, and located on the Wisconsin, or any where east of the Mississippi, the benefits anticipated by me to the Indians will be wholly lost; for any man who will reflect on the subject will see that, in a few years, the Winnebagoes must leave the whole of the Wisconsin country, and pass over to the west of the Mississippi.

Suppose a *pattern farm*, established on some well selected land west of the Mississippi, and under the direction of a *competent agriculturist*, with the necessary picked hands, and oxen and tools to the full amount of the appropriation; an example might be placed before the Indians leading to the happiest results. A farm should be so beneficially arranged and worked, as to show the largest products from the smallest possible quantity of ground. The necessary buildings of a permanent character should be first constructed, consisting of dwellings, stables, barns, and capacious root-houses; the farm enclosed with a good fence, and only so much land brought into cultivation as can be *well tended;* the crops well secured, and roots, &c., stowed away. Potatoes being easily raised, and much prized by Indians, should be raised in the largest possible quantity. During the winter and spring, when the Indian suffering is frequently great, those might be issued to such as came in, seizing the occasion to explain to them how they might secure much larger and constant supplies fron. no more labor than their women now use. Grounds adjoining, or in the vicinity of the farm, could then be broke for such Indians as would cultivate, and fenced; and if, from the tendence, there was any thing to justify it, the women might be instructed to excavate root-houses, for potatoes, &c., and buildings for corn cribs, and, in two or three years, they would perceive the benefit of having stores on which to depend, like the whites, in time of need; and would, from year to year, extend their cultivation, until, if possible, a change in their manner of living is effected?

In the case of the Indian school, I have long had a desire that the means of education should be extended to the Indians, and especially to the Winnebagoes who had been placed under my agency. In 1829, I endeavored to prevail on the commissioners to let a part of the annuity of eighteen thousand dollars go to a school; but as these annuities speedily find their way into the pockets of the traders, any thing calculated to lessen the amount they oppose as detrimental to their pecuniary interest, and the commissioners could not listen to my representations on the subject. In General Scott I found a man of literature, and much liberality in relation to the Indians; who not only listened to my first suggestions on the subject, but himself deeply entered into the subject, and placed it upon the most advantageous footing. If this measure, too, can be *carried out in the spirit of benevolence,* it has been conceived and introduced into the treaty, I anticipate the most happy results. Notwithstanding the opinion expressed in the report of the present honorable Secretary of War, at the present session of Congress, as to the melioration of the Indian race, I beg leave to submit a different one; and believe, that a patient examination of the plans adopted for effecting this object, and the *manner* in which they have been *executed,* as well as the difficulties thrown in the way of such an object by our own people, will readily account for the failures that have heretofore occurred.

In the south, from their local situation, white people could not be kept out of the Indian country. They freely mixed with them, and being mostly of the most objectionable part of the white population, who visited them to live upon their ignorance, they of course strove to counteract every effort t.. enlighten them.  Our northern and western Indians are so located that the whites can be entirely excluded should the wisdom of the Government resolve to do so.  Here, the traders, who, with their agents, are the most immoral, dissipated, and heartless people I know, are freely permitted to go into any part of the Indian country.  Their gains arise from the ignorance and vicious and savage habits of the Indians.  Let the Indians become civilized, and pursue the lives of civilized persons, and the fur trade is at an end so far as such civilization extends.  And I have several times heard the traders here deprecate every attempt to civilize the Indians, because it spoils them as hunters.

Let schools be established among the different tribes, the trade placed in the hands of the Government and conducted for their benefit, and the profits expended upon the civilization of the Indians, and all other white men, under *any pretence*, excluded from the Indian country, and then a fair experiment can be had.  Until then, such is the deleterious influence obtained by the traders over the minds of the savages, by the distribution of whiskey, that the best plans of amelioration, to succeed, must be directed by the most able, decisive, and independent hands; where the heart and affections can go along with the deepest conviction of right, and well grounded hopes of ultimate success amid all surrounding difficulties.

But such an institution, placed in the hands of a weak and irresolute individual, who has little belief of the possibility of success, and the whole is thrown away.

I sincerely trust these subjects will receive the most minute attention, as a grand effort to snatch a remnant of these wasting people from extinction.

In relation to the sixty thousand rations, one word.  At the time those rations were granted it was calculated that they would be issued on the west bank of the Mississippi; I now learn from some of the Indians they are to be issued at the portage of the Wisconsin.

Some Indians belonging to this agency informed me that they would want some part of the provisions, and that they should go to the portage in the spring.  Thus, instead of aiding the removal or migration of the Indians from the east to the west, it will, for a time, draw more Indians to the east.  If the rations are issued at the portage, very few will remove; but if sixty thousand rations are issued on the west of the Mississippi, numbers will migrate.  It would save expense to have these rations delivered on the west bank of the Mississippi, at or near the mouth of the Painted Rock creek, eight or ten miles above Prairie du Chien.  If advertised to be thus delivered, they could be delivered there as cheap as at this place, and cheaper than at the portage.  And, if notified, the agent at this place could receive and issue the rations at that point with no great trouble.

If the Winnebagoes are not early induced to migrate to the west of the Mississippi, by the union of every measure upon which the Government can operate, we may again, at no distant day, calculate on a rupture with them.  They cannot live on the Wisconsin without difficulties with the neighboring white settlements, and if left to make the experiment none but the fur traders will be benefited, and a few dependent on the Indian establishment.  And the fur traders *only* intend to *make money;* and whether the Indians live or die by drinking too freely of the whiskey given them is immaterial, if they first pay the rats.  This is not a feeling improperly ascribed to them, but avowed by their agent here; not in so many words, but he said, "*civilizing Indians spoiled them as hunters, and that if he did not give whiskey to the Indians others would, and, therefore, he would give whiskey rather than lose the fur.*"

I have hastily and fully submitted my opinions in the foregoing cases, from deep reflection heretofore entertained in relation to our Indian affairs in this quarter, and very respectfully transmit them to you. My desire to maintain the peace with the Indians placed under my agency, and a sincere desire to ameliorate, by every means in my power, the unhappy situation of the Indians, has induced me, under all the disadvantages, to lay this matter before you. Long acquainted with the Indians, and doubtless desirous to render them a permanent good, I am highly gratified to submit these views to the present honorable Secretary of War.

With high consideration and respect,

I have the honor to be, sir,

Your most obedient servant,

JOS. M. STREET,

*United States Indian Agent.*

The Hon. Secretary of the War Department.

———

Brown's Hotel, Washington City, *January* 28, 1833.

Sir: Having exhibited before you the authority under which we have been delegated, by the Cherokee nation, to visit the seat of Government, we will now take occasion to lay before you, for the consideration of the President, a brief view of the existing state of things, in relation to our national affairs, and also to make known the feelings of the Cherokee people. In doing so, it is not deemed necessary to go into a detailed narrative of the numerous circumstances attending the facts; nor are we disposed to enter into a prolix discussion of the justice and merits of those rights for which we have so earnestly sought the interposition of the protecting arm of the General Government. It is sufficient to state, that it has been the lot of our nation to differ in opinion with the constituted authorities of this Government, in regard to that system of policy having for its object the general removal of all the Indian tribes west of the river Mississippi; and that it has been our misfortune to find the President of the United States, entertaining views adverse to ours, upon the question of those rights which our nation claims, and heretofore have peaceably enjoyed, from time immemorial, and which have been solemnly recognized by the treaties now existing with the United States. In the course of these events, the State of Georgia assumed to herself the right to extend and exercise jurisdiction over all that portion of our territory called " the chartered limits of Georgia." The nature and effects of the laws adopted by her Legislature, to operate upon our people, are well known. Our nation being strenuously opposed to a change of location, and the officers of the Government having withheld the enforcement of the intercourse act of Congress, and the treaties for our protection, our nation was driven to the necessity of employing counsellors at law, for asserting our legal rights before the courts of the United States, and we have had the consolation, amidst our difficulties, to see that we have not been deceived in the opinion entertained of those rights, when the supreme judicial tribunal of the country decided that the laws of Georgia, extending jurisdiction over our territory, are repugnant to the laws, treaties, and constitution of the United States, and were null and void. Yet, with deep regret, have we witnessed and felt the illegal proceedings of Georgia, with increasing severity; at the same time, the protecting arm of the Federal Government withdrawn, and the annuity stipend, due to our nation by treaties, withheld; and from the mere claim of the right to exercise jurisdiction, the right of surveying, disposing of, and occupying our lands by force, have since been asserted by Georgia, and measures are now in train for the consummation of the unjust deed.

In this peculiar state of affairs, our nation, in the summer of the last year, received, through your department, certain propositions from the President, containing the basis upon which the Government was willing to negotiate a treaty for our territory east of the Mississippi; and, in reply thereto, the general council of the nation informed the President that the sentiments of the Cherokee people, on that subject, remained the same as has before been expressed, and that the basis of the propositions was objectionable, and that, owing to the peculiar state of things, the nation was in duresse; but let him remove all the difficulties complained of; and afford that necessary protection which had been solemnly guaranteed in our treaties, and then the exercise of that privilege which is so essential to freedom, would place the nation in a condition to reflect, speak, and act freely, &c. &c.

Sometime thereafter, a letter, directed to "the Cherokees east of the Mississippi," from Mr. Robb, the chief clerk of your department, was received, through the agent, acknowledging the receipt of this letter, and who stated that you were then, at that time, on a tour to Lake Erie, and to which place the letter had been forwarded, and that no doubt you would reply to it; but no further communication from you has since been received. Mr. Chester, however, under instructions from the department, attended our general council, in October last, and urged a reconsideration of the same propositions which had before been submitted and replied to; and who, as you have been apprized, was given to understand that a delegation would be appointed to attend to the business of the nation, before the Government of the United States, on all subjects relating to its interest.

Now, in the discharge of the duties entrusted to us, we ask leave to say that, notwithstanding the various perplexities which the Cherokee people have experienced, under the course of policy pursued towards our nation, they are unshaken in their objections to a removal west of the River Mississippi; and on the question of our rights, and the justice of our cause, their minds are equally unchangeable. However, we are fully sensible that justice and weakness cannot control the array of oppressive power; and when we anticipate the calamitous effects of such power, we do not fail to see, with equal clearness, that a removal, under existing circumstances, beyond that "Father of Rivers" in the west, would but produce consequences no less fatal. Therefore, we can never consent to be the instrument of a suicidal act to our nation's welfare and happiness. The dilemma of this momentous problem, then, must devolve upon the justice, the magnanimity, and the honor, of this great republic, to decide the ultimate issue. At our interview, the President, as well as yourself, took occasion to express deep solicitude, on the part of the Government, to adjust the difficulties which so much disturb the peace and tranquility of our nation.

Here you will please to allow us to repeat the expression of a corresponding desire on the part of our nation; and at the same time, to take the liberty of suggesting, for the consideration of the President, whether it would not be practicable for the Government to satisfy the claims of Georgia, through the individuals of that State, who may have drawn lots of land in our Territory, in the lotteries of that State, by granting them other lands of the United States, lying within the limits of the Territories and States of the Union, or in some other way. We would respectfully ask you, further, to state fully, the views and disposition of the President, how far, and in what manner, is he disposed to put a final end to the difficulties created by Georgia with our nation, and also, if the annuities due to our nation will not now be directed to be paid over to us as heretofore; likewise, please to inform us what disposition has been made of the lands reserved under the treaty of 1819, for the purpose of raising a school fund for our nation, and if sold, to state the amount of the proceeds; and also, the application made of the same.

With considerations of respect,
We have the honor to be,
Sir, your obedient servants,
JNO. ROSS,
R. TAYLOR,
JNO. F. BALDRIDGE, his x mark.
JOSEPH VANN.

The Hon. Lewis Cass,
*Secretary of War.*

---

Warsaw, Georgia, *January* 29, 1833.

Dear Sir: Some time in the month of July last, with my husband, we went to the Creek nation, to make a selection of a place, and an improvement on it; we did so, and remained on it until some time in September, when Mr. Rogers was taken very sick; we, however, remained until late in October; it was then thought expedient for us to return home. Mr. Rogers has ever since been confined, so that we have been unable to return. A letter just received from the Creek country states, that the whole of it is surveyed, and that my improvement fell upon another individual's claim older than mine, and the census taker had nearly completed taking the census of the nation, and I am fearful before I can reach the nation, the return of the census will be made. I therefore take this method to report myself to the department. I have two children; if their names are desired, I will hereafter give them.

I shall immediately proceed to the Creek nation, and make another selection, in conformity with the treaty. I hope our being providentially detained from the Creek nation, will not keep me out of a reservation.

My address is, Warsaw, Gwinnett, Georgia.

I have the honor to be, sir,
MARY ANN ROGERS.

To his honor Lewis Cass.

---

Washington, *January* 30, 1833.

Sir: I am requested by Mr. Jubal B. Hancock, living in the Choctaw country, to ascertain whether his name is registered among those who intend to remain and become citizens of the State, according to an article of the late treaty.

Please inform me, so that I can give the requisite answer.

Respectfully,

NATHAN GAITHER.

Hon. Lewis Cass.

---

To the Hon. Secretary of War.

We, the Seneca chiefs, being assembled at the council house, at Buffalo, in the State of New York, write to you, because, as the commissioner had said to us, that the Secretary of War has nominated or appointed me, that he commissioned me on this reason, an application has been made to the General Government it was desirable for you to sell your land; I will superintend over you the affair for the sale of your land to the pre-emption company. We replied to him: we have said that we have not said a word to have made an application to the Government to sell our land. As we have not intimated that we wish to sell our land, because we have such a small tract of land, it is sufficient for us to use it and no more; as we think that we shall remain here in the State of New York. We are determined not to remove from our country to the west. We are very glad that the President of the United States says he will not remove the Indians without their consent.

We hope that the treaties made between the United States and us, shall be fulfilled and always binding, and the protection which we claim shall not cease. And as we sincerely hope that the President shall arrest oppression which may be crept into our country, that has a tendency to exterminate our existence.

We herewith transmit a copy of a resolution passed by the general council of our nation, which will show the strength of our determination not to *remove*; and please present it to the President.

In testimony whereof, we have hereunto set our hands, this 31st day of January, in the year of our Lord one thousand eight hundred and thirty-three.

| | |
|---|---|
| YOUNG KING, | his x mark. |
| SENECA WHITE, | his x mark. |
| HENRY TWO GUNS, | his x mark. |
| BIG KETTLE, | his x mark. |
| JOHN SNOW, | his x mark. |
| GEORGE KENDUQUADEH, | his x mark. |
| LITTLE JOHNSON, | his x mark. |
| WHITE CHIEF, | his x mark. |
| DESTROY TOWN, | his x mark. |
| DANIEL TWO GUNS, | his x mark. |
| GREEN BLANKET, | his x mark. |
| JAMES STEPHENSON, | his x mark. |
| TALL PETER, | his x mark. |
| MARK CHARLES, | his x mark. |
| SKY CARRIER, | his x mark. |
| DOXTATOR, | his x mark. |
| JOHN HUDSON, | his x mark. |
| TOMMY JEMMY, | his x mark. |

Thompson S. Harris, *Secretary.*

We, the chiefs of the Seneca nation, being assembled at the council house, at Buffalo creek, and having an opportunity to consult respecting our welfare, respecting the prosperity of the chiefs, and of our people, considering that the pre-emption company do not cease to plead their right of pre-emption to these reservations, and to solicit the Seneca Indians to sell their lands; for this reason, we promise, covenant, and pledge ourselves, this day, that we will never sell said lands so long as we continue to be chiefs of said nation. And we further promise, that so long as our nations continue to exist, we will remain on these reservations, in the State of New York, now occupied by the said Seneca nation.

In testimony whereof, we have hereunto set our hands, this third day of November, 1832.

Done at Buffalo Creek Council House, in the county of Erie, in the State of New York.

| | |
|---|---|
| Seneca White | Chas. O. Real |
| Big Kettle | Green Blanket |
| Tunis Halftown | Mark Charles |
| Black Snake | John Look |
| George Killback | George Washington |
| Captain Jones | Jacob Black Snake |
| George Kenduquadeh | Young Chief |
| Tommy Jimmy | Hawwenause |
| Jack Snow | Kienteuk |
| George Deer | Destroy Town |
| John Snow | Tall Peter |
| Little Bread | Job Pierce |
| Blue Sky | Doxtator |
| Blacksmith | Little Johnson |
| Levi Halftown | John Snow |
| Jas. Robinson | Saml. Parker |
| Henry Two Guns | Jas. Stephenson |
| Sangonis Ransenah | Captain Snow |
| White Chief | Joseph Tequaneh |
| Samuel Gordon | Two Guns |
| John Hudson | Jimmy Johnson |
| Daniel Two Guns | Black Chief |
| John Pierce | John General |
| Young King | Blue Eyes |
| Corn Planter | White Seneca |
| Chief Warrior | Doaangwende |
| Long John | Thompson S. Harris. |

In presence of,  MARIS B. PIERCE.

---

SUPERINTENDENCY OF INDIAN AFFAIRS,
*Detroit, February* 1, 1833.

SIR: Your letter of the 16th October last, on the subject of the Ottawas of Maumee, reached Detroit during my absence at Green Bay, under instructions from the honorable the Secretary of War. Since my return, it has not been in my power to visit these Indians. The many duties which devolve upon me, and more particularly during the session of the legislative council, together with the intolerable state of the roads, have been such as to prevent me making the attempt.

Knowing the importance, however, if a treaty can be made, that it should be forwarded to Washington before the adjournment of Congress, I shall proceed to Maumee in the course of a week or ten days, and make the attempt. The roads are now passable, and the legislative council have on this day adjourned for three weeks.

On examining your letter first above alluded to, I find it is not so full as I could have wished. My letter of the 29th September had stated all that had occurred at Maumee in the council, and specified numerous reservations of land which they wished to make. The views of the department on this point would be very acceptable. The terms and mode of payment, &c. &c. should be laid down. And if, contrary to my expectation, these Indians should agree to go to the west of the Mississippi, I should know something more than I do with respect to the location of 40,000 acres. How shall it be described? You have access to all the treaties made of late granting lands in that quarter, I have not.

I shall be pleased to hear from you immediately on this subject, and enclosing a duplicate of your letter to me at Maumee, will oblige me much.

With great regard,

Your obedient servant,

G. B. PORTER.

The Hon. E. HERRING,
    Commissioner of Indian Affairs.

What shall I say to them about the money Lloyd withheld from them? See what is said about this in the proceedings of our council per my letter of 29th September.

February 2, 1833.

SIR: The information which you this morning imparted to me, of a sudden and unaccountable change in the disposition of the eastern Cherokees, to come to some speedy adjustment of the perplexing question which has so long harassed the Georgia and the Federal Government, is a source of deep regret. The allowance of fifty cents per acre for the whole of the Cherokee territory east of the Mississippi, as proposed by the President, to be made to those people, is, as I think, very liberal. Yet there are considerations involved in the general question, the importance of which cannot be estimated in dollars and cents; considerations which would justify, in my opinion, an allowance in gross of four millions, or even more than four millions of dollars.

If the hoped for adjustment cannot be effected, I submit for your consideration the propriety and expediency of authorizing, at the expense of the Government, an exploring party of the friendly part of the eastern Cherokees, to examine the country proposed as their future home. Some six or eight persons, to be selected by them from among themselves, to be accompanied by one or two white men of intelligence and moral worth, will be ample, and the expense would bear but a very small proportion to the object. Heretofore, the objection to emigration in detail from the eastern Cherokee country had much force in it; but by the extension of the jurisdiction of

Georgia over that part of the eastern Cherokee country which lies within the limits of that State, and the subsequent acquiescence of the General Government in the right so exercised by that State, I respectfully conceive the objection alluded to was deprived of all its force. A large portion, if not half of the eastern Cherokees, form a very strong party in favor of emigration. It is to be apprehended that even they will hesitate, if their request for permission to explore the country, a privilege which, they urge, has been, at the expense of the Government, allowed to all Indians who have emigrated, should be rejected, as such rejection may induce them to believe that the Government has reason to apprehend they would not be pleased with the location proposed to them. If permitted to explore the country, and a favorable report of it should be the result, inducing those now favorable to the proposed removal to emigrate thither, it would, in my opinion, not only give to emigration an impulse so powerful as to induce many who have heretofore stood in opposition, to throw themselves in the current, but, in the end, and at no distant period, leave the obstinate so few in number, as to deprive them of that imposing national character which they now imagine they possess. Besides, the obstinacy of those deluded people has involved both parties in difficulties adverse to the growth of their prosperity, tending to involve the whole in ruin and wretchedness. Those of them who have long labored to aid the views of the Government in the redemption of those people, by emigration from their present wretched condition, have some right to all the relief which it is competent for the Government to afford them.

I have the honor to be,

Respectfully,

Your obedient servant,

WILEY THOMPSON.

Hon. Lewis Cass.

---

INDIAN AGENCY, ROCK ISLAND,

*February* 3, 1833.

SIR: I have the honor to inform you that the intruders lately ordered from the Flint Hills, on the west bank of the Mississippi, on the land lately ceded by the Sacs and Foxes in their late treaty, have all left that side of the river.

By a report from S. D. Carpenter, esq., received yesterday, I learn that the intruders ordered off from Dubuque's mines, have not returned.

With great respect,

I have the honor to be,

Your obedient servant,

M. S. DAVENPORT,

*Indian Agent, Rock Island.*

Hon. Lewis Cass,

*Secretary of War.*

---

FORT GIBSON, *February* 5, 1833.

SIR: A steamboat arrived last evening with Governor Stokes. He is in good health, and a very agreeable gentleman. Our medals and flags come in the same steamboat safely and in good order. We have now been in council six days with the Cherokees and Creeks. Our progress is slow. I cannot yet say how the boundaries will be settled, the subject is attended with difficulties, but we hope to adjust it in a few days more.

Yours sincerely and respectfully,

HENRY L. ELLSWORTH.

Hon. LEWIS CASS,
     *Secretary of War.*

---

WASHINGTON CITY, *February* 5, 1833.

SIR: Having occasion for the use of some funds at the present moment, I have the honor to enclose you my account as special agent, &c., up to the 31st ultimo, and beg you will have the goodness to order its payment.

Very respectfully,

Your most obedient servant,

JAMES B. GARDINER,

*Special Agent, &c., Ohio Emigrating Indians.*

Hon. LEWIS CASS,
     *Secretary of War.*

---

UNITED STATES INDIAN AGENCY,
at *Prairie Du Chien, February* 6, 1833.

SIR: In my last I covered you my letter to Colonel Taylor, commanding at Fort Crawford, and his answer. A few days after, and before the ice in the river would permit us to make a movement, Lieutenant Beach came up, who parted with Mr. Davenport, agent at Rock Island, at Dubuque's mines, on the tract of country ceded by the Sac and Fox treaty of last September, at Rock Island, and from which you had ordered the removal of intruders, and informed Colonel Taylor and myself that Mr. Davenport met him and his party, by appointment, at Dubuque's, and that the intruders were all going off, at his request, peaceably, and on the 1st January, 1833 instant. Mr. Davenport addressed me the letter, marked A, in answer to one written him on the subject by Lieutenant Beach, in consequence of which information I have not proceeded any further, and now hand you this information.

My answer has been a little delayed by domestic calamity and personal ill health; and I am now scarcely able to write. Only a few weeks past, a son in his nineteenth year died; my wife is in extreme low health, and another son sick in bed.

I have the honor to be,

Sir, very respectfully,

Your most obedient servant,

JOS. M. STREET,

*U. S. Indian Agent.*

ELBERT HERRING, Esq.,
     *Com'r Indian Affairs,*

---

ROCK ISLAND, *January* 1, 1833.

SIR: Yours, of December, per Lieutenant Beach, has just been received. I am happy to inform you that the intruders on the west bank of the Mis sississippi have all evacuated the country, lately ceded to the United States. I thought it most advisable to use persuasive measures first, and am extremely glad that they have accomplished so much.

Some difficulty may hereafter occur, as I understand the *claimants* have sent on an *agent* to those mines, for the purpose of letting them out to such as may be willing to go over.

Should any commence depredations in this way, I suppose each individual will be amenable to the laws, and not merely the agent and claimants.

I should be pleased at all times to confer with you on matters relative to to the duties of my office, as they are altogether new to me.

Mrs. Davenport and family are well, and join me in presenting their respects to Mrs. Street and family.

With great respect,<br>
I am, sir,<br>
M. L. DAVENPORT.

Gen. J. M. STREET, *Indian Agent.*

P. S. Major Davenport would have sent before now the things left here, but for the want of opportunity. He will send them, however, by the first opportunity, steamboat or otherwise.

M. L. D.

---

HORN PRAIRIE, CHOCTAW NATION, WEST,<br>
February 6, 1833.

We, the treaty captains of Nittuckachee's district, take the liberty to address you. We are happy to inform you that our people are generally healthy at this time, though they have suffered much on account of the sickness last fall.

We are happy to inform you that our people are entirely satisfied with our new country. Enclosed you have a bill of our annuity for the present year, as made out by us, which we wish you to have purchased and delivered to us here, at Horn Prairie, on Red river, as soon as practicable, as our people are in great need of the articles in our bill. We think there is due us some money of the old school fund in the old nation, which we wish to have appropriated in the same kind of articles in our bill. We wish our annuity to be delivered here, as it is the most central part of the district. We have good winter and summer range for our horses. Timber is plenty, water good and plenty. We have objections to have our annuity delivered below Kiametia, (our people are generally poor); there is great deal of difficulty and expense in crossing Kiametia river. At Doaksville, where we have generally received our arms and articles mentioned in the treaty, our horses have suffered much, as there is no winter range. In fact, timber is scarce, and at times water is scarce.

We have to inform you that we have too many white traders in our country, we wish you to have them removed. There are Choctaws who are able and calculated to do business, but have no chance, on account of so many white traders being in our country. They have built a small town below Kiametia, consisting of white traders, with the exception of two. We are well aware of the difficulties that have taken place between the Choctaws and traders, in our old nation. We may agree to have a few traders in our country, but we do not wish to be crowded. We are, according to the title    Ad to have thirty-three captains, with uniforms. We are sorry to inform you that three of our treaty captains are dead. We wish their places filled by the following persons: Thomas Cuckee, in place of Horkuishomartarhen; Turkerhionettee, in place of Cowehoornah, his father; Ichargerhoomer, in place of Issaterhoomach. We, generally, have had medals given us by our former great fathers, as a token of great friendship between the Choctaws and the United States. We, therefore, petition to you, our present great father, to send us thirty-three small medals, three of them to be a size larger, also a large one for our beloved chief, Nittuckachee. We have left out some things of some importance to us in the treaty. We now humbly request of you to send us a drum, fife, and a flag, for the use of our district. We wish you to furnish us a blacksmith as soon as you can, as our people are destitute of farming utensils. It is getting late. We wish to cultivate our soil, and become farmers, as we are well confident that it is the surest way to make a living. We have no objection to our chief, Nittuckachee, as our ruler. We have nothing more to say at present, but remain your children.

| | |
|---|---|
| Iyacherhopia, | his x mark. |
| Pierre Juzan, | his x mark. |
| Tuscahalartee, | his x mark. |
| Hopiahoomah, | his x mark. |
| Hopiaachahubbee, | his x mark. |
| Purishaishtikkubbee, | his x mark. |
| Onubbee, | his x mark. |
| Chuallahoomah, | his x mark. |
| Hopiatubbee, | his x mark. |
| Cholaneattaha, | his x mark. |
| Nitterhoomah, | his x mark. |
| Ontickerhanaho, | his x mark. |
| Nuccaishtubbe, | his x mark. |
| Lakto, | his x mark. |
| Hopiaishtomukk, | his x mark. |
| Puurharnoomah, | his x mark· |
| Piperhocuttubbee, | his x mark. |
| Tikbernchahubbe, | his x mark. |
| Kannuuelachubbe, | his x mark. |
| Totanchahubbe, | his x mark. |
| Toousherbee, | his x mark. |
| Abarkerhubbe, | his x mark. |
| Hopiahunitter, | his x mark. |
| Big Axe, of Kuushba, | his x mark. |
| Inrokelawherhoomah, | his x mark. |

I certify that the above is the talk of the captains, at a council.

SAMUEL WORCESTER, *Sec.*

To our GREAT FATHER,
  *President United States.*

---

COUNCIL GROUND, NITTUCKACHEE,
  *Choctaw Nation, West, Feb.* 6, 1833.

A bill of annuity for Nittuckachee's district.

| | | | | | |
|---|---|---|---|---|---|
| 600 good large blankets | - | - | - | - | $1,000 00 |
| 12 pieces strouds | - | - | - | - | 350 00 |

| | | |
|---|---|---|
| 80 pieces domestic white - - - - | $300 00 |
| 80 Do checks - - - - - | 300 00 |
| 60 Do plaids - - - - - | 200 00 |
| 20 Do calico - - - - - | 140 00 |
| 1 fine frock coat laced with gold - - - | 40 00 |
| 1 fine pair pantaloons - - - - | 8 00 |
| 400 weeding hoes, good quality - - - | 120 00 |
| 200 axes - - - - - - | 350 00 |
| 150 iron wedges - - - - - | 140 00 |
| 25 grindstones - - - - - | 75 00 |
| 48 drawing knives - - - - - | 24 00 |
| 36 handsaws - - - - - | 20 00 |
| 48 4 quarter augurs - - - - - | 24 00 |
| 48 3 quarter do - - - - - | 18 00 |
| 12 cross cut saws - - - - - | 72 00 |
| 6 whip saws - - - - - | 48 00 |
| 1 bellows, anvil, and set blacksmith's tools - - | 50 00 |
| 1,000 pounds iron - - - - - | 80 00 |
| 200 pounds steel - - - - - | 37 00 |
| 6 papers ink powder - - - - | 1 00 |
| 1 ream writing paper - - - - | 2 00 |
| 50 small plough moulds - - - - | 50 00 |
| 130 4 gallon pots, casting - - - - | 195 00 |
| | $3,644 00 |

WINNEBAGO AGENCY,
*Waters of Sugar Creek, Feb.* 8, 1833.

SIR: I have the honor of informing you that a part of the Rock river band of Winnebagoes, are in this neighborhood, and although their conduct in general, appears to be good, yet I hear frequent complaints from the white inhabitants, of thefts committed on them by the Indians.

I have frequently warned them of the consequences, if they persisted in their depredations; but notwithstanding, an account has been handed me for lead ore, which they have stolen, and which they confessed to in my presence, (which I shall shortly forward to the department,) and another complaint of their having killed a number of hogs on the waters of the Pee-ke-toleka. I have great difficulty in pacifying the white people, and preventing them from commencing hostilities on the Indians. Most of the frontier inhabitants suffered greatly in the last war; are smarting under former grievances, and illy prepared to suffer further without redress of some kind. They say, to use their own language, "if Government will not protect them they will protect themselves."

The Indians profess to me a readiness to remove from the ceded country, when stipulated by treaty, yet withal, show a reluctance to go; they are making frequent inquiries of me when troops will be in the country, how many there will be, &c.

I am of the opinion that a portion of the ranging troops would be well employed on this frontier until after the removal of the Indians; the appear-

10‡

ance of military force will keep them quiet; without it I am fearful for the safety of our frontier inhabitants on the coming spring. I have done and shall continue to do all in my power to prevent difficulties between the white man and the Indian.

You will pardon me, sir, for again calling your attention to my accounts. My half yearly accounts, ending 30th September, leaving a considerable balance in my favor, (after deducting as will be seen, $500, for building an agency house, which was placed in my hands, and which is now chargeable to Government,) were duly forwarded to the department, and the receipt of them acknowledged; since which I have heard nothing further of them. From the extraordinary nature of the demands on me, and the peculiar circumstances attending the late Indian hostilities, as well as the fact of General Dodge having certified to many of my vouchers, I have no doubt but that they have passed, if not all, a portion of them, and the amount of that portion I should like to receive.

At the same time, I forwarded an estimate of funds, required for the purposes of my agency for the half year, ending 31st of March, 1833, I received a letter, informing me that funds were in the hands of Governor Porter, at Detroit. I wrote to Governor Porter, requesting the amount to be forwarded to me, both for my pay and the allowance on my requisition, since which time I have heard nothing of Governor Porter or the money.

I have made some advances in the present quarter for the purpose of purchasing provisions and presents, and paying transportation for Indians, but really am not able to support my agency much longer from individual funds. I have no doubt but that the department has been punctual; if so, there must be a lack of punctuality in some of its ramifications, or in the mail; let the case be as it may, I am at present the sufferer.

I shuold like to hear from my accounts speedily, and your early attention to them will confer a great favor.

Very respectfully, your obedient servant,
HENRY GRATIOT,
*Sub Indian Agent.*

Hon. LEWIS CASS,
*Secretary of War, Washington City.*

---

CREEK AGENCY, *February* 10, 1833.

SIR: I have frequently, of late, made communications to you respecting the affairs of the Creek Indians, with the hope that my suggestions might be of some service in the discharge of your many and important duties relative to that tribe.

The Indian nations you are well acquainted with generally; but yet there are particulars you must derive from some source or other.

The situation of this nation is at the present peculiar. They have no more land to sell, as a nation, and the whole of their lands is now individual property; and of this they are well advised. And this fact is not an agreeable one to the chiefs.

They are also informed they cannot remain here, surrounded and interspersed with a dense white population. The breach between the two parts of the nation is reconciled, and the only obstacle to a speedy removal consists in the parts of some of the head chiefs being still opposed to that meaure, and in making a disposition of their reservations.

I entertain the opinion that, at a moderate, but fair price, the reservations might now, or very soon may, be had by the Government.

How the Indians are to subsist the present year, I cannot imagine. Some of them are now sustaining themselves upon roots. They have, apparently, very little corn, and scarcely any stock. The game is gone, and what they are to do, God only knows. Nothing can preserve their property, or their existence, other than immediate removal in the country designed for them. By proper management they might become prosperous and happy.

I will add one thing more, and then turn aside from this gloomy future, to wit: several hundred barrels of flour were left here by the army, and I am informed thirty or forty barrels of it are partially spoiled, so as to be of no value to the Government; and if Col. S. C. Benton had the authority to give this spoiled flour to the most needy, it would, I have no doubt, save the lives of many, and ameliorate the sufferings of others. (The Euchee people near the town, the women and children in particular, are the most needy.)

We have, with all the means before us which we could command, investigated a great amount of claims, and in one or two days more will be able to prepare our report. But the whole of our proceedings make a part of this report, and will require at least one month or more severe labor of Major T. J. Abbott, the secretary of the board, to transcribe and forward the report and proceedings; and as the report would be of little service without the accompanying documents, I write this letter to advise you of the cause of the delay.

Major Abbott has completed the taking of the census of the lower towns. Major Parsons is not yet done with the upper towns, but thinks he can be in two or three weeks. The Indians are hard to collect, or hunt up, which causes great delay. I think the work will be faithfully performed.

The papers and claims which we have passed upon are, many of them, for large amounts, and altogether of great value to the claimants, and their transmission, by mail, unsafe. I, therefore, think if you were to order Major Abbot, who you can reach at this place, on to Washington, with the whole of our proceedings, and his and Major Parson's census roll, the measure would be a good one. And with his explanations and assistance, our work could soon be disposed of by the department. And if you wished to send the money out to pay the amount stipulated by the treaty to be paid, Major Abbott would be as trustworthy as any man alive, and would be a faithful agent in any trust whatever. I will remark, too much care cannot be bestowed in the payment of money to Indians. The whites cheat them, I believe, all they can, and some of them cheat each other as much as possible.

As the commissioners, after they agree upon their report, would be of no further service here, as the secretary of the board only could work, they will, to save expense to the nation, adjourn; and I shall set out for Claiborne, my home.

The extent of country covered by the upper towns of Creeks, is, perhaps, more extensive than that covered by the lower towns. I know your time is one of labor, and I will not, perhaps, trouble you soon again.

I have, &c.,

ENOCH PARSONS.

Honorable LEWIS CASS,
*Secretary of War.*

CHOCTAW AGENCY, *February* 10, 1833.

SIR: The undersigned, citizen of the old Choctaw nation, begs leave to address you on the subject of his claim for moving, at his own expense, from the old nation to this place. In the month of August, 1832, I applied to the emigrating agent for leave to enter two wagons and teams in the service of the United States, as I wished to bring them to the new nation with me; I urged the propriety of employing wagons belonging to citizens of the nation, in preference to those who came no farther than the Mississippi, as he would save the expense of the returning trip. He told me he certainly would give them the preference. Under this impression, I fitted out a first rate five mule team and a large five horse team, together with a one horse carriage to ride in, (not being able to ride on horseback.) I left the Tombeckbee on the 30th September; one of my wagons I loaded with my own effects, the other I loaded for seven Indian families. I arrived at the council ground on the 4th of October, the day appointed for the general rendezvous. I applied immediately to the agent to have my wagons registered. He told me he had appointed Captain Page to inspect and enter the wagons. I then went to Captain Page, who promised to inspect my wagons; but after keeping me in suspense five days, finally told me my wagons could not be received. I was then under the necessity of sacrificing one of my wagons, team, and falling on my own resources to get to my new home. I started from the Tombeckbee with seventeen head of horse, viz: two five horse teams, one carriage horse, four good brood mares, one first rate filly, and one stud horse. The filly got crippled at the council ground, and I had to give her away. I had three white men hired, two to drive my wagons, and one as an overseer. I had three negroes, (my family having emigrated in the first company.) On my arrival at the council ground, I was duly enrolled, and drew five days' rations for myself and ten work horses; my other horse I was not allowed any thing. Under these restrictions I left the company on the 11th of the month, and arrived at Fort Smith in twenty-three days. I brought with me thirteen head of horses; one wagon, one carriage, and six persons composed my company. I paid in ferriage, at the different crossing places, $33 75; my whole expenses amounting to about ninety dollars, exclusive of the provisions I started with. I claim payment for the load of Indian plunder I brought to the council ground; this claim the agent promised to pay, but has since refused it.

I will now beg leave to call your attention to that article in the Choctaw treaty relative to our cattle. Some time in the spring of 1832, I received a printed advertisement, signed, I think, A. Byrne, as agent appointed by the President, to value the Choctaw cattle. Colonel Byrne commenced at one of my neighbors, on the 24th, 25th, and 26th of May. He valued and sold all that could be there collected, and on the 27th, came to my pen, in order to commence on the 28th, agreeable to his advertisement. I had, at considerable expense, collected about five hundred head ready for valuation, when, to my astonishment, the agent informed me he had, the preceding evening, received an express from the Secretary of War, commanding him to stop all further valuation and sales until the Indians were ready to emigrate. Thus was I forced to turn my cattle adrift, and have never heard any thing further from Colonel Byrne. I wished to have given up to the Government twenty cows and calves, in exchange for cattle here, but am sadly disappointed. I estimate my loss, in non-compliance with the treaty,

at upwards of five hundred dollars; for, in the fall, when we were nearly ready to emigrate, our cattle could not be collected, and we had to sell them as they run.    I am, sir, respectfully,
Your obedient servant,
JNO. COLEMAN.
To the Honorable
The SECRETARY OF WAR of the United States,
Washington City.

---

BEDFORD, INDIANA, February 10, 1833.

SIR: I have the honor herewith to transmit to your department, the journal of occurrences kept by the conducting officers of the Seneca and Shawnee emigrating Ohio Indians, during their journey to the land of that tribe in the autumn of last year.    And also a column of remarks, showing the changes in the tribe during the route, as is directed in the printed "regulations."

I have been instructed by Mr. D. M. Workman, the conductor of the Senecas and Shawnees, to forward you these papers.
I have the honor to be,
Very respectfully,
Your most obedient servant,
DANIEL R. DUNIHUE,
Asst. Cond't. of Lewistown O. Ind.
To the Hon. SECRETARY OF WAR.

---

The following is a copy of the column of REMARKS added to the muster roll of the Seneca and Shawnee Ohio Indians, who have lately emigrated west of the State of Missouri, furnished the agent to whom they were consigned at their new homes.

Dated December 18, 1832.

Two men, while on the route, left the family of Civil John and joined the Shawnees.

Two also left the family of Totola and joined them.

One birth on the route, in Baptiste's family.

Louis Dougherty and family and John Dougherty and family joined the Shawnees, while on the route, with the exception of one woman, who is now with John Smith's family.

One of the men mentioned in the family of Coloshete did not emigrate.

One birth, on the route, in Setting Bear's family.

Joe White and family joined the Shawnees, while on the route.

One birth, while on the route, in the family of Peter Knox's son.

Powlas Brant left his family, while on the route.

Silversmith's son and wife were numbered in the family of the widow Turtle, but on the route separated from them.

One child died while on the route, belonging to the family of the Tall Man's widow.

By the various changes made during the route, it will be perceived that there are now but 220 persons.

DANIEL R. DUNIHUE,
Enrolling Agent.

*Journal of occurrences kept by the conductors of the* "LEWISTOWN DE-
TACHMENT" *of emigrating Ohio Indians, Senecas and Shawnees;
commencing on the 20th of August, 1832, and ending on the 13th of
December, 1832.*

August 20th, 1832. Agreeably to previous notice given them, the Senecas and Shawnee Indians this day assembled at Lewistown, Logan county,
Ohio, to receive rations. At their request, provisions for four days were
issued to them. The proper officers of this detachment were present, and
inspected the provisions and the issues, both of which were satisfactory.
The utmost harmony prevailed throughout the day; and in the evening, the
Indians returned to their homes, well satisfied with the manner of drawing,
and with the quantity and quality of their food. Each family drew separately.

Since there was no definite time set for the commencement of their journey, and their houses thought the most proper places for them to remain,
while rendered unwell from the effects of vaccination, it was considered
most expedient for them to continue their former manner of living, until
they should recover their health after being vaccinated, and a time fixed for
their departure.

Tuesday, August 21st. Civil John, the head chief of the tribe, and some
of the principal men were called together, by the request of Lieutenant
Lane, to ascertain whether there was a possibility of prevailing on them to go
by water. James McPherson was the interpreter. They say what they have
said before, that "they depended on Colonel Gardiner to carry their understanding of the treaty into effect. They are ready, willing, and anxious to
go, and always have been; but it is useless to try to persuade them to go by
steamboats." They say, that some of their old and infirm women say, " we
will not go in steamboats, nor will we go in wagons; but we will go on
horseback; it is the most agreeable manner for us; and if we are not allowed
to go so, we can, and will, remain here and die, and be buried with our relatives; it will be but a short time before we leave this world, at any rate,
and let us avert from our heads as much unnecessary pain and sorrow as
possible."

In the evening they departed, expressing a desire to hear the final conclusion of their great father, the President, and the Secretary of War, with
respect to the route which it is wished they should pursue. They ardently
hope that they will be permitted to go by land, on horseback.

Wednesday, 22d. The Indians remained at home to-day, and in the
evening sent word to their conductor, James McPherson, that they would
meet at his house to-morrow, for some purpose which they did not explain.

Thursday, 23d. The Indians met this morning, agreeably to their appointment of yesterday, and made known the business for which they assembled. It was this, namely: a young man, (one of their friends, and a
member of their band,) had just arrived from the Big Spring reservation,
to inform them, that the Indians of the Grand reservation were drawing up
writings in a secret manner, to establish a claim to a part of the avails arising from the Big Spring reservation, which were affirmed to be unjust by
the Indians of the Big Spring reservation, and by the Lewistown Indians,
their friends and relatives.

They (the Lewistown Indians) wished the interference of their friends, J.
McPherson, and Major Pool, the assistant agent, in their favor, and their co-

operation with Colonel Gardiner to protect their rights. They requested that Mr. Gardiner should be informed immediately of their claim, and exert himself to avert its deleterious effects to them and their property.

They were assured that they might rely upon the interposition of these officers in their favor, to protect their rights. They then departed for their homes in peace and confidence.

Friday, 24th. The Indians this day collected at a grove, near the house of James McPherson, and received rations for four days. Civil John said that the tribe should be assembled at his house, on Monday next, to be vaccinated.

Saturday, 25th. The Indians all remained at home to-day.

Sunday, 26th. To-day, also, the tribe remained at home.

Monday, 27th. This day Dr. Lord, with an assistant, proceeded to Lewistown, and vaccinated about one hundred and twenty of them; they were well pleased with the operation.

Tuesday, 28th. Dr. Lord vaccinated the remaining part of the Indians to-day. Provisions were issued for three days.

Wednesday, 29th. The Indians remained at their homes to-day.

Thursday, 30th. To-day also they remained at home.

Friday, 31st. Several of them took their horses to be shod to-day, to have them in readiness to start. Colonel Gardiner directed this to be done.

Saturday, September 1st. Several more of the Indians took their horses to be shod.

Sunday, 2d. The Indians remained at home to day. At night they made a feast, which is termed by them the "death feast," or *feast of death*. They celebrate, in feasts of this kind, the good and worthy qualities and actions of some deceased person of the tribe, and mutually and undisguisedly lament their death by tears and lamentation. They adopt some person in his place, for the purpose of perpetuating his name, and the memory of his actions.

Monday, 3d. The Indians assembled to-day, by order of Colonel Gardiner, to receive their blankets, tenting, and rifles, which were given to them. They appeared well pleased with them.

They were told by Mr. Gardiner to make every possible endeavor to be prepared to start in ten days. They said they would do so. They expressed great pleasure at hearing they were permitted to go by land, and that no delay in preparing was allowed. They said, that it was their desire to get to their destination as soon as possible. They fear that cannot be done before winter sets in; but they will endeavor to get there this season.

Tuesday, 4th. The Indians remained at their homes.

Wednesday, 5th. Several of them took their horses to get shod to-day.

Thursday, 6th. They continued making preparations to start.

Friday, 7th. To day they continued preparing.

Saturday, 8th. The Indians commenced delivering their chattel property to General J. McLane, the appraiser, for sale.

Sunday, 9th. They remained at home.

Monday, 10th. They continued delivering their property.

Tuesday, 11th. They commence assembling at Lewistown, in conformity with directions to that effect from James McPherson.

Wednesday, 12th. They continued assembling at Lewistown Some of them were engaged in taking more property to sell.

Friday, 14th. They were reminded of the necessity of being prepared by the appointed day to set off. Monday was appointed as that day.

Saturday, 15th. The Indians assembled to-day, and received the amount of money due them for their improvements, from Colonel John McElvain.

Sunday, 16th. They remained *principally* at Lewistown.

Monday, 17th. They received the proceeds of the sale of their property.

Tuesday, 18th. A part of them attended the funeral of Mrs. McPherson, who deceased yesterday, and whom the Indians had esteemed as a relative more than as a friend.

They say they will start to-morrow; they were reminded of the necessity of being ready, and promised to finish their arrangements to-day.

They have settled nearly all they owe in the neighborhood. Sixteen horses were distributed among them to-day.

Wednesday, 19th. Nearly all of them left Lewistown to-day, and encamped at the distance of ten miles.

Thursday, 20th. Those Indians who started yesterday proceeded to Hardin, a village nineteen miles from where they were encamped. The remainder travelled ten miles.

Friday, 21st. To-day those who arrived here first remained; and the balance of the tribe came up at night.

Saturday, 22d. By order of Colonel Gardiner, the Indians remained at their encampment to-day—order reigned.

Sunday, 23d. The detachment was ordered to march this morning. We encamped late in the evening at the distance of eighteen miles from Hardin.

Monday, 24th. We struck our tents at 8 o'clock, and marched to Greenville, fourteen miles; we could have gone farther, but a severe storm arose to prevent us.

Tuesday, 25th. Upon a solicitation of the principal chief and others, the Indians were permitted to remain in the camp long enough to dry their tents and blankets, which were wet in the rain yesterday.

At 11 o'clock we marched on, and at sunset, encamped at the distance of thirteen miles from Greenville, on the road towards Richmond, Indiana.

Wednesday, 26th. We struck our tents at 10 o'clock, and marched ten miles, being within four miles of Richmond; near which place we were ordered to remain by the superintendent, until further orders should arrive from him.

Thursday, 27th. The Indians remained at camp to-day.

Friday, 28th. Nearly all of the Indians went into town to-day; some to see the place, some to trade, and some to get intoxicated.

Saturday, 29th. A severe rain prevented them from leaving their encampment to-day.

Sunday, 30th. We were ordered, at 12 o'clock, by the superintendent, to march on immediately. By night, we succeeded in passing through Richmond, and two miles farther; making six miles.

Monday, October 1st. To-day some difficulty arose among the teamsters, which detained us until 11 o'clock; at which time we left the camp and proceeded through Centerville. Our start was so late, and the road being so muddy, that we travelled only seven miles.

Tuesday, 2d. Struck our tents at 9 o'clock, and marched thirteen miles and a half, where we halted for the night.

Wednesday, 3d. At 10 o'clock we commenced travelling, and at five gained the distance of fifteen miles.

Thursday, 4th. We commenced marching at 9 o'clock, and at 5, encamped at the distance of sixteen miles from our last encampment.

Friday, 5th. We started at 9, and passed Indianapolis two miles, making, to-day, eighteen miles.

Saturday, 6th. We remained in camp to-day. Our orders from the superintendent were, to remain near this place until he should direct us to proceed. In the evening, the superintendent arrived at Indianapolis.

Sunday, 7th. We received orders this morning to march a few miles. The Ottawa detachment is but a few miles in our rear. At two o'clock, we left the encampment, and marched eight miles.

Monday, 8th. We struck our tents at 9, and at 5, encamped at the distance of nineteen miles.

Tuesday, 9th. We travelled thirteen miles to-day, over a very bad road.

Wednesday, 10th. The Indians expressed an anxious solicitude to remain to-day to rest themselves and their horses, and to dry their tents and blankets, which were wet in a storm last night, &c., &c. Their wishes appeared so reasonable that they were granted the privilege of remaining.

Thursday, 11th. The detachment marched sixteen miles—no impediment.

Friday, 12th. We marched nineteen miles to the Wabash river.

Saturday, 13th. We were detained late in crossing the river. For the sake of economy, the horses were made to ford the river, while the most of the women and children were taken across in boats. The river was not low enough for it to be considered safe fording for any but men, or those who were good riders.

The detachment marched seven miles from the ferry, (Clinton.)

Sunday, 14th- We marched into Illinois to-day, and to the distance of eleven miles from our last encampment.

Monday, 15th. We started this morning about 7 oclock, and marched until dark, at a pretty rapid gait, which took us at the distance of twenty-seven miles. There was no water to be had between these two encampments, and the Indians were apprized the previous evening of this fact, and ordered to be prepared to start very early, that we might reach the Ambroise river.

Tuesday, 16th. At the request of the chiefs, and by permission of Col. Gardiner, the superintendent, the detachment remained on the encampment to-day for the purpose of refreshing themselves.

Wednesday, 17th. We started about 11 o'clock and marched 7 miles, to where we encamped. There is no water for twelve miles farther.

Thursday, 18th. One of the chiefs lost some of his horses, which detained us until 11 o'clock, when we left the encampment. In the evening, we encamped at the distance of twelve miles.

Friday, 19th. We marched twenty-one miles, having travelled late.

Saturday, 20th. This day, early, it commenced raining, and continued until noon, at which time all the tents were wet, and the horses were in the woods. We remained at the camp.

Sunday, 21st. We struck our tents at 11, and marched fourteen miles.

Monday, 22d. We started at 9 o'clock, and travelled late; we made the distance of twenty miles.

Tuesday, 23d. We travelled seventeen miles to-day; the roads were good, and the day fair. We encamped six miles west of Vandalia, Illinois.

11‡

Wednesday, 24th.    We travelled nineteen miles; we had an excellent road.

Thursday, 25th.    By order of the superintendent, the detachment remained stationary.    An express was sent by him to St. Louis for information respecting the prevalence of the cholera—the best place and manner of crossing the Mississippi river.    He addressed these inquiries to Governor Clark.

Friday, 26th.    Removed from the road, that travellers from St. Louis might not come among the Indians, for it is now understood that the cholera is prevailing there to a considerable extent.

Saturday, 27th.    The detachment remained in camp.

Sunday, 28th.    The Indians remained in camp; quietness was exhibited from every tent; good feeling abundantly prevailed throughout the day. The Indians have not for several days had an opportunity of procuring liquor; they consequently remain sober.

Monday, 29th.    We this day received orders to march, by Col. Abert, who assumed the future direction of the emigration on the 27th.

We started about 10 o'clock, and marched to the distance of fifteen miles on the road to Kaskaskia, where General Clark advised the superintendent to have this detachment of Indians taken across.

Tuesday, 30th.    In consequence of some of the principal men of the tribe being behind, the Indians refused to go until they should come up.    It was not till past noon that they arrived, and it was then too late to get to the next stream of water; so we were compelled to remain.

Wednesday, 31st.    We marched fourteen miles.

Thursday, November 1st.    A chief and his son were left behind yesterday to hunt for their horses, and have not yet come up.    The chiefs here refuse to leave him any farther behind.    They say that they are afraid that they are lost.    We were constantly compelled to remain for those behind.

Friday, 2d.    We struck our tents at 9 o'clock, and encamped at 5, having travelled seventeen miles.

Saturday, 3d.    We marched fourteen miles.

Sunday, 4th.    We travelled twenty miles, which brought us within four miles of the ferry, at the Mississippi, where we were to cross.

The conductor rode to Kaskaskia to see Colonel P. Menard, to whom he was directed by Colonel Abert for information respecting the route, and assistance in crossing the river.    In the evening, the conductor returned to camp.

Tuesday, 6th.    This morning the Indians proceeded to the ferry; the wind blew so severely that the ferrymen refused to cross.    It continued so all day.

Wednesday, 7th.    To-day about two-thirds of them were taken over, which occupied their time until dark.

Thursday, 8th.    The remaining part of the Indians were taken over to-day.

Friday, 9th.    The Indians remained at the camp, for the purpose of getting their horses shod.

Saturday, 10th.    The Indians had considerable difficulty in finding their horses.    We started late, and only travelled eight miles.

Sunday, 11th.    We travelled eighteen miles.

Monday, 12th.    We travelled seventeen miles.

Tuesday, 13th.    We travelled four miles, one west of the *mine of*

*Burton*, where we encamped for the purpose of having the remaining part of the horses shod.

Wednesday, 14th. We remained to-day for the purpose of getting horses shod, and giving the squaws an opportuuity of washing their clothes and blankets.

Thursday 15th. It was late this morning before the Indians could collect all their horses; we travelled only eight miles.

Friday, 16th. We travelled sixteen miles to the Merimack river.

Saturday, 17th. A family was left behind a day or two ago, which the Indians say they intend waiting for at this place.

Sunday, 18th. It rained all day, so much that the Indians would not start.

Monday, 19th. It was so cold that the Indians refused to travel. It snowed and blowed terribly.

Tuesday, 20th. A child died this morning, (the only death which has occured in this tribe,) which detained us until late. Some horses strayed away, which added to the delay. We travelled seven miles.

Wednesday, 21st. We travelled eighteen miles.

Thursday 22d. It rained and snowed so much that the Indians could not travel.

Friday, 23d. We marched fifteen miles.

Saturday 24th. We struck our tents at 8 o'clock, and marched until about 5. We made the distance of sixteen miles. The horses of two of the teamsters ran away, and their wagons were consequently left behind.

Sunday, 25th. A part of the detachment travelled ten miles, and the remainder continued stationary. The wagons which were left behind yesterday arrived in the evening.

Monday 26th. The Indians who remained behind yesterday, waiting for the teams, joined those in front.

Tuesday, 27th. We marched ten miles.

Wednesday, 28th. We struck our tents at 8 o'clock, and continued travelling until late in the evening, by which means we made the distance of eighteen miles.

Thursday, 29th. We travelled thirteen miles to the Gasconade.

Friday, 30th. The Indians remained to-day for the purpose of waiting for some of their brethren who are behind.

Saturday, 1st December. It commenced raining in the night, and continued all day, so that the detachment could not travel.

Sunday, 2d. We were compelled to cross a stream several times to day which nearly swam the horses; so that we were detained along the road so much that we travelled but eight miles.

Monday, 3d. We travelled 14 miles. One keg of powder and one hundred pounds of lead were given to the Indians to-day, by Lieutenant Lane, upon the condition that they should pay for it in game, which should be divided among all as other supplies of provisions.

Tuesday, 4th. We travelled twenty miles to-day. We started early, had a good road, and travelled late.

Wednesday, 5. We travelled thirteen miles to-day, which brought us to White river.

Thursday, 6th. We remained at the encampment for the purpose of refreshing the detachment.

Friday, 7th. About 11 o'clock we left the encampment and crossed White river, and marched nine miles beyond it, making ten miles to-day.

Saturday, 8th. We travelled twelve miles, to Gibson's fork of the Neosho.

Sunday, 9th. We travelled fifteen miles.

Monday, 10th. We travelled seven miles to day. We could have gone farther, but it was necessary to halt to get corn and meat.

Tuesday, 11th. We travelled thirteen miles.

Wednesday, 12th. We travelled eighteen miles.

Thursday, 13th. We travelled twelve miles to the Seneca agency.

I delivered the Indians into the care of Major Kennerly, the agent for the Senecas, agreeably to instruction. They will remain upon the land of their brethren, the Senecas, until an exchange of their tract of land is made, at which time they will remove to the piece given them.

I and my assistant, with the chiefs and others of our detachment, went to examine their tract which is situated west of the Neosho, and does not extend within less than five or six miles of it; but, in consequence of its being too high to ford, we were compelled to remain on the east side. There was no boat in which we could cross.

The resident Senecas say it cannot be cultivated; that there is scarcely any timber upon it, and but little good soil, and withal, entirely unadapted to their purposes.

Upon this representation, they refused going to see it, but they have since been over to make an examination of its advantages and disadvantages, but what their conclusion is I have not yet learned.

DANIEL M. WORKMAN,
*Conductor of Lewistown Emigrating Indians,*
By DANIEL R. DUNIHUE.

Mr. D. M. Workman instructed me to make out this copy and forward it on to the War Department, which I now have the honor of doing. It should have been sent on some time ago, but my recent arrival at home, and unavoidable business, has prevented me until the present time.

Very respectfully,
DANIEL R. DUNIHUE.

*February* 10, 1833.

---

SUPERINTENDENCY OF INDIAN AFFAIRS,
*Detroit, February* 11, 1833.

SIR: I have been requested to forward the enclosed memorial, praying that provision may be made for the valuation and payment of improvements which the Indians are obliged to abandon, under the treaty of Saginaw. The whole subject is so familiar to the honorable the Secretary of War, that I must refer to him for any further information you may require.

I am, very respecfully,
Your obedient servant,
GEORGE B. PORTER.

ELBERT HERRING, Esq.,
*Commissioner of Indian Affairs.*

*To the Honorable the Senate and House of Representatives of the United States in Congress assembled.*

The memorial of the undersigned, citizens of the Territory of Michigan, respectfully represents: That, at a treaty concluded at Saginaw, between the United States of America, by Lewis Cass, their commissioner, and the Chippewa nation of Indians, the sixth article of said treaty is in the words following, to wit:

"The United States agree to pay to the Indians the value of any improvements which they may be obliged to abandon, in consequence of the lines established by this treaty, and which improvements add real value to the land."

The improvements which the Indians are obliged to abandon, under this treaty, are considerable, and are among the first selections made in the country; they have, in some instances, been obliged to commence entirely anew, and have suffered from the consequences. The improvements on Green Point, on the Saginaw river, at Saline, on the Schiawasse river, and Fisher's village, of Grand Blanc, are among the first selections made in the country, and add real value to the land.

The undersigned memorialists therefore pray, that a law may be passed by your honorable body, granting relief to such Indians as are obliged to abandon their improvements; that the superintendent may be authorized to appoint commissioners to appraise the improvements, or to hire improvements made, of the same value, on their reservations. And your memorialists, as in duty bound, will ever pray.

*Dated at Saginaw, October 3,* 1832.

HENRY CONNOR,
THOMAS PIMPUEN,
E. S. WILLIAMS,
G. D. WILLIAMS,
A. WILLIAMS,
WILLIAM CONNER,
HENRY COMPEAN,
JACOB GRANT,
JOHN H. COMERS,
TROWBRIDGE,
LOUIS MAJOR.

*Indian Chiefs.*

| | |
|---|---|
| O-KE-MAW-KE-KI-TO, | his x mark. |
| KELCH-E-NO-TIN, | his x mark. |
| MUC-COO-COOCH, | his x mark. |
| KE-POO-TI-A-QUAW-TIN, | his x mark. |
| SHOW-O-NIP-E-NA-SE, | his x mark. |
| WAUB-E-TO-ANSE, | his x mark. |
| MONK-SAUB, | his x mark. |
| QUA-TOSH-E, | his x mark. |
| OC-QUE-WE-SANE, | his x mark. |
| MES-CO-PE-NA-SE, | his x mark. |
| SAW-WAW-BON, | his x mark. |
| SHIG-O-NA-GI-SHIG, | his x mark. |
| PA-MOS-U-GA, | his x mark. |
| WASH-U-AR, | his x mark. |

CHIM-E-TOSH,                     his x mark.
CHA-NIN,                         his x mark.
MES-SAW-BAY,                     his x mark.
CHI-CHIS-KA-WA,                  his x mark.

---

CREEK AGENCY, *February* 11, 1833.

SIR: The undersigned have been here since the 8th of January, investigating claims, and attempting to discharge the many duties heretofore assigned them by the War Department; and have, with much labor, waded through the great mass of claims which have been presented.

It will require at least one month or more labor of Major Abbott, Secretary of our Board, to transcribe the evidence and our proceedings, so that the same may form a part of our report, which report we shall by to-morrow have prepared.

Our continuance longer at this place would only increase the expense to the Government. We shall, therefore, as soon as we prepare our report, adjourn; and Major Parsons will proceed to complete the census roll of the upper towns, as soon as he can; Major Abbott having finished the lower towns.

Col. Crowell will remain here, at his residence, and E. Parsons will proceed to Claiborne, Alabama, his home.

The character and amount of the papers which we have examined, and the census rolls, would, in our opinion, authorize, in order to their safety, the ordering Major Abbot on to Washington, with the papers. Communications addressed to Major T. I. Abbott, would, for the time before stated, reach him at this place; and any matter you may wish to communicate to us, would reach either of us at our respective homes.

We have left Major Abbott to complete the work before mentioned, and if you concur in the opinion that it would be best for Major Abbott to bring on the papers, you will please so to inform him, as we did not choose to request Major Abbott to carry on the papers, but preferred submitting our opinion upon the fact to you, so that your discretion might be used upon the subject.

We are, &c.,
JOHN CROWELL,
ENOCH PARSONS,
B. S. PARSONS.

Hon. ELBERT HERRING,
*Commissioner Indian Affairs, Washington.*

---

SUPERINTENDENCY OF INDIAN AFFAIRS,
*Detroit, February* 11, 1833.

SIR: I am informed that General Street has written to the department, urging the necessity of the removal of the Winnebagoes west of the Mississippi; and the propriety of doing away with the sub-agency at Fort Winnebago. I know not whether this be so; but, as informed, I think it my duty to address you on the subject. He, or any other individual, must be ignorant of the country north of the Wisconsin, who would *try* to make the Secretary of War, (who has a perfect knowledge) believe that the Winnebagoes must go west of the Mississippi, to subsist. Nor is it the fact, as has been alleged, that their not going to that country is attributable to the influence of Mr. Paquette. I am decidedly of opinion that these Winnebagoes will never go west of the Mississippi to *remain*, as long as they can live north of the Wisconsin. During the winter season, some of them may go there to hunt. The Sioux are averse to their going to that country; and the Sacs will no doubt retaliate upon them, whenever an opportunity presents. The Winnebagoes are well aware of this, and have so stated. During my late visit to that country, when the Winnebagoes were assembled to receive their annuities, they spoke very decidedly on this subject. They were then making arrangements to move in large bodies to the Bar-ra-bo, and in that vicinity. Mr. Gratiot, the sub-agent, on Rock river, was present; and his Indians all intended going north of the Wisconsin. On the removal of these Indians his sub-agency will, I suppose, be done away with. But the duties and labors of the sub-agency at Fort Winnebago will be greatly increased. It is now, it seems to me, the most important post in this superintendency, because of its local situation, in the immediate vicinity of Indians disposed to be hostile. Under this view it was, that, when writing on another subject a few days since, I suggested the propriety of having an agency established by law at Fort Winnebago. No agent was ever better adopted to a situation than Mr. Kinzie. He has great influence over the Indians; and they are much attached to him. He speaks their language. When at the agency, I saw among his papers, a letter from the Secretary of the Commissioners, (General Scott and Governor Reynolds,) who concluded the treaty; and I enclose a copy of it for your perusal. But Mr. Kenzie cannot live on the good opinion of the world. His situation is different from that of any other agency. Living, as he does, in an Indian country, his house is the only one at which a stranger can stop, and he is, from this necessity, compelled to entertain a great number of persons during the year. The small salary which he receives will not enable him to live. Bread stuffs, provisions, and all the necessaries of life are very high there; and, to my surprise, I found that no order had ever been issued permitting him to be supplied by the commissary at the post, with provisions, &c , the same as officers of the army. The propriety of such an order is obvious; and I beg leave to urge it being made. If there be no prospect of an agency being established there, Mr. Kinzie will, I am of opinion, leave that place. And I assure you that I cannot now name any one to succeed him, who would be what a sub-agent there ought to be. This part of the subject. I trust, will claim the attention of the Secretary of War, whose intimate knowledge of all parts of this superintendency, and the material to make sub-agents of, will enable him to act with judgment and to the public advantage. He must be the right kind of a man, or else he had better not go to Fort Winnebago.

I enclose the copy of a talk I had with these Winnebago Indians. It was taken down in writing by Mr. Kinzie, and has been copied and forwarded to me since my return. Among other matters therein contained, it seems to me the complaint they make of not receiving their full proportion of the tobacco and salt stipulated by the treaty, is well founded. You have access to the pay rolls; and by ascertaining the number who are paid by General Street, at Prairie du Chien, and the number paid at Fort Winnebago, you can make a just apportionment of the fund to be sent to each agency. The complaint is, that much more than a fair proportion is sent to the Prairie.

The absolute necessity there is for supplying them early in the ensuing spring, with corn and provisions, is not too strongly represented by them. They could raise no corn during the past year, and they have nothing on which they can subsist. I hope this subject will claim the immediate attention of the department. The corn must be purchased at this place, or below us in Ohio, and sent up on the opening of the navigation. It must be done soon, or we cannot procure it.

On the subject first mentioned in this communication, I enclose the copy of a letter from Mr. Rolette, of Prairie du Chien. And since the receipt of this, I have received other information, which gives me to understand that Gen. Street has written to your department. I should be pleased to learn that it is not so.

I have the honor to be,

With great respect,

Your obedient servant,

G. B. PORTER.

The Hon. Elbert Herring,
   *Commissioner of Indian Affairs.*

---

*Memo. of a Talk held with the Winnebagoes, at Fort Winnebago, November 8, 1832.*

Little Elk, a Winnebago chief, addressed his excellency, Governor Porter, as follows:

Father: I have been selected by my nation, here present, to say a few words to you, that it may reach the ears of our great father, at Washington. We have been advised, by our father, (Mr. Kinzie,) to remain quiet; but some of our young people have not done so. We are ashamed of it, and our father is also. About four years ago, I saw our great father at Washington; he pointed out to us a good road, and we, (of the Ouisconsin and Fox rivers,) remained in that road. There are two bands in this nation: the Rock river band and Ouisconsin band. The former did not go to Washington to see our great father and to hear his words; therefore, did not take the right road; they were the ones who did wrong. When we went to Washington to see our great father, he there told us that we should be mixed with the whites. He then, at our request, appointed our friend here, (Mr. Kinzie,) our agent; we have found his words true; he has always given us good advice. Since I have heard my great father's words, they have ever been in my mind, and in the minds of those of Fox and Ouisconsin bands. No one can say otherwise than they have behaved well during all last summer. Since the Sacs and Foxes have been destroyed, we examined into the conduct of all our young men. They all showed us a clean hand and a clean heart. I hope, therefore, that the conduct of the tribes I represent may be made known to our father, the President, that he may take pity upon us, his red children, and alleviate our miserable condition. We want assistance in the way of provisions.

All our corn has been destroyed during the past summer; our only hope for the present is the chase: game is scarce; but I hope we will be able to make out to live till our great father can render us his aid.

Had it not been for Black Hawk and Prophet, the Rock river band would not have been engaged in staining our land with the blood of the whites.

It was some of *their* young men, who were related to the Sacs, that have caused all this trouble to our nation. Not long since we received a message from a great war chief (Gen. Scott) to attend at Rock Island. We went thither immediately. He told us that he had just come from the far east, and had been sent by his great father, the President. He examined into our conduct, and said he was pleased with our band's behaviour. He mentioned that some of our nation had taken up the hatchet against our friends, the whites; and that we must tell the truth about it, and tell him their names. Before we left this place for Rock Island, we heard that some of our young men of Rock river had behaved badly. As we had always delivered up our bad young men, when required by the whites, I thought it would not be right to do otherwise now. After we had complied with his wishes, he then told us that he wanted our land. He said, at the treaty of Prairie du Chien, a line had been drawn between us and the whites; that it was our fault if they came over it; that *he* wanted to make a *stronger* line—one that the whites would not go over. He did so; and if they go over this line, no line will stop them. He said that he was well pleased; that he had mentioned *two words* to us, and that we did as he desired. He told us that our father here, Mr. Kenzie, would soon pay us our money, and more next year. When at Rock Island, there were three claims presented against us. Our father (Scott) said he would see it paid. We thought that the money we should get, would be paid to us; but the whites want it all. They come to our father here (Mr. K.) with long papers, to take all our money. When we had no money, they never troubled us with their ugly papers. When I saw my great father at Washington, he told us how much money we should draw; he never mentioned to us any thing about claims. He advised us to make good use of our money. Even some of our traders here are digging up old claims, made by our grandfathers. I wonder what they think we are to do. We have but little, and that little they want, and to starve us. We have been waiting for some time here for our money, and our traders have also. We may lose all our fall hunts in consequence of it; and we will not, perhaps, reach our wintering grounds. The time has now past for laying up our winter's supply of provisions. Had it not been for our father here, (Mr. Kenzie) who has fed our women and children, and for a part of the 60,000 rations due us by the late treaty, which has been given to us, we should have starved. I hope, father, that you will tell our great father, the President, our condition, and for him to take pity upon us, his red children, in the spring; it is then we will want his support in provisions most. We want corn. I wish to mention another thing to you. The Indians at Prairie du Chien (about 500 souls) receive as much tobacco and salt as the Rock river bands and ours (about 3,800 souls.) Why is this? I think it ought to be divided equally. I hope it will be different hereafter. Our manner of living is different from the whites. You have good houses and good living: we have no such houses, and we have to hunt for our living.

*White Crow*, of Rock river, spoke as follows:

FATHER: I have a few words to say to you; father, I hope you will listen to me. I look upon you as our great maker. Ever since I can remember, I have followed the advice of the whites. I am in a very bad situation, as also our band. We have waited here long. Our American father has been a great while trying to purchase our lands; but we always told him we would not sell, unless the whole nation would consent. Some years ago we sold a

12‡

piece of land, because he told us we would be a great deal better off than ever we were before; but ever since, we have been worse off than we were before we sold any of our land. This spring, when the snow went off, the Sacs and Foxes came to us and said they were going to raise the war club against the whites, and wished to persuade us to join them. We said we could not, because we considered ourselves Americans. I soon after went down Rock river with this man, who has been our father and adviser (Mr. Gratiot) and we got to the American war chief's (Atkinson's) camp, and he told us to drive the Sacs back; but we could not; they wanted to bloody our land. When he (Atkinson) saw we could not get them off our land, he advised us to leave our land; to go away from our country, and to keep out of his way. We said we could not do that, as we had nothing to eat. He then said we should eat whatever we found in our country, in the way of cattle, hogs, &c.; but we told him we could not do so, as there would be claims enough presented against us, by the whites, at our payment. We thought it was only us that was foolish—that could tell *lies*—but I find that some of you whites are as good at it as many of our young men. Many of the whites are as bad as we are. They took all our corn, and many articles, as they passed our villages, and have even taken up the dead that were buried, and took off the blankets, &c., in which they were wrapped. Their conduct in this particular, father, has hurt the feelings of many of our young men. I have been told by some of the white chiefs that, as soon as the *fuss* would be over, we should be recompensed for our losses for corn, &c., they destroyed for us. I am looking for something to eat hereafter from our great father, the President. If we should not get something, we shall certainly lose half of our nation. We have been too far from our father here (Mr. Kinzie). We had only this one (Mr. Gratiot) to look to; and if something is not done for us, we will be in a very bad situation; and I still hold him fast by his hand. He has done too much for us, before he was appointed agent, for me to forget him. Things of that kind are not easily forgotten; and that is the reason I say I shall hold him by the hand. If any of our young men do wrong, I am always ready to deliver them up to the whites. As I have said, I always listen to your words, and those of our great father, the President. If any of our boys are in your hands now, it is the fault of the Sacs. Before they came into our country, we lived happily and peaceably; but as soon as they got into our land, they led some of our foolish boys wrong, and tore our country to pieces. A great many lies have been told on these boys, who are now in the fort. If I knew they were engaged in murdering, I would, with great pleasure, give them into your hands. As they have been suspected of murdering, I have given them up in that way. I hope they will be better treated, while in your hands, than they have been. They are badly off for clothing, they are freezing to death. They are only *suspected;* and until they are found guilty, they should not be treated as if they wished their death. If they are found guilty, I will not say a word; but, as it is, they suffer greatly. There will be a great many of their friends near here, who will supply them with fresh meat; and I hope they will allow us to give it to them. If our great father, the President, intends to do any thing for us, in the way of corn, we would wish our father (Mr. Gratiot) to have it, so that we can get it when we call for it.

My CHILDREN: I have listened, with great attention, to what you have said. I had come a long distance to hear and learn what your situation and condition were, and to see all your people. I regret, however, to find that we have not a clear sky, a bright sun, for our council. The smoke of happiness and the comforts of peace have forsaken you. The Great Spirit is displeased. I have had several councils lately—some beyond the Great Lakes, and several with the Menomonies, and Wabenokies, while at Green Bay. At all these, on each council day, the sky was clear, the sun bright, and the weather fine. Why is it that the Great Spirit is not equally propitious here? You know the cause. After all the kindness of your great father—disregarding his councils and advice, you have behaved badly; not the whole of your nation, but some of them. And after all the clemency and mercy extended to you by your great father, and the great war chief he sent among you, still you hesitate in doing right. You have, in consideration of his forgivenes, promised to surrender and deliver all up among you who were in any way concerned in the murder of our white men. You have not yet done so. Is it any wonder, then, that the Great Spirit is displeased with you? Your great father, the President of the United States, has great reason to be angry with you; but he pities you. He always speaks the *truth;* and he will be much dissatisfied with any of his red children who tell a *lie.* You have promised to deliver up all those of your nation, who were acting badly. You have not done so. You cannot expect that the Great Spirit will be appeased; that your great father's heart will be softened, until you can come in with clean hands, and tell the whole truth. Until you deliver up, not only the man you promised to bring in, but also the one we have heard of, and all others whom you know to have been in any way concerned in the outrages committed on our citizens; bring them all in, and thus exculpate yourselves. Each one of you, who is innocent, should feel an interest in the surrender of the guilty. You are right in supposing that these men, who have been committed, should not be considered guilty, until proved to be so. This is the rule of your great father. Every one is presumed innocent, until found guilty. Your men shall have a fair trial. I shall rejoice, if they can satisfy us that they are innocent. They would, in that event, be given up to you, and you would receive them among you as good men. But, when I say this, do not understand me that we intend letting them go clear if they be found guilty. Justice will require that they shall be punished as they deserve. The blood of our unoffending citizens cries aloud for vengeance. Those who are guilty must not expect to escape.

You say that your young men, who are in prison, are suffering with cold; that they have no blankets. I will attend to this. I shall go and see them, and take with me your father, (pointing to Mr. Kinzie,) and also the agent and father of your small band, (Mr. Gratiot,) and I shall take measures for bettering their condition, if I find what you say is correct Whatever you wish to give them, from time to time, must be done through your father here, (Mr. K.) You must not trouble the officers at the fort, but come to him, and whatever is right you should do, your father will have done according to your wishes. Remember what I say to you.

The fate of these men in prison should lead you to reflect and consider the consequences of such bad conduct. How was all this brought about? Let me tell you. Some years ago, your nation behaved badly; some of your men, at least, did so. You were filled with vanity and self-conceit. Because your great father, the President, did not at once send a great band of warriors to chastise you, to cut you to pieces, you vainly imagined he had not a sufficient force to punish you. He pitied your weakness; he disregarded your folly; and, for the purpose of convincing you of your errors, he sent for you, and invited your chiefs and head-men, to go to Washington to see him.   The first chief who spoke, (Little Elk,) was among those who went on.   I saw him there, and know the good advice he received from his great father.   He saw, with his own eyes, the great number of warriors his great father had, and how vain it would be for the Winnebagoes to attempt to contend with them.   On his return, he told his people (many of you who are present heard it) all he saw and heard; and I am pleased to find that so many of you have profited by it.   But, although invited, none of the Rock river band would go to Washington.   They did not believe what was told them, by those who went in 1828; turned a deaf ear to the good advice sent to them by their great father.   They now see the effect of such conduct.   By refusing to take good advice, evil came upon them. They forgot all the kindness which had been extended to them, and took bad advice from the Sacs.   Had they any cause for doing so?   Certainly not.

You all know that, after the treaty of Prairie du Chien, your great father faithfully fulfilled all the stipulations on the part of the Government of the United States.   Your money was sent to you regularly; you got your tobacco and salt; blacksmiths were provided, who did all your work; you had no cause of complaint.

When the Sacs behaved wrong, and made war upon our white people, your great father sent his war chiefs and warriors to chastise them.   One of his great war chiefs, General Scott, was also sent among them, and you all know what followed.   Where are these poor deluded Sacs and Foxes now? Look at their fate and learn wisdom from it.   Their chiefs and war chiefs are our prisoners; their women and children are rendered miserable.   Your great father has been informed that some of your Winnebagoes were concerned with these Sacs; he directed his great war chief to inquire whether this were true.   Your father here, (Mr. Kinzie,) and the father of the Rock river band, (Mr. Gratiot,) were instructed also to inquire into the matter. Some of you behaved honestly and well; came forward and told the truth; and when all was found out, you obligated yourselves, in the treaty with General Scott, to deliver them up.   You have not yet done so; you must do so, or you cannot, as I have already said, expect that your troubles will cease.

You complain that you have had to wait a long time for your money; and that you have suffered much in consequence of the delay; that you have lost your hunting season.   I regret to say it is all your own fault, and you should feel very thankful that you are allowed to have it even at this late period of time.   Your great father would have been fully justified in refusing to let you have one dollar.   Let me explain this to you: when you made the treaty at the Prairie, you promised to behave yourselves well; that you would not permit any of your people to make war upon the white men, or to kill them.   In consideration of these fair promises, you were to get money, &c.   When, therefore, *you* proved faithless, can you have any right longer to receive this money?   Certainly not.   Your great father had sufficient cause to drive you away, and to stop the payment of your annuity. But he pitied—he loved you.   He knew there were many good men among you, who obeyed his instructions, and remembered the good advice he gave you.   His heart was softened, and he did not think it right that, because some of your young men behaved badly, all of you should be punished.

He would not, however, send the money to you, until the necessary examination was made, and it was discovered who was in fault, and who were innocent. He was determined that no money should be paid to those who were concerned in any way with the Sacs. Your father here (Mr. Kinzie) was instructed not to pay any of these bad men or their families; they must not, therefore, be displeased with him. Their great father has directed it, and it must be done. Neither they nor their families can have any of the money brought here. As soon, then, as we heard from your father here that you were willing to obey the call of the great war chief, (Gen. Scott,) and to go to see him at Rock Island, and there enter into an engagement to surrender up those who were suspected of committing the murders and misdemeanors which he had heard of, the *money* was made ready for you at Detroit, and your friend the Chippewa (Major Forsyth) and I, made preparation for bringing it hither. But even then it seemed as though the Great Spirit were displeased. For twelve days the winds blew so much, that the vessel in which we were to sail could not get from Cleveland to Detroit; after it reached there, and while we are on board on our passage to Green Bay, storms, thunder, and lightning retarded our progress. Why was this so? You must see that there was something wrong. You cannot hope that all will be right until you come forward and tell the whole truth, and surrender the guilty who are among you. The money is now here, and your father may pay it to you to-morrow. But remember this is done on the promise which you now make, that you will, at once, bring those two men, and any others you know to be guilty. This, then, should satisfy you. It shows the goodness of your father (the President) in letting you have the money this year after you have given him so much trouble. But besides this, his great war chief has made a treaty with you upon the most fair, liberal, and generous terms; he has treated you better than you deserved. He has shown you that he is not only a good war chief, but a very good man. I have examined the treaty wh ch he made with you; it is all right. Behave yourselves well, and you will receive lasting benefits from it. Your money will come regularly to you as heretofore, and all that is stipulated by this treaty will be fulfilled. This war chief acted under the directions of your great father, who never speaks to his children with a forked tongue. He told you the truth when he said a line was now run between you and the white man that no one could step over. That the road would now be clear, and that you would be comfortable and happy if you followed his advice.

In regard to your necessities, which has caused him to issue, for your present subsistence, a considerable part of the rations, which, by the treaty, were to be delivered to you next spring, and your request that others may be provided for by that time, I can only add that the whole matter will be communicated to your great father, and I hope he may be enabled to grant your request; I shall recommend it to his particular attention. If possible, too, the attempt will be made to get some corn for you by spring; and should it be procured, of course the band under Mr. Gratiot will receive their just proportion, as they have requested, through the last speaker, (White Crow.)

There is, it seems to me, some injustice done you, in the distribution of the tobacco and salt provided for in the treaty. Your remarks are entitled to much weight; I shall endeavor to have justice done you. It pleases me to find that you pay so much attention to your own interests. Whenever any thing is not right you must speak of it to your father here, (Mr. Kinzie,)

and he will attend to it.   Your great father would not willingly wrong you.
But he is a great way off.   He has many agents, and they may sometimes
make a mistake; but whenever it is pointed out, it affords him pleasure to
rectify it.

There is a request which you make that is unreasonable, and it cannot be
granted.   You ask that your great father should pay the claims which are
presented for depredations committed by your people, for articles they
have got and the like, and that the claims may not be deducted from your
annuity.   This would be all wrong.   If one of you injure the property of
another, justice requires that you should pay for it.   But is there any
sense in supposing that your great father would pay for your bad conduct?
If you behave well, act uprightly, you will have no occasion to pay for any
claims of this kind; so as to claims for articles you have received, or which
you have purchased, you have got full value for the money they demand,
and every principle of honor and honesty requires that you should pay it.
In all matters of this kind, you should tell the truth.   It is the duty of your
father here (Mr. Kinzie) to receive these claims when handed to him, and
to present them to you.   If you know them to be right, you should admit
them at once.   You cannot expect to prosper, if you are dishonest.   It is
dishonest to refuse to pay a just claim; one that you know is correct.   On
the other hand, if an unfounded claim be presented, it is your duty to
refuse to allow it.   But you must not be displeased with your father here,
for making inquiry with respect to a claim of this kind, or any other, as I
have already said it is his duty to do so.   In presenting it to you, however,
you must not understand that he advises you to pay in every case.   He
never will urge you to allow a claim which he believes unjust.   I would
be better pleased with you, if you would place implicit confidence in your
father here.   You know how honest and true he is to your interests.   Some
of you went to Washington under his care, and the care of your friend, the
Chippewa, (Major Forsyth.)

Last summer, if you recollect, as now, you wished to persuade us that
you were our friends, and could show us a " clean hand," innocent of any
participation with, or knowledge of, the intentions of the Sacs.   You solicited, at that time, an interview with the Chippewa.   He, with your father
here, both of them are well known to you as your warm friends, met in
council; that you then requested the Chippewa to tell me, your father at
Detroit, all you said; that you held me tight by the hand, and desired your
father here to put your words down on paper, that your friend, the Chippewa, might carry it to me.   He told me all he and your father had said,
and I received by him the paper containing your talk.   I am sorry to say
*now*, that you have not behaved rightly; that you did not tell them all you
knew, but have deceived them.   Had you told them the truth, the Great
Spirit would not have got angry with you, and placed you in your present
troubles.   Your women and children would not, as they now are, have
been suffering for want of something to eat.   All this will be a good lesson
to you, and teach you hereafter always to tell the truth.   How do you
expect to be treated by the whites, after telling so many big lies?   They will
treat you like dogs, until you learn to behave better.   I expect to visit this
country again next year, and I hope your father here will have it in his
power to render me a good account of your behavior, and of your disposition to be good hereafter.

I have one more word to say to you, and that is about *whiskey*. If you look back upon your past conduct, up to this time, you will find that *whiskey* has caused more sorrow to your nation than the greatest enemy you have had to contend with. It is the poison of the red man; and so long as you permit it to come into your country, so long will you always be in trouble. Throw whiskey aside, behave well, and your nation will prosper.

I now hold you fast by the hand, and I hope the words which I have spoken to you will go into your ears, and never come out again.

---

FORT ARMSTRONG, ROCK ISLAND, *Sept.* 16, 1832.

SIR: The commissioners, who have just signed the treaty of this place with the Winnebago nation, take great pleasure in acknowledging the promptness with which you have brought the Indians of your deputation from Fort Winnebago to this place, and the efficient service you have been enabled to render the commissioners since your arrival, through the means of your local information and general acquaintance with Indian affairs, in the formation of the treaty.

On the part of the commissioners,

I have the honor to be, sir,

Your obedient servant,

RICHARD BACHE,
*Capt. Ord. and Secretary to the Commissioners.*

To JOHN H. KINZIE,
*Sub Indian Agent.*

---

PRAIRIE DU CHIEN, *December* 6, 1832.

DEAR SIR: From the short acquaintance I had with you, I think it my duty to notify you of any interference by person or persons in your superintendency. General Street, the Indian agent at this place, wrote a long letter to the War Department to have the Winnebagoes removed west of the Mississippi, and urging the extinction of the agency at Fort Winnebago, giving for reasons they still would be near the whites; and in his communication attributes their remaining north of Ouisconsin river to the influence of Paquette. Now, sir, to convince you of the absurdity of his communication, if the Winnebagoes should be removed west of this place, they would remain on the river, in the common highway, and trouble us much more than they would on the Ouisconsin, where they will see but few people. But, I have to remark, Gen. Street's son is a trader at this place, and has the store in the agency house. Rumor says father, son, and the sub-agent are all concerned. What motives can a man have in wishing himself additional trouble for the same pay? He certainly must wish to have them removed west of this to have payment of the whole annuities, and by that favor his son's trade, or their own, if the report is correct.

The Winnebagoes have a blacksmith allowed to them at this place: they prefer paying elsewhere than to take advantage of their blacksmith; and this man, who is in the pay of the United States, works three-fourths of his time for the citizens. All I state to you, can be substantiated.

Your most obedient servant,

JOSEPH ROLETTE.

To his Excellency G. B. PORTER,
*Governor of the Michigan Territory.*

House of Representatives, *Feb.* 12, 1833.

Sir: The enclosed is from a respectable man.   I do not know what attention, if any, should be paid to its suggestions.
I am, sir,
Your obedient servant,
S. BEARDSLEY.

Hon. Lewis Cass,
*Secretary of War.*

———

Vernon, *February* 6, 1833.

Dear Sir: Many of the Oneida Indians would go to Green Bay this spring, if they could be satisfied that the question relative to the peaceful enjoyment of their lands there was settled.   They are very incredulous as to it, and I have, therefore, at the solicitation of some of them, who wish to get as large a party as possible to go this spring, (which we have a great desire to promote,) thought it would be well for the President to send them some satisfactory evidence of the adjustment of these difficulties.   A communication from him, directed to the chiefs of the Oneida Indians at this place, would probably be very satisfactory to them.   They say there is nothing in the papers about it, and they will not believe the white men. Nothing short of a communication from their father, (as they style the President,) would seem to suffice.   Will you see the President on this subject?
Yours, truly,
J. WHIPPLE JENKINS.

Hon. S. Beardsley, *Washington.*

———

Wascissa, *February* 12, 1833.

Sir: Blunt visited me last night with a complaint that a trespass has been committed upon him by some Creek Indians; and that the white men have already commenced expelling the Indians from their cabins, and occupying them, under the pretext that he has sold his reservations.   In the stipulations made with Blunt, he was to be protected by the United States until prepared to migrate, the time for making all necessary arrangements being limited to two years.   I have referred Blunt to the Governor, who will no doubt attend to his case; but, believing as I do, that no effectual protection can be extended to the Indians on the Appalachicola, without the presence of a resident agent, who may be applied to, on all attempts to trespass on their rights, I take the liberty of again presenting the subject to your consideration.   I fear, unless active and immediate steps be taken with these impatient interlopers, much embarrassment may grow out of their acts, both to the Indians and the Government.   Their movements will unquestionably throw additional obstacles in the arrangements for removal, contemplated with the two other towns.   An additional agent cannot add much to the additional expense of the Indian Department, as his service may be commanded in assisting the removal of the Indians at the proper time, in the place of some other individual who would have to be employed for said purpose.   Should you conclude to make an appointment, I again present to your consideration, as a fit person, Mr. William Pope, now residing near the Indian towns, and whose name is on file in your office as an applicant for the place.

Respectfully, your obedient servant,

JAMES GADSDEN.

Hon. Lewis Cass,
*Secretary of War, Washington.*

———

Brown's Hotel,
*Washington City, February* 14, 1833.

Sir: Yours, in reply to ours, of the 28th ultimo, communicating the views of the President, has been maturely deliberated, and in duty to our nation we feel ourselves bound to respond to the same. We are told that the President looks with great anxiety and solicitation to our situation; that he knows our position is an embarrassing one, and that a change is called for by every consideration of present convenience and future security; and that the Government is desirous of entering into a satisfactory arrangement, by which all our difficulties will be terminated, and the prosperity of our people fixed upon a permanent basis. Yet we are assured that you are well convinced that these objects *can only be attained by a cession of our possessory rights* in Georgia, and by *our removal* to the country west of the Mississippi; that you can see no cause of apprehension, as we do, that such removal will be injurious, either in its immediate or remote consequences; a mild climate, a fertile soil, an inviting and extensive country, a government of our own, adequate protection against other tribes and against your own citizens, within a reasonable expectation, are freely offered to us. You cannot, therefore, see that the subject presents itself in the melancholy light in which we view it. You have also referred to the President's message to the Senate, of February 22, 1831, to show his views on the subject of the existing relations between the Indian tribes and the States in which they reside. In reviewing the principles upon which these views are predicated, we have been impelled to look into those upon which the primitive and conventional rights of the Cherokee nation have been recognized and established by the solemn acts of this Government. And it is with deep regret and great diffidence we are constrained to say, that, in this scheme of Indian removal, we can see more of expediency and policy to get rid of them, than to perpetuate their race upon any fundamental principle. Were it possible for you to be placed, or to imagine yourself for a moment to be in the peculiar situation in which we stand, with the existing treaties and laws, and the subsequent acts of the Government, all before your eyes, you cannot but feel and see as we do. It is impossible, then, for us to see, that by a removal to the country west of the Mississippi, all our difficulties would be terminated, and the prosperity of our people fixed upon a permanent basis. Would not a removal to the country west of the Mississippi, upon lands of the United States, by Indian tribes, under the provisions of the act of Congress, denationalize their character as distinct communities? By what tenure would such tribes occupy the lands to be assigned to them? Is not the fee simple title vested in and will be retained by the United States? What kind of a Government of their own, then, is designed for them to establish, and how is it possible for the United States to afford them more adequate

13‡

protection against your own citizens there, than where we are? These questions have never as yet been definitively settled down upon any fundamental law of Congress that we know of, and we cannot avoid believing that the present system of policy towards the Indians, is founded upon contingencies growing out of the interests and desires of the States, without regarding the permanent prosperity and happiness of the Indians. We intend no reflection upon the Government, in thus frankly communicating our views, but we deem it essential to a perfect understanding upon the subject. As to the climate, soil, and extent of the country, to which you have alluded, and the future propects of the Cherokees who are living there, our people are correctly informed on those points, from personal observations and otherwise. Withal, they have no wish to remove there. What, then, would be the consequence of a whole nation of people, driven by the force of necessity to leave their native land for a distant one, in a strange and inhospitable region, and there to experience the sad effects of injured disappointments? To what source could they seek indemnity for their injuries, and what tribunal will there redress their wrongs? for in vain have our nation appealed to the protecting arm of the General Government to fulfil treaty obligations; to shield our suffering people against illegal encroachments; and in vain will your supreme judicial tribunal have declared a verdict in favor of our nation, against the exercise of usurped power on the part of State authority. In the suggestions which we took the liberty to submit for the consideration of the President, that some practicable arrangement might be entered into between the United States and Georgia, to relieve our nation of its present embarrassments, we had entertained no doubt that, with a corresponding desire on the part of the General Government, such an arrangement could be effected, and, in that event, that Georgia would not be permitted to subject our people to the obedience of her laws, inasmuch as the Supreme Court of the United States had already pronounced the exercise of her jurisdiction over our territory and people, to be unconstitutional and void; and we are at a loss to see the grounds you have taken in arriving to the opinion that "we would still be subject to the laws of Georgia." We cannot subscribe to the correctness of the idea, which has been so frequently recurred to by the advocates of Indian removal, that the evils which have befallen and swept away the numerous tribes that once inhabited the old States, are to be traced to the *mere circumstance* of their contiguity to a white population; but we humbly conceive that the true causes of their extinction are to be found in the catalogue of wrongs which have been heaped upon their ignorance and credulity, by the superior policies of the white man, when dictated by avarice and cupidity. You appeal to our better feelings in regard to the situation of our people, and suggest that, under existing circumstances, some sacrifices may well be encountered in removing from a contact with the white population, in order to escape the fate which has swept away so many Indian tribes. Should the doctrine that Indian tribes cannot exist contiguously to a white population, prevail, and they be compelled to remove west of the States and Territories of this republic, what is to prevent a similar removal of them from there for the same reason? We can only plead, let equal justice be done between the red and the white man, and so long as the faith of contracts is preserved inviolate there will be no just cause for complaints, much less for aggressions on the rights of the one or the other, and that, so far as our (individually) sense of right, justice, and honor, will dictate to us a course to meet the wishes, the interest, and the permanent prosperity and happiness of our nation, that no pecuniary sacrifices or human sufferings ever so great, can or will deter us from encountering them.

Contrary to treaty stipulations and the intercourse act of 1802, there are numerous white families who have intruded upon the lands of our nation within the chartered limits of several of the adjoining States, and the repeated complaints made of the same to the agent, have not been regarded, and the trespassers, instead of being removed, have greatly increased in numbers, and are daily multiplying. We are constrained to bring this grievous subject before the department, that the evil be corrected.

In addition to these, there are others who threaten to overrun and dispossess our nation of its territory, under the sanction of State authority. Under the assumption of the right to exercise jurisdiction, it is known that Georgia has passed legislative acts to survey and draw a lottery for the occupation of our land, and which, in part, have been carried into effect; and without the timely interposition of this Government, will, doubtless, rob us of our lands.

Can this be permitted, or will the President extend the constitutional arm of the Government to save us from this impending calamity? His determination upon this delicate and important question, we most respectfully solicit. Also, if we are to understand, from your communication, that the propositions submitted through Mr. Chester, and which have been rejected by the general council of our nation, as containing the only basis upon which the Government will relieve our nation of the injustice of State oppressions. On the subject of our annuities you reply "that none are withheld from us;" "that the Government has engaged to pay certain annuities to the Cherokees, whether these are to be paid to persons representing the tribe, or the individuals composing it, as the treaties do not provide, the Government is at liberty to determine." The view you have taken of this subject is at variance with the true intent and meaning of those treaties, as all the former practice of the Government, in relation thereto, will show. The United States of America, through their commissioners plenipotentiary, entered into certain treaties with the chiefs, head-men, &c., of the Cherokee nation, who were duly authorized and empowered, by said nation, and in consideration for sundry cessions of land, there are certain annuities stipulated in those treaties to be paid to the Cherokee nation; and the usual practice of the Government, in paying those annuities, has always been through the United States agent, to the authorities of the Cherokee nation, and by them disposed of as the Legislative Council thereof think fit to direct for the public welfare. Upon the complaints of certain discontented chiefs of the upper Cherokee towns, to the Government, Mr. Jefferson, the then President of the United States, on the 4th day of May, 1808, spoke to them, in writing, thus: "You *complain* that you do not receive your just proportion of the annuity we pay your *nation;* that the chiefs of the lower towns take for them more than their share. My children, this distribution is made *by the authorities of the Cherokee nation,* and according to *their* own rules, over which *we have no control.* We do our *duty* in delivering the annuity to the *head-men* of the *nation, and we pretend to no authority over them, to no right of directing how they are to be distributed.*"

For the last thirteen years the Cherokee nation have had a treasurer, and into whose hands the annuities have been paid by the agent of the United States, and for the faithful performance of the duties assigned to this office, the treasurer has executed a bond, with ample security, in the penal sum fifty thousand dollars. The annuities due our nation, for the two last yea the agent has refused to pay them over to the treasurer as usual, notwithstanding the written request of the great mass of our people to do so; and upon his failing to induce the individuals of the nation to accept of this money, agreeably to the direction of the department, these annuities have since been deposited in the United States Branch Bank at Nashville, to the credit of the Treasurer of the United States. Under these circumstances, we felt justified in saying that our annuities are withheld from us. Since the unconstitutional proceedings of Georgia towards our nation, our public expenses have greatly increased, and, consequently, debts have been incurred, for the payment of which the faith of our nation stands pledged. And we trust the President will see, in this, good reasons for directing the annuities to be paid over to us, as heretofore, for we can see no possible advantage in the Government controlling the application of these annuities contrary to the interest and desire of our nation, where they constitute a debt from the United States to the Cherokee nation.

No complaints have ever been made to the Government, by our nation, against the dishonesty or misapplication of this annual stipend, by our own constituted authorities, on the contrary they have required the agent to pay it over as usual, and, without intending any reflection, we feel justified in saying that the Cherokee people feel as much respect for, and have as great confidence in the justice and integrity of their own public men, as they can possibly entertain towards the public agents of this Government in their nation.    With great respect,

We have the honor to be, sir,
Your obedient servants,
JOHN ROSS,
R. TAYLOR,
JOHN F. BALDRIDGE, his x mark.
JOSEPH VANN.

Hon. Lewis Cass, *Secretary of War.*

---

House of Representatives, *February* 17, 1833.

Dear Sir: I have the honor to enclose to you the copy of a letter received, by the Governor of North Carolina, from a citizen of Wilkes county, relating to depredations committed by intruders upon the lands in that part of the Cherokee nation which lies within the chartered limits of that State.

Governor Swain informs me that he had written to you upon the subject, which will have placed you in possession of his views.

Allow me to suggest, that, before the department takes any decisive steps, whether it would not be best to institute an inquiry into the precise state of the facts, through some *confidential agent*, which would enable you to judge more correctly as to the necessity of stationing a guard for the protection of that quarter.

Should you concur with me in this suggestion, I would intimate that General Thomas Love, of Macon county, would be an excellent selection to discharge the duties. The expense would be but trifling, as General Love resides near the nation, and is well acquainted with all the Indians of any notoriety in that part of the nation, as well as acquainted with the face of the country generally, and could, therefore, the more easily discern as to the *extent* of the injury complained of.

Very respectfully,    SAMUEL P. CARSON.
Hon. Lewis Cass, *Secretary of War.*

P. S. The President is personally acquainted with General Love, and is well aware of his capacity, to discharge the duties, should they be assigned to him.                                                        S. P. C.

---

WILKSBORO, *January* 29, 1833.

DEAR SIR: I am induced to write you a few lines on a subject which I conceive will be of some importance to the State of North Carolina, and I have been induced to make this communication to you by the solicitation of a number of the most respectable citizens in the western section of this State: it is in relation to the Cherokee lands within the jurisdictional limits of North Carolina. I have spent some time in that country within the last two months, and can assure you that the depredations that are now being committed on the Cherokee lands by intruders from Georgia, South Carolina, and Tennessee, are of the most aggravated nature; there is, at this time, more than one thousand intruders from those States, who are destroying the face of the soil, cutting down and killing all the valuable timber, and what is worse than all, they are depriving the natives and white citizens of all the benefits to be derived from the gold mines, which, I do assure you, is of much importance, as the gold lands within the limits of this State are the richest in the Union, and they certainly deserve the protection of the State; and if those intruders who are now in possession are permitted to remain there, the number will increase two fold as soon as the spring opens. I was astonished to find, on my arrival at Cocoa creek, that there were hundreds of men at work hunting gold; and from there until I reached the Georgia and Tennessee lines, I found the country full of those kind of intruders. But soon as I crossed over into Georgia and Tennessee, I found that the mines were protected by a suitable guard who were employed by the State authorities.

I have been requested to suggest to you the propriety of establishing similar guard for the protection of those mines; for you may rest assured, sir, that they are of immense value. To give you some small idea of the value of this country, I will merely state this one circumstance: I heard a gentleman of respectability and responsibility say, that he would give to the State of North Carolina $50,000 for one-half mile of the bed of Valley river; and this same individual is now engaged in cutting a canal to turn the water off, for the purpose of mining in the bed of the river. It is my opinion, as well as the opinion of almost every intelligent individual in this section of the State, that the portion of the country alluded to in my letter, deserves the immediate attention of the Executive protection; and we are of the opinion that should you think it prudent to establish an agency, or raise a guard to protect those mines, we would recommend, as a suitable person, to perform a duty of this kind, Major William E. Emmett, of this county, as he is well acquainted with the Indian character, from having been a great deal among them, and he would be better qualified to head a guard, or fill any military station, than any man in our knowledge, from his having been actively engaged in the United States army for several years. I have no doubt he would be willing to serve the State in any capacity by which he might render himself useful.

I would take it as a particular favor if you would address me a few lines, and inform me of what will be the probable course that you will pursue in relation to the Cherokee country, as I shall go there again in a few weeks, and the citizens will be very anxious to know what you may do in this matter.

I am, sir, yours,<br>Most respectfully,

Gov. Swain.                                   JOEL VANNAY.

---

MAUMEE, OHIO, February 18, 1833.

SIR: I lose no time in enclosing to you the treaty which I have this morning concluded with the Ottawas of the Maumee, for the cession of their lands on each side of the Miami river, of Lake Erie, and on the Miami bay. Not having received an answer to my letter of the 1st instant, asking for some further instructions, I have proceeded according to my own best judgment, and hope that what I have done will meet with the approbation of the department, and be ratified by the President and Senate of the United States. I found it impossible to effect a treaty without inserting the small reservations contained in this, amounting, in the whole, to but 2,560 acres. On much reflection, I am convinced it was right to allow them.

The tracts ceded contain 32,000 acres, agreeably to the description given of them in the treaties, by which they were originally set apart. Deducting therefrom the amount of these reservations, the balance would be 29,440 acres, for which I have agreed to pay one dollar per acre, amounting to $29,440. As these Indians had anticipated this sale by getting goods in advance, to the full amount of what the land was worth, they would listen to no proposition but that which yielded the most money to them. I endeavored, but without any the least effect, to persuade them to accept the very advantageous proposals contained in your letter of the 16th October last, in case they would wisely determine to go west of the Mississippi.

My account of the expenses incurred shall be transmitted as soon after my return home as possible.

With great respect,<br>Your friend, and obedient servant,<br>G. B. PORTER.

To the Hon. ELBERT HERRING,
Commissioner of Indian Affairs.

---

POLE CAT SPRING, CREEK NATION,<br>February 18, 1833.

SIR: The undersigned, head chiefs of the upper towns of the Creek nation of Indians, and national chiefs, make of you, and of their great father, the President, the following requests, which they hope will be in your power, and your pleasure, to award to them and their nation.

To wit: when you shall have examined the work of the commissioners in the investigation of claims, and a letter of the delegation of chiefs, from the upper towns, who attended the commissioners in said investigation, that you will order the money due under the treaty to be divided into two equal parts, first deducting six thousand dollars, said to be due Thomas Crowell, for money borrowed of him by the nation; and that one half of the remainder of the money shall be paid to the upper towns, as they in council shall direct, and so as to prevent the money of the people of the upper towns paying the debts of the people of the lower towns. The undersigned have satisfactory reasons for this request, and upon which to pray you to pay no regard whatever to the orders of the delegation of chiefs who attended the commissioners, in their presentation of a schedule of national claims. The said delegation consisted at first of equal numbers from the upper and lower towns, but, on the day this work of making national claims was done, two of the upper town chiefs were absent, and left the balance of power against us; and, moreover. we believe some of the upper town chiefs were bribed to do what they did.

And we ardently hope the whole of the money, and at least the part due to the upper towns, will be placed in the hands of General Enoch Parsons, to pay out according to the judgment the commissioners have passed, and the surplus, if any, as we may direct.

We believe General Parsons knows, better than any other man, the vile claims, and the proper disposition to be made of the money for the benefit of the nation, and we have entire confidence that he will do the Government and us justice; and if our request be granted, and he should betray the trust we repose, we will acquit the Government of all claim, but will add we have no fear of his cheating any party concerned, and believe the same justice cannot be done by any other person. He knows the claimants, and the foundation of the claims.

The above is done by us in general council, the date above, and we would prefer General Parsons should, at our own expense, go to Washington for the money, to the same being paid by any other person; but that is unnecessary, as the Government would place the funds with him. We know our just debts will exhaust the whole sum, without including fraudulent claims. We cause this letter to be signed with our names, and witnessed, so you may know it to be genuine.

| | |
|---|---|
| Ho-po-ithla Yoholo, | his x mark. |
| Ne-haw-loe-co Hobie, | his x mark. |
| Coosa Tustanugge, | his x mark. |
| Tuch-a-batcha Micco, | his x mark. |
| Mico Boiggaw, | his x mark. |
| Tam-athlaw Micco, | his x mark. |
| O-si Yoholo, | his x mark. |
| Tus-hatcha Micco, | his x mark. |
| Sos-ti Fixico, | his x mark. |
| O-si Hawgo, | his x mark. |
| Cho-gat-ta Fixico, | his x mark. |
| Spoak-okee Mico, | his x mark |
| Yoholo Mico, | his x mark. |
| Tuske-ne-haw, | his x mark. |
| Ah-chule Hargo, | his x mark. |
| Tom Anderson, | his x mark. |
| Tusta-nug Chopco, | his x mark. |
| Ah-haw-lock Hawgo, | his x mark. |
| Micco Yoholo, | his x mark. |
| Tallawaw Micco, | his x mark. |
| Ah-haw-locco-yi Yoholo, | his x mark. |

|                            |                |
|----------------------------|----------------|
| Coosa Micco,               | his x mark.    |
| Yoholo Hargo,              | his x mark.    |
| Talle-sa Fixico,           | his x mark.    |
| Hobie Hadka,               | his x mark.    |
| David Barnard,             | his x mark.    |

Witnesses present: WARD TAYLOR,
JUSTICE FORBES.

MAUMEE, OHIO, *Feb.* 18, 1833.

SIR. I enclose a memorial from the Ottowa Indians, of Maumee, with with whom I have been holding a treaty, complaining of the misunderstanding under which they labored when they concluded the treaty with Mr. Gardiner, in 1831. In my report to the department in September last, I stated the difficulty I anticipated in making a treaty on this account. This paper being presented to me now, I had a long conversation with Mr. Conner, and his certificate is annexed to their memorial. I cannot, from the representations made to me, doubt the Indians could not have understood Mr. Gardiner properly. To end the matter, the Government should pay them the money, so as to comply with the treaty as they supposed it was made. They are without a foothold in this region, and will soon be scattered before the winds. They cannot wait till the sales contemplated will take place. Should the Government comply with their request, the money had, perhaps, better be forwarded to me at Detroit. I shall be pleased to learn what disposition shall be made of the matter.

I am, very respectfully,
Your obedient servant,

G. B. PORTER.

ELBERT HERRING, Esq.,
*Commissioner of Indian Affairs.*

*To George B. Porter, Esquire, Governor of Michigan, and Superintendent of Indian Affairs.*

FATHER: We, the chiefs, and head-men of the Ottowa nation of Indians at Maumee, being assembled to hold a council with you, for the purpose, if possible, of making a treaty for the sale to the United States, of our two reservations, at and near the mouth of the river, and having heard what you had to say to us, beg leave to state, that, before we can make any new treaty, we must be satisfied about the treaty made with Mr. Gardiner, in August, 1831. T hat treaty, as it has been ratified and confirmed, and printed in your book, is not as we understood it, nor as it was interpreted to us. The way it was represented to us was this: Mr. Gardiner, in speaking about the land, offered to give us seventy cents per acre, besides paying for the improvements, and as we could not count, and, therefore, did not know to how much this would amount, Mr. Gardiner made the estimate, and said the money coming to us would be $40,000, besides the valuation of the improvements, which would amount to $2,000. Under the full belief that this sum of $40,000, exclusive of $2,000, for improvements, would be paid, consent was given to the treaty. Out of this sum, we agreed, as you will observe in the treaty, to pay our debts, amounting to about

$22,000, which would leave $18,000 coming to us, besides $2,000 for improvements; which money we calculated upon, and expected; for we had every reason so to do, and that, before this time, it would be paid to us. Besides this, Mr. Gardiner again and again promised us that the Government would deal with us in every way as favorably as with the Shawnees, for whose land a treaty had been made. As the treaty now reads, it appears, that instead of the seventy cents per acre, or $40,000, being applied first to pay our debts, and then the balance to ourselves, the lands are to be sold by the United States, and after deducting from the avails thereof, 70 cents per acre, exclusive of the costs of surveying, and $2,000 proposed to be advanced, as the valuation of our improvements, the balance is to be applied to pay the debts mentioned in the treaty, and the overplus, if any, to be applied to our benefit. We protest, as well on our own account, as on behalf of our brethren, who have gone west of the Mississippi, that this was not the treaty, and that we never did agree to any such thing. In this way, we would have got little or nothing for our land, as the result has shown. That the representation we make of the treaty is correct, we refer you to all our traders, and every one who was present at the treaty. Of this we wish you to inform yourself. Ask Messrs. John E. Hunt, John Hollister, Robert A. Forsyth, and all others who were present. Inquire particularly of Mr. Henry Connor, your interpreter. He was the interpreter at the treaty; and although we have never since spoken to him on the subject, relying on his known integrity of character, and convinced that he will tell the truth, we are willing to abide by what he will say.

We desire, therefore, that you will represent this matter to our great father, and obtain this money for us. We signed a paper and had it sent on to him long since, by the sub-agent at this place, but have received no answer. There are small debts which we justly owe that must be paid out of this money, as soon as you can get it. After that, it is to be divided between us and our brethren, who went west of the Mississippi. Before they parted from us a writing was made between us, stating the manner in which it is to be divided; one half to be for those who had gone or might emigrate, and the other for us who remain. We trust and hope that our great father, the President, and the Government will treat us as well as they did the Shawnees. They sent a deputation to Washington and represented the misunderstanding which existed in their treaty, as reported, and Congress gave them $30,000. We cannot suppose that this money will be withheld from us. But hope you will have pity on us, pay our debts stated in the treaty, give us the balance of $18,000, in such way as you think right, and we relinquish all the pretended excess or overplus, which might arise by the sale of the lands as provided for in the treaty. We ask this as our just due, and hope it will be granted.

*Maumee, Feb.* 15, 1833.

| | |
|---|---|
| Wau-se on-o-guck, | his x mark. |
| An-to-kee, | his x mark. |
| Ske-no, | his x mark. |
| Wau-bee-gai-keh, | his x mark. |
| Shaw-wa-no, | his x mark. |
| Ke-tuck-kee, | his x mark. |
| Aush-cush, | his x mark. |
| No-ten o, | his x mark. |

14‡

| Way-say-on, | his x mark. |
| Sass-Sair, | his x mark. |
| Nau-qua-gai-shick, | his x mark. |
| O-sage, | his x mark. |
| Mee-sau-kee, | his x mark. |
| Kin-ge-way-no, | his x mark. |
| An-ne-qua-to, | his x mark. |
| Meesh quet, | his x mark. |
| Sa-se-go-wan, | his x mark. |
| Pe-ton-o-quet, | his x mark. |

In presence of
JAMES JACKSON, *Sub-agent.*
LEWIS BEUFAIT,
CHAS. W. P. HUNT,
G. B. KNAGGS,
JAS. H. FORSYTH,
J. D. BEAUGRAND.

I hereby certify, that I have faithfully interpreted the above paper to the chiefs of the Ottowa band of Indians, whose names appear subscribed hereto, and that they acknowledge to have signed it for the purposes therein expressed.

HENRY CONNOR,
*U. S. Sub-agent and Interpreter.*

The undersigned have no hesitation in saying that the representation made in the foregoing paper, is correct, and there is no doubt that the under-standing of the Indians, at the time, as expressed in their intercourse with us, was as they have herein stated.

JOHN E. HUNT,
R. A. FORSYTH,
JOHN HOLLISTER.

I acted in the capacity of interpreter, at the treaty alluded to in the within memorial. I understood the arrangement to be as the Indians have therein expressed it, and accordingly so interpreted it to him.

HENRY CONNOR,
*U. S. Sub-agent and Interpreter.*

*Maumee, Feb.* 18, 1833.

---

COMMISSIONER'S OFFICE, FORT GIBSON,
*February* 18, 1833.

SIR: I have the honor of enclosing two treaties, concluded on the 14th instant, between the commissioners on behalf of the United States, and the Cherokee and Creek nations of Indians, west of the Mississippi. The proceedings in council, with the report of the commissioners thereon, will be made and forwarded to the department with as little delay as possible.

I am, very respectfully,
Your obedient servant,
S. C. STAMBAUGH,
*Secretary to Commissioners.*

Hon. LEWIS CASS,
*Secretary of War.*

House of Representatives, *February* 19, 1833.

Sir: Enclosed I send you a letter from General Enoch Parsons, in relation to the business in which he has been employed, in connexion with others, for some weeks past, at the Creek Agency. You will please to examine its contents, and do whatever you may think most proper under the circumstances. From the statement of General Parsons, I have no doubt it would subserve the interest of the Government for Mr. Abbott to come on here with the report and the documents on which it will be predicated. I should be glad to hear from you, in reference to the matter embraced in this letter. If not necessary to be filed in the department, please return it.

I have the honor to be,
Very respectfully,
Your obedient servant,
C. C. CLAY.

Hon. Lewis Cass.

P. S. I requested, some days ago, copies of certain accounts taken and reported upon claims of certain Creek Indians.

I am without any reply.

C. C CLAY.

---

Monticello, *February* 19, 1833.

Dear Sir: You will confer a favor on an humble citizen by answering the following questions:

Are there fractional surveys of the Creek lands in Alabama? If so, can an Indian take one of them? If an Indian is found out of one of their towns, will he be located where he is found? When will the Indians be located? Answers to the above will be thankfully received by

Your humble servant,
IRWIN LAWSON.

Hon. Lewis Cass,
Secretary of War.

---

Fort Wayne, *February* 20, 1833.

Dear Sir: I received a communication from the Commissioner of Indian Affairs, requesting further evidence of my having rendered professional services at the Miami treaty. I beg leave to submit the enclosed statements and certificates of Messrs. Marshall, Lewis, Hamilton, Forsyth, Ewing, Comparet, and Hanna, all of whom are personally known to the department.

The certificate of the commissioners might probably be had; but having disagreed with them, on account of their illiberality, I feel a delicacy in calling on them. I hope the accompanying statements will be satisfactory.

I have the honor to be,
Your very obedient humble servant,
L. G. THOMPSON.

Hon. Lewis Cass,
Secretary of War.

---

I do hereby certify that, during the pendence of the Miami treaty, I was informed by Chief Richardville, of that tribe, that Dr. L. G. Thompson was employed, at his and the Indians' request, by the commissioners, and have a perfect knowledge of Dr. Thompson's being actively employed from eighteen to twenty days, furnishing his own medicine; and, further, I called on Dr. Moffat with an Indian woman and child, who were unwell, and he directed me to Dr. L. G. Thompson, having no medicine himself; and I believe Dr. Thompson's claim is very reasonable.

JOHN FORSYTH.

*Fort Wayne, 20th February,* 1833.

---

INDIAN AGENCY, INDIANA,
*Logansport, February* 16, 1833.

I do hereby certify that at the late treaty of the Wabash, Indiana, Doct. L. G. Thompson, of Fort Wayne, was employed by the commissioners as a physician, and that sickness prevailed in the camp; that he rendered much service in administering and prescribing for the sick, and particularly for Mr. Peter Longlois, one of the interpreters, who was dangerously ill; that he served diligently and constantly for between sixteen and twenty days; that he had a very handsome practice at home, but, when requested, left it and came to camp; that I cannot say positively what such services are worth, but believe his account to be just; that the cholera was raging at Cincinnati and Detroit at that time; that between those two places and the treaty ground, there was a direct and almost daily communication; that great fears were entertained that it would reach the camp, grounded upon the said communication, the weather, the season, and unavoidable exposure of the persons in camp.

WILLIAM MARSHALL, *Indian Agent.*
Hon. ELBERT HERRING,
*Commissioner of Indian Affairs, Washington.*

---

INDIAN AGENCY, INDIANA,
*Logansport, February* 16, 1833.

SIR: I received yours of the 6th instant, and hasten to answer it. I know that, at the last treaty on the Wabash, you were employed by the commissioners, as a physician, for between sixteen and twenty days; that you rendered very essential services, particularly to Mr. Peter Longlois, one of the interpreters; indeed, you were very busily engaged the whole time; you had a very handsome practice at home, for it was sickly, and your coming to the treaty was, I verily believe, much to your disadvantage, yet your services were necessary, and you came. At that time, the cholera was raging at Cincinnati and Detroit to an alarming extent, and there was a direct communication constantly between those two places and the treaty ground, and a great many gentlemen were of opinion, from the weather, the season, and the exposure, that horrid disease would reach the camp.

You are at liberty to make use of this letter in any manner you may think proper; I also enclose you my certificate, which you are at liberty to use.

Col. Duret has gone to the city—we have nothing new here.

Respectfully,
Your obedient servant,
WILLIAM MARSHALL.

Dr. L. G. THOMPSON.

FORT WAYNE, *February* 20, 1833.

SIR: Dr. L. G. Thompson, of this place, informed me yesterday, that he had submitted to you, for your consideration, a claim for professional services, rendered during the pendency of a treaty with the Miami nation of Indians in September last, and that you had required some additional evidence of such services.

I can state that I called on one or two of the commissioners, and urged the propriety of his continuance during their negotiations with the Pottawatamie Indians, and I understood expressly from them that he was then in their employ; I believe, also, that the general opinion was that he had been engaged at the special instance and request of Chief Richardville.

As to the particular period or time he was engaged in the service, I cannot say, but suppose it to have been 19 or 20 days, and it seems to me that, for such services, taking into view the loss of practice at home, the fatigues incident to an exposed situation, that a liberal compensation should be allowed, of which, however, you are more competent to determine.

I am, very respectfully,
Your obedient servant,
SAM'L. LEWIS.

Hon. LEWIS CASS,
*Secretary of War, Washington.*

I concur in the above, so far as it relates to the time of the Doctor's being employed, and think a liberal compensation should be made him.
SAML. HANNA.

I recollect that Dr. L. G. Thompson assisted in his professional capacity at the late Miami treaty, about or near the time mentioned within, and concur in saying, that I think that a liberal compensation should be allowed him therefor.

W. G. EWING.

I concur in the above.

D. BURR.

I do hereby certify that Dr. L. G. Thompson was actively employed in rendering professional services at the Miami treaty, and think the bill he has submitted reasonable. FRANCIS COMPARET.

FORT WAYNE, *February* 20, 1833.

SIR: In reply to your query of what I know of the engagement made by the commissioners of the United States appointed to treat with the Miami Indians in the month of September last, for your professional services during their continuance on the ground, I have to state that it was generally understood that you were so employed by the commissioners, at the special request of Chief Richardville. As to the extent of your services, (my being much retired,) I could not be much acquainted with it. I was, however, personally known to your furnishing medicine to Chief Richardville, and attending, during a severe attack, on Joseph Richardville. I have no doubt you suffered a pecuniary loss in being from home during the time your practice being extensive here.

Your obedient servant,
ALLEN HAMILTON

Doctor LEWIS G. THOMPSON.

N. B. I cannot hesitate in saying that, under all circumstances, your claim of two hundred dollars is reasonable.

A. H.

---

INDIAN AGENCY, ROCK ISLAND, *Feb.* 22, 1833.

SIR: Yours of the 19th December, enclosing a copy of a letter from Joshua Pilcher, reached here during my absence to the river Des Moines, on a visit to the Indians, or would have been attended to earlier.

The explanation required by you relative to the Indian annuities of last year, was made, and forwarded to you on the 14th ultimo, which I hope is perfectly satisfactory. Some further explanation, by way of reply to Mr. Pilcher, may be necessary, in order that you may fully understand the whole matter.

*First,* his "surprise" at a measure "which will prevent them (the Indians) from ever seeing one dollar" of these annuities.

Why these expressions of sympathy and " inexpressible astonishment," &c., I know not, when Mr. Pilcher *knew* that the Indians *had received* their annuities, through their traders, whilst he was *acting* as agent. By reference to a copy of the receipts of the Indians, and the annexed remarks of the commissioners, (which, I presume, has been forwarded to you long since, by the superintendent at St. Louis,) you will perceive that the Indians did not expect or wish "*to see* a dollar" of their annuities, but were extremely anxious that they should be brought on for the purpose of satisfying those who had previously paid them. These accounts have been examined by me, and I have no hesitation in saying that they are reasonable and correct.

Again. The only possible way for the agent to get any voucher, will be, to affix "the names of such Indians," &c., and "get those *interested to certify* that the *money has been paid over to the Indians.*" How far Mr. Pilcher would act under similar circumstances in the manner he points out "as the only possible way" for the agent, is left to his own *honest intentions* to determine; but, for myself, I am governed only by motives which I am always willing for the world to know, and can assure you, from my conversation with the Indians during my late visit, that any other receipt that may be necessary, they will sign cheerfully when they come on in the spring.

Thus, you will see, that the fears entertained by Mr. Pilcher, the sympathy expressed, and his "inexpressible astonishment" about these annuities, are all groundless. The annuities are ready for the Indians whenever they come in. They can then make any disposition of the money they think proper.

With great respect,<br>Your obedient servant,<br>M. S. DAVENPORT,<br>*Indian Agent, Rock Island.*

ELBERT HERRING, Esq.,
   *Commissioner of Indian Affairs.*

---

INDIAN AGENCY, ROCK ISLAND, *Feb.* 22, 1833.

SIR: The day after I left here to execute the orders of the Indian Department in demanding the murderers of Martin, I was overtaken by an express from S. D. Carpenter, esq., whom I had appointed to superintend and report to me in case of persons returning to Dubuque's mines, stating that "from eighty to one hundred persons had gone over to Dubuque's mines, and were there engaged in mining, smelting," &c.

Without a small military force is established at those mines, it will be impossible to keep persons from intruding upon them.

With great respect,
I am, sir,
Your obedient servant,
M. S. DAVENPORT,
*Indian Agent, Rock Island.*

ELBERT HERRING, Esq.,
*Commissioner Indian Department.*

---

OFFICE BANK UNITED STATES,
*Washington, Feb. 23, 1833.*

SIR: I have succeeded in purchasing $30,000 Maryland five per cents. for the fund you mentioned. To enable me to pay for this and for any further sums that may offer, I would suggest that you advance me the whole sum that you wish invested. This course was pursued last summer by the Navy Department, when the Secretary authorized the purchase of stock for the pension fund.

I am, very respectfully,
Your obedient servant,
RICHARD SMITH, *Cashier.*

E. HERRING, Esq.,
*Sup't Indian Bureau.*

---

WASHINGTON CITY, *February 25, 1833.*

SIR: In compliance with your letter of the 6th instant, requiring me to submit to you a detailed report of my proceedings from the commencement of my appointment, and also a return, showing the number of Indians left in Ohio, their position, the reasons why they did not remove with the party taken by me, and my views respecting the propriety of removing them at the public expense, I have the honor to present the following statement.

Previously to my departure from this city, in April last, I received your verbal orders, under the sanction of the President, to proceed to the several Indian reservations, in the State of Ohio, as soon as practicable after my return home, for the purpose of notifying the respective tribes that the treaties formed with them had been ratified by the Government, and suitable arrangements would soon be made for their removal, and the supply of the various articles promised to them.

Accordingly, I set out on the 8th of May for the Indian towns, and soon afterwards held preparatory councils with the chiefs of the Senecas, Shawnees, and Ottoways. They appeared pleased with the prospects before them, and promised to use all possible diligence in putting their people in a state of readiness to meet the arrangements on the part of the Government. A question came up, however, in the course of these councils, which subsequently proved a prolific source of embarrassment and delay. During the negotiations with the several tribes, the Indians expressed a strong desire to be permitted to travel by land, and take their horses with them. They were assured that the Government would not object to this course, but would gratify all their reasonable wishes.

At the preparatory councils referred to, the subject was again mentioned, and I was reminded by the chiefs of the promises made to them during the pendency of their treaties. Knowing that *you* thought it inexpedient to remove them by land, I could now only promise them that I would communicate their requests to yourself and the President, and hoped they would still be permitted to remove in the way they most desired.

Before leaving the Indian country, I received your letter of the 17th May, which required me, as soon as I had completed "a tour among the several bands," to submit to the department a "*project* for the operations of the season," in which I was instructed to state the number and duties of the persons necessary to be employed as assistants in the emigration, and suggest the names of such as I might think proper to employ. I was further directed, to state *the route* which I thought should be taken, the number of parties which should move separately, the time they ought to assemble, the mode of supplying, and any other ideas which occurred to me, by which the Government would be enabled to direct in the best manner the general operations.

In accordance with these instructions, I prepared as much in detail as possible, "a project of operations for the season," embracing the several points referred for my consideration. This document was dated and transmitted on the 23d of June. I therein stated that, " in the exercise of the discretion confided to me in the printed instructions of the department, of the 15th ultimo, I have chosen the route *by land*, as most congenial to the habits and comfort of the Indians, and probably not much, if any more expensive to the Government." I considered it more certain, and less liable to sickness and accidents.

Before submitting my project, however, I addressed you a letter on the 2d of June, stating the wish of the Indians to travel by land; in referring to which, in your answer of the 21st of June, you say, "The President, with whom I have conferred on the subject, cannot accede to the propositions. General Gibson will advise you of the result."

On the 28th of June, General Gibson wrote me as follows: "On the subject of the removal by land, as again adverted to in your letter to me, I will remark, that the determination of the President remains unaltered. If they (the Indians) in reality entertain the fears to which you allude, you will endeavor to correct their impressions. Tell them of the rapidity and certainty with which they will travel; of the distresses to which the Senecas, who removed last year, were subjected; and use any other arguments which may occur to your mind; but, above all, say that the plan of removal by steamboat is unalterable."

In compliance with these orders, I went again among the Indians, and used every persuasion in my power to induce them to accede to the decision of the President. My efforts were utterly unavailing, and I so informed the Commissary General of Subsistence, in a detailed report of the 23d of July.

As the season advanced, I made a third attempt to change the determination of the chiefs and their people. But the cholera had, by this time, made its appearance in the steamboats on the lakes, and on the northern borders of Ohio, and the Indians became firmly resolved to remain on their lands another year, rather than run the risk of contracting the prevailing epidemic in traveling by water.

My own efforts were ably seconded by my several assistants, in their visits of business among the tribes; but their exertions were equally unsuccessful.

Believing, from my knowledge of the Indian character, and of the sinister influence exercised by some of the traders among the Ohio tribes, that it would be impossible to induce them to remove, by water, to St. Louis, in sufficient time to accomplish the remainder of their journey, (which must necessarily be by land) before the cold weather would prevent them from traveling, I felt anxious that the President should change his first decision, and permit the adoption of the land route.

Accordingly, I addressed the Commissary General of Subsistence on the subject, on the 23d of July, and requested that my letter might be laid before the President. I received an answer from the acting Commissary General, dated the 31st of July, and was informed that the President, the Secretary of War, and Commissary General were all absent from the city of Washington; but that the acting Secretary of War would transmit my letter to the President in Tennessee.

About the 10th of September, while in the vicinity of the Seneca Indians, I received a letter from the acting Commissary General, of the 1st of September, covering a letter from the President, dated at the Hermitage on the 17th of August, in which permission was given to remove the Indians by land.

During the whole of this time, that is, from the middle of May till the 10th of September, I was unable to make any efficient preparations, or to adopt any definite course in the removal. I did, indeed, at my own personal risk, order the purchase of seventy-five horses for the service, a few days before the receipt of the President's letter; but adopted this measure as the only possible means of removing the Indians during the year 1832, even with the consent of the President to take the route by land. The advanced period of the season rendered it extremely doubtful whether, with every practicable exertion and facility, we should be able to accomplish so long a journey, with such a mixed multitude of Indians of the worst habits, and so large a proportion of women and children among them.

The instructions to provide for the vaccination of the Indians were not received until the 10th of August. The matter procured in Ohio proved useless, and the attempt entirely failed. But the failure was not ascertained until it was too late to obtain new matter from Baltimore or this city.

The blankets, sheeting, and rifles, promised in the treaties, were not received until the 29th of August.

The payment of the sum of $19,000 to the Shawnees and Senecas, for their improvements, was not completed until the 14th of September. owing to the non-arrival of the money for that purpose.

The payment of the customary annuities to the Ottawas, was not made until after their arrival at the rendezvous, ten miles north of Piqua, on the 25th of September. This was owing to an inadvertence on the part of Gov. Porter, of Michigan

I have thus briefly stated the *principal* causes which delayed the final de-

15‡

parture of the expedition to so late a period as the 26th of September. But there were numerous other, and apparently unavoidable causes, which contributed to the delay; and were of a most vexatious and embarrassing nature. And to these may be added the proverbial indolence of Indians on such occasions, and the habitual and excessive intemperance of the half civilized bands, who have lived so long contiguous to the white settlements in Ohio.

For the sake of convenience, as well as to avoid collisions and quarrels on the way, each tribe or band was marched separately, and, as nearly as circumstances would permit, from ten to twenty miles apart. While passing through the populous settlements, it was found impossible to prevent the Indians from obtaining ardent spirits in such quantities as produced some serious disturbances and numerous detentions.

About the 1st of October, the several detachments crossed the western line of the State of Ohio, into Indiana. The precise number of the emigrants, I could never ascertain while on the march, in consequence of the constant intercourse between the tribes, their habits of visiting each other alternately, for days together, their practice of scattering along the road, or through the woods, or remaining in the villages where whiskey could be procured. Some seventy or eighty of the Shawnees remained at Wapaugh-konetta, after the main body had left the rendezvous, near Piqua, and Capt. Robb was ordered to return and bring them on. They did not overtake their detachment until we arrived within forty miles of the Mississippi. Nor could I, until now, tell the number of Shawnees who remained on the Hog Creek reservation, and refused to remove with their band. But I suppose the whole number removed last year from Ohio, to have been about eight hundred. The most of them travelled on horseback. A few had carriages and wagons of their own. The sick, the aged, and the decrepid who were unable to ride on horses, were carried in the public baggage wagons in a comfortable manner.

Until we arrived at Indianapolis, in Indiana, the Indians were supplied with rations, by contract, according to the printed regulations of the Department. But this mode, besides being by at least one-third the most expensive, and subjecting us to frequent frauds, could not be kept up, while on the march, without much inconvenience, delay, and uncertainty. It was, therefore, deemed expedient to order the necessary provisions to be supplied *in bulk*, on the requisitions of the respective conductors, when neither the assistant agent nor myself were present. Flour and meal were procured in bags or barrels, and beef or pork on foot. This was much more satisfactory to the Indians who selected their own distributors, and divided according to the *necessities*, and not the number of each family. They butchered the cattle, receiving the hide and tallow for their labor, with which they purchased coffee, sugar, spices, and other necessary articles for the sick and aged of their women. I soon became convinced of the sufficiency of the Indian ration, as fixed by the department, and while *rations* were issued according to *numbers*, many families had a large surplus of flour and beef, particularly the former, which they would sometimes sell to persons along the road, when prevented from putting it in the public wagons.

In the three detachments, there were about five hundred horses belonging to the Indians, and seventy-five purchased by the United States. The latter were very improperly selected, many of them incurably diseased, and most of them either too poor or too old for such service. They were not such as were ordered, and were purchased at a higher price than was stipulated by me. The consequence was, that the public horses, though fed with grain and hay, were unable to sustain the fatigues of the journey, and many of them died or failed on the road; while the Indian horses, with few exceptions, were kept in good traveling order, on tame and wild pasturage.

At Indianapolis, about the 5th or 6th of October, the disbursing agent gave me written notice, that he was "out of funds, and the emigration must stop" until money could be procured. He returned to Cincinnati for funds. I continued the march of the Indians without an hour's delay on this account. On the 24th of October, the front detachment arrived at the Hickory Grove, in Boyd county, Illinois, and within forty miles of St. Louis, a distance of more than two hundred miles, the whole of which was traveled in twenty days, with about eight hundred Indians and six hundred horses, supported principally on money *borrowed from the Indians themselves*. Here we remained for three or four days to recruit the horses, and await the return of an express I had sent to Gen. Clark, at St. Louis, to obtain information relative to the best route by which we could avoid the region infected with cholera, which was then prevailing with great malignity at St. Louis.

While thus detained, Col. John J. Abert, of the topographical engineers, came up with us, charged with instructions from you, relative to the future progress of the expedition. The disbursing agent arrived the next day, with a partial supply of money.

It is unnecessary, if not improper, for me, in this place, to advert to the circumstances which, in the opinion of the acting Secretary of War, rendered the interposition of Col. Abert necessary to the restoration of that harmony and concert of action essential to the success of the service. It is but just, however, to say that I found him a gentleman of the highest sense of honor, cool, firm, impartial, and intelligent; and in every respect adequate to the delicate and important duties assigned him. In what manner he executed the instructions of the department, his own reports, I have no doubt, will furnish the best and most ample testimony.

After I had received permission to return to my family in Ohio, Col. Abert expressed a wish that I should accompany him to the Mississippi, before relinquishing the charge of the expedition. I readily complied, and felt it a pleasure as well as a duty, to afford him every assistance in my power, in becoming acquainted with the numerous and complicated details of the service, which could only be learned by experience and practice. His own good sense, however, conciliating disposition, and energy of character, furnished the surest guaranty of his entire efficiency in performing the arduous duties he was about to undertake; and the result, I am happy to know, has fully realized my warmest anticipations.

Having accompanied Col. Abert to the eastern bank of the Mississippi, at Alton, and witnessed the crossing of the main body of the Indians, I left the expedition on the 2d of November, and returned to my residence, from whence I have had the honor to report to you for further orders.

I have considered it unnecessary to go further into the details of my proceedings than I have done, either as to the preparatory or the progressive measures, as they are already in the possession of the department, in the several communications which I have from time to time had the honor to address to yourself and the Commissary General of Subsistence: and to these I beg leave to refer you, particularly the following, and to ask that they may be appended to this report, whenever it shall become necessary to lay it before Congress, or the President:

First. My letters to you of the 22d and 27th of August, and 1st, 8th, and 21st of October, 1832.

Second. My letters to the Commissary General of Subsistence, of the 23d July, the 29th of August ,and the 3d and 8th of October, 1832.

Third. My letter to General William Clark, of the 25th of October, (herewith transmitted.)

It gives me much satisfaction to say, that, from the assistant agent, the conductors and assistant conductors, with a single exception, I received every support and assistance I could have wished or expected. They were faithful, efficient, and indefatigable in the discharge of their respective duties. Captain David Robb, the conductor of the Shawnee detachment, was unable to perform any active or laborious duty, by reason of infirmity and indisposition. It would have been better for the service if he had seen the propriety of resigning when first appointed.

In answer to your inquiries as to the number of Indians left in Ohio, their position, the reasons why they did not remove with the party taken by me, and my views respecting the propriety of removing them at the public expense, I have the honor to inform you that the number remaining, a great proportion of whom are women and children, is eighty-four. They belong to what is called the Hog Creek band of Shawnees, and are generally sober, discreet, and industrious persons. They determined to remain until next spring, rather than travel in company with the Shawnees of Waupaughkonetta, who, they believe, have treated them unjustly on several occasions, and might again defraud and quarrel with them on the way. When they made known to me their intention of remaining, I gave them no assurance that they would receive any assistance from the Government, if they did not remove at the same time with the rest of their brethren. But from their uniform good character, and the moral example they have always exhibited to their tribe, I think it would be just and proper that they should be assisted at the public expense, in their removal. And as they are defenceless against injury and imposition, and must pass through that part of the State of Illinois, where, from the unforgotten occurrences of the last year, a strong feeling of hostility exists against all Indians; I respectfully recommend that they may be placed under the charge and protection of some competent and experienced conductor, acquainted with the route, and capable of making purchases for them, and defending them against fraud and violence. They have horses and wagons of their own, and will, of necessity, as well as choice, remove by land.

I have the honor to be,
With great respect,
Your most obedient servant,
JAMES B. GARDINER,
*Special Agent and Superintendent.*

To the Hon. LEWIS CASS,
*Secretary of War.*

HICKORY GROVE, BOND COUNTY,
*Illinois, October 25, 1832.*

DEAR SIR: I have the honor to inform you, that I am thus far on my way from the State of Ohio, to the country west of the Missouri and Arkansas, with about eight hundred emigrating Indians, bands of three distinct tribes, the Senecas, Shawnees, and Ottawas, and marched in three detachments. The first detachment, composed of about two-thirds Senecas and one-third Shawnees, commonly called the "Lewistown Indians," about two hundred and fifty in number, are now encamped on the east fork of Shoal creek, two and a half miles east of this place.

The Ottawas, about one hundred souls, will probably arrive in this vicinity to-day.

The "Shawnees of Waupaghkonnetta and Hog creek," so called, consisting of about four hundred and fifty souls, will be up by to-morrow or next day.

In consequence of the want of the necessary preparations on the part of the Government, we were not able to start from the general rendezvous, in Shelby county, Ohio, until the 27th ultimo. Our march, since that time, has been constant, and as expeditious as the weather, the roads, and the health of the Indians would possibly admit.

With very few exceptions, the Indians are on horseback, and in *their own* wagons and carriages. We have seventy-five public horses and ten public wagons, to assist in the transportation of the baggage, and the conveyance of the aged, sick, and decrepid.

The Indians are generally healthy, and, so far, are contented and pleased with the prospect of reaching their new homes, before the severity of winter shall arrest their march. Many of them, it is true, have caused us much embarrassment and delay, in consequence of excessive intemperance, which, while passing through the populous settlements, we found it impossible to prevent. Of late, however, we have not been much annoyed from this prolific source of evil.

We have, as yet, received but ten thousand dollars, which sum, according to the report of the *disbursing agent*, was nearly exhausted in the preparatory measures, before we left the western line of Ohio. This gentleman left us at Indianapolis for Cincinnati, for the avowed purpose of procuring funds, and has not been heard of since.

From the time of leaving Indianapolis up to the present period, we have subsisted ourselves, the Indians, and about six hundred horses, principally on funds *borrowed from the Indians themselves!* Still, we have managed so as to prevent any real want, or any delay in our operations.

A great proportion of the emigrants, at least one-half, consists of women and children. Several of the former are very aged and infirm, and many of the latter helpless infants. A few deaths from cholera infantum, bad colds, dysentery, &c., have occurred on the road; but the number of *births* has at least been equal to that of the deaths.

When arrived at Vandalia, I confidently expected to receive some definite instructions from the War Department, relative to my future movements. I have not, however, received a solitary line from the Secretary of War, nor the Commissary General, since my departure from Ohio. The absence of those officers from the seat of Government has, I presume, caused the delay.

The prevalence of the cholera at St. Louis, with considerable virulence as we learn, has induced me to halt the line of emigration in this vicinity, for three cr four days, for the purpose of asking your advice and opinions as to my further progress at present. I trust you will excuse the liberty I thus take, under the embarrassing circumstances in which I am now placed. I have already informed the Secretary that, in the absence of instructions from him, I should throw myself upon you, as a safe and ready counsellor. And I have further requested him to authorize you to aid and direct me to the end of my journey, after reaching Missouri.

Deeply sensible of the responsibility which devolves upon me, as the superintendent of the emigration of Ohio Indians, I am extremely solicitous to exercise all possible prudence and caution, in preserving the lives and the health of the eight hundred defenceless human beings committed to my care. The policy of the Government is known to be as humane and munificent towards these people; and, as the instrument of that policy, I feel that I should be utterly without apology, if I rushed, unnecessarily and unadvisedly, into the region of a terrible malady, and thus expose to probable destruction so many of the human race.

I therefore respectfully ask your advice as to the proper *time*, and *place*, and *manner* of crossing the Mississippi; the route from thence, with *one* of the tribes, to the confluence of the Neosho and Arkansas rivers, and with the *other two*, to the southern side of the Kansas, above its junction with the Missouri; and the best and cheapest mode of supplying subsistence and transportation on the way. Would you advise me to cross the river as soon as possible? and, if not, *how long*, and *where* would you think it best to tarry? Should I not be furnished immediately with one or *two* experienced physicians? If so, can you send me such, or recommend me whom to employ? We have two hundred dollars worth of medicines, *badly selected;* but do not know how to use them on important occasions.

I trust we shall not long remain destitute of funds, unless the prevalence of the cholera at Cincinnati, of which we have just heard, shall delay or prevent the return of Lieutenant Lane, the disbursing agent.

I think it not improbable, from certain events which have occurred in the course of the emigration, that you may have already received some instructions from the Secretary of War, which may have an important bearing upon our future organization and movements. If so, will you have the kindness to inform me of the facts.

My regular express is now in the rear of the line, and I have no person I can depend upon, who can be spared long enough to convey you this letter. I therefore send it by Mr. McConnell, the postmaster of Vandalia, who has promised to deliver it to you in person. I respectfully request that you will send me your reply, *by express, as soon as possible.* The Indians are becoming extremely uneasy, from the exaggerated reports they have heard along the road; and it is important that their fears should be quieted as far as practicable.

I have the honor to be,
With the greatest respect,
Your most obedient servant,
JAMES B. GARDINER,
*Special agent and superintendent emigrating Ohio Indians.*
General Wm. Clark,
*Superintendent of Indian affairs, St. Louis.*

BROWN'S HOTEL, WASHINGTON CITY,
*February* 26, 1833.

SIR: The accompanying papers contain the proceedings of the Cherokee people, who reside within that portion of our territory lying within the chartered limits of Tennessee, at their public meetings held in consequence of certain rumor, in reference to the design of John Walker, junior, in coming on to this place, and as that individual has since arrived, and been some time in this city, and being uninformed of the specific objects of his visit; and, in order to meet the request of those of our fellow-citizens who have transmitted through us their protest against any improper interference or unauthorized action of said Walker, in regard to the affairs of the nation, we have deemed it our duty to lay the same before your department. It has ever been the desire of the constituted authorities of our nation, that harmony and good feeling should exist among the people, to secure the interest and welfare of the whole community, and, with this feeling, they have always endeavored to allay such excitements as are calculated to produce consequences of an unpleasant character.

With considerations of respect,
We have the honor to be, sir,
Your obedient servants,
JNO. ROSS,
JOSEPH VANN,
To the Hon. LEWIS CASS　　　R. TAYLOR,
*Secretary of War.*　　　JNO. F. BALDRIDGE, his x mark.

---

Whereas, it is rumored that John Walker, jr., has gone on to the city of Washington, with a view to make some arrangement with the Government of the United States, affecting our national rights, and in consequence of such reports, we, the undersigned, citizens of the Cherokee nation, within the chartered limits of the State of Tennessee, have deemed expedient and necessary, in order that we should be properly understood, and not misrepresented, to declare that John Walker, jr., has no authority from our nation, nor from the citizens of this portion of the nation, within the limits of Tennessee, to represent us in any manner whatever, and we do most solemnly protest against his entering into any arrangement whatever with the Government of the United States, affecting our rights as citizens of the Cherokee nation, as our delegation now at Washington City, Messrs. Richard Taylor, Joseph Vann, and John Baldridge, and our principal chief, John Ross, are the only properly authorized persons at Washington to represent us, and transact any business connected with the interest of this nation; and we do request our delegation, should it become necessary, to lay this protest before the proper department.

*January* 29, 1833.

| | | | |
|---|---|---|---|
| Benjamin Puden, | his x mark. | Philip Waters, | his x mark. |
| John Waters, | his x mark. | John Nelson, | his x mark. |
| Bullet Eye, | his x mark. | Richard Acorn, | his x mark. |
| Stand in the Water, | his x mark. | John Clubfoot, | his x mark. |
| Young Acorn, | his x mark. | James Coney, | his x mark. |
| Hamtrocker, | his x mark. | Jumping Boy, | his x mark. |
| Bird, | his x mark. | Ul Stuehee, | his x mark. |
| Chue-ty-ya-kee, | his x mark. | Pig in the Water, | his x mark. |

| Arch Acorn, | his x mark. | Beaver, | his x mark. |
| Pinch, | his x mark. | Young Jack, | his x mark. |
| Jack, | his x mark. | Green Ragis, | his x mark. |

Whereas, it is rumored that John Walker, jr., has gone on to the city of Washington, with a view to make some arrangement with the Government of the United States, affecting our national rights, and in consequence of such reports, we, the undersigned, citizens of the Cherokee nation, living in that part of the Cherokee nation within the chartered limits of the State of Tennessee, have deemed it expedient and necessary, in order that we should be properly understood, and not misrepresented, to declare that John Walker, jr., has no authority from our nation, nor from the citizens of this portion of the nation within the limits of Tennessee, to represent us in any manner whatever; and we do most solemnly protest against his entering into any arrangement whatever with the Government of the United States, affecting our rights as citizens of the Cherokee nation, as our delegation, now at Washington City, viz: Messrs. Richard Taylor, Joseph Vann, John Baldridge, and our principal chief, John Ross, are the only properly authorized persons at Washington to represent us and transact any business connected with the interest of this nation, and we do request our delegation, should it become necessary, to lay this protest before the proper department.

*January 29, 1833.*

| Samuel Candy, sen., | his x mark. | Bird, | his x mark. |
| Jefferson H. Conrad, | his x mark. | Tonah, | his x mark. |
| George Drumgould, | his x mark. | Pelekin Tiger, | his x mark. |
| Levi Timberleg, | his x mark. | Geo. Going Snake, | his x mark. |
| Bellows, | his x mark. | Two Fathom, | his x mark. |
| Arch Shell, | his x mark. | Bigbone Going | |
| Passby, | his x mark. | Snake, | his x mark. |
| Dirt Seller, | his x mark. | Eli, | his x mark. |
| Claw-acre, | his x mark. | Categaskey, | his x mark. |
| Running Wolf, | his x mark. | Whirlwind, | his x mark. |
| Wm. M. Nave, | | Beans & Hominey, | his x mark. |
| John Nave, | | Staff, | his x mark. |
| Read Bird, | his x mark. | Pigeon, | his x mark. |
| John Bogs, | his x mark. | Maxwell Chambers, | his x mark. |
| Four Killer, | his x mark. | | |

Whereas, it is rumored that John Walker, jun., has gone to the city of Washington, with a view to make some arrangement with the Government of the United States, affecting our national rights, and, in consequence of such reports, we, the undersigned, citizens of the Cherokee nation, living in that part of the Cherokee nation within the chartered limits of the State of Tennessee, have deemed it expedient and necessary, in order that we should be properly understood, and not misrepresented, to declare, that John Walker, jun., has no authority from our nation, nor from the citizens of this portion of the nation within the limits of Tennessee, to represent us in any manner whatever; and we do most solemnly protest against his entering into any arrangement whatever, with the Government of the United States, affecting our rights as citizens of the Cherokee nation, as our delegation, now at Washington City. viz: Messrs. Richard Taylor, Joseph Vann, John Baldridge, and our principal chief, John Ross, are the only properly authorized persons at Washington to represent us and transact any business connected with the interest of this nation; and we do request our delegation, should it become necessary, to lay this protest before the proper department.

*January 29th,* 1833.

| | | | |
|---|---|---|---|
| Going Snake, | his x mark. | Old Fields, | his x mark. |
| Sleeping Rabbit, | his x mark. | Anderson Springston, | |
| Coolah-chee, | his x mark. | Isaac Springston, | |
| Squirrel, | his x mark. | James Foreman, | |
| Bridge Maker, | his x mark. | Jessee Mesain, | |
| Deer-in-water, | his x mark. | Daniel McCoy, | |
| H. Martin, | | Wiley Bigbey, | |
| Michael Heldebrand, | | David Foreman, | |
| Peter Heldebrand, | | William Foreman, | |
| George Heldebrand, | | Samuel Foreman, | |
| James Heldebrand, | | Taylor Eldridge, | his x mark. |
| Lewis Heldebrand, | | Arch. Pathkiller, | his x mark. |
| Moses Heldebrand, | | Big Mole, | his x mark. |
| John Catron, | | William Blyth, | |
| Joshua Kirkpatrick, | | George Field, | |
| John Heldebrand, | | Israel Field, | |
| Thomas Foreman, | | Glover Thornton, | his x mark. |
| George Candy, | | Jack Foreman, | |
| George Bushy-head, | | James Vann, | |
| George Wilson, | | Young Wolf, | his x mark. |
| Path Killer, | his x mark. | Char-le-tee-hee, | his x mark. |
| Doctor, | his x mark. | Jesse Bushy-head, | |
| Johnson | his x mark. | Isaac Bushy-head, | |
| Cat, | his x mark. | Lewis Ross, | |
| Alexander Foreman, | | Charles Foreman, | |
| Stephen Ray, | | W. Wilson, | |
| The Cabin, | his x mark. | Archibald Wilson, | |
| James McDaniel | | Wilson Nivers, | |
| Bushy-head, | his x mark. | Johnson Foreman, | |
| Henry Seabolt, | his x mark. | Amos Thornton. | |
| Daniel Colston, | his x mark. | Ezekiel Biers, | his x mark. |
| Hair Conrad, | his x mark. | The Dry, | his x mark. |
| Thomas Mannow, | his x mark. | Johnson, | his x mark. |
| Joseph Spier, | his x mark. | Rafle Tier, | his x mark. |
| Tahchee-chee, | his x mark. | Deer Comer, | his x mark. |
| Thomas Fields, | his x mark. | Go Strait, | his x mark. |
| Alex. Drumgould, | his x mark. | Oo-he-chy, | his x mark. |
| Jackson R. Gourd, | his x mark. | Corntetle, | his x mark. |
| Choon-no-la-kah, | his x mark. | Hunter, | his x mark. |
| Scraper, | his x mark. | Slakin Girts, | his x mark. |
| Black Fox, | his x mark. | A-damsee-dle-ett | |
| Minte Watts, | his x mark. | Daniel P. Hopkins, | |
| Arch. Foreman, | | Crow Mocker, | his x mark. |
| James Spier, | his x mark. | Carvey, | his x mark. |
| Deer in Water, jr., | his x mark. | John Bacon, | his x mark. |
| Tee-sas-kee, | his x mark. | Samuel Coney, | his x mark. |

16‡

Whereas, it is rumored that John Walker, jr., has gone to the city of Washington, with a view to make some arrangements with the Government of the United States, affecting our national rights; and, in consequence of such reports, we, the undersigned, citizens of the Cherokee nation, within the chartered limits of the State of Tennessee, have deemed it expedient and necessary, in order that we should be properly understood, and not misrepresented, to declare that John Walker, jr., has no authority, from our nation, nor from the citizens of this portion of the nation within the limits of Tennessee, to represent us in any manner whatever; and we do most solemnly protest against his entering into any arrangement whatever with the Government of the United States, affecting our rights as citizens of the Cherokee nation, as our delegation now at Washington City, Messrs. Richard Taylor, Joseph Vann, John Baldridge, and our principal chief, John Ross, are the only properly authorized persons at Washington to represent us, and to transact any business connected with the interest of this nation; and do request our delegation, should it become necessary, to lay this protest before the proper department.

*January* 1, 1833.

| | | | |
|---|---|---|---|
| Wah hus-kee, | his x mark. | Young Dog, | his x mark. |
| Wah-num-kee, | his x mark. | Big Arse-te-hee, | his x mark. |
| Rivers, | his x mark. | Arch Spears, | his x mark. |
| Pike, | his x mark. | Young Bird, | his x mark. |
| Beaver Carrier, | his x mark. | John Long, | his x mark. |
| Caheunnee, | his x mark. | John Cag, | his x mark. |
| Jack Smoke, | his x mark. | Too-so-woo-la-tah, | his x mark. |
| The Squirrel, | his x mark. | Cau-na-too, | his x mark. |
| Ta-lah-skas-kee, | his x mark. | Sully, | his x mark. |
| Mike, | his x mark. | Good Dollar, | his x mark. |
| Soquitchee, | his x mark. | The Shadow, | his x mark. |
| Wattie, | his x mark. | The Kull, | his x mark. |
| Charles, | his x mark. | Big Plur, | his x mark. |
| Te-sais-kee, | his x mark. | The Beetter, | his x mark. |
| Kalo-woos-kee, | his x mark. | The Wolf, | his x mark. |
| Tah-yes kee, | his x mark. | Ground Squirrel | his x mark. |
| Wah-ta-too-kee, | his x mark. | The Wasp, | his x mark. |
| The Fish Tail, | his x mark. | The Drowning Bear, | his x mark. |
| The Hungry, | his x mark. | The Woman Killer, | his x mark. |
| Notuttah, | his x mark. | Tee-sah-tais-kee, | his x mark. |
| The Dew, | his x mark. | The Hungry Boy, | his x mark. |
| Skaya-too-kee, | his x mark. | The Thigh Hair, | his x mark. |
| Long Jaw, | his x mark. | Tick String, | his x mark. |
| The Otter Sifter, | his x mark. | George Squirrel, | his x mark. |
| Oo-lo-nah-stee-skee, | his x mark. | Ned Saunders, | his x mark. |
| Tom, | his x mark. | George Washington, | his x mark. |
| The Swimmer, | his x mark. | The Biter, | his x mark. |
| Alexander Ballard, | his x mark. | The Clab Board, | his x mark. |
| Charles, | his x mark. | Kah-kah-lo-ha-nah, | his x mark. |
| Skah-too-kah, | his x mark. | Nose Cutter, | his x mark. |
| Poor Shoat, | his x mark. | Alexander Pike, | his x mark. |
| Dick, | his x mark. | Chu-wa-loo-kee, | his x mark. |
| The Heavy Boy, | his x mark. | Dog in the Water, | his x mark. |
| Oo-kah tanee, | his x mark. | The Day Light, | his x mark. |

| | | | |
|---|---|---|---|
| Tunnahyee, | his x mark. | John Helterbrand, | his x mark. |
| Oo-la-ne-tah, | his x mark. | Michael Helterbrand, | his x mark. |
| Soldier, | his x mark. | Sam'l Helterbrand, | his x mark. |
| The Swimmer, | his x mark. | Peter Helterbrand, | his x mark. |
| Mouse Pain, | his x mark. | George Helterbrand, | his x mark. |
| Rain Crow Pain, | his x mark. | Dirt Seller, | his x mark. |
| Arch, | his x mark. | Sarney, | his x mark. |
| Going About, | his x mark. | Or gor-gill, W. Y., | his x mark. |
| Whinting, | his x mark. | The Biter, | his x mark. |
| Wats, | his x mark. | Standing About, | his x mark. |
| Forked Tail, | his x mark. | In the Night, | his x mark. |
| Snake Tail, | his x mark. | Isaac, | his x mark. |
| Drower, | his x mark. | Pigeon in the Water, | his x mark. |
| Black Fox, | his x mark. | King Fisher, | his x mark. |
| Scower, | his x mark. | Young Bird, | his x mark. |
| Weed, | his x mark. | The Cheater, | his x mark. |
| Tom Tit, | his x mark. | High Tail, | his x mark. |
| Big Mush, | his x mark. | The Bird, | his x mark. |
| Buffaloe Head, | his x mark. | Side Ways | his x mark. |
| The Blue Ray, | his x mark. | Get Up, | his x mark. |
| Standing Turkey, | his x mark. | Smoke, | his x mark. |
| Drowning Bore, | his x mark. | The Seed, | his x mark. |
| Rain Maker, | his x mark. | Coffee, | his x mark. |
| Levi James, | his x mark. | On the Stump, | his x mark. |
| John Borns, | his x mark. | Robert, | his x mark. |
| Dirt Buyer, | his x mark. | The Field, | his x mark. |
| The Hair, | his x mark. | The Crowing Bird, | his x mark. |
| Charles, | his x mark. | Horse Fly, | his x mark. |
| Sumorney, | his x mark. | | |

WASHINGTON, *February* 27, 1833.

SIR: On examining the maps in the General Land Office, I find no correct delineation of the boundary lines of the Cherokee lands, but there are, on the several maps of the States where those lands lie, a sketch of the lines, but which I consider very imperfect. However, that is the only guide by which I can make an estimate; and, therefore, have got the aid of Mr. Mills to make it, and which is as follows:

| | | | | |
|---|---|---|---|---|
| In the State of Alabama | - | - | - | 1,600,000 acres. |
| In the State of Georgia | - | - | - | 4,280,000 |
| In the State of Tennessee | - | - | - | 650,000 |
| In the State of North Carolina | - | - | - | 200,000 |
| | | | | 6,730,000 |

Although, by the maps which the above is taken from, the estimate seems to be about a fair one, yet I feel confident it is too large by nearly a million of acres, but may furnish you some idea of the contents of the Cherokee country.

With great respect, &c.,
JOHN COFFEE.

The Hon. SECRETARY OF WAR.

CHICAGO, ILLINOIS, *February* 28, 1833.

SIR: Herewith you will receive the petition of Jane Miranda, praying permission to sell one quarter section of land, reserved to her by the treaty of Prairie du Chien, of 29th July, 1829.

The facts set forth in the petition are true, and I am of the opinion that the prayer of the petitioner ought to be granted, as it would enable her to realize the benefit of the said reservation. The purchaser will give a fair equivalent for the land, and the payments will be made in good faith.

I have the honor to be,
Very respectfully, sir,
Your most obedient servant,
THOMAS J. V. OWEN,
*Indian Agent.*

His Excellency the PRESIDENT OF THE UNITED STATES,

---

CHICAGO, COOK COUNTY, ILLINOIS,
*February* 27, 1833.

SIR: The undersigned, your petitioner, obtained, at a treaty between the United States Government and the united nation of Ottaway, Pottawatamie, and the Chippeway Indians, of the Illinois, Milwakie, and Manatoouck rivers, holden at Prairie du Chien, in the Territory of Michigan, in the year of our Lord one thousand eight hundred and twenty-nine, a donation of land, consisting of one quarter section, on the Chicago river, above and adjoining a tract of land granted to Victoire Pothier, by the same treaty, and among other stipulations of the said treaty, it is agreed, that the said land, so obtained, as aforesaid, cannot be sold or otherwise disposed of without an assent of the President of the United States, and for the purpose of making the said donation available to your petitioner, she would pray your excellency to grant her permission to sell or otherwise dispose of it as may most conduce to her interest, and your petitioner will ever pray.

JANE MIRANDA, her x mark.

Witnesses to her signature,
R. A. KINZIE,
GHO. KERCHEVAL.

To his Excellency ANDREW JACKSON,
*President of the United States.*

---

SUPERINTENDENCY OF INDIAN AFFAIRS,
*St. Louis, March* 1, 1833.

SIR: I have the honor to enclose to you, herewith, a letter from Captain Pipe and other chiefs of the Delawares, lately emigrated from Sandusky, on the subject of the treaty entered into by them with Col. McElvain, the 3d August, 1829, stating *their* understanding of its provisions. Also, a letter of the same date from Major Cummins, communicating a statement of losses sustained by the same Indians whilst moving to their present lands.

I have examined the treaty with the Delawares, of 3d August, 1829, and find, therein, no stipulation of the kind, claimed by those Indians; nor have

I the means of ascertaining what was the understanding of the parties, apar^t from the treaty itself.

With regard to the losses sustained by those Indians in moving, I can only suggest, that, as the former Delawares, who emigrated from Ohio and Indiana, were remunerated for similar losses, it might not be inconsistent with strict justice to extend the same liberality to the present claimants. On the 9th May, 1828, an appropriation was made, of $1,000, to cover losses of a party of Delawares, and was paid to the claimants on the 27th April, 1829. (See abstract O, of accounts rendered to 30th June of that year.)

I have the honor to be,

With high respect,

Your most obedient servant,

**WILLIAM CLARK.**

Honorable E. Herring,
  *Commissioner of Indian Affairs.*

---

Delaware Agency, *February* 5, 1833.

Sir: There appears to be a misunderstanding between us and the treaty concluded at Little Sandusky, in the State of Ohio, on the 3d day of August, 1829, between ourselves and John McElvain, agent and commissioner on the part of the United States. We are informed by Richard W. Cummins, Indian agent, for the Delaware Indians, that, by said treaty, we are only entitled to receive three thousand dollars; two thousand paid at the time of making the treaty, and one thousand to be paid for the purchase of horses, clothing, and provisions, &c., as soon as we were prepared to move; all of which we acknowledge we have received.

We clearly understood, by said treaty, that we were to receive six thousand dollars for our nine sections of land; in confirmation of what we say, we refer you to Cornelius Wilson.

Your children hope you will look into this matter and let them know if it is a fact that we are to receive nothing more. When we were about to start we asked our agent, John McElvain, how much was coming to us, he answered, and said, not quite two thousand dollars; he then told us, when we were going to our new country, that we would see General Clark, who would attend to our business; that we would also have an agent; that the balance of our money would be paid to us by him, after we got to our new country.    Your friends and brothers,

CAPTAIN PIPE, his x mark.

WILLIAM MONTURE, his x mark.

ISAAC HILL, his x mark.

SOLOMON JONNICAKE, his x mark.

General William Clark,
  *Superintendent of Indian Affairs.*

---

Delaware Agency, *February* 5, 1833.

Sir: I beg leave to report to you the following property lost by Captain Pipe and party of Delaware Indians, (about thirty in number), on their journey from Little Sandusky, in the State of Ohio, to the Delaware lands on the Kansas river, which report is made entirely from the information received of Captain pipe and party.

*Property lost as follows, viz.:*

Captain Pipe lost three horses; a bay horse, small blaze in his forehead, worth seventy dollars, a brown horse worth fifty dollars, and a chesnut sorrel horse worth sixty dollars.

William Monture lost seven horses; one a black worth sixty dollars, a black horse worth fifty dollars, one sorrel horse worth forty dollars, a bay stud horse, white on his forehead and legs, worth thirty dollars, a bay horse, white mane, worth thirty dollars, a white mare, blind of one eye, worth twenty dollars, and a bay mare, white in her forehead, white legs, worth twenty dollars.

Isaac Hill lost one sorrel horse worth forty dollars.

John Hill lost three horses; one roan stud worth thirty dollars, one roan horse worth thirty dollars, one bay horse, white on his forehead, worth thirty dollars.

Cathen and the Butcher, two orphan children, lost a bay mare worth twenty dollars.

Young Armstrong lost two horses, one white horse worth fifty dollars, and a brown horse worth thirty dollars.

Black Racoon lost one bay horse, white on his face, worth forty dollars, and left at Sandusky two bake ovens and a ten gallon brass kettle, all worth fourteen dollars.

Thomas Hill lost four horses; one bay mare worth fifty dollars, one bay horse, white on his forehead and white legs, worth forty dollars, one brown horse worth thirty dollars, and a bay stud worth thirty dollars.

Winnahoca lost one roan mare worth twenty dollars.

Solo. Jonnicake lost one white mare worth thirty dollars, and a gun worth fifteen dollars.

George Williams lost one mouse colored mare, worth thirty dollars, and a big coat worth ten dollars.

Nancy lost one sorrel mare, one hind leg white, worth forty dollars.

The Indians say they were not allowed time to stay and hunt their horses; that their conductor told them that the Government would pay them for their losses; that it would be better to do so than to wait for them to hunt for their horses.

I am, sir, with high respect,
Your most obedient servant,
RICHARD W. CUMMINS,
*Indian Agent.*

Gen. WILLIAM CLARK,
*Superintendent of Indian Affairs.*

———

BROWN'S HOTEL, WASHINGTON CITY,
*March* 1, 1833.

SIR: I deem it proper to advise you that the delegation find it to be inconvenient to themselves to call on you this morning, for the purpose of waiting on the President, agreeably to your suggestion.

In consequence of which we have deemed it most proper to address the President a note, asking him to state at what time it will be most convenient to himself to see us on the business appertaining to the general concerns of our nation.

In behalf of the Cherokee delegation.

I am, sir, your obedient servant,

JOHN ROSS.

To the Hon. Lewis Cass,
*Secretary of War.*

---

House of Representatives, *March* 2, 1833.

Sir: Enclosed I send you a letter from a highly respectable merchant of Alabama, complaining that he has not had justice done him by the commissioners appointed to adjudicate upon claims against the Creek tribe of Indians. I refer to you his letter, so that, when the case comes before you, you can refer to Mr. C.'s statement.

I have the honor to be, respectfully,

SAMUEL W. MARDIS.

Hon. Lewis Cass,
*Washington City.*

---

Wetumpka, Alabama, *February* 9, 1833.

Sir: at the ratification of the treaty of 24th March, 1832, with the Creeks, their nation was indebted to me in the sum of $1,653 62, which their head-men and chiefs were desirous should be among the first sums paid, from the appropriation of $100,000 for the payment of their national debts. At the sitting of the commissioners, in January last, at Fort Mitchell, I called upon General Parsons and made known to him the circumstances of the case, and that as the chief men of the tribe felt under some obligations to me for favors extended to their people, and as they considered the debt national, they were desirous of making a draft in the most unexceptionable form, and desired his advice. He directed me to take the draft of any two or three of their head chiefs, including Tus-ke-ne-haw, directed to the Secretary of War, or to the commissioners, and in such form it would certainly be paid. Subsequently, Major Brodnax, of Georgia, proffered to accompany me to Neah Micco, the head-man of the lower Creeks, and obtain for me his signature; this, however, I deemed unnecessary, as General Parsons had directed me to have it signed by Tus-ke-ne-haw, and the next in rank to him, all of whom were anxious that my demand should be among the first liquidated. Accordingly, the principal men, and such as the commissioners gave me to understand were the only necessary ones, gave me a draft, (of which the following is a literal copy,) in presence of and witnessed by one of the commissioners.

[Copy.]

" The Secretary of War of the United States, or Commissioners under treaty of March, 1832, with the Creek nation, will please pay to Charles Crommelin, or bearer, sixteen hundred and fifty-three dollars sixty-two cents, for value received, by his releasing to us sundry demands against the Creek nation to the above named amount; as witness our hands, both for ourselves and for the Creek nation, this eleventh day of January, eighteen hundred and thirty three, the above being for demands originating previous to the treaty of March, 1832.

|                        |              |
|------------------------|--------------|
| TUS-KE-NE-HAW,         | his x mark.  |
| COOSA-TUSTA-MUGGA,     | his x mark.  |
| TUCK-A-BATCHA MICO,    | his x mark.  |

Witnesses present:
EDWARD AUGUSTUS McBRIDE,
GEORGE TAYLOR,
WM. McGILVERY, his x mark,
G. W. DILLARD,
B. S. PARSONS.

The original of the foregoing I deposited with the commissioners, and will be found among the documents transmitted by them to the Hon. Lewis Cass.

At the time of the meeting of the commissioners, as I have lately learned, Colonel John Crowell, or his agent or friends, procured drafts to be signed to a large amount, by Tus-ke-ne-haw for the *upper* Creeks and Neah Micco for the *lower*. Thus constituting (as was afterwards decided) such amounts nominally *national*, and contravening the real intent and interest of the nation itself. This proceeding, I am informed, was not suspected by two of the commissioners, the Messrs. Parsons, and, when auditing claims, was protested against by them; and that they would make it to appear in its proper light to the Secretary of War, who reserved to himself the ultimate revision of the claims presented. My claim was passed by the commissioners (and also by the committee of chiefs by them appointed) without a dissenting voice. Now, as large demands were preferred against the Indians, and, by a trifling informality, I may be deprived, for a time, of the whole or a part of my just demand, I take leave to ask of you, as a favor, should it suit your convenience, to name the circumstance to Mr. Cass, who, I am well assured, will act in the case as becomes his reputation for penetration and integrity.

I have the honor to be,
With great esteem and respect,
Your obedient servant,
CH. CROMMELIN.

Hon. SAMUEL W. MARDIS, *Washington.*

---

WASHINGTON CITY, *March* 4, 1833.

SIR: So much of the enclosed letter as is not erased, I take the liberty of referring to you, with a request that you will give me the desired information as soon as convenient.

Please return with your answer the letter of Mr. Alston.
Most respectfully,
Your obedient servant,
F. E. PLUMMER.

To Hon. LEWIS CASS,
*Secretary of War.*

SUPERINTENDENCY OF INDIAN AFFAIRS,
*Detroit, March* 4, 1833.

SIR: I enclose a copy of a letter received from John H. Kinzie, esq., subagent at Fort Winnebago, dated the 31st January, which has just come to hand.

You will find he notices the subject of provisions for the Indians, and informs me that the good intentions of the department cannot be realized, as there are not provisions sufficient at the post. It is needless for me to enlarge upon the subject; my views were given at length, in my letter to you of the 9th February. Provisions or corn must be had for them. I must also trouble you for the necessary information to enable me to answer his question, "Where is to be obtained the remaining part of the 60,000 rations stipulated by the treaty of Fort Armstrong?" Being alive to the situation of these Indians, and understanding, when in that country, that 20,000 rations had been left by General Scott, with Mr. Dixon, for distribution, I handed to him a letter, dated 8th November, 1832, a copy of which I enclose.

The subject of a more equal distribution of the annuity money, tobacco, salt, &c., between the Winnebagoes of General Street's and Mr. Kinzie's agencies, adverted to in my letter above referred to, of the 9th February, and by the Indians in council, you will also see is noticed by Mr. Kinzie in this letter, as well as the tobacco stipulated for in the late treaty.

His opinion in relation to the reports in circulation, about another Indian war, is entitled to great weight. From all the information I have received, I take pleasure in saying that I unhesitatingly concur with Mr. Kinzie.

I have the honor to be,
Very respectfully,
Your ob't. serv't.,
G. B. PORTER.

ELBERT HERRING, Esq.,
*Commissioner of Indian Affairs.*

---

SUB INDIAN AGENCY, FORT WINNEBAGO,
*January* 31, 1833.

SIR: I had the honor, some time since, of receiving a communication from the War Department, authorizing me to draw on the commissariat at this place, for one hundred and fifty barrels of flour, and one hundred barrels of pork, for distribution to Indians, should their wants require it.

The receipt of that communication has been acknowledged. Since then I have called on the commanding officer, (Col. Cutler,) and he has informed me, that quantity cannot be spared—that he has not over that supply on hand. As I know the Indians will be straitened for provisions in the spring, I have taken the earliest opportunity to advise you upon this subject, that measures may be taken to ameliorate the condition of those poor creatures.

Where is to be obtained the remaining part of the 60,000 rations stipulated by the treaty of Fort Armstrong? The Indians on Rock river, &c., will remove to this vicinity, and will expect to be supplied at this place.

As I shall (after June next) have almost twice as many Indians under my agency, I should suggest the propriety of the pay rolls of Prairie du Chien and this place, being referred to for an equal distribution of the annuity money, tobacco, salt, &c., to be divided among the Winnebagoes. With regard to the 1,500 pounds of tobacco, mentioned in the late treaty, it was *understood* that the Indians who had to *remove* were to receive it.

I mention these circumstances, that you may, if necessary, communicate it to the War Department before it be acted upon.

Very respectfully, sir,

Your obedient servant,

JNO. H. KINZIE,

*Sub-agent Indian Affairs.*

Governor PORTER.

P. S.—Many reports are in circulation respecting the prospect of another *Indian war.* For my part, I have never seen less to fear on that score than at present. All the principal men of the Winnebago nation, with whom I have conversed, are very anxious and desirous of remaining at peace. When I learn to the contrary, no time will be lost by me in making it known to the public.

Your obedient servant,

J. H. K.

AT THE INDIAN AGENCY,

*Fort Winnebago, November 8, 1832.*

SIR: Since my arrival at this place, I have understood that Major General Scott has instructed you to issue to the Winnebago Indians 20,000 rations, to be considered as a part of the 60,000 rations which, by his treaty made with them, were to be issued next spring. From my knowledge of the Indian character, and the information I have received, I take the liberty of saying, that it seems to me better to let them have as few of these 20,000 rations at present as possible. You well know how improvident these Indians are. Give all to them now, and they would not have a ration left in two weeks time. They can *now* get along very well without provisions. They will go out to their hunting grounds, and should the winter be open, there will be no necessity for giving these provisions to them until spring. In case the winter be severe, you will have to give some of them out. Still, I request it may be done sparingly. They will realize the benefits of them to the fullest extent, if they can be given to them in the spring, when the hardest pinch is felt. You know they always suffer most at that season.

In giving this advice and instructions, you must not suppose that I wish to interfere with any order which that most excellent officer (Gen. Scott) has given. I think I know him too well to believe, that he could, for a moment, so suppose. I am actuated by a sense of duty, as the Superintendent of Indian Affairs, and having the welfare of these Indians at heart. Mr. Kinzie and Mr. Gratiot concur in opinion with me.

Very respectfully,

Your obedient servant,

G. B. PORTER.

Mr. JOHN DIXON.

INDIAN AGENCY, CHICAGO,
*March 5, 1833.*

SIR: Your letter of the 18th January last, and accompanying extracts, were duly received; in answer to which I have the honor to state, that I have conversed with some of the most intelligent and influential chiefs of the Pottawatamie tribe on the subject of said letter, and am induced to believe that there would be but little difficulty in effecting an exchange of lands on fair and reasonable terms with these people; they are entirely averse to ceding the balance of their lands, but would, I have no doubt, exchange them for lands west of the Mississippi, provided they could be permitted to send a deputation of some of their principal men under the guidance of some individual in whom they would confide, to look at the country and ascertain what portion of it would please them best, and be most likely to contribute bountifully to their wants. Should this proposition be acceded to, they hope that measures may be adopted, and the means provided, to enable them to send a deputation for the purpose above mentioned, as early the present spring as practicable.

It seems to me that it would be advisable to indulge them in a request so reasonable. The expenses attending such an expedition would be very inconsiderable; and I am clearly of opinion that they would be unwilling to make any exchange until they are satisfied of the fact, that their new homes and country possessed advantages not inferior to those incident to the country they now occupy.

Your letter of the 5th of February is received; the suggestion therein contained will receive unremitting attention.

I have the honor to be, &c.,

TH. J. V. OWEN,
*Indian Agent.*

To ELBERT HERRING, Esq.,
*Indian Commissioner, Washington City.*

---

EXECUTIVE DEPARTMENT, MILLEDGEVILLE, GA.,
*March 5, 1833.*

SIR: The undiminished solicitude of the people of Georgia, upon the subject of the remaining Indian population within the limits of the State, make it my duty to renew our correspondence on the subject of the prospect before us, in regard to the anticipated arrangements with the Cherokees. What has been the issue or result of the visit of Ross and the rest of the Cherokee delegation to Washington? Is there any immediate prospect of an amicable and satisfactory arrangement with these people, so as to insure their removal in any reasonable time? If the rulers of the Cherokees will not let their people go, then we shall be under the necessity of urging the policy of providing for the removal of parties, towns, families, and individuals, as they may become desirous to emigrate. At this time, a large majority of the Indians in this State wish to remove; and if the door should again be opened to individuals, I entertain no doubt but that, under skilful and judicious management, they will nearly all accede to the liberal terms of the Federal Government, as heretofore proposed. Should you lose sight of effecting a treaty with the Cherokees, I have to request that you will do me the honor not to appoint agents, or determine on the details of any plan previous to affording me an opportunity of suggesting to you my views and observations on the subject. The whole of the difficulties and obstacles thrown in the way of a final and satisfactory adjustment of our Indian affairs, are of a kindred origin with other popular topics of excitement which distract the public mind. Demagogues are endeavoring to rule or ruin the country; but I still rely upon the good sense and virtue of the people, and when this reliance fails, my best hopes will be at an end.

With great respect, I am, &c.,

WILSON LUMPKIN.

Hon. Lewis Cass.

---

COLUMBUS, GEORGIA, *March* 5, 1833.

DEAR SIR: I have taken the liberty of addressing to you the following questions, believing you will readily respond to any questions that your official obligations will admit of, and if, in this letter, any thing is said which could be construed into a request to violate any official obligations, you will do me the justice to excuse it upon the ground of my ignorance of the duties of the department over which you have the honor to preside, as I am no lawyer, but a farmer: I proceed, then, most respectfully, to submit the question, whether the heads of families will be settled in the Creek nation on fractions situated on the rivers not containing a whole section or half section? Or, can land of such a quantity, situated in such a manner, be the subject matter of reservation to the Indians? Will those persons who have purchased the claims of the Indians, before the locations or reservations are made, be entitled to them after they are made? Your immediate attention to the above, if consistent with your official duty,

Will oblige,

PEARCE A. LEWIS.

Hon. Lewis Cass,
*Secretary of War, Washington City.*

---

CHEROKEE AGENCY, *March* 7, 1833.

SIR: About three weeks past, John Harnage, the son of Ambrose Harnage, an emigrant for the Arkansas, brought to this place five negroes and a wagon load of household stuff. He left them in my care, and returned with the wagon to aid his father in removing the balance of his family and property; and, on the 4th instant, James Foreman, the Indian sheriff, came to the camp and took away four of the negroes. It seems they were taken on an attachment, founded on a supposed judgment, which he expects Mr. Harnage may recover against him in a Georgia court, for selling a negro of Harnage's under the Cherokee law, after the Georgia laws were extended over that part of the Cherokee nation.

And on the next day Harnage arrived with his family, and states, that about twelve miles from this, James Foreman and a large company of Indians stopped his wagon in the road and took two of the likeliest of his negroes, making six in all, and worth from two to three thousand dollars. I sent Mr. Miller, the interpreter, and two others after them, to demand the negroes of both Foreman and Lynch; and if not given up, to require certified copies of the process by which they were taken, and the oath on which it was founded. He returned last evening, and reports, that he overtook Foreman and the negroes about twenty miles from this; that he demanded them of him, and that he agreed to give them up if Lynch would consent; Lynch was sent for, but refused.

They brought copies of all the papers, which are enclosed, with the request that you will direct what further measures I shall take in the case. An early answer is requested, as Harnage is here with a large family, on expense. He has agreed to take the commutation and transport himself and family; and if kept here until after the second Monday in May, it will be a serious loss to him, as he will lose the chance of making a crop the coming summer, besides the great risk of health by travelling so far by water in the warm season of the year; and should he await the trial in May, he has no expectation that an emigrant, and especially himself, who has always been in favor of the measures of the Government, and opposed to the ruling party in the nation, could get justice in their courts.

I have the honor to be,
Your obedient servant,
H. MONTGOMERY.
Elbert Herring, Esq.,
Commissioner of Indian Affairs

---

Washington City, March 8, 1833.

Sir: The subject of intrusion on the lands of the Cherokee nation, by the citizens of the United States, as you well know, is a fruitful source of unpleasant complaints.

The injuries sustained by our citizens, from this unlawful practice, within the chartered limits of Georgia, North Carolina, Tennessee, and Alabama, have been great, and are daily increasing. And, notwithstanding we have been so repeatedly assured by the department, that the intruders would be removed from our lands, by virtue of the intercourse act, where the State laws did not interfere with the exercise of authority, on the part of the General Government, yet, strange as it may seem to be, but it is nevertheless true, that these complaints have not been made to cease by any effectual order from the department to the agent. However, when we reflect and see that the agent (Colonel Montgomery) has himself countenanced and permitted his own son-in-law, John Hardwick, to reside in the nation, and to cultivate Cherokee lands in the vicinity of the agency, regardless to the remonstrances of our general council, it is a circumstance not so much to be wondered at that he should indulge other intruders, who have only followed the example of his son-in-law. From recent information, there are many white families who have removed into the nation, and are now intruding on our lands, within the chartered limits of Tennessee. To these facts we would respectfully call the attention of the department and urge that a speedy and effectual order be given for their immediate removal. Should you feel disposed to ascertain, from other sources, the truth of what we have stated, in relation to the conduct of the agent, and the situation of John Hardwick, we would respectfully refer you to Captain Day and Lieutenant Dancey, the disbursing officers, who were lately stationed at the agency. We take leave further to state, that there are some individual claims for improvements, abandoned on the lands ceded by the treaties of 1817 and 1819, which have never been valued and reported upon by the assessing agents. We would, therefore, request that you will authorize and direct the agent, or some other person, to have said claims collected and reported upon to the department, that the claimants may receive their just compensation for their improvements, agreeably to the stipulation of the aforesaid treaties.

We are, very respectfully,
Your obedient servants,
JNO. ROSS,
R. TAYLOR,
JOSEPH VANN,
JOHN F. BALDRIDGE, his x mark.

The Hon. Lewis Cass,
Secretary of War.

—————

March 9, 1833.

Dear Sir: I would be much obliged by your directing the requisition to issue for the sum you wished invested in stock. The seller of the $30,000 has been put to some inconvenience by the delay in forwarding the money.

Very respectfully,
Your obedient servant,
RICHARD SMITH, Cashier.

E. Herring, Esq.

—————

Fort Gibson, March 11, 1833.

Sir: You have already been advised of the intentions of the commissioners to hold a council with the Osage Indians, for the purpose of removing them further north, and making such provision for the tribe as to induce them to abandon their present pursuits, and, in the course of time, become an agricultural people. The commissioners convened at the Saline, on the 25th ultimo, agreeably to previous arrangement; but, in consequence of the sudden change and continued inclemency of the weather, the chiefs were unable to meet them before the 6th of the present month. All the chiefs and principal warriors of the nation were present. It was then ascertained that provisions were becoming scarce, and as the time, at first proposed to occupy in holding the council, had already expired, Colonel Chouteau gave the commissioners notice that he found it impossible to subsist the Indians but a few days longer at that place. Under these circumstances, and having a letter just received from the assistant commissary at Fort Gibson, informing that he had a large quantity of provisions, which he was anxious to give to the Osages, otherwise he would be compelled to sell them at auction, at a heavy loss to the Government, the commissioners agreed to adjourn the council to this place, provided the Indians would be satisfied with the change. Major Chouteau, the agent, who exercises great and salutary influence over this tribe, made known to them the decision of the commissioners, and the causes which led to it, and they agreed to come here to conclude the treaty contemplated by the council convened at the Saline. The commissioners returned to this place on Saturday last, and the agent and sub-agents of the Osages have just arrived with their party, about eight hundred in number.

It affords me pleasure to assure you that a happy termination of this council is anticipated. Colonel A. P. Chouteau and his brother, the agent, are apprized of the views of the commissioners, as recommended by the Government, and they will aid in carrying them into effect. With their counsel and influence, I believe the commissioners will be able to negotiate a treaty highly beneficial to these people, who are truly in a wretched situation, and honorable to the Government of the United States.

The commissioners have instructed me to inform you that, after the business of the present council is concluded, they intend to proceed northward, for the purpose of examining the country on the waters of the Kansas, Marie de Cygnes, and other rivers in that direction, in order to ascertain its capacity to sustain other tribes which the Government may feel desirous of removing to this country. They will not be able to leave this place before the beginning of April, and will not then go should instructions arrive, in the meantime from the department, directing their duties elsewhere during the ensuing summer. If such instructions should not prevent their expedition north, they expect to be in St. Louis about the 10th of May, there to await the further orders of the department.

Having no business pressing upon their attention, for some time after the Osage council, the commissioners respectfully ask permission to visit their homes during the summer months. They will remain at St. Louis for your answer to this request, and if granted, they will cheerfully visit the Choctaw academy, or the tribes on the western lakes, on their way home.

I am, very respectfully, &c.,
S. C. STAMBAUGH,
*Secretary to Commissioners.*

Hon. Lewis Cass,
*Secretary of War.*

---

Indian Agency, Indiana, *March* 11, 1833.

Sir: I received yours, of the 28th January, by the last mail, and notified each of the sub-agents of its contents, at their residence; they are both now and have been for some time at the eastward.

There are, sir, in about fifteen miles of this place, about two hundred of the Prairie Pottawatamies, headed by *Qui-qui-to,* their chief. They have been in the neighborhood for some time, and wish, in the spring, to remove west of the Mississippi, as soon as the grass is of sufficient growth to support their horses. Permit me, sir, to assure you they are strictly pious, and much beloved by all the whites in their neighborhood. They wish some person and my interpreter to go with them as far as the Big Water, if the Government will furnish them with a small outfit. I am confident they can be removed with much less than the usual expense. Qui-qui-to is a man calculated to do much good among the Indians; the conduct of his party gives him much influence with all the Indians. I have written to Governor Porter, in detail, upon the subject, and presume he will communicate with you.

You will pardon these suggestions; the whole subject is with the department.

I have the honor to be, sir,
Very respectfully,
Your obedient servant,
WILLIAM MARSHALL,
*Indian Agent.*

Hon. ELBERT HERRING,
*Commissioner of Indian Affairs.*

————

SUPERINTENDENCY OF INDIAN AFFAIRS,
*Detroit, March* 12, 1833.

SIR: I have the honor to enclose the copy (of so much as relates to this subject) of a letter, dated 25th February, from Gen. William Marshall, Indian agent at Logansport, Indiana. I can add nothing explanatory of what is stated in this letter; but if your department can spare the necessary funds, it seems to me it would be right to grant the request of these two chiefs and their bands. A very considerable prejudice, it is evident, exists in the minds of many of the inhabitants of Illinois against these Pottawatamies, and I am not surprised that the latter should wish to get away west of the Mississippi. I cannot tell how this feeling was got up against these poor Indians, but, at an early period last season, the white population acted as though they were determined that these Pottawatamies should be enemies *nolens volens.*

The several letters and reports I have made to you on this subject, have at least satisfied my mind that injustice has been done them.

Gen. Marshall's opinion and judgment on the point now before us, is entitled to much weight. Your answer will be anxiously expected by him.

Very respectfully,
Your obedient servant,
G. B. PORTER.

ELBERT HERRING, Esq.,
*Commissioner of Indian Affairs.*

————

INDIAN AGENCY, INDIANA,
*Logansport, Feb.* 25, 1833.

SIR: Some time in the month of December last, two Pottawatamie chiefs from the prairies in Illinois, with their bands, amounting to two hundred, came into the neighborhood of this place, in a very distressed situation, and asked permission to remain near this place until spring. They say, as soon as the grass is sufficiently high for their horses to subsist on, they wish to remove west of the Mississippi, if their great father, the President of the United States, will permit them, and give them some small assistance. They say all they ask is a few horses, a little provision, some white person, and an interpreter to go with them over the big water, and with Mr. Luther Rice, (my interpreter,) a full blooded Indian, well educated, and a good, pious man, to go as their interpreter.

When they arrived, I wished them to return again, but they refused;

stating that, during the late Sac difficulties, the white people destroyed all their corn, and the game had left the country, and they would certainly starve, and that some of the whites there were hostile towards them.

I assure you, sir, the chiefs and their whole band are strictly pious, and totally abstain from all kinds of intoxicating liquors, nor will they suffer any one who drinks to remain with them. They are very industrious, and hunt a great deal. I have been compelled to furnish them with a little bread; it is all they ask of me. The whites who are acquainted with them, speak very highly of them, and particularly of their principal chief, whose name is Qui-qui-to. He is daily making converts to his party, and there has not been a single case of intoxication since they have been here.

Qui-qui-to, after he has taken his party west of the Mississippi, wishes to return himself, and take another band with him. He possesses great influence with the Indians, and is calculated to do much good.

I am certain, sir, I could take my interpreter and remove these Indians at very little expense to the Government, should the department think it advisable. I have no doubt, should they be removed, a great many others would follow their example. Of this, however, sir, you are the better judge. Should you deem it advisable, be pleased to communicate the fact to the department.

> I have the honor to be, sir,
> Very respectfully,
> Your obedient servant,
> WILLIAM MARSHALL,
> *Indian Agent.*

His Excellency G. B. Porter,
*Sup. Indian Affairs, Detroit.*

---

SUPERINTENDENCY OF INDIAN AFFAIRS,
*Detroit, March 15, 1833.*

Sir: I have the honor to transmit herewith my accounts and vouchers for the expenses incurred in my negotiation with the Menomonie Indians, in conformity with instructions from the War Department, of September 11th, 1832, having concluded a final arrangement and treaty with them at Green Bay, on the 27th October, 1832.

> With great respect,
> Your obedient servant,
> G. B. PORTER.

Elbert Herring, Esq.,
*Commissioner of Indian Affairs.*

---

SUPERINTENDENCY OF INDIAN AFFAIRS,
*Detroit, March 16, 1833.*

Sir: I have the honor to enclose the copy of a letter from Thomas J. V· Owen, esq., Indian agent at Chicago, dated the 4th instant; in which he states that the Indians of his agency (Pottawatamies) are willing to exchange their lands for lands west of the Mississippi; and solicits means, &c., from the Government, to enable a deputation to view the country.

18‡

I should be pleased if the department would grant their request. The truth is, that these Indians were much dissatisfied with the late treaties made at Tippecanoe. The citizens around them were also dissatisfied; and, so far from allaying the hard feelings of these Indians, joined with them in their complaints. I was asked, when at Chicago, by these Indians assembled to meet me, why were all the commissioners taken from Indiana, instead of one from Indiana, one from Illinois, and one from Michigan; a part of the lands being in Illinois, and a part in Michigan? Why were not all the Pottawatamie nation invited and notified to attend the council? that the lands were owned in common by the whole Pottamatamie nation, and hence all should have been present, and one general treaty made for the cession of their lands, and the money should have been paid to the whole nation, with many other questions, showing their hard feelings. If their present request could be granted, it seems to me it would do much towards removing all these impressions. The distance is so inconsiderable from Chicago to the waters of the Mississippi, that the expenses of their deputation need not be much. That it is an object of great importance, that the Government should become possessed of their lands, cannot be doubted. This accomplished, the whole country from Lake Michigan, east of Green Bay; the lower Fox river and Lake Winnebago, and south of the last lake; the upper Fox river and Ouisconsin, to the Mississippi, would belong to the United States. As now situated, the valuable cession made to the United States by the Winnebagoes, under the treaty held by General Scott, loses much of its value, because the whole eastern side of it is bounded by the land of these Pottawatamies. Extinguish their title, and the whole country will soon be covered by our enterprizing citizens, and the Government be paid the price set upon it. Added to this, the Indians will all be removed from the extensive new settlements in Illinois, and from the country in which they caused so much trouble during the past year.

It may not be improper here to remark, that these Pottawatamies have been much enraged at the representations made against them by the authorities, as well as citizens of Illinois, from time to time, since the commencement of the hostilities last summer up to the present time. A very sensible letter from General William Marshall, our Indian agent in Indiana, dated June 5th, 1832, (a copy of which was forwarded by me to the Secretary of War, on the 15th of the same month,) very well describes the effects of the first proclamation of Governor Reynolds, in which he says: "I am of the opinion that the Pottawatamies and Winnebagoes have joined the hostile Sacs, and may all be considered as waging war against the United States." I mean not to reflect on Governor Reynolds. He acted, I am convinced, through the best motives. But I think this denunciation of the Pottawatamies was, to say the least of it, imprudent; and, I assure you, they have not forgotten it. Our friends who marched to Chicago during the war, know what the Indians said about it: "If we are to be treated as enemies, behave as we may, who can blame us for joining in with our brethren of the forest? But, remember we are suspected unjustly; and if any thing is done by our young men, it is not our fault. We are driven into it, and the whites must blame themselves." When at Chicago, I was surprised to find that they still felt sensitive on this point. From what I then learned, and all the examinations we have made since, I am convinced that, as a nation, great injustice has been done them. A sense of duty alone has induced me to present this matter for consideration, that it may have whatever weight it is entitled to, when the appointment of commissioners is made for holding a treaty with them. It is proper to add, that many of the citizens of Michigan, in the vicinity of Niles, join in their complaints against the commissioners who held the late treaties, because the reservation around the Carey mission was not included in the cession; and boldly say, that, if one of the commissioners had been from Michigan, it would have been otherwise. It is very desirable for the interests of this territory, that this reservation should be ceded to the United States, in case the Indians should feel disposed to part with it; and the appropriate time to ascertain this fact, and if possible obtain the land, will be when the treaty in contemplation shall be held. I think it, therefore, not only essential, but would claim it as a matter of right, that Michigan should have a commissioner to assist in making the treaty.

No more proper occasion will present for adding, that, with respect to the treaties lately held, I never was informed that they were to be held; that commissioners had been appointed, or who they were, or when they were to assemble; nor was I asked by the commissioners to have the Indians assembled; nor notified of the time or place fixed on for the council, nor afterwards informed that treaties had been made. Although a novice in the office of Superintendent of Indian Affairs, I have sometimes supposed that I ought at least to have been advised of what was going on within my superintendency. In making this remark, I disclaim all intention of a wish to have had any thing to do with the treaties. I was, at the time they were held, otherwise engaged, (profitably, I trust,) in reconciling the long existing dispute between the Menomonies and the New York Indians at Green Bay.

In expectation of receiving your instructions soon, that I may communicate them to Colonel Owen,

I am, with sentiments of much respect,
Your obedient servant,
ELBERT HERRING, Esq ,                        G. B. PORTER.
   *Commissioner of Indian Affairs.*

---

INDIAN AGENCY, CHICAGO, *March* 4, 1833.

DEAR SIR: Since my answer to your (unofficial) letter of the 25th January last, I have been requested by some of the principal chiefs of this agency, to say that they would be willing to exchange their lands in this country, for lands west of the Mississippi, on fair and equitable terms, and remove as soon as practicable, if the country is adapted to their wants and pursuits. As a previous condition, and for the purpose of ascertaining the fact, they ask of the General Government permission and the means of sending a deputation west of the Mississippi, under the guidance of some faithful and trustworthy individual, whom they might select, to assist them in selecting a country somewhere in the vicinity of the forks of the river Des Moines, being about the same degree of north latitude as the country they now occupy.        I have the honor to be,

Very respectfully, dear sir,
Your most obedient servant,
TH. J. V. OWEN,
*Indian Agent.*

To his Excellency G. B. PORTER, *Detroit.*

MONROE, *March* 18, 1833.

HONORED SIR: Our friend, the Hon. A. E. Wing, arrived safe at home on the 16th, at 5 o'clock in the morning, in good health. Mrs. Wing is in better health than she has been since she lived in this place. We were much pleased to learn that your health was good, and that of Mrs. Cass.

Mr. Wing informed me that my name was not in the treaty made by Mr. Gardiner, at the mouth of the Maumee river. The information astonished me how it had happened. I gave up a claim against these Indians of $1,200 for $200, and it was allowed and put in the treaty. I have requested Colonel John E. Hunt to write you on the subject, he was present; also a claim in the name of Francois Lavoy, which is assigned to me, as it was my goods that they owed him for.

Mr. Wing thinks that the mistake has been made by the clerks in copying the treaty. I hope you will pardon me for giving you this trouble, as a few lines is requested from you on the subject to let me know what to do about it.

Mrs. Anderson and Mrs. Warner Wing, wish to be remembered to Mrs. Cass and the young ladies; we are all in good health, and hope you enjoy the same blessing.

I am, with much respect,
Your obedient servant,

Hon. LEWIS CASS.          JOHN ANDERSON.

---

CHEROKEE AGENCY, *March* 19, 1833.

SIR: By the last mail I received your letter of the 27th ultimo, informing me that funds would shortly be remitted to me to pay for the improvements abandoned on the ceded lands in North Carolina, Georgia, and Tennessee. There is one circumstance connected with that case, on which I wish your advice and instructions. It is this: Messrs. A. McCoy and N. Hicks, two half-breeds, I understand have obtained from fifty-two of the claimants, powers of attorney to receive and receipt for their several proportions of it, and are to have and retain one-half for the great services which they were to render in obtaining their pay from the Government; and as the Indians have long laid out of their pay, and no services been rendered them by those men, nor any part of the payment advanced, it seems to me that it would be proper and right to pay it to the individuals only, if alive or in reach. Part of them have emigrated to the west, and have revoked the former powers of attorney, or given orders to other persons, and a few others have notified me not to pay it to McCoy and Hicks.

Will you be so good as to say what I shall do in the case?

Some two or three years since, the delegation, on their way to Washington, called at this office, and stated that the report made to the department had been lost or mislaid by the Committee on Indian Affairs, or otherwise, and obtained from me loan of the only copy kept in this office of these claims, with a promise to return it, which has not been done. Will you be so good as to forward, (with the money to pay them,) a list of the names of the claimants, with the sums allowed to each.

I have the honor to be,
Your obedient servant,

ELBERT HERRING, Esq.,          H. MONTGOMERY.
    *Commissioner of Indian Affairs.*

EXECUTIVE DEPARTMENT, MILLEDGEVILDE, GA.

*March 20, 1833.*

SIR: Having received no answer to my letter of the 5th instant, written to you on the subject of our Indian relations, and daily occurrences and manifestations of a mischievous and wicked opposition to our efforts, to settle and put to rest long standing inquietudes, which have grown out of our Indian relations, induce me again to request that I may hear from you on the subject. I wish to be informed fully of the result of your efforts to negotiate a treaty with Ross and his colleagues while at Washington. What is the present attitude, and the prospect before us? What are the remaining obstacles? and who are the agents now engaged to prevent a settlement of the existing perplexities? For myself, I have no delicacy of feeling towards men who are endeavoring to destroy the Government of our beloved country. And from the tone of the presses engaged in the cause of the enemies of the country, I can no longer entertain a doubt that efforts are making to continue the causes of excitement in Georgia, on the Indian subject as long as possible. To prevent false impressions being made on the public mind in this State, in regard to the course pursued by the Federal Executive, as well as myself, it will become necessary to lay the whole truth before the people. I can never consent, while I occupy my present position, to see the interest of the State sacrificed to promote the views of a political combination, who seem determined to rule or destroy the country.

Very sincerely,

Your obedient servant,

WILSON LUMPKIN.

Hon. LEWIS CASS,
*Secretary of War.*

---

EXECUTIVE DEPARTMENT, MILLEDGEVILLE, GA.

*March 21, 1833.*

SIR: After writing to you yesterday, I had the honor, in the evening, to receive your letter of the 12th instant, enclosing a copy of the proposed project for future operations on the Cherokee subject, which had been submitted to you by Major Currey.

I am by no means discouraged at your failure to succeed in bringing about an immediate treaty with the Cherokee delegation; your efforts are satisfactory to me, and will be so to the people of Georgia, when they are fully apprized of all the obstacles and oppositions, *open* and secret, which we have to encounter in this business. The plan of Major Currey, as a whole, I consider very good, and I have no doubt has been founded upon such observations and experience, as would never have occurred to a superficial observer. I have strong apprehensions that nothing can be effected shortly, in the nature of a general treaty. I fear that Ross, regardless of the interest of his people, has now thrown himself into the hands of the new opponents of the Federal administration. Unnatural and unreasonable as it may be, it is nevertheless true, that there are at this time a numerous combination of politicians, in this quarter, who will use every exertion to prevent the success of the public agents, who are now so earnestly engaged in trying to settle and adjust this long standing Indian controversy. But should the Indians, in council, refuse to accede to the liberal propositions of the Government, we will then succeed on Major Currey's plan, with some modifications.

First. I approve of the exploring expedition, but should not like to postpone opening the door to emigrants until the return of the exploring agents; because, as justly remarked by Major Currey, every new emigrant stimulates his friends and neighbors, more by example than can be done by any course of reasoning. Moreover, I know there are many of the Cherokees in Georgia who are very desirous to make their arrangements to remove to the west at the close of the present year; therefore, the present season should not be permitted to waste away, by any delusive plan, so as to prevent the emigration of those who are already anxious to go. Those who are opposed to the success of our efforts, will rejoice at having it in their power to say (for several months to come) that no success is attending our efforts to remove the Indians. They will endeavor to throw the blame on us for the obstacles thrown in our way by themselves. As to the details of the plan of emigration, and the means to be used in carrying it into effect, you shall hear from me more fully hereafter. I write in haste, and without that reserve which delicacy generally attaches to official correspondence. But if an apology be required, it must be found in the extraordinary occurrences of the times.

With great respect, &c.,
Your obedient servant,
WILSON LUMPKIN.

Hon. Lewis Cass.

---

Memorandum of an agreement made and sanctioned this 18th day of August, 1831, by the chiefs of the Wyandott nation of Indians, *witnesseth:*

That, whereas *Isaac Walker,* deceased, late of Upper Sandusky, in the county of Crawford and State of Ohio, (interpreter to said Indians,) was, by the treaty held at the Lower Rapids on the Maumee, on the 29th day of September, 1817, and, by the supplement to that treaty, held at St. Mary's, on the 17th September, 1818, entitled to a section of land, on the lands reserved by said nation at said treaties to contain six hundred and forty acres of land. And whereas the said Isaac, previous to his death, made a will, in which he bequeathed the above section of land to his only child, *Isaiah Walker,* to be located by his executor, with the permission of the chiefs of said nation; and in pursuance of the above request, we, the said chiefs, have given to *John Carey,* the executor of said *Isaac Walker,* permission to locate said section of land, to commence at the northwest corner of the strip of land, given at the supplementary treaty at St. Mary's (to connect the Cherokee boys' section with the Grand Reservation) and run east on the line of land of Joseph Chaffee, and the said Cherokee boys' section one mile, and south from the above corner on the line of the reservation one mile for the quantity, so that the said boundary shall contain six hundred and forty acres in a square form: to have and to hold the above described premises, with all the appurtenances thereunto belonging (with the permission of the President of the United States) to him, the said *Isaiah Walker,* and his heirs forever. And we bind ourselves and our successors in office faithfully to abide by the above grant; and the said Isaiah is at liberty now and at all times hereafter to enter on, and take possession of the above described premises for his own proper use and benefit. Given under our hands and seals the day and year above written, in the presence of

JOHN HICKS, his x mark.    [L. s.]
ROTUNDEN, his x mark.    [L. s.]
SAM-ON-DE-WAT, his x mark.    [L. s.]
PEACOCK, his x mark.    [L. s.]
SCRO-HE-WAS, his x mark.    [L. s.]

John McElvaine,
James Ranking,
  *Interpreters.*

I certify that the above instrument was fairly explained to the chiefs aforesaid, and that the same was executed by them in open council.

JOHN McELVAINE,
*Indian Agent.*

———

Symarktu, Crawford County, Ohio,
*March 22, 1833.*

Sir: The above is a copy of an article which I hold as *guardian* for *Isaiah Walker.* I send you the above copy in order to ascertain whether it can be sanctioned by the President, and, if sanctioned, whether it will be a permanent deed for said land, &c. If that should be the case, I will send the original article for his sanction. I have not entered on said land as yet, but if the grant is sanctioned by the President, I shall proceed to have the land improved for the benefit of the heir.

The above grant is located at the northwest corner of the reservation, on land which has not been improved by any of the nation, and entirely one side from the main body of their land, so that it will not interfere with the nation at all.

I wish you to inform me whether a *lease*, duly executed by the chiefs of the Wyandott nation, for any part of their reservation for a term of years, (say ten or twenty years) with an annual rent, would be considered by the department binding and valid, where it is conditioned that the *lessee* (in case the nation shall at any time sell their reservation) shall be bound to surrender said lease.

Please to give me an answer to the above as soon after the receipt of this as convenient.

Very respectfully,
Your most obedient servant,
JOSEPH CHAFFEE.

Hon· Lewis Cass.

PICKENSVILLE, ALABAMA, *March* 25, 1833.

DEAR SIR: I have been solicited by Mr. Wm. Mitchell, of this neighborhood, to make an inquiry of you involving much interest to him. For the purpose of the better enabling you to understand the nature of the inquiry, I will give you the whole circumstance relating to his case. In January, 1832, he moved into the Choctaw nation, and purchased of Gordon McGilbray, an Indian, permission to settle on land held, or intended to be held by the said McGilbray, under the fourteenth article of the late treaty with the Choctaws, and accordingly settled and made considerable improvement, under the belief that the claim would be good, and that in time the Indian would be able to give him a *bona fide* title. But during the spring and summer of last year, the Indian professed to have no such claim to land, and made arrangements to move west with his family, consisting of a wife and two small children. A speculator made the Indian an offer for his supposed claim of land, acquired under the said fourteenth article, which he accepted, and remained here with one child, but sent his wife and the other child west; and instead of remaining on, and cultivating the land upon which he lived and claims, in compliance with the conditions of the treaty, he has moved across the State line from Mississippi to Alabama, and is now living with his father, John McGilbray.

The speculator referred to has recently applied to the agent, Col. Ward, for the necessary certificate in favor of the said Indian, entitling him to a reservation of land under the said article, and has obtained it, who has given Mr. Mitchell written notice to leave the premises.

Now, Mr. Mitchell wishes to know of you whether Gordon McGilbray did have his name registered in due time to entitle him to a reservation of land under the said article or not. The object of the inquiry is this: Mr. Mitchell is an old and poor man, with a large family, and will not contend against an equitable claim, but will give immediate possession; but he is induced to believe that the certificate before referred to has been fraudulently obtained, *(if a genuine one.)*

An answer to this letter will confer a peculiar favor on this old man, as it may be the means of keeping him out of an expensive and litigious lawsuit with a hard hearted speculator.

I am, sir, most respectfully,
Your obedient servant,
GAB. FELDER.

To the Hon. LEWIS CASS.

---

WASHINGTON CITY, D. C., *March* 25, 1833.

SIR: I have the honor of enclosing a list of claims, made out at the time of paying the Choctaws west of the Mississippi, for their relinquished lands. These claims are founded, as you will perceive, upon the statement of the claimants themselves. In order to enable the department to refer with facility to the reservation books in the office of Indian Affairs, the claims are arranged upon rolls for each district, with a reference to the captain's company, and page of book. The Indians desire now to relinquish their lands, or, under their own view of their rights, they wish to be paid for their lands as relinquished, stating that they did, within the proper time, make their intention to relinquish known to Colonel Ward, whose duty it was to have returned them as relinquished to the department.

A list of all the Indians entitled to reservations, was left by me with Colonel Ward, in September, 1831, at the agency, in order to enable him to place the name of the person relinquishing upon the list opposite to his name and claim, in a column left for that purpose. This list, by order of the department, was forwarded by Colonel Ward immediately after the first day of January, 1832, before which time they were bound to relinquish, if at all. That some did relinquish, and have a right to expect pay, I have no doubt. The time, however, being past, it is for the Government to determine on the remedy. It is proper for me to state, that attempts have been made west to get pay for claims by those not entitled to them, and I think it also probable that some of the claimants may have sold their claims to white men, east, and wish to be paid as having relinquished. Would it not be well to require from the proper source, a list of claims purchased from the Indians, setting forth the location of the claim, with a showing where the Indian resided, when he sold his claim; with the advantage of this information, then to compare the proposed list of claims sold by them under that article of the treaty yet to be sanctioned by the President, with the pay-rolls for relinquished lands, frauds could be detected, and at the same time, the purchase of the white man sustained, if honestly made.

With respect, I am your obedient servant,

F. W. ARMSTRONG, *C. A. W.*

E. HERRING, Esq.
*Commissioner Indian Affairs.*

---

WASHINGTON CITY, *March 26,* 1833.

SIR: Susan (sometimes called Susannah) Graham claims the twenty eighth and the west half of the twenty-seventh sections of township fifteen, in range one east, situate in that tract of country ceded to the United States by the treaty of Dancing Rabbit creek, under, and by virtue of, the provisions of the 14th article of said treaty. Her name has been registered in the manner prescribed by the treaty, as appears from the report of Elbert Herring, esq., of the Bureau of Indian Affairs, made on the 10th of March, 1832, and enclosed to me under cover of yours of the same date. Mrs. Graham requests that the section and a half of land herein described, should be reserved from sale for her use. I request that this communication may be filed in the Bureau of Indian Affairs, War Department.

Most respectfully, your obedient servant,

F. E. PLUMMER,
*For, and at the request of, Susan Graham.*

Hon. LEWIS CASS,
*Secretary of War.*

---

WASHINGTON CITY, *March* 26, 1833.

SIR: I am desirous to know the number of Choctaws whose names are registered for reservations of land, under the provisions of the 19th article of the treaty of Dancing Rabbit creek.

1st. How many are entitled to one section of land, in consequence of having had in cultivation, during the year 1830, fifty acres or more.

19‡

2d. How many are entitled to three quarter sections of land, in consequence of having had in cultivation, during the year 1830, thirty acres, and less than fifty.

3d. How many are entitled to one-half section of land, in consequence of having had in cultivation from twenty to thirty acres.

4th. How many are entitled to one-quarter section of land, in consequence of having had in cultivation from twelve to twenty acres.

5th. How many are entitled to one-eighth of a section, in consequence of having had in cultivation from two to twelve acres.

This information is desired for the benefit of those Choctaws who are entitled to the benefits of the provisions of the article of the treaty before referred to. If the number of those whose names are registered for reservations, exceed the limitations prescribed in the treaty, the applicants are solicitous to know which of them will be excluded, in order that they may make application to the proper source for relief. I beg leave to refer you to the treaty for the stipulations and provisions contained in the 19th article, which will, in my humble opinion, enable you to discover the importance of the information to those interested.

Most respectfully,

Your obedient servant,

F. E. PLUMMER.

Hon. Elbert Herring,
    *Commissioner Indian Affairs.*

----

Washington City, *March* 27, 1833.

Sir: John Hacha, a native and citizen of the Choctaw nation of Indians, within the State of Mississippi, claims one-half section of land under, and by virtue of, the provisions of the 19th article of the treaty of Dancing Rabbit creek, made and entered into between the nation aforesaid, and the United States, on the 27th day of March, 1830. The land which he claims is known and designated as the east half of the northwest quarter, the west half of the northeast quarter, the west half of the southeast quarter, and the east half of the southwest quarter of section twenty-one, in township three, range ten, east. In support of his claim, I send you the enclosed documentary testimony, with a request that the same, together with this letter, be filed in the office of the Commissioner of Indian Affairs, and his name registered.

Most respectfully,

Your obedient servant,

F. E. PLUMMER.

Hon. Lewis Cass, *Secretary of War.*

----

The State of Mississippi, *Jones county:*

Before the undersigned, an acting justice of the peace in and for said county, personally appeared John Hacha, who, being duly sworn, on oath says, that he is a Choctaw Indian by birth, that he is the head of a family, and a housekeeper, and has been, from and before the 27th day of September, 1830; that he lives in that part of the State of Mississippi acquired from the Choctaw nation of Indians, by the treaty of Dancing Rabbit creek, made and entered into between said nation and the United States, on the 27th day of September, 1830; that he had in actual cultivation, within said territory, during the year 1830, twenty-two acres of land, (since ascertained to be on section No. twenty-one, township No. three, of range No. ten, east,) with a dwelling-house thereon, in which he resided.

JOHN HACHA, his x mark.

Sworn and subscribed before me, this 22d day of November, 1832.

THOMAS S. LOPER, *J. P.*

---

THE STATE OF MISSISSIPPI, *Jones county.*

Before me, the undersigned justice of the peace, personally appeared William Prine, a citizen of the county of Jones, and State aforesaid, who being duly sworn, deposeth and saith, that he is personally acquainted with John Hacha; that he is a Choctaw by birth; that he is the head of a family, and was a resident housekeeper, within that part of the territory acquired from the Choctaw nation of Indians, by the treaty of Dancing Rabbit creek, on the 27th day of September, 1830, and previous to that time; that he had in actual cultivation as much as twenty-two acres of land, or more, within the limits of said nation, with a dwelling-house thereon, during the year 1830, situated upon section No. twenty-one, township No. three, range No. ten, east. WILLIAM PRINE.

Sworn to, and subscribed before me, this 22d day of November, 1832.

THOMAS S. LOPER, *J. P.*

---

THE STATE OF MISSISSIPPI, *Jones county.*

Before me, the undersigned justice of the peace, in and for said county, personally appeared Stacy Collins, who, being duly sworn, deposeth and saith, that he is personally acquainted with Wm. Prine, of the county and State aforesaid, and that he is a man of integrity; any statement made by him on oath ought to be entitled to the fullest confidence.

STACY COLLINS.

Sworn to, and subscribed before me, this 22d day of November, 1832.

THOMAS S. LOPER, *J. P.*

---

THE STATE OF MISSISSIPPI, *Jones county.*

I, John Maffitt, clerk of the county court of Jones county, do hereby certify that Stacy Collins, whose name is signed to the foregoing certificate, is a man of respectability, and, as such, any statement made by him, whether on oath or otherwise, is entitled to full faith and credit.

Given under my hand and private seal (there being no official seal) this 22d day of November, 1832.

JOHN MAFFITT, *Clerk.* [SEAL.]

---

RISING SUN, *March* 27, 1833.

SIR: Your note of the 18th instant has been received, and its contents duly noticed.

I shall probably set out for the Indian country about the first of next month. Very respectfully,

A. C. PEPPER.

Hon. ELBERT HERRING.

DAYTON, *March* 27, 1833.

SIR: The enclosed account was sent to me at Washington, but did not reach there until after I had left the city. The claim belongs to Messrs. T. and W. Parrott, of this town. At their request, I enclose the account. They wish to know whether it will be allowed, and if so, what receipts or vouchers must be executed by them for the payment. I have also been requested to inquire whether the claim of Dr. John O'Ferral, for provisions for the emigrating Shawnees, has been allowed; and, also, when the annuities to that tribe will be paid, and who is the agent for that tribe.

I am, very respectfully,
Your obedient servant,
JOSEPH H. CRANE.

ELBERT HERRING, Esq.

---

FORT MITCHELL, *March* 27, 1833.

SIR: Ne-he-martler, one of the chiefs of the Seminoles, who received a reserve of two sections, has lost his certificate or grant. He now, and has for some time resided in the nation, (Creek,) and is anxious to sell his reserve. I have never seen it, but am informed it is valuable. He would like to know what Government would give for it. He wants another certificate forwarded, also, to this place, which he hopes to receive soon. If Government will give a fair valuation for it, I am authorized to say they can have it. Your attention will be respectfully acknowledged.

Your obedient servant,
NE-HE-MARTLER,
*By Luther Blake.*

ELBERT HERRING, Esq.,
*Indian Department, Washington City.*

---

MADISON COUNTY, ALA., *March* 27, 1833.

DEAR SIR: Enclosed you have the opinion of Mr. Silas Parsons, of Huntsville. My apology for the liberty is, that I am interested in the decision of the claims to the right of reservations in the cases alluded to. Some time after the treaty was made with the Creek Indians, I became desirous to settle in the country; and being informed that there was a small village of full blooded Creek Indians, within the Cherokee nation, who intended to remove over the line and claim their reservations, and then sell out and remove to the west of the Mississippi, I obtained the opinion of several gentlemen of legal ability, who all concurred in the opinion of their right to reservations; and believing, also, that the great object of the Government was their removal, I went to the village and made contracts with three of the heads of families, who proceeded with me and made their improvements, (say small cabins,) not interfering with the settlements of any other persons, either whites or Indians. The balance of the village, to the number of twelve heads of families, waited at the village for the return of the first three for their families, when they all proceeded to the country ceded. After travelling a few miles, they were stopped by a party of white men, who tied up and most inhumanly whipped some of them, and drove the whole party back. Those white savages then entered into a written contract with each other to whip or kill any white man who should offer aid to the Indians in obtaining reservations in the country. I should have made this address to you at an earlier date, but knowing that some Cherokee Indians resided within the Creek country, I waited to see whether or not they would be enrolled for reservations. On ascertaining that their application had been refused, I felt the more confirmed in my first opinion, that the claim of those poor, unfortunate, unoffending people, who have only the Government of the United States to look to for protection in their rights, would be recognized. I then made a plain and candid statement of the facts to Mr. Parsons, who wrote his opinion for me, which I send to you, not for a moment believing that it contains any thing new or unknown to yourself, but to show that, in making the attempt to settle the Indians and obtain their reservations at fair prices, I did not intend any thing but what was perfectly justifiable. I beg that you will give me your opinion on these claims at your convenience. The claim of Joseph Bruner has been purchased, and a selection made at Talledega. Will that purchase be ratified?

     I have the honor to be,

Most respectfully,<br>
Your obedient servant,<br>
WM. H. MOORE.

The Hon. Lewis Cass.

---

Wascissa, March 30, 1833.

Sir: I have to acknowledge the reception of your letter of the 18th ult., and shall, in my future negotiations with the two remaining Indian towns on the Appalachicola, be governed by the views therein expressed. In writing on that subject, it was to obtain more explicit instructions than those contained in a previous communication from the Secretary of War. I was not insensible to the "doubtful policy and practical difficulty" of such an arrangement as the younger chiefs were solicitous of making of their supposed interest in the reservation held in common with the older chiefs, not so willing at present to migrate.

Blunt's exploring party has returned and report favorably of the country to which he and his band proposed removing. The chiefs from the other towns who accompanied the expedition, seem much pleased, and have made such representations as may induce, in their opinion, Earchatimeco and Vacapasacy to listen more favorably to the propositions from our Government. They have invited me to visit, once more, their towns, and make another essay towards a negotiation. I shall, accordingly, leave this in a few days for that purpose, and hope to report to you a final and successful result.

Blunt has sought two or three interviews with me of late, all relating to subjects connected with the future execution of the engagement he has entered into for the removal of himself and followers west. As he is now anxious to commence the preparations necessary for his migration, it may be important to give to the Executive of the territory, some directions on the subject, Blunt requests, however, that I should, in the mean time, prefer to your department a petition for an advance of 400 dollars, from the sums hereafter to be paid him, to commence the building of boats, &c., necessary for his removal. I mentioned to him that from the stipulations of the treaty he was not to be paid any thing until ready to move, He is aware of this, and, therefore, only solicits the amount as a favor from peculiar circumstances and greater expense incurred by his exploring party than he had anticipated.   The petition is submitted to your consideration, with an expression of an opinion on my part that it would be *safe*, and might be *advantageous*, to make the advance.

Respectfully,

Your obedient servant,<br>JAMES GADSDEN.

ELBERT HERRING, Esq.,
*Office of Indian Affairs, Washington.*

---

CREEK NATION, *March* 30, 1833.

SIR: It has been represented to us, that some of the chiefs of the Tuckabatchee town, have requested you to place the $100,000 (which was appropriated by the late Creek treaty to pay the debts of the nation) in the hands of General Parsons, and for *him* to apply it to the payment of such debts as he might think proper.   The letter signed by these chiefs, was written by General Parsons,, and if it has been correctly represented to us, who as the *head chiefs*, of the *nation*, must enter our protest against such a course. During the investigation of claims, General Parsons seemed to be so much the friend of the Indians, that he not only scrutinized them, but objected to the payments of *some* claims, which the chiefs admitted as just and wished to pay; but now it seems his object was *self interest* instead of that of the Creeks.   We are the head chiefs of the nation, and was (as you will see) at the head of the delegation who acted with the commissioners during the investigation of claims presented to them, and it is our wish, as thus expressed by the delegation, that *all* the claims adopted by the *council* as national, should be first paid out of the national fund, and the balance sent to us as heretofore.

There are several just claims against the different towns, which have not been handed to the commissioners, which we intend to pay.

Our wishes, in relation to the disposal of the $100,000, have been fairly represented to the commissioners in writing; we, therefore, deem it unnecessary *again* to express them.

We will not pretend to recommend to you any individual to pay the money, but we must, for ourselves and our nation, protest in the strongest terms, it being put in the hands of General Parsons.

We are your friends and brothers,

NEHAH MICCO, his x mark,  } Of upper towns.<br>TUSKEHENHAW, his x mark, }

Signed in presence of
   RICHARD J. WADE and
   E. JOHNSON.
The Hon. LEWIS CASS,
   *Secretary of War, Washington.*

---

*March*, 1833.

A plan of operations for the removal of the Cherokees, east, to the country west of the Mississippi, respectfully submitted for the consideration of the honorable Lewis Cass, Secretary of War, under the following heads:
1st. An exploring party, to be fitted out at the expense of Government.

2d. The removal of life estates and fee simple reserves.

3d. Privilege of disposing of improvements to white men.

4th. Manner and time of paying for abandoned improvements.

5th. With the increase of emigration additional lands to be provided.

6th. Number of persons and quantity of baggage to each wagon.

7th. A company of regular troops under the direction of Indian agent.

1st. Should it appear obvious to the Indian agent, as well as the superintendent, that the principal chief and his party have agreed to call a council on their return home, merely to amuse the department and procrastinate other arrangements, an exploring party, consisting of one confidential Cherokee from each of the eight districts in the nation, to be fitted out, accompanied by one or two white men, as early as convenient, for the purpose of examining the lands already guaranteed to them, as well as so much of the adjacent territory as will make their full complement, bringing their country as nearly into a square or oblong square as possible, whose duty it shall be to report the result of their observations to the War Department, and also to the Cherokees, east, with a view to an acquisition of additional territory, as the tide of emigration may appear to require it, under the fifth section of this plan. Although your superintendent is aware that the leading men of the nation are already well informed as to the character of that country, still but few, if any, have explored it. Yet, while the most powerful party remain in opposition to western removals, they will, as he is persuaded, continue to countenance false reports, in order to discourage emigration. The weaker party having, most of them, been in time past, equally opposed to the policy of Government, and not having seen the country upon which, in the estimation of the ignorant, to found a substantial reason for changing, will be branded, as other advocates have been, with misrepresentation, falsehoods, toryism, &c., and their influence must thereby be greatly paralyzed; whereas, persuasions, after actual observation, would most probably, when used in connexion with surrounding circumstances, countervail in a high degree that deleterious influence. Such an expedition can be performed in three or four months, and will not cost the Government more than four or five thousand dollars. In the meantime, should the head-men be earnestly engaged in bringing about a treaty, the favorable report of this party would operate as a powerful auxiliary in accomplishing this desirable object with the common people, whilst, on the other hand, should their pledges to call a council, on their return home, be intended to mislead and delay other arrangements, their scheme would be rendered abortive by the facts collected in this expedition, and no time lost by their attempts at delusion.

2d. There is a class of Cherokees who, on account of their wealth and superior intelligence, exercise a controlling influence over the great body of this people, known as fee simple and life estate reservees, who, under the provisions of the treaty of 1819, section two, three, notified the Indian gent of a wish on their part to take reservation, within the territory seceded, to reside thereon permanently, and become citizens of the United States. This notification was a necessary condition upon which these reserves were granted. A portion of this class of people are becoming anxious to remove west; the remainder are opposed to emigration, and still continue to dissuade their countrymen from going; as they, by undertaking to become citizens of the United States, relinquish their interest in the Indian country;

the common principle of justice would debar them the privilege of disposing of these reservations for money, converting it to their own use, and afterwards removing and settling on the very same lands to which they had relinquished all claim, unless by the express consent of the contracting parties. And the General Government, being a party materially interested, never having given its consent, nor even been consulted, has, therefore, a right to remove these reservees, with their descendants, as intruders. But in order that they, as well as the most fastidious philanthropists, may find no cause of complaint against the department, it might be well to say, that by signifying to the agents of Government a wish, and enrolling previous to the 1st of January next, to join 'their brethren west, the Government will remove them on the same terms and conditions that others have been removed, or on the terms proposed at the last council. But should they fail to avail themselves of this offer, to be forthwith removed as intruders, after the date above specified.

3d. Where the State laws have not been extended, the emigrant, in addition to receiving pay from Government for his improvement, may dispose of the good will of the same to white persons or families until the State shall, by legislative enactment, dispose of them otherwise. If, within the limits of Georgia, where the Indian improvements will all shortly be held in expectancy by fortunate drawers, should said drawers, or persons purchasing of them, be disposed to pay the occupant for abandoning his improvement, it may be done, provided said occupant, with his family, will emigrate to the west, and, on the same principle, let the Alabama Cherokee make the best disposition he can of his improvements to white families. This plan, whilst it comes in contact with no State laws or regulations, takes no more money from the United States Treasury than is authorized by law, operates upon the avarice of the Indian, one of the most powerful and overruling passions of their nature, forming a spring, when' touched, impelling them to immediate action; that no improvement purchased by one Indian of another, after the 4th of March instant, shall be valued to the purchaser, unless residing thereon, or the person of whom it is purchased, shall also enrol and remove westwardly, and no improvement made by a white laborer appended to one made by an Indian, after the above specified date, shall be assessed by the appraising agents; neither should any improvement at any time made by a white man not intermarried with a Cherokee, be appraised, although an Indian may have come into possession of the same, either peaceably or forcibly; but where the Indian, so coming into possession, shall have made additional improvements, he shall, on enrolling himself, have that much appraised, to be paid for in the same manner with others.

4th. Where emigrants are indebted to white persons on *bona fide* contracts, made previous to their enrollment, or for necessaries purchased thereafter, and before their embarkation, the faith of the Government may be pledged, if requested by the debtor, at the discretion of the superintendent, to the amount of the valuation of the property abandoned; but in no case shall the emigrant be detained by one of his own countrymen, or his property seized to pay a debt due him. This last regulation is recommended, because it will operate as an inducement for the claimant to follow all payments for improvements to be made at the agency west, with the exception of just debts.

5th. In proportion to the number of removals, additional lands to be provided by the Government, until, as a nation, they shall be possessed of the same quantity of land in the west, as was occupied by them in the east, prior to the treaty of 1817. Previous to the treaty of 1828, the Cherokees claimed under the Government three millions of acres; by that treaty four millions more were given, on condition that they would receive those from the east disposed to join them in severalty. The numbers of acres claimed by the eastern, from the treaty of 1819, up to the present time, may be computed at seven millions, lying within the limits of the several States, so that when the whole of the remnant tribe is removed, to give them acre per acre, they will be entitled to three millions acres more. The number yet remaining east is estimated at from ten to twelve thousand souls; as one family goes west, their example begets a stronger disposition with those remaining to go also, than years of delay expended in argument and persuasion; hence the importance of opening the emigration, and thereby keeping alive that spirit, whilst at the same time the efforts of the Government may be more successfully directed to a general arrangement.

6th. The Cherokees being more wealthy, and having a greater quantity of clothing, bedding, farming utensils, &c., &c., than other tribes, I find, from actual experience, that two wagons, to fifty Cherokees, with thirty hundred weight of baggage, is by no means an extravagant allowance; and would, therefore, suggest the propriety of amending that part of the Commissary General's regulations, so far as it relates to the Cherokee removal.

7th. A company of regular infantry (*cavalry* if to be had) located near the eastern agency, under the direction of the Indian agent, to protect emigrants from improper detention and imposition from white men as well as Indians; to preserve good order among the party whilst assembling, and before their embarkation; and also to remove intruders from the country when necessary.

The foregoing is submitted as the best plan suggesting itself to your superintendent, which, if adopted by the department, in case of a failure, to effect a general or sectional treaty, must inevitably result in the removal of the whole tribe, with as little expense to the Government, a as treaty on the terms recently proposed.

Most respectfully,<br>I have the honor to be,<br>Your obedient servant,<br>BEN. F. CURREY.

Hon. Lewis Cass,
  *Secretary of War, Washington City.*

---

Cherokee Agency, *April* 1, 1833.

Sir: Enclosed I send you an abstract of disbursements, made in the first quarter of the current year, for emigration purposes only, (as nothing has been paid for ordinary or contingent purposes,) and an account current.

As an estimate was made, on the 31st December last, for the two first quarters of the present year, it is not deemed necessary to make another at this time.
Very respectfully,<br>Your obedient servant,<br>H. MONTGOMERY.

Honorable Elbert Herring,
  *Com'r of Ind. Aff's, Washington City.*

20‡

CHEROKEE AGENCY, *April 3,* 1833.

SIR: Some time since, Thomas Foreman, one of the Cherokee chiefs, returned to me a list of twenty-eight families who, he said, were intruders on Cherokee lands. On his list I found several who had permits from me to occupy improvements abandoned by emigrants and paid for by the Government. Those he insisted were intruding by clearing land and adding to the former improvements. There were, also, several who had been brought in by permits from the Treasurer of the nation. Those, I informed him, I had notified them I had nothing to do with. The balance I sent the interpreters round, with instructions to notify them to remove, and I understand that most of them are gone.

Those who have been adding to the valued improvements, by clearing land, I directed to desist until your pleasure was known upon that subject, which is requested, as a considerable part of the noise, about intrusion, is from that quarter.

There are several families who have been brought in by individual Indians, without permits from the national authorities, who claim the right to do so, about which I should like to have your instructions.

There is another individual case about which I feel a great delicacy, and would thank you for instructions.

When I came to this agency, having no other white family but myself and wife, I brought with me Mr. Hardwick, who had lately married our daughter, and agreed to pay him yearly wages to attend to my hands in the little farm, assist me in the office, and, when necessarily absent, attend to it for me. He and family are yet living with us, and, although we now cultivate separate fields, all is on the mile square, laid off by Col. Meigs, for the use of the agency, by order of the Government, (see Mr. McKenney's letter to me, on that subject, of the 1st October, 1825;) and, although Lewis Ross has, at least, two-thirds of the mile square in possession, yet I have been called on by John Ross to remove Mr. Hardwick, and, I have no doubt, for the sole purpose that Lewis Ross may occupy the improvement which he has made, and so get into possession the whole of the mile square, with the exception of a small corner on which I live.

As I have no sub-agent, I cannot get along well without Mr. Hardwick, but, if you so direct, he will remove.

I have again sent out notices to intruders to remove without delay, and hope by the time the troops arrive there will be none, or but very few to remove, except a set of vagabonds who, I understand, have taken possession of the barracks, made by the troops at Coquo creek, and are said to be digging for gold.

Very respectfully,
Your obedient servant,
H. MONTGOMERY.

Honorable ELBERT HERRING,
*Com'r of Ind. Aff's., Washington City.*

---

FORT GIBSON, *April 3,* 1833.

SIR: It gives me much pleasure in being able to inform you that the arrangement of the difficulties between the Creeks and Cherokees has given great satisfaction to both nations, and that the Seminoles are delighted with the country. We have assigned them between the Canadian river and the north fork of the same. The Senecas also express themselves much pleased with what we have done for them.

I regret, however, that we have not been able to carry into effect the benevolent views of the Government with the Osages. Our report to the department will enable you to judge of the cause of the failure.

We will proceed in a few days to examine the physical resources and situation of the country in which the commissioners designated or proposed to give them.

It is my private opinion that it is a matter of little moment to the Government to effect this exchange at all. My reasons for this opinion are these: an ample country has already been provided, by the late treaties, for the accommodation of the whole Cherokees, Creeks, and Seminole Indians. The whole Muscogee nation, and the Cherokees, have each, at least, 13,000,000 of acres secured to them. The Chickasaws will never consent to a northern location, and nothing will satisfy them but a place in the Choctaw country, and there is enough for both nations. So that, according to our instructions from the department, we have to make provision for the location of some remnants of tribes only from Ohio.

| | |
|---|---|
| From Ohio, Wyandots, about | 500 |
| Indiana and Illinois, say | 2,500 |
| If you please to add to this New York Indians | 6,000 |
| New England | 2,500 |
| Virginia | 47 |
| South Carolina | 450 |
| Quapaws (we ought not to forget) | 700 |
| | 12,697 souls. |

There is an unappropriated country between the Senecas, Shawnees, and Osages on the south, and the Piankeshaws, Weas, Kaskaskias, Shawnees, and Kanzas on the north, of about 15,000,000 acres, at least 3,000,000, we are informed, very good, on the East river, Neosho, and Choias de Cygnes. This tract will accommodate the above remnants of tribes, and place them contiguous to their old friends and kindred tribes. These tribes being small and near the white settlements, can here be well protected from the wild Indians in the west.

The only possible necessity for removing the Osages from the north is, that their present reservations may be needed to gratify the humor and rapacity of the Cherokees east. It is not necessary for their accommodation, the Cherokees well know; and if the Government were to give to the Cherokees what it would cost to remove the Osages, in addition to what they have offered, I believe the money would please them better than the land.

The Commissioners, I believe, all feel that it is very important to have an interview with the Government on this and many other important subjects. I believe the interests of the Government will be greatly promoted by such an interview, much more than the increased expense of a visit to Washington. We hope to receive instructions to that effect at St. Louis. My best respects to the President.

With great respect,
Your friend and servant,
J. F. SCHERMERHORN.

To the Hon. LEWIS CASS.

FORT GIBSON, *April* 3, 1833.

DEAR SIR: Before I left home last November, and not knowing how long it would be indispensably necessary to be absent, I drew two drafts on the War Department; one for two hundred dollars, payable to the cashier of the Branch Bank United States, Utica, in January last; and the other to the cashier of the Bank of Utica, payable in May next, for two thousand dollars. I will here state, that, after accepting my appointment at Washington, I travelled, in coming to this place in this Territory, the following distance, viz: three thousand three hundred and seventy-four miles. I arrived here on the 19th of December last. From this statement you will be able to determine what will be due me when my draft is payable, for services and travelling. I am not conversant with the manner of doing business at the different offices; and if there is any irregularity in the matter, you will please to overlook it and pay the same; and I will hereafter correct it. I will only further add, that as we have done holding treaties here until next fall, we will proceed in a few days to explore the country north and west, as far as the Kansas and Missouri rivers; after this, we shall proceed to St. Louis, where we hope to arrive between the middle of May and the first of June. I shall then have travelled about eight hundred or a thousand miles more.

With great respect,
Your most obedient servant,
J. F. SCHERMERHORN.
To the Hon. LEWIS CASS, *Secretary of War.*

———

GREENSBOROUGH, *April* 4, 1833.

SIR: By a clause in 19th article of the treaty of 1830, with the Choctaws, it is provided, that " children of the Choctaw nation residing in the nation, who have neither father nor mother, a list of which, with satisfactory proof of parentage and orphanage, being filed with the agent, in six months, to be forwarded to the War Department, shall be entitled to a quarter section of land, to be located under the direction of the President; and, with his consent, the same may be sold, and the proceeds applied to some beneficial purpose for the benefit of said orphans. "

I am desirous of ascertaining what number of orphans were registered in the department, under the foregoing provision; and whether the locations of their quarter sections have been made as provided for. If they have, how they are to be ascertained, and how they may be purchased. If not, whether the President would affix a price to the claim, and allow a purchaser to locate it when he chooses. An early answer to these inquiries will oblige
Your obedient servant,
THOMAS F. FOSTER.
Hon. LEWIS CASS.

———

FORT MITCHELL.

SIR: The majority of the commissioners appointed in behalf of the United States, to carry into effect in part the treaty concluded at Washington City in March, 1832, between the Government of the United States and the Creek nation of Indians, respectfully report:

That, pursuant to the notice given by them at Wetumpka, during their attendance at the general council there in September last, they again met the Creek nation of Indians assembled in council at this place; and, on Tuesday, the 8th of January, attended by a delegation of the principal Creek chiefs and head-men of the nation, proceeded to the discharge of the duties assigned them.

In conformity to the instructions of the department of June 27th, 1832, requiring the commissioners "to prepare, upon the representation of the chiefs of the nation, a schedule of the debts due by the Creeks; to collect such testimony, whether oral or written, as might be sufficient, in the opinion of the commissioners, to establish the justice of them; to transmit to the department the written evidence, together with a synopsis of the parole; to investigate the whole matter thoroughly; to take care that all fraudulent claims should be rejected; to procure assignments of ferries, bridges, and causeways, and assess their value; to obtain and forward transcripts of the judgments against Creek chiefs; statements of losses for which the Creeks suppose the United States to be responsible, with the evidence in their support; what improvements were made under the treaty of 1826, by whom, and their value; the names of the persons who suffered by being prevented from emigrating; the amount of their loss, &c.: to report the result, together with the opinion of the commissioners upon the whole matter, and all this as much in detail as possible;" the majority of the committee state that, to the utmost of their ability, they have zealously labored for the accomplishment of these various requisitions, and all other known wishes of the department relative thereto.

In relation to the numerous claims laid before them, the majority of the commissioners state that they, in conjunction with the delegation of chiefs above mentioned, (a list of whose names is herewith forwarded,) to the extent of their imperfect and limited means, carefully investigated the same; and, also, that while so doing, pursuant to further instructions from the department subsequent to the former, created and observed the line of distinction ordered to be drawn between claims for debts contracted, or purporting to have been due antecedent to the time of the ratification of the treaty. and debts purporting to be subsequent; and have denominated the claims of a date prior to the treaty, the first, and those of a later date, the second series. It having been required that the proceedings of the commissioners should, be "*as much in detail as possible,*" they deemed it essential that their report should present, in order to insure conformity to such requirement, copies of all the claims filed; the evidence in the said claims, both written and parole; and the opinion of the commissioners in each particular case, with their reasons for the same. The case numbered 188, first series, presents the schedule of the claims for certain improvements stipulated to be paid for under the treaty of 1826, together with the evidence pertaining to them, which is all that could be procured; and, it is presumed, owing to the extensive alterations made by the white settlers, all Indian signs and traces in that region of country being obliterated, that it is the best which can now be had. The number following, (189,) of the same series, is made up of a bundle of claims, marked from 1 to 131, for losses, &c., with their relative testimony. This is composed of affidavits and statements, made and taken *ex parte,* and is all that was adduced. The claims for the cost of voluntary emigration, and for losses accruing by reasons of not being permitted to emigrate after having been induced to make preparations so to do, having been presented irregularly and at different intervals during the council, are to be found interspersed with the rest of the claims, and numbered progressively, according to the order of their introduction. A statement has also been prepared of the number, names, and value, according to the best of the judgment of the commissioners, of the bridges, causeways, and ferries, the property of the Creek nation. Assignments of these to the United States, as far as could be ascertained, the nation has no intention of making, believing that they will be included by reservations, and, of course, become individual or private property. Besides those named, there are several other ferries on the Coosa river, the eastern landings of which are upon the Creek territory; but, under the impression that they were established by white persons, and not in the possession of, nor interfered with, by Indians, they were not enumerated with the others.

The course pursued by the commissioners, and by which they were governed in their investigations, was, to receive, in all cases, between Indians and white men, when the Indian charged with any debt or duty was present, the statement of the Indian by way of plea, and to use the same as a clue or guide whereby to conduct the examination. There being no mode by which, on account of the unenlightened condition of the Indians, and their ignorance of revealed religion, their consciences could be bound either by the sanction of an oath or otherwise, the commissioners did not think proper to allow of their testimony as altogether valid against white persons, or even in cases originating among themselves against each other, though, in cases of the latter class, they usually led to a satisfactory result. The commissioners had no power to compel the attendance of witnesses.

Some matters were examined into by the commissioners for the purpose of perpetuating testimony, others both for the satisfaction of the Indians and the information of the Government. *This* the majority of the commissioners felt it their duty to do, as they have reason for belief that much injustice is done the Indians, and many impositions practised upon them on account of their loose and unskilful method of doing business, and inability to preserve proper evidence of their transactions, whereby the same demand is not unfrequently with impunity urged more than once, and often times twice or thrice paid by them. The majority of the commissioners are also of the opinion that, for like reasons, similar frauds are successfully perpetrated upon the Government of the [United States, which, on many occasions, they believe to be troubled again and again with the same matters, varied only a little in aspect, which they have attempted to guard against, and prevent so far as their means empowered them.

The majority of the commissioners state that the interpreters used during the sitting of the council, were not of their own choosing, nor such as would have been preferred by them; they were Benjamin Marshall and Paddy Carr: a different selection, for various reasons, would have been more satisfactory; they were both from the lower towns, and both largely interested in many of the claims. Benjamin Marshall's, as will be shown by reference to the case numbered thirteen of the second series, is one of considerable amount, and which, though of a date subsequent to the treaty, was assumed as a national debt.

It will be observed that the majority of the commissioners, in some of their opinions, which are to be found annexed to the respective cases, (Col. John Crowell, one of the commissioners,) dissenting therefrom, whose dissenting opinion likewise appears, and who also dissents from this report) which said claims have been assumed as national, and by certain letters, &c., which are on file, requested to be paid, have said they thought that, in their present aspect, the same ought not to be paid, or their payment, at least for the present, suspended; and if paid ultimately at all, certainly not as national debts, nor out of national funds, and for reasons which are expressed in their aforesaid opinions which they refer to. The majority of the commissioners add that they have reason to believe that drafts, &c., are too frequently obtained from Indians when the *quid pro quo* is by no means proportionate, or where but little or a very inadequate consideration has passed between the parties. The dupes of their own ignorance, they are easily overreached, and in almost every instance where artifice is employed against them, their credulity renders them its easy victim. By a little cunning and manœuvreing, they are as easily managed in council, nor is it more difficult at *such times* to make them sanction, than at *others* to create such claims.

The day on which the chiefs, or so many of the delegates as attended on the occasion, decided upon what claims should be considered national, it appeared that they were governed by no other reason than that the signatures of the two principal chiefs of the nation, Ne-har-micco and Tus ke-he-ne-haw-thlock-o, (in English, the Fat King and Big Fellow,) were affixed to the papers without regard to the consideration, &c. This, at least in some instances, was sufficient, though it was by no means a criterion for others, bearing upon them the same stamp and imbued with the same dye of nationality, viz., the two names aforesaid, were wholly disregarded and passed over without ceremony.

Among the drafts assumed as national was the one above alluded to, namely, that of Benjamin Marshall, who was one of the interpreters for the council, and the assignee of J. H. Brodnax, although, in the opinion of a majority of the commissioners, the said John H. Brodnax had not made a sufficient or satisfactory showing of *consideration*, or that the debts alleged to constitute the basis of the claim had not previously been included in, and comprised part of, the *order* given by the Creek delegation at Washington City; and upon which order, from information of the department, he had already received the sum of $8,999 25 of the money accruing by the treaty to the Creek nation.

The debt also of Mr. Thomas Crowell, made national for causes stated in their opinion, the majority of the commissioners think should not be discharged out of the national funds; but, when paid, should be out of the money of the lower towns; so, too, of the claims of S. C. Benton. The inhabitants of the upper towns not having participated in any part of the benefits or consideration of the same, it would seem to be unjust to tax them with the burthen of their payment. The balance due upon the draft in favor of Barnard, and made national, the majority of the commissioners think, for like reasons, should be discharged out of the money of the upper towns.

The principal chiefs of the upper towns are desirous that the rule which, they affirm, has been long established, of paying over all public moneys of the nation by *moieties*, viz., one half to the upper, and one to the lower, should also, in this instance, (the payment of the $100,000,) be allowed to prevail; and, while in council, they filed their order to that effect, and which will be found with the other papers. The number of the inhabitants of the upper towns is, it is believed, the greater; therefore, to the lower towns no evil could result from such a course. By any other mode of payment it is but a scramble which part of the nation shall derive most advantage from the national money, or, in other words, which incur debt to the largest amount, and thereby absorb the most in the payment of it. The majority of the commissioners are of the opinion that it would be the better policy to pay these moieties in some place as nearly central as might be convenient to each of the two respective divisions of the nation; that is, to say the moiety or half pertaining to the lower towns, in some place nearly central to said lower towns, and so of the half pertaining to the upper towns, in some place nearly central to the same, leaving the precise spot, (subject, however, to the foregoing restriction,) to the discretion of the persons or agent paying the money, and giving sufficient public notice of the respective times and places of such payment. The fact of the agency being continued permanently at one place, and of payment of public money being made for any considerable length of time at one place, give rise to much eagerness and fruitful contrivance in those who are resident about it to procure for themselves, by some means or other, an appropriation of some part of it; and a majority of the commissioners, therefore, think that every precautionary measure that could, with propriety, be pursued for the prevention of fraud, either on the part of the whites or Indians, in the management of Indian affairs, the credit of the country requires that the Government should avail itself of.

While on this subject, the majority of the commissioners respectfully submit, that they are firmly of conviction that the payment of large amounts of money to the Indians is only an additional means and incentive to their corruption, and not at all counterbalanced by any perceptible good effect produced. If, with their assent, goods and merchandize, consisting of necessaries and such articles as might be suited to their wants and conditions, and conducive to their comfort, could be substituted, much advantage would be gained by it, and the improvement in their moral and physical condition, soon be manifest. If the Indians of this nation are not speedily removed, by emigration, it is evident that they must rapidly pass through every successive stage of human wretchedness and degradation to a lamentable extinction. Surrounded, as they now are, and interspersed with a white population, intemperate in habits, illiterate and idle, nothing but removal to some other country more propitious to their mode of life and manners can preserve them or the poor remnant of their property. If humanity, and a due regard to fellow-beings so helpless, should be allowed to have weight, assuredly the philanthrophy and magnanimity of the Government, in their behalf, is forcibly appealed to; and if *there be means* to ameliorate the miserable lot of so many thousands, and render them comparatively prosperous and happy, *money* certainly should interpose no obstacle and form, in an undertaking so great and christian-like, but a secondary consideration.

From every indication, the Indians here, for the most part, will be entirely prepared to emigrate whensoever they may be located upon their respective reservations of land, and have realized the value of the sale of them. For their sake, it is much to be desired that the Government of the United States could become the purchaser, but to this many difficulties are interposed. They are apprized that these reservations are private property, and belong to individuals; and the belief is prevalent, that if they permit the nation to dispose of them, that the proceeds will be converted into a national fund, and the particular individuals or owners deprived of the price of them. They know, too, that the circumstance of situation and fertility enhance their value, and the possessors of such as are superior in these respects, are unwilling, by a general sale, to share with the holders of inferior tracts, in a common or average price; to this is to be added, the influence of the interested whites about them. Land companies and adventurers, many of whom are engaged extensively in contracting with the Indians for lands, binding them in bonds to convey titles to their reservations, and bent upon every species of speculation, and whose sympathies for these deeply benighted and powerless savages, seem to be altogether merged in their cupidity.

The ill feeling and enmity which has so unhappily existed between this portion of the Creek nation, and the division of it settled west of the Mississippi, the commissioners have the pleasure to relate they have been instrumental in the healing of; and that a treaty of amity has been concluded between them, in which they have mutually pledged themselves to the observance of a lasting friendship; and, as an evidence of their sincerity, the parent nation have, by their own proper deed, granted and bestowed on the kindred tribe in Arkansas, five entire sections of land, out of the twenty-nine by the treaty reserved to them and placed at their disposal. The papers showing the facts are forwarded, to which reference is made for the illustration of the particulars.

The commissioners, believing that some of the claims brought before them were not properly within the sphere of their enquiry, declined an investigation of them. Of these, *some* had their origin in the McIntosh concerns, which they supposed had, or ought to have been adjusted by Col. Tutt; others they thought came more properly under the purview of the intercourse law.

Sundry letters and communications, signed by Indians, are filed and forwarded according to request, to which the commissioners refer for the contents.

During the setting of the council, a delegation of the principal chiefs and many others, head-men of the nation, for the space of three weeks or more, attended it, and were put to some expense for their support: they desired that the same should be mentioned to the paternal Government, and expressed a confident hope that the Government, in its liberality, would refund it.

For the preservation of order in the council room, and other purposes, it was found necessary to employ some person to act in the capacity of door-keeper or messenger; and to this intent Mr. Edward Crowell, of Fort Mitchell, was appointed. His term of service was from the 9th of January to the 24th, inclusive—amounting, in the whole, to sixteen days; for which it is thought the pay of five dollars per day would not be excessive.

The commissioners deemed it their duty to direct the secretary of the board to retain the whole of the original papers in his possession, except such as should be forwarded, until instructed in what other manner to dispose of them. Many of these papers, the commissioners have reason to believe, are forgeries; and many others, as their opinions will show, wholly unjust.

The secretary of the board, Maj. Thomas J. Abbott, has acted in that capacity from the commencement of the first session of the council, at Wetum-ka, in September last. He has skilfully and faithfully discharged the arduous duties of the office, and the commissioners think that five dollars

21‡

per day, for the number of days engaged in this service, and the allowance of his expenses, would be but reasonable compensation.

The commissioners met on the 8th of January ultimo, and having accomplished all they believed they had it in their power then to do, to prevent the further accumulation of expense to the Government, adjourned on the 12th day of February, and left Major Abbott to complete their report, by the addition of a full and perfect transcript of all the claims, evidence, &c., and the proceedings thereon; which, from their voluminous character, will require the active labor of some weeks in the performance; during which time he will remain here and be subject to the order of the department: all of which is respectfully submitted by the majority of the commissioners, who have the honor to subscribe themselves,

Sir, your obedient and humble servants,

ENOCH PARSONS.

B. S. PARSONS.

*By Thos. J. Abbott.*

Attest:    THOMAS J. ABBOTT,
*Secretary, &c.*

*April* 4th, 1833.

The undersigned, one of the commissioners appointed to perform certain duties connected with the Creek treaty of 24th March, 1832, having differed in opinion with a majority of the commissioners on some points assumed in their report, has the honor to submit the following dissenting opinions.

They have embodied into their report subjects which, in my opinion, did not properly belong to our official duties: I do not, therefore, deem it to be my duty either to concur or dissent to them in *this report*, but shall barely give my dissenting opinions to some of the most material points *assumed* in that report, and opinions given in the investigation of claims against the Creek nation.

I will premise that most of the claimants were not apprized that it would be required of them to prove the items which formed the consideration of *liquidated* demands, and, consequently, most of them were not prepared to do so; notwithstanding, the other commissioners went into the investigation of the consideration, and the schedule will show that witnesses, both white and red, were examined in many cases, as to the kind, quality, quantity, and prices of the articles which formed the consideration, and that, too, after the debtors had acknowledged the demand to be just.

I did not think an investigation of that kind at all necessary to a correct result, as well as an unnecessary waste of time, and, therefore, in all cases of *liquidated* demands, where the attesting witness proved the execution of the paper, and his testimony not invalidated, and the makers acknowledged it to be correct and just, and that they had received a valuable consideration, thought the claim fairly made out against the makers, and when for the use and benefit of a town, against that town.

It is proper I should state for your information, that it has been the practice for many years in this nation, for the national council first to determine what debts shall be paid out of the national funds, after which, the balance of any national money is divided among the different towns in proportion to the number of souls; hence has arisen a custom of each town to contract its own debts, which debts are paid out of the money belonging to that town alone, unless the national council chooses to adopt them as national.

It is true that both interpreters selected by the national council were from the lower towns, and were interested in some claims; but I cannot conceive how this circumstance could justify the other commissioners in believing that others would have been more satisfactory, since others were present, and requested to act in the cases in which Marshall and Carr were interested. I am well acquainted with these interpreters, and know them to be competent, and believe they acted faithfully. Carr's claim was a transaction between Indians alone, and the schedule will show that the debtors acknowledged it to be just, yet witnesses, both white and red, were examined as to the consideration. The claim of Marshall, assignee of Brodnax, was also acknowledged by the debtors to be just, and most of the consideration proven: nevertheless the other commissioners recommend its rejection, upon the supposition that part of the claims which formed the consideration might have been included in the claim for which Brodnax received pay at Washington. I do not think the facts of the case justify such a conclusion, and believe the claim fairly established, and ought to be paid out of the national funds, as ordered by the national council, and refer you to my controverted opinion in this case on the schedule. It will be perceived that I decline giving an opinion in the cases of Thomas Crowell and S. C. Benton, for reasons stated in the schedule, and shall barely remark, that these claims having been thoroughly investigated, and of long standing, and adopted by the council as national debts, ought to be paid out of the national fund, so likewise ought all others adopted by the council as such.

The other commissioners think some claims adopted by the council as national ought not to be paid, or, if paid at all, ought not to be paid out of the national funds; and say that claims are too frequently obtained without much consideration by stratagem, and that Indians are liable to be managed by the same cunning in council, and thereby induced to sanction or reject such claims. So far as the cases investigated and adopted by the council are concerned, I will remark, that I saw nothing like cunning or stratagem resorted to to induce the council to adopt them as national; indeed, it seemed to be apparent that there was no need of it, the council determined promptly, and without a dissenting voice.

In conclusion, I will remark, that there are many just claims against the Creek nation which were not presented for investigation, and others were withdrawn without being investigated, which claims the Indians intend to pay, or their proportion of them, out of the balance of the $100,000, after paying such claims as are adopted by them as national.

JOHN CROWELL.

Hon. Lewis Cass,
  *Secretary of War.*

The foregoing is a true copy of the original filed.
 Attest:       THOMAS J. ABBOTT,
              *Secretary, &c.*

---

Washington City, D. C., *April* 4, 1833.

Sir: I have the honor of reporting, in conformity with your verbal instructions to me of yesterday:—

First. That the various stipulations contained in the late Choctaw treaty, connected with the rights and interests of the Indians, have been complied with by the department, as far as is now practicable, except the precise matters here respectfully submitted.

Second. The treaty provides for *three* blacksmiths: I have employed but *two*, and they have been diligently engaged in working for the Indians for upwards of one year. I have not felt it my duty to employ the *third*, until after this fall's emigration, because, at this time, about one-third of the Indians of the nation are east of the Mississippi.

Third. The millwright, to be furnished for five years, has not been yet employed; nor will the nation, as I conceive, be entitled to his services until the emigration is completed.

Fourth. The three churches, when built, are to be used as expressed in the treaty, for school houses, until the nation shall erect others; it will therefore be impracticable to get those schools properly under way until after the churches are completed. They cannot be built until the nation is divided into districts, when it will be the duty of the authorities of the nation to point out the place in each district where the buildings are to be located. The Rev. Mr. Stirman, who was appointed a teacher some time ago, has been ordered to the nation, and I have stated to him that he can repair to Colonel Fulsom's settlement, where I believe the anxiety of the Indians for a school is so great that they will erect a temporary school house. I have not heard a word from him.

Fifth. The looms and wheels will be let out by contract this spring, as provided for by the commissary general of subsistence, in conformity with your wishes: two hundred and fifty wheels to be delivered at the agency in the first quarter of the next year, also one hundred looms; the remainder in the last quarter of the same year, and the first quarter of the year following. This arrangement, I have thought, will be in time for the wants of the Indians, as they are at present, and will be for some time, without houses to take care of them. The cards will be furnished in time for the foregoing articles.

Sixth. I will now call your attention to the subject of reservations, and refer you to a report made by me a few days ago, accompanied with certain rolls for the correction of errors, founded on the statement of the Indians, from which it appears that they claim the fifty cents per acre for relinquished lands, not to be found on the list returned by Colonel Ward. This subject will require the early attention of the department, because the Indians are now complaining.

Seventh. The chiefs and captains complain that I have granted permission to too many white traders to reside among them, and urge their right, under the 10th article of the treaty, to have them removed. I have seen two communications from them lately on the subject, one to the President, referred, and the other to Major Eaton. It is therefore my duty to give you fully my views on the subject, and at the same time put you in possession of the situation of the trade now in the nation.

I have examined attentively the article of the treaty under which I feel myself authorized to grant license, and, unless I am mistaken in the proper construction, it will be found that even the Indians themselves cannot trade without a written permit, which has to be granted by the authorities of the nation, and the authorities can only grant to those persons who are amenable to their laws; therefore, as a white man is not subject to their laws, they cannot grant to any but their own people. In the article referred to it reads, "or under the laws of the United States," which I take to be the intercourse law, authorizing the agent to grant license, taking bonds, &c. I will now proceed to give my views of the utility of the course pursued, which I conceive to be the only safeguard against the most unjust speculations, that otherwise would be practised on the common Indian. Allow those half-breeds to monopolize the trade, exclude the white traders, and you will place the poor Indian at their mercy, who, in fact, are unable: keep any thing beyond light goods, and if able, are unwilling to keep proper assortment.

The white traders, five in number, now in the nation, are compelled, by me, to be stationary, and are bound to keep a good assortment of goods, and by the regulations that are posted up on their doors, they are required to keep such groceries as are suitable for family purposes; as also such tools as are wanted by persons settling in a new country. They are positively forbidden to keep *stock* of any kind, except what is barely sufficient for their family wants. They are not allowed to cultivate a farm, or, indeed, grow any thing beyond family vegetables. They are forced to close their door on the Sabbath; and there exists a perfect knowledge, on their part, that *t* violation of the foregoing rules is a revocation of their license; upon whic₤ they are forthwith to leave the nation. By this course, there is fair com₤ petition, and the wants of the Indians are supplied upon as good terms a₤ they are below the line.

Eighth. I will now proceed to give the operation of the act of Congress, passed in July, 1832, prohibiting the introduction of spirits into the Indian country. Under the present order from the department, agents are bound to seize, no matter in whose hands, whatever may be found. This is all important; but after getting the poison into possession, you are obliged to place it into the hands of the military, or keep it yourself, and report to the department all the facts connected with the seizure.

In a conversation with the honorable senator, chairman of the Indian Committee, he expressed to me his belief, that the spirits, under the law, would be forthwith destroyed by the agents of the Government; and remarked, that it was so understood in the Senate between himself and the honorable senator from New Jersey, Mr. Frelinghuysen. The importance of destroying the spirits, whenever found, is too salutary in its effects to require argument; it is, therefore, for you to determine the course to be pursued.

Ninth. It now becomes me to protest against the quality of the powder furnished under the treaty by an arrangement with the Ordnance Department. This arrangement was not intended to put powder into the hands of the Indians wholly unfit for rifle purposes, or indeed for any thing else. But such is the fact; on the very day they drew their powder, after trying it, they would grumble, and go to the store and buy other powder. I am not willing that the Ordnance Department should get clear of a surplus of *bad* powder at the expense of the Choctaws and the faith of the Government.

The powder furnished my agency, and yet for issue, I hope will be turned over to the military in our own country, to be taken care of for the Ordnance Department, who should be charged with all the expenses in getting it to the Indian country west, refunding to the Choctaw appropriation the amount drawn by the Ordnance Department, from the Commissary General, for an article entirely unfit for use. For the reason stated, I am clearly of opinion that other powder should be furnished, with instructions to allow a portion of *good* powder, to satisfy such as have already drawn that which produces in a hunt but two things certain: first, a loss of time, and secondly, a loss of *lead.*

Tenth. I will, with due deference, make a few suggestions upon the subject of the school fund, which has been paid for twelve years to the missionary institution, under Mr. Kingsbury, in the old nation. The 6,000 dollars has been, for the present, I believe, surrendered to the nation by the missionaries. If so, would it not be important to establish a system of district schools out of the fund, for the balance of the time specified in the treaty under which it was appropriated? I have conversed, freely and fully, with all the chiefs on this interesting subject; and the most of the intelligent half breeds, who have any idea of the benefits of education, as to the utility of the system, which I here recommend in principle, without being able, at this moment, to go fully into the details proper to put the system fairly into operation.

1st. Divide the above amount into such salaries as would procure a teacher, having an industrious family, acquainted with spinning, weaving, &c.; let him settle in a neighborhood and keep a district school, at which the scholars would attend as at our own country schools. This teacher should be a farmer, and it should be made his duty to visit the families in his district, and instruct them in the arts of husbandry, and, as far as possible, create a spirit of emulation among them. Let the women of the country be authorized to visit the house of the teacher, where they could be instructed in matters of housewifery, learning to spin, weave, cut out and make their necessary garments. This teacher should be a pious, industrious man; if so, he would soon gain such influence over them as would, in my humble opinion, result in the most beneficial effects. He might be allowed a salary of 500 dollars, with the privilege of farming and raising stock; for this sum good men could be had. Reading, writing, English grammar, the use of figures, as far as the *Rule of Three*, would be all that should be taught at this school. The three schools provided for in the treaty will be of a higher grade; and the 40 youths to be educated under the treaty could be selected from those district schools, taking the most meritorious among them. I will here make a remark respecting the education of the youths alluded to, which is this: instead of sending them altogether to one institution, (no matter how good it may be,) would it not better insure their future usefulness to send them in numbers of 4 or 5 to different institutions, and in different parts of the United States? It is an admitted fact in the nation, that the keeping of a great number of boys together is only calculated to cherish and perpetuate habits and feelings that it is all important, if possible, to remove.

The ideas suggested are not new with me; and they are most respectfully submitted to you for your consideration.

The interest I feel for these unfortunate people makes me anxious that some change should take place, which will produce results more beneficial than the present plan of education. I do humbly conceive, that a well digested system upon something like the one here proposed, would, in the same time, and for the same sum, produce a very different state of improvement among the Choctaws, both in civilization and education; besides, their leaders are anxious for it, and will go into it with spirit. They are now decidedly opposed to large missionary establishments.

2d. The 6,000 dollars, thus divided, would give 12 schools, dispersed throughout the nation. The efforts of 12 good men, feeling, as they should, the deepest interest for the civilization and prosperity of the Indians, would do more good, in one year, to better their condition, than has been done in the last 12 years for the 72,000 dollars already paid by the nation east. The teachers could keep an account of the rise and progress of their respective districts, showing the probable number of acres in cultivation, the quantity of grain raised, &c. &c. He would be like a father to them, and an important adviser to these people, who soon form strong attachments for their friends and benefactors.

3rd. The unsettled state of the Choctaws makes it impossible, at this time, even to begin successfully the system of education; but it is to be hoped that in the course of twelve months they will form their new government west; when, whatever is practicable, connected with their future prosperity, can be carried into effect.

4th. One other remark, before I close this important subject. By pursuing this course with the forty youths to be educated under the treaty, they would return to the nation acquainted with the manners and customs of every part of the United States, all of which information could be concentrated at any time within their own country, by convening them; from which advantages the happiest results might justly be anticipated.

Eleventh. Under your order for the necessary supplies of such Indians as visit the agency on business, as well as for the accommodation of persons having business in the nation, I have permitted the widow McClellan to settle within half mile of the agency, to keep private entertainment, and t furnish the supplies, under your order, in conformity with the spirit which intends that provisions shall be procured from a third person, entirely disinterested. The widow, too, had a kind of permission or consent granted by the chiefs, when Colonel Gaines conducted a delegation of them west, as he informed me.

Twelfth. I have prevented Indians settling within the limits of a mile from the agency-house; and when they visit the agency, they are required to make known their business, and upon its being adjusted they distinctly understand that the agency is not intended as a rendezvous for them, to be fed at the expense of the Government.

Thirteenth. Twelve months ago, I placed in the department several petitions from the Choctaws, which will require the action of Congress before certain individuals can get their just claims under the treaty. In some instances the name of a person entitled to a reservation is given wrong, two cases of which are now within my recollection:—the father of Colonel Fulsom and Thomas Wall; I have received letters from them since I have been here on the subject. Last session being a short one, I told them that nothing could be done; but that at the approaching session, those petitions would be placed, by the honorable Secretary of War, before Congress. There is also a petition in favor of such of the Indians as received nothing under the cultivation act, and who had cultivated more than *two* and less than *twelve* acres.

Fourteenth. The annuity due the Indians under former treaties will, I presume, be paid west; and must be distributed under the rules governing former payments, and in conformity with the wishes of the three old chiefs and captains, signers of the treaty.

Nittecachee and his captains have petitioned the President for the payment of their portion in goods; and it is more than probable that the other districts may do the same. If so, would it not be best to aid them in getting their goods directly from the best market, affecting insurance to Fort Smith? The goods for many years have been purchased second or third-handed, coming to them at a heavy per cent. advance. They will be better satisfied to get their annuities in this way than in specie. The goods, too, blankets, domestics, and strouds, &c., with tools and such articles as are most necessary for them, will be much better than the money. Make it, however, the duty of the agent to see the articles equally divided among them. This will be the best mode of keeping out all sorts of traders, because it is for this money they hover over the Indian. With a view of illustrating the advantages of this mode of paying the annuity, I have the honor of referring you to my report, some days since, enclosing a bill of purchase from New Orleans for the sum of six hundred and nineteen dollars, in domestics, for five hundred and thirty-seven Indians. This will give to each from eight to twelve yards, according to the original cost of the domestic, which, if paid in money would give about $1.15, and if laid out by them in a store in the interior would purchase for them from two and a half to three yards of the same kind of goods; besides, when they receive money, it gives facilities to obtain whiskey. I am, therefore, decidedly in favor of this mode of payment, provided it be their wish.

Fifteenth. The public buildings at Fort Towson are upon a large scale, and it would be a saving of expense if storage could be furnished us until we complete our issues under the treaty; we have asked this accommodation, but it was not granted, in consequence of which, storage must be paid for at Doakes, four miles off.

If our *powder* could be kept in the magazine at the fort, it would be a great convenience to me, and much more secure for the public.

I have the honor to be
Your obedient servant,
F. W. ARMSTRONG, C. A.

Hon. LEWIS CASS,
    *Secretary of War.*

P. S. If this system for schools, or something like it, should be determined on, and the chiefs pleased with it when in operation, I feel almost confident that they would appropriate a sufficient sum to continue it, out of their annuity.

The plan for the public buildings in the nation will have to be furnished by the time they divide their country into districts, as provided for in the treaty.                                    F. W. A., C. A.

———

CHEROKEE AGENCY, *April* 4, 1833.

SIR: The enclosed letter from Mr. Walker has just been handed to me, and is enclosed for your information, that you may see to what means those delegates resort, to quiet the minds of their people; and it is to be feared they will, as heretofore, be but too successful, as I am informed that many of them are very much elated at the prospect of being again restored to their sovereignty and independence.

Of the story about the proffered bribe I had not heard before.

Very respectfully, your obedient servant,
H. MONTGOMERY.

Hon. ELBERT HERRING,
    *Commissioner of Indian Affairs, Washington City.*

HOPEWELL FARM, *April* 5, 1833.

DEAR COLONEL: I have not been able to ascertain the time appointed for the council; there are various accounts as to the time. I was informed on yesterday of John Ross's stating to the people, since his return, of the Government offering him a bribe of fifty thousand dollars, if he would consent to come into a treaty. I, therefore, wish you to make this inquiry of the department, because, if this is a fact, it certainly will go much to operate against the views of the Government. I have myself denied the assertion. Please make the inquiry, so as to have an answer before they call council.

&ast; &ast; &ast; &ast; &ast; &ast;

Mr. J. Vann asserts that the Government, next year, will buy out the fortunate drawers of Georgia, for the Indians, and let them remain. This story will be believed by such men as Mr. Vann himself. This must be one of *Ross's dreams*, which he has been relating to Vann. They also relate that all their former friends in Congress have advised them to remain, which I must believe to be false. I admit that there are some few of them wish them to engage in another important suit.

I wish you, in your letter to the department, to let me know if they will make any compensation to me for expenditures that I may make in effecting this important question. They, of course, will be very reasonable, and such as should be allowed. You know that I have been at some, and, of course, will be at considerable more. The expenses of all those meetings, when there was any, I have paid myself. I am not asking for it now; but you know that there is, and will be, more or less; and I wish their support while laboring for them; but if I did not believe it to be for the true interest and happiness of our common people, I assure you I would not advocate the cause. Your frined,

JOHN WALKER, JR.

Col. HUGH MONTGOMERY, *Cherokee Agency.*

---

HEAD OF COOSA, CHEROKEE NATION, *April* 5, 1833.

SIR: During the session of our last general council, a delegation was appointed to visit Washington City, for the purpose of endeavoring to obtain from the Government the protection for which, in vain, we have so long and ardently sought. This delegation, after an absence of some months, have returned to their nation, and a part of the undersigned have seen and read the communications which, in the discharge of the trust reposed in them, were addressed to you, and your replies to the same. In answer to the appeal made to the Executive, for the restoration to our people of those rights which the exercise of *State authority,* within our limits, have deprived them, they were referred to a message sent by the President to the Senate in 1831, upon a special call made by that body for information why the act of Congress of 1802, regulating trade and intercourse with the Indian tribes, &c., was not executed among the Cherokees, and were further informed, that the opinions of the President had undergone no change. A promise, however, was given for the removal of such citizens of the United States as have intruded upon lands within the chartered limits of Tennessee and North Carolina, disclaiming (according to the principles of the message alluded to) any authority to enforce the provisions of that act, within that portion of our territory over which the States of Georgia and Alabama have

22‡

extended their jurisdiction. Since the return of the delegation, a letter has been received by Mr. Ross, dated 14th March, and signed by "Elbert Herring, Office Indian Affairs." This letter acknowledges the receipt of a letter from Mr. Ross, of the 8th of March, and, as well as recollected, admits that we have experienced much hardship from intrusions; promises that a military force will shortly be ordered into the nation, from Charleston, to expel the intruders; and that the district attorney will be instructed, in case they return, to institute suits of prosecution, under the act of 1802, &c. The object, therefore, of this communication is, to ascertain the extent of the protection to be afforded by this military authority, under the pledge given by Judge Herring, in his letter to the delegation.

According to the reading of that letter, it is considered by many that the views of the Executive may have undergone a change; and that the action of this force will not be confined to any particular portion of our country; but that its blessings will be felt throughout. Under this view of the subject, considering the peculiar and unhappy condition of our people, it will not be a matter of surprise for you to learn that this favorable prospect has been hailed with feelings of much joy and gratulation. Aware, sir, how much we trespass upon your time, we would most respectfully inquire whether, indeed, our "Great Father" has thus kindly thought of us, and will thus kindly exercise those paternal feelings which some of the undersigned have often heard him express toward the Cherokees.

If we doubt the extent of this protection, it is only by taking in connection this with the letters from your department, to which we have already made reference.

A meeting of our general council will take place on the 13th of May, to deliberate on the affairs of the nation; and we trust that the information sought for will not be thought unworthy of the immediate attention of the department.

> With sentiments of high regard,
> We have the honor to be,
> Most respectfully,
> Your ob't. serv'ts.,
> JOHN RIDGE.
> W. S. COODEY.
> MAJ. RIDGE, his x mark.
> WILLIAM HICKS.
> JOHN FIELDS, his x mark.

Hon. LEWIS CASS, *Secretary of War.*

---

WASHINGTON CITY, D. C., *April* 6, 1833.

SIR: Since handing you my report of the 4th instant, I have received the enclosed petition from the captains of Colonel Leflore's district. The reason why they ask this amount to be allowed them, is, that under the general regulations for paying the annuities, the full amount must be equally distributed, each individual getting the same proportion.

The Choctaw chiefs have always been allowed to make certain district debts; and those debts, at their own request, first paid out of their annuity. These debts, usual for blacksmiths, &c., ought, I think, still to be settled in this way, because they do require a good many district expenditures not provided for in the treaty. For instance, when the millwright is employed under the treaty, they will want mills in each district. They should be allowed their own funds to complete those mills, as the United States will furnish nothing beyond the bare services of the workmen. Indeed, there are frequently good reasons for their making a *district debt*, as it is called. It must always, however, be shown, that the expenditure is for general purposes, and for the benefit of all, making it the duty of the agent to know well that fact before the funds are granted.

I have the honor of being
Your obedient servant,

F. W. ARMSTRONG, *C. A.*

Hon. Lewis Cass,
 *Secretary of War.*

P. S. I have reflected fully on the importance of the order given by me, establishing one mile as the proper limits, to protect the agency from being surrounded by Indians settling so near as to produce difficulty and inconvenience. I know well that, under the treaty, the agency is as much provided for as forts; for the convenience and protection of which, larger limits are given. I hope, therefore, that I will be sustained in my order; because, unless it is done by the department, to operate only on such as have settled since the order, and in contempt of it, my authority hereafter will, of course, be disregarded.

I have the honor to be
Your obedient servant,

F. W. ARMSTRONG, *C. A.*

---

We, the undersigned, head men and captains of Colonel Greenwood Leflore's district, agree to furnish a blacksmith and striker, to be paid out of our annuity. We further agree to pay the blacksmith thirty-five dollars per month, the striker also fifteen dollars per month. It is distinctly understood that we, the undersigned, bind ourselves to pay said blacksmith and striker our part of the money for their services, and furnish one thousand pounds of iron and one hundred pounds of steel, out of said annuity; the shop to be located on  , and coal-wood cut and burnt, ready for the smith.

In witness whereof, we have hereunto set our hands and seals this   day of January, A. D. 1833.

*Captains' names signed.*

| | |
|---|---|
| SILAS D. FISHER. | [ L. S. ] |
| THOS. HAYES. | [ L. S. ] |
| JAMES VAUGHN. | [ L. S. ] |
| EASTMAN LEMUN. | [ L. S. ] |
| CUPPITAHMHOOMAH, his x mark. | [ L. S. ] |
| RYATSKAYUBBE,   x | [ L. S. ] |
| JOHN FRASIER,   x | [ L. S. ] |
| CAPTAIN HOLITAHOMA, x | [ L. S. ] |
| CHATAMETTAHA,   x | [ L. S. ] |
| ADAM CHIRKMUBBEE,   x | [ L. S. ] |
| OKCHAYA,   x | [ L. S. ] |
| TOBALA,   x | [ L. S. ] |
| TUSKAHEMETTA,   x | [ L. S. ] |

IKEHARNAH,     his x mark.   [ L. S. ]
YOUTAH,             x       [ L. S. ]
JAMES SHIELDS.            [ L. S. ]
ANTHONY TURNBULL.       [ L. S. ]
WILLIAM LEFLORE.         [ L. S. ]

FORT WAYNE, INDIANA, *April* 6, 1833.

SIR: Yours of the 20th ultimo has been received. In your first communication on the subject of my allowance for services rendered at the Wabash treaty, you required a certificate of the commissioners, or other satisfactory evidence. I was of opinion that the certificate of the Indian agent, backed by the certificates of some six or eight other individuals, who, as men of character, were personally known to the Secretary of War, would have been sufficient; nor do I now wish to ask the commissioners for a certificate, after they have refused to lay the state of the case before the Secretary of War.

The simple fact is this: the commissioner, in the first place, appointed a physician by the name of Moffit, who was so intemperate that neither the white or red men had or could have any confidence in him; in consequence of which my appointment was urged by many who were in public employ. I was accordingly employed, and furnished all the medicine that was necessary on the ground. At the winding up of the matter, the commissioners seemed to think that the honor was sufficient, without any emolument. The certificate of General Marshall, the Indian agent, showed plainly that I was employed; that my services were necessary, and that I suffered a pecuniary loss at home, in consequence of my attendance there. This certificate is corroborated by a number of others. Much as I need pay for my services, I would rather give up my rights than be viewed by the commissioners as a supplicant. If it is really necessary to the recovery of my rights, that I shall again call on the commissioners, I shall call on them by a legal process, as that is the only way that I expect to receive justice of them. If the certificate of the Indian agent and the other statements forwarded tell, what will be satisfactory evidence other than the certificate of the commissioners?

I have the honor to be
Your obedient servant,
L. G. THOMPSON.

ELBERT HERRING, Esq.,
   *Commissioner of Indian Affairs.*

CREEK AGENCY, *April* 8, 1833.

SIR: The secretary to the Board of Commissioners for investigating claims against the Creek nation, who had been instructed to make out a fair copy of their proceedings, has (as he informed me) done so, and forwarded them to your department.

The object of this communication is to say to you, that the secretary has forwarded *his* copy, without permitting me to compare it with the original; nor will he leave in my possession the originals, stating that the majority of the commissioners gave him a written order to retain them. Now, sir, the secretary may have forwarded a correct copy; but it was proper that I, as one of the board (who is responsible to your department for the correctness of my conduct) should know that the copy was correct, more especially when it will be seen that I differed from the other commissioners in some important points, and made a separate report of our proceedings. I must therefore request, as an act of justice to myself, and the witnesses who gave testimony, to cause the original papers to be forwarded and compared with the secretary's copy, and demand of him the original report of the other commissioners. In addition to the claims, and the testimony taken in their support, there were a number of letters and other papers deposited with the secretary by the chiefs, with a request that they should be forwarded with our proceedings. It is due to the chiefs, therefore, to know whether they have *all* been forwarded. I have, &c.,

Hon. LEWIS CASS,        JNO. CROWELL.
  *Secretary of War.*

---

STAUNTON, VIRGINIA, *April* 9, 1833.

SIR: I handed to the honorable Secretary of War two letters, on business connected with my duties, on the morning I left the city. It is important that I should refer you particularly to them, from fear that the Secretary, in the great pressure of business constantly before him, should, for a time, overlook their reference to you.

I have thought often upon the propriety of not paying this year's annuity to the Choctaws until after this fall's emigration; indeed, I cannot see how it can be done, in justice to all, as it is impossible to ascertain the numbers on both sides of the Mississippi; therefore I am of the opinion that it will have to be deferred until January. After this year, the payments can be made as heretofore.

By reference to a provision in the treaty, it will be seen that $600 is granted them, to enable them to keep in the nation light horse. This sum was not, as I learn, paid last year by Colonel Ward; it will be proper to connect it with the amount due as annuity.

I hope the department will allow the Choctaws to pay district debts, for the reasons heretofore given by me in my report to the Secretary of the 6th instant.

In reference to letting them be paid in goods, as suggested by me, and petitioned for by them, I flatter myself it will be granted, from which course I think much good will result.

The funds proper to meet the demands due the Indians, for the objects stated, must be placed in the bank at Nashville, in time to meet your expectations, growing out of such instructions as you may think proper to give me hereafter.

I will feel much gratified to receive a written sanction of my course west, as Choctaw agent, having a particular reference to my detailed report made to the Secretary of War, touching the unfinished matters growing out of the treaty at Dancing Rabbit creek. I ask this, because the Secretary did, after reading it, approve of it; which approval he made known to me the evening I attended his office, at five P. M., in conformity with his own words, the day before I left the city. An early reply to this, at Knoxville, will confer a favor on     Your humble servant,

          F. W. ARMSTRONG, *C. A.*

ELBERT HERRING, Esq.,
 *Commissioner of Indian Affairs.*

WAUPAUGHKONETTA, *April* 10, 1833.

We sent you a letter some time since, by our friend Joseph Parks, stating that the Shawnee Indians now in Allen county, Ohio, were anxious to emigrate, and join their friends west of the Mississippi; and wishing that a sum of money, such as our father, the Secretary of War, might think us entitled to, might be placed in the hands of Joseph Parks, to assist us in removing. Since his return from Washington, he has informed us that our father has read our letter, and procured an appropriation for that purpose; for which favour he will please to accept our thanks. We have since conversed with all the Shawnees of our tribe, in this part of the country, and can assure our father that they are still anxious to remove and join their nation.

We wish to start on our journey as soon as the season and roads will permit, and hope that we will be enabled to go by the 15th or 20th of May, at farthest. We have sufficient money among us to purchase provisions and other necessaries, until we shall arrive at our new homes; and, on consultation with our friend Van Horne have thought it most advisable to use our own money on our journey, (for by some accident or misfortune we might lose it,) and we are entirely willing to do so, if our father, the Secretary of War, will send us, in writing, an assurance that we shall receive the amount of the appropriation which we understand has been made for our removal. When we arrive at our new homes, our friend Joseph Parks will bring such evidence to our father as will satisfy him that all the Shawnees of our nation have left Ohio, and joined their friends west of the Mississippi; and if our father will then place in his hands the 1,680 dollars, we shall be entirely satisfied, and will remember him with gratitude.

Very respectfully,
Your friends,

LITTLE FOX,              his x mark.
GEORGE WILLIAMS, his x mark.
QUILINA,                   his x mark.
PECULSE COE,          his x mark.
THOMAS B. VAN HORNE.

The Hon. LEWIS CASS,
    *Secretary of War.*

---

GENERAL LAND OFFICE, *April* 10, 1833.

SIR: I have to acknowledge the receipt of your letter of the 8th instant.

By the treaty concluded at Chicago, on the 29th of August, 1821, with the Ottawa, Chippewa, and Pottawatamie Indians, the following reservations in the cession south of Grand River, in Michigan Territory, were made for the use of the Indians, viz.

Three miles square at the Prairie Ronde village.

Six miles square at Mackasawbe.

Three miles square at the village of Matchebenashewish.

Four miles square at Natowasepe village.

The three first mentioned reservations having been ceded to the United States by the Pottawatamie's treaty of the 19th September, 1827, having been surveyed as public lands, the reservation at Notawasape village, does not appear to have been ceded to the United States at that time, and is the only reservation, with the exception of those for individuals, known to exist south of Grand River, in Michigan. Should you request it, a plat of that reservation will be furnished whenever required.

If the Natowasepe reservations belonged to the Pottawatamie Indian, even that is now the property of the United States; those Indians, by their treaty of the 27th October, 1832, having ceded to the United States all their lands in the States of Indiana and Illinois, and in the territory of Michigan, south of Grand River.

As furnishing the information required by you in relation to the unceded lands, situated west of and adjoining Lake Michigan, I enclose herewith a sketch, compiled from the maps in this office, showing what lands between the Lake and the Mississippi river have been ceded, and what now remain in the possession of the Indians.

As the treaty of 20th October last with the Pottawatamies of the Prairie and Kankakee, is considered as extinguishing all the Indian title southwest of Lake Michigan, in Illinois, the only unceded land in that State is believed to be the small tract in the northwest angle fronting on the lake.

I am, very respectfully, sir,
Your obedient servant,
ELIJAH HAYWARD.

Hon. Lewis Cass,
Secretary of War.

P. S.—As this office possesses all the information which is in the surveyor's offices, upon the subject of Indian reservations, I have not thought it necessary to write to the surveyors in relation to your letter.

---

## Memorandum.

The maps in the General Land Office do not furnish sufficient information to enable the office to mark, with accuracy, the bounds intended to be established by the 1st article of the treaty of the 21st September, 1832, with the Sac and Fox Indians. The best estimate of the side and rear lines of that cession gives 325 miles as the total length of those lines. The Mississippi front of the cession is estimated at 280 miles.

To survey the tract reserved for the use of the Indians by the 2d article of the same treaty, will require about 85 miles to be run.

In estimating the cost of making these surveys, it is thought that it would not be safe to calculate upon having it done for less than four dollars per mile.
General Land Office, 1st April, 1833.

---

General Land Office, April 10, 1833.

Sir: I have the honor to return the letter of Mr. Blake, in relation to the reservation of Nea Mathla, referred by you to this office.

By the additional article to the treaty made at camp Moultrie on the 18th of September, 1823, with the Florida Indians, a tract of two miles square, embracing Tuphulga village, on the waters of Rocky Comfort creek, was reserved for the use of Nea Mathla and his connexions, which is the only reservation known to have been made to that individual; and in relation to which I beg leave to refer you to the letters of the 7th of May, 27th of June, and 3d of September, 1828, from the War Department to this office;

by the last of which you will perceive that the department was of opinion
that the reservation might "be resumed and subject to locations or appropriations, as it would be had the reservation never been made, and of course
sold as other public lands in Florida."

The reservation was therefore included in the President's proclamation,
dated the 4th October, 1828, directing sales of the public lands at Tallahassee,
in the month of January, 1829.

It does not appear by the records of this office that any certificate was
ever issued in favor of Nea Mathla, for this reservation.

I am, very respectfully, sir,
Your obedient servant,
ELIJAH HAYWARD.

The Hon. ELBERT HERRING,
Commissioner of Indian Affairs.

---

INDIAN AGENCY, ROCK ISLAND, April 12, 1833.

SIR: Your letter of the 19th February reached here during my absence
to the Des Moines Rapids, to receive from Keo-kuck and other chiefs, four
of their people, who were given up for the murder of Martin, and hand
them over to the civil authorities for trial; which duty I have performed.

On the 22d of February last I informed you that I had the annuity
money on hand for the last year, "which was ready for the Indians as soon
as they came in."

Immediately on the receipt of your letter, enclosing J. Pilcher's, I called
on Messrs. Farnham and Davenport for the money, which was returned
forthwith. The Indians will not all get in before the 1st of May, when
their annuities will be paid them, and receipts taken according to instructions.

With great respect,
I have the honor to be
Your obedient servant,
M. S. DAVENPORT,
Indian Agent.

ELBERT HERRING, Esq.

---

SUPERINTENDENCY OF INDIAN AFFAIRS,
Detroit, April 12, 1833.

SIR: I have received, and read with great attention, your letter of the
30th ultimo, containing instructions relative to the Winnebagoes, and their
removal from the country ceded by the treaty of 15th September last. I
am not disposed to give trouble, but I consider it an imperative duty to
give you my views on this subject. When I look back at all the evils
which occurred in that region of country last summer, and call to mind the
many valuable lives which were sacrificed in the progress of an Indian war,
and count the expenses to which the Government was subjected, I cannot,
while holding the responsible office of Superintendent of Indian Affairs,
suffer any arrangement to be made with regard to the Indians under my
care which I disapprove, without remonstrating against it. I claim to
know more of these Winnebagoes than any other Indians. I have been
among them, and conversed with them individually and in little groupes,

day after day; met them in council; superintended the payment of their annuity money; and had with me the two respectable gentlemen, and their interpreter, who accompanied the deputation to Washington in 1828, to
each of whom they are greatly attached. Mr. Gratiot, the sub-agent at
Rock river, and Mr. Becquette, the son-in-law of General Dodge, Mr.
John Dixon, of Dixon's ferry, and several other respectable gentlemen,
were also there. The prisoners had been brought into the fort, and I visited them. I conversed freely with all the officers of the post, and the
gentlemen generally who had assembled at the payment. These facts are
mentioned, to convince you that I had an opportunity of becoming acquainted with the views and wishes of these Indians.

In my letter of the 11th of February, I stated, " I am decidedly of opinion that these Winnebagoes will never go west of the Mississippi to remain, as long as they can live on the north of the Ouisconsin. During the
winter season, some of them may go there to hunt. The Sioux are averse
to their going to that country, and the Sacs will no doubt retaliate upon
them whenever an opportunity presents. The Winnebagoes are well aware
of this, and have so stated. During my late visit to that country, when
the Winnebagoes were assembled to receive their annuities, they spoke very
decidedly on this subject. They were then making arrangements to move
in large bodies to the Bar-ro-bo, and in that vicinity. Mr. Grat:ot, the
sub-agent on Rock river, was present, and his Indians all intended going
north of the Ouisconsin."

I wrote to you again on the 4th of March, enclosing a letter from Col.
Kinzie, and referring to my former letter, (erroneously stating it to have
been dated the 9th of February, instead of 11th). The receipt of this letter of the 4th March has never been acknowledged. Your letter of the
13th March was a very satisfactory reply to that of 11th February: you say,
" It is not in the contemplation of the Government to press the removal of
the Winnebagoes west of the Mississippi. With them, it is optional to go
thither, or to their lands north of the Ouisconsin. The choice of their future abode in either region is left entirely to their own free will." Immediately after its receipt, I forwarded a copy of this letter to Col Kinzie.

You must, therefore, excuse me for saying that your letter of the 30th
March has taken me by surprize. The whole tenor of it seems to be predicated upon the idea that, by this treaty, the Winnebagoes agreed to remove to their lands west of the Mississippi; that, although this is not expressly stipulated, it was so understood; and you add, that this is " for the
permanent advantage of the Indians."

I do not pretend to interfere with what is adopted as the policy of the Government, although I cannot perceive the advantages which would be derived either to the Government or these Indians at present, by removing
them west of the Mississippi; nor do I see that any injury could arise from
their remaining on our side of the Mississippi, on their lands north of the
Ouisconsin. But thus much I do say, and I say it positively and knowingly, that these Winnebagoes do not suppose or believe, nor did they so
understand the treaty, that they were to go west of the Mississippi. On the
contrary, they have determined to go, and many of them have already gone
north of the Ouisconsin. The Indians of Colonel Kinzie's agency will locate generally in the vicinity of the Barabo, and those of Mr. Gratiot's in
a village on the north side of the Ouisconsin, which, I think, is opposite the

23‡

Sac prairie, about perhaps forty miles below Fort Winnebago. They are afraid present to go west of the Mississippi; some time must elapse before the Sacs will give up their intention of retaliation upon the Winnebagoes, and the Sioux are averse to their going there. The Indians on Rock river who intend, as above stated, to make their village on the north side of the Ouisconsin, opposite the Sac prairie, understood that their blacksmith shop on Rock river was to be removed to this village. They spoke of it frequently while at Fort Winnebago, in November. If, by the treaty, it is irrevocably fixed, that this shop shall be removed to the land granted to the nation on the west of the Mississippi, all I can say is, that they will be greatly disappointed; and that the establishment of it where there will be no Indians near, cannot conduce to the good of those for whom it has heretofore been kept up. They will also suffer, it seems, under the same misunderstanding in regard to the *provisions*. When it is admitted that it is optional with these Indians whether they go west of the Mississippi, or to their lands north of the Ouisconsin, is it fair to say that if you go to the one place you shall have rations, but if to the other you shall have none?

General Scott, after the making of the treaty, did not seem to view it in this light, for he gave an order to Mr. Dixon to issue 20,000 rations to those around him, all of whom, it was well known, would go north of the Ouisconsin. Be this, however, as it may, should many of them starve, (which, from their present situation, as by a letter to you of this date, appears likely,) because rations will not be delivered to them as they expected, and not at all unless they will agree to go west of the Mississippi, I have the consoling reflection that it is no fault of mine, and that I have done all I could to prevent it.

There will be no occasion for *force* in procuring the removal of these Indians from the land ceded, and I trust that it will not be thought of. Should you think it expedient to consult the Secretary of War on the subject, I am well convinced that he will assent to what I here state. By persuasion and kindness, these Indians may be induced peaceably and quietly to leave these lands, to which, for obvious reasons, they are much attached. But it is only necessary to let them *know* that *force* is to be used, in case they shall not remove by a certain day, and add to that that they must go west of the Mississippi, to bring about an immediate war, of a much more terrific character. I assure you, than we have for late years known. Excuse me, therefore, for suggesting that this idea of using force should be kept from the Indians, if possible.

I must protest against the injustice which will be done to these Indians of whom I have been speaking, by the manner in which you have directed the annuity money under this treaty to be paid. The treaty, you inform me, provides "that the payments on this account are to be made at Prairie du Chien and Fort Winnebago, in sums proportioned to the numbers residing most convenient to those places respectively," and then, to my surprise, you add, "that no accurate data exist in this office by which this proportion can be ascertained. The division for this year must therefore be equal."

When writing to you on the 11th of February, I stated, " you have access to the pay-rolls, and by ascertaining the number who are paid by General Street, at Prairie du Chien, and the number paid at Fort Winnebago, you can make a just apportionment of the fund to be sent to each agency. The complaint is, that much more than a fair proportion is sent to the prairie." I know no reason for changing my opinion. Exact certainty can be arrived at by examining the pay-rolls or receipts of Colonel Kinzie and General Street for the payment of their annuity money. Your answer to this part of my letter was, "that the unequal division in the appropriation, &c., between the different branches of the tribe, must have proceeded from ignorance or inadvertence. Attention will be given to correct this cause of complaint for the future;" by which I certainly had reason to expect that when you came to the apportionment of the annuity money under the late treaty, the proper means for making a just division would have been adopted. Under the treaty of Prairie du Chien, a similar division of the annuity money is provided for, viz., "18,000 per year at Prairie du Chien and Fort Winnebago, in proportion to the numbers residing within the most convenient distance of each place respectively." When a division was made of this for each agency, I believe Governor Cass and General Clark were both at Washington, and the arrangement was agreed to by them. $15,000 were assigned to Fort Winnebago, and $3,000 to Prairie du Chien, and in this manner the money has since been annually paid. Now, if it be just and proper under the old treaty that five-sixths of the money should be paid to our Indians, and one-sixth to General Street's, can it be right that a *moiety* of the money payable under the new treaty should go to Prairie du Chien? I might add, that our Indians are of the opinion that five-sixths of the $18,000 annuity is more than the Indians around the prairie should receive. I hope, therefore, that you will recal the decision which you have made, and instruct General Clark to refund the excess forwarded to him over and above the just proportion to which he is entitled.

The multifarious and heavy duties which the department have called on me to perform, make it necessary that I should arrange the funds for the year as soon as possible, and before I leave home; and hence I shall anxiously wait your determination on this matter.

I have the honor to be,
Very respectfully,
Your obedient servant,
G. B. PORTER.

ELBERT HERRING, Esq.,
*Commissioner of Indian Affairs.*

---

MONTGOMERY, *April* 12, 1833.

SIR: Your letter, under date 14th March, was received yesterday; and the wishes of the Government, so far as falls upon me, shall be immediately carried into effect.

You mention, that fresh complaints have been made to the department. I have to request the favor to be informed in what section of the country they are, and the names of the chiefs; the extent of country is great, and this information would be a saving of time and money to the Government. The spring term of the district court is near at hand, which will require my personal attendance. Your early attention to the above request is solicited.

Respectfully, &c.,
ROBERT L. CRAWFORD,
*U. S. Marshal.*

ELBERT HERRING, Esq.,
*Com'r. Indian Affairs.*

SUPERINTENDENCY OF INDIAN AFFAIRS,
*Detroit, April* 12, 1833.

SIR: I have just received a letter from Col. Kinzie, sub-agent at Fort Winnebago, dated March 15th, in which, among other things, he says, "All the Indians in this section of country are actually in a state of starvation. The winter has been very unfavorable. They have had no snow, and, in consequence, have not killed deer and bear enough to support them. They have subsisted mostly on acorns during this winter. They are coming in daily for something to eat; and I have been told, by a party who have just made their appearance, that two women had been left behind, unable to travel for want of food. Since my letter to you of the 31st January, Col. Cutler has examined his stores, and informs me that *half* of the amount of the 150 barrels of flour and 100 barrels pork directed to be issued to the Indians by the Secretary of War, can be spared. I have already made issues to them, and will render them all the aid in my power to relieve their wretched condition."

I write this to show you that I was right in stating to General Marshall (of which I informed you in my letter of the 5th) that I could not spare any part of the $500 sent to me for the relief of the Winnebagoes.

So soon as our navigation opens I will forward corn to Fort Winnebago, and thus relieve them.

Very respectfully,
G. B. PORTER.

ELBERT HERRING, Esq.,
    *Com'r. of Indian Affairs.*

---

JUMPER SPRINGS, TALLADEGA COUNTY,
*Alabama, April* 13, 1833.

SIR: Your letter of March 16th was received by last Friday's mail, and would have been acknowledged a week sooner, but for my absence from home. I regret, exceedingly, that among the white population who inhabit the Creek country, some, regardless of their own interest and their duty as good citizens of their country, continue to intrude upon Indian improvements. I do assure you that I have not failed to expostulate with such persons, and to warn them of the consequences of such conduct. It has had a good effect upon many, and but few in this section of the country are intruders. I will still continue to co-operate with the department in preventing intrusion or causing expulsion. I have had several conversations with individual chiefs since my last letter to you, in relation to sending their children to the Choctaw academy. My opinion is, that they will, in a short time, furnish the children. I have written again to the head chiefs on the subject, and shortly expect an answer.

Your letter of February 1st has been received, with an account of $50 in favor of Shohoke Hajo, certified by Noco Hajo. I have not yet obtained any evidence in support of the claim. The Indians say there is an Indian, by the name of Spohoke Hajo, that rendered services during the war. But this matter I will investigate farther; and if I can or cannot obtain evidence in support of the account, I will inform the department.

Will you do me the favor to inform me whether it is my duty to apply for, and receive, the books and papers of the former agency; and whether

I have any thing to do with the public property of the agency. If my appointment had been the same as Col. Crowell's, I should not have hesitated in applying both for the property and papers; but, as it was somewhat a different appointment, I was fearful of exceeding my authority in applying for either.

By a letter from the department, informing me of my appointment as sub-agent for the Creeks, my salary is fixed at five hundred dollars per annum, in addition to the per diem allowance for locating the Indian reservations. In a letter received subsequently from Mr. Mardis, he states that the President had fixed my salary at fifteen hundred dollars per annum. I should be glad to know certainly what my allowance will be, and whether it will be paid quarterly or not. I feel a delicacy in addressing the department on this subject, but, as a mistake on my part with regard to my salary may do me a serious injury, I have ventured to mention the subject to the department, as I have already, perhaps, advanced too far in expectation of receiving the $1,500 in quarterly payments. Would you be pleased to inform me whether I am allowed an interpreter as sub-agent. The Indians are frequently wishing to converse with me when I have no interpreter.

My opinion is, that it would be greatly to the advantage of the Creeks if they would sell all their lands to the Government. Many of them are now in distressed circumstances; they have no corn, game is scarce, and they are too indolent to work for a support. Companies of speculators are engaged in buying up their lands, and in a little time they will be the most unhappy, abject beings upon earth. In all my intercourse with them, I have endeavored to convince them of the impropriety of going in debt and drinking whiskey.    I am, &c.,
LEONARD TARRANT.

ELBERT HERRING, Esq.

———

SUPERINTENDENCY OF INDIAN AFFAIRS,
*Detroit, April* 13, 1833.

SIR: Your letter of the 2d inst. has been received. Having, in my letter of yesterday, written at length on the subject of the Winnebagoes, their removal from the ceded country, &c., I need here only add, that if you had referred to my letter of the 11th February you would have found my opinion, that after the removal of the Indians the sub-agency at Rock river would be unnecessary. I stated that I had been at Fort Winnebago, had seen and conversed with Mr. Gratiot, and the band of Indians under his charge, about their removal, &c. It is not necessary, therefore, that I should, on my arrival at *Green Bay*, make such inquiries as would enable me to determine the point. I had supposed that the knowledge acquired when among them, from Col. Kinzie, Mr. Gratiot, and the Indians themselves, was better than any thing I could hear at *Green Bay*, some two or three hundred miles from them. To meet that part of your letter, therefore, which states that a decision will be suspended until my report on this subject shall be received, please consider this letter as my report, that after the removal of the Winnebagoes the sub-agency at Rock river will be unnecessary.    I have the honor, &c.,
G. B. PORTER.

ELBERT HERRING, Esq.,
*Com'r. of Indian Affairs.*

CHICKASAW AGENCY, *April* 15, 1833.

SIR: Yours of the 25th ultimo has been received, and 1 shall, without delay, notify the chiefs of their obligation under the fourth article of the late treaty, and also your wishes and expectations upon that subject.

You were pleased to say that, if it should not be in my power to accompany them as their conductor, or that if they preferred some other person to conduct them, they are at liberty to employ him. I take pleasure in saying that, if I can possibly be spared from the agency, no personal considerations will prevent me from performing any service that may be of importance to the Indians or to the Government; but it is an unfortunate trait in the Indian character, and is certainly so with regard to the chiefs who rule this nation, that in the selection of white counsellors or agents for the transaction of business, a proper regard is not always had to qualification and responsibility. If they should select a person for that service whom I should have good reasons to believe was not disposed to promote the objects of the Government, and, as I might conceive, the vital interests of the Indians, in procuring them a home west of the Mississippi as early as possible; or should they select an irresponsible person that I could not believe would have a just regard to economy, and who would be remiss in accountability, it is respectfully submitted whether, under such circumstances, I should be justified in placing the funds in his hands for that service.

I have this day directed a publication to be made of the provisions of the late treaty with the Chickasaws, with respect to intrusions on their lands, and of the determination of the department to enforce them.

Should it be convenient for you to forward me a *printed* copy of the late treaty, it would afford me great convenience.

I am, with great respect,
Your obedient servant,
BENJ. REYNOLDS,
*Indian Agent.*

ELBERT HERRING, Esq.,
*Commissioner of Indian Affairs.*

---

TUCKEEBACHEE, *April* 16, 1833.

SIR: We are under the necessity of calling on our great father, the President, to allow some of our people land under the late treaty, as the gentlemen whom you have appointed to take the census of the people will not take the numbers of the persons for whom we are now about to apply. The circumstances are those, and the grounds upon which the persons appointed to take the census object: they were not immediately in the country at the time the treaty was made; they lived below Fort Mitchell, and near Fort Gains, on the Chattahoochie river. They long before the treaty made application to their relations in this country to come and bring them up. Their relations put it off from time to time, still intending to have them brought, until since the treaty. They are now here, and we are of the opinion that, through your friendly aid, our father, the President, will allow it to them. If those people are not allowed land, it will be a great injury to them, and they will be compelled to labor under great disadvantage. They are of this nation, and claim no other on the other side. Their numbers are hereto annexed.

We have the honor to be,
Your red children, &c.,

| | |
|---|---|
| TUSKEENAHAW, | his x mark. |
| HOPOETHE YOHOLO, | his x mark. |
| TUCKEEBACHEE MICO, | his x mark. |
| COOSA TUSTEMUGGEE, | his x mark. |
| LITTLE DOCTOR, | his x mark. |
| TUSTEMUGGEE MALLOW, | his x mark. |

*Names of heads of families and numbers.*

| | Males. | Females. | Total. |
|---|---|---|---|
| Wa-lue-yoholo, - | - 2 | 3 | 5 |
| Ho-law-te-mallow, | - 2 | 2 | 4 |
| Chat-le-mallow, - | - 2 | 3 | 5 |
| Tolledego-hajo, - | - 8 | 9 | 17 |
| Colehos-hajo, | - 1 | 1 | 2 |
| Net-ta-coma, | - 1 | 1 | 2 |
| | | | 35 |

COMMISSIONER'S OFFICE, FORT GIBSON, *April* 16, 1833.

SIR: In reference to the claims of the Cherokees west under the treaty of 1828, referred to us by the War Department, the commissioners would respectfully observe that, to avoid delay, they have requested Capt. Vashon, in whose capacity and integrity they have great confidence, to collect and arrange the vouchers and testimony upon which these claims are founded, so that they may all be presented at the same time, with the vouchers relied upon for their support. Owing to the great amount of payments to be made to the emigrating Cherokees, individually and by families, under their treaty, the labor of Capt. Vashon's agency is greater than that of any other agency west of the Mississippi, and the additional duties we now require will be more than he can perform without assistance. In conformity with the wishes of the department, the commissioners would recommend that the temporary agency of the Senecas be assigned to Capt. Vashon. This agency alone borders upon their tract of country. A final disposition of other tribes may hereafter make it expedient to place the Senecas under a different and nearer agency. The commissioners, in compliance with the earnest request of Capt. Vashon, respectfully recommend that he be permitted to employ, during the investigation of the claims, such an interpreter as he can confide in, together with a competent clerk, to enable him to investigate and properly arrange the claims, and to detect the frauds attempted to be practised upon the Government. With these additional aids, it is believed Capt. Vashon will be able to discharge the duties also of agent for the Senecas. Perhaps some of the above suggestions may be considered foreign to our immediate duties, but we feel confident in the merit of Capt.

Vashon, and disposed to accommodate him in the performance of his laborious duties.

We are, sir,
Your obedient servants,
MONTFORT STOKES,
HENRY L. ELLSWORTH,
J. F. SCHERMERHORN,
Commissioners.

S. C. STAMBAUGH, Secretary.

Hon. LEWIS CASS,
Secretary of War.

---

McCUTCHENVILLE, April 16, 1833.

SIR: By a special request from the pagan party of the Wyandots here, I write to you for some information relative to the prospect of sales of their lands to the General Government. They are becoming almost impatient to know something relative thereto. They are all in now from their winter's hunt, and are anxious to hear from you as it respects the sales of their lands.

The small band that made a treaty with Col. Gardiner, January 19, 1832, has not as yet received their pay for their improvements. You will please say when they may expect it, as they are in the want of it much.

I am, sir,
Your most obedient servant,
JOSEPH McCUTCHEN.

E. HERRING, Esq.

---

HUNTSVILLE, ALABAMA, April 18, 1833.

SIR: While attending the circuit court of Jackson county, in this State, last week, a rumor was received at Bellefonte, that *orders* had been given by the department over which you preside *for the removal of all white settlers within the limits of the Cherokee nation.* This intelligence came from some of those living in the nation, who had understood that a letter from the department to one of the principal men of the tribe, to that effect, had been received. As you may imagine, this information has thrown the settlers alluded to into a state of perfect consternation. Many of them have resided there one or more years undisturbed, and are consequently taken entirely by surprise. Some of them reside on places from which emigrating Indians have removed, after being paid for their improvements; and others have purchased improved places from the individuals by whom they were made. They have all, till now, been enjoying imaginary security under certain resolutions of our legislature, passed (as well as I recollect) in the fall of 1831, denying the authority of any power to disturb or remove those settled upon lands unoccupied by the Indians. I give the substance of the resolutions, not having them now before me: they may be found, however, in the pamphlet laws of the session which begun in November, 1831. Besides, the legislature has extended the laws of the State over the whole country claimed by Indians, and organized counties, appointed officers, and established courts; after which, we had entertained the opinion that military force would not be resorted to for the removal of supposed trespassers. Not having heard any intimation that a step of this nature would be taken be. fore leaving Washington, I have given the opinion that the rumor mention- ed above is unfounded. If I should be mistaken, and removals should take place at any time during the present year, incalculable distress and injury to many hundreds of our citizens will be the consequence. They have al- ready planted, or are engaged in planting their crops; and the season is too far advanced for them to find new homes, and raise the means of subsisting their families. I hope I shall be pardoned on this view of the subject, for asking a suspension of the order alluded to, if any such have been given, till time is afforded for presenting a more formal remonstrance; and, in the mean time, to be informed whether any orders have been issued; and if so, the nature of them.

I have the honor to be,
Very respectfully,
Your most obedient servant,
C. C. CLAY.

Hon. L. Cass.

---

SUPERINTENDENCY OF INDIAN AFFAIRS,
*St. Louis, April* 19, 1833.

SIR: I have the honor to acknowledge the receipt of your several letters of 16th March (two), one of 22d and one of 29th same month; two of the 1st, five of the 2d, and one of 3d April instant, which shall receive the pro- per attention.

The several treaties accompanying your communications of 2d instant have also been duly received. I shall communicate with the several agents, whose action will be necessary in effecting the objects of the department in relation to the prompt and faithful execution of those treaties.

The advance contemplated to be made to the Winnebagoes, to enable them to remove to the west side of the Mississippi, has not yet been forwarded to the proper agent; not having intended to do so until informed of the rati- fication of the treaty, which I expected would be accompanied by specific and full instructions on the subject, and which I will expect to receive when the funds are transmitted to me for that purpose.

I have been compelled to advance such of the annuities as are due to dis- tant tribes on the Missouri, in order to enable the agent to avail himself of the only means of transportation to his post. No funds have yet been re- ceived by me for the present year.

I have the honor to be,
With high respect,
Your most obedient servant,
W. CLARK.

Hon. E. HERRING,
*Commissioner Indian Affairs.*

---

ST. LOUIS, *April* 19, 1833.

DEAR SIR: Having completed my outfit, I shall leave this place to-mor- row, to complete the lines contemplated by the treaty of Prairie du Chien of 1830, and commenced by Major Boone. Should no material obstructions intervene, I hope to be able to complete these lines by the first of September; the closing point will leave me in the vicinity of the cession made by the Sac and Fox tribes of Indians to the United States at Rock Island in September last. Should you see proper to confer the appointment of surveyor on me, to run and mark the exterior lines of this purchase, I should not only be gratified, but would, as soon as the surveys were closed in which I am now engaged, proceed to run and mark the lines of the purchase made during the last season.

Any communication made to me on the subject will reach me through Gen. Street, at Prairie du Chien.

Very respectfully, I remain,<br>
Your obedient humble servant,<br>
JAMES CRAIG.

Hon. Lewis Cass.

---

Florence, Alabama, *April* 20, 1833.

Sir: Having returned to the agency through a populous section of the Cherokee country, and not being well assured of the intention of the leading men to recommend the acceptance or rejection of the terms proposed, and in order to communicate more satisfactorily with the department after passing the Georgia and Tennessee Indians, I concluded to visit those in Alabama. In doing this, I took charge of the Harnages as well as their negro property, a part of which had been seized; but, through the influence of your letter to the agent, and the indefatigable exertions of Mr. Miller, the United States' interpreter for the Cherokees, was recovered, and is now on its way below here to Arkansas.

In my tour, I have frequently met with copies of a letter to the principal chief from the department, on the subject of removing intruders, accompanied with assurances from himself, that their prospect for being reinstated, &c., are better now than at any period since the extension of the State laws.

Rumors are also afloat, countenanced by all those opposed to western removals, consisting of a medley of contradictions, as to the amount offered by the President and Secretary of War; the opinions of the President's friends with regard to the effect of the enforcing bill; the influence the delegation had exercised at the department in degrading the character of its agents, concluding with a declaration of a patriotic resistance on their part of all temptations held out by the General Government.

On the 16th of May next there is, however, to be a Cherokee council convened, where I am inclined to believe it would be proper for me to attend.

Should no decisive answer be given by the proposed council in favor of a treaty, you may rest assured they intend nothing less than an appeal to the judiciary, which will serve to amuse the ignorant for one or two years, and then, in case of a failure, which appears to me inevitable, they will again promise relief through a successive administration; thereby reducing their people to a condition equally as degrading as that experienced and quietly endured by the Catawba tribe, in South Carolina, unless some other plan is adopted for their removal than by general treaty.

In addition to the plan submitted by me, at the request of the honorable Secretary of War, I would suggest the propriety of increasing the western annuity, in a ratio with the emigration from the east. Also the policy of allowing the superintendent to employ intelligent Cherokees, paying so much per head for each one influenced by them to go westwardly.

One appraiser should be employed, who is well acquainted with the country, so as to be able to distinguish between improvements made by Indians and those by whites. I would, therefore, recommend the appointment of Jacob M. Scudder, esq., late Senator from Cherokee county, in the Georgia Legislature. His character entitles him to confidence, and his intelligence is calculated to make him useful in this service. Other appointments policy would seem to direct should be made from other States.

I have the honor to be,
Most respectfully,
Your very obedient servant,
BENJAMIN F. CURREY.

Elbert Herring, Esq.,
Commissioner of Indian Affairs.

---

Madison, 20th April, 1833.

Sir: I have just received from Col. Abel C. Pepper, Government agent for the removal of the Pottawatamies, a letter dated at Greensburgh, on his return home from the Indian country. He informs me that, on his arrival at Logansport, he found that a band of the Prairie Pottawatamies had assembled in that neighborhood, in the expectation of removing immediately; and that being destitute of provisions, he had issued them some, in the belief that it would be better to keep them embodied, than permit them to disperse. Two hundred and fifty-six had already enrolled themselves, and it was confidently expected that, by the 10th of May, the number would exceed 500. It seems to me that the present is an auspicious time to commence the removal of that tribe; and if you should be of this opinion, would it not be well to authorize the agent to provide for their removal immediately?

Yours, with great respect,
WILLIAM HENDRICKS.

Hon. Lewis Cass,
Secretary of War.

---

Columbus, Georgia, 20th April, 1833.

Sir: I have no doubt you are much troubled by hundreds of inquiries in regard to Creek lands, and it is with extreme reluctance that I add to your perplexity. There is, however, a matter now pending, of considerable consequence to a part of the Indians on the one part, and myself and a few of my friends on the other part. General Chilly McIntosh has been, for some time, engaged in enrolling Indians for emigration to the west, and now has a considerable number ready. Those Indians are now in a state of suffering, and McIntosh has not funds to carry them to their destined homes. He represents to us that the Creek nation has given to the western Creeks five of the twenty-nine sections of land mentioned in the treaty of 1832; that he is the representative of the western Indians, and proposes to sell to us those five sections, if we will furnish him with the necessary funds; to which proposition we have assented, upon condition that the trade will be recognised and ratified by the Government. The object of this is respectfully to ask you whether such a course would meet the approbation of your department: whether the gift of the five sections to the western Indians is recognised by the department. If not, what act is to be done by the nation, and how authenticated? Whether McIntosh is recognised as the representative of the western Indians? If not, can any act done by him or the nation here complete his authority? If so, what is that act, and how to be authenticated? If the sale to us will be good, how must it be made; in what form, and how authenticated? How are the locations to be made, and when may titles be obtained? An early answer is, you will perceive, highly necessary.

Respectfully,<br>Your obedient servant,<br>ELI S. SHORTER.

To the Hon. SECRETARY OF WAR.

————

CHEROKEE AGENCY, *April* 26, 1833.

SIR: Since my last, I have it from unquestionable authority, the delegation deny having ever promised to hold a council relative to the offers made by the Government. They say they were advised by Mr. Speaker Stevenson, that the present was an unsuitable time to listen to offers; that an offer of six millions of dollars was made by the Secretary of War; yet, relying on the virtue of the enforcing bill, they had declined giving this proposition a listening ear.

There will be a council held on the 12th May, but is believed the real object of the call is to rally and unite a general opposition to western removals.

*      *      *      *      *      *      *      *

Would it not be well to direct the Indian agent to exercise a sound discretion in withdrawing from the United States Bank so much of the annuity as proportionally belongs to, and may save the poor from distressing starvation?

In addition to the plan submitted by me for the removal of Cherokees, in the event a treaty is not concluded, I would suggest the policy of paying for missionary stands abandoned, where any considerable number of church members agree to remove west, placing the money in the hands of the agent, in trust, to be paid out for buildings and improvements of equal value there.

I have examined into the nature of Mr. Hardwick's (the son-in-law of Colonel Montgomery) right to live in the nation. The place he occupies was paid for out of the Government fund many years ago, and consequently, in strict justice and sound policy, should be tenanted by careful white people, and not again placed in a situation to fall into the hands of the Indians.

The removal of the fee simple and intelligent life estate reservees, as intruders, after the 1st January next, I am still more and more satisfied is an indispensable prerequisite to western removals, either by treaty or on the plan suggested to the honorable Secretary of War by me whilst at the city.

Richard Hinson, who returned to this country from Arkansas, has, with his family, gone back; would it not be well to instruct the agent west to pay his dues annually, by instalments, so as to save the Government from loss by any future attempts on his part at fraud?

The regular troops are here, and will, in a few days, under the direction of the agent, commence the removal of intruders.

I have the honor to be,
Most respectfully,
Your very obedient servant,
BEN. F. CURREY.

Elbert Herring, Esq.,
Com'r. of Indian Affairs.

---

Executive Office,
*Tallahassee, Florida, April* 27, 1833.

Sir: Governor Duval left this territory a few days since on a visit to his family, now in Kentucky, and in consequence, his duties as Governor of Florida have devolved upon myself. He will not probably return till late next fall.

I have the honor to acknowledge the receipt of your communication of the 12th instant, addressed to him respecting the Appalachicola Indians. No copy of the treaty of last fall, or any document relating to it, have ever been filed in the Secretary's office; but I have, since the receipt of your letter on yesterday, written to General Gadsden, who concluded the treaty, and shall probably see him in a few days, and obtain that precise and certain information neeessary for me to have, and which, although present at the signing of the treaty, and having a *general* recollection of its terms, I do not now sufficiently possess.

I do not anticipate any difficulty in getting off by the 1st of November, all those Indians of the Appalachicola towns, *whose chiefs signed the treaty last fall,* and those not included in the treaty will ultimately follow Col. Blunt, and may possibly be induced to go with him now. The agreement of the Seminoles to remove, will, I have no doubt, operate strongly upon Mulatto King (Vachapechasa) and Econchatimico, the two principal Appalachicola chiefs, who did not agree last fall, and who are yet said to be obstinate.

There are no official or other data in my possession from which I can at present make, as you request, " a statement showing the number of Indians that may *remain,* who are entitled to an annuity under the treaty of Camp Moultrie." The pay rolls of the agent, now on file, with his accounts, at Washington, furnish the best information on the subject at present in my power to render. I have adopted measures, however, to obtain more certain and authentic criteria, which, when received, I will transmit to you forthwith.

No efforts will be spared by me to carry into effect the views of the Government, as indicated in your communication, and I shall avail myself, as early as I can, of the benefit of a consultation with General Gadsden, in whose ability on this subject I have great confidence.

Without the slightest wish to evade the performance of any duty or to avoid responsibility, I would (solely because I consider it the best course) respectfully suggest the employment of General Gadsden as a special agent or commissioner, to make every arrangement necessary to get Col. Blunt and party off, under the treaty he concluded; the *advancement* to him forthwith of all the funds that may be called for, the investing him with power *to treat with those Indians who have not agreed to remove,* and with the fullest authority to exercise his discretion as circumstances may dictate.   In such case, all assistance that I can render him will be cheerfully and promptly given.   If, however, it should not be deemed necessary to appoint Colonel Gadsden, as I have suggested, every duty assigned to me will be fulfilled to the extent of my ability, and I shall on every opportunity seek his counsel.

I am, sir, very respectfully,
Your obedient servant,
JAMES D. WESTCOTT, Jr.

Hon. Lewis Cass,
  *Secretary of War.*

——————

Executive Office,
*Tallahassee, Florida, April 27,* 1833.

Sir: Major Phagan, (Indian Agent,) who accompanied the deputation of Seminole chiefs in their recent visit to the western Creek nation, under the treaty of Payne's landing, concluded last fall, has just arrived at this place, on his way to the agency, and made a report to me, which I have the honor to enclose.   I have given him the permission solicited.   In doing so I have been controlled not merely by the opinion that his arduous and valuable services for the last year entitled him to it, but also by the consideration that no other person (in my belief) could be of as essential service to the department as him, if at Washington, while the arrangements are being made for carrying the treaties into effect.   I have no hesitation in recommending him as the most proper person in Florida to go to the westward with the nation, and to assist in their removal; and I know Governor Duval concurs in this opinion.

As stated in another letter to the department, dated to-day, I shall see General Gadsden in a few days, and if, after consulting with him, it shall be deemed advisable, will again communicate to the department on the subject of the arrangements for the removal of the Appalachicola and Seminole Indians.

I have the honor to be,
Very respectfully,
Your obedient servant,
JAMES D. WESTCOTT, Jr.,
*Acting Governor of Florida.*

Hon. Lewis Cass,
  *Secretary of War.*

——————

Tallahassee, *April* 27, 1833.

Sir: I arrived here this morning, on my return from the journey commenced last September, with the deputation of Seminole chiefs to the western Creek nation.

The whole deputation have returned safely.   On yesterday I sent them from St. Marks, by water, to the agency.   I have the satisfaction of informing you that while at fort Gibson, after viewing the country assigned them by the United States' commissioners, the chiefs entered into a definitive treaty with the commissioners, by which the Seminole nation are to remove to the country assigned them, according to the treaty at Payne's landing. By this definitive treaty, of which I enclose a copy, it is expressly stipulated, that "the nation shall commence the removal to their new home as soon as the Government will make arrangements for their emigration satisfactory to them."

I shall on to-morrow return to the agency by land. After staying there perhaps a week, I wish to proceed to the city of Washington, in order to make a detailed report to the Government of matters connected with the visit of the deputation to the Creek nation, to settle my accounts with the Government for the journey, and to suggest many things, and advise with the Indian Department, and make arrangements for the speedy removal of the nation.

I hope they will all be got off by July or August at farthest. My absence from the agency will not exceed, at farthest, six weeks; and if in the meantime the annuity is received, it can be paid by Mr. Sheffield, the subagent, or retained till I return. I must therefore solicit a letter, giving permission to visit Washington for the purposes stated.

I have the honor to be,
Very respectfully,
Your obedient servant,
JOHN PHAGAN,
*Indian Agent.*

His Excellency, James D. Westcott, jr.
*Acting Governor, &c.*

---

Deansville, Oneida county, New York,
*April* 27, 1833.

Worthy Sir: The Brothertown Indians have understood that their location of 23,040 acres of land, on the east side of the Winnebago lake, has been confirmed to them by the Government of the United States, on the final ratification of the Menomonie treaty.

The Brothertown Indians are very desirous of having their land surveyed into suitable lots for farms, in the early part of this season, so that those who are now at Green Bay may remove on their lands as soon as possible. If the Government will permit them to go on and survey their lands as soon as possible, it will be greatly to their advantage. If they are permitted to survey the land, they expect to have one map and field notes sent to your excellency for the use of the Government, and one filed in the Secretary's office of the Territory of Michigan, and one for their own use.

It is very important that their land should be accurately surveyed into lots before they settle on it, and they are very impatient for the time when it will be proper for them to settle on the land on the east side of Winnebago lake, and they are now only waiting the permission of Government to go on and survey it.

May I have the pleasure of receiving the information as soon as it may suit your excellency's convenience?

Your most obedient servant,
THOMAS DEAN,
*Agent for the Brothertown Indians.*

His Excellency Lewis Cass,
*Secretary of War, Washington City.*

SUPERINTENDENCY OF INDIAN AFFAIRS,
*Detroit, April* 27, 1833.

SIR: I have the honor to inclose the copy of a letter just received from Colonel Kinzie, the sub-agent, at fort Winnebago, dated the 27th ultimo. The letter states so fully and clearly the object, that I need not recapitulate the contents.

There is, it seems to me, great weight in what these Indians say: that they are in a starving condition; that last year they could raise no corn because of the war; that if they remove to their new country they can raise no corn this year; but if permitted to remain on their present lands until fall, they could plant their corn, secure it in the fall, and remove comfortably and peaceably before winter would set in.

I know not what the Government intends doing with this country ceded, and of course mean not to interfere with their policy. But apart from this I would say, that as these Indians from the Winnebago and Green lakes are in the immediate vicinity of the Menomonies, and this part of their cession will of course be an Indian country, even should the Winnebagoes remove, no evil could result from granting their request.

Will you be so good as to direct a duplicate of your answer to this letter to Colonel Kinzie at Fort Winnebago. I may possibly leave Detroit for Green Bay before your letter will reach here.

Very respectfully, &c.
G. B. PORTER.

ELBERT HERRING, Esq.,
*Commissioner of Indian Affairs.*

---

FORT WINNEBAGO,
*Sub-Indian Agency, March* 27, 1833.

SIR: I have had a *talk* to day with some of the chiefs and head men of the Winnebagoes who reside south of Fox river, upon the subject of their having to remove from their villages on the 1st of June next. They are very anxious to get permission from their great father, the President, to remain there for this summer. They have presented me with a pipe for their great father, with these words: "Father, the pipe with us is an emblem of peace. It was given to us by our Great Spirit above, for to keep peace among his children below. It is used only by the good. We wish you, father, to take this pipe, and to send it with our words to our great father at Washington. We have brought it to you, knowing that it will have a clear road and bright sky to travel through, and we wish to hear from it before a great while. Tell our great father how we have suffered the past winter. He has taken pity on our women and children already, in supplying us occasionally with something to eat. We want him to continue good to us, and to permit us to cultivate our fields once more this summer, and it is all we ask. We wish to be better off next winter. We have not prepared now for a move. We have nothing to break up our land, and to make it good to plant our corn. The help which our great father is to give us will come too late for the time of sowing. Our old fields are ready made, and we wish to raise corn enough this year to last our women and children all next winter and part of next summer. Tell him we speak *strong*, and we want him to *think strong,* for our poor women and children. Our wish is for peace.

If our great father cannot grant our request we will then move.   Our families will then have to suffer, and we will be miserable for a great while."

The Indians who ask this indulgence of their great father, are principally from Winnebago and Green lakes.   They are peaceable Indians, and have not, to my knowledge, committed any depredations upon any white person since I have been among them.   They have asked me to let you know their *talk*, and to request you to intercede in their behalf.   I shall be glad to hear from you as soon as possible, that they may know the result of their application.

Very respectfully, &c.,<br>JOHN H. KINZIE,<br>*Sub-Agent Indian Affairs.*

His Excellency GEORGE B. PORTER, *Detroit.*

---

CINCINNATI, *April* 30, 1833.

SIR: I just write to inform you that the express (Mr. Forsyth) arrived at Fort Gibson previous to my departure from that place.   The board have concluded not to adjourn during the summer, but to continue their labors; and while my colleagues are examining the country, over which I have once passed, between Independence and Fort Gibson, I have, in compliance with the request of the board, undertaken to procure in the civilized west the necessary articles for the services under their late treaty; my services will be more useful here, and in the east a short time, than with the commissioners.

I have with me our report on the treaties made and councils held, and I shall visit Washington without delay, and return soon again to meet the board.   I wish very much for an opportunity to converse with yourself and Mr. Herring about some very important subjects relating to the Indian tribes.

In haste, I am,<br>Very sincerely yours,<br>HENRY L. ELLSWORTH.

Hon. LEWIS CASS,
*Secretary of War.*

---

CHEROKEE NATION, *May* 1, 1833.

SIR: I am well satisfied no terms can ever be made with this people whilst they have for their guide Ross, Martin, Taylor, Baldridge, &c., &c., who have but little interest in common with the great mass of the Cherokee tribe, and who manifest such total ignorance of the true character and condition of their subjects.   Nearly all the dominant party in this country are fee simple reservees, under the treaties of '17 and '19, and having pledged that they would reside thereon, permanently, as citizens of the United States, have no right in the nation, unless by the express consent of the General Government.   Policy and a regard to the true interests of the Cherokee people, would direct their removal as intruders after the 1st January next.

The delegation, it will be remembered, were informed in plain terms by the President, Secretary of War, and yourself, perhaps, that white people settled within the limits of the States which had extended their laws, could not be interfered with by the General Government; yet, the letter written by you to Ross on the subject of removing intruders, has been perverted by them, as applying equally to all parts of the country claimed by them, without regard to the jurisdiction of the States. Copies of this letter have been industriously circulated throughout the whole Cherokee settlements, conveying verbal information therewith, that the Secretary of War had, with the President, changed their policy on account of the "enforcing bill," &c. &c.

The council to be convened during this month will be but thinly attended, and a great meeting is to be promised in the fall, when nothing more can, from the course already taken by the leaders, be expected, than the appointment of a delegation to attend the next Congress, whose visit will, in all probability, be attended with no efficient steps towards a treaty. Indeed, the cry is already raised, " that Gen. Jackson will be out of office in the course of four years, *when Mr. Clay will do all that is asked of* HIM." And unless the country is threatened with depopulation by western removals from the different States, no general arrangement need be calculated on by this administration.

I am apprehensive John Walker, jr., has, at the suggestion of white men living in Tennessee, who are desirous of opening a field for speculation, adopted a new plan, which he will shortly submit to the department, making an arrangement, giving to each Cherokee a reservation of 640 acres of land, if he prefer remaining for the present; and if not he shall receive pay for his improvements by the Government, and emigrate on the plan heretofore pursued. It would, in my opinion, be altogether impolitic to allow reservations to any.

Vagabond white men are constantly intermarrying with squaws, who will oppose any terms, unless they themselves can be accommodated with reservations. Would it not be well to instruct your agents not to recognize them as citizens whose nuptials were celebrated after the 4th March last.

I have made an estimate of the greatest expense that can attend a removal on the plan submitted by me, to wit:

| | | | | | | | |
|---|---|---|---|---|---|---|---|
| Ten improvements, averaging | $10,000 | - | - | - | $100,000 |
| Twenty | do | do | 5,000 | - | - | - | 100,000 |
| Fifteen | do | do | 3,000 | - | - | - | 45,000 |
| Three hundred | do | do | 500 | - | - | - | 150,000 |
| Five hundred | do | do | 300 | - | - | - | 150,000 |
| Five hundred | do | do | 400 | - | - | - | 200,000 |
| One thousand | do | do | 200 | - | - | - | 200,000 |
| Six hundred | do | do | 100 | - | - | - | 60,000 |
| Blankets, kettles, guns, and tobacco | | - | - | - | 80,000 |
| Ploughs, axes and hoes | - | - | - | - | - | 10,000 |
| Transportation and subsistence of twelve thousand | - | - | 140,000 |
| Twelve months' subsistence after their arrival | - | - | 450,000 |
| Pay of officers, contingencies, &c. | - | - | 50,000 |

$1,735,000

The Cherokees claim, in the States east of the Mississippi, seven million two hundred thousand acres of land. There was estimated to be about 2,700 families in 1828. Two thousand six hundred and sixty-six acres of land would, on an average, belong to each Cherokee family. Since 1828, about two hundred families have enrolled and ceded to the Government all their right and interest in the nation east; reducing the whole number of acres above stated to six millions six hundred and sixty-six thousand acres. Let the enrolling system be carried on hereafter in the character of individual treaties, under such regulations and restrictions as the department may direct, exacting from each head of a family, and all others enrolling, a deed of cession for their proportional interest herein.

Under the Cherokee laws, as they now stand and have stood for many years past, each family has a right to clear and cultivate as much land as he pleases, so he does not go nearer than one quarter mile to his neighbor; and has a right to object to, and prevent his neighbor from improving or cultivating land within less than a quarter of a mile of his fence. When a Cherokee, by enrolling, surrenders to the Government all his right, title, claim, and interest in and to this country, has not the person holding as tenant under the General Government the same temporary rights of soil that were surrendered by the first occupant, at *least* until the State within whose limits the improvement may lie shall take jurisdiction over the same? In justice, it appears to me, the tenant should be protected in the enjoyment of these rights.

It is a matter of deep concern to those who have their eyes on the west, to be informed of the bounds set apart in the *late treaty*, defining the Cherokee limits in Arkansas by the commissioners.

Most respectfully,
I have the honor, &c.,
BENJ. F. CURREY.

Elbert Herring, Esq.,
*Commissioner of Indian Affairs.*

---

Wascissa, Jefferson County,
*May 1, 1833.*

Sir: Major Phagan spent the last night with me on his return to the Seminole agency. He has reported, he informs me, the successful result of his expedition to the west, leaving now nothing wanting but your instructions for the early removal of the Seminoles to the country allotted them on the Canadian fork. As the Major proceeds direct to Washington under a permit from the Executive of the Territory, you can personally communicate with him on those plans which may be deemed best for the transportation of the Indians to their new homes. I am inclined to the opinion, that after duly considering all the difficulties attending land and water conveyance, independent even of the repugnance the Indians have to the latter, that you will find the former most advisable. Should you adopt the water, a depot on the coast of Florida near the Indian location, (and the bay of Tampa alone affords an accessible point for large vessels,) would have to be established. The collecting the Indians at that point, the necessary preparatory expenses for doing so, the expense of delay, should the Indians be detained for the vessels, or of demurrage, should the vessels have to wait for them; the transhipment from sea vessels to steamboats, on the arrival of the former in the Mississippi, the probable detention of steamboats for the want of a concert of movement between them and the sea vessels, and the possible arrival of the latter in the Mississippi when the waters are too low for the former to ascend the Arkansas; are all obstacles of such a charac ter as may and will, in my opinion, be found to enhance the expense of water transportation considerably above that of a land route.

If the latter be previously selected through a settled and well supplied country, and the arrangements judiciously made, depots of provisions might be established at convenient distances, so that but few accompanying wa gons, and these principally to convey the children and infirm, would be necessary. The Indians could themselves afford great facilities with their horses, all of which they would wish to carry with them, and could not by water. They have generally a large stock of horses, and would very reluc tantly sell. An objection to the land route might be anticipated in the pos sible complaints for alleged depredations by the Indians on their march. But this can be prevented by making the chiefs responsible, and whose vi gilance will prevent irregularities. However, on this and other subjects you will derive from Major Phagan all the requisite information; he hav ing been designated by the Indians to accompany them, and their recom mendation having been responded to by the commissioners in the Indian territory, gives him a strong claim on the Government for being so em ployed. I have been prevented by an uncommon flood in the Appalachicola, interdicting all intercourse with its western banks, from visiting the Indians on that river, as I communicated was my intention in my last letter to you. I have been farther induced to postpone the contemplated interview until the return of Blunt from the Creek nation, where he has been invited, he informs me, to attend a council of the southern towns. They have it in agitation, if acceptable to the Government, to propose, as a substitute for the treaty you concluded with them, one on the conditions agreed with Blunt, and if accepted, to unite their fortunes with that chief, and remove with him immediately. I communicate, however, this information as I received it from Blunt, without any knowledge as to its correctness, or as to who may have first agitated the subject among the Creeks.

I feel very confident, however, that the two towns on the Appalachicola, the chiefs of which have hitherto been obstinate, will not long delay accept ing the condition offered them, and that all the Indians in the Territory of Florida may be removed within the next two years at furthest, provided the necessary appropriations be made by Congress.

Respectfully, your obedient,

JAMES GADSDEN.

Hon. Secretary of War.

———

Rankin, *May* 2, 1833.

Sir: For the information of those persons who are interested, I desire to be informed what course the individuals who claim land under the pro visions of the treaty of Dancing Rabbit creek must pursue, to secure their titles. That I may be the more distinctly understood, I take the liberty of propounding the following interrogatories, viz.:

Has any person been appointed to locate the land granted to orphans un der the 19th article of the treaty; and if so, who is he, and what are the nature of his instructions? Will the President permit them to locate their claims on any unimproved and unoccupied lands? What course must those persons who hold land under the 14th article of the treaty pursue, to have their claims reserved from sale? What testimony is it necessary for those who claim under the cultivation clause of the 19th article of the treaty to adduce, and before whom or what tribunal, in order to procure titles to their reservations? The answers to these interrogatories is respectfully requested, (if not in violation of any rule of the War Department,) for the benefit of those Indians who are interested. If the Government has established any rules or regulations in relation to the reservations, &c. granted to the Indians by the treaty, the manner of their location, &c., I should be pleased to be furnished with copies. If any person or persons have been appointed to locate any or all of the grants of land made by the treaty, or to attend to the business in any way, I should be pleased to be furnished with a copy of their instructions.

Please to address me at this place, (Rankin, Mississippi).

I am, sir, &c.,

F. E. PLUMMER.

Hon. Lewis Cass, *Sec'ry of War.*

---

SUPERINTENDENCY OF INDIAN AFFAIRS,

*Detroit, May 2,* 1833.

SIR: Under the 3d article of the treaty of Maumee, concluded on the 18th February last, there is due to Louis Beaufait seven hundred dollars. I know not what particular kind of voucher will be necessary to enable him to draw this amount. If it can be paid on his draft, which I enclose, it will oblige him very much. He is a most meritorious man, and the claim is correct and just. Should any other form of voucher be more proper, I will, on being instructed, have it prepared, and see it executed.

I also enclose the draft for $500 due to Henry Connor, as explained in the body of it, and shall be pleased if this amount can also be remitted. While at Maumee, and directly after the completion of the treaty, John Hollister & Co. gave a memorandum to Mr. Connor, which I hold, authorizing me to retain these $500, if the amount coming to them should be transmitted through me, and to pay it over to Mr. Connor, or, if they received it, that *they* would pay it to him. In answer to a letter from Mr. Connor, they say, in a letter received this day, that they have not drawn the money, and probably will not till July. He needs the money, and hence I ask it to be sent here.

I think it probable that three other persons named in the same article will expect to receive their money through me; and if not applied for at Washington, it had better be transmitted to me, viz.: Pierre Menard $400, John King $100, Louis King $56. These, with the moneys already committed to me to satisfy the claims in the third clause of this same article, can all be paid when I visit Maumee to pay the annuity.

Very respectfully, &c.,

G. B. PORTER.

ELBERT HERRING, Esq.,
  *Commissioner of Indian Affairs.*

---

POLE CAT SPRINGS, *May 2,* 1833.

SIR: I have the honor to report, that I have at length completed that portion of the census of the Creek tribe of Indians which pertains to that part of the nation denominated the Upper Towns, which will be found in part first of the book or census roll.

I left my house, in Jackson county, Alabama, on the discharge of this duty, on the 17th day of July last, and proceeded immediately on to Fort Williams to meet Colonel Pickett, who, I had been notified, would be my coadjutor in the business. At this place I neither found Colonel Pickett, nor any letter or message from him which might apprize me of the reasons of his nonattendance. From Fort Williams I directed my course to the house of Colonel Pickett, a distance of more than one hundred miles, and there learned, for the first time, that he had declined the acceptance of his appointment, and would not, therefore, be connected with me in the performance of its functions. Here I found a letter from Colonel John Crowell, then agent for the Creek Indians, requesting Colonel Pickett and myself to come to the agency, which I immediately complied with. On my arrival, Colonel Crowell and myself notified the Indians of the time at which their annuity would be paid, and also of the council which the commissioners would hold with them.

Major T. J. Abbott having been afterwards appointed in the place of Colonel Pickett, on receiving notification of the same, repaired to the agency, at which place he found me. On the day ensuing his arrival we set out together, in order to avail ourselves of the opportunity then afforded by the celebration of certain annual dances, called busks, which are attended by all the people of the respective towns belonging to the particular tribe, and by the Indians of the various tribes promiscuously, to present ourselves in our official capacity before the Indians thus collected, and thus in the best manner possible make ourselves known to, and our business understood by them. Shortly after our return from this tour, the other commissioner, General Enoch Parsons, my brother, reached Fort Mitchell; when, at the time appointed, we all, accompanied by the agent, Colonel Crowell, repaired to Wetumka, where we remained until the breaking up of the general council held there with the Indians. Of our proceedings on that occasion, the department has already been apprized by the report forwarded last fall by the commissioners.

After the dissolution of this council, Major Abbott and myself no longer acted in conjunction, but separately; I discharging the duties devolving upon me in the district of the upper, and he in the lower towns. We were in this manner engaged until we all again met in council with the Indians, on the 8th day of January last, at Fort Mitchell, which, from the great quantity and tedious nature of the business transacted, did not adjourn until the 12th of February. After which, I again set out to finish the taking the census of the upper towns, and have been up to this date thus employed, with the exception of five days, which I spent in attendance on a council of the Indians of the upper towns at Tuck-a-batch-ee. Major Abbott was also present at this council, and my brother, Enoch Parsons, notified and invited by the Indians; but owing to circumstances it was not in his power to attend. The object of this council was, to induce them to sell to the Government.

Major Abbott and myself, well knowing it to be the desire of a very great number of the common Indians immediately to emigrate, and to give such of the chiefs as were advocates for the same an opportunity of publicly expressing their sentiments, which they have hitherto been afraid to do; the extinction of their sovereignty over the country in which they lived, by the sale of their land to the United States, their reservations only excepted, and which were reserved to them as individual, and not as national property; the extension of the jurisdiction of the State of Alabama, and of the laws of the said State over them, together with the consequent extinguishment of their own law, and all other usages and customs connected with it, were carefully explained to them by Major Abbott, and probably would not have been without the effect of the object contemplated, but for the influence of a few of the principal chiefs, which again, together with the machinations of land speculators, prevailed. The time, however, I think, is not far off, ere they will regret and retract what they stated to be their intention, viz., of setting down and trying it a while.

On account of the continued fall of rain this spring, I have been much retarded by creeks and swamps, the creeks being in general swimming, and the swamps not unfrequently impassable. I had also to take the census of eight or ten of the towns a second time, in order to clear the rolls of the impositions which, by the connivance of the chiefs and the white men, (land speculators and their agents,) had been practised upon the Government, which was the cause of still further delay. It is more than probable, that there are many yet undetected, and which could not be found out without still protracting time, which, from the present late date, I did not feel warranted in doing.

Le Compere, the Indian youth, is not at school, and has no disposition to return to one: Barnard says he has education enough for him, and all attempts to alter their determination in this particular appear to be unavailing, and devoid of effect.

My account in form, together with receipts for money, &c. paid for interpreters, are enclosed; a draft for the amount of which, if allowed, be pleased to forward to the care of Captain William Walker, Montgomery, Alabama. All of which is respectfully submitted, by

Your obedient servant,<br>B. S. PARSONS.

Hon. Lewis Cass, *Secretary of War.*

---

Superintendency of Indian Affairs,<br>*Detroit, May* 3, 1833.

Sir: I have the honor to acknowledge the receipt of your letter of the 19th April, enclosing a copy of the appraisement of the improvements made by the Wyandot Indians on their reservations, and informing that the amount of the valuation of appraisers ($3,232 08), will be deposited to my credit, in the United States Branch Bank at New York.

I have directed Gen. McElvain to proceed and report as directed.

Very respectfully, &c.,<br>G. B. PORTER.

Elbert Herring, Esq.,
*Commissioner of Indian Affairs.*

---

Cherokee Agency, *May* 3, 1833.

Sir: A few days ago Col. Montgomery, being indisposed, requested me to enclose to you a letter to his address, from John Walker, jr., on the subject of Cherokee starvation and want.

Should the enrolling business be resumed on any plan shortly, humanity would appear rather to direct the rationing of this class so soon as they will come in and sign their relinquishment. The regular troops who are now in the nation could protect them from outrage, and, at the same time, keep them together until means are provided for their removal west.

Ross, Vann, Taylor, and Baldridge, have reported that your department, as well as the President of the United States, offered them eighty thousand dollars, as a bribe, to induce them to make a treaty, which was indignantly rejected.

Since their return home, Hilterbrand, who *was* in favor of a treaty, has been visited by Lewis Ross, at their instance, and changed.

Truth is perverted into falsehood, and falsehood made to wear the face of truth; and dishonesty is made to carry with it the appearance of honesty and virtue; and starvation, misery, and want get the name of peace and prosperity from these reservees; whilst that which *is not* is made to have an existence, and that which has a being is exhibited through a glass darkly.

The people groan under this kind of misrule, but through fear, without any great outbreaking murmurs, yet endure it all.

Coody, Ridge, Walker, Boudinot, Andrew Ross, the Griffins, some of the Adaires, Gwinnett, Miller, Spears, Wolf, McIntosh, and others, are anxious to make an arrangement with the Government, in the character of a new treaty. The plan submitted by me, with some slight alterations, would go down with most, if not all of these men, and their adherents.

I have the honor to be,
Most respectfully,
Your very obt. servt.,
BENJ. F. CURREY,
*Superintendent Cherokee Emigration.*

E. Herring, Esq.,
*Commissioner Indian Affairs.*

———

Waupaughkonetta, Ohio, *May* 3, 1833.

Sir: I have, agreeably to your instructions of the 5th ultimo, called on the Shawnee chiefs of this place, and ascertained it to be their wish that Joseph Parks should be appointed to conduct them to their new home. I have, therefore, as directed, obtained his bond, and also a receipt of the chiefs, which bond and receipt is herewith enclosed.

Parks' security is his brother and two Shawnee chiefs; although I would have much preferred it, had he got some one or more to have signed his bond who had a fixed residence in Ohio; but he could not obtain such without placing the penalty of the bond in their hands. However, the amount is well secured. Parks is worth five or six thousand dollars; his brother is worth at least two thousand; and the chiefs are worth from two to three thousand dollars. If, however, the department has any doubts as to the responsibility of the security, &c., Parks is, in that case, willing to defray the expense of the Indians to their new homes, and draw on the Government for the amount, after the accomplishment of their removal; but, at the same time, if it could be avoided, he would rather not do so.

It is considered best by Parks and myself, that a warrant should only be forwarded for one-half of the amount of the appropriation, and that the balance (eight hundred dollars) should be forwarded to the care of General Clark, to be paid to Parks when he reaches St. Louis.

As the Shawnees expect to set out about the 1st of next month, it is requested, as soon as convenient after the receipt of this letter, that the amount Parks is to receive, before he leaves Ohio, should be forwarded to him or myself, and enclosed to Columbus, as that is the best and nearest place to him to cash a warrant; and farther, it will be more convenient for me, as I consider it my duty to see that he obtains good funds, and to prepare him a book of blank receipts, &c. It is believed that about eighty-four Indians will emigrate with Parks. I will, however, after they are ready to set out, report the correct number.

In your letter of the 24th ultimo, with other things, you inform me that Parks is to be paid as interpreter up to the time he sets out for the west. I must, in order to make said payment, be authorized to draw for the amount.

The Big Spring Wyandots are anxious to be paid for their improvements. I, therefore, as soon as it is convenient, wish to be authorized to make said payment. When the amount is forwarded, a copy of the appraisement should be forwarded, and also about one hundred dollars to defray the expense of said payment.

I am, very respectfully,
Your most obedient servant,
JOHN McELVAIN,
*Agent for the Wyandots.*

Hon. E. HERRING,
*Commissioner Indian Affairs.*

P. S. Please forward the forty ($40) dollars I am entitled to, for making preparation for the removal of the Shawnees.

———

CLINTON, GREEN COUNTY, ALA., *May* 3, 1833.

SIR: Without the pleasure of a personal acquaintance with you, I take the liberty of requesting information from the President, through you, respecting the reservations allowed in the treaty with the Choctaw Indians, &c.

There was, I believe, a certain quantity of land set apart for schools, orphan children, &c., in that treaty, and to be disposed of by the President, or such person as he might appoint. I wish, sir, to purchase a settlement of land in that section of country, say one or more sections, provided I could have the selecting of the land, for which I am prepared to pay the cash, and willing to give a fair price.

I have no speculation in view, only wishing to make settlement in the country, and when I do, that for it to be on my own soil.

Any communication you may make me on the subject referred to, please to direct to me at the place this letter is wrote from.

With high regard for your public services,
I am, respectfully,
CHARLES GATES, JR.

Hon. LEWIS CASS.
26‡

DODGEVILLE, MICHIGAN TERRITORY, *May* 3, 1833.

SIR: On my arrival on this frontier, I found the people in a state of great alarm, from a belief that the Winnebagoes and Pottawatamies had united their strength to make an immediate attack, both on the frontiers of Illinois as well as this territory.   After a consultation with General Atkinson, I ordered Backus and Brown's companies of rangers to march to Hennepen, on the Illinois river, within fifty miles of Rock river, where I could march them to any part of the frontier, as the state and condition of the frontier people might require.   After seeing Mr. Kinzie and Mr. Gratiot, sub-Indian agents, I was led to the conclusion there was no just ground for alarm; and, after consulting with them, it was thought advisable to hold a talk with the Winnebagoes, and ascertain what their views were, and to signify to them the determination of the Government, as it respects their removal from the country they have ceded to the United States.   A copy of the talk held with the principal chiefs of Rock river is herewith enclosed.   The Winnebagoes are the most difficult Indians to understand I have ever been acquainted with; there is a stubborn sulkiness of disposition about them that I dont entirely know what it originates from.   I called their attention to the murderers who made their escape last fall from Fort Winnebago, to which they made no reply.   Some of the traders tell the Indians that, as they once delivered the murderers to the whites, by the laws of nations the whites must find the Indians and take them, and that they have nothing to do with them. Mr. Gratiot has seen four of the Indians on Rock river—the Indians who killed St. Vrain, the agent, among them.   It would quiet the minds of the people of the frontiers, if the eight murderers who made their escape could be brought to trial and punished.

There is a great unwillingness on the part of the Winnebagoes to leave the country they have ceded to the United States; and if they could avoid a compliance of their engagements with the United States, I think they would do so.   Captain Backus and Captain Brown will arrive on this frontier in a few days with the rangers.   Whether these two companies will be a force sufficiently imposing to oblige the Upper Rock river Indians to remove, I am unable to say; a few of the leading men will remove, but it is doubtful whether the greater part of them will not remain in the Rock river country.   The chiefs of the Winnebagoes appear to have less influence over their people than any Indians I am acquainted with.

I could think of no plan that appears more advisable than to call the chiefs together, and have their agents present with me in a conference with them.

I hope the steps I have taken, in relation to the Indians, will be approved by the War Department.

I have the honor to be,
With great respect,
Your obedient servant,
H. DODGE,
*Col. United States Dragoons.*

The Hon. LEWIS CASS,
*Secretary of War, Washington City.*

Memorandum of a Talk held at Four Lakes, April 29th, 1833, with the Winnebago nation of Indians, of Rock river.

Present, on the part of the United States, Colonel Henry Dodge, United States Dragoons; Henry Gratiot, Esq., and John H. Kinzie, Esq., United States sub-Indian agents for said nation. And, on the part of the Winnebagoes were present, *Whirling Thunder, White Crow, Little Priest,* Little Black Crane, and other chiefs and head men.

*Whirling Thunder* spoke as follows: Fathers! we are glad to meet you. As you (Colonel Dodge) have just returned from our great father at Washington, we feel anxious to hear the news; we have been looking for you a great while; we are badly situated, and wish much to hear what we are to do. It is for this reason we have come to meet you and our friends here (Mr. Gratiot and Mr. Kinzie) to hear the news. It is true, we bought considerable ammunition last fall; many of the whites believed it was for bad purposes, but not so; we bought it to enable us to subsist during the winter. Our women have broken their hoes in digging roots, &c. to live upon. We look upon you three as our fathers. We resemble children begging of their father for something to eat. We are all very anxious to remain on our lands for this season, that we may be able to raise wherewith to keep us from starving the ensuing winter.

*White Crow:* Fathers! you are a good chief (General Dodge) and we are happy to meet you. I have spoken to you in council before. There are four of you on whom we look to for justice. I mean Colonel Dodge, Mr. Gratiot, Mr. Kinzie, and General Street. Last summer we all met at Rock Island; I recollect what passed between us and General Scott. General Scott was sent to purchase our country; I said I had no objection. Many of my nation appeared to be dissatisfied; but that I think can easily be settled. A great deal of provisions has been promised to us, a part only has been delivered to us. If we were well supplied with provisions, we would not think it hard to remove from our country, but we know we will suffer; and it is for this reason we should like much to remain, for this season, in this country. I have nothing more to say. When you (General Dodge) left last fall, to see our great father, we were in hopes you would bring us good news when you returned, and that we would be permitted, by our great father, to remain on our lands another season.

*Little Priest:* Fathers! we are happy to see you to-day. I cannot speak different from what you have just heard from our chiefs, who have just spoken. We are anxious to hear what you have to say from our father the President. It is the desire of all the chiefs to come and see you, and to hear the news. The season is far advanced for us to make new fields. We beg that we may be permitted to remain in this country this season.

*Haw-paw-kwee-see-kaw* (a brave of Turtle Creek village): Fathers! my views are perfectly in unison with the other chiefs. We were glad to hear last fall when you left for Washington to see our great father. We were in hopes it would be for our good, and that we would be permitted to remain on this land for a season longer.

*Spotted Arm:* I cannot speak different from what you have just heard. My wishes accord with the rest of the chiefs who have spoken. I think like them.

*White Breast:* I have nothing to say more, than we have all been anxious for your return. You were never out of my mind, only when I was asleep. I hope you will all take pity upon us, and that we may be permitted to remain a little while longer on our lands.

*Crane:* I think as the others do who have just spoken. I hope you will take pity on our women and children. We wish to remain here another season.

*Little Black:* I did not wish to speak, because my mind is like those who have just spoken. I live at the village of the *Warrior*, on this lake. I have never injured any person.

Gen. Dodge addressed the Winnebagoes as follows: I have seen your great father, the President; his wish is, that his friends, the Winnebagoes, should live peaceably and happy. He sent his great war chief, Gen. Scott, last year, for the purpose of making a purchase of your country. His object was to separate you from the whites, and that a great river should be the boundary between you and the whites. That the treaty then made, a copy of which you have in your possession, has been ratified by your great father. All the stipulations in that treaty, on the part of the United States, will be complied with; the provisions, &c. promised, will be given. The President expects that you will comply with your part also. Our object now is, to have a fair understanding with you respecting your removal. I have heard, with regret, from your fathers present (Mr. G. and Mr. K.) that a report has been in circulation, that I was coming with a large force to destroy your nation. Those reports are not true, and without foundation. I have come here, as you see, with no armed men, except with a few of my neighbors, and Mr. Kinzie and Mr. Gratiot, your agents, to communicate freely with you, and to ascertain your views. Actions speak louder than words; words are mere empty sounds: you know me well. I have never disappointed you, and have always aided you in your treaties, and saw that justice was done you. The blood of your people has never been shed by our people on this frontier, except where you have joined with the Sacs, and when we have met you in battle. What has been the treatment we have received from you? *Your* people did aid, and shed the blood of our people. You have identified the murderers of our people, and delivered them up. They have escaped, and are living with you on Rock river. So long as the murderers are permitted to run at large, suspicion and a cloud of darkness will remain over your nation, until they are brought to justice. You have nothing to fear if you do right. To shed a drop of white man's blood will be the ruin of your nation. You have expressed a wish to see me. We here meet in friendship. The United States rangers will be here in a few days. They are not coming to make war upon you. These men are under the orders of Government. They are to keep peace between the white and red man, and to enforce a strict observance of the treaties made with the Government and Indians, and which it is expected will be fulfilled on their part. There is 20,000 rations of pork and flour at Fort Winnebago, on account of the treaty at Fort Armstrong. Knowing your present situation, we will take the responsibility of supplying you immediately with two hundred bushels of corn, in order to expedite your removal. Mr. Gratiot will bring you the corn. We understand that your great father, at Detroit, has about 500 dollars, to purchase corn, &c. for your wants. Mr. Kinzie has sent to your great father, at Detroit, for 300 bushels, to be distributed to the nation at Fort Winnebago; of which the Rock river Indians will be entitled to their proportion. The rations which are to be delivered on account of the treaty of last year are only for those who are obliged to emigrate.

With this corn, (a part of which you require for seed,) and the rations which will be given to you, I think will be sufficient for your support during the summer. Mr. Kinzie has received a letter from Gen. Clark, stating that he would send him now, if necessary, the 10,000 dollars which was stipulated to be given to you in September next, by the treaty of Fort Armstrong. Your chiefs, it seems, do not wish it at present, as you would prefer receiving your money all at one payment; say in the fall. You have now heard what I have to say; it is all I have to communicate. If any of you wish to speak to us, we are ready to listen to your words.

*Whirling Thunder:* I have listened to what you have said. I shall do as the whites wish. Had it not been for our red brothers, (the Sacs,) we would not be in our present troubles. We have always advised with you and our friends here (Mr. G. and Mr. K). You know well, father, that we have old people as well as you have. We will come up as far as we can with our canoes; and we hope our fathers here, Mr. Kinzie and Mr. Gratiot, will furnish us aid in transporting our canoes to the Wisconsin river. We have always looked upon you as our fathers; we will continue to do so as long as we live; and we hope, after we reach the Wisconsin, you will continue to see that justice will be done to us. We are not like your whites; we never provide for a rainy day. The sooner the corn can be delivered to us here, the better to enable our removal. We wish you three to interest yourselves on our behalf, and to get permission from our great father for us to hunt next fall on these lands. We think what you stated to us is the truth. We don't think you made it from your own head; it is from our great father at Washington, and we feel under many obligations to you for the interest you have taken for us. It is true many of our young men appear dissatisfied, but that is nothing. You may think that I am one of the great chiefs of the nation, but I am not. I have been requested by all the chiefs to speak thus to you. Fathers! our trouble now is, to get our canoes across to the Ouisconsin. I have nothing more to say.

*White Crow:* Fathers! you all consider me as one of the Rock river Indians. I belong to Winnebago lake. That which keeps me here is my wife, who is a Rock river woman. The friends of my wife persuaded me to remain with them, and to be their speaker. You request me now to visit my friends again. I will do so. I want you to send to our great father, and to get permission for me to hunt on Rock river next winter. I want you to speak *strong*. The young men can get along well in the new country, but the old men, like myself, cannot. We wish to hunt *small* game. As soon as I return home, I shall start for our *new home*. I do not know how many will follow me.

*Little Priest:* Fathers! I have nothing more to say than what has just been stated by my friend the *White Crow*: we consider ourselves as one person. I shall follow him.

Gen. Dodge: We have listened to your words. We know that your canoes ought to be transported across to the Ouisconsin. We shall endeavor to have it done for you. You ought to take with you as few canoes as will be necessary.

---

CREEK NATION, *May 5*, 1833.

SIR: We, the undersigned, chiefs of the Creek tribe of Indians, beg leave, through you, to make known to the United States Government that we have for many years past, and of right ought still to be continued, held and esteemed as principal chiefs of the said tribe of Indians, and as such 'are entitled, under the late treaty, to a section of land, having always heretofore acted as principal chiefs, and having been recognized as such by the Creek tribe of Indians for some time since the late treaty. A part of the principal chiefs assembled at the Tuckebache town, and for the purpose of speculation alone, concluded to make new chiefs, which they have accordingly done, to the great injury of us who are the regular head chiefs. They have appointed now, as chiefs, men who never held a station of any kind. We are informed that the commissioner is determined to register our names simply as heads of families, thus defrauding us of one half of our lands, giving us only one half section; and we are not the only sufferers by this new arrangement of chiefs, as the common heads of families are likely to be driven from their improvements (as we understand the chiefs will have, according to the instructions, the right of preference to location), and be located on land of the poorest quality, thereby defrauding them also of their rights. We further state that, since the treaty, a great many have become heads of families for the purpose of obtaining a reservation, and have imposed themselves upon the persons who were empowered to take the census; and others, who were entitled to a reserve as the heads of families, the husband has given in as a head of a family, and the wife as a widow and head of a family also. After stating these impositions, we contend, that as we were principal chiefs at the time of the ratification of the treaty, we are entitled to the rights guaranteed to us by that treaty, and respectfully request that you will have our names registered as principal chiefs of the Creek tribe or nation. We are fully persuaded that this change has been made at the instigation of white men, whose only motive is pecuniary aggrandizement, and not from any good will they have for the Indians. We are aware that the United States Government is frequently harassed from frivolous and unfounded complaints as regards our connexion with the whites, but ours is of a sound character, and sufficient proof can be procured in favor of what we claim, and we have nowhere to look for relief but to the United States Government.

ANTUSEE MICCO.
EFAR TUSTENUGGEE.
TUCKEBACHE-FIXICO.
COLOMA TUSTENUGGEE.

Hon. Lewis Cass.

P. S. I have been a chief for upwards of forty years over the Antusee town. I do further state that there are no less than twenty chiefs in the Tuckebache town agreeably to the present arrangement. Is this correct, or is it honest? It most assuredly is not. If treaties are binding, I have a vested right and will not surrender it. I have no doubt but justice would be administered to all of us if facts were known. We request you to make strict inquiry into our situation, and cause justice to be done without further difficulty or cost to us. I respectfully suggest to you the propriety of having this matter settled by the locating agent; I am told he is an honest man and will do us justice. I do not doubt Mr. Parsons' honesty, but I think him unqualified to discharge the appointment you have conferred upon him, therefore liable to be imposed on.

ANTUSEE MICCO.

FORT GIBSON, *May* 8, 1833.

SIR: The interests of the service upon which we are engaged seem to require that the business committed to us, during the summer, should be divided among the several members of the board.

You will, therefore, proceed to Washington, agreeably to the verbal instructions heretofore given you, with the proceedings of the Cherokee and Creek treaties, the Osage council, and the treaty made with the Seminoles, which you will lay before the Secretary of War.

You will explain to the Secretary the causes of the failure of the Osage treaty, and the prospect that yet remains of effecting a satisfactory arrangement with that tribe; and also bring before the department the whole business of the commission, as it has progressed, and the views of the board in relation to the removal of the whole Indian race to the country assigned them by the wisdom and benevolence of the Government.

It is desirable that you should join Mr. Ellsworth, if possible, before he leaves Washington, in order that you may make immediate arrangements to carry the Seneca treaty into effect. In making purchases for the erection of mills, smith shops, and the employment of workmen, you will use all possible precaution and economy. You are acquainted with the urgent necessities of these people, and we doubt not but you will use every exertion to have their wants satisfied in a judicious manner.

Should the President not deem it expedient that the commissioners should meet and treat with any of the northwestern Indians east of the Mississippi this fall, you will return as soon as practicable, and join the board at St. Louis, where we will endeavor to meet about the middle of July. In the mean time, one of us will endeavor to make an arrangement with the Quapaw Indians, now in the Arkansas Territory; and the other will view the country north of the Osage reservation, and meet the Pottowatamie delegation, agreeably to the instruction from the War Department.

We are, with respect,
Your obedient servants,
M. STOKES.
J. F. SCHERMERHORN.

To Col. S. C. STAMBAUGH,
*Secretary to the Board of Commissioners of Indian Affairs.*

---

*Journal of the proceedings of a Council held by the United States' Commissioners with the Osage Indians, commencing at the Great Saline, upon Neosho river, on the 25th day of February, 1833.*

*Monday, February 25.*—The commissioners, Montfort Stokes, Henry L. Ellsworth, and Jno. F. Schermerhorn, and Samuel C. Stambaugh, secretary, met in council at Colonel Chouteau's, Grand Saline.

Major P. L. Chouteau, United States Agent for Osages, informed the commissioners that an express had just arrived from *Clermont's* (principal or first chief of Osage nation) village, bringing intelligence that it would be impossible for the Osages to assemble at the Saline on this day, but that they would meet the commissioners in three or four days.

Board adjourned.

*Friday, March 1.*—The board in session. Major Chouteau, agent, reports the Osage chiefs all present, but that the inclemency of the weather will prevent the Osages from appearing to open the council to-day.

*Wednesday, March* 6 —The commissioners met the Osages in open prairie, near the Indian camp, and shook hands; agreed to meet next day in council.

Same day, Colonel A. P. Chouteau, agent for furnishing rations, informed the commissioners that provisions were becoming scarce in consequence of the great length of time occupied in bringing the Indians into council. And a letter received from Lieutenant Carter, assistant commissary at Fort Gibson, informing commissioners that he had a large quantity of provisions on hand not required for the troops, and which he was anxious to furnish for the use of the Osages, it was agreed, upon consultation, to adjourn the council to Fort Gibson, provided the chiefs would be satisfied with the change.

*Thursday, March* 7.—Major Chouteau, United States agent, laid the question of adjournment to Fort Gibson before the Osages, and upon consideration it was agreed to.

Same day, March 7, council adjourned to meet at Fort Gibson on Monday next.

*Monday, March* 11, 1833. The agent, sub-agents, and interpreters, with about eight hundred Osages, arrived at Fort Gibson, and met the commissioners at their quarters. It was agreed that the Osages should encamp on the west bank of the Neosho, opposite Fort Gibson, and that they would meet the commissioners in council on Wednesday next.

*Wednesday, February* 13.—The council met at the Osage camp; commissioners and all the chiefs of the Osage nation present.

A. A. Chouteau was selected to interpret from French to English; and the United States interpreter, Batisee, from Indian to French.

General Stokes, on behalf of the United States, then addressed the Osages as follows:

BROTHERS OF THE OSAGE NATION: We are glad to meet you again as friends, and we now hope to form such a treaty with you as shall be beneficial to your nation.

Brothers: We meet you by direction of your great father, the President of the United States. He has instructed us to assure you of his constant regard for your welfare, and his great desire to preserve peace between you and your neighbors.

Brothers: This cannot be done without you sincerely and faithfully aid in the wishes of your great father.

Brothers: We are directed to assure you, that all your treaties with the United States shall be fulfilled; and we are ready to see them fulfilled as soon as possible. We expect you to do the same on your part.

Brothers: It is known to you that, by your treaty with the United States, made at St. Louis in 1825, you have ceded to the United States the land upon which part of your nation are now living; that is to say, the whole of Clement's band and Requa's settlement. This land has been since ceded by the United States to the Cherokees, and it is necessary that our engagements should be complied with. For this purpose, we require that these bands should be removed as soon as convenient, that your nation should live together in one common country.

Brothers: We are directed by your great father, the President, to propose the removal of all the Osages from their present reservation. This removal is desired for the sake of preserving peace with your neighbors, and improving the condition of the Osages, by placing them in a more desirable country, alongside of their friends, the Kansas, with whom they were once united.

Brothers: This removal is not to be made without your free consent, and upon terms and conditions which shall be advantageous to all. We wish you to settle upon the lands between the Neosho and the country of the Kansas. Heretofore, you held your lands by treaty boundaries; but if you agree to remove, your great father will give you a patent for your land, by which you will forever hold them for you and your children, and not be disturbed by either white men or red men, so long as you remain a nation.

Brothers: These are the purposes for which we invited you to meet us here; and we are glad to see that you are come with confidence in the good intentions of your great father. We hope that the proposals we shall make will be satisfactory, for we have your welfare alone at heart.

Brothers: We want to hear you, and to know whether you are willing to remove upon such terms as will tend to your comfort and to the comfort of your wives and children. We wish to see you settled, that you may raise corn sufficient for your support. We wish to provide you with tools and articles to work your land; and we wish to assist you in becoming free, and exempt from the necessity of obtaining an uncertain subsistence by killing of game, to keep your wives and children from suffering. We are your friends; we want nothing from you, but to help you all we can; we will give you as much land (and better for you) as that you now live on, and will assist you in removing and beginning your settlements.

Brothers: We now want to hear you speak for the Osage nation. We cannot treat with you in separate bands. We, as the representatives of your great father, who know the kind feelings he entertains toward you, anxiously hope that the business commenced this day will end in making you a prosperous and happy people, and that you will be settled at last in a permanent home, where you will live in peace and friendship with all your red brethren west of the Mississippi.

Brothers: We want to hear your answer as soon as possible, as to whether you consent to an exchange of lands, in order that we may consider of the particular terms offered for your acceptance.

Major Chouteau, the agent, then spoke to the Osages as follows:

My brothers, as your friend and agent, I will say a word to you. You have heard what the commissioners have said, through your father here. He wants your answer, and I now want you to give it. If you want time to make up your minds, you can take time.

*Clermont,* first chief of the Osage nation, rose, and said: My fathers, I have listened and heard all you have said. Here are all my brothers and warriors sitting around me, who have also heard you. What you have proposed is a serious matter to us, and it may take us some time to give an answer. We would like to hear all you have to propose, and then we may be able to give you a final answer in a few days.

Commissioners inquired, do you want to hear all our propositions now, or will you first consider on what we have already proposed, and tell us first whether you are agreed to treat for removal at all, provided the terms we can offer will be satisfactory to your people?

Clermont replied: We will now consider what you have already said, and hear your other propositions to-morrow.

Adjourned till to-morrow, at 11 o'clock, A. M.

In council, Thursday, March 14: present as yesterday. Mr. Ellsworth then addressed the council as follows:

27‡

Brothers of the Osage nation: You have asked your great father to let you go to Washington to see him and mention your difficulties; he told you it was a great distance to travel, and promised to send commissioners to see you. We have now come, by his direction, to talk with you about those things which deeply concern your happiness. The Great Spirit who made us still watches over us, and we hope will preserve us while we are together.

Brothers: We come to you as friends; we have no motive but to do you good. Some white people may tell you that we want to get away your lands, and give you other poor lands for them; we tell you such men do not speak the truth; they are either interested, and advise you for their own corrupt purposes, or destitute of principle; they wish to make trouble; do not regard what they say. We rejoice that there are men in this country to whom you can look with confidence; men who have never deceived you. Your agent is one good man; your *brother*, Colonel A. P. Chouteau, who lives at the Saline, is another. The Mr. Chonteau, the present interpreter, and Mr. Requa, too, are your friends. In these you can have the fullest confidence; they know and understand all we tell you; go and ask them whether we advise you for good or evil; listen to their opinion; they will not advise you to do what we ask unless they believe it is for your *best* good. And let us ask you, why should we give you bad advice? we gain nothing by it; and your great father, who loves all his red children, told us to do you justice, and help you along; this is what your great father desires, and what we shall try to do. We tell you also, we have come to remain with you, and see done what we propose to you; if we return to visit our families we shall be back again very soon.

Brothers: You know, perhaps, that all the red men living east of the Mississippi are coming over to reside here. The Choctaws will occupy the country between the Red river and Canadian; the Cherokees and Creeks will occupy all the land between your reservation and the Choctaws; when all the Cherokees, Creeks, and Choctaws arrive here they will all be great nations, some of them three or four times as large as the Osage nation. On the north are located the Delawares, Shawnees, Piankeshaws, Weas, Kickapoos, and the Kanzas; on the east will be placed the Senecas and other tribes. So that you see very soon all the land west of the Missouri and Arkansas will be taken up and occupied by your red brothers. We will tell you now why they all come here: your red brothers do not like to live among white people. Your red brothers want to do different from the whites; and, therefore, your great father has so planned it, that all the red men will soon leave the States where white people live, and come over to this country. This country will always belong to the red man. No white man can ever be permitted to live in it, or trade in it, except by permission. This country will be protected by the soldiers from wild Indians, and all other folks that make you unhappy. And your great father has promised all the red men who come here that they shall be protected. No one shall fight them; no one shall steal from them; no one shall do them any harm. And now, should any one red man dare to kill or steal, that man will be punished. But we tell you frankly that we have not come here now to punish any of you, if you have done wrong. We come to make *peace*, and to advise you how you can avoid difficulties in future. A short time since Black Hawk, at the head of the Sacs and Foxs, and his warriors, thought they would fight and make war upon your father's white people. Your great father sent his oldiers and killed most of them. Black Hawk, Ke-o-kuck, and some thers were sent to prison; and I saw them in chains when I came here.

And now, brothers, let us tell you again, what will be the fate of all red men that make war either upon your white brothers, or an Indian in this country in friendship with your great father, and what will be the consequence of all the red people coming here to live. The game, the buffalo, the deer, the elk, &c., will be all killed or driven very far back to the mountains. You may be sorry for this: but would you not rather see your red brothers happy than to see them starve? Yes, the red man will come here, and the game will be scarce or gone entirely. And what will you do? You cannot depend upon hunting them. You cannot get skins to exchange for clothing and food. Your annuities will soon cease, and then what can support you? Something must be done, or you and your children will starve and die. We are all sorry to find you so poor and needy: but if some change is not made in your mode of living and pursuits, we believe you will all perish. We will now tell you, brothers, what you must do: you must depend upon agriculture and domestic manufactures; you must plough and plant corn, potatoes, pumpkins, beans; and you must teach your women to spin and make cloth. You will then be happy, and you will then become a great nation. How much happier would you be if you were all farmers; had a good snug log cabin to live in, where you could always be protected from the storm and cold; where you could have a cow to give you milk, oxen to work, and beaf to eat, and pigs to fatten for pork. You might all of you have a large crib of corn, and as many potatoes, pumpkins, and beans, &c. as you wanted. Look at your brothers, the Creeks and Cherokees; they have good houses and large fields of corn; they are not stronger than you; are they not happier than you? They think they are, and we think so too. The Cherokees and Creeks do not depend any longer upon the buffalo and deer. They hunt for amusement, and so may you when you become farmers, if you wish; but you will then much prefer home and your comfortable cabins to the fatigue and the danger of the chase. You may think the Pawnees and other Indians will attack you, if you are scattered about like the Creek and Cherokee farmers. You need not fear these wild Indians. Your great father will erect forts soon, and put soldiers in them, out on the Arkansas, Canadian, and Red rivers, west of your settlements; besides this, we are now trying to have a meeting with the Pawnees and Camanches, to make a peace; they have told us they wish to have a peace made with the Osages and other tribes, and make war no more. You may, therefore, be assured your great father will protect you in your farms, and no one shall hurt you; for your great father has a great many soldiers, who can, in a short time, kill all the wild Indians that hurt his red children here.

My brother who has spoken has told you we want to have you all collected together, and to exchange your present reservations for land lying north of the Neosho river. Some bad people have told you we want to place you out on the Smoky fork; this is not so; those that say so tell you what is not true. We wish to give you as good or better land than that which you now own. We wish to give you as much land as you now have. Your great father does wish that you will exchange your present land for other good land a little distance north. The distance is not great. You all know where the Neosho river runs. When you come to this river you will enter upon the land we offer you, and to this place many of you can go in one day. The land north of that river is said to be very good for corn, potatoes, wheat, pumpkins, grass, and other things.

Brothers: The Clermont's band and Requa's band must soon remove somewhere, and it will be about as easy to remove as far as the Neosho as anywhere else.   This is one reason why your great father wishes your removal to the land between the Neosho and Kanzas.   With the Kanzas you are acquainted; you speak the same language, and are united with them by marriage and by birth.   It is very desirable that you should be on land adjoining theirs, so that you may unite with them hereafter if you choose. The Cherokees, Choctaws, and Creeks have many warriors, and will be very powerful when they all come together.   If you and the Kanzas unite, you too will be powerful and strong.   Should you not remove, what will be your situation?   We shall place other tribes on the east and north of you; this we must do because there are many red men to live here, and all the land is wanted.   If we locate strangers around you, you might not agree with your new neighbors; they might be hostile to you, and certainly you would be separated from your old Kanzas friends; when, if you remove, you will be near your Kanzas friends, who will treat you well, because they love you.   You may think that you are willing to go, provided we will help you; and you will ask us "what we will do for you if you remove?"  We tell you we will help you all to build houses to live in; we will hire farmers to live among you, not only to advise you but to help you. We will help you to farm and plough your fields of corn; we will give you cattle, sheep, and hogs.   We will build you mills to grind your corn and wheat.   If you like wheat flour you can raise it abundantly, and the flour mill will grind it.   We will build you mills to saw your boards.   You can have schools.   We will give or build you school houses, and have the teachers reside among you, so that your children may live at home; and here let us say, that soon an Indian government will be formed here.   The Cherokees, and Creeks, Choctaws, and others will take a part in it; and will not the Osages too? If they wish to do this, some must learn to write and read, else you will not be equal to those around you.   We know you to be brave people, and can equal any others in learning as well as farming, if you try.

Brothers: You have fifty-four sections of land to be appropriated for education; this shall be converted into a fund for education, as soon as possible; in the meantime we will appropriate $2,000 a year for teachers for your children.  If any of you think that he has now a good house and farm, and will lose it if he goes away, for all these he shall be paid; and what we promise you we shall see done for you.   Should you fear suffering when you first remove, for the want of provisions, we tell you now again, if you agree to remove as soon as you can, and this you can do within a year, we shall, this spring, hire farmers to make fields on your new residence, and raise corn, potatoes, beans, pumpkins, &c. for you on your arrival.   But, in order to do all this it will require a great sum of money.   We propose to you to give you a large amount in cattle and farming utensils; besides this, to pay you, within twenty years, the value of your annuity of $1500 annually; the annuity is now perpetual.   It gives to each one about twenty-five cents a year; this is too small to divide.   But if this was paid sooner the amount would be large, and your great father thinks it would be better for you to have the value of the annuity paid sooner to aid you in farming, than to receive so little every year.   I wish to explain to you more fully, with regard to the annuity.   Your $1500 annuity gives each about twenty-five cents: suppose you had a sow to bring you pigs, and bring you fourteen pigs a year, would it not be better to have this sow and pigs now, than to have twenty-five cents in money for so many years?

Brothers: I have little more to say now. We hope you will be satisfied with our talk. If you do not understand us fully, tell us of it, and we will explain it to you. We wish to tell you plainly what is in our hearts; and ask you to tell us all that is in your hearts. Should you take our advice, and do as your great father wishes you to do, we shall also make you some valuable presents when you go home. I told you before that we were your friends. We shall not forsake you and leave you to perish with hunger and cold. We will go with you, if you wish it, to see the Kanzas after the treaty is made. We will look at the land with you, and if you desire it, ask the Kanzas to unite with you and make one great nation. What more can we do for you? And I can only add, that should you refuse to take our advice, and suffer from hunger and cold, while other red men around you are happy, remember, the reason why they are happy and you unhappy is, because they listen to our advice and you refuse it. We ask you now to go to your best friends and ask them what to do. We shall be happy to inform your great father how we met you here, and how willingly you took our advice, and complied with our wishes. If you try to please him he will always take care of you.

After Mr. Ellsworth had finished his talk, Major Chouteau, the agent, asked the Osages whether they wanted to hear all the propositions now, or reflect on what had already been said, and listen to the remainder to-morrow.

Clermont replied, that they wanted to consult on what they had already heard, and then he would hear all the propositions. He said they would prefer adjourning till to-morrow, as they were now tired.

Adjourned till to-morrow at 11 o'clock, A. M.

———

*Friday, March* 15, 1833. Council met: present as yesterday.

Mr. Schermerhorn, on behalf of the commissioners, submitted the following as their propositions to the Osages:

Articles of agreement and convention made and concluded at Fort Gibson, on the Neosho river, the     day of March, 1833, by Montfort Stokes, Henry L. Ellsworth, and John F. Schermerhorn, duly commissioned and appointed on the part of the United States, and the chiefs and braves of the Great and Little Osage nations of Indians.

Whereas, the Great and Little Osage nations, in former treaties with the United States, have ceded the greater part of their once extensive conntry; and, by so doing, they expected that it would become the residence of their white brethren, who would not interfere in their hunting grounds; but, instead of this, they have lately seen it settled by powerful nations of Indians; and in consequence of it, their game, on which they depended for a subsistence, has already become scarce, and must soon be destroyed; and being anxious to provide the means of subsistence for themselves, their women and children, as well as to live in peace with all their red brethren, the following articles of agreement and convention are made and concluded between the United States and the Great and Little Osage nations:

Article 1. The Great and Little Osage nations hereby cede, relinquish, and quit claim to the United States, all that certain tract of land by them reserved in their treaty concluded at St. Louis, June 2d, 1825, and is described as follows: beginning at a point due east of White Hair's village, and twenty-five miles west of the State of Missouri, pointing on a north and south line, so as to leave ten miles north and forty miles south of the point of said beginning, and extending west fifty miles in width, to the eastern boundary of the lands hereby relinquished or ceded by said tribes or nations.

Article 2. The United States, for and in consideration of the above cession of land by the Great and Little Osage nations of Indians, do hereby agree and covenant to give them, in exchange for the same, at least an equal quantity of land, to be bounded as follows: beginning at a point on Neosho river, sixty miles due west of the state line of Missouri, and thence running north, so that a direct line shall extend as far east as the eastern boundary of Kanzas' reservation, and on the north to be bounded by the Shawnees and Kanzas' lands; on the west by the twenty-third degree of longitude from Washington, and on the south by Neosho and Arkansas rivers, and a westerly line drawn between the two rivers. The reservation shall be surveyed and marked out at the expense of the United States, as soon as practicable; and the same shall be conveyed to them by patent, in fee simple, as a permanent home, as long as they exist as a nation and continue to reside on it. All persons connected with the agency, and such instructors and teachers as the President of the United States may permit, shall also reside here, and have the privilege of cultivating, without moles-tation or interruption, such lands as may be deemed necessary by them.

Article 3. The United States will build four dwelling-houses for the four principal chiefs of the said nations, in such part of their country as they may select. The Hopefield band shall be paid the amount at which their former improvements were valued; the Osages shall also be allowed the value of their present improvements in others of equal value in their new country. The widow of White Hair, on account of the uniform and firm attachment of her deceased husband to the United States, and as a mark of respect for his memory, shall have a comfortable house erected for her residence. All the stipulations of the United States in former treaties with the Osages shall be complied with, that have not already been fulfilled.

Article 4. In order to encourage the Osages to give up their wandering life, and no longer to make their dependence upon the precarious sub-sistence of the chase, and to induce them to engage in agricultural pursuits, and for the purpose of aiding them in cultivating the soil and raising stock, the United States agree that such chiefs as set the example, and induce their people to form agricultural settlements, shall be entitled to a yoke of cattle and farming utensils, and have a comfortable house erected for them; and if such settlements consist of fifty families or lodges, they shall be furnished by the United States with agricultural implements and stock to the amount of $2,000; and a proportionable amount if the number of families are greater or less than fifty. Each such settlement shall also be provided with a farmer, providing the same does not exceed twelve, to aid and instruct the Osages in every thing appertaining to farming business. The farmer shall have the stock and agricultural implements supplied by the Government under his special care, to see that nothing be squandered or destroyed, or any of the stock slain until it has so increased and multiplied that it can be done without damage; and he shall be accountable to the United States, through the agent, for the same. All such Osages as wish to build houses for their comfort and convenience, shall be aided and assisted in the same by persons acquainted with this business, at the expense of the United States. The settlements shall also be supplied with a sufficient number of blacksmiths, and their shops stocked with tools and materials to do the necessary work of the Osages. The United States will erect, for the accommodation of the Osages, eight patent railway corn mills, as soon after the removal as needed; also a saw-mill, and employ a hand to superintend the same. The farmers and other persons engaged to aid and instruct the Osages by this article, to be continued as long as the President of the United States shall deem necessary for the benefit of the Indians.

Article 5. The United States will cause to be selected, without further delay, the fifty-four sections of land reserved by the treaty of 1825 for education purposes, from the best and most saleable lands in the State of Missouri and Territory of Arkansas ceded by said treaty; and the same shall be disposed of by the President of the United States, in such manner as he may deem most advisable for the benefit of said fund; and the United States hereby appropriate $2,000 a year for the purposes of education, to be expended in the Osage nation, under the direction of the President of the United States, until the above lands are sold, and the amount thereof invested by the United States for the benefit of the Osages. The United States will also erect such school-houses and dwellings for teachers as may be deemed necessary in the different parts of the Osage nation.

Article 6. The United States further agrees to pay to the Osage nation $10,000 in full, for all the expenses of their removal, in provisions, or such articles as their necessities may require; the amount of $4,000 to be paid on the signing of the treaty, viz., three thousand bushels of corn, and the balance in merchandise, the receipt of which is hereby acknowledged; the remaining $6,000 to be delivered after their arrival in their new country: and the Osages hereby agree to remove within one year from this time.

Article 7. In order to relieve the Osages from their present embarrassments, in consequence of their depredations upon citizens of the United States and friendly Indians, their neighbors, which, by treaties with them, they have agreed shall be deducted from their annuities, the United States once more, and for the last time, agree to relieve them by paying all just demands upon them for depredations, provided they do not exceed $5,000, or if they can be settled for that amount; and on further condition that the Osages shall agree to abide by such general regulations as the United States may adopt for preserving peace among the different Indian nations, and promoting the welfare of them all.

Article 8. The United States agree, in lieu of all former annuities, and particularly to cancel the perpetual annuity, to pay to said nation $10,000 annually, for thirteen years, and $3,000 for seven years thereafter; the same to be paid in agricultural implements and domestic animals, or merchandise, at first cost, in the city of St. Louis, as the Osage nation may require.

Article 9. It is hereby agreed, on the part of the United States and the Great and Little Osage nations, that all articles in former treaties not modified and superseded by any part of this treaty shall remain binding and in full force upon the different parties to them.

Mr. Schermerhorn, in presenting the above propositions, commented at length upon each article, enforcing what had already been said, and concluded by presenting to the view of the Osages the following:

A schedule of the amount proposed to be given to the Osages by the present treaty:

1. They will receive much more land than is contained in their present reservations.

2. If they all adopt the agricultural life, they will receive,

| | |
|---|---|
| In farming implements and stock - - - - | $24,000 |
| Mills - - - - - - - | 4,000 |
| Merchandise and provisions, or whatever they may choose - | 10,000 |
| To pay depredations - - - - - - | 5,000 |
| | $43,000 |

Besides this, an annual expenditure for farmers, carpenters, blacksmiths, and schools, during the pleasure of the President of the United States, $10,000 a year.

By these means, in a short time, every family may have their own plantation, and houses built to live in. This does not include considerations offered to chiefs who shall commence agricultural settlements, and encourage their people to follow them, and which may amount to at least $5,000; and if they are willing and desirous to exchange their perpetual annuity for an annuity of twenty years, they will receive $3,000 a year for twenty years; or in other words, they will receive, for their perpetual annuity of $1,500 a year $60,000 in the course of twenty years.

After Mr. *Schermerhorn* sat down,

Clermont rose and said: Brothers, my chiefs and braves have heard what you have told us. If you have now told us all, we will consider it, and give you an answer hereafter.

The council then adjourned till to-morrow.

Saturday, March 16, 1833. Council met: present as yesterday.

Wautanego (the Fool): My fathers, we wish to have a friend to help us in this treaty; we can neither read nor write, but we have a friend here who can (Colonel A. P. Chouteau); we consider him a brother, and want him to assist us.

Governor Stokes replied: Brothers, you can have Colonel Chouteau to assist you; we consider him your friend and our friend. You can have any papers you want to examine at any time.

The principal chiefs of all the bands then rose, and expressed their satisfaction that Colonel Chouteau was permitted to assist them in their negotiations, as the whole Osage nation had confidence in him.

Governor Stokes: Brothers, we again say, we are glad you have selected your brother, in whom you have confidence, to assist you; we have confidence in him too. We want you all to hear and understand every thing we have to say, and your friend here can explain it. We hope you will now seriously deliberate upon the propositions we have made, and act prudently and wisely.

Mr. Ellsworth said, our brother has spoken the sentiment of us all.

Maj. Chouteau, agent, then said: My brothers, I feel glad that you have selected my brother to assist you, as I know he is your friend, and the friend of your great father. You have confidence in him, and so have our friends here. I must do my duty as the agent of the Government.

The council then adjourned till Monday.

*Monday, March* 18. The Osage chiefs notified the commissioners that they would not be ready to go into council before Wednesday.

*Wednesday, March* 20, 1833. Council met: present as before.

Clermont rose: My fathers, it is now four days since I heard your talk. My chiefs and braves will now speak, and I want you to listen.

Black Dog then rose, and said: My friends, since our chiefs have first shook hands with the Americans, a great many things were promised us, but never performed. You now again promise to make us a happy people, but I have never seen our people happy yet; and we are now afraid to agree to what you propose, for fear you will again deceive us: I have nothing more to say at present.

Clermont said that no more would not now speak from his town.

White Hair rose, and said: Fathers, hear all the chiefs and braves from my village. That land belongs to them. They will now speak, and I want you to listen.

Belle ban za, the head counsellor, then spoke as follows: Fathers, my chiefs want me to speak: I will do so, but I am lame and cannot rise. Fathers, the Osages were the first red men in this country who shook hands with the Americans; afterwards, we met in council to do business. When our chiefs went to Washington, our great father said he wanted to place us on an equality with the whites; but our old chief, White Hair, died without receiving this benefit, or without knowing how a white man lives. You see me; I don't look like a white man. Look at my buffalo robe; I am still an Indian. Since our chief saw our great father, we made another treaty, and the son of that chief (White Hair) was then a chief. I was at that treaty; it was made with a man between us and our great father (Gen. Clark). He said: My son, I have sent for you by your great father's orders; he wishes to make you happy, and protect your land for you; he wishes to settle you as white men; but the chiefs who made that treaty died without becoming like white men.

Fathers: You are good and wise men, and that is the reason I now tell you the Government has not fulfilled its promises to us. You see all these old people sitting here; their wigwams were once on the Missouri river; they were born there. But we have listened to the advice of our great father, and have left three towns on that account. Look at me; I am an Indian still, although I have followed your advice. Fathers, we have a very small piece of land now, and why do you want us to leave it? When I first heard of your coming to this country, I thought you were coming to help us and do us good; but now I have heard that you have come to take our last small piece of land from us. This is all I have to say to-day.

Adjourned till to-morrow.

Thursday, March 21. Council met at the commissioner's quarters.

Clermont addressed the commissioners: My fathers, you have written a paper, and I have seen it. Here are my chiefs and warriors, who have also just heard it read over carefully, and we will now go to our camp and consider upon it.

White Hair rose: My fathers and friends, my chief has shaken hands with you; it is the same as if I had done it. You say you are in a great hurry; we are so too. But you have come here to do business highly important to us, and we must give it due consideration. To-morrow we will give you an answer. We will now go to our camp, and to-morrow you will hear our propositions.

"Walking Rein," (principal chief of the Little Osages,) then said: My fathers, I have been many days here, but have not yet spoken. What our braves told you yesterday was true. My oldest brother went, with others,

28‡

to see our great father; he told him he should be happy. I afterwards went to see him, and he told me the same thing. But you see how old I am, and these promises are not fulfilled. I was at the last treaty we made with Gen. Clark, and he promised some things which have not been done for us.

The following chiefs and braves then rose, and corroborated what their head chiefs had said, all complaining that promises already made to them, by the General, had not been complied with, to wit: The Little Chief, Big Chief of Little Osages, San Sovil, Iron, Wau-bash-kan, (Little Osage,) Town-maker of Big Osages, and a warrior of Little Osages; they all said they had heard the propositions now again made by the General, and would consider them.

Governor Stokes then said: My brothers, we are glad to hear that you have taken our propositions into consideration. We hope you will consider them attentively, and that our negotiations will terminate satisfactory to you as well as to the Government. You shall receive no promises from us that will not be fulfilled. We will now adjourn, and expect to hear your answer to our propositions to-morrow.

Adjourned till to-morrow.

Friday, March 22d. Council met at Osage camp: all present.

Clermont rose: My fathers, I want to say a few words to you. Here is our interpreter, and he will tell you what I say. I bring this one, (presenting a young half-breed to the commissioner,) to hear whether he interprets true for me. I want you to hear my own words, and nothing but my own words. The Great Spirit has given us a fine clear day, and I will tell you the truth. My grandfather's town was first built far away north on Missouri; but our people quarrelled then, and my father came here, where I was born. Since my father came among the whites he has been very poor. I have had nobody, heretofore, to complain to; but I see you here to-day, and I will speak plainly. I want you to listen. The Great Spirit will judge whether I tell the truth. I see you four setting there. You did not come here of your own accord, but were sent. I believe some one who lives near here has written letters to bring you. I do not believe it is the wish of our great father that you are here. When the letter was written for you to come, none of my warriors saw it. I do not know what was in it. The small town I now live in belonged to my grandfather. My father went to St. Louis and sold it; and since that treaty I never received but a small part of our annuities. I want to know why we did not get the whole amount every year. But, without speaking of our annuity, I want to know why you have come here to remove us. I was born in the town I now live in, and don't like to leave it. I am now praying to you that I may be permitted to remain there. I have had these things on my mind, and I am afraid to make another treaty.

Lafolle (the Fool, a principal chief) rose, and said: Fathers, I have something to tell you too. The land of the Osages was once away off yonder, (pointing to the north). We had two chiefs, and I followed one of them here. We made a fire here, and I lit it. After we came here our chiefs went to see our great father. He has put something in my chiefs' heads. I believe he made a hole on the Missouri for our fire, and I came here. On the river I now live, a great many small streams meet. It is not long since our great father told us this country should be ours; that he was our father, and we should be Americans. But you see me, and I am not as he told me I would be. When I heard you were coming here, I expected our great fa-

ther had sent you to teach us to live as white people. But we have seen nothing yet of what our great father has promised.

Black Dog spoke: My fathers and friends, I will speak to you this day again.
My chiefs long ago shook hands with the Americans. These chiefs are
now dead, and they never followed the ways of the whites. You now
tell me I will be happy, but I cannot listen to that. Here we have a town;
I told you before we did not want to leave it, and I want you to help me to
remain. I don't wish to make a treaty with you to remove.

The following chiefs and warriors then rose, and told the commissioners
that they approved of what had just been said; they did not wish to make
a treaty to remove from their present homes; to wit: The "Mad Buffalo,"
"Wan Kee Shee," "War Eagle," of Clermont's town, the "Crazy Little
Osage," the "Night Auga bau be," (the one that cries,) "Mee tau ne gan,"
"Sun down," "Racoon Skin," the "Counsellor," "Nee hon ko shee,"
"Horse Thief," and "John Lafolle." The last speaker concluded by saying: "My fathers, all our people are crying for our town, and I pity them;
and I hope you will do so too. Fathers, if we have a child crying we take
pity on it; we hope, now that we are crying, you will take pity on us."

"Tolly," second chief of Clermont's town, rose and said: My fathers,
you have heard my braves, they have been crying to you. Here is our
home where I was born. When I rise in the morning, I can see where my
father is buried; I don't want to leave that home.

(Several warriors then spoke alternately, approving of what the chief
"Tolly" had said.)

White Hair then spoke: My fathers, the whites first opened the door of
my grandfather, "White Hair," and the Government made him a great
many promises. I don't believe they were all performed. A great many
were also made to my father, which were not fulfilled. The Osages have
always followed your advice till this day. I am only a boy, but my grandfather made me a chief. I don't think a father will give his son bad advice.
Here are the promises made to my grandfather, (handing a paper,) I have
not lost them.

The "Mad Chief" rose: My fathers, I am sorry to hear my brother talk
as he does to-day. I am crying for that. I am the only *old* chief left of
the White Hair family; the rest are all young. Here is a letter; you may
read it. I wish to do what my great father asks in this letter. (See letter
from Secretary of War, dated May 28, 1832.)

Belle ban zan, (head counsellor,) then spoke: My fathers, I want to
speak a few words to you. Here is my medal; it has on it the face of a
man who has pointed out a good road to me. Those who have spoken said
they were to see our great father; I have been there too. I have heard
what you have told us, and have considered it. It has been told you that
we are all one nation; but you see that we are divided. I think that we
should be but one nation; I am on a piece of land, too, that was laid off for
our people. This is our own. But I don't think you have given us bad
advice; and what you have asked us to do I hope will be done. There are
a great many Osages here. Several towns will take your advice.

The following chiefs and warriors then spoke, supporting what the head
counsellor had said, and agreeing to make a treaty, provided the terms
would be satisfactory, and old promises complied with, to wit: The "Little Chief," "Iron," "the Chief of Bell Hill," the "Terrible Warrior,"

" Young War Eagle," "Linaff," " Old Counsellor," "Walking Rein," "Little Osage Chief," the " Big Chief of Little Osages," " San Lan ree," "Little Osage," (a head warrior of Little Osages,) and " Wan bash Kan," (Little Osage counsellor,) who concluded as follows: " Fathers, the promises made to us heretofore have never been fulfilled. You see our people speaking with blankets; do you think they are happy? Our chiefs all died with little things to their flaps. I will die so too, perhaps. Try and help us, for we are very poor; of all these nations around you, you see no such fine looking warriors as ours; we are your handsome children; take pity on us.

The blind chief, (Old Missouri,) then said: My friends, I must speak; what you white people have told me has gone through my ears. Here is Clermont's (the chief's) people don't want to leave their lands; they say you have told lies. I am the only Missouri chief living among the Osages; and I am very old. You white people say we will be happy; I would sooner see it than hear talk of it. We are so poor, that when our children die we have not a blanket to wrap them in. You are the cause of bringing other Indians round us who make us so poor. You take our land to give it to other tribes. My fathers, you say we will hereafter be happy. I wish you would tell us what is to make us happy. We are told you are very good. Now I have come a great way to see you. I am blind, and very old. I hope you will give me a horse to ride home.

(Several other chiefs and warriors spoke, asking a further explanation of the propositions made by the commissioners.)

Tally's brother, blind chief of Clermont's band, then said: My fathers, I am very old, but every body here calls you father, and I will too. Our warriors ask you to keep our towns. If you can give it, I will then call you chiefs. Our great father put us in three towns, but our annuity money I never saw. The French and Spanish people laugh at us for holding so many councils. We are now on a small piece of land; there are six towns all touching each other. You talk about the land on Cane river; it is good for nothing, all prairie and no trees. If our great father wants to assist us to raise our families, the land we live on now would be best. We are surrounded by other nations, and we don't want any more to come near us.

Adjourned till to-morrow.

*Same evening*, *March* 22.—The Osage chiefs met the commissioners at their quarters, for the purpose of endeavoring to effect a compromise, by affording some explanation of the propositions already submitted.

The following letter was presented by Col. A. P. Chouteau, and read:

COMMISSIONER'S OFFICE,
*Fort Gibson*, *March* 22, 1833.

GENTLEMEN: I have good reasons for believing that an Osage, named "Stephen," educated at the Union Mission, is producing much mischief by giving bad counsel to Clermont's band. He declares to them that the Government has no right to compel this band to remove from the land they now occupy, and that you have no power to treat for their removal. Being very anxious that the views and wishes of the Government should be carried into effect, and fearing that improper influence, exciting the principal chief to resistance, may defeat it, I deem it my duty to report these facts to you, in order that you may adopt such measures on the occasion as you may deem expedient and proper.

Very respectfully,

(Signed)                    A. P. CHOUTEAU.
To the U. S. Commissioners.

Gov. Stokes, after the reading of the above letter, said: Brothers, we are very sorry that you have bad advisers among you, of which we have heard before, and still more regret that any misunderstanding has taken place between you and us. My colleague here has something to say on this subject, and will give you all the explanation and satisfaction in our power.

Mr. Ellsworth then addressed the Osages, particularly Clermont's band, from whom came, he said, the opposition to treat or remove from their present village. He told Clermont " that it was impossible that they could remain where they now are. If their great father was willing, he could not permit it. The land where Clermont's band now lives, has been given to another tribe; they have a paper telling them so, and your great father cannot take it. A treaty was made with your great father in 1825, by which you gave this land to him. In that treaty, the Osages gave up all the land except what was included in their reservations, upon which they agreed to remove. In consequence of this, your great father promised to pay you $7,000 annuity, which you have been receiving every year. And now let me ask you, who signed that treaty? Why the father whose son now objects to it was the first to sign it. Several others of the chiefs and braves of that band signed it; some of them are now here. Now will Clermont rise up and say, what his father done is not good? We trust, after this explanation, no one belonging to Clermont's band will say they have a right to remain; and if they remove at all, they may as well go to the country we offer as to their old reservation. You have said much about promises; we have only made you one promise yet; that was, that if you would come here we would feed you well. This we have kept. We will say one thing more. We have come here to do you good, and to remain here to see done what we promise; and we trust that when you meet us in this country hereafter, you will not charge us with having broken our promise. We cannot compel you to go from your reservation without your consent, but you *must* all move on that reservation. We hope, however, that the inducements we offer will induce you to remove."

Mr. Schermerhorn rose, and said: Brothers, what has just been spoken to you is the mind of us all. (Mr. Schermerhorn then went on to add explanations to what Mr. Ellsworth had said, and to show Clermont why annuities had not been received by him; that they were taken to pay claims against Osages for depredations. He also spoke in support of the propositions already presented.)

Clermont rose to reply, and presented " Stephen," to hear that he was correctly interpreted. Mr. Chouteau, the interpreter from French to English, sat down and refused to interpret.

Mr. Ellsworth then spoke, through " Bagette," an Osage half-breed: Brothers, we believe you are taking bad advice. The man standing before you (Stephen) is giving it. He has told you untruths. We have asked you to listen to your brothers, the Chouteaus, who have never deceived you, and not take bad advice.

Clermont again rose: My fathers, this is not a white man; he is an Osage; my sister is his mother. I bring him here, not as an American, to give me bad advice, but to hear whether my words are correctly interpreted. My fathers, I told you I had lost my property, and I will now tell you where I lost it. At first, our great father divided our money into three parts. Before my father died, "White Hair" was the cause of some mules being lost, and I had to pay for them. My brothers here know this is truth. I ask my brother Chouteau whether those chiefs (White Hair) paid me back these $1500? When Hamtramack was agent, there was some money to be paid us, and I did not get my part. I believe Colonel Arbuckle knows this. Of the money for the mules, $1500 has been kept from me; the agent here cannot say I ever received this money. My fathers, what I pay I remember. Here are some of our friends, the Creeks, who charged us with killing their cattle, and we paid for them. Some money was left with my brother, Major Chouteau, the agent, and he gave part to " White Hair," and part to " Little Osage Chief," but none to me. I have paid for the depredations committed for our people, and White Hair did not help me; but I helped him to pay for his. I think I have been wronged, and I wanted to tell you of it.

Chief orator of White Hair's band rose: My fathers, I am not going to speak to you, but to my brother Clermont. (He then went on to tell the chief, Clermont, that it was the agent *Hamtramack's* fault, that the money was not paid him.)

Governor Stokes then said: My brothers, we have heard what you have said, and you have heard us. We hope you will now go to your camp, and come into council to-morrow, prepared to do what is right.

Adjourned till to-morrow.

*Saturday, March* 23, 1833. Council met at Osage camp: all present.

Clermont and all the chiefs and principal braves of his band spoke in favor of remaining on the land they now occupy. Clermont concluded by saying: This town I do not wish to leave. I do not say so myself; but the nation our great father has sent here, (the Creeks,) have invited us to stay among them. Fathers, you want our village for another nation. Now, I will give you our annuity for one year and the land you offer us, to be permitted to remain. My young men have done some damage to our brothers, (the Creeks,) and I intend to pay for it.

The chiefs and principal braves of " White Hair" and the " Little Osage" bands expressed their willingness to make a treaty, provided they could agree with the commissioners upon terms.

The commissioners then addressed the chiefs, advising them to unite as one nation, and follow their advice to make a treaty.

Adjourned till afternoon.

Afternoon of same day, Osages would not come into council, but agreed to come on Monday next.

*Monday, March* 25, 1833. Colonel Chouteau announced to commissioners that the chiefs had not altered their determination, and that they would not go into council that day, but would meet to-morrow.

Adjourned till to-morrow.

*Tuesday, March* 26. Council met at Osage camp: all present.

Governor Stokes rose: My brothers of the Osage nation, we have been informed that you have held a council together for several days. We now want to know whether you have come to a determination about a treaty.

Clermont replied: My fathers, you have heard my answer many days ago. I will say a few words more. I will follow my great father's advice, and move to the town where some of my braves are gone, that is, to our reservation under treaty of 1825. I have already said I did not wish to go where you want to put me. I will make no treaty now, but will go and see my great father. Here is a man I have taken for my brother, (Colonel Chouteau,) he will take me to see my great father, who is my friend. (He then spoke to the Osages as follows:) My brothers and warriors, I now speak to all of you, to the whole Osage nation. You have heard my intention, as expressed to the commissioners. I do not know what you will do; but you have heard my determination.

"Lafolle," a principal chief, said: Fathers and friends, I am of the opinion expressed by my chief, who has just spoken. I wish him to go and see our great father.

Black Dog rose: My fathers and friends, Here is my chief; you have heard him speak; what he has said, I wish to be so. The land is the only good thing we have, and we are very poor. Our great father, you say, has sent you here, and you want our land for another nation. I suppose you owe them something, and wish to pay them with our land. Now, I believe our great father has much money; and if you owe these Indians any thing, pay them out of that money, and not with our land, which will make us poor and miserable. Fathers, I don't wish to touch the pen at this time. Here is our friend, Col. Chouteau; I wish to go with him and my chief to see our great father.

White Hair then rose, and said: My fathers and friends, you see we are not united; *Clermont* and other chiefs are not satisfied to leave their land. You have heard what *my* braves have said. I believe you come to do business in a correct way, and I don't want to change it. Here is our father, who has always been our friend. We selected him to help us with our treaty. What we have agreed upon, we want you to see to-day; then I have some other business which I want you to tell to my great father. But I want you to look at the paper, in the hands of our friend, (Col. Chouteau,) first, and I will then speak more.

Mr. Ellsworth spoke again, and said: Brothers, we will now propose a plan; that is, to make a treaty now, then you may go and see the land; if you like it, it is a treaty—if not, it is no treaty. If Clermont is satisfied with the land, he can go on it immediately, and need remove but once. And we wish to say to Clermont, that if he prevents this treaty, and goes on the reservations, he will be blamed for making his people unhappy. (He told Clermont he could not go to Washington, that his great father would send him back.)

Mr. Schermerhorn rose: Brothers of Osage nation, I rise only to let you know that I am of the same mind with my brother, on what he has said. The commissioners cannot grant Clermont's request to go to Washington. His great father has told him not to come—that it was a great distance, great expense, and we were sent to do all their business. It would look too much like children's play for him to go now, when we have been sent here. But we wish to preserve the peace and happiness of the Osage nation; and therefore, to remove all objections, we will make a conditional treaty; and if you then don't like the land we give you, it will be null and void. From what we have heard of the country, we are persuaded you will like it. The White Hair's people, and Little Osages, who lived there, are all willing to go.   We are therefore desirous that a treaty should be made at this time.

Mr. Ellsworth said: Brothers, I want to add one word more.   This is a very important matter.   You have all chosen one common friend, Colonel Chouteau; we advise you now to take his advice.

Lafolle again spoke: Fathers and friends, we have but a small piece of land now, and you come to buy it; we will not sell it.   You want to give us land further north, which every body knows is a poor country.   We don't want to speak further on the subject.

(After the same talk between the chiefs of the several bands, the council adjourned till afternoon.)

Afternoon of same day, council met.

Clermont spoke as follows: My fathers, I told you this forenoon that I thought a great deal of my land.   You say you will give me other land, but I don't want it; it is not good.   But if you want me to go and look at it, I will go.   You have promised my people something on the land you offer. If it is not good, will you give us what you offer, *for our benefit,* on the land we now live on; that is, on our reservations?

White Hair rose: My fathers, we have been talking together many days. I approve of what the chief has just said.   I think it good that we should look at the land together.   If we do not find it good, I want to know whether you will give us, on our present reservation, what we will demand of you in reply to your offer.   When we look at the land, we will make a treaty, if we find it good.

(Several other chiefs spoke; and it was agreed that the reply to the propositions made by the commissioners should be read.)

Col. Chouteau then rose, and presented the reply of White Hair's band, Little Osages, and others, to the propositions of the commissioners, read in council on the 15th instant.   The reply was read by the Secretary, as follows:

Answers to the Propositions of the United States Commissioners to the Osage nation.

*Proposition No.* 1 *and* 2.

Answer. The Osage nation agree to change and remove from their present reservation, provided the United States agree to convey to them, by patent, in fee simple, a country embraced within the following boundaries: "Beginning at the northeast corner of their present reservation, and run up and along the northern boundary of said reservation, until it strikes the Arkansas river; thence up and along said river to the Mexican line; thence along said Mexican line to a point where a due east course would strike the southwestern corner of the Kansas country; thence down the south boundary line of the Kansas country to where the same intersects the country occupied by the Shawnees; thence south of the western boundary of the Shawnees to the southwest corner thereof; thence due east along the southern boundary of the Shawness, until it strikes the northwest corner of the Pi-an-ke-shaw country; thence, running along the western boundary thereof, to its southwest corner; thence east, along said Pi-an-ke-shaw land, five miles, or to a point where a line due south will strike the place of beginning."

Should the Osage nation hereafter agree to divide the country hereby ceded or assigned to them, among individuals of the tribe, the Government shall grant a patent, in fee simple, to each individual for his share of land, in such manner and form as property is now vested in citizens of the United States.

### Proposition No. 3.

Answer. The Osages agree to accept the proposition to furnish houses for their four principal chiefs, equal, in value, to those they at present occupy, in accordance with the treaty of 1825. The United States will be required to pay for all improvements abandoned by the Osage nation, in consequence of their proposed removal, as well as the improvements heretofore abandoned by the band of Mo-na-pa-chy, who are to receive the valuation as already made. The Osages agree to the proposition of the commissioners to provide a comfortable house for the widow of White Hair; provided that a house of equal value to the widows of Clermont, Tally, Mona-pa-chy, and Thom-ga-mon-no, who were principal chiefs of the Osage nation, and have died since the treaty of 1825. They were all " firm in their attachment to the Government of the United States," and valuable as chiefs and counsellors to the Osage nation. The remaining part of proposition No. 3 is agreed to.

### Proposition and Article No. 4.

Answer. The Osages agree to proposition No. 4, to wit: That each chief or principal warrior that agrees to cultivate the soil shall be entitled to a yoke of cattle and farming utensils, and have a comfortable house erected to live in; and to receive in addition, provided a settlement is formed of fifty families or lodges, agricultural implements and stock to the value of two thousand dollars; likewise, four ox-carts, with four yoke of oxen, for each settlement; and a proportionable amount, if the families are greater or less than fifty.

The commissioners will perceive that the only alteration or change in this article is the word "*warrior*," and providing the ox-carts and oxen for the same. The Osage nation believe that the remaining part of the fourth article, providing farmers and mechanics, is too indefinite in its propositions. They require, in lieu of the proposition made by the commissioners, that twelve farmers shall be employed at the expense of the Government, for a period of ten years, or longer, if the President of the United States believes the necessity of the Osages should require it; and that there shall be employed, in addition to those already employed, for a like period with the farmers, three blacksmiths and one gunsmith. That houses and shops shall be erected for that purpose; the shops to be supplied with tools, iron, steel, and coal, and other materials necessary to carry on the same. Twelve mechanics shall be employed, at the expense of the United States, to assist in erecting the buildings provided for by this treaty, as well as to instruct the young men of the Osage nation who may be desirous of instruction in the mechanic arts; these mechanics to be employed for five years, or longer, at the discretion of the President of the United States.

The Osages accept of the eight patent railway mills and saw-mills, as proposed by the commissioners. The said mills to be erected immediately after their removal, and to be made by a mill-wright who is perfectly mas-

29‡

ter of his trade; and that competent hands be employed to superintend the same for five years. There shall also be provided by the Government, for the exclusive use of the saw-mills, a substantial ox-cart, with two yoke of oxen; and that houses shall be erected for the millers to reside in.

### Proposition or Article 5.

Answer. That part of the proposition relating to education purposes, stipulated for by the treaty of 1825, wherein fifty-four sections of land are reserved, the Indians assent to; but they believe their nation would be more benefited by receiving the two thousand dollars proposed to be appropriated for education purposes annually, until the reservations are sold, in articles of food and clothing; they therefore do not desire that the appropriation should be made.

### Proposition or Article 6.

Answer. The Osages agree to receive the $10,000 proposed by the commissioners for the expenses of their removal, in addition to $4,000 proposed to be given to them now; which they consider and receive as an evidence of the kind feelings of the United States toward the Osage nation, and which is to be delivered to them in merchandise at the signing of the treaty, and three thousand bushels of corn, to be delivered at the same time.

### Proposition and Article 7.

Answer. The Osages agree to this article, provided the United States agree to pay the just claims of other Indian tribes, and citizens of the U. States and Territories, that may have been incurred since the treaty of 1825. The validity of such claims to be decided by the United States Commissioners.

The Osage nation acknowlege to be justly indebted to their friend and brother Colonel Auguste P. Chouteau the sum of $3,000, which he has been kind enough to credit them, to keep their wives and children from perishing; and having no means to discharge the said debt, they require that the United States shall pay the same to the said A. P. Chouteau immediately upon the ratification of this treaty.

### Proposition or Article 8.

Answer. To satisfy the views of the United States, as well as to benefit their nation, the Osage chiefs agree to cancel their perpetual annuity of $1,500 by the payment of $3,000 annually by the United States for and during the space of twenty years, from and after the ratification by the President of this treaty, provided the annuity of $7,000, secured to them by their treaty with the United States made at St. Louis in 1825, be continued for the like period of twenty years, from and after the ratification of the aforesaid treaty, instead of computing it from the ratification of the aforesaid treaty. The Osage nation believe that justice and humanity will sanction this demand of an increased annuity, for the sacrifices they are about to make in giving up the last home of their fathers.

These annuities to be paid in stock, farming implements, merchandise, or money, at the option of the Indians; to be delivered at the Osage agency, at the risk and expense of the United States Government.

### Article 9.

Answer. The Osages agree to this article.

Should the aforesaid propositions of the Osages be agreed to and complied
with by the commissioners of the United States, the Osages will hereafter
propose some of minor importance to the Government of the United States,
but of great importance to the Osage nation.

After the above was read, Messrs. Ellsworth and Schermerhorn expressed their surprise that propositions so extravagant should be made, and said
they had no reply to make to them.

Governor Stokes rose, and said: Brothers of the Osage nation, we have
been here near thirty days in council, attempting to make a treaty, and a
considerable portion of your nation seem unwilling to treat on any terms.
We never saw these propositions till this moment, and we wish you to
meet us to-morrow at your camp, at 10 o'clock in the morning, when we
will talk further on the subject.

Adjourned till 10 A. M. to-morrow.

Wednesday, March 27, 1833, council did not convene, and agreed to
meet to-morrow morning at 10 o'clock.

Thursday, March 28, council met at Osage camp: all present.

Governor Stokes said: Brothers of the Osage nation, we meet you now
for the last time to convince you that we part as friends; my brother commissioners will say something to you, after which we will present you with
some medals of your great father, as a token of his friendship.

Mr. Schermerhorn then addressed the council as follows:

Brothers of the Osage nation: We have now been a whole month in council since we met you at the Saline. We informed you that your great
father had directed us to propose to you an exchange of your present reservation for lands a little north of you, so as to join your country with the
Kanzas, your younger brothers. Your great father, to effect this, consulted
your best interests, as well as that of all his red children. He has felt for
you and your women and children in their present condition, and has therefore offered to treat with you on the most generous and liberal terms, as the
treaty we have proposed to you fully shows. It appears from your talks
that about two out of three men have been willing to treat, viz., White Hair,
Little Osage, and Big Hill; but that Clermont and his followers were opposed,
first, because they would not remove on their reservation; and now, because they will remove no further. We think the main difficulty in refusing to treat was owing to the jealousies and oppositions among yourselves.
Some of you now tell us for the first time, that you will not treat on any
terms, until you examine the land with us; but the Little Osages, who know
the land well, and have heretofore lived on it, are still anxious to treat, as
also many of White Hair's people. But your great father does not wish to
treat with a part of the Osage nation, to make your divisions greater, but
with the whole, so that you may be more united than ever. He wishes to
heal your divisions and reconcile your difficulties, and not to increase them;
and therefore we cannot treat with you now.

It appears, however, that after having told us that you would not treat
with us on any conditions without viewing the land, that you and your
friend, Colonel A. P. Choutou, have had our propositions under consideration, and that you have so materially varied the very liberal offers of your
great father that no doubt he will be surprised to hear of it. We do not
want to deceive you, and therefore say to you, stay on your reservation until you are convinced that it is best for you to listen to and follow the

council of your great father.  We shall go and see the land before long, and you may also examine it if you think proper.  And when you are ready to accept the offers of your great father, you may tell us through your agent, and we will appoint a time to meet you.

You were told at the Saline, that if you would come to this place you should be well supplied with provisions, and that you need not be afraid here of the soldiers, and that while here you should be protected, and unmolested on your way home.  What we have said shall stand good; you shall not be detained or punished here.  But remember that by your treaties you are still accountable for all the violence and depredations you have committed, and you must answer for them.  Your great father will not suffer any of his own people or his red children to injure you, neither will he any longer permit you to injure them.  Your great father wishes you to cease from war and plunder, and to live in peace with all men, and it must be so.  He has said he will protect his people and all his red children, and he will do it.

If you have anything to say to us on any other subject we will hear you.

The chiefs said they had nothing more to say about making a treaty.

Governor Stokes then presented medals to the principal chiefs.  In placing the ribbon around the necks of the chiefs, Governor Stokes said: "This medal bears the likeness of your great father, the President of the United States.  It is given to you as a token of his friendship for you.  Wear it next your heart, and when you look at it, remember that he is your best friend."

After delivering some presents to the chiefs and principal braves, the council adjourned, *sine die.*

S. C. STAMBAUGH,
*Sec'y. Com. Indian Affairs.*

FORT GIBSON, *April* 2, 1833.

*Commissioner's Office.*

SIR: The department has been duly apprized of the council commenced with the Osages at the Saline, and the reason of adjournment to this garrison.  It only remains for the commissioners to communicate the progress since their return, and the result of their deliberations.

In conformity with our instructions, we consulted Col. A. P. Chouteau (as well as his brother the agent) as to the course to be pursued to obtain the object of the Government, and requested Col. Chouteau to aid the commissioners in effecting a treaty.  Col. Chouteau has long been the great friend and counsellor of the Osage nation, and the unlimited influence the Chouteaus seemed to possess over the nation, together with the assurance of a belief that a treaty could be made, induced the commissioners to intrust the management of the nation principally to them.  Indeed, such is their influence, that it would be difficult, if not impracticable, to make a treaty against their opinion.

The commissioners explained very fully the views and wishes of the Government, respecting the removal of the Osages to the land adjoining the Kanzas.  About two thirds of the nation appeared willing to treat.  The remaining one third, composed of Clermont's band, opposed making any treaty.  At first they declared their unwillingness to remove at all from their present residence, which is about fifty miles south of their reservation; and when they were told most positively that they must remove from their present village, they objected going farther north than their reservation, because the land we offered them was poor and unfit for cultivation. All those who live on the reservation were willing to leave it and make a treaty, and we were not a little surprised, that since it was about as easy for Clermont's band to locate themselves on the land we offered as on the reservation, that they should be alone to raise objections, and refuse the benefit we propose to confer upon them.

The commissioners, desirous to make amicable arrangements with all the bands, did not deem it advisable to conclude a treaty against the respectable minority of one third of the nation. Neither did the commissioners feel willing to abandon the hope of making a treaty hereafter, should it be deemed expedient. They, therefore, in order to remove the objections made by the minority, as well as to unite the nation in common consent, proposed to the Osages to examine the land offered, during the summer; to consider the proposition we had made; and if they should then desire to make the terms we have given the basis of a treaty, that they could notify us of their wishes. The commissioners beg leave to mention a few facts, in further explanation of the duration and consequent expense of the council. The Osages are a poor, almost naked and half starved people. The unexampled freshets in the fall swept away most of the corn and vegetables they had stored up for winter's use. The number of Osages is estimated by the agent at 6,000, and all but Requoius's band were suffering from the want of food when the council was called. This circumstance, connected with the deep interest felt in the issue of the meeting, brought together a larger number to be fed at the public expense than the commissioners had expected; and yet it may not be so much regretted that so many attended to divide the responsibility, when it is considered, that the sustenance of those here left a better supply for those at home.

The rations were issued daily upon the requisition of the agent, Major Chouteau, as he estimated their necessities. The commissioners have informed the department on the adjournment of the council, that there was a large quantity of provisions in the garrison, which would be sacrificed at auction, unless distributed to the Indians. The delay attending the council arose from several causes.

The Osage tribe have been divided by many jealousies and private feuds; some of the bands have lived quite remote, and Clermont's band has indulged a hope that Government would permit them to remain in their present village. Great rivalry as to rank has existed in the nation, and when all the bands were represented at the council, it was a matter of contest who should be head chief.

After the commissioners had made their proposition, an answer was requested. The Osages, with entire unanimity, appointed Col. Chouteau to act as their counsellor and adviser. Col. Chouteau, although he withheld the answer to our propositions until the close of the council, and after Clermont's band stated they would not treat at present, and assured the commissioners that the Osages had not demanded more in addition than what he believed the Government would readily allow, the commissioners could not but be surprised at the manifest difference when the answer was given. The demands of the Osages, although made, it is supposed, under expectation of some modifications, were altogether beyond what the commissioners expected, after the declaration of Mr. Chouteau. The quantity of land demanded was inadmissible, and the increase of annuities was directly in contravention of our instructions, which had been made known to Col. Chouteau. The additional annuity of $7,000, demanded for seven years, is made conditional upon the commutation of the perpetual annuity of $1,500. But the commissioners believe their offer to commute the perpetual annuity was sufficiently liberal. The commissioners regret not having been instructed more fully upon the principles which the department might deem equitable in the commutation of perpetual annuities. This subject is one of vast importance to the Indians, as well as to the Government. The offer of the commissions, after much deliberation, was made upon the basis of a four per cent. stock. Hence, the perpetual annuity of $1,500 is worth $37,500 in cash. The offer we made rejecting fractions was $3,000 annually for twenty years. Our instructions required us to extinguish, if practicable, the reservations of the Osages in the country allotted to the Cherokees. The purchase and possession of these reservations, by white people, at high speculative prices, together with the fact, that most of them are now under the control of Col. Chouteau, (the Osage counsellor,) induced the commissioners to avoid any connexion of the purchase of the reservations with the treaty. The reservations, it is supposed, must be considered (although obtained under a general treaty as private property) and can be disposed of without the consent of the Osage nation. When the proper time arrives to notify the holders of the invalidity of their purchase, and the impracticability of white citizens improving the lands, it is hoped that more equitable terms can be obtained for a relinquishment of the legal title. The commissioners informed the Cherokees that the Osage reservations were protected under the Cherokee treaty. To this opinion of the commissioners no objection was made by the Cherokees. The commissioners, however, told the Cherokees the Government were willing to extinguish the same, if hereafter it could be done on reasonable terms. If the eastern Cherokees remove, there will be a very favorable time to accommodate the principal chiefs with valuable locations on these reservations. Before, however, any thing is settled respecting the extinguishment of these reservations, or the commutation of the perpetual annuities, the commissioners anticipate the pleasure of a personal interview with the department, if practicable, or a further correspondence on these and several other very important subjects. The commissioners would only add, that the depredations of the Osages the past year have been very great, and if an indemnity is made by the Government, and charged to the annuity, the nation would be deprived of any payment for several years. The exhibition of the late military force of infantry and rangers at this garrison, during the Osage encampment, will, it is hoped, be productive of beneficial effects, especially as no opportunity was lost to advise the Osages, and warn them against the inevitable consequence of their unlawful conduct. The condition and improvement of this suffering tribe will receive the greatest consideration of the commissioners.

Very respectfully,<br>
Your obedient servants,<br>
MONTFORT STOKES.<br>
HENRY L. ELLSWORTH.<br>
J. F. SCHERMERHORN.

Hon. Lewis Cass, *Secretary of War.*

HIGHTOWER, FORSYTH, GA , *May* 6, 1833.

DEAR SIR: Necessity compels me to write to you on a subject which I had for some time omitted to do, under a belief that the circumstances which this letter will refer to would have been settled by Major Currey, the superintendent of Indian removals; but he has given me to understand that such could not be done, and I will here state the facts to you as they occurred, and rely on your department that justice will done.  John Downing, a half-blooded Cherokee, held in his possession near thirty negro slaves, part his own, but mostly belonging to two orphan nephews, which he also had charge of.  Some white men, there can be but little doubt from selfish motives, took it on themselves to administer on the estate of these orphan children, under the laws of Georgia.  I apprehend that the administrators intended to secure to themselves the whole of this property, as Indians could not be a party in court against white persons, by the laws of Georgia, and, consequently, could not recover their property by law.  I gave security for the delivery of the property to the administrators, in case the court sustained their administration, and returned the negroes, after they were seized on, to their proper owners.  An appeal was taken to the superior court, and before a decision was had, by authority of Major Currey, I enrolled Downing and the orphan children for Arkansas, and they and their property was removed to the west, except a negro girl, which was mortgaged to Ezekiel Beck, a mixed blooded Cherokee of respectable character and intelligence, for one hundred dollars.  Beck, being alarmed at the administration as above stated, removed the girl in that part of the Cherokee nation which lies in Alabama.  After the excitement about the administration had somewhat subsided, and the removal of the balance of Downing's negroes, this girl was brought back to this neighborhood.  Some short time before the court had decided on the legality of the administration, I advised Beck, if the administration was sustained, he had better remove the property out of the State.  Shortly after my interview with Beck, his uncle, Mr. Samuel Martin, from within the limits of Tennessee, was at Beck's house, and it was thought advisable that Martin should take the girl home with him, until the difficulty about Downing's property should be adjusted.  On the road, Major Currey met Martin with the negro girl.  The major informed me that he supposed all was not right, and he seized the girl and brought her to my house.  No remuneration had been made to Beck for the one hundred dollars loaned, for which he held a kind of mortgage on the negro.  Not many days after the negro was left at my house Beck came, apparently distressed that he had no security from the laws of Georgia, or the authorities of the United States.  I could not but sympathize for his condition, and I paid him fifty dollars which I had collected for Downing, and fifty dollars of my own money, believing that the Government would not remove the property until all just claims against it had first been settled; but it was removed without any regard to the lien held on the property by the mortgage, and no steps were taken by law to detain the property, as full faith was placed in the rectitude of the Government of the United States and its officers.  I advanced the money without the smallest interest to myself.  I did so solely to secure justice to an aggrieved man that knew not where to look for redress, and to sustain the good faith of the Government under whom I had been acting as enrolling and valuing agent.  You will please to excuse the length of my letter; I have stated all the particulars in order that all might be fairly understood. I only ask to be remunerated for the fifty dollars I advanced of my own money; and ask of you the favor to examine all the facts in regard to this business, and inform me of your determination relative thereto.

I am, &c.,

JACOB M. SCUDDER.

Hon. Lewis Cass,
 *Secretary of War.*

---

MILLEDGEVILLE, *May* 11, 1833.

Sir: I arrived at this place yesterday evening, having continued, without intermission, with the same mail wh ch left Washington with me. Hearing, on the road, that a convention was sitting at Milledgeville, I considered it too favorable an opportunity to be lost, for a diffusion of Judge Herring's explanation of his letter in relation to the Cherokees, and therefore persevered with the mail.

Soon after my arrival I saw Judge Wayne and General Thompson, of Congress. The former is president of the convention. He went with me this morning to see Governor Lumpkin, to whom I delivered the papers you had entrusted to me. He was much gratified with their contents, and remarked, that he had been so thoroughly impressed with the conviction that the letter of Judge Herring was never intended to have the meaning which had been given to it, that he had already pledged himself in letters and conversation to that effect, and he was now highly gratified in finding himself correct. He considered the explanation as in good time to prevent any serious effect from the first letter, as the Cherokee council did not sit until the 20th, and he would himself take some measures for diffusing a knowledge of the explanation.

I find it will be in my power to procure any facilities, in relation to funds, through the medium of the bank at Columbus.

There are many gentlemen here, at present, of intelligence, and well acquainted with Creek affairs, with several of whom I have had conversations. While they do not entirely discourage all hopes of making a treaty for the reservations, they, however, rather doubt our success.

The supposed Indian rights to these reservations have been purchased to a great extent, and the interest of these purchasers is opposed to a treaty, as it would oust them of their speculation. It is this interest with which we have to contend, and which is represented as formidable, from its influence over the Indians.

I shall leave this place to-morrow for Columbus.

I have the honor, &c.,

JOHN J. ABERT,
 *Lieut. Col. and Special Commissioner.*

Hon. Lewis Cass,
 *Secretary of War.*

---

ARKANSAS TERRITORY, NEW GASCONY, QUAPAW AGENCY,
 *May* 13, 1833.

RESPECTED SIR: This day Mr. Schermerhorn, United States Conmmissioner, entered into a supplementary treaty with the Quapaw tribe of Indians. He has given them, on the part of the Government, liberal terms. It had become necessary that they should be permanently settled, as many of them have been deprived of their improvements by the white settlers. In no instance were the whites the purchasers of the lands, as most of the land on which the Indians were settled had not been surveyed. Major Eaton, when Secretary of War, in a letter to Heckatoo, the head chief of the nation, wrote to him in the following words: "Your great father will suffer you to remain where you are until his white children shall want the land, or until a suitable country can be provided." The Indians are reduced to a very deplorable condition, and, I trust, are entitled to your fatherly care and protection. They have frequently requested me to appeal directly to you, as the father of the great American family, to see that something like justice should be done them. They transferred to the United States something like forty millions of acres of land, for a very small consideration, and have not, at this time, one foot of land on earth. By the treaty of 1825, the Quapaws were to be united with, and become a part of the Caddo tribe of Indians. They say that the Caddos refused to receive them into, or to extend to them any of the privileges of the tribe; that they assigned them a piece of land on Red river, that was subject to frequent overflow; that their crops were universally destroyed; that they were reduced to a perfect state of starvation; that many of the tribe literally starved to death. On the score of policy the Government will profit by the exchange, and their removal west of the Missouri line, or territorial line, or into the country set apart for the permanent settlement of the Indians, for the reason that the Red river country is well adapted to the raising of cotton, and when reclaimed, by the removal of the raft, will afford a dense white population. The Indians of course would be pressed to move, and would eventually be driven off. If an arrangement could be effected with the Mexican Government, so that the line would commence at latitude 32, on the Sabine, and take that parallel of latitude to a point where a due north course would strike the 100th degree of west longitude (from the city of London) on Red river, or the 23d west longitude from the city of Washington, the entire settlement in the now called Arkansas would be secured to the Territory, as well as a good sugar and cotton country would be added to our country.

By the approbation of Governor Pope, and under his written approval, and full powers from the chiefs of the Quapaw tribe of Indians, I visited Cantonment Gibson, in order to effect an arrangement with the commissioners for a permanent settlement of the Indians. I was received by the commissioners with kindness, and resided with them during my stay at the cantonment. Governor Stokes is a popular, and eminently qualified as a business man. He stands well with the officers and with the Indians in general.

Mr. Schermerhorn is perhaps as well qualified as any man in the Union, and is entirely devoted to business, and has collected and embodied a great deal of useful information, that I doubt not will be pleasing and satisfactory to your excellency when he makes his report. He is your personal and political friend. Colonel Stambaugh was very sick when he arrived here. Mr. Schermerhorn advised him to continue in the boat, as he might find it necessary to call in good medical aid.

Governor Stokes informed Mr. Schermerhorn that he would come on to

30‡

hold the treaty, but should any event transpire that would make it necessary to change his course, that he would sign any treaty that he might make.

There is one other small matter that much concerns myself. I would ask it as a favor, that your excellency would still extend to me your friendship, and that you will not suffer me to be removed in any future arrangement with the Indians.

I remain, with high regard,
Your excellency's
Most obliged humble servant,
RICHARD M. HANNUM.

To his Excellency ANDREW JACKSON,
*President of the United States.*

---

EXECUTIVE DEPARTMENT, MILLEDGEVILLE, *May* 13, 1833.

SIR: I have the honor to acknowledge the receipt of your letter of the 2d instant, together with the copies of the letters therein referred to, by the hand of Colonel Abert.

The course which you have adopted, and the means which you have afforded, to correct the false impressions which have been made upon the minds of the Cherokees and other deluded persons, meets my approbation, and is highly satisfactory.

I have made arrangements which will accomplish the desirable objects of having the contents of these papers made known to the Cherokees who may assemble in council. Moreover, with a view of correcting the misrepresentations which have been made, through the press and other channels, I shall take the liberty of having these communications laid before the public (i. e. your official letter, together with copies of the letters of Mr. Herring to the agents of the United States and the Cherokees). Under all the circumstances, I trust you will concur with me in regard to the propriety of the publication of these official letters. My agent, General Glasscock, who will attend the Cherokee council, will report to me the result; immediately after which you may expect to hear from me on the subject of our Cherokee affairs; and, if necessary, you shall have my views fully on the subject of emigration.

I have the honor to be,
Very respectfully,
Your obedient servant,
WILSON LUMPKIN.

Hon. LEWIS CASS,
*Secretary of War.*

---

MOBILE, *May* 13, 1833.

SIR: Your letter, directing that the investigation of claims, according to the treaty with the Creek Indians, should be transmitted by the mail, and that I should expedite that and the census, I had the honor to receive, after some delay, and immediately wrote to Major Abbott, requesting him to forward the work of the board of commissioners; and to Majors Abbott and Parsons, urging them to complete and forward the census as soon as possible.

Major Abbott wrote me, that upon the 4th of April he had, from Fort Mitchell, forwarded the operations of the commissioners, and that the census would soon follow.

The taking the census was, I believe, very troublesome; the ignorance of the Indians, their dispersed situation, habits, and the inclement winter, had occasioned much unavoidable delay.

I was astonished to learn from Major Abbott, that Colonel Crowell might have communicated your wishes to Abbott much sooner than I, who was upwards of two hundred miles from the place of investigation. When you shall have examined the facts disclosed before the board of commissioners, and by them to you, I hope you will perceive that there is good reasons for many of the requests made by the Upper Town chiefs, as to the payment of monies to their nation.

In Majors Parsons, Abbott, and myself, the Indians generally appeared to have some confidence, which, I hope, was not misplaced. I presume some of the Indians and whites concerned in particular matters may complain of us, but I hope the department will see we were endeavoring to do our duty to all concerned.

I have the honor to be, &c.,

ENOCH PARSONS.

E. Herring, Esq.,
*Commissioner of Indian Affairs, Washington.*

P. S. Major Parsons was compelled to retake the census in nine towns, to avoid frauds attempted to be practised upon him.

E. P.

———

Columbus, Georgia, *May*, 1833.

Sir: I have the honor to report, that that portion of the census of the Creek tribe of Indians which, after a division of the nation between Major B. S. Parsons and myself, it devolved on me to take, was completed early in January last, and is to be found in part second of the book or roll herewith forwarded, comprising a list of the heads of families, and enumeration of the population of what is denominated the Lower Towns. The division of country after this manner was made at the instance, and in consequence of the wish both of Gen. E. Parsons and of my coadjutor in the business, Major B. S. Parsons, to whom it appeared preferable; to the latter gentleman I also conceded the choice of divisions, who selected for himself the Upper Towns. The result of his labors, which are just completed, will be seen in part first of the book above alluded to.

A comparison of rolls being required, and Major Parsons being desirous that my work should be connected and appear under the same cover with his, I was necessarily detained some days after his was copied, in transcribing and transferring mine into the same book, and performing other acts essential for the completion of the whole.

In the performance of the duty entrusted to me by the department, I have endeavored, as impartially and conscientiously as possible, to carry into effect the instructions of the department transmitted for my guidance in the same, on the one hand vigilantly laboring to protect the rights of the Government, and preserve them from fraud, and on the other, likewise, con-

ceding to the tribe whatsoever might be made appear its due.  Owing to
the blended ignorance, credulity, and cunning of the natives, and schemes
of greedy speculators, the task has not been unattended by trouble or difficulty; but I trust, from the much care bestowed by me, I have succeeded
in the completion of it as happily as circumstances would allow.

I have likewise spent particular pains upon the orthography of the Indian
names, and in all instances used such letters in the spelling of them as would
perfectly express their sound, dividing them into syllables according to their
own mode of articulation, so as to insure, with ordinary attention, a proper,
or at least an intelligible pronunciation.  I have also avoided as much as
possible, the repetition of the like names in the same town, and to this end
have sometimes, with all the solemnity attendant on the ceremony, caused
the individual publicly and by the proper authority, to be named anew.
The name thus given is acknowledged by the party, and assumed as a war
name, by which he is even afterwards known and recognized.

I deem it necessary to refer the department to the case of Benjamin Marshall, United States interpreter for the Creek Indians; it is noted in page sixty
of part second, or census of the Lower Towns.  I would also state that there
are four or five cases of persons advanced in life, of both sexes, widows and
widowers, who have raised families, have still their own separate houses and
fields, and labor for themselves in their management and occupation, but
who, owing to the growth and marriage, or separate settlement of their
families, are left without any *permanent inmate* of their dwellings.  The
few persons thus circumstanced I enrolled, under the impression that they
came within the *spirit* and *meaning*, if not the *express* letter of my instructions, that it could not have been the intention of the department that
on such grounds they should be expelled in the evening of their life, helpless and destitute, from the home which was their only shelter, and which
had, perhaps, from infancy afforded them an asylum.  If, however, this
had been an error of judgment on my part, and the department will please
to inform me of it, I will furnish the names and notes of the cases, which
can then be erased.

In making out the roll of the principal chiefs, from the lists furnished me
by what is *styled the authorities of the tribe*, I found that the names of
forty-four only, instead of forty-five, to which number the lower towns are
entitled, were reported.  To have convened a council and procured the appointment of another at that protracted season, would have been the cause of
much delay.  I therefore thought it preferable respectfully to suggest to
the department a mode of supplying the omission which would obviate this
inconvenience, and which the tribe itself would readily acquiesce in, that is,
to fill the vacancy with one of three pretermitted chiefs, left out by a *few*
of the leading men from personal and invidious motives.  The names of
these three are John O-pou-ne, (of Che-haw-aw,) Col. John Stedham, (of
So-woe-o-lo,) and Tom-ac-micco, (of Thla-katch-ka.)

It was reported at Se-char-le-char, (the council at which the principal
chiefs were designated and chosen,) that the before named chiefs were in favor of a speedy emigration of the tribe west of the Mississippi, and were
exerting their influence amongst their respective people to inspire them with
sentiments favorable to the same.  This pretence was employed to excite a
prejudice against them, and was one of the means resorted to by *those* interested in keeping the tribe in their present residence to procure their exclusion.  They are all three men of influence, and have each of them some

claim to the favor of Government. To John O-pou-ne I feel under much obligation for the timely assistance lent me by him in procuring an interpreter after the death of Charles Scott, a half-breed, and the first employed by me. Scott and myself were much exposed to inclemency of weather; had oftentimes to pass streams, not fordable, by swimming, and to undergo many privations. Though a young and remarkably robust man, and inured by habit to hardship, he sunk under it, and after a short illness, thus prematurely and unexpectedly, became the silent tenant of the tomb. At this crisis, when it was all-important that I should have an interpreter capable, and that could be relied on, through the agency of O-pou-ne I was furnished with one whom I afterwards retained throughout, until the enumeration of the lower towns was completed. This service, rendered under such circumstances to me, I place upon the footing of a *public service*, and, therefore, present his claim first to supply the place of the forty-fifth chief. Col. John Stedham served in the army during the Creek war for some space of time, and had under his command a company of friendly Indians. He was at the affair of Kalebee under General Floyd, and at one or two others with the Seminoles. Tom-ac-micco also was at Washington in the winter of 1832, and composed one of the delegation who negotiated the treaty at that time, and is one of the signers of it. I would further suggest, that if the department deemed it proper to bestow upon *each* of the *three* an additional half section of land, the attempted injury against them would be repaired at comparatively trifling cost, and the malice of their enemies likewise disappointed.

I would conclude by stating that I left Tuscaloosa, my place of residence, on the 30th day of August, 1832, and have continued from that time to the present (two hundred and fifty-seven days, inclusive) in the service of the department, either engaged in the taking of the census of the Creek tribe, (i. e. the lower towns,) or in the capacity of secretary to the board of commissioners, &c., in the following manner, viz: about nine days at We-tum-ka: during the Indian council there in September last, I was employed in the capacity of secretary; also from the 7th January to 4th of April inclusive, (a space of eighty-eight days,) at which time the papers connected with the proceedings of the commissioners at Fort Mitchell, at the council held there in January and part of February last, were completed and forwarded to Washington; and from that date to the present in aiding Major Parsons in the completion of his work in the upper towns, and doing whatsoever remained to complete my own. To this is to be added all the previous time, the nine days at We-tum-ka excepted, which shows the exact time employed, particularly in each species of engagement, to wit: whole time employed from 30th August, 1832, to 13th May, 1833, two hundred and fifty-seven days, inclusive. The time employed as secretary at We-tum-ka, nine days, and at Fort Mitchell, eighty-eight days, making an aggregate of ninety-seven days, being deducted, leaves one hundred and sixty days; so that the time devoted to the taking of the census of the lower towns by me, and in aid of Major Parsons in the upper, amounts to  -  -  -  -  160 days
The time spent as secretary, to  -  -  -  -  97  do
                                                            ―――
Whole time  -  -  -  -  -  -  257  do

In my account, which is enclosed in form, not having any other basis whereon to found a charge, I have inserted the amount of the sum recommended to be allowed by the commissioners in their report, in consideration of the unremitted and severe labors which devolved upon me while acting as secretary, to wit, five dollars per day, and my expenses for board, &c. while thus engaged. If this sum is not such as may be allowed, the department will please alter and fix the rate at its pleasure.

I have also enclosed receipts for money paid to interpreters, including the whole hire of horses, finding provisions, &c., and defraying all other expenses incidental.

The department will please accept the tender of my thanks for their confidence in the bestowal of my former appointment, and should I have been sufficiently fortunate to have merited approbation in the manner in which I have discharged the duties of it, it will be a source of no inconsiderable gratification.

A draft for the amount of what may be found accruing to me, if forwarded to my address in Tuscaloosa, will, upon its arrival, to which place I am now hastening, and where I shall remain until I hear from the department, find me there.

Should the department have further use for my services, and be pleased in any capacity to require them, I should feel both happy and grateful for the further continuation and extension of its patronage. In the interim, permit me to subscribe myself,

Sir, very respectfully,
Your obedient humble servant,
THOS. J. ABBOTT.

Hon. LEWIS CASS,
*Secretary of War.*

# CENSUS OF CREEK NATION, EAST.

PART FIRST—TAKEN BY BENJAMIN S. PARSONS.

———

*Census of the principal Chiefs and Heads of Families of the Creek tribe of Indians, taken by virtue of the second article of the treaty concluded with that tribe at the City of Washington, March 24, 1832.*

| Names of the principal Chiefs. | Males. | Females. | Slaves. | Total. |
|---|---|---|---|---|
| **TUCKABATCHA TOWN.** | | | | |
| Juskenehaw | 1 | 1 | 10 | 12 |
| Hopoeithto Yoholo | 2 | 2 | 3 | 7 |
| Little Doctor | 4 | 2 | 8 | 14 |
| Mad Blue | 2 | 2 | – | 4 |
| Tuckabatcha Micco | 3 | 4 | 4 | 11 |
| Micco Buccar, or Old King | 2 | 1 | 1 | 4 |
| Tustunnugga | 2 | 1 | – | 3 |
| Nehawlocco Chopco | 1 | 1 | – | 2 |
| O. Sooch E. Micco | 3 | 3 | – | 6 |
| Ogillisa | 3 | 3 | – | 6 |
| Fushatchche Micco | 2 | 1 | – | 3 |
| Choquartla Fixico | 3 | 5 | – | 8 |
| Siash Yoholo | 1 | 3 | – | 4 |
| Bob Cornels | 2 | 1 | – | 3 |
| Sitckey Cornoles | 2 | 3 | – | 5 |
| Tom Martth Micco | 1 | 1 | – | 2 |
| Ahloc E. Yoholo | 2 | 1 | – | 3 |
| Tusconic Fixicco | 3 | 2 | 1 | 6 |
| Tussicke Holatta | 3 | 4 | – | 7 |
| David Barnard | 2 | 2 | 4 | 8 |
| | 44 | 43 | 31 | 105 |
| **TALLISEE TOWN.** | | | | |
| Tustanuggachopco | 3 | 1 | - | 4 |
| **CLEWWATHLA TOWN.** | | | | |
| Jim Boy | 2 | 5 | 5 | 12 |
| Sangty Micco | 2 | 2 | - | 4 |
| **HATCHACHUBBA TOWN.** | | | | |
| Hatchachachubba Tom | 3 | 5 | 1 | 9 |

CREEK CENSUS—Continued.

| Names of the principal Chiefs. | Males. | Females. | Slaves. | Total. |
|---|---|---|---|---|
| HICKORY GROUND TOWN. | | | | |
| William McGilvery - - | 2 | 1 | 25 | 28 |
| WEWOAKCAR TOWN. | | | | |
| Saughty Marlarhar - - - | 1 | 5 | - | 6 |
| WEGUFCAR TOWN. | | | | |
| Martawway Hargo - - | 1 | 2 | - | 3 |
| TOAKFARFCAR TOWN. | | | | |
| Neclepisa Hargo - - - | 2 | 1 | - | 3 |
| FISHPOND TOWN. | | | | |
| Tusconu Hargo - - - - | 2 | 4 | - | 6 |
| | 69 | 62 | 65 | 196 |
| KILIZA TOWN. | | | | |
| Spoak Oake Micco - - - | 3 | 2 | - | 5 |
| Quassad Hargo - - - - | 2 | 1 | - | 3 |
| UFOWLA TOWN. | | | | |
| Soholo Micco - - - - | 1 | 1 | 2 | 4 |
| Octearche Micco - - - | 2 | 5 | - | 7 |
| OAKFUSKA TOWN. | | | | |
| Manawway - - - - | 4 | 2 | - | 6 |
| Cotcher Emarthla - - - | 2 | 5 | - | 7 |
| HILLABE TOWN. | | | | |
| Clathlo Hargo - - - - | 2 | 2 | - | 4 |
| POCON TALLAHASSEE TOWN. | | | | |
| Spoak Oak Hargo - - - | 2 | 4 | 5 | 11 |
| HEMANHIE TOWN. | | | | |
| Tustanuggachopco - - - | 1 | 2 | - | 3 |

CREEK CENSUS—Continued.

| Names of Principal Chiefs. | Males. | Females. | Slaves. | Total. |
|---|---|---|---|---|
| Poscoaf Emathlar        -        -        - | 1 | 4 | - | 5 |
| Hobie Fefico    -    -    -    - | 3 | 1 | - | 4 |
| **TALLADEGA TOWN.** | | | | |
| Coosa Fixico   -    -    -    - | 4 | 4 | - | 8 |
| Cussetau Harjo  -    -    -    - | 2 | 2 | - | 4 |
| **CHEHAW TOWN.** | | | | |
| Inhelanis Hargo      -     -      - | 2 | 1 | - | 3 |
| Salotta (alias Emarthlar Yoholo) -    - | 4 | 2 | - | 6 |
| Fushatch Fixico  -    -    -    - | 3 | 5 | - | 8 |
| | 38 | 43 | 7 | 88 |

# CENSUS OF HEADS OF FAMILIES.

| Names of Heads of Families. | Males. | Females. | Slaves. | Total. |
|---|---|---|---|---|
| **THOLL THLO COE TOWN.** | | | | |
| Osfodock Mico    -    -    -    - | 2 | 2 | - | 4 |
| Holie    -    -    -    - | 1 | 2 | - | 3 |
| Illis Hargo    -    -    - | 1 | 2 | - | 3 |
| Clath Thlo Hargo    -    -    - | 5 | 4 | - | 9 |
| Tin Thlanis Hargo    -    -    - | 1 | 2 | - | 3 |
| Nehar Hargo    -    -    -    - | 4 | 2 | - | 6 |
| Emarthloche    -    -    -    - | 2 | 6 | - | 8 |
| Ogede Yoholo    -    -    -    - | 2 | 1 | - | 3 |
| Hotulga Hargo    -    -    -    - | 1 | 3 | - | 4 |
| O Sooch Fixico    -    -    -    - | 2 | 3 | - | 5 |
| Spoak Oak Hargo    -    -    - | 2 | 2 | - | 4 |
| Tuskege Emarthlar    -    -    - | 4 | 2 | - | 6 |
| Nocosec Emarthlar    -    -    - | 2 | 1 | - | 3 |
| Old Homis    -    -    -    - | 1 | 1 | - | 2 |
| Purse    -    -    -    -    - | 2 | 1 | - | 3 |
| Ossee Yoholo    -    -    -    - | 1 | 2 | - | 3 |
| Toaf Tulga    -    -    -    - | 2 | 2 | - | 4 |
| Tockcasa Hargo    -    -    -    - | 2 | 3 | - | 5 |
| Wocksee Hollata    -    -    - | 2 | 1 | - | 3 |
| Tallise Fixico    -    -    -    - | 2 | 1 | - | 3 |
| Talma Clues Fixico    -    -    - | 4 | 2 | - | 6 |

## CREEK CENSUS—Continued.

| Names of Heads of Families. | Males. | Females. | Slaves. | Total. |
|---|---|---|---|---|
| Emarthlocheharney | 4 | 2 | - | 6 |
| Feishatch Yoholo | 1 | 2 | - | 3 |
| Hoakchon Yoholo | 1 | 1 | - | 2 |
| Hotulga Hargo | 2 | 3 | - | 5 |
| Luchi Yoholo | 1 | 2 | - | 3 |
| Conchart Hargo | 2 | 3 | - | 5 |
| Wattabe Yoholo | 1 | 3 | - | 4 |
| Nehemarthloche | 3 | 3 | - | 6 |
| Chawilla Hargo | 1 | 1 | - | 2 |
| Neharlocco Hargo | 3 | 1 | - | 4 |
| Lifiif Hargo | 3 | 2 | - | 5 |
| Ronif Hargo | 3 | 2 | - | 5 |
| Ardock Hargo | 1 | 1 | - | 2 |
| Inho Mattahothlaboga | 6 | 3 | - | 9 |
| Tallisee Hargo | 1 | 1 | - | 2 |
| Tallola Hargo | 5 | 2 | - | 7 |
| Hopoithla Yoholo | 2 | 5 | - | 7 |
| Hospotark Hargo | 3 | 2 | - | 5 |
| Timmalock Huega | 1 | 1 | - | 2 |
| Ncharlockke Emarthla | 4 | 3 | - | 7 |
| Neharlockcoche | 2 | 4 | - | 6 |
| Megiska Hargo | 2 | 2 | - | 4 |
| Hobie Hargo | 1 | 1 | - | 2 |
| | 98 | 95 | - | 193 |
| Ematth Hargo | 3 | 2 | - | 5 |
| Echo Emarthlar | 3 | 1 | - | 4 |
| Wack Sehelattar | 2 | 1 | - | 3 |
| Fus Hargo | 1 | 1 | - | 2 |
| Ichme Yoholo | 1 | 1 | - | 2 |
| Kin Haw | 1 | 3 | - | 4 |
| Concharda Yoholo | 2 | 1 | - | 3 |
| Octipissee Yoholo | 1 | 1 | - | 2 |
| Yoholo Hargo | 3 | 4 | - | 7 |
| Osooch Emarthlar | 3 | 3 | - | 6 |
| Oakfuska Hargo | 2 | 1 | - | 3 |
| Osooch Hargo | 1 | 1 | - | 2 |
| Sodedar Hargo | 2 | 2 | - | 4 |
| Pauholse Yoholo | 1 | 1 | - | 2 |
| Illis Yoholo | 1 | 1 | - | 2 |
| Spoak Sak Yoholo | 1 | 1 | - | 2 |
| Immeearttee | 1 | 3 | - | 4 |
| Wigeda Hakie | 1 | 1 | - | 2 |
| Lolafega | 2 | 2 | - | 4 |
| Polly Gooldsby | 1 | 3 | - | 4 |

CREEK CENSUS—Continued.

| Names of Heads of Families. | | | | Males. | Females. | Slaves. | Total. |
|---|---|---|---|---|---|---|---|
| Po Narhoie | | | | 1 | 2 | - | 3 |
| Timmine Taftie | | | | 1 | 1 | - | 2 |
| Im Parsee | | | | 1 | 1 | - | 2 |
| Oakkie | | | | 4 | 1 | - | 5 |
| Suthlie | | | | 2 | 2 | - | 4 |
| Sinichhoie | | | | 2 | 2 | - | 4 |
| Sodakkie | | | | 1 | 1 | - | 2 |
| Mariah | | | | 1 | 1 | - | 2 |
| Par Sarkkie | | | | 1 | 2 | - | 3 |
| Tallisee Micco | | | | 2 | — | - | 2 |
| Archehatch Hargo | | | | 2 | 2 | - | 4 |
| Oakfuska Hargo | | | | 1 | 1 | - | 2 |
| Daniel Johnston | | | | 2 | 2 | - | 4 |
| Mihee Reed | | | | 2 | 1 | - | 3 |
| Rich·rd Tawin | | | | 3 | 3 | - | 6 |
| Osiani Har | | | | 2 | 1 | - | 3 |
| Tallin Har | | | | — | 2 | - | 2 |
| | | | | 62 | 59 | - | 120 |
| **TUCKABATCHE TOWN.** | | | | | | | |
| Betty Riley | | | | 1 | 1 | 6 | 8 |
| Och Hargo | | | | 4 | 3 | - | 7 |
| Norcos Hargo | | | | 3 | 1 | - | 4 |
| Cheboaf Hargo | | | | 1 | 1 | - | 2 |
| Ichhos Yoholo | | | | 4 | 2 | - | 6 |
| Poscove Emarthlar | | | | 1 | 1 | - | 2 |
| Nehawlocco | | | | 2 | 2 | - | 4 |
| Konep Soholo | | | | 2 | 2 | - | 4 |
| Coowarsart Hargo | | | | 1 | 3 | - | 4 |
| Sohos Hargo | | | | 2 | 3 | - | 5 |
| Tuckabatt Hargo | | | | 3 | 4 | - | 7 |
| Pawwas Hargo | | | | 2 | 2 | - | 4 |
| Spoakyea Yohoholo | | | | 1 | 1 | - | 2 |
| Tallisee Fixico | | | | 1 | 1 | - | 2 |
| Hojis Hargo | | | | 1 | 1 | - | 2 |
| Wocksee Soholo | | | | 1 | 1 | - | 2 |
| Clewathla Hargo | | | | 1 | 1 | - | 2 |
| Archule Hargo | | | | 1 | 1 | - | 2 |
| Coosistee Hargo | | | | 1 | 3 | - | 4 |
| Hopoitleg | | | | 2 | 3 | - | 5 |
| Choille Hardo | | | | 2 | 1 | - | 3 |
| Neharlocco Hargo | | | | 4 | 1 | - | 5 |
| Hobie | | | | 1 | 2 | - | 3 |
| Nehe Emaithlar | | | | 3 | 4 | - | 7 |
| Horthcbore Emarthalar | | | | 1 | 1 | - | 2 |
| Tuskenehaw | | | | 1 | 2 | - | 3 |

## CREEK CENSUS—Continued.

| Names of Heads of Families. | Males. | Females. | Slaves. | Total. |
|---|---|---|---|---|
| Clechon Emarthlar | 2 | 3 | - | 5 |
| Dick Cornels | 2 | 2 | 4 | 8 |
| Echo Hargo | 1 | 3 | - | 4 |
| Lobti Fixico | 1 | 2 | - | 3 |
| Fixico Hargo | 1 | 1 | - | 2 |
| Tuckabatch Yoholo | 1 | 1 | - | 2 |
| Sohololockco | 1 | 2 | - | 3 |
| Nehar Matta Hargo | 1 | 1 | - | 2 |
| Chechumma Hollatta | 2 | 2 | - | 4 |
| Hotulga Yoholo | 3 | 3 | - | 6 |
| Chehawmicco | 1 | 1 | 9 | 11 |
| Osar Hargo | 1 | 2 | - | 3 |
| Coegus Yoholo | 1 | 1 | - | 2 |
| Ottas Micco | 3 | 2 | - | 5 |
| Osick Hargo | 2 | 3 | - | 5 |
| Lucki Yoholo | 1 | 1 | - | 2 |
| Nehawlockcoche | 1 | 1 | - | 2 |
|  | 72 | 79 | 19 | 170 |
| Tommatth Hargo | 1 | 1 | - | 2 |
| Ichhos Fixico | 1 | 1 | - | 2 |
| Marhavie | 2 | 2 | - | 4 |
| Epar Sart | 1 | 1 | - | 2 |
| Immaharga | - | 2 | - | 2 |
| Littey | - | 2 | - | 2 |
| Holote Hoga | - | 2 | - | 2 |
| Cowockcoche | 2 | - | - | 2 |
| Conchad Hargo | 3 | 2 | - | 5 |
| Toatcarhos Emalthlar | 2 | 3 | - | 5 |
| Hillubba Hargo | 1 | 3 | - | 4 |
| Chostu Emasthlar | 2 | 2 | - | 4 |
| Tinthlannis Yoholo | 1 | 1 | - | 2 |
| Arhawloe Hargo | 1 | 1 | - | 2 |
| Fus Hargo | 1 | 1 | - | 2 |
| Sandul Fixico | 2 | 1 | - | 3 |
| Attasneharlocco | 1 | 1 | - | 2 |
| Kemarth Hargo | 2 | 3 | - | 5 |
| Cotchche Yoholo | 2 | 1 | - | 3 |
| Tallissee Fixico | 2 | 3 | - | 5 |
| Tuckabatcha Emarthlar | 1 | 1 | - | 2 |
| Oakfuska Hargo | 2 | 2 | - | 4 |
| Talmarsi Hargo | 2 | 3 | - | 5 |
| Chostie Fixico | 2 | 2 | - | 4 |
| Arthlon Hargo | 2 | 2 | - | 4 |
| Easaicco Hobie | 1 | 1 | - | 2 |

## CREEK CENSUS—Continued.

| Names of Heads of Families. | Males. | Females. | Slaves. | Total. |
|---|---|---|---|---|
| Cholocinlehaw | 1 | 2 | - | 3 |
| Socholladu | 1 | 1 | - | 2 |
| Cebutche | 2 | 2 | - | 4 |
| Chocheagar | 1 | 1 | - | 2 |
| Imbohoattie | 1 | 1 | - | 2 |
| Meathlar | - | 2 | - | 2 |
| Yoholo Fixico | 1 | 1 | - | 2 |
| Choquarttie Yoholo | 1 | 1 | - | 2 |
| Arpieharineachchaw | 2 | 1 | - | 3 |
| Nehar Hargo | 2 | 1 | - | 3 |
| Fushatch Yoholo | 2 | 1 | - | 3 |
| Fushatch Hargo | 2 | 1 | - | 3 |
| Ichchehaw | 1 | 1 | - | 2 |
| Chostu Fixico | 4 | 4 | - | 8 |
| Kenobie Yoholo | 2 | 2 | - | 4 |
| Osickhimnehaw | 2 | 3 | - | 5 |
| Micco Yoholo | 4 | 2 | - | 6 |
| Illis Heargo | 2 | 2 | - | 4 |
| | 68 | 73 | - | 141 |
| Suffocheche | 2 | 1 | - | 3 |
| Micco Hubbar | 2 | 1 | - | 3 |
| O. Connejar | - | 2 | - | 2 |
| Sehoga | 1 | 2 | - | 3 |
| Fushatehche Tustunneggee | 2 | 1 | - | 3 |
| Asleapar | 1 | 1 | - | 2 |
| Aschular | 3 | 2 | - | 5 |
| Yaskie | 3 | 1 | - | 4 |
| Lostu Yoholo | 3 | 3 | - | 6 |
| Sickfunga | 2 | 1 | - | 3 |
| Hotulga Fixico | 1 | 1 | - | 2 |
| Ceteg Waga | 3 | 2 | - | 5 |
| Eliza | 1 | 1 | - | 2 |
| Nancey Barnett | - | 2 | - | 2 |
| Peggy Sulivan | - | 2 | 10 | 12 |
| Soak Hulga | - | 2 | - | 2 |
| Nitta Boakcar | 1 | 1 | - | 2 |
| Dickson | 2 | - | - | 2 |
| Minggelleo Hargo | 1 | 2 | - | 3 |
| Pocarttie | 1 | 1 | - | 2 |
| Tockfolloat Kar | 1 | 1 | - | 2 |
| Charles Lane | 1 | 5 | - | 6 |
| George | 4 | 2 | - | 6 |
| Mock Tar | 2 | 1 | - | 3 |
| Sock Too Ca | 1 | 2 | 1 | 4 |

## CREEK CENSUS—Continued.

| Names of Heads of Families. | Males. | Females | Slaves. | Total. |
|---|---|---|---|---|
| Fiaiga | - | 3 | - | 3 |
| Coosa Yoholo | 1 | 2 | - | 3 |
| Carphoak Kie | 1 | 1 | - | 2 |
| Konohega | - | 3 | - | 3 |
| Con Chad Emarthlar | 4 | 1 | - | 5 |
| Tallarlothahargo | 1 | 3 | - | 4 |
| Pas Koaf Hargo | 1 | 4 | - | 5 |
| Yoholo Hargo | 1 | 4 | - | 5 |
| Hargo Yoholo | 1 | 2 | - | 3 |
| Clewathla Fixico | 1 | 1 | - | 2 |
| Nehar Tustanug Hargo | 4 | 1 | - | 5 |
| Istimloſo Hoga | 1 | 2 | - | 3 |
| Timneota | 1 | 2 | - | 3 |
| Sally | 3 | 2 | - | 5 |
| Chekesawbie | - | 2 | - | 2 |
| Hondalla | 1 | 1 | - | 2 |
| Sinnegiga | 3 | 1 | - | 4 |
| Tilla Hoakie | 2 | 3 | - | 5 |
| | 68 | 75 | 11 | 154 |
| Toholiga | 1 | 3 | - | 4 |
| Timmonie | - | 2 | - | 2 |
| Nehaw Mattu Sick Micco | 2 | 2 | - | 4 |
| Spoak Oak Hargo | 1 | 1 | - | 2 |
| Sehikitliga | 1 | 2 | - | 3 |
| Arbohie | - | 3 | - | 3 |
| Fogishoie | - | 2 | - | 2 |
| Temi Aulca | 1 | 1 | 3 | 5 |
| Tefarhoie | - | 2 | 2 | 4 |
| Yawhar Hargo | 2 | 2 | - | 4 |
| Hchiche | 1 | 1 | 4 | 6 |
| Tin Chawway | - | 2 | 2 | 4 |
| Chelock Hargo | 1 | 1 | - | 2 |
| Fushatch Hargo | 1 | 1 | - | 2 |
| Hillis Fixico | 1 | 5 | - | 6 |
| Echostu Yoholo | 2 | 2 | - | 4 |
| Littishie | 1 | 1 | - | 2 |
| Walthleiga | 1 | 1 | - | 2 |
| Saltheiga | 2 | 2 | - | 4 |
| Chulock Hargo | 1 | 1 | - | 2 |
| Soak Tanieche | 1 | 1 | - | 2 |
| Yoholoche | 1 | 1 | - | 2 |
| Ar. Koniga | 2 | 1 | - | 3 |
| Yohobiegaw | 1 | 1 | - | 2 |
| Ho Tannie | - | 2 | - | 2 |

CREEK CENSUS—Continued.

| Names of Heads of Families. | | | | Males. | Females. | Slaves. | Total. |
|---|---|---|---|---|---|---|---|
| Spo Koncharlocco | · | · | · | 3 | 1 | · | 4 |
| Spoakogie Micco | · | · | · | 1 | 4 | · | 5 |
| Ofunniga | · | · | · | 1 | 3 | · | 4 |
| So Yarna | · | · | · | · | 2 | · | 2 |
| Im Pollartdie | · | · | · | · | 2 | · | 2 |
| Yarnar Saw | · | · | · | 1 | 1 | · | 2 |
| Chechummie Hargo | · | · | · | 2 | 1 | · | 3 |
| Pocheisse | · | · | · | 1 | 1 | · | 2 |
| Echowastise Hargo | · | · | · | 2 | 1 | · | 3 |
| Toatkarbie Emarthlar | · | · | · | 1 | 3 | · | 4 |
| Wetooak Kar Hargo | · | · | · | 2 | 1 | · | 3 |
| Nehar Yoholo | · | · | · | 1 | 1 | · | 2 |
| Folot Hogie | · | · | · | 3 | 1 | · | 4 |
| Conchart Yoholo | · | · | · | 2 | · | · | 2 |
| Tenawhinnehar | · | · | · | 1 | 3 | · | 4 |
| Esarho Kie | · | · | · | · | 2 | · | 2 |
| Isparlart Kie | · | · | · | · | 2 | · | 2 |
| E. Pock Kalodiga | · | · | · | 1 | 2 | · | 3 |
| | | | | 46 | 74 | 11 | 131 |
| Howiche | · | · | · | 1 | 1 | · | 2 |
| Timmosie | · | · | · | 1 | 1 | · | 2 |
| Arhawloc Fixico | · | · | · | 1 | 4 | · | 5 |
| Anny Sullivan | · | · | · | 1 | 2 | 7 | 10 |
| Homer Cornels | · | · | · | 2 | 1 | · | 3 |
| Timfull Hoga | · | · | · | · | 2 | · | 2 |
| Barrant Duboise | · | · | · | 4 | 2 | 4 | 10 |
| Fitz Tarkie | · | · | · | · | 2 | · | 2 |
| Chebiehar | · | · | · | 1 | 1 | · | 2 |
| Anny Cornoles | · | · | · | 2 | 3 | 6 | 11 |
| Ottis Fixico | · | · | · | 3 | 2 | · | 5 |
| Eachhos Fixico | · | · | · | 1 | 1 | · | 2 |
| Cotchchar Fixico | · | · | · | 2 | 4 | · | 6 |
| Tiheache | · | · | · | 1 | 1 | · | 2 |
| Ar Clegega | · | · | · | 3 | 3 | · | 6 |
| Holitchchar | · | · | · | · | 2 | · | 2 |
| Viney | · | · | · | · | 2 | · | 2 |
| Tom Low | · | · | · | 3 | 2 | · | 5 |
| Emarthloche | · | · | · | 1 | 2 | · | 3 |
| Warlocco Hargo | · | · | · | 2 | 1 | · | 3 |
| Edarthlie | · | · | · | 1 | 1 | · | 2 |
| Sinnoche | · | · | · | · | 4 | · | 4 |
| Yoholo Micco | · | · | · | 1 | 2 | · | 3 |
| Esiega | · | · | · | 2 | 1 | · | 3 |
| Enolickhogar | · | · | · | 1 | 2 | · | 3 |

## CREEK CENSUS—Continued.

| Names of Heads of Families. | Males. | Females. | Slaves. | Total. |
|---|---|---|---|---|
| Hoith Uga | 1 | 1 | - | 2 |
| Coosa Fixico | 1 | 3 | - | 4 |
| Toneche | 1 | 1 | - | 2 |
| Chedoakkee | 1 | 1 | - | 2 |
| Sogeapie | 2 | 1 | - | 3 |
| Co Yar | 1 | 1 | - | 2 |
| Tosehoke | 2 | 1 | - | 3 |
| Anny | 2 | 1 | - | 3 |
| Nancy | 1 | 2 | - | 3 |
| Gil Car | 1 | 2 | - | 3 |
| Mariah | - | 3 | - | 3 |
| Coeiga | 2 | - | - | 2 |
| Fequarthlar | 2 | 2 | - | 4 |
| Peggy | 1 | 1 | - | 2 |
| Betsey | 1 | 1 | - | 2 |
| Snow | 1 | 2 | - | 3 |
| Major | 1 | 1 | - | 2 |
| Arius Hargo | 1 | 2 | - | 3 |
| Togal Kar | 1 | 1 | - | 2 |
| | 57 | 76 | 17 | 150 |
| Solippa | 1 | 2 | - | 3 |
| Lucy | 2 | 1 | - | 3 |
| Luiza | 1 | 1 | - | 2 |
| Sawhos Kie | - | 3 | - | 3 |
| Sourcolie | 2 | 1 | - | 3 |
| Sarhoie | 1 | 2 | - | 3 |
| Simmarhoaktie | 2 | 1 | - | 3 |
| Tardegie | — | 2 | - | 2 |
| Tatlouwar Hargo | 1 | 1 | - | 2 |
| Tallissee Emarthlar | 3 | 2 | - | 5 |
| Tom Marth Yoholo | 2 | 1 | - | 3 |
| David Walker | 1 | 2 | 6 | 9 |
| Susan | - | 2 | - | 2 |
| Sinemomeachar | - | 2 | - | 2 |
| Hocoske Emarthlar | 1 | 3 | - | 4 |
| Sarginhea | - | 2 | - | 2 |
| Luchi Yoholo | 3 | 2 | - | 5 |
| Ho Tarbie | - | 2 | - | 2 |
| Sehineithlar | 2 | 2 | - | 4 |
| Cowassa Micco | 1 | 3 | - | 4 |
| Midogie | - | 2 | - | 2 |
| Fullega | - | 2 | - | 2 |
| Timmiskakie | - | 2 | - | 2 |
| Holodega | 1 | 1 | - | 2 |

GREEK CENSUS—Continued.

| Names of Heads of Families. | Males. | Females. | Slaves. | Total. |
|---|---|---|---|---|
| Ohounga - - - - | 2 | 1 | - | 3 |
| Moslie - - - - | 2 | - | - | 2 |
| Honithbie - - - - | - | 2 | - | 2 |
| Marbejar - - - - | 1 | 1 | - | 2 |
| Sam Clark - - - - | 1 | 4 | - | 5 |
| Fi Eacheche - - - - | 2 | 2 | - | 4 |
| Hospo Tock Hargo - - - | 1 | 4 | - | 5 |
| Archehatch Fixico - - - | 1 | 3 | - | 4 |
| Coosahopoiethly - - - | 2 | 1 | - | 3 |
| Toufkice - - - - | 1 | 1 | - | 2 |
| Tallissa Hopoithly - - - | 3 | 1 | - | 4 |
| Cologie - - - - | 1 | 1 | - | 2 |
| Poster - - - - | 1 | 1 | - | 2 |
| Sinnargoftie - - - - | - | 2 | - | 2 |
| Tohokourga - - - - | - | 3 | - | 3 |
| Harclophokie - - - - | 1 | 1 | - | 2 |
| Hogubie - - - - | 1 | 2 | - | 3 |
| Argitthlie - - - - | - | 2 | - | 2 |
| Tom Barnett - - - - | 2 | 1 | - | 3 |
| Timmohie - - - - | 1 | 1 | - | 2 |
| | 47 | 78 | 6 | 131 |
| Gillissinnehar - - - - | 1 | 2 | - | 3 |
| Cheharhargo - - - - | 1 | 1 | - | 2 |
| Hoparla Hargo - - - - | 2 | 3 | - | 5 |
| Micco Yoholo - - - - | 2 | 2 | - | 4 |
| Tuckabatcha Fixico - - - | 2 | 2 | - | 4 |
| Timmarnokee - - - - | 3 | 1 | - | 4 |
| Nehawlocco - - - - | 1 | 2 | - | 3 |
| Tockonockke - - - - | 1 | 1 | - | 2 |
| Timmeleche - - - - | 2 | - | - | 2 |
| No Ko Le Yoholo - - - | 1 | 2 | - | 3 |
| Micco Ylocco - - - - | 1 | 1 | - | 2 |
| It Kudde Hargo - - - | 3 | 1 | - | 4 |
| Nockhoiega - - - - | 1 | 1 | - | 2 |
| Sucky - - - - - | - | 2 | - | 2 |
| Hochehatchche Hargo - - | 3 | 3 | - | 6 |
| Fullega - - - - | 1 | 1 | 1 | 3 |
| Losti Hargo - - - - | 1 | 1 | - | 2 |
| Oakfusca Hargo - - - | 3 | 1 | - | 4 |
| No Ko Sille - - - - | 3 | 3 | - | 6 |
| Timmar Sau - - - - | 1 | 2 | - | 3 |
| Tussickkecharga - - - | 1 | 1 | - | 2 |
| Yosboskaw - - - - | 1 | 1 | - | 2 |
| Osoochche Yoholo - - - | 4 | 4 | - | 8 |

## CREEK CENSUS—Continued.

| Names of the Heads of Families. | Males. | Females. | Slaves. | Total. |
|---|---|---|---|---|
| Tarbos Hargo - - - - | 1 | 2 | - | 3 |
| Megiskar Hargo - - - | 2 | 3 | - | 5 |
| Arharloc Hargo - - - - | 2 | 3 | - | 5 |
| Seeheiga - - - - - | 2 | 1 | - | 3 |
| Ho Tulga Hargo - - - - | 1 | 3 | - | 4 |
| Samuel Smith - - - - | 5 | 2 | 7 | 14 |
| Cooswar Sart Hargo - - - | 1 | 3 | - | 4 |
| Ochis Hargo - - - - | - | 2 | - | 2 |
| Sobieithlee - - - - | - | 2 | - | 2 |
| Salliwar - - - - - | 1 | 1 | - | 2 |
| Sehoathla - - - - - | - | 2 | - | 2 |
| Tarheethle - - - - | 1 | 2 | - | 3 |
| Sarbeechche - - - - | 2 | - | - | 2 |
| Cleeikka - - - - - | 2 | 1 | - | 3 |
| Arlarhokar - - - - | - | 3 | - | 3 |
| Hoakchon Hargo - - - - | 2 | - | - | 2 |
| Huchetarheathlar - - - - | 1 | 1 | - | 2 |
| Pim McQueen - - - - | 1 | 1 | - | 2 |
| Wise Kar - - - - | 3 | 2 | - | 5 |
| Tiwiheagar - - - - | 1 | 2 | - | 3 |
| Ahseiquar - - - - | 1 | 3 | - | 4 |
| | 71 | 74 | 8 | 153 |
| Cheharlebogar - - - - | 3 | 4 | - | 7 |
| Talloaf Hargo - - - - | 5 | 2 | - | 7 |
| Arkihe - - - - - | 1 | 1 | - | 2 |
| Yawuejar - - - - - | - | 2 | - | 2 |
| Ichhoice - - - - - | - | 2 | - | 2 |
| Lif Tif Hargo - - - - | 1 | 1 | - | 2 |
| Ebuckalatkar - - - - | - | 2 | - | 2 |
| Tim Hea Char - - - - | 1 | 1 | - | 2 |
| Archuloc Hargo (2d of same name,) - | 1 | 1 | - | 2 |
| Spanny Fixico - - - - | 3 | 1 | - | 4 |
| Tommy Yoholo - - - - | 2 | 1 | - | 3 |
| Seo Mar - - - - - | 1 | 1 | - | 2 |
| Cooista - - - - - | 1 | 2 | - | 3 |
| Arbicco Hargo - - - - | 1 | 2 | - | 3 |
| Sodeclunne Hargo - - - | 3 | 2 | - | 5 |
| Emarthlar Hatka - - - - | 1 | 1 | - | 2 |
| Hospodark Fixico - - - | 2 | 2 | - | 4 |
| O. Sar Fixico - - - - | 1 | 1 | - | 2 |
| Hoakchon Fixico - - - - | 1 | 1 | 2 | 4 |
| Ararttu Hargo - - - - | 2 | 1 | - | 3 |
| Nehe Emarthlar Yoholo - - - | 1 | 1 | - | 2 |
| Archular Yoholo - - - - | 3 | 1 | | 4 |

CREEK CENSUS—Continued.

| Names of Heads of Families. | Males. | Females. | Slaves. | Total. |
|---|---|---|---|---|
| Ubockholattar - - - - | 2 | - | - | 2 |
| Par Sarga - - - - | 3 | 1 | - | 4 |
| Tallesse Hargo - - - - | 1 | 2 | - | 3 |
| Toney - - - - - | 2 | 2 | - | 4 |
| Illishothlebogar - - - - | 2 | 3 | - | 5 |
| Sogarttu Hargo - - - - | 1 | 1 | - | 2 |
| Ispohie - - - - - | - | 2 | - | 2 |
| Cowegus Hargo - - - - | 4 | 1 | - | 5 |
| Coosa Hargo - - - - | 2 | - | - | 2 |
| Mecco Hargo - - - - | 4 | 1 | - | 5 |
| Tallowar Micco - - - - | 3 | 1 | - | 4 |
| Sarnar - - - - - | 1 | 1 | - | 2 |
| Spoakoak Fixico - - - - | 2 | 1 | - | 3 |
| Molly - - - - - | - | 2 | - | 2 |
| Yarginna Fixico - - - - | 1 | 1 | - | 2 |
| Tallowar Tustunnugga - - - | 2 | 3 | - | 5 |
| Tuskie Hargo - - - - | 2 | 3 | - | 5 |
| Chawoccala Fixico - - - | 2 | 1 | - | 3 |
| Tinchobocca - - - - | 1 | 1 | - | 2 |
| Starlocca - - - - - | 2 | - | - | 2 |
| Cotchchegar - - - - | 1 | 1 | - | 2 |
| Seieche - . - - - | 2 | - | - | 2 |
| | 74 | 61 | 2 | 137 |
| Sawhie - - - - - | 1 | 1 | - | 2 |
| Arkiehegar - - - - | - | 2 | - | 2 |
| Sam Low - - - - - | 2 | 2 | - | 4 |
| Soshoie - - - - - | 1 | 1 | - | 2 |
| Tustenug Holie - - - - | 1 | 3 | - | 4 |
| Konip Hargo - - - - | 2 | 1 | - | 3 |
| Oakchannar - - - - | 2 | - | - | 2 |
| Tomger Cornels - - - - | 1 | 1 | - | 2 |
| Liley - - - - - | 1 | 1 | 1 | 3 |
| Mistaharka - - - - | 1 | 1 | - | 2 |
| Holattar - - - - - | - | 3 | 7 | 10 |
| Tokoie - - - - - | - | 3 | - | 3 |
| Oche Hargo - - - - | 1 | 1 | - | 2 |
| Octtearche Yoholo - - - | 1 | 1 | - | 2 |
| Cuwarla Emarthlar - - - | 1 | 1 | - | 2 |
| Sucky Cornels - - - - | 1 | 5 | 22 | 28 |
| Betty Cornels - - - - | 1 | 1 | 23 | 25 |
| Maisth Yar - - - - | - | 2 | - | 2 |
| Jim - - - - - | 1 | 1 | - | 2 |
| Toatcarhossa - - - - | 4 | 2 | - | 6 |
| Judy Tooly - - - - | 1 | 2 | 2 | 5 |

## CREEK CENSUS—Continued.

| Names of Heads of Families. | Males. | Females. | Slaves. | Total. |
|---|---|---|---|---|
| John McQueen, (free negro) | 2 | 2 | - | 4 |
| Spokos Yoholo | 1 | 1 | 3 | 5 |
| Old Buffalow | 2 | - | - | 2 |
| Sokoliga | 1 | 1 | - | 2 |
| Zachariah McGirth | 1 | 2 | 7 | 10 |
| Tin Galla | 1 | 1 | - | 2 |
| Intuckhoie | 1 | 1 | 10 | 12 |
| Elizabeth Cornel | 1 | 2 | - | 3 |
| Octearche Fixico | 3 | 2 | - | 5 |
| Homahoda | 1 | 2 | - | 3 |
| Tohartu | 2 | 1 | - | 3 |
| Jenney | 1 | 2 | - | 3 |
| Tuckabutcha Emarthlu | 1 | 1 | - | 2 |
| Enehar Fixico | 3 | 1 | - | 4 |
| Juba, (a free negro) | 6 | 4 | - | 10 |
|  | 50 | 58 | 75 | 183 |
| OTTISEE TOWN. |  |  |  |  |
| Ottisse Micco | 4 | 3 | - | 7 |
| Yoholo Micco | 2 | 1 | - | 3 |
| Coosa Micco | 1 | 4 | - | 5 |
| Fushatchche Micco | 1 | 3 | - | 4 |
| Octoha Micco | 2 | 2 | - | 4 |
| Otulgu Emarthlar | 5 | 6 | - | 11 |
| Spoakoak Tustanugga | 2 | 3 | - | 5 |
| Cotchchar Tustunnugga | 3 | 3 | - | 6 |
| Hoboyacha | 2 | 2 | - | 4 |
| Conip Yoholo | 2 | 3 | - | 5 |
| Tustanuc Hargo | 4 | 4 | - | 8 |
| Thlantalle Emarthlar | 6 | 1 | - | 7 |
| Othleboboie Emarthlar | 3 | 1 | - | 4 |
| Oakfuska Yoholo | 3 | 2 | - | 5 |
| Nokose Emarthlar | 1 | 2 | - | 3 |
| Ottissi Emarthlar | 1 | 3 | - | 4 |
| Osawwe Emarthlar | 1 | 2 | - | 3 |
| Euehar Micco | 5 | 2 | - | 7 |
| Euehar Emathlar | 2 | 2 | - | 4 |
| Parhose Hargo | 1 | 1 | - | 2 |
| Tuckabatcha Hargo | 2 | 2 | - | 4 |
| Tommy Hargo | 1 | 2 | - | 3 |
| Thlaththlo Fixico | 2 | 2 | - | 4 |
| Coosa Fixico | 1 | 1 | - | 2 |
| Octearche Hargo | 2 | 2 | - | 4 |
| William Jugant | 1 | 1 | - | 2 |
| Ispanny Hargo | 1 | 1 | - | 2 |
| Archule Hargo | 6 | 2 | - | 8 |

CREEK CENSUS—Continued.

| Names of Heads of Families. | Males. | Females. | Slaves. | Total. |
|---|---|---|---|---|
| Thlautal Fixico - - - - | 1 | 1 | - | 2 |
| Ossee Yoholo - - - - | 1 | 1 | - | 2 |
| Hoboeger Yoholo - - - | 3 | 2 | - | 5 |
| Talmachus Hargo - - - - | 5 | 2 | - | 7 |
| Tuskenehaw - - - - | 5 | 1 | - | 6 |
| Chofolope Hargo - - - - | 4 | 3 | - | 7 |
| Cocchu Yoholo - - - - | 1 | 1 | - | 2 |
| Tustunnugga Emarthlar - - - | 2 | 3 | - | 5 |
| Yakinhar Fixico - - - - | 2 | 4 | - | 6 |
| Lostar Hargo - - - - | 1 | 1 | - | 2 |
| Coosistu Hargo - - - - | 1 | 1 | - | 2 |
| Micco Powugar - - - - | 1 | 1 | - | 2 |
| Liftif Hargo - - - - | 2 | 1 | - | 3 |
| Toatkarbie Hargo - . - | 3 | 1 | - | 4 |
| Konip Fixico - - - - | 2 | 4 | - | 6 |
| | 101 | 90 | - | 191 |
| Neharthlocke Emarthlar - - - | 4 | 1 | - | 5 |
| Arlocco Yoholo - - - - | 4 | 2 | - | 6 |
| Hillabbee Hargo - - - - | 1 | 1 | - | 2 |
| Cuegus Harg - - - - | 2 | 1 | - | 3 |
| Konip Emarthlar - - - - | 2 | 2 | - | 4 |
| Oler Hargo - - - - | 2 | 1 | - | 3 |
| Uppahle Emarthlar - - - | 4 | 2 | - | 6 |
| Lumhe Hothlehoboc - - - | 3 | 1 | - | 4 |
| Cheloke Hargo - - - - | 2 | 2 | - | 4 |
| Neharlocco Hargo - - - | 3 | 2 | - | 5 |
| Spoak Hargo - - - - | 3 | 2 | - | 5 |
| Micco Oboyuche - - - - | 2 | 2 | - | 4 |
| Fushatcha Hargo - - - - | 2 | 5 | - | 7 |
| Owar Talega - - - - | 3 | 1 | - | 4 |
| Atarhar Fixico - - - - | 1 | 2 | - | 3 |
| Arfos Hargo - - - - | 2 | 2 | - | 4 |
| Chulocke Yoholo - - - - | 3 | 3 | - | 6 |
| Poscoaf Hargo - - - - | 2 | 1 | - | 3 |
| Nocotilla Hargo - - - - | 3 | 1 | - | 4 |
| Arharle Emarthlar - - - | 1 | 2 | - | 3 |
| Micco Yoholo - - - - | 2 | 2 | - | 4 |
| Hillabba Fixico - - - - | 2 | 1 | - | 3 |
| Ichhos Hargo - - - - | 1 | 1 | - | 2 |
| Arbywe Hargo - - - - | 1 | 1 | - | 2 |
| Cowie Hargo - - - - | 4 | 4 | - | 8 |
| Studdy Hargo - - - - | 1 | 1 | - | 2 |
| Arharloc Hargo - - - - | 1 | 1 | - | 2 |
| Icche Hargo - - - - | 1 | 1 | - | 2 |

CREEK CENSUS—Continued.

| Names of Heads of Families. | Males. | Females. | Slaves. | Total. |
|---|---|---|---|---|
| Conchart Hargo - - - - | 1 | 1 | - | 2 |
| Oecaske Fixico - - - - | 1 | 1 | - | 2 |
| Sohoega - - - - - | 1 | 2 | - | 3 |
| Stemmofunnatkee - - - | 1 | 1 | - | 2 |
| Halliegie - - - - | 3 | 2 | - | 5 |
| Tisquar - - - - | 2 | 1 | - | 3 |
| In Lar Kie - - - - | 1 | 1 | - | 2 |
| Teto Hoga - - - - - | - | 3 | - | 3 |
| Timmarhobocca - - - - | - | 2 | - | 2 |
| Sucky - - - - - | 1 | 1 | - | 2 |
| Folot Hoga - - - - | 2 | 1 | - | 3 |
| Timmedliege - - - - | 1 | 1 | - | 2 |
| Sarchinhoga - - - - | 1 | 1 | - | 2 |
| Istarhokie - - - - | 2 | 2 | - | 4 |
| Yokeche - - - - | - | 2 | - | 2 |
| Cowega - - - - - | 1 | 3 | - | 4 |
| Isholatta - - - - | 3 | 4 | - | 7 |
| Fullogiga - - - - | 2 | 3 | - | 5 |
| Lindojar - - - - | 1 | 1 | - | 2 |
| | 79 | 73 | - | 152 |

TALMACHUSSA TOWN.

| | | | | |
|---|---|---|---|---|
| Oppanga - - - - | 1 | 1 | - | 2 |
| Talmarta Tustunnugga - - - | 1 | 3 | - | 4 |
| Hoboy Hatka - - - | 3 | 1 | - | 4 |
| Hellubba Tustunnugga - - - | 2 | 2 | - | 4 |
| Ufalla Tustunnugga - - - | 1 | 1 | - | 2 |
| Hoboyis Hunnegigo - - - | 2 | 1 | - | 3 |
| Isfunny Tustunnugga - - - | 3 | 2 | - | 5 |
| Coha Le Emarthlar - - - | 1 | 1 | - | 2 |
| Arhar Micco - - - - | 3 | 2 | - | 5 |
| Coleme Tustunnugga - - - | 1 | 2 | - | 3 |
| Fi Yoholo - - - - | 1 | 4 | - | 5 |
| Hoboithlar Hargo - - - | 1 | 2 | - | 3 |
| Athlow Hargo - - - - | 3 | 2 | - | 5 |
| Oackchon Emarthlar - - - | 2 | 3 | - | 5 |
| Cubbitchchar Hargo - - - | 1 | 2 | - | 3 |
| Ascohe Emathlar - - - | 2 | 1 | - | 3 |
| Konip Emathlar - - - | 2 | 1 | - | 3 |
| Ispanny Hargo - - - - | 2 | 3 | - | 5 |
| Arharlock Fixico - - - | 1 | 3 | - | 4 |
| Luchi Yoholo - - - - | 2 | 1 | - | 3 |
| Choforloap Hargo - - - | 1 | 1 | - | 2 |

CREEK CENSUS—Continued.

| Names of Heads of Families. | Males. | Females. | Slaves. | Total. |
|---|---|---|---|---|
| Chofoloap Hargo (2d of same name) - | 2 | 1 | - | 3 |
| Oche Emarthlar      -      -      - | 1 | 2 | - | 3 |
| Concharta Yoholo    -      -      - | 1 | 1 | - | 2 |
| Tus Kenehatcha      -      -      - | 1 | 1 | - | 2 |
| Cobbitchche Yoholo  -      -      - | 1 | 1 | - | 2 |
|                                     | 48 | 53 | - | 101 |
| Yoholo Emarthlar    -      -      - | 1 | 1 | - | 2 |
| Carchar Yoholo      -      -      - | 2 | 1 | - | 3 |
| Kolis Lelinenehar   -      -      - | 2 | - | - | 2 |
| Woc See Yoholo      -      -      - | 2 | 1 | - | 3 |
| Ubalat Kar    -     -      -      - | 1 | 2 | - | 3 |
| Setarwe       .     -      -      - | 1 | 2 | - | 3 |
| Satta Yachche -     -      .      - | - | 2 | - | 2 |
| Mo Thalche    -     -      -      - | - | 2 | - | 2 |
| Sofila Maga   -     -      -      - | - | 3 | - | 3 |
| Soco Yalth Hoga     -      -      - | 1 | 1 | - | 2 |
| Sally    -    -     -      -      - | 1 | 1 | - | 2 |
| Mahegar       -     -      -      - | 1 | 1 | - | 2 |
| Masic         -     .      -      - | - | 2 | - | 2 |
| Te Yar Mic    -     -      -      - | - | 2 | - | 2 |
| Sinho Misar   -     -      -      - | 2 | 1 | - | 3 |
| Sachmho Ka    -     -      -      - | 1 | 1 | - | 2 |
| Mehar Kee     -     -      -      - | 1 | 1 | - | 2 |
| Mahegar (2d of same name)   -    - | 1 | 1 | - | 2 |
| Istiman Sie   -     -      -      - | - | 2 | - | 2 |
| Soquaga       -     -      -      - | 2 | 1 | - | 3 |
| Woc Seholattar -    -      -      - | 3 | 3 | - | 6 |
| Nehar Fixico  -     -      -      - | 1 | 3 | - | 4 |
|                                     | 23 | 34 | - | 57 |

CLE WALLA TOWN.

| Mecco Chopco   -     -      -      - | 2 | 2 | - | 4 |
|---|---|---|---|---|
| Micco Emarthlar      -      -      - | 4 | 1 | - | 5 |
| Lar Tar Micco  -     -      -      - | 2 | 2 | - | 4 |
| Ufawla Tustunnuggy   -      -      - | 1 | 1 | - | 2 |
| Talledega Tustunnuggy -     -      - | 2 | 1 | - | 3 |
| Fushatchche Micco    -      -      - | 1 | 1 | - | 2 |
| Micco Hargo    -     -      -      - | 4 | 2 | - | 6 |
| Wocse Hargo    -     -      -      - | 1 | 4 | - | 5 |
| Holoc Ke Yoholo      -      -      - | 2 | 2 | - | 4 |
| Tallessee Hopocethly -      -      - | 5 | 3 | - | 8 |
| Toat Kis Hargo -     -      -      - | 2 | 3 | - | 5 |
| Cochche Yoholo -     -      -      - | 1 | 1 | - | 2 |

CREEK CENSUS—Continued.

| Names of Heads of Families. | Males. | Females. | Slaves. | Total. |
|---|---|---|---|---|
| Ufawla Hargo        -      -      -      - | 2 | 2 | - | 4 |
| Inclannis Hargo     -      -      -      - | 3 | 3 | - | 6 |
| Pawhos Hargo        -      -      -      - | 2 | 4 | - | 6 |
| Micco Chatta        -      -      -      - | 1 | 5 | - | 6 |
| Clan Tal Fixico     -      -      -      - | 4 | 3 | - | 7 |
| Nehar Yoholo        -      -      -      - | 2 | 3 | - | 5 |
| W. J. Shumo         -      -      -      - | 4 | 1 | 12 | 17 |
| Leboth Ka           -      -      -      - | 2 | 2 | - | 4 |
| Peggy Elliott       -      -      -      - | - | 2 | - | 2 |
| Tatth Hocar         -      -      -      - | 1 | 3 | - | 4 |
| Betsey              -      -      -      - | 1 | 1 | - | 2 |
| Fitz Tugga          -      -      -      - | 2 | 4 | - | 6 |
| Hickcoiega          -      -      -      - | 1 | 3 | - | 4 |
| O Sook Fixico       -      -      -      - | 2 | 1 | - | 3 |
| Smed    -      -      -      -      - | 1 | 2 | - | 3 |
| Cabick Ke Yoholo    -      -      - | 1 | 1 | - | 2 |
| Putit Sar           -      -      -      - | 1 | 3 | - | 4 |
| Mithlanaga          -      -      -      - | 4 | 2 | - | 6 |
| Fuckoske            -      -      -      - | 1 | 1 | - | 2 |
| Istinliga           -      -      -      - | - | 2 | - | 2 |
| Holattie Emarthlar  -      -      - | 1 | 4 | - | 5 |
| Chocolis Hargo      -      -      - | 2 | 3 | - | 5 |
| Wegede Hoga         -      -      - | 2 | 2 | - | 4 |
| Cochchar Micco      -      -      - | 4 | 2 | - | 6 |
| Talmachus Hargo     -      -      - | 1 | 3 | - | 4 |
| Pawhos Fixico       -      -      - | 2 | 1 | - | 3 |
| Larna   -      -      -      -      - | 1 | 1 | - | 2 |
| Coeega              -      -      -      - | 2 | 1 | - | 3 |
| Pin Hargo           -      -      -      - | 2 | 1 | - | 3 |
| Chull Yoholo        -      -      -      - | 4 | 3 | - | 7 |
| Nitta   -      -      -      -      - | 2 | 2 | - | 4 |
| | 85 | 94 | 12 | 191 |
| Isfanny Yoholo      -      -      -      - | 4 | 2 | - | 6 |
| Nabothche Yoholo    -      -      - | 2 | 2 | - | 4 |
| Yokepohiga          -      -      -      - | 1 | 2 | - | 3 |
| Lothte Yoholo       -      -      -      - | 3 | 1 | - | 4 |
| Arbithke Hargo      -      -      - | 3 | 5 | - | 8 |
| Micco Halka         -      -      -      - | 5 | 2 | - | 7 |
| Cochcha Fixico      -      -      - | 1 | 1 | - | 2 |
| Hathlon Hargo       -      -      - | 2 | 4 | - | 6 |
| Arparee Emarthlar   -      -      - | 1 | 1 | - | 2 |
| Miccoborge          -      -      -      - | 2 | 2 | - | 4 |
| Fed     -      -      -      -      - | 1 | 1 | - | 2 |
| Lartatiee           -      -      -      - | 2 | 2 | - | 4 |

CREEK CENSUS—Continued.

| Names of Heads of Families. | Males. | Females. | Slaves. | Total. |
|---|---|---|---|---|
| Cochchar Yoholo (two of same name) - | 1 | 1 | - | 2 |
| Homaheedar - - - - | 1 | 4 | - | 5 |
| Heardith Kar Hargo - - - | 1 | 1 | - | 2 |
| Woe See Yoholo - - - | 2 | 1 | - | 3 |
| Tus Conar Fixico - - - | 1 | 2 | - | 3 |
| Hillubba Emarthlar - - - | 1 | 1 | - | 2 |
| Hinneheer Emarthlar - - - | 2 | 2 | - | 4 |
| Ochoiega - - - - | 1 | 2 | - | 3 |
| Yarhar Fixico - - - - | 4 | 2 | - | 6 |
| Fixico Hargo - - - - | 2 | 3 | - | 5 |
| Hillis Fixico - - - - | 2 | 1 | - | 3 |
| Sanny Fixico - - - - | 3 | 2 | - | 5 |
| Mundarla - - - - | 1 | 3 | - | 4 |
| Coosobobouthla - - - | 2 | 3 | - | 5 |
| Coosa Hargo - - - - | 2 | 4 | - | 6 |
| Hie Oakke - - - - | 1 | 3 | - | 4 |
| Isfanny Emarthlar - - - | 2 | 1 | - | 3 |
| Hemar Hargo - - - - | 2 | 2 | - | 4 |
| Tallise Micco - - - - | 5 | 1 | - | 6 |
| Ichhos Fixico - - - - | 2 | 1 | - | 3 |
| Cubbieachche Emarthlar - - - | 2 | 1 | - | 3 |
| Fushatchche Hargo - - - | 3 | 2 | - | 5 |
| Konip Fixico - - - - | 1 | 1 | - | 2 |
| Sodesa - - - - | 3 | 2 | - | 5 |
| Cubbreachche Fixico - - - | 3 | 3 | - | 6 |
| Cochcherhothlobore - - - | 2 | 1 | - | 3 |
| Istajargo Hargo - - - - | 2 | 1 | - | 3 |
| Istickafunna Yoholo - - - | 2 | 1 | - | 3 |
| Emarthlar Yoholo - - - | 2 | 3 | - | 5 |
| Tusconar Hargo - - - | 3 | 1 | - | 4 |
| Watup Hoboye - - - | 2 | - | - | 2 |
| Cochchar Hargo - - - | 1 | 1 | - | 2 |
|  | 91 | 82 |  | 173 |
| Osse Yoholo - - - - | 1 | 1 | - | 2 |
| Fucktalusta Hargo - - - | 2 | 2 | - | 4 |
| Istooliga - - - - | 1 | 2 | - | 3 |
| Talmarse Fixico - - - | 3 | 1 | - | 4 |
| Yarhar Emarthlar - - - | 5 | 4 | - | 9 |
| Hargo Yoholo - - - - | 1 | 1 | - | 2 |
| Wolga - - - - | 1 | 2 | - | 3 |
| Talloaf Yoholo - - - | 2 | 1 | - | 3 |
| Arfus Hargo - - - - | 4 | 6 | - | 10 |
| Nocosiccar - - - - | 2 | 6 | - | 8 |
| Choquartta Hargo - - - | 4 | 3 | - | 7 |

33‡

| Names of Heads of Families. | Males. | Females. | Slaves. | Total. |
|---|---|---|---|---|
| Echo Hargo - - - - | 2 | 2 | - | 4 |
| Chuwostu Yoholo - - - - | 1 | 1 | - | 2 |
| Carbietche Emarthlar - - - | 2 | 1 | - | 3 |
| **TAUWAR SA TOWN.** | | | | |
| Efar Tustunnugga - - - | 1 | 2 | - | 3 |
| Ottise Yoholo - - - - | 3 | 1 | - | 4 |
| Chofoloap Hargo - - - | 2 | 1 | - | 3 |
| Poiethla Hargo - - - - | 2 | 3 | - | 5 |
| Slath Slo Hargo - - - - | 1 | 5 | - | 6 |
| Spanny Fixico - - - - | 1 | 3 | - | 4 |
| Coe Hargo - - - - | 1 | 2 | - | 3 |
| Echo Hargo - - - - | 3 | 2 | - | 5 |
| Luche Yoholo - - - - | 2 | 1 | - | 3 |
| Cowar Larda Hargo - - - | 3 | 1 | - | 4 |
| Chos Hargo - - - - | 2 | 1 | - | 3 |
| Nokocilla Hargo - - - | 2 | 3 | - | 5 |
| Coliga Yoholo - - - - | 1 | 5 | - | 6 |
| Poscoaf Hargo - - - - | 4 | 1 | - | 5 |
| Octtearche Yoholo - - - | 1 | 1 | - | 2 |
| Emarthlar - - - - | 2 | 1 | - | 3 |
| Oakchon Yoholo - - - | 2 | 1 | - | 3 |
| Conip Fixico - - - - | 3 | 3 | - | 6 |
| Hoakchi Yoholo - - - | 2 | 1 | - | 3 |
| Micco Emarthlar - - - | 1 | 1 | - | 2 |
| Tockasa Hargo - - - - | 1 | 2 | - | 3 |
| Tallesi Fixico - - - - | 3 | 2 | - | 5 |
| Choccharholattar - - - | 1 | 3 | - | 4 |
| | 75 | 79 | | 154 |
| Albudda Hargo - - - - | 1 | 1 | - | 2 |
| Lemarparharmiga - - - | 2 | 1 | - | 3 |
| Ocinhee - - - - | 1 | 1 | - | 2 |
| Esomiche - - - - | 1 | 2 | - | 3 |
| Arholiga - - - - | - | 2 | - | 2 |
| Tingarqu - - - - | 1 | 2 | - | 3 |
| Oaklarpissa Yoholo - - - | 2 | 1 | - | 3 |
| **AUTANGA TOWN.** | | | | |
| Hargie Yoholo - - - - | 1 | 1 | - | 2 |
| Alabama Emarthla - - - | 2 | 1 | - | 3 |
| Harpie Emarthlar - - - | 2 | 2 | - | 4 |
| Sarwanwo Hargo - - - | 2 | 2 | - | 4 |

CREEK CENSUS—Continued.

| Names of Heads of Families. | Males. | Females | Slaves. | Total. |
|---|---|---|---|---|
| Tal Marse Emarthlar | 2 | 1 | - | 3 |
| Hobie | 1 | 2 | - | 3 |
| War Thloc Yoholo | 4 | 2 | - | 6 |
| War Lar Hargo | 4 | 3 | - | 7 |
| Echo Fixico | 5 | 2 | - | 7 |
| Choakchart Fixico | 2 | 4 | - | 6 |
| O. Soochcha Hargo | 2 | 1 | - | 3 |
| Sohotie Fixico | 2 | 2 | - | 4 |
| Tallige Hargo | 1 | 1 | - | 2 |
| Samuel Hale | 2 | 3 | - | 5 |
| Joshuah W. Harman | 2 | 2 | - | 4 |
| David Hale | 5 | 3 | 2 | 10 |
| Seaborn F. Jones | 1 | 1 | 1 | 3 |
| Charles Elliott | 3 | 5 | - | 8 |
| Polly Miles | - | 2 | 1 | 3 |
| Edward James | 3 | 3 | - | 6 |
| Charles Weatherford | 2 | 1 | 11 | 14 |
| Coegus Hargo | 3 | 1 | - | 4 |
| Micco Hatka | 4 | 2 | - | 6 |
| Tabossole Fixico | 1 | 1 | - | 2 |
| Ottis Hargo | 2 | 2 | - | 4 |
| Tushatch Yoholo | 1 | 2 | - | 3 |
| Ochas Hargo | 3 | 2 | - | 5 |
| Coowar Sart Micco | 1 | 2 | - | 3 |
| Octiarche Hargo | 1 | 2 | - | 3 |
| Chon Hargo | 2 | 2 | - | 4 |
| Cubbreachche Hargo | 2 | 2 | - | |
| Konip Hargo | 1 | 2 | - | 3 |
| | 77 | 74 | 15 | 166 |
| Mocolus Tuska | 2 | 1 | - | 3 |
| Ufaula Hargo | 3 | 2 | - | 5 |
| Conchart Yoholo | 1 | 2 | - | 3 |
| Tosohoboyhatka | 2 | - | - | 2 |
| Fixico Hargo | 1 | 2 | - | 3 |
| Echo Yoholo | 3 | 1 | - | 4 |
| Tallise Hargo | 5 | 2 | - | 7 |
| Tussickki Hargo | 1 | 4 | - | 5 |
| Tallamarse Hargo | 1 | 1 | - | 2 |
| Nehar Yoholo | 2 | 1 | - | 3 |
| Simmie | 1 | 1 | - | 2 |
| Fachejie | 1 | 1 | - | 2 |
| Sopreie | 2 | 2 | - | 4 |
| Ethlama | 1 | 1 | - | 2 |
| Arfistar | 2 | 1 | - | 3 |

## CREEK CENSUS—Continued.

| Names of Heads of Families. | Males. | Females. | Slaves. | Total. |
|---|---|---|---|---|
| Clemarlth Hargo | - | 2 | - | 2 |
| Iockhomiga | 1 | 2 | - | 3 |
| Tuwiga | 3 | 3 | - | 6 |
| Marlitchcha | 1 | 2 | - | 3 |
| Ehar Thlar | 2 | 1 | - | 3 |
| War Thlocco Hargo | 2 | 2 | - | 4 |
| George Stiggins | 2 | 7 | 6 | 15 |
| | 39 | 42 | 6 | 87 |

### TALLISEE TOWN.

| | Males. | Females. | Slaves. | Total. |
|---|---|---|---|---|
| Arhaulochargo | 1 | 4 | - | 5 |
| Tallouwar Micco | 4 | 1 | - | 5 |
| Hopoithlo Yoholo | 2 | 3 | - | 5 |
| Sandy Jusong | 1 | 1 | - | 2 |
| Neharlocco | 2 | 2 | - | 4 |
| Echhosti Hargo | 4 | 3 | - | 7 |
| Tuskenehaw | 1 | 1 | - | 2 |
| O Sooch Hargo | 1 | 1 | - | 2 |
| Archuloc Hargo | 1 | 1 | - | 2 |
| Wac Se Micco | 4 | 1 | - | 5 |
| Parhas Fixico | 3 | 2 | - | 5 |
| Woc Sehotattar | 1 | 2 | - | 3 |
| Noko Silla | 3 | 3 | - | 6 |
| Sockasa Fixico | 1 | 1 | - | 2 |
| Nehaw Hargo | 3 | 2 | - | 5 |
| Arhawloc Fixico | 1 | 1 | - | 2 |
| Spinny Hargo | 3 | 2 | - | 5 |
| Coosista Hargo | 3 | 1 | - | 4 |
| Echo Fixico | 2 | 2 | - | 4 |
| Micco Yoholo | 1 | 1 | - | 2 |
| George | 1 | 1 | - | 2 |
| Nekose Emarthlar | 1 | 3 | - | 4 |
| Echo Emarthlar | 3 | 1 | - | 4 |
| Spanny Fixico | 3 | 1 | - | 4 |
| Echo Hargo | 2 | 3 | - | 5 |
| Arbiock Hargo | 1 | 1 | - | 2 |
| Chuwastiliga | 2 | 3 | - | 5 |
| Nokas Hargo | 1 | 1 | - | 2 |
| Miccoche | 1 | 1 | - | 2 |
| Archule Hargo | 1 | 1 | - | 2 |
| Neharbotte Hargo | 1 | 1 | - | 2 |
| Ebockie | 1 | 1 | - | 2 |
| Ho Tulga Yoholo | 1 | 1 | - | 2 |
| Tussicya Hatk | 2 | 2 | - | 4 |

CREEK CENSUS—Continued.

| Names of Heads of Families. | Males. | Females. | Slaves. | Total. |
|---|---|---|---|---|
| Conu Yoholo - - - - | 4 | 1 | - | 5 |
| Sumar Lee - - - - | 1 | 2 | - | 3 |
| Emarthlar Hatka - - - | 3 | 2 | - | 5 |
| Coosista Emarthlar - - - | 1 | 1 | - | 2 |
| Conchadda - - - - | 2 | 2 | - | 4 |
| Ichcarkau - - - - | 1 | 2 | - | 3 |
| Narcomie - - - - | 1 | 1 | - | 2 |
| Konip Hargochoche - - - | 1 | 1 | - | 2 |
| Tallowwar Fixico - - - | 3 | 1 | - | 4 |
| | 81 | 69 | | 150 |
| Tallowdeg Micco - - - - | 1 | 1 | . | 2 |
| Yarharhargo - - - - | 2 | 1 | . | 3 |
| Ufacola Fixico - - - - | 1 | 1 | . | 2 |
| Cockchar Fixico - - - - | 1 | 2 | . | 3 |
| Spoakoak Fixico - - - - | 2 | 2 | . | 4 |
| Parwasse Yoholo - - - - | 1 | 2 | . | 3 |
| Yoholo Hargo - - - - | 3 | 2 | . | 5 |
| Illis Fixico - - - - | 1 | 1 | . | 2 |
| Hollattar Emarthlar - - - | 1 | 1 | . | 2 |
| Oackchon Hargo - - - - | 2 | 2 | . | 4 |
| Tuskeag Hargo - - - - | 1 | 1 | . | 2 |
| Immarmieke Yoholo - - - | 1 | 1 | . | 2 |
| Hatlarda - - - - - | 1 | 1 | . | 2 |
| Carbreachche Hargo - - - | 2 | 2 | . | 4 |
| Hopoie - - - - - | 2 | 1 | . | 3 |
| Tussiggayar Hargo - - - | 1 | 3 | . | 4 |
| Timmarlastiche - - - - | 1 | 1 | . | 2 |
| Cochchi Yoholo - - - - | 1 | 1 | . | 2 |
| Tallintisiggayar - - - - | 2 | 2 | . | 4 |
| Nokoshargo (2d of same name,) - - | 1 | 1 | . | 2 |
| Tusconer Fixico - - - | 1 | 3 | . | 4 |
| Micco Emarthlar - - - | 2 | 2 | . | 4 |
| Octtiarche - - - - | 1 | 1 | . | 2 |
| Hobiehatka - - - - | 2 | 1 | . | 3 |
| Maholiie - - - - | 1 | 1 | . | 2 |
| Charboaf Hargo - - - - | 2 | 3 | . | 5 |
| Nokosiggar - - - - | 3 | 2 | . | 5 |
| Echhas Fixico - - - - | 2 | 2 | . | 4 |
| Simlummie - - - - | - | 3 | , | 3 |
| Wolega - - - - - | 1 | 1 | . | 2 |
| Nulhega - - - - - | 1 | 2 | . | 3 |
| Sarwonhie - - - - | 2 | 2 | . | 4 |
| Conohie - - - - | 1 | 1 | , | 2 |
| Nauk Kar - - - - | 1 | 1 | . | 2 |

## CREEK CENSUS—Continued.

| Names of Heads of Families. | Males. | Females. | Slaves. | Total. |
|---|---|---|---|---|
| Tobothliga - - - - - | 3 | 1 | . | 4 |
| Lawgische - - - - - | - | 2 | . | 2 |
| Tustanug Fixico - - - - | 1 | 1 | . | 2 |
| Larbieajar - - - - - | - | 2 | . | 2 |
| Illindur - - - - - | 1 | 1 | . | 2 |
| Isfanniskar - - - - | 2 | 1 | . | 3 |
| Clesarttie - - - - | 1 | 2 | . | 3 |
| Sarginnar - - - - | 2 | 1 | . | 3 |
| Itole Hogar - - - - | 1 | 1 | . | 2 |
| Gie Sick - - - - - | - | 2 | . | 2 |
| | 59 | 68 | | 127 |
| Starhokie . . . . | 1 | 2 | . | 3 |
| Tecumgie . . . . | 1 | 2 | . | 3 |
| Toharkie . . . . | 1 | 2 | . | 3 |
| Saddetojie . . . . | 3 | 1 | . | 4 |
| Ar Sabogie . . . . | 1 | 1 | . | 2 |
| Mis Tar Ta . . . . | 1 | 2 | . | 3 |
| Micconubbar . . . . | 1 | 2 | . | 3 |
| Sarwehogar . . . . | 1 | 2 | . | 3 |
| Ottasa Yoholo . . . . | 1 | 4 | . | 5 |
| Sarlieakkie . . . . | 1 | 2 | . | 3 |
| Immeha . . . . | 1 | 1 | . | 2 |
| Intobieheach Kar . . . . | - | 2 | . | 2 |
| Woboga . . . . | 4 | 3 | . | 7 |
| Mundarla . . . . | - | 2 | . | 2 |
| Hardoapkar . . . . | 1 | 1 | . | 2 |
| Sarnarhie . . . . | - | 2 | . | 2 |
| Ottis Micco . . . . | 3 | 1 | . | 4 |
| Moaktarnie . . . . | - | 2 | . | 2 |
| Yartarwa Hargo . . . . | 2 | 2 | . | 4 |
| Tallesse Micco . . . . | 2 | 1 | . | 3 |
| Talmachiss Hargo . . . . | 1 | 2 | . | 3 |
| Sarnarithoice . . . . | 2 | 2 | . | 4 |
| Isstuddie . . . . | 1 | 5 | . | 6 |
| Kinhar . . . . | 1 | 2 | . | 3 |
| Cheek Copkar . . . . | 2 | 3 | . | 5 |
| Homiedoattie . . . . | 1 | 2 | . | 3 |
| Marlarliga . . . . | 3 | 2 | . | 5 |
| Yehonie . . . . | 1 | 1 | . | 2 |
| Koneethlar . . . . | 2 | 1 | . | 3 |
| Istimmie Fitz Tarkie . . . | - | 2 | . | 2 |
| Sarkoliga . . . . | 2 | 3 | . | 5 |
| Nar Sic Tar . . . . | - | 2 | o | 2 |
| Hopoithleana . . . . | - | 2 | . | 2 |

CREEK CENSUS—Continued.

| Names of Heads of Families. | Males. | Females. | Slaves. | Total. |
|---|---|---|---|---|
| Ohartarlie | - | 2 | . | 2 |
| Tarfarlot Hoie | 1 | 2 | . | 3 |
| Iskarbotkie | - | 3 | . | 3 |
| Simmarttome | 1 | 1 | . | 2 |
| Simhulga | 3 | 3 | . | 6 |
| Pop Huck Kar | - | 2 | . | 2 |
| Spokeokee Yoholo | 2 | 1 | . | 3 |
| Emarthlo Chopco | 2 | 1 | . | 3 |
| Talmarkeloche | 2 | 1 | . | 3 |
| Wiguickcha | 1 | 1 | . | 2 |
| Tasconer | 3 | 4 | . | 7 |
| | 56 | 87 | | 143 |
| Sarbarhoie | 2 | 2 | - | 4 |
| Stimmissa | — | 2 | - | 2 |
| Yarbohoie | 2 | 2 | - | 4 |
| Hockkarboyiega | 1 | 1 | - | 2 |
| Tal Hoakkie | 2 | 3 | - | 5 |
| Chockkiepar | — | 3 | - | 3 |
| Kinhariecha | 1 | 1 | - | 2 |
| Tarlargie | 2 | 3 | - | 5 |
| Miathlar | 1 | 1 | - | 2 |
| Stinkarbarkie | 1 | 3 | - | 4 |
| Hiedega | 1 | 2 | - | 3 |
| Monlarbiejar | 1 | 2 | - | 3 |
| Simmitkolee | 1 | 1 | - | 2 |
| Ottis Fixico | 3 | 1 | - | 4 |
| Coosaneharlocco | 1 | 1 | - | 2 |
| Archularchopco | 1 | 1 | - | 2 |
| Arwiebie | 1 | 1 | - | 2 |
| Yillesee Micco | 2 | 3 | - | 5 |
| Hobungar | 1 | 1 | - | 2 |
| Conchaddalocco | 3 | 1 | - | 4 |
| Kocluis Hargo | 1 | 1 | - | 2 |
| Taginnar | 1 | 1 | - | 2 |
| Osourer | 2 | 3 | - | 5 |
| Fullodie | 1 | 1 | - | 2 |
| Tuckabatcha Fixico | 2 | 2 | - | 4 |
| Sekosar | 1 | 1 | - | 2 |
| Luwiga | 2 | 1 | . | 3 |
| Osse Yoholo | 3 | 2 | - | 5 |
| Nokiejar | — | 3 | - | 3 |
| Ufawla Hargo | 1 | 1 | - | 2 |
| Kinnesar | 2 | 5 | - | 7 |
| Arlock Fixico | 3 | 2 | - | 5 |
| Arpithki Yoholo | 1 | 2 | - | 3 |

CREEK CENSUS—Continued.

| Names of Heads of Families. | Males. | Females. | Slaves. | Total. |
|---|---|---|---|---|
| Tuckabacha Fixico (2d of same name)    - | 3 | 1 | - | 4 |
| Tussickkia Hargo    -    -    - | 3 | — | . | 3 |
| Fus Hacha    -    -    -    - | 3 | 4 | - | 7 |
| Chuwilla Hargo    -    -    .    - | 2 | 3 | - | 5 |
| Tomma Emarthlar    -    -    - | 2 | 2 | - | 4 |
| Coekkonarhar    -    -    -    - | 1 | 2 | - | 3 |
| Arharlocco Yoholo    -    -    - | 2 | — | - | 2 |
| Odis Hargo    -    -    -    - | 2 | 1 | - | 3 |
| Cockchar Micco    -    -    -    - | 2 | 1 | - | 3 |
| Chimmarkoakkie    -    -    - | 1 | 2 | - | 3 |
| Kinhiche    -    -    -    - | 1 | 1 | - | 2 |
|  | 69 | 77 |  | 146 |
| Chogartta    -    -    -    - | 2 | 1 | - | 3 |
| Cobbick Yoholo    -    -    -    - | 2 | 1 | - | 3 |
| Coossar Hargo    -    -    -    - | 1 | 1 | - | 2 |
| Osooch Yoholo    -    -    -    - | 2 | 1 | - | 3 |
| Tockco Hila    -    -    -    - | 1 | 1 | - | 2 |
| Socerbola    -    -    -    - | — | 2 | - | 2 |
| Polly    -    -    -    - | — | 2 | - | 2 |
| Tuckabatch Emarthlar    -    -    - | 1 | 1 | - | 2 |
| Simmecar    -    -    -    - | 1 | 1 | - | 2 |
| Chos Yoholo    -    -    -    - | 2 | 1 | - | 3 |
| Sehojackcha    -    -    -    - | 1 | 1 | - | 2 |
| Cussutar Hargo    -    .    -    - | 2 | 3 | - | 5 |
| Fitztarkie    -    -    -    - | 2 | 3 | - | 5 |
| Osolosee    -    -    -    - | — | 2 | - | 2 |
| Tommy Yoholo    -    -    -    - | 1 | 2 | - | 3 |
| CHEHAW TOWN. |  |  |  |  |
| Parhos Fixico    .    .    .    . | 5 | 1 | - | 6 |
| Nokos Hargo    .    .    .    . | 3 | 2 | - | 5 |
| Spoak Oak Hargo    .    -    . | 2 | 3 | - | 5 |
| Noscop Fixico    .    .    .    . | 5 | 1 | - | 6 |
| Chogarttie Yoholo    -    .    .    . | 2 | 1 | - | 3 |
| Nolthbob Emarthloche    .    .    . | 2 | 4 | - | 6 |
| Charley    .    .    .    . | 4 | 2 | - | 6 |
| Noscop Hargo    .    .    .    . | 4 | 4 | - | 8 |
| Thlathlo Yoholo    .    .    .    . | 1 | 1 | - | 2 |
| Clis Sarhoice    .    .    .    . | 1 | 1 | - | 2 |
| Tusconu Hargo    .    .    .    . | 4 | 5 | - | 9 |
| Connathlar    .    .    .    . | 1 | 1 | - | 2 |
| Sofullega    .    .    .    . | 1 | 1 | - | 2 |
| Talloaf Hargo    .    .    .    . | 5 | 2 | - | 7 |
| Homega    .    .    .    . | 1 | 2 | - | 3 |
| Simmarla    .    .    .    . | 2 | 1 | - | 3 |

### CREEK CENSUS—Continued.

| Names of Heads of Families. | Males. | Females. | Slaves. | Total. |
|---|---|---|---|---|
| Cockladiga . . . . | 2 | 1 | - | 3 |
| Jack . . . . | 1 | 2 | - | 3 |
| Cauphiga . . . . | 2 | 2 | - | 4 |
| Otehia . . . . | 1 | 1 | - | 2 |
| Nochicha . . . . | 1 | 1 | - | 2 |
| Slarhoie . . . . | — | 3 | - | 3 |
| Matta . . . . | 1 | 1 | - | 2 |
| | 69 | 66 | | 135 |
| Ekingar . . . . | 1 | 2 | - | 3 |
| Marthlohie . . . . | 3 | 1 | - | 4 |
| Warga . . . . | 1 | 1 | - | 2 |
| Billy . . . . | 2 | 1 | - | 3 |
| Summer . . . . | 2 | 1 | - | 3 |
| **TUSKEEGA TOWN.** | | | | |
| Hillubba Hargo . . . . | 2 | 1 | - | 3 |
| Nehar Micco . . . . | 2 | 1 | - | 3 |
| Ottis Hargo . . . . | 2 | 2 | 17 | 21 |
| Nokose Emarthlar . . . | 1 | 1 | - | 2 |
| Osir Hargo . . . . | 2 | 4 | - | 6 |
| O Gilla Ser . . . . | 1 | 1 | - | 2 |
| Parhos Fixico . . . . | 2 | 2 | - | 4 |
| O Gillisinnehar . . . . | 2 | 3 | - | 5 |
| Nehelocco . . . . | 1 | 2 | - | 3 |
| Samuel Manack . . . . | 2 | 1 | - | 3 |
| Emathlar . . . . | 2 | 2 | - | 4 |
| Chulocco Hargo . . . . | 4 | 2 | - | 6 |
| Octiache Emarthlar . . . | 2 | — | - | 2 |
| Hotulga Emarthlar . . . | 2 | 2 | - | 4 |
| Konip Emarthlar . . . | 3 | 2 | - | 5 |
| Casseetar Hargo . . . . | 2 | 2 | - | 4 |
| Cockche Yoholo . . . . | 1 | 3 | - | 4 |
| Tallowwar Hargo . . . | 1 | 4 | - | 5 |
| Coosa Fixico . . . . | 3 | 2 | 3 | 8 |
| Echo Fixico . . . . | 1 | 3 | - | 4 |
| Micco Hatka . . . . | 3 | 2 | 13 | 18 |
| Joseph Goowin . . . . | 1 | 2 | - | 3 |
| James McGilvary . . . . | 1 | 2 | - | 3 |
| Colemie Tushamugga . . . | 1 | 1 | - | 2 |
| Ocoiehooche . . . . | 1 | 3 | - | 4 |
| Octiarche Hargo - - - - | 1 | 1 | - | 2 |
| Charche Yoholo - - - - | 1 | 1 | - | 2 |
| Lewes Manuck - - - - | 3 | 2 | - | 5 |

34‡

CREEK CENSUS—Continued.

| Names of Heads of Families. | Males. | Females. | Slaves. | Total. |
|---|---|---|---|---|
| Nokos Fixico - - - - | 1 | 3 | - | 4 |
| Echo Hargo - - - - | 1 | 1 | - | 2 |
| Konip Hargo - - - - | 1 | 2 | - | 3 |
| Tinthannis Hargo - - - - | 3 | 2 | - | 5 |
| Micco Yoholo - - - - | 2 | 3 | - | 5 |
| Micco Hargo - - - - | 2 | 1 | - | 3 |
| | 69 | 72 | 33 | 174 |
| Carworbie - - - - | 1 | 2 | - | 3 |
| Oackchon Hargo - - - - | 2 | | - | 2 |
| Billy - - - - | 1 | 1 | - | 2 |
| Dick - - - - | 1 | 1 | - | 2 |
| Francis - - - - | 1 | 1 | - | 2 |
| Sandy - - - - | 1 | 1 | - | 2 |
| McIntosh - - - - | 1 | 1 | - | 2 |
| Sister - - - - | 1 | 1 | - | 2 |
| Tarwarhie - - - - | 2 | 2 | - | 4 |
| Sarnarhie - - - - | 1 | 1 | - | 2 |
| Sally Car - - - - | — | 2 | 2 | 4 |
| Chocolarga - - - - | — | 2 | - | 2 |
| Suthoyie - - - - | 1 | 1 | - | 2 |
| Tarwarsickkie - - - | 1 | 1 | - | 2 |
| Nancy - - - - | — | 2 | - | 2 |
| Warnarhieya - - - - | — | 2 | - | 2 |
| Settonhoeeka - - - - | 1 | 2 | - | 3 |
| Timmeteeche - - - - | — | 4 | - | 4 |
| Nelly - - - - | — | 2 | - | 2 |
| Moseley - - - - | — | 2 | - | 2 |
| Dick, (2d of same name) - - - | 1 | 2 | - | 3 |
| Thlanarkie - - - - | 1 | 1 | - | 2 |
| Polly McGilvery - - - | 1 | 2 | - | 3 |
| Polly Cane - - - - | - | 3 | - | 3 |
| Rose Sa - - - - | 1 | 3 | - | 4 |
| Fannar - - - - | 2 | 2 | - | 4 |
| Sintha - - - - | 2 | 2 | - | 4 |
| Rachael - - - - | - | 5 | - | 5 |
| John Ward - - - - | 1 | 3 | - | 4 |
| Con Charta - - - - | 1 | 1 | - | 2 |
| Hanna McGirth - - - | 1 | 2 | - | 3 |
| Iackopie - - - - | 1 | 1 | - | 2 |
| Mary, (a free negro) - - - | 2 | 3 | - | 5 |
| | 29 | 61 | 2 | 92 |

CREEK CENSUS—Continued.

| Names of Heads of Families. | Males. | Females. | Slaves. | Total. |
|---|---|---|---|---|
| COOSAWDA TOWN. | | | | |
| Micco Hatka - - - - | 3 | 2 | - | 5 |
| Cochchar Hargo - - - - | 1 | 1 | - | 2 |
| Nokosickar - - - - | 1 | 1 | - | 2 |
| Coloche Emarthlar - - - | 1 | 1 | - | 2 |
| Nehar Fixico - - - - | 2 | 3 | - | 5 |
| Tommy Yoholo - - - - | 2 | 1 | - | 3 |
| Eckhos Hargo - - - - | 3 | 3 | - | 6 |
| Archi Yoholo - - - - | 2 | 2 | - | 4 |
| Emarthloche - - - - | 1 | 1 | - | 2 |
| Albuddar Hargo - - - - | 1 | 1 | - | 2 |
| Toatkartoche - - - - | 1 | 1 | - | 2 |
| Nehar Hargo - - - - | 1 | 1 | - | 2 |
| Cussictar Hargo - - - - | 1 | 1 | - | 2 |
| Nosiccar Hargo - - - - | 1 | 1 | - | 2 |
| Mitteetarkee - - - - | 2 | 2 | - | 4 |
| Ospodark Hargo - - - - | 1 | 1 | - | 2 |
| Samuel Sizemore - - - - | 1 | 1 | - | 2 |
| Sinnoche - - - - - | 1 | 1 | - | 2 |
| Siecokie - - - - - | 1 | 1 | - | 2 |
| Fushatch Yoholo - - - | 1 | 1 | - | 2 |
| Connorhie - - - - | - | 2 | - | 2 |
| Hathla - - - - - | 1 | 1 | - | 2 |
| Soccooche - - - - | — | 2 | - | 2 |
| Molly - - - - - | — | 3 | - | 3 |
| Inhokie - - - - - | — | 2 | - | 2 |
| Konip Hargo - - - - | 2 | — | - | 2 |
| Talliah - - - - - | — | 2 | - | 2 |
| Tunhoie - - - - - | — | 4 | - | 4 |
| Charhie - - - - - | — | 2 | - | 2 |
| Tallika - - - - - | 1 | 1 | - | 2 |
| Nancy - - - - - | — | 2 | - | 2 |
| Sekena - - - - - | — | 2 | - | 2 |
| | 32 | 50 | | 82 |
| CUBIHATCHA TOWN. | | | | |
| Peter Anderson - - - - | 2 | — | - | 2 |
| Mutteachkar - - - - | 1 | 1 | - | 2 |
| Sucky - - - - - | 1 | 2 | - | 3 |
| Samarerkly - - - - | 1 | 2 | - | 3 |
| Solodega - - - - - | 2 | 2 | - | 4 |
| Thomas Barefoot - - - | 4 | 3 | - | 7 |
| William McGirth - - - | 3 | 3 | 2 | 8 |
| Benjamin Walker - - - | 2 | 2 | - | 4 |

CREEK CENSUS—Continued.

| Names of Heads of Families. | Males. | Females. | Slaves. | Total. |
|---|---|---|---|---|
| Thomas Peegeon - - - - | 2 | 3 | - | 5 |
| Betsy Peeogeon - - - - | — | 2 | - | 2 |
| Finnehar - - - - - | 1 | 1 | - | 2 |
| Carbiethcar - - - - | 1 | 1 | - | 2 |
| Joseph Peeggieon - - - - | 2 | 3 | - | 5 |
| Patta - - - - - | 4 | 1 | - | 5 |
| Conchart - - - - | 3 | 2 | - | 5 |
| Chucules Hargo - - - - | 2 | 1 | - | 3 |
| Tawossa Micco - - - - | 2 | 1 | - | 3 |
| Pin Hargo - - - - | 1 | 1 | - | 2 |
| David Piegeon - - - - | 2 | 3 | - | 5 |
| Chonatkar - - - - | 1 | 1 | - | 2 |
| Thickhannick - - - - | 1 | 1 | - | 2 |
| William Walker - - - - | 3 | 2 | 32 | 37 |
| Mary Wills - - - - | — | 2 | - | 2 |
| Good Day - - - - | 2 | 2 | - | 4 |
| Arwattalega - - - - | 1 | 1 | - | 2 |
| Mahaley Tooley - - - - | 1 | 3 | 2 | 6 |
| Vardy Jolly - - - - | 1 | 4 | - | 5 |
| Slarhie - - - - - | 4 | 2 | - | 6 |
| Homer Hargo - - - - | — | 2 | - | 2 |
| Siohbie - - - - - | 4 | 2 | - | 6 |
| Widdow Cornels - - - - | 1 | 1 | 10 | 12 |
| Littokie - - - - - | 1 | 1 | 3 | 5 |
| Betsy, (a free negro) - - - | 3 | 4 | - | 7 |
| Tewkonar Harjo - - - - | 1 | 1 | - | 2 |
| Temeethieche - - - - | 1 | 1 | - | 2 |
| Talmarse Yoholo, (alias same) - - | 1 | 2 | - | 3 |
| | 59 | 65 | 49 | 173 |

THLOBTHLOCCO TOWN.

| | | | | |
|---|---|---|---|---|
| Arthlee . . . . . | 2 | 1 | - | 3 |
| Ocheenar . . . . | 1 | 1 | - | 2 |
| John Marshall . . . . | 1 | 1 | 5 | 7 |
| Funny . . . . . | 4 | 1 | - | 5 |
| Sin Pieka Barnard . . . | 3 | 3 | - | 6 |
| Chegartta Tustanugga . . . | 3 | 2 | - | 5 |
| Chocolo Hathka . . . . | 1 | 1 | - | 2 |
| Noco Se Yoholo . . . . | 1 | 4 | - | 5 |
| Tulwe Tustanugga . . . | 3 | 1 | - | 4 |
| Tusnic Charta . . . . | 5 | 1 | - | 6 |
| Micco Hatka . . . . | 2 | 1 | - | 3 |
| Sinnarthlar . . . . | 1 | 1 | - | 2 |
| William Barnard, (2d same name) . | 2 | 1 | . | 3 |

CREEK CENSUS—Continued.

| Names of Heads of Families. | Males. | Females. | Slaves. | Total. |
| --- | --- | --- | --- | --- |
| Chocottie | 3 | 1 | - | 4 |
| Har Hie | 1 | 2 | - | 3 |
| Parsco Hargo | 1 | 4 | - | 5 |
| Lepos See | 1 | 1 | - | 2 |
| Hackhallowa | 1 | 2 | 14 | 17 |
| Yelcor Hargo | 1 | 2 | - | 3 |
| Sortie Hoie | 1 | 2 | - | 2 |
| Cono Fixico | 1 | 1 | - | 2 |
| Asho Liga | — | 2 | - | 2 |
| Nehe Yoholo | 2 | — | - | 2 |
| Hotulga Hargo | 1 | 1 | - | 2 |
| Ofulgar | 1 | 1 | - | 2 |
| Parsartie | 1 | 3 | - | 4 |
| Chewaste Hargo | 1 | 1 | - | 2 |
| Tommy Yoholo | 1 | 2 | - | 3 |
| Cheloak Hargo | 1 | 1 | - | 2 |
| Finne Tega | 1 | 1 | - | 2 |
| Sattuck Hargo | — | 2 | - | 2 |
| Muccowiga | 1 | 1 | - | 2 |
| Math Seth Tar | — | 2 | - | 2 |
| Tussickeholattar | 1 | 1 | - | 2 |
| Yoholo Hargo | 1 | 2 | - | 3 |
| Fus Hargo | 1 | 3 | - | 4 |
| Timmoholiga | — | 2 | - | 2 |
| Sannar Hoga | — | 3 | - | 3 |
| Sintaggaha | 2 | 2 | - | 4 |
| Ofockcha | — | 2 | - | 2 |
| | 54 | 66 | 19 | 139 |
| Milgar | 1 | 1 | - | 2 |
| Hotul Fixico | 1 | 1 | - | 2 |
| Fecolike | 2 | 1 | - | 3 |
| Fashotie | — | 2 | - | 2 |
| Arseoakie | 2 | 1 | - | 3 |
| Ashounhoga | 1 | 1 | - | 2 |
| Sallijabba | 1 | 1 | - | 2 |
| Arharsway | 1 | 1 | - | 2 |
| Hoyarna | 1 | 1 | - | 2 |
| Te Higa | 1 | 1 | - | 2 |
| Tobothkie | — | 2 | - | 2 |
| Betsy | 1 | 1 | - | 2 |
| Arnoche | 1 | 1 | - | 2 |
| Yothliga | — | 2 | - | 2 |
| Tommy Emarthlar | 2 | — | - | 2 |
| Soccokika | — | 3 | - | 3 |

CREEK CENSUS—Continued.

| Names of Heads of Families. | Males. | Females. | Slaves. | Total. |
|---|---|---|---|---|
| Spanny Tustanugga - - - | 2 | 1 | - | 3 |
| Osarenehar - - - - | 1 | 2 | - | 3 |
| Setemarsa - - - - | — | 2 | - | 2 |
| Cely - - - - - | — | 3 | - | 3 |
| Sucky - - - - - | 2 | — | - | 2 |
| Tommy Hargo - - - - | 1 | 2 | - | 3 |
| Isfarka - - - - - | 2 | — | - | 2 |
| Atlochi - - - - - | 2 | — | - | 2 |
| Suffoniga - - - - - | 1 | 1 | - | 2 |
| Talladeg Hargo - - - - | 2 | 1 | - | 3 |
| | 28 | 32 | | 60 |

LUCHIPOGA TOWN.

| | Males. | Females. | Slaves. | Total. |
|---|---|---|---|---|
| Chuloc Tustanugga - - - | 4 | 3 | - | 7 |
| Chiocome Micco - - - - | 2 | 3 | - | 5 |
| Micco Legar - - - - | 1 | 1 | - | 2 |
| Oakchart Yoholo - - - - | 2 | 1 | - | 3 |
| Conchart Emarthlar - - - | 3 | 4 | - | 7 |
| Eachhos Hargo - - - - | 2 | 4 | - | 6 |
| Fus Hargo - - - - | 2 | 4 | - | 6 |
| Artup Hargo - - - - | 2 | 3 | - | 5 |
| Nehar Yoholo - - - - | 2 | 3 | - | 5 |
| Ardiecan Hargo - - - - | 2 | 3 | - | 5 |
| Tallaharsa Hargo - - - - | 2 | 2 | - | 4 |
| Colelame Hargo - - - - | 2 | 2 | - | 4 |
| Fixico Hargo - - - - | 4 | 2 | - | 6 |
| Nehar Hargo - - - - | 2 | 2 | - | 4 |
| Hogillise Hargo - - - - | 2 | 3 | - | 5 |
| Neharlocco Yoholo - - - | 6 | 3 | - | 9 |
| Warla Emarthlar - - - - | 4 | 4 | - | 8 |
| Octiarchi Emarthlar - - - | 1 | 2 | - | 3 |
| Ichcleachwarche - - - - | 2 | 3 | - | 5 |
| Wocse Yoholo - - - - | 1 | 1 | - | 2 |
| Cochchar Hargo - - - - | 2 | 2 | - | 4 |
| Coegus Hargo - - - - | 3 | 1 | - | 4 |
| Nelson - - - - - | 2 | 5 | - | 7 |
| Nolocco Hargo - - - - | 3 | 3 | - | 6 |
| Oser Micco - - - - | 1 | 3 | - | 4 |
| Hillubba Hargo - - - - | 2 | 1 | - | 3 |
| Cowoccoche Emarthlar - - - | 6 | 3 | - | 9 |
| Losti Yoholo - - - - | 4 | 3 | - | 7 |
| Nokos Fixico - - - - | 2 | 2 | - | 4 |
| Octiarche Yoholo - - - - | 1 | 2 | - | 3 |
| Ottes Fixico - - - - | 3 | 3 | - | 6 |

### CREEK CENSUS—Continued.

| Names of Heads of Families. | Males. | Females. | Slaves. | Total. |
|---|---|---|---|---|
| Fuckta Lusta - , - - - | 1 | 1 | - | 2 |
| Wacse Hargo - - - - | 5 | 3 | - | 8 |
| Fushatchche Tustanugga - - - | 1 | 1 | - | 2 |
| Coe Hargo - - - - | 1 | 1 | - | 2 |
| Kinnehar - - - - | 2 | 1 | - | 3 |
| Poitt Hargo - - - - | 2 | 1 | - | 3 |
| Chis Le Hargo - - - - | 2 | 1 | - | 3 |
| Yarkinhar Micco - - - - | 2 | 2 | - | 4 |
| Cucchart Fixico - - - - | 2 | 1 | - | 3 |
| Oakfulga - - - - - | 3 | 1 | - | 4 |
| Tulga Yoholo - - - - | 2 | 1 | - | 3 |
| Hillis Hargo - - - - | 1 | 1 | - | 2 |
|  | 101 | 96 |  | 197 |
| Tallisee Yoholo - - - - | 3 | 1 | - | 4 |
| Cubbitch Hargo - - - - | 1 | 1 | - | 2 |
| Fushatchcha Fixico - - - | 1 | 1 | - | 2 |
| Coe Emarthlar - - - | 1 | 1 | - | 2 |
| Emarthloche - - - | 1 | 4 | - | 5 |
| Efar Yoholo - - - - | 2 | - | - | 2 |
| Arsehiga - - - - | 1 | 2 | - | 3 |
| Octe Arche Fixico - - - | 1 | 1 | - | 2 |
| Octe Arche Hargo - - - | 1 | 1 | - | 2 |
| Miccochohoconoce - - - | 1 | 1 | - | 2 |
| Tallope Yoholo - - - - | 1 | 2 | - | 3 |
| Innehar Fixico - - - - | 1 | 1 | - | 2 |
| Iemarmie Fixico - - - - | 1 | 1 | - | 2 |
| Concharthargochule - - - | 2 | 1 | - | 3 |
| Talladega - - - - | 1 | 2 | - | 3 |
| Thlath Thlo Hargo - - - | 2 | 3 | - | 5 |
| Ne Emarthlar Hargo - - - | 1 | 1 | - | 2 |
| Micco Fixico - - - - | 2 | 2 | - | 4 |
| Echoarchular - - - - | 3 | 3 | - | 6 |
| Tallise Hargo - - - - | 2 | 1 | - | 3 |
| Mickeya - - - - | 2 | 3 | - | 5 |
| Connarhische - - - - | - | 2 | - | 2 |
| Searthlibie - - - - | - | 2 | - | 2 |
| Billy - - - - - | 1 | 2 | - | 3 |
| Moheah - - - - - | 3 | 3 | - | 6 |
| Ichhos Micco - - - - | - | 2 | - | 2 |
| Cha Sartie - - - - | 1 | 3 | - | 4 |
| Mohiga - - - - - | 1 | 1 | - | 2 |
| Ichhohea - - - - - | 1 | 2 | - | 3 |
| Fil To Parsa - - - - | - | 2 | - | 2 |
| Argissa - - - - - | - | 2 | - | 2 |

## CREEK CENSUS—Continued.

| Names of Heads of Families. | Males. | Females. | Slaves. | Total. |
|---|---|---|---|---|
| Farmome - - - - - | - | 4 | - | 4 |
| Ehattau - - - - - | 1 | 2 | - | 3 |
| Ohiatkar - - - - - | 1 | 1 | - | 2 |
| Yarnoga - - - - - | - | 3 | - | 3 |
| Hich Iga - - - - - | - | 3 | - | 3 |
| O Tekar - - - - - | 1 | 3 | - | 4 |
| Marquehokie - - - - | 1 | 3 | - | 4 |
| Chocolocco - - - - | 1 | 1 | - | 2 |
| Wottoga - - - - - | - | 2 | - | 2 |
| Hichcoge - - - - | 1 | 4 | - | 5 |
| Clechummeholattar - - - | 1 | 1 | - | 2 |
| Kingarhie - - - | 1 | 1 | - | 2 |
| Chochehogar - - - - | - | 2 | - | 2 |
| | 46 | 84 | | 130 |
| Carbet Tunny - - - - | 1 | 1 | - | 2 |
| Cobbescha - - - - | 1 | 2 | - | 3 |
| Miocco - - - - - | - | 2 | - | 2 |
| Hargo - - - - - | - | 3 | - | 3 |
| Con Sippie - - - - | 1 | 1 | - | 2 |
| Sago Ya - - - - - | 1 | 2 | - | 3 |
| Caty - - - - - | 2 | 1 | - | 3 |
| Sofunga - - - - - | - | 2 | - | 2 |
| Im Farlinnar - - - - | 1 | 1 | - | 2 |
| Sardirche - - - - | - | 2 | - | 2 |
| Oaklarna - - - - | 1 | 1 | - | 2 |
| Sundilla - - - - | 1 | 2 | - | 3 |
| Inhe Yar Hargar - - - | 1 | 1 | - | 2 |
| Jimmy - - - - | 1 | 2 | - | 3 |
| Lucy Lusta - - - | - | 2 | - | 2 |
| Ficeco Yatcha - - - - | - | 2 | - | 2 |
| Sarwe Yaga - - - - | - | 2 | - | 2 |
| Matlega - - - - - | 1 | 2 | - | 3 |
| Sally - - - - - | 1 | 3 | - | 4 |
| Simmo Siar - - - - | 1 | 1 | - | 2 |
| Ticcarhie - - - - - | 2 | 3 | - | 5 |
| Arbutchcha - - - - | - | 2 | - | 2 |
| Nancy - - - - - | - | 2 | - | 2 |
| Carpuggy - - - - - | - | 3 | - | 3 |
| Ninor - - - - - | 4 | 1 | - | 5 |
| Lindy - - - - - | - | 2 | - | 2 |
| Osunnie - - - - - | - | 2 | - | 2 |
| Tohatta - - - - - | 1 | 1 | - | 2 |
| Inmindie - - - - - | 1 | 2 | - | 3 |
| Inheachkar - - - - | 1 | 1 | - | 2 |

## CREEK CENSUS—Continued.

| Names of Heads of Families. | Males. | Females. | Slaves. | Total. |
|---|---|---|---|---|
| Clarhola - - - - - | 1 | 4 | - | 5 |
| Ubocla Tiga - - - - | 1 | 2 | - | 3 |
| Sehallatter - - - - | - | 2 | - | 2 |
| Tiarkkie - - - - - | 1 | 2 | - | 3 |
| Coiegar - - - - - | 3 | 1 | - | 4 |
| Oakchartcoche (2d of same name) - | 2 | 1 | - | 3 |
| Miccocharttie - - - - | 1 | 1 | - | 2 |
| Archule Hargo - - - - | 4 | 1 | - | 5 |
| Micco Marhe - - - - | 1 | 1 | - | 2 |
| Palat Kar - - - - - | 3 | 2 | - | 5 |
| Atbithliga - - - - - | 1 | 1 | - | 2 |
| Innarthnar - - - - | 1 | 2 | - | 3 |
| Jimmy (2d of same name) - - | 3 | 2 | - | 5 |
| Narboche - - - - - | 1 | 2 | - | 3 |
| | 46 | 77 | | 123 |
| Soap Kar - - - - - | 1 | 1 | - | 2 |
| Sear Karbie - - - - | - | 3 | - | 3 |
| Big Luey - - - - - | 1 | 3 | - | 4 |
| Tallithoei - - - - - | 1 | 3 | - | 4 |
| Sehega - - - - - | 1 | 1 | - | 2 |
| Tackeathto - - - - | - | 2 | - | 2 |
| Cochchar Emarthlar - - - | 2 | 1 | - | 3 |
| Melauway - - - - - | 1 | 2 | - | 3 |
| Hepsy - - - - - | 1 | 3 | - | 4 |
| Ichhos Fixico - - - - | 2 | 4 | - | 6 |
| Tucktarnieche - - - - | 4 | 1 | - | 5 |
| Pin Garleachkar - - - | 1 | 1 | - | 2 |
| Faclodega - - - - - | 1 | 1 | - | 2 |
| Archcha - - - - - | 1 | 2 | - | 3 |
| Markeathlar - - - - | 3 | 2 | - | 5 |
| Hantlaw - - - - - | 1 | 3 | - | 4 |
| Chue Emarthlar - - - - | 1 | 1 | - | 2 |
| Neharlocco Fixico - - - - | 3 | 3 | - | 6 |
| Fushachcha Hargo - - - - | 2 | 2 | - | 4 |
| Ichhoie - - - - - | - | 3 | - | 3 |
| Rose - - - - - | - | 2 | - | 2 |
| Betsey - - - - - | 1 | 1 | - | 2 |
| Arwelugga - - - - | - | 2 | - | 2 |
| Neharloccoche - - - - | 3 | 1 | - | 4 |
| Aranegg - - - - - | - | 2 | - | 2 |
| Cockwelarga - - - - | 1 | 2 | - | 3 |
| Lila - - - - - | - | 2 | - | 2 |
| Coosa Mattlo - - - - | 5 | 5 | - | 10 |
| Chearhar - - - - - | 2 | 1 | - | 3 |

35‡

CREEK CENSUS—Continued.

| Names of Heads of Families. | Males. | Females. | Slaves. | Total. |
|---|---|---|---|---|
| Siney      .        .        .        .        . | - | 2 | - | 2 |
| Mocquagor        .        .        .        . | - | - | - | - |
| Harry      .        .        .        .        . | 2 | 2 | - | 4 |
| Mutt Teagar        .        .        .        . | 3 | 2 | - | 5 |
| Hopoieathla Micco        .        .        . | 1 | 2 | - | 3 |
|  | 45 | 70 |  | 115 |

SOUGAHATCHCHA.

| | | | | |
|---|---|---|---|---|
| Ho Tulga Hargo  .        .        .        . | 4 | 5 | - | 9 |
| Arhawlocco Fixico        .        .        . | 1 | 1 | - | 2 |
| Micco Hargo        .        .        -        . | 2 | 1 | - | 3 |
| Tockcopaumigga  .        .        .        . | - | 3 | - | 3 |
| Oakfuska Yoholo  .        .        .        . | 1 | 4 | - | 5 |
| Osu Hargo        .        .        .        . | 3 | 1 | - | 4 |
| Itcotta Hargo    .        .        .        . | 2 | 2 | - | 4 |
| Arharloc Ficco    .        .        .        . | 3 | 2 | - | 5 |
| Tal Marsa        .        .        .        . | 2 | 1 | - | 3 |
| Lippoa Hargo        .        .        .        . | 1 | 2 | - | 3 |
| Epar Hargo        .        .        .        . | 2 | 4 | - | 6 |
| Coosar Fixico    .        .        .        . | 1 | 3 | - | 4 |
| Robin   .        .        .        .        . | 2 | 2 | - | 4 |
| Cheloakkie        .        .        .        . | 1 | 1 | - | 2 |
| Suppoie  .        .        .        .        . | 1 | 1 | - | 2 |
| Lof Tar Hargo        .        .        .        . | 1 | 2 | - | 3 |
| Chunnegas        .        .        .        . | - | 2 | - | 2 |
| Ho Tulga  .        .        .        .        . | 2 | 1 | - | 3 |
| Kin Haw  .        .        .        .        . | 2 | 2 | - | 4 |
| Tarpokeenar        .        .        .        . | 1 | 2 | - | 3 |
| Simmaharga        .        .        .        . | 3 | 2 | - | 5 |
| Starhega  .        .        .        .        . | 1 | 1 | - | 2 |
| Mishoyar .        .        .        .        . | - | 3 | - | 3 |
| Tunmy   .        .        .        .        . | 1 | 2 | - | 3 |
| Marla    .        .        .        .        . | 2 | 2 | - | 4 |
| Choti Yoholo        .        .        .        . | 3 | 2 | - | 5 |
| Tusconer Hargo   .        .        .        . | 1 | 3 | - | 4 |
| Big Bob  .        .        .        .        . | 4 | - | - | 4 |
| Yar Tap Yoholo   .        .        .        . | 2 | 1 | - | 3 |
| Toganie  .        .        .        .        . | 1 | 1 | - | 2 |
| Thomas H. Gray  .        .        .        . | 2 | 1 | - | 3 |
| Hargi Gie Yoholo        .        .        .        . | 3 | 2 | - | 5 |
| Hobie    .        .        .        .        . | 6 | 3 | - | 9 |
| Tustanuggo Hogo        .        .        .        . | 2 | 4 | - | 6 |
| Inchungar .        .        .        .        . | - | 4 | - | 4 |
| Tussickia Kargo  .        .        .        . | 1 | 3 | - | 4 |

CREEK CENSUS—Continued.

| Names of Heads of Families. | Males. | Females. | Slaves. | Total. |
|---|---|---|---|---|
| Leneuppie | - | 3 | - | 3 |
| Tusconer Fixico | 1 | 5 | - | 6 |
| Fullodiga | 2 | 3 | - | 5 |
| Suf Falopkar | 1 | 2 | - | 3 |
| Ho Gillar Sar | 6 | 1 | - | 7 |
| Yathlar | 2 | 1 | - | 3 |
| Sothtarfixico | 5 | : | - | 5 |
| | 81 | 91 | | 172 |
| Hopoithla Hargo | 2 | 2 | - | 4 |
| Kieatar | 1 | 2 | - | 3 |
| Spanyhathlocco | 2 | 2 | - | 4 |
| Tommy Hargo | 4 | 3 | - | 7 |
| Woc Sa Fixico | 2 | 2 | - | 4 |
| Arhegega | - | 2 | - | 2 |
| Tallip Yoholo | 1 | 2 | - | 3 |
| Tenhollattar | - | 4 | - | 4 |
| Chuyarholo | 1 | 3 | - | 4 |
| Octarche Yoholo | 1 | 2 | - | 3 |
| Tohingarkar | 1 | 2 | - | 3 |
| Narthlegar | - | 2 | - | 2 |
| Konip Yoholo | 4 | 3 | - | 7 |
| Losti Micco | 1 | 4 | - | 5 |
| Oneippolar | - | 5 | - | 5 |
| Cubbreackche Emarthlar | 2 | 3 | - | 5 |
| Octto Yoholo | 2 | 1 | - | 3 |
| | 24 | 44 | | 68 |

UFAULA TOWN.

| | Males. | Females. | Slaves. | Total. |
|---|---|---|---|---|
| Lotte Yoholo | 2 | 2 | - | 4 |
| Tubtamey Hargo | 3 | 2 | - | 5 |
| Tussickie Hargo | 2 | 1 | - | 3 |
| Skinissogo | 1 | 2 | - | 3 |
| Tylar | 2 | 4 | - | 6 |
| Arbicca | 1 | 3 | - | 4 |
| Sally Townsend | 2 | 2 | - | 4 |
| Dannel Townsend | 2 | 2 | - | 4 |
| Chis Sa Hargo | 1 | 7 | - | 8 |
| Kinnehar | 1 | 3 | - | 4 |
| Spoakoak Micce | 3 | 4 | - | 7 |
| Miccochopco | 3 | 1 | - | 4 |
| Nehaulocco Hargo | 3 | 1 | - | 4 |
| Fixico Hargo | 2 | 1 | - | 3 |

## CREEK CENSUS—Continued.

| Names of Heads of Families. | Males. | Females. | Slaves. | Total. |
|---|---|---|---|---|
| Concharta Emarthla | 1 | 1 | - | 2 |
| Innehar Fixico | 3 | 1 | - | 4 |
| Arlon Yoholo | 2 | 1 | - | 3 |
| Athlon Hargo | 1 | 1 | - | 2 |
| Letketiga | 1 | 1 | - | 2 |
| Benny | 3 | 2 | - | 5 |
| Undul Hargo | 2 | 1 | - | 3 |
| Miccochohoconoce | 3 | 1 | - | 4 |
| Yarbothta | 2 | 2 | - | 4 |
| Illegaby | 2 | 1 | - | 3 |
| Ne Oak Kie | 4 | 4 | 2 | 10 |
| Albuttuche | 3 | 1 | - | 4 |
| Daniel G. Watson | 1 | 1 | - | 2 |
| Coosar Micco | 2 | 1 | - | 3 |
| John | 1 | 1 | - | 2 |
| Osenubbar Hargo | 1 | 2 | - | 3 |
| John Smith | 5 | 5 | - | 10 |
| Mista Hoga | 1 | 2 | - | 3 |
| Tallip Yoholo | 1 | 1 | - | 2 |
| Nokocille | 1 | 4 | - | 5 |
| Chu Yoholo | 2 | 2 | - | 4 |
| Atbuddar Hargo | 3 | 1 | - | 4 |
| Tuckabatcha Hago | 1 | 2 | - | 3 |
| Istalocher | 1 | 1 | - | 2 |
| Choccalegar | 2 | 2 | - | 4 |
| Oche Hargo | 2 | 1 | - | 3 |
| Surwarnoak Hargo | 1 | 2 | - | 3 |
| Par Foslega | 2 | 1 | - | 3 |
| Charley | 2 | 2 | - | 4 |
| | 84 | 83 | 2 | 169 |
| Choegar Hargo | 2 | 1 | - | 3 |
| Tomeleachar | 1 | 2 | - | 3 |
| Callander | - | 2 | - | 2 |
| Hodissa | 1 | 1 | - | 2 |
| Ubi Heacher | - | 2 | - | 2 |
| Talleachar | 1 | 1 | - | 2 |
| O Gillissinnehaw | 1 | 2 | - | 3 |
| Somileager | 3 | 1 | - | 4 |
| Tustanugger Emarthlar | 1 | 1 | - | 2 |
| Moholiytar | 2 | 2 | - | 4 |
| George Scott | 2 | 2 | - | 4 |
| Cane Yoholo | 2 | 1 | - | 3 |
| O Looch Hargo | 1 | 1 | - | 2 |

CREEK CENSUS—Continued.

| Names of Heads of Families. | Males. | Females. | Slaves. | Total. |
|---|---|---|---|---|
| Ufawla Hargo - - - | 2 | 1 | - | 3 |
| Sodedunna Harjo - - - | 1 | 4 | - | 5 |
| Ararti Hargo - - - | 1 | 2 | - | 3 |
| Lostar Fixico - - - | 4 | 2 | - | 6 |
| Efur Tustarlugga - - - | 2 | 2 | - | 4 |
| Sogoie - - - - | 1 | 1 | - | 2 |
| Algonie - - - - | | 2 | - | 2 |
| Concharta Fixico - - - | 1 | 3 | - | 4 |
| Coegus Hargo - - - | 1 | 2 | - | 3 |
| Logo Harjo - - - | 1 | 2 | - | 3 |
| Wocsa Micco - - - | 2 | 3 | - | 5 |
| Yarbackheefee - - - | 1 | 1 | - | 2 |
| Micco Harjo - - - | 1 | 3 | - | 4 |
| Tenatth Harjo - - - | 4 | 2 | - | 6 |
| Tommy Yoholo - - - | 2 | 1 | - | 3 |
| Chebarney - - - | 1 | 2 | - | 3 |
| Cuffee Harjo - - - | 3 | 1 | - | 4 |
| Nehawlocco - - - | 2 | 1 | - | 3 |
| Sammy - - - - | 1 | 2 | - | 3 |
| Ottes Yoholo - - - | 2 | 1 | - | 3 |
| Ogillissa Harjo - - - | 2 | 1 | - | 3 |
| Talladig Harjo - - - | 2 | 2 | - | 4 |
| Billy - - - - | 1 | 1 | - | 2 |
| Tarsarjega - - - | 1 | 2 | - | 3 |
| Ottis Harjo - - - | 2 | 2 | - | 4 |
| Oharthy - - - | 1 | 4 | - | 5 |
| Yoholo Chopco - - - | 2 | 1 | - | 3 |
| Parscoaf Harjo - - - | 1 | 2 | - | 3 |
| Toni Carr - - - | 2 | 1 | - | 3 |
| Tic Tunniche - - - | 1 | 2 | - | 3 |
| Charles Merril - - - | 2 | 1 | - | 3 |
| | 67 | 76 | - | 143 |
| Chowasti Fixico - - | 1 | 2 | - | 3 |
| Sarwaccoche - - - | 1 | 2 | - | 3 |
| Wocse Harjo - - - | 1 | 3 | - | 4 |
| Ufawla Chopco - - - | 3 | 1 | - | 4 |
| Joseph P. Cook - - - | 1 | 2 | - | 3 |
| Chocchar Micco - - - | 2 | 1 | - | 3 |
| Ufawla Micco - - - | 2 | - | - | 2 |
| Lef Til Harjo - - - | 2 | 2 | - | 4 |
| Owelocca - - - | 1 | 2 | - | 3 |
| Mahoga - - - | 2 | 1 | - | 3 |
| Arlichchar - - - | 2 | 1 | - | 3 |
| Tusconer Harjo - - - | 1 | 2 | - | 3 |

## CREEK CENSUS—Continued.

| Names of Heads of Families. | Males. | Females. | Slaves. | Total. |
|---|---|---|---|---|
| Fox | 1 | 1 | - | 2 |
| Meheachar | 2 | – | - | 2 |
| Chuwasti Harjo | 2 | 2 | 2 | 6 |
| Mar Tap Harjo | 2 | 1 | - | 3 |
| Fus Harjo | 2 | 1 | - | 3 |
| Fushatchcha Harjo | 2 | 1 | - | 3 |
| Sofalofkar | 1 | 3 | - | 4 |
| Sarhire | 2 | 1 | - | 3 |
| Hosulga Harjo | 2 | 1 | - | 3 |
| Poster | – | 2 | - | 2 |
| Nokole Earthlar | 2 | 1 | - | 3 |
| Michheicha | 1 | 2 | - | 3 |
| Cowar Sarda | 1 | 2 | - | 3 |
| Owottaliga | 1 | 2 | - | 3 |
| In Git Talfar | 1 | 1 | - | 2 |
| Chissa Yoholo | 1 | 2 | - | 3 |
| Mackar Samiga | - | 3 | - | 3 |
| Tockkarsa Harjo | 1 | 2 | - | 3 |
| Sinda | - | 3 | - | 3 |
| Simmothoie | - | 2 | - | 2 |
| Cochchar Harjo | 1 | 1 | - | 2 |
| Iswegar | 2 | 2 | - | 4 |
| Sopuck Kala | 1 | 1 | - | 2 |
| Jimmy | 2 | 1 | - | 3 |
| Chearlie | 1 | 2 | - | 3 |
| Ottis Micco | 1 | 2 | - | 3 |
| Itcarcha Yoholo | 4 | 2 | - | 6 |
| Otta Sa | 1 | 1 | - | 2 |
| Lottome | - | 2 | - | 2 |
| Carbeeachar Fixico | 1 | 2 | - | 3 |
| Parhos Yoholo | 2 | 4 | - | 6 |
| Sinimargarkie | 1 | 1 | - | 2 |
|  | 59 | 74 | 2 | 135 |
| Inhalhagar | 1 | 1 | - | 2 |
| Stowarhie | 1 | 1 | - | 2 |
| Possom Bubbie | 1 | 2 | - | 3 |
|  | 3 | 4 |  | 7 |

### HATCHCHECHUBBA TOWN.

| | | | | |
|---|---|---|---|---|
| Tallissi Tustanugga | 2 | 2 | - | 4 |
| Isfanny Harjo | 1 | 1 | - | 2 |
| Ufawla Emarthlar | 1 | 2 | - | 3 |

## CREEK CENSUS—Continued.

| Names of Heads of Families. | Males. | Females. | Slaves. | Total. |
|---|---|---|---|---|
| Wocsa Harjo - - - - | 3 | 3 | - | 6 |
| Chulocco Yoholo - - - | 2 | 2 | - | 4 |
| Tockkosar Micco - - - | 2 | 2 | - | 4 |
| Tussicke Yar - - - - | 3 | 3 | - | 6 |
| Nehaw Yoholo - - - - | 2 | 2 | - | 4 |
| Isfanny Emarthlar - - - | 2 | 3 | - | 5 |
| Konip Fixico - - - - | 2 | 1 | - | 3 |
| Coosisla Harjo - - - - | 1 | 2 | - | 3 |
| Tommy Tustunnugga - - - | 4 | 3 | - | 7 |
| Arthlon Harjo - - - - | 1 | 2 | - | 3 |
| Archule Fixico - - - - | 2 | 2 | - | 4 |
| Octearche Yoholo - - - | 3 | 1 | - | 4 |
| Albudda Earthlar - - - | 1 | 1 | - | 2 |
| Tallissie Harjo - - - - | 2 | 1 | - | 3 |
| Tallowwar Emarthlar - - - | 2 | 2 | - | 4 |
| Watco Yoholo - - - - | 2 | 1 | - | 3 |
| Nehar Fixico - - - - | 3 | 1 | - | 4 |
| Coowarsart Yoholo - - - | 2 | 1 | - | 3 |
| Tuskega Emarthlar - - - | 2 | 1 | - | 3 |
| Tockkasar Harjo - - - | 1 | 3 | - | 4 |
| Coegus Harjo - - - - | 1 | 1 | - | 2 |
| Nokos Harjo - - - - | 3 | 2 | - | 5 |
| Arwatteliga - - - - | 2 | 2 | - | 4 |
| Wocsee Yoholo - - - - | 2 | 2 | - | 4 |
| Micco Harjo - - - - | 4 | 1 | - | 5 |
| Tallissa Yoholo - - - - | 2 | 1 | - | 3 |
| Micco Yoholo - - - - | 2 | 1 | - | 3 |
| Chuwasti Micco - - - - | 1 | 1 | - | 2 |
| Lofti Micco - - - - | 1 | 1 | - | 2 |
| Cochos Harjo - - - - | 1 | 1 | - | 2 |
| Noko Silla - - - - | 2 | 2 | - | 4 |
| Clechumma Hollarta - - - | 3 | 1 | - | 4 |
| Arbickko Harjo - - - - | 1 | 1 | - | 2 |
| Uewocco Harjo - - - - | 1 | 1 | - | 2 |
| Tallis Toga - - - - | 1 | 1 | - | 2 |
| Talmarse Harjo - - - - | 1 | 1 | - | 2 |
| Wartoeco Harjo - - - - | 1 | 1 | - | 2 |
| Chuwastie Emarthlar - - - | 1 | 1 | - | 2 |
| Hopie Youcha - - - - | 1 | 1 | - | 2 |
| Conchart Yoholo - - - - | 1 | 1 | - | 2 |
| | 80 | 67 | | 147 |
| Soteete Yoholo - - - - | 1 | 1 | - | 2 |
| Meathlar - - - - | 1 | 1 | - | 2 |
| Hinnehawwotoliga - - - | 1 | 1 | - | 2 |

CREEK CENSUS—Continued.

| Names of Heads of Families. | Males. | Females. | Slaves. | Total. |
|---|---|---|---|---|
| Holof Tar - - - | 1 | 1 | - | 2 |
| Soiecha - - - | 1 | 1 | - | 2 |
| Sotta - - - | 1 | 1 | - | 2 |
| Sodedunna Emarthlar - - | 1 | 1 | - | 2 |
| Simmihoie - - - | — | 2 | - | 2 |
| Sehoboth Clarna - - | 1 | 1 | - | 2 |
| Jochehar - - - | 1 | 1 | - | 2 |
| Tehiga - - - | 1 | 2 | - | 3 |
| Sumer Harjo - - - | 2 | 2 | - | 4 |
| Honieha - - - | 2 | 1 | - | 3 |
| Coiega - - - | — | 4 | - | 4 |
| Secoliga - - - | — | 2 | - | 2 |
| Atloc Harjo - - - | 1 | 1 | - | 2 |
| Loftie Yoholo - - - | 2 | 1 | - | 3 |
| Cligumma Emarthlar - - | 4 | 4 | - | 8 |
|  | 21 | 28 |  | 49 |

HICKORY GROUND TOWN.

| | | | | |
|---|---|---|---|---|
| Tallissee Fixico - - | 1 | 1 | - | 2 |
| Cooser Holueathlar - - | 3 | 1 | - | 4 |
| Powhos Yoholo - - | 3 | 2 | - | 5 |
| Konip Harjo - - | 2 | 2 | - | 4 |
| Cooper Pack - - | 4 | 2 | - | 6 |
| Coachchos Micco - - | 2 | 1 | - | 3 |
| Nehawlocco - - | 1 | 2 | - | 3 |
| Holofter Emarthlar - - | 1 | 1 | - | 2 |
| Chuwasti Fixico - - | 1 | 1 | - | 2 |
| Fushatch Yoholo - - | 5 | 2 | - | 7 |
| Chokola - - | 1 | 3 | - | 4 |
| Tallissee Micco - - | 4 | 3 | - | 7 |
| Illis Fixico - - | 3 | 1 | - | 4 |
| Cussetar Fixico - - | 5 | 2 | - | 7 |
| Nokosie Emarthlar - - | 2 | 1 | - | 3 |
| Coonoo Fixico - - | 1 | 2 | - | 3 |
| Sintha Yoholo - - | 1 | 1 | - | 2 |
| Cusseatar Harja - - | 1 | 1 | - | 2 |
| Chuwa Yoholo - - | 1 | 1 | - | 2 |
| Carwocta Harjo - - | 2 | 2 | - | 4 |
| Spoak Oak Harjo - - | 2 | 1 | - | 3 |
| Sulga Emarthlar - - | 3 | 1 | - | 4 |
| Emarthlar Harjo - - | 2 | 2 | - | 4 |
| Jenny Redmouth - - | 1 | 1 | - | 2 |
| Emarthloche - - | 1 | 1 | - | 2 |
| Chule Harjo - - | 1 | 1 | - | 2 |
| Peggy - - | 2 | 1 | - | 3 |

CREEK CENSUS—Continued.

| Names of Heads of Families. | Males. | Females. | Slaves. | Total. |
|---|---|---|---|---|
| Arhalocco Fixico | 2 | 1 | - | 3 |
| Chule Harjo (second of same name) | 2 | 1 | - | 3 |
| Hotulga Harjo | 1 | 1 | - | 2 |
| Osooch Harjo | 1 | 1 | - | 2 |
| Powwas Harjo | 1 | 1 | - | 2 |
| Powhos Emarthlar | 1 | 3 | - | 4 |
| John Barr | 2 | — | - | 2 |
| Sucky McGeehe | 4 | 2 | - | 6 |
| Nobotchchi Yoholo | 1 | 2 | - | 3 |
| James McFarland | 1 | 1 | - | 2 |
| John McFarland | 1 | 2 | - | 3 |
| Chochatuphoga | 2 | 2 | - | 4 |
| Chuwasti Harjo | 1 | 1 | - | 2 |
| Hotulga Harjo | 2 | — | - | 2 |
| Nocoosic Harjo | 2 | — | - | 2 |
| Chissic Yoholo | 2 | 3 | - | 5 |
|  | 82 | 60 |  | 142 |
| Tuckabatcha Yoholo | 1 | 2 | - | 3 |
| Poith Harjo | 2 | 2 | - | 4 |
| Fushatchcha Harjo | 2 | 1 | - | 3 |
| Milly | 2 | 3 | - | 5 |
| Echo Fixico | 2 | 1 | - | 3 |
| Mocktoga | — | 3 | - | 3 |
| Peggy Durant | 1 | 2 | - | 3 |
| Saru Harjo | 1 | 1 | - | 2 |
| Nehaw Harjo | 1 | 1 | - | 2 |
| Clahiga | 2 | 1 | - | 3 |
| Noko Silla Fixico | 2 | 1 | - | 3 |
| Nitbihiga | 2 | 1 | - | 3 |
| Cubieache Emarthlar | 2 | 1 | - | 3 |
| Nehaw Fixico | 1 | 2 | - | 3 |
| Fiefar | 1 | 1 | - | 2 |
| Clath Thloche | 1 | 1 | - | 2 |
| Sarhoie | 2 | 2 | - | 4 |
| Soffo Lofta | 1 | 1 | - | 2 |
| Supparga | 2 | 3 | - | 5 |
| Tinchocolocco | 1 | 1 | - | 2 |
| Simmarsie | 2 | 2 | - | 4 |
| Oche Harjo | 2 | — | - | 2 |
| George Tallisse | 1 | 1 | - | 2 |
| Nahoga Ward | — | 2 | 13 | 15 |
|  | 34 | 36 | 13 | 83 |

## CREEK CENSUS—Continued.

| Names of Heads of Families. | Males. | Females. | Slaves. | Total. |
|---|---|---|---|---|
| **WEWOAKKAR TOWN.** | | | | |
| Ufawla - - - - - | 1 | 1 | - | 2 |
| Tuskiga - - - - - | 1 | 1 | - | 2 |
| Tuskenehaw - - - - | 1 | 1 | - | 2 |
| Peter - - - - - | 1 | 3 | - | 4 |
| Billy - - - - - | 3 | 2 | - | 5 |
| Contal Emarthlar - - - - | 3 | 1 | - | 4 |
| Thlath Thlo Harjo - - - | 2 | 1 | - | 3 |
| Chuwasti Harjo - - - - | 2 | 2 | - | 4 |
| Innehaw - - - - - | 2 | 1 | - | 3 |
| Octiarche Fixico - - - - | 1 | 1 | - | 2 |
| Octiarche Micco - - - - | 1 | 2 | - | 3 |
| Henarhinnehaw - - - - | 1 | 3 | - | 4 |
| Enotenugga - - - - | 1 | 2 | - | 3 |
| Charley - - - - - | 2 | - | - | 2 |
| Tulge Ycholo - - - - | 2 | 3 | - | 5 |
| Chuwaste Micco - - - - | 3 | 1 | - | 4 |
| Nehar Fixico - - - - | 2 | 2 | - | 4 |
| Emarthloche - - - - | 2 | - | - | 2 |
| Homer Karkie - - - - | 2 | 2 | - | 4 |
| Oakfuska Yoholo - - - | 1 | 2 | - | 3 |
| Arlock Harjo - - - - | 1 | 2 | - | 3 |
| Konip Yoholo - - - - | 2 | 1 | - | 3 |
| Nehar Yoholo - - - - | 2 | 1 | - | 3 |
| Arlock Fixico - - - - | 2 | 2 | - | 4 |
| Hinneharche - - - - | 2 | 1 | - | 3 |
| Arharlocco Emarthlar - - - | 3 | 2 | - | 5 |
| Parhiega - - - - - | 1 | 1 | - | 2 |
| Narkie Tar - - - - | 1 | 1 | - | 2 |
| Yoholo Harjo - - - - | 2 | 1 | - | 3 |
| John - - - - - | 1 | 1 | - | 2 |
| Hospotarkie - - - - | 2 | 1 | - | 3 |
| Logar Harjo - - - - | 1 | 1 | - | 2 |
| Simmunniche - - - - | 1 | 1 | - | 2 |
| Albuttar Harjo - - - - | 1 | 2 | - | 3 |
| Oche Hargo - - - - | 1 | 1 | - | 2 |
| Arhaw Yoholo - - - - | 2 | 2 | - | 4 |
| Hishohear - - - - | 1 | 1 | - | 2 |
| Charley (2d of same name,) - - | 1 | 1 | - | 2 |
| Mathliga - - - - - | 1 | 1 | - | 2 |
| Choakcharinnehair - - - | 1 | 1 | - | 2 |
| Cittaheachkar - - - - | 1 | 1 | - | 2 |
| George - - - - - | 1 | 2 | - | 3 |
| | 64 | 59 | | 123 |

CREEK CENSUS—Continued.

| Names of Heads of Families. | Males. | Females. | Slaves. | Total. |
|---|---|---|---|---|
| Halwikar - - - - - | 1 | 1 | . | 2 |
| Socowiga - - - - - | 1 | 1 | . | 2 |
| Tihoga - - - - - | 1 | 2 | . | 3 |
| Coak Fixico - - - - | 2 | 2 | . | 4 |
| Nehau Harjo - - - - | 1 | 2 | . | 3 |
| Iswiga - - - - - | 2 | 2 | . | 4 |
| Fulga Fixico - - - - | 2 | 2 | . | 4 |
| Willa - - - - - | 1 | 1 | . | 2 |
| Coiega - - - - - | 1 | 1 | . | 2 |
| Silluphogar - - - - | 1 | 1 | . | 2 |
| Imbohie - - - - - | 2 | 1 | . | 3 |
| Johnny - - - - - | 2 | 2 | . | 4 |
| Narboche Emarthlar - - - | 1 | 1 | . | 2 |
| Nehegis Emarthlar - - - | 2 | 2 | . | 4 |
| Charley (3d of same name) - - | 1 | 3 | . | 4 |
| Miliga - - - - - | 1 | 1 | . | 2 |
| Par Fartkar - - - - | 1 | 1 | . | 2 |
| Mar Tharga - - - - | 1 | 1 | . | 2 |
| Simhoie - - - - - | 1 | 1 | . | 2 |
| Figa - - - - - | 1 | 1 | . | 2 |
| Oleheacha - - - - | 1 | 1 | . | 2 |
| Pefonthoche - - - - | 1 | 3 | . | 4 |
| Woc Se Harjo - - - - | 3 | 2 | . | 5 |
| Hegatchcha - - - - | 1 | 1 | . | 2 |
| Tarhoie - - - - - | 1 | 1 | . | 2 |
| Coo Sar Harjo - - - - | 1 | 1 | . | 2 |
| Sihega - - - - - | 1 | 1 | . | 2 |
| Simmarhie - - - - | 1 | 1 | . | 2 |
| Simmehoga - - - - | 1 | 1 | . | 2 |
| Fic Somiega - - - - | 2 | 1 | . | 3 |
| Wulgar - - - - - | 1 | 1 | . | 2 |
| Sohiah - - - - - | - | 2 | . | 2 |
| Im Parsa - - - - - | 1 | 2 | . | 3 |
| Chearharjo - - - - | 1 | 1 | . | 2 |
| Sallicega - - - - - | 1 | 2 | . | 3 |
| Isfanny Hargo - - - - | 1 | 1 | . | 2 |
| Howonhar - - - - | 1 | 3 | . | 4 |
| Tommy - - - - - | 1 | 3 | . | 4 |
| Toatkis Harjo - - - - | 3 | 3 | . | 6 |
| Litkar - - - - - | 2 | 3 | . | 5 |
| Ulsegar - - - - - | 2 | 1 | . | 3 |
| Maltho Yar - - - - | 2 | 1 | . | 3 |
| Timmowockar - - - - | 1 | 3 | . | 4 |
| Nocos Harjo - - - - | 2 | 2 | . | 4 |
| | 58 | 71 | | 129 |

## CREEK CENSUS—Continued.

| Names of Heads of Families. | Males. | Females. | Slaves. | Total. |
|---|---|---|---|---|
| Urharnega - - - - - | 1 | 4 | - | 5 |
| Ubullartkar - - - - | 2 | 2 | - | 4 |
| Cu Hargo - - - - - | 1 | 1 | - | 2 |
| Emarthlar Yoholo - - - - | 3 | 1 | - | 4 |
| Narboche Fixico - - - - | 2 | 1 | - | 3 |
| Colgus Fixico - - - - | 2 | 1 | - | 3 |
| Mat Hoga - - - - - | 1 | 1 | - | 2 |
| Pinmi Emarthlar - - - - | 1 | 1 | - | 2 |
| Culgus Fixico, (2d of same name) - - | 2 | 1 | - | 3 |
| Yoholoche - - - - | 1 | 2 | - | 3 |
| Tuskege Emarthlar - - - | 2 | 2 | - | 4 |
| Lokoliga - - - - - | 3 | 1 | - | 4 |
| Wocleholo - - - - | 1 | 1 | - | 2 |
| Tommy Emarthlo - - - | 1 | 1 | - | 2 |
| | 23 | 20 | - | 43 |

### POCHISHACKCHA TOWN.

| Names of Heads of Families. | Males. | Females. | Slaves. | Total. |
|---|---|---|---|---|
| Cowassart Emarthlar - - - | 1 | 2 | - | 3 |
| Tustanugga Emarthlar - - - | 3 | 1 | - | 4 |
| Neharchehanng - - - - | 1 | 3 | - | 4 |
| Tuscarhobie - - - - | 3 | 2 | - | 5 |
| Yoholo - - - - - | 2 | 2 | - | 4 |
| Nokos Harjo - - - - | 1 | 1 | - | 2 |
| Powhos Micco - - - - | 3 | 1 | - | 4 |
| Innehaw Fixico - - - - | 3 | 3 | - | 6 |
| Cusseetar Yoholo - - - - | 3 | 1 | - | 4 |
| Mortar Harjo - - - - | 2 | 2 | - | 4 |
| Tinthlannis Harjo - - - - | 2 | 2 | - | 4 |
| Powhos Yoholo - - - - | 1 | 1 | - | 2 |
| Hilbubba Harjo - - - - | 1 | 1 | - | 2 |
| Nehaw Yoholo - - - - | 1 | 1 | - | 2 |
| Torchintuska - - - - | 1 | 1 | - | 2 |
| Oackchon Yoholo - - - - | 1 | 1 | - | 2 |
| Panthe Yoholo - - - - | 1 | 2 | - | 3 |
| Cobbiecha Yoholo - - - - | 1 | 1 | - | 2 |
| Moctu Harjo - - - - | 1 | 1 | - | 2 |
| Sarthla - - - - - | 1 | 1 | - | 2 |
| Ospotask Harjo - - - - | 1 | 1 | - | 2 |
| Toatkis Harjo - - - - | 1 | 1 | - | 2 |
| Moclus Yoholo - - - - | 2 | 1 | - | 3 |
| Nittarday - - - - - | 1 | 2 | - | 3 |
| Neharwo Tulgar - - - - | 1 | 2 | - | 3 |
| Nehaw Harjo - - - - | 1 | 1 | - | 2 |
| Nehawlocco Yoholo - - - | 1 | 1 | - | 2 |
| Narboche Yoholo - - - - | 1 | 1 | - | 2 |

CREEK CENSUS—Continued.

| Names of Heads of Families. | Males. | Females. | Slaves. | Total. |
|---|---|---|---|---|
| Stimmartulka   -   -   -   - | 1 | 1 | - | 2 |
| Tommy Harjo   -   -   -   - | 2 | 1 | - | 3 |
| | 45 | 42 | - | 87 |
| POCKENTALLEHASSE TOWN. | | | | |
| Lofter Fixico   -   -   -   - | 2 | 3 | - | 5 |
| Hospartok Harjo   -   -   - | 2 | 3 | - | 5 |
| Woxc Harjo   -   -   - | 4 | 1 | - | 5 |
| Passcove Harjo   -   -   - | 1 | 2 | - | 3 |
| Pothle Yoholo   -   -   - | 1 | 4 | - | 5 |
| Powis Harjo   -   -   - | 2 | 3 | - | 5 |
| Oswitch Yoholo   -   -   - | 1 | 1 | - | 2 |
| Coehas Fixico   -   -   - | 3 | 2 | - | 5 |
| Ubocka   -   -   -   - | 1 | 2 | - | 3 |
| Neharlocco   -   -   - | 2 | 3 | - | 5 |
| Tulge Yoholo   -   -   - | 1 | 1 | - | 2 |
| Ispoke Yoholo   -   -   - | 1 | 4 | - | 5 |
| Tuckabatchei Yoholo   -   - | 1 | 1 | - | 2 |
| Watgue Yoholo   -   -   - | 2 | 2 | - | 4 |
| Nocose Harjo   -   -   - | 2 | 7 | - | 9 |
| Corser Harjo   -   -   - | 2 | 2 | - | 4 |
| Narboche Fixico   -   -   - | 4 | 3 | - | 7 |
| Parhose Fixico   -   -   - | 2 | 1 | - | 3 |
| Figintuskaw   -   -   - | 2 | 1 | - | 3 |
| Fose Harjo   -   -   - | 2 | 2 | - | 4 |
| Mihegee   -   -   -   - | — | 4 | - | 4 |
| Tallip Harjo   -   -   - | 1 | 1 | - | 2 |
| Kotchar Fixico   -   -   - | 1 | 6 | - | 7 |
| Chechun Fixico   -   -   - | 2 | 3 | - | 5 |
| Sehegigau   -   -   -   - | 1 | 4 | - | 5 |
| Stifley   -   -   -   - | 1 | 2 | - | 3 |
| Choe Marthlar   -   -   - | 2 | 1 | - | 3 |
| Masey   -   -   -   - | 1 | 3 | - | 4 |
| Appeok Harjo   -   -   - | 2 | 2 | - | 4 |
| Sannecogu   -   -   - | 1 | 1 | - | 2 |
| Asan Harjo   -   -   - | 5 | 2 | - | 7 |
| Talwar Fixico   -   -   - | 1 | 1 | - | 2 |
| Muntallar   -   -   -   - | — | 3 | - | 3 |
| Sofwelarkey   -   -   - | 1 | 1 | - | 2 |
| Choharjo   -   -   -   - | 3 | 2 | - | 5 |
| Iswarke   -   -   -   - | 1 | 2 | - | 3 |
| Konip Fixico   -   -   - | 2 | 2 | - | 4 |
| Allockgoege   -   -   - | 1 | 1 | - | 2 |
| Pinemarthlar   -   -   - | 2 | 2 | - | 4 |

CREEK CENSUS—Continued.

| Names of Heads of Families. | Males. | Females. | Slaves. | Total. |
|---|---|---|---|---|
| Sitkolargey - - - - | 2 | 1 | - | 3 |
| Simmome - - - - - | - | 2 | - | 2 |
| Chewaste Fixico - - - - | 1 | 2 | - | 3 |
| Narboche Yoholo - - - - | 4 | 3 | - | 7 |
| Athoigey - - - - - | 1 | 1 | - | 2 |
| | 74 | 100 | | 174 |
| Neharmarto Harjo - - - | 1 | 3 | - | 4 |
| Neharlocco Harjo - - - - | 1 | 5 | - | 6 |
| Oswitch Micco - - - - | 1 | 1 | - | 2 |
| Sewachee - - - - - | 3 | 1 | - | 4 |
| Alletega - - - - - | 2 | - | - | 2 |
| Tustemnuckcooche - - - | 3 | 2 | - | 5 |
| Osfolie - - - - - | 1 | 1 | - | 2 |
| Yoala - - - - - | 2 | 1 | - | 3 |
| Suckinarna - - - - | - | 2 | - | 2 |
| Kolise Emarthlar - - - - | 1 | 1 | - | 2 |
| Seer Sitlia - - - - | 1 | 1 | - | 2 |
| Sparni Harjo - - - - | 1 | 1 | - | 2 |
| Tosokko - - - - - | - | 4 | - | 4 |
| Konip Yoholo - - - - | 2 | - | - | 2 |
| Tonogey - - - - - | 1 | 1 | - | 2 |
| Talwar Harjo - - - - | 1 | 1 | - | 2 |
| Harparye - - - - - | - | 2 | - | 2 |
| Talmas Harjo - - - - | 2 | 1 | - | 3 |
| Talmas Fixico - - - - | 2 | 2 | - | 4 |
| Foshatch Fixico - - - - | 1 | 1 | - | 2 |
| Holofter - - - - - | 2 | 2 | - | 4 |
| Chelok Harjo - - - - | 2 | 1 | - | 3 |
| Kenarye - - - - - | - | 4 | - | 4 |
| Oketawpos Harjo - - - - | 2 | 2 | - | 4 |
| Parlock Fixico - - - - | 8 | 1 | - | 9 |
| Warlock Micco - - - - | 3 | 1 | - | 4 |
| Talse Harjo - - - - | 3 | 2 | - | 5 |
| Cho Yoholo - - - - | 1 | 2 | - | 3 |
| Nocosee Emarthlooche - - - | 1 | 2 | - | 3 |
| Osarharjo - - - - - | 2 | 2 | - | 4 |
| Ohaskee - - - - - | 1 | 1 | - | 2 |
| Kulgar - - - - - | 1 | 3 | - | 4 |
| Timiethle - - - - - | - | 2 | - | 2 |
| | 52 | 56 | | 108 |

WEOGUFKA TOWN.

| | | | | |
|---|---|---|---|---|
| Cufsetan Harjo - - - - | 3 | 2 | - | 5 |
| Sekithlia - - - - - | 1 | 2 | - | 3 |

CREEK CENSUS—Continued.

| Names of Heads of Families. | Males. | Females. | Slaves. | Total. |
|---|---|---|---|---|
| Osar Harjo - - - | 1 | 3 | - | 4 |
| Kowelocko - - - | 1 | 1 | - | 2 |
| Tuckabatche Harjo - - - | 1 | 1 | - | 2 |
| Isparhole - - - | 1 | 1 | - | 2 |
| Talledeeg Fixico - - - | 2 | 1 | - | 3 |
| Oktearche Fixico - - - | 2 | 3 | - | 5 |
| Yoholo Emarthlar - - - | 2 | 2 | - | 4 |
| Otlese Fixico - - - | 2 | 1 | - | 3 |
| Nehar Marthte Emarthlar - - | 2 | 1 | - | 3 |
| Kochus Micco - - - | 2 | 2 | - | 4 |
| Watque Yoholo - - - | 1 | 1 | - | 2 |
| Hillis Fixico - - - | 2 | 2 | - | 4 |
| Okeche Emarthlar - - - | 1 | 2 | - | 3 |
| Fuckhia - - - | 1 | 1 | - | 2 |
| O Yettick Yoholo - - - | 1 | 2 | - | 3 |
| Nettiga - - - | 1 | 1 | - | 2 |
| Cho Yoholo - - - | 1 | 1 | - | 2 |
| Archoole Harjo - - - | 3 | 2 | - | 5 |
| Lofter Yoholo - - - | 2 | 2 | - | 4 |
| Kowe Harjo - - - | 1 | 4 | - | 5 |
| Hillabe Emarthlar - - - | 1 | 1 | - | 2 |
| Talse Fixico - - - | 2 | 2 | - | 4 |
| Chugotte Fixico - - - | 1 | 3 | - | 4 |
| Satelohe - - - - | 1 | 1 | - | 2 |
| Archewyche - - - | 1 | 1 | - | 2 |
| Mannogey - - - | 1 | 1 | - | 2 |
| Sotche Mitche - - - | 1 | 1 | - | 2 |
| Mittecawle - - - | 1 | 1 | - | 2 |
| Tithlegey - - - | 1 | 1 | - | 2 |
| Billy - - - - | 1 | 1 | - | 2 |
| Kochus Harjo - - - | 2 | 2 | - | 4 |
| Cubeche Emarthlar - - - | 1 | 2 | - | 3 |
| Tonnoechar - - - | 1 | 2 | - | 3 |
| Watte - - - - | 1 | 1 | - | 2 |
| Timmortee - - - | - | 2 | - | 2 |
| Hihatchco - - - | 2 | 1 | - | 3 |
| Abicco Harjo - - - | 2 | 1 | - | 3 |
| Isfarne Yoholo - - - | 2 | 2 | - | 4 |
| Emarthloothe - - - | 2 | 2 | - | 4 |
| Supingulgey - - - | 1 | 1 | - | 2 |
| Immomi - - - | 1 | 1 | - | 2 |
| | 60 | 68 | - | 128 |
| Fallaty - - - - | 1 | 1 | - | 2 |
| Arwampky - - - | 1 | 1 | - | 2 |

## CREEK CENSUS—Continued.

| Names of Heads of Families. | Males. | Females. | Slaves. | Total. |
|---|---|---|---|---|
| Okechi Harjo       -      -      - | 2 | 2 | - | 4 |
| Powhose Emarthlar  -      -      - | 4 | 3 | - | 7 |
| Chewasti Harjo     -      -      - | 3 | 1 | - | 4 |
| Cuwattelogar       -      -      - | 3 | 3 | - | 6 |
| Kobbitchar Fixico  -      -      - | 1 | 1 | - | 2 |
| Koegus Harjo       -      -      - | 3 | 3 | - | 6 |
| Toske      -      -      -      - | 1 | 1 | - | 2 |
| Pothlehela         -      -      - | 1 | 2 | - | 3 |
| Woxe Harjo         -      -      - | 2 | 2 | - | 4 |
| Cobbitchey Harjo   -      -      - | 3 | 4 | - | 7 |
| Cheeho Poya        -      -      - | 2 | 1 | - | 3 |
| Chee Fixico        -      -      - | | | | |
| J. Egey    -      -      -      - | 1 | 2 | - | 3 |
| Talse Yoholo       -      -      - | 3 | 2 | - | 5 |
| Klannogey          -      -      - | 2 | 1 | - | 3 |
| Tussekear Harjo    -      -      - | 2 | 1 | - | 3 |
| Neetske Yoholo     -      -      - | 2 | 2 | - | 4 |
| Albutter Harjo     -      -      - | 1 | 1 | - | 2 |
| Timmawway          -      -      - | 2 | 3 | - | 5 |
| Yartikar Harjo     -      -      - | 3 | 1 | - | 4 |
| Thlathle Yoholo    -      -      - | 3 | 1 | - | 4 |
| Conatkee Marthlar  -      -      - | 5 | 2 | - | 7 |
| Chear Harjo        -      -      - | 2 | 3 | - | 5 |
| Fucktelustu Yoholo -      -      - | 2 | 3 | - | 5 |
| Okechoy Fixico     -      -      - | 3 | 3 | - | 6 |
| Tucko Sar Hargo    -      -      - | 3 | 1 | - | 4 |
| Keegew Fixico      -      -      - | 5 | 1 | - | 6 |
| Letif Harjo        -      -      - | 1 | 1 | - | 2 |
| Susey      -      -      -      - | 1 | 1 | - | 2 |
| Tewarhobotte       -      -      - | 1 | 2 | - | 3 |
| Tewarthu Harjo     -      -      - | 1 | 1 | - | 2 |
| Lofter Fixico      -      -      - | 5 | 2 | - | 7 |
| Yoholo Harjo       -      -      - | 1 | 2 | - | 3 |
| Nocose Harjo       -      -      - | 2 | 1 | - | 3 |
| Hemar Harjo        -      -      - | 2 | 3 | - | 5 |
| Jimmy      -      -      -      - | 4 | 1 | - | 5 |
| Oswitch Emarthlar  -      -      - | 4 | 2 | - | 6 |
| Arhalle Emarthlar  -      -      - | 1 | 1 | - | 2 |
| Okejuske Harjo     -      -      - | 1 | 2 | - | 3 |
| Sehelarche         -      -      - | 1 | 1 | - | 2 |
| Farnehar Harjo     -      -      - | 1 | 1 | - | 2 |
| Chuwille Harjo     -      -      - | 1 | 1 | - | 2 |
| | 95 | 76 | - | 171 |

CREEK CENSUS—Continued.

| Names of Heads of Families. | Males. | Females. | Slaves. | Total. |
|---|---|---|---|---|
| Echim Emarthlar | 1 | 1 | - | 2 |
| Setaule | 1 | 1 | - | 2 |
| Miattubba | 2 | 1 | - | 3 |
| Senauhe | 2 | 2 | - | 4 |
| Micque Yoholo | 3 | 2 | - | 5 |
| Ocheharjo | 2 | 3 | - | 5 |
| Hoharlockoharjo | 1 | 2 | - | 3 |
| Norbocheharjo | 1 | 1 | - | 2 |
| Talseharjo | 1 | 1 | - | 2 |
| Klarsose | 3 | 1 | - | 4 |
| Cinnuggome | 3 | 2 | - | 5 |
| Nortumga | 1 | 1 | - | 2 |
| Efustegey | 1 | 1 | - | 2 |
| Kotchar Yoholo | 1 | 2 | - | 3 |
| Simesau | 3 | 2 | - | 5 |
| Koneseharjo | 1 | 1 | - | 2 |
| | 27 | 24 | | 51 |

TOAK-PAF-KAR TOWN.

| Names of Heads of Families. | Males. | Females. | Slaves. | Total. |
|---|---|---|---|---|
| Spookoak Yoholo | 1 | 2 | - | 3 |
| Ishallotta | 1 | 1 | - | 2 |
| Coefar | 1 | 1 | - | 2 |
| Hoakchose Harjo | 1 | 2 | - | 3 |
| Holattar Emarthlar | 1 | 1 | - | 2 |
| Mathlar | 1 | 2 | - | 3 |
| Tommy Yoholo | 1 | 1 | - | 2 |
| Arlocco Yoholo | 1 | 2 | - | 3 |
| Tobatth Harjo | 1 | 1 | - | 2 |
| Yath Hoga | 1 | 1 | - | 2 |
| No Boftichi | 1 | 1 | - | 2 |
| Echo Harjo | 2 | 2 | - | 4 |
| Tuckabatcha Yoholo | 1 | 3 | - | 4 |
| Sihoke | 2 | 1 | - | 3 |
| Oche Yoholo | 1 | 2 | - | 3 |
| Saunie | 2 | 1 | - | 3 |
| Tuckabatcha Fixico | 2 | 1 | - | 3 |
| Hillubba Emarthlar | 2 | 2 | - | 4 |
| Hillubba Nehaulocco | 1 | 1 | - | 2 |
| Choccocohie | 1 | 1 | - | 2 |
| Fulhoegar | 1 | 1 | - | 2 |
| Pin Harjo | 1 | 2 | - | 3 |
| Sofholokie | 1 | 1 | - | 2 |
| Spooage Emarthlar | 2 | 2 | - | 4 |
| Mat Touiecha | 1 | 1 | - | 2 |
| Simmihoie | 1 | 1 | - | 2 |

CREEK CENSUS—Continued.

| Names of Heads of Families. | Males. | Females. | Slaves. | Total. |
|---|---|---|---|---|
| Katey | 1 | 1 | - | 2 |
| Emarthlo Harjo | 1 | 2 | - | 3 |
| Arlocche Fixico | 2 | 1 | - | 3 |
| Allojar | 2 | 1 | - | 3 |
| Sisepy | 1 | 1 | - | 2 |
| Clocastar Harjo | 1 | 1 | - | 2 |
| Nithloche | 1 | 1 | - | 2 |
| Emarthlar Yoholo | 2 | 1 | - | 3 |
| Illis Fixico | 1 | 1 | - | 2 |
| Pinjeg | 1 | 1 | - | 2 |
| Wotco Yoholo | 2 | 1 | - | 3 |
| Polly | — | 2 | - | 2 |
| Ubucklart Hoga | 2 | 1 | - | 3 |
| Spoakoga Fixico | 2 | 1 | - | 3 |
| Spoakoak Harjo | 1 | 1 | - | 2 |
| Talladig Micco | 2 | 1 | - | 3 |
| Peggy | — | 3 | - | 3 |
| | 54 | 58 | | 112 |
| Ni Cey | — | 2 | 1 | 3 |
| Lotticha | 3 | 2 | - | 5 |
| Sarfarchkar | 2 | 1 | - | 3 |
| Snockaftar | 1 | 2 | - | 3 |
| Hopiejar | 1 | 1 | - | 2 |
| Lotty | 2 | 1 | - | 3 |
| Jimmy | 1 | 1 | 1 | 3 |
| Hannah | 1 | 2 | - | 3 |
| Carphogar | 1 | 1 | 1 | 3 |
| Cubbieache Fixico | 1 | 3 | - | 4 |
| Arthlonhoe | 1 | 1 | 1 | 3 |
| Coo Sar Fixico | 2 | 2 | - | 4 |
| Choakchart Harjo | 1 | 2 | 1 | 4 |
| Timmonie | 2 | 1 | - | 3 |
| Fushatch Emarthlar | 3 | 3 | - | 6 |
| Cochchar Harjo | 1 | 2 | - | 3 |
| Fittodick Harjo | 1 | 2 | - | 3 |
| Cettiarche Harjo | 2 | 1 | - | 3 |
| Cusse Tarharjo | 1 | 3 | - | 4 |
| Sattarwickcha | 1 | 2 | - | 3 |
| Tuskenehau | 2 | 2 | - | 4 |
| Ottis Fixico | 2 | 1 | - | 3 |
| Ufaula Fixico | 2 | 1 | - | 3 |
| Seathliejar | 1 | 2 | - | 3 |
| Wocseholattar | 1 | 2 | - | 3 |
| Rosey | 2 | 2 | - | 4 |

CREEK CENSUS—Continued.

| Names of Heads of Families. | Males. | Females. | Slaves. | Total. |
|---|---|---|---|---|
| Cheloke Harjo - - - - | 1 | 2 | - | 3 |
| Ottis Sa Emarthlar - - - | 2 | 1 | - | 3 |
| Tettargie - - - - - | 1 | 2 | - | 3 |
| Arlocfixico - - - - | - | 2 | - | 2 |
| Mistahar Kie - - - - | 1 | 2 | - | 3 |
| Arginnar - - - - - | 1 | 2 | - | 3 |
| Coluneme Harjo - - - - | 1 | 3 | - | 4 |
| Talmarsi Fixico - - - - | 2 | 1 | - | 3 |
| Millarttie - - - - - | - | 4 | - | 4 |
| Tobathle Harjo - - - - | 1 | 2 | - | 3 |
| Starfulhoie - - - - | 2 | 1 | - | 3 |
| Tallowarharjo - - - - | 1 | 2 | - | 3 |
| Chucoottalige - - - - | 3 | 1 | - | 4 |
| Homiga - - - - - | 2 | 2 | - | 4 |
| Cobbichcharharjo - - - - | 1 | 2 | - | 3 |
| Co Sirnockcheharjo - - - | 2 | 2 | - | 4 |
| Cochchar Fixico - - - - | 1 | 3 | - | 4 |
| Occowie - - - - - | 2 | 2 | - | 4 |
| | 62 | 81 | 5 | 148 |
| Yoholoche - - - - | 2 | 2 | - | 4 |
| No Ko Se Yoholo - - - - | 4 | 2 | - | 6 |
| Charley - - - - - | 2 | 3 | - | 5 |
| Cowo Sartharjo - - - - | 2 | 1 | - | 3 |
| Tarbohie - - - - - | 2 | 2 | - | 4 |
| Mar Bockkie - - - - | 1 | 2 | - | 3 |
| Stinnoga - - - - - | 1 | 1 | - | 2 |
| Locher Yoholo - - - - | 2 | 1 | - | 3 |
| Clechummeharjo - - - - | 2 | 2 | - | 4 |
| Choquartta Yoholo - - - | 2 | 3 | - | 5 |
| Lif Tifharjo - - - - | 2 | 2 | - | 4 |
| Toboisholattarharjo - - - | 1 | 3 | - | 4 |
| Ubothlar - - - - - | 2 | 2 | - | 4 |
| Efar Emarthlar - - - - | 2 | 2 | - | 4 |
| Tusconer Harjo - - - - | 3 | 1 | - | 4 |
| Hilbubba - - - - - | 1 | 2 | - | 3 |
| Molly - - - - - | 1 | 2 | - | 3 |
| Esloche - - - - - | 1 | 1 | - | 2 |
| Talhomatta - - - - | 1 | 1 | - | 2 |
| Cubbichche Yoholo - - - | 3 | 1 | - | 4 |
| Timmecogjey - - - - | 2 | 1 | - | 3 |
| Emarthloche - - - - | 1 | 2 | - | 3 |
| Wox Se Yoholo - - - - | 2 | 1 | - | 3 |
| Chugarttie Yoholo - - - | 1 | 1 | - | 2 |
| Narboche Emarthlar - - - | 2 | 2 | - | 4 |

CREEK CENSUS—Continued.

| Names of Heads of Families. | Males. | Females. | Slaves. | Total. |
|---|---|---|---|---|
| Molly (two same name)  -    -    - | 1 | 1 | - | 2 |
| Wewoke Yoholo  -    -    -    - | 2 | 2 | - | 4 |
| Chuswarti Yoholo     -    -    - | 2 | 2 | - | 4 |
| Martup Harjo   -    -    -    - | 2 | 1 | - | 3 |
| Tilliechar     -    -    -    - | 2 | 1 | - | 3 |
| Chuwilla Harjo  -    -    -    - | 1 | 1 | - | 2 |
| Cit Tunwie    -    -    -    - | 2 | 4 | - | 6 |
| Hilbubba Micco   -    -    -    - | 2 | 3 | - | 5 |
| Etia      -    -    -    - | 1 | 1 | - | 2 |
| Coosarbecha    -    -    -    - | 1 | 1 | - | 2 |
| Simotta    -    -    -    - | 2 | 2 | - | 4 |
| Lache Harjo    -    -    -    - | 3 | 1 | - | 4 |
| Tehibocco    -    -    -    - | 1 | 1 | - | 2 |
| Simbohega    -    -    -    - | 1 | 1 | - | 2 |
|  |  |  |  |  |
|  | 68 | 65 |  | 133 |

SOCKOPARTOY TOWN.

| Names of Heads of Families. | Males. | Females. | Slaves. | Total. |
|---|---|---|---|---|
| Domothti Harjo   -    -    -    - | 2 | 2 | - | 4 |
| Noklis Harjo    -    -    -    - | 4 | 2 | - | 6 |
| Nehemarthte Fixico   -    -    - | 2 | 1 | - | 3 |
| Nehar Harjo    -    -    -    - | 1 | 2 | - | 3 |
| Nehodi     -    -    -    - | — | 2 | - | 2 |
| Koegus Yoholo   -    -    -    - | 2 | 2 | - | 4 |
| Chofolope Yoholo    -    -    - | 2 | 1 | - | 3 |
| Moklus Fixico    -    -    -    - | 2 | 1 | - | 3 |
| Contul Harjo    -    -    -    - | 1 | 2 | - | 3 |
| Oswitch Harjo    -    -    -    - | 3 | 1 | - | 4 |
| Narbocche Fixico    -    -    - | 2 | 2 | - | 4 |
| Toffor Fixico    -    -    -    - | 1 | 2 | - | 3 |
| Mehar     -    -    -    - | 1 | 1 | - | 2 |
| Hathlun Harjo    -    -    -    - | 1 | 2 | - | 3 |
| Alabama Emarthlar    -    -    - | 1 | 1 | - | 2 |
| Nese      -    -    -    - | 2 | 1 | - | 3 |
| Chooye Yoholo   -    -    -    - | 2 | 2 | - | 4 |
| Thlathlo Yoholo   -    -    -    - | 2 | 1 | - | 3 |
| Sofer     -    -    -    - | 1 | 2 | - | 3 |
| Teharlofte    -    -    -    - | 1 | 1 | - | 2 |
| Wunnawhe    -    -    -    - | 1 | 1 | - | 2 |
| Nehar Yoholo    -    -    -    - | 1 | 2 | - | 3 |
| Talmachus Harjo -    -    -    - | 4 | 2 | - | 6 |
| Sanclathlo    -    -    -    - | 1 | 2 | - | 3 |
| Mantallegey    -    -    -    - | 1 | 2 | - | 3 |
| Marthloloby    -    -    -    - | 2 | 1 | - | 3 |
| Isfulhoge    -    -    -    - | 1 | 2 | - | 3 |
| Judy      -    -    -    - | 1 | 1 | - | 2 |

CREEK CENSUS—Continued.

| Names of Heads of Families. | Males. | Females. | Slaves. | Total. |
|---|---|---|---|---|
| Yarhar Harjo . . . | 1 | 1 | - | 2 |
| Sotieachter . . . | 1 | 1 | - | 2 |
| Kono Harjo . . . | 3 | 1 | - | 4 |
| Sawfichegay . . . | 1 | 1 | . - | 2 |
| Hetulgey Harjo . . . | 1 | 2 | - | 3 |
| Chooli Yoholo . . . | 1 | 2 | - | 3 |
| Albitter Harjo . . . | 2 | 1 | - | 3 |
| Memaltley . . . | 2 | 1 | - | 3 |
| Moklus Emarthlar . . . | 1 | 2 | - | 3 |
| Fosehatche Fixico . . . | 2 | 2 | - | 4 |
| Usse Yoholo . . . | 2 | 1 | - | 3 |
| Talwar Fixico . . . | 1 | 2 | - | 3 |
| Konip Harjo . . . | 3 | 1 | - | 4 |
| Ohechoy Fixico . . . | 2 | 1 | - | 3 |
| Kiemulga Emarthlar . . | 2 | 1 | - | 3 |
| Konis Harjo . . . | 2 | 1 | - | 3 |
| | 72 | 65 | | 137 |
| Cussete Emarthlar . . . | 1 | 1 | - | 2 |
| Tewiee . . . | 2 | 1 | - | 3 |
| Autus Yoholo . . . | 2 | 2 | - | 4 |
| Lothoe . . . | - | 2 | - | 2 |
| Choowasti Emarthlar . . | 1 | 1 | - | 2 |
| Tussekearchartie . . . | 2 | - | - | 2 |
| Talsi Harjo . . . | 2 | 1 | - | 3 |
| John . . . | 3 | 1 | - | 4 |
| Enehe Emarthlar . . . | 3 | 1 | - | 4 |
| Sinne . . . | 1 | 1 | - | 2 |
| Ko Emarthlar . . . | 2 | 1 | - | 3 |
| Ischehe . . . | 2 | 1 | - | 3 |
| Hotalke Emarthlar . . . | 2 | 3 | - | 5 |
| Tustunnuckee . . . | 1 | 1 | - | 2 |
| Holulge Yoholo . . . | 1 | 2 | - | 3 |
| Kowe Harjo . . . | 3 | 3 | - | 6 |
| Nocosi Ekar . . . | 2 | 2 | - | 4 |
| Liji . . . | 1 | 1 | - | 2 |
| Stouwagge . . . | 2 | 1 | - | 3 |
| Tomarth Yoholo . . . | 1 | 1 | - | 2 |
| | 34 | 27 | | 61 |
| FISH-POND TOWN. | | | | |
| Sappeloke . . . | - | 2 | - | 2 |
| Talope Harjo . . . | 2 | 2 | - | 4 |
| Tabbassoler Harjo . . . | 2 | 2 | - | 4 |

CREEK CENSUS—Continued.

| Names of Heads of Families. | Males. | Females. | Slaves. | Total. |
|---|---|---|---|---|
| Kochud Fixico | 2 | 1 | - | 3 |
| Istarfulhogey | 2 | 1 | - | 3 |
| Nanbickcooche | 1 | 2 | - | 3 |
| Mihelatchee | 2 | 2 | - | 4 |
| Sofpefoteheige | — | 3 | - | 3 |
| Pokateke | 2 | 1 | - | 3 |
| Mittalhege | 1 | 2 | - | 3 |
| Illis Harjo | 2 | 3 | - | 5 |
| Stunihieteley | 2 | 3 | - | 5 |
| Stuckitligey | 1 | 1 | - | 2 |
| Parhose Emarthlar | 4 | 2 | - | 6 |
| Chufficnigey | 3 | 2 | - | 5 |
| Okichoy Micco | 2 | 2 | - | 4 |
| Homulga | — | 2 | - | 2 |
| Hokunnee | 1 | 2 | - | 3 |
| Hillabee Harjo | 2 | 1 | - | 3 |
| Kiwassart Harjo | 2 | 2 | - | 4 |
| Arsemehoke | 1 | 2 | - | 3 |
| Woxe Emarthlar | 2 | 1 | - | 3 |
| Tuckabatchee Harjo | 2 | 1 | - | 3 |
| Arlock Harjo | 1 | 1 | - | 2 |
| Agingathee | 1 | 1 | - | 2 |
| Istemiheke | 1 | 1 | - | 2 |
| Susey | 1 | 2 | - | 3 |
| Martar Harjo | 2 | 2 | - | 4 |
| Thlathlo Harjo | 2 | 2 | - | 4 |
| Sawwihicky | 2 | 1 | - | 3 |
| Fegathle | 2 | 2 | - | 4 |
| Koegis Yoholo | 1 | 2 | - | 3 |
| Nisey | 1 | 2 | - | 3 |
| Osar Harjo | 2 | 1 | - | 3 |
| Simwarhe | 2 | 1 | - | 3 |
| Harselolocke | 1 | 2 | - | 3 |
| Jim | 2 | 1 | - | 3 |
| Immoligey | 3 | 3 | - | 6 |
| Hogillis Micco | 1 | 3 | - | 4 |
| Sartarhoe | 1 | 2 | - | 3 |
| Chasechart Harjo | 2 | 1 | - | 3 |
| Monolitcha | 2 | 1 | - | 3 |
| Artiscookchartee | 1 | 3 | - | 4 |
|  | 69 | 76 |  | 145 |
| Niholubbee | 2 | 1 | - | 3 |
| Timawfuslegey | 1 | 2 | - | 3 |
| Cufsetau Harjo | 1 | 2 | - | 3 |

CREEK CENSUS—Continued.

| Names of Heads of Families. | Males. | Females. | Slaves. | Total. |
|---|---|---|---|---|
| Micco Subba - - - | - | 2 | - | 2 |
| Illis Fixico - - - | 3 | 1 | - | 4 |
| Okechun Harjo - - - | 2 | 2 | - | 4 |
| Spoke Oke Harjo - - - | 1 | 1 | - | 2 |
| Litke - - - - | 1 | 1 | - | 2 |
| Ismogigey - - - | 1 | 2 | - | 3 |
| Chooele Harjo - - - | 2 | 1 | - | 3 |
| Neharlockcooche - - - | 3 | 1 | - | 4 |
| Sofonfaggey - - - | - | 2 | - | 2 |
| Tockosa Harjo - - - | 3 | 1 | - | 4 |
| Tallabicker - - - | 2 | 1 | - | 3 |
| Parhose Harjo - - - | 2 | 1 | - | 3 |
| Kobbia - - - - | 1 | 2 | - | 3 |
| Tuckabatche Fixico - - | 2 | 1 | - | 3 |
| Letif Harjo - - - | 2 | 1 | - | 3 |
| Timhigey - - - | 1 | 2 | - | 3 |
| Willey - - - | 1 | 1 | - | 2 |
| Chouwar - - - | 1 | 2 | - | 3 |
| Hotulge Harjo - - - | 1 | 2 | - | 3 |
| Echarse Harjo - - - | 3 | 2 | - | 5 |
| Pouhosehobiegey - - - | 3 | 1 | - | 4 |
| Betsey - - - | 1 | 2 | - | 3 |
| Har Plocko Yoholo - - | 2 | 2 | - | 4 |
| Osar Harjo, (2d same name) - - | 2 | 1 | - | 3 |
| Chofelope Harjo - - - | 1 | 2 | - | 3 |
| Dickey - - - | 1 | 2 | - | 3 |
| Artus Fixico - - - | 2 | 1 | - | 3 |
| Melinda - - - | - | 3 | - | 3 |
| Pin Harjo - - - | 1 | 2 | - | 3 |
| Isshawway - - - | - | 3 | - | 3 |
| Kontul Fixico - - - | 1 | 2 | - | 3 |
| Tennorgit - - - | 1 | 2 | - | 3 |
| Tokalle - - - - | - | 3 | - | 3 |
| Oktiarche Emarthlar - - | 2 | 2 | - | 4 |
| Tuskehenehaw - - - | 2 | 1 | - | 3 |
| Peggy - - - - | 2 | 1 | - | 3 |
| Cuegotto Harjo - - - | 2 | 1 | - | 3 |
| Timmonehicke - - - | 2 | 1 | - | 3 |
| Tiack Setche - - - | 2 | 1 | - | 3 |
| Enehe Emarthlar - - - | 2 | 1 | - | 3 |
| Simmuttee - - - | 1 | 3 | - | 4 |
| | 60 | 72 | | 137 |
| Tin Thlanis Harjo - - - | 1 | 3 | - | 4 |
| Warlocco Harjo - - - | 2 | 3 | - | 5 |

## CREEK CENSUS—Continued.

| Names of Heads of Families. | Males. | Females. | Slaves. | Total. |
|---|---|---|---|---|
| Tobbothkie - - - | 1 | 1 | - | 2 |
| O Sooch Fixico - - - | 1 | 2 | - | 3 |
| Woxse Emarthlar Harjo - - | 1 | 1 | - | 2 |
| Timmithliega - - - | 1 | 2 | - | 3 |
| Inneharwoccoligar - - - | 1 | 4 | - | 5 |
| Neharlocco - - - | 1 | 2 | - | 3 |
| Afochchege - - - | 2 | 2 | - | 4 |
| Nehar Harjo - - - | 2 | 1 | - | 3 |
| Legar - - - - | 1 | 2 | - | 3 |
| Echo Fixico - - - | 1 | 2 | - | 3 |
| Stimmarbohie - - - | 2 | 1 | - | 3 |
| Octtiarche Fixico - - - | 2 | 1 | - | 3 |
| Choakchartinnehar - - - | 4 | 1 | - | 5 |
| Oclubpise Fixico - - - | 2 | 5 | - | 7 |
| Sally - - - - | 1 | 1 | - | 2 |
| Nithligar - - - | 2 | 1 | - | 3 |
| Ubiathley - - - - | - | 3 | - | 3 |
| George - - - - | 2 | - | - | 2 |
| Yarhar Harjo - - - | 1 | 4 | - | 5 |
| | 31 | 42 | | 73 |

### OAK-TAW-SAR-SEY TOWN.

| Names of Heads of Families. | Males. | Females. | Slaves. | Total. |
|---|---|---|---|---|
| Ho Tulga Yoholo - - | 2 | 3 | - | 5 |
| Archuloc Harjo - - | 2 | 1 | - | 3 |
| O Gillasey Harjo - - | 3 | 3 | - | 6 |
| Nocos Fixico - - | 1 | 2 | - | 3 |
| Chuwasti Fixico - - | 2 | 3 | - | 5 |
| Osooche Harjo - - | 2 | 4 | - | 6 |
| Mallitkar - - | 2 | 2 | - | 4 |
| Arharloc Fixico - - | 1 | 2 | - | 3 |
| Stinmelike - - | 1 | 2 | - | 3 |
| Pin Emarthlar - - | 3 | 1 | - | 4 |
| Oak Taw Saw Sey Harjo - | 2 | 2 | - | 4 |
| Muckharsey - - | 1 | 2 | - | 3 |
| Wigejar - - - | 1 | 2 | - | 3 |
| Talwar Fixico - - | 2 | 2 | - | 4 |
| Nocos Harjo - - | 2 | 1 | - | 3 |
| Oche Yoholo - - | 2 | 2 | - | 4 |
| Tushehichche - - | 3 | 3 | - | 6 |
| Ho Tulga Fixico - - | 1 | 1 | - | 2 |
| Chular Harjo - - | 1 | 1 | - | 2 |
| Mat Socharkie - - | 3 | 1 | - | 4 |
| Wotco Yoholo - - | 2 | 2 | - | 4 |
| Suppinco Uga - - | 1 | 3 | - | 4 |
| Mittiheachar - - | 1 | 1 | - | 2 |

CREEK CENSUS—Continued.

| Names of Heads of Families. | Males. | Females. | Slaves. | Total. |
|---|---|---|---|---|
| So Kar Harjo - - - - | 2 | 2 | - | 4 |
| Emarthlar Harjo - - - - | 3 | 2 | . | 5 |
| Tommy Yoholo - - - - | 2 | 1 | - | 3 |
| Clechumme Harjo - - - | 4 | 2 | - | 6 |
| Elitdiga - - - - | 2 | 2 | - | 4 |
| Illis Harjo - - - - | 1 | 2 | - | 3 |
| Coakchoy Fixico - - - | 2 | 1 | - | 3 |
| Emarthlo Yoholo - - - | 2 | 3 | - | 5 |
| Ho Tulga Harjo - - - | 1 | 2 | - | 3 |
| Tulwar Harjo - - - - | 2 | 2 | - | 4 |
| Talmarlehinnehar - - - - | 3 | 1 | - | 4 |
| | 65 | 66 | | 131 |

OAK-CHOY TOWN.

| | | | | |
|---|---|---|---|---|
| Chuwasti Yoholo - - - | 1 | 3 | - | 4 |
| Coegus Harjo - - - - | 1 | 3 | - | 4 |
| Ottis Fixico - - - - | 1 | 2 | - | 3 |
| Talwar Harjo - - - - | 2 | 2 | - | 4 |
| Oakche Harjo - - - - | 2 | 1 | - | 3 |
| Talmarsewottiligga - - - | 1 | 2 | - | 3 |
| Nocos Fixico - - - - | 2 | 2 | - | 4 |
| Conchart Yoholo - - - | 1 | 3 | - | 4 |
| Nehotosee - - - - | 1 | 2 | - | 3 |
| Chofolop Harjo - - - | 4 | 2 | - | 6 |
| Talloppoche - - - - | 2 | 1 | - | 3 |
| Sodedunne Harjo - - - | 2 | 2 | - | 4 |
| Tannachhohe - - - - | 1 | 2 | - | 3 |
| Starthle - - - - - | 3 | 3 | - | 6 |
| Toharte - - - - - | 1 | 3 | - | 4 |
| Coemarlth Fixico - - - | 2 | 2 | - | 4 |
| Nocos Harjo - - - - | 1 | 2 | - | 3 |
| Wwoakki Yoholo - - - | 2 | 1 | - | 3 |
| Kokke Yoholo - - - - | 1 | 2 | - | 3 |
| Billy - - - - - | 3 | 1 | - | 4 |
| Yet Tashokie - - - - | 1 | 2 | - | 3 |
| Narboche Harjo - - - | 2 | 1 | - | 3 |
| Sithlogache - - - - | - | 2 | - | 2 |
| Woliga - - - - - | 1 | 2 | - | 3 |
| Oakfuska Harjo - - - | 1 | 4 | - | 5 |
| Nehar Fixico - - - - | 2 | 1 | - | 3 |
| Mawwarhie - - - - | 1 | 2 | - | 3 |
| Ubiheach Kar - - - - | 1 | 2 | - | 3 |
| Talthhoie - - - - | 2 | 1 | - | 3 |
| Timliga - - - - | - | 2 | - | 2 |
| Fus Harjo - - - - | 3 | 2 | - | 5 |

38‡

CREEK CENSUS—Continued.

| Names of Heads of Families. | Males. | Females. | Slaves. | Total. |
|---|---|---|---|---|
| Powhosharjo        -    -    -    - | 1 | 2 | - | 3 |
| Conchart Fixico   -    -    -    - | 3 | 3 | - | 6 |
| Niharneattooche   -    -    -    - | 2 | 1 | - | 3 |
| Cono Harjo         -    -    -    - | 5 | 1 | - | 6 |
| Ichhokie   -    -    -    -    - | 2 | 1 | - | 3 |
| Toho Yarha         -    -    -    - | 2 | 1 | - | 3 |
| Talmochus Harjo   -    -    -    - | 2 | 2 | - | 4 |
| Hotulga Harjo      -    -    -    - | 2 | 1 | - | 3 |
|  | 67 | 74 |  | 141 |

OSELARNEBY TOWN.

| | Males. | Females. | Slaves. | Total. |
|---|---|---|---|---|
| Oakclabpissa Harjo      -    -    - | 3 | 2 | - | 5 |
| Konip Fixico    -    -    -    - | 3 | 2 | - | 5 |
| Emarth Harjo    -    -    -    : | 3 | 1 | - | 4 |
| Nocos Harjo     -    -    -    - | 3 | 2 | - | 5 |
| Oakchoy Harjo   -    -    -    - | 1 | 3 | - | 4 |
| Emarthla  -    -    -    -    - | 2 | 1 | - | 3 |
| Contal Harjo    -    -    -    - | 2 | 2 | - | 4 |
| Osi Yoholo      -    -    -    - | 3 | 1 | - | 4 |
| Oclus Yoholo    -    -    -    - | 3 | 1 | - | 4 |
| Tustanugga      -    -    -    - | 1 | 3 | - | 4 |
| Fushatch Fixico  -    -    -    - | 2 | 2 | - | 4 |
| Spoakoak Harjo  -    -    -    - | 3 | 1 | - | 4 |
| Ubi Harjo       -    -    -    - | 2 | 1 | - | 3 |
| Efar Harjo      -    -    -    - | 1 | 3 | - | 4 |
| Arloc Fixico    -    -    - .    - | 3 | 2 | - | 5 |
| Tuckabatcha Emarthlar   -    -    - | 2 | 3 | - | 5 |
| Powhos Harjo    -    -    -    - | 2 | 2 | - | 4 |
| Cockchar Fixico  -    -    -    - | 2 | 3 | - | 5 |
| Oakfuska Emarthlar      -    -    - | 1 | 3 | - | 4 |
| Wollocco  -    -    -    -    - | 1 | 3 | - | 4 |
| Mallodiche      -    -    -    - | 1 | 2 | - | 3 |
| Nogoche  -    -    -    -    - | 1 | 2 | - | 3 |
| Liftif Yoholo   -    -    -    - | 1 | 2 | - | 3 |
| Osi Yoholo      -    -    -    - | 1 | 2 | - | 3 |
| Tinthlannis Harjo -    -    -    - | 1 | 3 | - | 4 |
| Ogete Yoholo    -    -    -    - | 3 | 1 | - | 4 |
| Pinharja   -    -    -    -    - | 4 | 3 | - | 7 |
| Narboche Fixico  -    -    -    - | 2 | 4 | - | 6 |
| Skinnia    -    -    -    -    - | 2 | 2 | - | 4 |
| Cheewaste Fixico -    -    -    - | 2 | 2 | - | 4 |
| Choquartta Fixico -    -    -    - | 3 | 2 | - | 5 |
| Chicellumgo     -    -    -    - | 1 | 2 | - | 3 |
| Fieshatcha Yoholo      -    -    - | 3 | 1 | - | 4 |
| Tumallot Harjo  -    -    -    - | 1 | 2 | - | 3 |

## CREEK CENSUS—Continued.

| Names of Heads of Families. | Males. | Females. | Slaves. | Total. |
|---|---|---|---|---|
| Oswitch Harjo - - - - | 2 | 2 | - | 4 |
| Ochimmega - - - - | 2 | 1 | - | 3 |
| Cheeyar Yoholo - - - - | 3 | 1 | - | 4 |
| Oakchon Harjo - - - - | 2 | 1 | - | 3 |
| Mannarche - - - - | 1 | 2 | - | 3 |
| Narboche Emarthlar - - - | 4 | 2 | - | 6 |
| Chofelope Yoholo - - - - | 1 | 2 | - | 3 |
| Yarkin Harjo - - - - | 1 | 2 | - | 3 |
| Cochis Emarthlar - - - - | 1 | 2 | - | 3 |
| | 87 | 86 | | 173 |
| Echo Harjo - - - - | 1 | 4 | - | 5 |
| Talmarse Harjo - - - - | 1 | 3 | - | 4 |

### HATCHET CREEK TOWN.

| Names of Heads of Families. | Males. | Females. | Slaves. | Total. |
|---|---|---|---|---|
| Artee Harjo - - - - | 2 | 2 | - | 4 |
| Ochee Harjo - - - - | 2 | 3 | - | 5 |
| Isparne Fixico - - - - | 2 | 4 | - | 6 |
| Letif Emarthlar - - - - | 2 | 3 | - | 5 |
| Woxey Emarthlar - - - | 2 | 4 | - | 6 |
| Isparne Yoholo - - - - | 2 | 3 | - | 5 |
| Ewyche - - - - - | 2 | 3 | - | 5 |
| Yatik Harjo - - - - | 2 | 3 | - | 5 |
| Tuskonar Fixico - - - - | 2 | 2 | - | 4 |
| Emarthlar - - - - - | 1 | 2 | - | 3 |
| Hikoege - - - - - | 1 | 2 | - | 3 |
| Chooille Hargo - - - | 3 | 2 | - | 5 |
| Hogillishenehaw - - - - | 2 | 3 | - | 5 |
| Chao Watteliggey - - - - | 2 | 4 | - | 6 |
| Nocose Yoholo - - - - | 2 | 2 | - | 4 |
| Cho Fixico - - - - | 3 | 1 | - | 4 |
| Fichonay - - - - - | 2 | 2 | - | 4 |
| Sokoleche - - - - - | 2 | 2 | - | 4 |
| Hopichopko - - - - | 3 | 3 | - | 6 |
| Kotchar Micco - - - - | 1 | 2 | - | 3 |
| Oswitcher Harjo - - - - | 2 | 2 | - | 4 |
| Kono Harjo - - - - | 1 | 2 | - | 3 |
| Powose Emarthlar - - - | 3 | 1 | - | 4 |
| Woxeyholarte Emarthlar - - - | 1 | 3 | - | 4 |
| Telijah - - - - - | 2 | 2 | - | 4 |
| Tokkosar Harjo - - - - | 1 | 2 | - | 3 |
| Narpooche - - - - | 2 | 1 | - | 3 |
| Chochitto Harjo - - - - | 1 | 3 | - | 4 |
| Ischelawhe - - - - | 1 | 2 | - | 3 |

## CREEK CENSUS—Continued.

| Names of Heads of Families. | Males. | Females. | Slaves. | Total. |
|---|---|---|---|---|
| Samoche . . . . . | – | 3 | - | 3 |
| Nocose Emarthlar . . . . | 2 | 1 | - | 3 |
| | 58 | 81 | | 139 |
| Simmonauhe . . . . | 2 | 1 | - | 3 |
| Sallottiga . . . . . | 2 | 1 | - | 3 |
| Matmiegey . . . . | 1 | 1 | - | 2 |
| Cholocko . . . . . | 1 | 3 | - | 4 |
| Honipfixico . . . . | 1 | 3 | - | 4 |
| Konoe Yoholo . . . . | 1 | 2 | - | 3 |
| Osarharjo . . . . | 2 | 1 | - | 3 |
| Ninechee . . . . . | 2 | 1 | - | 3 |
| Sopokey . . . . . | – | 3 | - | 3 |
| Parse Yoholo . . . . | 2 | 2 | - | 4 |
| Isfarneharjo . . . . | 1 | 3 | - | 4 |
| Chofolopeharjo . . . . | 3 | 1 | - | 4 |
| Choemarthlar . . . . | 2 | 2 | - | 4 |
| Hillis Yoholo . . . . | 3 | 1 | - | 4 |
| Osi Yoholo . . . . | 2 | 2 | - | 4 |
| Mickkuntuskau . . . . | 3 | 1 | - | 4 |
| Hanlothoe . . . . | 1 | 1 | - | 2 |
| Choowastiharjo . . . . | 2 | 2 | - | 4 |
| Allumehegey . . . . | 1 | 2 | - | 3 |
| Choogotteharjo . . . . | 2 | 2 | - | 4 |
| Parhoseharjo . . . . | 1 | 2 | - | 3 |
| Lofterfixico . . . . | 2 | 1 | - | 3 |
| Nehartogar . . . . | 1 | 2 | - | 3 |
| Tom Echee . . . . | 2 | 1 | - | 3 |
| Tommyfixico . . . . | 2 | 4 | - | 6 |
| Choogottefixico . . . . | 3 | 2 | - | 5 |
| Arhose . . . . . | 1 | 1 | - | 2 |
| Yattefixico . . . . | 2 | 1 | - | 3 |
| Tallip Yoholo . . . . | 3 | 1 | - | 4 |
| Talemarseharjo . . . . | 2 | 1 | - | 3 |
| Eu Fanleefixico . . . . | 1 | 2 | - | 3 |
| Woxe Yoholo . . . . | 1 | 1 | - | 2 |
| Timmohowe . . . . | – | 3 | - | 3 |
| Kushimhokey . . . . | 2 | 1 | - | 3 |
| Affenokey . . . . | 2 | 1 | - | 3 |
| Intarseke . . . . | 1 | 1 | - | 2 |
| Kolummeharjo . . . . | 2 | 2 | - | 4 |
| Segithley . . . . | 1 | 1 | - | 2 |
| Sihegey . . . . | 2 | 1 | - | 3 |
| Passcove Yoholo . . . . | 1 | 2 | - | 3 |
| Hocose Ekar . . . . | 2 | 3 | - | 5 |

CREEK CENSUS—Continued.

| Names of Heads of Families. | Males. | Females. | Slaves. | Total. |
|---|---|---|---|---|
| Simminnot - - - - | 1 | 1 | - | 2 |
| Sallodegit - - - - - | 2 | 2 | 1 | 5 |
| Thlathlo - - - - - | 1 | 1 | - | 2 |
| | 71 | 73 | 1 | 145 |
| Timmo Yatche - - - - | 2 | 1 | - | 3 |
| Fixico Yoholo - - - - | 3 | 3 | - | 6 |
| Far Emarthlar - - - - | 2 | 4 | - | 6 |
| Cho Yoholo - - - - | 2 | 2 | - | 4 |
| Sisseber - - - - - | 2 | 1 | - | 3 |
| Yoke Satchee - - - - | 2 | 2 | - | 4 |
| **EMARHETOWN.** | | | | |
| Parhose Emarthlar - - - | 2 | 4 | - | 6 |
| Choharjo - - - - | 3 | 4 | - | 7 |
| Chofolopeharjo - - - - | 2 | 1 | - | 3 |
| Yarhar Emarthlar - - - - | 3 | 6 | - | 9 |
| Tabbassolarharjo - - - - | 3 | 2 | - | 5 |
| Maw O Key - - - - | 1 | 1 | - | 2 |
| Isfanarteeligger - - - - | 2 | 1 | - | 3 |
| Talamarse Yoholo - - - - | 2 | 2 | - | 4 |
| Pokherharjo - - - - | 2 | 2 | - | 4 |
| Emarthlarathe - - - - | 2 | 1 | - | 3 |
| Kosar Micco - - - - | 2 | 4 | - | 6 |
| Tallip Yoholo - - - - | 1 | 2 | - | 3 |
| Seho Marharjo - - - - | — | 2 | - | 2 |
| Pin Emarthlar - - - - | 1 | 1 | - | 2 |
| Talse Emarthlar - - - - | 2 | 1 | - | 3 |
| Farharjo - - - - - | 4 | 1 | - | 5 |
| Lopegey - - - - - | 1 | 4 | - | 5 |
| Hotalleemarthlar - - - - | 4 | 2 | - | 6 |
| Chewastifixico - - - - | 1 | 1 | - | 2 |
| Echoemarthlar - - - - | 1 | 2 | - | 3 |
| Chokatekar - - - - | — | 2 | - | 2 |
| Kosarfixico - - - - | 2 | 1 | - | 3 |
| Tilliffe - - - - - | 1 | 2 | - | 3 |
| Suelartar - - - - - | 2 | 2 | - | 4 |
| Sohallege - - - - - | 2 | 1 | - | 3 |
| Totallege - - - - - | 2 | 1 | - | 3 |
| Talmarsefixico - - - - | 3 | 1 | - | 4 |
| Talhomarte - - - - | 2 | 2 | - | 4 |
| | 66 | 69 | | 135 |

## CREEK CENSUS—Continued.

| Names of Heads of Families. | Males. | Females. | Slaves. | Total. |
|---|---|---|---|---|
| Eneharfixico      -      -      -      - | 1 | 1 | - | 2 |
| Spokeoke Emarthlar      -      -      - | 1 | 2 | - | 3 |
| Konippe Emarthlar      -      -      - | 2 | 1 | - | 3 |
| Halway      -      -      -      - | 2 | 2 | - | 4 |
| Holarte Emarthlar -      -      -      - | 2 | 2 | - | 4 |
| Choolitter Emarthlar      -      -      - | 1 | 1 | - | 2 |
| Mahonegey      -      -      -      - | 1 | 1 | - | 2 |
| Meokese   -      -      -      -      - | — | 4 | - | 4 |
| Innoegey   -      -      -      -      - | 1 | 1 | - | 2 |
| Semarthlar      -      -      -      - | — | 2 | - | 2 |
| Tihogey   -      -      -      -      - | 1 | 1 | - | 2 |
| Stinsehogey      -      -      -      - | 2 | 1 | - | 3 |
| Tewathhele      -      -      -      - | 2 | 1 | - | 3 |
| Mehogey   -      -      -      -      - | 1 | 1 | - | 2 |
| Nocoseilleharjo      -      -      -      - | 1 | 2 | - | 3 |
| Cho Yoholo      -      -      -      - | 3 | 2 | - | 5 |
| Chewastiharjo      -      -      -      - | 3 | 1 | - | 4 |
| Kohasse Emarthlar      -      -      - | 2 | 2 | - | 4 |
| Yoholoche -      -      -      -      - | 1 | 2 | - | 3 |
| Simmehode      -      -      -      - | — | 2 | - | 2 |
| Nehomarthte Fixico      -      -      - | 1 | 2 | - | 3 |
| Hillis Fixico      -      -      -      - | 1 | 1 | - | 2 |
| Nehethle   -      -      -      -      - | 1 | 2 | - | 3 |
| Simmohquager      -      -      -      - | 2 | 4 | - | 6 |
| Chanege   -      -      -      -      - | 3 | 1 | - | 4 |
| Chewik  Harjo      -      -      -      - | 2 | 2 | - | 4 |
| Toney      -      -      -      -      - | 1 | 1 | - | 2 |
| Toger      -      -      -      -      - | — | 2 | - | 2 |
| Pin Emarthlar      -      -      -      - | 1 | 1 | - | 2 |
| Kiheuchee -      -      -      -      - | — | 2 | - | 2 |
|  | 39 | 50 |  | 89 |

### KIAMULGATOWN.

| | | | | |
|---|---|---|---|---|
| Cho Yoholo      -      -      -      - | 1 | 3 | - | 4 |
| Albet Emarthlar   -      -      -      - | 1 | 2 | - | 3 |
| Chimhoker      -      -      -      - | — | 2 | - | 2 |
| Walgey      -      -      -      - | 1 | 2 | - | 3 |
| Sehoeigey -      -      -      -      - | — | 2 | - | 2 |
| Chockoegee      -      -      -      - | — | 2 | - | 2 |
| Nocose Harjo      -      -      -      - | 2 | 3 | - | 5 |
| Yarkin Harjo      -      -      -      - | 2 | 1 | - | 3 |
| Tonehare   -      -      -      -      - | 3 | 1 | - | 4 |
| Eneharwoppeligger      -      -      - | 2 | 3 | - | 5 |
| Chofee Harjo      -      -      -      - | 2 | 4 | - | 6 |

CREEK CENSUS—Continued.

| Names of Heads of Families. | Males. | Females. | Slaves. | Total. |
|---|---|---|---|---|
| Chewasti Yoholo - - - - | 2 | 1 | - | 3 |
| Cho Emarthlar - - - - | 2 | 1 | - | 3 |
| Flejum Emarthlar - - - | 2 | 1 | - | 3 |
| Tuski Harjo - - - - | 1 | 1 | - | 2 |
| Nicka - - - - | - | 2 | - | 2 |
| Somichchar - - - - | 1 | 1 | - | 2 |
| Tommy Harjo - - - - | 2 | 2 | - | 4 |
| Nehe Harjo - - - - | 2 | 2 | - | 4 |
| Sittehigey - - - - | 1 | 3 | - | 4 |
| Tahhagiepe - - - - | 1 | 1 | - | 2 |
| Martowar Harjo - - - - | 1 | 1 | - | 2 |
| Tuskonar Fixico - - - - | 2 | 2 | - | 4 |
| Artus Micco - - - - | 2 | 4 | - | 6 |
| Hoboy Fixico - - - - | 1 | 2 | - | 3 |
| Enehe Emarthlar - - - - | 1 | 1 | - | 2 |
| Choekar Harjo - - - - | 2 | 2 | - | 4 |
| Koegus Yoholo - - - - | 1 | 3 | - | 4 |
| Cho Fixico - - - - | 1 | 1 | - | 2 |
| Kowasneholocco - - - - | 3 | 2 | - | 5 |
| Talsi Harjo - - - - | 1 | 4 | - | 5 |
| Fuffachachegey - - - - | - | 3 | - | 3 |
| Thlathle Yoholo - - - - | 1 | 1 | - | 2 |
| Emarth Harjo - - - - | 4 | 1 | - | 5 |
| Archoolok Harjo - - - - | 1 | 3 | - | 4 |
| Kotchar Micco - - - - | 1 | 1 | - | 2 |
| Arch Yacubby - - - - | 1 | 1 | - | 2 |
| Stallote Emarthlar - - - | 1 | 1 | - | 2 |
| Emarthloche - - - - | 1 | 1 | - | 2 |
| Klechumma Harjo - - - | 2 | 2 | - | 4 |
| Pathlechubby - - - - | 1 | 1 | - | 2 |
| Oketo Yoholo - - - - | 2 | 1 | - | 3 |
| | 59 | 78 | | 137 |
| Powhoe - - - - | 1 | 1 | - | 2 |
| Athloche - - - - | 1 | 1 | - | 2 |
| Nehe Yoholo - - - - | 1 | 1 | - | 2 |
| Micco Harjo - - - - | 1 | 1 | - | 2 |
| Onobboche - - - - | 1 | 2 | - | 3 |
| Tommy Hokete - - - - | 1 | 1 | - | 2 |
| Illis Harjo - - - - | 2 | 2 | - | 4 |
| Coweta Tuskenehaw - - - | 3 | 3 | - | 6 |
| Hillis Yoholo - - - - | 2 | 1 | - | 3 |
| Negisko Harjo - - - - | 3 | 1 | - | 4 |
| Kontalle Emarthlar - - - | 3 | 1 | - | 4 |
| Stunlarthpar - - - - | 2 | 3 | - | 5 |

CREEK CENSUS—Continued.

| Names of Heads of Families. | | | | Males. | Females. | Slaves. | Total. |
|---|---|---|---|---|---|---|---|
| TALLEDEGA TOWN. | | | | | | | |
| Fosehatchei Fixico | - | - | - | 3 | 5 | - | 8 |
| Narche Micco | - | - | - | 2 | 3 | - | 5 |
| Neharlocco | - | - | - | 2 | 1 | - | 3 |
| Imboarfigo | - | - | - | 4 | 1 | - | 5 |
| Kono Fixico | - | - | - | 4 | 3 | - | 7 |
| Tofulhoge | - | - | - | 1 | 2 | - | 3 |
| Kunchart Emarthlar | - | - | - | 1 | 3 | - | 4 |
| Kochus Harjo | - | - | - | 2 | 2 | - | 4 |
| Fittodick Harjo | - | - | - | 2 | 3 | - | 5 |
| Ligi Yoholo | - | - | - | 3 | 2 | - | 5 |
| Hotose | - | - | - | 1 | 1 | - | 2 |
| Albet Emarthlar | - | - | - | 1 | 2 | - | 3 |
| Talamarse Emarthlar | - | - | - | 2 | 2 | - | 4 |
| Sannitko | - | - | - | 2 | 2 | - | 4 |
| Koegus Harjo | - | - | - | 1 | 2 | - | 3 |
| Sesypar | - | - | - | 1 | 2 | - | 3 |
| Arpecooche Harjo | - | - | - | 3 | 2 | - | 5 |
| Harlock Yoholo | - | - | - | 2 | 1 | - | 3 |
| Karpickchar | - | - | - | 2 | 1 | - | 3 |
| Sallargey | - | - | - | 1 | 1 | - | 2 |
| Tallarne Fixico | - | - | - | 1 | 1 | - | 2 |
| Nabbe Emarthlar | - | - | - | 3 | 2 | - | 5 |
| | | | | 65 | 62 | | 127 |
| Hogillisenehaw | - | - | - | 1 | 1 | - | 2 |
| Ohukobbe | - | - | - | — | 2 | - | 2 |
| Tarfoligey | - | - | - | 3 | 1 | - | 4 |
| Simoparye | - | - | - | 1 | 3 | - | 4 |
| Okeolarpisse Fixico | - | - | - | 1 | 1 | - | 2 |
| Yoholo Yarjo | - | - | - | 2 | 2 | - | 4 |
| Allok Fixico | - | - | - | 1 | 4 | - | 5 |
| Cle Harjo | - | - | - | 1 | 1 | - | 2 |
| Kono Harjo | - | - | - | 2 | 3 | - | 5 |
| Iepe | - | - | - | 2 | 1 | - | 3 |
| Suwarhe | - | - | - | 1 | 1 | - | 2 |
| Tintlawbe | - | - | - | 1 | 1 | - | 2 |
| Mawegey | - | - | - | 1 | 1 | - | 2 |
| Pin Harjo | - | - | - | 3 | 2 | - | 5 |
| Tommy Emarthlar | - | - | - | 3 | 1 | - | 4 |
| Archooli Harjo | - | - | - | 1 | 2 | - | 3 |
| Slikay | - | - | - | 3 | 3 | - | 6 |
| Semohargay | - | - | - | 2 | 1 | - | 3 |
| Yoholo Micco | - | - | - | 2 | 2 | - | 4 |

CREEK CENSUS—Continued.

| Names of Heads of Families. | Males. | Females. | Slaves. | Total. |
|---|---|---|---|---|
| Nokesawah - - - - | 2 | 1 | - | 3 |
| Kunchart Harjo - - - - | 1 | 2 | - | 3 |
| Siamege - - - - | 2 | 1 | - | 3 |
| Okefuske Harjo - - - - | 5 | 2 | - | 7 |
| Littejacke - - - - | 1 | 1 | - | 2 |
| Cussetaw Yoholo - - - - | 3 | 1 | - | 4 |
| Seegey - - - - | 1 | 2 | - | 3 |
| Chewasti Fixico - - - - | 1 | 2 | - | 3 |
| Micconubbe Harjo - - - | 3 | 1 | - | 4 |
| Koutal Harjo - - - - | 2 | 3 | - | 5 |
| Waggeche - - - - | 2 | 1 | - | 3 |
| Nocose Yoholo - - - - | 2 | 3 | - | 5 |
| Iegey - - - - | — | 2 | - | 2 |
| Cussetau Fixico - - - - | 1 | 1 | - | 2 |
| Isfarne Yoholo - - - - | 3 | 1 | - | 4 |
| Stuntlobbe - - - - | 1 | 2 | - | 3 |
| Emarthlochawne - - - - | 1 | 2 | - | 3 |
| Yettik Harjo - - - - | 3 | 1 | - | 4 |
| Salhoe - - - - | — | 2 | - | 2 |
| Ewynokke - - - - | — | 2 | - | 2 |
| Efar Emarthlar - - - - | 1 | 1 | - | 2 |
| Mannogecher - - - - | 1 | 2 | - | 3 |
| Albitter Harjo - - - - | 1 | 2 | - | 3 |
| Kotchar - - - - | 1 | 1 | - | 2 |
| Chawnegar - - - - | 1 | 1 | - | 2 |
| | 70 | 73 | | 143 |
| Oche Yoholo - - - - | 1 | 2 | - | 3 |
| Choille Harjo - - - - | 4 | 2 | - | 6 |
| Fihoge - - - - | 1 | 3 | - | 4 |
| Mallear - - - - | 1 | 1 | - | 2 |
| Saltpoye - - - - | 1 | 1 | - | 2 |
| Tuskochunknar - - - - | 2 | 1 | - | 3 |
| Passcove Harjo - - - - | 1 | 1 | - | 2 |
| Cearbihe - - - - | 2 | 1 | - | 3 |
| Choekar Harjo - - - - | 1 | 2 | - | 3 |
| Cholokoke Harjo - - - - | 4 | 2 | - | 6 |
| Nehar Fixico - - - - | 1 | 2 | - | 3 |
| Fultolehogar - - - - | 1 | 3 | - | 4 |
| Pollothogar - - - - | 2 | 1 | - | 3 |
| Okechun Harjo - - - - | 1 | 2 | 4 | 7 |
| Ottus Harjo - - - - | 2 | 3 | - | 5 |
| Choe Emarthlar - - - - | 2 | 1 | - | 3 |
| Tofolotehokar - - - - | 1 | 2 | 5 | 8 |
| Yathleche - - - - | 1 | 1 | - | 2 |

CREEK CENSUS—Continued.

| Names of Heads of Families. | Males. | Females. | Slaves. | Total. |
|---|---|---|---|---|
| Hoeah - - - - - | - | 2 | 2 | 4 |
| Emarthlar - - - - | 4 | 3 | - | 7 |
| Joke - - - - - | 1 | 2 | - | 3 |
| Clewalla Harjo - - - - | 4 | 4 | - | 8 |
| Innokiegey - - - - | 1 | 1 | - | 2 |
| Konatke Emarthlar - - - | 3 | 1 | - | 4 |
| Micco Emarthlar - - - - | 2 | - | - | 2 |
| Tobias O'Kelly - - - - | 2 | 1 | - | 3 |
| | 46 | 45 | 11 | 102 |
| CON-CHARTETIE TOWN. | | | | |
| Oakchoy Fixico - - - | 2 | 3 | - | 5 |
| Cilleboy Emarthlar - - - | 4 | 1 | - | 5 |
| Ho Tulga Fixico - - - | 1 | 1 | - | 2 |
| Kolip Harjo - - - - | 2 | 1 | - | 3 |
| Tustanugeigie - - - - | 1 | 1 | - | 2 |
| Ocullote Rie - - - - | 1 | 1 | - | 2 |
| Tallip Harjo - - - - | 1 | 2 | - | 3 |
| Socoliga - - - - | 1 | 1 | - | 2 |
| Emarth Harjo - - - - | 2 | 2 | - | 4 |
| Fuskene - - - - | 3 | 2 | - | 5 |
| Farney Fixico - - - - | 1 | 3 | - | 4 |
| Artotie - - - - | 1 | 1 | - | 2 |
| Searfoche - - - - | 2 | 1 | - | 3 |
| Mima - - - - - | 1 | 1 | - | 2 |
| Talwar Harjo - - - - | 2 | 1 | - | 3 |
| Conchart Fixico - - - | 3 | 1 | - | 4 |
| Thlathlo - - - - | 1 | 1 | - | 2 |
| Eliza - - - - - | 1 | 1 | - | 2 |
| John - - - - - | 2 | 1 | - | 3 |
| Jim - - - - - | 1 | 1 | - | 2 |
| Nokose Fixico - - - - | 3 | 2 | - | 5 |
| Talladig Fixico - - - - | 2 | 2 | - | 4 |
| Toatkohos Emarthlar - - - | 1 | 4 | - | 5 |
| Loney - - - - | 1 | 1 | - | 2 |
| Tocarlie - - - - | 2 | 1 | - | 3 |
| Arfuskee - - - - | 2 | 1 | - | 3 |
| Ottishobie - - - - | 1 | 1 | - | 2 |
| Billy - - - - - | 2 | 1 | - | 3 |
| Daniel Bruner - - - - | 4 | 4 | - | 8 |
| Mosey - - - - - | 2 | 1 | - | 3 |
| Emarthlar Harjo - - - - | 5 | 2 | - | 7 |
| Peggy - - - - - | 2 | 1 | - | 3 |
| Sallihoga - - - - | 2 | 2 | - | 4 |
| E Toat Yoholo - - - - | 3 | 1 | - | 4 |

CREEK CENSUS—Continued.

| Names of Heads of Families. | Males. | Females. | Slaves. | Total. |
|---|---|---|---|---|
| Petise - - - - | 1 | 2 | - | 3 |
| Arhollee Emarthlar - - - | 3 | 1 | - | 4 |
| Nancey - - - - | 1 | 1 | - | 2 |
| John Steel - - - | 2 | 2 | - | 4 |
| Washington - - - | 1 | 2 | - | 3 |
| Will - - - - | 1 | 1 | - | 2 |
| Montallieja - - - | 1 | 3 | - | 4 |
| Tallip Harjo - - - | 1 | 1 | - | 2 |
| Ecey - - - - | 1 | 2 | - | 3 |
| | 77 | 66 | | 143 |
| Cheewasti Harjo - - - | 5 | 2 | - | 7 |
| Oswitch Fixico - - - | 2 | 3 | - | 5 |
| Cheewille Harjo - - - | 2 | 1 | - | 3 |
| Hishoiga - - - | 1 | 1 | - | 2 |
| Warhieja - - - | 1 | 1 | - | 2 |
| Powhose Emarthlo - - - | 3 | 1 | - | 4 |
| Stimmothhoie - - - | 1 | 4 | - | 5 |
| Cussetar Fixico - - - | 3 | 1 | - | 4 |
| Konip Emarthlo - - - | 2 | 3 | - | 5 |
| Tallisse Yoholo - - - | 3 | 1 | - | 4 |
| Sally - - - - | 1 | 2 | - | 3 |
| Hotulga Yoholo - - - | 3 | 1 | - | 4 |

CHEARHAW TOWN.

| | | | | |
|---|---|---|---|---|
| Conchasta Micco - - - | 1 | 4 | - | 5 |
| Octiarche Harjo - - - | 4 | 3 | - | 7 |
| Micco Nubbar - - - | 2 | 1 | - | 3 |
| Talle Harjo - - - | 3 | 4 | - | 7 |
| Starhosie - - - | 5 | 1 | - | 6 |
| Sofa - - - - | 1 | 1 | - | 2 |
| Selitca - - - - | 4 | 3 | - | 7 |
| Sammy - - - - | 4 | 1 | - | 5 |
| Coewa - - - - | 1 | 2 | - | 3 |
| Cle Harjo - - - | 3 | 2 | - | 5 |
| Woxsee Harjo - - - | 3 | 2 | - | 5 |
| Arloc Harjo - - - | 5 | 2 | - | 7 |
| Archelislie - - - | 2 | 1 | - | 3 |
| Sockuppoky - - - | 2 | 1 | - | 3 |
| Sockhulga - - - | 2 | 1 | - | 3 |
| Cuecar Harjo - - - | 1 | 1 | - | 2 |
| Socoleja - - - | 5 | 3 | - | 8 |
| Talmarse Harjo - - - | 2 | 1 | - | 3 |
| Hilliche - - - | 3 | 2 | - | 5 |

CREEK CENSUS—Continued.

| Names of Heads of Families. | Males. | Females. | Slaves. | Total. |
|---|---|---|---|---|
| Loloc Kie . . . . | 2 | 1 | - | 3 |
| Watpo Harjo . . . . | 1 | 2 | - | 3 |
| Thinkin Tuska . . . . | 2 | 3 | - | 5 |
| Ossarga . . . . | 1 | 2 | - | 3 |
| | 88 | 68 | | 156 |
| To Yol Kie . . . . | 1 | 1 | - | 2 |
| Towhallop Rie . . . . | 1 | 1 | - | 2 |
| Tewoxholattie . . . . | 1 | 1 | - | 2 |
| Yoke Sar Sa . . . . | 1 | 2 | - | 3 |
| Hebilthinnehar . . . . | 2 | 3 | - | 5 |
| Sinemattieheche . . . . | 3 | 1 | - | 4 |
| Suthoie . . . . | 1 | 1 | - | 2 |
| Jimmy . . . . | 1 | 1 | - | 2 |
| Kingehar . . . . | 1 | 2 | - | 3 |
| Sock Ke Ka . . . . | 1 | 2 | - | 3 |
| Se Rubie . . . . | 1 | 3 | - | 4 |
| Pin Emarthlar . . . . | 2 | 2 | - | 4 |
| Luchirharjo . . . . | 3 | 3 | - | 6 |
| Arsinbutharjo . . . . | 1 | 2 | - | 3 |
| Ioake . . . . | 1 | 1 | - | 2 |
| Tallise Yoholo . . . . | 4 | 2 | - | 6 |
| Pi Ker . . . . | 1 | 1 | - | 2 |
| Kidgotco . . . . | 1 | 3 | - | 4 |
| Lindubba . . . . | 1 | 3 | - | 4 |
| O Clubpissaharjo . . . . | 3 | 2 | - | 5 |
| Cotteeharjo . . . . | 4 | 4 | - | 8 |
| O Se Yoholo . . . . | 1 | 3 | - | 4 |
| Suck Harjo . . . . | 1 | 3 | - | 4 |
| David Madhog . . . . | 1 | 1 | - | 2 |
| Nicey . . . . | 1 | 1 | - | 2 |
| Kinhar . . . . | 1 | 1 | - | 2 |
| James Kelly . . . . | 4 | 4 | - | 8 |
| Tomtarga . . . . | - | 2 | - | 2 |
| Milligey . . . . | 1 | 1 | - | 2 |
| Kloslitko . . . . | 1 | 1 | - | 2 |
| Koue Harjo . . . . | 1 | 1 | - | 2 |
| Sehitchhar . . . . | 2 | 1 | - | 3 |
| Arsooche Emarthlar . . . . | 4 | 4 | - | 8 |
| Kinnaith Harjo . . . . | 3 | 2 | - | 5 |
| Alligkargey . . . . | 1 | 1 | - | 2 |
| Istuffunfuckee . . . . | 1 | 2 | - | 3 |
| Sheoffunnargey . . . . | 1 | 1 | - | 2 |
| Talladig Harjo . . . . | 2 | - | - | 2 |
| Soseper . . . . | 1 | 1 | - | 2 |

## CREEK CENSUS—Continued.

| Names of Heads of Families. | Males. | Females. | Slaves. | Total. |
|---|---|---|---|---|
| Kohomer . . . . . | 2 | - | - | 2 |
| Owhygee . . . . . | 1 | 1 | - | 2 |
| Istohitchchego . . . . | 1 | 1 | - | 2 |
| Loney . . . . . | 1 | 1 | - | 2 |
| Kontal Emarthlar . . . | 2 | 1 | - | 3 |
| | 69 | 75 | | 144 |
| Nicose Emarthlar . . . | 3 | 3 | - | 6 |
| Skimmowe . . . | 4 | 3 | - | 7 |
| Folegey . . . . . | - | 4 | - | 4 |
| Sally . . . . . | - | 2 | - | 2 |
| Laueche . . . . | 3 | 2 | - | 5 |
| Sochatabicher . . . | - | 2 | - | 2 |
| Tustunnuch Harjo . . . | 2 | 2 | - | 4 |
| Tuckabatchee Harjo . . . | 4 | 2 | - | 6 |
| Late . . . . . | 2 | 1 | - | 3 |
| Yarhar Marthlar . . . | 1 | 2 | - | 3 |
| Chockolock Harjo . . . | 3 | 1 | - | 4 |
| Hillis Harjo . . . . | 4 | 4 | - | 8 |

### CHOCKOLOCKO TOWN.

| | | | | |
|---|---|---|---|---|
| Jim Fife . . . . . | 8 | 8 | 7 | 23 |
| Yoholo Emarthlar . . . | 1 | 2 | - | 3 |
| Chofixico . . . . | 1 | 4 | - | 5 |
| Iswarhe . . . . | 2 | 3 | - | 5 |
| Myeper . . . . . | 1 | 2 | - | 3 |
| Timanolgo . . . . | 3 | 1 | - | 4 |
| Widow Wolf . . . | 1 | 2 | - | 3 |
| Tallasse Harjo . . . | 1 | 1 | - | 2 |
| John Leisco . . . . | 1 | 6 | - | 7 |
| Sally Kogee . . . . | 1 | 2 | - | 3 |
| Billy Fife . . . . | 3 | 2 | - | 5 |
| Beaver . . . . . | 3 | 2 | - | 5 |
| Isfarneoboy . . . . | 1 | 2 | - | 3 |
| Okechum Yoholo . . . | 4 | 4 | - | 8 |
| Tussekiarholofter . . . | 3 | 2 | - | 5 |
| Tussekearartke . . . | 1 | 3 | - | 4 |
| Isfarne Yoholo . . . | 1 | 1 | - | 2 |
| Chehan Harjo . . . | 3 | 3 | - | 6 |
| Clechumme Harjo . . . | 3 | 2 | - | 5 |
| Mollecher . . . . | 1 | 2 | - | 3 |
| | 69 | 82 | 7 | 158 |

CREEK CENSUS—Continued.

| Names of Heads of Families. | Males. | Females. | Slaves. | Total. |
|---|---|---|---|---|
| Tuskonarharjo | 5 | 3 | – | 8 |
| Kochimnar | 2 | 2 | – | 4 |
| Kotockia | 3 | 3 | – | 6 |
| Mathhode | - | 4 | – | 4 |
| Lautubba | 2 | 1 | – | 3 |
| Tikkoegey | 2 | 1 | – | 3 |
| Tillo | 1 | 1 | – | 2 |
| Letif Harjo | 2 | 3 | – | 5 |
| Tommy Emarthlar | 2 | 1 | – | 3 |
| Fokealateke | 1 | 3 | – | 4 |
| Totch Yan Hargo | 1 | 1 | – | 2 |
| Itchko | 3 | 2 | – | 5 |
| Pouheelustee Harjo | 5 | 1 | – | 6 |
| Arpecooche Emarthlar | 2 | 1 | – | 3 |
| Emarthlar Harjo | 3 | 1 | – | 4 |
| Oho Yoholo | 3 | 4 | – | 7 |
| Sally | 2 | 2 | – | 4 |
| Pinekar | 2 | 2 | – | 4 |
| Pouhose Yoholo | 1 | 1 | – | 2 |
| Chewasti Harjo | 5 | 3 | – | 8 |
| Harlockhobia | 4 | 2 | – | 6 |
| Nocoseekar | 2 | 1 | – | 3 |
| Artuskonubbe | 4 | 5 | – | 9 |
| Wathlar | 1 | 1 | – | 2 |
| Osiar Harjo | 1 | 1 | – | 2 |
| Chinnabee | 3 | 2 | – | 5 |
| Lofterfixico | 2 | 2 | – | 4 |
| Hotulgefixico | 5 | 2 | – | 7 |
| Sathoe | 1 | 2 | – | 3 |
| Hiocke | - | 3 | – | 3 |
| Tommy Heathle | 1 | 2 | – | 3 |
| Kotcharfixico | 3 | 2 | – | 5 |
| Pothleboya | 2 | 3 | – | 5 |
| Okechoy | 2 | 1 | – | 3 |
| Fixico Yoholo | 1 | 2 | – | 3 |
| Seoth Lego | 3 | 3 | – | 6 |
| Okqua Harjo | 1 | 2 | – | 3 |
| Cho Yoholo, (2 of same name) | 1 | 1 | – | 2 |
| Fixico Harjo | 1 | 4 | – | 5 |
| Simmeofke | 2 | 3 | – | 5 |
| Simanalt | 1 | 5 | – | 6 |
| Isfarne Emarthlar | 8 | 5 | – | 13 |
| Pouhose Harjo | 3 | 4 | – | 7 |
| Hobaua | 2 | 2 | – | 4 |
| | 101 | 100 | | 201 |

CREEK CENSUS—Continued.

| Names of Heads of Families. | Males. | Females. | Slaves. | Total. |
|---|---|---|---|---|
| Tussekear Micco - - - - | 1 | 2 | - | 3 |
| Kotcharharjo - - - - | 2 | 3 | - | 5 |
| Kethligey - - - - | 2 | 2 | - | 4 |
| Papkofixico - - - - | 1 | 1 | - | 2 |
| Omalegey - - - - | 1 | 1 | - | 2 |
| Chewaste Yoholo - - - - | 3 | 4 | - | 7 |
| Cilharjo - - - - | 1 | 4 | - | 5 |
| Teoboskie - - - - | 2 | 1 | - | 3 |
| Artusharjo - - - - | 2 | 1 | - | 3 |
| Osi Yoholo - - - - | 1 | 2 | - | 3 |
| Iskowabbe - - - - | 2 | 4 | - | 6 |
| Hotulgeharjo - - - - | 2 | 2 | - | 4 |
| Holarhimehar - - - - | 2 | 2 | - | 4 |
| Choemarthlar - - - - | 3 | 2 | - | 5 |
| Konoharjo - - - - | 1 | 1 | - | 2 |
| Holige . . . . | 1 | 1 | - | 2 |
| Seyologey . . . . | 2 | 2 | - | 4 |
| Sawhoe . . . . . | 1 | 3 | - | 4 |
| Karpiccharemarthlar . . . | 3 | – | - | 3 |
| Chittokone . . . . | 2 | 2 | - | 4 |
| Ischieche . . . . | 1 | 4 | - | 5 |
| Sathliegey . . . . | 1 | 1 | - | 2 |
| Wotkopie . . . . | 1 | 1 | - | 2 |
| Tatle Fife . . . . | 1 | 1 | - | 2 |
| Imjitterharjo . . . . | 3 | 4 | - | 7 |
| Powo Switchee . . . . | 1 | 1 | - | 2 |
| Simannottogey . . . . | 2 | 1 | - | 3 |
| Yohololock . . . . | 2 | 2 | - | 4 |
| Sohobbe . . . . | 1 | 1 | - | 2 |
| Hannah . . . . . | 2 | 1 | - | 3 |
| Hoosarhoboy . . . . | 1 | 1 | - | 2 |
| Holarteemarthlar . . . . | 3 | 2 | - | 5 |
| Moclewhobia . . . . | 1 | 1 | - | 2 |
| Sisse Yoholo . . . . | 3 | 1 | - | 4 |
| Fixicoharjo (2d of the same name) . | 1 | 2 | - | 3 |
| Oswitchfixico . . . . | 2 | 2 | - | 4 |
| Artusfixico . . . . | 1 | 2 | - | 3 |
| Mehogirt . . . . . | 1 | 3 | - | 4 |
| Choowi Yoga . . . . | 1 | 1 | - | 2 |
| Artolothlo . . . . | 5 | – | - | 5 |
| Konipfixico . . . . | 1 | 1 | - | 2 |
| Nehaw Yoholo . . . . | 1 | 1 | - | 2 |
| Hoister . . . . | 1 | 1 | - | 2 |
| Charley . . . . | 1 | 2 | - | 3 |
| Stimopoge . . . . | 4 | 4 | | 8 |
| | 77 | 81 | | 158 |

CREEK CENSUS—Continued.

| Names of Heads of Families. | | | | Males. | Females. | Slaves. | Total. |
|---|---|---|---|---|---|---|---|
| **TALLASE-HATCHEE TOWN.** | | | | | | | |
| Talgisharharjo | - | - | - | 3 | 2 | . | 5 |
| Choemarthlar | - | - | - | 2 | 2 | . | 4 |
| Lofterharjo | - | - | - | 3 | 1 | . | 4 |
| Talsenehelocko | - | - | - | 3 | 1 | . | 4 |
| Nocoseilleharjo | - | - | - | 2 | 1 | . | 3 |
| Fuskeharjo | - | - | - | 1 | 2 | . | 3 |
| Koweharjo | - | - | - | 2 | 1 | . | 3 |
| Talledegfixico | - | - | - | 2 | 3 | . | 5 |
| Coohopoya | - | - | - | 2 | 1 | . | 3 |
| Letifharjo | - | - | - | 1 | 2 | . | 3 |
| Nocose Yoholo | - | - | - | 2 | 1 | . | 3 |
| Narpooche Yoholo | - | - | - | 1 | 2 | . | 3 |
| Oktiarcheemarthlar | - | - | - | 1 | 2 | . | 3 |
| Wagooche | - | - | - | 2 | 1 | . | 3 |
| Woxeharjo | - | - | - | 1 | 3 | . | 4 |
| Choekarharjo | - | - | - | 1 | 3 | . | 4 |
| Choocheharjo | - | - | . | 1 | 2 | . | 3 |
| Nocoseharjo | - | - | - | 3 | 1 | . | 4 |
| Pielusterharjo | - | - | - | 3 | 1 | . | 4 |
| Kobbich Yoholo | - | - | - | 1 | 2 | . | 3 |
| Konip Yoholo | - | - | - | 2 | 1 | . | 3 |
| Littefixico | - | - | - | 2 | 1 | . | 3 |
| Miccoharjo | - | - | - | 2 | 2 | . | 4 |
| Cussetawfixico | - | - | - | 1 | 1 | . | 2 |
| Karpiecharfixico | - | - | - | 2 | 3 | . | 5 |
| Artus Yoholo | - | - | - | 3 | 2 | . | 5 |
| Lofti Yoholo | - | - | - | 2 | 1 | . | 3 |
| Tustunnuckee | - | - | - | 1 | 2 | . | 3 |
| Chehauharjo | - | - | - | 3 | 2 | . | 5 |
| Jupinkalge | - | - | - | 3 | 3 | . | 6 |
| Kotcharharjo | - | - | - | 1 | 2 | . | 3 |
| Jesse Hill | - | - | - | 2 | 3 | . | 5 |
| Okefuskefixico | - | - | - | 2 | 2 | . | 4 |
| Okechumemarthlar | - | - | - | 2 | 2 | . | 4 |
| Neheyeskoharjo | - | - | - | 2 | 3 | . | 5 |
| Totekahafseemarthlar | - | - | - | 2 | 2 | . | 4 |
| Kotcharomartooche | - | - | - | 1 | 2 | . | 3 |
| Wiege | - | - | - | 2 | 2 | . | 4 |
| Hogotte Yoholo | - | - | - | 4 | 1 | . | 5 |
| Talse Yoholo | - | - | - | 2 | 3 | . | 5 |
| Kunchart Yoholo | - | - | - | 2 | 2 | . | 4 |
| Cho Ye Yoholo | - | - | - | 1 | 5 | . | 6 |
| | | | | 81 | 81 | | 162 |

## CREEK CENSUS—Continued.

| Names of Heads of Families. | Males. | Females. | Slaves. | Total. |
|---|---|---|---|---|
| Chofolope Yoholo        - - -     | 1 | 1 | - | 2 |
| Tommy Fixico       -  -  -  -     | 2 | 1 | - | 3 |
| Cho Harjo        -  -  -  -        | 4 | 5 | - | 9 |
| Saualbubbechay      -  -  -  -     | 2 | 3 | - | 5 |
| Okechoy Harjo      -  -  -  -      | 1 | 6 | - | 7 |
| Clo Harjo -      -  -  -  -        | 1 | 4 | - | 5 |
| Ottus Fixico      -  -  -  -       | 2 | 2 | - | 4 |
| Pathhe Harjo      -  -  -  -       | 3 | 1 | - | 4 |
| Morhoeille      -  -  -  -         | 1 | 3 | - | 4 |
| Konip Fixico, (2d same name)  -  - | 4 | 2 | - | 6 |
| Thomas Foster      -  -  -  -      | 1 | 1 | - | 2 |
| Nocosealay Harjo -  -  -  -        | 2 | 3 | - | 5 |
| Stoiehokarse      -  -  -  -       | 1 | 1 | - | 2 |
| Stimmarte      -  -  -  -          | — | 2 | - | 2 |
| Tewonnogey      -  -  -  -         | — | 3 | - | 3 |
| Chilto Yoholo      -  -  -  -      | 2 | 2 | - | 4 |
| Yoholo Miccooche      -  -  -      | 2 | 1 | - | 3 |
| Marfolotehoke      -  -  -  -      | — | 2 | - | 2 |
| Monnothoe      -  -  -  -          | 1 | 3 | - | 4 |
| Siam Hoge      -  -  -  -          | 1 | 2 | - | 3 |
| Hospotok Harjo      -  -  -  -     | 4 | 5 | - | 9 |
| Kowassat Harjo      -  -  -  -     | 1 | 1 | - | 2 |
| Powhose Harjo      -  -  -  -      | 3 | 4 | - | 7 |
| Hobithtustunnukee      -  -  -     | 1 | 1 | - | 2 |
| Efar Emarthlar      -  -  -  -     | 1 | 2 | - | 3 |
| Sally      -  -  -  -  -           | 1 | 1 | - | 2 |
| Jack Fish -      -  -  -  -        | 1 | 3 | - | 4 |
| Coffee      -  -  -  -  -          | 2 | 1 | - | 3 |
| Charles Steel      -  -  -  -      | 1 | 1 | - | 2 |
| Henry Clay      -  -  -  -         | 1 | 1 | - | 2 |
| Sinkawhe -      -  -  -  -         | 1 | 1 | - | 2 |
| Okechoy Harjo, (2d same name)  -  - | 2 | 3 | - | 5 |
| Tefulgar   -      -  -  -  -       | 3 | 1 | - | 4 |
| Tulga Emarthlar -      -  -  -     | 1 | 1 | - | 2 |
| Fixie Harjo, (3d of same name)  -  - | 2 | 2 | - | 4 |
| Choalay Harjo      -  -  -  -      | 1 | 1 | - | 2 |
| Sukay      -  -  -  -              | — | 2 | - | 2 |
|  | 57 | 79 | | 136 |

### RABBIT TOWN.

| | Males. | Females. | Slaves. | Total. |
|---|---|---|---|---|
| Sallycoga -      -  -  -  -        | 3 | 3 | - | 6 |
| Artus Yoholo      -  -  -  -       | 1 | 1 | - | 2 |
| Konip Harjo      -  -  -  -        | 2 | 3 | - | 5 |
| Holofter Chopko -      -  -  -     | 2 | 3 | - | 5 |
| Okechoy Harjo      -  -  -  -      | 1 | 2 | - | 3 |

40‡

CREEK CENSUS—Continued.

| Names of Heads of Families. | Males. | Females. | Slaves. | Total. |
|---|---|---|---|---|
| Tommy Yoholo Chopko - - - | 1 | 2 | - | 3 |
| Artushopoethele - - - - | 1 | 2 | - | 3 |
| Sattoparchu - - - - | 1 | 1 | - | 2 |
| Washington - - - - | 2 | 2 | - | 4 |
| Hoiche - - - - | 1 | 2 | - | 3 |
| Hinnip Fixico - - - - | 2 | 2 | - | 4 |
| Chokofus Harjo - - - - | 1 | 1 | - | 2 |
| Talofe Hargo - - - - | 2 | 2 | - | 4 |
| Jimmy - - - - - | 1 | 2 | - | 3 |
| Echarge Emarthlar - - - | 2 | 3 | . | 5 |
| Rabbit - - - - - | 2 | 3 | . | 5 |
| Pole Cat - - - - - | 1 | 1 | . | 2 |
| Simmenottee - - - - | 2 | 2 | . | 4 |
| Micco Yoholo - - - - | 1 | 1 | . | 2 |
| Maddupenehar - - - - | 1 | 1 | . | 2 |
| Hiamarhe - - - - - | 1 | 1 | . | 2 |
| Hillabee Harjo - - - - | 3 | 1 | . | 4 |
| Charcogee - - - - | 2 | 1 | . | 3 |
| Hosarhalla - - - - | 1 | 2 | . | 3 |
| Kosar Harjo - - - - | 1 | 1 | . | 2 |
| Nawbutse Yoholo - - - - | 1 | 1 | . | 2 |
| Wesehar - - - - - | 2 | 1 | . | 3 |
| Nocoseothlepoya - - - - | 2 | 2 | . | 4 |
| Odenigey - - - - - | 1 | 2 | . | 3 |
| Wyke - - - - - | 1 | 2 | . | 3 |
| Anne - - - - - | 1 | 1 | . | 2 |
| Somier - - - - - | 1 | 2 | . | 3 |
| Nehar Harjo - - - - | 2 | 4 | . | 6 |
| Sumawlegay - - - - | 2 | 2 | . | 4 |
| Klesothke - - - - | 1 | 1 | . | 2 |
| Lucy - - - - - | 1 | 1 | . | 2 |
| Chockolock Harjo - - - | 2 | 1 | . | 3 |
| Arslidde - - - - - | — | 2 | . | 2 |
| Sisokee - - - - - | 1 | 1 | . | 2 |
| Arbicker Harjo - - - - | 1 | 1 | . | 2 |
| Sally - - - - - | 2 | 4 | . | 6 |
| Watkoshacko - - - - | 1 | 1 | . | 2 |
|  | 60 | 74 |  | 134 |
| Mocktuska - - - - | 1 | 1 | . | 2 |
| Pollege - - - - - | 2 | 1 | . | 3 |
| Richard Rush - - - - | 2 | 1 | . | 3 |
| Wailocko Harjo Chopko - - - | 2 | 1 | . | 3 |
| Choke Charter - - - - | 5 | 3 | . | 8 |
| Talamarsi Emarthlar - - - | 1 | 1 | . | 2 |

CREEK CENSUS—Continued.

| Names of Heads of Families. | Males. | Females. | Slaves. | Total. |
|---|---|---|---|---|
| Tussekiae Harjo - - - - | 1 | 1 | - | 2 |
| Katey - - - - - | 1 | 1 | - | 2 |
| Hillo - - - - - | 1 | 1 | - | 2 |
| Billy - - - - - | 2 | 3 | - | 5 |
| Sylarcogga Harjo - - - - | 2 | 1 | - | 3 |
| Sorwejacke - - - - | - | 2 | - | 2 |
| Kotchar Fixico - - - - | 1 | 1 | - | 2 |
| Ehomarter - - - - | 1 | 1 | - | 2 |
| Yolechar - - - - | 1 | 1 | - | 2 |
| Micco Chopko - - - - | 1 | 1 | - | 2 |
| Johnny - - - - - | 1 | 2 | - | 3 |
| Ninnehe Emarthlar - - - | 2 | 2 | - | 4 |
| Okechoy - - - - - | 3 | 2 | - | 5 |
| Tallase Fixico - - - - | 1 | 4 | - | 5 |
| Issworne Harjo - - - - | 1 | 1 | - | 2 |
| Choloepo Yoholo - - - - | 1 | 2 | - | 3 |
| Kosehatch Emarthlar - - - | 1 | 5 | - | 6 |
| Ehiemarthlooche - - - - | 1 | 1 | - | 2 |
| Sukey - - - - - | 1 | 1 | - | 2 |
| Isfarne Emarthlar - - - | 1 | 1 | - | 2 |
| Hardushonebe Emarthlar - - - | 3 | 3 | - | 6 |
| Nocose Switchee Harjo - - - | 1 | 1 | - | 2 |
| Sohonea - - - - - | 1 | 3 | - | 4 |
| Choille Harj - - - - | 2 | 2 | - | 4 |
| Isfarne Yoholo - - - - | 3 | 2 | - | 5 |
| Powhose Harjo - - - - | 3 | 2 | - | 5 |
| Kot Harjo - - - - | 3 | 1 | - | 4 |
| | 53 | 56 | | 109 |

ARBICCOOCHE TOWN.

| | | | | |
|---|---|---|---|---|
| Cubbitche Harjo - - - - | 1 | 5 | - | 6 |
| Clocusco Micco - - - - | 2 | 2 | - | 4 |
| Cobbiechcha Micco - - - | 1 | 2 | - | 3 |
| Oakfuska Micco - - - - | 1 | 1 | - | 2 |
| Chawoccala Micco - - - | 1 | 2 | - | 3 |
| Ogillis Micco - - - - | 3 | 1 | - | 4 |
| Neharlocco Harjo - - - - | 1 | 1 | - | 2 |
| Oakfuska Harjo - - - - | 2 | 2 | - | 4 |
| Tulge Emarthlar - - - - | 3 | 1 | - | 4 |
| Coosar Fixico - - - - | 2 | 1 | - | 3 |
| Oakfuscache Micco - - - | 4 | 1 | - | 5 |
| Folote Harjo - - - - | 2 | 3 | - | 5 |
| Oakchoy Harjo - - - - | 2 | 2 | - | 4 |
| Coosar Harjo - - - - | 3 | 3 | - | 6 |
| Alloway Harjo - - - - | 1 | 1 | - | 2 |

## CREEK CENSUS—Continued.

| Names of Heads of Families. | Males. | Females. | Slaves. | Total. |
|---|---|---|---|---|
| Benne | 2 | 1 | - | 3 |
| Fittalliga | 1 | 2 | - | 3 |
| Conchart Emarthloche | 1 | 3 | - | 4 |
| S Spanny Harjo | 2 | 4 | - | 6 |
| Powhos Yoholo | 2 | 1 | - | 3 |
| Talwar Harjo | 1 | 3 | - | 4 |
| Talmarsey | 2 | 1 | - | 3 |
| Cothboboegar | 3 | 1 | - | 4 |
| Woxsi Hargo | 2 | 3 | - | 5 |
| Liftif Harjo | 3 | 1 | - | 4 |
| Konip Harjo | 1 | 2 | - | 3 |
| Allabudder | 4 | 1 | - | 5 |
| Cotch Yarholo | 2 | 3 | - | 5 |
| Yarhar | 1 | 3 | - | 4 |
| Talmarse Harjo | 2 | 1 | - | 3 |
| His Augu | 1 | 2 | - | 3 |
| Sarwarney Harjo | 2 | 2 | - | 4 |
| Echo | - | 2 | - | 2 |
| Isfiga | 1 | 1 | - | 2 |
| Micco | 2 | 1 | 1 | 4 |
| Cheharne | 2 | 1 | - | 3 |
| Fittar Harjo | 1 | 1 | - | 2 |
| Isfanny Emarthlar | 3 | 1 | - | 4 |
| Neharmarthloche | 1 | 1 | - | 2 |
| Micco Yoholo | 2 | 2 | - | 4 |
| Neharlocco | 1 | 1 | - | 2 |
| Inneharcochokecone | 1 | 2 | - | 3 |
| Inneharliccoche | 1 | 1 | - | 2 |
| | 76 | 76 | 1 | 153 |
| Sittawega | 3 | 1 | - | 4 |
| Oakchoy | 2 | 1 | - | 3 |
| Ottishobie | 1 | 1 | - | 2 |
| Kiemarth Harjo | 4 | 1 | - | 5 |
| Channeke | 1 | 2 | - | 3 |
| Clewathla Harjo | 2 | 1 | - | 3 |
| Arsarhie | 1 | 2 | - | 3 |
| Ilickchar | 1 | 2 | - | 3 |
| Chisse Micco | 2 | 2 | - | 4 |
| Arloc Harjo | 1 | 3 | - | 4 |
| Nehemarta Micco | 2 | 2 | - | 4 |
| Oakchon Harjo | 1 | 2 | - | 3 |
| Powhos Emarthlar | 1 | 2 | - | 3 |
| Channehe (two same name) | 2 | 1 | - | 3 |
| Ichhos Harjo | 1 | 3 | - | 4 |

CREEK CENSUS—Continued.

| Names of Heads of Families. | Males. | Females. | Slaves. | Total. |
|---|---|---|---|---|
| Nehe Yoholo | 1 | 3 | - | 4 |
| Tussickkie | 1 | 3 | - | 4 |
| Toth Yarkie | 1 | 2 | - | 3 |
| Conchart Yoholo | 1 | 3 | - | 4 |
| Isfehoka | 1 | 1 | - | 2 |
| Tarfulhoakkey | 1 | 1 | - | 2 |
| Nocus Harjo | 2 | 2 | - | 4 |
| Octearche Emarthlar | 3 | 2 | - | 5 |
| Tallise Tustanuggy | 2 | 2 | - | 4 |
| O Gillisinnehar | 1 | 3 | - | 4 |
| Arloc Fixico | 2 | 2 | - | 4 |
| Isfarney Fixico | 2 | 1 | - | 3 |
| Taskenehar | 1 | 1 | - | 2 |
| Ehere | 3 | 1 | - | 4 |
| Ho Tulga Harjo | 1 | 4 | - | 5 |
| Suggenar | 1 | 2 | - | 3 |
| Chofe Micco | 3 | 1 | - | 4 |
| Teungar | 1 | 2 | - | 3 |
| Nokosilla Harjo | 2 | 2 | - | 4 |
| Falinniche | 1 | 1 | - | 2 |
| Coegus Yoholo | 1 | 2 | - | 3 |
| Tommarth Harjo | 2 | 1 | - | 3 |
| Immeter | 3 | 1 | - | 4 |
| Charlo Harjo | 2 | 2 | - | 4 |
| Spoakoak Harjo | 2 | 1 | - | 3 |
| Archule Harjo | 2 | 2 | - | 4 |
| Ocoweah | 2 | 2 | - | 4 |
| Imboadega | 1 | 1 | - | 2 |
| So Lockka | 1 | 3 | - | 4 |
| | 72 | 80 | - | 152 |
| Echomie | 1 | 2 | - | 3 |
| Istimmeehungotta | - | 3 | - | 3 |
| Socklodega | 1 | 2 | - | 3 |
| Hoaktechartekey | 2 | 2 | - | 4 |
| Watta | 1 | 1 | - | 2 |
| Tuskege | 5 | 2 | - | 7 |
| Cowocko Harjo | 2 | 2 | - | 4 |
| Talmarse Emarthlar | 2 | 1 | - | 3 |
| Ottis Fixico | 1 | 4 | - | 5 |
| Hillubba Harjo | 1 | 4 | - | 5 |
| Chofe Emarthlar | 1 | 2 | - | 3 |
| Micegar | - | 2 | - | 2 |
| Osooch Emarthlar | 1 | 2 | - | 3 |
| Tuskege, (2d of same name) | 2 | 1 | - | 3 |

CREEK CENSUS—Continued.

| Names of Heads of Families. | Males. | Females. | Slaves. | Total. |
|---|---|---|---|---|
| Emarthlar   -   -   - | 2 | 1 | - | 3 |
| Minnarkie   -   -   - | 1 | 2 | - | 3 |
| Yafega   -   -   - | - | 3 | - | 3 |
| Asfolega   -   -   - | - | 4 | - | 4 |
| Coegus Harjo   -   - | 4 | 3 | - | 7 |
| Nokohatch Emarthlar   - | 2 | 2 | - | 4 |
| | 29 | 45 | | 74 |
| HITCHO-PAR-TAR-GA TOWN. | | | | |
| Eufaula Fixico   -   - | 2 | 2 | - | 4 |
| Iscalike Harjo   -   - | 3 | 2 | - | 5 |
| Holarter Emarthlar   - | 1 | 4 | - | 5 |
| Okechun Harjo   -   - | 2 | 1 | - | 3 |
| Eufaula Harjo   -   - | 3 | 2 | - | 5 |
| Chusse Harjo   -   - | 1 | 1 | - | 2 |
| Mahoe   -   -   - | - | 2 | - | 2 |
| Liley   -   -   - | 1 | 2 | - | 3 |
| Tommaofdose   -   - | - | 2 | - | 2 |
| Samson Grayson   - | 2 | 1 | - | 3 |
| Otuggebiegy   -   - | 2 | 4 | - | 6 |
| Charles Miller   -   - | 2 | 3 | - | 5 |
| Allannia   -   - | 2 | 2 | - | 4 |
| Dove   -   -   - | 2 | 3 | - | 5 |
| Micque Yoholo   - | 1 | 1 | - | 2 |
| Hillis Harjo   -   - | 4 | 4 | - | 8 |
| Issehogey   -   - | 1 | 1 | - | 2 |
| Emarthlar Chopko   - | 1 | 1 | - | 2 |
| Iscowobbe   -   - | 4 | 3 | - | 7 |
| Innoger   -   - | 1 | 3 | - | 4 |
| Sutenokey   -   - | 2 | 4 | - | 6 |
| Stunocher   -   - | - | 3 | - | 3 |
| Tyler   -   -   - | 1 | 2 | - | 3 |
| Hatchee   -   - | 4 | 3 | - | 7 |
| Harlock Yoholo   - | 5 | 3 | - | 8 |
| Lottokehoger   -   - | 3 | 3 | - | 6 |
| Holofter   -   - | 2 | - | - | 2 |
| Davy   -   -   - | 1 | 1 | - | 2 |
| Iskonokke   -   - | 1 | 1 | - | 2 |
| Taloke   -   - | 2 | 1 | - | 3 |
| Elijah Carr   -   - | 4 | 1 | 2 | 7 |
| Alexander Tutt   -   - | 5 | 2 | - | 7 |
| Soomer   -   - | 2 | 1 | - | 3 |
| Istemuneathliggy   - | 1 | 1 | - | 2 |
| Yoholo Emarthlar   - | 2 | 1 | - | 3 |
| Milly   -   -   - | 1 | 2 | - | 3 |

CREEK CENSUS—Continued.

| Names of Heads of Families. | Males. | Females. | Slaves. | Total. |
|---|---|---|---|---|
| Nehar Yoholo - - - | 2 | 2 | - | 4 |
| Yarhar Harjo - - - | 2 | 1 | - | 3 |
| Intussekia - - - | 1 | 2 | - | 3 |
| Tommy Harjo - - - | 1 | 1 | - | 2 |
| Choole Yoholo - - - | 1 | 2 | - | 3 |
| | 78 | 81 | 2 | 161 |
| Pin Emarthlar - - - | 2 | 2 | - | 4 |
| Poscharter - - - | 1 | 4 | - | 5 |
| Spokeoke Harjo - - - | 3 | 3 | - | 6 |
| Sopliga - - - - | - | 2 | - | 2 |
| Mahoe, (2d of same name) - - | 1 | 1 | - | 2 |
| Artus Fixico - - - | 2 | 4 | - | 6 |
| Sawhoe - - - - | 1 | 1 | - | 2 |
| EKUN-DUTS-KE TOWN. | | | | |
| Oktiarcheholartar - - - | 1 | 2 | - | 3 |
| Ortus Micco - - - | 1 | 1 | - | 2 |
| Kolumme Harjo - - - | 2 | 1 | - | 3 |
| Clechumme Harjo - - - | 1 | 2 | - | 3 |
| Nehar Harjo - - - | 1 | 2 | - | 3 |
| Hoboya - - - - | 2 | 1 | - | 3 |
| Lojar Harjo - - - | 3 | 2 | - | 5 |
| Arwattelegger - - - | 2 | 1 | - | 3 |
| Arche - - - - | 4 | 1 | - | 5 |
| Karpicchar Emarthlar - - | 2 | 1 | - | 3 |
| Ivy Scott - - - | 1 | 2 | - | 3 |
| Peter - - - - | 2 | 3 | - | 5 |
| Rabbit - - - - | 2 | 1 | - | 3 |
| Suttarway - - - | 1 | 2 | - | 3 |
| Jegey - - - - | 3 | 1 | - | 4 |
| Morfoloke - - - | 2 | 1 | - | 3 |
| Sam - - - - | 1 | 2 | - | 3 |
| Kininhatchee - - - | 2 | 1 | - | 3 |
| Wiga - - - - | 1 | 2 | - | 3 |
| Sohilegey - - - | 1 | 2 | - | 3 |
| Tonnickkega - - - | 1 | 3 | - | 4 |
| Yoholo Micco Gee - - - | 2 | 1 | - | 3 |
| Seannockee - - - | 1 | 2 | - | 3 |
| Closerhail - - - | 1 | 2 | - | 3 |
| Hobothlener - - - | 1 | 1 | - | 2 |
| Ubeletche - - - | 1 | 1 | - | 2 |
| Kunchart Hargo - - - | | | | |
| | 52 | 58 | | 110 |

## CREEK CENSUS—Continued.

| Names of Heads of Families. | | | Males. | Females. | Slaves. | Total. |
|---|---|---|---|---|---|---|
| Ubeleche | - | - | - | 1 | 1 | - | 2 |
| Hillabee | - | - | - | 2 | 1 | - | 3 |
| Isfiatte | - | - | - | 2 | 1 | - | 3 |
| Martin | - | - | - | 2 | 2 | - | 4 |
| Kenalt Harjo | - | - | - | 2 | 1 | - | 3 |
| Tustunnuckee Emarthlar | - | - | 2 | 2 | - | 4 |
| Steyathlige | - | - | - | - | 2 | - | 2 |
| Micky | - | - | - | 1 | 1 | - | 2 |
| Seathliga | - | - | - | 2 | 1 | - | 3 |
| Stimoathhelegey | - | - | - | - | 2 | - | 2 |
| Stohia | - | - | - | 1 | 1 | - | 2 |
| Sufficklumga | - | - | - | - | 2 | - | 2 |
| Sawhoia | - | - | - | - | 2 | - | 2 |
| Bruce | - | - | - | 1 | 2 | - | 3 |
| Billy Scott | - | - | - | 5 | 2 | - | 7 |
| John Kily | - | - | - | 3 | 1 | - | 4 |
| Albetter Harjo | - | - | - | 3 | 1 | - | 4 |
| Okechoy Harjo | - | - | - | 2 | 2 | - | 4 |
| Sehobia | - | - | - | 1 | 5 | - | 6 |
| Istimmihika | - | - | - | 1 | 1 | - | 2 |
| | | | 31 | 33 | | 64 |

### HIL-LA-BEE-TOWN.

| | | | | | | |
|---|---|---|---|---|---|---|
| Yoholo Wyger | . | . | . | 3 | 6 | - | 9 |
| Hotulga Hargo | . | . | . | 3 | 2 | - | 5 |
| Chokechart Emarthlar | . | . | 4 | 1 | - | 5 |
| Carpidchar Yoholo | . | . | 1 | 2 | - | 3 |
| Lodige | . | . | . | 2 | 1 | - | 3 |
| Sawwanne Harjo | . | . | 3 | 2 | - | 5 |
| Sammy | . | . | . | 2 | 1 | - | 3 |
| Arsarholer | . | . | . | 2 | 3 | - | 5 |
| Martowar Harjo | . | . | 2 | 2 | - | 4 |
| Yakkuphoe | . | . | . | 2 | 1 | - | 3 |
| Alsicher | . | . | . | 1 | 3 | - | 4 |
| Senochehoe | . | . | . | - | 3 | - | 3 |
| Fixsumhoge | . | . | . | 1 | 2 | - | 3 |
| Emarthlar Yoholo | . | . | 1 | 2 | - | 3 |
| Ohoyaume | . | . | . | 1 | 2 | - | 3 |
| Jacob | . | . | . | 1 | 2 | - | 3 |
| Nocose Yoholo | . | . | 3 | 3 | - | 6 |
| Otchchiegey | . | . | . | 1 | 2 | - | 3 |
| Yarhar Emarthlar | . | . | 1 | 2 | - | 3 |
| Talwar Harjo | . | . | . | 1 | 2 | - | 3 |
| Pokolo Marthlar | . | . | 3 | 2 | - | 5 |

CREEK CENSUS—Continued.

| Names of Heads of Families. | Males. | Females. | Slaves. | Total. |
|---|---|---|---|---|
| Phil Grayson - - - - | 4 | 4 | - | 8 |
| James Grayson - - - - | 2 | 2 | - | 4 |
| Isfarne Yoholo - - - - | 1 | 2 | - | 3 |
| John - - - - - | 1 | 2 | - | 3 |
| Stingarbocke - - - - | 1 | 2 | - | 3 |
| Sehatke - - - - - | 1 | 1 | - | 2 |
| Tustunnuckcechopko - - - | 1 | 2 | - | 3 |
| Susey - - - - - | — | 2 | - | 2 |
| Farharjo - - - - - | 3 | 1 | - | 4 |
| Alloche - - - - - | 1 | 2 | - | 3 |
| Nehar Fixico - - - - | 4 | 2 | - | 6 |
| Allock Yoholo - - - - | 2 | 2 | - | 4 |
| Hohofale - - - - - | 1 | 3 | - | 4 |
| Slokefduske Micco - - - | 2 | 4 | - | 6 |
| Enehemarthlooche - - - | 1 | 2 | - | 3 |
| Kurpicchar Emarthlar - - | 2 | 1 | - | 3 |
| Watko - - - - - | 2 | 2 | - | 4 |
| Tolofeharjo - - - - | 2 | 1 | - | 3 |
| Summijache - - - - | 2 | 1 | - | 3 |
| Albetterharjo - - - - | 3 | 3 | - | 6 |
| Ischimbe - - - - - | 1 | 3 | - | 4 |
| | 75 | 90 | | 165 |
| Hope - - - - - | 2 | 2 | - | 4 |
| Jim - - - - - | 2 | 1 | - | 3 |
| Mickheher - - - - | 3 | 1 | - | 4 |
| Sotokalka - - - - | 2 | 1 | - | 3 |
| Timaissege - - - - | 1 | 2 | - | 3 |
| Ocheharjo - - - - | 2 | 2 | - | 4 |
| Fiarholo - - - - | 3 | 1 | - | 4 |
| Pinkey - - - - - | 1 | 2 | - | 3 |
| Tuske Micco - - - - | 2 | 2 | - | 4 |
| Rabbit - - - - - | 6 | 3 | - | 9 |
| Tuckabatcheeharjo - - - | 2 | 2 | - | 4 |
| Charley - - - - - | 4 | 3 | - | 7 |
| Low Jacky - - - - | 5 | 4 | - | 9 |
| Konsat Fixico - - - - | 1 | 5 | - | 6 |
| Talse Fixico - - - - | 2 | 1 | - | 3 |
| Sallarse - - - - - | 1 | 2 | - | 3 |
| Lartarharjo - - - - | 3 | 3 | - | 6 |
| Osiftkiga - - - - - | 1 | 2 | - | 3 |
| Eupolika - - - - - | 2 | 1 | - | 3 |
| Kotchar Yoholo - - - | 2 | 3 | - | 5 |
| Eastinnoge - - - - | 2 | 1 | - | 3 |
| Mehejiga - - - - - | 1 | 3 | - | 4 |

41‡

CREEK CENSUS—Continued.

| Names of Heads of Families. | | | | Males. | Females. | Slaves. | Total. |
|---|---|---|---|---|---|---|---|
| Timmohoe | - | - | - | 1 | 2 | - | 3 |
| Simmoliga | - | - | - | 2 | 1 | - | 3 |
| Wox Emarthlar | - | - | - | 2 | - | - | 2 |
| Cuwalla Harjo | - | - | - | 1 | 1 | - | 2 |
| Woxe Yoholo | - | - | - | 1 | 1 | - | 2 |
| Midoga | - | - | - | — | 3 | - | 3 |
| Tussekehatke | - | - | - | 2 | 2 | - | 4 |
| Mehoke | - | - | - | 1 | 3 | - | 4 |
| Summulte | - | - | - | 1 | 1 | - | 2 |
| Ismudiga | - | - | - | 1 | 2 | - | 3 |
| Sawannoge | - | - | - | 2 | 1 | - | 3 |
| Jack | - | - | - | 1 | 2 | - | 3 |
| Kolchar Micco | - | - | - | 1 | 2 | - | 3 |
| Istohiege | - | - | - | 1 | 1 | - | 2 |
| Argarke | - | - | - | 2 | 1 | - | 3 |
| Tawwelarke | - | - | - | 1 | 1 | - | 2 |
| Charlebe | - | - | - | 1 | 2 | - | 3 |
| Letif Harjo | - | - | - | 1 | 2 | - | 3 |
| Konchart Emarthlar | - | - | - | 2 | 1 | - | 3 |
| Solotte | - | - | - | 1 | 1 | - | 2 |
| Tommy Yoholo | - | - | - | 1 | 2 | - | 3 |
| Lithoke | - | - | - | 3 | 2 | - | 5 |
| | | | | 79 | 81 | | 160 |
| Eufaula Micco | - | - | - | 3 | 1 | - | 4 |
| Ihitchy | - | - | - | - | 3 | - | 3 |
| John Calhoun | - | - | - | 2 | 1 | - | 3 |
| Karboke | - | - | - | 3 | 1 | - | 4 |
| Mieatche | - | - | - | 1 | 1 | - | 2 |
| Chogillis Harjo | - | - | - | 3 | 2 | - | 5 |
| Fukteluste | - | - | - | 4 | 4 | - | 8 |
| Woxe Harjo | - | - | - | 1 | 4 | - | 5 |
| Mehoger | - | - | - | 3 | 3 | - | 6 |
| Tobaccoman | - | - | - | 1 | 1 | - | 2 |
| Talse Emarthlar | - | - | - | 4 | 1 | - | 5 |
| Chokohay | - | - | - | 3 | 1 | - | 4 |
| Cochus Harjo | - | - | - | 2 | 1 | - | 3 |
| Enehar Emarthlar | - | - | - | 2 | 2 | - | 4 |
| Kosarharjo | - | - | - | 4 | 2 | - | 6 |
| Owarhiche | - | - | - | 1 | 1 | - | 2 |
| Talma | - | - | - | - | 3 | - | 3 |
| Mickemawler | - | - | - | 1 | 4 | - | 5 |
| Choeche | - | - | - | 2 | 4 | - | 6 |
| Issoolege | - | - | - | 2 | 2 | - | 4 |
| Konchart Yoholo | - | - | - | 2 | 2 | - | 4 |

CREEK CENSUS—Continued.

| Names of Heads of Families. | Males. | Females. | Slaves. | Total. |
|---|---|---|---|---|
| Mistoweke - - - - | 5 | 3 | - | 8 |
| Chofixico - - - - | 1 | 1 | - | 2 |
| Coosa Yoholo - - - - | 3 | 1 | - | 4 |
| Neligey - - - - | 3 | 1 | - | 4 |
| Sothlitche - - - - | 2 | 1 | - | 3 |
| Jim (2d of same name) - - - | 2 | 1 | - | 3 |
| Ben - - - - | 3 | 1 | - | 4 |
| Imbalade - - - - | - | 3 | - | 3 |
| Sandy Grayson, senior - - - | 1 | 1 | - | 2 |
| Nelly - - - - | - | 2 | - | 2 |
| Little John - - - - | 6 | 5 | 14 | 25 |
| John Grayson - - - - | 1 | 2 | - | 3 |
| Tegarsumer - - - - | 1 | 3 | - | 4 |
| Lizzy Grayson - - - - | 2 | 2 | 21 | 25 |
| Sinnoga - - - - | - | 3 | 1 | 4 |
| William Grayson - - - - | 3 | 5 | - | 8 |
| | 77 | 79 | 36 | 192 |

NOHOHUNT, THE GARTSNAR TOWN.

| | Males. | Females. | Slaves. | Total. |
|---|---|---|---|---|
| Awwodollega - - - - | 1 | 1 | - | 2 |
| Kaney - - - - | 1 | 2 | - | 3 |
| Kinnothoee - - - - | 2 | 1 | - | 3 |
| Tommy Harjo - - - - | 1 | 1 | - | 2 |
| Long Jim - - - - | 3 | 3 | - | 6 |
| Pallatche Harjo - - - - | 3 | 3 | - | 6 |
| Sockkogiaga - - - - | 2 | 2 | - | 4 |
| Neharlokokochokone - - - | 2 | 1 | - | 3 |
| Awche Yoholo - - - - | 2 | 1 | - | 3 |
| Sawgoeiga - - - - | - | 3 | - | 3 |
| Molly - - - - | - | 2 | - | 2 |
| Fiechar - - - - | 1 | 1 | - | 2 |
| Tucktalusta Harjo - - - - | 2 | 2 | - | 4 |
| Ifarny Yoholo - - - - | 2 | 1 | - | 3 |
| Echo Emarthlar - - - - | 2 | 1 | - | 3 |
| Tussiggie Micco - - - - | 1 | 1 | - | 2 |
| Nokose Yoholo - - - - | 2 | 1 | - | 3 |
| Neharlocco Emarthlar - - - | 1 | 2 | - | 3 |
| Chissee Yoholo - - - - | 1 | 3 | - | 4 |
| Linder - - - - | 1 | 1 | - | 2 |
| Tallisse Harjo - - - - | 1 | 1 | - | 2 |
| Lotkar - - - - | 1 | 3 | - | 4 |
| Clardeche - - - - | 1 | 1 | - | 2 |
| Yarhar Harjo - - - - | 2 | 1 | - | 3 |
| Charboiejar - - - - | 2 | 2 | - | 4 |
| Konebe Emarthlar - - - - | 5 | 1 | - | 6 |

### CREEK CENSUS—Continued

| Names of Heads of Families. | Males. | Females. | Slaves. | Total. |
|---|---|---|---|---|
| Echo Yoholo | 2 | 4 | - | 6 |
| Ossehiga | 2 | 2 | - | 4 |
| Big Sol | 3 | 3 | - | 6 |
| Nehic | 1 | 1 | - | 2 |
| Tomma Fixico | 1 | 1 | - | 2 |
| Nocosilla Harjo | 2 | 1 | - | 3 |
| Istoholiga | - | 2 | - | 2 |
| No Kos Harjo | 1 | 1 | - | 2 |
| Ahoga | 1 | 2 | - | 3 |
| Asquehoka | - | 3 | - | 3 |
| Fushatchchahoboiethly | 4 | 2 | - | 6 |
| Condal Yoholo | 2 | 1 | - | 3 |
| Hulgar | 1 | 3 | - | 4 |
| Tulmadogo | 1 | 3 | - | 4 |
| Charbie Fixico | 3 | 2 | - | 5 |
| James Hutton | 1 | 2 | 1 | 4 |
| | 67 | 75 | 1 | 143 |
| Castercharcoche | 1 | 4 | - | 5 |
| Cascharcojee | 2 | 2 | - | 4 |
| Holeannar | 1 | 3 | - | 4 |
| Iscarkie | 2 | 2 | - | 4 |
| Miccochopco | 2 | 3 | - | 5 |
| Arbicco Yoholo | 1 | 1 | - | 2 |
| Yoholo Harjo | 1 | 1 | - | 2 |
| Fushatchchaneharlocco | 2 | 1 | - | 3 |
| Innehoga | 2 | 2 | - | 4 |
| Kalunda | - | 3 | - | 3 |
| Fushatchche | 1 | 1 | - | 2 |
| Homerhar Kie | 1 | 2 | - | 3 |
| Yoholo Micco | 3 | 1 | - | 4 |
| Neheau | 2 | 1 | - | 3 |
| Gilcowigie | 1 | 2 | - | 3 |
| Narpooch Emarthlar | 2 | 4 | - | 6 |
| Ihobie | 2 | 2 | - | 4 |
| Thlath Thlo Harjo | 3 | 2 | - | 5 |
| Oweweligau | 1 | 1 | - | 2 |
| Neharke | 1 | 2 | - | 3 |
| Osarharjo | 1 | 2 | - | 3 |
| Neharlocko Harjo | 2 | 1 | - | 3 |
| Ottersinnehaw | 2 | 2 | - | 4 |
| Talmochus Harjo | 1 | 1 | - | 2 |
| Chitto Harjo | 2 | 1 | - | 3 |
| Simhoya | 2 | 1 | - | 3 |
| Tup Harjo | 2 | 1 | - | 3 |

CREEK CENSUS—Continued.

| Names of Heads of Families. | Males. | Females. | Slaves. | Total. |
|---|---|---|---|---|
| Coosayoholo - - - - | 2 | 1 | - | 3 |
| Wille - - - - - | 1 | 1 | - | 2 |
| Conchadda Micco - - - - | 2 | - | - | 2 |
| Conchatharjo - - - - | 4 | 2 | - | 6 |
| Old George - - - - | 1 | 1 | - | 2 |
| Sukeharharjo - - - - | 2 | 4 | - | 6 |
| Tustunnuckee Emarthlar - - | 4 | 5 | - | 9 |
| Tinlannisharjo - - - | 4 | 2 | - | 6 |
| Paddy . . . . | 1 | 1 | - | 2 |
| Kotchar Fixico . . . . | 1 | 1 | - | 2 |
| Sauhoe . . . . | — | 2 | - | 2 |
| Sukeharharjo (2d of same name) . | 2 | 4 | - | 6 |
| Haffaubofeharjo . . . | 4 | 2 | - | 6 |
| Coosaneharlocco . . . | 3 | 2 | - | 5 |
| Arbicharjo . . . - | 2 | 3 | - | 5 |
| Tommoge . . . . | — | 2 | - | 2 |
| Tibbiega . . . . | 2 | 1 | - | 3 |
| | 78 | 83 | | 161 |
| Fichiliga - - - - | — | 2 | - | 2 |
| Lucy - - - - - | — | 3 | - | 3 |
| Arsawhamicco - - - - | 1 | 1 | - | 2 |
| Coosa Yoholo (2d of same name,) - | 2 | 1 | - | 3 |
| Alpetterharjo - - - - | 1 | 2 | - | 3 |
| Sawhocharga - - - | - | 2 | - | 2 |
| Emarthlooche - - - - | 2 | 2 | - | 4 |
| Tussicayachada - - - - | 2 | 2 | - | 4 |
| Cooistaharjo - - - - | 1 | 1 | - | 2 |
| Saccoarga - - - - | 1 | 2 | - | 3 |
| Arsitche - - - - | 1 | 1 | - | 2 |
| Sparneemarthlar - - - - | 4 | 1 | - | 5 |
| Koncharteemicco (2d of same name) - | 3 | 2 | - | 5 |
| Pokolifke - - - - | 1 | 1 | - | 2 |
| Yobirchchar - - - - | 1 | 2 | - | 3 |
| Hillabeefixico - - - - | 1 | 1 | - | 2 |
| Katey - - - - - | 1 | 1 | - | 2 |
| Yannitscha - - - - | 1 | 1 | - | 2 |
| Warlokoharjo - - - - | 1 | 1 | - | 2 |
| Fiathoke - - - - - | 1 | 1 | - | 2 |
| Yoholomecco (or Charley) - - | 3 | 2 | - | 5 |
| Cussetanharjo - - - - | 1 | 1 | - | 2 |
| Emarthlartustunnuckee (2d of same name) - | 1 | 1 | - | 2 |
| Sally - - - - - | 1 | 1 | - | 2 |
| Hannah - - - - - | 1 | 2 | 1 | 4 |
| Billinga - - - - - | 2 | 1 | - | 3 |

## CREEK CENSUS—Continued.

| Names of Heads of Families. | Males. | Females. | Slaves. | Total. |
|---|---|---|---|---|
| Fixico - - - - - | 1 | 2 | - | 3 |
| Tallaseneharlocko - - · | 1 | 2 | - | 3 |
| Nocose Emarthlar - - - | 1 | 1 | - | 2 |
| Tonohe - - - - - | 2 | 1 | - | 3 |
| Neharlocko - - - - | 1 | 1 | - | 2 |
| Nehamartta - - - - | 2 | 1 | - | 3 |
| Chittoharjo - - - - | 2 | 1 | 2 | 5 |
| Sukey - - - - - | 1 | 1 | - | 2 |
| Sawbopode - - - - | 1 | 2 | - | 3 |
| Arwalke - - - - | - | 4 | - | 4 |
| Chawbofemicco - - - - | - | 2 | - | 2 |
| | 46 | 56 | 3 | 105 |

### CORN-HOUSE TOWN.

| | | | | |
|---|---|---|---|---|
| Artusharjo - - - - | 1 | 2 | - | 3 |
| Oggede Yoholo - - - - | 2 | 2 | - | 4 |
| Nokose Yoholo - - - - | 1 | 2 | - | 3 |
| Hospotokharjo - - - - | 1 | 2 | - | 3 |
| Tiarche Yoholo - - - - | 1 | 2 | - | 3 |
| Ninoneheagar - - - - | — | 3 | - | 3 |
| Tussechichopko - - - - | 3 | 2 | - | 5 |
| Hobicfixico - - - - | 3 | 1 | - | 4 |
| Dick - - - - - | 3 | 1 | - | 4 |
| Neharloccooche - - - - | 2 | 1 | - | 3 |
| Kotcharharjo - - - - | 1 | 2 | - | 3 |
| Okkolodega - - - - | 2 | 1 | - | 3 |
| Okcosneharlocko - - - - | 2 | 1 | - | 3 |
| Tiarchefixico - - - - | 1 | 1 | - | 2 |
| Ottusmicco - - - - | 2 | 2 | - | 4 |
| See Hoga - - - - | 1 | 2 | - | 3 |
| Chokchartee Emarthlar - - | 2 | 2 | - | 4 |
| Chocowasharjo - - - - | 3 | 1 | - | 4 |
| Willie - - - - - | 3 | 4 | - | 7 |
| Sewarlothoga - - - - | 4 | 4 | - | 8 |
| Sawwanwahharjo - - - | 1 | 2 | - | 3 |
| Chelockchafixico - - - | 1 | 2 | - | 3 |
| Yarfkeemarthlar - - - | 2 | 2 | - | 4 |
| Chewastoharjo - - - - | 1 | 2 | - | 3 |
| Sistice - - - - - | 1 | 2 | - | 3 |
| Idiccoharjo - - - - | 2 | 2 | - | 4 |
| Hoslupke - - - - | 2 | 1 | - | 3 |
| Simmahoga - - - - | 2 | 1 | - | 3 |
| Okekoskaharjo - - - - | 2 | 2 | - | 4 |
| Tommygiga - - - - | 3 | 1 | - | 4 |

CREEK CENSUS—Continued.

| Names of Heads of Families. | Males. | Females. | Slaves. | Total. |
|---|---|---|---|---|
| Yarhar Harjo    -    -    - | 1 | 2 | | 3 |
| Hoyanhoe    -    -    - | | | | |
| | 59 | 60 | | 119 |
| KIALEGE TOWN. | | | | |
| Oktiarche Harjo    -    -    - | 1 | 3 | - | 4 |
| Oke chun Yoholo    -    -    - | 2 | 1 | - | 3 |
| Arbicco Yoholo    -    -    - | 1 | 2 | - | 3 |
| Echo Yoholo    -    -    - | 1 | 2 | - | 3 |
| Fosehatchee Fixico    -    -    - | 1 | 1 | - | 2 |
| Homaraithlee    -    -    - | — | 2 | - | 2 |
| Smegar    -    -    -    - | 1 | 2 | - | 3 |
| Ubackcalardega    -    -    - | 1 | 2 | - | 3 |
| Fullegockwegie    -    -    - | 2 | 2 | - | 4 |
| Clea Harjo    -    -    - | 2 | 1 | - | 3 |
| Ulga Hargo    -    -    - | 2 | 2 | - | 4 |
| Nehar Fixico    -    -    - | 1 | 2 | - | 3 |
| Neharlocko Harjo    -    -    - | 1 | 1 | - | 2 |
| Nartop Harjo    -    -    - | 2 | 1 | - | 3 |
| Kotcharmicco    -    -    - | 3 | 2 | - | 5 |
| Kimul Harjo    -    -    - | 2 | 2 | - | 4 |
| Narboche Yoholo    -    -    - | 1 | 1 | - | 2 |
| Konepe Emarthlar    -    -    - | 3 | 3 | - | 6 |
| Sawney Fixico    -    -    - | 1 | 4 | - | 5 |
| Tuskegehopoethele    -    -    - | 1 | 1 | - | 2 |
| Hopoethe Harjo    -    -    - | 1 | 1 | - | 2 |
| Te Marthlar    -    -    - | 1 | 3 | - | 4 |
| Thlathlo Emarthlar    -    -    - | 1 | 2 | - | 3 |
| Loftie Harjo    -    -    - | 1 | 2 | - | 3 |
| Tussicyi Harjo    -    -    - | 1 | 2 | - | 3 |
| Chowasti Fixico    -    -    - | 1 | 2 | - | 3 |
| Koegee    -    -    -    - | 1 | 2 | - | 3 |
| Chogartte Harjo    -    -    - | 2 | 2 | - | 4 |
| Holcassie    -    -    - | 1 | 1 | - | 2 |
| Fosehatchee Yoholo    -    - | 4 | 2 | - | 6 |
| Yoholo Wegar    -    -    - | 2 | 3 | - | 5 |
| Tuskeeg Harjo    -    -    - | 2 | 1 | - | 3 |
| Hosparlok Harjo    -    -    - | 3 | 1 | - | 4 |
| Terchokhoga    -    -    - | 1 | 1 | - | 2 |
| Iepe    -    -    -    - | 3 | 3 | - | 6 |
| Sathoigee    -    -    - | 1 | 1 | - | 2 |
| Toffo Fixico    -    -    - | 2 | 3 | - | 5 |
| Sofuckhoe    -    -    - | 2 | 1 | - | 3 |
| Arhaule Emarthlooche    -    - | 2 | 2 | - | 4 |
| Nulcobiegee    -    -    - | 1 | 1 | - | 2 |

CREEK CENSUS—Continued.

| Names of Heads of Families. | Males. | Females. | Slaves. | Total. |
|---|---|---|---|---|
| Towasse Emarthlar . . . | 1 | 1 | - | 2 |
| Okechoy Fixico . . . . | 4 | 2 | - | 6 |
| | 67 | 76 | | 143 |
| Tuckabatchee Yoholo . . . | 2 | 3 | - | 5 |
| Sinkenha . . . . | 1 | 3 | - | 4 |
| Coosahomer . . . . | 3 | 2 | - | 5 |
| Talmas Harjo . . . . | 1 | 2 | - | 3 |
| Talmachris Harjo . . . | 1 | 2 | - | 3 |
| Karpicchar Yoholo . . | 1 | 2 | - | 3 |
| Sawginga . . . . | 1 | 2 | - | 3 |
| Hotulge Yoholo . . . . | 2 | 1 | - | 3 |
| Arboketiga . . . . | 1 | 2 | - | 3 |
| Archoole Harjo . . . . | 3 | 2 | - | 5 |
| Yoholo Mico . . . . | 2 | 3 | - | 5 |
| Ohholodegee . . . . | 2 | 1 | - | 3 |
| Fosehatchee Emarthlar . . | 2 | 2 | - | 4 |
| Kenalth Harjo . . . . | 1 | 3 | - | 4 |
| Konip Harjo . . . . | 1 | 3 | - | 4 |
| Tuckabatchee Emarthlar . | 1 | 3 | - | 4 |
| Coosi Yoholo . . . . | 2 | 2 | - | 4 |
| Spokeokee Yoholo . . | 2 | 2 | - | 4 |
| Thlathlo Harjo . . . . | 2 | 3 | - | 5 |
| Fitdig Harjo . . . . | 2 | 2 | - | 4 |
| Tarmathlamicco . . . . | 2 | 2 | - | 4 |
| Neharlocco . . . . | 2 | 1 | - | 3 |
| Tuskonar Harjo . . . | 2 | 2 | - | 4 |
| Koki Yoholo . . . . | 1 | 2 | - | 3 |
| Nehemarto Fixico . . . | 1 | 1 | - | 2 |
| Cleachumme Yoholo . . | 2 | 2 | - | 4 |
| Sawfutchco . . . . | 2 | 1 | - | 3 |
| Sparnehobic . . . . | 1 | 3 | - | 4 |
| Talmarse Yoholo . . . | 1 | 3 | - | 4 |
| Muttallegee . . . . | 1 | 2 | - | 3 |
| Talla Yoholo . . . . | 2 | 1 | - | 3 |
| Parhose Harjo . . . . | 1 | 2 | - | 3 |
| Jegar . . . . . | 1 | 2 | - | 3 |
| Ottis Fixico . . . . | 1 | 3 | - | 4 |
| Sittaheechche . . . . | 2 | 1 | - | 3 |
| Nargaffiege . . . . | 1 | 2 | - | 3 |
| Tarpins Harjo . . . . | 1 | 2 | - | 3 |
| Yoholo Harjo . . . . | 1 | 2 | - | 3 |
| Sally . . . . . | 1 | 2 | - | 3 |
| Ottis Harjo . . . . | 2 | 2 | - | 4 |
| Oktiarche Fixico . . . | 2 | 1 | - | 3 |

## CREEK CENSUS—Continued.

| Names of Heads of Families. | Males. | Females. | Slaves. | Total. |
|---|---|---|---|---|
| Emarthlar Yoholo - - - | 1 | 4 | - | 5 |
| Tommy Yoholo " - - | 1 | 3 | - | 4 |
| Pin Harjo - " - - | 2 | 2 | - | 4 |
| | 66 | 94 | | 160 |
| Somarlige - " - | 1 | 1 | - | 2 |
| Tallasee Emarthlar - - " | 3 | 1 | - | 4 |
| Hotalke Harjo - " - | 3 | 3 | - | 6 |
| Chowasti Harjo - " - | 2 | 1 | " | 3 |
| Inluckhoe - - - " | 1 | 2 | " | 3 |
| Osarhinhan - - " | 2 | 1 | - | 3 |
| Spokeoke Fixico - - " | 2 | 2 | " | 4 |
| Kotchar Fixico - " - | 1 | 2 | - | 3 |
| Yoholo Harjo - " " | 1 | 3 | - | 4 |
| Mokkasomga - - " | 2 | 1 | " | 3 |
| Nubbe Emarthlar - - " | 1 | 2 | " | 3 |
| Timfulhoge " - " | 2 | 2 | - | 4 |
| Thlokus Harjo - " " | 1 | 2 | " | 3 |
| Arlok Fixico - " " | 3 | 2 | - | 5 |
| Osooche Harjo - - - | 2 | 1 | 2 | 5 |
| Fiegiga - - - " | 3 | 2 | - | 5 |
| Sosaw - - " - | 1 | 1 | - | 2 |
| Sawwonnoga - " " | 2 | 2 | " | 4 |
| Harlotte Emarthlar - - " | 3 | 2 | - | 5 |
| Michoge - - " " | 1 | 2 | - | 3 |
| Vicey - - " - | 1 | 1 | - | 2 |
| Foloppo Harjo - - - | 3 | 2 | " | 5 |
| Fixico Harjo - - " | 1 | 1 | - | 2 |
| Yodicko Yoholo - - - | 2 | 4 | - | 6 |
| Mauwolaw - - - | 2 | 1 | - | 3 |
| Sutchica - - " - | 2 | 1 | - | 3 |
| Chowasti Yoholo - " - | 2 | 1 | - | 3 |
| Archooley Yoholo - " - | 2 | 1 | - | 3 |
| Poethley Yoholo - " - | 2 | 2 | - | 4 |
| Chocolis Harjo - - " | 3 | 1 | | 4 |
| Kenalth Yoholo - - " | 2 | 2 | - | 4 |
| Tuskiyaw Harjo - " - | 3 | 2 | - | 5 |
| Kolchchar Harjo - " - | 1 | 1 | - | 2 |
| Narboitch Harjo - " - | 3 | 2 | - | 5 |
| Arbicco Fixico - - " | 2 | 1 | - | 3 |
| Sitchchodica - " " | 1 | 2 | - | 3 |
| Chofolope Harjo - " " | 4 | 2 | " | 6 |
| Hoboethlaneche - - - | - | 3 | - | 3 |
| Poosa Harjo - - " | 2 | 2 | " | 4 |
| Hoboilthla - " " | 2 | 1 | " | 3 |

## CREEK CENSUS—Continued.

| Names of Heads of Families. | Males. | Females. | Slaves. | Total. |
|---|---|---|---|---|
| Timmowelarga   -   -   -   - | 1 | 2 | . | 3 |
| Charlo Harjo   -   -   -   - | 1 | 2 | . | 3 |
| Kunchart Fixico  -   -   -   - | 4 | 1 | , | 5 |
| Fosehatchee Harjo   -   -   - | 3 | 1 | . | 4 |
|  |  |  |  |  |
|  | 86 | 74 | 2 | 162 |
|  |  |  |  |  |
| Sockkoska Harjo -   -   -   - | 2 | 2 | . | 4 |
| Arstacoathle   -   -   -   - | 1 | 1 | . | 2 |
| Simmarbokar   -   -   -   - | 1 | 1 | . | 2 |
| Sawohiche   -   -   -   - | 1 | 2 | . | 3 |
| Ossee Yoholo   -   -   -   - | 3 | 3 | . | 6 |
| Passcove Harjo   -   -   -   - | 2 | 1 | . | 3 |
| Yawholoche   -   -   -   - | 3 | 1 | . | 4 |
| Sinmiechar   -   -   -   - | 1 | 3 | . | 4 |
| Osey Yoholo   -   -   -   - | 1 | 1 | . | 2 |
| Ararte Harjo   -   -   -   - | 2 | 1 | . | 3 |
| Spokeoke Harjo   -   -   -   - | 2 | 1 | . | 3 |
| Timmanarfeege   -   -   -   - | 1 | 1 | . | 2 |
| Chogatta Fixico   -   -   -   - | 2 | 2 | . | 4 |
| Suddedunna Harjo   -   -   - | 1 | 3 | . | 4 |
| Cussetan Fixico   -   -   -   - | 3 | 1 | . | 4 |
| Fosehearga   -   -   -   - | 1 | 3 | . | 4 |
| Miccopoelthe Emarthlar -   -   - | 3 | 1 | . | 4 |
| Stussehoga   -   -   -   - | — | 3 | . | 3 |
| Micco Emarthlar -   -   -   - | 2 | 1 | . | 3 |
| Ottesey Yoholo   -   -   -   - | 1 | 2 | . | 3 |
| Yarhar Harjo   -   -   -   - | 3 | 2 | . | 5 |
| Hokechi Emarthlar   -   -   - | 2 | 1 | . | 3 |
| Talmarse Fixico   -   -   -   - | 3 | 2 | . | 5 |
| Lofty Fixico   -   -   -   - | 1 | 2 | , | 3 |
| Cosratlarbeegea   -   -   -   - | 1 | 1 | . | 2 |
| Nocose Yoholo   -   -   -   - | 3 | 1 | . | 4 |
| Arsarliche   -   -   -   - | 2 | 1 | . | 3 |
| Oche Harjo   -   -   -   - | 2 | 1 | . | 3 |
| Isparne Yoholo   -   -   -   - | 2 | 1 | . | 3 |
| Enehe Emarthlar -   -   -   - | 2 | 4 | . | 6 |
| Osooche Yoholo   -   -   -   - | 2 | 1 | . | 3 |
| Stimmolthhoe   -   -   -   - | 1 | 1 | . | 2 |
| Mistihe   -   -   -   - | 1 | 1 | . | 2 |
| Ochis Harjo   -   -   -   - | 1 | 2 | . | 3 |
| Carcar   -   -   -   - | 1 | 3 | . | 4 |
| Tuckabatchee Fixico   -   -   - | 1 | 1 | . | 2 |
|  |  |  |  |  |
|  | 61 | 59 |  | 120 |

CREEK CENSUS—Continued.

| Names of Heads of Families. | Males. | Females. | Slaves. | Total. |
|---|---|---|---|---|
| CHATTOKSOFKE TOWN. | | | | |
| Ishatuphogey - - - - | 2 | 2 | - | 4 |
| Hoboethele - - - - | 1 | 2 | - | 3 |
| Nocose Harjo - - - - | 2 | 2 | - | 4 |
| Chucle - - - - | 2 | 2 | - | 4 |
| Neharlocco - - - - | 2 | 2 | - | 4 |
| Harlotharke - - - - | 1 | 3 | - | 4 |
| Wat Grayson - - - - | 1 | 1 | - | 2 |
| Sandy Grayson, jr. - - - | 1 | 2 | - | 3 |
| Rachael Spiller - - - - | 1 | 2 | 2 | 5 |
| Walter Grayson, jr. - - - | 2 | 2 | - | 4 |
| Osar Harjo - - - - | 2 | 2 | - | 4 |
| Pikar - - - - - | 1 | 2 | - | 3 |
| Nelly - - - - - | 1 | 3 | - | 4 |
| Cocheerhar - - - - | 1 | 2 | - | 3 |
| Fanny - - - - - | — | 4 | - | 4 |
| Charley - - - - - | 1 | 2 | - | 3 |
| Sannoker - - - - - | 2 | 1 | - | 3 |
| Cauuphogee - - - - | 1 | 1 | - | 2 |
| Sofickhonia - - - - | 2 | 2 | - | 4 |
| Enehe Marthlar - - - - | 2 | 1 | - | 3 |
| Cho Fixico - - - - | 2 | 2 | - | 4 |
| Iyarhome - - - - - | 2 | 2 | - | 4 |
| Hothlepoya - - - - | 1 | 3 | - | 4 |
| Kotcharyoholo - - - - | 2 | 1 | - | 3 |
| Fosehatchee Harjo - - - | 1 | 2 | - | 3 |
| Helulge Emarthlar - - - | 3 | 2 | - | 5 |
| Chockihe - - - - - | 2 | 1 | - | 3 |
| Yarhar Harjo - - - - | 2 | 2 | - | 4 |
| Kolumme Harjo - - - - | 2 | 1 | - | 3 |
| Yoholo Chopko - - - - | 2 | 3 | - | 5 |
| Iyarhome, (2d of same name) - - | 1 | 2 | - | 3 |
| Fosehatcheeopoethele - - - | 2 | 3 | - | 5 |
| Tarbothte - - - - - | 2 | 1 | - | 3 |
| Fose Harjo Locco - - - | 2 | 2 | - | 4 |
| Hotulge Harjo - - - - | 1 | 3 | - | 4 |
| Fistarke - - - - - | 1 | 1 | - | 2 |
| Hilkarsicga - - - - | 1 | 2 | - | 3 |
| Tarlitte - - - - - | — | 2 | - | 2 |
| Tediche - - - - - | 2 | 2 | - | 4 |
| Miccochopko - - - - | 1 | 2 | - | 3 |
| Artus Fixico - - - - | 4 | 1 | - | 5 |
| Okhotie - - - - - | 2 | 2 | - | 4 |
| | 66 | 82 | 2 | 150 |

CREEK CENSUS—Continued.

| Names of Heads of Families. | Males. | Females | Slaves. | Total. |
|---|---|---|---|---|
| Tommy Harjo      -      -      -      - | 1 | 2 | - | 3 |
| Saemitte         -      -      -      - | 1 | 2 | - | 3 |
| Sholtte          -      -      -      - | 2 | 1 | - | 3 |
| Pin Harjo        -      -      -      - | 1 | 1 | - | 2 |
| Eneharchokone    -      -      -      - | 3 | 2 | - | 5 |
| Coosa Emarthlar  -      -      -      - | 1 | 1 | - | 2 |
| Yarcooche        -      -      -      - | 2 | 3 | - | 5 |
| Sinhomarharke    -      -      -      - | — | 2 | - | 2 |
| Allithoka        -      -      -      - | 2 | 2 | - | 4 |
| Martup Yoholo    -      -      -      - | 1 | 3 | - | 4 |
| Meharke          -      -      -      - | 3 | 2 | - | 5 |
| Kingajha         -      -      -      - | 1 | 1 | - | 2 |
| Tuntunnuck Harjo      -      -      - | 4 | 1 | - | 5 |
| Eginnatcha       -      -      -      - | 1 | 2 | - | 3 |
| Mothlathfiga     -      -      -      - | 1 | 1 | - | 2 |
| Tulse Mico       -      -      -      - | 1 | 1 | - | 2 |
| Hitsigey         -      -      -      - | 2 | 1 | - | 3 |
| Istofigee        -      -      -      - | — | 2 | - | 2 |
| Osooch Harjo     -      -      -      - | 1 | 2 | - | 3 |
| Narlooche Yoholo      -      -      - | 1 | 1 | - | 2 |
| Talmarse Harjo   -      -      -      - | 2 | 2 | - | 4 |
| Sallunda         -      -      -      - | 1 | 1 | - | 2 |
| Tustunnuckee     -      -      -      - | 1 | 3 | - | 4 |
| Sudde Micco      -      -      -      - | 1 | 2 | - | 3 |
| Charoker         -      -      -      - | 3 | 1 | - | 4 |
| Sowygay          -      -      -      - | 1 | 2 | - | 3 |
| Neharlocko Harjo      -      -      - | 1 | 2 | - | 3 |
| Cussetanopotheehele   -      -      - | 3 | 3 | - | 6 |
| Choanelar        -      -      -      - | 1 | 3 | - | 4 |
| Tussekiar Harjo  -      -      -      - | 1 | 1 | - | 2 |
| Charley (second of same name)    -      - | 3 | 2 | - | 5 |
| Simmehogey       -      -      -      - | 1 | 2 | - | 3 |
| Yoholo Harjo     -      -      -      - | 2 | 2 | - | 4 |
| Konechart Yoholo -      -      -      - | 3 | 1 | - | 4 |
| Emarthloche      -      -      -      - | 1 | 1 | - | 2 |
| Littie           -      -      -      - | 1 | 1 | - | 2 |
| Cho Fixico (second of same name)     - | 2 | 1 | - | 3 |
| O Swich Emarthlar     -      -      - | 2 | 2 | - | 4 |
| Hotalke Yoholo   -      -      -      - | 1 | 1 | - | 2 |
| Oktiarche Harjo  -      -      -      - | 2 | 1 | - | 3 |
| Semmihoke        -      -      -      - | 1 | 1 | - | 2 |
| Larboniche       -      -      -      - | 1 | 2 | - | 3 |
| Lotter Harjo     -      -      -      - | 1 | 2 | - | 3 |
| Fosehatch Fixico (third of same name)  - | 2 | 2 | - | 4 |
|  | 67 | 74 |  | 141 |

## CREEK CENSUS—Continued.

| Names of Heads of Families. | Males. | Females. | Slaves. | Total. |
|---|---|---|---|---|
| Sannickkogee | 1 | 2 | - | 3 |
| Fosa Harjo | 2 | - | - | 2 |
| Tewalle | 3 | 2 | - | 5 |
| Choolittal Emarthlar | 4 | 1 | - | 5 |
| Iste Marthlar | - | 2 | - | 2 |
| Isfarne Fixico | 3 | 1 | - | 4 |
| Sokkosarby | - | 2 | - | 2 |
| Sekoige | - | 2 | - | 2 |
| Echo (or Judy) | 1 | 2 | - | 3 |
| Hekarse Harjo | 3 | 2 | - | 5 |
| Cusse Yoholo | 2 | 3 | - | 5 |
| Sobbokeido | 1 | 1 | - | 2 |
| Simwokigo | 1 | 1 | - | 2 |
| Fose Yoholo | 1 | 2 | - | 3 |
| Soharte | 3 | 1 | - | 4 |
| Nocose Harjo | 2 | - | - | 2 |
| Harhar Emarthlar | 3 | - | - | 3 |
| Isnargofte | 1 | 2 | - | 3 |
| Sedoie | 1 | 2 | - | 3 |
| Ischokolargee | - | 3 | - | 3 |
| Tewarwike | 1 | 1 | - | 2 |
| Oktiarche Yoholo | 1 | 2 | - | 3 |
| Iskarnè | 1 | 1 | - | 2 |
| Timmondelechar | - | 3 | - | 3 |
| Talofe Harjo | 2 | 1 | - | 3 |
| Simmarte | - | 3 | - | 3 |
| Kotchar Harjo | 5 | 1 | - | 6 |
| Sally | 2 | 2 | - | 4 |
| Horarnochche | 1 | 3 | - | 4 |
| Chiloke Harjo | 2 | 2 | - | 4 |
| Konchart Fixico | 1 | 1 | - | 2 |
| Notchomiche | 1 | 1 | - | 2 |
| Karbitch Yoholo | 2 | 1 | - | 3 |
| Sowwarhegatche | 3 | 2 | - | 5 |
| Hobo Emarthlar | 2 | - | - | 2 |
| Oktiarche Emarthlar | 2 | 4 | - | 6 |
| Nocose Harjo | 3 | 2 | - | 5 |
| Nockehere | 1 | 2 | - | 3 |
| Martutter | 2 | 3 | - | 5 |
| Kale | 1 | 1 | - | 2 |
| Semarke | 3 | 3 | - | 6 |
| Sauhosiga | 3 | 3 | - | 6 |
| Iskarde | 3 | 1 | - | 4 |
| Talmarse Emarthlar | 1 | 1 | - | 2 |
| | 75 | 75 | | 150 |

## CREEK CENSUS—Continued.

| Names of Heads of Families. | Males. | Females. | Slaves. | Total. |
|---|---|---|---|---|
| Tunnie - - - - - | 2 | 2 | - | 4 |
| Hoegeeche - - - - | - | 2 | - | 2 |
| Stinkarke - - - - | 4 | 2 | - | 6 |
| Kowokkoche Harjo - - - | 2 | 1 | - | 3 |
| Mico Harjo - - - - | 2 | 1 | - | 3 |
| Cloppolega - - - - | 3 | 1 | - | 4 |
| Neharloccooche - - - - | 1 | 1 | - | 2 |
| Ogillise Harjo - - - - | 1 | 1 | - | 2 |
| Tinney - - - - | 2 | 1 | - | 3 |
| Fosehatch Emarthlar - - - | 2 | 2 | - | 4 |
| Hokefuske - - - - | 1 | 1 | - | 2 |
| Sawhofiga - - - - | 1 | 3 | - | 4 |
| Sohale - - - - - | - | 2 | - | 2 |
| | | | | |
| TAL-LIP-SE-HO-GY TOWN (near Barnett's.) | | | | |
| Oktiarche Fixico - - - | 2 | 4 | - | 6 |
| Chofolope Harjo - - - - | 2 | 4 | - | 6 |
| Yoholo Harjo - - - - | 2 | 1 | - | 3 |
| Nocose Harjo - - - | 1 | 5 | - | 6 |
| Osar Harjo - - - - | 3 | 2 | - | 5 |
| Arsosar - - - - | 2 | 3 | - | 5 |
| Easteecharco Micco - - - | 3 | 3 | - | 6 |
| Talope Harjo - - - - | 2 | 1 | - | 3 |
| Milleger - - - - | - | 3 | - | 3 |
| Allike - - - - - | 1 | 2 | - | 3 |
| Yarhar Harjo - - - - | 1 | 1 | - | 2 |
| Isfarne Fixico - - - - | 2 | 1 | - | 3 |
| Tallolooche - - - - | 3 | - | - | 3 |
| Charlo Harjo - - - - | 1 | 1 | - | 2 |
| Osiar Yoholo - - - - | 2 | 1 | - | 3 |
| Sikittawa - - - - | 1 | 2 | - | 3 |
| Clokecaster Harjo - - - | 1 | 1 | - | 2 |
| Iscowoppe - - - - | 3 | 2 | - | 5 |
| Yokecha - - - - | 1 | 2 | - | 3 |
| | 54 | 59 | | 113 |

Total of the population of the upper towns, including negroes - 14,142
Deduct the number of negroes, slaves - - - - 445

Indians - - 13,697

I do hereby certify, that the above census has been taken by me, and that this roll is as correct as I have been able to make it.

*May* 1, 1833.                                    B. S. PARSONS.
Sworn to before me,                  JAS. W. ARMSTRONG, *J. P.*

*Census of the Principal Chiefs and Heads of Families of the Creek
tribe of Indians, taken by virtue of the second article of the treaty concluded with that tribe at the city of Washington, March 24th, 1832.*

At a General Council of the lower towns of the Creek tribe of Indians
held at Seecharlitchar, on the 29th day of November, 1832, the following
persons were designated and acknowledged as Principal Chiefs, (viz.)

| Names of the Principal Chiefs. | Males. | Females. | Slaves. | Total. |
|---|---|---|---|---|
| **CUSSETAW TOWNS.** | | | | |
| Nehar Micco | 5 | 6 | 4 | 15 |
| Tuskehenehaw Chooley | 1 | 1 | 1 | 3 |
| Arparlar Tustunnuckee | 3 | 2 | - | 5 |
| Isfarne Emarthlar | 3 | 4 | - | 7 |
| Okefuske Yoholo | 2 | 5 | - | 7 |
| Tuckabatcheeharjo | 1 | 3 | 1 | 5 |
| Efar Emarthlar | 2 | 4 | 11 | 17 |
| Cussetau Micco | 2 | 1 | - | 3 |
| Nicco Chartee | 1 | 2 | - | 3 |
| Easteecharco Chopko | 1 | 1 | - | 2 |
| **COWETA TOWNS.** | | | | |
| Kotchar Tustunnuckee | 1 | 2 | - | 3 |
| James Island | 4 | 4 | - | 8 |
| Efar Tuskenehaw | 1 | 2 | - | 3 |
| Absolom Islands | 1 | 1 | - | 2 |
| Jacob Beavers | 2 | 3 | - | 5 |
| Talmarse Harjo | 2 | 2 | - | 4 |
| Charlo Harjo Cochokone | 3 | 2 | - | 5 |
| Emarthlar Harjo | 1 | 2 | - | 3 |
| Joseph Marshall | 4 | 2 | 16 | 22 |
| | 40 | 49 | 33 | 122 |
| **THLAKATEKA (OR BROKEN ARROW.)** | | | | |
| Seeokoba | 1 | 1 | - | 2 |
| Honeseharjo | 3 | 3 | - | 6 |
| Konippe Emarthlar | 3 | 1 | - | 4 |
| Yufkar Emarthlarharjo | 2 | 2 | - | 4 |
| **EUFAULA.** | | | | |
| Fosehatchee Emarthlar | 2 | 4 | - | 6 |
| Kepar Yar Tustunnuckee | 3 | 1 | - | 4 |

CREEK CENSUS—Continued.

| Names of the Principal Chiefs. | Males. | Females. | Slaves. | Total. |
|---|---|---|---|---|
| Enehar Tustunnuckee . . . | 3 | 1 | - | 4 |
| Tustunnuck Harjo . . . | 2 | 1 | - | 3 |
| **CHEHAWAH.** | | | | |
| Yoholo Harjo . . . . | 1 | 7 | 3 | 11 |
| Kotchar Harjo . . . . | 4 | 1 | - | 5 |
| Johnny Chopko . . . . | 3 | 2 | - | 5 |
| **EUCHEE.** | | | | |
| Timpooche Barnard . . . | 3 | 1 | 3 | 7 |
| William Barnard . . . . | 4 | 5 | 11 | 20 |
| Ponaker Thloco . . . . | 4 | 5 | - | 9 |
| **OSWITCHEE.** | | | | |
| Oktiarche Emarthlar . . . | 1 | 1 | - | 2 |
| Oswitchee Emarthlar . . . | 2 | 3 | - | 5 |
| Tuckabatchee Fixico . . . | 3 | 2 | - | 5 |
| **TOLOWARTHLOCKO.** | | | | |
| Nehar Thlocco . . . . | 3 | 3 | - | 6 |
| Enehar Tuskehenehaw . . . | 2 | 4 | 1 | 7 |
| **CHEWOCOLEE, (EUFAULA.)** | | | | |
| Woxe Micco . . . . | 1 | 2 | - | 3 |
| | 50 | 50 | 18 | 118 |
| **HITCHETEE.** | | | | |
| Enehar Emarthlar . . . | 3 | 3 | - | 6 |
| Tunnechee . . . . | 1 | 3 | - | 4 |
| **SOWOCCOLO.** | | | | |
| Neah Micco . . . . | 2 | 2 | - | 4 |
| Parhose Emarthlar . . . | 3 | 2 | - | 5 |

CREEK CENSUS—Continued.

| Names of Heads of Families. | Males. | Females. | Slaves. | Total. |
|---|---|---|---|---|
| **HATCHEECHUBBA.** | | | | |
| Tallase Micco - - - - | 4 | 1 | - | 5 |
| | 13 | 11 | | 24 |
| **EUFAULA.** | | | | |
| Molezar Grace - - - - | 2 | 3 | 15 | 20 |
| Thleparka - - - - | 1 | 1 | - | 2 |
| Okefuskee Yoholo - - - | 2 | 1 | - | 3 |
| Hothlepoya Harjo - - - | 1 | 3 | - | 4 |
| Elsey Perryman - - - - | — | 2 | - | 2 |
| Okechun Harjo - - - - | 3 | 1 | - | 4 |
| Kepiaw Harjo - - - - | 1 | 1 | - | 2 |
| Harharlock Harjo - - - - | 1 | 1 | - | 2 |
| Eneharjiskar Harjo - - - | 4 | 1 | - | 5 |
| Nocoseille Harjo - - - - | 3 | 3 | - | 6 |
| Yarhar Harjo - - - - | 2 | 3 | - | 5 |
| Thlathloche Emarthlar - - - | 3 | 2 | - | 5 |
| Ninnechoppa Harjo - - - | 4 | 2 | - | 6 |
| Unmar Emarthlar - - - | 2 | 1 | - | 3 |
| Okefus Tustunnuckee - - - | 1 | 1 | - | 2 |
| Fickalumkar - - - - | 2 | 2 | - | 4 |
| Harpekaw Fixico - - - | 2 | 3 | - | 5 |
| Letif Harjo - - - - | 1 | 2 | - | 3 |
| Harharlokfixico - - - - | 1 | 2 | - | 3 |
| Shenarhe - - - - | 2 | 1 | - | 3 |
| Cchoefolowar - - - - | 5 | 3 | - | 8 |
| Tustunnuckee Fixico - - - | 2 | 1 | - | 3 |
| Echo Harjo - - - - | 2 | 2 | - | 4 |
| Etommy Tustunnuckee - - - | 2 | 1 | - | 3 |
| Nocose Yoholo - - - - | 1 | 1 | - | 2 |
| Okeamalga Marlar - - - | 1 | 2 | - | 3 |
| Echoille Harjo - - - - | 2 | 1 | - | 3 |
| Kotchar Harjo - - - - | 3 | 2 | - | 5 |
| Othlarhoche - - - - | 1 | 5 | - | 6 |
| Ontallaharjo - - - - | 4 | 3 | - | 7 |
| Talopie - - - - | 1 | 2 | - | 3 |
| Woxefixico - - - - | 1 | 4 | - | 5 |
| Kotchar Fixico - - - - | 4 | 2 | - | 6 |
| Konchart Harjo - - - - | 2 | 2 | - | 4 |
| Tolofeharjo - - - - | 1 | 1 | - | 2 |
| Parhose Emarthlar - - - | 1 | 3 | - | 4 |
| Hoteseharjo - - - - | 2 | 2 | - | 4 |
| Woxeharjo - - - - | 5 | 2 | - | 7 |

43‡

## CREEK CENSUS—Continued.

| Names of Heads of Families. | Males. | Females. | Slaves. | Total. |
|---|---|---|---|---|
| Alhoaitchee      -      -      -      - | 3 | 1 | - | 4 |
| Parhose Micco      -      -      -      - | 1 | 1 | - | 2 |
| | 82 | 77 | 15 | 174 |
| Seminole -      -      -      -      - | 2 | 1 | - | 3 |
| Miarke      -      -      -      -      - | 1 | 2 | - | 3 |
| Tiukse      -      -      -      -      - | 1 | 1 | - | 2 |
| Tefutshoe, (alias Fanny)      -      -      -      - | — | 2 | - | 2 |
| Otalke Harjo      -      -      -      - | 2 | 2 | - | 4 |
| Othlemarte Fixico      -      -      - | 2 | 1 | - | 3 |
| Woxeholartar      -      -      -      - | 1 | 3 | - | 4 |
| Paskofar   -      -      -      -      - | 1 | 1 | - | 2 |
| Echo Fixico      -      -      -      - | 1 | 1 | - | 2 |
| Talargey  -      -      -      -      - | 1 | 1 | - | 2 |
| Welarkee -      -      -      -      - | 2 | 1 | - | 3 |
| Homejay -      -      -      -      - | 1 | 2 | - | 3 |
| Fosehatchee Fixico      -      -      - | 2 | 1 | - | 3 |
| Sowpersarlle      -      -      -      - | 1 | 1 | - | 2 |
| Korpikchar Harjo -      -      -      - | 2 | 4 | - | 6 |
| Eneharthlocko Yoholo      -      -      - | 2 | 2 | - | 4 |
| Emarme Harjo      -      -      -      - | 4 | 1 | - | 5 |
| Woxe Micco      -      -      -      - | 1 | 2 | - | 3 |
| Tuskenehaw      -      -      -      - | 3 | 1 | - | 4 |
| Eneharthlocko Harjo      -      -      - | 3 | 5 | - | 8 |
| Othlemarte Tustunnuckee -      -      - | 2 | 2 | - | 4 |
| Kotchar Micco      -      -      -      - | 3 | 1 | - | 4 |
| Fose Harjo      -      -      -      - | 1 | 1 | - | 2 |
| Sokotarhay      -      -      -      - | — | 3 | - | 3 |
| Oche Harjo      -      -      -      - | 3 | 1 | - | 4 |
| Homarhite      -      -      -      - | 1 | 1 | - | 2 |
| Osehitchee      -      -      -      - | 4 | 3 | - | 7 |
| Sokethliche      -      -      -      - | 1 | 2 | - | 3 |
| Istimyke  -      -      -      -      - | 1 | 3 | - | 4 |
| Sukithlige      -      -      -      - | 1 | 2 | - | 3 |
| Singkoahoge      -      -      -      - | 3 | 1 | - | 4 |
| Suckolumhay      -      -      -      - | — | 2 | - | 2 |
| Thlarkenarhay      -      -      -      - | 1 | 2 | - | 3 |
| Temoyaothliche   -      -      -      - | 1 | 1 | - | 2 |
| Arpecooche Emarthlar      -      -      - | 3 | 1 | - | 4 |
| Timpooche      -      -      -      - | 1 | 1 | - | 2 |
| John Perryman   -      -      -      - | 1 | 1 | - | 2 |
| Siarkay      -      -      -      -      - | 2 | 2 | - | 4 |
| Karpikchar Emarthlar      -      -      - | 3 | 1 | - | 4 |
| Pelishartkee (a Euchee Indian)      -      - | 1 | 1 | - | 2 |

CREEK CENSUS—Continued.

| Names of Heads of Families. | Males. | Females. | Slaves. | Total. |
|---|---|---|---|---|
| Yarhar Fixico, (a Euchee) - - | 2 | 2 | - | 4 |
| Kotchar Micco, (a Euchee) - - | 1 | 5 | - | 6 |
| | 69 | 74 | | 143 |
| Nocose Yoholo, (a Euchee) - - | 2 | 1 | - | 3 |
| Honitshoochee - - - - | 1 | 1 | - | 2 |
| Woolhoeche . . . . | 1 | 1 | - | 2 |
| Nowhothlikay . . . . | 1 | 2 | - | 3 |
| Kunchartee Fixico . . . | 2 | 1 | - | 3 |
| Holarte Marthlar . . . . | 3 | — | | 3 |
| Tustunnuckee Emarthlar . . . | 1 | 1 | - | 2 |
| Yarkay - . . . | 1 | 1 | - | 2 |
| Seyekiche . . . . | 2 | 1 | - | 3 |
| Nokose Ekar . . . . | 1 | 1 | - | 2 |
| Nehartoko . . . . | 1 | 1 | - | 2 |
| Cheloko Harjo . . . . | 1 | 1 | - | 2 |
| Fiyoholo · . . . . | 2 | 1 | - | 3 |
| Solitchchee . . . . | 1 | 1 | - | 2 |
| Totekiss Harjo . . . . | 1 | 2 | - | 3 |
| Tokolthka . . . . | 2 | 1 | - | 3 |
| Eufaula Harjo . . . . | 3 | 1 | - | 4 |
| Charnaliche . · . . | 1 | 2 | - | 3 |
| Tolaway Harjo . . . . | 2 | 2 | - | 4 |
| Okechun Holartar. . . . | 1 | 2 | - | 3 |
| Chokartke Harjo . . . · | 1 | 1 | - | 2 |
| Inchokikey . . . . | 1 | 1 | - | 2 |
| Echonarche Harjo . . . | 2 | 1 | - | 3 |
| Yufka Emarthlar . . . . | 3 | 2 | - | 5 |
| John Robeson . . . | 1 | 1 | - | 2 |
| Hilton, (alias Tustunnuckee Chopko) . | 1 | 1 | - | 2 |
| Neharthlockokochokone . . . | 2 | 2 | - | 4 |
| Easteecharko Harjo . . · | 2 | 1 | - | 3 |
| Kosar Harjo . . . . | 1 | 1 | - | 2 |
| Chuckfolikay . . . . | 1 | 1 | - | 2 |
| Echo Emarthloche . . . | 2 | 1 | - | 3 |
| Jukharkay . . . . | 2 | 1 | - | 3 |
| Niltoechee . . . . | — | 2 | - | 2 |
| Thlarheheega . . . . | — | 2 | - | 2 |
| Shehartartee . . . . | — | 2 | - | 2 |
| Tarsahokay . . . . | 2 | 1 | - | 3 |
| James Perryman . . . . | 1 | 1 | - | 2 |
| Miik Chay . . . . | 1 | 3 | - | 4 |
| Honichay . . . . | 1 | 2 | - | 3 |
| Billy Umkar . . . . | 2 | 1 | - | 3 |
| Koncharteelokko . . . | 1 | 1 | - | 2 |

## CREEK CENSUS—Continued.

| Names of Heads of Families. | Males. | Females. | Slaves. | Total. |
|---|---|---|---|---|
| Sokoseke Harjo | 1 | 2 | . | 3 |
| Echo Ekar | 3 | 1 | . | 4 |
| | 61 | 56 | | 117 |
| Echo Yoholo | 3 | 4 | . | 7 |
| Holartar Micco | 3 | 2 | . | 5 |
| Charkee | 1 | 1 | . | 2 |
| Tarleche | 1 | 1 | . | 2 |
| Follarhe | 1 | 1 | . | 2 |
| Palochay | 1 | 1 | . | 2 |
| Sciepe | 1 | 1 | . | 2 |
| Sarpehee | 1 | 1 | . | 2 |
| Tiechoa | 2 | 1 | . | 3 |
| Larteche | 3 | 1 | . | 4 |
| Limpekay | 1 | 1 | . | 2 |
| Marhechikay | 1 | 1 | . | 2 |
| Ben Burgess | 3 | 2 | . | 5 |
| Harpiarkar Micco | 2 | 1 | - | 3 |
| Mochusseege | 1 | 1 | - | 2 |
| Cheiskar | 2 | 1 | - | 3 |
| Otake | 3 | 2 | - | 5 |
| Nineomartehoparye | 2 | 2 | - | 4 |
| Seoparkey | — | 2 | - | 2 |
| Senipke | 1 | 1 | - | 2 |
| Supefartikay | 1 | 1 | - | 2 |
| Mokosekochokone | 2 | 3 | - | 5 |
| Eneharthlock Emarthlar | 2 | 2 | - | 4 |
| Tarsekegee | 1 | 1 | - | 2 |
| Chokoeche | 1 | 3 | - | 4 |
| Marpokay | 2 | 1 | - | 3 |
| Lucy Burgess | 1 | 1 | - | 2 |
| Legey | 1 | 1 | - | 2 |
| Choolekooswar | 3 | 4 | - | 7 |
| Futche | 1 | 1 | - | 2 |
| Sartethlekay | 1 | 1 | - | 2 |
| Emonarye | — | 2 | - | 2 |
| Salfokelohitchee | — | 3 | - | 3 |
| Harpoeche | 1 | 1 | - | 2 |
| Ticktoneche | 1 | 1 | - | 2 |
| Talwhoyilete | 1 | 2 | - | 3 |
| Esarpar Harjo, (a Euchee) | 3 | 1 | - | 4 |
| Narsitte | 1 | 3 | - | 4 |
| Kosar Yoholo | 3 | 1 | - | 4 |
| Sparne Fixico | 1 | 2 | - | 3 |
| Miotla | — | 3 | - | 3 |

CREEK CENSUS—Continued.

| Names of Heads of Families. | Males. | Females. | Slaves. | Total. |
|---|---|---|---|---|
| Okechemikay - - - - | 1 | 3 | - | 4 |
| Nittarhe - - - - | 2 | 2 | - | 4 |
| | 63 | 71 | | 134 |
| Sarthlotheka - - - - | 2 | 2 | - | 4 |
| Awtakar - - - - - | 1 | 3 | - | 4 |
| Fickhonia - - - - | 2 | 2 | - | 4 |
| Sattehiga - - - - - | 2 | 2 | - | 4 |
| Tehege - - - - - | - | 3 | - | 3 |
| Sinelache - - - - | 2 | 1 | - | 3 |
| Parhela - - - - - | 1 | 3 | - | 4 |
| Sceekar - - - - - | 1 | 1 | - | 2 |
| Salechar - - - - - | 1 | 2 | - | 3 |
| Yelka Harjo - - - - | 3 | 1 | - | 4 |
| Tustunnuckkochokone - - - | 3 | 1 | - | 4 |
| Hopaiuchee - - - - | 2 | 2 | - | 4 |
| Artus Harjo - - - - | 3 | 3 | - | 6 |
| Oktiarche Marthlar - - - | 3 | 3 | - | 6 |
| Tustunnuckee Chooley - - - | 4 | 1 | - | 5 |
| Klaromarta Tustunnuckee - - | 4 | 2 | - | 6 |
| Tokkose Marthlar - - - | 5 | 3 | - | 8 |
| Honap Emarthlar - - - | 4 | 3 | - | 7 |
| Yarhar Emarthlar - - - | 2 | 2 | - | 4 |
| Thlathlo Fixico - - - - | 3 | 3 | - | 6 |
| Nocoseille Tustunnuckee - - | 2 | 2 | - | 4 |
| Oktiarche Harjo - - - - | 5 | 1 | - | 6 |
| Otulke Marthlar - - - - | 3 | 2 | - | 5 |
| Talwar Fixico - - - - | 1 | 3 | - | 4 |
| Nokose Harjo - - - - | 1 | 2 | - | 3 |
| Fosehatcheeolar - - - - | 3 | 2 | - | 5 |
| Kotchar Harjo - - - - | 2 | 2 | - | 4 |
| Emarthlar Harjo - - - - | 1 | 3 | - | 4 |
| Sfarne Harjo - - - - | 3 | 1 | - | 4 |
| Tukkose Harjo - - - - | 2 | 1 | - | 3 |
| Charle Marthlar - - - - | 3 | 2 | - | 5 |
| Emarthlar Charlee - - - | 2 | 1 | - | 3 |
| Chewasti Harjo - - - - | 1 | 1 | - | 2 |
| Oyanhoye - - - - | - | 2 | - | 2 |
| Sarpohar - - - - | 2 | 2 | - | 4 |
| Tokharkay, (a Euchee) - - | 1 | 2 | - | 3 |
| Okkoltartay, (a Euchee) - - | 1 | 1 | - | 2 |
| Chapela, (a Euchee widow) - - | - | 2 | - | 2 |
| Sparne Emarthlar - - - | 1 | 1 | - | 2 |
| Wartoole Burgess - - - | 2 | 2 | - | 4 |
| Wokieka - - - - - | 1 | 1 | - | 2 |

## CREEK CENSUS—Continued.

| Names of Heads of Families. | Males. | Females. | Slaves. | Total. |
|---|---|---|---|---|
| Konippe Emarthlar     -     -     - | 1 | 4 | . | 5 |
| Talmochus Harjo     -     -     - | 3 | 2 | . | 5 |
|  | 89 | 85 |  | 174 |
| Wayle   -     -     -     -     - | 2 | 1 | . | 3 |
| Cowpucka     -     -     -     - | 3 | 1 | . | 4 |
| Lumheothlepoya   -     -     -     - | 4 | 1 | . | 5 |
| Mistohome     -     -     -     - | 1 | 1 | . | 2 |
| Sole Harjo     -     -     -     - | 1 | 2 | . | 3 |
| Scoo Ray     -     -     -     - | 3 | - | . | 3 |
| Woxe Yoholo     -     -     -     - | 2 | 3 | . | 5 |
| Karharlartay     -     -     -     - | 1 | 1 | . | 2 |
| Kowokhoge     -     -     -     - | 1 | 1 | . | 2 |
| Nethlar kotay     -     -     -     - | 1 | 1 | . | 2 |
| Allumhar     -     -     -     - | - | 4 | . | 4 |
| Yarhar Harjo     -     -     -     - | 1 | 2 | . | 3 |
| Stemonarke, (wife of Major Hardridge) | 1 | 1 | . | 2 |
| Stemelindar     -     -     -     - | 3 | 1 | . | 4 |
| Lizzy Burgess     -     -     -     - | 1 | 3 | . | 4 |
| Lewya   -     -     -     -     - | 1 | 2 | . | 3 |
| Aleka, (alias Ellee Burgess)     -     - | 2 | 2 | . | 4 |
| Loamhiche, (alias Harry)     -     - | - | - | . | - |
|  | 29 | 28 |  | 57 |
| SOWOCCOLO. |  |  |  |  |
| Col. John Stidham     -     -     - | 1 | 1 | 20 | 22 |
| Sally Stidham     -     -     -     - | - | 1 | 19 | 20 |
| Shemothelioche   -     -     -     - | 3 | 2 | . | 5 |
| Jack Stidham     -     -     -     - | 1 | 1 | . | 2 |
| Michael Stidham  -     -     -     - | 1 | 1 | . | 2 |
| William Stidham  -     -     -     - | 1 | - | 3 | 4 |
| Micco Marhe     -     -     -     - | 1 | 2 | . | 3 |
| Neharlockoyoholo     -     -     - | 3 | 5 | . | 8 |
| Emarthlarharjo   -     -     -     - | 5 | 1 | . | 6 |
| Olarte   -     -     -     -     - | 1 | 2 | . | 3 |
| Parhoscharjo     -     -     -     - | 1 | 2 | . | 3 |
| Nartowarke     -     -     -     - | 1 | 1 | . | 2 |
| Chokotenehar     -     -     -     - | 2 | 3 | . | 5 |
| Sallotka   -     -     -     -     - | 1 | 2 | . | 3 |
| Kuntallaharjo     -     -     -     - | 2 | 1 | . | 3 |
| Kotchar Yoholo   -     -     -     - | 2 | 4 | . | 6 |
| Tukkosarfixico   -     -     -     - | 2 | 1 | . | 3 |
| Okechun Harjo    -     -     -     - | 3 | 3 | . | 6 |
| Oktiarche     -     -     -     - | 1 | 1 | . | 2 |

CREEK CENSUS—Continued.

| Names of Heads of Families. | Males. | Females. | Slaves. | Total. |
|---|---|---|---|---|
| Miccoche . . . . . | 1 | 3 | . | 4 |
| Harparke . . . . . | 2 | 1 | . | 3 |
| Marsehilpe . . . . | 2 | 1 | . | 3 |
| Tetarke . . . . . | 1 | 2 | . | 3 |
| Klohe . . . . . | 1 | 2 | . | 3 |
| Thlarparla . . . . . | 3 | 1 | . | 4 |
| Alpetterharjo . . . | 1 | 2 | . | 3 |
| Chokoteharjo . . . . | 1 | 1 | . | 2 |
| Tarharye . . . . . | 1 | 1 | . | 2 |
| Saifercheke . . . . | 2 | 1 | . | 3 |
| Parne . . . . . | 1 | 1 | . | 2 |
| Sukolike . . . . . | 1 | 2 | . | 3 |
| Arwatteliggo . . . | 4 | 1 | . | 5 |
| Cowupka . . . . . | 1 | 1 | . | 2 |
| Tarkoseyoholo . . . | 2 | 3 | . | 5 |
| Heparke . . . . . | 1 | 1 | . | 2 |
| Assoneharjo . . . . | 1 | 3 | . | 4 |
| Hartshoyay . . . . | 2 | 2 | . | 4 |
| Yarhar Tustunnuckee . . | 2 | 2 | . | 4 |
| Posikay . . . . . | 1 | 1 | . | 2 |
| Arhemarhe . . . . | 1 | 2 | . | 3 |
| Tarkosemarloche . . . | 1 | 2 | . | 3 |
| Homararthle . . . . | 2 | 1 | . | 3 |
| | 67 | 71 | 42 | 180 |
| Yarhar Emarthlar . . . | 3 | 1 | . | 4 |
| Letika . . . . . | 1 | 3 | . | 4 |
| Archerhine . . . . | 1 | 1 | . | 2 |
| Sumike . . . . . | 1 | 2 | . | 3 |
| Fixico Emarthlar . . . | 1 | 1 | . | 2 |
| Mohiatke . . . . . | 1 | 2 | . | 3 |
| Koyeche . . . . . | - | 2 | . | 2 |
| Ethlomar . . . . . | 1 | 1 | . | 2 |
| Kesasse . . . . . | 3 | 2 | . | 5 |
| Ismarta . . . . . | 1 | 1 | . | 2 |
| Echarye . . . . . | 1 | 1 | . | 2 |
| Tommy Yoholo . . . | 1 | 2 | . | 3 |
| Shemeke . . . . . | 1 | 1 | . | 2 |
| Klarhoye . . . . . | 2 | 2 | . | 4 |
| | 18 | 22 | . | 40 |

COWYKA, a branch of SOWOCKCOLO.

| | | | | |
|---|---|---|---|---|
| Yoholo Micco . . . . | 5 | 2 | . | 7 |
| Emarthlar Tustunnuckee . . . | 1 | 3 | - | 4 |

CREEK CENSUS—Continued.

| Names of Heads of Families. | Males. | Females. | Slaves. | Total. |
|---|---|---|---|---|
| Emarthloche | 2 | 2 | . | 4 |
| Chottomiccoche | 3 | 3 | . | 6 |
| Kesehatcheemarthlar | 1 | 3 | . | 4 |
| Poforete | 1 | 3 | . | 4 |
| Parsockemarthlar | 2 | 2 | . | 4 |
| Okeolarthlenehar | 3 | 3 | . | 6 |
| Harlike | 1 | 2 | . | 3 |
| Okepisharjo | 1 | 1 | . | 2 |
| Olartarmeecooche | 2 | 1 | . | 3 |
| Mesepe | 3 | 3 | . | 6 |
| Tuppeyeche | 1 | 1 | . | 2 |
| Okeolartharjo | 2 | 3 | . | 5 |
| Yarharlarne | 4 | 1 | . | 5 |
| Ottose | 2 | 3 | . | 5 |
| Esarke | 1 | 1 | . | 2 |
| Tollarlarke | 1 | 1 | . | 2 |
| Chartoluste | 1 | 1 | . | 2 |
| Charley | 2 | 3 | . | 5 |
| Semenoke | 1 | 2 | . | 3 |
| Tallaseeharjo | 1 | 1 | . | 2 |
| Tarhoyilete | 1 | 1 | . | 2 |
| Kenike | 2 | 2 | . | 4 |
| Kioge | 2 | 1 | . | 3 |
| Fanny, wife of Scar Hardridge | 2 | 1 | . | 3 |
| Archewe | 1 | 3 | . | 4 |
| Leteche | 1 | 1 | . | 2 |
| Kiyarle | - | 2 | . | 2 |
| Fosehatchee Yoholo | 2 | 2 | . | 4 |
| Passkoveharjo | 1 | 2 | . | 3 |
| Soltheye | 1 | 2 | . | 3 |
| Yattowarharjo | 2 | 2 | . | 4 |
| Koweharjo | 4 | 1 | . | 5 |
| Charloharjo | 1 | 1 | . | 2 |
| Homarhocathle | 3 | 1 | . | 4 |
| Oyarfopeke | 3 | 1 | . | 4 |
| Thlathloharjo | 1 | 1 | . | 2 |
| Wuncharnarsee | 1 | 2 | . | 3 |
| Georgeehotke | 1 | 1 | . | 2 |
|  | 70 | 72 |  | 142 |
| Yanose | 1 | 2 | . | 3 |
| Ben | 1 | 2 | . | 3 |
| Karparye | 1 | 3 | . | 4 |
| Hitchhoye | - | 2 | . | 2 |
| Markte alias Warkarpoochasse | 2 | 1 | . | 3 |
|  | 5 | 10 |  | 15 |

CREEK CENSUS—Continued.

| Names of Heads of Families. | Males. | Females. | Slaves. | Total. |
|---|---|---|---|---|
| HATCHEECHUBBA. | | | | |
| Nocose Yoholo | 3 | 2 | . | 5 |
| Fose Yoholo | 1 | 1 | . | 2 |
| Tustunnuckeeharjo | 2 | 2 | . | 4 |
| Kunchartee Yoholo | 3 | 2 | . | 5 |
| Shehiya | 4 | 2 | . | 6 |
| Fosehatch Emarthlar | 3 | 1 | . | 4 |
| Cowpuktoharjo | 2 | 2 | . | 4 |
| Tokkoseharjo | 1 | 1 | . | 2 |
| Karpikche Marthlar | 4 | 2 | . | 6 |
| Chokoteharjo | 3 | 1 | . | 4 |
| Kosarharjo | 1 | 1 | . | 2 |
| Kosiste Yoholo | 2 | 1 | . | 3 |
| Semanarlake | 1 | 1 | . | 2 |
| Yoholoharjo | 1 | 2 | . | 3 |
| Hoteseharjo | 1 | 1 | . | 2 |
| Klarsecharwe | 1 | 3 | . | 4 |
| Stintochepohe | 1 | 1 | . | 2 |
| Sarsar | 1 | 1 | . | 2 |
| Cowupika | 1 | 1 | . | 2 |
| Milthhoya | 1 | 1 | . | 2 |
| Tuckabatcheharjo | 2 | 1 | . | 3 |
| Warlar | 1 | 2 | . | 3 |
| Tukkonosar | 3 | 2 | . | 5 |
| Klasarhoye | 1 | 2 | . | 3 |
| Sarharnoke | 1 | 4 | . | 5 |
| Klarsoharwe | . | 4 | . | 4 |
| Partarke | 2 | 2 | . | 4 |
| Yohologe | 2 | 2 | . | 4 |
| Semoppehoye | 1 | 1 | . | 2 |
| Shofarharke | 1 | 1 | . | 2 |
| | 51 | 50 | | 101 |
| PALOCHOKOLO. | | | | |
| Tustunnuck Harjo | 4 | 3 | . | 7 |
| Kotchar Micco | 2 | . | . | 2 |
| Tolowar Micco | 1 | 4 | . | 5 |
| Hoparyoche | 3 | 1 | . | 4 |
| Hotulke | 2 | 2 | . | 4 |
| Kunchartharjo | 3 | 4 | . | 7 |
| Foseharjo | 2 | 2 | . | 4 |
| Timmarleche | 1 | 2 | . | 3 |
| Tokkosarharjo | 3 | 1 | . | 4 |
| Chokkoliche | 1 | 1 | . | 2 |
| Lowwechar | 1 | 1 | . | 2 |

44‡

CREEK CENSUS—Continued.

| Names of Heads of Families. | Males. | Females. | Slaves. | Total. |
|---|---|---|---|---|
| Homarhodar . . . . . | 1 | 2 | . | 3 |
| Yokone . . . . . . | 1 | 1 | . | 2 |
| Muttehika . . . . . | 2 | 1 | . | 3 |
| Seenitcha . . . . . | 2 | 1 | . | 3 |
| Upiechiche . . . . . | 1 | 1 | . | 2 |
| Chetiyike . . . . . | 1 | 3 | . | 4 |
| Yolthhoeche . . . . . | 2 | 3 | . | 5 |
| Taskeke . . . . . | 1 | 4 | . | 5 |
| Harthlisya . . . . . | 1 | 1 | . | 2 |
| Saffolotehoke . . . . . | 1 | 3 | . | 4 |
| | 36 | 41 | | 77 |
| TOLOWARTHLOCKO, a branch of Paklochokolo. | | | | |
| Nocosiekar . . . . | 3 | 1 | . | 4 |
| Tussekiemarthlar . . . . | 2 | 4 | . | 6 |
| Neharthlockoharjo . . . | 5 | 3 | . | 8 |
| Kotcharharjo . . . . | 1 | 1 | . | 2 |
| Farharjo . . . . | 2 | 1 | . | 3 |
| Stemetache . . . . | 1 | 1 | . | 2 |
| Tolowarharjo . . . . | 2 | 1 | . | 3 |
| Chocoteyoholo . . . . | 1 | 1 | . | 2 |
| Tukkosar Yoholo . . . . | 3 | 2 | . | 5 |
| Yoholo Chopko . . . . | 3 | 3 | . | 6 |
| Harpiukharjo . . . . | 3 | 2 | . | 5 |
| Chewastarye . . . . | 2 | . | . | 2 |
| Yartowarharjo . . . . | 1 | 1 | . | 2 |
| Chockhoelar . . . . | 2 | 1 | . | 3 |
| Emarthlar . . . . | 3 | . | . | 3 |
| Klarsarye . . . . | 1 | 1 | . | 2 |
| Tarpocheche . . . . | 1 | 1 | . | 2 |
| Choharjo . . . . | 2 | . | . | 2 |
| Hesarke . . . . | 1 | 1 | . | 2 |
| Tuthlepooche . . . . | 1 | 1 | . | 2 |
| Sarhoye . . . . | 2 | 2 | . | 4 |
| Folotika . . . . | 1 | 1 | . | 2 |
| Martarye . . . . | 1 | 1 | . | 2 |
| Tarlartege . . . . | 1 | 2 | . | 3 |
| Thlarpe . . . . | . | 4 | . | 4 |
| Chintarle . . . . | 2 | 1 | . | 3 |
| Sueloka . . . . | 1 | 1 | . | 2 |
| Honeseharjo . . . . | 1 | 1 | . | 2 |
| Pisshoketa . . . . | 1 | 3 | . | 4 |
| Sholotehoka . . . . | . | 2 | . | 2 |
| Fiitshoya . . . . | 1 | 2 | 1 | 4 |
| Chatto Micco . . . . | 3 | 1 | . | 4 |

CREEK CENSUS—Continued.

| Names of Heads of Families. | Males. | Females. | Slaves. | Total. |
|---|---|---|---|---|
| Tohowallapika . . . . | 1 | 1 | . | 2 |
| Parlarthley . . . . | 1 | 3 | . | 4 |
| Chowhoye . . . . | 2 | 1 | 5 | 8 |
| Yelkaharjo . . . . | 3 | . | . | 3 |
| Kotcharfixico . . . . | 3 | 2 | . | 5 |
| Honesar . . . . | 1 | 2 | . | 3 |
| Selarchee . . . . | 2 | 2 | . | 4 |
| Sutsaharkar . . . . | 1 | 3 | . | 4 |
| Tukosar Micco . . . . | 3 | 5 | . | 8 |
| | 71 | 66 | 6 | 143 |
| Yarkinhar Miccooche . . . | 1 | 1 | . | 2 |
| Arsimhoye . . . . | 1 | 1 | . | 2 |
| Sehechepe . . . . | 1 | 1 | . | 2 |
| Litchar . . . . | 1 | 1 | . | 2 |
| Issheweloya . . . . | . | 3 | . | 3 |
| Okepis Yoholo . . . . | 2 | . | . | 2 |
| | 6 | 7 | | 13 |

HITCHETEE.

| | Males. | Females. | Slaves. | Total. |
|---|---|---|---|---|
| Nulkarpucke Tustunnuckee . . | 1 | 1 | - | 2 |
| Tustunnuk Chopko . . . | 2 | 1 | - | 3 |
| Otalka Tustunnuckee . . . | 3 | 1 | - | 4 |
| Kochokoneharjo . . . . | 2 | 2 | - | 4 |
| Neharharjo . . . . | 2 | 2 | - | 4 |
| Okeolarthleharjo . . . . | 4 | 2 | - | 6 |
| Neharthlocko . . . . | 3 | 2 | - | 5 |
| Chonekay . . . . | 2 | 3 | - | 5 |
| Chokoteyoholo . . . . | 3 | 1 | - | 4 |
| Honeseharjo . . . . | 3 | 1 | - | 4 |
| Yartowarharjo . . . . | 1 | 1 | - | 2 |
| Sikkomaryhe . . . . | 2 | 2 | - | 4 |
| Nepike . . . . | 1 | 2 | - | 3 |
| Sowartarle . . . . | 2 | 2 | - | 4 |
| Semunnutskay . . . . | 1 | 3 | - | 4 |
| Parchese . . . . | 2 | 1 | - | 3 |
| Warcholey . . . . | 3 | 1 | - | 4 |
| Nittiheche . . . . | 3 | 1 | - | 4 |
| Chocotemarthlar . . . . | 4 | 3 | - | 7 |
| Hosiche . . . . | 2 | 1 | - | 3 |
| Mihetechay . . . . | 1 | 1 | - | 2 |
| Hesparhe . . . . | 2 | 1 | - | 3 |
| Thlarlike . . . . | 2 | 1 | - | 3 |
| Klochopike . . . . | 1 | 3 | - | 4 |
| Arpiuckharjo . . . . | 3 | 1 | - | 4 |

## CREEK CENSUS—Continued.

| Names of Heads of Families. | Males: | Females. | Slaves. | Total. |
|---|---|---|---|---|
| Timholartike | 1 | 3 | - | 4 |
| Tukkosarharjo | 1 | 2 | - | 3 |
| Tokothlike | 3 | 1 | - | 4 |
| Shemarharke | 2 | 2 | - | 4 |
| Money | 2 | 2 | - | 4 |
| Yothlike | 3 | 1 | - | 4 |
| Arsepooche | 2 | 4 | - | 6 |
| Yarkarmikay | 4 | 1 | - | 5 |
| Melintay | 1 | 1 | - | 2 |
| Satarhike | 3 | 2 | .. | 5 |
| Meliya | 1 | 1 | - | 2 |
| Ninnechuppaharjo | 3 | 2 | - | 5 |
| Tihoye | 1 | 3 | - | 4 |
| Charleche | 1 | 1 | - | 2 |
| Mullitke | 1 | 1 | - | 2 |
| Warkike | 3 | 3 | - | 6 |
|  | 85 | 70 |  | 155 |
| Pokche | 3 | 1 | - | 4 |
| Hospotokharjo | 3 | 2 | - | 5 |
| Lippe | 2 | 2 | - | 4 |
| Futsharye | 1 | 1 | - | 2 |
| Teseoke | 1 | 1 | - | 2 |
| Sally | 1 | 1 | 18 | 20 |
| Losannah | - | 1 | 2 | 3 |
| Seharparyay | 1 | 2 | - | 3 |
| Palparhoke | 1 | 2 | - | 3 |
| Kolarshartay | 1 | 1 | - | 2 |
| Dimsey | 1 | 1 | - | 2 |
| Staparharke | 1 | 1 | - | 2 |
| Sattehike | - | 2 | - | 2 |
| Welokoeche | - | 2 | - | 2 |
| Chojar | 1 | 1 | - | 2 |
| Seeartoochee | 3 | 1 | - | 4 |
| Chuckhike | 1 | 3 | - | 4 |
| Semetetarye | 1 | 1 | - | 2 |
| Sofoliya | 1 | 1 | - | 2 |
| Kinhe | 1 | 2 | - | 3 |
| Hosikay | 2 | 1 | - | 3 |
| Iskoyeche | 1 | 3 | - | 4 |
| Sumikey | 2 | 1 | - | 3 |
| Larhowe | 1 | 1 | - | 2 |
| Winey | 1 | 1 | - | 2 |
| Isfoleche | 1 | 1 | .. | 2 |
| Cussetawharjo | 1 | 1 | - | 2 |

CREEK CENSUS—Continued.

| Names of Heads of Families. | Males. | Females. | Slaves. | Total. |
|---|---|---|---|---|
| Oktiarcheharjo . . . . | 3 | 2 | - | 5 |
| Sowarke . . . . . | 2 | 3 | - | 5 |
| Pity . . . . . | - | 2 | - | 2 |
| Nokefarke . . . . | 1 | 1 | - | 2 |
| Stewunharye . . . . | 1 | 1 | - | 2 |
| Tomiche . . . . | 1 | 1 | - | 2 |
| Arkoyike . . . . | 3 | 2 | - | 5 |
| Arseche . . . . . | 2 | 1 | - | 3 |
| Holotoke . . . . . | 2 | 2 | - | 4 |
| Temihethle . . . . | 1 | 1 | - | 2 |
| Daniel Gray . . . . | 2 | 1 | - | 3 |
| Archewyche . . . . | 2 | 1 | - | 3 |
| Micoharjo . . . . | 3 | 2 | - | 5 |
| Towwarkeeche . . . | 1 | 1 | - | 2 |
| Yartoochi . . . . . | 1 | 1 | - | 2 |
| Pufhikay . . . . . | 4 | 4 | - | 8 |
| | 62 | 64 | 20 | 146 |
| Kunchartee . . . . | 3 | 1 | . | 4 |
| Kussarhole . . . . | 1 | 1 | . | 2 |
| Fossehatch Yoholo . . | 3 | 2 | . | 5 |
| Chokoteharjo . . . | 3 | 3 | . | 6 |
| Sathoye . . . . | 3 | 1 | . | 4 |
| Tosarlarye . . . . | — | 2 | . | 2 |
| Marteke . . . . | 1 | 1 | . | 2 |
| Timpoche . . . . | 1 | 1 | . | 2 |
| Mishoyo . . . . | — | 2 | . | 2 |
| Sarpuckoleche . . . | 1 | 2 | . | 3 |
| Marwetinne . . . . | 1 | 1 | . | 2 |
| | 17 | 17 | . | 34 |

HIHAJE, (a branch of the Hitchetee).

| Names of Heads of Families. | Males. | Females. | Slaves. | Total. |
|---|---|---|---|---|
| Tustunnucckee . . . | 1 | 2 | . | 3 |
| Chochemike . . . . | 1 | 1 | . | 2 |
| Kosarharjo . . . . | 5 | 2 | • | 7 |
| Sarhopethle . . . . | 2 | 1 | . | 3 |
| Bucke . . . . . | 1 | 1 | . | 2 |
| Issey . . . . . | 1 | 1 | . | 2 |
| Killey . . . . . | 3 | 1 | . | 4 |
| Murwelarkay . . . | 1 | 1 | . | 2 |
| Klarsaryay . . . . | 1 | 3 | . | 4 |
| Artallaryay . . . . | 1 | 3 | . | 4 |
| Markoeche . . . . | 1 | 1 | . | 2 |
| Suckpagekay . . . . | - | 4 | . | 4 |

## CREEK CENSUS—Continued.

| Names of Heads of Families. | Males. | Females. | Slaves. | Total. |
|---|---|---|---|---|
| Fallarlay . . . . . | . | 4 | . | 4 |
| Yarneshe . . . . . | 2 | 2 | . | 4 |
| Mistarwar . . . . . | 2 | 2 | . | 4 |
| Sofe . . . . . | 1 | 1 | . | 2 |
| Hannah, (widow of Eupolika, a free black woman) . . . . | . | 3 | . | 3 |
| | 22 | 32 | | 54 |
| HOTALLEHOYARNAR. | | | | |
| Charley Tustunnuckee . . . | 1 | 3 | . | 4 |
| Folunke . . . . . | 3 | 2 | . | 5 |
| Tarfer . . . . . | 1 | 3 | . | 4 |
| Thlathloharjo . . . . | 2 | 2 | . | 4 |
| Seeliche . . . . . | 1 | 1 | | 2 |
| Yatko . . . . . | 1 | 2 | | 3 |
| Yarfkar . . . . . | 2 | 1 | . | 3 |
| Semersey . . . . . | 1 | 1 | . | 2 |
| Thlarsemeawkey . . . . | 1 | 2 | . | 3 |
| Nittarharse . . . . | 2 | 1 | . | 3 |
| Sowwieke . . . . . | 1 | 1 | . | 2 |
| Seeotiche . . . . . | 2 | 1 | . | 3 |
| Pinkale . . . . . | 1 | 3 | . | 4 |
| Motta . . . . . | 1 | 1 | . | 2 |
| Challoe . . . . . | 1 | 2 | . | 3 |
| Muttakar . . . . . | . | 3 | . | 3 |
| Lomarhokar . . . . | 1 | 3 | . | 4 |
| Merseho . . . . . | 1 | 1 | . | 2 |
| Timfoleechkar . . . . | 2 | 2 | . | 4 |
| Senokkar . . . . . | 1 | 2 | . | 3 |
| Sechocke . . . . . | . | 2 | . | 2 |
| Sattakar . . . . . | 1 | 3 | . | 4 |
| Euparhoythle . . . . | 2 | 3 | . | 5 |
| Scisse . . . . . | 1 | 1 | . | 2 |
| John Sims . . . . . | 1 | 1 | 6 | 8 |
| Timfolochiche . . . . | 1 | 1 | . | 2 |
| Yarskar . . . . . | . | 2 | . | 2 |
| | 32 | 50 | 6 | 88 |
| CHEHAWAH. | | | | |
| John Oponnee . . . . | 3 | 1 | 19 | 23 |
| Nocose Yoholo . . . . | 2 | 4 | . | 6 |
| Harpiukharjo . . . . | 2 | 1 | . | 3 |
| Neharthlocko . . . . | 3 | 1 | . | 4 |
| Karpicchar . . . . | 3 | 2 | . | 5 |
| Letifharjo . . . . . | 2 | 1 | . | 3 |
| Ingkootar . . . . . | 1 | 1 | . | 2 |

CREEK CENSUS—Continued.

| Names of Heads of Families. | Males. | Females. | Slaves. | Total. |
|---|---|---|---|---|
| Okee Tustunnuckee, (alias Washington) . | 3 | 3 | . | 6 |
| Kochokonarharjo . . . . | 4 | 7 | 7 | 18 |
| Kotcharharcooche . . . . | 2 | 3 | . | 5 |
| Kesehatch Yoholo . . . . | 2 | 4 | . | 6 |
| Thlarhike . . . . . | 3 | 2 | . | 5 |
| Howolichay . . . . | 2 | 2 | . | 4 |
| Ninneomarthlar Tustunnuckee . . | 3 | 2 | . | 5 |
| Chehawharjo . . . . | 2 | 2 | . | 4 |
| Eupoyithle . . . . | 4 | 4 | . | 8 |
| Yarkar Mitche . . . . | 2 | 4 | . | 6 |
| Tuskonarharjo . . . . | 1 | 1 | . | 2 |
| Iskoyou . . . . . | 3 | 2 | 6 | 11 |
| Fulloharjo . . . . | 2 | 2 | . | 4 |
| Futcher . . . . . | 2 | 2 | . | 4 |
| Chokartefixico . . . . | 1 | 2 | . | 3 |
| Tewokarle . . . . . | 2 | 2 | . | 4 |
| Esarpar . . . . . | 1 | 1 | . | 2 |
| Timfulkar . . . . . | 2 | 1 | . | 3 |
| Talopethlocko . . . . | 3 | 1 | . | 4 |
| Sapparharkar . . . . | 3 | 1 | . | 4 |
| Lotay . . . . . | 2 | 2 | - | 4 |
| Mochusse . . . . | 1 | 2 | - | 3 |
| Neharthlockoharjo . . . | 1 | 2 | - | 3 |
| Taylor . . . . . | 2 | 1 | - | 3 |
| Chiley . . . . . | 1 | 1 | - | 2 |
| Noche . . . . . | 1 | 1 | - | 2 |
| Sockposarte . . . . | 1 | 2 | - | 3 |
| Keselar . . . . . | 1 | 1 | - | 2 |
| Kiarpike . . . . . | 2 | 1 | - | 3 |
| Kowosay . . . . . | 1 | 1 | - | 2 |
| Seleeko . . . . . | 1 | 2 | - | 3 |
| Echoharjo . . . . . | 1 | 1 | - | 2 |
| Kussarme . . . . . | 1 | 1 | - | 2 |
| Eupusser . . . . . | 1 | 1 | - | 2 |
| | 80 | 78 | 32 | 190 |
| Sarpulse . . . . . | 1 | 1 | - | 2 |
| Sartokkarke . . . . | 2 | 3 | - | 5 |
| Eley . . . . . | 1 | 1 | 11 | 13 |
| Scihethle . . . . | 1 | 1 | - | 2 |
| Sinarhothle . . . . | 1 | 1 | - | 2 |
| Towallarpoke . . . . | 1 | 2 | - | 3 |
| Saffolotehoke . . . . | 1 | 1 | - | 2 |
| Lihakar . . . . . | 2 | 4 | - | 6 |
| Tarlkey . . . . . | 2 | 1 | - | 3 |
| Harlothoke . . . . | 1 | 1 | - | 2 |

## CREEK CENSUS—Continued.

| Names of Heads of Families. | Males. | Females. | Slaves. | Total. |
|---|---|---|---|---|
| Sechetoke . . . . . | 2 | 3 | - | 5 |
| Tikar . . . . . | - | 3 | - | 3 |
| Tofopike . . . . . | - | 3 | - | 3 |
| Yolthhokar . . . . | 2 | 2 | - | 4 |
| Sathoye . . . . . | - | 5 | - | 5 |
| Temokarke . . . . | - | 2 | - | 2 |
| Letey . . . . . | 3 | 3 | 5 | 11 |
| Liley . . . . . | - | 2 | 5 | 7 |
| Somechar . . . . | 3 | 2 | - | 5 |
| Singkarye . . . . | 1 | 1 | - | 2 |
| Yekeeseho . . . . | 2 | 1 | - | 3 |
| Parley . . . . . | 1 | 2 | - | 3 |
| Timpokietay . . . . | 2 | 2 | - | 4 |
| Nokitchkar . . . . | 1 | 1 | - | 2 |
| Osooch Yoholo . . . | 1 | 4 | - | 5 |
| Lappootike . . . . | 3 | 2 | - | 5 |
| Efolo Yoholo . . . . | 1 | 1 | - | 2 |
| Tewuckharye . . . . | 4 | 2 | - | 6 |
| Nartalley . . . . | 1 | 2 | - | 3 |
| Narpharjo . . . . | 4 | 1 | - | 5 |
| Futshiye . . . . | 2 | 3 | - | 5 |
| Kelissar . . . . | 6 | 1 | - | 7 |
| Yatho . . . . . | 1 | 1 | - | 2 |
| Esarkey . . . . | 2 | 1 | - | 3 |
| Semartoke . . . . | 1 | 2 | - | 3 |
| Tieche . . . . . | 1 | 2 | - | 3 |
| Lucky . . . . . | 1 | 2 | - | 3 |
| Weloseho . . . . | - | 2 | - | 2 |
| Toharte . . . . | 1 | 1 | - | 2 |
| Parnokowelarke . . . | 3 | 2 | - | 5 |
| Keney . . . . . | 1 | 1 | - | 2 |
| Kowe . . . . . | 1 | 2 | - | 3 |
| Soparkar . . . . | 1 | 1 | - | 2 |
| | 65 | 81 | 21 | 167 |
| Dial, (alias Tiole,) . . . | 1 | 1 | 6 | 8 |
| Klarfulke . . . . | 4 | 1 | 2 | 7 |
| Thlewarley . . . . | 1 | 1 | - | 2 |
| Fanny . . . . . | 2 | 1 | - | 3 |
| Peke . . . . . | - | 2 | - | 2 |
| Hehunkar . . , . | - | 2 | - | 2 |
| Judy . . . . . | - | 2 | - | 2 |
| Sandy Perryman, (a free Black,) . | 3 | 2 | - | 5 |
| | 11 | 12 | 8 | 31 |

CREEK CENSUS—Continued.

| Names of Heads of Families. | Males. | Females. | Slaves. | Total. |
|---|---|---|---|---|
| OSWICHEE, (on the Chattahooche River.) | | | | |
| Parhose Emarthlar . . . | 4 | 2 | - | 6 |
| Foseharjo . . . . . | 1 | 1 | - | 2 |
| Charley Emarthlar . . . | 3 | 3 | 2 | 8 |
| Efuloharjo . . . . | 1 | 1 | .. | 2 |
| Opioke Yoholo . . . | 1 | 2 | - | 3 |
| Yorkey . . . . | 3 | – | - | 3 |
| Chocoteharjo, or Jacob, . . . | 3 | 3 | - | 6 |
| Nehar Yoholo . . . . | 3 | 1 | - | 4 |
| Konofixico . . . . | 1 | 3 | - | 4 |
| Tuckabatche Yoholo . . . | 2 | 2 | - | 4 |
| Choarchooche . . . . | 4 | 6 | - | 10 |
| Thlathlofixico . . . | 2 | 4 | - | 6 |
| Intosarkey . . . . | 1 | 1 | - | 2 |
| Thlockposwar . . . . | 2 | 2 | - | 4 |
| Toppusharjo . . . . | 1 | 1 | - | 2 |
| Sehokar . . . . | 2 | 1 | - | 3 |
| Tewassoomme . . . . | 1 | 1 | - | 2 |
| Cho Emarthlar . . . . | 2 | 4 | - | 6 |
| Challar . . . . | 1 | 1 | - | 2 |
| Kinkehe . . . . | 2 | 1 | - | 3 |
| Atkecharwe . . . . | 1 | 2 | - | 3 |
| Hiekiche . . . . | 1 | 1 | - | 2 |
| Ekiske . . . . | 2 | 1 | - | 3 |
| George (or Georgy) . . . | 1 | 1 | - | 2 |
| Nilcup Yoholo . . . . | 3 | 1 | - | 4 |
| Kolleseharjo . . . . | 1 | 2 | - | 3 |
| Marfolote . . . . | 2 | 2 | - | 4 |
| Oparye . . . . | 5 | 1 | - | 6 |
| Kelissarharjo . . . . | 1 | 1 | - | 2 |
| Chooeley . . . . | 2 | 2 | - | 4 |
| Itcharwike . . . . | 1 | 2 | - | 3 |
| Chiarye . . . . | 1 | 1 | - | 2 |
| Tartoseke . . . . | 2 | 1 | - | 3 |
| Penote . . . . | 1 | 1 | - | 2 |
| Shemelar . . . . | 1 | 1 | - | 2 |
| Chockkoeche . . . . | 1 | 1 | - | 2 |
| Oaspartokfixico . . . . | 1 | 2 | - | 3 |
| Spokeokeharjo . . . . | 1 | 1 | - | 2 |
| Charmelar . . . . | 1 | 1 | - | 2 |
| Chefarle . . . . | 1 | 1 | - | 2 |
| Tewattarche . . . . | 1 | 1 | - | 2 |
| Sappohokar . . . . | 1 | 1 | - | 2 |
| | 72 | 68 | 2 | 142 |

CREEK CENSUS—Continued.

| Names of Heads of Families. | Males. | Females. | Slaves. | Total. |
|---|---|---|---|---|
| Tekinkar . . . . . | 1 | 1 | - | 2 |
| Talmochasharjo . . . . | 1 | 1 | - | 2 |
| Hochepe - . . . . | 1 | 1 | - | 2 |
| Hohike . . . . . | 1 | 1 | - | 2 |
| Yumkar . . . . . | 1 | 1 | - | 2 |
| Sockharlofekay . . . . | 1 | 3 | - | 4 |
| Feharyhe . . . . . | 1 | 1 | - | 2 |
| Isfoleche . . . . . | 1 | 1 | - | 2 |
| Chocksehokar . . . . | 2 | 2 | - | 4 |
| Sally . . . . . | 2 | 4 | 1 | 7 |
| Thleniya . . . . . | — | 2 | - | 2 |
| Thlarlarke . . . . . | 1 | 1 | - | 2 |
| Atupike . . . . . | — | 2 | 1 | 3 |
| Honetar . . . . . | 2 | 1 | - | 3 |
| Ochote . . . . . | 2 | 2 | - | 4 |
| Katey . . . . . | 3 | 2 | 4 | 9 |
| Otarke . . . . . | 1 | 2 | - | 3 |
| Stingkarke . . . . | 1 | 4 | - | 5 |
| Folotike . . . . . | 2 | 2 | - | 4 |
| Chokkothle . . . . | 2 | 1 | - | 3 |
| Sarpehe (or Old Billy) . . | 1 | 1 | - | 2 |
| Farlennar . . . . | 5 | — | - | 5 |
| Marlosetar . . . . | 1 | 1 | - | 2 |
| Sowhosekar . . . . | 2 | 2 | - | 4 |
| Fulleche . . . . . | — | 4 | - | 4 |
| Tenarsey . . . . . | 1 | 2 | - | 3 |
| Sattarhike . . . . | 1 | 2 | - | 3 |
| Osokey . . . . . | 1 | 1 | - | 2 |
| Singcoolkar . . . . | 1 | 1 | - | 2 |
| Arsenoche . . . . | 2 | 2 | - | 4 |
| Lumhiche . . . . . | 1 | 1 | - | 2 |
| Arswelarkey . . . . | 1 | 1 | - | 2 |
| Konepe Marthlar . . . | 1 | 1 | - | 2 |
| Sockhollar . . . . | 2 | 1 | - | 3 |
| Tallehechar . . . . | 1 | 1 | - | 2 |
| Letifharjo . . . . . | 1 | 2 | - | 3 |
| Tethlekar . . . . . | 2 | 2 | - | 4 |
| Ehomer . . . . . | 2 | 2 | - | 4 |
| Stehechepe . . . . | — | 2 | - | 2 |
| Emarthlarthlocko . . . | 2 | — | - | 2 |
| | 54 | 64 | 6 | 124 |

OSWITCHEE,
*On the waters of Opillike Hatchee.*

| | | | | |
|---|---|---|---|---|
| Oktiarcheharjo . . . . | 1 | 1 | - | 2 |
| Shockhoethlar . . . . | 1 | 1 | - | 2 |

CREEK CENSUS—Continued.

| Names of Heads of Families. | Males. | Females. | Slaves. | Total. |
|---|---|---|---|---|
| Yoholoharjo        .    .    .    . | 1 | 1 | - | 2 |
| Konipharjo         .    .    .    . | 3 | 3 | - | 6 |
| Choloke Emarthlar       .    .    . | 2 | 3 | - | 5 |
| Harpikcharharjo    .    .    .    . | 1 | 1 | - | 2 |
| Fekiye       .    .    .    .    . | 1 | 1 | - | 2 |
| Alpetterharjo      .    .    .    . | 2 | 1 | - | 3 |
| Cheparne     .    .    .    .    . | 2 | 1 | - | 3 |
| Sowwarheche        .    .    .    . | 1 | 2 | - | 3 |
| Koweharjo          .    .    .    . | 1 | 3 | - | 4 |
| Parchesehoye       .    .    .    . | 1 | 1 | - | 2 |
| Polly        .    .    .    .    . | . | 3 | - | 3 |
| Nehemarthlar       .    .    .    . | 2 | 4 | - | 6 |
| Tarsarye     .    .    .    .    . | 2 | 2 | - | 4 |
| Starhoyar    .    .    .    .    . | 2 | 1 | - | 3 |
| Fotchko      .    .    .    .    . | 1 | 2 | - | 3 |
| Sekiyarpe    .    .    .    .    . | 2 | 1 | - | 3 |
| Chockkarthle       .    .    .    . | 1 | 1 | - | 2 |
| Ishoniyay    .    .    .    .    . | 1 | 1 | - | 2 |
| Upowhothle         .    .    .    . | 1 | 2 | - | 3 |
| Sarpokole    .    .    .    .    . | . | 3 | - | 3 |
| Ismaryar     .    .    .    .    . | 2 | 2 | - | 4 |
| Summarle     .    .    .    .    . | 2 | 2 | - | 4 |
| Fixico       .    .    .    .    . | 2 | - | 1 | 3 |
| Tosey        .    .    .    .    . | 1 | 1 | - | 2 |
| Chockkarye         .    .    .    . | 6 | 1 | - | 7 |
| Scehelarpike       .    .    .    . | 1 | 3 | - | 4 |
| Larpkar      .    .    .    .    . | 2 | 1 | - | 3 |
| Etohone      .    .    .    .    . | 2 | 1 | - | 3 |
| Kowokkooche        .    .    .    . | 2 | 1 | - | 3 |
| Arstote      .    .    .    .    . | 1 | 1 | - | 2 |
| Hoochkarpe         .    .    .    . | 2 | 1 | - | 3 |
| Folartechar        .    .    .    . | 2 | 1 | - | 3 |
| Ishoye       .    .    .    .    . | 2 | 1 | - | 3 |
| Chewastiooche      .    .    .    . | 1 | 2 | - | 3 |
| Sokkepokar         .    .    .    . | 1 | 1 | - | 2 |
| Seethlefarke       .    .    .    . | 1 | 3 | - | 4 |
| Thlarhoethle       .    .    .    . | 2 | 1 | - | 3 |
|  | 61 | 62 | 1 | 124 |
| Polly-harye        .    .    .    . | 1 | 2 | - | 3 |
| Ispeye       .    .    .    .    . | 1 | 2 | - | 3 |
| Homarhote          .    .    .    . | 2 | 1 | - | 3 |
| Seeharnikay        .    .    .    . | 2 | 3 | - | 5 |
| Pulparhooche       .    .    .    . | 2 | 2 | - | 4 |
| Titarke      .    .    .    .    . | 2 | 1 | - | 3 |

CREEK CENSUS—Continued.

| Names of Heads of Families. | Males. | Females. | Slaves. | Total. |
|---|---|---|---|---|
| Tolowarharjo | 1 | 1 | - | 2 |
| Fopechay | 1 | 1 | - | 2 |
| Narharfitay | 1 | 2 | - | 3 |
| Fickhoniye | 2 | 1 | - | 3 |
| Martarye | 1 | 2 | - | 3 |
| Lowso | 1 | 1 | - | 2 |
| Sukey | 1 | 2 | - | 3 |
| Lekotehar | 2 | 2 | - | 4 |
| Hoyiche (or Sally) | 1 | 1 | - | 2 |
| Niteley | 2 | 1 | - | 3 |
| Kolcharyoholo | 1 | 3 | - | 4 |
| Marhoeke | 1 | 1 | - | 2 |
| Islotte | 4 | 1 | - | 5 |
| Omararthle | 2 | 2 | - | 4 |
| Chimlar | 1 | 1 | - | 2 |
| Okemulke Emarthlar | 4 | 3 | - | 7 |
| Soaster | 2 | 5 | - | 7 |
| Thlockpuse Emarthlar | 3 | 1 | - | 4 |
| Sathoyiche | 2 | 1 | - | 3 |
| Hocharche (or Jenny) | 1 | 2 | - | 3 |
| Hitchhokay | 2 | 1 | - | 3 |
| Sockarkey | 2 | 1 | - | 3 |
| Sceatarwe | 4 | 1 | - | 5 |
| Piecheche | 1 | 2 | - | 3 |
| Nocoseille | 1 | 1 | - | 2 |
| Harharlokharjo | 1 | 1 | - | 2 |
| Parheche | 1 | 1 | - | 2 |
| Sinhikatke | 1 | 1 | - | 2 |
| Mittehose | 2 | 2 | - | 4 |
| Thlesarhowe | 4 | 1 | - | 5 |
| Mattoye | 2 | 1 | - | 3 |
| Islotkey | 2 | 1 | - | 3 |
| Tewarhar | 1 | 3 | - | 4 |
| Yattekar | 1 | 1 | - | 2 |
| | 73 | 66 | | 139 |
| | | | | |
| Timfulheechkar | 1 | 1 | - | 2 |
| Aryarlar | 1 | 1 | - | 2 |
| Nartomiche | 3 | 5 | - | 8 |
| Usley | 1 | 1 | - | 2 |
| | 6 | 8 | | 14 |

EUCHE (on the waters of the Chatahouchee.)

| | | | | |
|---|---|---|---|---|
| Yarharharjo | 1 | 3 | - | 4 |
| Kolchar Tustunnuckee | 6 | 3 | - | 9 |

CREEK CENSUS—Continued.

| Names of Heads of Families. | Males. | Females. | Slaves. | Total. |
|---|---|---|---|---|
| Harlockyoholo | 2 | 1 | - | 3 |
| Tustunnuckharjo | 1 | 1 | - | 2 |
| Cussena Barnard | 4 | 6 | 6 | 16 |
| Tustunnuckeechopke | 1 | 2 | - | 3 |
| Tustunnuckeechartee | 2 | - | - | 2 |
| Mullekey | 3 | 1 | - | 4 |
| Yowwethlar (or Ben) | 2 | 2 | - | 4 |
| Yatarsarlthay | 1 | 1 | - | 2 |
| Konkarlthharnay | 1 | 2 | - | 3 |
| Attelay | 2 | 2 | - | 4 |
| Eulohotay | 2 | 3 | - | 5 |
| Touhonay | 1 | 3 | - | 4 |
| Akkoteelhay | 2 | 1 | - | 3 |
| Suckkequarhar | 6 | 2 | - | 8 |
| Sanheharparquarhar (or Sam Brown) | 3 | 1 | - | 4 |
| Yattarkohowe | 4 | 2 | - | 6 |
| Tesharsarltharnay | 2 | 2 | - | 4 |
| Killekohethlarnay | 1 | 2 | - | 3 |
| Charkkoyarthlay | 2 | 1 | - | 3 |
| Yartekotər | 2 | 2 | - | 4 |
| Akkohaintletay | 2 | 3 | - | 5 |
| Songteelhay | 3 | 2 | - | 5 |
| Shooquarhar | 1 | 2 | - | 3 |
|  | 63 | 58 | 6 | 127 |
| Eufarkowe | 1 | 1 | - | 2 |
| Artarkohenay | 2 | 1 | - | 3 |
| Tarsarlthay | 2 | 1 | - | 3 |
| Quarhay | 4 | 2 | - | 6 |
| Artho | 2 | 1 | - | 3 |
| Kayhartanay | 4 | 1 | - | 5 |
| Wiunkquarhar | 1 | 1 | - | 2 |
| Yustaahartunne | 2 | 1 | - | 3 |
| Kartarhailthyona | 2 | 2 | - | 4 |
| Sarko-oontkoonthlenay | 3 | 2 | - | 5 |
| Skarke | 3 | 2 | - | 5 |
| Tartekoneshay | 3 | 1 | - | 4 |
| Hatappefar | 2 | 1 | - | 3 |
| Suyarnay | 1 | 1 | - | 2 |
| Shushiye | 2 | 1 | - | 3 |
| Sharkhowithlarnay | 1 | 3 | - | 4 |
| Sharltenay | 1 | 1 | - | 2 |
| Tayownstaynay | 2 | 1 | - | 3 |
| Kelefassa | 2 | — | - | 2 |
| Topinlaartinney | 2 | 1 | - | 3 |

CREEK CENSUS—Continued.

| Names of Heads of Families. | Males. | Females. | Slaves. | Total. |
|---|---|---|---|---|
| Kekoko-oonthlarna (alias John) | 1 | 3 | - | 4 |
| Kowetinnay | 1 | 2 | - | 3 |
| Koushonay | 3 | 2 | - | 5 |
| Koathhenchenay | 1 | 2 | - | 3 |
| Shackunshar | 5 | 1 | - | 6 |
| Teekoonstornay | 3 | 2 | - | 5 |
| Yarkoethlar | 1 | 1 | - | 2 |
| Sarkehay | 3 | 1 | - | 4 |
| Shearkoa | 3 | 4 | - | 7 |
| Tukkarhowe | 3 | 2 | - | 5 |
| Sheatsyar | 3 | 2 | - | 5 |
| Ourche | 2 | 4 | - | 6 |
| Kolay | 2 | 5 | - | 7 |
| Gim Barnard (or Fulloke) | 3 | 3 | 3 | 9 |
| Tothleyarkar | 1 | 2 | - | 3 |
| Kekoupornay | 2 | - | - | 2 |
| Koholay | 3 | - | - | 3 |
| Karlokkohohonay | 1 | 1 | - | 2 |
| Koartay | 1 | 1 | - | 2 |
| Hetarkoway | 1 | 1 | - | 2 |
| Shupparke | 3 | 2 | - | 5 |
| Tartefar | 2 | 3 | - | 5 |
| Scharhooye | 2 | 1 | - | 3 |
| | 92 | 70 | 3 | 165 |
| Kahartenay | 1 | 2 | - | 3 |
| Lite Sims | 2 | 1 | 2 | 5 |
| Tar Karhootay | 1 | 2 | - | 3 |
| Yarlikhowenay (or Nancy) | 1 | 4 | - | 5 |
| Kartarlay | 1 | 1 | - | 2 |
| Kooachyar | 2 | 1 | - | 3 |
| Kongseyear | 2 | 3 | - | 5 |
| Tailtheyournay (or Margaret Barnard) | - | 3 | - | 3 |
| Scittarsharthlenay | 1 | 1 | - | 2 |
| Harriet Barnard | - | 2 | 1 | 3 |
| Kowntyowaynay | 1 | 1 | - | 2 |
| Tappenay | 1 | 3 | - | 4 |
| Essawarney | 2 | 4 | - | 6 |
| Yowwithtannay | 1 | 3 | - | 4 |
| Tetarye | 2 | 1 | - | 3 |
| Okkoahonay | 1 | 1 | - | 2 |
| Satarkhoway | 1 | 1 | - | 2 |
| Tarkarkoutlarnay | 1 | 3 | - | 4 |
| Sarkhayhay | - | 2 | - | 2 |
| Jenny Barnard | 1 | 3 | - | 4 |

## CREEK CENSUS—Continued.

| Names of Heads of Families. | Males. | Females. | Slaves. | Total. |
|---|---|---|---|---|
| Tarkharnay  .    .    .    . | 1 | 2 | - | 3 |
| Pakhoethlar  .    .    .    . | 1 | 1 | - | 2 |
| Kitty Barnard  .    .    .    . | - | 2 | 4 | 6 |
| Konelewethlar  .    .    .    . | - | 3 | - | 3 |
| Nanny Barnard  .    .    .    . | 2 | 4 | 6 | 12 |
| Kotong  .    .    .    .    . | 1 | 1 | - | 2 |
| Toby Brown  .    .    .    . | 1 | 1 | - | 2 |
| Milly Brown  .    .    .    . | 1 | 1 | - | 2 |
| Jack Barnard  .    .    .    . | 1 | 2 | - | 3 |
| Koarpay  .    .    .    .    . | 2 | 1 | - | 3 |
| Fatsharwiney  .    .    .    . | 2 | 1 | - | 3 |
| Unnarwilley  .    .    .    . | 2 | - | - | 2 |
| Atorfar  .    .    .    .    . | - | 2 | - | 2 |
| Empethle .    .    .    .    . | 1 | 1 | - | 2 |
| Shouwarney  .    .    .    . | - | 2 | - | 2 |
|  | 37 | 66 | 13 | 116 |

### HIGH LOG (*Euchee.*)

| Names of Heads of Families. | Males. | Females. | Slaves. | Total. |
|---|---|---|---|---|
| Micco Chooley (or Euchee King)  .    . | 4 | 2 | - | 6 |
| Sarlthenay  .    .    .    . | 1 | 3 | - | 4 |
| Unkhar  .    .    .    .    . | 3 | 2 | - | 5 |
| Towlay  .    .    .    .    . | 1 | 1 | - | 2 |
| Pillar  .    .    .    .    . | 8 | 4 | - | 7 |
| Koyka  .    .    .    .    . | 2 | 1 | - | 3 |
| Sekohowenay  .    .    .    . | 2 | 1 | - | 3 |
| Chawkinney  .    .    .    . | 8 | 2 | - | 10 |
| Charquarhar  .    .    .    . | 2 | 1 | - | 3 |
| Cowunkethlannay .    .    .    . | 3 | 1 | - | 4 |
| Owwingkay  .    .    .    . | 3 | 2 | - | 5 |
| Fawfawnay  .    .    .    . | 3 | 2 | - | 5 |
| Kowekethlar  .    .    .    . | 3 | 1 | - | 4 |
| Kokonay  .    .    .    .    . | 2 | 3 | - | 5 |
| Topholtharnay  .    .    .    . | 2 | 2 | - | 4 |
| Eachenay  .    .    .    . | 2 | 1 | - | 3 |
| Karhay  .    .    .    .    . | 1 | 1 | - | 2 |
| Arsaywenay  .    .    .    . | 2 | 3 | - | 5 |
| Enhokeway  .    .    .    . | 2 | 7 | - | 9 |
| Arkollay  .    .    .    .    . | 2 | 1 | - | 3 |
| Arkofar  .    .    .    .    . | 3 | 1 | - | 4 |
| Sarkoontenay  .    .    .    . | 2 | 4 | - | 6 |
| Tukkose Marthlar  .    .    . | 1 | 1 | - | 2 |
| Kowykenay  .    .    .    . | 2 | 1 | - | 3 |
| Attelaway  .    .    .    .    . | 2 | 5 | - | 7 |
| Sarhontailthletay .    .    .    . | 3 | 3 | - | 6 |
| Sarkofar  .    .    .    .    . | 3 | 7 | - | 10 |
| Welartay  .    .    .    .    . | 2 | 1 | - | 3 |

## CREEK CENSUS—Continued.

| Names of Heads of Families. | Males. | Females. | Slaves. | Total. |
|---|---|---|---|---|
| Pedewithlar - - - - | — | 3 | - | 3 |
| Yarlafar - - - - | 1 | 1 | - | 2 |
| Chacharhay (or Johnny) - - - | 1 | 2 | - | 3 |
| Pohay - - - - | 2 | 1 | - | 3 |
| Ulawithlar - - - - | 2 | — | - | 2 |
| Sarkotannay - - - - | 3 | 2 | - | 5 |
| Takomeparnay - - - - | 2 | 1 | - | 3 |
| Yarkontenay - - - - | 4 | 1 | - | 5 |
| Hathekokay - - - - | 3 | 4 | - | 7 |
| Howykar - - - - | 1 | 1 | - | 2 |
| Eukolaykokowethlarnay - - | 4 | 1 | - | 5 |
| Koinsaw (alias old Brown) - - | 3 | 1 | - | 4 |
| | 95 | 82 | | 177 |
| Sheatsyar - - - - | 2 | 1 | - | 3 |
| Parkohongkay - - - - | 2 | 1 | - | 3 |
| Sicakharlay - - - - | 4 | 2 | - | 6 |
| Koyukewhay - - - - | 2 | 1 | - | 3 |
| Tarsakohowe - - - - | 4 | 3 | - | 7 |
| Tarwinay - - - - | 2 | 2 | - | 4 |
| Pethlenay - - - - | 2 | 3 | - | 5 |
| Yarstarkonthley - - - | 1 | 1 | - | 2 |
| Sartewarnay - - - - | — | 3 | - | 3 |
| Tarfannay - - - - | 1 | 1 | - | 2 |
| Konsharnay (or John) - - - | 4 | 3 | - | 7 |
| Tarkhowethlar - - - | 2 | 2 | - | 4 |
| Keartenay - - - - | 2 | 3 | - | 5 |
| Toashtoo - - - - | 1 | 1 | - | 2 |
| Arlowe - - - - | 2 | 1 | - | 3 |
| Siutonay - - - - | 3 | 4 | - | 7 |
| Kawponay - - - - | 2 | 3 | - | 5 |
| Kartarkenay - - - - | 3 | 2 | - | 5 |
| Kointhlenay - - - - | 1 | 2 | - | 3 |
| Parkenay - - - - | 2 | 1 | - | 3 |
| Siufarkontenay - - - | 3 | 1 | - | 4 |
| Thlarkowe - - - - | 3 | 2 | - | 5 |
| Uwarkay - - - - | 2 | 2 | - | 4 |
| Poteharnay - - - - | 1 | 1 | - | 2 |
| Kolenchenay - - - - | 1 | 2 | - | 3 |
| Sarkarhenthlungkay - - - | 2 | 1 | - | 3 |
| Tesharkoonshear - - - | 6 | 3 | - | 9 |
| Kowethlarcheer - - - | 3 | 1 | - | 4 |
| Kahay - - - - | 2 | 5 | - | 7 |
| Sukkarkoethlar - - - | 4 | 1 | - | 5 |
| Aparnay - - - - | 1 | 1 | - | 2 |

CREEK CENSUS—Continued.

| Names of Heads of Families. | Males. | Females. | Slaves. | Total. |
|---|---|---|---|---|
| Yarkhar | 4 | - | . | 4 |
| Thlarkonsharnay | 1 | 1 | . | 2 |
| Seetartay (alias Davy) | 1 | 1 | . | 2 |
| Kohuahanay | 2 | 1 | . | 3 |
| Shooutar | 2 | 1 | . | 3 |
| Wetearchsharnay | 1 | 1 | . | 2 |
| Yarimpethle | 1 | 2 | . | 3 |
| Tarkontay | 4 | 4 | . | 8 |
| Hachhachownfair | 4 | 3 | . | 7 |
| Uparkewethlar | 1 | 2 | . | 3 |
| Sawutonay | 5 | 1 | . | 6 |
| Tarfonnay | 1 | 1 | . | 2 |
| | 97 | 78 | | 175 |
| Tarshelay | 1 | 1 | . | 2 |
| Takkotenay | 3 | 5 | . | 8 |
| Konekar | 1 | 1 | . | 2 |
| Ukowethlar | 1 | 2 | . | 3 |
| Susoonay | 2 | 1 | . | 3 |
| Kawlehechoonay | 4 | 1 | . | 5 |
| Kosarhe | 3 | 2 | . | 5 |
| Yartarhay | 2 | 1 | . | 3 |
| Thlarhimpar | 4 | 2 | . | 6 |
| Konchenay | 1 | 1 | . | 2 |
| Kawkautonay | 1 | 2 | . | 3 |
| Pokoway | 2 | 2 | . | 4 |
| Setarkoanthsarnay | 1 | 1 | . | 2 |
| Sayukehaw | - | 2 | . | 2 |
| Kokenay | 3 | 1 | . | 4 |
| Uwarkalay | 1 | 2 | . | 3 |
| Karhenay | 1 | 1 | . | 2 |
| Temarshehar | 5 | 5 | . | 10 |
| Sarkoway | 2 | 2 | . | 4 |
| Osooche Tustunnuckee | 2 | 2 | . | 4 |
| Thlowethlar | 4 | 1 | . | 5 |
| Thlarkoonkare | 3 | 2 | . | 5 |
| Teotay | 2 | 3 | . | 5 |
| Yatsarkonkahanay | 2 | 5 | . | 7 |
| Sitharlay | 2 | 2 | . | 4 |
| Kekol y | 3 | 3 | . | 6 |
| Koho yarkanay | 2 | 3 | . | 5 |
| Kowayhaynay | 3 | 1 | . | 4 |
| Sokinhay | 5 | 2 | . | 7 |
| Sawchoonay | 3 | 1 | . | 4 |
| Sarwe (alias Joe) | 1 | 1 | . | 2 |

46‡

CREEK CENSUS—Continued.

| Names of Heads of Families. | Males. | Females. | Slaves. | Total. |
|---|---|---|---|---|
| Tarthluckquarhar . . . | 1 | 2 | - | 3 |
| Kasay . . . . | 4 | 2 | - | 6 |
| Tarkhayhanay . . . | 1 | 2 | - | 3 |
| Shackon Sharnay (alias Toby) . . | 1 | 2 | - | 3 |
| Kohowe . . . . | 2 | 1 | - | 3 |
| Hokkekotehar . . . | 2 | 2 | - | 4 |
| Koshaywe . . . | 3 | 2 | - | 5 |
| Kotennay . . . | 1 | 4 | - | 5 |
| Kottowayge . . . | 1 | 1 | - | 2 |
| Koholartay . . . | 1 | 1 | - | 2 |
| Yattarlay . . . | 2 | 4 | - | 6 |
| Tarthlarnay . . . | 1 | 1 | - | 2 |
| | 90 | 85 | | 175 |
| Ushoone . . . | 3 | — | - | 3 |
| Yattarar Kongkoonay . . | 1 | 2 | - | 3 |
| Kartarnay . . . | 1 | 1 | - | 2 |
| Koongkannay . . . | 1 | 4 | - | 5 |
| Karpekowethlarnay . . | 1 | 1 | - | 2 |
| Soantonnay . . . | 4 | 1 | - | 5 |
| Killaykowe . . . | 2 | 1 | - | 3 |
| Kartethlarnay . . . | 1 | 2 | - | 3 |
| Shyarponay . . . | 1 | 2 | - | 3 |
| Pokohotay . . . | 1 | 3 | - | 4 |
| Koesoin Kasheer . . . | - | 2 | - | 2 |
| Kowethlarnay . . . | 3 | 2 | - | 5 |
| Ochoutar . . . | 1 | 2 | - | 3 |
| Soote Athe . . . | 1 | 4 | - | 5 |
| Toshetannay . . . | 1 | 3 | - | 4 |
| Tarsowenay . . . | 3 | 1 | - | 4 |
| Tolaytay . . . | 1 | 4 | - | 5 |
| Sarkarhaintto Kanay . . | 1 | 1 | - | 2 |
| Kopofonay . . . | 2 | 4 | - | 6 |
| Arkosay . . . | 2 | 2 | - | 4 |
| Tongsarfare . . . | 1 | 1 | - | 2 |
| Koarstoosheer . . . | 2 | 1 | - | 3 |
| Hokketaitinney . . . | 1 | 1 | - | 2 |
| Killekarthlonay . . . | 2 | 2 | - | 4 |
| Teerharwhittenay . . . | 2 | 2 | - | 4 |
| Sentewar . . . | 3 | 4 | - | 7 |
| Hothlolay . . . | 1 | 2 | - | 3 |
| Kossay . . . | 3 | 1 | - | 4 |
| Karlarkarhewothlay . . | 3 | 6 | - | 9 |
| Wilklarchar . . . | 2 | 2 | - | 4 |
| Kashtonay . . | 3 | 3 | - | 6 |

CREEK CENSUS—Continued.

| Names of Heads of Families. | Males. | Females. | Slaves. | Total. |
|---|---|---|---|---|
| Chooarwekossay . . . | 3 | 2 | - | 5 |
| Kearhaylaykonay . . . | 3 | 1 | - | 4 |
| Peathle . . . . | 1 | 1 | - | 2 |
| Toshespannay . . . | 2 | 5 | - | 7 |
| Shoofkey . . . | 2 | 1 | - | 3 |
| Sharkanay . . . . | 2 | 0 | - | 2 |
| Utehay . . . . | 1 | 1 | - | 2 |
| Taykokitsharnay . . . | 3 | 3 | - | 6 |
| Tuntaywethlar . . . | 1 | 2 | - | 3 |
| Hiutarnay . . . | 2 | 2 | - | 4 |
| Chearchoofarnay . . . | 3 | 3 | - | 6 |
|  | 78 | 89 |  | 167 |
| Hokowethlarlay (alias Euchee Jim) . | 1 | 2 | - | 3 |
| Tarkenay . . . | 1 | 1 | - | 2 |
| Sikehiyar Thlarnay . . | 3 | 3 | - | 6 |
| Kollay . . . . | 2 | 2 | - | 4 |
| Lartar . . . . | 1 | 1 | - | 2 |
| Kowarnay . . . | 1 | 2 | - | 3 |
| Koyartalay . . . | 2 | 1 | - | 3 |
| Chotaysharlay . . . | 2 | 1 | - | 3 |
| Tarseakkonklay . . . | 2 | 3 | - | 5 |
| Kohoquarthlarnay . . . | 1 | 1 | - | 2 |
| Eleyontar . . . | 2 | 1 | - | 3 |
| Kowethlarshar . . . | 2 | 1 | - | 3 |
| Weche . . . | 1 | 1 | - | 2 |
| Kolawnenay . . . | 2 | 4 | - | 6 |
| Sarkoofarnay . . . | — | 2 | - | 2 |
| Tarkhehe . . . | — | 2 | - | 2 |
| Cussela Harjo . . . | 2 | — | - | 2 |
|  | 25 | 28 |  | 53 |

CUSSETAW (on little Euchee Creek).

| | Males. | Females. | Slaves. | Total. |
|---|---|---|---|---|
| Kosar Hopoethle . . | 2 | 2 | - | 4 |
| Thlarsarway . . . | 1 | 2 | - | 3 |
| Mary (wife of Joseph Wheeler) . | 1 | 1 | - | 2 |
| Amanda (wife of James Callahan) . | 1 | 1 | - | 2 |
| Tustunnuckee . . . | 1 | 4 | - | 5 |
| Wilse . . . . | 2 | 1 | - | 3 |
| Emarthlar Harjo . . . | 2 | 4 | - | 6 |
| Intenarse Hoye . . . | 2 | 1 | - | 3 |
| Posulle . . . | 2 | 2 | - | 4 |
| Neharthlocko . . . | 1 | 3 | - | 4 |
| Miskeyartehe . . . | 1 | 2 | - | 3 |
| Weketar . . . | 1 | 1 | - | 2 |

CREEK CENSUS—Continued.

| Names of Heads of Families. | Males. | Females. | Slaves. | Total. |
|---|---|---|---|---|
| Hiar Yarkar | 1 | 1 | - | 2 |
| Sally, wife of Fieldin Scroggins | 1 | 1 | 15 | 17 |
| Mayoke | - | 1 | 1 | 2 |
| Sallarke | 2 | 4 | - | 6 |
| Polly Fitzgerald | 1 | 2 | - | 3 |
| Kottarthlar (or Joseph Brown) | 2 | 1 | - | 3 |
| Tarsehoke | 1 | 1 | - | 2 |
| Thlockoechee | 3 | 3 | - | 6 |
| Hadkis Harjo | 3 | 2 | - | 5 |
| Mooske | 2 | 1 | - | 3 |
| Paddy Carr | 2 | 5 | 35 | 42 |
| Fanny Lovett | - | 1 | 30 | 31 |
| Lithoke | - | 1 | 1 | 2 |
| Arswelarke | - | 1 | 1 | 2 |
| Scintarthle | 2 | 1 | - | 3 |
| Kochusse | 1 | 2 | - | 3 |
| Konoyarhikar | 2 | 1 | - | 3 |
| Warsohole | 1 | 1 | - | 2 |
| Welarkoochee | 1 | 1 | - | 2 |
| Mullomike | 2 | 1 | - | 3 |
| Joseph Carr | 1 | 3 | 21 | 25 |
| Sarkoyeche | 1 | 3 | - | 4 |
| Tarkoehepe | 4 | 2 | - | 6 |
| Sikey | 1 | 2 | - | 3 |
| Sarhotosey | 2 | 1 | - | 3 |
| Parhose Fixico | 1 | 1 | - | 2 |
| Mitteche | 1 | 1 | - | 2 |
| Isfarne Emarthlar | 1 | 2 | - | 3 |
| | 56 | 73 | 104 | 233 |
| Lucy Mims | 1 | 1 | - | 2 |
| Harpe | 1 | 1 | - | 2 |
| Chofullwar | 1 | 1 | - | 2 |
| Humharke | 1 | 2 | - | 3 |
| Harwokhoke | 1 | 1 | - | 2 |
| Honith Larte | - | 2 | - | 2 |
| Sarkarparle | 1 | 2 | - | 3 |
| Thleparle | 1 | 1 | - | 2 |
| Satteloye | 1 | 1 | - | 2 |
| Fullkar | 1 | 2 | - | 3 |
| Kunchartee | 3 | 1 | - | 4 |
| Melehocho | 1 | 3 | - | 4 |
| Nowur | 2 | 2 | - | 4 |
| Arpeka Tustunnuckee | 1 | 1 | - | 2 |
| Artus Harjo | 2 | 1 | - | 3 |
| Harpar | 1 | 1 | - | 2 |

CREEK CENSUS—Continued.

| Names of Heads of Families. | Males. | Females. | Slaves. | Total |
|---|---|---|---|---|
| Artarye   -   -   -   -   - | 1 | 4 | - | 5 |
| Sowwarne   -   -   -   - | 2 | 2 | 1 | 5 |
| Arlummar   -   -   -   - | 1 | 1 | - | 2 |
| Hotalke Tustunnuckee   -   -   - | 1 | 2 | - | 3 |
| Tussinne   -   -   -   - | 4 | 1 | - | 5 |
| Far Micco   -   -   -   - | 2 | 2 | - | 4 |
| William (son of Efar Emarthlar)   - | 1 | 1 | - | 2 |
| Fahlinniche (or Old Tom)   -   - | 4 | 2 | - | 6 |
| Siffoliye (or Skiney)   -   - | 1 | 1 | - | 2 |
| Muncharye   -   -   - | 1 | 2 | - | 3 |
| Thlarheche   -   -   -   - | 1 | 1 | - | 2 |
| Kenihe   -   -   -   -   - | — | 2 | - | 2 |
| Lopukkar   -   -   -   - | 1 | 1 | - | 2 |
| | | | | |
| CUSSE-TAW (on Tolarnulkar Hatchee.) | 39 | 45 | 1 | 85 |
| Okefuske Tustunnuckee   -   -   - | 1 | 1 | - | 2 |
| Harharlock Harjo   -   -   - | 1 | 1 | - | 2 |
| Saffoloke   -   -   -   - | 2 | 2 | - | 4 |
| Tulka Fixico   -   -   -   - | 4 | 1 | - | 5 |
| Talwar Tustunnuckee   -   -   - | 2 | 1 | - | 3 |
| Sceho Kay   -   -   -   - | 2 | 1 | - | 3 |
| Nehar Harjo   -   -   -   - | 5 | 3 | - | 8 |
| Yartakar Harjo   -   -   -   - | 1 | 3 | - | 4 |
| Nocoseille   -   -   -   - | 1 | 1 | - | 2 |
| Hulle   -   -   -   - | 1 | 2 | - | 3 |
| Thlarye   -   -   -   - | 2 | 3 | - | 5 |
| Sarpoke   -   -   -   - | 5 | 1 | - | 6 |
| Arkinarway   -   -   -   - | 1 | 1 | - | 2 |
| Woolle Kay   -   -   -   - | 3 | 3 | - | 6 |
| Omiyiche   -   -   -   - | 2 | 2 | - | 4 |
| Narttar   -   -   -   - | 1 | 1 | - | 2 |
| Hetuppe   -   -   -   - | 2 | 1 | - | 3 |
| Pelelar   -   -   -   - | 2 | 1 | - | 3 |
| Micco Fixico   -   -   -   - | 1 | 1 | - | 2 |
| Hosar Yoholo   -   -   -   - | 1 | 1 | - | 2 |
| Chewasti Micco   -   -   -   - | 3 | 5 | - | S |
| Micco Hadke   -   -   -   - | 1 | 1 | - | 2 |
| Chumiyarke   -   -   -   - | 2 | 2 | - | 4 |
| Sarhoparye   -   -   -   - | 3 | - | - | 3 |
| Karzonar   -   -   -   - | 1 | 1 | - | 2 |
| Tonokay   -   -   -   - | 2 | 1 | - | 3 |
| Cho Fixico   -   -   -   - | 1 | 1 | - | 2 |
| Scemarlar   -   -   -   - | 1 | 1 | - | 2 |
| Nokefar Yoholo   -   -   -   - | 1 | 1 | . | 2 |
| Chofe Harjo   -   -   -   - | 1 | 1 | - | 2 |

CREEK CENSUS—Continued.

| Names of Heads of Families. | Males. | Females. | Slaves. | Total. |
|---|---|---|---|---|
| Tulse Harjo | 2 | 3 | - | 5 |
| Tatholo | 1 | 1 | - | 2 |
| Letekar | 1 | 1 | - | 2 |
| Futche | 2 | 3 | - | 5 |
| Konepe Emarthlar | 1 | 2 | - | 3 |
| Faster | 2 | 3 | - | 5 |
| Tehechar | 1 | 1 | - | 2 |
| Arweheke | 1 | 1 | - | 2 |
| Honiche | 1 | 1 | - | 2 |
| Timarlarkoeche | 1 | 2 | - | 3 |
| | 69 | 63 | | 132 |
| Jenny | - | 2 | - | 2 |
| Sfarne Fixico | 3 | 1 | - | 4 |
| Tioposiche | 2 | 1 | - | 3 |
| Sarparkey | - | 2 | - | 2 |
| Sallartkey | 1 | 1 | - | 2 |
| Alteekar | 3 | 2 | - | 5 |
| Misse | 1 | 1 | - | 2 |
| Kotolar | 4 | 3 | - | 7 |
| Klaritshoye | 1 | 1 | - | 2 |
| Arlockoeche | 2 | 3 | - | 5 |
| Arwarhe | 1 | 1 | - | 2 |
| Benny | 1 | 1 | - | 2 |
| Metehose | 2 | 2 | - | 4 |
| Ohhomolike | 1 | 2 | - | 3 |
| Arharthley | 1 | 1 | - | 2 |
| Sokoyikay | - | 2 | - | 2 |
| Scehokechec | 3 | 2 | - | 5 |
| Klarseharwe | 1 | 1 | - | 2 |
| Slincharneleke | 2 | 2 | - | 4 |
| Okechun Harjo | 3 | 1 | - | 4 |
| Tallehechar | 1 | 1 | - | 2 |
| Harpethlar | 1 | 1 | - | 2 |
| Tommy Harjo (alias Mokoke) | 3 | 3 | - | 6 |
| Chiskotchooley | 2 | 1 | - | 3 |
| Yoholo Chopko | 3 | 1 | - | 4 |
| Saffolotehoke | 3 | 3 | - | 6 |
| Eupokkolotike | 2 | 2 | - | 4 |
| Sowwelarke | 1 | 2 | - | 3 |
| Nocose Yoholo | 2 | 3 | - | 5 |
| Wike | 2 | 1 | - | 3 |
| Woxeholartar | 4 | 4 | - | 8 |
| Talmarse | 1 | 1 | - | 2 |
| Fixico Harjo | 3 | 3 | - | 6 |

CREEK CENSUS—Continued.

| Names of Heads of Families. | Males. | Females. | Slaves. | Total. |
|---|---|---|---|---|
| Marfolote . . . . | 1 | 1 | . | 2 |
| Karpicchar Emarthlar . . . | 4 | 1 | . | 5 |
| Narchume . . . . | 4 | 4 | . | 8 |
| Koziste . . . . . | 1 | 2 | . | 3 |
| Dick Spiller . . . . | 1 | 1 | . | 2 |
| Tulgiskarmicco . . . . | 2 | 1 | . | 3 |
| Okefuskemicco . . . . | 2 | 2 | . | 4 |
| Artus Emarthlar . . . . | 4 | 3 | . | 7 |
| Nocose Harjo . . . . | 1 | 1 | . | 2 |
| Thlathlo Emarthlar . . . | 4 | 3 | . | 7 |
| | 84 | 77 | | 161 |
| Istecharhowe . . . . | 1 | 1 | . | 2 |
| Klarheche . . . . | 1 | 2 | . | 3 |
| Sammy . . . . . | 1 | 2 | . | 3 |
| Cussetaw Harjo . . . | 3 | 1 | . | 4 |
| Ochesemicco . . . . | 3 | 2 | . | 5 |
| Ekarse Harjo . . . . | 1 | 2 | . | 3 |
| Kotchar Micco . . . . | 2 | 1 | . | 3 |
| Holiche, (alias Sarah) . . . | . | 1 | 4 | 5 |
| Haryokkuppe . . . . | 1 | 1 | . | 2 |
| Okeelissar . . . . | 2 | 1 | . | 3 |
| Alpetter . . . . . | 2 | 1 | . | 3 |
| Kunhadkemicco . . . . | 1 | 3 | . | 4 |
| Haruposekar . . . . | 2 | 3 | . | 5 |
| Spokeoke Harjo . . . . | 2 | 2 | . | 4 |
| Arliche . . . . . | 1 | 2 | . | 3 |
| Isfarne Harjo . . . . | 2 | 3 | . | 5 |
| Yelkar Harjo . . . . | 1 | 2 | . | 3 |
| Harlotte . . . . . | 2 | 1 | . | 3 |
| Tewartotchee . . . . | 4 | 4 | . | 8 |
| Nochowe . . . . | 1 | 1 | . | 2 |
| Sawwiheke . . . . | 3 | 3 | . | 6 |
| Tokulle . . . . . | 1 | 1 | . | 2 |
| Kuntalle . . . . . | 1 | 1 | . | 2 |
| Pekholigey . . . . | 1 | 2 | . | 3 |
| Pekfartke . . . . | 3 | 1 | . | 4 |
| Letike . . . . . | 2 | 1 | . | 3 |
| Etote . . . . . | 1 | 1 | . | 2 |
| Fosehatchee Tustunnuckee . . | 1 | 1 | . | 2 |
| Litkotaryar . . . . | 1 | 1 | . | 2 |
| Tarseheyar . . . . | 1 | 4 | . | 5 |
| Yarhar Emarthlar . . . | 2 | 3 | . | 5 |
| Mistekarye . . . . | 2 | 3 | . | 5 |
| Weketarke . . . . | 1 | 1 | . | 2 |
| Sokkoliche . . . . | 1 | 1 | . | 2 |

CREEK CENSUS—Continued.

| Names of Heads of Families. | Males. | Females. | Slaves. | Total. |
|---|---|---|---|---|
| Okechi Yarholo . . . . | 1 | 1 | - | 2 |
| Sarhulle . . . . | 1 | 1 | - | 2 |
| Tommy Emarthlar . . . | 1 | 1 | - | 2 |
| Scarche . . . . | 3 | 1 | - | 4 |
| Smarhe . . . . | 2 | 3 | - | 5 |
| Sowwonney . . . . | 2 | 2 | - | 4 |
| Chokolarkey . . . . | 1 | 2 | - | 3 |
| Hothlarser . . . . | 1 | 2 | - | 3 |
| Itsharpe . . . . | 1 | 1 | - | 2 |
| | 67 | 74 | 4 | 145 |
| Istemarcharnar . . . . | 1 | 1 | - | 2 |
| Kofar, (a Euchee) . . . | 3 | 3 | - | 6 |
| Yotso, (do) . . . | 1 | 2 | - | 3 |
| Yikehonay, (do) . . . | 3 | 1 | - | 4 |
| Temosehar . . . . | 7 | 3 | - | 10 |
| Yarhar Harjo . . . . | 1 | 1 | - | 2 |
| Ekarsarme . . . . | 2 | 1 | - | 3 |
| Kunchartee Emarthlar . . . | 3 | 1 | - | 4 |
| Welaykarpe . . . . | 1 | 1 | - | 2 |
| Nehar Tustunnuckee . . . | 2 | 2 | - | 4 |
| Sokoyiye . . . . | 1 | 1 | - | 2 |
| Tolofehar . . . . | 1 | 1 | - | 2 |
| Artotekar . . . . | 1 | 1 | - | 2 |
| Seeapeliche . . . . | 1 | 1 | - | 2 |
| Kartarpar . . . . | 2 | . | - | 2 |
| Yartekar . . . . | 2 | . | - | 2 |
| CUSSETAW, ON OPILLIKEE HATCHEE, TAL-LASSEE TOWN. | 32 | 20 | | 52 |
| Tustunnuckee Harjo . . . | 1 | 3 | - | 4 |
| Parhose Yoholo . . . | 3 | 4 | - | 7 |
| Pokar . . . . | 1 | 2 | - | 3 |
| Arstarchkar . . . . | 1 | 1 | - | 2 |
| Neharthlocko Harjo . . . | 1 | 4 | - | 5 |
| Charse Harjo . . . . | 3 | 3 | - | 6 |
| Marme . . . . | 1 | 1 | - | 2 |
| Misteharye . . . . | 1 | 3 | - | 4 |
| Micco Harjo . . . . | 1 | 1 | - | 2 |
| Loomhe . . . . | 1 | 1 | - | 2 |
| Holocharke . . . . | 1 | 1 | - | 2 |
| Karpickchar Tustunnuckee . . | 2 | 2 | - | 4 |
| Wickey . . . . | . | 2 | - | 2 |
| Yehoethlar . . . . | 1 | 2 | - | 3 |

CREEK CENSUS—Continued.

| Names of Heads of Families. | Males. | Females. | Slaves. | Total. |
|---|---|---|---|---|
| Chickelrafkar . . . . | 1 | 1 | - | 2 |
| Lochopekar . . . . | 1 | 2 | - | 3 |
| Miarke . . . . . | 1 | 2 | - | 3 |
| Kar Yokar . . . . | 2 | 1 | - | 3 |
| Chenarwe . . . . | 1 | 1 | - | 2 |
| Tommy . . . . . | 1 | 1 | - | 2 |
| Larhowe . . . . . | 2 | 1 | - | 3 |
| Mothlokar . . . . | 2 | 1 | - | 3 |
| Istemechar . . . . | 1 | 1 | - | 2 |
| Isfarne Yoholo . . . . | 2 | 3 | - | 5 |
| Kisselar . . . . . | 1 | 1 | - | 2 |
| Fenoye . . . . . | 1 | 1 | - | 2 |
| Yarficchar . . . . | 1 | 1 | - | 2 |
| Osooche Yoholo . . . . | 2 | - | - | 2 |
| Imponarye . . . . | 1 | 2 | - | 3 |
| Pikkoligay . . . . | 2 | 1 | - | 3 |
| Martowar . . . . | 1 | 1 | - | 2 |
| Narnokome . . . . | - | 2 | - | 2 |
| Arswokkar . . . . | 1 | 1 | - | 2 |
| Hoyarhike . . . . | 3 | 1 | - | 4 |
| Wiketar . . . . | 1 | 2 | - | 3 |
| Siyechiche . . . . | - | 2 | - | 2 |
| Soharleche . . . . | - | 2 | - | 2 |
| Futsharke . . . . | 1 | 3 | - | 4 |
| Harlock Harjo . . . . | 1 | 2 | - | 3 |
| | 47 | 66 | | 113 |
| Pinkarle . . . . . | 1 | 1 | - | 2 |
| Koair, (a Euchee) . . . | 1 | 3 | - | 4 |
| Sarhow Yay, (do) . . . | 1 | 3 | - | 4 |
| Linte . . . . . | 1 | 3 | - | 4 |
| Hitchetee Emarthlar, (alias Toney) . | 3 | 1 | - | 4 |
| Nokayguy . . . . | 2 | 1 | - | 3 |
| Hehotay . . . . | 1 | 1 | - | 2 |
| Narhothlekay . . . . | - | 2 | - | 2 |
| Sanoche . . . . | 2 | 2 | - | 4 |
| Temarsaryay . . . . | 3 | 1 | - | 4 |
| Sarkoeche . . . . | 1 | 1 | - | 2 |
| Fose Harjo . . . . | 1 | 1 | - | 2 |
| Billy Barnett . . . . | 2 | 1 | - | 3 |
| Kuntal Emarthlar . . . | 2 | 3 | - | 5 |
| Loseetarnee . . . . | 1 | 4 | - | 5 |
| Sokelarpike . . . . | 3 | 2 | - | 5 |
| Arstimfieche . . . . | 1 | 1 | - | 2 |
| | 26 | 31 | | 57 |

CREEK CENSUS—Continued.

| Names of Heads of Families. | Males. | Females | Slaves. | Total. |
|---|---|---|---|---|
| CUSSETAW (on Chowwokolohatchee.) | | | | |
| Neharhungcose - - - | 4 | 4 | - | 8 |
| Hotese Harjo - - - | 2 | 1 | - | 3 |
| Tusconar Emarthlar - - - | 4 | — | - | 4 |
| Talwar Tustunnuckee - - | 1 | 2 | - | 3 |
| Salchemeche - - - | 1 | 2 | - | 3 |
| Yartowar Harjo - - - | 1 | 3 | - | 4 |
| Towwike - - - | 4 | 1 | - | 5 |
| Kotunne - - - | 1 | 3 | - | 4 |
| Tiechiche - - - | 1 | 1 | - | 2 |
| Elese - - - | 1 | 1 | - | 2 |
| Charley - - - | 1 | 1 | - | 2 |
| Homarlike - - - | 3 | 1 | - | 4 |
| Ewunnar - - - | 2 | — | - | 2 |
| Hotolokey - - - | 2 | 2 | - | 4 |
| Yolthkar - - - | 1 | 2 | - | 3 |
| Somihoye - - - | 4 | 1 | - | 5 |
| Harwolike - - - | 1 | 2 | - | 3 |
| Tingkartehi - - - | 1 | 2 | - | 3 |
| Kite - - - | 1 | 2 | - | 3 |
| Kohosarke - - - | 1 | 2 | - | 3 |
| Lowskey - - - | — | 3 | - | 3 |
| Hohoyilete - - - | 4 | 2 | - | 6 |
| Sallecharke - -· - | 1 | 2 | - | 3 |
| Homarhite - - - | 2 | 1 | - | 3 |
| Harwyheche - - - | 1 | 5 | - | 6 |
| Kesehelar - - - | 2 | 2 | - | 4 |
| Fotchar - - - | 1 | 4 | - | 5 |
| Ulkar - - - | 1 | 2 | - | 3 |
| Soktehike - - - | 1 | 1 | - | 2 |
| Talledega - - - | 1 | 1 | - | 2 |
| Tetar - - - | 2 | 1 | - | 3 |
| Kelissar Harjo - - - | 7 | 1 | - | 8 |
| CUSSETAW (at Secharlitcha.) | 60 | 58 | | 118 |
| Neharthlocko - - - | 1 | 1 | - | 2 |
| Tolowar Micco - - - | 1 | 1 | - | 2 |
| Micco Yoholo - - - | 2 | 2 | - | 4 |
| Oktiarche Emarthlar - - | 2 | 3 | - | 5 |
| Cussetaw Harjo - - - | 2 | 1 | - | 3 |
| Hitchetee Tustunnuckee - - | 1 | 1 | - | 2 |
| Kosar Micco - - - | 1 | 1 | - | 2 |
| Yoholo Emarthlar - - - | 2 | 1 | - | 3 |
| Oche Harjo - - - | 1 | 3 | - | 4 |
| Nehar Yoholo - - - | 1 | 2 | - | 3 |

CREEK CENSUS—Continued.

| Names of Heads of Families. | Males. | Females. | Slaves. | Total. |
|---|---|---|---|---|
| Miccooche | 1 | 2 | - | 3 |
| Kotchar Yoholo | 1 | 2 | • | 3 |
| Tommy Harjo | 1 | 2 | - | 3 |
| Woksok Harjo | 3 | 4 | - | 7 |
| Misteharke | 2 | 1 | - | 3 |
| Okechun Yoholo | 1 | 2 | - | 3 |
| Emarthlooche | 2 | 2 | - | 4 |
| Chokotenehar | 2 | 1 | • | 3 |
| Alper | 1 | 1 | - | 2 |
| Chocote Yoholo | 1 | 1 | - | 2 |
| Tolowar Harjo | 1 | 1 | - | 2 |
| Sowumke | 1 | 2 | - | 3 |
| Toparchartee | 1 | 1 | - | 2 |
| Harfuckche Micco | 2 | 1 | - | 3 |
| Yarpe (a Euchee) | 2 | 2 | - | 4 |
| Tuckabatchee Harjo | 1 | 1 | - | 2 |
| Parhose Harjo | 2 | 2 | - | 4 |
| Tulmarse Harjo | 3 | 1 | - | 4 |
| Oyunnepe | 1 | 1 | - | 2 |
| Minottar | 1 | 1 | - | 2 |
| Arsonuck Tustunnuckee | 2 | 1 | - | 3 |
| Arsamar | 1 | 1 | - | 2 |
| Sofoteke | 1 | 1 | - | 2 |
| Chocote Harjo | 2 | - | - | 2 |
| Mesukke | 1 | 1 | - | 2 |
| Karle | 1 | 1 | - | 2 |
| Harparlar Harjo | 1 | 1 | - | 2 |
| Fenoke | 1 | 1 | - | 2 |
| Fosehatcha Yoholo | 3 | 2 | - | 5 |
| Istinhopier | 2 | 2 | - | 4 |
| | 59 | 58 | | 117 |
| Setepike | 1 | 1 | - | 2 |
| Karsarnar | 1 | 1 | - | 2 |
| Kotarhe | 1 | 1 | - | 2 |
| Thlockupar | 1 | 1 | - | 2 |
| Yichepoke | 1 | 1 | - | 2 |
| Tiyarhe | 1 | 1 | - | 2 |
| Kolomemarthlar | 1 | 1 | - | 2 |
| Thlarwolar | 1 | 1 | - | 2 |
| Hethlockoechee | 2 | 1 | - | 3 |
| Arnarchomar | 1 | 1 | - | 2 |
| Pefartke | 1 | 2 | - | 3 |
| Salloster | 1 | 1 | - | 2 |
| Pela | 2 | 2 | - | 4 |

## CREEK CENSUS—Continued.

| Names of Heads of Families. | Males. | Females. | Slaves. | Total. |
|---|---|---|---|---|
| Sally . . . . . | 1 | 2 | - | 3 |
| Lowpoochke . . . . | 1 | 1 | - | 2 |
| Tefarhoethle . . . . | 1 | 1 | - | 2 |
| Ninnarhaychar . . . . | 1 | 2 | - | 3 |
| Intarney . . . . . | 1 | 2 | - | 3 |
| Wartarpachay . . . . | 1 | 2 | - | 3 |
| Mesele . . . . . | — | 2 | - | 2 |
| Tothleko . . . . | — | 3 | - | 3 |
| Tarnechay . . . . | — | 2 | - | 2 |
| Tokothlar . . . . | — | 2 | - | 2 |
| Ismomachey . . . . | 1 | 1 | - | 2 |
| Marheche . . . . | 2 | 1 | - | 3 |
| Hoketonche . . . . | 1 | 2 | - | 3 |
| Tumkey . . . . | 1 | 1 | - | 2 |
| Kosarpokete . . . . | 1 | 1 | - | 2 |
| Arlekonkyarna (a Euchee) . . | 1 | 2 | - | 3 |
| Timehotay (a Euchee) . . | 2 | 1 | - | 3 |
| Charlthenay (ditto) . . . | 1 | 3 | - | 4 |
| Tustunnuckcooche . . . | 2 | — | - | 2 |
| Chokechartinehar . . . | 3 | — | - | 3 |
| Kinhiche . . . . | 2 | 4 | - | 6 |
| Markalkar . . . . | 1 | 1 | - | 2 |
| William Low . . . . | 3 | 4 | - | 7 |
| | 42 | 55 | | 97 |

CUSSETAW, on Osenubba Hatchee, or Tuckabatchee Harjo's Town.

| | | | | |
|---|---|---|---|---|
| Yartekar Tustunnuckee . . . | 3 | 4 | - | 7 |
| Tommy Micco . . . . | 1 | 1 | 1 | 3 |
| Thlathlo Tustunnuckee . . . | 2 | 2 | - | 4 |
| Satchemike . . . . | 2 | 3 | 1 | 6 |
| Chewasti Fixico . . . . | 2 | 1 | 3 | 6 |
| Emarthlar Yoholo . . . | 1 | 1 | - | 2 |
| Fuckelustee . . . . | 2 | 2 | - | 4 |
| Yoholo Charne . . . . | 1 | 1 | - | 2 |
| Alpetter Emarthlar . . . | 4 | 1 | - | 5 |
| Emarthlar Hadke . . . . | 4 | 4 | - | 8 |
| Tussekiar Harjo . . . . | 2 | 2 | - | 4 |
| Thlathlo Emarthlar . . . | 2 | 1 | - | 3 |
| Kolchar Harjo . . . . | 1 | 5 | - | 6 |
| Tolowar Harjo . . . . | 4 | 2 | - | 6 |
| Sfarne Emarthlar . . . . | 3 | 3 | - | 6 |
| Tofoke . . . . | 2 | 1 | - | 3 |
| Nocose Harjo . . . . | 1 | 2 | - | 3 |
| Salletike . . . . | 1 | 3 | - | 4 |

## CREEK CENSUS—Continued.

| Names of Heads of Families. | Males. | Females. | Slaves. | Total. |
|---|---|---|---|---|
| Senar (Grayson) - - - | 1 | 1 | - | 2 |
| Kiselarnee - - - | 1 | 1 | - | 2 |
| Chomechiche - - - | 1 | 2 | - | 3 |
| Cholar Fixico (alias Dan'l Asbury) - | 1 | 2 | - | 3 |
| Chocote Yoholo - - - | 1 | 1 | - | 2 |
| Legey - - - | 1 | 2 | - | 3 |
| Homihechar - - - | 1 | 1 | - | 2 |
| Saryar - - - | 3 | 2 | - | 5 |
| Ponnarker - - - | 1 | 1 | - | 2 |
| Kunchartee - - - | 1 | 1 | - | 2 |
| Micco - - - | 1 | 1 | - | 2 |
| Klarposekar - - - | 1 | 1 | - | 2 |
| Choney - - - | 1 | 1 | - | 2 |
| Siar - - - | 1 | 1 | - | 2 |
| Enehoche - - - | 2 | 2 | - | 4 |
| Salloster - - - | 1 | 1 | - | 2 |
| Chokelarnee - - - | 4 | 1 | - | 5 |
| Starchockkarthle - - - | 2 | 1 | - | 3 |
| Enehar Fixico - - - | 2 | — | - | 2 |
| Oaspartarke - - - | 1 | 1 | - | 2 |
| Neharthlocko - - - | 2 | — | - | 2 |
| | 69 | 64 | 5 | 136 |
| Dicky - - - | 1 | 1 | 1 | 3 |
| Stemisarke - - - | 1 | 1 | - | 2 |
| Sallarte - - - | 1 | 1 | - | 2 |
| Temesepe - - - | 1 | 1 | - | 2 |
| Tustunnuckhothlepoya - - | 2 | — | - | 2 |
| Tarpolar - - - | 1 | 1 | - | 2 |
| Martulkey - - - | 1 | 1 | - | 2 |
| Stemartehike - - - | 1 | 1 | - | 2 |
| Sceto - - - | 1 | 1 | - | 2 |
| Stemarhoye - - - | 3 | - | - | 3 |
| Tarseyo - - - | 1 | 1 | - | 2 |
| Hulle - - - | 1 | 1 | - | 2 |
| Lowsethlocko - - - | 1 | 2 | - | 3 |
| Tiakey - - - | 1 | 2 | 1 | 4 |
| Sallarke - - - | 1 | 1 | - | 2 |
| Billy (Grayson) - - - | 1 | 1 | - | 2 |
| Lowsey - - - | 1 | 1 | - | 2 |
| Lartechoyar - - - | 1 | 1 | - | 2 |
| Fullhoeche - - - | 1 | 1 | 1 | 3 |
| Harpealthkar - - - | 1 | 1 | - | 2 |
| Pahlochokolo - - - | 2 | - | - | 2 |
| Simme - - - | 1 | 1 | - | 2 |
| Telostige - - - | 1 | 1 | - | 2 |

CREEK CENSUS—Continued.

| Names of Heads of Families. | Males. | Females. | Slaves. | Total. |
|---|---|---|---|---|
| Yiye - - - - - | 2 | - | - | 2 |
| Tekulkkar - - - - | 1 | 1 | - | 2 |
| Parhose Yoholo - - - | 2 | - | - | 2 |
| Honilete - - - - | 1 | 1 | - | 2 |
| Saffaryike - - - - | 1 | 1 | - | 2 |
| Sarharche - - - - | 2 | - | - | 2 |
| Nocofite - - - - | — | 2 | - | 2 |
| Stillepika Chartee - - | 2 | - | - | 2 |
| Pulsey - - - - | 2 | 1 | - | 3 |
| Lizey - - - - | 2 | 1 | - | 3 |
| Marley - - - - | 2 | 1 | - | 3 |
| Polly - - - - | 1 | 1 | - | 2 |
| Timharkar - - - | 2 | 2 | - | 4 |
| Sally - - - - | 1 | 1 | - | 2 |
| Sothleko - - - - | 1 | 2 | - | 3 |
| Semarwar - - - | — | 2 | - | 2 |
| Niche (or Hokolose) - - | — | 2 | - | 2 |
| Kiche - - - - | 2 | - | - | 2 |
| Koehoke - - - - | 1 | 1 | - | 2 |
| | 52 | 41 | 3 | 96 |
| Stemarpowike - - - | 1 | 1 | - | 2 |
| Charne - - - - | 1 | 2 | - | 3 |
| Koloomme - - - | 2 | 2 | - | 4 |
| Koherse Emarthlar - - | 2 | 3 | - | 5 |
| Inlummarley - - - | 3 | 2 | - | 5 |
| Hothliche - - - | — | 2 | - | 2 |
| Yarhar Emarthlar - - | 1 | 1 | - | 2 |
| Kolar - - - - | 2 | - | - | 2 |
| Somiye - - - - | 2 | 2 | - | 4 |
| Singkarke - - - | 1 | 2 | - | 3 |
| Simfoloke - - - | 1 | 1 | - | 2 |
| Tommythlocko - - - | 1 | 2 | - | 3 |
| Larnar - - - - | — | 2 | - | 2 |
| Temarlitte - - - | — | 3 | - | 3 |
| Robert Rogers (a Cherokee missionary,) - | 1 | 2 | - | 3 |
| | 18 | 27 | | 45 |

CUSETAW, (near West Point,) or TUSKEHE-NEHAW CHOOLEY'S TOWN.

| | | | | |
|---|---|---|---|---|
| Charlisse Tustunnuckee - - - | 1 | 1 | - | 2 |
| Karfe (or Coffee) - - - | 3 | 2 | - | 5 |
| Fosehatchee Emarthlar - - | 1 | 1 | - | 2 |
| Koharthlock Emarthlar - - | 2 | 3 | - | 5 |
| Efar Tustunnuckee - - - | 1 | 1 | - | 2 |

CREEK CENSUS—Continued.

| Names of Heads of Families. | Males. | Females. | Slaves. | Total. |
|---|---|---|---|---|
| Choloke Harjo - - - - | 1 | 1 | - | 2 |
| Cheletarle - - - - | 1 | 2 | - | 3 |
| Yoholo Harjo - - - - | 2 | 3 | - | 5 |
| Cheloke Yoholo - - - - | 5 | 1 | - | 6 |
| Chocote Harjo - - - - | 1 | 1 | - | 2 |
| Checosey - - - - | 1 | 3 | - | 4 |
| Tullihechar - - - - | 2 | 2 | - | 4 |
| Fosehatchee Micco - - - | 1 | 2 | - | 3 |
| Moxemichiche - - - - | 1 | 2 | - | 3 |
| Kotchar Tustunnuckee - - - | 2 | 3 | - | 5 |
| Kowokkooche - - - - | 3 | 1 | - | 4 |
| Tolowarharjo - - - - | 2 | 3 | - | 5 |
| Towarlikar - - - - | 1 | 1 | - | 2 |
| Echarse Yoholo - - - - | 3 | 2 | - | 5 |
| Tintarche - - - - | 1 | 1 | - | 2 |
| Shattarthlike - - - - | 1 | 1 | - | 2 |
| Tarthlumme - - - - | 2 | 1 | - | 3 |
| Pinharjo - - - - | 1 | 1 | - | 2 |
| Klarsarte - - - - | 2 | 3 | - | 5 |
| Choolarfixico - - - - | 1 | 1 | - | 2 |
| Cussetawharjo - - - - | 1 | 2 | - | 3 |
| Kosar Yoholo - - - - | 3 | 1 | - | 4 |
| Karpiccharharjo - - - - | 1 | 1 | - | 2 |
| Hospartarke Emarthlar - - - | 1 | 3 | - | 4 |
| Harfoloteche - - - - | 2 | 1 | - | 3 |
| Cussetawfixico - - - - | 2 | 3 | - | 5 |
| Harkooniche - - - - | 1 | 2 | - | 3 |
| Narcoseekar - - - - | 3 | 2 | - | 5 |
| Yarkinhar Micco - - - | 1 | 1 | - | 2 |
| Koweharjo - - - - | 2 | 2 | - | 4 |
| Harpiuk Harjo - - - - | 1 | 1 | - | 2 |
| Temethlar - - - - | 1 | 1 | - | 2 |
| Washington - - - - | 2 | 1 | - | 3 |
| Kolar - - - - | 1 | 1 | - | 2 |
| | 64 | 65 | | 129 |
| Sotay - - - - | 1 | 1 | - | 2 |
| Hillabeeharjo - - - - | 1 | 1 | - | 2 |
| Chewastiharjo - - - - | 1 | 2 | - | 3 |
| Thlathloharjo - - - - | 2 | 1 | - | 3 |
| Nocosefixico - - - - | 1 | 2 | - | 3 |
| Tulseharjo - - - - | 3 | 1 | - | 4 |
| Chiskarlikar - - - - | 3 | 1 | - | 4 |
| Harkitte Yoholo - - - - | 2 | 7 | - | 9 |
| Harkealthkar - - - - | 1 | 2 | - | 3 |

CREEK CENSUS—Continued.

| Names of Heads of Families. | Males. | Females. | Slaves. | Total. |
|---|---|---|---|---|
| Semarhechike - - - | 1 | 1 | - | 2 |
| Eufoolike - - | 2 | 1 | - | 3 |
| Sintihoke - - - | 1 | 1 | - | 2 |
| Harkunne - - - | 1 | 1 | - | 2 |
| Karpikchar Fixico - - | 2 | - | - | 2 |
| Tulwike - - - | 1 | 1 | - | 2 |
| Eufaula Harjo - - - | 1 | 1 | - | 2 |
| Totekis Harjo - - - | 2 | 1 | - | 3 |
| Staffokolotikey - - - | 1 | 1 | - | 2 |
| Emartoko - - - | 1 | 1 | - | 2 |
| Pefarthoeche - - - | 1 | 1 | . | 2 |
| Lucy - - - | 1 | 1 | . | 2 |
| Nocoseekarchopko - - | 1 | 1 | . | 2 |
| Warkernufkar - - - | 1 | 1 | . | 2 |
| Katey - - - | 1 | 2 | . | 3 |
| Polly - - - | 2 | 3 | . | 5 |
| Tempoeche - - - | 1 | 1 | . | 2 |
| Iskoeche - - - | 1 | 1 | . | 2 |
| Arkoeke - - - | - | 2 | . | 2 |
| Fullhoeche - - - | 1 | 1 | . | 2 |
| Scepoke - - - | - | 3 | . | 3 |
| Funfucke - - - | 1 | 1 | . | 2 |
| Sarchekarlarfikay - - - | - | 2 | . | 2 |
| Harhopiye - - - | 1 | 1 | . | 2 |
| Sappeley - - - | 1 | 3 | . | 4 |
| Chockey - - - | 1 | 2 | . | 3 |
| Hotosey - - - | 1 | 1 | . | 2 |
| Markey - - - | 1 | 1 | . | 2 |
| Chockkohoye - - - | - | 2 | . | 2 |
| Howwarligey - - - | - | 2 | . | 2 |
| Suttinhalthkey - - - | 1 | 1 | . | 2 |
| Poketucke - - - | 1 | 2 | . | 3 |
| Harthlarkar - - - | 3 | 1 | . | 4 |
| Sokkonarhe - - - | 1 | 1 | . | 2 |
|  | 50 | 64 |  | 114 |
| Scetoholartike - - - | 1 | 1 | . | 2 |
| Sowwikey - - - | 1 | 1 | . | 2 |
| Yartoweche - - - | - | 2 | . | 2 |
| Sarhockkar - - - | 1 | 1 | . | 2 |
| Siyehartar - - - | 1 | 1 | . | 2 |
| Semokape - - - | 1 | 1 | . | 2 |
| Hokose - - - | 1 | 1 | . | 2 |
| Tarsekeek Harjo - - - | 1 | 1 | . | 2 |
| Scehocharche - - - | 2 | 1 | . | 3 |

CREEK CENSUS—Continued.

| Names of Heads of Families. | Males. | Females. | Slaves. | Total. |
|---|---|---|---|---|
| Chokefoliye | 1 | 2 | - | 3 |
| Harhoyepe | 1 | 1 | - | 2 |
| Eschowwe | 1 | 1 | - | 2 |
| Siarho | 1 | 2 | - | 3 |
| Yopo | 1 | 1 | - | 2 |
| Sokkarche | 1 | 1 | - | 2 |
| Nickey | 1 | 1 | - | 2 |
| Lecharkar | 1 | 1 | - | 2 |
| Artorechi | 1 | 1 | - | 2 |
| Sinechar | — | 3 | - | 3 |
| Harparlar Harjo | 3 | 1 | - | 4 |
| Thlarnoche | 1 | 1 | - | 2 |
| Tarpley | 1 | 1 | - | 2 |
| Thlarnucke | 1 | 1 | - | 2 |
| Sappoke | 1 | 1 | - | 2 |
| Foster | 1 | 2 | - | 3 |
| Notchkarye | — | 2 | - | 2 |
| Yoolthhoeche (or Sally) | 1 | 2 | - | 3 |
| Honecharke | 1 | 1 | - | 2 |
| Harharlokolartar | 1 | 1 | - | 2 |
| Totekarharse | 1 | 1 | - | 2 |
| Toloto | 1 | 1 | - | 2 |
| Holetikay | 1 | 1 | - | 2 |
| Nocoseible (or Charley) | 1 | 1 | - | 2 |
| Yarmarse | 1 | 1 | - | 2 |
| Kochusse Emarthlar | 2 | 4 | - | 6 |
| Nancy | — | 2 | - | 2 |
| Yo Motchekar | 1 | 1 | - | 2 |
| Siketeche | 1 | 1 | - | 2 |
| Narsetoye (or Lucy) | 1 | 1 | - | 2 |
| Sefolike | 1 | 1 | - | 2 |
| Yartoko | 2 | 2 | - | 4 |
| Kiyarke | 1 | 1 | - | 2 |
| | 43 | 55 | | 98 |
| Chockfullkar | 2 | — | - | 2 |
| Sinthlarhe | 1 | 1 | - | 2 |
| Nocose Yoholo | 1 | 1 | - | 2 |
| Temarliche | 2 | 1 | - | 3 |
| Jackson | 1 | 1 | - | 2 |
| Encemarthlooche | 1 | 1 | - | 2 |
| Jimey Holloway | 1 | 1 | - | 2 |
| Harsikke | 1 | 1 | - | 2 |
| Klarseechee | 2 | 1 | - | 3 |
| Thlartache | — | 2 | - | 2 |
| Sfarno Tustunnuckee | 1 | 2 | - | 3 |

48‡

## CREEK CENSUS—Continued.

| Names of Heads of Families. | Males. | Females. | Slaves. | Total. |
|---|---|---|---|---|
| Hokoekar - - - - - | 1 | 1 | . | 2 |
| Talmarse - - - - - | 2 | 2 | . | 4 |
| Sistothle - - - - - | 1 | 1 | . | 2 |
| Sekar - - - - - | 1 | 1 | . | 2 |
| Tarseho - - - - - | 1 | 1 | . | 2 |
| Supokarlartike - - - - | 2 | — | . | 2 |
| Tumtarke - - - - - | 1 | 1 | . | 2 |
| Kenar - - - - - | 1 | 1 | . | 2 |
| Yarhar Emarthlar - - - | 1 | 1 | . | 2 |
| Tenarkar, (or Sam McIntosh) - - | 1 | 1 | . | 2 |
| William Moore - - - - | 3 | 4 | . | 7 |
| Semike, (or Mary) - - - | — | 2 | . | 2 |
| Anne - - - - - | — | 2 | . | 2 |
| | 28 | 30 | | 58 |
| (EUFAULA, on Chowokolohatchee, a branch of Lower Eufaula on the Chattahoochee and its tributary streams.) | | | | |
| Holartar Tustunnuckee - - - | 2 | 2 | . | 4 |
| Nehar Fixico - - - - | 1 | 1 | . | 2 |
| Kotchar Harjo - - - - | 3 | 3 | . | 6 |
| Chamishoye - - - - | 2 | 2 | . | 4 |
| Melowike - - - - | 2 | 1 | . | 3 |
| Fickhoniye - - - - | 3 | 2 | . | 5 |
| Fickchockhiye - - - - | 1 | 2 | . | 3 |
| Talope Yoholo - - - - | 2 | 1 | . | 3 |
| Necose Yoholo - - - - | 2 | 2 | . | 4 |
| Fiksoomikey - - - - | — | 2 | . | 2 |
| Inletikey - - - - | 3 | 1 | . | 4 |
| Isfarne Harjo - - - - | 1 | 1 | . | 2 |
| Hoyarnechar - - - - | 2 | 1 | . | 3 |
| Konip Harjo - - - - | 2 | 2 | . | 4 |
| Kotchar Tustunnuckee - - - | 2 | 2 | . | 4 |
| Stemokoye - - - - | — | 2 | . | 2 |
| Talowar Harjo - - - - | 1 | 2 | . | 3 |
| Emarthlar Tustunnuckee - - - | 2 | 1 | . | 3 |
| Sufarchiye - - - - | 2 | 2 | . | 4 |
| Cholar Fixico - - - - | 3 | 1 | . | 4 |
| Istemoharye - - - - | 3 | 2 | . | 5 |
| Nocose Harjo - - - - | 1 | 1 | . | 2 |
| Folotikey - - - - | 1 | 2 | . | 3 |
| Pokeide - - - - | 4 | 2 | . | 6 |
| Woxe Yoholo - - - - | 2 | 2 | . | 4 |
| Semehosar - - - - | 2 | 2 | o | 4 |
| Stemokoeke - - - - | 2 | 1 | . | 3 |
| Saffokolote - - - - | 2 | 2 | . | 4 |
| Totarligay - - - - | 4 | 1 | . | 5 |

## CREEK CENSUS—Continued.

| Names of Heads of Families. | Males. | Females. | Slaves. | To'al. |
|---|---|---|---|---|
| Neharthlocko Emarthlar | 3 | 1 | - | 4 |
| Arstote | 1 | 2 | - | 3 |
| Sinhonithle | 3 | 1 | - | 4 |
| Yofke Emarthlar | 3 | 2 | - | 5 |
| Eliza | — | 3 | - | 3 |
| Osooche Harjo | 2 | 3 | - | 5 |
| Neharthblockchopko | 2 | 2 | - | 4 |
| Homarhe | 2 | 2 | - | 4 |
| | 73 | 64 | | 137 |
| Arlitshoye | 1 | 2 | - | 3 |
| Marsehe | 3 | 2 | - | 5 |
| Siepe | 1 | 1 | - | 2 |
| Yarhar Tustunnuckee | 2 | 1 | - | 3 |
| Seeharparhoye | 1 | 2 | - | 3 |
| Okelissar | 4 | 1 | - | 5 |
| Seeharne | 6 | 1 | - | 7 |
| Enarhenehar | 2 | 1 | - | 3 |
| Chote | 1 | 3 | - | 4 |
| Stehechepe | — | 2 | - | 2 |
| Lowsooche | — | 2 | - | 2 |
| Hoyanhoye | 2 | 2 | - | 4 |
| | 23 | 20 | | 43 |

### COWETA, KOOCHKALECHA TOWN.

| Names of Heads of Families. | Males. | Females. | Slaves. | To'al. |
|---|---|---|---|---|
| Tuskenehaw | 1 | 2 | - | 3 |
| Hathlan Harjo | 2 | 3 | - | 5 |
| Holartar, (alias Col. Blue) | 3 | 2 | - | 5 |
| Okechunhotartee | 2 | 2 | - | 4 |
| Parhose Harjo | 3 | 2 | - | 5 |
| Kowokooche Yoholo | 1 | 1 | - | 2 |
| Yartekar Harjo | 3 | 2 | - | 5 |
| Harpekooche | 1 | 1 | - | 2 |
| Thomas Carr | 1 | 2 | 10 | 13 |
| Harharlok Emarthlar | 1 | 1 | - | 2 |
| Seeharye | 1 | 1 | - | 2 |
| Chockkothle | — | 2 | - | 2 |
| Seeharparye | 1 | 1 | - | 2 |
| Chopokeskar | 1 | 1 | - | 2 |
| Kowe | 3 | 2 | - | 5 |
| Chisse | 1 | 1 | - | 2 |
| Simmar | 1 | 1 | - | 2 |
| David Marshall, (alias Kowemarthlar) | 4 | 2 | 1 | 7 |
| Yarhar Emarthlar | 1 | 2 | - | 3 |
| Lotoke Riche | 2 | 3 | - | 5 |

## CREEK CENSUS—Continued.

| Names of Heads of Families. | Males. | Females. | Slaves. | Total. |
|---|---|---|---|---|
| Harparlarharjo | 3 | 4 | - | 7 |
| Otulkeharjo | 2 | 2 | - | 4 |
| Fosehatch Yoholo | 1 | 2 | - | 3 |
| Echo Emarthlar | 2 | 3 | - | 5 |
| Passcove Micco | 4 | 2 | - | 6 |
| Kotiley | 2 | 1 | - | 3 |
| Sakko Yohoke | 1 | 3 | - | 4 |
| Holartarharjo | 2 | 1 | - | 3 |
| Coquette | — | 3 | - | 3 |
| Penikke | 1 | 1 | - | 2 |
| Harletharye | 1 | 3 | - | 4 |
| Nanny | 2 | 1 | - | 3 |
| Meter, (wife of Nero, a free black,) | — | 4 | - | 4 |
| Chepunthlocko | 2 | 2 | - | 4 |
| Solatlar | 1 | 1 | - | 2 |
| Lenite | 1 | 1 | - | 2 |
| Scehokar | 1 | 3 | - | 4 |
| Sonarne | 1 | 1 | - | 2 |
| Hunchartee Emarthlar | 1 | 1 | - | 2 |
| Shenarye | 1 | 2 | - | 3 |
| | 62 | 75 | 11 | 148 |
| Salloompe | 2 | - | - | 2 |
| Metarthle | 1 | 1 | - | 2 |
| Sennarchike | 1 | 2 | - | 3 |
| Misse | 1 | 2 | - | 3 |
| Nowkar (alias Polly) | 1 | 3 | - | 4 |
| Iskunne | 2 | 1 | - | 3 |
| Charmelikay | 1 | 1 | - | 2 |
| Timpoeche | 1 | 2 | - | 3 |
| Hosparke | - | 2 | - | 2 |
| Klarseho Yilete | 2 | 1 | - | 3 |
| Hopoye | 1 | 1 | - | 2 |
| Isaac Brown, alias Harsote | 3 | 1 | - | 4 |
| Harlarsehene | 2 | 1 | - | 3 |
| Someche | - | 2 | - | 2 |
| Artarwe | 1 | 1 | - | 2 |
| Sarme | - | 3 | - | 3 |
| Chum Yoholo | 1 | 1 | - | 2 |
| Fose Emarthlar | 3 | 1 | - | 4 |
| Nickey | 1 | 1 | - | 2 |
| Nocose Yoholo | 2 | 2 | - | 4 |
| Spokey | 1 | 2 | - | 3 |
| Scetinhocke | 1 | 2 | - | 3 |
| Kotchar Yoholo | 2 | 1 | - | 3 |
| Temarke | - | 3 | - | 3 |

## CREEK CENSUS—Continued.

| Names of Heads of Families. | Males. | Females. | Slaves. | Total. |
|---|---|---|---|---|
| Foolechiche . . . . | 1 | 2 | - | 3 |
| Tomorrow . . . . | 1 | 1 | - | 2 |
| Sockpeachkey . . . . | — | 3 | - | 3 |
| Yarkey . . . . | 1 | 4 | - | 5 |
| Wunnelikay . . . . | 1 | 1 | - | 2 |
| Charmelikay . . . . | 2 | 1 | - | 3 |
| Nunno . . . . | 1 | 1 | - | 2 |
| Tarsekar . . . . | 4 | 2 | - | 6 |
| Fosehatchee Marthlar . . . | 2 | 2 | - | 4 |
| Kowokkooche Harjo . . . | 1 | 1 | - | 2 |
| Klarseharwe . . . . | 1 | 2 | - | 3 |
| Chiskarlikar . . . . | 1 | 1 | - | 2 |
| Semehechiche . . . . | 2 | 1 | - | 3 |
| Tarholar . . . . . | 1 | 1 | - | 2 |
| Pakey . . . . . | 1 | 1 | - | 2 |
| Kimarme . . . . | 1 | 1 | - | 2 |
| Sehoparye . . . . | 1 | 1 | - | 2 |
| Kunchart Yoholo . . . . | 2 | 1 | - | 3 |
| | 53 | 64 | | 117 |
| Polly (an Indian woman,) - - | 2 | 1 | - | 3 |
| Polly, (half negro, and having a negro slave for a husband, named John) - - | 1 | 1 | 1 | 3 |
| Lowsey - - - - - | 1 | 1 | - | 2 |
| Looskooche - - - - | 1 | 2 | - | 3 |
| Karpikchar Yoholo - - - | 1 | 4 | - | 5 |
| Benjamin Marshall* - - - | 2 | 4 | - | 6 |
| | 8 | 13 | 1 | 22 |
| COWETA, (on Toosilkstorkoo Hatchee.) | | | | |
| Henry Marshall - - - | 1 | 3 | 2 | 6 |
| Matthew Marshall - - - | 3 | 2 | - | 5 |
| William Marshall - - - | 1 | 1 | 1 | 3 |
| Old Mrs. Marshall (alias Hits Kartay) - | — | 2 | 3 | 5 |
| James Marshall - - - | 1 | 1 | 6 | 8 |
| Lucy Marshall - - - | 1 | 1 | 1 | 3 |
| Josey Marshall - - - | 1 | 1 | - | 2 |
| Thomas Marshall - - - | 1 | 4 | 2 | 7 |
| Chofolowar - - - - | 2 | 2 | - | 4 |
| Yarhar Larnee - - - | 1 | 1 | - | 2 |
| Fixico Harjo (alias Buck,) - - - | 1 | 1 | - | 2 |

* Benjamin Marshall the United States interpreter, for the Creek nation of Indians, having already by the late treaty had a special reservation of land asigned him, and having presented himself before me, and asserted a right to be enrolled as the head of a family, in order to be put in possession of the quantum of land reserved to heads of families respectively, I deemed it my duty to note his case, and submit the same to the determination of the department.                                                    T. J. A.

CREEK CENSUS—Continued.

| Names of Heads of Families. | Males | Females | Slaves. | Total. |
|---|---|---|---|---|
| Karlar | 3 | 1 | - | 4 |
| Isfarne Micco | 3 | 2 | - | 5 |
| Charsehehenear | 1 | 2 | - | 3 |
| Parhose Yoholo | 1 | 2 | - | 3 |
| Tuckayjar | 2 | 2 | - | 4 |
| Kiselarne | 2 | 2 | - | 4 |
| Suffurche | 1 | 1 | - | 2 |
| Yekeheney | 1 | 1 | - | 2 |
| Lowey | 2 | 3 | - | 5 |
| Klaisewikey | 1 | 1 | - | 2 |
| Wunhokey | 2 | 3 | - | 5 |
| Scisse | 1 | 2 | - | 3 |
| Karsattar | 1 | 1 | - | 2 |
| Winey | - | 3 | - | 3 |
| Yoholooche | 1 | 1 | - | 2 |
| Pullsiche | 1 | 1 | - | 2 |
| Billy Reddick (a free black) | 1 | 1 | - | 2 |
| | 37 | 48 | 15 | 100 |

### COWETA (on Warkooche Hatchee.)

| | Males | Females | Slaves. | Total. |
|---|---|---|---|---|
| Nehar Yoholo | 3 | 2 | - | 5 |
| Thlarkar | 3 | 2 | - | 5 |
| Hopiye | 1 | 2 | - | 3 |
| Helase Tustunnuckee | 1 | 1 | - | 2 |
| Tulse Fixico | 1 | 1 | - | 2 |
| Arfulhokar | 1 | 1 | - | 2 |
| Mechar | 1 | 2 | - | 3 |
| Tommy | 1 | 1 | - | 2 |
| Timfiyay | 1 | 1 | - | 2 |
| Sumhooeche | - | 2 | - | 2 |
| Kowokkooche | 1 | 1 | - | 2 |
| | 14 | 16 | - | 30 |

### COWETA (on Hallewokke Yoaxarhatchee.)

| | Males | Females | Slaves. | Total. |
|---|---|---|---|---|
| Charse Harjo (alias Mad Beaver) | 2 | - | - | 2 |
| Hiepooche | 2 | 3 | - | 5 |
| Mockparlarte | 3 | - | - | 3 |
| Oktiarche Harjo | 1 | 3 | - | 4 |
| Melikke | 1 | 2 | - | 3 |
| Mehechar | 2 | 1 | - | 3 |
| Semarhome | 1 | 2 | - | 3 |
| Talope | 1 | 1 | - | 2 |
| Archarko | 2 | 1 | - | 3 |
| Choolarchopko | 1 | 2 | - | 3 |
| Nocose Harjo | 2 | 2 | - | 4 |

CREEK CENSUS—Continued.

| Names of Heads of Families. | Males. | Females. | Slaves. | Total. |
|---|---|---|---|---|
| Tunte            -    -    -    - | 1 | 1 | - | 2 |
| Fixico           -    -    -    - | 3 | 2 | - | 5 |
| Karpikchar Micco     -    -    - | 4 | 2 | - | 6 |
| Sarlarye         -    -    -    - | 2 | 1 | - | 3 |
| Foseharchooche   -    -    -    - | 3 | 1 | - | 4 |
| Necose Yoholo    -    -    -    - | 1 | 3 | - | 4 |
| Narnokike        -    -    -    - | 2 | 1 | - | 3 |
| Nocose Ekar      -    -    -    - | 2 | 1 | - | 3 |
| Cho Harjo        -    -    -    - | 3 | 2 | - | 5 |
| Cho Koleetkar    -    -    -    - | 2 | 3 | - | 5 |
| Chewasti Micco   -    -    -    - | 2 | 1 | - | 3 |
| Parlharmeche     -    -    -    - | 2 | 1 | - | 3 |
| Chokkoke         -    -    -    - | 2 | 1 | - | 3 |
| Nitte            -    -    -    - | 1 | 2 | - | 3 |
| Warloko Yoholo   -    -    -    - | 1 | 4 | - | 5 |
| Elar             -    -    -    - | 1 | 1 | - | 2 |
| Tohokoniche      -    -    -    - | 1 | 2 | - | 3 |
| Spetar           -    -    -    - | 1 | 1 | - | 2 |
| Thlockpuswar     -    -    -    - | 2 | 1 | - | 3 |
| Sockarle         -    -    -    - | 1 | 1 | - | 2 |
| Hospartok Harjo  -    -    -    - | 2 | 1 | - | 3 |
| Soksomke         -    -    -    - | 1 | 1 | - | 2 |
| Inche            -    -    -    - | 1 | 1 | - | 2 |
| Skarte           -    -    -    - | 1 | 1 | - | 2 |
| Arlicheche       -    -    -    - | 1 | 1 | - | 2 |
| Konoke           -    -    -    - | 1 | 1 | - | 2 |
| Chartee          -    -    -    - | 1 | 2 | - | 3 |
| Hiyokechee       -    -    -    - | - | 2 | - | 2 |
| Archickille      -    -    -    - | - | 2 | - | 2 |
|  | 63 | 61 | - | 124 |
| Arlarhokar       -    -    -    - | 1 | 1 | - | 2 |
| Atchetoke        -    -    -    - | 1 | 1 | - | 2 |
| Fistukke         -    -    -    - | 2 | 1 | - | 3 |
| Nulcuppooeche    -    -    -    - | - | 2 | - | 2 |
| Chootee          -    -    -    - | 1 | 1 | - | 2 |
| Semothleche      -    -    -    - | 3 | 1 | - | 4 |
| Sphiyike         -    -    -    - | 1 | 1 | - | 2 |
| Hoyineche        -    -    -    - | 1 | 1 | - | 2 |
| Futsharharke     -    -    -    - | 1 | 3 | - | 4 |
| Stemartoomhe     -    -    -    - | 1 | 1 | - | 2 |
| Cheparne         -    -    -    - | 1 | 1 | - | 2 |
| Losechopko       -    -    -    - | 1 | 1 | - | 2 |
| Woxe Harjo       -    -    -    - | 1 | 1 | - | 2 |
| Tolofe Harjo     -    -    -    - | 1 | 1 | - | 2 |

CREEK CENSUS—Continued.

| Names of Heads of Families. | Males. | Females. | Slaves. | Total. |
|---|---|---|---|---|
| Mihecharke - - - - | 1 | 2 | - | 3 |
| Sowwarkeche - - - - | 1 | 1 | - | 2 |
| Sohekiche - - - - | 1 | 2 | - | 3 |
| Harne - - - - | 1 | 1 | - | 2 |
| Harwarsike - - - - | 2 | 1 | - | 3 |
| Losey - - - - | 1 | 1 | - | 2 |
| Intulkar - - - - | 1 | 1 | - | 2 |
| Tuskarnoongke - - - | 1 | 1 | - | 2 |
| Chowwechiche - - - | 1 | 1 | - | 2 |
| Archokohay - - - - | 1 | 1 | - | 2 |
| Kussarharme - - - - | 1 | 1 | - | 2 |
| Thlarfieke - - - - | 2 | 2 | - | 4 |
| Sonartooke - - - - | 2 | 1 | - | 3 |
| Kussumkar - - - - | 1 | 1 | - | 2 |
|  | 33 | 34 |  | 67 |
| Cow-e-ta, at Cho-lose-parp Kar, or Kotch-ar Tus-tun-nuckee's Town. |  |  |  |  |
| Emarthlar Cochokone - - - | 2 | 2 | - | 4 |
| Arsomik Harjo - - - | 2 | 2 | - | 4 |
| Stowike - - - - | 4 | 1 | - | 5 |
| Pin Harjo - - - - | 2 | 2 | - | 4 |
| Hosar Harjo - - - - | 3 | 3 | - | 6 |
| Sfarne Fixieo - - - - | 2 | 2 | - | 4 |
| Tommy Harjo - - - - | 1 | 1 | - | 2 |
| Harfarle Harjo - - - - | 3 | 3 | - | 6 |
| Hotulke Yoholo - - - - | 4 | 1 | - | 5 |
| Yarkinhar Fixico - - - | 1 | 3 | - | 4 |
| Okefuske Harjo - - - | 2 | 3 | - | 5 |
| Kosiste Emarthlar - - - | 2 | 3 | - | 5 |
| Nocoselooche - - - | 1 | 1 | - | 2 |
| Artus Harjo - - - - | 2 | 1 | - | 3 |
| Konip Harjo - - - - | 1 | 2 | - | 3 |
| Thlarseleetkar - - - | 2 | 4 | - | 6 |
| Inthlarnis Harjo - - - | 2 | 1 | - | 3 |
| Charse Fixico - - - | 3 | 1 | - | 4 |
| Fosehatchee Emarthlar - - | 2 | 2 | - | 4 |
| Narcoye - - - - | 1 | 2 | - | 3 |
| Punwe - - - - | 2 | 2 | - | 4 |
| Fi Yoholo - - - - | 3 | 1 | - | 4 |
| Micco Narhe - - - - | 4 | 1 | 5 | 10 |
| Alpetter Harjo - - - | 1 | 1 | - | 2 |
| Foseharchooche - - - | 1 | 1 | - | 2 |
| Echarse Yoholo - - - | 1 | 1 | - | 2 |
| Iswokechar - - - - | 1 | 1 | - | 2 |
| Konip Yoholo - - - | 2 | - | - | 2 |

## CREEK CENSUS—Continued.

| Names of Heads of Families. | Males. | Females. | Slaves. | Total. |
|---|---|---|---|---|
| Chockhoethlar . . . . | 1 | 1 | - | 2 |
| Arsalar . . . . | 1 | 1 | - | 2 |
| Helis Fixico . . . . | 1 | 1 | - | 2 |
| Hothleharye . . . . | 1 | 1 | - | 2 |
| Soffinheche . . . . | 1 | 1 | - | 2 |
| Tolowar Harjo . . . . | 1 | 1 | - | 2 |
| Enehe Marthlar . . . . | 1 | 1 | - | 2 |
| Oche Harjo, (alias Johnny) . . | 1 | 1 | - | 2 |
| Pethleke . . . . | 1 | 1 | - | 2 |
| | 66 | 57 | 5 | 128 |
| Charlo Fixico . . . | 2 | 1 | - | 3 |
| Soyarkarpe . . . . | 2 | 2 | - | 4 |
| Okechun Harjo . . . . | 1 | 1 | - | 2 |
| Futsharlike . . . . | 1 | 1 | - | 2 |
| Coweta Harjo . . . . | 1 | 1 | - | 2 |
| Cheparne . . . . | 1 | 1 | - | 2 |
| Molly, (or Mary, a half negro) . . | 3 | 1 | - | 4 |
| William Powell, (alias Chofeharjo) . | 1 | 3 | - | 4 |
| Lucy Powell, (alias Lucy Hadke) . | 1 | 1 | - | 2 |
| Martha Powell, (alias Lucy Larner) . | - | 2 | - | 2 |
| Tetiche . . . . | 1 | 2 | - | 3 |
| Mitchel Kinnard, (alias Toppar Loache) . | 1 | - | 9 | 10 |
| Yarharhokete . . . . | 1 | 1 | - | 2 |
| Hoyunhoe . . . . | - | 2 | - | 2 |
| Enehar Fixico . . . . | 1 | 2 | - | 3 |
| Tunnarle . . . . | 2 | 1 | - | 3 |
| Sehechepe . . . . | 2 | 3 | - | 5 |
| Tilliche . . . . | 1 | 1 | - | 2 |
| Hitchhoye . . . . | 1 | 1 | - | 2 |
| John Island . . . . | 2 | — | - | 2 |
| Lekocthiche . . . . | 1 | 1 | - | 2 |
| Efar Fixico . . . . | 1 | 1 | - | 2 |
| Sattikothe . . . . | 1 | 2 | - | 3 |
| Chekose . . . . | 1 | 3 | - | 4 |
| Saltarwe . . . . | 2 | 1 | 10 | 13 |
| Chisse Harjo . . . . | 1 | 1 | - | 2 |
| Chofullwar . . . . | 1 | 3 | - | 4 |
| Choole Harjo . . . . | 1 | 1 | - | 2 |
| Parlarche Harjo . . | 2 | - | - | 2 |
| Okparlartay . . . . | 1 | 1 | - | 2 |
| Seniche . . . . | 1 | 3 | - | 4 |
| Cussetaw Tustunnuckee . . . | 3 | 2 | - | 5 |
| Kowokkooche Harjo . . . | 2 | 1 | - | 3 |
| Starharye . . . . | 1 | 1 | - | 2 |

49‡

## CREEK CENSUS—Continued.

| Names of Heads of Families. | Males. | Females. | Slaves. | Total. |
|---|---|---|---|---|
| Chisse      -      -      -      -      -      - | 1 | 1 | - | 2 |
| Watte      -      -      -      -      - | 1 | 1 | - | 2 |
| Thlenitkar      -      -      -      - | 2 | - | - | 2 |
| Osooche Emarthlar      -      -      - | 1 | 1 | - | 2 |
| Jake Thlinar      -      -      -      - | 2 | - | - | 2 |
| Ekesey      -      -      -      -      - | — | 2 | - | 2 |
| Lowsethlocko      -      -      -      - | — | 3 | - | 3 |
| Hosiche      -      -      -      -      - | 1 | 2 | - | 3 |
| Tehopeye      -      -      -      - | 1 | 1 | - | 2 |
|  | 53 | 59 | 19 | 131 |
| Arsarwe      -      -      -      -      - | 2 | 1 | - | 3 |
| Kiselarnee      -      -      -      - | - | 2 | - | 2 |
| Narhole      -      -      -      -      - | 1 | 1 | - | 2 |
| Nokesarwarle      -      -      -      - | — | 2 | - | 2 |
| Islotke      -      -      -      -      - | 2 | 3 | - | 5 |
| Scetotartikey      -      -      -      - | — | 3 | - | 3 |
| Istinhethliche      -      -      -      - | — | 2 | - | 2 |
| Looswar      -      -      -      -      - | — | 2 | - | 2 |
| Hun Hoye      -      -      -      - | — | 2 | - | 2 |
| Seliche      -      -      -      - | 2 | 3 | - | 5 |
| Fenar      -      -      -      - | 1 | 1 | - | 2 |
| Notepoke      -      -      -      - | 2 | 3 | - | 5 |
| Parlarluckar      -      -      -      - | 1 | 2 | - | 3 |
| Halhoker      -      -      -      - | — | 2 | - | 2 |
|  | 11 | 29 | - | 40 |

### THLAKATCHKA, OR BROKEN ARROW.
### WETUMKA, OR EUCHEE HALCHEE.

| Names of Heads of Families. | Males. | Females. | Slaves. | Total. |
|---|---|---|---|---|
| Tomac Micco      -      -      -      - | 1 | 1 | 2 | 4 |
| Karpikchar Yoholo      -      -      - | 1 | 1 | - | 2 |
| Fixico Harjo      -      -      -      - | 2 | 1 | - | 3 |
| Nehar Yoholo      -      -      -      - | 2 | 3 | - | 5 |
| Tuskonar Fixico -      -      -      - | 1 | 2 | - | 3 |
| Yarhar Harjo, alias Tom Brown      -      - | 2 | 1 | - | 3 |
| Thlewarle Emarthlar      -      -      - | 1 | 5 | - | 6 |
| Tulse Fixico      -      -      -      - | 1 | 1 | - | 2 |
| Harparlar Harjo      -      -      -      - | 1 | 1 | - | 2 |
| Yarkinhar Fixico      -      -      - | 1 | 1 | - | 2 |
| Fose Harjo      -      -      -      - | 4 | 1 | - | 5 |
| Tarse Keek Harjo      -      -      - | 1 | 1 | - | 2 |
| Yoholo Harjo      -      -      -      - | 3 | 5 | - | 8 |
| Sunte      -      -      -      -      - | 1 | 1 | - | 2 |
| Harharlock Harjo      •      • | 2 | 2 | - | 4 |

## CREEK CENSUS—Continued.

| Names of Heads of Families. | Males. | Females. | Slaves. | Total. |
|---|---|---|---|---|
| Itchar Yoholo | 4 | 1 | - | 5 |
| Archolok Harjo | 1 | 1 | - | 2 |
| Lochar Harjo | 1 | 1 | - | 2 |
| Holartar Fixico | 1 | 2 | - | 3 |
| Neharthlockochopko | 1 | 1 | - | 2 |
| Woxehotartar | 3 | 2 | - | 5 |
| Spokeokee Emarthlar | 3 | 4 | - | 7 |
| Holartar | 1 | 1 | - | 2 |
| Kowarthlocko Harjo | 1 | 1 | - | 2 |
| Kolchar Tustunnuckee | 1 | 1 | - | 2 |
| Towasse Micco | 1 | 1 | - | 2 |
| Echarse Yoholo | 1 | 1 | - | 2 |
| Tussekaryar Harjo | 4 | 1 | - | 5 |
| Totekarharse | 1 | 1 | - | 2 |
| Kowokkooche Harjo | 1 | 2 | - | 3 |
| Ninnechoppar Harjo | 3 | 4 | - | 7 |
| Tulmarse | 1 | 3 | - | 4 |
| Marparharke | 3 | 1 | - | 4 |
| Temesekar | 1 | 1 | - | 2 |
| Efar Tustunnuckee | 4 | 2 | 3 | 9 |
| Kowok Emarthlar | 1 | 1 | - | 2 |
| Iskinhar | 1 | 1 | - | 2 |
| | 63 | 61 | 5 | 129 |
| Fi Yoholo | 3 | 1 | 1 | 5 |
| Tommy Harjo | 2 | 1 | - | 3 |
| Tukko Harjo | 1 | 2 | - | 3 |
| Tulse Yoholo | 1 | 1 | - | 2 |
| Hoholikarme | 1 | 1 | - | 2 |
| Tolofe Harjo | 2 | 3 | 1 | 6 |
| Cheparne | 2 | - | 3 | 5 |
| Mekoli Ray, alias James Berryhill | 1 | 1 | - | 2 |
| Fosehatchee Harjo | 2 | 1 | - | 3 |
| Hothlemarte Harjo | 1 | 1 | - | 2 |
| Koekus Yoholo | 1 | 1 | - | 2 |
| Choolar Fixico | 1 | 1 | - | 2 |
| Fucktelustee, alias Black Dirt | 1 | 4 | 9 | 14 |
| Lucylocko, wife of R. Royster, a white man | 1 | 2 | - | 3 |
| Isfulhoke | 1 | 1 | - | 2 |
| Kenarye | 3 | 2 | - | 5 |
| Klissarwike | 1 | 1 | - | 2 |
| Toje | 1 | 1 | - | 2 |
| Honechiche | 1 | 1 | - | 2 |
| Pochus Micco | 2 | 2 | - | 4 |
| Coweta Harjo | 1 | 1 | - | 2 |

CREEK CENSUS—Continued.

| Names of Heads of Families. | Males. | Females. | Slaves. | Total. |
|---|---|---|---|---|
| Tunole - - - - - | 1 | 2 | - | 3 |
| Yartuf Harjo - - - - | 2 | 1 | - | 3 |
| Nehemarthlar - - - - | 2 | 1 | - | 3 |
| Cheekkar. - - - - - | 1 | 2 | - | 3 |
| Kose Yoholo - - - - | 2 | 5 | - | 7 |
| Arsoethlar - - - - | 1 | 1 | - | 2 |
| Woxe Emarthlar - - - - | 2 | 4 | - | 6 |
| Sehoyiche - - - - | - | 2 | - | 2 |
| Yarkinharchopko - - - | 1 | 1 | - | 2 |
| Spokeoke Yoholo - - - | 4 | 2 | - | 6 |
| Sarche - - - - | 1 | 1 | - | 2 |
| Seenar - - - - | 1 | 1 | - | 2 |
| Senechiche - - - - | 2 | 1 | - | 3 |
| Kotchar Yoholo - - - | 1 | 1 | - | 2 |
| Shockhonochiche - - - | 1 | 1 | - | 2 |
| Aipetter Harjo - - - | 2 | 1 | - | 3 |
| Marhosar - - - - | 1 | 1 | - | 2 |
| Sehomarleche - - - - | 1 | 1 | - | 2 |
| Kelissar Harjo - - - | 2 | 1 | - | 3 |
| Holthley - - - - | 1 | 1 | 2 | 4 |
| Chatto Miccooche - - - | 2 | 3 | - | 5 |
| Narkoitage - - - - | - | 2 | - | 2 |
| | 61 | 65 | 16 | 142 |
| Istemosiye - - - - | 1 | 1 | - | 2 |
| Choille Harjo - - - | 2 | 1 | - | 3 |
| Kochus Yoholo - - - | 1 | 3 | - | 4 |
| Fosehatch Yoholo - - - | 2 | 1 | - | 3 |
| Chickey - - - - | 1 | 1 | - | 2 |
| Sarney - - - - | 1 | 1 | - | 2 |
| Sockeparke - - - - | 1 | 1 | - | 2 |
| Mulleetkar - - - - | 1 | 1 | - | 2 |
| Archee Yoholo - - - | 3 | 3 | - | 6 |
| Yarkinhar - - - - | 3 | 2 | - | 5 |
| Tulse Harjo - - - - | 1 | 1 | - | 2 |
| Chowwokoloneharthlocko - - | 3 | 2 | - | 5 |
| Isfarneharjo - - - - | 1 | 1 | - | 2 |
| Emarthlar Charharne - - | 1 | 2 | - | 3 |
| Dickey - - - - | 2 | 1 | - | 3 |
| Hoyanechar - - - - | 1 | 1 | - | 2 |
| Tulmarse Emarthlar - - | 1 | 4 | - | 5 |
| Teoporehoke - - - - | 1 | 1 | - | 2 |
| Lowsarchooley - - - | 1 | 1 | - | 2 |
| Lowsotekar - - - - | 1 | 1 | - | 2 |
| Arkoye - - - - | 1 | 2 | - | 3 |

CREEK CENSUS—Continued.

| Names of Heads of Families. | Males. | Females. | Slaves. | Total. |
|---|---|---|---|---|
| Lintooche | 5 | — | - | 5 |
| Ischotekar | 1 | 3 | - | 4 |
| Chisse Harjo | 2 | 1 | - | 3 |
| Teyarmike | 2 | 1 | - | 3 |
| Kotcharhar Chooche | 1 | 3 | - | 4 |
| Tus Konar Harjo | 2 | — | - | 2 |
| Micooche | 2 | 1 | - | 3 |
| Sokkolatekar | 1 | 1 | 4 | 6 |
| Choof Yake | 1 | 1 | - | 2 |
| Stimmarhotartike | 1 | 2 | - | 3 |
| Lowskiyarlay | 1 | 1 | - | 2 |
| Sathlokey | 1 | 1 | - | 2 |
| Hillabee Harjo | 2 | 4 | - | 6 |
| Cheyolowske | 1 | 2 | 3 | 6 |
| Tooltooke | 2 | 2 | - | 4 |
| John Carr | 2 | 8 | 3 | 13 |
| Potter | 3 | 1 | - | 4 |
| Lucy Prince (a free black) | 1 | 1 | - | 2 |
| Johnathan Isaac (a free black) | 1 | 1 | - | 2 |
| Jack (a free black) | 1 | 1 | - | 2 |
| Nancy (a free black) | 1 | 1 | - | 2 |
| | 64 | 69 | 10 | 143 |

THLAKALCHKA.

| | | | | |
|---|---|---|---|---|
| Yarkinhar Micco | 1 | 1 | - | 2 |
| Harcholock Harjo | 1 | 1 | - | 2 |
| Thlockpusware | 1 | 1 | - | 2 |
| Yarhole Emarthlar | 2 | 3 | - | 5 |
| Minotta (alias John) | 1 | 1 | - | 2 |
| Hatchkeyee | 1 | 2 | - | 3 |
| Chalhoyar | 1 | 1 | - | 2 |
| Homar Hotay | 1 | 1 | - | 2 |
| Fose Harjo | 1 | 1 | - | 2 |
| Hechar | 1 | 1 | - | 2 |
| Letekar | 2 | 1 | - | 3 |
| Sinhoyarnechar | 1 | 1 | - | 2 |
| Kuntalle | 1 | 1 | - | 2 |
| Billy | 1 | 2 | - | 3 |
| Nocoseekar | 1 | 1 | - | 2 |
| Fosehoketee | 1 | 1 | - | 2 |
| Meharke | 1 | 1 | - | 2 |
| | 19 | 21 | | 40 |

## CREEK CENSUS—Continued.

| Names of Heads of Families. | Males. | Females. | Slaves. | Total. |
|---|---|---|---|---|
| THLAKALCHKA, (Koteofar.) | | | | |
| Talmarse | 1 | 1 | - | 2 |
| Holthharse | 4 | 2 | - | 6 |
| Fosehatchee Emarthlar | 1 | 1 | - | 2 |
| Okeolasse Emarthlar | 2 | 3 | - | 5 |
| Sarpulparke | 2 | — | - | 2 |
| Karpikchar Harjo | 1 | 1 | - | 2 |
| Nocose Harjo | 1 | 1 | - | 2 |
| Arnarkoeche | 4 | 1 | - | 5 |
| Hoosar Harjo | 2 | 2 | - | 4 |
| Parsuk Harjo | 3 | 1 | - | 4 |
| Yarpetar | 1 | 1 | - | 2 |
| Hoketalarne | 1 | 2 | - | 3 |
| Isparle | 2 | 1 | - | 3 |
| Litketarthle | 2 | 1 | - | 3 |
| Okekooske Harjo | 3 | 2 | - | 5 |
| Kootchars Emarthlar | 3 | 3 | - | 6 |
| Sowwarheeche | 5 | 2 | - | 7 |
| Hofooniche | 2 | 2 | - | 4 |
| Kotchar Harjo | 2 | 4 | - | 6 |
| Sarlecche | 1 | 2 | - | 3 |
| Lartar Micco | 1 | 1 | - | 2 |
| Arseho | 1 | 1 | - | 2 |
| Sowikay | 1 | 1 | - | 2 |
| Simmunnarte | 1 | 1 | - | 2 |
| Singkarke | 1 | 1 | - | 2 |
| Munchunnunnichar | 1 | 1 | 2 | 4 |
| Holearnar | 3 | — | - | 3 |
| Woxe Harjo | 2 | — | - | 2 |
| | 54 | 39 | 2 | 95 |
| THLAKALCHKA CHOLOCKOMINNE, or HORSE PATH TOWN. | | | | |
| Woxe Harjo | 4 | 1 | - | 5 |
| Tallasse Tustunnuckee | 3 | 1 | - | 4 |
| Hotulke Emarthlar | 1 | 3 | - | 4 |
| Chopofe Micco | 4 | 1 | - | 5 |
| Koparthlocko Fixico | 2 | 3 | - | 5 |
| Neharthlock Emarthlar | 1 | 1 | 3 | 5 |
| Holartar Yoholo | 1 | 1 | | 2 |
| Harharlock Micco | 2 | — | - | 2 |
| Micccoche | 2 | 3 | - | 5 |
| Miccothlocko | 1 | 1 | - | 2 |
| Tefarharke | 2 | 2 | - | 4 |

CREEK CENSUS—Continued.

| Names of Heads of Families. | Males. | Females. | Slaves. | Total. |
|---|---|---|---|---|
| Chokarte - - - - - | 1 | 4 | - | 5 |
| Chopofe Harjo - - - - | 1 | 3 | - | 4 |
| Tarsekiar - - - - - | 2 | 1 | - | 3 |
| Warthlocko - - - - | 2 | 1 | - | 3 |
| Hopoealth Harjo - - - - | 2 | 1 | - | 3 |
| Hospar - - - - - | 3 | 2 | - | 5 |
| Chike - - - - - | 1 | 2 | - | 3 |
| Thlewarle Harjo - - - - | 4 | 3 | - | 7 |
| Honupper - - - - | 1 | 1 | - | 2 |
| Chofolowar - - - - | 3 | 4 | - | 7 |
| Holthkopiche - - - - | 2 | 2 | - | 4 |
| Tommy Harjo - - - - | 1 | 1 | - | 2 |
| Chewastarye - - - - | 1 | 4 | - | 5 |
| Johnny Thlocko, (alias Johnny Thompson) | 1 | 1 | - | 2 |
| Nocosekar - - - - | 3 | 3 | - | 6 |
| Ligoche - - - - - | 1 | 2 | - | 3 |
| Coweta Harjo - - - - | 2 | 5 | - | 7 |
| Chisse - - - - - | 2 | 2 | - | 4 |
| Homarlarnee - - - - | 1 | 3 | - | 4 |
| Talmochus Harjo - - - - | 3 | 2 | - | 5 |
| Chitto - - - - - | 1 | 1 | - | 2 |
| Pen Harjo - - - - | 3 | 1 | - | 4 |
| Tulse Fixico, (alias John Danely) - | 2 | 1 | - | 3 |
| Hosar Harjo - - - - | 1 | 1 | - | 2 |
| Kochus Harjo - - - - | 3 | 2 | - | 5 |
| Marke - - - - - | 1 | 1 | - | 2 |
| Nocoseaaly - - - - | 1 | 3 | - | 4 |
|  | 72 | 74 | 3 | 149 |
| Thlockmarlike - - - - | 1 | 3 | - | 4 |
| Talladega - - - - - | 1 | 1 | - | 2 |
| Hatchkisse - - - - | 2 | 2 | - | 4 |
| Mieter - - - - - | 2 | 2 | - | 4 |
| Yelka Harjo - - - - | 1 | 1 | - | 2 |
| Choolar Fixico - - - - | 4 | 2 | - | 6 |
| Nitey - - - - - | 1 | 2 | - | 3 |
| Seehoyar - - - - - | 1 | 1 | - | 2 |
| Eufaula Micco, (alias Wm. Massey) - | 1 | 2 | - | 3 |
| Sparse - - - - - | 3 | 1 | - | 4 |
| Semarpoke, (alias Tommy) - - | 2 | — | - | 2 |
| Sarye - - - - - | 1 | 1 | - | 2 |
| Yarkinhar - - - - | 1 | 1 | - | 2 |
| Cheparne - - - - - | 1 | 1 | - | 2 |
| Simmartulkar - - - - | 2 | 4 | - | 6 |
| Fose Harjo - - - - | 1 | 2 | - | 3 |

CREEK CENSUS—Continued.

| Names of Heads of Families. | Males. | Females. | Slaves. | Total. |
|---|---|---|---|---|
| Tulseharjo - - - - | 1 | 2 | - | 3 |
| Cholotekar - - - - | 1 | 1 | - | 2 |
| Tarskeke Micco - - - - | 2 | 1 | - | 3 |
| Sattote - - - - - | 1 | 1 | - | 2 |
| Tolofeharjo - - - - | 1 | 1 | - | 2 |
| Thomas Berryhill - - - | 1 | 2 | - | 3 |
| William Berryhill - - - | 6 | 5 | - | 11 |
| Eli Berrryhill - - - - | 2 | 1 | - | 3 |
| John Berryhill - - - | 1 | 1 | - | 2 |
| Thomas W. Berryhill - - - | 2 | 1 | - | 3 |
| Ben Posey - - - - | 4 | 4 | - | 8 |
| Oktiarche - - - - | 1 | 1 | - | 2 |
| Litke - - - - - | 1 | 1 | - | 2 |
| Homarharye - - - - | 1 | 1 | - | 2 |
| Hiyekene - - - - - | 1 | - | 2 | 3 |
| Nimrod Doyell - - - - | 2 | 1 | - | 3 |
| Jackson Doyell - - - - | 1 | - | 1 | 2 |
| Muscogee Doyell - - - - | — | 1 | 1 | 2 |
| Sekestee - - - - - | 1 | 1 | . | 2 |
| Scekealthlar - - - - | 2 | - | . | 2 |
| Tomeshe - - - - - | 1 | 1 | . | 2 |
| Shehote - - - - - | 1 | 2 | . | 3 |
| Kotcharchooche - - - - | 1 | 1 | . | 2 |
| Farlumkar - - - - | 1 | 1 | . | 2 |
| Tarkozar - - - - - | 1 | 1 | . | 2 |
| Pin Ekar - - - - - | 1 | 1 | . | 2 |
| Marhokole - - - - | 2 | 1 | . | 3 |
| | 65 | 60 | 4 | 129 |
| Naroalthkar - - - - | 1 | 1 | | 2 |
| Tarchockhoyilete - - - - | 1 | 1 | . | 2 |
| Harwiekar - - - - | 1 | 1 | . | 2 |
| Yoalthkar - - - - | 3 | 1 | . | 4 |
| Nanny Miller - - - - | — | 1 | 2 | 3 |
| Nanny - - - - - | 1 | 4 | . | 5 |
| Nokerfite - - - - | 1 | 1 | . | 2 |
| Homarye - - - - | 1 | 1 | . | 2 |
| Sowwiheke - - - - | 1 | 2 | . | 3 |
| Fummo - - - - - | 1 | 1 | . | 2 |
| Slowarke - - - - | 1 | 1 | . | 2 |
| Chocksehoke - - - - | — | 2 | . | 2 |
| Winey - - - - - | — | 2 | 3 | 5 |
| Ogiffe - - - - - | 1 | 1 | . | 2 |
| Lucy Chartee - - - - | - | 2 | . | 2 |
| Timoke - - - - - | - | 2 | . | 2 |

CREEK CENSUS—Continued.

| Names of Heads of Families. | Males. | Females. | Slaves. | Total. |
|---|---|---|---|---|
| Soharye - - - - - | - | 2 | - | 2 |
| Pitchy - - - - - | - | 3 | - | 3 |
| Fickiyeche - - - - | 1 | 1 | - | 2 |
| Scetiyeye - - - - - | - | 2 | - | 2 |
| Kisse - - - - - | 1 | 1 | - | 2 |
| Ponihe Ro - - - - | 1 | 1 | - | 2 |
| Kooloosar - - - - | 1 | 2 | - | 3 |
| Tarkonarfkar - - - - | 3 | 3 | - | 6 |
| Tohicheche - - - - | - | 3 | - | 3 |
| Seetarne - - - - - | - | 2 | - | 2 |
| Gideon Arthur - - - - | 1 | 3 | - | 4 |
| | 21 | 47 | 5 | 73 |

THLAKATCHKA AND OKEFUSKA ECHEE SE HO-
GEE TOWN, on the waters of the Tallapoosa.

| | | | | |
|---|---|---|---|---|
| Micco Foseke - - - - | 4 | 2 | - | 6 |
| Nehorfixico - - - - | 1 | 1 | - | 2 |
| Karpikcharharjo - - - | 2 | 3 | - | 5 |
| Hillabeefixico - - - - | 1 | 2 | - | 3 |
| James Moore - - - - | 2 | 3 | 11 | 16 |
| Katey Moore - - - - | 1 | 3 | 1 | 5 |
| Peggy Moore - - - - | 1 | 1 | 1 | 3 |
| Nancy Moore - - - - | 1 | 1 | 1 | 3 |
| John Moore - - - - | 1 | 1 | - | 2 |
| Harpecooche Emarthlar - - - | 1 | 1 | - | 2 |
| Yelkaharjo - - - - | 2 | 4 | - | 6 |
| Tustunnuckkooche - - - | 2 | 1 | - | 3 |
| Thlathloharjo - - - - | 3 | 2 | - | 5 |
| Harparlarharjo - - - - | 5 | 2 | - | 7 |
| Enfanlaharjo - - - - | 6 | 2 | - | 8 |
| Siliche - - - - - | 2 | 1 | - | 3 |
| Chooille - - - - - | 2 | 4 | - | 6 |
| Kosarharjo - - - - | 3 | 5 | - | 8 |
| Karpikcharnicco - - - | 3 | 2 | - | 5 |
| Sokpolotke - - - - | 3 | 2 | - | 5 |
| Imparlarte - - - - | 1 | 1 | - | 2 |
| Parhoseharjo - - - - | 2 | 2 | - | 4 |
| Osoochharjo - - - - | 2 | 3 | - | 5 |
| Tommy Miccooche - - - | 1 | 1 | - | 2 |
| Artusneharthlocko - - - | 3 | 2 | - | 5 |
| Archoolehargo - - - - | 3 | 1 | - | 4 |
| Nocose Yoholo - - - - | 2 | 2 | - | 4 |
| Tommy Fixico - - - - | 3 | 1 | - | 4 |
| Nocose Emarthlooche - - - | 2 | 1 | - | 3 |
| Hillabeeharjo - - - - | 2 | 2 | - | 4 |

CREEK CENSUS—Continued.

| Names of Heads of Families. | Males. | Females | Slaves. | Total. |
|---|---|---|---|---|
| Hopoethleyoholo . . . . | 1 | 2 | - | 2 |
| Miyepar . . . . . | 1 | 1 | - | 2 |
| Euparletikay . . . . | 1 | 1 | - | 2 |
| Pin Rey . . . . . | 2 | 2 | - | 4 |
| Konip Yoholo . . . . | 1 | 1 | - | 2 |
| Sfarneharjo . . . . | 2 | 2 | - | 4 |
| Kunchartee . . . . | 2 | 1 | - | 3 |
| Warsokete . . . . | 1 | 2 | - | 3 |
| Yufke Emarthlarharjo . . . | 3 | 4 | - | 7 |
| | 81 | 74 | 14 | 169 |
| Itemoligey . . . . . | — | 2 | - | 2 |
| Yarho Kar . . . . . | 1 | 3 | - | 4 |
| Fulsetoko . . . . . | 3 | 1 | - | 4 |
| Tommyharjo . . . . . | 2 | 2 | - | 4 |
| Stingkarke . . . . . | 2 | 1 | - | 3 |
| Notchkar . . . . . | 2 | 2 | - | 4 |
| Cheose . . . . . | 1 | 2 | - | 3 |
| Maryoke . . . . . | — | 2 | - | 2 |
| Artassar . . . . | 2 | 1 | - | 3 |
| Wyche . . . . . | 1 | 1 | - | 2 |
| Spokeokeharjo . . . . | 2 | 1 | - | 3 |
| Inmunnarleechar . . . | 1 | 1 | - | 2 |
| Okechumharjo (alias) Simon . . | 3 | 3 | - | 6 |
| Imfittarharjo . . . | 1 | 3 | - | 4 |
| Tarkoosooche . . . . | 3 | 2 | - | 5 |
| Talofeharjo . . . . | 1 | 3 | - | 4 |
| Nocosehatchee . . . . | 1 | 1 | - | 2 |
| | 26 | 31 | | 57 |

| | |
|---|---|
| Total of the population of the lower towns, including slaves, | 8,522 |
| Deduct the number of slaves, . . . . | 457 |
| Which leaves the number of Indians . . . | 8,065 |

In addition to the foregoing, the two following names have been reported to me, (by the chief,) of individuals to whom they have assigned one half section each of the twenty-nine sections of land, reserved by the 6th article of the treaty, and left at the disposal of the tribe, viz.:

George Grayson, half section; Winchester Doyle, half section.

I do hereby certify that the above census was taken by me, and that this roll is as correct as I have been able to make it.

*May* 13, 1833.                    THOMAS J. ABBOTT.

Sworn to before me, THOMAS J. MARTIN, I. C. C. R C.

NEW GASCONY, ARKANSAS TERRITORY,
*May* 14, 1833.

SIR: I acknowledge the receipt of your letter of April 6, respecting a draft drawn on the War Department for a quarter's salary. I will endeavor, to the best of my abilities, to obey your instructions in every matter pertaining to the duties of my office. Gov. Pope has left the Territory for Kentucky. I was told that Secretary Fulton was confined to his house by sickness, which is my apology for writing this letter. Gov. Pope placed in my hands fifteen hundred dollars, Quapaw money, which I paid over to the Indians, and took their receipt. He placed in my hands a further sum of one thousand dollars, a donation from the Government. I paid, out of that sum, three hundred and fifty dollars to Antoine Barraque. I paid Joseph Duchasin (order in favor of A. Barraque) seventy dollars, as part of the salary due him as interpreter. I retained in my own hands one hundred and fifty dollars, by the written request of the chiefs, and the approbation of Gov. Pope, to visit the commissioners on Indian business. I did not charge one cent for three trips up and down the river to receive and exchange the money, and for the purpose of making my report to Gov. Pope. The sub-agency is kept about one hundred and twenty miles below the Rock, and near the Indians. There are forty-one Indians yet to pay. The chiefs made a mistake in giving in the number, which deranged the whole calculation. I have sent out Indians to notify the remainder to come in and receive as much of the donation as will put them on a par with the other Indians. The chiefs are desirous that the balance of the money be kept to pay expenses in exploring their new country, and marking out the route, which will be pretty much through the woods. If the exploring expedition should meet your approbation, the money will be kept for that purpose. If you do not approve the expedition, I think it will be prudent to lay the money out for clothing for the poor of the tribe. Last fall, when laboring under severe bodily sickness, I made out a statement for Gov. Pope, as to the situation of the tribe. He stated to me that he forwarded the communication to the War Department. I was very much surprised, as I intended it only for his own eye, to found a letter on to the department. The communication was made in his own house, and at a time when I was incapable to write. I well knew, from the goodness of his heart, he would pardon any omission that might arise in consequence of bodily disability.

So soon as I am instructed, I will forward my account properly authenticated. I presume Gov. Pope has forwarded to the department the receipts taken from the Indians, as well as Antoine Barraque's receipt. Gov. Pope directed me to pay Duchasin's order, and Mr. Schermerhorn to detain the balance of the money in my hands for the purpose of meeting the expenses of the exploring expedition.

I am, with great respect,
Your humble servant,
RICHARD M. HANNUM.

To ELBERT HERRING, Esq.,
*Commissioner of Indian Affairs.*

TALLADEGA COUNTY, ALABAMA,
*Jumper Springs, May* 15, 1833.

SIR: Having received information that the census of the Creeks is taken and forwarded on to the department, and that the surveys will soon be completed, I deem it necessary to apply to the department for additional instructions.

And first, permit me to inquire if it will be my duty to correct the errors of those who have taken the census; and if so, who are properly considered heads of families? Are those persons who have become heads of families since the treaty was concluded, entitled to reservations? Are white men and free negroes who have been long residents of the country entitled to lands?

Some of the Indians have several wives, who sometimes live in different towns, and at a considerable distance from each other; they are allowed by the Indians to own property, not subject to the control of their husbands, and from the facility with which they can at any time dissolve their marriage contracts, it will be extremely difficult to determine who amongst them will be entitled to reserves. Please instruct me on that subject.

Where Indian improvements are on fractional sections, not so large as a half section, what is to be done in such cases? Some of those fractions are really valuable, and those who live upon them would relinquish their claims to any overplus, rather than take their reservations elsewhere.

Will it be proper, where circumstances seem to require it, to make the locations east and west, as well as north and south, viz., may the locations be so made as to give the reservee a north or a south half, as well as an east or a west half section?

When at Fort Mitchell, in conversation with Eficmatla, one of the chiefs who signed the treaty, he said he had understood that it was my opinion that the Indians would have to take their reservations where the largest part of their improvements were at the time the treaty was concluded. I replied, that that was my opinion, and gave him my reasons for thinking so; he insisted that I was mistaken, and requested me to write for information on that subject, and said the President told him to direct his people to select good places, and remove to them, and that they would be entitled to them. I mentioned the subject to Colonel Crowell; he said that it was so, and that he himself heard the President tell Eficmatla to do so, and that numbers of Indians had, on the faith of what their chiefs had told them, already removed and made improvements. I met Benjamin Marshall, who was, as he told me, moving his sister from her old to a better place. Please write to me on that subject.

Many of the Indians, I have no doubt, have been induced to remove and make improvements by interested white men, who design to purchase their claims; but it is also true that a great many have done so of their own accord, with a view to better their situations. Many, however, still remain where they resided when the treaty was made, and some of them will obtain lands almost entirely worthless.

In some parts of the nation, the Indians living in little villages have already agreed amongst themselves (where the lines of the surveys include more than one of their improvements in one half section) who shall relinquish their claims. But those who have given up their claims, have made improvements elsewhere, and mostly on tracts contiguous to those they had relinquished, being anxious to reside in the same neighborhood, which was originally formed for social purposes, and which is generally composed of individuals some way related to each other. These people, if it were possible (according to my instructions, and the provisions of the treaty) to gratify, I should be anxious to do it. But when I explain to them the treaty on this subject, they seem dissatisfied, and many of them have been induced to believe, by interested and designing white men, that I have it in my power, if I were so disposed, to give them their places, and frequently tell them that if they or their friends had the appointment I have, they should have them. I mention this as one of the many means which is resorted to to render the Indians dissatisfied with me; and though in some instances they have partially succeeded, I have no idea that their success will be of long continuance. One thing, however, I do know, and that is, that I am not unconscious of the high responsibility of my station, and the anxiety I feel to be serviceable to the Indians, and to discharge the duties of my appointments to the satisfaction of the department, and to merit the approbation of his excellency, the President; and to do this, all the art I shall use will be to do right, and deceive none of the parties.

If ever there was a people exposed to the machinations of speculators, it is the Creeks. A relation of the means resorted to in order to induce them to sell their lands to individuals, and to prevent them from selling to Government, would astonish the department, and fill the patriotic bosom of our Chief Magistrate with indignant disgust; suffice it to say, that the Indian character and disposition are indefatigably studied; the Government is complained against, its agents assailed in various ways, influential white men who have married natives are engaged, even the laws are pressed into their service, the Indians are at one time flattered and caressed, at another they are threatened and alarmed. I would say more, but I have trespassed already upon the patience of the department, and will conclude by observing, that if I am not deceived, they have already overdone the matter, and many of the Indians begin to understand them, and seem inclined to sell to Government. There are so many reasons which might be urged in favor of their selling to the Government, that I cannot but believe that if the proper means were used, they would see the great advantage which it would be to them, and hesitate no longer.

With great respect, &c.,<br>
LEONARD TARRANT.

Elbert Herring, Esq.

---

Pickensville, Alabama,<br>
May 15, 1833.

Sir: Your answer of the 22d of April to my letter of inquiry, dated 23d March last, has been received. It gave the information desired, for which Mr. Mitchell feels truly thankful. But upon one point you were not as clear as is desirable, that is, in speaking of McGilbry; you have not used the Christian name, and as there are three Indians claiming land under the 19th acticle of the late Choctaw treaty of that name, it is now desirable to ascertain whether John Turner and Gordon McGilbry have all had their names duly registered; and if not, which one is not named upon the record. An answer to this letter will, I think, terminate in the friendly adjustment of existing differences.

Respectfully, yours,<br>
GAB. FELDER.

Hon. ELBERT HERRING,
*Office of Indian Affairs.*

---

COLUMBUS, *May* 16, 1833.

DEAR SIR: The land reserved to me by the last treaty between the Creek Indians and the United States Government has been much trespassed on and injured during the present year, by the laborers of the intendant and commissioners of the town of Columbus, who are engaged in procuring lumber to build a bridge across the Chattahooche river, the western abutment of which must necessarily be placed on my land, and those men, as well as others, are now trespassers upon and have already very much injured the land by felling timber, &c.

How are these evils to be remedied? I am advised that unless I had received the patent from the Government, acknowledging and establishing my right, that I cannot adopt any measures of redress in my own name. If this is true, I desire the Government to interpose its power for the preservation of my rights, by punishing those who have trespassed, removing trespassers, and preventing the intendant and commissioners of Columbus from placing a bridge on my land, unless they will allow me an equal interest in it, by paying off half the expense of building, &c. Otherwise, to issue the patent, and forward it, addressed to me at this place, by mail, as early as possible, so as to enable me to avail myself of such remedies as the laws of Georgia, Alabama, and the United States will afford me for the redress of present and past injuries. On this subject I feel much solicitude, and therefore earnestly desire immediate information relative to it.

Very respectfully,<br>
Your most obedient serv't.,<br>
B. MARSHALL.

ANDREW JACKSON,
*President of the United States.*

---

COLUMBUS, GEORGIA, *May* 17, 1833.

SIR: I have not yet heard a word from the joint commissioner, nor do I find any one here who knows where he lives. I presume, however, that a duplicate of the instructions were sent to him, and that he will repair to the agency after receiving them.

My hopes of making a treaty and of purchasing the reservations have somewhat increased. Although we shall certainly meet with a strong opposition from those who have speculated upon these inchoate rights of the Indians, yet there is also a large population of highly respectable men who have disapproved of these speculations, but who are anxious to come in as fair purchasers under the Government, and who will lend their aid and influence in effecting a treaty.

An obstacle in the minds of the Indians is, that these reservations are matters of individual profit, and do not go in the hands of the nation or chiefs, and are, therefore, of personal advantage. I have removed this by the remark, that I was willing to stipulate in the treaty that those entitled to reservations should receive the price which might be agreed upon to be paid for them. And to lessen the apprehensions of those who had speculated, I have also said that their interests, to the amount of bona fide payments, would also be protected. Many laugh, however, and I see plainly that a second Yazoo business is contemplated. However, an apprehension of this will not deter me, as I will make a treaty if I can on proper terms, and leave any result of this kind to the courts.

It will probably not be in my power to have a meeting of the nation earlier than the 10th of June, at which time I shall pay off the annuities, and also try to arrange a treaty.

It is of extreme importance to the State of Alabama that we should succeed, as it will avoid those obstacles to settlements which will result if these lands are monopolized by speculators; and, as far as I can ascertain, the most extensive speculations yet made are by citizens of Georgia.

I have, &c.,

J. J. ABERT,
*Lt. Col. Top. Eng.*

Hon. Lewis Cass,
*Secretary of War.*

---

Columbus, *May* 17, 1833.

Sir: Having ascertained this morning that McIntosh was about thirty miles off, in the Creek nation, and an opportunity offering, I shall, in the course of the day, send the letter to him which you committed to my care. As it was an open letter, I added to it a note that I was in this town, and could be consulted on the subject of the letter if he thought it desirable. My reasons for this note were, because I understood that he had already gone to some extent in his arrangements for removing, probably, about five hundred Indians, and because of the following expression in your letter: you say "If you have, however, made any progress in the business, you will suspend further operations; the department, &c." Now, as I do not suppose that you intended by this sentence to discountenance any arrangements which McIntosh had already made, under the authority of your letter of the 11th of February, which would be both a breach of good faith and of good policy; but as your letter of the 4th May might be so interpreted, I deemed it advisable to add the note above alluded to, that I might advise to a course which, while it avoided the evil of such a result, might also stay the further prosecution of a business which the department was desirous to suspend.

It is all important at present that we should preserve to every chief who is friendly to the system of emigration his stand with the nation. For if to the opposition to the contemplated treaty, which we shall assuredly experience from the whites, we add that of a vexed and mortified feeling among the chiefs, we shall certainly fail. Now, if the arrangements which McIntosh has already made, under the authority of your letter of the 11th of February, are to be suspended or countermanded, (for it amounts to the same thing,) it will place him in the attitude of having acted without the authority of the department, or of having that authority withdrawn after his course of action had commenced. Either view of the case cannot fail to depress his personal stand with his people, lessen his influence, and probably destroy any desire he may have to promote the present wishes of the Government.

Believe me to be, &c.,

J. J. ABERT,

*Lt. Col. Top. Eng.*

ELBERT HERRING, Esq.,

　　*Com'r of Ind. Aff's., Washington City, D. C.*

---

COLUMBUS, GEORGIA, *May* 18, 1833.

SIR: Since my letter to you, of yesterday, I have seen Chilly McIntosh. I brought a letter for him from Judge Herring, in relation to the business with which he was charged, and sent it him yesterday, but he had not received it. I told him of my anxiety to see him, in order to explain the letter, lest he might suppose it as intended to arrest all his proceedings under his authority, from the department, in relation to the party about to emigrate. I assured him, after mentioning the contents of the letter, that its object was not to put a stop to what he had done, not to defeat the arrangements he had already made, but merely to limit him to the extent of his present proceedings.

To this extent the faith of the Government was unquestionably pledged, and his standing as its agent compromitted.

He replied, that as far as he had gone he must be sustained, or his life was hazarded. That he had acted in accordance with his authority, and if it were now withdrawn, he would be viewed as one who had deceived his friends, or who had lost the confidence of the Government. In either case his situation would be very critical, and his influence at an end. He added, that he had about 300 Indians engaged to emigrate, had already established depots of provision, and had mortgaged his whole private fortune for means to defray his expenses, and that to stop now was out of the question. I told him on no account to stop, but to persevere to the extent of his present engagements, and if desirable by him, I would give him a letter to that effect. He then remarked, that he was very destitute of funds, and wished to know if some portion of what was to be allowed to him could not be furnished, and that he had fixed the 10th of June for the commencement of his march. I replied that I would write to you on the subject, and have an answer by that time.

You were mistaken in your impression that these Indians were to have a meeting on the 18th. They have not been called together, and do not meet unless so called. Marshall, the interpreter, tells me that at least 20 days are necessary to give notice and collect for a council. I shall go to the agency to-day, and send out notice for a council to be held on the 10th of June. I requested McIntosh to attend the council. He is an active and intelligent fellow, and the zealous advocate of emigration. He assured me that in his opinion a great majority of the Indians had sold their rights. That white agents were throughout the nation using every artifice to induce the Indians to sell. That the usual price for a half section was 15 dollars, and the Indians came under bonds to convey, and contracts to reside on the land for the five years required by the treaty. That, in his opinion, with proper arrangements, upwards of 5,000 might be induced to emigrate this season. That the mass of them were literally suffering for food. Entirely unsettled in their views, worked upon and furnished with drink by the whites, every thing they had, even their ration of meal, was carried to the grog shop; and, with but few exceptions, all planting or cultivation neglected. That, in consequence, if some active arrangements for emigration were not made, their sufferings during the ensuing winter would be excessive. Conscious of this, he considered a large mass of them ready to emigrate, and could be induced to move soon after the council, if an agent were ready to conduct them. I take the liberty of presenting this opinion to your serious consideration. I had heard of the wretchedness of this people; of their dilapidated towns, and neglected fields, from other sources, and believe the representations of McIntosh to be correct. He says, and I believe it, that a delay of effort to induce emigration until the next season, will only increase their wretchedness and the embarrassment of the Government.

I should like to receive from you some intimation of the extent to which the Government is disposed to go in the purchase of these reservations. There are, perhaps, a few which cannot be obtained, as I have heard of one section right for which 5,000 dollars has been refused. The improvements were on choice ground, and these would fix the location. Some one or two more may be similarly situated, but generally they will not be so very valuable. It has occurred to me, that an offer of 50 cents the acre for the 90 chief reservations, and 25 cents the acre for the balance, including the 29 sections of the 6th article, would probably secure the purchase of the whole, except the exceptions above stated. Estimating the heads of families at 4,000, which I do from tolerable authority, the quantity of acres and the cost would be as follows:

| | | | | | | |
|---|---|---|---|---|---|---|
| 90 sections, | = | 57,600 acres, | at 50 cents, | | $28,850 | 00 |
| 29 " | | 19,360 " | " 25 " | | 4,840 | 00 |
| 4,000 half " | | 1,280,000 " | " 25 " | | 320,000 | 00 |
| | | | | | $352,640 | 00 |

I doubt if the purchase will be made at less than the rates above stated, and purchasers of rights could be secured for all bona fide payments, to the extent of the price of each section; these payments chargeable on each section or half section; and the balance to be paid to the Indians who might be entitled to the land.

I have just seen a Mr. Elliott, a citizen of this place, who has been employed under McIntosh to aid in enrolling his band for emigration. He has been throughout the Creek nation lately, and assures me that but for the efforts of the speculators, thousands of the Indians could now be induced to emigrate, and that if we succeed in making a treaty, they will move in mass by the fall. The argument of the speculators or their agents to induce the Indians to remain is, that if they go they will get nothing for their lands. He says that the report that a locating and certifying agent had been appointed also operated against immediate emigration, as it served to show that the Government was taking steps for the immediate execution of the treaty of March, 1832, and the Indians were therefore waiting for the issue. I begged him to correct this report, as I believed that Mr. Tarrant had only been assured that he might expect such an employ. But on reading the letter to Mr. Tarrant of the 3d of May, (a copy of which is among the papers committed to me,) a day after the date of our instructions as commissioners, no notice whatever is taken of the desire of Government to purchase these reservations, or of the fact that commissioners were appointed for that purpose; but, on the contrary, an evident system is developed for carrying into effect the treaty of 24th March. Observe the following: "In addition to your pay as sub-agent, you will be allowed, as heretofore informed, five dollars per day as locating agent, when your services commence in making the selection of reservations. After the reservations shall have been located, you will be appointed certifying agent, for the purpose of ascertaining and reporting as to the fairness of contracts with the Indians for the sale of their lands. On this subject you will be more particularly instructed when your appointment shall be announced to you." Need I comment upon this quotation, to show all the evil effects which we may experience from it? It is really tantamount to a declaration that no confidence is entertained in our success, or no wish that we may succeed. It will be known; such things are always known; and I cannot yet say to what extent it may embarrass us. I shall, however, write immediately to Tarrant, and let him know that commissioners have been appointed to treat for these reservations.

McIntosh has this morning called with the letter alluded to in the forepart of this communication, and which he had just received. He says that he should interpret it as countermanding all that he had been authorized to do, and the effect would be to brand him as a liar with the tribe, destroy all his stand, and hazard his life for the supposed deception. I assured him that, in my opinion, no more was meant by the letter, than to limit his efforts to the extent he had already gone under the authority of the letter of the 11th of Februarp. That to that extent he ought to complete his undertaking. He requested of me a letter to that effect, and I shall give him one. The subject is not immediately under my cognizance; but it is one which, in addition to the inconvenience which may ensue to McIntosh himself, involves also, to my judgment, the honor and plighted faith of the department, and will therefore justify the responsibility which I may find necessary to take upon myself.

I have &c.,<br>
J. J. ABERT,<br>
Lt. Col. Top. En.

Hon. Lewis Cass.

---

OFFICE OF SUPERINTENDENT OF INDIAN AFFAIRS IN FLORIDA.

Tallahassee, May 18, 1833.

Sir: On yesterday, Colonel Blunt, the principal chief of the Appalachicola Indians, and who made the treaty with Colonel Gadsden last fall, visited me, in compliance with a notice I had previously sent him. He states to me that himself, and all the Indians named in the treaty, will get off by the 20th of July. As I am acquainted with his arrangements, I have no doubt he will be ready by that time. The transmission of the funds to pay the $10,000, and the commutation of the annuity, &c., is therefore necessary as soon as possible. Great difficulty and trouble occurs from the manner in which funds are generally transmitted to this superintendency. Drafts on New Orleans, Mobile, or Charleston (and especially the latter places) should never be sent us; we cannot get them cashed in specie here without paying a discount of one and a half per cent., and those for large sums we cannot sell. Drafts on New York here will generally command a premium, (which the government would save) in exchange for current bank notes, of two per cent., and can be cashed for specie, at par, at our banks. In order to prevent difficulty, I would again renew the suggestion in my letter a few days since, to the Secretary of War, that authority from the department *to draw on it*, for the amount to be paid to Blunt and his Indians, be given to Colonel Gadsden or myself. I shall visit Blunt's town to-morrow, to ascertain the precise number of his Indians entitled to the annuity under the treaty of Camp Moultrie, and also of those that remain, their quota for this year being then to be paid to them, and I will advise the department thereof forthwith.

Blunt requests me to write for his son, at the public Indian school in Kentucky. It is necessary he should be here before the 20th of July. As the Seminoles are going off also, the seven other Indian boys from Florida could all be sent home at the same time. I have, however, requested Colonel Gadsden to write to the department on this subject.

Colonel Blunt delivered me the enclosed letter from Mr. Littlebury Jones, a highly respectable citizen residing near him; and I received that from Mr. Pope, the temporary sub-agent (also enclosed) a day or two since. I have no doubt of the truth of the robbery, and it renders a visit by me to Blunt's town more advisable.

I had hoped Colonel Gadsden would have been able to have gone over with me, and have concluded a treaty with the remaining chiefs, but he cannot. I visited him three days since for the purpose of consultation, and will use such proper efforts as are in my power to get them to consent to go next fall.

I am, sir, very respectfully,
Your most obedient servant,
JAMES D. WESTCOTT, Jr.,
*Acting Superintendent.*

Hon. Lewis Cass,
*Secretary of War.*

—————

*May* 10, 1833.

Dear Governor: I wish you to furnish me with all the instructions necessary to govern me in the discharge of my duty as sub-agent. The treaty with them would be of service to me in these controversies, which are many of small matters, but there has one occurred lately of serious nature. Colonel Blunt went into the woods for the purpose of hunting his cattle, and during his absence, two ruffians, by the name of Philip Oakes and John Rolls, attacked his house, broke down the door, entered with large sticks or clubs, assaulted his family, robbed the house of the most valuable articles, and about seven or eight hundred dollars in cash. I have been down to see about it, but as there was no proof but that of the Indian woman, I have taken out a search warrant, and placed it in the hands of an officer to search for the property, with the hope of finding some part of it, so as to lead to a discovery. There has been several other depredations on them; some I have succeeded in settling, others I have written J. K. Campbell on the subject some days ago. I wish you would answer this as soon as practicable, as I am much perplexed with these lawless ruffians.

In haste,
Your obedient servant, &c.,
WM. S. POPE.

Wm. P. Duval, *Governor of Florida.*

BLUNTSTOWN, *May* 16, 1833.

DEAR SIR: I am at this place, and have been for some weeks, making a crop here, and on the island two miles distant from this. Colonel Blunt, a few days since, has been robbed of seven hundred dollars in cash, and about two hundred in goods and clothing. It is well understood, at this place, that George Stafford, John Rolls, and Philip Oakes have robbed him. I yet hope I shall be able to get a part or all of his money. Not only his money, and goods, and clothes have been stolen, but violence to Mrs. Blunt and family. The outlaws must be gotten off. I refer you to Stephen Richards for the truth of every thing I say. Colonel Blunt, to my knowledge, as I wrote his letters, has sent to the sub-agent, Judge Pope, to come to this place. He came once; his presence, I know, was much wanted. Blunt can't get him again. Blunt, as well as myself, thinks he is afraid of these robbers. Blunt has been neglected, as I think, by him, and Blunt told me so himself. I will render Blunt, or the agent, every assistance I can, as I expect to be at this place the greater part of my time. Colonel Blunt is entirely dispirited, and has abandoned the idea of making a crop this year. Not only his money and goods, &c. have been stolen, but several attempts have been made to steal his negroes. Some of them are now in the woods, and I know they are in great danger of being taken off. I refer you to Mr. Richards for the truth of this and every thing I write. This, I think, is a very favorable time to get the Indians off to Texas. Blunt first suggested this idea to me; it is Blunt's wish to get off fifty or sixty Indians forthwith. He is without money, having his stolen, and relies on you and Colonel Gadsden to supply him. Not only the money, goods, and Blunt's negroes stolen, and attempts to steal his negroes, but Blunt's wife, and several of the Indian women have been taken out of their houses by force     *     * by Stafford, Oaks, and Rolls, as I am told by Blunt himself. Stafford has taken a very good horse belonging to an Indian, Jack Amelia, under a pretence that he had bought him of Colonel Blunt's servant, Bob, and has sold him; this can be proven by white men. As I believe I could say many more things to you; but let me refer you to Mr. Richards and Colonel Blunt himself for the balance.

Yours respectfully,

L. H. JONES.

Governor DUVAL.

---

COLUMBUS, GEORGIA, *May* 19, 1833.

SIR: Since my letter to you of the 18th instant, I have had an interesting conversation with a gentleman of great respectability and intelligence, and belonging to a company which has been engaged in purchasing the Indian rights under the treaty of March, '32. He speaks with perfect fairness and candor on the subject, and assures me that his interests are too much involved against our success for him to do less than oppose the treaty. He thinks that his company alone have purchased upwards of 700 rights. That in many cases they have given 1,500 dollars for a right, in many more 1,000, and that he is well satisfied that the aggregate amount which will in this way be paid to the Indians, will much exceed any aggregate which the Government could give. That they have proceeded in the most open, fair, and legal methods in their purchases, and will resort to all fair and legal methods to sustain themselves, should the Government effect a treaty. He thinks the

Indian could sell his rights under the treaty; and in cases in which he has sold, can be compelled to perfect all consequent acts. He admitted that in many cases rights had been disposed of for from 15 to 20 dollars, but in all these the lands were worth no more, and that the competition was so great and so actively pursued, that he is fully convinced the Indians have been gainers by the system.

He frankly remarked to me that he did not believe that the chiefs dared to sell their reservations. That they returned home in fear of their lives from the last treaty, and if they were to make one now, which would produce the embarrassments which certainly would follow to all those who had sold, they would in all probability be massacred. He says that unusual pains have been taken to apprise the Indians of their rights, of the obligations they come under by selling, and of the consequences if they attempted to avoid them. And that as certain as we made a treaty, and the Indians attempted to emigrate, *ne-exeats* would be issued against all who had sold, and they would by that means be retained upon the land, in order to protect the rights of purchasers.

He not only corroborated the opinion of McIntosh, that a majority had sold, but thinks it is only a small minority which has not.

He corrected me in the opinion that the purchasers were generally Georgians, by stating that, of his personal knowledge, by far the greater part were Alabamians.

I have now presented to you in my several letters the views and difficulties of both sides of this case, as well as I have been able to collect them.

The great object of the Government is, I presume, to hasten this emigration, and not to repossess itself of lands which it had yielded up to the Indians; but as a means, two methods present themselves for effecting this object.

One, by purchase under a treaty, as you have advised.

The other, by securing under a treaty the rights of *bona fide* purchasers.

The first is perfectly within the powers with which we are invested, but it is extremely doubtful in its success, and it will probably be attended with very embarrassing consequences to both the Indians and the Government, and would rather retard the system of emigration.

The second is without our powers, and of course we cannot treat upon it; but if we were to fail in the first, the second would be a means of effecting a most rapid emigration, as the interests of all parties would be united on that object.

I limit myself in this summary exhibition of the two plans, under the circumstances of the present case, as their more detailed consequences will suggest themselves more readily to one so well informed as yourself on these subjects, than to me.

I have the honor, &c.,

J. J. ABERT,
*Lieutenant Colonel Topographical Engineers.*

Hon. Lewis Cass,
*Secretary of War.*

COLUMBUS, GEORGIA, *May* 20, 1833.

SIR: My intention is not to inundate you with letters in this way all the time, but what I have to say in relation to the treaty must be said without delay, or you will not have time to advise or direct us before we shall be obliged to act; on this account, my ideas may not come to you as well digested as they ought, but I hope sufficiently clear to be comprehended.

You may have already inferred from my remarks that I do not contemplate a treaty upon a basis of annuities. I have every reason to believe that one cannot be made on this basis. The basis must be that of a purchase, by which the price will result to the advantage of whatever Indian may be entitled to a section. Without this understanding, no Indian could be induced to treat, as the reservations are viewed as matters of personal rather than of national property. Nor is it probable that ever, on this basis, we shall succeed, unless we are able, also, to stifle the opposition, if not secure the cooperation of those who have speculated. This may possibly be done by securing the speculators against all loss for the amounts which they have actually paid, with interest and expenses, as there is perhaps some little alarm among them about the titles ultimately, and many, I think, would rather avoid the delay and litigation which a treaty might occasion. The disappointment in the Indian, in not receiving from the United States as much as individuals had bargained to pay him, might be appeased by the argument that he could not give a good title for the land.

My arrival here, with the avowed object of treating for these reservations, has created a good deal of what the French call a sensation. And my course being candid and pleasant with every one, has made me somewhat of a centre of information and remarks from all sides, and the result has been, to induce me to believe that we may possibly make a treaty for the reservations on the following principles:

1st. To purchase the reservations at an average price per acre.

2d. This price to be paid to the Indian who would have been entitled to the land.

3d. To charge each Indian who has sold and is entitled to a section with whatever payments he may have received on account of his section, and to pay to him only the balance which may be due after such charge, and to refund the amount so charged to the individual who may have paid it to the Indian.

There is no danger that these payments will overrun a reasonable average per acre, for although the prices to be ultimately paid by purchasers are in many cases considerable, as stated in my last letter, yet the amounts actually paid are generally small.

4th. To secure to purchasers the interest upon the amounts actually paid, and the expenses which they have been at in effecting the purchases.

These perhaps would not constitute correct charges upon the reservations, although they would upon the Creek lands, generally. We should probably have to define these expenses to be those of the salaries and expenses of agents actually employed, and of deeds, bonds, acknowledgments, &c., or obtain some average rate per section from those who have speculated, as an adequate allowance.

It is probable, and barely probable, that we may make a treaty upon the foregoing principles, and that probability rests more upon the fears of those who have bought sections that we may make a treaty against their exertions, and thereby expose them to what may result in entire loss, or certainly in much difficulty, than in any desire to yield their expectations of profit. And yet, however the provisions for their security are, I believe no more than justice to those who have speculated on the faith that the treaty would be left undisturbed.

But you will perceive this plan abandons the usual system of annuities. The circumstances of the case, however, are totally different from such as usually exist; and if encountered successfully, it can only be done, in my opinion, by a course different from that usually pursued.

Yet, as our instructions for the purchase are limited to the system of annuities, you will readily perceive that if these remain unaltered, there is, as far as my judgment on such matters is worth a thought, no great prospect of success.

I must account for my writing alone on this subject, from the fact that I have not yet seen General Parsons. He lives about 250 miles from this place. I sent a duplicate of the instructions to him soon after my arrival, which he may probably by this time have received.

I have already ascertained that I can procure specie to any amount I may want, from the banks in this place, for my checks upon Savannah.

Very respectfully, &c.

J. J. ABERT,
*Lieut. Colonel Topographical Engineers.*

Hon. Lewis Cass,
Secretary of War.

---

Columbus, Georgia, *May* 22, 1833.

Sir: I had an interview yesterday at the agency with several of the Creek chiefs, at which I explained the object of my visit, and the necessity that their chiefs and head men should be called together at an early day; at farthest by the 10th of June. I also informed them that I wished no more called together than were necessary to transact the business of the payments, and attend to any propositions which might be made in relation to a sale of the reservations to the United States. I told them also that I wished the place of meeting to be in the vicinity of the agency. They replied, that two or three of the chiefs were not then present; and that it was necessary, according to their custom, to consult these also. That they would see them in a day or two, and would try and have my wishes complied with.

I think it highly probable that a meeting will take place by the 10th, and that, in four or five days after, we shall be able to transact business.

And I am assured by all persons, Indians and white men, that the meeting will be very numerously attended. The business itself will require the attendance of great numbers, for if it should be decided that the annuities have to be paid "to individuals," and I should have, in consequence, to "take the receipts of heads of families," these heads of families must be present, and you are, no doubt, already aware, from the returns of the census, of their number.

If to this probability of a large concourse, from the very nature of the business to be transacted, we add the probabilities resulting from curiosity, from the feeling prevalent with many that it will be the last meeting of the kind held this side of the Mississippi, from the consideration with many that these meetings are days of jubilee, where friends from a distance meet, and where the poor and friendless are fed, and from the known custom with these people to attend such meetings with their families, you will perceive that we may have many to feed.

Your instructions state that "I may distribute to the Indians, when assembled, a small quantity of provisions, proportioned to their number, and the period they will be kept together." I know of no other proportion on such occasions, than that of a ration to each Indian over a certain age, and shall, therefore, adopt that as a rule. But as I am satisfied that the number will exceed what you appeared to anticipate, in a conversation with me before my departure from Washington, I have made the foregoing remarks.

It appears to me incompatible with the position which the United States is desirous of maintaining with these people, and subversive of a proper influence, to deny provisions to all who may attend on such occasions, although the number may exceed that which, with strict propriety, the nature of the business to be transacted would justify.

But if we keep these people in a good humor, and make an arrangement about the reservations which shall quiet the fears of both Indian and speculator, and there should be an acceptable agent on the spot, or soon there, to attend to the business, I have no doubt that vast numbers of them would emigrate in a short time. Captain Page, of the army, and formerly employed on a similar duty with the Choctaws, would, I believe, be a very acceptable agent for this purpose with the Creeks.

I have not yet seen Mr. Tarrant; but in Colonel Crowell, who lives at the agency, I have found a gentleman of candor and intelligence, and of much experience in these matters, and knowledge of the present feelings among the Indians. He says he doubts if we can make a treaty on any other basis than that of paying to each Indian the price of his reservation.

In relation to payments "for the losses for the improvements, and for persons who suffered from not emigrating," you say that I must in no case pay to a white man upon the order of an Indian. I am disposed to think that this restriction will oblige me to leave many of these claims unsettled.

I have, &c.,
J. J. ABERT,
*Lieutenant Colonel Topographical Engineers.*

Hon. LEWIS CASS,
*Secretary of War.*

----

HEAD OF COOSA, CHEROKEE NATION,
*May 22, 1833.*

SIR: In pursuance of a resolution of the General Council, which terminated its cession on the 20th instant at Red Clay, I hasten to transmit you herewith, for the information of the President, certain resolutions adopted by the council, as an expression of its sentiments on the public affairs of this nation. In laying them before the President you will please to permit me, through you, to assure him that the *peace and happiness* of the Cherokee people require repose, by removing the perplexing difficulties which have so long disturbed their welfare; and that whilst a course of irritating excitement is kept up, the distresses of the nation may be increased; but yet, it is evident that the object desired to be attained can never be realized by the observance of it. Should the reasonable expectation of the council be favorably regarded by the President, and all further proceedings suspended, he may rest assured that no effort, on my part, shall be wanting in co-operating with the proper authorities of this nation for the adoption of measures with the view to a final termination of all difficulties. To insure a calm deliberation upon this important subject, it is indispensably necessary that harmony and tranquillity should prevail among the people. You will, therefore, please to advise me of the determination of the President on the subject as soon as convenient.

I have the honor to be, sir,

Your obedient humble servant,

JOHN ROSS.

Hon. Lewis Cass, *Secretary of War.*

---

*Whereas* the several communications, embracing the correspondence between the late delegation to Washington and the honorable Secretary of War, in reference to the public affairs of this nation, having been read in general council, and the principal chief having fully stated, in the presence of said delegation, the several conversations had with the President and Secretary on this subject, the following resolutions be, and they are hereby, adopted as an expression of the sentiments of the council in relation thereto:

*Resolved by the committee and council in general council convened,* That the position maintained by the delegation in the support of the rights of this nation be, and is hereby, approved.

*Resolved,* That the council view with regret the evasive and unsatisfactory manner in which the honorable Secretary has replied to the several subjects introduced before him by the delegation. The question of our national rights having been so clearly recognised and established by every department of the General Government, and as defined by various subsisting treaties, laws enacted in the spirit of those treaties, and decisions of the Supreme Court of the United States, the Cherokees cannot but feel with deep regret and sensibility the evil consequences arising from the oppressions by State authorities, and the entire suspension of fulfilment, on the part of the Government, of those solemn pledges, so repeatedly made, for their protection.

*Resolved,* That, under existing circumstances, the nation is in a state of duress, and that, until removed, it cannot properly exercise that freedom of deliberation and action so desirable and necessary for the final termination of present difficulties; and being convinced that the country west of the Mississippi, to which the Government has invited the removal of the nation, is such as cannot better the future prospects and welfare of the Cherokees, as a nation, under the present unsettled policy of the Government in relation to the Indian tribes; and should they be compelled by the force of circumstances, contrary to every principle of justice and humanity, to leave the "land of their fathers," the council can determine no other alternative, promising relief, than a removal beyond the limits of the United States. But having confidence yet in the good faith of the Government of the United States, and no desire to remove west of the Mississippi, nor to leave the limits of the United States, and being solicitous to have a speedy termination of present difficulties;

*Resolved*, That the basis and terms of the late propositions offered by the Government being objectionable, and aware of the limited powers of the President, it is deemed inexpedient for the nation at present to determine, as a final resort, that course necessary to be pursued, until some further action of the ensuing Congress in relation to this important matter.

*Be it further resolved*, That if the President will cause all further illegal proceedings on the part of Georgia and Alabama to cease, within the limits of this nation, and will suspend further proceedings through the agents of the Government, the proper authorities of this nation, with a view to the final termination of all difficulties, will adopt such measures as will bring before the General Government at the next session of Congress this subject, upon such fair and honorable principles as, in their opinion, justice and magnanimity will not fail to sanction.

*Be it further resolved*, That the principal chief be, and he is hereby, requested to transmit a copy of the foregoing resolutions to the honorable Secretary of War, for the information of the President of the United States.

In General Council, Red Clay, C. N., May 20, 1833.

WM. ROGERS,
*Clerk to Committee.*
A. McCOY,
*Clerk to Council.*
RICHARD TAYLOR,
*Prest. Nat. Committee.*
GOING SNAKE,
*Speaker of Council.*

Approved:
JOHN ROSS, *Principal Chief.*

---

ST. LOUIS, Mo., *May 22*, 1833.

DEAR SIR: You have been informed before this, by the arrival of Colonel Stambaugh at Washington, that we left Fort Gibson for the purpose of holding a treaty with the Quapaws, but that the state of his health would not permit him to await the result of the council with them. I have the pleasure now to inform you, that I have entered into a treaty with them on the part of the United States, and that in a few days I will forward an abstract of the treaty and the talk, &c. The treaty itself I wish to retain, to give the other commissioners an opportunity to add their signatures to it, if they approve of it. For the expenses of the council and presents, in part, I have drawn a draft on the Secretary of War for $179 87¼, in favor of Mr. Barraque, or order. Had I, however, known as much as I do now of the difficulties of accepting the individual draft of one of the commissioners, I should at least have hesitated before I did it, although I think that the public business ought not to suffer for the want of any nice formalities in these matters. I may, however, be under the necessity of doing the like again, as I am here now alone and I think it doubtful whether Governor Stokes will be able at this season of the year, first on account of the high water, and next on account of the flies, to meet me at Fort Leavenworth, as he contemplated when Colonel Stambaugh left him.

I arrived here yesterday, and had the pleasure of receiving your communications, both official and unofficial, and I assure you they gave me much satisfaction to find that you had interested yourself so much in our affairs.

Governor Clark, the superintendent of Indian affairs, received me very kindly, and informed me that the Pottawatamies have not yet gone on to explore
the country. I shall delay here for them ten days, and then proceed up the
Missouri to do what I can to expedite our business, which I know the President has much at heart. I am fully persuaded it was indispensably necessary that the commissioners, or some of them, should have a personal interview with the department of Indian affairs, and I hope, therefore, that the
visit of Messrs. Ellsworth and Stambaugh will be productive of much good.
                    With great respect, &c.,
                            J. F. SCHERMERHORN,
                                    *Comm'r West.*
Hon. ELBERT HERRING, *Comm'r Ind. Affairs.*

---

                                            *May 23, 1833.*

SIR: Yours under date 10th instant is this day received, and I deputed
Mr. A. H. Sommerville to repair forthwith to the Creek nation, with instructions to execute the several orders and instructions received from the
War Department, relative to intruders upon the Creek lands. Mr. Sommerville is a prudent and energetic man, and the interest of the Government
nor those of the Indians will be in the least degree compromitted.
                    Very respectfully, &c.,
                            ROBT. L. CRAWFORD,
                                    *United States Marshal.*
Hon. LEWIS CASS, *War Department.*

---

                    CHEROKEE AGENCY, *May 23, 1833.*

SIR: On Monday the 13th instant the council, on account of the inclemency of the weather, as well as for the want of a quorum to do business,
did not meet.
    On the following day, the committee and council met. They were ad-
dressed by Mr. Ross. His object appeared to be to reconcile the Cherokees
to the opinion that the President of the United States had the same right
and power, by virtue of his office, under the various laws, treaties, and decisions of the Supreme Court, to estop the jurisdiction of the several States
over the Cherokee settlements that he had to suppress practical nullification
in South Carolina. Reference was made most particularly to the President's
proclamation, and the bill providing further for the collection of the revenue.
Then followed the reading of the correspondence between the delegation,
the President and Secretary of War; when Mr. Ross informed the company that much had passed verbally, and he would on the next day, after
consulting his colleagues, report all that was important to be communicated.
    On Wednesday the council met according to adjournment. Mr. Ross
having heard of the arrival of an express from the department, through
Milledgeville, Georgia, did not proceed with his promised narrative, and the
day passed off without any public remarks relative to the condition of the
Cherokee people in their relations with the States or General Government.
    On Thursday, after the meeting of the committeemen and counsellors,
Ross observed, after some preliminary remarks, the Secretary of War had
offered them $2,500,000 for their country, provided they would agree to
remove themselves and provide their new homes; that the President had

offered them $2,700,000 for all their country east, excepting the North Caro-
lina part; saying he was not under the same obligations to extinguish the
Indian title there that he was in the other States. Ross said he asked the
President if he was not bound equally to that State as he was to Tennessee and Alabama; to which the President replied he *was*, but that that part
of the Cherokee country was of no real value. The President then requested him to throw off all etiquette, and say at once what they were willing to
take for the whole country. He declined fixing a price. The President
then observed he would give three millions of dollars, provided they would
leave their country, as the Chickasaws had agreed to do, providing a home
for themselves and paying for their own removal and subsistence. He replied, he was not authorized to treat, but that was not the worth of the gold
mines in Georgia. He observed they had talked also about the annuity
which he said had been improperly withheld from the nation, and the Secretary of War had promised to pay it to the national authorities, if the
people would, in their collective capacity, request it; that on this subject he
had promised to give an answer after the meeting of the council. He said
he had asked the President why the Government could not as well purchase
out the interest of the fortunate drawers in Georgia, and let *them* emigrate
westwardly. To which the reply was, this would not, even if consented to,
relieve the Cherokees from the operation of State authorities. He then inquired, if you cannot protect us under such circumstances, how can protection against similar evils westwardly be afforded? The President's answer
was not satisfactorily explained, and Mr. Ross said he then informed him,
if they were compelled by the force of circumstances to leave their birthright, they would never consent to settle within the limits of the United
States. The President advised them earnestly, whatever they done, never
to think of going beyond the limits of the United States.

He then observed, after the passage of the enforcing bill, he had, in a letter of the 8th March, renewed his application for the removal of intruders, and
the letter which he had received from Judge Herring of the 14th March was
in reply; that on receiving it he had understood it as referring to the whole
Cherokee settlements, and that a change had taken place in the views of the
Executive with regard to Cherokee relations after the passage of that bill.

In his narrative he was evidently embarrassed, which, I am informed, is
very unusual with him. This confusion may have proceeded from a knowledge that he and the rest of the delegation had previously made statements
that it would not do for him to repeat there, and a fear that what fell from
his lips on that occasion might be contradicted by the most authentic evidence.

The enclosed petition, was on that evening presented to Mr. Ross by Mr.
Coody, his nephew, and a member of the executive council, which was dis-
cussed before that body, composed of Ross, Major Ridge, Lowry, Coody,
and Waters; the latter of whom being absent, there was a division for two
days, Ross and Lowry on one side, and Coody and Ridge on the other.
This discussion resulted in a compromise, by which Ross and Lowry agreed,
if they would not now press the matter before the national committee and
council, they would answer the petition at the October council, where it is
expected there will be an immense concourse of people, and they would afterwards be governed by their decision.

In the meantime, Gen. Glasscock arrived with various communications
from the Governor of Georgia, forwarded at the request of William Hicks

ex-principal chief, and others of the Cherokee tribe, consisting of a plan of removal, furnished, at the request of the Secretary of War, by myself; a copy of a letter from the President to the Governor, as well as several from the Secretary of War, which were shown to the executive committee and some of the members of the national committee and council, believing it might be the means of opening their eyes more fully to the real situation of the country, and lead to a favorable determination, if not at that time, perhaps at the regular council in October next.

On Monday the 20th, resolutions, drafted by Mr. Ross, were read and passed, in substance as follows, by a silent vote.

Approving the conduct of the delegation, declaring the Secretary of War evasive and unsatisfactory in his various replies to the several questions submitted by them for his decision; objecting to the country west of the Mississippi, without a more settled policy on the part of the General Government towards the different tribes, as well as to the propositions submitted at sundry times as a basis upon which to conclude a treaty; obligating themselves, if the President will cause to cease the illegal operation of the State laws, and suspend the efforts of the agents of the Government to bring about a western removal, the proper authorities will attend the next Congress; memorialize that body, and should it determine the States have a right to jurisdiction over the Cherokee settlements, they will come to immediate terms satisfactory to the Government; but in the alternative they are compelled by the force of circumstances to a western removal, they will go beyond the limits of the United States; referring to laws, treaties, &c., which they regretted to say the General Government had failed to execute for their protection; ordering a copy of these resolutions to be furnished the President of the United States, through the Secretary of War. These resolutions, a copy of which had been promised me, were not spread upon the journals.

John Ridge, who had read a letter addressed to him and others from the department a few days before, and depicted, in an eloquent and impressive manner, the forlorn situation of the country, demanded that these resolutions should be made a matter of record, which was consented to; but his attention being turned for a moment or two towards his father, who was by this time addressing the crowd in an adjoining grove, Judge Taylor snatched the resolutions from the clerk's table, and joining John Ross, they rode off in great haste, leaving no track or trace of the resolutions further than they rested on the memory of the auditors.

Should these resolutions be of a different import from the above, when they reach the city, it is desired, by those friendly to a treaty, that the original, with a copy of the letter enclosing it, be furnished them, through me, for their inspection, and Ross's further exposure.

In their various conversations, the delegation denied making any promise to even consider the propositions of the Secretary and President; but that their report was to be confined exclusively to the annuity business.

Old Major Ridge is the greatest orator in the nation; he dismissed the meeting, after giving a concise and well arranged history of their present condition, compared with what it had been; the probability of their being called on in a few months, for the last time, to say whether they will submit always to the evils and difficulties every day increasing around them, or look for a new home, promising them freedom and national prosperity; advising them to bury party animosity, and in case they should conclude to seek a new home, to go in the character of true friends and brothers.

It is the opinion of the treaty party, that it would be well for me to continue travelling through the country, in order to counteract any misrepresentations that may be attempted through the faithlessness of the opposite party.

Past experience has shown that Ross and his party hold no pledge sacred; and lest his object in the recent compromise may be only to baffle the Government, it might be well to commence enrolling the names of those willing to treat, with a pledge that if no treaty is effected during this fall or early in the next winter, of a general or partial character, they are to be transported, subsisted, &c. &c., as the emigrants have been heretofore, paying them one-fourth of the value of their improvements on their being mustered at the agency for a final departure, but securing to them an equal participation in all the rights and benefits arising out of any *bonus*, annuities, &c., that may be allowed the nation under any final arrangement at the time they relinquished their proportional interest in the country.

Until the meeting of the late council, the treaty party were depressed in spirits, seeing the predominance of falsehood over truth. Yet the communications by *express* from the department, of the 1st May, united with the statements of the Indian agent; also those of the United States interpreter, who arrived at the council ground on the 16th, from an excursion with the regulars removing intruders; and the papers forwarded by the governor, through General Glasscock, had a most happy effect, in diminishing the influence of Ross's falsehoods, and promoting the prospects of a final adjustment of the Cherokee question.

There is so little reliance to be placed on any promise made by the Cherokee chiefs, I am in hopes no exertion will be relaxed by the States or General Government at their request; for it would only give new hopes to a restoration of all that has ever been called for, and be the means of defeating the views and wishes of the Executive, with regard to their future happiness.

Allow me to suggest the policy also of declining to correspond with John Ross, or any of the present ruling dynasty, composed as it is of reservees principally. Let the President prepare a talk for the whole Cherokee people, and appoint commissioners to meet them on the 2d Monday in October next to deliver it, clothed with full powers to treat on any terms that would be granted at Washington; instructed and empowered to *eject reservees* and *their* descendants, *while men intermarried* with Cherokees, as well as all *enrolled emigrants* who have heretofore registered their names and received any portion of Government bounty, that may be found interfering to prevent a treaty.

For this important trust, I suppose the commissioners west of the Mississippi would be directed to attend. If not, I would name General John Coffee, of Alabama, John McLean, of the Supreme Court bench, or General Call, of Florida, and Colonel Hugh Montgomery, as most likely to effect the object desired. If the Government can get its consent to let a part of Washington and Crawford counties go, there is no question but a general treaty could be concluded on the ground.

A treaty made at Washington City I believe would not be satisfactory to the people. *No reservations should be granted under any circumstances.*

As things now stand, should the commissioners come from the west, followed by such of the chiefs as are disposed to encourage a reunion of the eastern and western Cherokees, I believe it would have a much happier effect than sending out from this country an exploring party, who, unless selected by the nation, would be charged with bribery; and if selected by the nation before the people are ripe for a treaty, would be most likely to give a prejudiced account through *fear*, or a desire to please the dominant party.

I have the honor to be,

Very respectfully, &c.,

BEN. F. CURREY.

ELBERT HERRING, Esq.,
*Commissioner of Indian Affairs.*

---

*Red Clay, May 15, 1833.*

*To the Honorable Committee and Council, in general council convened*

The undersigned citizens of the nation having taken into serious consideration the peculiar and unhappy condition of their country, and believing, so far as they are informed, that the present course of policy pursued by the authorities of the nation will not result in the restoration of those rights of which they have been deprived, and being unable to understand the reasons which influence the perseverance in a course of measures which promise, in their opinion, every thing but a speedy and favorable adjustment of existing difficulties, respectfully solicit the attention of your honorable bodies to this important subject, and to give to the people of the country a full and clear view of their present condition, and to define the foundation of those hopes of protection so often expressed of late, but which the undersigned cannot comprehend.

It must be obvious to you, that the affairs of this nation have been brought to a crisis never before known or anticipated by its citizens generally. And believing, as they do, that the preservation and perpetuation of the Cherokees, *as a nation*, should be the first and greatest object to be cherished by every friend of liberty, they trust that those upon whom the confidence of the people have been bestowed, will prove themselves worthy of their nation, and capable of conducting its affairs as the exigencies of circumstances may require for the general welfare.

W. S. GOODEY, *of the Executive Council.*
JOHN WALKER, Jr.
JOHN MILLER, *U. S. Interpreter.*
WM. HICKS, *Ex. Principal Chief.*
E. BOUDINOT, *former Editor of the Phenix.*
JESSE MAYFIELD.
J. STARR.
JOHN WEST.
JACK SPEARS.
ELI HICKS.
JOHN McDANIEL.
JOHN FALLING WATER.
CHARLES H. VANN.
ROBERT RODGERS.
WILLIAM RODGERS.
RILEY THORNTON.
ISAAC BUSHYHEAD.
D. R. COODY.

DANIEL GRIFFIN.
MAJOR RIDGE, *of the Executive Council.*
JOHN FIELDS, Jr.
JACK GRIFFIN.
EZEKIEL STARR.
EDWARD FOREMAN.
L. WATIE.

David Vann and John Ridge, being members of the national committee, did not sign this petition, but were pledged on its coming before that body to advocate the measure contemplated.

--------

St. Louis, *May* 24, 1833.

DEAR SIR: I arrived here on 21st instant, after concluding a treaty with the Quapaws on the 13th, for their removal to the Indian territory west of the State of Missouri, to lands to be assigned by the commissioners. An abstract of the treaty, with the talk, &c. in council, I will forward as soon as I can prepare them. I have drawn on you, sir, for the amount of expenses and presents at the council, in favor of Mr. Barraque, which I trust will be paid at sight.

The commissioners found it would be useless for the Pottawatamies to visit them at Fort Gibson, since there were no lands that could be assigned them south of the Delawares. They therefore concluded to meet their delegation on the Missouri river. When I arrived here I could obtain no intelligence from them of General Clark, as to their expected arrival.

I was informed last night, by Aaron Finch, esq., of Indiana, to whom I was introduced by Paymaster Major Kirby, of New York, that on the 15th instant he saw Mr. Marshall, their agent, who stated that there was some dissatisfaction among the chiefs who were unacquainted with Colonel Pepper, which would probably delay the exploring party some time. He urged me to visit them, and thought that I might probably remove their difficulties and expedite their movements. He was also anxious that I should have an interview with the agent and some of the chiefs of the Miamies; and thought that such information as I could communicate to them of the country intended for their permanent home, would facilitate a treaty with the Miamies this summer. Since the commissioners have suspended their other business to attend to the Pottawatamies, and I have nothing specially claiming my attention here, I have concluded to accompany Mr. Finch to-day, on his return to Indiana, in order to do what I can to expedite the movements of the Pottawatamies. I trust, sir, this course will meet your approbation, as I wish only to promote the service in which I am engaged, with whatever labor it may be attended.

Colonel Stambaugh has, before this, communicated to you the reason why Governor Stokes did not accompany him to meet the Quapaws, as agreed upon by the commissioners. I fear the difficulties of the journey at this time, on account of the high waters and the flies, will prevent his meeting me at Fort Leavenworth, as contemplated by him. Since I have given up all idea of returning this summer, I shall employ my time in promoting the service in which I am engaged to the utmost of my power. Make my best respects to the President.

With great respect,
Your obedient servant,
J. F. SCHERMERHORN,
*Commissioner west.*

To the Hon. LEWIS CASS,
*Secretary of War.*

P. S. DEAR SIR: Should the Government think proper to purchase from the Pawnees the country south of the Platte, west of the Missouri, according to the views communicated by Major Dougherty, I wish you would inform the commissioners at this place, with definite instructions on the subject. On my return from Indiana I shall immediately proceed up the Missouri, unless otherwise instructed.

The commissioners have not received any treaties but those in the volume of Indian treaties. Will you have the goodness to forward to them at this place, immediately, all the subsequent treaties with the Indians, and also all other public documents calculated to throw light on the different subjects on which they are required to report.

With respect,
J. F. SCHERMERHORN.

---

OFFICE BANK UNITED STATES,
*Washington, May* 24, 1833.

SIR: I have just received the certificate for the last purchase of Maryland five per cent. stock, and I now enclose my account of purchases for your department, the certificates of stock, and the letters from the treasurer of the western shore of Maryland, showing the rates purchased at.

I am, sir, very respectfully,
Your obedient servant,
RICHARD SMITH, *Cashier.*

E. HERRING, Esq.,
*Superintendent of Indian Affairs.*

---

APPALACHICOLA, FLORIDA, *May* 25, 1833.

SIR: The writer of the within certificate is the reputed agent of one or more extensive land companies in Texas, and had, I was informed, a day or two since, on visiting the Indian towns on this river, made considerable difficulty with those chiefs and Indians who were making arrangements for going to Texas, under the treaty concluded by Colonel Gadsden last fall. Through the agency of Captain Seth Love, who will deliver you this, he was dissuaded from pursuing this course any farther, and gave the enclosed to be used in dispelling the dissatisfaction and difficulty his statements had caused. I have retained copies for service here, and have transmitted the original for the use of the department, if occasion should arise therefor.

I am, sir, respectfully,
Your obedient servant,
JAMES D. WESTCOTT, Jr.,
*Acting Governor of Florida.*

Hon. LEWIS CASS,
*Secretary of War.*
53‡

APPALACHICOLA, *May* 25, 1833.

Having understood that it is reported I have thrown some difficulties in the way of the emigration of the Indians to Texas, to prevent any misunderstanding, I would state, that from all the information obtained, the part assigned to the Indians is without the limits of the grants claimed and owned by the Galveston Bay and Texas Land Company of New York; therefore respectfully request that nothing I have said may be so construed as to mar their emigration, but, on the contrary, to facilitate it.

A. H. FALCONER.

Witness: SETH LOVE.

---

SUPERINTENDENCY OF INDIAN AFFAIRS,
*May* 27, 1833.

SIR: I have the honor to acknowledge the receipt of your several letters of 5th, 6th, and two of 8th, 9th, 11th, and two of 27th of April; three of 4th, 6th, 9th, and 13th May, instant; all of which have received due attention.

Your letter of the 8th April, approving my nomination of Major Pilcher, came too late to enable me to avail myself of his services; he has been for some time unemployed, and, having been accustomed to an active life, he could no longer brook the delay which was preying upon his health; he therefore accepted an appointment in the service of the American fur company, to conduct a portion of their trade in the Upper Missouri, although with an understanding (as he informed me) that he should quit their service should he be offered a permanent appointment in the Indian department, for which he conceives himself better qualified.

Under this deprivation of the services of a man so well qualified, and which I had calculated upon, I employed Captain William Gordon (a gentleman formerly engaged in the fur trade of the Upper Missouri), to deliver the merchandise and agricultural implements to the Shawnees, Delawares, Kickapoos, and other tribes, who were parties to the Castor Hill treaties of last fall. This gentleman is intelligent, has a perfect acquaintance with the Indian character, as well as a general knowledge of business; I consider myself fortunate in having procured his services, and hope the measure will be approved.

Some difficulty has arisen, as I am informed, between the exploring party of Pottawatamies, from Indiana, and the gentleman (Colonel Pepper) who was to have accompanied them.

The Rev. Mr. Schermerhorn, who was here at the time, has gone to those Indians, and will endeavor to effect the views of the government in regard to their removal. I furnished him with a talk to the Pottawatamies, and confidently hope he will be enabled to obviate the difficulty which appears to have arisen.

Your request with regard to the eighty-four Shawnees from Ohio, under their interpreter, Mr. Parks, will be particularly attended to.

I have the honor to be, with great respect,
Your most obedient servant,<br>WILLIAM CLARK.

Hon. E. HERRING,
*Commissioner Indian Affairs.*

IRWINTON, CREEK NATION, ALABAMA,
*May* 27, 1833.

DEAR SIR: We, with other citizens living in the Creek nation, desirous of ascertaining whether pre-emption rights will be allowed here, should it become Government land, wish you would have the goodness to give us your opinion respecting it, and whether a person cultivating land on one quarter section, and not living on the same, will hold a pre-emption over another who afterwards makes improvements on the same quarter section, and living with his family thereon; or whether they will both hold a pre-emption, each entitled to a certain quantity of the quarter section. You will confer a favor on us and the citizens of this place, by transmitting to us so much of the law relative to pre-emption rights as will instruct us what is necessary for an individual to hold a pre-emption, and the quantity of land they will be entitled to.

Very respectfully, &c.,
W. & A. LYMAN.

Hon. LEWIS CASS, *Sec'ry of War.*

P. S. All communications to be forwarded to Columbus, Georgia, as there is no post office open in this place.

---

COLUMBUS, *May* 28, 1833.

I have been called on by Mr. Benjamin Marshall to write you in relation to his reserve, opposite the town of Columbus. He wishes me to remind you of the conversation which took place when making out the details of the treaty. It was mentioned that his reserve was to be governed by the surveyor's lines; when Marshall observed, that if it was to be so governed, he might lose his mills: then you agreed that it should be run out so as to include his improvements entire, if they could be included, running one mile up and down the river, going back for quantity.

Now, should the mills not be included, Marshall will lose all his labor on the premises, and several thousand dollars paid out in the workmanship of the property; and also lose the most valuable part of his improved lands. I will refer you to the Hon. Samuel W. Mardis, who opposed the passage of a bill which had passed the Senate, giving one acre of land to the town of Columbus for the abutment of a bridge, upon the ground that a treaty had been concluded a few days before, giving the land which the abutment would embrace to Benjamin Marshall; therefore, the bill was lost in the House of Representatives. Marshall has sold the reserve for thirty-five thousand dollars to white persons and is anxious to receive his pay and remove west, but is now only detained in consequence of not receiving a patent, which is withheld, as he represents, owing to a petition from the citizens of Columbus, representing some dissatisfaction to the location. Should the abutment not fall on Marshall's reserve, it will certainly fall on another Indian; and why such complaints are made I am at a loss to know, without the citizens have purchased from the other Indian, and in that case the United States cannot be benefited. I wish you would write me on the subject; it would confer a singular favor on Marshall.

I have the honor to be,
Most respectfully, yours,
JNO. H. BRODNAX.

To the Hon. the SECRETARY OF WAR.

Fort Wayne, Indiana,
*May 29, 1833.*

Sir: Your letter of the 24th ultimo has been received, and in reply, I have to say that the commissioners appointed to hold a treaty with the Miami Indians (and at whose request I rendered the services for which I asked the department to allow me a reasonable compensation) live in different parts of this State. So soon as I was informed by the department that they had not certified the facts as they agreed to, I addressed each of them a letter, requesting them to lay the state of the case before the department, to which communications I received no answers.

I then requested a friend of mine, who had an opportunity of seeing two of the commissioners, to confer with them on the subject. He informed me that he had an interview with them, and that they told him they were compelled to employ me, and that if I did not take fifty dollars they were determined that I should have nothing, and refused to make a certificate.

Now, sir, were not my pecuniary circumstances embarrassed, I would let the matter rest here, but necessity compels me to ask for my due. I know that the amount claimed will not compensate me for the sacrifices I made in order to comply with the request of the commissioners. I think the certificates of the Indian agent, and various other gentlemen, (most of whom are personally known to the Secretary of War,) are amply sufficient to substantiate my claim. If the department thinks, after examining these certificates, and taking all things into consideration, my claim exorbitant, I am willing they should curtail it. If any further statement is necessary, (aside from the certificate of the commissioners to substantiate my claim,) inform me, and I can get certificates or affidavits as strong as holy writ. Please write me soon.

I have the honor to be
Your most obedient servant,

L. G. THOMPSON.

Elbert Herring, Esq.,
*Commissioner of Indian Affairs.*

P. S. I would refer the department to the commissioners themselves; they will not answer my letters; probably they would be more courteous with the department.

L. G. T.

---

Connersville, Indiana, *May 30, 1833.*

Sir: I have, agreeably to the request of the Secretary of War, as expressed in your letter of the 23d March last, taken a tour through the Indian territory, and have conversed with the principal chief Richardville, and others of the chiefs and traders, and from all the information I have been enabled to gather, am of opinion that the Miami tribe of Indians will sell all their lands situate north of the Wabash, and part of the reserve south of the Wabash, if proper persons are appointed to negotiate with them in September, when they convene to receive their annuity. I think that if some one or two persons with whom the chiefs had an acquaintance, and in whose integrity they can confide, were appointed in conjunction with Governor Porter, they would succeed in effecting this desirable object, as from what I can glean they are favorably predisposed.

I have the honor, very respectfully,
To be your obedient servant,
JOHN McCARTY.

Hon. Elbert Herring,
    *Office Indian Affairs, Washington.*

---

Executive Department, Georgia,
*Milledgeville, May 31, 1833.*

Sir: Before this reaches you, you will have learned through other channels the result of the late Cherokee council. You will also have discovered the use which I have made of the means which you were so kind as to afford me to dispel the delusions imbibed by the Cherokees, through the false statements of bad men and evil counsellors. From the report of General Glasscock, (who attended the council as my agent,) and letters which I have received from Major Currey, special agent of the United States, I entertain no doubt of the good effects which have and will result from what transpired at the late council. It has afforded a favorable opportunity, which has been well improved both by the agents of the Federal and State Governments, to enlighten the minds of the Cherokee people by the force of truth and documentary evidence, which will hereafter prevent the recurrence of practising upon them gross and deceptive falsehoods, in regard to the real state of their present affairs. Every thing is now harmonious and well understood upon this subject between the agents of the Federal and State Governments; and the important duty which now presents itself is, to use to the best advantage the means under our control, in bringing to the most speedy and happy issue the great and benevolent object of removing the Indians beyond the limits of the States, the only hope of rescuing them from speedy extermination. Circumstances now place much of the responsibility of what remains to be done in regard to the Indians who still remain in Georgia upon the authorities of the State. The present administration of the Federal Government has performed every duty in endeavoring to fulfil the compact of 1802. What remains to be done, depends very much upon a judicious management of State authority. Under this view of the subject, I hope I shall not be considered as assuming too much in mingling my efforts with yours in accomplishing the same desired object.

I concur with Major Currey and General Glasscock in believing that the business of enrolling names *in favor of a treaty*, should be commenced throughout the Cherokee country, with a condition, if no treaty is concluded during the ensuing fall, or early in the winter, they shall be removed on the terms proposed by the President to the Cherokees, through Mr. Chester, guaranteeing to them, as well as all those who have preceded them, an equal share of any compensation or annuity which may hereafter be secured by those remaining, by any final arrangement which may be made by the Government. Also, that they shall have their proportion of the three years' annuity, now due them, before their departure hence, and be entitled to their proportion of the moneys arising from the sale of the twelve miles square, under the treaty of 1819, for the benefit of schools in the eastern nation. I deem it unnecessary to enter upon further particulars at this time,

having heretofore signified my general assent to the plan submitted to you
by Major Currey, whose judgment in these matters I consider entitled to
much weight and consideration. I am clearly of opinion that enrolling
agents ought immediately to be appointed, and pardon me for saying, great
caution in their selection should be observed, for much will depend on
their weight of character and standing in the country.

I am, sir, with great respect,
Your obedient servant,
WILSON LUMPKIN.

Hon. LEWIS CASS,
    *Secretary of War.*

---

COLUMBUS, GEORGIA, *June* 2, 1833.

SIR: It has not been in my power to have an earlier day assigned for the
meeting of the council than the 19th of June. The chiefs held out for some
hours with great pertinacity for a more distant day, the middle of July, or
a notice of forty-five days, alleging as reasons, old customs, and the dif-
culty of preparing for the council, and of getting together in less time.
I insisted upon a notice of twenty days. After much unmeaning talk, and
being confident that they could conveniently assemble in that time, I told
them that twenty-five days was the longest notice I could admit; and if they
would not agree to meet in that time, I should pay off the claims and leave
them to wait for their annuities. This brought them to terms, and made the
19th of June the day. The agency was also agreed upon as the place.

Finding that many persons were anxious to have the privilege of feeding
these Indians at the council, I deemed it the best course to give public notice
for proposals, and have concluded a contract at seven and a quarter cents
the ration. I shall economise the expenditure under this head, by allowing
of no issues but such as I shall require in writing, and paying for no more
than shall be receipted for by an agent to be appointed by me for that purpose. By these means it will be in my power to control the expenditure,
which will, however, I think, with all the care I may bestow upon it, exceed your expectations.

My hopes of making a treaty still maintain themselves, on the supposition
that you may think proper to extend our powers. I have already explained
to you in former letters my reasons for doubting our success on the principle of annuities. I have spoken entirely of annuities, because the interest
upon any gross sum for the reservations amounts to about the same thing.
The Indians are so possessed with the impression that the treaty of March,
1832, guarantied individual rights to chiefs and heads of families, that I do
not believe any proposition in which this guarantee is not recognised
will be entertained. I am so assured by many intimate with their
opinions, and anxious to apprise me of them. They tell me that whatever
is to be paid for these lands, must be to the individuals who will be entitled
to reservations, or the Indians will not consent to a treaty; and that the
amounts which have been paid by speculators for rights must be guarantied
to them, or they will not consent; and I assure you, sir, that the influence
of these speculators is so great over the Indians, operating through their
agents, and in every imaginable way, that to succeed, we must either obtain their consent, or neutralize their opposition.

The Indians think their lands worth the Government price, one dollar and a quarter per acre, and that this amount ought to be paid for them. I am induced to believe that the reservations would average that price, if sold at auction. I heard to-day that they were disposed to treat for such a price, and would probably attend the council prepared to make such an offer. Now, as the object is not to make money out of them, you see there is a probability of a treaty. This price is the maximum of their expectations; we may bargain for less.

There is another view of this case, which I will briefly state. It is to guarantee to the Indian who may become entitled to a reservation whatever that reservation might sell for, the United States being the guardian of the Indian, and authorized to make the sale.

In either case, however, the amount actually paid by speculators will have to be secured.

Similar opinions have been expressed to you in previous letters; they are repeated now as evidence that continued observation since has tended to confirm them.

As the council will not be in session till the 19th, and as several days will be occupied in making the payments, which I shall endeavor to arrange before we enter upon the treaty, there is time for additional instructions, should you deem it advisable to furnish us with any.

In relation to the plan of these Indians moving themselves west of the Mississippi, which is alluded to in your instructions about the treaty, I deem it a duty to assure you, that in my opinion it will terminate in loss of time and utter disappointment. They are incapable of such an effort, and of the arrangements and foresight which it requires. Nor have they confidence in themselves to undertake it. They fear starvation on the route; and can it be otherwise, when many of them are nearly starving now, without the embarrassment of a long journey on their hands. A people who will sell their corn in the fall for twenty-five cents a bushel, and have to buy in the spring at a dollar, or dig roots to sustain life; a people who appear never to think of to morrow, are not a people capable of husbanding the means, and anticipating the wants of a journey, with women and children, of eight hundred miles. Every spot of good hunting groud, every storm, every trivial accident, will occasion days of delay; and join to these their general listless, idle, lounging habits, their love of drink, which will keep them in its vicinity while they have a shilling to procure it, and what can be expected if the emigration is left to themselves? They need the unceasing exertions of a vigilant and intelligent agent, to urge them forward, and to supply their wants, to protect and encourage them; and without some such agent, I have but little faith in the success of Indian emigrations.

With these Creeks, distracted and unsettled as they now are, it might be advisable to have one agent, well acquainted with them, with authority and means to organize them, in small parties of not less than 500, and so soon as a party is assembled, to send it off under a white conductor. Probably three or four such parties might be moved by the fall, and then probably the whole could be induced to move in a body. With some similar arrangement, I believe that in less than eighteen months every Creek might be west of the Mississippi. But if arrangements for emigration are delayed much longer, there is danger that many of them become so contented with their dependent position, that they will never move.

I am not aware that any objections exist in Washington to the employment of Colonel Crowell, late agent; but judging of him from what I have seen and what many highly respectable and influential gentlemen of this place have said to me, I doubt if one better qualified for the place of principal agent can be found.  He is energetic, intelligent, well acquainted with these Creeks, and generally liked by them, and fully impressed with the belief that the preservation of the Indian depends upon his emigration.

You cannot well have an adequate idea of the deterioration which these indians have undergone during the last two or three years, from a general state of comparative plenty to that of unqualified wretchedness and want.

The free egress into the nation by the whites; encroachments upon their lands, even upon their cultivated fields; abuses of their persons and property; hosts of traders who, like locusts, have devoured their substance and inundated their homes with whiskey, have destroyed what little disposition to cultivation the Indians may have once had; and I am most credibly informed, that the corn crop of this season, of Indian culture, if ever so favorable in its returns, will not be sufficient to feed more than one quarter of them. The wretchedness which must flow from such a condition of things is truly melancholy to contemplate, unless the General Government interposes in some liberal and efficient manner.  Emigration would feed and at the same time remove them; but fed they must be, or numbers of them will starve. And if their expectations from their reservations were quieted, one of the great barriers to emigration would be removed.

In a word, sir, from all that I have seen and heard, emigration is the last and only hope of self-preservation left to these people; and were they as fully impressed with that opinion as I am, they would give away their lands and go.  They are brow-beat, and cowed, and imposed upon, and depressed with the feeling that they have no adequate protection in the United States, and no capacity of self-protection in themselves.  They dare not enforce their own laws to preserve order, for fear of the laws of the whites. In consequence, more murders of each other have been committed in the last six months than for as many previous years; and the whites will not bring the offender to justice, for he, like Iago, no matter which kills, sees in it his gain.          Most respectfully, &c.,

J. J. ABERT,
*Lieut. Colonel Topographical Engineers.*

Hon. Lewis Cass,
  *Secretary of War.*

---

GENERAL LAND OFFICE, *June 5, 1833.*

SIR: As the surveyor of the lands ceded by the Chickasaw treaty concluded at Pontitock creek on the 20th and 22d of October last will not be able to proceed with accuracy in surveying the southern portion of that cession, until the line forming the southern boundary of that cession, and which is also the northern boundary of the Choctaw cession of 1830, at Dancing Rabbit creek, is definitely fixed, I beg leave to call your attention to the 13th article of the Chickasaw treaty relating to this subject, and request that you will advise me whether any measures have been taken by the War Department, with a view to the establishment of that boundary.

With great respect, &c.,
ELIJAH HAYWARD.

Hon. Lewis Cass,
  *Secretary of War.*

CREEK AGENCY, *June* 6, 1833.

SIR: I have duly received your letter of the 20th of May, enclosing a communication from several chiefs of the Creek nation, complaining of injustice to themselves by the election of other chiefs, by which they will lose their rights to entire sections of land under the treaty, and directing me to examine into the matter.

This is but one of the many abuses under the treaty of March, '32, which has come to my knowledge, all of which ought, in my opinion, to receive the most careful investigation before the Government finally acts in the making of the locations.

The investigation should go into the whole of these reputed abuses, and it is not in my power, nor in that of any other man, to make it in a manner that will do justice to himself and to the Government, without bestowing upon it many weeks of labor, and traveling into every town of the nation. Nor in my opinion is any stranger to these people qualified for the task. He may have the intelligence, the industry, and the firmness which this duty will require, but unless these qualifications are guided and enlightened by a general personal knowledge of the Indians, and of their condition at the time. and previous to the treaty, he will be as liable to imposition as the individual who took the census, and be more likely to confirm his errors than to correct them.

If I might be allowed to suggest a mode of making this investigation, it would be this: to send the list of chiefs and heads of families, which has been returned to the Government, to some one here who has not been engaged in the taking of the census, and require of him to investigate it, and report upon it, giving his reasons in detail in all cases in which his opinions shall differ from the original return. Upon these two returns the department might act with some confidence of acting correctly.

I have already stated the qualifications which, in my opinion, ought to be possessed by the individual who may be charged with this investigation; and have also, in a former letter, spoken favorably of the late agent, Colonel Crowell. For the situation therein alluded to several might be found as competent as himself, but for the investigation herein recommended I feel bound to say, that were the choice with me it would fall upon him in preference to any one else.

The duty will be very laborious, and ought to be well paid for; and if done by Crowell will, in my opinion, be done faithfully; and if done faithfully, unless I have been much misinformed, it will give offence to many whose hopes of profit depend upon any thing else than a faithful fulfilment of the treaty.

In justice to Colonel Crowell I will add, that from him I have received no information in relation to any abuses or impositions in taking the census. My information on this subject was obtained while at Columbus, and from sources which I deemed entitled to credit.

Most respectfully, &c.,

J. J. ABERT,
*Lieut. Colonel Topographical Engineers.*

JOHN ROBB, Esq.,
   *Chief Clerk War Department.*

54‡

CREEK AGENCY, *June* 6, 1833.

SIR: I have explained to Mr. Thomas Crowell your remark in relation to his claim under the fourteen hundred dollars appropriation.

Mr. Crowell's claim originates in an advance of money made by him to Benjamin Hawkins, who had a power of attorney from the Indians west of Mississippi, to receive what was due to them under the appropriation.

Hawkins being in this quarter, and in want of money, applied to Mr. Crowell to advance to him the amount upon a transfer of the power, which would enable Mr. Crowell to receive the money when it should be sent on. He declined doing so until he had consulted the commissioners, who gave their countenance to the transaction, and promised the Messrs. Parsons (Col. Crowell declining to act, it being a case of his brother's) to notice it in their report to you.

I have seen the transfer of the claim; it has to it the names of General Parsons and Mr. Abbott, as witnesses.

I have also seen Hawkins and Chilley McIntosh on the subject. They both assured me that it was a just claim on the part of Mr. Crowell, for an adequate consideration, and to him alone was the money now due.

Respectfully, &c.,

J. J. ABERT,

*Lt. Col. Top. Eng'rs.*

Honorable LEWIS CASS, *Secretary of War.*

---

TALLADEGA COUNTY, ALABAMA,

*Jumper Springs, June* 7, 1833.

SIR: Your letter of the 22d April was not received until this week, owing to a mistake in directing it to Montevallo.

I will make known, without further delay, the secretary's determination to stop speculation in certificates of every description issued to the Indians. I have transmitted a copy of your letter to the editor of the Planters' Gazette, in Montgomery, for publication, and will, by letters and advertisements, communicate this intelligence to those places in the Creek country, where the white people have not the advantage of newspaper information. It shall also be made known to the Indians through their chiefs.

Respectfully, &c.,

LEONARD TARRANT.

ELBERT HERRING, Esq.

---

TUSCALOOSA, *June* 7, 1833.

SIR: From the representations of Chilley McIntosh, I was induced last winter to believe that his visit to the old Creek nation was for purposes of a nature mutually advantageous to the two divisions of the Muscogee people, and that the accomplishment of the same would be alike desirable, as well to those within the limits of this State as to those settled beyond the Mississippi. I was likewise induced to believe, from the statements of the said Chilley, that it, perhaps, would not be impolitic in the Government of the United States to permit the said Chilley to remove by emigration a number of his friends and relations, who, he said, were greatly desirous of *joining* he western Creeks, and that immediately; and to allow the persons thus emigrating the privilege of receiving from the locating agent, through persons appointed by them as their attorneys for that purpose, the investiture of the lands to which they might, as heads of families, by reservation under the late treaty, be entitled.

Under such impression, I wrote a letter on the subject, at the instance of McIntosh, addressed to you, the same being signed by him, whereby he became clothed with certain delegated powers, of the extent of which I have not become apprised, but which I am assured he is using to the great injury of the credulous and simple Indians.

He styles himself emigrating agent; has appointed sub-agents or assistants, which latter leave untried no means (as I have been informed and verily believe) of accomplishing and carrying into effect plans for their own special purposes, matured in common between *them* and the companies of land speculators with whom they are connected.

The Indians are induced to enrol to emigrate by every possible artifice; not so much to procure their emigration, and so subserve the wishes of the Government in this particular, (which would seem to be mere matter of indifference to them,) but to procure their powers of attorney to receive from the locating agent their reservations of land; by which said powers, from the manner in which they are drawn up, (which purport to be irrevocable,) they are authorized to make what disposition of the said land they please; to sell, rent, or otherwise dispose of the land at their own option, for *much*, or for *little*, any wish, &c. afterwards, on the part of the Indian, the rightful owner, to the contrary notwithstanding. At one time reports are circulated that to those who enrol, make powers, &c., at a certain period and place, wagon loads of silver will be distributed; at another, the *vast wealth* contained in the *vaults* of the Columbus banks, Georgia, are kept in reserve for them. So infatuated were these poor deluded people by the rumors, that on one occasion, I am told, numbers did actually resort to a place called West Point, (in Georgia,) on the west side of the Chattahooche river, to share these wagon loads of silver; and that, to silence their discontent at their disappointment, the subterfuge of the riches of the banks was then resorted to.

It is much to be regretted that all the agents who have acted under the authority of the Government have not acted correctly. To the abuses committed by some of them some of the difficulties in Indian affairs have owed their origin. The confidence of the Indians in the Government, and in the upright agents of the same, suffers greatly from such causes, and to them is chiefly owing a great share of the abuses alluded to.

I deemed it my duty, on receiving information of those proceedings, to inform the department of the same; and therefore respectfully suggest the propriety of recalling, as early as practicable, the powers given to McIntosh, who is either the *dupe* or the *tool* of a set of heartless speculators, and thus save a few of these poor, ignorant, and deluded people from being swindled out of their rights, and ruined, under cover of authority from the Government.

Very respectfully, &c.,
ENOCH PARSONS.

ELBERT HERRING, Esq., *Com'r Indian Affairs.*

Columbus, *June* 8, 1833.

Dear Sir: I this day received a letter from the department, upon the subject of my reserve, and I should have rested perfectly satisfied of the intention of the Government to do me ample justice, unless led away by false statements from some persons in this section, who were disappointed in not being able to purchase it of me. The reserve was laid out under the direction of General Coffee, and run according to the treaty, making the starting point half way between my mills and the house; this being the proper starting point, in my opinion, and the opinion of Colonel Brodnax, the surveyor. I would have run much lower down than I did, and took in all my improvements, but I was desirous of making the starting point as near the centre as possible. Some attempts, of late, I understand, have been made to prove that the mills are not mine. I am somewhat astonished at this course, for it is notorious, that I have always owned these mills, having had them built myself. I wish the Government to advise me if any attempts of this kind are making. I am suffering a good deal of injury on account of not getting my patents.

The whole difficulty that has originated about this matter proceeds from the fact of the bridge having been put on my reserve. I have understood that the parties who have taken such a stand in this matter against me, have an Indian to locate upon the reserve, and have bought him out; these are the facts which can be established; but I have never thought for a moment that the Government intended to change the survey, for the Government certainly must see that the reserve was laid off in strict conformity to the articles of the treaty.

Very respectfully, your servant,
B. MARSHALL.

Hon. Secretary of War.

---

Creek Agency, *June* 8, 1833.

Sir: I have received your letter of the 22d of May, enclosing a communication from Mr. Moore, in relation to the right to reservations of certain Creek Indians, who have been residing among the Cherokees.

I will make the inquiry you request, but I fear it will not prove successful, for the want of the names of the Indians or heads of families concerned.

Very respectfully, &c.,
J. J. ABERT,
*Lieut. Col. Top. Eng's.*

D. Kurtz, Esq.,
*Act. Com. Ind. Affairs.*

---

Office Indian Agency,
*Michilimackinac, June* 10, 1833.

Sir: I have this day received the circular letter of the department of the 6th of May, containing instructions for carrying into effect the laws prohibiting the introduction of ardent spirits into the Indian country.

It is the purpose of this letter to suggest that the execution of the laws would be facilitated by having the grant of land embraced in Wayne's treaty, "on the main to the north of the island, or on the strait between Lakes Huron and Michigan," surveyed, so as to enable the agents to determine with certainty the portion of country "to which the Indian title has not been extinguished."

It is provided by the treaty, that whenever the United States shall think proper to survey and mark out the boundary of the ceded lands, they shall give timely notice to the Indians, that they may appoint persons to be present, to see that the lines are run according to the grant.

I have, &c.,

HENRY R. SCHOOLCRAFT, *I. A.*

E. HERRING, Esq.,
    *Com. Ind. Affairs, Washington.*

---

GRATIOT'S GROVE, MICHIGAN TERRITORY,
*June* 12, 1833.

SIR: On the 27th of April last, Col. Dodge, J. Kinzie, esq., and myself, met the principal part of the Rock river band of Winnebagoes at the Four Lakes, and had a talk with them respecting their removal. They expressed a willingness to remove across the Ouisconsin, but would require the aid of the United States in crossing their canoes from the waters of Rock river to those of the Ouisconsin, a distance of about twelve miles; and would also require the remainder of the rations coming to them (twenty thousand) by treaty stipulations. Those rations Mr. Kinzie informed me could not be procured immediately, and in order to facilitate their removal we promised them two hundred bushels of corn, and teams to assist them in crossing their canoes and baggage.

The corn I purchased in Galena, the nearest, in fact only point where it could be had; and on the 15th of May issued it to them at the Four Lakes, and commenced their removal. The principal men and thirty lodges crosses at this time. Man Eater and his party were up Rock river, and are, as I am informed, now at Fort Winnebago, and will, I presume, make arrangements for crossing from there.

During the past winter and spring I had frequent talks with them respecting their removal, and always advised them to cross the Mississippi, where game is abundant; and by going fifty or sixty miles back from the river, where they would find buffalo and elk, and on the water courses beaver; none of which game are in the country they have left. At present, they are determined to go no further than the north bank of the Ouisconsin, and will make their village at a place called the Sac Prairie, where there was formerly an Indian field. One great object of the Indians, since they had to remove this season, was to do so soon as possible, that they might make their fields and plant their seed; and we agreed to furnish them with the means, for the double purpose of accommodating them and taking them when they intimated a wish to go; all which I hope will meet the approbation of the department.

On the eve of their departure, they extinguished all their old fires, and kindled a new one, procured by the friction of two sticks of wood, which they "hoped would burn clear and make them happy." They then held a "Grand Medicine Dance," at which they expected, and I made them some presents. From unforeseen events, my accounts of presents and of contingencies have run up in the present quarter to nearly what I anticipated or estimated for the last half year. During the time of the Indian alarm last spring, I was compelled to make large presents to Whirling Thunder, a chief, and other Indians, to get them to accompany me to Turtle village and other Indian encampments, which I thought it my duty to visit, in order to ascertain if there was any foundation for the reports in circulation, and, in order that I might not be deceived by appearances, I left two confidential men at suitable stations to watch them, and report to me their movements.

I regret that it becomes necessary to trouble you again in relation to my public accounts. I have heard nothing from them since you informed me they were handed over to the Third Auditor. I feel a great anxiety to have them speedily arranged.

On the 24th of March last, I drew on Gov. Porter for nine hundred and ninety dollars, agreeably to form and instructions, which drafts have not as yet been heard from. The cause I cannot divine. The delay is unaccountable. I will therefore beg your attention to my affairs: besides the advances I have made of private funds for the purposes of Government, my pay for the last five quarters is still in arrear.

With much respect, &c.

HENRY GRATIOT,

*Sub-Indian Agent.*

ELBERT HERRING, Esq.,
  *Washington City.*

---

CREEK AGENCY, *June* 12, 1833.

SIR: I have duly received your letter of the 1st, limiting the expense of feeding these Indians at the contemplated council.

And remain, sir,

Your obedient servant,

J. J. ABERT,

*Lieutenant Col. Topographical Engineers.*

E. HERRING, Esq.,
  *Comm'r Indian Affairs.*

---

SUPERINTENDENCY OF INDIAN AFFAIRS,

*St. Louis, June* 12, 1833.

SIR: By last evening's mail I received a letter from Col. John H. Kinzie, sub-agent at Fort Winnebago, by which it appears that all the Winnebagoes have moved to the north of the Ouisconsin, with the exception of a few families on Rock river.

The information received from Mr. Kinzie has very much changed my views as to the propriety of the contemplated operations on the west of the Mississippi. Should the Winnebagoes not move to the lands which they acquired by the late treaty, I would not advise the erection of the school buildings or establishment of a farm so distant from the body of the tribe, as those establishments might be subject to the hostile incursions and insults of any other tribe with whom they might be in difficulties. The effect of the example intended for their benefit by the establishment of a farm would be lost, and the assistance in agriculture would avail them but little unless furnished near their residence.

General Street left this a few days ago, provided with the means of carrying into effect the stipulations of the late Winnebago treaty, relating to assistance in agriculture, the establishment of the school, together with such other provisions of same treaty as properly came within his sphere of action.

The annuity of $5,000 also directed by your instructions of 2d April to be paid through him, was paid accordingly. Yet by Mr. Kinzie's letter it would appear that the number of Indians within General Street's agency only amount to about one-sixth of the whole nation. If this statement is correct, the apportionment made by the department would not be in conformity with its established rules. Judging from General Street's payment of annuities last year, the receipts would only show five hundred and ninety one Indians, (although some may not have made their appearance,) whilst the number reported by Mr. Kinzie amounts to 3,947.

Under all these circumstances, I consider it my duty to write to General Street, and instruct him to stay all operations regarding the late treaty until I hear from you on the subject.

I have the honor to be,
With great respect,
Your most obedient servant,
WILLIAM CLARK.

Hon. ELBERT HERRING,
Com'r. of Indian Affairs.

UNITED STATES SUB-INDIAN AGENCY,
Fort Winnebago, May 29, 1833.

SIR: I have the honor to acknowledge the receipt of your letter of the 2d instant, informing me of the disposition of the annuity money, &c. due the Winnebagoes, agreeably to the late treaty with them.

Had the commissioner of Indian affairs been aware of the intention of the emigrating Winnebagoes, he would no doubt have arranged the division of those items differently, and agreeably to the number of individuals at each agency, as exhibited in the pay rolls of Prairie du Chien and of this place, respectively. The Winnebagoes do not intend to remove west of the Mississippi, nor was it contemplated by them when they sold their country. They have a vast extent of good country north of Ouisconsin, where a large portion of their nation have resided for a number of years. The Rock river Indians wish to remain near them, and they determined, when at the treaty last fall, to locate themselves between *Prairie des Sacs* and the Barnebault river, on the Oui-consin. Since then they have selected the country between Devil's lake (near the Ouisconsin) and the Barnebault, which brings them within from eight to fifteen miles of this agency. Many have already reached their intended location, and are preparing their corn fields accordingly.

They will never go west of the Mississippi to reside. A part of them only will resort to that country during the *winter* season, to make their winter *hunts,* and retire in the spring. I think it best that they should remain north of the Ouisconsin, for this reason; our citizens are flocking to the Dubuque's mines and vicinity, and if the Winnebagoes remove to their land west of the Mississippi, it will be placing them in the same relation to the miners that they heretofore have been. Their contiguity to the Sacs. who re unfriendly to them, would tend to create constant disturbances. By being north of the Ouisconsin, they will be away from any white population, and from any tribe of Indians to incite them to mischief. Should the present arrangement not be changed with regard to the provisions, the Indians in this vicinity will suffer much.

It is not to be expected that they will go all the way to Prairie du Chien for provisions. If they should, they will be under the necessity of abandoning their cornfields. Provision should never be issued to them in *bulk*; they are so improvident that they would not take the trouble to transport it any distance; and many would be induced to exchange it for ardent spirits. These and many other facts I need not explain. Your knowledge of the Indian character would lead you to all these reflections. The blacksmith's shop they wish to have continued among them.

Any instructions you may give me in relation to the Winnebago Indians, agreeable to the treaty stipulations, shall be attended to. I have received directions to that effect from Governor Porter.

The Indians of Fox river, Winnebago, and Green lakes, &c., have all moved to the Barnebault and vicinity, a stream which empties into the Ouisconsin about four miles below this place. There are several villages upon its banks; the nearest is eight miles, the most distant eighteen from here. A new village is being established sixteen miles above this on the Ouisconsin; and also one on the Fox river (north) about twenty miles from here.

I understand that there still remain on head of Rock river a few families. They will no doubt leave that country as soon as they learn that force will be resorted to.

After these explanations, I hope you will be able to make the necessary assignment of funds to be sent to me for agricultural purposes, &c., &c. The tobacco should all be sent here agreeable to the treaty, as it is for the emigrating Indians.

The number of persons of the Winnebago nation paid by me last fall is as follows: Men 1,086; women 1,307; and children 1,554: total 3,947 souls. Will you be kind enough to inform me of the number of Winnebagoes paid by General Street last fall. I am anxious to know the number of souls in the nation.

> With great respect and esteem,
> Your obedient servant,
> JOHN K. KINZIE,
> *Sub-Agent Ind. Affairs.*

Gen. WILLIAM CLARK,
    *Sup't Ind. Affairs, St. Louis, Mo.*

---

HOPEWELL FARM, C. N., *June* 13, 1833.

SIR: I should have written you before now had not Major Currey informed me that he had given you the particulars of our last council. You see that it has terminated as I had before told you. I well knew that the propositions of the Government would not be made known to our people by the delegation, and Ross's advice is, still to keep firm and united; but has said, if they can get no relief by next year, that he will advise the people to come into a treaty, sell out, and leave the limits of the United States. He would be in favor of selling for money, by which he could have the distributing of the cash; but the Government should never suffer such impositions;

they should have more regard for their welfare, than to suffer such fraud practised upon the ignorant part of our community. I am in favor of opening a general emigration, and at the same time receive names of all those who are disposed to become citizens of the different States, excepting Georgia, and say that there shall be a life estate of 640 acres of land to the head of each family, and 160 to each child, by their forever relinquishing any further claim to the Cherokee lands west. But should those reservees ever become dissatisfied, and wish to join their brothers in the west, let the Government pay them for such improvements as they may have made, and remove them and provide for them as they would for those who went by enrolment; and let the Government possess the lands. There could be no speculation in this plan, and it would be giving all the privilege of exercising their own free will. There are many who would be in favor of remaining; it would be a hard matter to deprive them of their interest, merely because they were not disposed to follow the nation. Many are much in favor of this plan; and those who have been opposed to reservations heretofore, would willingly consent for them to be allowed in this way. I think it right that there should be made equitable propositions; this, I think, would effect the desired object.

Major Currey informed me that he had recommended sending out commissioners during the summer. If the office of emigration is not opened, I would be in favor of the plan, and would recommend General Coffee, of Alabama, R. J. Meigs and Colonel Turk, of Athens, Tennessee, as suitable persons to send out as commissioners. They have the confidence of the people in this country, and would know better how to get along with our people than those unacquainted. I would refer you to H. L. White, of Knoxville, for the character of those two gentlemen I have recommended.

The annuity money should be sent on, or you should instruct our agent to make a purchase of some grain and have it distributed for the annuity, for our people are in a state of starvation. There was a Cherokee about 40 miles below this went to his neighbor and proffered his horse for seven bushels of corn. One of my neighbors had some grain to spare. I drew orders on him in favor of the Cherokees, so far as their proportionable part of the annuity; and he furnished them with corn, and I promised him that you would, when informed of this fact, direct the agent to draw upon the department for the amount of grain furnished, or instruct the agent to pay the amount. I consulted Colonel Montgomery and Major Currey on the propriety of the plan, and they both advised me to do so, believing that when you was informed of this fact that you would have the amount paid; and unless you instruct our agent to have grain procured for them I think many of them will starve.

There are some Cherokees who enrolled under the treaty of 1817, who are violently opposing the views of the Government. One of these men attended a meeting that I had called, with a company armed for the purpose of taking my life; but it rained and raised the water courses so the day before, that I was not able to reach there, or I suppose the attempt would have been made. These persons cannot be considered any thing more than intruders; and I think that you should instruct our agent to notice such persons, and if they continue their course, to remove them out of the limits of the nation. They are urged by some of our leading men; they are promised protection in this country, if they will act for them; otherwise they would be removed, for our council, a few years since, passed a resolution that they should leave the limits of the Cherokee nation. I went to see those persons since, and informed them that if they ever made another attempt that they would be removed by the agent.

I should like to know what plan will be adopted by the Government; a good plan would be, not to suffer those men living under the jurisdiction of Georgia and Alabama to represent the Cherokee nation. If this could be done, which I suppose you have the right to do, a treaty could be effected immediately. There is but little confidence in *   *   *   *, he is as changeable as the Washington climate.

With sentiments of high regard, &c.,<br>
JOHN WALKER, jr.

To the Hon. ELBERT HERRING,
  *Superintendent Indian Affairs*

---

GENERAL LAND OFFICE, *June* 14, 1833.

SIR: By the enclosed extract from a letter of Governor Carroll, of Tennessee, to this office, dated 4th instant, you will perceive that an unavailing application has been made to him for a copy of the plat and field notes of the southern boundary of the Chickasaw cession of October, 1818; and as it is very important that the surveyor of the Chickasaw cession of 1832 should have a copy of those documents, I will thank you, in case they are in your office, to furnish me with them as soon as convenient.

I am, very respectfully, sir,<br>
Your obedient servant,<br>
JNO. M. MOORE,<br>
*Acting Commissioner.*

ELBERT HERRING, Esq.,
  *Commissioner Indian Affairs.*

---

*Extract of a letter dated 4th June, 1833, from Governor Carroll, of Tennessee, to the Commissioner of the General Land Office.*

"I have received your communication of the 20th May, requesting me to furnish you with a certified copy of the plat and field notes of the survey of the southern boundary of the lands ceded by the treaty of the 19th of October, 1818, with the Chickasaw Indians; and in reply, inform you that a diligent search has been made in the Secretary of State's Office for those papers, but they could not be found.

"As General Winchester, the commissioner who run the line, was appointed by the General Government, his return was doubtless made to some of the departments at Washington."

---

SUPERINTENDENCY OF INDIAN AFFAIRS,<br>
*St. Louis, June* 15, 1833.

SIR: I had the honor to enclose you on the 12th instant a copy of Mr. Kinzie's letter to me of the 29th May; since which, having learned other particulars regarding the intended movements of the Winnebagoes, which coincide with my own views in relation to their settlement north of the Ouisconsin, I would beg leave to recommend the establishment of their school at a place called Grand Gré, or "Trout Spring," eight miles north-east from Prairie du Chien, and about three from the Ouisconsin. A beautiful site can be selected at that place also for a farm.

As far as I am at present advised, I am of opinion that the provisions intended for the Winnebagoes should be sent to Fort Winnebago, where they could be issued with sufficient convenience to those who have moved, and who are entitled to receive them, and will request the quartermaster at Prairie du Chien, in whose charge the provisions are, to send them to Fort Winnebago, to be issued on the requisitions of Col. Kinzie, the sub agent, to whom I have written on the subject.

I have the honor to be,
With high respect, &c.,
WM. CLARK.

Hon. ELBERT HERRING, Esq.,
Commissioner Indian Affairs.

GENERAL LAND OFFICE, June 17, 1833.

SIR: Your letter to the commissioner, of the 8th instant, has been duly received, wherein you state that Col. George W. Martin has been appointed by the department to locate reservations under the 19th article of the treaty with the Choctaws of September 27th, 1830, and request that the commissioner will direct copies of the plats of the one hundred and twelve townships, and fractional townships, which have been surveyed, to be prepared and forwarded to Col. Martin.

It devolves upon me to advise you that with the present force at the disposal of this office it will be impracticable to comply with your request, and that the surveyor general of Mississippi will not be enabled to furnish such extra copies within any *reasonable* time. The surveyor is already required to prepare *triplicate* plats of the public surveys, and until such *triplicates* are completed, a fourth set cannot be ordered.

Under these circumstances it will be advisable, and indeed indispensably necessary for Col. Martin to make references to the plats in the office of the surveyor general, at Washington, Mississippi; which office is directed by a law of the last session of Congress to be removed to *Jackson*, or to the land offices of the northeastern and northwestern districts. The President has designated a town recently established on the Yellow Busha, (a stream tributary to the Yazoo,) which is situated within about three miles of the old missionary establishment at Elliott, as the seat of the land office for the northwestern district. The town is, I believe, named Tuscahoma. He has designated the town of *Columbus*, on the Tombeckbee, as the seat of the land office for the northeastern district.

The necessary instructions preparatory to the opening of these offices have been given. The officers have not as yet received the late advice of the President's designation of the *sites* for those offices.

The first step to be observed by the officers will be to obtain the township plats from the surveyor general. Col. Martin may, in the meantime, decide whether it would be more convenient to make reference at the office of the surveyor general, or at the district land offices.

I would further remark, that in the location of the numerous reservations under various Indian treaties heretofore made, it has never been customary to furnish copies of plats to the Indian agents. They have always obtained the information to be afforded by the plats, by reference either to the surveyor's office or the district land office.

I have to request that you will have the goodness to furnish this office with a copy of the instructions to Col. Martin as soon as your convenience will admit.

I am, very respectfully,
Sir, your most obedient servant,
JNO. M. MOORE,
*Acting Commissioner.*

ELBERT HERRING, Esq ,
*Commissioner of Indian Affairs.*

---

MARSHAL'S OFFICE, *June* 18, 1833.

SIR: The order countermanding the instructions of March 14th, relative to the removal of intruders from the lands ceded by the Creek tribe of Indians, has been suspended, agreeably to the instructions of May 7th.

Very respectfully, &c.,
ROB'T. L. CRAWFORD,
*United States Marshal.*

ELBERT HERRING, Esq.,
*Commissioner Indian Affairs.*

---

CHICKASAW AGENCY, *June* 19, 1833.

SIR: For the purpose of carrying into effect the object of your instructions of the 25th and 29th of March last, I have visited the old and ruling chiefs of this nation, at their respective homes, the better to impress upon each of their minds that, if they wish to save their people as a nation, the absolute necessity of using every exertion in their power to obtain a home for them beyond the Mississippi, and of their obligation to do so under the late treaty. During the trip, I have taken the statements of eight of the old chiefs, relating to the boundary line between them and the Choctaws, which will be forwarded to you in a few days.

Soon after my return, a messenger from the king was sent to inform me that, in consequence of the late talk I had given them, when passing through the country, he had called a council of all his principal men, to meet at Major Levi Colbert's, on the 7th of June, with a request that I should attend, with a copy of the treaty, and from which I have just returned. The council continued six days, during which time I endeavored to explain the provisions of the treaty, and told them what you expected from them, and that the survey of their lands was about to commence, and would soon be in market, and the white people settled among them, and probably make corn the next year; that if they wished to save their people, it was time in earnest to seek some place to settle thereon; that the funds were ready to defray their expenses in hunting a new home, to purchase it, to remove there, and support them the first year; and that their father, the President, expected them to act like men, and save their people from ruin, and that he was at all times prepared to assist them. After much consultation they requested me to say to you that they were sensible of the necessity of finding and procuring a new home for their people, and that every exertion should be used to do so; but that the cholera was prevailing on all the western waters to an alarming extent; that some of their people had lately been at Mississippi, trading, and died with the disease; that they did not think it safe to set out until the sickly season has passed; but that they would be prepared and go so soon as the season would permit, and hoped to be able to make a favorable report before the surveys of the lands were completed.  I have tried to impress on their minds the necessity of appointing their most intelligent and business men for this service, and those in whom full confidence may be placed.  They insist that I shall accompany them.  I know of nothing to prevent, should I be able to close the accounts of my agency up to the last of September by that time.  The months of October, November, and December, are favorable for traveling in this climate, and I presume would be sufficient time to do all that could be done.

The chiefs in council requested that I should not pay the annuity for four or five weeks to come, as their people was all in the habit of attending the payment; that if it was paid earlier, their crops would be lost; and that it would be much to their damage to assemble them until their corn was worked. They, at the same time, requested me to ask of you permission to pay it to the chiefs, for the purpose of buying them a new home.  I used every argument I could against making the request.  I told them that the treaty had provided the funds to pay for a new home so soon as they would find one, and that the annuity was the money of their people; that there was a great failure in their last crops; that many of their people had gone in debt for the means of living, with the promise of paying when they received their annuity, and that their people would be distressed if the annuity was not divided among them.  I also said to them, that I felt a delicacy in making the request, as I knew that a similar one had been made last winter by their delegation in Washington.  Should you not grant their request, please direct me to be governed by my former instructions, in the distribution of their annuity.

I have no doubt, from what I have learned since I left the council, that the old chief, Levi Colbert, has been flattered into the belief that, by taking with him twenty thousand dollars, it would enable him to buy a country for his people, from the Caddo Indians, who live south of Red river.

Very respectfully,<br>Your obedient servant,<br>BENJ. REYNOLDS,<br>Indian Agent.

Hon. E. Herring.

---

Chickasaw Agency, June 20, 1833.

Sir: Enclosed is a statement of eight of the old and ruling chiefs of the Chickasaw nation, taken separately, agreeable to your instructions of the 25th and 29th of March last.  I regret that I was not able to collect a more satisfactory history of the subject; and that I have not been able to find some old and intelligent chief who had been at the Tunica Old Fields.  I also, at the request of Major Levi Colbert, enclose the statement of a very old and intelligent Choctaw marked A, and a paper marked B, copied from a paper in the possession of Maj. Colbert at his request.  I have lately been in that part of the country where it is supposed the line will pass, and have no doubt that there are many settlements made within the Chickasaw country by the whites, who believe that they are within the Choctaw country; and I have no doubt that some of the Choctaws who have taken reservations, will be found to be within the Chickasaw country. It may be proper to remark that I have used all the means in my power to ascertain the locality of the Tunica Old Fields; and, from the best information I have been able to receive, they are situated about eighteen miles (by water) below Helena, Arkansas Territory, on the east side of the Mississippi, and about one and a half miles from its margin, and show the marks of an ancient village.

Very respectfully,<br>
Your obedient servant,<br>
BENJ. REYNOLDS,<br>
*Indian Agent.*

Hon. ELBERT HERRING,
    *Commissioner of Indian Affairs.*

---

CHICKASAW NATION, *May* 18, 1833.

In-mub-be, a chief of the Chickasaw nation, says, that he has heard it asserted by old people the Chickasaws and Choctaws had a long war, caused by a dispute concerning their boundaries, and that an old Choctaw chief, who was then the ruler of his people, came to the Chickasaw old towns, and said that he had come to make peace; that he had measured the ground from his town, the Oke-tub-be-hah creek, and from thence to the Chickasaw town; and that the Oke-tub-be-hah was half way between the two towns. It was then agreed the said creek should be the line between the two nations, from its mouth to its source; from thence a direct course to the Tunica Old Fields, on the Mississippi.

---

CHICKASAW NATION, *May* 12, 1833.

Samuel Lely, a chief of the Chickasaw nation, says, that since his recollection there have been several attempts to mark the line between the Chickasaws and Choctaws, as agreed upon at the conclusion of the old war; and a dispute arose as to which branch of the Oke-tib-be-hah should be the line; and at one time it was agreed that the high land between the two main forks should be the line; and when the high land was traced it struck the old Natchez road about one mile south of Wall's old place; to run from thence a straight course to the Tunica Old Fields, on the Mississippi: since his recollection, the Choctaws contended for all of the Tunica Old Fields; but the Chickasaws maintained that it has been long understood that they were to be divided between the two nations; and that his understanding has always been that the dispute was settled in that way.

---

CHICKASAW NATION, *May* 18, 1833.

Ish-te-ho-to-pa, king of the Chickasaw nation, says, that the line between his nation and the Choctaws had been settled on long before he assumed the functions of king of the Chickasaw people; and that he understood that it was to commence at the junction of Oke-tub-be-hah creek with the Tombig-bee, and run up the main branch of Oke-tub-be-hah to its source, to the Tunica Old Fields, on the Mississippi.

He has never seen the Tunica Old Fields, nor does he know how far they are below the mouth of the St. Francis river.

---

CHICKASAW NATION, *May* 18, 1833.

Col. George Colbert, a chief of the Chickasaw nation, says, that during the agency of Samuel Mitchell, he was, with others, appointed to settle the line between his people and the Choctaws, and that they met Puckshe nubby and Ochumma, on the part of the Choctaws, and they agreed that the line should be as follows, viz.:

Beginning at the junction of Oketubbehah creek with the Tombigbee, and running up said creek to the main fork of Noosahcheyah; thence on the high land, between the forks, to a blazed tree on the old Natchez road, about one mile south of Wall's old place; thence on a direct line to the Tunica Old Fields, on the Mississippi. He says there was some dispute between the two nations as to the place where the Old Fields laid on the Mississippi, and that the Choctaws contended for all the Old Fields; but the dispute was referred to Puckshenubby and Ochumma, on the part of the Choctaws, who agreed that the Old Fields should be divided. He never has seen the Tunica Old Fields, but has always understood that they were situated on a high point of land below the mouth of the river St. Francis; and that the place derived its name from a tribe of Indians who once lived there, but who have long since become extinct. He further says that the tradition of his people is, that long since the Chickasaws and Choctaws waged war with each other on account of a dispute concerning their lands and boundaries, and when peace was made the above described line was agreed upon as the boundary between the two nations. He says it was not the custom of Indian tribes to mark the lines that divided the lands of each other, but their boundaries called for water courses, ridges, or the half-way ground between their towns, as they all lived in towns as late as his recollection; and, in that manner, the boundaries were fixed between his people, the Choctaws, Creeks, and Chickasaws.

---

CHICKASAW NATION, *June* 12, 1833.

Captain William McGilvery, a chief of the Chickasaw nation, says that he always understood that the line between the Choctaws and Chickasaws began at the mouth of Oketubbehah, and run up the same to a large bend; thence a straight course to a marked tree, one mile south of Wall's old place, on the old Natchez road; thence a straight line to the Tunica Old Fields, on the Mississippi. There was no dispute about the line in old times; but the young chiefs have made a contention as to the locality and identity of the place known by the name of " Tunica Old Fields." He has never been at the Tunica Old Fields, but has heard of them since a boy.

---

CHICKASAW NATION, *June* 12, 1833.

Bahacah, a chief of the Chickasaw nation, says that it was agreed to between the Choctaw and Chickasaw nations, that the boundaries between them should begin at the mouth of Oketubbehah, and run up the same to its head, and thence a straight line to the Tunica Old Fields, on the Mississippi river.

He says that he is a very old man; and, when a boy, the Choctaws and Chickasaws had a long war, at the close of which they walked the ground between the two nations, and that the Oketubbehah creek was found to be the half-way point between the two nations, and was agreed upon as the line, to its head; and then a straight course towards the sunset, until it would strike the Mississippi at the Tunica Old Fields. He further says, that he has never seen the Tunica Old Fields; nor did he ever know, until late years, that there existed a dispute about its locality.

---

CHICKASAW NATION, *June* 12, 1833.

Tomchico, a chief of the Chickasaw nation, says that the Chickasaws and Choctaws had a long war, when he was a very small boy; that his chief was by the name of Piomuttahhah, the name of the Choctaw chief he does not recollect. That they were set to war with each other by the French, who lived at New Orleans and Pensacola, and that his people went to Charleston and got powder, lead, and arms, from the white people there; and that after a long war the old Choctaw chief met the Chickasaw chief and made peace, and agreed that the line between them should begin at the mouth of Oketubbehah, and run up to its head, and then a straight course to the Tunica Old Fields; and that the warriors on each side should not cross the line to hunt. He does not know how long since the line was marked at the old Natchez road; but it has been a great while since it was settled that far, and that it has been marked some further towards the Mississippi; and, after the line was fixed, there was no dispute by the old people who are now dead and gone. But the new chiefs who have come into power have had some disputes as to the locality of the Tunica village, or Old Field, on the Mississippi. He further states, that he never has seen the Old Field himself.

---

CHICKASAW NATION, *June* 12, 1833.

Major Levi Colbert, (principal chief of the Chickasaw nation), says, that many years ago there was a dispute between the Chickasaws, Choctaws, Creeks, and Cherokees; and their father, the President, requested them to have a meeting of the four nations, and settle the boundaries between them; and that a meeting was called at the Chickasaw Old Fields, that none of the Cherokees met, and but two Creeks; but a great many of the Choctaws convened, and in a full council of the Chickasaws and Choctaws, they agreed to appoint three commissioners on the part of each nation, who should fix upon and divide the boundaries between them, and that it should be permanent; and that the commissioners met and agreed to begin at the mouth of the Oketubbehah creek, and run up the main branch to a bend, two or three miles east of the old Choctaw "Long Town Path," now the Natchez road; thence a strait line to the blazed tree, on said path, about one mile south of Wall's old place; thence a straight line to the Tunica Old Fields on the Mississippi; he says there was no dispute between his nation and the Choctaws about the line, until a few years ago. That the Choctaws of late pretended that the Tunica Old Fields were a few miles higher up the river than the place which we had always claimed; that he has always understood that the Tunica old fields were about thirty miles by water below the mouth of the river St. Francis, at a high point of land on the Mississippi.

He says, that the Chickasaws permitted a white man to live at the "Old Fields" many years ago, for the purpose of keeping a canoe to convey his people across the Mississippi to hunt, and that the Choctaws never disputed their right to do so.

———

## A.

### CHICKASAW NATION, June 12, 1832.

Tah-um-ba, (a Choctaw,) says he is an old man, and has long lived with the Chickasaws; that he is a relation of the old Choctaw king (Fren-che-mah-stubbe); that it was one of the last requests of the old king, the lines as fixed on should remain between the two nations undisturbed; that he understood it was to begin at the junction of the Oke-tubbe-hah creek, and run up the said creek to its source; and thence a strait line to the Tunica Old Fields, on the Mississippi. He was many years ago at the Old Fields, but does not know how far they are below the mouth of the St. Francis river, for he knows but little about miles, and that he went by land along a trail, leading from Levi Peroy's to that place; that the place was generally known when he was young, and that there was no dispute about it till late days.

———

## B.

### HOLOKY, CHICKASAW NATION,
### October 22, 1832.

We, the undersigned, do hereby certify and acknowledge that the true and just line between the Choctaw and Chickasaw nations begins at the mouth of Oke-tubbe-hah, and runs up it until it gets to the mouth of Noo-sah-che-yah; then up that Creek to a large round swamp, where Noo-sah-che-yah makes a considerable bend towards the Chickasaws; at that point it takes out on the south side near a large pond, keeping a direct course to a grove of large pine on the ridge, about one mile beyond Wall's old stand on the Natchez road; thence a westwardly course to a point on the Missis-sippi river, well known by the name " *Tunica village*."

In witness, we hereunto set our hands and seals.

| | |
|---|---|
| HUCK-TO-HUN-TUBBE, | his x mark. |
| HAM-YOU-TUBBE, | his x mark. |
| KUSH-KAK-BEEN-UM-PO-LO, | his x mark. |
| PAH-SHINK-NOW-WOB-NAH, | his x mark. |
| KAH-BE-PO-YEA, | his x mark. |
| SHO-MOUNTA, | his x mark. |
| LOCK-IT-TUBBEE, | his x mark. |
| IM-MAH-LE-CHA, | his x mark. |
| TAN-LEY, | his x mark. |

———

INDIAN AGENCY,
*Rock Island, June 20, 1833.*

SIR: Enclosed is a speech of Keo-kuck, made prefatory to the payment of the annuities due the Sacs and Foxes, in 1832, in presence of the several officers stationed at Fort Armstrong.

56‡

You will perceive that Keo-kuck urges the payment of their annuity money to the chiefs and head men of the nation, that they may expend it for the good of the whole. The whole nation were unanimous in this recommendation; and I am clearly of opinion that this course would have a much better effect than any other. It would give to the chiefs more power and influence; make them more respected, and render their people much more tractable, obedient, and respectful.

The object of the Government in distributing annuities among them is certainly laudable and humane; but is entirely frustrated by the *mode* of distribution. The evil consequences, as portrayed by Keo-kuck, attendant upon the present manner of distribution, are strictly true in every particular. The chiefs appear to have no other object to serve, nor ambition to gratify, than the prosperity of their nation. They are in no better situation than the rest of their people. They share with them in all things; and, so far as I can discover, never appropriate any thing extra to their own use. I do, therefore, earnestly recommend the appeal of these people to the consideration of the Executive.

With the highest respect, &c.,
M. S. DAVENPORT, *Ind. Agt.*

ELBERT HERRING, Esq.,
    *Com'r. Ind. Affairs.*

————

At a full council of the Sacs and Foxes, held at the Indian agency at Rock Island, on the 1st day of June, 1833, convened for the purpose of paying the annuities of 1832:

Keo-kuck, the principal chief of the Sacs, said: My father, Our great father, the President, and the other head men of the Government, certainly do not know our customs, or they would not require us to do things over the second time. Last summer he sent General Scott here to have a talk with us; we talked with him on the other side of the river, and afterwards at this place. He made me get up to talk. He then told me the President had great confidence in me, and if I wanted any thing, he had no doubt would grant my request. I told him then about this money, and I expected that every thing had been settled as I arranged it with him.

I told him also that I wanted our annuity money to be in the control of the chiefs and braves of my nation. It is the wish of all my people, as expressed to him then, and reiterated again and again to you. If this were done we would have strength to manage every thing for the good of our people. This request has been made to our great father in writing, but refused. I now wish this talk written down as I speak it, in presence of all my nation, and sent to our great father.

My father, there is but a small portion of these annuities coming to each of us; and this mode of distributing it *individually* would ruin my people, as there are many among them who would take their money and buy *whiskey*, instead of such articles of necessity as they would otherwise receive.

Last summer, when General Scott was here, we signed a paper for this money, which had been paid to us by our trader in provisions, ammunition, clothing, and other necessaries, which were found requisite to restrain some of our young men from joining Black Hawk's party, as well as to support our families. We waited a long time for our money to come on, that we might pay it to him ourselves; but were forced to go out to hunt for the subsistence of our families before it arrived. We then gave him the paper, and told him when the money came to present it to you, and get the money. We thought then that every thing was settled; but now we see the money returned again. We don't understand what this means. We are surprised to find that every thing has to be done over again.

I wish you to write so that the President may know that it is the wish of all my people that the chiefs, braves, and warriors receive their money hereafter, and distribute it for the good of the whole.

In regard to this money, all my people present will sign your papers and take their proportion of the money, which belongs to our trader. They have received goods for it, every man, woman, and child in the nation. My people all know and acknowledge that they have received goods for this money; and we hope that our great father will hereafter have our annuities paid to the principal men of the nation, that they may use it for the good of all their people.

Poi shiak, a Fox chief, said: My father, I repeat what Keo-kuck has said to you; my people all desire that our annuity money be paid as he has requested. I hope this speech will go to the President, and the request of our people be granted. I have no more to say now, but when I go to see our great father I will tell him all about it.

Wa-pel-lo, a Fox chief, said: My father, my people all wish their annuities paid as Keo-kuck has requested. I hope his speech will go straight to our great father, and that we may hear from him soon.

---

CREEK AGENCY, *June* 24, 1833.

Sir: I have the honor to acknowledge the receipt of your letter of the 12th, enclosing papers in relation to the claims of the Cherokees, Ridge and Vann.

The agent, Judge Tarrant, has been here for several days, and is still here, and ready to render me any service in his power. He appears to me to be a faithful, informed, and firm officer.

We have not yet been able to get the Indians in council, but expect to do so to-morrow. The prospect of a treaty is not very flattering.

Very respectfully, &c.,
J. J. ABERT,
*Lieut. Col. Topographical Engineers.*

E. HERRING, Esq.,
*Commissioner Indian Affairs.*

---

MARSHAL'S OFFICE, So. DIST. ALA.,

*June* 25, 1833:

SIR: Yours under date 3d instant came to hand during my absence from this place.

The instructions of March 14th were suspended by an order dated May 7th. Previous to the receipt of the order of May 7th I had despatched an agent, Mr. Sommerville, into the nation, for the purpose of executing the order of March 14th. I have this day despatched Mr. J. Austill to the ceded lands, with the necessary instructions. This delay has occurred in consequence of the cholera raging in our section of country; I was desirous of getting into the country. The frequent failure of mails has also added to the delay. Mr. Austill is an active, energetic man; and I feel no doubt but that every intruder will be removed in a short time.

Very respectfully &c.,

ROBERT L. CRAWFORD.

Hon. Lewis Cass,
   *Secretary of War.*

---

CHEROKEE AGENCY, *June 27*, 1833.

SIR: On my return to this point, yesterday, from an excursion into the interior of the nation, by the receipt of the enclosed letter from Mr. Hendrix, an emigrant, who, with his family, went to Arkansas during the spring of 1832, my attention is called to an omission, on the part of the appraisers, to make return of the valuation of his abandoned improvements to the War Department.

By reference to their book, which is in my possession, the following entry is found in the hand writing of Major Davis, one of the appraisers.

*lliam Hendrix's improvement on Long Swamp, Georgia, viz.:*

| | |
|---|---|
| One dwelling house $55 00, one double stable $20 00   -   - | $75 00 |
| Two cabins, $20 00 each, $40 00; two corn cribs, one $10, the ther $15 00 -   -   -   -   -   -   - | 65 00 |
| One other cabin $20 00, one lot $10 50, one do. $3 00, one do. $2 00, one do. $3 00   -   -   -   - | 38 50 |
| Twenty-two apple trees, at $1 00, $22 00; ninety peach trees, at 75 cents, $67 50   -   -   -   -   - | 89 50 |
| Thirty-three acres of low ground, at $8 00 per acre   -   - | 264 00 |
| | $532 00 |

I, William Hendrix, a Cherokee, having enrolled myself for Arkansas, do hereby relinquish all my right and title to all the improvements valued to me under the treaty of May 6th, 1828, as well as all my interest in the Cherokee nation east of the Mississippi, to the President of the United States, and his successors in office, the title to which I do warrant and defend from me, my heirs or assigns for ever.

his
WILLIAM + HENDRIX.
mark.

Test: J. M. C. MONTGOMERY,
  WM. M. DAVIS.

I was present, and aided in the measurement of the lands abandoned, and feel satisfied the improvements were worth the sums affixed to each respectively. Should it be considered absolutely necessary this return should be made out by the appraisers, over their own proper signatures, it can be done yet. I cannot believe this will be required, as they are separated, and a considerable distance from this point; and from the entry and inscription on their book, that the improvement had been placed on the *roll*, am evidently of opinion that they have already performed that duty.

If the above abstract, from the book of the appraisers, will justify the department in approving the valuation, be so good as to inform me whether the amount thereof will be directed to be paid Mr. Hendrix by the agent west; or, in case that should be considered improper, what course must be pursued.

Most respectfully,
I have the honor to be,
Your obedient servant,
BENJ. F. CURREY.

Elbert Herring, Esq.,
*Commissioner of Indian Affairs.*

The within is a correct abstract from the appraisers' book; the entry in the hand writing of Major Wm. M. Davis, one of the appraisers, an the relinquishment attested by both of the appraisers.
H. MONTGOMERY, *Indian Agent.*
*June* 27, 1833.

———

Fork of the Illinois River,
*Cherokee Nation, April 22,* 1833.

Sir: I have made application to Mr. Vashon, agent of Western Cherokee nation, for the value of the improvement I left in that nation, and he tells me my name is not registered on the document. I communicate these lines to know the reason why it is not. I hold the writing you gave me of the value of my improvement, with your name signed to it. I write this letter by advice of the agent, who thinks, perhaps, that you have made a mistake some way, and wants to give you a chance of rectifying the same.
Yours, &c.,
WM. HENDRIX.

Mr. B. F. Currey.

———

Cherokee Agency, *June* 28, 1833.

Sir: Some time since (being unwell) I asked Major Currey to enclose you a letter from Mr. J. Walker to me, upon the subject of the annuity due the Cherokees, and to state to you that if a few thousand dollars was remitted to me, it could be paid out to them individually, and that it might be the means of preventing a great deal of suffering amongst the poorer class of the Indians. I have not received an answer to that letter, nor seen any to him upon that subject; and as the calls of those poor wretches are day by day repeated and increasing, and their suffering, in many parts of the nation, extreme for want of bread, and grain very scarce and not to be had without money, which they have not, nor any other way to get it, I hope I shall be excused for again asking your attention to that subject.

It is a fact, that notwithstanding the flaming reports of missionaries and some of the chiefs, about the improved state of the Cherokees, that they are becoming poorer every year, (I mean the full-blooded Indians,) and this year they are in a state of wretchedness bordering on starvation, and but for the friendly assistance rendered them by Mr. Walker (at his own risk) many of them must have suffered ere this.

If you would send me the balance of the annuity due this nation for the year 1831, which was deposited in bank, $5,989 67, and authorize me to pay to each family that would apply for it the several sums due them for 1831, '2, and '3, this would make a sum to each family worth calling for. I have no doubt but that sum would soon be paid out, in spite of all the chiefs and their officers could do to prevent it, and the poor Indians in a great measure relieved from their present distress, and perhaps some lives be saved.

I am, sir, with high respect,<br>Your obedient servant,<br>H. MONTGOMERY.

Hon. Elbert Herring,
*Commissioner Indian Affairs, Washington City.*

---

Cherokee Agency, *June* 28, 1833.

Sir: Communications of the 16th May and 6th June have been duly received.

I returned to this place on the 26th instant, off a tour through the Indian settlements. Many of the common people appear to be contented, resting in anticipation their leaders will do something for them at the national council in October next. Their suffering from poverty is great. Six Cherokees out of ten, who had been driven by hunger to the forests for plants, &c., upon which to subsist, a few days ago died in the valley towns; it was by using a poisonous plant for salad.

I believe a majority of the Cherokees would receive their annuity at this time if they had that privilege. Calls are constantly made on the agent to know when it may be expected.

On next Wednesday there is to be a council held in the Ancoa district, to which all parties are invited. The proceedings there will be an indication of what the chiefs intend doing, as it is called under their directions. Ten or fifteen days ago John Fields, a treaty man, was assaulted and badly wounded, by a party opposed to terms. I had them arrested and bound over to appear at the Floyd circuit court, to answer for their misconduct. This was considered necessary to ensure the future safety of all who may hereafter avow themselves favorable to the same measure.

I have the honor to be,<br>Most respectfully,<br>Your very obedient servant,<br>BEN. F. CURREY.

Elbert Herring, Esq.,
*Commissioner Indian Affairs.*

---

Creek Agency, *June* 29, 1833.

Sir: I have the honor to acknowledge the receipt of your letter of the 17th instant.

The errors in the census, to which I alluded in mine of the 6th, were those of excess in the number of heads of families. The general impression is that these are much beyond a correct result, say from 1,500 to 2,000; and they were occasioned by frauds practised by the Indians upon those employed in taking the census, and which only an intimate knowledge of the Indians could have enabled them to avoid.

We are to receive an answer to-morrow to our proposal for a treaty, but I doubt its being favorable. While those people are within the reach of the white influence in this quarter, and while that influence is against us, our success is not probable. Yet I believe the great mass of the chiefs came to this meeting disposed to treat, and if they had been left to themselves, would have made a treaty.

Should we find no better result within our control, we will endeavor to keep the subject alive, by advising the appointing of a delegation to meet at a future day, at some place to be designated by the President. The President can then accede or comply, and the matter will be left no worse than we found it.

Very respectfully, &c.,
J. J. ABERT,
*Lieut. Col. Top. En.*

JOHN ROBB, Esq.,
*Acting Secretary of War.*

---

*Extract of a letter from Samuel Gwin to Honorable Lewis Cass, Secretary of War.*

CLINTON, *June* 30, 1833.

"I returned a few days past from a trip through the northwest land district, embraced in the late Choctaw purchase at Dancing Rabbit Creek.

Not knowing who would have the locating the reserves, floats, &c., in the nation, and being satisfied that great frauds *were in contemplation* on the United States, and believing that these claims would have, at last, to pass through my hands, I have drawn up a circular, giving my views fully on every point in the treaty touching the reserves &c., which will, in a few days be published. To save the United States from those contemplated frauds, I have been strict in requiring evidence where frauds could occur. I have been among the speculators, have heard their plans and intentions, and it is upon this information that much of my circular is based. The Indian cannot be injured, if he gets the land given him at the treaty; or at least, he cannot ask for more. The speculators wish to change it to better lands and places for towns. I shall send you a copy as soon as they are printed, and would take it as a favor to correct any errors, in fact, that you may discover when comparing it with the treaty. I have taken this course solely with a view to cut up a set of speculators, who are attempting to change every Indian settlement right where the land is not good.

I would thank you also for a copy of all those who have listed themselves with the agent, as pointed out in the treaty, having such a quantity of land in *actual cultivation* in 1830, *and a house* on it, and any other claims a register of which is in your department.

An attempt is now made to put off the sales in the late purchase, until this fall year. If this succeeds, it will be the most ruinous act that could be done. These claims are now fresh in the recollection of many persons, and can be corrected; but once let this evidence be removed, and there is no barrier to prevent frauds, and it would be better to give up the whole country to the speculators, without further trouble. I pledge myself in one month to close every reserve, float, and settlement right, if authorized so to do. Let it be known that there is no shuffling, and all will be right, and can be easily done. Every township that is surveyed should be brought into market at as early a day as practicable. Until this is done, there will be no end to those claims; but the moment a sale is announced, they will forthwith close the matter.

Another reason which is given for wishing the sales postponed is, to give time to locate the orphans' claims. A delay on this account is entirely unnecessary, and not called for by the claimants. If an agent is appointed to locate these claims, he can do it in a short time; but should the President determine to sell these claims at the Government price at once, and vest the proceeds in stocks, which, by the by, will be better for the orphans, why it will be still less cause of delay in the sales."

---

CREEK AGENCY, *July 2, 1833.*

SIR: I have this day drawn a draft on you in favor of J. G. Worsham, for two thousand nine hundred and one dollars forty-five cents, being the amount of his account for furnishing the Indians, at the late council, with provisions. And shall also draw one in a few days in favor of General Enoch Parsons, for five hundred and sixty one dollars and sixty cents, the same being the amount of his account for services as commissioner, under the orders of the War Department of the 2d May last.

Very respectfully, &c.,

J. J. ABERT,
*Lieut. Colonel Topographical Engineers.*

HEN. LEWIS CASS,
*Secretary of War.*

---

CREEK AGENCY, *July 3, 1833.*

SIR: I shall leave this place to-morrow for Columbus, where I shall be detained a few days in bringing my money transactions to a close, after which I shall return to Washington.

We have failed in our efforts to make a treaty. A more detailed account of this duty will be presented in a few days in a joint report.

Very respectfully, &c.,

J. J. ABERT,
*Lieut. Col. Topographical Engineers.*

JOHN ROBB, Esq.,
*Acting Secretary of War.*

---

CREEK AGENCY, ALABAMA,
*July 3, 1833.*

SIR: The undersigned commissioners appointed to treat with the Creek Indians, have the honor to report:

That we caused these Indians to be assembled on the 19th ultimo, and have been in council with them ever since.

That on the first day and at a very full council of chiefs and head men, we exposed to them, as clearly as in our power, their present position, their course in selling their presumed rights to land, the character of the greater part of their sales, and the consequences which, in our judgment, would inevitably follow. We alluded, also, to the threats which we had understood had been held out against them, and to the efforts which we understood had been made, and were making daily, to lessen the weight of what we might feel authorized to say to them. Then, as briefly as was consistent with a clear expression of our views, we exposed to them the basis upon which we were willing to treat for the purchase of the reservations provided for in the treaty of 24th March, 1832.

This basis was, that we would recognize the right of individuals of their nation to separate sections and half sections of land, agreeably to the treaty of '32.

That these should then be ceded to the United States, and the United States would obligate itself to bring them into market at an early day, and to pay to each individual entitled to a section or half section under the treaty of '32, whatever his particular section or half section should be sold for. That these payments should be made periodically, say one fourth at a time, in order to avoid the entire waste of all their means, which we feared would follow if the whole amount were paid at one time; and also, in order to enable individuals to have adequate means of making themselves comfortable after arriving at their new homes, in addition to their customary annuities.

We also intimated that we should expect in return that the treaty would stipulate some specified period for emigrating; but that while the emigration was progressing and until completed, they should be allowed the undisturbed occupation of the reservations; and if desired by them, as we knew what threats had been held out against them, we would agree to a stipulation in the treaty, obligating the United States to defend them by an agent, in all suits brought against them on account of the sales and contracts into which they had so unadvisedly entered.

These general principles were explained at the time they were made, in much detail, and frequently afterwards, and were illustrated by every argument and suggestion which appeared to us adapted to have them clearly understood; and to impress upon the Indians the evident disinterested feeling of the United States in relation to any profit from the land, the evident deplorable condition in which their own folly had placed them, and their utter inability to extricate themselves.

That we frequently produced strong impressions upon them, and favorable to the philanthropic views of the Government, we have every reason to believe; but these were not allowed to acquire strength by reflection or time, but were rapidly removed by the actively operating interest of those who were opposed to our success, and who replaced, in their stead, sentiments of mistrust and apprehension.

Our efforts were continued without abatement of zeal, although with some desponding feeling, and were also well sustained by many of our friends until the 30th of June; when, in consequence of an intimation to that effect from the chiefs, we attended them to receive their answer to the proposals.

We met accordingly in full council, and received their answer in writing, and which accompanies this report. This answer, as you will perceive, declines acting upon our proposals, and is tantamount to a refusal to enter into any treaty in relation to the reservations.

We deem it our duty to state to you, that we have no doubt this answer

57‡

was dictated by the white interest involved in speculations upon these reservations; and that it is also our opinion, if these Indians had been left to themselves, they would have given a favorable ear to our proposals, and have made a treaty: they were, however, not allowed a moment's rest, but the most untiring, and if we may acquiesce in a common belief at the council, the most unjustifiable means were resorted to, in order to induce them to decline the treaty. On these accounts we consider them rather to be pitied than condemned.

After receiving their answer, and assuring them that it would be submitted to the President, and expressing our regret that they had so completely closed the door to the friendly and protecting hand which had been extended towards them; we then again, under the aspect of farewell advice, brought as directly to their feeling and knowledge as in our power, their true situation, and the ruin and desolation which they were about to bring upon themselves. Impoverished by law suits, punished for offences which they were not aware they had committed; subject to laws they could not comprehend, and at complete variance with all their habits and notions of right, without a place to call their home, for the land which they had not sold to the United States, they had most inconsiderately, and as far as in their power, sold to individuals: they would soon, if indulged in the wish they had expressed, of having their rights located, be without a shelter, and dependent upon the charity of their white neighbors. That they were fast verging to this point, their rapid impoverishment ought to convince; and also that in their answer they were now urging it upon the President to strike from beneath their feet their sole remaining home here, while they declined permitting him to lead them to the new home assigned to them west of the Mississippi.

We urged them to reconsider their reply; not so completely to shut the door as they had now done, and at least to expunge from it the request so fraught with their own ruin. But although we have heard of many opinions among them regretting the reply, and acknowledging their perplexity and apprehensions, yet it was left in our hands as we now submit it to you.

We frequently brought to their minds the advantages of their new homes, west, where twelve millions of acres of land were assigned to them, and where they could exercise their own laws and customs, unrestrained by any other than the paternal authority of the United States, where the interference with them by the whites could be controlled; where they would be a distinct, and might again become a great people; and where aided by the efforts of the United States, their progress in improvement and civilization would be undisturbed and certain.

These and various other remarks were made to them in a language adapted to their capacities, and to an easy interpretation. But although at times we appeared to convince and evidently satisfied them that their prosperity was at an end where they were, yet we could not prevail.

The general character of the bargains which have been made with the Indians may be inferred from the notice which was served upon us, and which accompanies this report.

The object of this notice was to protect the presumed rights of the purchasers, and to prohibit a sale on the part of the Indian, or a purchase on the part of the United States, to the extent of the names attached to the notice.

We will not trouble you with a detail of the many reports which have come to our knowledge of the methods which have been adopted, in order to induce the Indians to sell, or of the impositions said to have been practised in the sales themselves; we would rather, for the honor of human nature, believe that these reports are erroneous, and at least will forbear to embody them in an official paper, while we are yet in want of conclusive testimony in relation to them. We will merely say on this subject, that we think them sufficient to justify the most scrutinizing examination, when the officer ordered to locate the reserves shall be placed on his duty.

We do not mean by these remarks to impugn the character of all the purchases. Many of them have no doubt been fairly made, and will endure the test of the most severe investigation.

But the singular improvidence of these people is of itself a serious cause of regret, and will tend, we have no doubt, to cast a shade over many a correct sale. Instances have come to our knowledge of their disposing of obligations worth 400 dollars, given by responsible and honorable men, for the trifling consideration of five or six dollars, thus parting with their half sections of land for about twenty-five dollars; the cash advanced in the first instance being about twenty dollars. Against such improvidence, no adequate system of protection can easily be adopted.

In a word, sir, after giving to this subject the most careful consideration, we are forced to the conclusion, that there is no other way of saving these Indians from the ruin which hangs over them, and of preserving to them a reasonable share of the proceeds of their reservations, than by the United States becoming the purchaser, and exercising that guardianship over those proceeds which both humanity and public policy dictates.

We do not presume to advise in a case which may be considered as involving the obligations of a treaty, but merely to give opinions resulting from facts which came under our personal observation, and in this spirit we will add, that we doubt if 100 Indians of this nation will own a tract of land within six months after the locations are made; or if at that time they will have as much of the proceeds of the sales as will buy them a bushel of corn.

In relation to their emigration west, we believe that many of them are disposed to go, and probably several large parties could be induced to start the ensuing fall and winter, if arrangements were made to conduct them, and to feed them on the way. But we doubt their ability to conduct themselves. We also doubt the economy, if not the practicability, of the plan of moving the whole nation in a body. There is not that bond of common feeling among them which would be an inducement to such a plan. Entire towns might be prevailed upon to move at once; or one or two adjacent towns having habits of family intercourse. But generally the several towns are strangers to each other, with different customs, and in some cases different languages.

The abuses which these Indians suffer, under color of the law, in the way of damages, and of taxes for costs, equals, if it does not exceed the stories which we have heard in relation to their land sales, and are rapidly divesting them of their property, and reducing them to a state of abject poverty. Their helpless ignorance, their generally good character, (for they are a well disposed people,) their honesty of purpose, and general honesty of conduct, instead of establishing claims upon good feelings, seems rather to expose them to injuries. Their weaknesses receive no compassion, and their very helpless ignorance but renders them the more liable to wrongs.

We see no remedy to their condition but in emigrating west; and it would be better for them to abandon their lands for nothing (as they are now said to be doing) and to move, than to remain under their present circumstances.

We do not mean by this opinion, however, to recommend a system which would at the same time throw their lands into the hands of those whose speculations are said to be so deservedly obnoxious to severe reproach.

Our system would be by a treaty which would preserve these Indians from their present unfortunate position, in relation to their lands, and which would place the United States in the breach. With the Government these claimants might contend; and if they succeeded, the Indian would at least be assured of the value of his land in the known good faith of the United States. But this can be effected only by the consent of the Indians; and that, in our opinion, is not to be obtained while the negotiation is conducted within the reach of the white influence involved in the speculations.

We state the facts as they appear to us, and leave it to the Government to adopt the remedy.

Towards the termination of the council we received from the chiefs the enclosed letter, in relation to balances said to be due them under certain previous treaties. As we are not intimate with the merits of these claims, we merely limit ourselves to bringing the subject to your notice, with the opinion that it should be acted upon, and an appropriation made; the payment of the same ought to be made to the chiefs of the different towns, and the money divided in proportion to the population of each town. And to put at rest all cavil on this subject among the Indians, it ought to be so provided for in the law making the appropriation.

Having heard that a civil officer has arrived at this place with authority to remove certain intruders, specified by name, we take the liberty respectfully to state, that we doubt the benefit of any such partial action. And in relation to the question of removing intruders generally, it has been so long delayed, and now involves the happiness of so great a number of families, we also doubt the advantage of any action of the Government, except in cases in which intruders have entered upon the cabins, or cultivated or enclosed fields of the Indians.

Our explanation in council on this subject countenanced the opinion that the right to remove intruders was now limited to such cases, and to all after the locations were made, to the extent of those locations.

Having in the course of our report alluded to the sufferings and losses of these people under the color of the law, we are of the opinion that immense sums of money might be saved to them, and great personal injuries avoided, if some person were employed to defend them, and whose duty it should be to see that they received that protection which the laws of the State, when correctly administered, undoubtedly extend to them. We have no doubt that if timely attention had been given to the suits which terminated in judgments exceeding an amount of eight thousand dollars, and lately paid by the United States, that this amount would have been reduced to less than two thousand.

Having thus briefly exposed our course and observations, we have merely to add the assurance of the regret we feel at the failure which has attended our efforts in a cause involving, in our opinion, the happiness of these people, and to a great degree the prosperity of this State.

Respectfully submitted.

ENOCH PARSONS, ⟩ *Commissioners.*
J. J. ABERT, ⟩

To the Hon. LEWIS CASS,
    *Secretary of War, Washington City, D. C.*

---

COUNCIL GROUND, NEAR CREEK AGENCY,
*June* 30, 1833.

BROTHERS: The head chiefs of the Creek nation, in council assembled, a few days ago received your talk in relation to a sale of the reservations provided for in the late treaty between the United States and Creek nation of Indians, which the chiefs have had under consideration; and, after a thorough investigation among the tribes, have to give the following answer:

Last September, in council at Wetumpkee, we wrote a letter to the Secretary of War, stating to him, when experience would teach us that a removal beyond the Mississippi would be to our interest, we would give our father, the President, an answer to that effect. We are perfectly satisfied with the present treaty, if it had been carried into effect. We are not disposed to enter into any further treaty with the United States, and sincerely request the treaty already made complied with.

We have frequently informed our father, the President, of the many trespasses his white children have made upon us, but he has given a deaf ear to our complaints. Our people are of the same opinion now as they were at Wetumpkee last September; they say they have no land to sell to the United States.

Before we quit our answer, we must entreat you to intercede with our great father to hasten the locations of our land. We are anxious to know our rights, and to carry into effect all and every part of the treaty made; and as we said at Wetumpkee, when we believe it our interest to move west, will communicate it to the President. Any thing short of such a communication from us to him will be entirely useless.

Accept of our best wishes.

We are your red brothers,

    NEAH MICCO,        his x mark.
    JAMES ISLAND,       x
    COEHAH TUSKENUCKEE, x
    TUCKE-BACHE HADJO,   x
    TUCKE-BACHE MICCO,   x
    COOSA TUSKENUCKEE,   x
    SA-LA-TEE,          x
    DAVID BARNARD,     x
    NEAH-THLOCCO-OPOES,   x
    JOHN STIDHAM,      x
    JOHN OPONNY,       x

To Colonel ABERT and General PARSONS.

CREEK AGENCY, *July* 1, 1833.

We, the head chiefs of the Creek nation, in general council assembled, would respectfully call your attention to, and ask your interference in our behalf, so far as to cause the treaties that have heretofore been made with us to be complied with.

You will doubtless recollect that, according to the treaty at Fort Jackson, the United States stipulated to pay the Creek nation for damages sustained and property lost by our people during the late war. You may also recollect, that after the loss of Colonel Hawkins's papers, and prior to the report of General D. B. Mitchell on these claims, an appropriation was made by Congress, which was supposed would be sufficient to cover these claims; but, as by reference to the report of General Mitchell, and a letter of General Pinckney, it will be found it was by far too small, and leaves a considerable balance due our people under that treaty.

Also at the treaty of the Indian Springs, $250,000 of the amount stipulated to be paid us for our land by the United States was set apart to pay the claims of citizens of the State of Georgia against the Creek nation; which amount, as by reference to the board of commissioners, by far exceeds the claims that were allowed, and consequently left a considerable balance unexpended in the hands of the Government. These claims are of long standing; and your own recollection, as well as the documents referred to, will incontestibly establish their justice.

We respectfully request that you would present these facts to the Congress of the United States, and ask an appropriation that will be adequate, on an examination, for the adjustment of our claims under these treaties.

|  |  |
|---|---|
| NEAH MICCO, | his x mark. |
| TUCKABACHIE MICCO, | x |
| TUSKA-NEW-HAU, | x |
| NEA-COCK-O-OPALA, | x |
| COOSA TUSTANUGGEE, | x |
| TUCKABACHIE HADJO, | x |
| COTCH-A-TUSTANUGGEE, | x |
| TUCK-E-NUCK EMATLA, | x |
| JAMES ISLAND, | x |
| JOHN STIDHAM, | x |
| MAJOR BARNARD, | x |
| EFI EMATLA, | x |
| FOSHATCH EMATLA, | x |
| SOL-HAR-TA, | x |
| HANA EMATLA, | x |
| JACOB BEARNES, | x |
| TUF-FA-LA-EMATLA, | x |
| TOMAH MICCO, | x |

Signed in presence of us:
    LEONARD TARRANT,
    NATHAN RICE.
    PADDY CARR,  } *nterpreters.*
    B. MARSHALL, }
To the PRESIDENT OF THE UNITED STATES.

*June* 19, 1833.

GENTLEMEN: Understanding that you are authorized by the President of the United States, and instructed to make and enter into a treaty with the chiefs and head men of the Creek nation of Indians in the State of Alabama, for the purchase of all the individual reserves secured (by the last treaty made and entered into between said tribe of Indians and the United States) to each head of a family, we beg leave to notify you that one hundred and forty-seven Indians, whose names are hereunto annexed, were, at the time of making said treaty, heads of Indian families, and each entitled to a reserve of land; that M. W. Perry and Company have fairly, and for a valuable consideration, purchased from said Indians respectively their said reserves, and taken obligations in the form hereunto annexed; and that the said M. W. Perry and Company have made heavy advances to each one of said Indians in part payments of said lands, and are ready to pay the balance of the purchase money in each case, agreeable to the contract. Should any purchase be made by you under your present appointment, you are notified to exclude from said purchase the reservations aforesaid. It is not by any means *necessary*, yet it is due to Messrs. M. W. Perry and Company to add, that in making said purchases they had no wish to embarrass the Administration in regard to its policy towards the Indians, nor did they believe that they were doing so; which nonbelief was induced from a deliberate examination of said treaty, the laws of Alabama recognizing the validity of Indian contracts, the same laws abolishing all official distinctions in said tribe, and the acquiescence of the General Government in regard thereto; and particularly by letters received some months ago from the honorable Secretary of War by individuals of Columbus, Georgia, intimating that the General Government could have no motive in wishing to purchase the Indian lands, as private purchasers were coming forward with sufficient spirit to ensure the Indians a fair price for their lands. Should the Government, however, purchase such lands from the pretended chiefs of said tribe, when by the laws of the State there are no such chiefs, and when the validity of those laws have been admitted by Government, should the individual vested rights of private Indians be divested by the acts of unauthorized agents, and especially should such a purchase be made to the injury of Messrs. M. W. Perry and Company, after express notice of their previous purchase for a valuable consideration, then it will become necessary for them to prevent, by the proper process, the removal of any of said Indians out of said State until the said contract be executed.

The conveyances are subject to your inspection, if desired.

M. W. PERRY & CO.,

*Pro personæ.*

To Colonel ABERT and General E. PARSONS.

[Annexed to this paper were the names of one hundred and forty-seven Indians.]

---

FORT MITCHELL, *July* 3, 1833.

DEAR SIR: I reached this place to-day, for the purpose of getting a detachment of troops to remove such of the intruders as are troublesome to the Indians, and those that have taken possession of Indian improvements without giving compensation for the same. There are at this time three thousand settlers upon the Indian lands, and although the greater proportion of them are civil enough to the Indians, yet they disturb them by bringing in large stocks of cattle, horses, and hogs, which lead theirs astray; and they have lost a great proportion of their stock in this way. I will confine myself, for the present, to such as the chiefs require should be driven out.

It does not appear possible to keep those people out after they have been removed, unless the troops are furnished with horses to ride. The extent of country is great, and it will be necessary to keep the troops moving all the time. Thirty horses would be quite sufficient, and do more good than one hundred men on foot.

I have the honor, &c.,<br>
J. AUSTILL,<br>
Deputy Marshal.

Hon. Lewis Cass,
    *Secretary of War.*

United States Indian Agency,<br>
At Prairie du Chien, July 3, 1833.

Sir: Your letter of the 29th March last did not reach this agency until the 15th May, although I was before that time in possession of yours of 6th of April.

Having descended to St. Louis for the Winnebago annuities, I did not see your letter of the 29th March, until a few days past; I then addressed Captain Legate in relation to the subject, and received for answer his letter marked (A) , since which I have not heard from him or Mr. J. P. Sheldon. I shall hold myself in readiness to fulfil the requisitions of the Government.

In the second section of the act of Congress enclosed, is the following enactment: " It shall be lawful for the *President of the United States* to direct the Indian agents at Prairie du Chien and Rock Island, or either of them, when offences against said act shall be committed on lands recently acquired by treaty from the Sac and Fox Indians, to execute and perform all the duties required by the said act to be performed by the marshals, in such mode as to give full effect to the said act, in and over the lands acquired as aforesaid." I wish to ask, *is it not necessary to the legality of any act of mine under this law, that,* in the language of the act, *the President of the United States should direct me to act ?* I ask for information, and to call your attention to a re-examination of the language of the act.

With high respect, &c.,<br>
JOS. M. STREET,<br>
U. S. Indian Agent.

To the Hon. Elbert Herring,
    *Commissioner of Indian Affairs.*

United States Lead Mines, Galena,<br>
June 20, 1833.

Sir: I have the pleasure to acknowledge the receipt of your note of the 13th instant, relative to intruders upon the lands on the west bank o th Mississippi river.

I had previously received a letter from T. B. Burnett, esq., sub-agent, upon the same subject. I have not yet received the special instructions from the Commanding General, referred to in his letter.

I have instructed Mr. J. P. Sheldon, the assistant superintendent of the lead mines, who is stationed in that section of the country, to report to you and to the Indian agent at Rock island, the names of all persons hereafter found on the land recently ceded by the Sac and Fox Indians, who are not authorized to be there under the laws and regulations for leasing the lead mines.

I am informed that Mr. George W. Harrison is there, surveying land under the authority of the private claimants, at what is called Dubuque's mines.

Respectfully, &c.,

THOS. LEGATE.

General J. M. STREET,
    *U. S. Indian Agent, Prairie du Chien.*

---

TALLADEGA COUNTY, JUMPER SPRINGS, ALABAMA,
*July 5,* 1833.

SIR: Your letters of May the 3d and 6th, and of June the 12th, have been received; and in answer to yours of the 3d permit me to state, that the frequent applications of the Indians on various subjects connected with their welfare, such as an examination of their claims against the Government, how and when they are to be located, and who amongst them are entitled to reserves, whether they are authorized to sell their reserves, &c.; and what is remarkable, the Indians and white people in this country have almost to a man taken my advice, which I am pleased to see has been, in every respect, in conformity with the instructions given Colonel J. J. Abert. I believe I may safely state, that twenty purchases of reservations have not been made in this country. They wish to consult me in regard to their private accounts, in relation to receipts and acquittances, and in what manner they are to act in order to recover what is due them from individuals, and how they are to seek redress when they have been beaten and abused by the whites, their property levied on for the debts of another, (which, I am sorry to say, is frequently the case,) and various other subjects too numerous to mention. And although I have carefully avoided taking any part in their private concerns, and have not interfered with the operations of the laws of the State, I have thought it my duty to advise them in all cases, what was the proper course for them to pursue. I have frequently had to mount my horse and hunt up an interpreter, not knowing what was wanting until one was found; and the Indians have frequently returned home without making their business known for want of an interpreter.

I mention these circumstances to the department, that it may determine whether an interpreter would be necessary to me or not. My expenses for interpreters to the present time does not exceed twelve dollars. My expenses as sub-agent have been considerable. I have twice visited Fort Mitchell, and was absent from home several weeks, and on expense the whole time, paying frequently two dollars a day for my board, &c. But if it was the intention of the department that my salary should cover all expenses, I did accept the appointment, and have no right to complain.

58‡

I have executed the bond required, and sent it on for approval. Colonel Crowell has promised to forward the books and papers belonging to the office to this place.

I have addressed the district attorney on the subject contained in the twelfth section of yours of the 6th.

I regret exceedingly that the commissioners failed to make a treaty with the Indians, the consequence of which must terminate in their utter ruin. I am of opinion that a treaty might have been made, if it had not been for the powerful influence of the land speculators. Colonel J. J. Abert gave great satisfaction in the discharge of his duties. All parties, the Indians and the different claimants, both the successful and unsuccessful, declared themselves satisfied with the course he pursued.

I am sorry to say that General Parsons was not so successful. Charges and insinuations injurious to his reputation as a commissioner were industriously circulated against him. It was reported that he did not wish to make a treaty; and that he was concerned with William Walker in purchasing land from the Indians; that he was partial in the examination, and in his report upon the claims of individuals. It was said that he was an old land speculator, and had oppressed the poor in his own country in order to make money, and therefore could not feel so sensibly as he expressed himself for the injuries done to the Indians. Such insinuations and reports were, no doubt, circulated to injure General Parsons, and to prevent a treaty.

I have the honor, &c.,

LEONARD TARRANT.

Elbert Herring, Esq.

———

Wascissa, *July* 6, 1833.

Sir: Since my return from the Appalachicola, I have received a communication from Mr. Herring, of the Office of Indian Affairs, at Washington, authorizing me to draw for the remaining sum of $10,000 stipulated to be paid to Blunt and his sub-chiefs, when they shall have commenced the removal of their whole party.

In the negotiation which I have lately concluded with the upper bands on the Appalachicola, I had supposed that my agency as commissioner to treat with the Florida Indians had terminated, and that the execution of the treaties with them necessarily devolved on the executive of the territory, as ex-officio superintendent of Indian affairs. There is an evident propriety in this, which cannot have escaped your judgment, as the known and recognized authority of the Governor would greatly assist him in the capacity of agent in executing the terms of the treaties concluded. If my duties in the $10,000 payment were limited simply to the payment of the amount to Blunt, it might be performed without any trouble to me, or much inconvenience to that chief and his party, by riding sixty miles to receive it. But it would probably be at considerable hazard, until some authorized agent had seen to the faithful execution on the part of Blunt of all the obligations imposed by his agreement with the United States. This duty I could not attend to at any time without great prejudice to my private concerns, which have already suffered from the frequent absences under temporary Indian duties from my home. In addition, the season appointed for Blunt's removal, (for I have had no agency in the arrangement,) would be exceedingly injudicious at any year, being in the midst of disease on the river, and storms on our coast; but peculiarly hazardous at this time, when the cholera has made its appearance on that river, and has exiled from the port the Indians will have to embark from a majority of them who had not fallen victims to the disease. September, October, or November, would be the most desirable months for the executive of the territory, as agent for Indian affairs, to attend to the removal of Blunt and his party; and I again repeat, that it might not be found prudent to pay Blunt until the agent has every assurance of the fulfilment on his part of all the conditions of the treaty.

I have written to Mr. Westcott, the acting Governor of Florida, that I will give him a draft for the $10,000 I am authorized to draw for, whenever he is prepared to receive it; but as it seems from Mr. Herring's communication, as well as from late conversations with Mr. Westcott, that he is very unwilling to attend to the execution of these treaties; should the postponement for removal, as suggested above, be acceded to on your part, his excellency will be here, or by advice might be required to be at his post in time to attend to duties so intimately connected with the public interests of the Territory he has been called to govern.

I know not how to estimate the labor encountered and the services rendered under the commission under which I have been acting ever since November last. In the late visit to the upper towns on the Appalachicola, independent of the floods, such as have never been before witnessed in this quarter, and the almost impassable roads encountered, I have returned with a fever which has confined me many days to my bed, and the ruin of a matched carriage horse, whose place I had to supply by purchase before I could get home. In fact, the seemingly temporary duties, as exhibited by my temporary and frequent absences alone from home, have constituted but a very minor part of the duties and vexations which have unavoidably fallen upon me as commissioner to treat with the Indians in Florida, arising from a constant correspondence with agents and confidential individuals willing to promote the objects of Government, connected with frequent troublesome and expensive visits from chiefs at my own house, and interested individuals, who, assuming an influence over the Indians, were incessantly seeking interviews with me for the purpose of volunteering their services to forward a negotiation, which their own interference was alone retarding. Indeed, if my per diem of eight dollars as commissioner was continued to me, (to include transportation and other expenses,) from the 15th November, when I last closed my accounts with Government, to the 18th of June, the date of concluding the late treaty with the upper bands, it would not be more than an adequate compensation for the trouble, expenses, and difficulties I have been exposed to, independent of the injury my private affairs have suffered from my occasional absences, and oft repeated interruptions at home from my private obligations, holding at the same time myself always ready to obey any call to treat from the Indians. I am at a loss, therefore, how to make out an account from the above exhibit of the duties I have had to perform, in virtue of my commission to treat with the Indians. If not constantly negotiating with them, my frequent consultations with deputations, my correspondence, interruptions, &c., with the incidental expenses attending the same, have been equivalent to almost constant employment, superadded to charges I have had occasionally to meet for subsistence of Indians in Tallahassee, and at the treaty ground. I submit, however, an account in blank for you to fill up with what amount you may think just, as full compensation to me individually, as well as to cover the expense of transportation and other charges to which I have been exposed in providing for and subsisting Indians in their frequent consultations with me.

I remain respectfully,
Your obedient servant,
JAMES GADSDEN.

The Hon. LEWIS CASS,
Secretary of War.

The amount awarded me I will thank you to remit, enclosed to me at Lepona post office, Jefferson county, Florida, by a check, if convenient. on the receiver of public moneys in Tallahassee; otherwise, a check on either New Orleans or Charleston will be equally acceptable.

---

LOGANSPORT, INDIANA, July 6, 1833.

SIR: The band of Indians under Quach Quach Tah, their chief, has been left under my charge. Colonel Pepper, the special agent for the emigration, has gone west with the exploring party; and we only wait the arrival of the disbursing officer, when the emigration will start.

The object of this communication is to redeem a promise I made to the band under my care, that I would request through you, that their annuity be forwarded west for them, and to be disbursed by Governor Clark. At the same time they wish Col. Owen, the agent at Chicago, informed of the same, as this party received their payment at that agency heretofore.

This band is composed of 256 souls, and may possibly be increased before we depart. A copy of the muster roll will be forwarded to the Commissary General of Subsistence in a few days.

Please address me at Fort Leavenworth.

Very respectfully,
Your obedient servant,
LEWIS H. SANDS,
Assistant Agent removal Pottawatamies.

ELBERT HERRING, Esq.,
Com'r. of Indian Affairs, Washington City.

---

GENERAL LAND OFFICE,
July 5, 1833.

SIR: I have the honor to return the plat of the southern boundary of the State of Tennessee, as run under the 6th article of the Chickasaw treaty, of the 19th October, 1818, received with your letter of the 2d April last, accompanied by the letter from General Winchester, upon the subject, subsequently obtained from your office.

I am, very respectfully,
Sir, your obedient servant,
JNO. M. MOORE.

The Hon. ELBERT HERRING,
Commissioner of Indian Affairs.

---

CLINTON, July 7, 1833.

DEAR SIR: Enclosed you will receive a publication that I have felt it my duty to make, to satisfy the numerous inquiries daily made to me on the subject of the Indian reserves and floats under the late Choctaw treaty.

I submit these remarks to you, that you may compare them with the provisions of the treaty, and if I am in error on any point, I wish to be corrected.

It is important that these claims should be disposed of at as early a day as practicable, as every day's delay tends to embarrass the closing of them.

I have no doubt attempts will be and are making, to change many of the settlement claims to other lands that please the present holders more.

I would advise the closing all these claims as early as practicable. I hope you will examine the enclosed, and correct it in all the material points, and return the same.

I am, very respectfully,

Your obedient servant,

SAMUEL GWIN,

*Register N. W. District, Mi.*

(The paper enclosed, as referred to above, has been lost or mislaid.)

---

*Extract of a letter from Jeremiah Austill to the Secretary of War, dated July 8, 1833.*

" I have been in this part a few days, with a detachment of troops, for the purpose of enforcing your instructions. The Indians complain of * * * as being obnoxious, quarrelsome, and abusive to them, and having threatened their lives, if they came about him; and they complain of * * * and * *, for having burnt up their cabins and threatening their lives if they came about them or upon their premises. Those persons have not taken possession of any cleared land of the Indians, yet they prevent the Indians who are entitled to reservations, but have not located themselves, from settling where they had commenced building. I have determined to remove them forthwith from the nation, and to deliver their crops to the chief of the town, and to burn their buildings. Those persons threaten me with the civil law, and to punish the Indians if they enter the places held by them. Unless I have some power to punish those that are removed for returning again into the nation, in a more summary way than to send to Mobile for a process against them, it will be impossible to keep them out. If I have authority to arrest them, and bind them over to court, and to return the bonds to court, upon which the district attorney may prosecute, they may be kept out.

" You will, no doubt, be informed of the conduct of the settlers through other sources. I have no apprehension of doing less than my duty, and I hope not to do more than will be approved by the Government."

---

*July 9, 1833.*

BROTHERS: I wrote my great father a letter on the 28th December, 1831, to inform him of our unhappy and unsettled condition, and received for answer a letter from our good friend Maj. Eaton, Secretary of War, informing me that it would do our great father pleasure to do every thing in his power to contribute to the quiet and happiness of his red children; and that he was not at liberty to give us a country to live in; the great council has that power, and that he would bring our case before them; and that our father will suffer us to remain until his white children shall want the land, or until a suitable country can be provided.

We settled on land unsurveyed or unsold by the Government, and paid horses for building us cabins, and cleared our land, and fenced it at great la-

bor for the want of proper tools to work with.  The land, in almost every
instance, was taken from us by our white brethren, without paying us one
cent for it.  We have lost our labor, and had not a foot of land to raise us
corn.  We appealed to our sub-agent Richard M. Hannum; he candidly
informed us that he had only power to expostulate with those that were doing us unjustice; that he had represented our situation to the Secretary of
War, who informed him that our ultimate fate would be referred to the
United States commissioners; and that they had no power to permanently
fix us in any State or organized territory; and that when we removed it
would be into the Indian country, or return to the Caddoes.  We therefore
solicited him to go to Cantonment Gibson to endeavor to procure us a home.
He stated to us that he had no power; but if Gov. Pope consented, he would
go.  We requested him to wait on Gov. Pope; he accordingly did so; and
informed us when he returned that the Governor wrote to the commissioners in our behalf.  One of the commissioners visited us, and we made a new
treaty with him.  Since the treaty was made, bad birds have come in among
us, some of the drunken Choctaws, who have made some of our people unhappy; they have told them that the country was poor and cold, and that
we [would] be killed by the Osages.  Some time ago there was a Quapaw
Indian came from the Caddoes and told us that the agent sent for us to re
turn: we paid no attention to him, since which time another Quapaw has
come in, and states that he was sent by the agent to tell us to return; that
he would furnish us with provisions, and pay us fourteen hundred dollars,
money that he had in his hands of ours.

If he has the money he ought to have paid it long ago; or if he sent for
us he ought to have acted openly and candidly, and clothed his messenger
with proper power.  He was the bearer of only a rough scrawl directed
to the chiefs, without any signature.  Our nation, to a man, would have
been glad to remain here if we would have been permitted to remain in
peace; and as such we represented our desire to our sub-agent, who has done
every thing in his power to protect us, and render our condition happy and
prosperous; but our nation, to a man, was opposed to return to the Caddoes;
we were there already and experienced but misery and death; we sacrificed
our all by that unjust and unhappy treaty made with Mr. Crittenden.

We appeal to you, our great father, to put a stop to the underhanded
means made use of on Red river to induce us to return.  If we are compelled to return there our tribe will become extinct; but if it is the intention of the Government to compel us to return to the Caddoes, we trust your
excellency will empower some person to enter into a new arrangement with
us.  We are willing to surrender our annuity for a gross sum, to be vested
in stock, or to be paid in a given time.  We are too much scattered already.
I doubt not, if we could all be collected together, we would be five hundred
in number.  Our sub-agent directed us to repair back on the Bayou Milton,
entirely out of the white settlement.  We opened little clearings the last
spring.  The high rise of the waters has covered our little crops.  We are
entirely left destitute of every means of support; we therefore pray that we
may be provided with money and provisions out of any thing that may be
coming to us, to relieve our present wants.

I dictated this letter myself; it has been interpreted to me after; it con-

tains my opinion, and the opinions of my brothers, as near as I can express it.
I remain your dutiful son,

HECKATON, his x mark.

Signed in presence of                                   *Quapaw Chief.*
JOHN D. SHAW.

To my Great Father, THE PRESIDENT OF THE UNITED STATES;
or, in his absence, TO THE SECRETARY OF WAR.

---

SHAWNEE, JACKSON COUNTY, MISSOURI,
*July* 9, 1833.

SIR: Please to accept my sincere thanks for your prompt favor of 18th of June, in answer to my letter of May 23, in relation to the school appropriation for the Kickapoos.

It now becomes my duty to ask leave respectfully to state that the Baptist society, with which I have the happiness of being connected, are also anxious to locate a mission among the Ottoes and Omahas, near to or at the agency of Maj. Jno. Dougherty, on Missouri river, a few miles above the great Platte river. By the treaty of Prairie du Chien, July 15, 1830, provision was made for education, and I beg leave to request that such amount of that provision as you shall deem expedient, be entrusted to the board of managers of the Baptist General Missionary Convention for the United States, to be applied according to directions of the Government.

From copies of two letters from Maj. Dougherty, United States Indian agent, dated October 30, 1831, and July 7, 1833, herewith enclosed, you will infer the favorable dispositions towards the enterprise both of the agent and the Indians; and the desire of the latter that their portion of those education funds be applied as above requested.

Let me further request that your answer to this be made to Reverend Lucius Bolles, D. D., corresponding secretary, &c., Boston, Massachusetts.

Now, sir, please indulge me in saying that I believe the prospect of rendering lasting benefits to the Indians was never half so flattering as it is at this time, in this Indian territory; and in proportion to those promising appearances should be our efforts to do them good. I mention this with the greater felicity, as I write to one who, in providence, has been placed at the *helm* of Indian affairs, and I doubt not with a heart breathing " good will" to that unhappy people.

I am, sir,
With great respect,
Your obedient servant,
ISAAC McCOY.

ELBERT HERRING, Esq.,
*Commissioner of Indian Affairs, Washington, D. C.*

---

FORT LEAVENWORTH, *July* 7, 1833.

DEAR SIR: I have the pleasure to acknowledge the receipt of your communication of the 9th ultimo, stating that the Baptist Board of Missions for the United States have it in contemplation to establish a school, and other missionary operations, among the Ottoes and Omahas, and other Indians near them; and you accompany the statement of that fact by a request, that permission be granted said board to locate a school within the limits, and perhaps at or near the seat of my agency, for the benefit of those Indians.

In reply, permit me to say, that your request meets with my sanction and that the board will receive my hearty co-operation in all matters tending to further their benevolent designs, in improving the moral condition of the Indians placed under my charge.

The subject of establishing schools among the Ottoes and Omahas has, for some time past, been frequently spoken of by the chiefs of those tribes, and has frequently, by them, been made the object of special request. Two of the principal chiefs of the Ottoes, and the principal chief of the Omahas, together with several of their head men, are now with me. Mr. Lykins, one of your society, made known to them this morning, in my presence, the object which your request embraces, at which they were not only much pleased, but expressed a strong desire to see your operations commence among them. They have heretofore expressed, and, doubtless, yet entertain a wish, that the amount secured to them for school purposes, by the treaty of Prairie du Chien of the 15th July, 1830, should be applied to schools in their own immediate neighborhood, in order that its benefits might be more generally enjoyed by the whole tribe. What course the Government will feel disposed to take as it regards the future application of that fund, I am not prepared to say; but I hope, however, that your society may meet with such aid, which, together with the laudable exertions of judicious and competent teachers, as will insure their ultimate success.

I am, very respectfully,
Your obedient servant,
JOHN DOUGHERTY,
*Indian Agent.*

Rev. Isaac McCoy.

———

CANTONMENT LEAVENWORTH, *October* 30, 1831.

SIR: In obedience to your instructions of 26th May, 1831, relative to sending a boy from the Omaha, and one from the Ottoe and Missouri tribes, to the Choctaw academy, near Georgetown, Kentucky, I have conferred with their principal men on the subject, and advised them to do so. I apprised them of the manner, and by whom that academy is conducted. They requested one day to consult among themselves on the matter, and promised an answer next morning. Accordingly, the Jatan chief of the Ottoes, and Big Elk, of the Omahas, returned, and requested me to say to you, that they were fully sensible of your kindness towards them, in offering to instruct their children, for which they returned you and their great father their sincere thanks; but that they are unwilling to send off, to so great a distance, a single child, alone, without some one who could converse in its own language to accompany it; because the child would soon forget its own tongue, and become estranged even from its father and mother, be ashamed of their poverty, and abandon them in their old age. They also requested me to say to you, that they are truly anxious to have their children instructed in the ways and manners of their white brothers, and that, in their own opinions, the best and most suitable mode of accomplishing this object would be, to send among them a teacher to reside with and learn them to read, write, and work like white men; and, further, they wished me to inform you, that a missionary, who has been long in the habit of teaching young Indians these several arts, had sent them word he was anxious to establish himself, or some one of his people, among them for that purpose, and that they are extremely anxious to see him located in that way, at some suitable point in their country ; and whatever amount their great father might have the goodness to allow them, for the education and instruction of their children, and they sincerely hoped both you and him would take pity on them, and have it expended in that way. The Big Elk and Jatan both expressed a wish that you would be pleased to communicate to them, as early as convenient, your views and wishes on this subject.

Very respectfully,
J. DOUGHERTY,
*Indian Agent.*

Gen. WILLIAM CLARK,
*Superintendent of Indian Affairs.*

---

COLUMBUS, GEORGIA, *July* 11, 1833.

SIR: I have just reached home, after being absent near four weeks, and upon my arrival was informed by several of my friends, that at the last meeting of the Creek Indians, with the agents of the government, some charges were made against me which demand an investigation. I have not been able to learn who were my accusers, or of what specific acts I was accused. The charges are, however, stated to have been previously sent to your department, and to have created some impression there. It is a fact well known, never concealed, but made as public as possible, that soon after the ratification of the last Creek treaty, I employed Dr. John S. Scott to purchase, for him and myself jointly, Indian reservations. I have had, personally, nothing to do in the purchases, for I know but little about the Indians or their mode of doing business. Under the above arrangement Scott purchased one hundred and seventy-one reservations, and we have paid, in advance, an average of something over ten dollars each, the balance payable when titles shall be perfected, and in every instance, by the terms of the contract, the Indian is put under an obligation to emigrate so soon after the perfecting of titles as the Government is prepared. The contract, *in every* instance, (as I am informed, and believe) was fairly made, the consideration reasonable, and the Indian then, and yet, *fully satisfied*. These facts, I fear not to say, will be fully supported, whenever our purchases come to be examined into by any *honest and unprejudiced* agent of the Government. In this I never supposed, for a moment, that we were acting contrary to the wishes or policy of the administration. I saw that by the terms of the treaty each Indian head of a family was entitled to a reservation, that the integrity of the Government was pledged to make the locations, that the reservee was entitled to sell, *by the approbation of the President*, which consent I could not presume would be withheld, unless where fraud had been practised.

Recently, when Colonel Abert came to the nation with instructions to make a treaty with the chiefs for all the reservations, and was instructed not to exclude from its operation those already purchased, I determined at once to defeat the treaty if possible, and gave notice in person, to the agent, of my intention. In this I acted not only for myself, but as counsel for Benjamin P. Tarver and several others, who were in my situation. I saw in all this nothing to reproach myself with when done; it has the approbation of my judgment yet, and has and would be acted over if occasion called for it. But I am wandering from my purpose. It seems, as far as I can learn

59‡

that I stand accused before you of some unfairness and fraud in these contracts, and with having written a letter to Scott, or some one else, containing evidence of fraud. I respectfully ask you to favor me with whatever charge has been made, the person by whom made, and a copy of any letter of mine, of the character alluded to, which may be in your department. Any such charge is false, and cannot be supported but by *perjury*, and any such letter is a *forgery*. I am an American citizen; my character is dear to me, although I fill but a small space in the public eye; and I hold it to be my clear right to ask a compliance with this respectful application. This whole Indian business is now any thing but pleasant to my feelings, for it is about to bring (nay has brought) me in collision with the administration, whose general policy and course has commanded and received my approbation. I have no doubt that many *busy bodies*, with fair professions on their lips, but with corruption and malice in their hearts, have had much to say upon the subject of Indian speculations to you and to the President. But such men, who stab in the dark, who will not come out openly, and who keep themselves curtained, are entitled to but little respect, and should be heard with caution. Let an issue in any way be made up between the accuser and the accused, and their exposure will be completed. I venture now to say, that if all their names can ever be made public, I convict some of them of having endeavored to get into some one of the much abused companies, and were rejected, and many others of having either made, or attempted to make purchases, upon terms much more unfavorable to the Indian than those of the companies. Much has been said of the enormous profits that will be made should the purchases hold good, and of the large monopolies of land that will be created. All this has nothing to do with the question of *legal right;* but on the part of Scott and myself, and I am authorized also by my client, Benj. P. Tarver, to include his one hundred and sixty odd purchases, will be willing to investigate each one of our purchases before the agent, Colonel Abert, to pay the Indian in his presence, to satisfy him perfectly, to have the reserves (if approved as to fairness) conveyed to the Government at sixty-two and a half cents an acre to be paid to us. The payments to and from us to be cash down. This will effectually destroy both the enormous profits and monopolies. In such an event, of course, no other or further purchases will be made by either of said parties. Before any purchase was ever made, in which I have any interest, I sought, through our members in Congress, and every other channel within my reach, for information upon the subject, but could obtain none to induce me, for a moment, to believe that any *fair* purchase would be disregarded. Should any one in which I have an interest turn out to be fraudulent, no agent of the Government will be more willing or prompt in rejecting it than myself, but fair ones will not be surrendered.

Respectfully, your obedient servant,<br>
ELI S. SHORTER.

To the Hon. Secretary of War.

P. S. In regard to the above proposition, as to Scott and myself, I must add a condition, that there shall be secured to us the two reserves which we will designate, and which were purchased at $500 each, we, of course, to pay for them.

---

Cherokee Agency, *July* 11, 1833.

Sir: I have the honor to acknowledge the receipt of yours of the 22d ultimo, by last mail, giving the views of the President on the project submitted for the removal of the Cherokees, and the determination of the department consequent thereon.

Enrolling books have been prepared, in accordance with your instructions, and Colonel Montgomery, the Indian agent, is engaged in rendering all the aid in his power. None have enrolled yet. * * * *, who has for so long a time been urging the opening of emigration for all, has shrunk from the responsibility of signing his name or taking the lead either in favor of the terms submitted to the Cherokee people by the President, or on the terms proposed in the event no treaty is made.

I suggested, some time since, to the department that perhaps * * * * had fallen into the arms of speculators in the white settlements; his course of late confirms that opinion; he is, however, a reservee under the treaty of 1819, and his situation precarious, depending on the opinion of the Attorney General.

It has been intimated by zealots here, that a case would be made for the Supreme Court shortly, keeping the Indians in suspense until towards the termination of General J.'s administration, and then it would be an easy, matter to detain them for the balance of his term.

You request me to communicate freely on subjects calculated to ameliorate the condition of this people, and advance the benevolent views of the Government.

Enclosed I transmit to you the suggestions of the Cherokee agent, whose intimate knowledge of Indian Affairs, from long experience, has led him to the conclusions contained in the communication marked A, in all of which I agree with him most heartily.

The assistants authorized to be selected by Governor Lumpkin have not yet reported themselves; but as soon as they do, instructions will be given, and interpreters furnished, agreeably to the views of the department.

It is uncertain how the plan adopted will succeed, as we have not had time to make a fair trial. In the course of a few weeks we will be able to communicate more satisfactorily on this head. Should the opinion of the Attorney General be in favor of removing the reservees, they will have no time left to conjure up mischief or lay new plans, by which to destroy or render more miserable their deluded followers.

I have the honor to be,
Most respectfully,
Your very obedient servant,
BEN. F. CURREY.

Hon. John Robb,
   *Acting Secretary of War.*

---

**A.**

Sir: At your request I embody below such suggestions as I believe ought to be made to the Government:

1st. The Indians generally, and especially the half breeds, cannot get off, (and of course will not enroll,) unless a part of the price of their improvements is paid them before they set out. They are all indebted, and most of them as much, and many of them more, than they are worth, improvements and all. They ought, therefore, to be paid at least one-half on embarcation: this is one inducement which has always been held out to them, and without which you will not get along well.

The proportion of the three year's annuity, now due them, ought to be paid on enrollment; this they are at present in absolute want of.

The Indians ought to be assured positively that no reservations would be allowed, and more especially those, and their descendants, who have previously had reservations (should they not be turned out as intruders). From this quarter comes our strongest and almost only opposition.

There is another class which ought not to be neglected, (and many of them have had reservations,) I mean white men who have married or taken up with Indian women; many of them are mere vagabonds, who have come into the nation and taken reserves merely for sake of the reservations, and some of them are the most violent and clamorous opponents of the administration and the measures of Government. These ought all to be driven out of the nation unless they emigrate with their Indian families by a given day, say first of January next.

Yours,

H. MONTGOMERY.

Major CURREY.

---

WASHINGTON CITY, July 11, 1833.

DEAR SIR: On a recent visit to the Pottawatamies, of Indiana, I was solicited by several gentlemen of that State to effect, if possible, a treaty with the Miami Indians for the lands still owned by them. In consequence of this I sent a private messenger and collected the chiefs at the forks of the Wabash, when I had an interview with them. After stating to them the views and the wishes of the Government, I proposed to them to treat for their lands in Indiana. They gave me assurances that they would certainly treat with me and General William Marshall for the part of their lands, and may be for the whole. I think the whole may be obtained, if proper measures are pursued.

According to the best information I can obtain, the Miamies have in their several reservations upwards of 800,000 acres. From what I have seen, and from the best information I can obtain, the lands are among the best in the State, and will find a ready sale, at a considerable advance of the Government price. I think a treaty may be made on the following conditions:

1. By giving them about 1,000,000 acres west of the Mississippi.

2. By removing them, and supporting them one year after their removal, at the expense of the United States.

3. By allowing them about $400,000, or fifty cents per acre, for their lands; a very considerable portion of this to be expended west in improvements, agricultural implements, and domestic animals, and the balance in limited annuity of 20 years.

4. The Indians to give immediate possession of all the lands, for ten miles on each side of the Wabash immediately, and to remove as soon as possible, say not to exceed five years.

A treaty on the above basis, can be effected, I believe, by making use of the following means:

1. To grant about 40 sections of land to chiefs and principal and influential Indians.

2. To confirm Richard Ville's (principal chiefs) grants by the nation to him at the forks of the Wabash.

3. To give to the chiefs, as personal annuities, in addition to their distributive share of the annuities of the nation, about $1,000.

4. To remove the agency to the forks of the Wabash, which is the most convenient and central point for the Indians and agent to do the business of the nation.

I would also recommend to the department that the agent, General Marshall, be instructed to purchase for the Government the reservations made to individual Indians by the treaty of 1832. The Indians are selling them to speculators for a trifle, although I believe the treaty confers nothing but an *individual Indian title*, and consequently they cannot sell but to the United States.

With great respect,
Your obedient and humble servant,
J. F. SCHERMERHORN,
*Commissioner west.*

Hon. Lewis Cass,
*Secretary of War.*

---

NEAR WEST POINT,
*Creek nation, Chambery County, July 12, 1833.*

DEAR SIR: I have had a serious time here for several days with the intruders. Charges have been preferred against a number of whites, some for intrusion, and others for abusing the Indians and disturbing the peace and harmony of the nation. I gave them all orders to remove forthwith from the nation, unless they gave full satisfaction to the Indians for the damages done them. The settlers held a meeting for the purpose of raising a force sufficient to drive me and the troops off, and after raising a part of the number deemed sufficient to effect their purpose, I entered their ranks and advised them to desist, or I would instantly set fire to every farm held by those taking up arms, and if I could raise troops enough, send them as prisoners to Mobile; whereupon they yielded, and I believe are now mostly well satisfied, for the chiefs, apprehending danger from them if they were driven out, consented that they might remain until their crops were gathered, upon condition that those who had trespassed should pay what should be deemed a sufficient compensation, or to give up the improvements claimed or made by the Indians. So far all has been settled in one or the other of these arrangements. I shall proceed on until all are quiet.

I believe that I could effect the removal of most of the Indians next season for I have been much among them, and they have great confidence in my good feeling towards them, and for their welfare.

I have the honor to be
Your obedient servant,
JEREMIAH AUSTILL,
*Deputy Marshal, Alabama.*

The Hon. Lewis Cass,
*Secretary of War.*

---

WARREN COUNTY, ILLINOIS,
*Forty miles south from Rock Island, July 12, 1833.*

My former communication was not intended to introduce a correspondence; but the reply has brought things to my knowledge of which I had not thought before, to wit: that the depredations committed on us by the Indians was owing to the wrongs done to them; but to this, sir, I must in every form and shape plead not guilty. I was one of the first settlers in this county, perhaps the tenth family, the Indians were very numerous at that time, 1828, and as to small matters behaved themselves honestly; no difficulties ever took place between us; in the cold they were lodged in our houses; they were fed at our tables without asking or thinking of pay, yet they frequently killed our hogs and cattle, which were carried off immediately; they frequently stole our horses, but these last were often recovered, either by a small fee or by watching their camps awhile, though many were never recovered, as it was scarcely possible to identify the thief, when application was made for that purpose; nor do I believe that in a single instance, in our part of the country, was ever a fraud practised on them, only by the licensed traders. I do know, that if we ever bought an article from them we paid them as much or more than we paid the traders; but the fact is here, the traders view the advances of the whites as an indirect attack on their interest; for, as they are preparing splendid on the river, if the Indians have to retire so must they also, and being all members of the fur company, they are at war with the removal of the Indians; and they and their dependents do most of the business of our principal towns, and of course give a tone to the pulse of public opinion. Being in Cincinnati not long since on some business, some statements were made as positive facts, which to my positive knowledge had not the color of truth; and what must it be when it would arrive at Washington, either by speech or print. Far as we are from our Government, we are as far from the wish to wrong or deceive any; we live on our farms, and if suffered to conduct them in peace, we live independent of either the Indians or their agents or traders; but for them to be permitted to kill our hogs and cattle, steal our horses, and butcher our citizens, in the most wanton and cruel manner, in the face of open day, with a high hand, and scarcely brought to a mock trial, and instead of the rope are greeted by the trader—a fine warrior, brave men—is past endurance, which was lately the case with the murderers of Martin.

We hoped this spring the new purchase over the river would soon be settled, and the Indians prevented from crossing the Mississippi; but as soon as they had got their corn planted they were ordered off by the agent, and the place again left to the Indians; and now they are just as freely and frequently on this side as ever, for this three years past, and no doubt but they will possess themselves of the corn planted by the whites. I have frequently seen, this spring, one hundred at Phelp's, trading this side the river, and every day more or less.

Accept, sir, the unfeigned respects of your obedient servant,
JOHN CALDWELL.

To his Ex'cy Lewis Cass,
Secretary of War.

---

Columbus, *July* 13, 1833.

DEAR SIR: I have commenced improving a section of land in the Choctaw nation, with the expectation that it may be given to my two grand children, Alexander and Ebenezer Pitchlynn, whose parents are dead, and they have been left destitute and poor. I write to you, believing that you will give me all the information you can upon this subject. If you are not authorized to do something in this matter, please write me to whom I must write for information, that I may know whether or not it is necessary for me to improve the lands with the prospect of having it secured to the children. By writing me upon this subject you will much oblige your friend.

Very respectfully, &c.,

JOHN PITCHLYNN.

P. S. I also wish to be appointed guardian for the children.    J. P.

N. B. You will much oblige me by presenting this letter to my old friend, General A. Jackson.    J. P.

---

St. Louis, *July* 13, 1833.

Sir: I have the honor to inform the department of my safe arrival at this place. Governor Stokes is also here. The board will leave this in a few days for Fort Leavenworth, where they will complete the arrangements for meeting the tribes on the Missouri, in conformity with their instructions.

Governor Stokes and myself have drawn, through the United States Bank, a draft for $1000, dated 13th of July, at sight, on the Secretary of War, and shall probably draw $500 more before we leave. Perhaps it may not be exactly correct for only *two* of the commissioners to draw; but as Mr. Schermerhorn has returned home on a visit, and our outfit must be provided here, the majority of the board have presumed to make the necessary drafts, which it is hoped will be duly honored, as being indispensable to the progress of the commissioners.

Most respectfully, yours,

HENRY L. ELLSWORTH.

Hon. Lewis Cass,
    *Secretary of War.*

---

Know all men by these presents, that we, the undersigned, chiefs and headmen of the Western Creek nation, in full council assembled, do make, constitute, and appoint Chilley McIntosh and Robert Tiger our true and lawful attorneys, for us and in our names to locate and sell five sections of land, given to us by the Eastern Creeks, and to compound and agree for the same, and to do all other acts concerning the premises, as fully in every respect as we could or would do were we personally present.

In witness, we have hereunto set our hands and seals, this seventeenth day of April, one thousand eight hundred and thirty-three.

| | |
|---|---|
| ROLLY McINTOSH, | x [seal.] |
| FUSH-HATE-HY MICCO, | x [seal.] |
| BENJAMIN PERRYMAN, | x [seal.] |
| COW-WOC-CO-CHEE EMARLO, | x [seal.] |
| ISPOAK-OAK HARJO, | x [seal.] |
| JOHN RANDALL, | x [seal.] |
| CORSER YOHOLO, | x [seal.] |
| HILLEBEE TUSCANUGGEE, | x [seal.] |
| SAMUEL MILLER, | x [seal.] |
| HOLATTER THELOCKO, | x [seal.] |
| ESTER-CHARCO HARJO, | x [seal.] |

TUS-KAE-NE HAH,                          x [SEAL.]
CHA-COTEE TUSTANUGGEE,     x [SEAL.]
POWES HARJO,                             x [SEAL.]
GISKERLIGER EMARLO,           x [SEAL.]

Witness: JOHN CAMPBELL, *Agent Creek.*
   K. LEWIS,
   JOHN HAMBLY, *Acting Interpreter.*
   ELI JACOBS, *Clerk.*

GEORGIA, *Muscogee county.*

I, Gerard Burch, deputy clerk of the superior court of said county, do hereby certify that the above and within are true copies of power of attorney made by the chiefs and head men of the western Creek nation to Chilley McIntosh and Robert Tiger; and Chilley McIntosh and Robert Tiger, agents of the western Creek nation, their deed for five sections of land to Benjamin Hawkins and John Milton taken from the records of the clerk's office of the superior court of said county of Muscogee. Given under my hand and private seal, having no seal of office, this 15th day of July, 1833.
      GERARD BURCH, *Dep. Clk.* [SEAL.]

GEORGIA, *Muscogee county:*

This indenture made this first day of June, in the year of our Lord one thousand eight hundred and thirty-three, between Chilley McIntosh and Robert Tiger, acting as agents, agreeably to the power of attorney hereunto annexed, of the western Creek Indians of the one part, and Benjamin Hawkins and John Milton, of said State, of the other part, witnesseth, that the said Chilly McIntosh and Robert Tiger, agents of the western Creek Indians, according to and for the purposes of the power of attorney hereunto annexed, for and in consideration of the sum of two thousand dollars, to them in hand paid, at and before the sealing and delivery of these presents, do grant, bargain, sell, alien, convey, and confirm, unto the said Benjamin Hawkins and John Milton, their heirs and assigns, all the five sections of land, giving to the said western Creek Indians, referred to in the power of attorney, hereunto annexed, and those they represented by the eastern Creek Indians, for and in consideration of peace with them, agreeably to a treaty recently made between said last mentioned Indians, by their delegates and chiefs, and Lewis Cass, commissioner, on the part of the United States, were to receive twenty-nine sections of land, according to the sixth article of said treaty, of which the five sections above mentioned and hereby conveyed are a part, with the rights and appurtenances thereunto belonging, and with all the rights relative thereto, that they, the said western Creeks are rightfully entitled to, from said contract with the said eastern Creek Indians: to have and to hold the said sections of land and rights incident thereto, unto the said Benjamin Hawkins and John Milton, their heirs and assigns forever, and to their own proper use in fee simple; and the said Chilly McIntosh and Robert Tiger, acting as agents aforesaid of the said western Creek Indians, according to the power of attorney hereunto annexed, the said bargained premises unto the said Benjamin Hawkins and John Milton will warrant and for ever defend the right and title thereof against themselves, and against the claim of all other persons whatever.

In testimony whereof, the said Chilly McIntosh and Robert Tiger, agents as aforesaid, have hereunto set their hands, and affixed their seals, the day and year above written.

CHILLY McINTOSH, [SEAL.]
*Agent Western Creek Indians.*
ROBERT TIGER, his x mark, [SEAL.]
*Agent Western Creek Indians.*

Witness: GERARD BURCH,
GRIGSBY E. THOMAS, *J. S. C. C. C.*

---

GEORGIA, *Muscogee county:*

Know all men by these presents, that we, Chilly McIntosh and Robert Tiger, acting as the agents of the western Creek Indians, agreeably to the power of attorney hereunto annexed, have this day bargained and sold, and conveyed to Benjamin Hawkins and John Milton, for and in consideration of the sum of two thousand dollars, the receipt is hereby acknowledged, the five sections of land thereunto referred, and have executed a deed to them therefor; and that, whereas, they doubt our authority in right or that of the nation to sell and convey the same until they shall be located.   Now know ye, that we, as agents as aforesaid, Chilly McIntosh and Robert Tiger, obligate said western Creek Indians, ourselves as their agents, to said Benjamin Hawkins and John Milton, in the sum of twenty thousand dollars, to execute other and legal titles to them for said sections after their location, if the deed already on this day made shall not be adjudged valid; or if after the location they desire another deed, and will surrender that already given, or to their assigns.

In witness whereof, we have hereunto set our hands, and affixed our seals, the first day of June, in the year of our Lord one thousand eight hundred and thirty-three.

CHILLY McINTOSH, [SEAL.]
*Agent Western Creek Indians.*
ROBERT TIGER, his x mark, [SEAL.]
*Agent Western Creek Indians.*

Signed, sealed, and delivered in presence of
GERARD BURCH,
GRIGSBY E. THOMAS, *J. S. C. C. C.*

GEORGIA, *Muscogee county:*

I, Gerard Burch, deputy clerk of the superior court of said county, do certify that the above is a true copy bond, made by Chilly McIntosh and Robert Tiger, agents of the western Creek nation, to Benjamin Hawkins and John Milton, taken from the record of the clerk's office of the superior court of said county.

Given from under my hand and private seal, having no seal of office, this 15th July, 1833.

GERARD BURCH, *Dept. Clk.* [SEAL.]

---

CHEROKEE AGENCY, *July* 15, 1833.

SIR: It is a matter of concern with many Cherokees, and, to satisfy their inquiries on the subject, I have taken the liberty to assure them that the party enrolling for the west shall have a representative voice in the formation of a treaty, proportioned to their comparative numerical force.

60‡

I have also observed to some few individuals, that the Government will have no objection to paying honorable men a fair compensation for services rendered in bringing this important question to a speedy termination; their pay to be proportioned to the services.

Should the department approve of the above, it will give a considerable impulse to the conditional enrollments now in progress.

I have the honor to be,
Most respectfully,
Your very obedient servant,
BEN. F. CURREY.

ELBERT HERRING, Esq.,
*Commissioner Indian Affairs,*

---

*Extract of a letter from Gen. William Clark, dated July* 15, 1833.

SIR: I avail myself also of this occasion to transmit you a letter of the 24th June from General Street, on the subject of the Winnebago treaty of last year.

Hon. ELBERT HERRING,
*Com. of Ind. Affairs, Washington City.*

---

U. S. INDIAN AGENCY,
*At Prairie du Chien, June* 24, 1833.

SIR: Mr. P. Chouteau handed me your letter of the 12th instant. Its contents are noted, and the several requisitions will be duly observed.

Regulated by the treaty engagements in my intercourse with the Indians, you need not have apprehended a payment of the annuities *before they are due;* and my Indians are not in the habit of making *any demands of me.* An intercourse established in confidence, and continued in deep affection, has no recurrence to such measures. The 3d article of the treaty of the 15th September, 1832, stipulates for the payment of ten thousand dollars to the Winnebago nation, at Prairie du Chien and Fort Winnebago, annually, for twenty-seven successive years; the first payment to be made in September, 1833. In relation to the first proportion of the ten thousand dollars annuity, there will be no necessity of acting upon it *now,* as there is sufficient time for you " to receive instructions from the department," and know whether the " late information with regard to the movement of those Indians" (from Mr. Kinzie) will induce a change of measures that had been so well considered and wisely adopted for the benefit of the Indians and the peace of the frontiers.

After the receipt of your letter, I addressed a communication to the department at Washington, containing a full and faithful view of the subject. Having had the honor personally to present some of these views to you re- cently, I am induced to hope you will, from a conviction of their propriety and vital importance, aid my endeavors to procure the prosecution of the plans indicated by the department in the letter of the Commissioner of Indian Affairs at Washington to you of the 2d of April last. If some measures are not pursued to withdraw the Indians from the Wisconsin, and induce them to migrate to the west of the Mississippi, a constant military force will be necessary to prevent a rupture. Settled, as under the present mistaken views they now are, on the north bank of the Wisconsin, with the whites on the south bank, difficulties can only be prevented by force; for the starving Indians on the north will appropriate the plenty of the whites on the south bank of a small river, and bloodshed and the consequent horrors and expenses of savage war will ensue. I am at a loss to conjecture why the progress of the school should also be arrested. The 4th article of the treaty of 15th September, 1832, expressly stipulates that the school shall be "some where *near Fort Crawford or Prairie du Chien.*" This is for the benefit of the *whole nation,* intended to be conducted under the superintendence of a competent person, and in a situation easily accessible to the higher officers in the Government, that its management and progress might be ascertained from personal inspection, which the treaty provides for.

I know, and have long since advised the department, through your office, that * * * would strenuously oppose the migration of the Winnebagoes of the south of the Wisconsin to the west of the Mississippi; that the agent of the American fur company *here* would exert all the materials he could operate upon to prevent the removal, as it would interfere with the fur trade with the lower Sioux, who hunt on the land given to the Winnebagoes. The interpreter at Fort Winnebago is in the pay of the fur company, and, with * * * is exerting his influence to induce these Indians to make villages on the Wisconsin, below and near the Portage. A reference to my correspondence for the last six or eight months will show that I have apprised the department of this, and that these Indians would attempt to remain on the ceded lands, and would only remove upon the appearance of a military force in the country; that then a removal would take place to the north of the Wisconsin. This has occurred, as a knowledge of Indians and the manœuvres that were in operation to thwart the measures of the Government enabled me to foresee it would. This influence would (had the Government permitted) have retained these Indians a little longer on the ceded country, and now will be exerted to prevent their removal to the country designed for their reception by the United States.

If prevented from migration by the same sordid influence and misguided councils, these Indians will be kept hanging around the agency at the Portage to starve, or be fed at the expense of the United States, until their sufferings will be greater than they can bear, and a rupture with the whites now settled on the south of the Wisconsin, shall demonstrate the impracticability of Indians in a savage state and whites living in such immediate proximity.

On the 28th January last I submitted my views in relation to the Indians, growing out of the treaty of 1832, to the department, and received for answer that they should receive due consideration; and I was gratified to receive the copy of a letter to you, for my instruction and guide, from the Commissioner of Indian Affairs at Washington, dated 2d April, 1833. The pervading features and leading measures of that document have their origin in that spirit of high benevolence that no contracted personal projects or pecuniary interests can control. In examining the plan indicated by the department, I cannot believe a system of measures so ably deleniated, so highly advantageous to the Indians, and calculated, in their operations and maturity, to sustain the peace of the frontiers upon a permanent basis of reciprocal benefits and advantages, will be abandoned. And what is the consideration for which the abandonment of these measures are asked? It is to enable the Indians to oppose the plans of the Governmenat for their removal to the west.

The United States have no wish to possess their lands; they are not wanted; but to prevent constant disturbance with the whites; and to enable the United States beneficially to pursue measures provided in the treaty, for the information, improvement, and general amelioration of the present ignorant, degraded, and suffering state of these Indians. The success of these measures; the cultivation of the Indian mind and the Indian character, rescues them from the rapacious hands of the traders and the heartless speculator, and clothes them with an independence unknown in their wild ungoverned state. Though free to roam the woods as they list, the Indians in the vicinity of the whites, and in awe of their power, are the mere slaves of the unprincipled white population engaged in the Indian trade. From this thraldom, it is the duty as it is to the interest of the Government of the United States to liberate the Indians, and gradually elevate them to a higher moral and political standard.

In the letter of the 2d April, before referred to, the department directs the payment of $5,000 of the annuity under the 3d article of the treaty of 1832, to be made at Praire du Chien, thereby drawing a portion, at least, of the Rock river Indians beyond the sphere of the misguided influence operating on them; and giving the agent here an opportunity of correctly impressing their minds with the benevolent views of the Government in their favor; for the events of the last year must have convinced the most sceptical, that there is an influence exerted at this agency over the Indians, for the benefit alike of the United States and the Indian. And that although, in the distribution of money and other disbursements, an influence is felt and acknowledged at the agency at Fort Winnebago, that influence was not made to withdraw the Indians from a connection with the hostile Sacs and Foxes last summer, nor was it beneficially felt to any extent, until the entire defeat of the hostile Indians.

The same letter directs the expenditure of the school and agricultural appropriations to be made within this agency, and west of the Mississippi. This letter was written after an examination of my letter of the 28th January; and it is clearly intimated in that letter, these measures were superinduced from a conviction that they would tend to lead the Indians to follow the established plans of the Government, in relation to Indians; views, I will add, originating in an extensive, well digested plan of benevolence, having for their object the improvement of the Indians, their permanent happiness and prosperity, and consequent security of our frontiers. Is it reasonable to suppose the department will advise the entire abandonment in this quarter of these great and interesting objects? can they consent to the sacrifice of half a nation of Indians, to glut the cupidity of a few white men?

I have no personal or pecuniary interest involved in this matter, apart from a deep sense of responsibility as a man and an officer.

With great respect,
I am, sir, your most obedient servant,
JOSEPH M. STREET,
U. S. Indian Agent.

Gen. Wm. Clark,
Superintendent Indian Affairs, at St. Louis.

UNITED STATES INDIAN AGENCY,
*At Prairie du Chien, July* 18, 1833.

SIR: Deeply impressed with the correctness as well as the importance of the opinions I entertain in relation to the removal of the Indians, I am impelled by a high sense of duty to the Government I serve, and the Indians under my charge, to present every thing calculated to throw light upon this important subject, however I may differ in my views from other officers in the Indian department.

I herewith cover you a letter (marked A) from a practical man of sound discrimination, long a trader with these Winnebagoes on Rock river. He is an American, opposed to giving whiskey to Indians, had the confidence of General Atkinson during the late Indian difficulties, and went the whole route with his army.

The removal breaks up his trade, as he does not mean to follow the Indians. Yet his honest good sense is apparent in his letter. I have many other evidences of the correctness of views heretofore pressed on the department, and of a systematic plan to defeat the objects of the Government, and prevent the removal of the Winnebagoes to the west of the Mississippi. I shall hereafter press another subject, glanced at in this letter; the ruinous mode of payment of annuities to the Indians. The *money payment* has been effected by the traders, through agents and interpreters, either in their interest, or negligent of the interests of the Indians, and the high moral responsibilities of the station they occupied. The Indians have no fixed determination on the subject. And if the Government would change the payment, as an experiment, the benefits would be so discernable to the Indians, that it would ever after be urged by all Indians *while sober.*

The Winnebagoes south of the Wisconsin have for years been studiously kept from visiting me, and a party who came here a few days past said they were told *I was their enemy,* and *had been the cause of the loss of their country on Rock river.* These Indians came to see me, and this morning 35 of them, with about 100 from Pine river, on the Wisconsin, have taken provisions and gone over to the west of the Mississippi, to explore the country and fix on a place of residence.

The Indians from Rock river, after being here two days, and drawn provisions, expressed their surprise at receiving any thing, and my kind treatment and friendly talk.

They said: " Father, we were told you were not the friend of the Winnebagoes on Rock river. That you would treat us like bastards, and send us off hungry. That at Rock Island you caused our country to be sold. You had long wanted our country, and told the Winnebagoes if they did not sell their country, the whites would take it for nothing. And that the country west of the Mississippi (we were told) belongs to the Sioux, and it was not our great father's, the President's, to give to us. If we went there the Sioux would kill us. They were resolved not to give up their land.

" Father, we now know the first is not true. You have given us plenty to eat, and powder and lead to hunt; your words are good, and we will examine for ourselves. We know some lies have been told us. You say the land is good and full of game; we will go and see it, and shall then know whether all is true we have heard of you. You tell us the country does not belong to the Sioux; that our great father has told you to go and show it to us, and put us on it, as our home, and that no other nation shall disturb us. If they do, and we come to you, our great father will send his soldiers to protect us. We know some lies have been told us, for we have seen your face, and we are pleased with you. Your words are good, and you have been kind to us.

"Father, General Dodge has hunted us from lake to lake like deer; we could not hide from him; we wanted to remain where we were. We have looked at the country on the Wisconsin; it is poor, and there is not much meat and no fur skins, and there is too many Indians there already. We can't live there; but General Dodge would not let us remain on Rock river; and when we got hungry, some of us said let us go and see this father at Prairie du Chien, and now we are glad we have done so; our hearts are happy.

"Father, we wish you to give us some more provisions to eat while we are looking at the country, for fear we may starve before we see any game. We will go in the morning."

About one hundred and thirty-five have gone over in this party, and from one hundred and twenty to two hundred of the Indians of the Mississippi are now in that country.

Could I get to see and converse with the Rock river Indians, I have no doubt I can get nearly half of them over by next spring. I have as yet been successful in every attempt I have been directed to make to effect the views of the Government with the Indians, when not opposed by men in the employment of the Government.

I am aware that my letters and communications on this subject get to the members of the American fur company; how I am unable to say, yet the fact is certain. Whole passages of my letters have been repeated to persons here nearly verbatim, from my letters to the department. But as I speak fearlessly what I believe of all and every person, when my duty prompts, I have considered it no further than to mention it to you, believing such things ought not to be.

Most of the Indian news from Fort Winnebago reaches this place through letters from the sub-agent there, to the officers and members of the American fur company here. During the disturbances of last year, Mr. Kinzie's letters to them brought us the information of what was doing there. For to me he did not write on the subject.

With great respect,
I have the honor to be,
Sir, your most obedient servant,
JOSEPH M. STREET,
*U. S. Indian Agent.*

The Hon. ELBERT HERRING,
*Commissioner of Indian Affairs.*

P. S. I should have mentioned that after sending 36,000 rations to this place, General Clark has ordered them to be sent to Fort Winnebago, I am informed; so that should many of the emigrating Indians come to see me, I shall have nothing for them to eat. *No part of the 60,000 rations are left to be issued here,* if these are removed. As yet, the assistant commissary has not been able to obtain conveyance for them, and if he succeeds, (which I doubt,) it will be at an exorbitant rate, as there are no boats on the river. It would be in every point of view to the interest of the United States to direct the issue of these provisions here; and I hope you will do so.

I am, respectfully,
Your most obedient servant,
JOS. M. STREET, *U. S.. Indian Agent.*

A.

Dixon's Ferry, Illinois, *July* 8, 1833.

Dear Sir: Ever since the late treaty at Rock Island, I have been constantly endeavoring to get the Winnebagoes to remove peaceably across the Mississippi, above Prairie du Chien. In the forepart of the winter they appeared willing to go, but this spring they tell me the Sioux will not permit them to occupy the country called the Neutral Ground. Whether this is true or not I cannot tell, but think it may be a fabrication, put in circulation by the basest part of creation in the vicinity of Fort Winnebago. I have just returned from them, where I witnessed such scenes produced by the whiskey pedlars as is calculated to make an American blush for his country. If they remain there they are destined to become the most miserable beings in human shape. Cannot something be done to remove them? Will not the Government, on a proper representation, take such measures as will prevent any men not of good character from going amongst them? The evil of granting licenses to men of infamous character, and whose principal aim appears to be to set them against the American people and Government, should no longer be tolerated. As an agent, as a philanthropist, and a christian, the public have a right to expect much at your hands, for I am persuaded that nothing stands between them and civilization but the whiskey traffic, which can only be prevented by their removal; and *that*, I assure you, may be easily accomplished.

With respect,
Your obedient servant,
JOHN DIXON.

General Joseph M. Street,
*Indian Agent, Prairie du Chien, M. T.*

A correct copy from the original in my office, July 18, 1833.
JOS. M. STREET,
*United States Indian Agent.*

Cherokee Agency, *July* 18, 1833.

Sir: I am sorry to have to inform you that    *    *    * ,
notwithstanding all his professions of friendship to the Government, has not only not enrolled himself, but has, ever since the emigration opened, been doing all he can to prevent others from doing so.

When Major Currey received your orders, Mr. Walker was from home; and as we for some time past had reason to doubt the sincerity of his professions, we concluded to decline opening the books until the Saturday following, and in the meantime the major called on him and showed him the instructions. He made some frivolous objections, and took out Mr. Miller, the interpreter, and advised him not to enrol, and the next morning called at the office; and fearing that he might make a plea that he had been slighted by not having the first offer, we then asked and insisted on him to head the roll; but he refused, and every day until the meeting persuaded and prevented all he could from enrolling. This information is given in order that the Government may see how much confidence they ought to place in the professions of    *    *    . For myself, I am fully convinced that sole object all the while has been his own aggrandizement and interest; and as those wishes were not gratified last winter, he seems now determined that the Government shall feel his weight by doing all the harm he can.

I hope, however, that his influence will not last long, as the Indians begin to see his object, and he must soon fall. We have enrolled but four families yet, but I have the pleasure to inform you that those are among the most respectable in the neighborhood.

Very respectfully,
Your obedient servant,
H. MONTGOMERY.

Hon. Elbert Herring,
Commissioner of Indian Affairs, Washington City.

------

St. Louis, Missouri, July 20, 1833.

Sir: In your general instructions to the commissioners of Indian affairs west, you refer us to Colonel A. P. Chouteau as a person possessing much information concerning Indians and their affairs, and who would freely communicate with the commissioners on the subject of their duties, and who enjoyed the confidence of the Government. On my arrival at Fort Gibson I met with Colonel Chouteau; and pending our negotiations with the Creeks and Cherokees, and subsequently in our conferences with the Osages, I had frequent consultations with him on the subject of Indian affairs. I found Colonel Chouteau, upon all occasions, every thing which the instructions from the War Department had led me to expect. He possesses more correct information relative to Indians and their affairs than any person I have met with west of the Mississippi; and certainly has more influence, and enjoys the confidence not only of the Osages but of the Creeks and Cherokees, than any other man in this country. The reason is obvious. He interests himself upon all occasions to see justice done, not only between the tribes themselves, but also between them and the whites. He has communicated with candor, upon all suitable occasions, the information necessary for us in our intercourse with the Indians; and his services, if they could be obtained, would be of incalculable advantage to the Government. His whole life has been passed with the various tribes west of the Mississippi; and his acquaintance with the Panis, the Camanches, and the Ricarees, is little less than that with the Osages, with whom he has mostly lived and traded. It is much to be regretted that he is not officially employed, and his being overlooked is matter of surprise and regret to many of the friends of the present Administration. If it arose from his being an Indian trader, that objection is now done away, for it is within my knowledge that he has parted with his interest in that concern.

My two colleagues, for causes which they cannot satisfactorily explain, have taken up an unfounded prejudice against Colonel Chouteau, which has already embarrassed our proceedings, and may (if persisted in) finally prevent the success of some of the important objects of our appointment.

I feel no disposition to denounce my colleagues, or either of them. Their intentions, I am willing to believe, are good; but either they or myself greatly misapprehend the benevolent views of the Government towards the Indians, especially those who are permanently settled or to be settled west of the Mississippi.

I cannot nor will not believe, until otherwise convinced, that we were sent here to render the condition of the Indians more uncomfortable than we found them, by removing them to worse lands than they now occupy, and then attempt to justify the measure by calling it a *good bargain* for the United States.

Colonel Chouteau incurred the displeasure of my colleagues, because he was as unwilling as myself to have the Osages removed to a poor naked prairie, destitute of timber, and much nearer to their enemies, the Panis, than they now are.

The object of the Government of the United States with regard to the Osages, as expressed in our instructions, is to remove them to lands adjoining the Kanzas, and to encourage and assist them in agricultural pursuits. The treaty of exchange which was offered to them, and which they rejected, was not calculated to promote these objects. I have lately been three weeks with the Osages in their towns, and have seen a part of the country to which it is proposed to remove them. It is poorer and more destitute of timber and water than any country occupied by Indians west of the Mississippi; and instead of holding out a sufficient inducement for them to follow agriculture for a support, they were refused the payment of their just debts, which they earnestly besought us to provide for. This conduct I cannot approve of towards the Osages, from whom we have received so great a cession of valuable land, including part of the State of Missouri, a great part of the Territory of Arkansas, and almost the whole country on which we are now settling the southern emigrating Indians. We have got all this vast territory from the Osages, and for annuities less in proportion than those given to any other nation.

It surely does not comport with the views of the Government of the United States, nor accord with the feelings of the American people, to deal out hard terms towards the Osages, from whom we have received such large and valuable concessions.

I have much pleasure in stating to you that General Clark perfectly coincides with me in the propriety of pursuing a liberal and enlarged policy towards the Osages; and no man is a better judge of the value and extent of their cessions to the United States, which he had a great share in procuring.

If the Osages had known at the time the value of the country they were ceding, and how important the possession of it was to the United States, and the prices other Indians were obtaining for their lands, they might have secured enough to have made them a prosperous, independent, and a happy nation. Instead of this they are very poor. Their annuity, exclusive of powder and lead, would not procure them blankets for half their population. And their whole annuity for two years would not pay their just debts, mostly incurred for the absolute necessities of life. This I aver to be their present condition; and they are obliged to go three times a year to hunt buffalo, to prevent their wives and children from starving; and when they are compelled to fight the Panis and Camanches, on every excursion to the buffalo grounds. The Osages are a high-minded, generous nation; but if they are not cherished and protected by the Government of the United States, they must become extinct, by their continual wars in order to procure food.

It is with some reluctance that I run the risk of incurring the resentment of the missionary societies scattered over this country; but duty to the Government, whose servant I am, compels me to say that, so far as relates to their establishment in this country, their conduct has not contributed to further the interests of the United States, nor has it been beneficial to the Indians; their teaching and instructions being more particularly directed towards the promotion of religion than to the concerns of agriculture, or to wants of common life, are not likely to change savages into useful members of an Indian community. If an Indian youth understood all the complicated doctrines of religion, and was turned back to his nation without knowing how to raise a crop or to kill game, of what benefit has his education been to his nation or to himself? I have witnessed that he becomes one of the most useless and degraded members of his tribe.

Whatever may be the peculiarities of the Indian character, you know, sir, that they are not fools; and that they readily distinguish between the useful and the useless members of their community. They have generally, in this country, expressed a wish to have the missionary establishments discontinued. The Creeks will not have them, and the Cherokees and Osages wish to get rid of them. Some of the missions are mere money making establishments, where they build mills, cultivate lands by the aid of slaves and hirelings, and raise cattle to the number of five hundred at one mission; where they have not a dozen scholars of any description, and where they would not give a starving Indian one meal of victuals to save his life without pay. These are facts coming within my own observation. I should not complain of this, if they were not incessantly interfering with our business and with the agencies.

Our quarters in times of the most urgent business are crowded with missionaries and itinerant preachers, who are spies, watching and reporting every act of the agents of Government, which does not accord with their ideas of rectitude.

　　　*　　　　*　　　　*　　　　*　　　　*　　　　*

I cannot believe, sir, that you will be influenced by the charges of these hypocritical informers. However meritorious some of the missionaries may be, it is a fact, that others will never be satisfied unless they get the management of Indian affairs west into their own hands; and nothing prevents them from denouncing every Government agent west, who is not subservient to their views, but the fear that their ambitious schemes would be discovered and frustrated.

I have extended this communication to an unusual length, and yet have not said half of what I wished to make known on matters relating to our immediate duties.

No man, sir, knows better than yourself the absolute necessity of making presents to Indians at all times of public conference. If the agents of the Government appear to act parsimoniously or niggardly, it gives the Indians a mean and contemptible opinion of the authority of the agents and of the power of the Government, and they will not listen to or respect them. But if the Indians are treated with a liberal hospitality, such as they exercise towards one another, according to their means, it gives them a proper idea of the power and great resources of the Government, on which they may safely rely for protection and support; and they will readily listen to promises which they have an assurance will be fulfilled.

This influence upon Indians, by a liberal policy, I have observed in all my intercourse with them for many years, and the same effect cannot have escaped your notice.

Now if we are to pay out of our appropriation the cost of presents, and the expense of holding conferences and talks, preliminary to the making treaties, our means will be too limited to do any thing essentially beneficial to the Government in that respect. The sum of ten thousand dollars was put into the hands of General Clark for the expenses of the late treaty at ————, and he actually expended six thousand dollars of that sum. It must therefore be obvious to you, that, with our scanty means, we cannot hold intercourse with one half of the tribes whose situation demands our attention.

For my own part, having determined to touch no public money but my own compensation, I had not calculated how far our funds were exhausted. Having devoted my whole time and attention to my public duties, I have not even learned how our expenses of living and traveling are to be settled.

You will pardon, my dear sir, the freedom with which I have given my opinions of men and measures in this communication. They are given without disguise, as the honest convictions of my mind, and without having any other motive than an ardent desire to fulfil the duties enjoined on me by the Government, as far as my limited abilities will enable me.

I am, dear sir, with great respect and personal esteem,

Your obedient servant,

M. STOKES.

The Hon. Lewis Cass,
Secretary of War.

————

Washington, *July* 22, 1833.

Sir: I have the honor to lay before you the accounts of Gen. Enoch Parsons, Col. John Crowell, and Mr. Edward Crowell, for services under the commission for adjusting Indian claims. They are left in blank, to be filled up by the department.

Very respectfully, &c.,

J. J. ABERT,
Lieut. Col. Top. Eng.

D. Kurtz, Esq.,
Acting Commissioner Indian Affairs.

————

United States Indian Agency,
At Prairie du Chien, July 24, 1833.

Sir: Notwithstanding the withdrawal of the means calculated to induce a speedy migration of the Winnebagoes to the west of the Mississippi, I have the pleasure to announce to you, that one hundred and eighty-six Winnebagoes have come down the Wisconsin, reported to me for migration to the "new limits" prescribed to them on the west of the Mississippi, received provisions and small supplies of powder and lead, and have *gone over with all their families to select permanent homes for their future residence.* In addition to these, several parties have gone across the country, by land, on horses, and have crossed to the west of the Mississippi, near the upper Ioway river and the *battle ground*, intending to come and see me after locating their families, and leaving their horses in good grass.

Winnoshuk, a principal man of the Winnebago nation, has gone over with 40 or 50 persons to examine for a place to establish a village on the Red Cedar river. The Indians that have visited me intend to send runners back after they see the country; and I have no doubt that by the use of proper exertions at least one third of the nation will be on the west of the Mississippi by next June. If the department will determine to look to the west, and cast its weight and influence with those who are exerting themselves to produce permanent settlements west of the Mississippi, the migration of the Indians is no longer questionable. Not only have all those whom I have been able to see migrated, but they have sent word to the portage for their friends to follow. Let the department enable me to see and talk to these Indians, and a removal will be readily effected.

These that have gone over are from Turtle river, an eastern tributary of Rock river, the prophet's town, and near lake Korquemong, or Rock river. At the moment I am writing there cannot be less than 250 or 300 Winnebagoes west of the Mississippi; these all, mostly, or near half, from the Indians of my agency, living on the Wisconsin. Finding the numbers pressing from the south, they have determined to migrate. The other half are Indians from the south of the Wisconsin.

When I had written this far, I was handed your letter to Gen. Clark, of the 27th June. I deeply regret the delay in the school, which I humbly conceive was not required by the state of things as then reported to you. The school was fixed by treaty near Prairie du Chien, or Fort Crawford. To meet this requisition, the school will necessarily be obliged to be established on the east of the Mississippi. The bold rocky shores of the west of the Mississippi, at this point, for many miles, would prevent the erection of a school on that shore, near either Prairie du Chien or Fort Crawford. This I deem unimportant, as the children would not be in a situation exposed to the settlers, or to any danger from the use of ardent spirits. I had selected an eligible site, within one mile of Prairie du Chien, and three miles from the Fort. The village would be three and a half or four miles distant, though the Prairie would come within one mile. The land belongs to the United States, and a reservation might be made to prevent the too near approaches of settlements. The surrounding country, at the distance of three or four miles, all belongs to the Winnebago nation. Should you, on a review of this subject, think that the school might progress, the buildings might yet be considerably forwarded this winter or fall. I feel confident I should be enabled by the spring to report so large a migration to the west as to justify the progress with a farming establishment.

With your letter, I received orders to pay John H. Kinzie 3,500 dollars, of the 8,000 from Gen. Clark. I shall hold myself ready to do so, yet he will be unable to pay this money to the proper Indians, as you perceive from my letter that numbers have already migrated to the west, and before the change can take place some hundreds more will be west of the Mississippi. But it will make no difference. Those who attended at the payment, 29th June, at the portage, say it was the most shameful scene they ever witnessed. The poor creatures who pass here, migrating, are naked, and some wounded. Several were killed at the portage. A letter I had the honor to cover you last mail, will give you some idea of the abominable proceedings. I have never had any such here. In that letter you will see the opinion of a plain, sensible, disinterested man, well and long acquainted with *these Indians*, as to the prospect of removing them. The difficulty lies in the white men and half breeds amongst the whites, and not in the Indians. The American fur company's agents, and their overwhelming moneyed influence, with the whites, and whiskey influence with the Indians, in that quarter, has heretofore been too powerful for a single handed individual, who, from the arrangements of the department, could not operate at that point.

I freely and fearlessly express my deep convictions, though I am aware that through some unknown channels all my plans, and especially all my declarations as to the men in the employment of the American fur company, in my letters to the department, are known to these men. Last spring one of them read an extract from a letter he had received, corresponding with one I had written to the department, and the agent of the company here said he knew all I had written about them and the migration of the Winnebagoes, and *I would be defeated.*

With great respect, (in extreme haste,)

I have the honor to be your ob't serv't.,

JOS. M. STREET,

*United States Indian Agent.*

The Hon. ELBERT HERRING.

---

TALLADEGA COUNTY, ALABAMA,

*Mardisville, July 25, 1833.*

SIR: The Indians, within a few days since, have presented to me a number of small accounts against the United States, which they say they were directed to do by Gen. Parsons. I received their papers, filed them, and promised to write to the department for information on the subject.

Many of their accounts are no doubt inadmissible; and the certificates and affidavits which they have filed to support their claims are informal in many cases, owing to the ignorance of the justices of the peace who have taken the affidavits, and the ignorance of those persons who make the certificates.

Their accounts consist of stolen property, and losses sustained by them in dealing with the white people. The evidences they produce are unliquidated notes and accounts, the certificates of Indians, and white men's affidavits, &c.

Please inform me whether such accounts and claims are admissible; and if so, what evidence will be required to establish them. Perhaps it would be better to give me instructions on accounts in general, as I am informed they have more to present.

If I am entitled by law to the treaties and laws in relation to the Creek Indians, please forward them to me.

I am, &c.,

LEONARD TARRANT.

ELBERT HERRING, Esq.

---

HOPEWELL FARM, C. NATION, *July 26, 1833.*

SIR: I received yours in answer to my letter of the 13th June, in which you have given me the plan proposed for enrolling of our people. I have been somewhat disappointed in the plan; for this plan differs considerably from the one I saw drafted out, which you informed me would be adopted in case the nation did not come to a treaty at our last council.   The pening of the emigration upon any plan will be of an advantage in bringing the parties to unite in a treaty.   The exploring party should have been granted. We intended to petition the President for that privilege; but Maj. Currey advised the Secretary of War not to grant it, after encouraging our people to petition, and promising his aid in getting it granted.   We then gave it up, believing that it would not be granted.   Major Currey visited me a few days ago for the purpose of enrolling of me, which I did not feel a willingness to go into at this time, nor did I think it advisable for me to do; for those who are the most influential, and have been in favor of a treaty, should keep out, in order to urge the propriety of coming into a general treaty; for, if all the treaty making party were to enrol, their influence would be entirely destroyed with all, excepting with those who have enrolled.   They need no encouragement; they have already given their assent.   Under these considerations, I have advised some of the most influential men of our party to keep out until after the council this fall; at which time we intend to make a strong effort to compel the chiefs to come to some terms by which the subject may be brought to a close; and should we fail, many of them will enrol.   But very little will be done until after that time, as I believe there would be no difficulty in getting the matter closed by an individual treaty. They are generally disposed to go into one, if it could be had.   I was informed a day or two since, by a friend, of Major Currey's intention of reporting me to the department as being unfriendly to a treaty, as he expressed.   If so, I can say to you that it is entirely false, let it be expressed by who it will.   He has said that I was under a promise to you to enrol, and that it was through my influence that it was opened, which you know not to be so.   But it has all originated from the circumstance of my not enrolling.   If his object is to force people into measures, he will succeed but slowly.   I am sorry that he has taken such a course against the friends of a treaty.   Mr. Coodey and myself have been riding through the country, advising the people to take the matter into consideration, and prepare their minds for a treaty at the fall council.   I think it more than probable that we will be able to effect a great deal in the time.   I am fearful that Major Currey is doing much injury in threatening to drive off all white men married among us, all reservees, and those enrolled under the treaty of 1817. Your agents should be more mild, and never use any thing like force. I write you this merely to contradict any false report that may be made to you by any one; and you will find me unchangeable in my course; for I have given the subject a mature consideration, and it is the only course for us, if we wish to be saved as a people, viz., a removal west.

I am, &c.,

JOHN WALKER, Jr.

Elbert Herring, Esq.,
     *Superintendent Indian Affairs.*

---

Extract of a letter from Jeremiah Austill, Deputy Marshal, to the Secretary of War, dated

*July* 26, 1833.

" I am sorry to say that the condition of the Indians was most deplorable, nor can they be relieved from their distressing condition.      *      *
I have not removed.   The two first have many claims upon the Indians for goods sold them, and they have threatened if removed to sue every

one, and that no favors should be extended to them.  I have informed the Indians it is better to submit to those men for the present, than to be sued in the State courts; and as to    *    *    *    , he has become a speculator in Indian land claims, and a partner of the intruders below this; and at this time has the Indians completely in his power—many of them in his debt, and they are in great dread of him.  He had learned that orders had been given for his removal, and when I reached there the chiefs stood in such fear of him that they not only requested that he should remain in the nation, but many of the intruders had taken the fields of the Uphawlee Indians, and drove them from the river.  Those who were driven off last season had returned and connected themselves with    *    *    *    , in such a manner that if they were put out, it would subject the Indians to greater difficulties than they are now in.  They have compelled the Indians to give up their farms, and to consent to take rents; and although they are thus compelled into measures, there is no redress, for those people exercise the State laws over them to an alarming extent.  The officers of the State have in some cases issued false precepts, and executed them upon the Indians.  False accounts are made out; the Indians seized and put in jail, and compelled to surrender all they have, either their land claims or their property.  And how this species of fraud and villainy is to be obviated I am unable to say, unless the Indians leave the country.  I find that a large proportion are disposed to leave the country as soon as possible.  I have little doubt but one half of all the Indians could be taken off next spring. I have in traveling among them urged the necessity of their departure, and that if the Government was disposed, I would take all that would leave next spring; and several chiefs declared they would go with me, so soon as the Government settled their claims for their lands; that they were ready to sell, either to the Government or individuals.  The Government should guard against one  *  *  *  and  *  *  *  they stand in enmity towards each other—both trying to fleece the Indians; and they reveal what each other has done.  They have obtained bonds for nearly all the valuable lands below here; and one half of the Indians are not aware that it is for their lands, as many have already informed me.  One case came before me, below: Several familes were living on the same bluff, it being a desirable place to live, having fine water and lying convenient to rich river lands. Some Indians who lived there were driven off, and their houses burnt up; and about twelve months since, when I was here, the citizens of the place,  *  *  *  and others, together with  *  *  *  put a half breed upon the place to claim it, and for him to consent to their remaining there; and he, it appears, as well as one other, had sold his claim to the place; and  *  *  *  had compelled the chiefs to say this half-breed ( * * * ) had a right to the place.  I had the chiefs brought before me, to say whether he had any claim to it or not, and who had the best right to it; that it was their duty to do justice to their people, and to say who had the best right to it.  They then informed me that one  *  *  *  had the best right to it; that this Indian, and several more of his family lived there, and that the white people had run them off and burnt up their houses. The number of the fraction, if I recollect right, is fraction south 33, township 11, range 29; and, although pine land, would sell well.  The site is handsome, and would now command a good price.  I am threatened with the State law and put at defiance by many of the intruders if they are removed. I shall, however, proceed on, and remove all the intruders, and such as are troublesome to the Indians, regardless of their threats, so far as it can be done with safety to the Indians.

It is well, perhaps, to say something more of * * *. When it was found that the persons living upon the bluff spoken of had taken it by forcible means, I ordered them all off, and intended to burn up all their houses, upon which * * * informed the chiefs that if the people were driven off and the place burnt up, he would have them killed and all the Indians put in jail. Knowing that it was in his power, as things now stand, I made the best possible compromise, at the request of the chiefs, and suffered them to remain until further orders. Should you write, be pleased to direct to Montgomery, Alabama.

------

CHICKASAW AGENCY, *July* 26, 1833.

SIR: In obedience to your instructions of the 25th March last, I gave notice on the 15th of April following, in the newspapers printed in Tuscumbia and Florence, of Alabama, of Columbus, Mississippi, and Memphis, Tennessee, and also had a number of hand bills struck and distributed in the nation, warning all persons against settling on the Indian lands, and notifying those already settled to move off, or they would be proceeded against.

After waiting until the 4th of June, and finding that there were many intruders who disregarded the notice given, I addressed a letter to the United States marshal of the State of Mississippi, advising him of my instructions, and of the course I had pursued. A copy of his reply is herewith enclosed. I presume no further proceedings will be had on this subject until further instructions are received from you.

Some of the more intelligent half-breeds and Indians have employed white men to improve their reservations, in order that they may receive the advantages held out in the fifth article of the late treaty; and so far as I have been able to learn, the persons thus employed are orderly citizens, and have expressed their willingness to remove from the Indian lands, should they be considered intruders. Your instructions on this subject will be thankfully received.

I also enclose to you the copy of a proposition which has been submitted to the chiefs of this nation; and from what I have been able to learn, they will be able to see the country offered, should they not be able to make an arrangement with the Choctaws for a home for their people. They have constantly urged me to go with them in search of a new home, and I have promised to do so if in my power.

You will please direct me as to the course I shall take in relation to the proposition; and should they conclude to send their delegation to see the country the ensuing fall, whether or not it would meet your approbation for me to accompany them.

Since my return from Washington last spring, I have spent most of my time in traveling through the nation, and have seen all the ruling chiefs at their own houses, and most of their intelligent warriors, and have pressed upon them the necessity of using every exertion to procure a home in the west for their people, and they have promised to do so, but seem at a loss how to proceed; and I am well satisfied that without great exertions on the part of the Government, they will not provide themselves a new home until their surplus lands are sold, and the white people settled amongst them to their ruin.

With great respect,
Your obedient servant,
BENJ. REYNOLDS,
*Indian Agent.*

Hon. ELBERT HERRING,
   *Commissioner of Indian Affairs, Washington.*

---

RAYMOND, MISSISSIPPI, *July* 6, 1833.

SIR: Your letter, dated Chickasaw Agency, of 4th ultimo, some short time since came to hand, and would have been acknowledged earlier, but on account of indisposition.

I have carefully noted the particulars of your communication, and am at a loss what course to pursue, officially, in regard to the Chickasaw intrusions, in the absence of some special instructions from the Commissioner of Indian Affairs, or from some of the departments of Government having in charge the preservation of the treaty. My best reflections on the subject have induced the belief, that my attention to the particular part of the treaty infracted would be called thereto by the Government, and that I would be ordered when and how to scour the country and remove the intruders. I have never been furnished with the treaty, nor do I distinctly know its stipulations. Will you be kind enough to inform me how and in what manner I am to act, and whether I should proceed to visit the nation until further ordered, and my duty specially pointed out in the particulars.

Respectfully, your most obedient servant,
SAMUEL W. DICKSON.
*Marshal, W. D.*

To BENJ. REYNOLDS, *Indian Agent.*

---

*Chickasaw Agency, July* 14, 1833.

The subscriber has a power of attorney, duly and properly authenticated, from Chambers and Padilla, to sell and dispose of four millions of acres of land, in the province of Texas, lying between the one hundred and one hundred and second degrees of west longitude from London, and bounded as follows, viz., commencing at the point, west, where the twenty border league between the republics of Mexico and the United States, terminating upon the north bank of the Red river of Natchitoches, where the twenty-third degree of longitude west of Washington City crosses said river: running from thence north with said degree to within twenty leagues of the Arkansas river: thence westwardly parallel with said river Arkansas to the twenty-fifth degree of west longitude from the said City of Washington: thence due south with said degree to the north bank of said Red river: thence down the same with its meanders to the point of commencement. Said grant was obtained by Padilla and Chambers from the republic of Mexico on the 12th of February, 1830, under the condition of having the same settled in accordance with the colonization laws of the same.

The subscriber is anxious to sell the whole of said grant to the Chickasaw tribe of Indians for a reasonable consideration, provided the same should

62‡

please them on examination. He will not ask or demand one cent until the patent is delivered vesting in them a fee simple right, and they put in peaceable and quiet possession of the same by the republic of Mexico: the patent and title shall be such as shall be approved by them and by the President of the United States. Should the Chickasaws, after examination, wish said grant to be extended east across the twenty border leagues so as to adjoin on the west the lands of the United States, the subscriber pledges himself to have the same so extended; all of which shall be done so soon as practicable after the contract shall be made.

WM. K. HILL.

---

WASHINGTON, July 27, 1833.

SIR: I have the honor to lay before you my accounts and vouchers for the disbursements lately committed to me, and remain

Very respectfully, &c.,<br>J. J. ABERT,<br>Lt. Col. T. E.

D. KURTZ, Esq.,
Act. Com. Ind. Aff.

---

CASS COURT HOUSE, GEORGIA,<br>July 28, 1833.

SIR: On this day Colonel Harding was selected by the Government to aid in the business of enrolling. He has had the necessary instructions, and will be furnished a faithful interpreter.

The reservees and white men intermarried with Cherokees only have to be advised by the department of the determination to remove them by the first of January, in order to ensure their undivided exertions to effect a treaty before that period.

**** is doing all in his power to defeat the policy of taking names favorable to a treaty. The fact is, he never intended going west until he could reap the benefits of another reservation.

William Hicks, past principal chief, is my interpreter, and is listened to with great attention. The exertions of John Miller, interpreter for the agent, will have a happy effect, who enrolled with Hicks, McIntosh, and others.

Although no great number have yet enrolled, the prospect is that at least one-fourth of the nation will enroll.

Under the treaty of 1817 about five hundred families enrolled and relinquished their interest in this country, a part of whom received full pay therefor, whilst others received only a part. Would it not be proper for me to notify them also to prepare for a winter removal? Their opposition has been and is still felt to a considerable extent. The rules of justice and principles of humanity require at present the most prompt and energetic action, by which to close this question and ensure the future happiness and prosperity of the Cherokees.

I have the honor to be,<br>Most respectfully,<br>Your very obedient servant,<br>BENJAMIN F. CURREY.

To ELBERT HERRING, Esq.,
Commissioner of Indian Affairs.

P. S. On Mr. Ross's return from the city last spring, he stated that Mr. **** had said that State would be satisfied if the general Government would pay the fortunate drawers for their claims. This was at the time considered so futile and groundless as not to require notice; but since the enrolling books were opened, the Phœnix has, in order to prevent persons from adopting the plan proposed by the department, appealed to the people of the United States to carry this measure of theirs into effect. For the Executive to suggest to them through me the utter impracticability of effecting this purpose would have a tendency to remove opposition on that score.

Very respectfully,

B. F. CURREY.

---

HEAD QUARTERS EASTERN DEPARTMENT,
*New York, July* 30, 1833.

SIR: I do myself the honor to enclose, for the consideration of the department, a letter from Ke-o-kuck, the principal chief of the Sac and Fox confederacy of Indians. I think it entitled to great consideration, and hope the wishes of the chiefs and head men will be complied with.

After the commissioner had signed the treaty with those Indians last fall, Ke-o-kuck stated in full council that it was the desire of the confederated nation, that in future their annuities should be paid in the manner stated in the accompanying letter; and Governor Edwards and myself, commissioners, promised to make a recommendation to that effect. I think we did so in one of our joint letters to the department; but not having copies of those communications by me, I cannot speak with confidence. At the time the request was made, (in full council,) I demanded, through the interpreter, whether the nation had any objection to the proposed manner of future payments, and all silently assented to it.

If Ke-o-kuck should request to visit Washington, I hope he may be gratified.

I have the honor to be, sir,

Your obedient servant,
WINFIELD SCOTT.

Hon. L. CASS, *Secretary of War.*

---

ROCK ISLAND, *June* 25, 1833.

MY FATHER: When the treaty was signed last September at Rock Island, I discovered that it was not stipulated to whom the annuities were to be paid. I spoke to you in full council by the wish of my nation, and requested that the annuities should be paid to the chiefs and head men of the nation—those who signed the treaty and sold you the land. My father, you promised to let our great father know our wishes, and we understood you that they would be complied with; since which the money we signed the paper for last fall has again been brought and distributed to all the individuals of the nation, who were required to sign the papers again; but all of them have paid the money over for the goods and provisions that were furnished us for our support during our difficulty. The portion coming to each individual was very small, only $1 25, and would have been of no benefit to them if they had not followed our advice; many would have purchased whiskey for their money, which would have done them no good.

My father: I call on you to befriend our nation. It is in your power to make us happy, by having our annuities paid as requested.

My father: The chiefs, head men, and myself have worked hard, and have made our village clear; we have dispersed the black clouds that darkened our sky, and now all looks happy. We have buried the dead; we have clothed the widow and orphan, and provided for them.

In full belief that we should have the control of our annuities, as you promised, we have, by the wish of our nation, appropriated money to pay three *attorneys*, (who were recommended by the superintendent and agent,) to defend some of our young men who were tried on a charge of murder. We have purchased powder for our hunt; have had rifles made to order; axes made by Collins, which have been introduced in the place of the tomahawk; purchased clothing and provisions, and distributed the whole among my people. For all which I have pledged myself, as well as all the chiefs and braves of my nation, to see it paid.

My father: We now ask you to assist us in fulfilling our engagement. We know that you will help us, because we have done all for the good of our nation. I speak for the Foxes as well as the Sacs; their chiefs, all the nation wish me to do so.

My father: The chiefs have nothing for themselves more than the rest; they share the same with all their people.

My father: I told you that if we ever had any difficulty again, I would call on you, when you promised to assist us. I remember your advice, and will follow it. All our nation remember you with gratitude. Our women and children speak of you often; they look upon you as a father. I have requested my great father, the President, to permit me to come to Washington. I hope I shall see you there. I would be pleased to hear from you.

KE-O-KUCK.

To Major General WINFIELD SCOTT.

I certify that the foregoing is a correct interpretation of a letter dictated by Ke-o-kuck to General W. Scott.

ANT. LE CLAIR,<br>
*Indian Interpreter.*

---

SUPERINTENDENCY OF INDIAN AFFAIRS,<br>
*St. Louis, July* 30, 1833.

SIR: My bill of exchange of this date, in favor of Henry S. Coxe, esq., cashier of the branch bank of the United States at this place, or order, for six thousand dollars, is on account of the purchase of corn for the Sacs and Foxes, under the 10th article of their treaty of 21st September, 1832, and under appropriation of 2d March, 1833; and which, when paid, will be chargeable to me on that account.

I have the honor to be,<br>
With the greatest respect,<br>
Your obedient servant,<br>
WILLIAM CLARK.

Hon. LEWIS CASS, *Secretary of War.*

CREEK NATION, *July* 31, 1833.

DEAR SIR: I have to report one of the most unpleasant cases that has occurred. A number of the chiefs complained of Hardiman Owens, who lives 20 miles from Fort Mitchell, and he says has recently been appointed postmaster. I came to his house two days since, and informed him that there were many charges against him, that of taking their fields from them and killing their hogs, horses, and beating the Indians in a most cruel manner; all of which were proved by the Indians and several white persons. I then ordered him to leave the nation; he replied he would die before he left. I left, however, to visit the Tuckabatchee town, and move him on my return. Soon after leaving, the chiefs came after me and begged me not to leave them; that he had drawn his knife on them, and swore he would kill some of them. I returned with a command, and arrested him. He then begged, and promised to leave in peace. I let him go, and proceeded on about 15 miles, and was again overtaken by the Indians, stating that he had followed them, and threatened he would burn their houses and kill all those who dared to come upon the fields taken by him. I then returned, and met him on the road, and he ordered me to keep off from his place. I replied that the troops were returning, and he had better leave before they arrived. He went back home and sent his family off, and set a mine in his house; and when we reached there he very politely asked us to walk in. I was in advance about fifty paces of the command; and when in the act of riding up to the gate, an Indian called, and stated that there was powder in the house. I turned my horse to leave, and Owens ran out in the rear. I called to the men to come up and arrest him, if possible, but not to enter the house; and in a few seconds it blew up; but fortunately no one was injured. We gave chase, but he escaped in the pursuit; he snapped a gun on me.

We had not left the place one mile before he returned, swearing he would kill me on sight, and some half dozen Indians. I have therefore directed the Indians to take him, if possible; and if he returned among them, to shoot him down. I have sent another detachment after him, who are now absent; he also stated that but for several persons behind me, he would have shot me before he sprung the mine.

He is the most daring man I have ever met with, and one of the most dangerous. The Indians are in great alarm, and beg of me not to leave them unless he is taken. In all other cases I have had no difficulty—compelling such as are peaceable to pay rents and damages for their intrusion upon the Indians' fields; and a few who have been troublesome, and for stealing and killing stock, have been removed.

I have the honor, &c.,

JEREMIAH AUSTILL,
*Deputy Marshal.*

Hon. LEWIS CASS,
*Secretary of War.*

N. B. The detachment has returned, and inform me that he was surrounded by them, but drew his arms, and when in the act of firing upon the sergeant, one of the men shot him.

TALLADEGA SPRINGS, IN TALLADEGA COUNTY, *July* 31, 1833.

DEAR SIR: You will permit the commissioners whose names are hereunto annexed to represent to you, in a brief manner as possible, the object of this their communication. We were appointed by an act of our Legislature, approved January 12, 1833, entitled an act for the organization of certain new counties therein named, "commissioners to locate the permanent seat of justice for the county of Talladega;" a county formed of a part of the late Creek purchase in this State. Our county is one which promises to be a home to the opulent, fashionable, and gay; and consequently has induced, and will encourage thousands to settle in it speedily. The great and unrivalled flux of emigrants into our country prompts us to represent to you the impossibility of locating the seat of justice now, without through you, the Government will countenance our object. The act above referred to enjoins on us, after procuring by good and sufficient title a lot of land whereon to locate the seat of justice, to perform the duty.

Now it is manifest to you that the performance of the duty will be impossible, until our Government either purchases the lands from the Indians, or proceed to locate them on their respective selections. We, by the authority we had, have selected a site whereon to locate the seat of justice in conformity with the act in every respect, with the exception that we have not, nor can we purchase the land of the Indian who resides on the half section which includes the site. The Indian is willing, yea, desirous to sell his interest to us, if he could do so legally.

Could we procure said site by bona fide conveyance, the speedy prosperity and population of our county and village would be unparalleled.

The situation of said site is the most eligible, beautiful, nearest the centre in our county, well watered, pleasantly undulating, abundantly spacious, fertile, and admirably well adapted to the rearing of an elegant and wealthy town.

To the end of our object we therefore, in behalf of the real interest of our fellow citizens, the prosperity of our county, as the interest also of the Indian Tamleachy Fife, who is living on the land we have chosen, most earnestly solicit your kind interference, either in authorizing Mr. Tarrant, the locating and certifying agent, to make that special location, or devising some other mode of enabling us to accomplish our purpose.

We are willing to pay the Indian's demand, which shall be a fair value, and so considered by the agent and the President.

Please answer us immediately on receipt of this, and much oblige
Your obedient servants, &c.,<br>
HUGH G. BARCLAY,<br>
HENRY CARTER,<br>
A. J. CRAWFORD,<br>
JESSE TIPTON.

To the Hon. LEWIS CASS,
    *Washington City.*

----

ST. LOUIS, MISSOURI, *August* 5, 1833.

SIR: I have been so little with either of my colleagues lately, that I must be excused for making my reports and other communications separately, and upon my own responsibility, leaving it to my colleagues to do the same, and leaving it to the department to place the proper estimate upon each communication. With this preliminary explanation, I shall from time to time give to the department such information as I deem relevant to the duties assigned to the commissioners of Indian affairs west.

A part of my business at this place was to examine into the office of General William Clark, superintendent of Indian affairs. It was the only place where I could obtain correct information of the precise situation and location of the many tribes under his superintendence, and of others with whom we have no agencies, and but little connexion.

I found General Clark disposed at all times, and upon all occasions, to furnish either written or verbal information necessary for our government, in relation to our negotiations with the Indians west. His office is well kept, and discreetly managed. Maps and sketches of the western country are made in the office, as fast as the situation of the unsettled and unexplored country west is ascertained. Copies of all important letters and documents relative to Indian affairs, and to those concerned in their management, are accurately made, and readily furnished to the commissioners whenever required. I should have been deficient in my knowledge, and of my duty as a commissioner, if I had not visited this office, and had access to the maps and papers kept here. I mean that part of my duty which requires a knowledge of the permanent, as well as the temporary location of the Indians. The office may be termed a *bureau of information*, not only relative to Indian affairs, but of much that pertains to the history of this western country, and it is kept in such order and regularity, that information upon any particular subject may be referred to at all times without difficulty. It is much to be regretted that a similar office has not been established for the superintendence of the Indians settled on the Arkansas and on Red river, where the Government has been led into errors for the want of necessary information.

In my examination into the business of General Clark's office, the nature and extent of the duties of the clerks employed therein necessarily came under my observation, and I am convinced that the compensation allowed to the second clerk, (Mr. McGuire,) is entirely disproportioned to his services, which are laborious and important. I would therefore earnestly recommend that he be allowed at least eight hundred dollars per annum, to commence with the present year. This was the salary of the lower grade of clerks in the public offices at Washington when I was there, from 1816 to 1823, and the services of Mr. McGuire here are more laborious and equally important with those employed in the public offices at higher salaries. I am the more desirous for this increase of pay to Mr. McGuire, as I am informed that unless it should be made equal to a decent support, the superintendent will not be enabled to retain him, and his services at this time are indispensable. On inquiry of General Clark, I find that he has heretofore recommended this advance of pay for Mr. McGuire. Exclusive of other duties, his services are necessary in drawing and correcting the imperfect maps of the country west of the State of Missouri and territory of Arkansas. It is needless, sir, to deceive ourselves by placing too great a reliance upon the works of celebrated men. The map of Mr. McCoy, to my certain knowledge, is incorrect, and his report more so. Some of your predecessors in office have been deceived by misinformation relative to the country assigned to the Indians, and the Government was greatly embarassed for the want of correct information in making the treaties of 1826 with the emigrating Creeks, and that of 1828 with the Cherokees. I am much mistaken if the Government acted upon sufficient information in ceding the extensive and immensely valuable territory to the Choctaws, or in the inadequate provision made to the Quapaws. These, sir, are matters well known to you, and they are only mentioned in the hope that, to avoid similar inconveniences in future, the department will, by all the means in its power, obtain the best information as to the real situation of the country designated for the permanent home of the Indians. A general and correct survey of this country will not probably be made for many years, and in the mean time, we must depend upon maps and charts fabricated from the verbal reports of traders and travellers from time to time, as this information is acquired. For this purpose, I think the services of Mr. McGuire, under the direction of General Clark, are important to the Government, and on this account I feel much interest in his being retained in office. I am apprehensive that in more than one instance the commissioners have recommended the removal of public agents for no other purpose than to make room for meddling applicants, equally objectionable as those removed. I have not dabbled in this uncharitable business, nor shall I do so, unless I plainly see that the Government is to be benefited by the change. From papers and certificates which I have examined, I am led to believe that the charges preferred against * * * * * * * originated more from religious zeal and bigotry than for a regard to truth and the public interests. This country, sir, is overrun by a set of needy itinerant preachers, whose interference is not calculated to further the views of the Government in their management of the Indians, so far as I have construed those views on this subject. This, sir, is my candid opinion; and I have no doubt that some of these officious enthusiasts will denounce me for speaking thus freely. It is not probable that their numbers will be diminished, but rather increased, inasmuch as new and needy disciples are annually taught and sent forth to seek a *living some how or some how;* and it is not practicable, or perhaps proper to attempt to prevent their introduction into the country. All I ask, and all I wish is, that their mistaken zeal may not be suffered to influence and counteract the benevolent views of the War Department so as to injure the public service. There is another subject which I must be excused for mentioning. Having determined (on accepting my present appointment) not to touch a cent of public money except my own compensation, I have been too remiss in not attending to the disposition of the funds placed in our hands. I really thought every thing was going on well, and that no extravagant or unnecessary expense had been incurred, except some trifles which had been ordered from New Orleans before I joined the commissioners. Upon a more strict examination, which necessity compelled me to make, I discover that in less than one year we have drawn for more than the amount of the appropriation, and still many necessary expenditures are unprovided for, besides a large portion of my own compensation unpaid. I deserve no indulgence in this behalf. I must suffer for my negligence in not attending more particularly to the distribution of the funds; but there are many, very many important objects of public interest that must be provided for. No man in the United States knows better than yourself the absolute necessity of providing for Indian presents in all conferences for making treaties or other regulations. They must be conciliated by presents, or intimidated by force. The latter mode of treating has, I hope, been abandoned, and the former, I trust, will be provided for. It

is impossible, with our limited means, to visit, or have a successful intercourse with the various tribes whose situation requires our attention.  I
have heretofore too much neglected to examine into the manner in which
our funds have been exhausted, and considering my joint responsibility on
that score, it is no matter what inconvenience I suffer.  But the success of
our efforts to perform the duties assigned us, and to fulfil the expectations of
the Government, absolutely requires a further appropriation for this service.
I am led to believe that this is no unreasonable demand, when I perceive in
all the late treaties, and in the laws for carrying them into effect, the large
sums appropriated for similar purposes.

I have nothing to add at present, and beg you to accept the assurances
of my very great respect.

M. STOKES.

The Hon. LEWIS CASS,
    *Secretary of War.*

---

*Extract of a letter from Jeremiah Austill to the Secretary of War,
dated Tuckabatchee, August 5, 1833.*

"I reached this town three days since, and the head chiefs have called a
council, and have requested me to have all the whites removed from this
section of the nation, and particularly those who have come within their town
fences contrary to their wishes.  It appears there are not less than sixty or
eighty persons now farming within the town fence, or rather the four towns
below the falls on Tallapoosa.  The most of those persons have rented of
the Indians, contrary to the orders of the chiefs, and the balance have put
in cultivation the lands which the Indians use for grazing their horses within
the town fence, all of whom the chiefs insist shall be removed.  But such
is the spirit of resistance amongst the intruders, that it appears to me that a
rebellion must take place.  * * * of Alabama, who has recently presided
in the Creek county, has persuaded the settlers that the chiefs have no authority over the towns, and that if they have, the consent of one Indian to
come within the town to cultivate his field is sufficient, and that he will
have me punished by law if I remove them.  Thus many have been led
astray.

I have urged the chiefs to consent that those persons might remain until
their crops were gathered; they refuse, alleging that they gave them warning before they came in.  I have determined, however, to suspend further
proceedings until I hear from you.  The command with me consists of one
lieutenant and thirty men, which are not sufficient to remove those here
without much danger, and I have no doubt there would be blood shed; not
only our lives are threatened, but many of the Indians, if the orders are enforced."

---

TUCKABATCHEE TOWN, *August 6, 1833.*

DEAR SIR: In my communication of yesterday, I omitted one fact, in
relation to the intruders, which proves the necessity of preventing the

whites from renting any of the Indian fields. I have learned that in many instances the intruders have threatened the lives of the Indians intruded upon, if they complained or informed upon them to me. Several instances of this kind have been passed over without my knowledge, and the Indians are threatened here; and some of the Indian countrymen are threatened if they do not prevent the Indians from complaining. Such is the state of things here, and I hope they may not exist long.

I have the honor, &c.,

JEREMIAH AUSTILL,
Deputy Marshal, S. D. A.

Hon. Lewis Cass.

---

Choctaw Agency, Mi., August 6, 1833.

Sir: Upon examining the books at the agency office, I find my name not entered on the register kept by Colonel Ward, agent for Choctaws. The agent says that he recollects that I told him to enter my name for a citizen, to remain five years. I have five children over 10 years of age, and three under. You will be pleased to look in the book returned to your office and see if my name is not entered. Should it not be entered for the five year stay, what is to be done in the case?

Your obedient humble servant,

LEVI W. CROWELL.

---

Washington, August 6, 1833.

Sir: I have the honor of returning to your office certain communications, and their enclosures, in relation to the Creek census, and to rights to reservations, with the assurance that it was not in my power, when in that country, to make a satisfactory investigation of the cases.

Allow me respectfully to recommend that these papers be sent to Judge Tarrant, the agent; and at the same time, in justice to that officer, to say, that the duties which his situation imposes upon him, are very inadequately compensated by his present salary.

Very respectfully, &c.,

J. J. ABERT,
Lt. Col. T. Eng.

D. Kurtz, Esq., Act. Com. Ind. Affairs.

---

Washington, August 6, 1833.

Sir: I have the honor to return to you the papers sent to me, relating to the claims of the Cherokee chiefs, Ridge and Vann, against the Creek nation.

These individuals did not offer to support their claims; and as, upon inquiry, it appeared that they had been already amply paid for their services, I did not press their claims upon the Creek nation.

Gen. Parsons informed me that one of these claimants had received five thousand, and the other six thousand five hundred dollars.

Very respectfully, &c.,

J. J. ABERT,
Lt. Col. Top. Eng'rs.

D. Kurtz, Esq., Act. Com. Ind. Affairs.

McCUTCHENVILLE, *August* 8, 1833.

Sir: I have the pleasure in saying now to you, that, in all probability, the remaining band of Wyandot Indians in Ohio will be ready to make and conclude a treaty with the Government this fall.

I have been doing all that was in my power, under authority of an appointment from the Hon. John Robb, of the date of 29th August last, to make preparations for a treaty with the remainder of said band.

I have met with difficulties that no doubt you are well aware of; that is, in the way of making preparations for Indian treaties that have reserves within the bounds of any State.

The pagan party of the above named tribe are still determined to dispose of their lands here. I will take the liberty to enclose to you a statement of some of the most responsible Indians in the Wyandot nation, which you are, if you see fit, at liberty to take a copy, and then have the goodness to enclose the original to me.

I am, sir,

Your most obedient servant,

JOSEPH McCUTCHEN.

Hon. E. HERRING.

---

TUSCAHOMA, WASHINGTON Co., *August* 9, 1833.

Sir: I am just in receipt of a communication from the War Department relative to my agency in locating and registering the claims provided for in the treaty made at Dancing Rabbit creek.

Notwithstanding my desire to commence my official duty, I shall be constrained to defer acting until I hear further from the department, for reasons herewith assigned.

1st. When there is a plurality of claimants on the same tract of survey, will it not be proper to give a preference to the oldest occupant (when it can be established who is oldest)? And what course is best to be pursued with regard to the minor claims or claimants; shall I locate them on similar lands nearest and adjoining?

2d. In locating the several claims, for instance, thus alluded to in 14th article of the treaty, where it provides the lands of the child shall adjoin the location of the parent, shall I be confined to lateral lines of survey, or otherwise; for instance, covering or adjoining?

3d. When a tract or claim has been divided by line of survey, leaving the house in one section and most of the improvement in another, will the claimant be allowed to take part in two sections, so as to include the whole of his improvement? Or should the claimant prefer relinquishing the house and taking the residue of the improvement, will he be permitted to do so?

4th. Should the claim be so prejudiced as to be entirely worthless, may he be permitted to have land of *same value*, if such should be contiguous and adjoining the improvement at or near his residence, notwithstanding he should cross a sectional line to accomplish it?

Permit me here to mention that Col. Leflore (in behalf of his people) is very firm and positive in his demands of favorable constructions by the department, of all the clauses contained or embraced in the third and fourth interrogatories as above stated.

He says "he ever objected to a rigid construction of the treaty relating to these cases, and claims redress under the latter clause of the 18th article of the treaty, which reads when ' well-founded doubts shall arise it shall be construed most favorable towards the Choctaws.' " He further says, "many have already abandoned their reserves, which have been or would be rendered worthless under a rigid construction of the treaty, (as regards ruling them, to take their claim in the section containing a respective part of their improvements, regardless of its including *any portion of good land*,) believing it a matter of design in the Government to take the good land and leave them that which was valueless. The claims affected by surveys, and now held, are not very numerous, but he feels desirous that justice may be done, confidence restored and sustained; feeling great solicitude that his people may go west imbibed with full confidence and a just regard for our Government."

5th. In locating and registering such claims as are on fractional tracts of survey, will the claimant be ruled to sectional lines of survey; or will the river be considered a natural boundary, and the claims to be located on the same side of the river on which the improvements are?

6th. There are many of the reservees gone west, having abandoned their claims; what is to be done in such cases?

7th. I am uninstructed as to the manner contemplated by the department n the location of the orphan claims. Shall these be located as floats, or otherwise, to be confined to districts, &c.?

I am required by the department to "establish such prominent marks upon each reservation as will show its extent and boundary." I shall forthwith call on the surveyor general for the requisite plats, maps, &c., on which I shall mark the extent, boundary, &c. of the several claims at the time of registering the same, believing it the most correct and satisfactory mode.

8th. In locating the three quarter section claims, shall the claimant be ruled to the sectional lines of survey in all instances, that is, to be compelled to take three quarters in the same section (with his improvement)?

I am of opinion the most correct mode in locating floats where there are more than one applicant for the same tract, it should be determined by lottery, unless when the float has been owned by one making improvements, &c., since the treaty. Should the department have further communications to offer for my better government than at present, they would be most direct by Rankin, unless the route contemplated in the Chickasaw treaty should go into operation, and in that event via the Chickasaw nation to my residence, near Tuscahoma and Chocchuma. I am equally distant from either.

Very respectfully,
Your obedient servant,
GEO. W. MARTIN.

Honorable Lewis Cass,
    *Washington City.*

N. B. I shall use my best exertions; and hope to receive an answer to this, that I may commence my duties the earliest practicable moment.

------

Washington, Tennessee,
*August* 14, 1833.

Sir: The subject of the Cherokee lands is producing some degree of interest, in anticipation of the meeting of the General Assembly of Tennessee in September next; and as I feel an anxious desire in that body to promote the just and liberal views of the administration of the General Government in relation to this subject, I have *ventured,* after a consultation with Colonel Standifer, to address you upon the matter. The laboring people of this State are becoming desirous that our jurisdiction and laws should be extended to our southern limits. I am myself in favor of the policy, and will so go in our Legislature] But, independent of the propriety of the measure in itself considered, I learn that a strong party in the State of Georgia, under the banners of nullification, *will* endeavor, and perhaps are endeavoring to embarrass the progress of the administration in reference to the Cherokee lands, under "the plea" of the 5th section of the *"enforcement bill."*

Will you, my dear sir, take the trouble of an interview with the President on the subject of this letter, and let me have his opinion upon the policy of the course I propose to pursue, in its connection with the views of the administration on our Indian relations. An account somewhat full from your pen will be highly acceptable, and, Colonel Standifer doubts not, would have its due and proper weight in the enactment of such a law by the General Assembly of Tennessee, as would in its consequences operate favorably to the emigration of the Cherokees west of the Mississippi.

Please direct an answer to Nashville.

I have the honor, &c.,

THOS. J. CAMPBELL.

Hon. Lewis Cass.

---

TALLADEGA COUNTY, ALABAMA,
*Jumper Springs, August* 15, 1833.

SIR: Your letters of the 20th ultimo were received last mail, one containing an answer to a part of mine of the 15th May last, in relation to a conversation I had with Efiematly. The treaty is plain on this subject; and I am satisfied I done wrong by writing about it, though at the request of the chief.

In reply to the other letter of the same date, I am compelled to say, that one of the commissioners at least has been much and grossly imposed upon by the Indians. My acquaintance not being so extensive with the lower Creeks, I cannot speak so certainly of the other; but on a reference to a synopsis of the census, I discover that the number of heads of families, in proportion to the whole number of inhabitants, is greater in the lower than in the upper towns; I am therefore of opinion that both have been imposed upon, and that to a considerable extent.

I do not wish to be understood as conveying an opinion that the commissioners connived at these impositions, or that they were culpably negligent in the performance of their official duties; but only that it is an undeniable fact that they have been imposed upon; neither do I believe that the Indians are alone to blame in this matter. They have been prompted to it by a despicable set of people, who are always basely interfering in the affairs of the Indians, and seeking, by a thousand dishonorable means, to ingratiate themselves into their favor.

The department may be assured that due diligence on my part will be used to detect these intended frauds, that their consummation may be prevented in locating the Indian reserves.  I am doubtful whether it will be correct to give them a north or a south half, as well as an east or a west half section.  It is the wish of a great many to take their reserves in the north or in the south part of the section, by dividing it east and west.  I mentioned this subject in my letter of May last, which was not noticed in yours of June the 12th.  It was probably overlooked in the press of business.

My official bond is herewith enclosed.

I am, sir, respectfully,

Your obedient servant,

LEONARD TARRANT.

Elbert Herring, Esq.,
     *Washington.*

———

St. Louis, *August* 15, 1838.

Sir: It may be considered and certainly is presuming much for me to offer my opinions and advice to a department of the Government so well supplied with information, and conducted by one so eminently qualified to avail himself of the advantages which that information affords.  But, sir, it has been an invariable rule with me in the discharge of my public duties for the last forty-five years, to fulfil to the utmost of my limited capacity the wishes and directions of those who have entrusted me with public employments.  I have observed by the public papers, that a late attempt to treat with the Cherokees for their lands in North Carolina, Tennessee, and Georgia and Alabama, has failed.  I am not sorry for this failure at this time, for it is a matter known to me that no treaty with the Cherokees east of the Mississippi, without the aid and concurrence of those west, would be either satisfactory to the nation or to the United States.  By the treaty of 1828, the Cherokees west are bound to receive and provide for the emigrants who may choose to remove under the provisions of that treaty.  They continue to act under this obligation with great reluctance; but the moment you make a new treaty with the Cherokees east of the Mississippi, no matter what it may stipulate for the benefit of the emigrants, the Cherokees west will withdraw all countenance or protection in their power, except so far as the emigrants are able to purchase lands and habitations, or other privileges, as other strangers.  The Cherokees west claim to be the *Cherokee nation*, and they are certainly so to be considered in every point of view.  I would therefore recommend to you, sir, that in any future attempt to make a treaty, the Cherokees west be invited to send representatives to aid in such stipulations as they may approve.  Without this precaution, it will be impossible to preserve their unity as a nation; and it appears by our instructions, that it is a great object of the Government not only to closely unite the different bands of the same nation, but to endeavor to unite kindred nations, having the same manners and speaking a similar language.  It is in furtherance of these parental and benevolent views of the Government that I have made this communication, and I am not without fears that we shall have many difficulties in accomplishing this part of our instructions.  A restless and ambitious chief of the Kickapoos, named Kishko, has already given us some trouble by refusing to join the remainder of the tribes to settle on the lands assigned them by the Government near Fort Leaven worth. Kishko controls about forty-five families, and is now with the Kanzas. We shall endeavor to reconcile him and his band to the provisions of the treaty. I must again be excused for adverting to the subject of presents to the Indians. There is not a company or even an individual trader who does not find it his interest to precede his negotiations by presents; and I have seen in my intercourse with the Indians, that in all talks they show their contempt towards the public agents who have not the means, by suitable presents, to convince them of the power, the liberality, and resources of the Government. The American fur company alone give to the western tribes upwards of four thousand dollars a year in presents; and without this donation their trade would not be worth pursuing. And shall the Government of the United States have less liberality, less discernment, and more limited means to negotiate with wild and uninformed Indians than a trading company? You may make an unsatisfactory treaty by the display of an imposing military force; but you know, sir, that there can be no permanently satisfactory negotiations with the Indians of the far west, without the reconciling aid of presents.

Is it not to be regretted that your commissioners, in this respect, have less power and more limited means than your superintendent of Indian Affairs? I have consulted Gen. Clark on this subject, and he is decidedly of opinion with me, that to attempt a treaty with the Pawnees and Camanches of the great western prairie, without suitable presents *in hand*, would be totally useless and ineffectual. The half civilized Indians east of the Mississippi may rely on paper promises, because they know that those promises will be complied with. But the first question of a Camanchee, a Pawnee, or a Blackfoot, is—what have you got to give me? It is rather humiliating to say nothing, nothing but promises. They will not listen to a talk upon such conditions. Independent of the little squabbles and misunderstandings we have settled and have to adjust with the Creeks, the Cherokees, the Osages, the Delawares, Mahas, the Ioways, and the Kickapoos, we have to hold conferences, and endeavor to give an influence to the Government, among more than one hundred thousand Camanches, Pawnees, Auricaras, Crows, Knistineaux, Assinniboins, Sioux, Gros Venires; and if possible the Blackfeet, besides the inferior tribes of Mandons, Minatarus, Tete de Coupé, Gens de Periche, Solaux. Can it be expected, sir, that, with the limited means at our disposal, we can accomplish any thing beneficial to the Government? For myself, I can say that I have not touched a cent of our appropriation, not even the amount of my compensation; and I can crawl along with my colleagues, in receiving, if not earning our per diem allowance. But this, sir, is not suitable to my disposition. I wish to do something towards fulfilling the expectations of the Government by whom we were appointed; I wish to bring all the Indians between the Mississippi and the Rocky Mountains under some kind of control or influence of the Government. This can only be done by annuities or presents. If we do not want their land, still an annual present will teach them to listen to their great father, as a friend interested in their welfare. We know, sir, that the United States have promised protection and security to the emigrating tribes. How is this promise to be fulfilled? The Camanches and Pawnees are the Arabs of the Prairies, living sometimes in the United States and sometimes in Texas. To threaten these people with war, they would laugh at it. Where can you find them? They regularly follow the herds of buffalo. The only way to have an influence is, to call them in annually to some of our military posts, to receive an annuity or a suitable present. Whenever Indians receive a gratuity from Government, no matter in what shape, they immediately evince a respect for that Government. In no other way can they be operated upon, until they are placed in a situation to be controlled by a military force. To tell them that it is their interest to be at peace, is to persuade them to give up a portion of their income obtained by plunder. I have thus, sir, taken the liberty of giving you my own views of the policy to be pursued towards the Indians of the far west. It remains for the Government to pursue such plans as may be deemed expedient and proper. I shall do all in my power to comply with such instructions as I may receive.

I am, sir, with great respect,
Your obedient servant,
M. STOKES.

The Hon. Lewis Cass,
    *Secretary of War.*

--------

Dumfries, *August* 15, 1833.

Sir: When I last saw Mushulatubbe, the old Choctaw chief, he handed me the enclosed instrument of writing, to present to the President in person. This I never intended to do but only through the proper channel. It will be seen by the agent, that for the paltry consideration of three little negroes, a debt to Doctor Hand of Columbus (a medical bill) of $100, the assumption to pay a debt to a man named Neville for $65 and $50 in cash, Mr. Daniel W. Wright, then a partner of Messrs. Hatch and Hand, obtained two of the best floating sections of land in the Choctaw purchase, worth at the time of the agreement, according to the evidence of Major Peter P. Pitchlynn, $2,000 each, and subsequently worth upwards of $3,000 each, or $6,000 for the two; Colonel Folsom sold his at $3,500 each.

The agreement is witnessed by Colonel Ward and Middleton MacKay, interpreter. Colonel W. Since then, in the presence of Colonel W. Armstrong, declared he was not advised of the terms of the agreement at the time he witnessed it.

The agreement being evidently a fraud, I did not fail to let Mr. Wright know that the case would be reported, together with that of Molly Nail and Robert Nail. We had been friends; he being a man of fascinating manners it was impossible to avoid his flattery and friendship, and which he abundantly dispensed towards a man he wished to use. It was my fate to experience this; for, as soon as the new agents come on, he so hedged himself under their influence that he was able, in a newspaper statement, to refer to Major F. W. Armstrong for the correctness of his conduct in regard to his land speculations with the Indians. I replied to him, and sent him word that as soon as we met the matter must be settled to my satisfaction. He, however, did not return through Mississippi, but, being at Natchez, he took the route by New Orleans and Mobile.

Wright is a popular man, and there are so many in Mississippi inculpated in fraudulent purchases of Indian lands, that his conduct on that score does not in the least detract from his reputation. I have good grounds for believing that Major Armstrong's hostility to me was owing, in fact, to an impression that I had infringed on his prerogatives as Indian agent. The indignities he heaped on me from the moment of our meeting until the period of our separation, was sufficient to produce exasperation in any man; and to be driven from the service at a single breath, and accused falsely of drunkenness, (I have certificates to prove the charge false,) and then, sir, to be ordered out of his presence and treated as a slave set on shore in disgrace—the course I pursued was inevitable. I pray you, sir, to excuse my troubling you with these remarks, it being impossible to refrain availing myself of the opportunity to lay before you the case of Mushulatubbe, and to add, as I am bound to believe, the causes which led to my removal from the emigration service.

I was advised by a friend of yours to send you the agreement. I recollect several other cases, among which are the heirs of Middleton Mackay, and also of Billy Hays, a captain.

I am, sir,

Your obedient servant,

WM. S. COLQUHOUN.

Hon. Lewis Cass.

---

State of Mississippi, *Choctaw Nation.*

Know all men by these presents, that the following contract has this day been entered into between Daniel W. Wright, of the county of Monroe and State aforesaid, and Mingo Mushulatubbe, a chief of the Choctaw tribe of Indians, now resident in said State, witnesseth: That whereas a treaty was concluded and signed a few days since between the chiefs, captains, and head men of said tribe of Indians, and John H. Eaton and General John Coffee, commissioners on the part of the United States, by which treaty, among other provisions, the said Mushulatubbee has reserved to him two sections of land, to be located on any unimproved or unoccupied lands in said nation. Now, it is agreed by the parties to these presents, for themselves, their heirs, executors, or administrators, that, in the event of said treaty being ratified by the President and Senate of the United States, that the said Wright is to pay to the said Mushulatubbee three negroes, viz.: two boys, to be between the ages of fourteen and thirty years of age, and a girl between the age of twelve and twenty years of age, to pay a debt due from him to Dr. John H. Hand of one hundred dollars, pay a note of his, with the said Wright as security, executed this day to a man by the name of Neville, and due the first day of December next, for $65 and $50 in cash, estimated at one dollar and twenty-five cents per acre; all to be delivered and paid upon ten days' notice, at the agency house in said Choctaw nation, whenever the said Mushulatubbee shall make, or cause to be made to the said Wright, a good and sufficient title in fee simple to said reserves of six hundred and forty acres each. For the faithful performance of the terms and true meaning of this contract, the parties to these presents hereby bind themselves one to the other, them and each of them, their heirs, executors, administrators, and assigns, in the sum of three thousand dollars.

In testimony whereof, we have hereunto set our hands and affixed our seals, this 7th day of October, 1830.

D. W. WRIGHT,    [seal]

MUSHULATUBBEE. [seal.]

Test:

W. Ward, *A. C. N.*

M. Mackey, *U. S. Interp.*

64‡

Sir: Having already submitted to the department a report in detail of the course pursued in making the payments under the late Creek treaty, I have now the honor to lay before you, a report upon other matters embraced in your instructions of the 2d May last.

First in order is the school fund and the plan under which it can be best applied to its intended object.

You remark " that two modes present themselves; one to select some of the Indian youths, and to send them to a proper institution, where their education will be attended to; and the other, to establish schools in their country. Each of these plans has its advantages and disadvantages, and perhaps it would be best to apply a portion of the appropriation to each; that is, to give to the young men a higher education than they could obtain at home, and thus prepare them for teachers and other useful avocations, and to establish common schools for the tuition of the other children."

Anxious to obtain a knowledge of the views of the Indians on this interesting subject, I had occasionally conversations with several of the principal chiefs, but it was not in my power to bring the matter before the nation in council until towards the termination of its session. The council remarked, that it was not prepared to give any decisive opinion upon the two different modes, but it was evidently disposed to prefer the establishment of primary schools among themselves, in which their boys could be educated under the eyes of their friends, to the mode hitherto adopted of selecting a few boys and of sending them to academies at a distance, and exclusively among white people. I found this opinion also to prevail with those chiefs with whom I had private conversations on the subject; and the desire to be very general among the Indians, that if a plan of primary or common schools were adopted, it should not be connected with any missionary establishment.

Before entering upon an examination of these two different modes, it may be well to remark, that the great policy of the Government is now to remove and to concentrate these several Indian tribes (which are east) upon the borders of our settlements west of the Mississippi. There lands are assigned to them as permanent homes, and the faith of the Government is pledged in the most solemn manner that of these lands they shall not be again dispossessed. This pledge constitutes a prominent feature in all the late treaties for emigrating the several tribes, and the action of the Government in relation to these tribes must hereafter have in view that pledge, and its necessary consequences.

But as the Government can no more stay the tide of time than it can stay the path of white empire west, so does its solemnly plighted faith require it to look forward to that period when these pledged rights to the Indians will be encroached upon, and when it will have to sustain them upon the lands now allotted them. To accomplish this object, and to maintain its faith, it becomes a necessary part of the policy of the Government in relation to the Indians, that when this period of encroachment by the whites shall arrive, and the demand for extended organized government west be greater than the government can well resist, that these Indians shall have attained that degree of moral and intellectual improvement which shall justify their being received as members of our great political family, and their being entitled to all the rights and privileges of free and responsible citizens.

Whatever system of education be therefore adopted in relation to these tribes, must have this humane and magnanimous policy steadily in its view;

and a choice between any modes of education is to be or should be determined only as either has a greater tendency to promote this desirable and necessary object.

Regarding, then, this object as a guiding principle, I will hazard a few remarks upon the two modes of education proposed, prefacing that the subject being new to me, you will on that account extend a lenient eye over the crudeness of my reflections upon it.

The first separates the boy from his nation and friends at that age, generally, when notions of morality and propriety are apt to be adopted. He loses, by his separation, all knowledge of his own people, and they of him; acquires other habits, and becomes, in his feelings and intelligence, much elevated above his tribe; becomes also a stranger to the house and customs of his parents and to his nation, and is equally unknown to the youths of his country, rising into manhood with him, and whom he is intended by his education to control and to instruct.

In all amusements, trials of skill, and sports of his people, in all their athletic games, so eminently in their minds the test of superior abilities, and in fact the sole basis of acknowledged superiority among them, he is found an inferior, from a want of an exercise in them, and fails, therefore, in acquiring a moral ascendancy over his people by the sole means upon which moral ascendancy is to be acquired with them. He becomes, therefore, in their estimation an inferior man, and is neither sought as a leader in war, a director of a great hunt, a valuable adjunct in any of their athletic games, or as an able adviser in council. For this last he wants a knowledge of their traditions and customs, and exhibits on these an inferiority to the common Indian.

His intelligence and intellectual acquirements (of the learning of the whites) may be superior, but this gives to him no advantages with a people purely physical, and entirely incapable of estimating or appreciating his acquirements, and jealous of their own pre-eminence.

His education may have exposed to him the moral depravity of his tribe, the folly of habits at war with reason, and of customs in violation of decency. But he stands a solitary observer, incapable of reforming others, as he possesses neither the requisite influence or weight of character; nor has he the materials upon which his more refined moral notions can make any impression. He feels himself alone in the land of his fathers, without a friend or suitable associate.

Shall he return to the white people, who have so unfitted him for remaining among his own? With these he would not be received as an equal, and as an inferior he is unwilling to be received. He finds himself, therefore, a solitary being, incapable of doing good to others, and rendered inefficient and unhappy by the very education intended to increase both his influence and happiness. This feeling operates upon his own judgment to the prejudice of the education he has received, and his example operates to lessen its value in the minds of his own people. For a time, perhaps, he may resist the effects of his depressing position, but sooner or later becomes familiar with a course of life at first so obnoxious to him. Finding that his wife must be taken from the very race whose habits he deplores, and his children be brought up according to those habits, he feels the folly of an education which merely made him an isolated and useless being, and, from apathy or despair, becomes one of the common mass; and too frequently a consciousness of his own degeneracy occasions him to descend even below the condition of the most rude and most depraved of his own tribe.

Such I believe has been the result, with very few exceptions, of the plan of selecting a few boys and of sending them off to be educated. Experience is against it, and exceptions are so very rare, that they may be considered only as melancholy proofs of an erroneous system.

And how can it be otherwise? Can a few solitary individuals reform a people, unless that people be capable of appreciating the reform proposed? or unless those individuals possess the moral energy and influence, and physical means, adequate to coerce their reform into practice? Now, with our Indians, neither of these necessary conditions exist. The mass is incapable of appreciating the advantages which the educated individual can unfold to it, and the individual is entirely destitute of any power to coerce his views into adoption.

Already has this plan been pursued to no inconsiderable extent, and for many years both by the Government and by philanthropic individuals, but we still find the Indians, as a people, as barbarous and uncivilized as they were when this country was first discovered.

Under these circumstances, then, the system for improving the Indians which is based upon the mode of occasionally bestowing an academic education upon a few selected boys, is as erroneous in its theory as it has proved inefficient and unsatisfactory in its practice.

The other plan, of establishing common schools among them, and of having the boys partially educated under the eyes of their parents, has been tried, I believe, only to a limited extent. This trial has been with the Cherokees, and its advantages have been manifested by the general condition of that people, which is considered more improved than that of any other Indian people with whom we have intercourse.

If it is admitted that the way to improve a people is to operate upon the general mass, it must follow, that the more any system of education is diffused the more universally will that mass be acted upon by it, and consequently the more will that people be improved. Now if in a nation, such as the Creeks for instance, comprising, with those west of the Mississippi, about 25,000 souls, a system were adopted which should bestow the mere ability of reading upon the majority of the rising generation, 'it would do more towards the general improvement of that people than could possibly be effected by giving an academic or college education to some half dozen boys; and, by enabling this majority to read, it would so enlarge their minds, and so increase their capacity to judge of the advantages of intellectual improvement, that it would give standing and influence to the few who might be educated in academies, and afford some foundation for their usefulness.

Admitting, however, that this might not be the case, and that the system were confined, in the first instance, to the most simple elementary instruction, that of reading only; it cannot, I think, be doubted that such an acquirement, possessed by the rising generation, would so manifest the benefits of education, that its advantages could easily, in the succeeding generation, be bestowed upon a far greater number, and even be extended to writing and to some knowledge of arithmetic.

The condition of these Indians, without exception, is such that it is necessary for each family to labor physically for its own support. It must cultivate its own bread stuffs and attend to its own herds, or hunt for food, or for means which it can traffic for food. A system of improvement, to be useful, should be adapted to their condition. And as improvements create artificial wants, these, in return, by exposing the advantages of intellectual acquirements, would, from the necessity of the case, coerce the latter more generally upon society.

Would the professions of the lawyer, the physician, or the divine, be followed by civilized men, if the state of society did not call for their exercise, and its wants sustain those who pursued them in their exclusive devotion to these professions? Would the manufacturer or the merchant pursue his vocation, if he did not find in it his advantage in administering to the complicated wants of society? The occupations are consequent upon the improved condition of society, and society must be in a state to sustain them, or they could not exist. Now, then, in a people still in a hunter state, still in what may be considered the most rude condition of man, what advantage can accrue to them by bestowing a complicated education upon a few of their members? It absolutely unfits these members for the society in which they must live, and is a wasting of time in acquiring that which is useless to the individuals themselves, and unfits them for harmonizing with the people of whom they must form a part.

Of what avails to these individuals their academic acquirements, when they must hoe their own corn, tend their own herds, hunt their own game, or starve? Of what avails their intellectual advantages, when the very time spent, and habits adopted in obtaining them, only diminish the physical energies upon which they must depend for actual sustenance, and when the very condition of the society of which they form a part, can never call those advantages into action?

The higher branches of education are what I hope you will not suppose me capable of objecting to. But why? Because such education improves the moral and physical condition of society. But in a society in which this higher order of education can produce no such results, but operates to the injury of him who possesses it, why should one hesitate in such a case to say that such an education is worse than useless? The great object before us is to improve the general condition of the Indian tribes, and not to have a few phenomena of their race " to point a moral or adorn a tale."

Education, to be of advantage to a people, must be adapted to their state, and within their capacity to use and to appreciate. And, as before remarked, to be efficient as a means of improving that people, it must be generally diffused among them.

What would be the condition of our own society, if the only means of education were those which colleges afford, and the only instructed individuals were those who could meet the expenses of a college course? If we go back in our own history to that state of society, we shall then find the white man a semi-barbarian; and pursuing that history to the present period, we must place the origin of general intelligence, and of the great and rapid strides to our present state of civilization, to the establishment of common schools. Is it not singular, then, that we should pursue with the Indians a system at war with universal experience, and that we should still pertinaciously adhere to a plan which exhibits the Indian, after all our boasted efforts, the same unimproved being he was a century past. This last fact alone ought to create doubts of the propriety of the plan heretofore pursued, and can leave us to draw but one of two conclusions: either that the Indian is incapable of being civilized, or that we have pursued a plan radically defective.

The first is truly a melancholy conclusion; and if correct, would justify an abandonment of these sons of the forest to themselves; extending towards them only the most simple rights of humanity, occasional supplies of food, that their annihilation might not be the result of absolute starvation. The second opens the animating prospect, that by altering our plan, the remnants of this once powerful, and always chivalric people, may yet be preserved to adorn civilized society.

The great courage of the Indian, his proud independence of character, an intellect admitting of a high degree of improvement, are elements upon which, in my opinion, judicious and steadily directed efforts could not fail to operate with great advantage, and to produce in the end the most gratifying consequences.

But these efforts, to be of any avail, must be upon some general plan; must be directed upon the great mass of Indian society. We must improve generally and gradually, and not pour the full glories of a noonday sun upon weak and purblind eyes. We must remove by degrees the veil of darkness which hangs over them, and not, by suddenly rending it asunder, destroy all hope, by presenting at one view the entire abyss over which he has to pass. We must avoid filling his mind with despair, by opening at one prospect the difficulties of the road, and the great distance of the goal to be attained.

Now, to accomplish this great object, and for which we are held accountable to the world and to our own posterity, is the duty and the policy of the present day. We are rapidly emigrating these Indians, and concentrating them at places from which, if there is truth or honor in the pledged word of a nation, they cannot be again removed. With this emigrating policy, then, there must be connected a well digested system of gradually improving and civilizing these Indians, or the pledge of the nation has a cloak of insincerity over it. We know that the white settlements will encroach upon these guaranteed lands, and we know that when these settlements become numerous, the Indian must be incorporated in them, or must be removed farther west. If the Indian should then be as unimproved as now, he cannot be incorporated, but will have to be removed in despite of all our solemn national pledges. Is it not then due to the sincerity of those pledges, that, hand in hand with this system of emigration should go a system for the improvement of the Indian, and for preparing him for that incorporation into our great body politic, which a regard to our own sincerity requires us to admit as the ultimate policy of the present period.

As the most powerful, as the only efficient means of accomplishing this policy, is, in my judgment, a system of common schools, couple it, if you please, with instruction in the more simple arts; but let the means which will enable the Indian to appreciate those arts be the great fulcrum of our efforts.

Intelligence must precede a civilization of national habits, for it is only from the convictions of reason that we abandon the worse for the better. Reason must therefore be enlightened, that it may be able to choose; and in the improvement of a people, that reason must be the reason or mind of the mass. Upon this mass, then, should all our exertions be directed. What lever so powerful, what means so efficient for this purpose, as a system of common schools? It spreads its blessings and its advantages gently and imperceptibly, but certainly, over the whole community.

I am also disposed to recommend that these common schools should be under some general supervision of the chiefs themselves. It would be calling in the aid of that pride of self-control so strong in the Indian character.

This supervision would, without doubt, be very rude and imperfect in the first instance; but as the plan would foster personal consequence, to which none are more sensible than Indian chiefs, it would call forth their attention and care, and in the end interest the whole nation in the preservation and consequences of the schools.

Connected with the school system ought to be a gradual introduction of rights of property. One of the greatest elements of civilization is the doctrine of *meum* and *tuum*—ideas of individual property and of individual right, beyond things of merely personal appendage, and of protection without personal violence in their possession.

I will venture to assert, that the history of no people yet discovered exhibits them in any other than the most rude condition, with whom there was not recognised a right of property in the individual or family to the particular portion of soil which they cultivated; a right which could not be intruded upon without some equivalent, and which gave to the cultivator all the profits of his labor, and acknowledged a right of succession in his posterity.

Once establish the system of common schools, and have these notions of property recognized by any barbarous people, and the great work of civilization is begun upon a solid basis; upon a basis of gradually increasing intelligence, and acknowledged inviolability of private right. We know that among ourselves the system of common schools is the pride and boast of our country, and that the portion of it which possesses this system in the greatest perfection, is the most celebrated for its intelligence, morality, order, industry, and prosperity. Why should we not, therefore, extend the advantages of this system to the savage whom we are desirous to civilize? The great principles of human nature, the great springs of human action, are the same in savage as civilized man. Why, then, should we hesitate in the adoption of a plan for improving the one, which has been found so efficacious in the improvement of the other?

I do not mean by these remarks to advise an abandonment of the plan of academic education for a few boys, but merely and clearly to say, that if one only of these plans is to be pursued, that alone of common schools among the Indians themselves is deserving of the patronage of the Government, or adapted to produce any general beneficial effects. It would, however, be highly advantageous to preserve both plans, and to select from the common schools a few clever and intellectual boys for the academy.

The school instruction should, of course, be in our language. That of the several tribes, as with all barbarous people, is extremely limited, having sounds and names only for their few wants and simple ideas. As those wants and ideas become extended, their language will exhibit its inadequacy, and so many terms from our own will have to be adopted, that it will ever be a complicated and imperfect mode of expression. The better way will be at once to diffuse among them the knowledge of an adequate language, and of the one pervading the country to which they belong, and of which they are at some future day to form a part.

It is a question, however, of no small degree of interest, whether any system, having for its object the improvement of these Indians, ought or can be successfully adopted with those tribes which yet remain east and within the chartered limits of a State.

Viewing their condition as I do, as incapable of improvement while surrounded by, and subject to an unlimited intercourse with the whites, I consider their removal and permanent location west as a necessary preliminary step. They must first be placed beyond the reach of intercourse with the whites, or where that intercourse can be prohibited or controlled by the United States, or all efforts at their improvement will be abortive.

The whites are the chief causes of the corruptions and debaucheries of the Indian, and are their instructers in most of the arts of knavery and fraud with which they are reproached. From these, therefore, they must be separated, or their improvement is hopeless.

Besides, as their entire removal west is inevitable, or their rapid destruction if they remain, no system of improvement with those who yet remain east of the Mississippi could be brought to any maturity before their removal or extinction as a people would take place, and of consequence, no advantage could result from it.

The Indians have no desire that any missionary system should be connected with their schools. I have found among them a very general and strong repugnance to those establishments; and, judging from my own observations, or from what I could gather on the subject, I am inclined to the opinion that they have done more harm than good.

A man to be a missionary should possess a matured mind, should have a profound knowledge of human nature, and much strength of judgment; should study carefully the notions, habits, and superstitions of the people he seeks to improve, and should offer as little direct violence to these as possible, if he expects to amend them. He should, in a few words, be a man of exemplary piety; of much experience with, and knowledge of mankind, and have all his learning and sentiments under the guidance of sound practical sense.

Unfortunately, however, youth and ardent zeal have been considered as desirable qualifications in the missionary, if not the sole that were inquired into; and he has been selected for these, which, to my judgment, are unequivocal evidence of his entire unfitness for the duty.

Zeal without experience only leads to those shocking absurdities with which the history of missionaries so much abounds, and to those truly deplorable disappointments which have resulted not only from missionary efforts in our own country, but throughout all Asia. We may forgive its errors because that zeal is in a holy cause; but this forms no reason why we should encourage its action, when the effects are only to injure that cause.

Those whom age and judgment have qualified are better provided for, and do not seek such employ. But until to a suitable age and maturity of judgment we can also find united the zeal which will covet the duty, it is better, far better, both for the cause of religion and of the people to whom these missionaries are sent, that the practice should not be encouraged.

An Indian is as strongly possessed with the excellence of his own moral code as we are of ours, and it is only by opening to his plain but strong common sense the superior practical advantages of ours that we can expect his adoption of it. The simple elementary doctrine of justice and morality he can readily comprehend; but the points of our religion, which are articles of faith, are totally beyond any course of reasoning comprehensible to him, or adapted to his present intellectual state. They are treated by him either as ridiculous fables, or as a doctrine not intended for the Indian. He remarks upon them, therefore, either as a jest, or replies that "there is a different God and a different religion for the Indian and the white man."

We see also in this, that even for the cause of religion it is necessary to have a foundation of some intellectual improvement. And it may not be amiss to bear in mind how far the chosen people of God were themselves improved, before He thought them fit to receive the mystery and revelations of our present belief. And from this example we may draw no invaluable lesson of the course we should pursue, when we seek to pour into unenlightened minds the full doctrines of christianity.

Without going into any details on this part of the report, of one fact I feel well assured, that, be the cause what it may, missionary establishments are highly obnoxious to our Indians. To connect these, therefore, with a school system, would probably also render the latter obnoxious, and occasion its advantages to be neglected.

In this, as in all other matters connected with the moral improvement of man, we should pursue the path into which facts and experience will lead, if we are desirous of success; and guided by these, there is a strong probability that we will succeed. The teachers ought unquestionably to be moral and exemplary men, and if possible, in all cases, married men. And if a knowledge of some mechanic art and of plain farming were possessed by them, their value would be considerably enhanced.

As a highly important adjunct to the cause of civilization, there ought to be established among the Indians, by law, some form of an organized government, recognizing, in the first instance, their own existing system as its basis, which, by offering no violence to their customs, would encounter little if any opposition from its apparent usurpation.

As to the question of right to pass such a law, it is to my mind a very simple one.

They are a savage people, within our jurisdiction, under our guardianship, and incapable of protecting and of improving themselves. They are a conquered people, morally and physically conquered, and dependent upon our forbearance for actual existence. They are a people to whom also we are desirous of fulfilling the duty of faithful guardians, and of preparing them at some future day for the management of their own concerns and for becoming a part of our own body politic. On these grounds, therefore, and of what is due to them as well as to ourselves, we possess the right of regulating their general political condition. And in the prosecution of this right, I should not hesitate, first, as a means of establishing it among them, of incorporating in a law their general system of government, and then of requiring that law to be respected among themselves. The principle is sufficiently established by the States which have extended their laws over the Indian tribes within their limits: the practical defect in these cases, and the causes of all the discontent to them among the Indians, is the complete inadaptedness of those laws to the condition of the people over whom they are extended.

The government of the Indians, as far as I have been able to investigate it, is of a republican character, under the authority of chiefs. These chiefs are elected and hold their offices during good behavior, as it is in the power of the electors at any time to break a chief. Their authority is much respected; nor is there any people who pay more respect, or submit more absolutely to their established laws. They possess, therefore, fine elements for good government—a habitual veneration for their public officers and for their laws. A general recognition of their own system by the United States, in the form of a law, would give to it additional force, and to their officers increased respect, and accustom the whole people to a supervisory guardianship in all matters, upon which their improvement so essentially depends.

65‡

An important auxiliary to establishing a preponderating influence by the United States would be the paying of an annual stipend to the head chiefs of each tribe. It would make them, also, agents of the United States, and propitiate their aid and influence in furthering the views of the United States, in relation to the general improvement of the tribes, and to a gradual introduction of ameliorations in the forms of their government, which their improving condition would require and bear.

It is a subject which will call for the most careful digestion and examination; but, at the same time, it is one which will have to be attended to; for the time has now arrived, as once before remarked, when measures will have to be adopted having as their ultimate object the acknowledgment of these people as a part of our political community. Our respect for our own national integrity, our respect for the great cause of humanity, and our regard for the reputation which our Government shall maintain in the eyes of posterity, alike call upon us for an immediate, a devoted, and a judicious attention to this interesting question.

In anticipation of the subject, I will respectfully suggest the propriety of calling upon the agents of every tribe which has been emigrated west, and of those tribes also which are our neighbors, and are resident upon the reserved territory, for information in relation to the present existing government of the tribes under their care.

The inquiries of these agents ought, I think, to be directed towards the following points:

How the chiefs are chosen, what is their relative authority and duties, and what the tenor of their offices. How their laws are made, how executed, and in what way a knowledge of them is preserved.

What are their laws, criminal and civil.

What are the acknowledged customs in relation to rights of property, real and personal, and the rights of testators and heirs, and matrimonial rights.

With any information adapted to throw light upon the forms of government with the several tribes, their laws, criminal and civil, and the customs which affect their civil relations with each other. They have organized governments, and systems of criminal and civil law, and it is information upon these which it is now so desirable and so necessary to possess.

But whatever system may be adopted of schools and of government with the Indians, it is evident that its success will greatly depend upon the vigilance and intelligence of the principal agents with the several tribes. These must be men capable of appreciating its advantages, zealous in establishing its influence, and exclusively devoted to its ultimate accomplishment. Without such agents, the best digested system will progress but feebly; and to obtain such, the compensation to each must be of an amount to command the necessary qualifications, and to justify their exclusive devotion to the ultimate object of the system. In vain may information be collected, judicious systems be digested, and able laws be passed, if a false economy shall coerce the immediate and practical supervision of these into disqualified and incompetent hands.

The condition of the property of the agency, into which I was directed to examine was highly commendable. The dwelling house, outbuildings, garden, and fencing were all in good order. Col. Crowell, the late agent, had enclosed a large space for a garden, upon which he had bestowed much labor and expense. He had planted a great many vines, having quite an extensive vineyard, and also a large nursery. The grape appeared to flourish in that soil; and this experiment of the colonel may be considered successful, and flattering to his judicious management.

The department seems to consider the expenses of blacksmiths and of an interpreter with the Creeks as rather unnecessary. Upon these subjects I will take the liberty of remarking, that in addition to the blacksmiths in the pay of the United States, the Creeks have found it necessary to employ several others, whom they have paid as a national expense, out of their annuity. The whole of these are found to be rather insufficient for their wants, and I saw no reason, if the necessities of the case are to be considered, why the expenses under this head, hitherto borne by the United States, were not as obligatory upon the United States now as heretofore.

And it may also be remarked, that the more the attention of these people is directed to domestic and agricultural pursuits, the greater will be their wants for the services of the blacksmith.

True, it may be said that turning of their attention also increases their ability for meeting such expenses from their own resources. Yet, this is a kind of reasoning which they do not appreciate, and which they cannot reconcile with their ideas of a becoming course in a great, or liberal, or patronizing government. The privation would also fall with most severity upon the more destitute, which are the greater number, and would, I am satisfied, do essential harm, and be a subject of more annoyance to the nation generally than an absolute reduction of their annuity. Conveniences of this character, long enjoyed by the whole nation, and valued by the whole, create more obnoxious sentiments by withholding them than can possibly be estimated by amount of their cost.

There is, however, an abuse connected with these blacksmiths' establishments which requires immediate attention and correction. The white squatters and intruders claim the right of having their work done at these shops; not only the right, but a preference over an Indian. They also use the iron of the Indian, and rarely pay either for that or the labor. This conduct has already created some disturbances, and was the subject of complaint to me on the part of the Indians. I promised to bring it to your notice.

Orders should, I think, be issued, prohibiting these blacksmiths for doing any work for a white man, unless at their option, when there was no work for an Indian in hand, and when the white man furnished his own iron.

The question in relation to the continual employ of an interpreter depends, I think, entirely upon another, namely, whether or not the Government means hereafter to hold any intercourse with these people as a nation. If it does, it is proper that an interpreter, in the pay of the Government, should be always at its command. If it does not; of course his employ is unnecessary.

In my late intercourse with these Indians, I employed Benjamin Marshall, and found him a faithful and well informed man, and an able interpreter. His influence was so actively exercised in behalf of the wishes of the Government, that in order to neutralize it, reports were circulated that he was bribed by me, and therefore not to be trusted by his people.

The treaty stipulations, to which your instructions also called my attention, are those in relation to the census, and to the method of locating the land rights.

Of the census I will remark, that I found it extremely difficult to obtain satisfactory information, and soon ascertained that the subject was beyond the means and time then at my disposal correctly to investigate. In conversing, however, with all parties, as well those opposed to the treaty we were directed to make, as those in favor of it, I found a very general opinion prevailing, that the census was in excess about 2,000 in the class of heads of families entitled to half sections of land.

This excess, it was said, had been occasioned by impositions practised upon the persons charged with the taking of the census, and which to detect required a more intimate knowledge of the Indians, as existing when the treaty of March, '32, was made, than they possessed.

These impositions may be classed under the following heads:

1. Cases in which individual Indians had passed themselves off frequently under different aspects and names. An interpreter informed me that he had personal knowledge of an Indian who, (in one town,) by altering his appearance, changing his name, and borrowing different children for the occasion, had passed himself off several different times, and expected several different land rights under his different names.

2. Cases in which individuals long living as one family had, since the treaty, separated themselves, located themselves upon choice spots in separate cabins, and were entered as separate heads of families.

3. Cases in which individuals had (since the treaty) taken several different wives, located them in different cabins, and had entered each as a separate head of a family.

There was another abuse practised to a great extent, but the tendency of which was not to increase the number of the census. This was cases in which Indians, who, at the time of the treaty of '32, and after it, lived together in settlements or towns, and by the treaty were to have their rights located in a body. These, when the supposed advantages of the treaty were pointed out to them, separated into distinct settlements of one individual or family each, locating themselves in cabins upon choice and hitherto unoccupied lands.

From these remarks it will be seen that before a location of a section takes place, the right of the individual claiming it under the census needs investigation.

From the character of the impositions said to have been practised upon the officers who took that census, the necessity that this investigation should be made with the aid of some one well acquainted with the condition of the Indians at the time the treaty was made, is as evident as that of the investigation itself. And the propriety of joining in the commission for locating some one so informed, is, to my judgment, equally unequivocal. Without such a course, I would recommend that no investigation should be made; for unless the commission is organized of materials capable of detecting the errors supposed to exist, it would be worse than useless to form it, and would be viewed in that country as an effort to cover and sanction errors, while the ostensible object was to expose them.

The duties of investigating and locating could be carried on at the same time, and the necessity of more than one being employed upon them is also apparent, from the extent of the duties and the time they will involve.

The location being made, the right in the Indian thereby becomes unequivocally vested, and his ability to dispose of his land, and to insure, with the approbation of the President, a good title to the purchaser completed.

Upon the subject of the locations you remark: "It is desirable, should no arrangements for emigrating be made with the Indians, that such a system with respect to the locations and the transfer of them may be adopted as will be just and satisfactory to the Indians, and as will guard them against such fraudulent attempts as, we have no reason to doubt, will be made to procure the assignment of their rights."

The article in the treaty of March, 1832, which appears to have the most direct reference to this subject, is the third. This provides (after survey, census, selection and location of the 2d are made,) that "these tracts may be conveyed by the persons selecting the same to any other person for a fair consideration, in such manner as the President may direct. The contract shall be certified by some person appointed for that purpose by the President, but shall not be valid till the President approves the same. A title shall be given by the United States on the completion of payment."

The questions, therefore, of a "fair consideration," of the "manner" in which the Indian may convey, and of the form of the contract, are subject to the approbation of the President, and without his approbation the contract cannot be valid.

The right, also, of the Indian to convey his tract is consequent upon the fact of "selecting the same;" and the right of selecting is consequent upon the facts of the census and the location of the tracts. These two last facts not having yet been consummated, the whole question still remains within the supervisory directions of the President; for no valid sale can be made until a right of selling exists; and no conveyance or contract can exist, upon which the approbation of the President can be bestowed, to give it validity, as the preliminary conditions or facts upon which that approbation can be demanded or bestowed have not yet been ascertained.

The question, therefore, in relation to the right of sale in the Indians, remains as it was on the day after the treaty was made, and may be treated under that aspect.

This opinion, therefore, with your instructions, will govern me in the few remarks I may have yet to make.

The important points for consideration are,

1st. That the Indian shall obtain a "fair consideration" for his land, and

2d. That the payment of this consideration shall be so guarded that he shall receive it in a way to benefit him without prejudice to the just rights of the purchasers.

As I do not consider any average price for these lands would be a "fair consideration" to the owner of each tract, to whom these words undoubtedly refer, I shall not occupy your time by any remarks upon that plan. Some other plan must then be adopted than that of an average price; and, to my judgment, there are but three other modes deserving of any consideration.

1st. That of the decision of the certifying and locating agents, upon offers which shall be made to them on the ground, and where employed in locating.

2d. That of the decision of commissioners, distinct from their certifying and locating agents, upon their view of the ground and of the offers which shall be made to them.

3d. Or the locations being made, and the name of each owner attached to his particular tract, the whole at a given day, or part at different days and different places, to be brought into public market, and sold at public auction.

Objections may be brought against these different modes. To the first, that combinations may exist between the agents and the purchasers; but these may be guarded against by the characters of the agents. That the duty of surveying and locating will require their whole time, and this duty necessarily procrastinated, if the attention of the agents is divided upon the additional duty of judging of the offers and affixing the prices. That it will be an extremely unpleasant and responsible task, which, however faithfully fulfilled, will entail upon the agents much personal hostility from competitors; and be it never so impartially executed, will be the subject of invidious accusation, and an excuse for inundating the department with complaints, in order to stay the final approbation of the Executive, and will ever remain a cause of discontent and dissatisfaction.

The second mode is liable to all the objections which may be brought against the first, except those emanating from the time required, and from divided attention.

To the third may also be objected the fear of combinations among bidders, and a general repugnance which I found had been impressed upon the Indian mind to sales in this way. This repugnance, however, rested entirely from an apprehension of combinations among bidders, and was created as a means of opposing our propositions on the part of the United States for these reservations, which embraced the mode of selling by public auction.

For myself, I fear no ill effects from any combinations among bidders.

Individuals in great numbers are now waiting and anxious to purchase in open market from Georgia, South Carolina, North Carolina, Virginia, Tennessee, and Alabama. They claim an equal chance in obtaining these lands, are ready to encounter an equal risk, and deprecate, justly, any mode which shall not open the market alike and equal to all.

Beside, there is no greater danger of combinations in this than in any other way; in fact there is less, as the competitors will be greater in number, watching each other and strangers to each other, or so disconnected that combinations of the whole are hardly probable, and unless of the whole could not well be pernicious. And after all, over the whole, there still remains the supervisiory approbation of the President, necessary to the validity of the sale, and which could be withheld in cases of unequivocal combinations.

The plan would also entirely exempt the agents from unpleasant imputations, and the Executive from after embarassing complaints.

I do not reason upon the supposition that all the purchasers are to combine in order to obtain the lands in a fraudulent way; if I did it would be equally against any mode of selling them. My reasoning is only in favor of the plan least liable to be affected by presumed combinations, and therefore the least objectionable.

Upon the whole, then, sir, as the result of my judgment, I acknowledge myself in favor of the mode of selling these lands by auction in open market, and more likely than any other of doing justice to the Indian, by obtaining for him a " fair consideration," and of giving general satisfaction to the purchasers.

The second question for consideration in relation to these sales is to secure the purchase money to the Indian in a way to benefit him without prejudice to the just rights of the purchaser.

The prices at which these lands shall sell must also be considered as covering all the value of the improvements upon them; and an interesting object on the part of the Government, nay, I say an act of justice due from it to the Indian, is to see that the purchase money shall be so preserved, that the Indian may be enabled with its aid to establish himself equally comfortably in his newly assigned home west of the Mississippi.

The singular improvidence of the Indian is such that we know, if left to himself, he will foolishly waste all his means; and then, if removed west, his destitute condition will throw him back into a more barbarous state than even he now is, without a cabin, without domestic utensils, without farming implements, or the means of procuring either. It is a debt therefore which the Government owes to itself, as the guardian and sole reliance of these Indians, and which it also owes to its own philanthropic plans for his improvement, that they at least should not deteriorate; and that it should interpose its supervisory power to obstruct any plan in which deterioration constitutes a necessary concomitant.

This plan in the present case will be merely to prevent an idle and useless wasting of the " fair consideration " which the Indian is to receive for his land.

The purchaser having agreed upon his price, and that price being approved, it cannot possibly occasion to him any difference to whom that price is paid; nor as he could be required to pay the whole at once, if it should be required of him, in periodical instalments. He is willing to pay the stipulated consideration, and all he wants in return is the title and possession of the land.

Under this view of the case, then, the Indian may be benefited, and the purchasers in no way wronged or embarrassed.

To effect these desirable objects I would, therefore, recommend that the consideration money should be paid to an agent of the United States, on behalf of the Indian, in such periodical instalments as the Executive might prescribe in the form of the conveyance and contracts, and be by the United States held for the use of the Indian or his heirs, and repaid to him in the manner most conducive to his benefit and to the great object which the Government has in view.

This method of selling and of ascertaining the "fair consideration" by public auction, together with the plan of making the United States the agent (in the form of the conveyance or contract) for receiving the consideration money, are the only means in my opinion which can be pursued without an entire disregard of the wants and condition of the Indian, without greatly injuring the Indian in the execution of the treaty, which was intended for his benefit, and without an abandonment on the part of the United States of an important feature in its Indian policy.

Respectfully submitted.

J. J. ABERT,
*Lieut. Col. T. Eng'rs. and Com.*

Hon. Lewis Cass, *Secretary of War.*

---

Fort Mitchell, *August* 19, 1833.

Dear Sir: I received your favor of the 6th instant a few days since, and I herewith enclose you copies of the powers of attorney given to Benjamin Hawkins, and transferred by him to me.

The claimants living in Arkansas, believing that the money would be sent here, gave to Benjamin Hawkins powers of attorney to collect it for them.

Hawkins, finding the money had not been sent on to pay the claims, proposed to me to purchase them. I refused to do so until we should go before the commissioners, then in session, and they would say to me that the claim was a good one, and the transfer would be legal, and that they would in their report request the money to be sent here. All this was done, and General Parsons, you will see, is a witness to the transfer.

If they did not mention this in their report I presume they forgot it. You recollect you saw Hawkins, and he stated to you that I had paid him the money, and that he had settled with the claimants in Arkansas.

If any farther evidence is necessary, they can get it by addressing a letter to the agent in Arkansas, and get him to give them the facts.

I have the original powers in my possession.

Yours respectfully,<br>THOMAS CROWELL.

Col. J. J. ABERT,
    *Washingon City.*

------

Know all men, by these presents, that I, Jane Carr, of the western Creek nation, do by these presents make, ordain, constitute, and appoint Benjamin Hawkins my true and lawful attorney, to act for me, and in my name to ask, demand, sue for, and receive of and from all and every person that may have or authorized by the United States Government to defray the expense of those Creeks that emigrated and paid their own expenses to this country, the said Benjamin Hawkins is hereby fully authorized by me to receive and receipt for all moneys that is due to me by the United States Government for defraying my own expenses in emigrating to this country.

Given under my hand and seal this 31st day of August, one thousand eight hundred and thirty-two; and also to receive pay for my improvements that I left.

JANE CARR.

Test:
CHILLY McINTOSH,
STEPHEN HAWKINS.

Endorsed as follows, to wit:

I endorse the within power of attorney to Thomas Crowell, and authorize him to receive and receipt for me, for any money that he may be paid by the General Government on account of the same.

BENJAMIN HAWKINS.

Test:
THOMAS J. ABBOTT,
ENOCH PARSONS.

Know all men, by these presents, that I, Susanah McIntosh, of the western Creek nation, do by these presents make, ordain, constitute, and appoint Benjamin Hawkins, of the same place, my true and lawful attorney, in my name, to ask and demand of every person or persons that is authorized by the United States Government to pay for defraying my expenses in emigrating from the old Creek nation to this country; and to receive and receipt for the same as if I were personally present myself.

Given under my hand and seal, one thousand eight hundred and thirty-two.

SUSANAH McINTOSH, her x mark.

Witness:
CHILLY McINTOSH,
STEPHEN HAWKINS.

And endorsed as follows, to wit:

I endorse the within power of attorney to Thomas Crowell, and authorize him to receive and receipt for the same, for any money he may be paid by the General Government on account of the same.

Test: BENJAMIN HAWKINS.
Thomas J. Abbott,
Enoch Parsons.

----

GENERAL LAND OFFICE, *August* 20, 1833.

Sir: The Secretary of War having advised the Treasury Department that Col. Geo. W. Martin has been appointed to locate the reservations provided for in the treaty with the Choctaws of September 27th, 1830, with the exception of those for orphans, the location of which has been assigned to William Trahern, esq.; and that those gentlemen have been directed to make duplicate returns of their proceedings to the proper land offices. I am instructed to require you to withhold from sale, all the lands which may be reported to you by either of those gentlemen, as Indian reservations, under the aforesaid treaty. These tracts must be marked on your plats and tract books, as being reserved for the respective reservees; and at the close of each month you will forward to this office one of the duplicate returns with which you will be furnished by the agents. Upon this return you will certify that the lands therein mentioned have been marked upon your plats and tract books. Should you discover any errors in those returns, or be apprised of any facts which should be made known to the Executive before the reservations are finally acted upon, you will accompany the returns by such statement thereof as may be necessary.

I am, &c.,

ELIJAH HAYWARD,
*Commissioner.*

To the REGISTER OF THE LAND OFFICE,
*At Augusta, Chocchuma, Columbus, and Mount Salus, Mississippi.*

----

GENERAL LAND OFFICE, *September* 10, 1833.

Gentlemen: From representations recently received by the President of the United States, there is reason to apprehend that all the locations of land stipulated to be reserved for the benefit of certain individuals of the Choctaw tribe of Indians, by treaty between the United States and the said tribe, concluded at Dancing Rabbit creek on the 27th day of September, 1830, may not be duly perfected and made known at the proper land offices, on or before the respective periods for the opening of the sales, as designated and prescribed in the proclamation bearing date the 12th of August last. In consequence, whereof, I am charged by the President to authorize and direct you to withhold from public sale such tracts or portions of the land so proclaimed to be sold at your office as the United States agents for locating the reservations on behalf of the Choctaws shall indicate to you as necessary and proper to be withheld from sale, in order fully to carry into effect the intentions of the treaty.

66‡

In order that this instruction may not have any prejudicial effect on the public sales, it is requested that you will regard it as *confidential* until the day of sale.

I am, &c.,

JOHN M. MOORE,
*Acting Commissioner.*

To the REGISTER,
*At Mt. Salus, Columbus, Augusta, and Chocchuma, Miss.*

P. S.  George W. Martin is the general agent, and Col. William Trahern the agent for locating the orphan reserves.

---

SUPERINTENDENCY OF INDIAN AFFAIRS,
*St. Louis, August* 20, 1833.

SIR: I have the honor to transmit herewith, a report of William Gordon, esq., provisional sub-agent, of the 12th instant.

This report is of a character to well merit the attention of the department; embracing, as it does, subjects of no ordinary stamp; and it evinces a determination and capacity, on the part of Mr. Gordon, to perform the duties of the office to which he has been appointed, creditable to him, and which bid fair to be highly useful to the service.

Respectfully, I am, sir,

Your obedient servant,

WILLIAM CLARKE.

Hon. ELBERT HERRING,
*Commissioner Indian Affairs, Washington City.*

---

ST. LOUIS, Mo., *August* 12, 1833.

DEAR SIR: I have the honor to report for your information, that I have discharged the duties confided to my care, and as directed in your instructions of the 14th May last, as far as practicable.

On my arrival at Fort Leavenworth with the goods which you had purchased and directed to be appropriated to the payment of the annuity due to the Kickapoo Indians, under the stipulations of the treaty of Castor Hill, of 26th October, 1832, I found that the Indians had determined, either from their own reflection, or from the unwarrantable interference of other persons, not to receive them in any part or at any prices in the payment of the annuity due them. To the interference of others I must attribute that determination, though of course I have no positive proof of the fact.

I represented to the Kickapoos that the goods had been purchased as you considered by their own particular request, and certainly for their own exclusive benefit; that they had been brought to them at very considerable expense; that they were as well suited to their wants as they could possibly get in their own vicinity, and at far cheaper rates; they, however, persisted in refusing them. Under this state of things I had resort to the plan directed by you to be pursued, in your communication of 14th June, and raised the requisite funds by drafts on you. I made the payment to them on their lands on the 20th July.

I made the payment to the Delawares of Cape Girardeau, in the goods which you had given me charge of for that purpose, on the 25th June. The

Delawares received their annuity in goods, expressing the highest satisfaction at their quality and prices.

The duties which you confided to my charge and execution would have been performed at a much earlier date but for the temporary difficulty which I have mentioned in regard to the Kickapoos, and to the great and continued fall of heavy rains, which kept the roads in an impassable state for a considerable length of time after my arrival in the vicinity of the Indians for whom the goods were intended. This latter cause created much delay, and greatly increased expense.

The agricultural implements for the Kaskaskias, Peorias, Weas, and Piankeshaws, I delivered, agreeably to your instructions, to Maj. R. W. Cummins, United States Indian agent, near his agency; those for the Kickapoos I delivered to them, and took their receipts.

As the result of my observations in that country, I will state that the Kickapoos are generally satisfied with their removal and location, with the exception of some thirty or forty families, the immediate adherents of the chief Kishco. They express much dissatisfaction, and I am inclined to believe would do so let the main band be located where it might. I feel confident that the difficulty, in regard to the subject, is the result of the individual jealousy of Kishco, of the influence of the other principal chiefs, and that he estimates and opposes the consolidation of the different bands exclusively by the standard of his own selfish policy and ambition.

The other bands of Indians amongst whom my official duties called me appeared in a very flattering state of prosperity and contentment, affording the most unequivocal evidence of the wise policy of removing them beyond the limits of the States and Territories.

The relations subsisting between the different nations is obviously of the most friendly and intimate character. One instance alone of a different feeling fell under my observation. I allude to a difference between the Delawares and Pawnees. The latter, it appears, had committed some depredations on the former, some fifteen or eighteen months ago, for which the Delawares fitted out, during my visit among them, a war party, for the purpose of redressing themselves. They were told to submit their grievances to the Government, and that proper redress would no doubt be afforded them. They replied that they had long ago done so, and as the Government had evinced no disposition to interfere, they felt authorized to resort to their own means. This war party consisted of about twenty men, and had not returned when I left their country.

I feel it my duty to inform you that I am thoroughly convinced, from my own observation in part, but mainly from information derived from others, in which I put the most implicit reliance, that the laws regulating intercourse with the Indians, so far as relates to the introduction of ardent spirits into the Indian country, have been violated by particular persons, in the course of the present year, to a considerable extent; nor can I see how the evil is to be corrected without a resort to some more efficient means than those which have been heretofore adopted. I would here take occasion to say, that the means for carrying into effect those laws ostensibly committed to the keeping of the different agents in whose superintendency the offence might be committed, are and of necessity must be inefficient. In the first place, an outfit on horses, which may carry in its double distilled state liquor amounting to from twenty to thirty gallons per horse, may be fitted out at any point near the frontier; in this way any number of horses, or even wagons, may be loaded and despatched for the Indian country. In this case the fact would be known to the agent, who, having observed nothing, would follow or not according to his own discretion; and if he did follow, would the party in possession of the spirits submit his kegs or packages to his inspection, unless he presented a force sufficient to command a compliance with his intentions? No, sir; the smuggler would present his license, would state to the powerless agent that he had passed all the posts at which he recognized the right of any one to interfere. Upon these specious but false pretexts he would proceed, and leave the agent to find his way back and make his report of the facts, of which he was certain himself, but could not absolutely prove by any one else. I believe that it often occurs that Indian agents neglect to do what they might do, merely from the fact that in the attempt to discharge some of their most important functions, and from the force of circumstances failing in it, they thus reason: that a small one is not worth attending to; and besides, he would probably feel some compunction in prosecuting one man for a small offence, when he knew that another had committed the same to a far greater extent. Another way in which whiskey might be taken into the Indian country, and probably it is, is this: a boat may produce false bills of lading or invoices; it may not appear from either that she contains any ardent spirits; the agent or officer whose duty it might be to examine her, thus imposed upon, would give her a *superficial* examination and let her pass, under the honest conviction that she contained nothing objectionable. But, sir, this conveys to my mind no positive or satisfactory evidence that she contains none; it may be secreted in the interior of packages, in barrels ostensibly containing flour or biscuit, or in a thousand ways which would not be observable without the most scrutinous examination. Since I have reported my impressions of the existence of the abuse, I feel it my duty to give my views of what I consider the only efficient means of preventing its practice. In the first place, no land expedition should be allowed to enter the Indian country in any other way than on the condition of reporting to some military officer or Indian agent beyond the frontier. The officer or agent should be positively instructed to examine closely every package; and further, if the examining officer should afterwards suspect from any circumstance that he has been duped, or the laws in any way violated, he should, if an agent. be authorized to call on the nearest military post for a force sufficient to follow and make the necessary investigation; and this should be conducted in the most secret manner possible, for to give the least publicity to the intention would assuredly defeat its own object. The same rule should govern if a military officer were to make the examination.

Boats and their cargoes should be made to undergo the same rigid investigation. In this way, if one or two detections should be made, which I am inclined to believe could be easily done, and the offender made to suffer the most rigid penalty of the law, the evil would immediately cease. Without the adoption of this, or some other equally efficient course, the laws prohibiting the introduction of spirits had as well be repealed. Indeed, justice would seem to require that they should be, for the trader who conforms to their requisitions is injured, and the one who violates them with impunity is benefited.

Before concluding this report, which is already longer than I could have wished, a sense of duty impels me to state my unequivocal belief of the injurious tendency of allowing missionaries to locate themselves among the

Indians, without the adoption of some restrictions which do not appear in practice to exist. It is charitable to believe that some of them are actuated from the best and purest motives; but experience and observation lead irreristibly to the conclusion that a majority of them are governed by considerations of unworthy personal interest. In many cases where they have been permitted to locate themselves among a nation to a very useless extent, and more particularly if they consist of different denominations, the harmony and good feeling of the Indians have been very injuriously affected. Another consequence highly detrimental to the interests of the Indian is this: that they will in a very few years, if allowed to prosecute their views in their own way, monopolize a great proportion of their best lands, to say nothing of the present destruction of timber, &c. I know not, sir, whether complaints on this head ever reach your ears from the Indians; but be assured they do exist. Another and last objection which I shall state, is the adverse influence which they sometimes exercise to the interests of the agent, and through him the Government. The agent must conform to the will of the missionaries, or the influence of the missionary will be brought to bear against the agent.

This delicate subject I have adverted to with reluctance, but from a paramount sense of duty.

I have the honor to be, sir,
Your obedient servant,
WM. GORDON,
*Pr'l Sub-Agent Indian Affairs.*

Gen. WM. CLARK, *Sup. Ind. Affairs.*

---

LOWNDES COUNTY, MISSISSIPPI, *August* 20, 1833.

DEAR SIR: Some new and interesting movements are getting on foot by land speculators respecting the lands to be granted to the heads of Choctaw families under the fourteenth article of the late treaty concluded at Dancing Rabbit. A construction is placed upon this article which seems to me to be foreign from its letter, and highly fraudulent against the Government, which I understand is to be carried into effect by appealing to the sympathies of the Government in behalf of the Indians under the eighteenth article, which stipulates that the treaty shall be construed in the most favorable manner towards the Indians, when, in truth, they will not in the least be benefited. Their construction is this: that the treaty fixes the location of 640 acres for the head of the family at the reputed place of residence, and that then the locations for the children are in the nature of floats; for instance, suppose an Indian to have eight unmarried children entitled to one half section each, that instead of locating for *them* the half section lying around and adjoining that of the parent, they will be permitted to commence anywhere adjoining the parent, and run off in any direction in solid column or diagonal, by quarter or half sections, so as to secure all the most valuable land, not only in the immediate vicinity, but for several miles off. The facts that have come to my knowledge are these: the head of a certain Choctaw family and his unmarried children are said to be entitled to six sections of land; they have made an unconditional and bona fide sale to a speculator at one dollar per acre, to take effect at the expiration of five years from the ratification of the treaty; the land upon which they live is fine oak and hickory land, but the speculator, not being satisfied with what is good, covets a large fertile prairie lying several miles off, which will bring to the Government at least five dollars per acre; and secondly, that the land to be granted under the provisions of said article wholly belongs to the parent, and no part of it to the children; therefore, the head of the family having eight children entitled to one half section each, is properly and legally the owner of the whole, and thus being solely seized of five sections, has full authority, when he has lived upon the land five years after the ratification of the treaty, to consummate the sale now made, disregarding any claim that the children might have. Thus these poor Indian children are to be defrauded out of the boon given them by the Government, if this construction is not in accordance with the true meaning of the treaty, for the benefit of white men. Will it be permitted?

That you may understand more clearly the manner in which these claims are intended to be located, I have enclosed a rough sketch, representing the State line, township and sectional lines, residence, and intended locations.

For the purpose of preventing frauds against the Government, Indian children, and emigrants, I thought best to inform the War Department that an attempt will be made upon the sympathies of the Government, representing the poverty of the Indians, and that the land which they must receive under the strict letter of the treaty is not fit for cultivation; that benevolence ought to be exercised towards them, and that they ought to be permitted to locate their land elsewhere, and according to the sketch I have enclosed. But, sir, I do assure you, that in this there is a *wolf* in *sheep's clothing;* the Indians are not to be benefited, because, as I have before said, they have made an unconditional sale; and that, too, to the very men who are intending to excite the sympathies of the Government; thus, by stratagem and hypocrisy, enrich themselves and depress the Indians; for one dollar per acre is much less than the value of the land upon which they now live. I would suggest one other important idea respecting settlement or cultivation rights, granted under the 19th article: that where an Indian has in cultivation a certain quantity of land, he is entitled to a proportionate quantity to include the reputed residence; a large quantity of reservations of this kind have likewise been sold to speculators. And it is not uncommon, when the surveys have been made, that a corner stake stands near the house, the house upon a poor tract; by moving the stake a few rods, the house is then represented as being of a different quarter or half section, of much more, and sometimes of intrinsic value. If entries of this description of claim are permitted to be made without a watchful eye on the part of the Government, frauds of no small magnitude may be committed. I would, therefore, suggest the propriety of compelling all land claimants under Indian titles to take the county surveyor, and particularly point out their claim, by him to be surveyed and returned to the registers of the several land offices; and also, that a commissioner be appointed for each land district, with specific instructions how to locate the several reservations. I would point out other means of intended fraud, but having seen the able publication of Major Gwinn on the subject of Indian claims, perceived that it was laid before you, and that it contains most if not all the means of preventing frauds, both against claimants and the Government.

Some of my neighbors and myself are deeply interested in the mode by which the claims under the fourteenth article will be located, because we have emigrated here, and under great difficulties, privations, and hardships, have made valuable improvements upon the public domain, with a view of purchasing them at the land sales; and if these speculators are permitted to run the locations of their claims in any direction, so as to designedly cover the improvements made by emigrants at a remote distance from the Indians, when there is an abundance of good unoccupied land adjoining the location of the heads of families, we will find it to our advantage to cease improving and give possession; this we would the more readily do if it were to the advantage of the Indians. Will you please give me an answer as soon as circumstances will permit, stating the manner of locating these claims; because if they are located according to the enclosed draft, some of our improvements will be taken, and the season is advancing when we should be making preparations elsewhere for a crop next year. A compliance will much oblige yours and many friends of the administration.

Respectfully,<br>GAB. FELDER.

Hon. ELBERT HERRING.

P. S. Direct your answer to Pickinsville, Alabama.

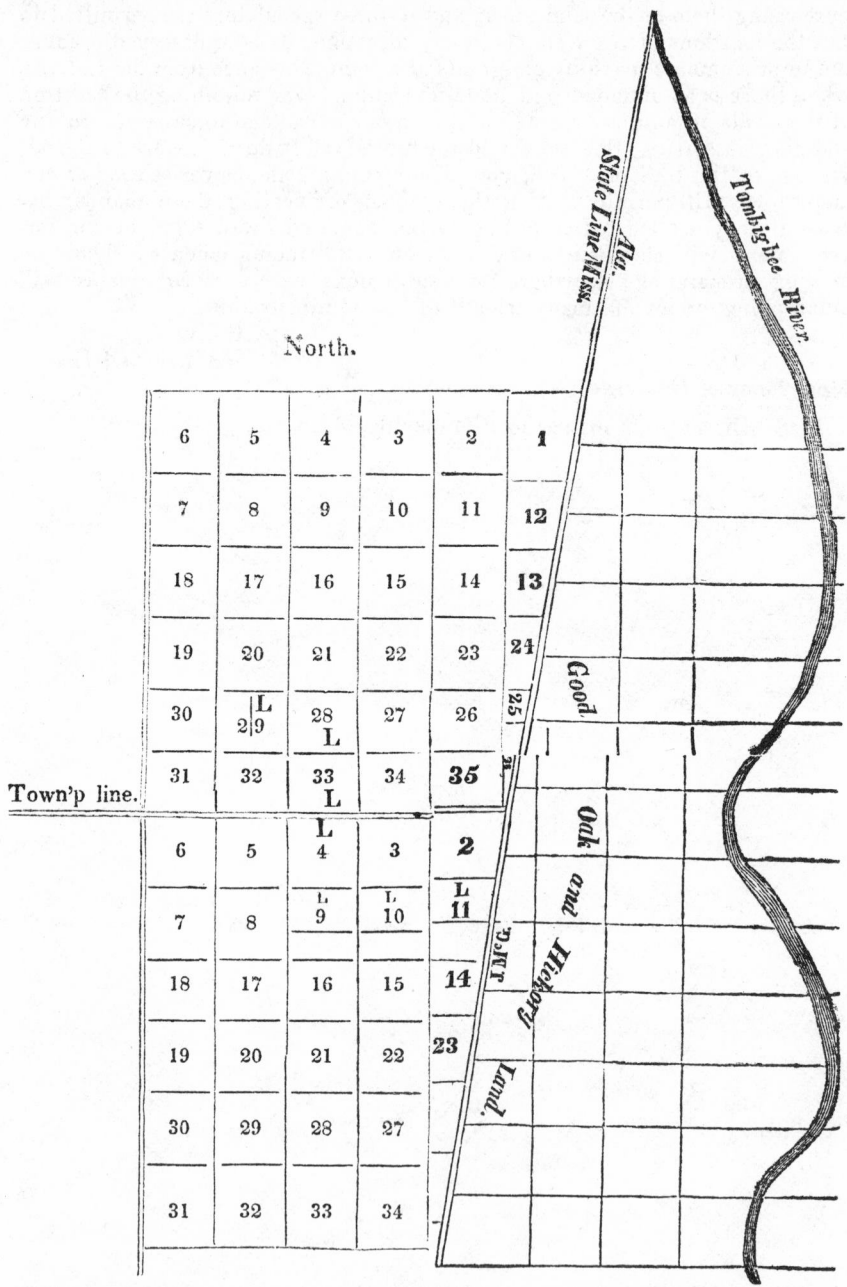

This sketch represents four fractional townships, two lying in Alabama and two in Mississippi. John McGilbry lives in Alabama, on the fraction upon which is marked J. McG. I am not acquainted with the numbers of the sections in Alabama; but they design coming into Mississippi, and entering the north halves of 11, 10 and 9, the west half of section 4, the whole of sections 33 and 28, and the eastern half of section 29; all of which are marked with L. This may not present the entries correctly, but it clearly exhibits the plan and design.

Executive Department,
*Tuscaloosa, August* 20, 1833.

Sir: An attempt by the deputy marshal of the southern district of Alabama to remove an individual by the name of Owen from premises alleged to belong to an Indian, has resulted in the death of the supposed trespasser. A detachment of United States soldiers, on the requisition of the deputy marshal, was placed under his direction, and the deceased was shot by one of these soldiers. The frequent incursions of this officer, with an armed force, among our inhabitants residing in the country acquired from the Creek Indians, with the purpose of settling disputes between them and the Indians, have produced very general dissatisfaction, which, since the killing of Owen, has risen to an excitement, that if not quieted will lead to excesses equally unpleasant to the General Government and to the authorities of this State.

It is not my purpose to show that the conduct of the marshal was improper, or that an offence has been committed against our laws, but to request that the Government refer the complaints of the Indians to a tribunal less objectionable than that of the marshal with an armed soldiery.

At the last session of the General Assembly of this State, the whole of the Creek country within the limits of the State was laid off into counties, which were organized so as to give full and complete effect and operation to our laws. It was understood that no objection would be raised by the Government to its settlement by the white people, provided they abstained from intruding upon the reservations secured to the Indians by the treaty of the 24th of March, 1832. The fifth article of that treaty, by obvious construction, permits settlements upon any of the lands ceded except reservations, "after the country is surveyed and the selections made." The Indians, therefore, cannot resort to these settlements as a ground of just complaint, and it would not be difficult to show that intruders, even upon selections, cannot legally be removed by the marshal. I lay it down as a correct position, that when the Government has disposed of its lands, all disputes and controversies relating to their title, or to the right of possession, are referable only to the judicial tribunals of the country. I do not deem it necessary, however, to discuss this point at present, relying as I do upon the disposition of the President to cause the treaty to be carried into effect by such means only as are clearly authorized by the constitution and laws.

Encouraged by the treaty, by the laws of the State, and by the express permission of the Government to settle upon and occupy these lands, a population has moved upon them equally respectable with that of other sections of the State, and to which, in point of numbers, the Indians bear but a small proportion. In their present situation they cannot be regarded as a distinct tribe, for as such they have disappeared and been lost in the large community now in possession of their ancient birthright. They are permitted by the treaty to sell their reservations, with the approbation of the President, and it is quite notorious that many of them have sold and otherwise disposed of them. They have entered into contracts with their white neighbors, as well in relation to other matters as their lands, and upon inquiry it will be found that in many instances their dissatisfaction and complaints arise out of these contracts. In these cases it will not be pretended that any authority can be conferred on the marshal to interfere. They form

67‡

the proper subjects of judicial investigation, and our courts are competent, and at all times open to decide them.

By the laws of this State, whenever an individual is entitled to the possession of lands, he can, by a summary proceeding before a justice of the peace, expel an intruder or trespasser within a few days. I transmit herewith our statute on that subject. It has for many years been in force, and has fully accomplished the purposes for which it was intended.

Whatever may be the opinion of the President as to the powers of the Government to eject intruders by force, without the forms of law, I am persuaded that, under existing circumstances, he will concur in the opinion that this law will be equally effectual, and that the marshal, at the head of a band of armed soldiers, in the bosom of a peaceable, orderly, and quiet society, cannot, and should not be permitted to settle questions that are in their character strictly and properly legal.

With distinguished consideration,
I have the honor to be, sir,
Your obedient servant,
JOHN GAYLE.

Hon. Lewis Cass,
        Secretary of War.

----

CHOCTAW NATION, WEST, *August* 20, 1833.

DEAR SIR: A proper regard to my own interests, and a sense of duty to my family, form my apology for troubling you with this communication. In the second article of the supplement to the late treaty between the United States Government and the Choctaw people, my name is inserted as one entitled to a gratuity of a section of land. The location of the land is to be fixed by my residence and improvement, a condition which cannot be complied with. From the time I left my father's house, which was soon after my return from the school in Kentucky, I have never resided within the limits of the Choctaw country. I left my father at the time of my marriage, and after that, until I removed to this country, I resided constantly with my father-in-law, a white man, living near, but without the limits of the Choctaw country, and I never had, or pretended to have any improvement in that country. There were two other persons, *McDonald* and *Jones*, whose names are embraced in the same article with mine, who were known never since their childhood to have resided in the Choctaw country, and were, on that account, provided with floating reservations. My case was about being represented to the commissioners while this article was under consideration, when a similar provision would probably have been made for me, but the business having been suddenly interrupted by a disturbance among the people it was neglected. My claims were thought to be quite as good as those of the persons above named, while they were entirely disconnected from any participation in the affairs of the Choctaw nation, until the subject of the treaty came up, when they were known to be unfriendly to the principal treating chief, Colonel Leflore. I had constantly, since my return from Kentucky, held the office, and performed the duties of a captain of the northwest district, near the line of which I resided; had sustained my chief, Colonel Leflore, in the measure of treating, and exerted what influence I possessed among my warriors to effect it. When the removal commenced, finding that I could not dispose of my claim in its present shape, and knowing that Government was anxious to get the people off, I started among the first, and done what I could to assist the agents of Government, under whose direction I acted. While almost every person provided for by the treaty realized the value of their several donations previous to leaving the old country, many of whom by the employment of the proceeds in planting in this country have doubled the amount, I am in a worse situation than I was previous to the treaty—on a new place, without the means of making comfortable improvements. The favor I have now to ask is, that you would have the goodness to advise me what will be the probable issue of my claim. I can do nothing with it in its present shape, and I know not where to apply for aid. There is no agent of Government here to whom I can apply, and if there was, he could not probably satisfy my inquiries. Thinking that Congress could grant the necessary relief, I sent last session to Mr. Plummer, the Representative of Mississippi, a petition, praying that my claim might be made a floating reservation in the northwest district, accompanied with the certificates of my chief and such of the agents of Government for the removal as I could see. I observed from the papers that it was presented, but not having heard of it since, I conclude that it was dismissed as an improper application. I am now inclined to think that my case presents a question of construction by the President, or other proper officer, whose decision will be regulated by the 18th article of the treaty. Although the subject of this communication may be considered by others as very trifling, it is of vast importance to me, and you will do me an act of kindness, which I shall remember with gratitude, by giving it the necessary attention.

I should be glad to receive a communication, either from yourself or from some person to whom you may most properly refer the matter, addressed to me at Vicksburg, Mississippi, from whence it will be forwarded to m﹐ as soon as convenient. I have been for more than a year endeavoring to dispose of it to a person who will purchase it if it is constituted a floating reservation in the district in which I was captain. I am extremely anxious to close the sale.

Yours, very respectfully,<br>S. D. FISHER.

Hon. L. Cass, *Secretary of War.*

<hr>

### At the Forks of the Wabash,

*August* 22, 1833.

Sir: Since my arrival at this place, I have learned, with regret, tha Gen. Marshall, the Indian agent, has been put to much inconvenience, and been greatly embarrassed by the conduct of the commissioners who negotiated the treaties with the Pottawatamies last year. It became necessary, in the commencement of their negotiation, that sundry little matters should be given out as presents. Gen. Marshall and Col. Owens were accordingly directed to procure and deliver whatever was necessary, in this way, not exceeding in amount $5,000. The request that they should do so appears, as I am informed, on the journal of proceedings. As it was within Gen. Marshall's agency, the labor and responsibility devolved on him. He accordingly purchased and delivered to the amount of about

$1,400; and in the confusion and irregularity which took place in closing their business, the commissioners did not make any provison for reimbursing to Gen. Marshall this money. Having made the purchases, he was of course liable to pay, and has been compelled to pay. The papers and vouchers for this disbursement, he informs me, were given to Gen. Tipton, when he went on to Washington last fall, that he might effect an arrangement by which he (Gen. Marshall) would be relieved. Nothing was done; and, unfortunately for him, the papers were left with Gen. Tipton's other papers at Washington, as he informs Gen. Marshall. That these are the facts I have no doubt. I have deemed it best to communicate them to you, and to receive your instructions with regard to it, before I proceeded to carry into effect the stipulations contained in the third article of the treaty made (at Tippecanoe) on the 26th of October, 1832. The goods provided for in this article have been purchased, and these, with the $20 000 in specie, will be prepared for delivery to the Indians by the 1st day of October. Gen. Marshall has expended his own means, under direction of the agents of the Government, and he must be made whole. In what way it can most readily be done will be for you to say. And, as I shall be on the ground, and can thereby more readily arrange it, or get at all the facts, I will be pleased to receive your instructions as soon as convenient. May I add, that I wish a duplicate of your letter made, the one to be directed to me at Detroit, the other at Logansport.

It affords me great pleasure to have it in my power to say that, notwithstanding the difficulties that were lately raised around Gen. Marshall, he retains the entire confidence of the Indians, and the public generally, and is in my opinion a valuable and useful agent, and an estimable man.

With great regard and esteem,<br>Your obedient servant,<br>G. B. PORTER.

The Hon. Lewis Cass,
    *Secretary of War.*

---

INDIAN AGENCY,<br>*Chicago, August 24, 1833.*

SIR: By the first article of the treaty of Tippecanoe, of the 25th October, 1832, the Pottawatamie tribe of Indians ceded to the United States a tract of country included within certain described boundaries, and by the second article of same treaty, the commissioners of the United States and Indians agreed that there should be reserved from the cession aforesaid certain described tracts, to individual Indians and half breeds. The treaty is entirely silent in relation to the President's approbation to the sale or lease of any of said reservations. Under these circumstances, the question arises, whether these people can legally sell their reservations to individuals wishing to purchase, either with or without the consent of the President, or whether the right of purchase is vested alone in the General Government. Under the firm conviction that, upon the ratification of the treaty, the party became vested absolutely with a *bona fide* title, and had full power to convey, I have in a few instances sanctioned the sale of these reservations, knowing that the purchase was made in good faith, and that the grantor had received for his land a fair equivalent. The cases alluded to are, first, the sale of Mix-e-manny to Richard S. Hamilton, of one section, to include the village of said Mix-e-manny; and secondly, the sale of Claude Lofrombaise to John H. Kenzie and David Hunter, of one section on Thorn creek.

I have just been told that these purchases would be viewed by the department as a direct violation of the twelfth section of the intercourse act of 1802, and that the purchasers were guilty of a misdemeanor, and were liable to punishment by fine and imprisonment.

I was always of opinion, and still am, that the section of the act referred to was intended to prohibit persons from going into the country the Indian title to which had not been extinguished by treaty, as provided by the constitution, and buying, leasing, or otherwise obtaining a grant of land from any Indian nation or tribe of Indians; or to illustrate more fully my views, suppose that, before the cession of the tract of country in question. A had purchased a section of land of an Indian, he unquestionably would have violated the law, because the Indian having no title to the land other than an interest in common with the tribe, he could not legally convey, and the white man purchasing under such circumstances would assuredly act in direct violation of that section referred to. But where individual reservations have been made within the boundary of a ceded tract, either to a pure Indian or a half breed, by treaty stipulation, and with the consent of authorized commissioners, and the chiefs of the tribe, here the original Indian title becomes extinct, and the individual, in my opinion, obtains a title in severalty, and is vested with full power to convey. If, however, I have misconstrued the law, and erred in sanctioning the sale of these reservations, I must ask the indulgence, not only of the head of Indian Affairs, but of the President and the Secretary of War, to impute it to the want of a proper understanding of the true meaning of the law referred to. May I hear from you, as soon as convenient, on this subject.

I have the honor to be,<br>Very respectfully, your most obedient servant,

ELBERT HERRING, Esq.,           TH. J. V. OWEN.
*Indian Commissioner, Washington City.*

---

WASHINGTON, August 27, 1833.

SIR: In the instructions of the War Department of the 2d of May last, in reference to the payments lately made by me, allusion is had to a claim of Mr. Thomas Crowell upon "the fourteen hundred dollars allowed to those Indians who have emigrated west at their own expense."

In the frequent conversations which I had with Mr. Crowell on this subject, I became satisfied that his claim had not been understood at Washington, but as I had not the means for adjusting it, nor the necessary authority, I contented myself with advising him to furnish me with a detailed statement of the case, and with copies of his powers of attorney. I have now the honor of submitting to you the statement, and copies of the powers, which were received by me this morning.

The reference in the statement to conversations between myself and Hawkins on this subject is strictly correct.

Very respectfully, &c.,<br>J. J. ABERT,

DANIEL KURTZ, Esq.,           *Lieut. Col. Top. Eng.*
*Acting Commissioner Indian Affairs.*

SELENA, *August 29*, 1833.

SIR: The enclosed communication was handed a few days since, and should have been forwarded immediately, but was detained on account of a very severe indisposition, and which is my only apology for its detention.

Very respectfully, &c.,

R. L. CRAWFORD,
*Marshal Southern District Alabama.*

Hon. LEWIS CASS,
*Secretary of War.*

———

TUSCALOOSA, *August 20*, 1833.

SIR: Since you have been engaged in executing your orders from the War Department, in relation to intruders upon Indian settlements and reservations, a general dissatisfaction has been created among our citizens residing in the counties of Macon, Chambers, and some others, and complaints have reached me from highly reputable sources. Since the death of Owen the excitement has been considerably increased, and I am apprehensive that, unless the mode of proceeding adopted by the Government to investigate the claims and grievances of the Indians be abandoned, the people in that quarter will be driven into excesses that will be equally unpleasant to the authorities of the General Government and of this State. I am convinced that the investigation of Indian rights, titles, &c. by an armed force, in the bosom of a civil and peaceable society, is not only improper, but is wholly unauthorized by the constitution and laws of this State, and by the constitution of the United States. The President does not desire to incommode our citizens, or to protect the Indians by any other means than such as are sanctioned by the laws, and I feel confident that he will direct the troops to be withdrawn as soon as a communication, which will be despatched by the first mail, reaches him. I have to request, therefore, that you will abstain from any further interference until an answer to that communication is received.

I am, &c.,

JOHN GAYLE.

To R. L. CRAWFORD, Esq.,
*Marshal South. Dist. Alabama.*

———

CHEROKEE AGENCY, *August 30*, 1833.

In order to be ready to send off emigrants at the proper period, two appraisers should be ordered to report themselves for service about the 1st of November.

And lest a portion of the pay should be indispensable, in order to enable the emigrants to get off, I would suggest the propriety of getting an appropriation of at least three hundred thousand dollars at as early a period as Congress can be procured to make it, to pay for abandoned improvements. The fact of there being no appropriation for this purpose operates very much against enrollments.

Should you consider it proper to furnish me a copy of the reported survey, by the United States commissioners, of the country laid off west for the

Cherokees, it might be of infinite service at the council, which convenes
October 10th.

Should it be considered politic, myself and the Indian agent will attend
that council.  It might be well to direct the agent to have the troops in the
neighborhood of the council ground, and should any interference be attempted to thwart the views of Government by citizens of the United
States, to have them arrested; also to keep ardent spirits off the ground.

> Very respectfully,
> I have the honor to be
> Your most obedient servant,
> BENJ. F. CURREY.

Elbert Herring, Esq.,
  *Commissioner of Indian Affairs.*


P. S.  In article eight of the treaty of 1817 provision is made for the
heads of Indian families wishing to become citizens of the United States
to have six hundred and forty acres laid off, on territory then or that might
thereafter be seceded; the register of whose names to be kept open, &c.
Under this article several families had their names registered, some of whom
are disposed to continue on the lands yet unceded, provided the Secretary
of War shall decide their claim to be a good one.  But in the event the
decision is against them, then, in that case, they will go west and join their
brethren.  Be good enough to have this question considered as early as
practicable, and advise me of the result.

> Very respectfully, yours, &c.,
> BENJ. F. CURREY.

------

Office of Superintendent of Indian Affairs,
  *In Florida, Tallahassee, Sept.* 1, 1833.

Sir: I have the honor to acknowledge the receipt of the communications
of the Indian office, dated the 9th and the 17th ultimo, directed to Governor
Duval.  He is yet absent, and the duties thereby imposed of course fall
upon myself.

The first communication relates to the removal of the Appalachicola Indians.  In my last letter to the department on this subject, I stated my belief that *Blunt* would be ready to go off by the 20th of July.  The sickness on the river, and other circumstances, have caused a disappointment
in that regard.  Since then (the second week in August) I went over to
Appalachicola, having appointed a meeting at Mr. Pope's, the sub-agent's
house, and I sent word to *Blunt* and his second chief to attend, in order to
ascertain how matters stood, &c.  *He* did not attend, but sent some of his
chiefs with Davy, who made a variety of excuses, and gave many reasons
for not having got ready as they promised.  I conversed with these chiefs
fully, and wrote to Blunt by S. Richards, the interpreter, urging him to
get off, &c.  I have the honor to enclose you his answer, and also a letter
from a Mr. St. John, a respectable young man, clerk in a store on the
river.

Their letters contain the substance of what the chiefs told me.  I shall
continue to urge them by every proper means in my power to get off forthwith; but from all I can learn, I must say now, I am doubtful of such result

*this fall.* No news has been yet heard from Blunt's son in Kentucky. He is very anxious, especially as report states that there have been several deaths among the Indian youths in the school. He should be sent home as soon as possible. I would advise the purchase for him of the boat he requests in his letter. There is one, he says, on the river, which he has in view. Something should be done in regard to the robberies committed upon him. It is not for the superintendent to decide whether Blunt is or is not entitled to (as he claims in his letter) remuneration from the Government for these robberies. He relies upon the guarantee in the treaty of Camp Moultrie of the peaceable possession of the reserves. I have no doubt that he lost the money and goods he alleges. Every possible effort was adopted to bring the perpetrators of this outrage to punishment, and they were apprehended, but escaped from the custody of the officer. I enclose you a copy of a proclamation I issued for them.

Rawls, one of the robbers, after his apprehension, confessed the offence fully. I have a copy of his written examination. Stafford and Oaks fled to Alabama; but the latter was pursued by some persons from whom he had stolen a horse; and shot dead in the woods. Oaks has fled to Texas. But thirty or forty dollars of money and goods were recovered, nor is there any probability of any more being got. The instruction of the department as to his claim is respectfully requested. The communication of the 17th above mentioned, relative to Maj. Phagan and the public moneys, occasions me to go to the Seminole agency tomorrow, to pay the annuity, &c. I have paid the Appalachicola Indians some time ago, but the payment of the others has been delayed *for his return.* I am informed, however, the Indians want it, and have therefore considered it best to down go at once; and Mr. Sheffield, the sub-agent here, being sick, the duty is imposed upon me personally.

I enclose to the department a letter from Col. R. H. Long, of Jackson county, Florida, respecting some negroes in Econchattemicco town, in the Appalachicola, claimed by Hawkins, an Arkansas Indian. Mr. Pope, the sub-agent's account of the business, disagrees with Col. Long's in some respects. He is now absent, on leave for a few weeks, in New Orleans, on important private business of his own, and on his return will make a written report. From the slight examination I have made, I am inclined to think the claim of Hawkins, the Arkansas Indian, is just and valid. The sale to Milton I consider a sham, to afford facilities for their recovery merely. I would respectfully suggest that the decision of the matter be directed to be referred (as has heretofore been the course of the Department of War in respect to disputes as to slaves claimed by Indians in East Florida) to the summary examination of the judge of the district of West Florida.

I am, very respectfully, sir,
Your most obedient servant,
JAMES D. WESTCOTT, Jr.,
*Secr'y and Acting Gov'r and Acting Sup't, &c.*

Hon. E. Herring,
*Indian Commissioner, &c.*

BLUNTSTOWN, *August* 12, 1833.

DEAR SIR: I received your letter today by Mr. Richards, and am very sick, and could not come as I sent you word by my second chief yesterday. I am getting ready to go away as fast as I can. My people have been very sick this summer, and I have been delayed by it. I am going to build fifty canoes to move in. I have several built. I wish to go in this way. To get a vessel will cost too much money. I am afraid a great many of my people wont go with me. One third or more will stay. The reason is, because Walker and Chattimico have agreed to stay, and because Col. Gadsden's treaty says they shall be protected and have land. John Yellow Hair and several others wanted to go with me, but I can't take them now. They don't get any pay for going with me. I thought Col. Gadsden and you were going to get other Indians to go with me, and to make such a treaty, but you do not do so. I have been a friend to the whites, and the others have not, and now the whites go on their side. I am much hurt at this. My people are very much dissatisfied. Walker has one of my negroes now, and will not give him up. Several of my men have joined his town since the treaty. I will come and see you next month, and talk with you fully on this subject. I want Gen. Jackson to give me a whaleboat, which can be bought here for sixty dollars. I can get ready this fall, and will go, but Government must pay me my money that was stolen from me; it was seven hundred dollars in cash, and about one hundred and fifty dollars in goods. I will send you a list. Grace has stolen my negro and two horses. I want pay for them also. I do not want to go till these are settled, and my son returns home. I send you this, and will tell you my mind more fully when I see you.

JOHN BLUNT, his x mark.
DAVID ELLIOTT, his mark.
STEPHEN RICHARDS, *Interpreter*.

His Excellency JAMES D. WESTCOTT,
    *Acting Governor of Florida, Tallahassee.*

---

ASPALAGA, *August* 17, 1833.

DEAR SIR: Col. Blunt is here, and wishes me to write you respecting his removal to the country selected by him. He is ready and willing to abide his agreement with the Government, but seems dissatisfied with the arrangement Col. Gadsden has made with Walker, Pachassee, and those Indians that choose to remain in their reserves, subject to the laws of Florida. Many, nay a great portion of his men, in consequence of the privilege extended to Walker, seems to prefer removing to his town, subject to the same laws with Walker, than to go with Blunt to the Texas. It has caused a great deal of dissatisfaction among his men, and is likely to retard his removal. He wishes to know the truth of the matter, and know too whether Walker and the Indians that flock to his standard will be permitted to remain undisturbed upon their lands, while he, Blunt, who has always acted fairly and honorably, will be compelled to remove with only a small portion of his men. His negroes, likewise, in consequence of this rumor, are deserting him, and say they are determined not to go with him. He says Col. Gadsden promised to assist him in securing this property until he should be out of the reach of the bad *white men* and Indians, who are persuading his negroes to desert him. Blunt is still willing to remove, but wants your assistance in securing his negroes, and compelling the other portion of his men to abide the agreement he has made.   He seems to think it rather unfair that privileges should be allowed *Walker* that have been denied him, when he has always been the friend of the white men, and has listened to their talk, and to the talk of their great father.   He has been preparing his boats for the purpose of removing, but the fever prevailing in his town to a great extent is likely to put them back some.   He is determined to remove as soon as possible, and would like to know something definite relative to *those* Indians remaining *who* choose to take sides with " Walker."   He does not seem to comprehend it.   He would have come up to Pope's, agreeably to your request, to see you, but his child was so sick he could not leave home.   He wishes you to write him, and direct to this office.

Most respectfully,<br>
JOHN S. JOHN,<br>
*For Col. John Blunt.*

James D. Westcott,
   *Acting Governor of Florida.*

---

Mariana, *August* 14, 1833.

Dear Sir: I regret very much that it was not in my power to see you when you were in Jackson.   Indeed, I did not expect that you, with your family, would have passed without giving us one of your *old fashioned calls.*   I had heard that it was your intention to visit Jackson county, and deferred submitting a matter of business to you until I could see you.   In this I was disappointed, as I did not hear of your being in the county until you were gone.   My object was and is to bring before you a claim which has lately been put in my hands against some negroes now in the possession of Econchattimicco, the Indian chief residing near Brown's Ferry.

Col. Milton, the owner of the claim, has proceeded in the matter thus far.   He had an interview with Econchattimicco, at which I was present, with Capt. Isaac Robinson.

The Indian chief, with great honesty, gave to us the nature of his claim through his own interpreter and Col. Hawkins, the interpreter of the western Creeks.

His statement amounted to this: That the negroes belonged to an Indian by the name of Fulcharge; that Fulcharge and his brother agreed that when either of them died the property of each should be held by their children— that is to say, that Fulcharge's children should hold his own property; that afterwards Fulcharge died, leaving a son by the name of Cotcherharjochapco, who was then very young; that after Fulcharge's death, his brother (whose name I have forgotten) took possession of the property, to take care of it for his brother's child; that after this Fulcharge's child or children treated his or their uncle badly, and he would not give up the property to Fulcharge's son; subsequently the brother died, and before his death asked him, Econchattimicco, to take possession of the property; that some short time after the death of the brother he took possession of these negroes, and that he had no other claim on them, &c., &c.

I do not pretend here to give you the whole matter of Econchattimicco's saying, or of the proceeding which took place at and subsequently to this interview, as much has been said by some persons in relation to the matter utterly destitute of the truth, but give barely the grounds of the claim, as I know that if you do any thing in the matter it will be from a full knowledge of all the facts, substantiated by proof.

Then, to proceed with Col. Milton's title. By the death of Fulcharge Cotcherharjochapco, his son, became entitled to the negroes. He conveyed, for the sum of $3,000, to Benjamin Hawkins his claim to the negroes. Benj. Hawkins, for the like valuable consideration, conveyed to Col. Milton, the present claimant.

I will here state, from my knowledge of Col. Hawkins, who is a half breed Indian, whose character is conspicuous in the history of the country, and better known to the President of the United States as a distinguished warrior, and intelligent and honorable man, and of Col. Milton, that I do not believe that either of them would press an unjust claim upon any one. The claim has been presented to the sub-agent, but having been irritated on the subject by unfounded reports, we defied his power to interfere. Resort was then had to the process of attachment, but the marshal refused to serve it, unless by the permission of the sub-agent, he having a few days before given orders to the Indians to resist the marshal, or any other white men, should he come on the reserve. Upon application to the sub-agent he refused his permission to the marshal to enter the reserves and make a levy. No levy of consequence was made.

My object is now to present the matter to you as the chief of the department of Indian affairs in the territory. It may be more proper that I should go through the only agent known in the law (except the Executive), Major Phagan; but I am almost forbid in this attempt from the distance at which he resides.

As my only object in this matter is having justice done between the parties, and such only is the wish of my client, I would, with your Excellency's views of the proper direction to be given to the case, that an investigation may be had therein; if before you, when and where it will be agreeable to meet you, that the proof may be exhibited; if before Major Phagan, that I may be enabled to communicate with him on the subject. Before the sub-agent, residing near these reserves, I could not go, for the very reason that I can see no law giving him such power, or even authorizing an appointment. In this, however, I may be wrong; and if so, should be much gratified to be convinced of my error, by reference to the page and section. With sentiments of high esteem, yours, &c.,

RICHARD H. LONG.

James D. Westcott,
*Acting Governor of Florida, Tallahassee.*

I desire to be understood by your excellency that my views in relation to the reserves are entirely at variance *now* with the decision of the court in Fayette county, and should be perfectly willing to meet the question anywhere. But our decision is before us, and until reversed, shall act in obedience to it.

Will you please to give me an answer as soon as practicable, that I may pursue another remedy, if I am remediless before you.

R. H. LONG.

———

Choctaw Agency, *September* 1, 1833.

Sir: A communication from the office of Indian Affairs, bearing date 5th of November, 1832, was received after my return west of the Mississippi, stating that, in consequence of the reduced number of the Choctaws, the appointment of Colonel Ward as agent would be discontinued after the 31st of December, 1832, and requesting me to perform such duties of an agent as the few remaining Choctaws may require.

I am now actively engaged in preparing for the emigration, and have been solicited by the Indians to have some blacksmith work done for them; they have a number of axes to repair, with a few small wagons, and some horses to shoe; and as they have had no smith this year, I have taken the liberty of employing one for a month, with a striker, to use the tools belonging to the Government, and to furnish some iron and steel; which, under the circumstances, I hope you will approve. Had time permitted I would first have advised you. The expense of every description will not exceed one hundred dollars, and I would respectfully ask that sum to be remitted, or ordered to be paid through one of the disbursing agents now here. The Indians all pass by this place to emigrate, and do and will send their axes far and near to repair; to them it is a matter of great importance. It is believed there is yet some six or seven thousand Indians to remove. There is a strong party opposed to emigrating; but I hope to remove these prejudices by a council which I am to have with them in a few days. Be pleased to answer this, as I wish to set out about the 1st of October.

Respectfully, your obedient servant,

WM. ARMSTRONG,
*Superintendent Choctaw Removal.*

ELBERT HERRING, Esq.,
*Commissioner of Indian Affairs.*

---

WASHINGTON, *September 2, 1833.*

SIR: I enclose you the treaty made by the commissioners with the Seminole delegation at Fort Gibson, in March last, assigning the Seminole nation a country west of the Mississippi, with the proceedings in council upon that subject. The basis of this arrangement is fully explained in the late treaty with the Creek Indians, and the report of the commissioners of April 2d, submitting it to you for the consideration of the President and Senate; and it is unnecessary for me to do more now on this point than call your attention to these papers. I will, however, take the liberty of respectfully urging the speedy removal of the Seminoles from Florida to the new home provided for them in the Creek country, by this treaty. The land allotted to them is of the very best quality in the territory, and was selected by themselves after a long and careful examination, made with the advice and assistance of the commissioners, after the conclusion of the Creek treaty. This arrangement may therefore be considered a happy confirmation of all the engagements made between the United States and Seminole tribe, with respect to their location west of the Mississippi river. But you are aware of the superstitious feeling of these people. You know, too, how easily those feelings can be operated upon by designing men; and there may be *some* men, having influence over these people, who may from selfish motives advise them not to accept the liberal provision made for them by the government, should their removal be postponed any length of time. Hence, in my opinion, the sooner they can be removed the better; to which subject I very respectfully call your attention. A copy of the Seminole treaty was forwarded to you immediately after it was concluded in March last, which I presume you received in due time.

I am, very respectfully,
Your obedient servant,
S. C. STAMBAUGH,
*Sec. Com. Ind. Affairs.*

Hon. LEWIS CASS,
*Secretary of War.*

---

WESTERN CREEK AGENCY, *September* 4, 1833.

SIR: I have to solicit your attention to the case of the teamster, which, I discover by the voucher that the comptroller has sent me, has been reduced to fifty cents per day; this would not board and clothe a man in this country. Boarding is from twelve to fifteen dollars per month; and a good field hand cannot be got for less than fifteen dollars per month, and his boarding and washing found him. A good steady teamster that can be relied on cannot be had for less than a dollar per day, when he boards himself. Mr. Ballard has quit the employment some time since, believing that he could do better than he would by getting a dollar per day in the public service.

I have therefore, sir, most respectfully to solicit a reconsideration of this matter, in order that this young man, who is a very trusty honest one, may have justice done him.

General Chilly McIntosh a few days since reported a party of emigrants, consisting of sixty persons, part of which was brought in last spring by Benjamin Hawkins, and the rest, amounting to upwards of forty, was brought on by General McIntosh; and as I have had no instructions as to what manner this year's provisions are to be supplied, I am completely at a loss how to proceed. I understand there will a great many come on this fall on their own account, and they are all anxious to draw provisions so soon as they arrive.

There has been upwards of one hundred cases of cholera at Fort Gibson within the last two months; but it has now entirely subsided, without having one solitary case in the Creek nation, but the Creeks are unusually sickly for the last month with bilious fevers.

I have the honor to be,
Sir, respectfully,
Your obedient servant,
JOHN CAMPBELL.

ELBERT HERRING, Esq.,
*Commissioner Indian Affairs.*

---

LEXINGTON, *September* 5, 1833.

SIR: I enclose to you for the information of the President, a letter just received from the widow of the man who was killed by the regular troops, in their attempt to remove him from the lands possessed by the Creek Indians in the State of Alabama. Owen was a native of Georgia, and of the county in which I reside. His friends are numerous, and very respectable; his father died in the service of the country, and was considered a highly valuable officer in the army commanded by General Floyd, in the expedition against the Creek Indians.

I passed the place of Owen's residence in the month of June last, and understood that he had a very fine crop growing. I suppose that the object of Mrs. Owen's application to the President is to have some compensation made her by the Creek Indians for the loss of that crop. Mrs. Owens is left without property, with a family of children, whom she is unable to provide for, from a chronic disease of the most unfortunate kind. Permit me to request your attention to her case, and if she is entitled to any redress for the injury she has sustained, that it be afforded her through your interference.

Very respectfully, your obedient servant,<br>
GEORGE R. GILMER.

Hon. LEWIS CASS.

---

CHEROKEE AGENCY, Sept. 5, 1833.

SIR: The annuity which you directed me to promise as an inducement to the Indians would have a much happier effect if ordered to be paid on their enrollment. From three to five thousand dollars will be required for this purpose during the present fall and approaching winter.

No treaty need be calculated on from present appearances until the reservees are made to know they are mere tenants, at the will of the General and State Governments, and those who have heretofore enrolled and received a part or full pay for their right here are taught by practice to believe they too will be compelled to comply with their voluntary engagements.

Authority from the department to say the enrolling party shall have a certain proportion of their money for improvements before they embark, in the event there is no treaty, will very much encourage the enrollment of influential men, most of whom cannot get off without some cash to pay their debts.

Be good enough to write me fully on these various subjects at an early period, as the public interest requires that they should be informed without delay.

I have not, owing to a tumor on my leg, been able to ride for several days. I hope, however, to be fit for service, by care and attention, as early as the 10th instant.

The exertions of the dominant party to prevent present enrollments are unequalled by past experience.

I have the honor to be,<br>
Most respectfully,<br>
Your very obedient servant,<br>
BENJ. F. CURREY.

ELBERT HERRING, Esq.,
Commissioner Indian Affairs.

It would be well also for the enrolling party to have assurances that they will be entitled to a representative voice in a treaty, and be at the city during the early part of the winter.

---

CHEROKEE AGENCY, Sept. 6, 1833.

SIR: The enclosed letter was left in this office on yesterday by Mr. Bean, with the request that I would enclose it to you, and accompany it with such remarks as I thought proper

I can only say for Mr. Bean than he is an honest man, and son-in-law to Colonel Starr, who has always supported the measures of the Government in relation to the Cherokees; he has a very numerous family, and is very desirous to get them off to the Arkansas, and Mr. Bean and family with the rest.

If it is believed by the Government that Mr. Bean's claim is good to the reservation I would suggest whether it would not be proper for the Government to pay him for it, so that he may get off with those of the family who are going to the west in the course of the fall or winter.

I have to request that you will favor me with an answer to this letter as soon as convenient.

Very respectfully,
Your obedient servant,
H. MONTGOMERY.

Hon. E. HERRING,
Sup. of Indian Affairs, Washington City.

---

CHEROKEE AGENCY, Sept. 5, 1833.

SIR: Under the 8th section of the treaty of 1817, which says, "to each and every head of an Indian family residing on the east side of the Mississippi river, on the lands that are now or may hereafter be surrendered to the United States, the United States do agree to give a reservation of six hundred and forty acres of land, &c." I entered for a reservation within the limits of the unceded territory in the right of my wife, who is a half breed Cherokee, including my residence thereon. I have continued to reside ever since with my family, complying with the requisition of that article.

Will you be so good as to inform me through the agent whether I can enjoy the same without any further treaty stipulation.

Very respectfully,
Your obedient servant,
JOHN BEAN.

---

WASCISSA, July 6, 1833.

SIR: Indisposition, contracted from my late visit to the Indian towns on the Appalachicola, has prevented my enclosing you before this a final arrangement made with the two remaining Indian bands on said river. My letters for twelve months past have reported to you the obstinacy and indisposition of the chiefs of those towns to treat for a removal on any conditions. Having at a very early period communicated to them the wishes of the Executive of the United States on this subject, exposed the liberality of the Government to them, and explained to them their true interests, I had conceived it most advisable to leave the chiefs to their own reflections, under a conviction that at the proper time, and when convinced that the other Indians generally intended to move, they would readily accede to the propositions I was prepared to make them. A few weeks since I received, through the hands of the acting Governor, a communication signed by the principal chiefs of both the bands, stating their willingness to treat with me if I would revisit their towns; I lost no time in riding to the sub-agent, nearly equidistant from both Econchattimicco and Mulatto King's reserves, and inviting the principal chiefs to meet me there; I found to my disappointment, however, that the chiefs either did not rightfully comprehend the communications which had been made me, with the sanction of their signatures, or were unwilling to yield to the obligation I considered that arrangement had imposed on them.

I found in the course of a consultation or talk that a strong prejudice existed on the mind of Econchattimicco, Mulatto King, and other sub-chiefs, against Blunt, and a very great distrust of the interpreter Richards. It was on this account they stated that they had hitherto declined meeting me by invitations to places where the chiefs and the interpreter were to be present. I mentioned to them that it was a matter of indifference to me, as commissioner, who interpreted, if the Indians were satisfied; and having ascertained that they would listen to propositions, provided they were communicated through interpreters in whom they reposed confidence, I permitted them to nominate the two whose names are affixed to the treaties; the one Jim Walker, a colored man, who resides in Mulatto King's town, and has been long used by him as his interpreter; the other a half breed, grandson of Econchattimicco, and who was for a short time employed by Governor Duval as interpreter at Tallahassee. In the course of a long talk I discovered that the above chiefs were as much indisposed to treat for a removal as ever; that the difficulties of effecting a negotiation with them had increased by delay. They have been exposed, ever since the question was first agitated, to so many disagreeing talks from unauthorized individuals; have been secretly influenced by so many who hoped in the negotiation to profit by the terms concluded on; and have listened to so many contradictory tales of the Creeks and Seminoles, consenting to and again refusing to remove, that they have become distrustful of that event, and without that event they could on no conditions be persuaded to migrate. In addition, they have individually been told that the Creeks had made treaties on more favorable terms, and were now realizing fortunes by the sale of the land the Government had given them.

To reconcile these conflicting opinions by inducing them to yield to any distinct proposition for removal was impossible, so long as there was a doubt in their minds as to the Creeks and Seminoles moving. To leave them without effecting any thing, was only exposing the chiefs Econchattimicco and Mulatto King to the influence of those individuals, and rumors which had already so distracted their minds. I deemed it, therefore, after some reflection, and much consultation with the Indians, that the agreement signed and concluded on was, upon the whole, the most advisable arrangement to be made. It would at once quiet the minds of the Indians, and remove them from the injurious influences to which I have alluded; and it could not but in time fulfil the objects of Government, either by removing the Indians to where they can be protected, or by the voluntary relinquishment on their part of the protection guaranteed to them under the stipulations of previous treaties. I feel assured, however, that they will ultimately negotiate under the last stipulations of their compact, relinquishing their lands, and coming in as parties to the treaty of Payne's landing. There can be no difficulty on this subject, for they are a component part of the Seminole nation, were parties to the treaty of Camp Moultrie; and in the additional article in that treaty, by which reservations were made them on the Appalachicola, the Government reserved the right of ordering them within the Seminole limits whenever it thought proper to do so. The difficulties hitherto thrown in the way of negotiation by Econchattimicco and Mulatto King, were evidently with a view of ascertaining, with certainty, that the Seminoles and Creeks really intended to migrate, and with the belief that delay would secure to them the most favorable terms. They now have, should they migrate, the right of selection between selling the sections to be laid for them and paying their own expenses, or of receiving $3,000 and having their expenses paid. After they have tried the land market, and consulted freely with those who are their best friends, they will find that the latter proposition is the most favorable. I cannot believe they will ultimately (should the Seminoles remove) conclude to remain in the country and come under the laws of Florida; for they have too much understanding not to foresee the evident consequences of such subjection. They want but time, and when convinced of the removal of the Seminoles, we may rest assured they will follow. In the mean while I have suggested, and the suggestion has been well received, that each of the bands send one or two young chiefs with the first migrating party of Seminoles, to examine for themselves the country on which they may be permanently located, if so disposed. I had deemed it best (the present reservations having been but imperfectly located, in consequence of the high waters on the Appalachicola, at the time they were marked and from their lines interrupting the regularity of our Government survey) that the lands awarded them under the new stipulations should conform to those surveys. The quantity, (3) three sections, owing to the sinuosity of the river, will probably be verynearly as much in quantity as is contained in the whole of the reservations. Were the lands brought into market at this time they would not, at the maximum, command more than $5 the acre, or $9,600 for each band, an amount somewhat within what the Government would have been compelled to allow, under stipulations similar to those concluded with Blunt.

I have now closed my agency with the Indians, and, as the service has been one accompanied neither with profit nor pleasure, my only gratification must depend upon the approbation with which those services have met by the Executive of the United States, and yourself as minister of the department to which those services appertain.

Respectfully, your obedient servant,

JAMES GADSDEN.

Hon. Lewis Cass.

---

Talladega County, Alabama,
*Mardisville, September 7, 1833.*

Sir: The enclosed is a communication received but a short time before the mail leaves for Georgia. The bearers were two Eche se-ho-ga Indians. As soon as I could obtain an interpreter they urged me to send the paper on to the department, and stated that their people wished to start to the Chickasaw country before cold weather. I am somewhat acquainted with Major Webb, and have understood he is a man of respectability. I have, however, no doubt but what he is engaged in purchasing Indian reservations.

I am, &c.,

LEONARD TARRANT.

Elbert Herring, Esq.

69‡

ALABAMA, *Creek Nation.*

We the undersigned, chiefs of the Eche-se-ho-ga town and heads of creek families, entitled to reserves under the late treaty made at Washington city, in March 1832, have come together this 3d day of September, in open council, and have agreed to request Judge Tarrant, our agent, to inform our father, the President, that all who are hereunto subscribed of our town, together with some of other towns, heads of Creek families, all of whom are our relations, that we wish to emigrate this fall to the Chickasaw nation; and that we met together this spring past, and appointed a delegation to go to the Chickasaw nation; which delegation has returned, and has obtained the consent of the chiefs of that nation for us to remove there for the present as they are all our family connexions in that nation, and that we are anxious to get together, so that when they emigrate to Arkansaw, then we will go with them; and also to inform our father, the President, we wish to start in sixty days or less, if we can get off; and that we are in debt here, and cannot remove without making some arrangements with our reserves to settle our debts. We wish our father, the President, to suffer us to appoint an agent or attorney of our acquaintance, who is Major John C. Webb, who is known to our agent to be a man of character and of good standing, in whom we have the utmost confidence from long acquaintance, who will be duly and legally authorized by your sanction to act generally every way on our part, in disposing of our lands by legal power of attorney, and by your honor sanctioning this request. Our agent or attorney will be duly authorized to settle all our debts out of the proceeds of our lands, which will go before him, and acknowledge and order him to pay them; and by this arrangement our creditors will consent for us to go without any interruption. Our attorney will make us such advances as we need for our passage, and we wish him to purchase us some horses, to transport our children and baggage, otherwise we wish to provide our own passage, and receive our fifteen dollars before we start, or when we get to Arkansaw, if our father, the President, would prefer to pay it there; but we wish our father, the President, to order us located before we start. But should it not be convenient for us to be located before we start, our attorney will be duly authorized to receive our certificates of location. as he is well acquainted with all our old homes, and can show the locating agent each residence we leave. But if our father, the President, thinks we should be chargeable on the Government more than the provisions of the treaty, we assure him it is not the case; we wish to go there on account of all our relations being there, who emigrated from this nation, and if he chooses to withhold from us our fifteen dollars a head for our passage, our blanket, and rifle, and one year's provisions till we reach Arkansas, he can do so, as our friends have good crops, and will let us have corn low there. We wish to inform our father the sooner we leave here the better for us; therefore, through our agent we wish our father to sanction this request. We appoint Tus-tee-nug-u-chee, a open council, to carry this to our agent, Judge Tarrant. By your attention to this you will confer a favor on your care.

| | Marks. | No. in family. | | Marks. | No. in family. |
|---|---|---|---|---|---|
| Cobicher Harjo, chief, | x | 5 | Opith Harjo, chief, | x | 6 |
| Hillabo Fixico, chief, | x | 6 | Ich hos Eholar, chief, | x | 7 |
| Arbenecher E Marthler, | x | 5 | Tus ke nah, | x | 7 |

| | Marks. | No. in family. | | Marks. | No. in family. |
|---|---|---|---|---|---|
| Soe pa lat ea, | x | 5 | Yer ho cah, (widow,) | x | 3 |
| Tomey Harjo, | x | | Nones holt la bouyer, | x | 4 |
| Oah fus ka micho, | x | 4 | O si a Hollar, | x | 3 |
| Tomey Micho, | x | 2 | Sim olt ler, (widow,) | x | 2 |
| Slath lo Harjo, | x | 4 | Par li ga, do | x | 3 |
| Tomey Fixico, | x | 4 | Tom dach a, | x | 2 |
| Ogellesee Harjo, | x | 2 | Ar bich er Harjo, | x | 3 |
| Chillocco Harjo, | x | 6 | Oe che E Martler, | x | 4 |
| Yelgar Harjo, | x | 9 | As das ho boillee, | x | 3 |
| Echo Ely Harjo, | x | 6 | Hart wili chu, | x | 5 |
| Oc ta tach Ehollar, | x | 2 | Ar yul ka, | x | 5 |
| Imbulatta, | x | 2 | Con chart fixico, | x | 2 |
| Pow us Harjo, | x | 4 | Ka la, | x | 2 |
| Car lo car, | x | 3 | So kar ka, (widow,) | x | 2 |
| No us C Ehollar, | x | 5 | Narch car, do | x | 3 |
| So har ta, (widow,) | x | 6 | Che u see, do | x | 3 |
| U faw la Harjo, | x | 9 | Ar tay lee, | x | 1 |
| War sueta, | x | 3 | O nup sicher, | x | 1 |
| Tus ta nug u chee, | x | 3 | My E par, | x | 1 |
| Tomey Ehollar | x | 3 | Oak fus ka Harjo, | x | 1 |
| Tuck ma liga, (widow,) | x | 6 | Coosa Harjo, | x | 2 |
| Ter ne a, do | x | 5 | Salley Go a, | x | 2 |
| I am a, do | x | 3 | Slab e cher, | x | 1 |
| E sum gah do | x | 2 | War har, | x | 7 |
| Lar tu gu, do | x | 7 | So har ta, | x | 6 |
| Tim nea, do | x | 3 | Hoo loo, | x | 3 |
| Lar boo day, do | x | 5 | Tus E ke ah Harjo, | x | 1 |
| Me ton o la, do | x | 2 | Mut ti li ga, | x | 1 |
| S Parsey E Martler, | x | 3 | Ben Harjo, | x | 2 |
| Ar fafi car, | x | 2 | O we ghack ee, | x | 2 |

**Aggregate,** 236

Signed in presence of us

JOHN P. MOORE, *Interpreter.*
JAMES MOORE, his x mark, *Interpreter.*

Test: FRANKLIN McLEMORE,
PETER DUDLEY.

---

RUSSEL COUNTY, ALABAMA, NEAR COLUMBUS,
*September 8, 1833.*

We beg permission to call your immediate and earnest attention to a subject of deep interest to us, and to many other persons who are in our situation; but we shall content ourselves with a short and plain statement of our own cases. We respectively have farms on the west side of the Chattahoochee river, and within the limits of the Creek nation. We obtained possession by the free and voluntary consent of *all* the Indians who were interested; we have held, and yet hold possession in the same way, not *one* of the Indians, so far as we know or believe, being dissatisfied; we have built our own houses, made extensive clearings, and now have valuable crops both of corn and cotton ready to gather.

In none of the previous orders of the Government against intruders have we been included, or attempted to be molested; but we are just now *informed* that new orders have been given by your department to the marshal of Alabama, for the removal of *all* settlers upon the Creek lands, and that those orders are to be immediately executed.

We have never believed our possession to be disapprobated either by the Indians or the General Government; and certainly it has not been to the *injury* of either, for the improved value of the property will be an ample compensation to its ultimate owner for the use we have made of it.

One of us has cleared every foot of the land he cultivates, and pays this year nearly one dollar per acre rent for the privilege; two others have cleared theirs with the exception of a small quantity which they rented from the Indians in a large field, at an extravagant rate, a great part of which field is uncultivated by the Indians this year; and the fourth pays such rent as has been satisfactory to the owner for the two last years, and of which he does not now complain. The loss and inconvenience which must be sustained by us, in the event of such orders being so enforced, will be at once obvious to you, for our cotton crops cannot possibly be gathered and removed for some time to come. If *any one* Indian complains that he has not received a sufficient compensation for the use of his field, we are perfectly willing to pay respectively such additional sum as may be considered just and fair by any discreet agent of the Government. We therefore appeal to your sense of justice, and earnestly request that your orders to the marshal may be so modified as to secure justice to each party, and to allow us time peaceably to save and gather our crops, and then to remove our hands and property, if such should be the pleasure of the Government.

We are, sir, respectfully,
Your obedient servants,
EDW. CURRY,
A. ABERCROMBIE,
JAMES WADSWORTH,
J. G. WORSHAM.

To the Hon LEWIS CASS,
    *Secretary of War.*

---

DISTRICT ATTORNEY'S OFFICE, MOBILE, ALABAMA,
*September* 8, 1833.

SIR: I received by this morning's mail your letter of the 26th ultimo, stating that you were directed by the President to request me to institute prosecutions under the act of Congress of the 3d March, 1807, against all persons subjecting themselves to its penalties by intruding upon the lands ceded to the United States under the treaty with the Creek Indians of March 24th, 1832; also enclosing a copy of the opinion of the Attorney General on this subject, together with a copy of the letter of instructions you addressed to the marshal of this district for his direction and government; and directing me to take the necessary arrangements to institute prosecutions against all persons whose names may be reported to me by the marshal. In reply thereto, permit me to state that I will take, at the earliest period, the necessary measures to carry *into effect* (I trust) those instructions. The marshal and his deputies are, however, temporarily absent from this city in the discharge of their duties, and some little time may elapse before I shall be placed in possession of such information as may enable me to institute such proceedings as may lead to the conviction of the intruders upon the lands above mentioned.

I have the honor to be, very respectfully,
Your obedient servant,
JNO. ELLIOTT.

Hon. LEWIS CASS,
    *Secretary of War.*

———

CLINTON, *September 9, 1833.*

DEAR SIR: Your letter of the 20th ultimo was received to-day. I am required to withhold from public sale such lands as Colonel Martin and Mr. Trahern may designate as reservations, or orphan claims, under the treaty with the Choctaw Indians.

It has been suggested that probably the disposition contemplated by the instructions, of the orphans' lands, is not the best for them. Many of this class are yet minors, and will be so *five years* hence. If the land is reserved in the name of *each orphan*, and subject to his disposal alone, will it not be necessary for them to have guardians, especially after the expiration of five years, when these lands will be subject to taxation? The President is authorized by the treaty to sell them if he deems it best to their advantage. Now what I would suggest is, that they be disposed of in the same manner that the "Choctaw school lands" are in this district. Let them be offered at public sale, and if not sold, be subject to private sale as other lands, keeping a separate account and deposite of the same. This will surely be to the advantage of the orphans, as there scarcely ever will be a time when the lands are in greater demand than at this moment.

I only suggest the above for the consideration of the President, believing that it would, if adopted, save the Government much trouble, and be of singular advantage to the orphans in a pecuniary point of view. I expect the sales will be very fully attended and extensive. Great preparations are making to attend, and the speculators are completely disappointed.

I am now laboring under a high fever; was taken last night. It was my intention to leave this tomorrow, but will be detained a few days longer under the operation of medicine. You will in future address all communications for Mr. Sterling and myself to "Chocchuma," care of postmaster at Rankin, Holmes county, Mississippi. We will have to employ an express to carry them from thence to the office.

I am, respectfully,
Your obedient servant,
SAMUEL GWIN.

ELIJAH HAYWARD, Esq.,
    *Commissioner General Land Office.*

Mr. Fitz has not yet furnished me with the field notes of any of the townships, and is uncertain when he can.

———

GENERAL LAND OFFICE, *September 10, 1833.*

SIR: I have the honor to advise you that the surveyor of public lands in Alabama has transmitted to this office a connected plat of the surveys of the country recently acquired from the Creek Indians; also diagrams of those portions of the Coosa and Tallapoosa districts which can be immediately proclaimed for sale, should the President deem it now expedient to issue his proclamation.

The maps are herewith submitted for your inspection, with a request that you will have the goodness to cause them to be returned.

With great consideration,<br>
Your obedient servant,<br>
JNO. M. MOORE,<br>
Acting Commissioner.

Hon. Lewis Cass,
    *Secretary of War.*

---

Washington City, September 10, 1833.

Sir: I have the honor of enclosing to you a copy of the report made to the commissioners by Kendall Lewis and Frederick Sangrain, who were appointed to value and appraise certain inprovements of the Creek Indians who would be compelled to remove, in conformity with the provisions of the treaties concluded between that tribe and the United States at Fort Gibson, on the 14th February, 1833. I also enclose the report of Captain Nathan Boone, of his *field notes* of a survey of the boundary line between the Creek and Cherokee Indians, as settled by their late treaties with the United States, with a map of the survey.

As the running of the "boundary line between the Creeks and Cherokees," and the "valuation of the Creek improvements," were made under the directions of the Commissioners of Indian Affairs, in accordance with the stipulations of the treaties of 14th February, 1833, I have been instructed to lay the reports before you, in order that they might be brought, with the *proceedings in council,* before the President and Senate, should you deem it necessary, in presenting the treaties for confirmation.

I have the honor to be,<br>
Very respectfully,<br>
Your obedient servant,<br>
S. C. STAMBAUGH,<br>
Secretary to Commissioners Indian Affairs.

---

Valuation on Canadian.

Daniel Kennard—
    1 dwelling-house, 16 feet square, 20 dollars; 1 do. 12 do.,
      11 dollars; 114 rails, 1 dollar 14 cents, -   -   - $32 14

David Miller—
    1 dwelling-house, 16 feet square, 15 dollars; 1 do. 12 do.,
      11 dollars, -   -   -   -   -   -   26 00

ohn Wynn—
    1 dwelling-house, 25 dollars; 1 corn crib, 8 dollars; 1 kitchen,
      12 dollars; 2,300 rails, 23 dollars; 6 acres cleared land,
      18 dollars, -   -   -   -   -   -   86 00

Mohaio Po Chu—
    1 dwelling-house, -   -   -   -   -   -   6 00

John Herod—
    1 dwelling house, 22 dollars; 6 acres cleared land, 18 dollars;
      2,630 rails, 26 dollars 30 cents, -   -   -   -   66 30

Samuel Herod—
    2 acres cleared land, 6 dollars; 900 rails, 9 dollars, -   - 15 00

Talso Hargo—
 1 dwelling-house, 15 dollars; 1 do., 10 dollars; 2 acres cleared
  land, 6 dollars; 550 rails, 5 dollars 50 cents, - - $36 50
Kendall Lewis—
 1 dwelling-house, 76 dollars; 1 store do., cellar, passage and
  shed, 140 dollars; 1 corn crib, 6 dollars; 1 hen-house, 6
  dollars; kitchen, 7 dollars 50 cents; 4 acres cleared land,
  12 dollars; 2,648 rails, 26 dollars 48 cents; 54 peach trees,
  20 dollars 25 cents, - - - - - 294 23

*Powis Hargo's town.*

Powis Hargo—
 2 dwelling houses, with passage, 33 dollars; 2,893 rails, 28
  dollars 93 cents; 6 acres cleared land, 18 dollars; 1 corn
  crib, 5 dollars; 1 hen-house, 2 dollars, - - - 86 93
Hoppoy Hargo—
 1 house, 12 dollars; 1½ acres cleared land, 4 dollars 50 cents;
  265 rails, 2 dollars 65 cents, - - - - 19 15
Unessa Tus Tus Nugee—
 1 house, 5 dollars; 400 rails, 4 dollars; 1 acre cleared land,
  3 dollars, - - - - - - 12 00
Echebe—
 1 house, 13 dollars; 1 hen-house, 3 dollars; 1,500 rails, 15 dollars; 4 acres cleared land, 12 dollars; - - - 43 00
Eueha Fixeco—
 1 house, 10 dollars; 1 corn crib, 3 dollars; 1,300 rails, 13
  dollars; 2 acres cleared land, 6 dollars, - - 32 00
Mad Fish—
 1 house, 15 dollars; corn crib, 6 dollars 50 cents; 5 acres
  cleared land, 15 dollars; 3,200 rails, 32 dollars; 1 house
  (belonging to his mother), ten dollars; - - 78 50
Mad Beaver—
 1 house, 11 dollars; 1 corn crib, 3 dollars; 2 acres cleared land,
  6 dollars; 500 rails, 5 dollars, - - - 25 00
Mistaharke—
 1 house, 14 dollars; 1 crib, 6 dollars; 2 acres cleared land,
  6 dollars; 300 rails, 3 dollars, - - - 29 00
Tomma Hargo—
 1 house, 12 dollars; 1 crib, 3 dollars; 840 rails, 8 dollars 40
  cents; 1½ acres cleared land, 4 dollars 50 cents, - 27 90
Hospetack Hargo—
 1 house, 15 dollars; corn crib, 6 dollars; 1,900 rails, 19 dollars;
  5 acres cleared land, 15 dollars, - - - 55 00
Attoc Kee—
 700 rails, 7 dollars; 1½ acres cleared land, 4 dollars 50 cents, 11 50
Tom ma E ha o ba—
 1 house, 16 dollars; 2 acres cleared land, 6 dollars, - 22 00
Fi I ga—
 1 house, 13 dollars; 2 acres clearing, 6 dollars, - - 19 00
Chilo Kee—
 1 house, 15 dollars; 1 do., 7 dollars; 1 crib, 7 dollars; 2800
  rails, 28 dollars; 4 acres clearing, 12 dollars, - - 69 00
Otalka Fixeco—
 2 acres clearing, 6 dollars; 1600 rails, 16 dollars, - 22 00

Enola—
  3 acres clearing, 9 dollars; 474 rails, 4 dollars 74 cents; 1
    house, eight dollars,    -    -    -    -    $21 74
Wa Ha Cholk Hago—
  1 house, 12 dollars; 2 acres clearing, 6 dollars; 1,200 rails $12,    30 00
Fush Hatchchee u Holee—
  1 house, 15 dollars; 1 do, 8 dollars; 1 crib, 4 dollars; 1,500
    rails, 15 dollars; 5 acres clearing, 15 dollars,    -    -    57 00
Leda—
  1 house, 10 dollars; 1 crib, 5 dollars,    -    -    -    15 00
Catch Tawee—
  1 house, 18 dollars; 1 acre clearing, 3 dollars; 500 rails, $5,    26 00
Na Na O Mate—
  1 house, 9 dollars 50 cents; corn crib, 3 dollars 50 cents; 2,410
    rails, 24 dollars 10 cents; 6 acres clearing, 18 dollars,    -    55 10
olla O Ha, (Arkansas)—
  3 acres clearing, 9 dollars; 500 rails, 5 dollars,    -    -    14 00

### *Arkansas.*

Toma Yoco—
  1 camp and corn crib, 3 dollars; 500 rails, 5 dollars; 1½ acres
    clearing, 4 dollars 50 cents,    -    -    -    -    12 50
Thlee I Ke—
  1 house, 12 dollars; 1 corn crib, 2 dollars; 1,860 rails, 18 dol-
    lars 60 cents; 6 acres clearing, 18 dollars,    -    -    50 60
Letif Hargo—
  1 house, 14 dollars; corn crib, 12 dollars; 2,100 rails, 21 dol-
    lars; 7 acres clearing, 21 dollars,    -    -    -    68 00
Tomma Gogee—
  1 house, 16 dollars; 1 corn crib, 4 dollars; 2,410 rails, 24 dol-
    lars 10 cents; 6 acres clearing, 18 dollars; 14 peach trees,
    3 dollars 75 cents,    -    -    -    -    -    65 85
Miica—
  1 house, 8 dollars; 1,136 rails, 11 dollars 36 cents; 2 acres
    clearing, 6 dollars,    -    -    -    -    -    25 36
Cite Kichee—
  1 house, 8 dollars; corn crib, 5 dollars; rails 12 dollars; 3½
    acres clearing, 10 dollars 50 cents,    -    -    -    35 50
O I Hatca—
  1 house, 8 dollars; 1 corn crib, 5 dollars; 2 acres clearing, 6
    dollars; rails 11 dollars,    -    -    -    -    30 00
Bear Head—
  1 house, 11 dollars; 1 crib, 4 dollars 50 cents; rails 10 dollars;
    1 acre clearing, 3 dollars,    -    -    -    -    28 50
Deer Liver—
  1 house,    -    -    -    -    -    -    -    12 00
To-lo-la Hoca—
  1 house, 7 dollars; 1 crib, 5 dollars; hen house, 2 dollars;
    1½ acres clearing, 4 dollars 50 cents,    -    -    -    18 50
Assenapa Harjo—
  1 house, 7 dollars; 1 corn crib, 5 dollars,    -    -    12 00
Sima—
  1 house, 14 dollars; 1 do., 6 dollars; 1 do., 2 dollars; 1½ acres

clearing 4 dollars 50 cents; rails 3 dollars 60 cents; 23 peach
trees, 8 dollars 62½ cents, - - - - $38 72
Hopey Hargo—
   1 eamp, 2 dollars; corn crib, 3 dollars; rails, 2 dollars; 1 acre
   clearing, 3 dollars, - - - - - 10 00
Yallo Harjo—
   1 house, 10 dollars; 1 do., 8 dollars; 1 crib, 4 dollars; 1 do.,
   2 dollars; 10 peach trees, 3 dollars 75 cents; rails, 15 dollars 20 cents; 2½ acres clearing, 7 dollars 50 cents, - 50 45
Gonna—
   I house, 12 dollars; 1 do., 10 dollars; 25 peach trees, 9 dollars 37½ cents; rails, 3 dollars 61 cents; 3 acres clearing,
   9 dollars - - - - - - - 43 98½
Missa—
   1 house, 11 dollars; 2 acres clearing, 6 dollars; rails, $3 50 cents, 20 50
Tus-kee-gee Harjo—
   House, 8 dollars; 2 do., 7 dollars; rails, 10 dollars 98 cents;
   1½ acres clearing, 4 dollars 50 cents, - - - 30 48
Aulis Yo-ho-lo—
   1 house, 13 dollars; 1 crib, 3 dollars; 4 peach-trees, 1 dollar
   50 cents; rails, 8 dollars; 2½ acres clearing, 7 dollars 50 cents, 33 00
Sinta Likee—
   1½ acres clearing, 4 dollars 50 cents; rails, 8 dollars, - 12 50
Sac Kee—
   1 house, 9 dollars; 1½ acres clearing, 4 dollars 50 cents; 13
   peach-trees, 4 dollars 87½ cents; rails, 8 dollars, - - 26 37½
Hilibue E Mathla—
   1 house, 20 dollars; 2½ acres clearing, 7 dollars 50 cents;
   6 peach-trees, 2 dollars 25 cents; rails, 4 dollars, - 33 75
Halph Harjo—
   1 house 15 dollars; 1 crib, 5 dollars; 4 acres clearing, 12 dollars; rails, 9 dollars; 18 peach trees, 6 dollars 75 cents, - 47 75
Opia Meco—
   1 house, 8 dollars; 1 do., 4 dollars; one acre clearing, 3 dollars;
   rails, 2 dollars 81 cents; 10 peach-trees, 3 dollars 75 cents, 21 56
Simmon Tallee—
   1 house, 8 dollars; 2 do., 11 dollars; 70 peach trees, 26 dol.
   25 cents; rails, 10 dollars; 3 acres clearing, 9 dollars, - 64 25
Suctala Lottigo (woman)—
   2 houses, 16 dollars; 1 corn crib, 2 dollars; rails, 3 dollars;
   1 acre clearing, 3 dollars, - - - - 24 00
Jonna (woman)—
   1 house, - - - - - - - - 10 00
Lasla—
   1 house, 10 dollars; rails, 2 dollars, 1 acre clearing 3 dollars 15 00
Gipa—
   1 house, 7 dollars 50 cents; 2 acres clearing, 6 dollars; rails,
   8 dollars - - - - - - - 21 50
Okee Las E Mathla—
   1 house, 11 dollars; 1 corn crib, 8 dollars, - - 19 00
Little Mad Tiger—
   1 house, - - - - - - - 10 00

Dina—

    1 house, 10 dollars; 1 crib, 3 dollars; rails, 9 dollars; 1 acre clearing, 3 dollars,  -   -   -   -   - $25 00

Talle Chick Harjo—

    1 house, 7 dollars; 1 crib, 5 dollars; 1 acre clearing, 3 dollars; rails, 5 dollars,  -  -  -  -  - 20 00

Temmisse—

    1 house, 8 dollars; 2 acres clearing, 6 dollars; 10 peach trees, 3 dollars 25 cents; rails, 10 dollars,  -  - 27 25

  Town, fields, and fence, belonging to the following:

Ispoic, Tocalla, Mynialee, Estercharco—

    3½ acres clearing, 10 dollars 50 cents; 1,000 rails, 10 dollars 20 50

Mister Blake—

    1 house, 6 dollars; 1 acre clearing, 3 dollars; rails, 4 dollars 50 cents,  -  -  -  -  - 13 50

Satkee—

    Rails, 7 dollars; 1½ acres clearing, 4 dollars 50 cents; 5 peach trees, 1 dollar 87½ cents, -  -  -  - 13 37½

Ucettia Youla—

    1 house, 9 dollars; 1 do. 6 dollars,  -  -  - 15 00

Holock Harjo—

    1 house, 8 dollars; rails, 6 dollars 40 cents; 1 acre clearing, 3 dollars, -  -  -  -  -  - 17 40

Leda—

    1 house, 8 dollars; rails, 2 dollars 40 cents; 3 peach trees, 1 dollar 12½ cents; ¼ acre clearing, 1 dollar 50 cents,  - 13 02½

Cussela Harjo—

    1 house, 14 dollars; rails, 5 dollars 60 cents; 1½ acres clearing, 4 dollars 50 cents; 8 peach trees, 3 dollars,  -  - 27 10

Fos Harjo—

    1 house, 7 dollars; 2 acres clearing, 6 dollars,  -  - 13 00

*On Verdigris.*

Ben Perryman—

    2 houses, 22 dollars; 1 corn crib, 7 dollars; 1 house, (daughter's,) 9 dollars; 11 acres clearing, 33 dollars; 1 do. and crib, 20 dollars; 35 peach trees, 13 dollars 12½ cents; rails, 37 dollars; 200 rails and 1 house on Grand river, 17 dollars, 158 12½

Tomma—

    1 house,  -  -  -  -  -  -  - 9 00

Dicky—

    2 acres clearing,  -  -  -  -  -  - 6 00

Fox—

    Rails, 1 dollar 50 cents; 1½ acres clearing, 4 dollars 50 cents, 6 00

Hillebe Tustenuga—

    1 house, 18 dollars; 2 do. 18 dollars; 3 cribs, 7 dollars; 9½ acres clearing, 28 dollars 50 cents; 17 peach trees, 6 dollars 37 cents; 3,800 rails, 38 dollars; 1 milk-house, 2 dollars, 117 87½

Deer Foot—

    1 house, with shed, 8 dollars; rails, 1 dollar,  -  - 9 00

E Pat-o-he—

    1 house, 5 dollars; 1 crib, 3 dollars; rails, 4 dollars,  - 12 00

Hitch Hatch Harjo—

    1 house, 8 dollars; rails, 15 dollars; 2 acres clearing, 6 dollars, 29 00

Suc Hago—
    1 house,  -   -   -   -   -   -   -    $6 00
Lee Hee Chee—
    1 house, 6 dollars; 1 crib, 2 dollars 50 cents; 1 shed, 1 dollar;
      rails, 7 dollars; 2 acres clearing, 6 dollars,   -   -   22 50
Hopiac Harjo Chopco—
    1 house, 4 dollars; 1 crib, 2 dollars; rails, 2 dollars    -   8 00
James Hardrage—
    Rails, 41 dollars 20 cents; 10½ acres clearing, 31 dollars 50
      cents; 1 house, 10 dollars; 1 do. with shed, 10 dollars;
      1 do. 8 dollars; 1 do. 6 dollars; 1 do. 5 dollars; 3 corn
      cribs, 5 dollars; 1 crib, 4 dollars 50 cents; 1 house, 15
      dollars; 2 kitchens, 10 dollars; 3 cribs, 8 dollars; 91 peach
      trees, 34 dollars 12½ cents; house and rails, on Grand river,
      25 dollars,   -   -   -   -   -   - 213 32½
Benjamin Hawkins—
    1 double house, floored, hewed, &c., 150 dollars; 1 kitchen,
      8 dollars; 1 smoke-house, 7 dollars; 2 houses, 20 dollars;
      1 house, 8 dollars; 2 do. 8 dollars; 1 corn crib, 8 dollars;
      1 stable, 6 dollars; rails, 22 dollars 50 cents; 3 acres clear-
      ing, 9 dollars; 300 square logs for mill, 150 dollars; 100
      round do. do. 25 dollars,  -   -   -   -   - 421 50
Polly Hardrage—
    1 house, 13 dollars; 1 do. 9 dollars; 1 do. 8 dollars; 1 crib,
      3 dollars; 2 acres clearing, 6 dollars; 1 do. 1 dollar; rails,
      16 dollars,  -   -   -   -   -   - 56 00

### Arkansas.

Cormathlee Chu—
    1 house, 8 dollars; 1 do. 15 dollars; rails, 1 dollar 50 cents, 24 50
Bushahead—
    3 acres cleared land, 9 dollars; 800 rails, 8 dollars,  -   - 17 00
Susanna McIntosh—
    1 house, 30 dollars; 1 do. 25 dollars; 1 do. 8 dollars; smoke-
      house, 4 dollars; 1 house, 20 dollars; 1 do. 15 dollars;
      1 corn crib, 8 dollars; 1 house, 20 dollars; 1 do. 15 dollars;
      1 do. 4 dollars; 1 do. 8 dollars; 1 do. 9 dollars; 20 acres
      cleared land, 60 dollars; 20,800 rails, 28 dollars,   - 254 00

    Whole amount,   -   -   -   -   $ 3,801 58½

    The above valuation of the improvements of the Creek Indians east of
the present boundary line between them and the Cherokees west, assigned
by their treaty with the United States, February 14th, 1833, and according
to the provision of said treaty, made by Kendall Lewis, of the Creek nation,
and Frederick Sangrain, a citizen of the United States, appointed by the
Commissioners of Indian Affairs for that purpose.

### Certificates.

    We hereby certify upon our honor, that, according to our best belief, the
above valuation of the Creek improvements is just and equitable.
                                   K. LEWIS.
                                   F. SANGRAIN.
                                   *April* 17, 1833.

I hereby certify, that I accompanied the persons above appointed to appraise the Creek improvements; and that, in my opinion, they have made an honest and judicious valuation of them.

J. F. SCHERMERHORN,<br>
Indian Commissioner west

A true copy.
    S. C. STAMBAUGH,
        Sec'y Commissioners.

---

CHOCTAW AGENCY, September 11, 1833.

SIR: I have just returned from the lower district, and find here Mr. Martin, the agent selected to locate the land claims under the late treaty with the Choctaws. Mr. Martin has shown me his instructions, in which he is directed to apply to me and Colonel Ward for a copy of the register of those entitled to land under the cultivation section. The register in the possession of Colonel Ward is in part destroyed. I acted as an agent in taking the census and examining the fields in Mushulatubbee's district, which was returned to the War Office. Before Mr. Martin can act, he will have to be furnished with a copy of those entitled to land, as will appear by the books returned by my brother, F. W. Armstrong, and also a list of those who have relinquished their land to the Government on which payment in part was made west Mississippi last winter. The books will show the locality of the land, and enable the agent to discharge his duty. The lands are advertised for sale, and knowing that not a moment is to be lost, I have taken the liberty of addressing you on the subject.

Respectfully,<br>
Your obedient servant,<br>
WM. ARMSTRONG,<br>
Sup't Choctaw Removal.

Hon. LEWIS CASS,
    Secretary of War.

---

CHOCTAW AGENCY, September 11, 1833.

SIR: I am at this place in discharge of the duties as agent for locating the reservations made at the treaty at Dancing Rabbit Creek, and have made application for copies of the registers of said reserves (as per instructions of the War Department) preparatory to locating the same.

But I am much disappointed in not being able to procure such copies and information as seems to have been anticipated by the department; Colonel Ward says there are no entire and perfect copies of the registers of reservations retained here, and advises me to apply to the department, &c.

I shall procure such papers here as may enable me to proceed in the locating, but I am certain the work cannot be done in a complete and perfect manner unless I am furnished with a more full register, as the one here is incomplete.

I wrote the department requiring further instructions, on the 9th August; I am also desirous to hear from the department on the several interrogatories therein mentioned.

I am, very respectfully,<br>
Your obedient servant,

The Hon. LEWIS CASS,
    Secretary of War, Washington City.
GEO. W. MARTIN.

N. B. The register here has been torn, and is extremely imperfect, as I am informed and believe.

Fort Mitchell, Ala., *September* 11, 1833.

Sir: I presume you hear much about the buying of Indian reserves; fair contracts; the killing of Owen, &c. Permit me, sir, to inform you on these subjects. Many, from motives of speculation, have bought Indian reserves fraudulently in this way; take their bonds for titles; pay them ten or twenty dollars in something they do not want, and take their receipts for five times the amount. If the land be of no value they are not bound to take it, but if it is they are bound to let them have it. I know some of their reserves that I am authorized to give two thousand dollars for. Not knowing the value of land, the Indians have been persuaded to sell for five hundred dollars, taking their pay in nothing, or in that which is of no value to them. I am extremely anxious for them to sell to the Government, even should they get but half price. And I have no doubt but the Indians will treat, and shortly, too, if the Government will pursue the course she has taken, which is to remove intruders; but if it should not be left with the Indians to say who are intruders, their lives are in danger, should they do so. At this time they (intruders and speculators) are raising volunteers to resist our Government force. They make much noise about killing Owen; he ought to have been killed. It has also given the Indians great confidence in the General Government. It is nothing but nullification. I shall use my best efforts to arrange a treaty before Congress meets, unless they are located, which I hope will not be done.

I have the honor, &c.,
LUTHER BLAKE.

Hon. Elbert Herring,
*Washington City.*

---

Choctaw Agency, *September* 11, 1833.

Sir: I feel it my duty to say to you that I am not yet in possession of the necessary papers and information as will enable me to locate the Indian reserves made at Dancing Rabbit Creek.

When I am furnished with such necessary requisites, I will lose no time in doing what devolves on me in this matter. I have, as yet, neither *maps*, *full instructions*, nor, what is of the utmost importance, the *register* made by Major Armstrong, or the agent at this place, nor can I procure one short of Washington City. This is entirely important for me to have before I can possibly make the locations alluded to in the treaty.

I am, very respectfully,
Your obedient servant,
GEO. W. MARTIN.

Gen. Andrew Jackson,
*President U. S., Washington City.*

---

St. Louis, *September* 11, 1833.

Dear Sir: Mr. Sprague returning to Washington affords me a favorable opportunity of writing you a few lines concerning the land belonging to the half breed Sac and Fox Indians.

General Clark, in giving instructions to the surveyor (Mr. Sprigg) for surveying the land, directed him to lay out one mile square at the foot of the Rapids des Moines, on the Mississippi; also a mile square at the head of the same rapids, the former intended for a town, and the latter is claimed under a *pretended* or unconfirmed Spanish grant.

This situation is an important spot, and the right of title had best be de-termined on before the division of the land takes place. Permit me, there-fore, to solicit your friendly influence to have the United States commission-ers, *now sitting here*, to act on that claim; and should they not confirm the title to the present claimants, for it to be reserved as a town site, and laid off in lots, as I presume the *lower town will be.* In low water the steam-boats cannot pass that rapid, and are compelled to unload at those two places, which makes those situations more valuable than any other part of the reservation—distance fifteen miles.

It is remarkable how slow the preparatory steps are for making the di-vision of that land, and where the fault lays I cannot find out; no public no-tice has yet been given for the claimants to prove their right, which cer-tainly is important before the division takes place; and, in this particular, I beg leave to refer you to the Sac and Fox chiefs' letter sent to the honora-ble John H. Eaton, Secretary of War, dated 30th July, 1829, and witnessed by their agent, Thomas Forsyth, esq.

I have talked with many of the claimants respecting the division of that land; they agreed that my letter to you, dated 29th October, 1829, contained the best plan for an equitable division.

A petition will be sent to the next Congress praying that a title in fee may be given them to their land; may we not hope for your powerful influ-ence to obtain this and some other small requisitions therein prayed for, for want of a title; it will prevent permanent and useful residenters.

I am, sir,<br>
Very respectfully,<br>
Your humble servant,<br>
JNO. W. JOHNSON.

Hon. Lewis Cass, *Secretary of War.*
N. B. Please to write me on receipt of this.

---

General Land Office, September 11, 1833.

Sir: In reply to an inquiry from this office upon the subject, you advised this office under date of the 9th of June last, that the agent for the Choctaws had been directed to obtain the opinion of the Choctaw chiefs, as to the cor-rectness of the line between them and the Chickasaws as established by the treaty of 1830; and I now have to request that you will inform me whether any information has been received by you upon that subject since the date of that letter, as I have this day received a letter from the Surveyor General, stating that it is very important that this line should be defined as soon as practicable.

With great respect, sir,<br>
Your obedient servant,<br>
JOHN M. MOORE,<br>
Acting Commissioner.

Hon. Elbert Herring,
    *Commissioner of Indian Affairs.*

---

Choctaw Agency, September 14, 1833.

Sir: I have the honor to acknowledge the receipt of yours of the 30th August last, requesting me to act in valuing the improvements and other property belonging to the board of American missions within the Choctaw purchase. I will endeavor to perform this duty as early as practicable, and report as directed. The several missionary stations are located in the three districts of the nation, at some distance apart. I shall, however, notify Mr. Kingsbury, who, I understand, is the agent for the board, and proceed immediately.

I took the liberty of writing to the Secretary of War by last mail, in reference to what would be proper to furnish Mr. Martin with (the agent) for locating the land under the treaty. This I done, because in Mr. Martin's instructions he had been directed to call on me with Col. Ward for a register, &c. I was one of the agents who took the census and surveyed the fields under the cultivation section in the Choctaw nation, which was returned by my brother, F. W. Armstrong, to the War Department. A copy of those who were entitled to land by cultivation will have to be furnished Mr. Martin, which copy will show the locality and quantity of land; also, a copy of those who relinquished their lands to the United States; as also a copy of those who registered to remain five years, and become citizens. The register of those entitled to land, left by F. W. Armstrong with Col. Ward, was left exposed, and, indeed, a leaf or two lost. Mr. Martin took it with him to Chocchuma, and I presume will act as far he can until he receives other instructions.

Seeing the lands advertised for sale, and the time so short for Mr. Martin to make return in, must be my apology for addressing you at all on the subject. The citizens of this State are deeply interested in the proper location of these claims. I hope, however, I have been anticipated, and that the copies as above have been, before this, sent to Mr. Martin.

Respectfully,
Your obedient servant,
WM. ARMSTRONG,
*Sup't Choctaw Removal.*

To ELBERT HERRING, Esq.,
*Commissioner, &c., Washington.*

---

CHOCCHUMA, MI., *September* 15, 1833.

SIR: I received on the 8th instant, and *not till that time,* a communication from D. Kurtz, esq., Acting Commissioner, &c., dated the 8th of August last, advising me that "the President of the United States has directed that the lands ceded to the United States by the treaty of Dancing Rabbit Creek shall be offered at public sale on the third Monday in October next; that it is necessary the location of the reservations provided for in that treaty should be completed and entered in the proper land office prior to that date;" and, he adds, "you are therefore directed to proceed without delay to execute this duty." Immediately on the receipt of this communication, I proceeded to the old agency, a distance of one hundred and twenty miles from my residence, to obtain from Col. Ward or William Armstrong, esq., copies of the register of the different "classes of reservees in the three districts," as directed in your instructions of the 26th June last. The result of my application enabled me only to procure a partial and very defective register, of which you have been advised by my communication of the 11th instant.

i

You promised in your instructions of the 26th of June last, to forward, to the care of ₁General Coffee, copies of the township maps of survey which are deemed necessary to the better discharge of my duty. I have again to repeat that I am not yet furnished, notwithstanding the most urgent request which I have made by letter both to the registers and surveyor general. I, however, still hope a short time will, from some quarter, put me in possession of them. The want of these maps, the defect in the register just referred to, although great barriers to the quick and correct discharge of the duties assigned me, still I have not deemed them of sufficient magnitude to delay my entering immediately on the locations of the claims referred to in the treaty and your instructions. I therefore, on the 14th instant, deemed it proper to open my office for the reception of applications to locate reservations, and have proceeded accordingly. The time is so limited between this and the public sale, that it will be impossible for me to go around and locate *on the ground* all the reservations provided for under the treaty, as seem to be contemplated by your instructions of the 26th June last.

Upon reference to your instructions, the President's proclamation, offering the lands for sale, and the treaty, it is clearly the object of all that the officer charged with the settlement and location of the different reservations, improvement claims, and five years' stay claims, allowed under the treaty, shall so manage as at least to exclude from sale all such claims justly entitled under the treaty; otherwise great injustice would result to the honest claimant, and much inconvenience possibly to the Government: as, in such a contingency, the result would be, petitions to Congress for redress, which could not be denied upon an honest claim; which might require other provisions to be hereafter made less advantageous to the Government. With this view of the subject, and in the absence of further instructions from your department, I find myself much embarrassed as to the proper course for me to pursue. The time of the public sale is so near at hand that it will be impossible for me to go on the *ground* and make the locations of all the claims allowed under the treaty, previous to the day of sale, and embraced under your instructions. I must then either proceed to locate on the ground as many of the claims as I can previous to the public sale, and register them as instructed, leaving the balance unattended to and liable to be offered at public sale, or adopt such other course as may seem best calculated to effect what I conceive to be the spirit and object of your instructions, thereby excluding from sale all reservations allowed under the treaty, and so manage the business that I can, consistently with the rights of the Indians and the obligations of the Government, hereafter proceed to locate on the ground all such claims. Some judicious course, like this, will enable the Government to exclude from sale, just at hand, the lands of all just claimants under the treaty; and will enable me hereafter, when locating on the ground, to correct and cause to be entered on the township maps, as contemplated by your instructions and the President's proclamation; the reservations of all just claimants, and, at the same time, rejecting all such claimants as may have claimed lands not intended to be embraced and granted to them by the treaty.

I have condensed the instructions which I have received from the War Department and the General Land Office in the form of a circular, for the benefit of those interested, a copy of which I herewith enclose.

I have the honor to be, &c.,

GEO. W. MARTIN, *Agent.*

Hon. LEWIS CASS, *Secretary of War.*

## To those who claim Reservations under the Treaty of Dancing Rabbit Creek.

By a communication from the War Department, under date of July 23, which was not received until the 5th of August last, I learned that I was appointed to make the selections and locations of the reservations of lands granted to the Choctaws under and by virtue of the provisions of the treaty of Dancing Rabbit Creek, made and entered into on the 27th of September, 1830, between the United States of America and the Choctaw nation of Indians. It was contemplated by the department, before I proceeded to the discharge of the duties required of me, that I should be furnished with the plats of all the townships of land within that district of country ceded by the treaty aforesaid, which have been surveyed; and also with copies of the register of all persons entitled to land under the same. I have not yet been furnished with any of the plats of survey, and with but imperfect copies of the registers. By a communication from the War Department, dated August the 8th, which I received on the 8th instant, I am informed that the President of the United States has directed the lands ceded by the treaty aforesaid to be offered at public sale, to commence on the third Monday in October next, and that it is necessary for the reservations provided for under the treaty to be located prior to the day of sale; and I am directed to proceed without delay to execute the duty required of me. My instructions seem to require of me to go in person on the ground and examine the improvement and lines of survey, corner posts, &c. of each local reservation claimed under the treaty. This I am unable to do before the day of sale. For the information of those interested, I have prescribed the following rules and regulations to be observed in presenting claims under the treaty, and in making locations, which are as nearly in conformity with my instructions as the circumstances of the case will permit.

I will open an office in each land district within that tract of country ceded by the treaty aforesaid, for the purpose of receiving applications and registering the names of applicants for reservations as soon as practicable, and keep the same open until the day set apart for the commencement of the sales in each district. In the northwestern district the office will be opened at Elliott, in the northeastern district at Columbus, in the Augusta district at Augusta, and in the Mount Salus district at Clinton.

The applicants must proceed to the place designated in their respective districts prior to the day of sale, and adduce to the agent, or such person as may be appointed to represent him, satisfactory proof that he or she is entitled to a reservation of land under the treaty, designating the numbers of the reservation so claimed. The name of the reservee will then be registered, the number of the section, half section, quarter section, or other quantity to which he may be entitled, marked on the plat of survey in the proper land office, and the land reserved from sale.

The reservations granted to heads of families, under the 14th article of the treaty to those who desire to remain five years and become citizens, will be bounded by sectional, half sectional, or quarter sectional lines of survey; and so located as to include the improvement of the head of the family at the time of the making of the treaty, or a portion of it. The half sections and quarter sections allowed for their children must adjoin the location of the parent.

71‡

The reservations granted under the 3d and 4th clauses of the 19th article of the treaty will also be bounded by sectional and quarter sectional lines of survey, and so located as to include that part of the improvement which contained the dwelling house of the head of the family at the time of the making of the treaty.  When the dwelling house of two or more persons entitled to reservations under this article shall be included within the same section, half section, or quarter section, they will be so located as to take such legal subdivisions of adjacent sections as will give to each reservee his claim in as square a form as practicable; thus, if different improvements are so situated upon the same section or subdivision of a section as to allow the parties by taking legal subdivisions to retain that part of their respective improvements containing their dwelling houses, they will have to take such legal subdivisions together with such adjacent lands as may be necessary to give the required shape and contents to their claims.  If, however, two or more reservees have settled upon and improved the smallest legal subdivision of a section, and thus rendered it impracticable to make a division of the improvements by the selection of legal subdivisions, they will have to make an arrangement among themselves as to the manner in which their reservations are to be located.  If they cannot agree among themselves, they will be permitted to cast lots for the same, and those who lose their improvements take the quantity to which they are entitled out of the adjacent lands.  Where a reservation based upon an actual improvement falls on a fraction, and that fraction is short of the number of acres to which the reservee is entitled, he will be allowed to make up the complement from the adjoining fraction, provided that the subdivision which may be located to complete the quantity be so designated as to give the entire reserve a square form.  If the contingency should happen contemplated in the latter part of the fourth clause of the 19th article, that the number of reservees should exceed the number provided for, the chief of the proper district will be called on to decide who shall be excluded.  Captains entitled to less than a section, who claim an additional half section under the 5th clause of the 19th article, must locate the same on lands adjoining their improvements and dwelling house.

Those claiming local reservations granted to them by name in the treaty or the supplement thereto, in designating the boundaries of their claims, will have to be governed by the rules prescribed in the particular clause under which they claim.  Those persons claiming floating reservations granted to them by name in the treaty or supplement, will be permitted to locate the same on any lands which were unoccupied and unimproved at the time of the making of the treaty, unless confined by the treaty to a particular district.  In making the locations they will be confined to, sectional, half sectional, or quarter sectional lines of survey, and will not be permitted to cross sectional, half sectional, or quarter sectional lines.  If they locate them on fractional sections, they will be compelled to take such fraction, if less than the complement, in full satisfaction of the whole quantity claimed under such floating reserve.  In no case whatever can a floating claim be divided.  Where application is made at the same time to locate two or more floating claims of equal size on the same tract of land, the same course for the adjustment of the matter as is prescribed in case of conflicting claims under the 3d and 4th clauses of the 19th article will be pursued as near as practicable, and all conflictions will be settled in the same manner.  Where application is made at the same time to locate two or more floating claims of different sizes, the largest will have the preference; thus, a section will have precedence over a half section, and a half section be preferred to a quarter section, &c.

In all cases the claim will be confined within the section lines of the section run and marked by the surveyor of the United States, and will not be permitted to go into an adjoining section or fraction unless the quantity of land or the terms of the treaty in which the grant is made requires or authorizes it to be done.

I intend to examine on the ground after the sales the several local reservations, if it should be deemed necessary to a final adjustment and settlement of the claims, before I return a register thereof to the War Department, or adopt such other course as I may be instructed to pursue in relation thereto.

It is important that every claimant should in person or by his agent attend promptly to his interest and make his application, particularly describing the land claimed within the time prescribed, in order to exclude his land from sale. I have thus given explicitly my views, and the substance of the instructions to me, which I hope will be satisfactory to all interested. If any additional information is desired in relation to any clause of the treaty which I have inadvertently omitted, I will take a great pleasure in giving it on application. It is the intention of the President, as well as the War Department and the undersigned, in making the locations of the several reservations granted under the treaty, to conform to the letter and spirit of that instrument in every particular, and to construe the same, wherever well founded doubt shall arise and any discretionary power is to be exercised, "favorably towards the Choctaws."

GEO. W. MARTIN,
*Agent for locating Indian Reservations.*

---

CHOCTAW AGENCY, *September 17, 1833.*

SIR: I reached this place on the 12th instant with my family. The first duty to be performed was to carry into effect the instructions given me by you, in relation to the taking of the testimony contemplated in the late treaty with the Chickasaws, and upon which the President is to determine the precise line to be established between the Choctaws and Chickasaws; and in which the Choctaws are deeply concerned, differing from the opinion of the Chickasaws as expressed in the treaty, wherein they say that the Choctaws having treated, "they, the Choctaws, have now no interest in the decision of the question." It will be recollected that many reservations have been sold by the Choctaws as provided for in their treaty, and white men are now living on them, having paid their full valuation. Should the line be established as contended for by the Chickasaws, the United States will have paid for relinquished lands surrendered by the Choctaws, and the white man will have his reservation swept from him, because many Choctaw settlements will be found within the limits laid down in the Chickasaw treaty: all this will be right if they do not own the lands. But it is strange that the Choctaws should have mistaken such a place as what is now called Nelson's Bluff, on the Hatchie or main Yazoo river. Nelson is provided for in the Choctaw treaty specially; and at the time of the treaty at Dancing Rabbit creek lived at a place where he had made improvements, having the best house in the nation.

He attempted to make himself rich by going to the very bluff on the Hatchie, and making a settlement subsequent to the treaty. He did make this settlement, him and his family. Now I would ask, is it probable Nelson would have done this on Chickasaw land? Certainly not.

His bluff is particularly pleasing to the Chickasaws, because it is likely to be a prominent point, and indeed the only good landing near the head of navigation on the Yazoo, in the work I done in the old nation. Nelson is confined to his old dwelling.

In this way it is that I have become so well satisfied that the Chickasaw line was not understood by the Choctaws as coming south to include that point.

For the reasons stated, I deem it my duty to apprise you that the testimony cannot be taken until several of the leading chiefs, now east, arrive here.

Colonel Leflore and David Folsom are at present on the east side; when they arrive, with some old chiefs, I will, without delay, forward the testimony complete.

I presume the President will not wish to decide the question without their testimony, being acquainted with them as men of great intelligence, connected with affairs of the nation. I will add further, that sickness is so great through this country at this time, that it is impossible to get together even the old chiefs that are here; it is truly distressing to be obliged to witness the situation of those persons now in this neighborhood; almost every person is sick, at least not one well family. It is so with the whites who are about the agency.

I have the honor to be
Your obedient servant,
F. W. ARMSTRONG, C. A.

Elbert Herring, Esq.,
    Commissioner of Indian Affairs.

---

Corinth, Heard County, Ga., *September* 17, 1833.

Sir: I have an idea of settling on the public lands of Alabama (now in the occupancy of the Creek Indians,) adjoining to this county, and will be thankful to know from you if I settle on land not claimed by the Indians whether I will be dispossessed before the sale of the land or not; a settlement on unoccupied lands will only enhance the value at public sale, which I presume the Government will not object to.

If you conceive from the treaty that I will be considered as an intruder, I will decline moving until the sale. Observance of this will much oblige me.

Respectfully,
    THOMAS WOOD.

Hon. Lewis Cass, Esq.,
    *Washington City.*

---

Otoe Village, on the Platte River, *September* 18, 1833.

Sir: I have the honor to inform you of my safe arrival at this place last evening. I found the Otoes well, and just returned from their hunt; they have received me with respect, and treated me with great hospitality. I

propose holding a council with them to-morrow. I shall proceed with as little delay as possible to the Pawnee village, about eighty miles west. It is my present intention to take a delegation of the Otoes and Pawnees to Fort Leavenworth, to make peace with the neighboring tribes, with whom they are at war. My own health is feeble; before I had fully recovered from the cholera I was attacked by the fever and ague, but I am now recovering, and I trust shall have strength to discharge the important duties of the mission.
I am yours
Obediently and sincerely,
HENRY L. ELLSWORTH.

Hon. E. Herring,
        *Indian Commissioner.*

---

NASHVILLE, *September* 20, 1833.

DEAR SIR: I have just seen a letter from William Armstrong: he says "the people of Mississippi are all in uproar on account of the sales of land in October; arising from the circumstance that the cultivation claims secured under the treaty are not reserved from sale." Major Martin, whom you sent to locate the orphan claims, has not been able to do any thing, because the report made by F. W. Armstrong of the cultivation claims under the treaty has not been sent to him. One was left with the agent, Colonel Ward, but is so torn and mutilated as to be of no service; and, until he is advised where those claims are, the orphan reservations cannot be made. To quiet "this uproar," you had better, from the report of F. W. Armstrong, have all those cultivation claims marked down upon the plat of survey by the commissioner, Mr. Hayward, and sent speedily to Major Martin. The plat, too, should be forwarded to the register in Mississippi, and be instructed not to sell any of these cultivation Indian claims.

I doubt much if there will be time for this; and if not, rather than the confusion spoken of should take place, would it not be well to postpone the sales?

I write in haste, and to keep you all out of scrapes and difficulties. Indeed, so prevailing is the idea with the people that the price of the public lands will be reduced at the next Congress, that dissatisfaction is expressed about the sales at this time.
Your's,
J. H. EATON.

Hon. LEWIS CASS,
        *Secretary of War, Washington City.*

---

DUMFRIES, *September* 20, 1833.

SIR: Your attentive acknowledgment of my letter, enclosing Mushulatubbee's conveyance to D. W. Wright, I duly received, but have deferred replying to until now. In order to a fair and equitable adjustment of the numerous contracts for floating claims and reserves, I will submit a few facts analogous of the whole, and from which I hope the War Department will be able in part to reach the cunning land speculator in his strongest hold. In a majority of cases, a small advance was made by the citizen to the Indian for his possession, say from a quarter to one tenth the amount agreed on as the price, the balance to be paid when the President ratified the sale. Promissory notes were given to the Indians, to be paid when the title became perfect. A *bona fide* deed and warranty, with an acknowledgment of the receipt of the whole purchase money, is given by the Indian, who emigrates forthwith to Arkansas: the purchaser, as soon as he can, sells the land to an emigrant settler, and he, perhaps, to some one else; indeed it may go through half a dozen transfers before the ratification, and, consequently, before the money is due to the Indian. The first purchaser, by a few successful operations, realizes a fortune, leaving the Indian to seek him where he can find him, and the last purchaser in danger of losing his land and improvements honestly obtained and paid for.

Mushulatubbee's two sons (full blood Indians), James and Hiram King, were allowed a section each at the treaty (at their father's old place on the great military road leading to Lake Pontchartrain, a most valuable location). Messrs. Wright, Hatch, and Hand, of Columbus, had formed a sort of combination or connexion to speculate in claims. Old Mushalatubbee was with them a great *habba shela* (friend), and together with the two floating sections, they got Mushulatubbee's sons' two sections before mentioned, for which they gave three young negroes. Pending this transaction, Messrs. Gravil and Grant Lincicum, of Columbus, informed me that squire *Magbee*, or Macbee, who knew that the said negroes were free, colleagued with a lawyer Tucker, of Columbus, to extort money out of Colonel Townsend, who brought the negroes from Tennessee or Kentucky, and sold them to the said company, Wright, Hatch, and Hand. Of the six negroes sold to Mushalatubbee five of them were free, and the sixth purchased from Grant Lincicum. The said free negroes were the offspring of a free woman that accompanied a family from near Hagerstown, Maryland, to Kentucky, many years ago. But to return to Tucker and Macbee: they went to Townshend and threatened to make the discovery, unless he would give them five hundred dollars; he agreed to do it, and gave his note accordingly; but when it became due he refused to pay it on the ground of bribery and extortion. They sued him in the court at Columbus: the trial came before Judge Nichols, and perhaps few cases have occurred where the enormity of the crime was viewed with less concern. It was said that Wright and Co. took back these negroes and put others in their places, but not believed. James King having been hurried off with them to Arkansas long before the emigration commenced; and Messrs. Lincicum, also Peter Pitchlynn, told me that it was only a sham, that the negroes (except one of them drowned in the river Polsau) were eighteen miles from Fort Smith. Wright, a few days after the treaty, took a deed for Robert Nail's claim for a half section; Robert was then about eighteen years old; it was to be paid for as soon as the sale was ratified by the President. Robert and his mother had great confidence in Wright, and of course would sign any paper he required of him. Supposing, therefore, as soon as the emigration commenced he could get the money, he applied for it, and was told he would not pay him, but would place the money in the hands of Major Pitchlynn. He continued to baffle Robert with this as long as I remained in the nation. Wright & Co. had taken, I understand, a conveyance bond from the old interpreter, Middleton Mackay, for his great from Congress given in lieu of his reserve, which was not valuable. Mackay told me he had never received any thing from them, and merely promised to give them the refusal. Mackay and his wife died of cholera on the road between Memphis and Little Rock. I have no doubt some one has set up a claim for Mackay's donation, and I am as certainly sure he never sold it. The claim of Captain Billy Hayes (a Choctaw) came directly under my notice. Nored and McNutt agreed to give him $700, viz., $300 on the 1st of September, 1831, and $400 more on the 1st of January, 1832. McNutt left for Arkansas with the emigrants; Nored remained, and paid Hayes $276; the agreement was left in my hands, and I gave it to Major Armstrong, who told me he had left it with Colonel Ward at the old agency. Nored refuses most positively to pay the balance, on the ground that Captain Hayes was not allowed as much land as he expected. Nored lives on the place, eighteen miles northeast of Doakstand. I hope he will be made to pay to Billy Hayes' heirs every cent before any title is given him. The land is richly worth the money. A good house on it, a large enclosure, and 480 acres.

Colonel James McDonald, an educated Choctaw, was provided for in the treaty, and subsequently drowned himself in Pearl river, near Jackson. Robert Jones, a relation of McDonald, told me that Judge Caldwell, of Clinton, had obtained from McDonald's mother (his rightful heir) the claim for a paltry, or at least a consideration far short of its value.

In reference to the latter part of your letter I ought only to say, " The account of my injuries and wrongs are rather long and the particulars tedious;" but in using this apology I do not abandon the task of recounting, to those who feel interested for me, the whole subject matter thereof, and by which, although not justifiable in any law, yet decidedly so by those who have heard and believed my statement of the transaction. It is matter of astonishment to myself and friends how I have encountered so many difficulties, and what has been the cause of it; my own impression is that it has ever been my misfortune to meet with oppression, and to resist it to a degree beyond the necessity of the case. During my service in the army and elsewhere for the Government, I have disbursed near a hundred thousand dollars; I was among the first commissaries appointed after the establishment of the commissariat; I have letters in the archives of the War Department showing my promptitude as a volunteer in the time of the war, and of my general character for capacity and integrity through life; I can procure ample testimonials from an extensive acquaintance in the different parts of the country where I have resided; I defy any one to bring a charge of fraud or peculation against me in more than twelve years' public service; my misfortunes are therefore rightfully ascribed to an irresistible impulse of passion, almost as fatal to my peace and happiness as the worst of offences. I did not think I should ever offend again when that best of men, Major Eaton, listened to my wrongs and gave me employment, and I did use every precaution to avoid collision with any person—but I am growing tedious, and will only add, as I am rather under the *ban*, that I hope you will look on my case with a more favorable view hereafter than the first impression induced you to do; and that I may not despair at some future period of being restored to the confidence of all my friends.

I am, sir, very respectfully,

Your most obedient servant,

WM. S. COLQUHOUN.

Hon. Lewis Cass,
*Secretary of War.*

CLAIRBORNE, *September* 21, 1833.

DEAR SIR: Although I am well aware of the importance of time to your Excellency, and of the little that can be conveniently abstracted by you from the momentous concerns of state, yet, considering the subject matter of my letter as not altogether foreign from these concerns, but connected with them, and of import to the public welfare, I deemed it my duty, with the knowledge that I possessed of the state of things commented on, to lay a few facts before you, and respectfully to solicit towards them a small portion of your attention.

Through the medium of the newspapers I lately became apprised that it was the intention of the Government to expel from the limits of the Creek Indian nation *all persons* (otherwise styled intruders) who might have settled themselves on the public lands therein without discrimination, and that such were the instructions transmitted to the United States marshal from the Department of War. This caused the situation in which a very numerous and respectable body of the upright and honest citizens of Alabama, who under peculiar circumstances have removed there, would be placed to present itself to my view; and conceiving that by possibility some of the circumstances connected with this subject might have been misconceived, or not fully understood, I have believed it, as already remarked, my duty to invite your attention to the same, and hope I shall not be considered as unnecessarily officious in so doing.

First. The settlements made in the Creek Indian country by our people have been under the sanction and laws of the State, which pledge the faith of the State that the same is lawful, and that their possessions shall be peaceable.

Secondly. The whole Creek nation has, by the Legislature of the State, been erected into counties, and courts have been constituted for and held in them. The necessary officers, such as judges, clerks, sheriff, &c., have also been elected, and have entered upon and discharged their various functions by virtue of commissions duly issued by the authority of the State, and with every legal form. Besides this, all other acts and things have been done that are essential to their speedy civil and political organization.

Thirdly. The continued inaction and supineness of the General Government in relation to the expulsion of these settlers, and the letter of the honorable Secretary of War to some of the members of Congress of this State, have been construed into an acquiescence on the part of the Government and assent to their settlement.

I am fully informed that many of the settlements upon the Indian lands have been made in shameful and flagrant despite and violation of every principle of humanity or justice; that neither the social hearth nor sanctuary of home has been respected or held sacred, and that the unfortunate Indian possessor has even been forcibly expelled to make room for such ruthless occupancy; but I am happy to be enabled to say, that this is not the case in all instances of settlements, nor by any means general; the country, from long and continued accession of comers, must now possess a population of some thousands; of the number, more than three fourths are honest, peaceable and industrious, and have acquired their possessions, if improved at all, on the property of an Indian, by rent, or other species of contract, or have made their own improvements upon vacant, unoccupied, and unclaimed lands; and not a few of these latter have been made with a view of permanency of possession, if possible, by purchase at the land sales from the Government, or otherwise, and therefore are extensive and valuable. Numbers of this class of settlers, if removed as contemplated, being an occurrence to them, from the previous course of the Government, so unlooked for and unlikely to happen, must suffer severe and excessive pecuniary loss; while the *poorer sort*, who have in a manner expended almost their *little all* to establish themselves in their newly acquired residences, will be irretrievably ruined.

That the duty of the Government to comply with the obligations of the treaty of 1832, and carry the same into effect in good faith, is imperative, I am not ignorant of; but I have ventured to entertain the belief (whether with temerity or correctly I respectfully submit) that such settlers as had, for fair equivalents, either rented Indian lands or made their own improvements upon such untenanted lands as should not be found to be included in Indian reservations, were not, by the terms of it, required to be removed; for, by the treaty, all lands not covered by such reservations become public lands, and consequently vest in the United States, and are, as a matter of course, to be occupied and sold by the United States as the property of the same.

The large and valuable improvements made by the settlers, the Creeks, in the event of their expulsion, though but for a temporary period, would take a malignant delight in destroying, as well on account of their depth of ignorance and barbarism, as of their innate and inexorable hate of the white men. The first token of a general removal of our citizens would be to them the joyful signal for their savage triumph, and the furious burst and ebullition of their unrestrained and demoniac feeling. Nothing would be respected or regarded, whether the premises of friends or foes; all would alike be doomed to ruin. The conflagration of burning dwellings and enclosures, the indiscriminate erasure of every trace and sign of civilization and refinement, would but add rich zest to their barbarian thirst for destruction. In such an event much time must elapse before the country could again be made to assume its flourishing aspect, or recover its present degree of improvement. In the Talladega valley particularly, where there is a dense population, and comparatively but little timber, and where much of that little has already been appropriated by the settlers to the purposes of building and enclosing, new forests would have to spring up, and fresh timber be produced, before the lands could come again into cultivation extensively: so that from such a measure as that of a general and indiscriminate expulsion of the settlers, whether intruders upon Indian premises or not, no accurate calculation can be made of the deep and lasting evil that must of necessity ensue.

Amongst the settlers no doubt there has been much impediment thrown in the way of the Government, as well as by the companies of land speculators, in regard to its views of the further treating with Indians for their reservations, by their belief that to bargain with the Indians themselves would probably be the surest and cheapest method of acquiring fee-simple titles to their settlements. Nevertheless, whatever may have been their proceedings in this particular, it can now make no alteration in things; the question must, at this crisis, recur to the condition or position of the State, in regard to its extension of its laws over the ceded territory, its assumption of jurisdiction, and faith pledged to its citizens, of protection, &c.

It is sufficiently well known that the obstructions to a treaty, having for its basis the *emigration* of these Indians, are many, and have been for the most part interposed by a few of the chiefs under the influence of certain *whites resident in that country*, entertaining views heretofore disclosed, and of *which influence* they would *make the most*, and dispose of at the highest advantage, by the arts of *white traders and dealers*, who would detain them until they had swindled out of them the veriest remnant of their property, and by the numerous and greedy companies of land speculators. But, notwithstanding this formidable array, I do not despair, despite of all effort by such an *unholy alliance* to the contrary, of the possibility of such a treaty being made, though certainly not without some sacrifice and concession to the principals amongst these actors. Some fifty or hundred perhaps of *special reservations* would have to be granted; and possibly some *white men*, under the guise of Indian covering, would have to be made the ultimate donees or patentees of them. High prices, too, peradventure, might have to be paid; but what, I would respectfully urge, are all these compared with the commotion and difficulty likely in the present disturbed state of things to be produced, on the one hand by the relative condition of the white and red men, on the other the State. The *Governor's letter* to the Department of War, and the attitude of the nullification faction, who have abandoned the flag first unfurled by them, and taken shelter under the standard of State rights, will of course enlist and congregate to their side most of the settlers who may be forcibly ejected, and thus add a vast accession to their party.

These things are to be understood as alluded to, not *in terrorem*, but as a mere exposition of facts; and I feel warranted in saying that a delegation of chiefs, authorized and invested with full powers to treat, could be selected, and go then to Washington, and a treaty made and concluded before our citizens settled in that district of country could gather in and secure their crops; a privilege which, it would seem from the instructions of the marshal, as laid before the public, has been extended to them; possibly by this means occurrences may be prevented which, should they, unhappily for the peace of the community, be permitted to transpire, all must sincerely and deeply deplore.

I think that by the means of the two Crowells, (John and Thomas,) Major William Walker, and a few others, such a delegation of chiefs might be had, and beyond a doubt certainly, could the parties named be induced by the *cement* of *interest*, (perhaps in the form of special reservations to such Indians as they might fix upon,) to act together. Major Walker, as an Indian countryman, or head of a Creek family, is himself, under the treaty, entitled to a reservation with the rest. This I am certain he would be ready to give up and sacrifice for the common good; for I must do him the justice to say, from all that I know of him, and so far as in all these transactions I have seen him tested, that whether it was made his peculiar interest or not he would act correctly; nor would it be necessary to resort to particularity of means to win or keep him in the course of uprightness and rectitude. His deportment at the *late attempt to treat* with the Creeks furnishes proof ample enough on that head.

Should the Government deem a course of this kind proper to be pursued, (and with deference I suggest it for reflection,) I think arrangements might be entered into; the greatest difficulty in the way being the little unanimity and friendship existing between Major Walker and the Crowells. This, however, might be remedied and removed, in my opinion, as to the *latter* at least, in the manner proposed.

My inducement to address you on this matter has been the possibility, at this critical juncture, of rendering some small service to my country, and that only. Should any thing, therefore, herein submitted have that tendency, the end in view will have been fully attained, and my object answered. The course I have pursued will, I hope, prove offensive to none; and my motives, however much misrepresented or mistaken by others, by yourself, at least, be rightly understood and appreciated.

With my best wishes for your welfare and health, I have the honor becomingly to subscribe myself, with high respect,

Your excellency's

Most obedient and humble servant,

E. PARSONS.

Gen. ANDREW JACKSON,
*President of the United States.*

---

FORT MITCHELL, ALABAMA,
*September 21, 1833.*

HONORABLE SIR: At the request of the Indian chiefs, I propose to suggest to you their wishes and views relative to the propriety of an immediate removal of the intruders beyond the limits of the Creek territory.

Intruders on their lands, they say, are innumerable; and they have been very solicitous that the selection of their occupancy should be on the most choice part of the country. Now, whether they have trespassed on the reserve of an individual Indian or not, it is quite evident they have on the Indians at large, insomuch as those very lands are taken up, and consequently cannot be occupied by the Indians. And even some of these intruders have not contented themselves with as much of the good land as they can cultivate, but have enclosed large bodies of land, to the entire exclusion or prohibition of an Indian locating his reserve where he would wish.

To obviate this, and render it as free from difficulty as probably the nature of the case will admit, I, at their instance, proposed to suggest to you the propriety of an *immediate removal*, and that without *discrimination*, every white person not duly authorized to act on their respective duties from the Government, beyond the limits of the nation. For they (the Indians) think *all* others must be *directly intruders*, insomuch as there is not yet known any authority from which they might become lawfully entitled to the land. We further suggest the propriety of this course of procedure for several reasons, one of which we will mention. If a discriminate course is adopted, where will the line of demarkation be drawn? Shall time legalize their intrusion? It will further be adopting a precedent replete with ostensible grounds for complaint by those that are or will be removed, if in fact there can be, with that distinction, an intruder found within the nation, for they admit there are none, if it is left to them, but what will find a mediator either through fear or bribery.

With high respect, &c.,

TANT WILLIAMSON.

Hon. LEWIS CASS, *Secretary of War.*

MOBILE, *September* 22, 1833.

DEAR SIR: Your orders and the opinion of the Attorney General have been duly received, and their contents shall be strictly obeyed, to the best of my ability. There is one point of your instructions that I may have placed an incorrect construction upon, and that is where you say, " before a resort is had to actual force, and where force is applied, it will be limited to the actual removal of the intruders from the ceded territory." In the second place I am required to transmit the names of all persons who shall hereafter intrude upon, *or who now live upon the ceded land and refuse to remove, &c.* It appears in the first place that force is to be used if actually necessary, and in the second it is not; but if they refuse to obey, resort is to be had to civil process. My view of the subject is this, that upon refusal to remove force shall be used, and if they return again, then to prosecute them.

_If I am therefore in error of the true intent of your order, please correct me. Leave will be granted to all those intruders who have compromised with the Indians under my presence, and with my consent, until they gather their crops. This course was adopted for the interest of the Indians, and that the settlers might reap a proportion of their labor, believing that if they were removed at the time, the settlers would destroy the crops after I had left, or commit some violence upon the Indians. The settlers in the Tuckabatchee towns are differently situated; they came invested in most cases, and in a proportion took forcible possession against the express orders of the chiefs. I shall therefore proceed to remove them in a few days hence.

I have the honor, &c.,

JEREMIAH AUSTILL,
*Deputy Marshal.*

Hon. LEWIS CASS, *Secretary of War.*

---

COLUMBUS, *September* 22, 1833.

SIR: In pursuance of the course laid down in my letter to you of the 15th instant, I have established offices and appointed assistants at the several land offices, for the reception and filing of applications in the several districts, namely, William Dowsing, esq., at Columbus, William Houze, esq., at Augusta, R. H. Sterling, esq , at Elliott, and George B. Dameron, esq., at Mount Salus, who are authorized to receive and place on file for registration all such claims as may be presented, and come under the rules prescribed and furnished them, a copy of which is herewith enclosed. I intend visiting each office prior to the day of sale, for the purpose of examining the claims presented, and to register and reserve from sale such claims as are filed, and shall come under the provisions of the treaty, and in conformity with my instructions from your department.

I have the honor to be, &c.,

GEORGE W. MARTIN.

Hon. LEWIS CASS, *Secretary of War, Washington City.*

Marshal's Office, So. Dist. Alabama,
*Mobile, September 23, 1833.*

Sir: Your instructions under date 26th August, came to hand during my absence from this place.

The death of H. Owen has created a considerable degree of excitement in some sections of the country, and I am informed that persons have offered their names for enrollment, in the event of the settlers being removed from the Creek lands, and that companies are already forming for the purpose of resistance.

I believe that there are but few intruders at this time in the nation except that class who were allowed to remain agreeably to your letter to Messrs. Clay, Mardis, and Moore, and which constitutes a part of my instructions.

I have written to the commanding officer at Fort Mitchell, requesting him to inform me when the company of troops ordered recently to that place arrive; as yet I have heard nothing from him.

I deem it unsafe to go there without a sufficient force, as well to enforce obedience to the laws as protection to myself. So soon as I learn that the company has reached Fort Mitchell, Mr. Austill will leave this for the purpose of removing those persons who are excepted in your letter to Messrs. Clay, Mardis, and Moore.

A company of cavalry would do much more service than infantry.

The fifth and sixth paragraphs of your last instructions I am somewhat at a loss to know how to act. In the fifth you say, that where force is applied, it shall be limited to the actual removal of intruders from the ceded territory; and in the sixth paragraph you say, that should they refuse to remove agreeably to your requisition, you will report the names of all, together with the names of witnesses necessary to prove the fact.

I request to be instructed whether those persons who have been removed by actual force are to be returned to the district attorney, together with all those who now live upon the lands and refuse to remove, for very few will remove unless by force; every one who have settled there are immediately concerned, and hence the impossibility of obtaining witnesses.

I anticipate considerable difficulty in removing that class of intruders who are allowed to remain until their crops are gathered.

I shall give notice for them to remove by the fifteenth day of January, which will give them sufficient time to gather their crops; numbers of them have large cotton farms made upon their own improvements.

Those who have intruded upon the Indians' fields, and are otherwise obnoxious to them, I shall have removed forthwith.

Threats have been made to shoot me, or any deputy I may send for the purpose of removing them.

The removal of all persons from the ceded lands will occasion great distress and loss of property to those who have made their own improvements.

I am at a loss, also, to know what to do with those whiskey sellers; they have all settled in the woods, and made a small improvement of their own, and do not interfere with the Indian improvements.

Those persons who made their own improvements, and were allowed to remain till their crops are gathered, will some of them remove peaceably, the majority will not.

Respectfully, &c.,
ROBERT L. CRAWFORD.

Hon. Lewis Cass, *Secretary of War.*

LOUISVILLE, BARBOUR COUNTY, ALA.,
*September 25, 1833.*

SIR: I have been called upon by the citizens of Irwinton to address you a note respecting the late instructions from you to the marshal of the southern district, and the attorney general's opinion on the subject of intruders on the public lands. I was one of the commissioners appointed to designate that place for a place of deposite, &c. The commissioners were only authorized to select a place on the Chattahoochie river to the nearest point; we accordingly done so without interfering with any Indian improvement. The Legislature of this State passed that act in 1829, and in the spring of 1830 it was settled, and the chiefs of that town gave peaceable possession to the citizens, and they settled there under the belief that when there was a treaty effected with the Indians the land would belong to the Government, and that they would buy the land and make an equal distribution of the land, each one to pay a proportionable part of the purchase money; but to their astonishment there was a treaty made, and the Indians were allowed reserves, but they have been good enough to suffer them to remain this long, and now they are said to be intruding on the Government; and agreeably to the attorney general's opinion, no Indian chief can permit any white person to stay in the nation without the consent of the Government. And I wish to know of you if the Indian chiefs will permit them to stay in that village, if the Government would suffer them to remain: should they be forced away it will be a ruination to many of them. Be so good as to answer me as soon as convenient.

I remain, &c.,
Your obedient servant,
**F. W. PUGH.**

Hon. LEWIS CASS.

———

MARDISVILLE, TALLADEGA COUNTY, ALA.,
*September 26, 1833.*

SIR: The enclosed certificate contains all the evidence which I consider of importance, and which can be obtained here in relation to the claims of certain Creek Indians, residents of the Cherokee country, and who are alluded to in the letter of Wm. H. Moore to the Secretary of War, dated March 29, 1833. Though I am of opinion that it is quite conclusive against the claimants, I am not sufficiently acquainted with the laws, customs, and usages of the Creeks, to say positively how long Creek Indians may be absent from their country, and residents of other countries, before they disfranchise themselves. But this much I do know, that all the Indians living in the country have to contribute to the support of their government, and instead of a tax they cultivate the fields of their town chiefs, and the public fields which are contiguous or around their town houses.

Now, as these Indians have been absent and actual residents of the Cherokee country for a series of years, and have not contributed to the support and maintenance of the government, community, or whatever else it might be termed, and as the Cherokees who reside in this country, and have been residents here for a number of years, have been registered by the census taken as well as white men and free negroes, I am of opinion they are not entitled to reservations under the provisions of the late treaty.

Those Cherokees alluded to by Wm. H. Moore, and who were not registered by the commissioners appointed to take the census, were living near the line which separates the Cherokee from this country; but when the surveyors surveyed this country they were taken into the Creek country or cession, but had always before considered themselves living in their own country, as they did not know exactly where the line was; of course, as they always considered themselves as residing in their own country, and no doubt contributed to its support, and acknowledged no other, they had no right to be enrolled; nor can this circumstance be urged as a reason why the Creeks who have resided for a number of years near fifty miles within the acknowledged limits of the Cherokee country should be allowed to return and obtain reservations here.

What is unnecessary and nugatory in the enclosed certificate was put there because Selochtalochta, or General Chinnabie, would have it so. I complied with his wishes, as I knew it would neither prejudice nor favor the claims of the claimants with the department. He requested me to inform the President that he was alive and well, and very much his friend, &c. &c.

I have the honor to be,
Very respectfully,
Your obedient servant,
LEONARD TARRANT.

Elbert Herring, Esq.

---

State of Alabama, Talladega,
*September 23,* 1833.

We do hereby certify that those Indians living in the Cherokee country, and who were brought into this country by William Moore to claim reservations under the late treaty, are not entitled by our laws and usages to any benefits to which the Creeks are entitled by the said treaty.

We further certify that they were enemies to the whites and to us during the late war, and that we consider them bad Indians, and that we do not want our father, the President, to listen to their complaints, as they are not considered by us members of our community.

We further certify that, according to our laws, all Creeks remaining in any other Indian country, and having renounced their own country, whether they live in the Choctaw. Chickasaw, or Cherokee countries, are not entitled by our laws to any reservations in this country.

We further certify that it is our opinion they have no wish to go to Arkansas, but that they want to get our lands to sell them, and to return to the Cherokee country. We wish our father, the President, to believe that it is our sincere opinion that they never would have applied for reservations here if they had not been influenced by the white people and half blooded Cherokees. We wish further to state to our father, the President, that at the conclusion of the war our father, the President, then commanding the whites and Indians, directed all the Indians that had run off to other nations of Indians to return and settle in their own country, and that such Indians as returned we acknowledged again as members of the Creek family; but that such as remained and would not return we consider as forfeiting all rights and privileges amongst us.

We further state, if our father the President was to acknowledge the claims of these people, it would be against our wishes.

And we further state that their returning here without our consent was the reason why our countryman, or Tallassehatchy, whipped and drove them back to the Cherokee country.

Given under our hands the date above.

|                        | SE-LOCH-TA,             | his x mark. |
|                        | FOSE HATCHY FIXICO,     | his x mark. |
| Attest:                | JAMES FIFE,             | his x mark. |

WM. KELLY, *Interpreter.*
JOHN BOX.
H. B. HAMILTON.

---

TALLADEGA, *September 27, 1833.*

DEAR SIR: Although unpleasant to be intrusive, I have again to call your attention to the subject of the claims of a few of the Creek tribe who live in the limits of the Cherokee nation. You was kind enough to state to me, in answer to my former note, that the subject was referred to Col. Abert for investigation. I waited patiently to hear from the decision, and was at length informed by a confidential friend of Mr. Tarrant that he had received the instruction. I came to this place expecting that the agent would give me the proper information as to the nature of proof, and all the information that I might expect from the Government; but to my surprise he refused to say any thing on the subject, and went so far as to misrepresent the place that he was then going to, in order to prevent my attending at the the same place, although to others he said he was to procure for the Government the views of the chiefs as to the acknowledgment of those Indians. He did not know their names, place of residence, or any other fact about them, and gave no opportunity for them to be heard by the chiefs; and a fact I am ready to prove is, that he took with him, and called on for witnesses and evidence, the very persons who are implicated in the charge of whipping those Indians, and who had formed themselves in a company to whip from the country all white men who aided the Indians, and that he knew them to be such. I can prove that Judge Tarrant has uniformly been opposed to those claims, and that he has expressed too much solicitude on the subject to be an impartial umpire. I stand prepared to prove those Indians to be native Creeks, and that they have never been expelled from the nation, and that they have never been recognised as a part of the Cherokee tribe; and unless they are provided for in the Creek nation that they have no claim elsewhere. I do hope the Government will not decide against those persons from Judge Tarrant's statements, as I can prove that Chimby, one of the chiefs, came after me, and wished me to attend at his town; but I had not the smallest thought from Tarrant's statement that he would be there. I hope that a fair investigation may be had; and that the charge of speculation may not be heard, unless indeed it may *proceed from a pure fountain.*

With great respect,
I have the &c. &c.,
WM. H. MOORE.

The Hon. LEWIS CASS.

NILES, N. T., *September 28, 1833.*

DEAR SIR: I have the pleasure to inform you that I have just returned from the treaty at Chicago with the Pottawatamies, which I was requested to attend on the 10th instant by Governor Porter and Colonel Owen, two of the commissioners. In consequence of a little detention at Buffalo, to see the Seneca chiefs who had requested an interview with me, and a severe storm on Lake Erie, I did not arrive at Chicago until the 22d instant. On my arrival, I found very little progress had been made towards effecting the objects of the Government with these Indians. They had utterly refused for several days to sell any of their lands; it.was however believed, that the lands situated in Illinois might yet be obtained, although they were very reluctant to part even with those.

The day after my arrival I had a private interview with Caldwell and Robinson, two of their principal chiefs, and to whom the Indians had committed the whole negotiation on their part. I opened to them the views of the Government with regard to the removal of the Indians, and pointed out to them the advantages which would result to their people; and also gave them a description of the lands west of the Mississippi, and suggested that they might obtain from the Government as much land west as they still possessed east of the Mississippi. They finally agreed to negotiate for all their lands west of Michigan lake, supposed to contain 5,000,000 acres, for an equal quantity on the Missouri, extending from the Nodaway to the Boger river, and east to the west line of the State of Missouri and the lands of the Sacs and Foxes. To this the commissioners agreed, and gave them also $1,000,000, which is to be paid in removal and support for a year, agricultural-improvements, schools, debts, goods, annuities, &c. &c., the usual detail of treaties; the lands west to be assigned for the use and benefit of the united Chippewa, Ottoway, and Pottawatamie nations. The St. Joseph and Nottawaysippi Indians still refused to treat for their reservations when I left there on the 26th instant, immediately after the signing of the treaty.

\*　　　\*　　　\*　　　\*　　　\*　　　\*　　　\*

I leave here on Monday for Fort Wayne. The Miami treaty is appointed for the 8th October. I hope to be able to give you a favorable account of our success in that negotiation. I am too much fatigued to write any more to-night, having rode sixty miles on horseback yesterday, and therefore must defer much which I might say until I arrive on the Wabash.

With great respect,
Your obedient servant,
J. F. SCHERMERHORN.

To the Honorable ELBERT HERRING,
*Commissioner.*

---

CHICAGO, *September 28, 1833.*

SIR: I have the honor to transmit for your perusal, the better to enable you to decide upon the request that I shall make, the copy of a treaty and supplementary articles concluded on the 26th and 27th instant with the united nations of Chippewa, Pottawatamie, and Ottoway Indians.

You will perceive the cession embraces all their land on the west shore of Lake Michigan, and all owned by them in Michigan Territory, south

73‡

of Grand river, without a reservation. The treaty will be transmitted as soon as the pressure of my avocations will permit me to close the schedules attached to it.

These Indians are thoroughly imbued with the spirit of emigration. From the issue of this negotiation and the feeling it has generated among them, I anticipate confidently a favorable result to my intended effort with the Miamies, whom I shall meet on the 8th October. The example will, I doubt not, produce an impression upon all the Indians remaining decidedly advantageous. I am equally confident in the belief that while these impressions are yet fresh, propositions would be readily entertained by the owners of the reservations of land retained by the Tippecanoe treaties of October 26th and 27th, 1832, to cede them to the United States, and join their brothers in their pilgrimage to the west. Not a foot is reserved to them by the treaty we have just concluded. Thus this whole country may probably be altogether relieved from any serious impediment to its entire settlement, by the removal of a population which will always embarrass and retard it; while, at the same time, the policy of the Government, in respect to its Indian intercourse, will have been advanced to an important extent.

Under these circumstances, I feel impelled by my sense of duty to submit to the consideration of the department the expediency of following up the policy of the Government while the time is propitious, by authorizing an immediate negotiation to be had with these people for their reserves under the two treaties aforesaid. As I shall have these Pottawatamies assembled at the Tippecanoe mills, to receive their money and goods, the attempt to procure a cession of these reservations can be made without any expense to the Government. They embrace almost every valuable spot of land in that country; for, without these groves of timber and water privileges, what are the prairies worth?

If the views I have taken the liberty to suggest meet the approbation of the department, I have the honor to request that an authority and instructions to me may be immediately prepared and transmitted to the post office at Maumee, with directions to the postmaster to forward them to me by express at the Forks of the Wabash. The letter can reach me in this way in eight days after it is mailed at Washington.

I am, in very great haste,
With considerations of much regard,
Your obedient servant,
G. B. PORTER.

Honorable LEWIS CASS,
  Secretary of War.

---

NEAR JONES'S BLUFF, SUMPTER Co., ALA.,
September 29, 1833.

DEAR SIR: I am and have been a citizen for twelve years and more on the territory ceded to the United States by the Choctaw people at Dancing Rabbit Creek, in September, 1830. (Previous to my settling in this country, I served three years and five months as a regular soldier in the United States army, the most of the time in active service in the last war.) Under the 14th article of that treaty I entered, or had my name entered on the agent's (Colonel Ward) books within the prescribed time, as one who wished to become a citizen of the United States. I had at that time a wife and four little children under ten years of age living with me: these are all that I entered with Colonel Ward—for which I have his certificate; but I had at that time another child, my first born, a son, at the Choctaw Academy in Kentucky; and being unskilled in the art of constructing treaties, and as he was not immediately under my roof at the time of giving in the rest, I ignorantly failed to name him. These facts I can well establish. Now, one inquiry I wish to make is, whether I can obtain land for this other child, by satisfactorily establishing his existence now and at the time of the treaty, and a development of the circumstances of his name being neglected. If so, you will oblige an humble individual by seeing me righted in this particular. Now there are a great many white people settled on the Choctaw purchase—some four or five on the land which, in good faith, I must get—and they endeavor to shake my faith in the Government, by saying that white men married to Choctaw women were not considered by Government as the heads of Choctaw families; and the treaty was so worded in order to cut white men with Indian families out of land. This, I know, was not the intention or understanding of the contracting parties at the time, for inquiries were made at the time of the United States Commissioners upon this head, and they did unequivocally state, that white men married to Choctaw women were considered as Indians, and would be entitled, under the treaty, to all the privileges and benefits of other Choctaws. You will confer a favor upon me by giving me your opinion upon this head.

Another inquiry I wish to make is, whether a claimant will be allowed to take fractional sections, or quarter sections, in lieu of whole ones. Our late agent had, for some time previous to going out of office, been in the habit of stimulating very freely, so much so that I thought he was liable to do business rather loosely; and I have been actually informed that he has failed to enter names when he was applied to to do so; and I have understood that he has lost a part of the names that he registered. Should this be the case, what remedy has the claimant? Will his certificate set the claim to rights? Or will it be sufficient evidence for the locator to lay off the claim? You will oblige me by informing me if my name is on the list transmitted to your office, and whether it is as one claiming a citizenship. I have the agent's certificate to this effect; but if he has lost any names, it is possible mine may be among them. Another, and the last inquiry is, what way are we to get rid of those persons who are settled upon our lands, and cutting down and destroying our timber, and clearing it up in little spots, in a very injurious manner?

Your very humble servant,<br>JACOB DANIEL.

Lewis Cass.

P. S. Please inform me whether Antonio Parish's name is on your list. He is a brother-in-law, and an old brother soldier, who served with me in the last war.

N. B. Please write me immediately, and direct your letter to Daniel's Prairie, Green County, Alabama.

EXECUTIVE OFFICE, TALLAHASSEE, *Sept.* 30, 1833.

SIR: Communications from the War Department have instructed me (as you have heretofore been advised) to attend to the fulfilment of the treaty you concluded with Col. Blunt and other of the Indian chiefs, on the Appalachicola river, last fall.

I had once all in my power to promote the views and interests of the Government in relation to this subject, but deeply regret to find I meet with considerable difficulty. In fact (as I have advised the Secretary of War), I have no idea that Blunt will be able to get one-fiftieth part of his people to go with him; and I have a strong doubt whether he will not abandon, or try to abandon the treaty, and stay at home; and I am quite certain he cannot be got off this fall.

I have transmitted to the department his letter, and advised the Secretary of War of the substance of his verbal communications to me; and the character of the obstacles existing are, therefore, fully known at Washington.

The principal difficulties have originated in the agreement with the upper towns, concluded by you this summer, as it has been represented to Blunt and his Indians. These I have endeavored to obviate, but without effect. Without having any certain or definite information of the particular terms of that agreement, I find myself at a loss to explain away some of the objections urged; and as no copy has been filed in this office, I have to request that if you have a copy thereof in your possession, that you will transmit it by the next mail. It is greatly to be regretted, as you concluded the treaty with Col. Blunt, you could not superintend the execution of it. I have great doubts, as the matter now stands, whether any advantage will result to the Government. I should be gratified if you could yet undertake the superintendence of the execution of the treaty; although I think, even in such a case, you will not succeed as favorably as was anticipated when concluded.

On your visiting Tallahassee, if you wish, I will show you copies I have retained of Blunt's letters to me, and memoranda of conversations with him, and copies of other letters received by me, which I have communicated to the War Department. I have thought perhaps it might be advantageous to the Government to state to you the situation of the business, as you may, perhaps, suggest some course to the department more proper than I have indicated should be pursued.

JAMES D. WESTCOTT, JR.

Col. JAMES GADSDEN, *late Com'r., &c.*

————

TALLADEGA, *October* 1, 1833.

SIR: At a public meeting, composed of about one hundred and fifty of the citizens of this county, the following address was unanimously adopted, and I was selected to communicate it to your department.

Respectfully, your obedient servant,

H. H. WYCHE.

*To the Secretary of War:*

SIR: Your instructions of August 26th to the marshal of the southern district of Alabama have produced a state of uncertainty and suspense ruinous to many, and very injurious to all of our citizens settled on the land lately purchased of the Creek Indians.

There are, at a moderate computation, thirty thousand souls now inhabiting the Creek purchase liable to removal under your instructions. We do not pretend to claim any positive right to the land; but we would respectfully suggest that the practice of the Government, from its organization to the present day, has been such as virtually to invite the citizens to settle and improve the waste lands.

Under the belief that this policy would still prevail, we have settled on the Creek land, and many of us under circumstances which will involve us in irretrievable ruin should we be now removed. We do not expect or wish the Government to violate the treaty concluded with the Indians, but we hope it will be executed on a plan that will save our citizens from ruin.

The reports made by the public officers as to the injury done the Indians by the white settlers cannot apply to the great body of the people. The citizens of this county we know have pursued a different course. They have been engaged in opening and preparing the waste land for cultivation, without intruding on the Indians, or in any manner interfering with their interests. That there may be individuals who have ejected Indians we are not prepared to deny; but these instances we know must be very limited in number, and the individuals can be removed without much difficulty.

The Government is aware of the ruin and distress which will inevitably result from the breaking up and disorganizing of a whole community at once. Should, however, the Government consider itself bound to remove the whites, as necessary to a faithful execution of the treaty, it is requested that all the information on the subject may be furnished us which can be communicated with propriety.

Without intending or wishing to interfere with the administration of the government, we will suggest that, if consistent with its policy, an immediate location of the Indians may avert much anticipated distress.

*Talladega County, Ala., September 28, 1833.*

———

SUNBURY, OHIO, *October 2, 1833.*

DEAR SIR: Agreeably to the instructions of the Secretary of War, given early last spring, by which I was directed to ascertain during the then coming summer whether the Wyandots had altered their minds in regard to ceding their lands, &c., I have, therefore. after much opposition and trouble, been able to bring my inquiries to a close, but not to such a one as I had anticipated.

As I stated in a recent communication to the department, I immediately on my return to Ohio commenced the inquiry with the chiefs and leading men of the tribe, which, at first, was treated coolly, and seemed to create but little interest with them; but, by frequent and cautious conversations held with them, I at length made it a matter of importance to them, and in a short time all the chiefs except two, in all nine, became favorable to the measure, as follows: The head chief, Warpole, and three others, became anxious to conclude a treaty; three agreed with them, but were unwilling to treat until the nation was consulted; and two of the chiefs opposed the measure in toto.

The chiefs in favor of selling strove for a long time to satisfy their associates opposed to them that it was to the interest of their people to emigrate; but failing to do so, they at length agreed to submit the question to a general council, and to abide its decision, which met on the 26th ultimo; and, after much debate and warmth, it was found that nearly two-thirds of the tribe voted against selling and emigrating.

When the principal chief found he was left in the minority, and that he had been deceived, a number voting contrary to what they had told him they would do, he became exasperated, and publicly proclaimed 'that he was not to be duped and outdone; that, notwithstanding he was in the minority, still he would conclude a treaty for the whole or a part of the reservation, and that he would, with all who were willing to join him, emigrate to the west.

This declaration threw those opposed to him in great consternation and confusion, and threats were thrown out by them that they would arrest and break him for opposing the will of the majority; but he being a man never known to be intimidated, and never to fail in carrying his point in the nation, at once treated their threats with contempt; and he the next morning expressed the same determination to a delegation who waited on him to know whether he had recanted.

At the time of the meeting I was lying very sick with the fever, and had it not been so I think it is likely the result would have been different. After the close of the meeting the chiefs reported to me the result, which was in substance as related; and the head chief then repeated what he had said at the close of the national council—that he wished commissioners to be appointed as soon as convenient to treat with them; and the next chief in rank was opposed to it, so the council broke up with angry feelings.

A few days afterwards I understood that another expression of the nation was shortly to take place, but which I shall not be able to attend, having come to this place to recover my health, as no medical aid could be had at Sandusky. And perhaps it is as well to let them counsel for the present among themselves, as much heretofore has been said by myself and others in respect to their situation, &c.

You can have but little idea how much this tribe is in the way, and of the anxiety of the respectable part of the citizens residing around and near to the reservation to get rid of these Indians, and for the Government to use every means in its power to obtain a speedy cession of their lands, &c. &c.

This reservation is situate in the heart of a fertile and populous part of Ohio; and as long as it remains the property of the Indians, so long must the citizens of Crawford county labor under many inconveniencies, one of which is, their present seat of justice being upwards of thirty miles from many of them. This is not all; many more might be enumerated, but it is considered useless to do so, as the department is better able to judge of this matter than I am of pointing them out.

Now the question is, what course is best calculated to remedy the evil complained of, and to save a remnant of this tribe from the ruin which awaits it in its present location? From every information the department has received in relation to this matter, it is rational to suppose that it has but little encouragement even to make a formal attempt at present to treat with these Indians, as it might fail, after going to considerable expense and trouble. This might be the case; but at the same time I do think a trial ought to be made, and that a treaty with this tribe might be brought about; but it will take time and money to accomplish it; and also liberal and extensive powers ought to be given to the commissioners appointed for that purpose. This reservation has become valuable, and I have no doubt but it would bring an average of from two to three dollars per acre.

I have become almost satisfied that a purchase cannot be made of the chiefs alone: therefore, the only course to be pursued, in my opinion, is to assemble every head of a family, and to feed and act sociably with them for a time, and for the commissioners to say to them that they are sent by their great father to hold a friendly talk with them in relation to their critical situation; that their possessions is not the object of their mission; that the only object their great father had in view in sending them was to promote their happiness, and that alone; that they were directed by him to give them time to consider of the message they were directed to deliver to them; and at the same time, as occasion may offer, to make use of every argument calculated to gain their friendship and to bring them to a knowledge of their true situation, carefully avoiding to say any thing to arouse their passions, or that would lead them to believe that their lands were the sole object in view. If this course don't succeed, the commissioners then ought to take a more rigid one.

It is useless, and I think worse than useless for any one to say any thing more to the chiefs, or to any other one of the tribe in relation to a treaty, unless he has full power to conclude one; as such a course, owing to the whims and changing disposition of these Indians, seems only to be calculated to embarrass rather than to bring the matter to a close, as it only goes to make them more familiar and careless, and to think lightly of the subject. My reasons for so saying are, these Indians several times appeared willing to treat, and in a few days they were quite the reverse. This is in some measure owing to the influence that certain lazy, worthless men have over them, who make use of every means to prevent their removal; as they can, as long as the Indians remain, make an easy living out of them by selling them intoxicating liquor; and, indeed, do more—accummulate property by this degrading and ruinous traffic. This is easily done, as an Indian, when he is moderately intoxicated, would part with his last blanket or horse for a quart of whiskey.

Therefore, the course I have recommended I think the only one most likely to succeed, as it would prevent these characters from interfering while concluding a treaty. But whether it is best to make an attempt forthwith or to defer it until next spring, is left to the department to decide. At the same time, if the department should consider the course recommended to be the true one, I would then recommend that it delay operations for a short time, in order first to ascertain whether something favorable may not grow out of the late council, and the determined stand the principal chief has taken towards concluding a treaty, as it would be much better for the Indians to make application to sell than for the Government to purchase.

All of which is most respectfully submitted, by
              Your most obedient servant,
                                        JOHN McELVAIN,
Hon. E. Herring,                          *Wyandot Agent.*
   *Com. Indian Affairs, Washington.*

---

                                   Sunbury, Ohio, *October 2, 1833.*

Dear Sir: I neglected to mention, before I closed my letter of this date, that so certain is a Mr. Garrett, who is married to a quarter blood, and a

Mr. Walker, a quarter blooded Wyandot, that the Wyandots will emigrate within a year or so, that they are willing and anxious to go ahead and make some preparations for the tribe by the time it may arrive, such as to erect mills, &c., and that in the section of country examined by the Wyandot delegation the winter before last.

This they are willing to do, provided the Government gives its permission, and renders them some aid. This step would go far towards drawing the Wyandots to that country, as these men are their particular friends; and if permission is given to them, mills will be erected next season. These men wish an answer as soon as it is convenient to forward one, as they wish to be off forthwith, if permission is granted, and upon such terms as will justify them in the undertaking.

It was as much as I could do to write these communications, not yet having recovered from the fever I contracted at Sandusky while paying the annuity; therefore I hope that my blunders may be overlooked. And if I shall fail to forward my annual reports (which I am now making out) in time, it will be owing to sickness, and no other cause; and if I fail I must request the department not to attach any blame to me for neglect of duty; but at the same time I hope I shall within a few days be able to make out and to forward said reports; but if I do not fast recover it will be out of my power to do so, as I can set up but a few minutes at a time.

Your obedient servant,<br>
JOHN McELVAIN,<br>
Wyandot Agent.

Hon. E. Herring,
    *Com. Indian Affairs.*

---

Executive Department, Tuscaloosa, Oct. 2, 1833.

Sir: I have the honor to acknowledge the receipt of your letter of the 5th ultimo, together with the accompanying documents. They have been examined with the deliberate attention due to the subject to which they relate.

In mine of the 20th August the objects I had principally in view were, to suggest to the President a mode of proceeding for the protection of the Indians in their posessions and reservations more congenial to the spirit of our institutions than that of sending among our citizens an armed force, and to call his attention to the irregularities inseparable from its employment, in executing the stipulations of the treaty, of which the killing of Owen is an instance.

I did not advert to the condition of the settlers upon such parts of the "ceded territory as were not included in the selections of the Indians," nor attempt to show that they had any right, founded either upon their claims to the indulgence of the Government or the laws of the land, to remain. It was impossible for me to anticipate the order contained in your letter to the marshal of the 26th August, directing the expulsion of our whole white population from the ceded territory. I beg leave, therefore, to submit for the consideration of the President my views upon this new and unexpected state of things, still trusting, with undiminished confidence, that, upon a review of the whole subject, he will find ample room to rescind this measure, which, I am constrained to believe, is one of uncalled for and unnecessary severity.

In looking over that portion of the documents furnishing complaints against the settlers, which you did me the honor to enclose for my inspection, I was at once led to the conclusion that the determination to remove them had been produced mainly, if not exclusively, by the information contained in the letters of Mr. Austill, written in the months of July and August. All these documents, except the letters referred to, and one from some of the chiefs of the 20th December last, are of date anterior to your communication to our delegation in Congress of the 8th December, 1832, giving permission to " those persons who obtained peaceable possession of the lands on which they live, &c. to occupy these tracts till the several selections are made." It appears that the injuries complained of before this period were more numerous, frequent, and aggravated than any which have been inflicted since. Mr. Austill has adopted the plan, it seems, of reporting to the War Department individual cases of intrusion, and when they are summed up they do not amount to any considerable number.

It is true that the tenor and complexion of his letters are calculated to make an unfavorable impression of the settlers generally, but it is obvious that his prejudices are very strong, that his feelings had become excited, and that a correct representation of their character, or of the true condition of the Indians, is to be obtained from some other source. If you have been led to form, from the letters of this gentleman, an unfavorable opinion of the great body of these people, I beg leave to assure you that it is utterly erroneous and unjust. Nine tenths of them have not interfered with the Indians; and in the upper counties, which are the most populous, not a whisper of dissatisfaction has been uttered.

The country in question, as you have been advised, has been laid off into nine counties, by an act of our General Assembly, and organized so as to put the entire machinery of our State Government into full and complete operation. This measure was adopted as well in conformity with the known views and wishes of the President as in pursuance of the constitution of the State of Alabama. Several of these counties contain a population of six or eight thousand souls, and the aggregate amount will not be short of twenty-five thousand.

The great object of the settlers this year has been to raise a sufficiency of corn and other provisions to supply the wants of the next season, and also to obtain the necessary quantity of cattle, hogs, and other stock. It is well known that the first business of settlers in a new country is to exchange their transportation for the means of subsistence, and this has actually been done by the greater portion of the population of the Creek nation. Their wagons, carts, horses, &c. are gone, and very many cannot possibly leave the country within the time specified in your instructions to the marshal.

The agricultural labors of these people have been crowned with success; and their crops of corn, peas, potatoes, &c. will place them, during the ensuing year, above the difficulties produced by the scarcity of the last.

Imagine for a moment the almost total destruction of these crops, the loss of most of the stock, and the wretched and destitute condition of thousands of women and children, and you will have a faithful picture of the scene which your orders, if executed, will spread over this entire region.

It seems to me that the obligations resting upon the President to avert from this large community so dire and overwhelming a calamity, are as "imperative in their character" as any which have been assumed by the

74‡

Government in the Creek treaty. At least, they interpose considerations of equal weight, I should suppose, with those by which it has been induced to overlook these obligations until the present time.

It is not to be lost sight of that these people do not stand in the light of intruders who have settled upon the public lands, and continued their settlements against the orders of the Government. As before remarked, since your letters to Col. King and others of the 8th December last, all who were then in the country had permission to remain until the selections were made. This you say was given, as it doubtless was, "upon the presumption that the country would be surveyed and the selections made before it would be time to put in another crop; and also in the belief that no inconvenience or injury would result to the Indians." You further observe that, "in both these expectations there has been a disappointment."

The delay in making the locations was not produced by any of the settlers, and the injuries complained of have been inflicted by but few. If the first cause of disappointment be matter of complaint, the sin does not lie at their door; and if offences have been committed, justice demands that the perpetrators alone should be punished.

The fifth article of the treaty of March, 1832, requires "that all intruders upon the country hereby ceded shall be removed therefrom in the same manner as intruders may be removed from other public land until the country is surveyed and selections are made, &c." For "the manner of removal you refer to the act of Congress of the 3d of March, 1807, and take for granted that, in all cases of settlement upon the public land the employment of military force may be resorted to." I have no disposition to question the constitutionality of this act, but I doubt the correctness of your construction.

It was not the intention of Congress in passing the act of 1807 to restrain persons from settling the public lands who had no object in view beyond their cultivation.

Any one who is conversant with the fraudulent claims which individuals, as well as companies, had set up to large tracts of land, before and at the period when the act in question was passed, will find no difficulty in perceiving that the principal, if not the only purpose of Congress, was to prevent them from obtaining possession, by which they expected to give strength and validity to their claims. The Yazoo purchase, effected by a fraudulent contract with the State of Georgia, embraced thirty-five millions of acres. It was believed by those interested in this contract, that they would be in a situation to contend with the Government with better prospects of success, if they could succeed in making settlements upon the territory they had purchased. It was their object to decide the controversy by suits at law, and to this end they had determined to place themselves in the attitude of defendants, by taking possession of the tract of country in which the county of Madison, in this State, is situated.

The act of 1807 was framed to counteract the views of these and other fraudulent claimants, and to prevent such persons only from making settlements as entertained the design of opposing the policy of the Government, as indicated in the rules and regulations established by Congress respecting the territory of the United States.

This view is confirmed by the fact, that as often as the settlers upon whom the act was to operate are mentioned, their claims are also adverted to, and the severest penalty denounced against them in the forfeiture of these claims.  All persons who had made settlements previous to the passage of the act are permitted to remain, provided they will sign a declaration that they do not lay any claim to the land, and do not occupy the same by virtue of any *claim* derived from any person whatever, and provided, also, they will yield quiet *possession* to any person who may purchase of the United States.  If they refuse to submit to these conditions, the marshal, at any time after the first of January, and after three months' notice, is authorized to remove them, and they incur the penalty of one hundred dollars, and imprisonment not exceeding six months.  The evidence to be furnished against those who may be indicted, among other things, is the certificate of the register that their *claims* to the lands they had occupied had not been recognized and confirmed by the United States.

Those who make settlements after the passage of the act, at the discretion of the President may be removed by the marshal, and they forfeit all title to whatever *claim* they may have which shall be vested in the United States.

A recital of the several acts of Congress passed in relation to persons who have occupied and cultivated the public lands, will confirm the opinion still more conclusively, that that body did not intend to prevent their cultivation, and that this was not the evil sought to be remedied by the act of 1807.

By the act of the 10th May, 1800, "each person who before the passage of the act shall have erected or begun to erect a grist mill or saw mill upon any of the lands herein directed to be sold, shall be entitled to the pre-emption of the section including such mill, at the rate of two dollars per acre."

By the act of the 5th of February, 1813, "every person, or the legal representatives of every person who has actually inhabited and cultivated a tract of land lying in either of the districts established for the sale of the public lands, in the Illinois Territory, which tract is not claimed by any other person, and who shall not have removed from said territory, every such person and his legal representives shall be entitled to a preference in becoming the purchaser from the United States of such tract of land at private sale."

By the act of 12th April, 1814, "every person and the legal representatives of every person who has actually inhabited and cultivated a tract of land lying in that part of the State of Louisiana which composed the late territory of Orleans, or the Mississippi territory, which tract is not rightfully claimed by any other person, and who shall not have removed from the said State or Territory, shall be entitled the right of pre-emption in the purchase thereof."

By the act of 22d April, 1826, "every person, or the legal representatives of every person who, being either the head of a family or twenty-one years of age, did, on or before the first day of January, 1825, actually inhabit and cultivate a tract of land situated in the territory of Florida, which tract is not rightfully claimed by any other person, and who shall not have removed from the said Territory, shall be entitled to the right of pre-emption in the purchase thereof."

By the 5th section of the same act, "every person, or his or her legal representatives, comprised in the list of actual settlers reported to the Commissioner of the General Land Office by the register and receiver for the district of Jackson Court House, in the State of Mississippi, under the authority of an act of Congress, entitled an act, &c., not having any written evidence of claim to land in said district, and who, on the 3d day of March, 1819, did actually inhabit and cultivate a tract of land in said district, not claimed, &c., shall be entitled to the right of pre-emption on becoming the purchaser of the United States of such tract of land." (See Gordon's Digest, from which these extracts are taken.)

Each of these acts embraced settlers in a particular State or territory, and were generally passed in anticipation of the sales of the public lands. But the act of 1830 is more general in its provisions, and includes all persons whatever who had settled upon the public domain.

By that act it is provided, "that every settler or occupant of public lands prior to the passage of this act who is now in possession and cultivated any part thereof in the year 1829, shall be, and he is hereby authorized to enter with the register of the land office for the district in which such lands may lie, by legal subdivisions, any number of acres not more than 160, or quarter section, to include his improvement, upon paying to the United States the then minimum price of the land."

Here is a continued succession of acts embracing and running through a period of thirty years, all conferring upon the settlers the valuable privilege of pre-emption. They show beyond dispute, that during this time it was the settled policy of the Government to encourage our citizens to settle and occupy the public lands, that this class of our population has always been esteemed highly meritorious, and that the exclusive right to purchase at private sale has been extended to them in consideration of, and as a reward for the services they have rendered by these settlements in testing the value and productiveness of the soil, and in affording facilities to purchasers to examine it.

These acts have been passed, with the exception of that of 1800, subsequently to 1807, and if it be a crime to cultivate the public land, the Government has suborned our citizens to its perpetration, by offering them large rewards, and conferring on them valuable privileges.

If, then, the settlement of the waste lands of the United States is not unlawful of itself, according to the spirit, true intent, and meaning of the act of 1807, the President cannot properly exert the discretionary power conferred on him for the removal of settlers, unless he has good reasons to apprehend that they intend preferring a claim to the land they occupy, or in some other respect opposing the acts of Congress for the disposal of the public domain, or interfering with and defeating "the rules and regulations respecting the territory of the United States." Nothing of this kind has been done by our people who have settled in the country ceded by Creek Indians. They "designate no boundaries thereon by marking trees, or otherwise," nor have they any intention to withhold it from any person or persons who may purchase of the United States. Their only object is, to occupy their settlements until they shall be offered for sale, and then to go into the market upon equal terms with other persons. The "manner," therefore, of removing occupants who settle upon the public lands with no design but to cultivate them is not by military force.

A treaty, like an act of Congress, is the supreme law of the land only when it is made in pursuance of the constitution of the United States. If it trenches upon the admitted jurisdiction of a State, or violates the constitutional rights of a citizen, it is not law, can impose no obligation on our people, and will be declared null and void by the legally constituted authorities.

Such is believed to be the character of that part of the 5th article of the Creek treaty, by which the Government has undertaken to remove by force all intruders upon the occupations of the Indians, "until the country is surveyed, and the selections made," and also, to remove them in the same manner from these selections, "for the term of five years from the ratification of the treaty," &c. The Indians, while they retained their character of a tribe, had an unqualified indefeasible right to their immediate improvements. The second article of the treaty not only confirms this right of possession until the selections are made, but after that period adds to it a fee simple title. The article referred to requires that a "census of these persons shall be taken, under the direction of the President, and the selections shall be made so as to include the improvements of each person within his selection, if the same can be made; and if not, then all the persons belonging to the same town entitled to selections, and who cannot make the same so as to include their improvements, shall take them in one body in a proper form." When more persons reside in a town or neighborhood than can receive their complement of land at these places, a portion of them will remain, and the others will receive their allotment in a body elsewhere; so that in every instance the possession of the improvements continues with the Indians not subject to the control of the Government, from the ratification of the treaty until the selections are made, and afterwards indefinitely.

It is obvious, therefore, that these improvements are not public land, and it is equally clear that the reservations, after they are located, will become the private property of the individuals to whom they may be assigned.

The Government has no present or future interest in such of the selections as will include improvements. They are the private property of the persons in possession, who are in no respect whatever dependent on the will or permission of the Government for its enjoyment. If any agent of the United States were to attempt the removal of one of these people entitled to have his selection around his improvements, it cannot be doubted that the district court, or the courts of this State would interpose their authority for his protection.

Whence, then, is the power derived to regulate or control the possession of these improvements? If the Indians choose to rent their fields, they only use the privilege common to every citizen; and if a white person obtains peaceable possession under a contract of this kind, he cannot be removed by military force, without a total disregard of the constitution of the United States. If a citizen can be thus forcibly and unceremoniously expelled from his possessions, the sword has already cut out from that instrument the clause which declares that no person shall be deprived of his "property without due process of law."

But intruders are to be removed by force from the selections, "for the term of five years from the ratification of the treaty," &c. After the Indians are put in possession of these tracts, ninety of which are to contain 640 acres, and the others 320 acres each, they will certainly cease to be public land. Not only the right to occupy, but the right to sell is secured by the treaty; and if there is any reason for contending that the improvements before the reservations are located are not private property, there will be none afterwards.

The constitution of the United States, in limiting the powers of the General Government in relation to the public domain, is too explicit to admit of doubt—it is, that " Congress shall have power to dispose of and make all needful rules and regulations respecting the territory or other property of the United States."

When these lands are sold or otherwise disposed of, its authority ceases, and it has no more or greater power to regulate their future possessions, or punish for trespasses than any other landholder. The Government may make a contract with our citizens conferring what title it chooses, but the contract is to be enforced and the title protected by the courts, and not by its own direct action. One hundred years might with equal propriety have been inserted in the treaty, and there was the same authority for extending the power of removal to all subsequent purchasers that there was to the Indians.

That the Indians within the limits of this State are citizens thereof, and subject to its laws in every respect, cannot be questioned, at least by the General Government. The treaty with these people is nothing more than a contract with so many citizens of Alabama.

Suppose an agreement had been entered into with eight resident citizens of the county of Montgomery, acting for themselves, and also as the agents of one hundred of their neighbors, by which the Government, besides conveying to each 640 acres of land, had stipulated to remove by force for five years all persons who might intrude upon any of these tracts. It is quite apparent that such stipulation, as well as any attempt to carry it into effect, would be an unwarrantable interference with matters which can be regulated alone by the laws of the State, and a palpable encroachment upon its jurisdiction. And yet this case is precisely similar in principle to the one under consideration.

If the General Government have the right to regulate the conduct of our people in relation to their land, if it can rightfully expel a citizen who trespasses upon the landed possessions of his neighbor by the summary interposition of a military guard, without even the forms of military investigation, what is there to restrain it from the exercise of the same power in relation to trespasses upon personal property. From this the transition would be easy to taking cognizance of all irregularities, misdemeanors, and crimes, the right to punish which has heretofore been considered as belonging exclusively to the State tribunals. If, by the treaty making power, the ordinary operation of our laws upon the persons and property of our own citizens can be suspended, as will be the case if the fifth article of the treaty is executed in the mode prescribed in your late order to the marshal, the whole field of State jurisdiction may be considered as occupied, and State sovereignty, the reserved rights of the States, &c. are but unmeaning sounds, totally unworthy of serious consideration.

I know that these terms are used by many as mere cant expressions, and that they have been brought into disrepute by the extravagant pretensions and absurd doctrines of a sister State; but they imply things that are still worth preserving, and as long as the blessings of this Union are justly appreciated, they will command the best and highest exertions of the patriot. It is often difficult to trace with precise accuracy the boundary which separates the jurisdiction of the State and Federal Governments. We can at all times, however, determine nearly where it lies. But this treaty is for giving it a new direction. It crosses the line designed in the constitution at right angles, and runs into the very heart and centre of our domestic concerns.

But, sir, there is another view of this subject, which will expose in a light still more glaring the utter incompatibility of this treaty with the jurisdictive rights of the State of Alabama.

As before-observed, the right of extending our laws over the country from which our people are ordered to be expelled is admitted to the fullest extent. This necessarily implies the right of employing the means that are indispensable to its exercise. What are those means? As enumerated in the constitution of this State, and the laws made in pursuance thereof, they are, that the State shall be laid off in counties and convenient circuits; that the circuit court shall be held in each county at least twice in every year; that the counties shall be divided into small districts, in each of which there shall be appointed two justices of the peace and two constables; that there shall be in each circuit a judge of the circuit court, who shall reside in his circuit; that there shall be for each county a judge of the county court; that there shall be also in each county a sheriff, clerks of the circuit and county courts, a coroner, notaries public, commissioners of roads and revenue, &c.; and that there shall be summoned, previous to every circuit court, a competent number of grand and petit jurors, and a like number of petit jurors for the county courts. All these ministers of our laws are required to reside in the counties to which their offices belong. These are the ordinary means by which our State Government is put in operation, and effect given to our laws. And yet the late instructions to the marshal absolutely prohibit the use of any of them.

The General Government has not only admitted the right of Alabama to extend her jurisdiction over the ceded territory, but it has invited and encouraged such extension by sundry documents, to which it is unnecessary to refer. No sooner, however, is the country organized, and all necessary steps taken to this end, than an armed force is collected on the banks of Chatahoochee, for the purpose of expelling from this large and flourishing section of the State all "white persons," including of course all civil officers and other persons whose agency is necessary to the execution of our laws. We will have no power to punish any offences committed by the Indians, or to subject them in any respect to the restraints of the law, because our courts will have been suppressed in all the counties in which they reside. Now, sir, if your order be carried into effect, will not an instance have occurred in our country, and the first instance, too, of the government of a State being put down and destroyed in nine of its counties by military force? Will not the alarming spectacle be exhibited of the laws of one of the States of this Union, in their ordinary operation, being compelled to yield, in a time of profound peace, to the dominion of the sword, to give way to the capricious will of a deputy marshal, whose favorite modes of punishment seem to be the conflagration of dwellings and the application of the bayonet?

I respectfully request that this project, so fatal in its tendency to civil liberty, and so directly subversive of the acknowledged rights and sovereignty of the State of Alabama, be abandoned. I protest against it as an unconstitutional interference with our local and internal affairs, and as a measure of revolting injustice and oppression towards that portion of our inhabitants who have not injured the Indians. Put away, sir, the sword, which has been unnecessarily and too hastily drawn against this large and unoffending community. It is the appropriate arbiter in contests of ambition, but not in questions of constitutional right. It is not to be forgotten, that the American people, on a recent occasion, pronounced emphatically, that questions of jurisdiction between the foreign and domestic branches of our Government are to be settled by the tribunal which the constitution vests with the power of expounding the laws.   To these tribunals I appeal on behalf of the good people of this State.

Very respectfully,

I have the honor to be, sir,

Your obedient servant,

JOHN GAYLE.

Hon. Lewis Cass,.

Secretary of War, Washington City.

---

N. E. Land District, Mississippi, *October* 3, 1833.

Sir:.I presume that Col. George W. Martin has apprized you of the course he has taken in relation to the location of Indian reserves, viz., the appointing of an acting agent at each land office, for the purpose of registering Indian reserves; and, inasmuch as he has conferred the appointment on *me*, for this district, I feel it my duty to consult you upon such subjects as are presented to me, about which I may be in difficulty.   The case which I wish to present to you is the following:

Col. David Folsom (a half breed Choctaw) has purchased an Indian reserve of three quarters of a section.   He has also purchased another reserve of one quarter section, making a whole section.   Both of those Indians lived on the same section, on which was a missionary establishment, where the Rev. Mr. Byington resided, and at present resides.   The buildings and improvements are pretty good.   The colonel has applied to me to register his two reserves covering that establishment.   I have not thought proper to comply with his wishes, and he says he will contend.   You will please give me specific instructions in reference to this subject as soon as practicable.   It is also in contemplation by a certain gentleman, I am informed, to sweep *Mayhew* in the same, or nearly in the same manner.

I entertain but little doubt of being able to register all the reserves within this district before the sales of the land.

You are aware of the importance of an early response to this without a suggestion on my part.

Your obedient servant,

WM. DOWSING, *Register*.

Hon. Elijah Hayward,

Commissioner General Land Office,

Washington City.

---

Marshal's Office, Mobile, *October* 3, 1833.

Sir: In the execution of the several instructions received from you, relative to removal of intruders from the Creek lands, I have advertised, in three journals, that all persons who are on those lands, who have made their own improvements, to remove so soon as their crops are gathered; and that time is fixed on the 15th day of January next.   It will enable those who have planted cotton time sufficient to gather and secure all.   I am informed (not officially) that it is the intention of the Executive of this State to issue a process in nature of an action of trespass for every person who is removed by me.   I am well satisfied that something of the kind will be attempted.

There are several counties laid off in the Creek country, and regular terms of courts are holden.   I have to request the favor to be instructed in the manner I shall act, should process be issued; and I have no doubt they will be, whether I shall suffer the sheriff to execute them upon me or not. If it is right they should, I will yield.   I should dislike to be tried by those who are entirely interested, and more particularly in those counties embraced in the Creek country.   There are a great number of persons who have settled on the Creek lands, and they have more or less connexions in the different sections of the State; and the excitement that prevails, in consequence of their removal after their crops are gathered, is very great.

I hear of no complaints now of persons molesting the Indians in their improvements.   It would be very desirable if some course could be pursued in carrying the treaty into effect without military aid, or the marshal, or his deputy.

Some say that the instructions of the Government have been executed with too much exactness or rigor; others say, that partiality has been shown; and I confess that I was unable, in many cases, to act as justly between the parties as I could wish, because I found it impossible to arrive at facts.

If consistent with the views of the Government, it would be well if some one could be appointed to reside in some convenient part of the nation, and settle the differences between the whites and Indians.

The distance from this to the nearest part of the Creek lands is near two hundred miles.   An act of intrusion might take place, and I may not hear of it for a considerable time.

I have no doubt but a great saving would be made to the Government, both in time and money.   A just conception of your instructions of 28th August is had by me, relative to that class of intruders who are to remain until their crops are gathered.   Yours of the 16th ultimo, accompanied by the copy of a letter to Messrs. Currey, Abercrombie and others, is also received.

Very respectfully, &c.,<br>R. L. CRAWFORD,<br>*U. S. Marshal.*

Hon. Lewis Cass, *Secretary of War.*

---

FORT MITCHELL, ALABAMA, *October* 4, 1833.

SIR: The enclosed communication is from a respectable citizen of Alabama, now living in the Indian country, who requests that I would address you in behalf of the white intruders; but presuming that the Government have decided on the course to be pursued towards these people, I deem it almost unnecessary for me, at this late period, to make any comments on their situation.

I beg leave, however, to remark, that although I believe a majority of the intruders to be   *   *   *   , yet there are many good men amongst them; and that their indiscriminate removal will cause serious distress in many poor but worthy families; yet it would, I fear, be a most difficult and delicate matter to make the selection; besides, unless the whole are removed, it would be almost as well not to remove any.

My views in relation to the situation and removal of the intruders were freely expressed in more than one communication, addressed to the General-in-Chief, about a year ago, when I was the commanding officer at this post; to which I beg leave to refer you, should you think them worthy of your notice.

I have the honor to be,
Most respectfully, sir,
Your obedient servant,
P. WAGER,
*Major United States Army.*

To the Honorable Lewis Cass,
*Secretary of War, Washington city.*

---

Macon County, Ala., *September 24, 1833.*

Sir: I see in the marshal's instructions from Colonel Cass, that the settlers are all to be removed from the Creek territory, which, if put in force, will prove destructive to a great many persons; in fact, it will be an injury to all living in the country. The settlers are well satisfied that the Government does not wish to harass them wantonly; but that the Government has been misinformed of the true situation of the settlers and Indians there can be no doubt. The complaints made of the settlers to Government have been caused from designing persons, such as wish to speculate off of the Indians, and knowing, if the whites are not removed, their opportunity for speculation will not be so good. And another thing, no doubt, that will have a tendency to injure the settlers is, that there have been reports circulated that they intended to resist the Government troops; and I understand that it is reported at Fort Mitchell that I have two hundred volunteers for that purpose. I assure you, sir, it is every word false. If there is a volunteer within the limits of this nation I do not know it; in fact I do not believe it. It is true there has been some meetings of the citizens, for the purpose of getting or trying the Executive of this State to interpose; and even those meetings I have not attended. I do not demand it as a right, but ask it as a favor, for you to write to Colonel Cass, stating how matters stand, and request that the orders may not be put in execution until the Executive of this State can have an opportunity of making a true statement of affairs here to the Government. The settlers know the land belongs to the Government, and that they have no right to remain on it without permission from the Government. After the Government is apprised how matters really do stand, and it then thinks it expedient to put us out, we will go without a murmur. A letter from you to Colonel Cass upon this subject would no doubt greatly benefit the settlers. If an apology is necessary for this intrusion, my situation with that of many others is a sufficient one.

Respectfully, your humble servant,
THS. S. WOODWARD.

Major Philip Wager,
*Fort Mitchell, Ala.*

P. S. The President himself has seen too many of the hardships of a new settled country to remove us, if he knew our true situation and the cause of the complaints made against us.                          T. S. W.

OTOE VILLAGE, ON THE PLATTE RIVER,
*October* 4, 1833.

SIR: I have the honor to transmit, through your department, a petition from the Omahaw Indians to their great father. The Omahaws reside about 60 miles west of the Missouri, on the Elkhorn; their number is estimated at 1800; their present location is on a prairie, with few agricultural advantages. I have urged them to locate themselves on the Missouri, where there is fine land and timber; they have readily consented to this, and are anxious to give up the chace, and pursue an agricultural life. They reside in their village but a short time; in the spring they plant a little corn, and spend the summer on the buffalo ground; they return in the fall to gather the crop, if any there be, and spend the winter on the bottoms of the Missouri; the chiefs have been divided on the subject of location, but are now unanimous.

Their consent to abandon their old village is the best evidence of the sincerity of their professions. Their story is simply told in their petition, and will, I trust, induce Congress to grant some assistance.

I did not feel willing to enter into a treaty obligatory on the United States to pay money, as the gratuity could so properly be referred to the discretion of the government.

I would most respectfully recommend an appropriation sufficient to purchase agricultural implements, some stock, also furnish two farmers, and erect a corn mill. The agreement of the Omahaws not to consider aggressions from neighboring tribes as cause of war, but to refer the difficulty to some umpire appointed by the President, is one important step towards civilization.

I have only to add what I have remarked to you before, that the game is fast disappearing, and that the Indians are brought to this certain alternative, to *till the ground or starve.* They cannot become farmers without instruction and assistance. The present seems a favorable moment to bestow charity on the unfortunate aborigines. I rely with much confidence on the civilization of this tribe, if adequate means are used.

I am, most respectfully,
Your obedient servant,
HENRY L. ELLSWORTH.

To the Hon. E. HERRING,
*Indian Commissioner.*

---

*To our Great Father, the President of the United States.*

The chiefs and warriors of the Omahaw tribe of red men, in behalf of our tribe, humbly represent, that the Omahaws reside far up the Missouri river; that they are the friends of the white men, and love to open their ears to the advice of their great father.

The Omahaws are a brave people, and were once numerous and happy; they are now few and unhappy.

Once there were buffalo, elk, and deer in abundance; but the white men have killed some, and our red brothers who have come from the east to live here are killing what is left. The game is almost gone What shall we do? Must we die so soon? Our great father has sent us a good father, Mr. Ellsworth, to talk to us. He has told us we must work and cultivate the ground, and then we shall be happy. Our agent, Mr. Dougherty, has told us the same many times. It is a good talk for us, but we have no cattle, and know not how to work as the white men do; we send to our great father, who takes care of his red children, to ask him to give us some farmers to tell us how to work; some cattle and agricultural implements, some potatoes and other seeds to plant, and then we will not go to the chace, but live at home and work as our great father tells us to do. We are willing to locate ourselves on our lands, where our great father thinks best for us to live for agricultural purposes. Our father and friend who has talked to us here has told us to send our children to school, that they may learn to read and write, as white boys and girls do. This we like very much, and wish our great father would send us some teachers to live in our villages, and we will send our children to school, for we want to have them learn.

Our father here tells us not to make war any more, for you want all the red men to live in peace; but if we have any difficulty with neighboring tribes, to refer the matter in dispute to some arbiter whom you shall appoint to settle the same: this we are willing to do. We have done.

Will not our great father help us, that we may be again happy, that we may once more have enough to eat, and our women and children not starve and die when the cold winter comes?

Dated at Otoe village, on the Platte river. this third day of October, 1833.

OMPABLONGA, or BIG ELK, *1st Chief.*
BIG EYES, *Chief.*
IRON EYES, *Chief.*
AGA HA, *Money Chief.*
WAY RUGARON, *Chief.*
WAH COO RA, *a Brave.*
NEGOSH SLUDAY, *a Brave.*

Signed in presence of
HENRY L. ELLSWORTH,
EDWARD ELLSWORTH.

---

WASCISSA, *October 5, 1833.*

SIR: I rise from a bed of sickness to enclose you a copy of an agreement made with Mulatto King and Tustenuggy-Hajo in June last. That concluded with Econchattemicco is verbatim the same, substituting the name of that chief where Mulatto King and Tustenuggy-Hajo's appear. I did not suppose that these documents, until duly ratified, could be considered as records, or could be even admitted as such in your office, unless received through the Department of War, or I should have furnished you copies as I returned through Tallahassee from the Appalachicola. Indeed, I am not in the habit generally of retaining copies of such instruments, as you well know from a reply of mine to a previous application made by you in relation to the other agreements I was an instrument in making. It is now accidentally that I find myself in possession of the first or rude draft of the contract which was finally acceded to by the upper towns on the Appalachicola.

I regret very much " when you had it once in your power to promote the views and interests of the Government" in relation to the execution of the treaty with Blunt, you had not done so, as you would have relieved yourself of the difficulties of which you now complain, and may have prevented the injurious consequences now very unreasonably attributed to the agreements made with Mulatto King and Econchattemicco. Why should they produce the probable results of which you speak? Or why should they be permitted to be obstacles to the faithful compliance, on the part of Blunt, with an agreement which he voluntarily made, I might almost say forced upon the commissioner of the United States.

When I commenced my negotiations with the towns on the Appalachicola, I refused positively to treat with *either separately*. Several-ineffectual attempts were made to get the chiefs and warriors to assemble, the two upper towns invariably evading the call. Blunt still continued importunate, pressing me to treat with him separately. It was finally agreed between us, that he would make one more effort to assemble the chiefs of the two upper towns, and to meet me in Tallahassee in October last; and to aid him in his object, the Governor actually gave an order to Econchattemicco and Mulatto King to assemble at his house at the time appointed. You know the result. Blunt and his chiefs appeared with but one individual—Hye Tyger, from Mulatto King's towns; and he came more as the bearer of a letter from the chiefs Econchattemicco and Mulatto King, declining to meet me, and stating positively their unwillingness to sell their reserves or to remove from the country. I still felt unwilling to treat with Blunt separately; but he made the appeal, which was strong. That the upper towns could not, he was persuaded, be induced to treat; that the chiefs were obstinate fools, incapable of seeing their true interests; and that it was cruel to make him suffer for their stubbornness; that he was convinced he could no longer live in peace and quietness near the white people; that he would never consent to come under their laws, and was willing to migrate if I would treat with him alone, and let the other towns follow their course. I did so, and have given this detail of facts that you may correctly judge how far Blunt has any pretext for asserting (if he has so asserted) that the late agreement with Econchattemicco and Mulatto King present any just obstacles to the faithful compliance, on his part, with what he has *voluntarily and solemnly* obligated himself to perform.

I had an interview with Blunt some three or four weeks since, in Tallahassee, and he certainly did not convey to me the impressions which it seems you have derived from his conversations and written communications. He informed me that he was active in building boats, and making other preparations for migrating; that he could not go, however, as early as was expected of him, and would not, at all events, depart before his *son* was returned to him. He further stated that he would expect from Government payment for the robbery committed on him. I gave him no encouragement on this subject. He intimated that you had promised he should be repaid, and that he should expect it. I recollect your once expressing an opinion to me that Blunt could be compensated for his loss under a construction placed by you on one of the articles of the treaty of Camp Moultrie. I thought not; but desirous that he should, if possible, recover the sum stolen, I suggested that you should submit the subject to the Secretary of War. If, however, you have communicated this legal opinion to Blunt, you will find it a very hard task to make him discriminate *between a mere opinion and a positive promise* by the agent of Government that he should have the money returned him. At the close of the interview, Blunt complained of his people deserting to, and being protected in the upper, and particularly Mulatto King's town. I did not consider a subject so easily corrected of much moment.  By what authority does Mulatto King or Econchattemicco presume to admit within the limits of their reserve, or to extend protection to any others than those permitted by treaty to remain with them?  The late contract made with them certainly extends no such privilege.  A resident agent on the Appalachicola was strongly recommended by me, for the express object of preventing collisions between the towns, and to correct the very evil now complained of.  This was always anticipated by me, (for I was not blind to the growing hostilities between the chiefs of the upper and lower towns,) and which would have occurred with or without the conclusion of the late agreement with Econchattemicco and Mulatto King.

The correction of the evil, and that very effectually, is in the power of the Executive of the territory.  The chiefs of the upper towns should be immediately called to account, and compelled to surrender up, or drive from their limits, every Indian from Blunt's town, and held responsible for the repetition of the offence.

A breaking of the late agreement made with them by the Government refusing to ratify it, may be one punishment threatened; and if that should fail them, the penalty in the additional article of the treaty of Camp Moultie may be held *in terrorem* over them, by which the General Government reserved to itself the power of ordering the chiefs and their followers within the limits of the Seminole territory, if their conduct on their reserves was not such as to meet with its approbation.

In seeking, sir, for the real obstacles to a satisfactory adjustment of Blunt's treaty, you will probably find that they lay much more concealed than the possible effects of the agreement made with Econchattemicco and Mulatto King.  Blunt's ruling passion may have escaped your observation. I have long suspected that he has been anxious to promote the desertion of his people, with the exception of the few he is most devoted to.  Early in the winter Cochran's family, he reported, were taken from him and carried to the Creek nation.  Now the complaint is, that his people are seeking the protection of Mulatto King in consequence of the late agreement, when the agreement gives that chief no such authority.  The object is obvious. Blunt, when his plans are matured, will remove, and with those who remain at the time on his reserve.  His reserve will then be surrendered to the United States, and he will claim the 10,000 dollars, the whole amount stipulated to be paid, with the pretext that it was not by his acts, but by those of the Government that he was prevented from complying with the obligations of removing the whole number of souls on the reserve when the stipulation was made.  I am no prophet, but this is the game, or I am much deceived.

Your letter only confirms me on the correctness of the views I took, that the Executive of the territory was the proper person to carry into effect the different Indian treaties made within the limits of his Government.  Most of the obstacles in the way of execution, are such as his gubernatorial authority can alone remove; and it was from this conviction, and this alone, and not from any desire to shift on others difficulties and responsibilities I was bound to meet myself, that induced me to decline your suggestion that I should accept of a special commission to execute the treaty with Blunt.  Within the limits of the territory the execution of treaties had generally devolved on the Governors as *ex-officio* superintendents of Indian affairs; and had the Secretary of War deemed it advisable to change the practice, I presume he would not have waited for an application from any individual.

I have submitted my opinions on the subject of your letter with the candor and disinterestedness which has invariably characterized my intercourse with you. Not over confident in my own judgment, I am unwilling to obtrude it upon others; but where solicited, I will cheerfully submit my suggestions to be acted on by the more mature judgment of others. My state of health will not, I am satisfied, permit me prudently to leave home for several weeks. If, however, it is of any consequence, or it would be at all satisfactory to you to communicate your correspondence with the Department of War on the difficulties encountered in executing the treaty made with Blunt, we can appropriate a day or two to the object, if you could conveniently spend that time at my house.

I am, respectfully,

Your obedient servant,

JAMES GADSDEN.

His Excellency J. D. WESTCOTT.

---

HUNTSVILLE, *October* 8, 1833.

DEAR SIR: I have just returned from an excursion of three weeks through the counties of Blount, St. Clair, and Jackson. At St. Clair, two weeks ago, I met the first intelligence of your instructions to the marshal of the southern district of Alabama, in reference to the settlers of the territory recently acquired from the Creek Indians.

Be assured your letter, and the opinion of the Attorney General, have produced much excitement and alarm, not only amongst those who reside in the Creek territory, but amongst our citizens generally. Until your instructions were made known, no apprehension of any such measure was entertained by those who had settled upon and occupied any of those lands peacefully and without trespassing on the improvements in the actual possession of the Indians. They, and indeed our citizens generally, had supposed, according to the terms of the treaty, and the tenor of your letters of the 8th December last to myself, and other members of the delegation from Alabama, and your letter of instructions to the Cherokee agent of the first of May last, (a copy of which you did me the honor to enclose to me, in reply to mine of the 18th April,) that they would be exempt from the operation of military force or even civil process.

All the difficulties and dissatisfaction of the Indians have doubtless arisen from the reckless conduct of a few lawless individuals, who have forcibly driven Indians from their improvements, and perhaps some of those engaged in speculation. These bear an incalculably small proportion to the mass of the population who reside in the ten counties carved out of the new territory by our last legislature. The counties of Benton and Talladega border on St. Clair. While at Ashville, the seat of justice of the latter, I saw respectable gentlemen from both the former, from whom I learned that, according to the census recently taken under the authority of the State, Benton contains a population of thirty-three hundred white souls, and Talladega about four thousand. It is estimated by intelligent and respectable gentlemen, who have travelled through those new counties, that they contain in all a population of from twenty-five to thirty thousand souls. It is unnecessary for me to attempt a description of the distress and ruin which would be inevitable, if there should be a removal of all those people pursuant to your order. Many of them have emigrated hundreds of miles, from North and South Carolina, Georgia, Kentucky, and Tennessee, as well as from the longer settled parts of this State. Should they be permitted to gather their crops, which constitute almost their sole means of subsistence for the next year, they cannot remove them, nor can they sell them, for if all are removed, who will there be in the country to purchase? Again, the corn crop of Alabama is a short one; it is believed by many that it will command five dollars per barrel before midsummer; should this number, or any great proportion of them, crowd into the older counties, how can they be preserved from starvation? These hints will be sufficient to convey to your mind some idea of the dismay, distress, and utter ruin to thousands of our citizens which must attend the execution of your orders to the marshal of the southern district.

Another consideration, which deserves notice, arises from the fact that ten counties have been organized principally, if not wholly from this new territory, and judicial and ministerial officers have been sent or appointed amongst them. The laws of our State may be considered in as full operation in those counties as in any other portion of the State. Although the opinion of the Attorney General seems to contemplate the employment of military force to accomplish the removal of these citizens, I do not so understand your instructions to the marshal, and earnestly hope I am not mistaken. I presume, *as the President does not think he has the constitutional right to remove settlers or intruders from Indian territory, over which the laws of a State may be extended, by military force.* he would not be disposed to exercise such power in removing such persons from a tract of country to which the Indian title is extinguished, and over which the laws are also in full force. The Attorney General remarks, " It can hardly be supposed, by any one, that the United States have not the same right that an individual possessed, to defend their lawful possessions by force against a trespasser. Must they surrender up the public property whenever lawless violence attempts to seize upon it?" Those remarks seem to suppose the existence of a case altogether different from the real one. I should not deny the right of the Government to defend its possessions as far as an individual may lawfully do. If the Attorney General intended to be understood, *that an individual can lawfully expel by force even a trespasser, after he is in quiet possession,* I think, *with due deference, he would find himself unsustained by authority.* But the individuals whose removal is the subject of consideration are not now entering upon this territory; they are already in quiet possession, and at the worst, in my humble judgment, must be considered tenants at will.

It is unnecessary, however, to discuss the legal principles which may be involved. My chief object, both as a friend of the Government and the people, was to bring to your view the real state of the question, and to suggest a remedy which might, in some degree, obviate difficulties. It appears to me that the operations of the Government might be confined to mere civil process. I should be sorry to see even that urged with much haste or rigor. In the meantime, a sufficient additional number of agents might be employed to locate the Indian reservations in the shortest practicable time; which, when done, would supersede all necessity for a removal of settlers who are peaceful, and not trespassers on the improvements actually in the possession of Indians.

I persuade myself that these hasty suggestions will be received with a degree of indulgence corresponding with the friendly and respectful spirit in which they are offered. I am far from the attempts or desire to obtrude my views unnecessarily or improperly either upon the President or yourself; for each of whom, I may be permitted to say, I have ever cherished the most friendly regard and the most profound respect.

I shall be much gratified to hear from you in reply, when your conveni- ence may permit.

I have the honor to be, sir,
Most respectfully,
Your obedient servant,
C. C. CLAY.

Hon. Lewis Cass,
*Secretary of War.*

———

FRANKFORT, KENTUCKY, *October* 8, 1833.

SIR: On yesterday I had the honor to receive your communication, in which I am informed of my reappointment to appraise the Cherokee im- provements within the chartered limits of Georgia. I have concluded to accept of the appointment, and shall report myself accordingly at the time and place prescribed in your letter.

I have the honor to be,
Very respectfully,
Your most obedient servant,
WM. M. DAVIS.

Hon. Lewis Cass,
*Secretary of War,*
*Washington City.*

———

COMMISSIONER'S OFFICE,
*Fort Leavenworth, October,* 1833.

SIR: Enclosed herewith is the talk with the Pawnee nation, which pre- ceded the treaty of cession heretofore transmitted.

Yours respectfully,
HENRY L. ELLSWORTH,
*U. S. Commissioner.*

Hon. E. HERRING,
*Indian Commissioner, Washington.*

———

COUNCIL WITH THE PAWNEE NATION OF THE PLATTE RIVER,
*October* 9, A. D. 1833.

(Mr. E.) FRIENDS AND BROTHERS OF THE PAWNEE NATION: The Great Spirit has kindly permitted us to meet this day. I have come a great dis- tance to see you. I am happy to behold your four bands all meet together like brothers. I thought it best to ask you to assemble here, though I in- tend visiting each of your villages before I return home. Your great father has sent me to talk to you. Listen to what I have to say. Your great father lives a long distance from you, yet he loves you as well as the Osages and Delawares who live nearer, and he is equally desirous for your happiness as theirs. Your great father wants all his red men to live in peace, and make war no more. He does not believe that *you* prefer war to peace, but will be disposed to make a settlement of all difficulties, and shake hands with your enemies. Yourselves and the Delawares have long been at war. You have claimed that the Delawares trespassed upon your lands. When your great father gave the Delawares their land, he did not know that you claimed any part of it. He is very anxious to remove the difficulty, and is willing to aid you in agriculture and give you goods, if you will cede to him the land lying south of the Platte river. You have land enough that is good without this. Your father will permit you during his pleasure, with other friendly Indians, to hunt on the land you cede, while it remains unassigned to any tribe. Your great father knows the game is every year becoming scarcer, and will soon be gone. When the game is gone, what will you do? You must cultivate the ground, or starve. The Otoes and Omahaws, with whom I have talked, have agreed to give up the chase, work on their land, build themselves log houses, raise cattle, corn, beans, potatoes, squashes, and other things. You are nearer the buffalo than they are, but the buffalo will soon be a great distance from you. You will I am sure be happier at home than at the chase, if you can have enough to eat. Now, if you are willing to work on the land, your great father will give you farmers to assist you. He will give you cattle and hogs, and with a few breeding hogs you will be supplied with abundance of pork, if you do not kill the pigs too soon. He will give you axes, hoes, and ploughs. He will give you mills in which you can grind with horses, all your corn. He will give you schools, where your children may learn to read and write like white men's children. Other red men are learning their children, and I wish the Pawnee children to know as much as the rest. He will give you blacksmiths to reside in your villages. All these things will make you happy. But you cannot enjoy these advantages unless you remain in your villages, and protect your blacksmiths and teachers. When peace is made with the Delawares and Osages, there will not be much danger. I hope a peace will soon be made with the Sioux. Your great father will do it as soon as he can, if you are willing. I am your friend. I came to do you good. I will not deceive you. You have a good friend here, Mr. Dougherty, your agent. He loves you, and will not tell you to do any thing wrong. Ask his advice, if you doubt what to do. Your great father thinks Mr. Dougherty a good man, so do I. You have also your old friend, Mr. Passin; ask his advice. Brothers, I am sorry to know that the Delawares have destroyed this village. You have, however, rebuilt it. I am sorry, too, that your enemies have killed any of your nation. I hope peace will soon be made, and you will have war no more; and that your women and children can remain safely in your villages when the warriors are absent at the chase. Tell me all that is in your hearts. I have done.

Head chief of the nation (of the Grand Pawnee band.) My father: I accede to what you ask; I am glad to accept the proposition; I am glad that our great father knows where we live, and pities us, and is agoing to help us. For my part, I am not only willing but glad to accept the proposition. My father, I am in hopes things will now be changed; that the whites will not do as they have done. They go *around* us to get to the mountains and Mexico, because they fear us; but now I hope they will come to us as to a *home*. All the Pawnee chiefs have heard what you say. I now speak for all those young men you see crowding the door. They desire peace, and will eat out of the same bowl with all nations. My father, we have been, as it were, like men travelling, sick, weary, and dying; but your arrival and the words spoken to us have resuscitated all. We are all glad at what you say, and hope you will make it good. What I have said to you is true. I thank you, my father, for what you do for us, and hope you will send the proffered aid as soon as possible. We view your promises as certain truth; as much so as if we had the substance of them now in our hands. At present we look like persons who have passed through a burning prairie. We are black, our robes are dirty; but I hope we shall soon dress like other people. We are poor, and in great need of what you offer. All the chiefs and braves on this side I have conversed with, and I believe they think as I do, and will be under great obligations to you. Let us know, my father, what you will do for us. All are anxious to see the treaty. You have come a great ways, and have come to do us good. We would be glad could you commence giving us some of those good things next spring. Look at these dirty and greasy people, my father; they surely need your help. Blacksmiths, my father, we should like near at hand. It is a great distance to go to Missouri for little things. I am glad, of course, to have a shop anywhere, but would like it nearer. I thank you, my father; all the squaws and children thank you; it is a great day of rejoicing among them. I speak for my village: all its inhabitants are glad; and though we never saw you before, we love you at first sight. You desire of us exactly what we wish ourselves. You cannot want peace more than we do. My father, I find nothing more to say. I am so glad that I have forgotten half what I had laid up to tell you.

Little Chief Tappaye band. My father: What my chief has said are the exact sentiments of my own breast. I am willing to abandon the chase and the land for what you offer. My village is not here, but on my return I will tell my people all that you have said.

Mole-in-the-face, Chief Repub. village. My father: I have nothing further to say. My relations have spoken, and I perfectly agree with them.

Spitfire, chief Pawnee Loups. My father: The chiefs who preceded me have all spoken the truth; and I only remark, if you wish that land, my father, it is yours—take it. I am anxious to become acquainted with you. You, my father, (Mr. Dougherty,) believe that the Master of Life put you on this earth to help us red skins. I am glad you have come to help us; and I hope you, my father, (Mr. Ellsworth,) will commence in the spring, that we may have plenty to eat. We get into difficulties oftentimes by going to the south and meeting white people. I hope we shall now see them coming to our village. Heretofore the whites used to steal around in passing us, but now it will not be so. I am glad, my father, and will repeat all you have said to my young men. I feel happy, my father, and those young men you see feel like laughing. I hope from this time they will laugh, and cry no more. We would like to know when we may expect the things you promise us. We are now all going to the hunt again, and in an opposite direction from you, still we shall think of you; and I hope that some of those good things will be forthcoming on our return from the hunt in the spring.

Mr. Ellsworth, in conclusion. I have a few more words to say. Brothers: It makes my heart glad to find you take the advice of your great father so readily. I have not only heard all you have said, but have had it committed to paper. You have asked me when you shall receive your annuities. I have made a treaty with the Otoes, and shall now make one with you, and it will be sent on to your great father. If he thinks it is right, as he probably will, he will send on the annuities. I wish to say a few words respecting the farmers, &c., &c. Your great father will give farmers and blacksmiths in your villages immediately, if you will stay and protect them from hostile bands. If all the villages will not stay and protect the persons and property offered them, that village which does so shall receive its portion of the annuities and advantages. If the Pawnees will leave a party to protect the farmers, &c., your great father will give twenty-five guns to each village, to help to protect them from hostile bands. Your great father wishes you to select a few from each village to accompany me down when I return to Fort Leavenworth, and make peace. You may consider the subject. A treaty will be ready for you to sign in the morning. In the meantime, let me say, this is a happy day, and an ox will be killed to give you a feast. To-morrow, also, some goods will be delivered to *this* village; and then I proceed to the other villages, and carry them their portion.

I certify the above to be a true copy from record.

EDWARD A. ELLSWORTH,
*Secretary pro tem.*

---

CHEROKEE AGENCY, *October* 10, 1833.

SIR: I have now on hand only about five hundred and ninety blankets, and some few of them are so much injured by the rats and moths as to be worth but little, and not to answer the purpose for which they were intended; and should the emigration progress as well as from present prospects we have a right to expect, there will be needed in the course of this winter and spring at least from eight to twelve hundred more; and as they can be laid in on better terms in the eastern than in the southern cities, I have to request that you will have them purchased and forwarded before the emigrants set out, say before the last of January next.

It is my opinion, founded on that of all the merchants in this vicinity, that the cheapest and most practicable means of transportation is from Baltimore in wagons; this is the way they bring all their dry goods. They also inform me that wagons are to be had at all times in Baltimore. They also say that full loads are always required, say 4,000 pounds, which I should suppose would require from 1,000 to 1,200 blankets.

Of the other articles, viz., guns and kettles, I have a sufficient stock for the present year, and tobacco can be bought as cheap here as anywhere.

Of our progress in the enrolling business Major Currey no doubt advises you from time to time.

Very respectfully,
Your obedient servant,
H. MONTGOMERY.

ELBERT HERRING, Esq.,
*Commissioner of Indian Affairs, Washington City.*

MISSISSIPPI, LOWNDES COUNTY, *October* 10, 1833.

DEAR SIR: I am requested to write you as agent for John McGilbry and Taner McGilbry, who have taken citizenship as Choctaws under the provisions of the treaty of Dancing Rabbit creek, agreeable to the fourteenth article of said treaty. Application was made through me to Major Dowsing, who is acting as agent for locating reservations of said treaty: the location was wished by the Indians to adjoin the parent by a connexion of one half mile, and connect one on the other in that way throughout; this was objected to by the acting agent as contrary to his instructions from the principal agent Col. Martin. I have consulted several men learned in law, who give it as their opinion that they were entitled to run their land in any way so as to adjoin the location of the parent. Is there any doubt as regards their location? if there is, is it not a well founded doubt on the part of the Choctaws? I will refer you to that clause of the treaty where it is expressed that where any well founded doubt arises as to the construction of the treaty, the most favorable shall be given to the Choctaw: this does certainly give the right claimed by the Choctaws. If you are not the proper officer of the Government that should be applied to on this subject for information, will you be so good as to lay this statement before them for instructions, and forward them to me as soon as possible.

There are a few settlers who have settled on this land who are endeavoring to prejudice the Government against the Indians and their rights. It is understood by the Indians that one of them, *Gabriel Felder*, has wrote a remonstrance to your department against their locating their lands agreeable to the most favorable construction of said treaty, adding that it was only advantageous to a speculator. If this is the case, I can assure you it is without foundation, and should take it as a singular favor to be furnished with a *copy of that letter.* I have no fear that such would go to the prejudice of the Indians, as I have every confidence that ample justice will be dealt out to those unfortunate people; and that as regards the location, no speculator will be benefited or injured in that event.

Be so good as to advise me on this subject as early as possible.

There appears to be one more difficulty in this location: the State line between Alabama and Mississippi running through the improvements, a part is wanted on each side which we wish to be advised on. I hope that *Mr. Felder* will not be countenanced in his nullification notions, who not only wishes to nullify the laws and treaty, but the rights of those unfortunate Indians.

The Indians urge me to press on you for a construction of their treaty, and to advise them through me as soon as possible, as they wish to know before the lands are sold.

I am, sir,
Your obedient servant,
THOMAS D. WOOLDRIDGE.

To the Hon. LEWIS CASS,
*Secretary of War.*


P. S. I enclose you a map of the land wanted; they are all entitled to six sections and a half of land, including Gordon McGilbry's claim; those marked R is the land claimed by the McGilbrys; those marked R embrace all of the improvements owned by the whole of them.

Please address your letter to Pickensville, Alabama.

6  5  4  3  2  1

7  8  9  10  11  12

18  17  16  15  14  13

19  20  21  22  23  24

30  29  *R* *R* *R* *R* 28  *R* 27  26  25
*R* *R* *R*

31  32  *R* *R* *R* *R* *R* 33  34  *R* *R* 35  *R* *R* 36
*R*

6  5  *R* 4  *R* 3  *R* 2  *R* 1 *R* *R*
*R* *R*

7  8  9  *R* 10  *R* 11  12

18  17  16  15  14  13

19  20  21  22  23  24

30  29  28  27  26  25

31  32  33  34  35  36

*Mississippi*  *Alabama*  *Tombuckly River.*

Section 28, and northwest ¼ of 27, and northeast ¼ of 23, is wanted for Turner McGilbry, and two children under ten years of age. Section 35 and west half of section 34, for Gordon, and two children under 10 years of age.

Fractional ½ section 1 in Alabama, southwest ¼ of section 2, north half 11, northeast ¼ of 10, southeast ¼ of 3, and west ½ of 3, northeast ¼ of 4, east half of 33, and northwest ¼ of 33, northeast ¼ of 32, and southeast ¼ of 29, for John McGilbry, and four children over ten years of age, and two under.

You will see by the map that it is nearly in a body. It would be an extreme hard case to confine them to the river and river swamps. We think they are entitled to the location as laid down by the treaty; and Col. Trahern, who was locating a few days since, orphan claims, gave it as his opinion that they were entitled to those lands, and respected their claims.

> Yours respectfully,
> THOMAS D. WOOLDRIDGE.

Columbus, *October* 12, 1833.

Sir: According to instructions received from the Office of Indian Affairs, I have completed the locations of the orphan children of the Choctaw nation in the northwestern and northeastern land districts. The time being too short to accomplish the whole of the orphan claims before the ensuing sales at the different land offices, therefore in the southeastern district I have not made any selections, but will do so as soon as practicable.

     I have the honor to be,
        Very respectfully,
          Your obedient servant,
            WILLIAM TRAHERN,
             *Agent Choctaw Orphan Children.*

Hon. Lewis Cass,
   *Secretary of War.*

———

Washington, *October* 14, 1833.

Sir: Having perused the instructions you had contemplated issuing to Mr. Bright and myself, in relation to the location of the reservations under the Creek treaty, I beg leave to assure you of my grateful feelings to both the President and yourself, for this renewed evidence of your confidence.

Under the permission which you have allowed to me, I will respectfully suggest the following modifications:

1st. That, in reference to myself, in lieu of the compensation stipulated in those instructions, I shall be allowed all my expenses upon my own certificate on the amount.

2d. That in addition, after the duty is completed, the department will allow to me such compensation for this duty as its sense of justice will dictate. Upon this I rely with the utmost confidence.

3d. That all my present pay and allowances should go on. These are necessary to the support of my family during my absence.

4th. That we might be allowed to pay the assistants employed to locate under us not exceeding five dollars per day, including all expenses. We can control this expenditure by stipulating the number of locations which shall be considered as a day's work.

5th. To be allowed a clerk, who may be taken from this place, but whose compensation should be limited at five dollars per day, including all expenses, as I know a very competent gentleman who is willing to go on these terms.

6th. And that we should be allowed discretion over expenses of a contingent character, not connected with our individual expenses, such as interpreters, means of transporting about our maps and papers, and purchase of stationery.

7th. Query. Shall we be furnished with the views of the department, as explained in its correspondence to Judge Tarrant and others, in relation to persons entitled to reservations; or is it intended that we should exercise our own discretion and judgment of the treaty on these subjects? I believe the department has decided that the habitations of the Indian shall be the improvement to guide the location. Now it is frequently the case that the Indian has cultivated a piece of good bottom land, while he has fixed his residence upon a distant, barren, but healthy sand hill. To choose his residence for his reservation would in such cases be injustice, and the apprehension of such a course was a subject of much discontent when I was in that country last summer.

Respectfully submitted.

J. J. ABERT,
*Lieut. Col. Top. Eng'rs.*

Hon. LEWIS CASS,
    *Secretary of War.*

---

CHICKASAW AGENCY, *October* 14, 1833.

SIR: I have this day drawn on the honorable the Secretary of War in favor of Messrs. C. T. and H. Barton, of Tuscumbia, Alabama, for three thousand dollars, which I respectfully ask to be duly honored and charged to my account.

The amount is for outfit and expenses of a Chickasaw delegation, which will set out on the 16th instant in search of a new home west of the Mississippi; and which sum is to be reimbursed out of the sale of their lands, and agreeably to your instructions of the 25th March, 1833.

It is impossible for me at this time to make an estimate of the sum necessary for this service. The delegation is to consist of twenty-one chiefs and captains, a portion of whom have been provided with the necessary outfit at Tuscumbia, Alabama. The balance are to be supplied at Memphis, Tennessee. But an accurate account of all expenses will be rendered at the close of the trip.

At an early day I discovered that no movement would be made unless the chiefs were made sensible of the situation of their people, and that unless they sought some place of retreat, their people must dwindle to nothing; and from their constant solicitation I have consented to be their conductor and their cashier. They have also employed Colonel William Hunter, of Tennessee, and Milton Grey, of Alabama, to accompany us; and I take pleasure in saying that they are worthy men, and will use every exertion in their power to promote the service in which they are engaged.

Upon a consultation with the chiefs, we shall proceed direct to Cantonment Towson, for the purpose, if possible, out of the abundance of the Choctaw country to obtain a home for this people. Should that fail, we must be governed by circumstances. Be pleased to write me, directed to Cantonment Towson, giving me your advice and instruction.

Before I cross the Mississippi at Memphis, I expect to address you on other subjects connected with the interests and prosperity of this people; and shall from time to time advise you of our progress and prospects.

Very respectfully, sir,
I have the honor to be
Your obedient servant,
BENJ. REYNOLDS,
*Indian Agent.*

ELBERT HERRING, Esq.,
    *Commissioner of Indian Affairs, Washington City.*

77‡

CHICKASAW AGENCY, *October* 14, 1833.

SIR: I have this day drawn on you in favor of Messrs. C. T. and A. Barton, of Tuscumbia, Alabama, for three thousand dollars, which I respectfully ask to be duly honored, and charged to my account. The amount is for outfit and expenses of a Chickasaw delegation, who will set out on the 16th instant, in search of a new home west of the Mississippi, and which sum is to be refunded out of the funds arising out of the sales of their lands under the late treaty. The bill was drawn in conformity with instructions from the Commissioner of Indian Affairs, dated the 25th March last.

I have the honor to be,
Very respectfully, sir,
Your obedient servant,
BENJ. REYNOLDS,
*Indian Agent.*

To the Hon. LEWIS CASS,
    *Secretary of War.*

---

KNOXVILLE, *October* 15, 1833.

DEAR SIR: Last spring I sent some hands to Talladega county, Alabama, and in the course of the summer raised a crop, to which it was my purpose this fall to move my family; and I am now within a few weeks of setting out with my family for that country.

I spent nearly all summer there myself; and in that time made selection of a place to settle, and erected some cabins for the accommodation of my family, to which I intend removing, unless interdicted by your order.

Having been pretty much out of the channel of news, I have not seen the direction which it is said you have given in relation to the settlers in the Creek nation; but have heard it spoken of as a determination to remove the settlers from the Creek nation.

The place I have selected is at the Indian town Conjarda, about three miles below the place where the Jackson Trace from Fort Strother to Talladega battle ground crosses Chockolocko creek, and am settled on a place that will pretty certainly fall in the reserve of the Indian Pinehill; and I am settled within a few hundred yards of the Indians' dwellings.

Before I attempted to settle there, I obtained the consent and approbation of Pinehill to erect cabins, and live where my cabins are built, and I was not to interrupt his cleared land; but there was enough of land for me to clear, which engagement I intend to fulfil.

When I left that country, I believe Pinehill, and all the other Indians about me, were perfectly contented with me, and neighbored with me as pleasantly as white people would have done.

I have not bought any reserve, or the chance of any reserve, nor do I intend so to do until I am satisfied it will meet the approbation of the Federal Government—though I bought an improvement adjoining for one hundred dollars, on which no Indian resides, nor has any Indian any cleared land on the quarter section on which my improvement is situated.

I have been thus explicit, that you may understand the matter and comprehend my views.

So far forth as I may have it in my power to aid the Government in the removal of the Indians, if permitted to remain there, the department may rely on my exertions tending to that object.

My purpose is to solicit leave of the department over which you have the honor·to preside, to remain at Conjarda so long as I shall not incommode the Indians or the Government; and with that permission I have no fears of any discord with the natives.

I view the settlers in that country as tenants at sufferance of the Government, and that they have not any right to remain in that country beyond what is derived from the *tacit* or express consent of the Government; and as such, I declare to you, so soon as I shall know that it is the will of the Government that I must abandon any possession, I shall do so without murmur, or the semblance of opposition or resistance. Opposition or resistance I cannot make, because I do not see right on which it can be based.

These are the views I have; and they are frankly declared, because they are believed to be based on solid foundation.

It may be sport for others, whose rights and interest are not to be affected thereby, to embroil the settlers and Government; but, sir, it will be sad pastime to those whose interest and prospects are thereby to be engulphed.

So soon as the reserves are laid off, if my being located at Conjarda shall be found prejudicial to the interests of the Government or the Indians, I will not be found in the way of either, if permitted to remain.

If a statement of my character will be acceptable to the department, I will request Messrs. White and Grundy, of the Senate, Blair, Bunch, Lea, Standifer, Bell, Polk, Johnson, &c., of the House, all of whom are personally acquainted with me, to submit such statements thereof as they may esteem proper.

I shall be at Rogersville for some three or four weeks, where it would be pleasant to learn the will of the department.

I have the honor to be, dear sir,<br>Your obedient servant, &c. &c.,<br>P. PARSONS.

To Hon. Lewis Cass,
 *Secretary of War.*

---

Choctaw Agency, *October* 15, 1833.

Sir: I have the honor of forwarding, through you, to the proper officer, my accounts for the second and third quarters; also my estimate for the three last quarters of the present year, together with a general estimate for 1834. By a reference to them it will be seen that I have not included anything due the Choctaws under treaties previous to the one made at Dancing Rabbit Creek, September, 1830, because I do not officially know anything about annuities paid east, except the portion of the one paid the Indians here, amounting to $619, the receipt for which accompanies these accounts, and which will relieve me from the charge of that amount standing against me, as noted in the statement of my accounts from the Second Comptroller's office.

I have conversed with such of the captains and chiefs as are here, upon the plan proposed in your communication in relation to schools, &c. They are much pleased; and so soon as the nation can assemble in council, under the new treaty, their approbation will be had to the plans, when the school houses will be forthwith built.

We had with us, from Philadelphia, a reverend gentleman belonging to the Baptist church, sent here by the Baptist Board of Foreign Missions, Mr. Charles E. Wilson. I handed him your answer to my report to the Secretary of War, of April last. He read it, and expresses himself much gratified at the proposed plan, as a basis for the education and civilization of the Choctaws. He has been teaching here about four months, during which time he has applied himself to the study of the dispositions, habits, and customs of the Choctaws, from which to form a proper opinion as to the results that may be calculated on by persons making efforts for their prosperity and happiness.

I am much pleased to have the concurrence of a gentleman towards whom every person that knows him in the country feels the fullest confidence in what he says. His patience and amiability of character suits him particularly for the objects of his mission. He believes in the determination of the Government to better, if possible, the situation of the Indians; and in place of souring their minds against the President, Secretary of War, and officers of the United States acting for them, he is to be found establishing, as far as is practicable, a confidence which has been unfortunately lost between the Indians and the Government, owing to bad advice from some quarter or other, which it is not necessary for me even to attempt to point out at this time. I will therefore suggest the propriety of placing this school fund to my credit in the Nashville Bank, so that the school houses can be built early in the winter or spring.

It becomes my duty to refer to the course of Mr. Stirman. I presume, in compliance with my order of February last, he repaired to the Mountain Fork settlement; from thence to this place, where he remained a few days, and left without making any report, or asking leave of absence. The Indians say he could have got a school house in the neighborhood; and, if so, he might have been teaching, although on a small scale.

I feel it my duty, as agent, to protest against his being paid.

The 20th article of the late treaty contemplates three teachers for twenty years; it is, therefore, impossible that Mr. Stirman's time can be deducted from this provision in the treaty. The $2,500 will be paid for teaching, and will, I suppose, commence with the first annuity of $20,000, say from the 1st day of January, 1834, when the Choctaw emigration ceases, and from which time a Government will be established amongst them, in conformity with the late treaty.

I wish the annuities due the Choctaws for 1833 to be placed in the Nashville Bank, because the funds now in my possession are deposited there.

The light horse fund of $600 will be wanting soon. It will be seen, by reference to my estimates, that I have requested $1,000 for provisions. The explanation necessary is as follows: The chiefs and captains must necessarily be convened several times next year, to put into operation their new government; besides, there will be two annuities to pay in 1834

To make these payments in dollars and cents to each individual, will take several weeks. Should the Indians determine on having money, they must be fed; and it is for the department to point out in what way this is to be done, if to be done by the United States.

Immediately after the arrival of the Indians from the east, I will inform you, agreeable to your instructions to me, in what mode they wish to be paid their annuity. It is proper that I should here state that the Indians who received a portion of the annuity in domestics, say that they never got as much before in their lives, and are delighted at it, because families of ten got 100 yards, a child getting ten yards. This has astonished them, and they ask why it was never done before.

I flatter myself that after the Indians get settled, and we get fairly into operation in this nation, that the rise and progress of the Choctaws will be a source of pleasure to every person friendly to their prosperity. I have, in a former communication, given the reasons why the receipts for arms, axes, &c. &c., were not forwarded.

They are taken in companies, and we have to leave the receipts open, because the Indians are constantly arriving from their old nation, and have to be arrayed, as far as practicable, under their captains, and have their articles furnished them.

My account will, for this quarter, I think, close all the treaty supplies, except looms and wheels.

Since my letter of September 20th, informing you of the bad health of this country, I am sorry to say that the sickness has not in the least abated in this quarter. The physician whom I employed is now himself at the point of death; and scarcely a man of any color, near this place, has escaped entirely.

The vaccine matter which was sent by the department, I regret to say, has not taken effect in a single instance.

Very respectfully,
Your obedient servant,
F. W. ARMSTRONG,
*C. Agent.*

ELBERT HERRING, Esq.,
*Commissioner of Indian Affairs.*

---

GENERAL LAND OFFICE, *October* 16, 1833.

SIR: The enclosed is a copy of a letter of instruction to the registers and receivers of the land offices in Mississippi, for those districts embracing the territory ceded by the Choctaw Indians, issued from this office on the 30th ultimo, at your suggestion, and with the approbation of the President.

I have the honor to be,
Very respectfully,
Your obedient servant,
ELIJAH HAYWARD.

Hon. LEWIS CASS,
*Secretary of War.*

---

GENERAL LAND OFFICE, *September* 30, 1833.

GENTLEMEN: On the 10th instant instructions were issued to you to withhold from the approaching sales of public lands in your district such tracts or portions of the lands proclaimed to be sold, as the United States "agent for locating the reservations on behalf of the Choctaws shall designate to you as necessary and proper to be withheld from sale, in order to carry into effect the intentions of the treaty."

I am directed by the President to enclose, for your information, a copy of an instruction from the War Department to the locating agent, George

W. Martin, dated 27th instant, from which you will perceive that, owing to some misunderstanding, the copy of the register of the names of the Choctaw Indians entitled to reservations has not been received by the agent, and that another copy is preparing to be transmitted.

Inasmuch as from the circumstance stated the locating agent may find it necessary to withhold from sale a greater body of land than was first supposed to be necessary, I am charged by the President to say to you, that you are authorized to withhold from public sale *as many townships or fractional townships, in contiguous bodies or otherwise*, of the land proclaimed, as the agent may designate as necessary to accomplish the intentions of the treaty. You are requested to give public notice accordingly.

I am, very respectfully,
Your obedient servant,
JOHN M. MOORE,
*Acting Commissioner.*

To the LAND OFFICE *at Mount Salus, Columbus,
Augusta, and Chocchuma, Mississippi.*

---

JASPER, EAST TENNESSEE, *October* 18, 1833.

DEAR SIR: Being very desirous to get correct information touching the late purchase of the Creek Indians, and not knowing how to succeed otherwise than by application to you, I hope you will not consider this an intrusion.

You know it is the duty of all Governments to use all proper means to promote the felicity of the body politic over whom they preside, and that object being accomplished, in some degree, by the happiness of any particular individual, it is also our duty to promote that, when it is consistent with the public weal.

Therefore, I make the application with confidence, for I do consider that not only my comfort, but that of a rising family depends, in a great degree, on the success of this application. Please, therefore, answer the following interrogatories:

Why are the settlers to be removed off the Creek lands? Does the order for removal embrace *all*, or only those who have intruded on Indian possessions? Has the country yet been surveyed? Have the Indians yet taken their reservations? If they have not, when will they do so? When the Indians have taken their reservations, will the whites be permitted to settle in the country, if they intrude not on the Indians? By attending to the above letter, you will confer a particular favor on

Yours, respectfully,
ED. L. WOODWARD.

Hon. LEWIS CASS.

---

MONTGOMERY, SOUTHERN DISTRICT ALABAMA,
*October* 23, 1833.

SIR: In the execution of the instructions from the War Departmen relative to the removal of intruders from the Creek lands, I met with considerable difficulties, particularly from the State authorities. The Governor has issued his proclamation, which I herewith enclose.

I verily believe a removal of the settlers from those lands, at this time, will create a difference between the General and State Governments which will be not easily settled, and particularly should there be more blood shed, which will inevitably be the case in the removal.

The number of intruders who have taken forcible possession of Indian improvements are very few, not exceeding, I think, eighteen or twenty; whereas the number of persons who have peaceably made their improvements amounts to several thousands.

Could distinction be made between the settlers, it would be very desirable; the distress occasioned by a general removal would be immense; hundreds of persons have removed there who have nothing left, and no means to remove with. This statement is made with the view of letting the Executive know the true state of this business. The excitement which at this time exists is very great, and I believe that they are determined to make common cause of it. They are holding meetings throughout those new counties, and passing resolutions, and resistance will be made. The Executive of this State has had the militia organized in those counties.

A bill of indictment has been found against Mr. Austill and some of the United States troops, and *casas* are issued.

Under the Governor's proclamation I am liable, and no doubt will be indicted, if I attempt to remove a single person.

I had requested the commanding officer at Fort Mitchell to furnish me with fifty men, to be at Pole Cat Springs on the 18th instant. Yesterday he informed me that he did not have ammunition sufficient in the event of a conflict between the settlers and troops, and he had no doubt that such would be the case. Should more blood be shed, under the circumstances I have thought it most prudent to await your instructions on this subject. I do not wish to risk my life without full protection, and I have no doubt but attempts will be made by some persons, because among an ignorant set of persons they seem to think that I am the cause of all their troubles; but I fear more from the State authorities than any thing else.

I believe that a few designing white men who have influence over the chiefs have caused the Indians to complain; and some white men who have Indian wives are also concerned, in order that they may have a better chance of buying the Indian reserves.

There is no doubt but in some cases the Indians have been shamefully abused, but I do not believe their injuries have been near so great as have been represented by them.

I had a conversation a few days since with Colonel William R. King, our Senator. He mentioned that if a distinction could be made, that nothing could have a greater tendency towards allaying the excitement that now exists. I have seen a number of the persons who reside there. They say that if a distinction could be made, so that those who have made their improvements could remain, that they would pledge themselves to give every exertion to have those who have taken forcible possession expelled.

The force at Fort Mitchell is not sufficient, in any event, to carry the instructions into effect.

Very respectfully, &c.,<br>ROBT. L. CRAWFORD,<br>United States Marshal.

Honorable Lewis Cass,
  *Secretary of War.*

EXECUTIVE DEPARTMENT,
*Tuscaloosa, October 23, 1833.*

SIR: I have received to-day by express from the honorable P. T. Harris, one of the circuit judges of this State, sundry documents establishing the fact, that all attempts by the civil officers to investigate the circumstances in relation to the killing of Owen have proved unavailing, and that the process of the court has been set at defiance by the commanding officer at Fort Mitchell. I transmit copies of the whole of these despatches for the consideration of the President, and respectfully request that you will advise me of his determination on the subject at an early period.

I have the honor, &c.,
JOHN GAYLE.

Honorable LEWIS CASS,
*Secretary of War.*

---

CIRCUIT COURT, *October Term*, 1833.

STATE OF ALABAMA, *Russel county:*

The grand jurors for the county of Russel, and State aforesaid, on their oath present, that James Emmerson, late of the county aforesaid, known as a soldier in the United States army, not having the fear of God before his eyes, but being moved and seduced by the instigation of the devil, on the thirteenth day of October, in the year of our Lord one thousand eight hundred and thirty-three, with force and arms, in the county aforesaid, in and upon one Hardeman Owen, in the peace of God, and of the State of Alabama then and there being, feloniously, wilfully, and of his malice aforethought, did make an assault, and that the said James Emmerson, with a certain gun called a musket, of the value of ten dollars, then and there being charged with gunpowder and a leaden bullet, which gun he, the said James Emmerson, in both his hands then and there had and held at, against, and upon him, the said Hardeman Owen, then and there feloniously, wilfully, and of his malice aforethought did discharge and shoot off, and that the said James Emmerson, with the leaden bullet aforesaid, by force of the gunpowder aforesaid, out of the gun aforesaid, by him the said James Emmerson, so as aforesaid discharged and shot off him, the said Hardeman Owen, in and upon the right side of the head of him, the said Hardeman Owen, then and there feloniously, wilfully, and of his malice aforethought, did strike, penetrate, and wound; the said bullet, so discharged and sent forth as aforesaid, passing through the head of him the said Hardeman Owen, giving to the said Hardeman Owen then and there, with the leaden bullet aforesaid, out of the gun so as aforesaid discharged and shot off, in and through the head of him the said Hardeman Owen, one mortal wound of the breadth of one inch, and of the length of six inches, of which said mortal wound the said Hardeman Owen then and there instantly died; and that James King and Frank Borger, both soldiers of the United States army, and five others, to the jurors unknown, all late of said county, feloniously, wilfully, and of their malice aforethought, then and there were present aiding, abetting, assisting, comforting and maintaining the aforesaid James Emmerson to do and commit the felony and murder aforesaid, in manner aforesaid, and in form aforesaid. And as the jurors aforesaid, upon this their oath aforesaid, do say that the said James Emmerson, Frank Borger, and James King, and the five others to the jurors unknown, then and there feloniously, wilfully, and of their malice aforethought, in manner and form aforesaid, did kill and murder the said Hardeman Owen, against the peace and dignity of the State of Alabama.

And that one David Manning, a Lieutenant in the United States army, late of said county, and one Jeremiah Austill, late of said county, not having the fear of God before their eyes, but being moved and seduced by the instigation of the devil, in the county aforesaid, before the said murder was committed in form aforesaid, to wit, on the thirteenth day of October, in the year aforesaid, in the county aforesaid, did feloniously, wilfully, and maliciously incite, move, procure, aid, counsel, hire, and command the said James Emmerson, James King, and Frank Borger, and the five others (to the jurors unknown), the said murder in manner and form aforesaid, to do and commit against the peace and dignity of the State of Alabama.

WM. D. PICKETT,
*Solicitor Eighth Circuit.*

CIRCUIT COURT, *October Term,* 1833.

STATE OF ALABAMA, *Russel county:*

I do hereby certify the within indictment, together with the endorsement, to be a true copy from the original bill on file in my office.

B. G. G. A. LUCAS, *Clerk.*

The State *vs.* James Emmerson, James King, Frank Borger, David Manning, Jeremiah Austill, and others—*Murder.*

*Prosecutor,* George Elliot.

Witnesses: David Bord, Drury Spain, Jephtha Fanning, Eli Couch, George Stone, John Benton.—A true Bill. A. ABERCROMBIE, *Foreman.*

RUSSEL COURT HOUSE, ALA.,
*October* 14, 1833.

SIR: I am advised through the medium of the " Globe," at Washington City, official paper of the administration, and from other high and respectable sources, that the commanding officer at Fort Mitchell has been instructed to afford to our civil authorities all proper facilities for putting the case of the killing of Hardeman Owen in a train for legal investigation. The Circuit Court of Alabama for the county of Russel is now in session, and a bill of indictment against the perpetrator or perpetrators of that act will this day be prepared. In pursuance of those instructions I have thought proper, from a sense of duty, respectfully to ask at your hands the aid required; and to facilitate this object, that the detachment of soldiers who were present at the killing of Owen be delivered over to the sheriff of this county.

The reason why this is deemed necessary is owing to the difficulty of ascertaining the name or names of the persons who committed the act, as no one was present it appears but the file of soldiers; or this may be dispensed with if you will be good enough to furnish the State with the name or names in question, and with the witnesses who will prove the fact.

Respectfully, &c.,
WM. D. PICKETT,
*Solicitor Eighth Judicial Circuit.*

Major JAMES S. MCINTOSH.
78‡

CIRCUIT COURT, *October Term*, 1833.

STATE OF ALABAMA, *Russel county:*

To the Sheriff of the said county, greeting: You are hereby commanded, without delay, to take the body of Major James McIntosh, if to be found in your county, and bring him forthwith before the Honorable the Judge of the Circuit Court for the county of Russel, now in session, to answer the said court for a contempt of the same.

Herein fail not, and have you then and there this writ, with your endorsement thereon..

Bevel Lucas, clerk of the Circuit Court for Russel county, this 15th of October, 1833.

B. G. G. A. LUCAS, Clerk.

Issued 15th October, 1833.

The State vs. James McIntosh.

SHERIFF'S RETURN.

I went to the fort and called on the defendant; he swore I should not take him. I am satisfied if I had made the attempt it would have been at the risk of my life. That defendant was commanding officer at the fort, and had sworn on yesterday he would not surrender up any one in the fort.

E. D. CROWELL,<br>Sheriff Russel county.

*October* 16, 1833.

---

FORT MITCHELL ALA., October 15, 1833.

SIR: In reply to your communication of yesterday, informing me that you have been advised through the medium of the Globe at Washington city, the official paper of the administration, and from other highly and respectable sources, that the commanding officer at Fort Mitchell has been instructed to afford to our civil authorities all proper facilities for putting the case of the killing of Hardeman Owen in a state for legal investigation, I have to inform you that I have received no instructions relative to the case above cited, and I apprehend that I will not, from the simple fact that the soldier who shot Hardeman Owen was in the lawful execution of his duty. I must, therefore, decline your invitation to deliver to the sheriff of this county the detachment of soldiers who were present at the time that Owen was killed.

Had any officer or soldier of my command unlawfully used violence or committed any offence against the persons or property of any citizen of the United States, such as is punishable by the known laws of the land, no one would have been more ready or willing, upon legal application duly made, to use their utmost endeavors to deliver over such accused person or persons to the civil magistrate.

I am, Sir, very respectfully, &c.,

J. S. McINTOSH,<br>Major Brevet Fourth Infantry Commanding.

To WM. D. PICKETT, Esq.,
    *Solicitor 8th Judicial Circuit.*

CIRCUIT COURT, *October Term*, 1833.

THE STATE OF ALABAMA, *Russel County:*

This day came Eli Couch, in open court, and maketh oath that he resides at Fort Mitchell; that he knows Sergeant Francis Borger, James King, and James Emmerson; that they are soldiers in the fort, and under the command of James S. McIntosh; that he has seen them in the fort within one or two days past, and almost daily for the last five or six months; that they are generally there on duty; that when he went with the sheriff of Russell county with process against them, that they were absent from the said fort, while all the other soldiers, he believes, were present.

Sworn to in open court, the 16th October, 1833.

B. G. G. A. LUCAS, *Clerk.*

CIRCUIT COURT, *October Term*, 1833.

THE STATE OF ALABAMA, *Russel County:*

This day came Samuel C. Benton, in open court, and makes oath that he lives at the fort, and knows Frank Borger, James King, and James Emmerson, soldiers of the United States army, at said fort, under the command of Major James McIntosh; that he has seen them, or some one or two of them there as late as the 13th instant; that they are there generally on duty, and have been for some time past.

Sworn to in open court, 16th October, 1833.

B. G. G. A. LUCAS, *Clerk.*

CIRCUIT COURT, *October Term*, 1833.

THE STATE OF ALABAMA, *Russel County.*

I do certify the foregoing to be true copies of the originals now on file in my office.

B. G. G. A. LUCAS, *Clerk.*

*October* 17, 1833.

---

RUSSEL COURT HOUSE, *October* 17, 1833.

SIR: To your excellency, as chief magistrate of the State of Alabama, I enclose copies of a correspondence between the solicitor general of this circuit and the commanding officer at Fort Mitchell, the affidavit of the sheriff of this county, the affidavits of two gentlemen by the name of Benton and Couch, (both of whom reside at or near Fort Mitchell,) the attachment which issued for the arrest of Maj. McIntosh for a contempt of the court, with the sheriff's return thereon, and the bill of indictment against David Manning and others for the murder of Hardeman Owen. By an examination of the letter of Major McIntosh, it is obvious that the soldiers who were present at the killing of Owen were at Fort Mitchell when that letter was written; and that the persons for whom subpœnas were issued were secreted at the time the sheriff was permitted to search within the fort for them, is established by his (Benton's) and Couch's affidavits. From all the papers herewith sent, you will perceive that the process of the courts is set at defiance, and that without some assistance we shall have to submit to the military authority which has been established at Fort Mitchell. You can readily imagine if the officer commanding refused to give up the soldiers as witnesses, that we cannot expect them to be surrendered to the mandatory process of the court, when that process is intended to bring them before the civil tribunals, to answer to the violated laws.   He has already determined "that the soldier who shot Hardeman Owen, was in the lawful execution of his duty;" and from this decision there can be no appeal, unless the arm of the State is put forth to protect the courts.   It need not be stated to your excellency that the common soldier is but the mere machine in the hands of the officer; and you can, without difficulty, see that there is too much reason to believe that the apprehensions of the sheriff are too well founded.   You will also perceive that the *posse comitatus* is entirely insufficient to afford adequate protection to the court and its officers.   It only remains, then, for your excellency to apply the proper remedy, and place at the disposal of the sheriff a sufficient force to command respect to the laws.   Until this be done, or the United States troops removed, it will be in vain to attempt to enforce the criminal laws in any case where they may be interested.   In closing this communication I will only add, that the court has received every aid in his power from Col. Pickett, who has been diligent in ferreting out the testimony, and active in his exertions to bring to justice those who have been charged with the murder of Owen.

I am, with great respect, &c.,

P. T. HARRIS.

To Governor of Alabama.

Circuit Court, October Term, 1833.

The State of Alabama, *Russel County:*

Personally appeared Edward Crowell, sheriff of said county, in open court, who, being duly sworn, deposeth and saith, that on the 14th instant he had placed in his hands, by order of said court, subpœnas for Frank Borger, James Emmerson, James King, and David Manning, officer and soldiers of the United States army, under command of Major James S. McIntosh, at Fort Mitchell in said county; that he proceeded to the quarters of the major, and told him he had certain processes for the individuals above named and wished to serve them.   His reply was, "I'll be damned if I give up a man."   After he had put up his horse and returned, the major, upon ascertaining the papers were not to take the persons, but merely subpœnas, affiant was permitted to search the fort, but could not find any one of them; that he succeeded in serving the subpœna on Lieutenant David Manning out of the fort; he replied, "I shall not go."   That on the 15th instant a capias, in the nature of an attachment for contempt of said court, against the said Major McIntosh, was placed in his hands by the clerk of said court; that he again proceeded to the fort and the place where the major was, and told him he had a capias to take him to court.   He replied, "You shall not touch me;" at the same time saying he had not treated the court with contempt, and that said court had no authority to take him. That the reason he did not attempt to take his person when he had the capias was because it would have endangered his life by so doing.

That he is satisfied any attempt he may make to serve process on said soldiers, or upon the said major will be resisted, and prove useless.   That the power of the county is insufficient to execute process on said persons, situated as they are with arms, and protected by the fort.

Sworn to in open court, October 17, 1833.

ED. CROWELL, *Sheriff R. C.*

I hereby certify the foregoing to be a true copy from the original on file in my office.

B. G. G. A. LUCAS, *Clerk.*

*October* 17, 1833.

---

WEST CHEROKEE NATION, AGENT'S OFFICE,
*October* 25, 1833.

SIR: In obedience to the instructions of 10th May last, I have the honor to transmit, herewith enclosed, a list of the claims for spoliations under treaty of 1828, remaining unpaid (per list transmitted by the department, as submitted by my predecessor in 1828), exhibiting the number, name, and amount due to each claimant, with an abstract of the proof in support of each claim annexed, as filed therewith by my predecessor prior to the treaty of 1828. I do not think that any of them can now be rejected; they all appear to have been officially and satisfactorily investigated by my predecessor, reported to and approved of by the department, and accordingly their payment subsequently provided for by treaty stipulation. The existing deficit might have been obviated by a just apportionment of the sum stipulated; but the incautious payment of a large amount of the claims at the department, without affording me the information solicited by my letter of 17th October, 1831, upon the subject of the list of claims for spoliations obtained from the office of my predecessor, seems to be the cause why any deficit now exists; and therefore I think it would now appear inexpedient to charge the remaining unsettled claims with any deficit thereby created, or to hold the nation accountable therefor. The remark on your list No. 2, that $50 is marked paid, on my former list, to U-kot-a-hi, claim No. 78, appears to be a mistake. The claim No. 79, George Morris, is marked $50 paid, (on the copy retained by me,) but was not deducted in payment of said claim to J. Drew, per list transmitted.

The department states, " the claims presented by Mr. Webber for spoliations committed by the Osages have been paid;" meaning thereby, I presume (as your list No. 1 does not exhibit any payment made to Webber), the draft drawn by me in his favor, 21st February, 1832, for $4,311 58, which included a separate statement of the settlement of claims on account of Osage spoliations, amounting to $691 33; and accordingly that portion of the draft was made payable on said account.

I also transmit, herewith enclosed, a list of all claims settled by me and made payable by draft, or otherwise, out of the stipulation for spoliations under the treaty of 1828.

The list No. 1, transmitted the by department, exhibits the payment of claims, on account of spoliations, under the treaty of          $6,347 00

And the settlements made by me on said accounts amounts to          1,288 33

Which, together with the enclosed list of unsettled claims, amounting to          -          -          -          -          -          -          1,383 00

exhibits a deficit of $258 39, to enable the department to effect a final settlement of the claims as reported by my predecessor, and to exclude renewed applications.

The circumstances which led to the existence of this deficit seem to dictate some further provision for that additional amount, rather than permit a further increase of the long existing dissatisfaction occasioned by delay of payment.

Permit me here to beg leave to solicit the attention of the department to the payment of Spring Frog's old claim, as promised by the department's letter of 8th November, 1832. The last time the old gentleman called on me he appeared to be greatly mortified and grieved that he had still to wait longer for payment.

Most respectfully, sir,

Your most obedient servant,

GEO. VASHON,

*Indian Agent Cherokees West.*

ELBERT HERRING, Esq.,
    *Commissioner Indian Affairs.*

---

MONTGOMERY, SOUTHERN DISTRICT ALABAMA,

*October* 26, 1833.

SIR: I enclose you a copy of a letter which I have received from Major McIntosh at Fort Mitchell; it will show a true state of things in the Creek country.

My situation is a delicate one—the instructions of the Government on one side, and the State authorities on the other.

I am informed that the Government has directed warrants to be issued against me, in the event of a single removal.

Please to instruct me on this subject as early as may be convenient.

Very respectfully,

Your obedient servant,

ROBT. L. CRAWFORD,

*U. S. Marshal, Southern Dist. Alabama.*

Hon. LEWIS CASS,
    *Secretary of War.*

---

DETACHMENT HEAD QUARTERS,

*Fort Mitchell, Alabama, October* 15, 1833.

SIR: Your communication, requesting me to order a detachment of fifty men to meet you at the Pole Cat Springs by the 18th instant, was duly received.

From the great excitement in the State, owing to the killing of Hardeman Owen and of the intended removal of intruders from the Indian lands, there is reason to apprehend that difficulties will occur between the United States troops and the intruders. Should more blood be shed in the ejectment of these people, it may eventuate in a general rupture between the State and the General Government; and in the event of such a state of affairs, I have not that supply of ammunition on hand that I could wish, but have sent to Augusta arsenal, Georgia, for an additional supply, which I am in daily expectation of receiving. There are several communications in this post office from the War Department addressed to yourself; it is possible that these instructions may contain information relative to the removal of intruders, which might delay the movement of the command to some future period, when the whole of the intruders might at one and the same time be removed beyond the Indian territory. I must therefore request that you will visit us before the troops are put in motion. I will expect to see or hear from you by return mail.

I am, sir, respectfully,

Your obedient servant,

J. S. McINTOSH,

*Maj. Bt. Fourth Infantry Commanding.*

To R. L. CRAWFORD, Esq.,
United States Marshal; or

J. AUSTILL,
Deputy Marshal, Montgomery, Alabama.

P. S. Be on your guard; the civil authorities have issued a warrant to arrest you for the killing of Owen.

J. S. M.

---

FORT GIBSON, *October* 27, 1833.

SIR: By our instructions, we are directed to report some general plan for the Government of the Indians west of the Mississippi. Being deprived of the counsel and assistance of either of my colleagues, I have deemed it my duty to submit my own views on the subject, leaving it to my colleagues to offer theirs.

I beg leave here to remark, that the separation of the Indian Commissioners west is not to be attributed to me, or to any arrangement of mine. Ever since I joined the commission, I have been either at my post, or visiting the different agencies, as required by our instructions. Mr. Schermerhorn has been absent since May last; upon what business it is no part of my duty, and less of my inclination to inquire.

Upon the arrival of Mr. Ellsworth at St. Louis he found me too much indisposed to accompany him to Fort Leavenworth. We had some business to settle at that place with the Shawnees, and a band of the Kickapoos, headed and controlled by a chief named Kishko: I consented to follow as soon as my health permitted, and did so.

But, on arriving at the Shawnee, the Delaware, and Kanza agencies, and conversing with these agents, I found that Mr. Ellsworth had left Fort Leavenworth two weeks before my arrival. His object was to collect the Pawnees and Camanches of Red river, who have been in the habit of committing robberies and murders on the Santa Fe road.

This interview, with these Arabs of the great prairie, would be very desirable, and has been enjoined upon us by our instructions; but my own opinion is, that Mr. Ellsworth might as well attempt to collect last year's clouds as to collect the Pawnees and Camanches at this time, and under present circumstances. They are all out on their fall hunt; they are at war with the Delawares, the Shawnees, and the Osages, who are now out upon the same great western prairie; and they are compelled for their own safety to keep their bands together. In addition to this they are greatly enraged at this time, having had one of their villages burned, and their corn cut down and destroyed by a war party of the Delawares. I have not heard from Mr. Ellsworth since his departure from Fort Leavenworth, but I have no confidence in the success of the expedition. I earnestly hope I may be mistaken in my opinion.

Before I enter upon the task of designating the outlines of a form of government for the Indian nations west of the Mississippi, permit me to state some of the difficulties that must attend all negotiations with the western Indians. Heretofore, all the treaties with the Indians east of the Mississippi, and many of the treaties with those west, have been for the purchase of lands, mostly for the benefit of white settlers. So far as I am acquainted with the country west, there is but a small portion of it which the United States want for any purpose. It all lies west of the Arkansas and Missouri boundary line, beyond which I hope there will never be a white settler.

This small portion of land not yet purchased lies south and east of the river Platte, and joining Pawnee Mahas, Pawnee Republicans, and two other little bands of Pawnees on the Platte. The right to this country is claimed by the Pawnees of the Platte, and if purchased by the Government might serve to locate some of the emigrating Indians.

During the seven years that I was in the Senate of the United States, whenever an Indian treaty was presented for confirmation, the first inquiry was, how much land have we acquired? what did it cost; and what is it worth?

I myself have been among those who urged these considerations previous to a vote for ratification. What will now be the inquiry? The Government has set apart the lands west of the Arkansas and Missouri, as a permanent home for the red people, where they may be happy and contented, and increase in numbers like the people of the United States; where they may rest secure from further intrusion, and a remnant of the original owners and possessors of this great continent be preserved in their color and distinction as a people. The case as to treaties is completely changed. When an Indian treaty is presented, the questions will again be asked—How much land have you purchased? What did it cost? How much is it worth; and for whose benefit was it purchased?

The answer to this last question must be—We purchased it for the benefit and comfort of our red brethren: we have given it to them without money and without price. And moreover, you must furnish them with ploughs; with hoes; with axes; with cattle; with looms, spinning-wheels, cards, &c. &c., to enable them to pursue an agricultural life for the support of themselves, their wives and children. What commissioner can sustain himself, after the signature of such a treaty? And yet it is a part of our instructions so to provide. Again, in pursuance of our duty, and in conformity with the benevolent views of the Government, we are instructed to report and recommend a system of regulations for securing the peace and harmony of the western nations. The Government has promised them protection and security. This cannot be done without a considerable expense for many years to come.

Will Congress provide the means for carrying the benevolent views into effect for the benefit of the Indian race?

With these preliminary remarks, I will candidly give my opinion as to the best mode of providing a government for the Indians, until they shall be so far civilized and enlightened as to govern themselves.

*Form of government for the Indians south of the Missouri river.*

There shall be a Governor to reside at the military post.

He shall have power to call the representatives of the different Indian nations to a general council, whenever any difficulties in their affairs require it. He shall have power to demand murderers and robbers from the respective nations under his superintendence, and to have them arrested by the military, whenever they are refused to be given up.

The offenders must be tried at the military post, by the head chiefs of three nations, to be summoned by the Governor; none of whom shall belong to the nation injured, or the nation to whom the offender belongs. The sentence of the chiefs must be executed without appeal or pardon. When claims are made by one nation for property stolen or destroyed by another, they must be settled by the arbitration of the Governor, the commandant of the military post, and three chiefs summoned from nations not concerned in the offence.

The Governor, in conjunction with the commandant of the military post, must of necessity be sub-dictators in cases of hostility between two nations; for if a powerful nation, such as the Choctaws, the Creeks, the Cherokees, or the Osages, should make war upon a weak nation, such as the Senecas, the Piankeshaws, or the Quapaws, the weaker nation would be exterminated before the pleasure of the President of the United States could be known. The strong arm of the General Government must interfere to save the weaker nation until the will of the President of the United States shall be made known. It was with much difficulty that Colonel Arbuckle and myself prevented hostilities between the Cherokees and Osages last May. The peace of the different nations has been guaranteed by the United States, and it must be preserved by summary means. The conduct of the Governor and military commandant must be submitted to the President of the United States, and his approval be obtained, or the parties removed from office or otherwise punished, as Congress may direct.

The internal concerns of each nation may be regulated by themselves. They are now very good in some of the nations.

When Congress enacts a law giving the authority herein set forth, the Governor shall summon the chiefs of all the nations with whom the United States have intercourse south of the Missouri, to signify their acceptance or rejection of this Government. If a majority of the nations accept it, they will of course be bound by it. If a majority reject it, Congress will make other provision.

A council of the representatives of the different nations shall annually meet at the military post, for the purpose of settling their affairs, adjusting their differences, and proposing such alterations in the scheme of government as they may deem proper. The number of the different nations is easily ascertained, and they shall be represented in the general council, according to their numbers. This voting in national affairs by representatives in proportion to their numbers, will cause some of the weaker nations to unite with others in order to increase their weight in the general council, and be productive of much good. These propositions are predicated upon a supposition that the United States must keep up a military establishment in this country for many years, which must be the case, in order to afford protection to the emigrating Indians, which the Government has promised, and most assuredly will fulfil.

## *The Expense.*

The Government of the United States will furnish provisions for the representatives and arbitrators, whenever they assemble at the military post on national business; and they will not insist upon any further compensation.

I am convinced that a majority of nations south of the Missouri may be induced to sanction these or similar regulations. With the nations north of the Missouri I am not well enough acquainted to judge what will suit them. If Congress shall deem it proper to have but one government for all the nations west of the Mississippi, it will be for them in their wisdom to point out a more proper and comprehensive plan. But my opinion is that the nations north and south of the Missouri cannot be brought to unite in the same form of Government: their manners and customs are very different; and the distance from the 49th degree of north latitude to the Red river is too great for the representatives to meet with convenience at any central point; whereas the nations from the Red river to the Missouri can meet at Fort Gibson, the head of steamboat navigation, without inconvenience. None of them would have to travel more than five hundred miles, through a level country, and not impeded by any great water course.

This southern government would include the great nations of the Choctaws, Creeks, and Seminoles, Cherokees, Osages, Shawnees, Delawares, Kanzas, Kickapoos, Pawnees; Mahas; besides the smaller nations of the Senecas, Quapaws, Pienkeshaws, Peorias, &c., and also the Pottawatamies, if they settle south of the Missouri.

I have ascertained that if this scheme of Government shall be adopted, a cession of land of six miles square, or more, can be obtained from the Cherokees. Indeed, it would have been ceded by the last treaty, if Mr. Schermerhorn had not stated that Government wanted it for the purpose of establishing a seminary for the education of preachers. The Indians will not give land for any such purposes.

If this government is established, it is intended that all the annuities shall be paid here to the Indians themselves. Great impositions have been practised by many of the agents, in the payment of annuities. But when the money or goods is paid in the presence of the assembled nations, it will give universal satisfaction.

Thus, my dear sir, I have given you my views of the best manner in which the enlarged and benevolent intentions of the General Government towards the Indian tribes may be carried into effect.

It will be for the President of the United States, for yourself, and for Congress to decide upon what course shall be pursued in this important concern.

I have the honor to be,
With great respect,
Your obedient servant,
M. STOKES.

Hon. LEWIS CASS.

———

WESTERN CREEK NATION,
*October* 27, 1833.

SIR: The chiefs and head men of the Western Creeks gave to Chilly McIntosh and Robert Tiger a power of attorney, bearing date 17th April, 1833, giving them jointly the power to sell five sections of land, given by the Eastern Creeks to those who reside west of the Mississippi, in January last, which land was not sold by them. Since the return of McIntosh and Tiger to this country, we have understood that Benjamin Hawkins has sold the whole five sections given to our nation; he has acknowledged to have sold one half for his own benefit. He has never had any power given him by the proper authorities of this nation to sell any part, nor in any way to interfere in the sale of the land at all. We, therefore, the principal chiefs and head men of the Western Creek tribe, do enter our protest against the proceedings of Hawkins in the sale of the land; and also do revoke the power of attorney given to Chilly McIntosh and Robert Tiger, and all other powers of attorney that may be produced prior to the date of this. We request that you will locate the five sections of land given to this nation, and hold and defend the same from any person or persons who may have purchased the same until there shall come an agent properly authorized, by the proper authorities of this nation, to demand the same for the benefit of the Western Creeks.

We also wish you to make known the proceedings of Hawkins to the Secretary of War, in order that no fraud may be practised on us.

We respectfully request that you will write to us, and let us know, as soon as possible, what has been done with the land, so that we may know how to proceed.

Very respectfully,
Your friends and brothers,

| | |
|---|---|
| ROLEY McINTOSH, | his x mark. |
| TUSK-HATCHE-MICCO, | his x mark. |
| BENJ. PERRYMAN, | his x mark. |
| CO-WOCK-COCHE EMARLO, | his x mark. |
| IS-POAK-OAK-HARJO, | his x mark. |
| HOS-PO-TOCK-HARJO, | his x mark. |
| SAMUEL MILLER, | his x mark. |
| POWES HARJO, | his x mark. |
| WARLOCK HARJO, | his x mark. |
| GISKER-LIKER-MICCO, | his x mark. |
| JOHN RANDALL, | his x mark. |
| CORSER YOHOLO, | his x mark. |
| HOLATTER THLOCKO, | his x mark. |
| EASTER-CHARCO-HARJO, | his x mark. |
| SAMUEL PERRYMAN, | his x mark. |
| TUSKA-ENE-HAH, | his x mark. |
| CHACOTEE-TUSTENUGGE, | his x mark. |
| TUCK-A-BATCHE-HARJO, | his x mark. |

Done in the presence of
JOHN CAMPBELL, *Agent Creeks.*
ELI JACOBS, *Clerk.*

To LEONARD TARRANT, Esq.

---

CLAIBORNE, *October* 27, 1833.

SIR: By the mail of the 24th October, I had the honor of receiving yours bearing date the 8th ult. preceding, together with the documents enclosed.

It would appear, from some of the expressions contained in yours of the above date, that my letter to his excellency the President of the United States was understood to be predicated upon a supposition on my part that not only such settlers in the Creek Indian country as had by force or fraud ejected Indians from their fields and habitations, and otherwise intruded upon their possessions or improvements, were to be immediately removed from the said country, but also *all others* at the same time with them. If my letter would bear any such construction it must be owing to some omission or mistake which I by no means intended. I think I stated that my information, relative to the intentions of the Government in this particular, was obtained through the medium of the *newspapers;* of course, after a perusal of the instructions of the Secretary of War to the United States Marshal, it is scarcely to be conjectured that I could have remained in ignorance of the distinction drawn between the two classes of settlers, and of the order for the unceremonious removal of the one, and the extension of time for the gathering and securing of crops, &c. granted in favor of the others. I might not have thought it necessary, perhaps, to have expressed all this substantially in writing, but deemed that I had been sufficiently explicit, at least to show that the whole *was understood.* It was by no means in relation to this *general or promiscuous immediate removal* that my remarks were intended to be directed, as from some expressions in yours it appears was in part supposed, but against the necessity of *removing at all* such honest and peaceable settlers *as had made their own improvements,* without intrusion upon Indian rights or possessions, and without in any manner injuring or interfering with them. These were the points which I intended to present respectfully to your notice, and which I thought with sufficient precision I had done. The number of these I also stated to be three fourths of the whole number of settlers in the nation, and which I believe to be much below their real estimate.

In compliance with what you state to be the wishes of the Government, I will endeavor to ascertain whether a delegation of Creek chiefs willing to treat for the sale of their reservations can be selected, and if possible get up such an one, and either send or accompany them to Washington. I shall immediately be up and doing, and leave no becoming means untried for the insuring of the object, for upon it I think much depends the peace and tranquillity of the country. As early as practicable I will make communication to you of the result.

With sentiments of high respect,

I subscribe myself, sir,

Very respectfully, yours, &c.,

ENOCH PARSONS.

JOHN ROBB, Esq.,
 *Acting Secretary of War.*

---

SHAWANOE, JACKSON COUNTY, Mo., *Oct.* 28, 1833.

DEAR SIR: I have understood that in exchanging lands with the Osages, it has been proposed to give to them all the unappropriated land between their present reservation on the south and the lands of Weas, Ottawas, Shawanoes, and Kanzas, on the north. Having examined in person almost all parts of this Indian territory, I beg leave to say that the above measure would deprive the Pottawatamies, Miamies, Ottawas, and all other northern bands, of suitable locations. They would have to be placed north of the Delawares and Kickapoos, and in an undesirable tract of country, and in the country which heretofore has been deemed more suitable for the Winnebagoes and Sacs and Foxes than for others. The Miamies would be separated from their kindred, the Weas; and the Pottawatamies and Ottawas would be separated from their kindred Ottawas.

This measure would also frustrate the plan of Secretary Eaton (which I hope Government will not abandon) of reserving a portion of that central tract of country for Government purposes, and as a seat of government for the Indian territory.

The plan of removing the Osages in order to make room for southern Indians originated with Secretary Eaton, who contemplated locating them alongside of the Kanzas; those two tribes speaking the same language, and being virtually the same people. I beg leave to say that, by observation of places and people in this country, I am confirmed in my opinion that his plan was judicious.

Most respectfully, sir,
Your humble and obedient servant,
ISAAC McCOY.

Hon. Lewis Cass,
    *Secretary of War.*

---

Fayetteville, *Oct.* 29, 1833.

Sir: Your favor of the 15th instant, informing me of my selection for the purpose of making the locations authorized to be made for the Creek Indians, by virtue of a treaty concluded with that tribe on the 24th of March, 1832, was this day received. I accept the appointment, and will repair, without delay, to Fort Mitchell; and hope, by a strict attention to the duties confided to me, not to disappoint the confidence reposed in me by my unsolicited appointment.

Very respectfully, &c.,
JAMES BRIGHT.

Hon. Lewis Cass,
    *Secretary of War.*

---

Memphis, Tennessee, *Oct.* 31, 1833.

Sir: I have this day drawn on the Department of War, in favor of Cowan and Bias, for one thousand dollars, for outfit and expenses of a Chickasaw delegation now on their way to the west in search of a new home for their people; and which sum is to be refunded out of the moneys arising from the sales of their lands.

Please honor and pay the same, and charge to account of
Your obedient servant,
BENJ. REYNOLDS,
*Indian Agent.*

Hon. Lewis Cass,
    *Secretary of War.*

In General Council at Red Clay, C. N.,

*October* 31, 1833.

Sir: We take occasion to report through you for the information of the President of the United States, that John Ross, the principal chief of this nation, together with Messrs. Richard Taylor, Daniel McCoy, Hair Conrad, and John Timson, are delegated to represent this nation on a mission before the Government of the United States at Washington City at the next session of Congress, on all subjects touching the rights and interest of the same, with a view to a final termination of existing difficulty. And in order to meet the expenses of said delegation, we call upon you to pay over to Mr. Richard Taylor the sum of thirty-five hundred dollars, out of the annuities due to this nation by treaties with the United States; and his receipt for the same will be your sufficient voucher.

Very respectfully,

Your obedient servants,

 R. TAYLOR, *President of Council.*
 JOSEPH VANN,
 RICHARD FIELDS,
 JAMES DANIEL,
 JOHN TIMSON,
 W. W. BOWLING,
 THOMAS FOREMAN,
 DAVID VANN,
 SAMUEL GUNTER,
 JNO. FOX BALDRIDGE,
 OLD FIELDS,
 HAIR CONRAD,
 GEORGE STILL,
 GEORGE BLAIR,
    *Members of Committee.*

WILLIAM ROGERS, *Clerk N. Committee.*

 GOING SNAKE, *Speaker of Council.*
 JOHN WATTS,
 JAMES SPEARS,
 SLEEPING RABBIT,
 YOUNG GLASS,
 CHUMUKOH,
 TH. BARK,
 GEO. CHAMBERS,
 A. CAMPBELL,
 TAHQUOT,
 E. DUNCAN,
 SOFT SHELL TURTLE,
 WALKING STICK,
 BEAN STICK,
 WHITE PATH,
 TIS A TU KEE,
 JAMES FOSTER,
 CHURVOLOOKEE,
 CHARLES,

JOHN WAYNE,
SITUAKEE,
PETER,
SWEET WATER,

*Members of Council.*

JNO. ROSS, *Principal Chief.*
GEORGE LOWRY, *Assistant P. Chief.*
GEORGE M. WATERS,
MAJOR RIDGE, his x mark,

*Executive Committee.*

A. McCoy, *Clerk N. Council.*

To Col. Hugh Montgomery,
    *United States Agent.*

---

Louisville, Barbour County,

*October* 31, 183

Sir: I received your letter of the 12th instant, and was rejoiced to hear from you that no time would be lost in locating the Indians; and also saw your letter to Governor Gayle, stating the reason that the Indians had not been located before this time was owing to the great fraud that was imposed on the agents in executing that duty. I have seen several respectable gentlemen living in the lower part of the Creek country, and have conversed with them on the subject of fraud being practised on the Government, and told me that it was carried on to great extent. Some of them had been living in that part of the nation for three years, and had become acquainted with most of the Indians, and many of the young females among them, people that lived with other heads of families in the same house, give in to the agent as head of a family who claimed young white persons as husbands who lived in Georgia; and many other instances where there were grown persons living in one house, they would all give in as a head of a family. I asked them what portion of the Indians' claims for land was wrong; and they said that they thought from what they saw, that nearly one third were impositions in the lower district. I will state that it is hard to prevent those frauds, except the locating agent is acquainted with those Indians.

Be so good as to answer me when the Indians will be located, so that I may make known to the citizens living in the Creek country, as they are always anxious to hear from the War Department.

I remain, sir,
Your most obedient servant,
F. W. PUGH.

Hon. Lewis Cass,
    *Secretary of War.*

---

Montgomery, Alabama,

*October* 31, 1833.

Sir: Your letter, under date 10th instant, was received by yesterday's mail, enclosing a copy of a letter from John Simms and Little Simms.

ᶠ The removal of the settlers from the Creek lands, I fear, will eventuate in a general rupture between the General and State Governments. I have concluded to wait until I hear from you again. The excitement, in consequence of the order for a general removal, is great indeed, and the Executive of this State appears determined to aid them. He has directed the county officers to be vigilant, and to issue warrants against me, should I remove a single one, or molest them in any way.

Very respectfully,

ROBT. L. CRAWFORD,
*United States Marshal.*

Hon. Lewis Cass,
Secretary of War.

----

Mardisville, Talladega County, Ala.,
*October* 31, 1833.

Sir: Your letters of the 26th and 28th ultimo have been duly received, and it gives me pleasure to know that the department is satisfied with my reply to a letter written by D. Kurtz the 24th of July last. All high minded and honorable men will do right if they know how, and cannot endure, without the most painful feelings, the suspicion of having wilfully acted wrong.

My situation at present is truly unpleasant. Reports are continually circulated amongst an agitated and almost distracted people, that my representations to the Government have been the cause of the late orders from the department for the removal of settlers from the Creek country. A meeting has been gotten up in Macon county, in the Creek country, and in their last resolution they charge the agents of the Government and a few white men living among the Indians with having exerted an unfriendly influence amongst the chiefs against the settlers. The last charge, as relates to myself, is utterly false; and no exception to individuals holding appointments under the Government is made.

Very respectfully, &c.,

LEONARD TARRANT.

E. Herring, Esq

----

Macon County, Alabama, *Nov.* 1, 1833.

Sir: I received your letter of the 15th October last, in which you state that Major Wager had transmitted to the War Department a letter of mine, written to him on the subject of intrusions on the Creek lands. It is true I did write to that officer upon the subject of the settlers in this county, and requested of him, as a favor, to step forward in behalf of a large and respectable number of citizens whose conduct I know had been greatly misrepresented to the General Government; believing, at the same time, that Major Wager's knowledge of both whites and Indians would enable him to make as correct a statement as to the true state of things here as any that had been written previous on the subject; knowing, too, that any communication from him to the department would be true if stated on his own responsibility, which has not been the case in every instance. Had my acquaintance with you been such as would have authorized it, I would have written to you instead of Major Wager; but, inasmuch as you have been pleased to write me on the subject, I must beg the indulgence to state a few facts that, if not known, should be made known to the President.

In the 'first place, it must be recollected that, from the death of Col. Hawkins until the jurisdiction of Alabama was extended over the Indians, this country, with few exceptions, has been infested with a corrupt set of men. Even men that the Government placed here, placing implicit confidence in their honesty, have acted unfairly and dishonorably both with the whites and Indians. Money has been their object, regardless of any obligation they were under to the Government, or their duty towards the whites and unfortunate Indians. Some of those persons are here yet, and they want more money; but, in consequence of the large number and respectability of the present inhabitants, they have not the same opportunities to practise such frauds as they could easily do in former times. Their only alternative now is to complain to the Government, in the name of the Indians, of injuries done them by the settlers, in order that the whites may be removed, so as it will enable them to carry on with the greater facility their old trade for the remaining few years that the Indians may remain. The objects of these men are too well known here to admit of a doubt. They calculate that the Government, from the complaints that have been made against settlers, would drive the whites from the country and wherever the Indian reservations are known, there can be no opposition in the purchase of them. I have seen an extract of a letter from Col. Crowell to the department, in which he states that he had seen the chief of some one of the towns, (which town is not mentioned in the extract,) and that the chief had given him a distressing account of the Indians; that they were hiding in the woods, without the means of subsistence, afraid to meet the intruders, who treated them cruelly, &c. It is possible the Indian made the above statement to Col. Crowell, but I hardly believe it probable that Col. Crowell thought the statement to be true when he communicated it to the department. At all events, I will take the responsibility on myself to say nine tenths of that statement is false. The letter of Col. Crowell, no doubt, has had an unfavorable bearing on the settlers; and that that letter, with some written by John Brodnax for some of the chiefs whom he has an undue control over, have, I presume, been one of the principal causes of the order for the removal of settlers. As to Col. Crowell, his situation when he received the appointment of Indian agent, and the property now in possession of those whom he has had about him, will show the course he has pursued with the Indians; but for Mr. Brodnax I must say something, as I see he has played himself off on those who made the treaty as an Indian interpreter. It is possible he may have played himself off as a gentleman. If he has done so, I assure you he has not acted in his true character. Among those who are acquainted with him he has lost all reputation for telling the truth, (if he ever had any,) and only retains his influence over the ignorant Indian with his duplicity and money that he has swindled from them.

Gen. Parsons, a commissioner of the Government, could long since have effected a treaty with the Indians but for the unfortunate influence of this man, Brodnax, and a few others that have lain behind the curtain and pushed him forward. And could a treaty have been made, it would have warded off the calamity that now threatens thousands of unoffending women an:

children.  Gen. Parsons is known to the President, and is known to be strictly honest.  To him I appeal as to the correctness of my statements, if the President himself is not well enough acquainted with me to give full credit to my assertions.

In conclusion, permit me to make one request: that is, for the General to send two or more disinterested officers among us; let them see and report the true situation of both whites and Indians.  Were there but few settlers this would or might look like importuning, but when you come to look at the number and respectability of the inhabitants, and the inevitable loss of property that will be sustained in the event of your orders being carried into execution, I cannot believe you will think the request illiberal.  I speak the truth when I say to you that I have as many acquaintances, both among whites and reds, as any one residing in the country; and that I know, of my own knowledge, a large majority of the Indians are anxious the settlers should remain.  I know the President must have a warm side for frontier settlers, and if they cannot look on him as a friend who are they to look to?  If I may be permitted to answer, I would say none.  I have no doubt if the President can be assured that the Indians do not wish the removal of the whites, the present unhappy situation of the settlers would be at an end, and prevent difficulties that might otherwise take place between the General Government and Alabama.  The plan I propose is easy, and I think fair; at least it will greatly accommodate the settlers.  Gen. Parsons resides in Alabama; Col. Twiggs can reach here in four days from New Orleans, and Major Wager is already here; all three men of undoubted veracity.  The reason why I have taken the liberty to name these gentlemen, they are honest, they have judgment, they can reach this point with ease, and they are also better acquainted with the country and the manners and customs of its inhabitants than any officers of my acquaintance.  My situation, with that of many others, I hope will be a sufficient apology for writing this.

Very respectfully,<br>Your obedient servant,<br>THOS. S. WOODWARD.

Hon. Lewis Cass.

P.S.  The greatest evil that can befal the Indians is to locate them on the tracts of land designated for them; for in that event there will be thousands of impositions practised upon them that the Government cannot prevent.  If a treaty could be effected, and their money paid to them in Arkansas, it would be doing them the greatest favor that could be bestowed upon them.  I say what I know to be the fact in this case.

T. S. W.

---

Suggsville, Clarke County, Ala., Nov. 2, 1833.

Dear Sir: Having, on a recent occasion, as the head of a Creek family, offered my name to Maj. Parsons while taking the census of the Creek tribe of Indians, and the same being rejected on account of the nature of his instructions, the color of my skin, &c., he could not recognize me as an Indian, therefore could not take my name; but believing me to be entitled to land, evinced some concern on my account; and in a very friendly manner advised me to address your honor on the subject in a letter, confining myself scrupulously to the truth, and lay before you the particulars of my claim, adding that he had not the least doubt but that you would at once instruct him to consider and receive me as the head of a Creek family and claimant under the treaty. And having determined to adopt this course, in order that you may be more particularly acquainted with the nature and extent of my claim, it is necessary that I should inform your honor that I am included in the number of those persons holding land under the treaty entered into at Fort Jackson, on the 9th August, 1814, between General A. Jackson, on behalf of the United States, and the chiefs, &c. of the Creek nation, on the part of their own people, and that this claim has never fully come to the knowledge of the proper authorities for their examination. First, then, I would ask your attention to this part of my claim, it being the oldest. At the time of the general confusion which divided our people, and resulted in a civil war in the bosom of our once happy country, I am proud to say that I was on that side called the friendly party; took an active part during the war in favor of the United States, by connecting myself with the troops from the Mississippi in the neighborhood of Fort Mims, in the walls of which some of my dearest relatives had sought to shelter themselves from the enemy; but, alas, they shared the fate of all who were butchered by the merciless hands of our own countrymen. I acted as a volunteer; was on various expeditions against the hostile part of my country, and shared in the general suffering incident to an army in the wilderness; and being settled in that part of the country ceded to the United States by the treaty at Fort Jackson, I availed myself of the opportunity, under the first article of that treaty, (which provides for chiefs and warriors settled in the section of country above named, in these words: " Provided, nevertheless, that where any chief or warrior of the Creek nation, who shall have been friendly to the United States during the war, and taken an active part therein, shall be within the territory ceded by these articles to the United States, every such person shall be entitled to a reservation of land within the said territory of one mile square, to include his improvement as near the centre thereof as may be, which shall insure to the said chief or war- rior," &c.) to present my claim, as a warrior, for one section of land, with the evidences to establish the same to Gen. Mitchell, who was the agent appointed for that purpose.

On this occasion the General said that he did not think as I did; that I was entitled only to one half section, on the ground that I did not live on the tract claimed by me previous to the war. I, in some degree, pressed the propriety of his recording my claim for one section, and he as often re- fused. Finally, my being ignorant of the best manner of procedure, and also thinking that, by acceding to his propositions, my right to the balance of the section could not be affected thereby, I signed it with much reluc- tance. I cannot think of charging this agent with any other view than that of strict propriety, but will let his acts speak for themselves, and sub- mit for your consideration a few observations relating thereto. He was instructed by the General Government, in a very particular manner, to take the evidences that should be offered with each claim; and when he was satis- fied as to the validity thereof, to put such immediately into peaceable pos- session of the same; but in all cases where a doubt should remain in his opinion, to transmit the same, with the evidence by which they might be supported, to the President, Secretary, &c. for final decision. Now, had General Mitchell, after making up his opinion in regard to my claim, have recorded the same with the evidences, and had transmitted them to the proper authority, accompanied with any remarks that he may have thought necessary, I should have been satisfied; for then all the evidences advanced by me to establish the legality of my right to one mile square, would have received that attention from the General Government to which it is yet so justly entitled, by which a final and satisfactory decision would have been made, and relieved me at this time from the necessity of troubling your honor, at least on this part of my claim.

It is more than I know, whether, in admitting a part of my claim, and refusing to register the other, he has assumed any authority, or merely mistaken the proper use of those with which he was clothed; but this much I know, that one mile square of land has been granted to me by a solemn treaty; and because my claim has never been made known in full to the Government, I have only as yet received a part of it. In questioning the propriety of the conduct of any one, I wish to be extremely cautious, and more particularly so of that of an officer in whose care a National Government had confided the transaction of business of importance. But when this becomes necessary, we should recollect that the best of judges, with the purest intention, is yet liable to err. That this may have been the case in the present instance, I am ready to admit, yet the duty that impels me to examine into and point out defects is, nevertheless, impressive.

I would then say, that to compare the instruction of Gen. Mitchell with his rejecting a part of my claim, we find that they do not agree; for I offered him a claim for one section of land, with more than a shadow of evidence to support it, and he positively refused to take it. How could the Government give me land on which they knew nothing of my claim? That they should, through some channel, have been made acquainted with it, is indisputable; but to extend the examination somewhat further into the details of this case, and admit his authority (which could only have been assumed) for deciding in all cases, we will discover that his only objection, which has already been named, cannot be supported by that instrument which gave this right to me. It was intended by that treaty to give all those who had been friendly and active during the war, a home—a spot of their native soil, to plant their corn and repose their wearied limbs; and could I be made to believe that, because I was not now stationary, and tied down to that very spot for years before the treaty, my right should be forfeited, I should unhesitatingly be forced to enter into some unfavorable conclusion with regard to the intention of this great republic towards her less prosperous neighbors. But not so; the evidences of humanity, that exalts the character of a nation, have been too strongly marked in her movements toward our people to warrant such a belief. The section on which I lived at the time of the treaty, and claimed, has the Alabama river running immediately through it, dividing it into two fractions, one of which contains 510 acres, the other about 80; the rivers taking up the balance of 50. It is ten miles up the river from the place of my birth, the same having been reserved for Lachlin Durant, a brother of my mother. Although my section is divided into such unequal parts, if any difference exists in value, it is in favor of the least. Notwithstanding the opinion of the agent, in registering my claim, he allowed me to extend it on the whole of the first named fraction, and the same has been confirmed to me. I now claim 130 acres, it being the balance of my claim under this head for one mile square.

I now respectfully solicit your attention to the second part of my claim. Having been entreated by my friends and relatives living in that part of the

Creek nation lately ceded to the United States to go and live among them, as many had done who held reserves in the same neighborhood with me, I came to the conclusion to do so, knowing that my right to live in and enjoy all the privileges in that part of the country was the same as with any other Indian in the nation. So, in December, 1831, I commenced an improvement in the Tookabache town, on the Talapoosa river, where I have continued to improve and cultivate ever since. By this it will be seen that I settled in that part of the country previous to its being conveyed to the United States by the late treaty, and being entitled to all the privileges of citizenship, and having a wife and four children, I claimed, as the head of a Creek family, one half section of land, under the second article of a treaty made at the city of Washington 26th March, 1832, between Lewis Cass, on the part of the United States, and the Creek Indians, which reads, "and every other head of a Creek family to select one half section each." In laying before you an account of my claims, I wish to be confined exclusively to plain simple matters of fact; and that you may be the more certain of the reality of this, I will assure your honor that no other agency has been employed in this communication but my own head, hands, and pen. I have before mentioned that my name, as a claimant of land, was offered to Major Parsons, and rejected, because my skin is some fairer than a part of my countrymen; and perhaps he discovered that I was not brought up exactly in the Indian style; and my wife not being an Indian woman, might have had a share of influence in directing his opinion. The truth is, I feel no injustice done me by Major Parsons, if his instructions were such as not to justify him in the belief that my name was entitled to a place on his list; he undoubtedly does honor to his office to exclude such. However, I do not, nor does he by that circumstance think my claim less legal, because in the same way of reasoning, if the Indians were never to relinquish their right to the soil, and were to remain throughout a great period of time under the Government of a white population, continually mixing with them, and improving the color of their skin, it is certain that in the course of time the old would die, and in like manner would their color pass away, with all other distinguishing character of the Indian; and for this progression of things in their natural order, the birthright of their descendants must be for ever forfeited. No, no; this cannot be the decision of a wise government.

Tuskina and others of the chiefs were present and advocated my side, but to no purpose. Major Parsons very justly took the names of three of my brothers as claimants of land, (Wm. McGirth, David and Benjamin Walker,) on account of their having Indian wives. He says they are heads of Creek families; this is all true, and I must add that I am the head of a Creek family too; and I am persuaded that I will be able to satisfy you on this point.

Every free man or woman who, having been born in the limits of the Creek nation, and being recognised as descendants of that tribe, whether full blooded or mixed, have always had a right to marry whom they pleased of any other nation, and introduce them into their own country, clothed with all the right, title, and privileges of any of its citizens. This being admitted, it follows that mine is bound to be a Creek family; and so long as they continued to hold the country, so long did my family and I have the right of living in the nation. I was born and principally brought up in it, and if I am not so very red, perhaps my ancestors were; and if they had a right to the soil, I have also, for the Indians like their children too well to cast them off on account of their color. So it is evident that, agreeably to the usages of our people, I have an unquestionable right to a claim, and the high opinion that I entertain of the authorities of the United States gives me assurances that they will do every possible justice to the cases now submitted for their examination.

Be pleased to excuse the liberty I have taken in calling your attention to my claims, and trespassing so much on your patience, by endeavoring to explain their nature. I respectfully solicit your perusal of them: not that I expect you to give me land on the mere authority of these lines, but admitting that what they contain can be satisfactorily established. Your honor can decide, and will confer a very singular favor by placing me in possession of the result of your investigation, and the information necessary for the course to be pursued.

I have lived to see more than forty years, and feel disposed to pass the balance of my days in the country that gave me birth; and perhaps some others of our countrymen may do the same; but I think it probable that before a very distant day the majority now in Alabama will follow our brethren to the west; and the propriety of this course is too plain to be resisted, when we take a view of all the circumstances connected with the situation of our country at present.

The United States has the best of reasons to wish the acknowledgment of no other national government power within her limits that might possibly be used prejudicial to her interests, and hence the necessity of extending her laws completely over her territories, that all may be compact, united, and enabled to give that facility to all her internal operations that circumstances might make necessary; this being effected in our country by a treaty in which it is presumable that our people has had full compensation made them for their possessions.

It only remains now for them to consider their interest in this matter; and, as they appear slow as yet in adopting the good customs of the whites, and so ready to take up with all those that do not improve their condition, my sincere prayer is, that they may at all times view their white neighbors as friends; and that so soon as convenient, they may direct their attention toward the home secured to them, there to join their brethren, and commence with renewed activity the great work of cultivating the inviting soil and their intellectual powers.

I have the honor to be, very respectfully,
Your obedient and humble servant,
Hon. Lewis Cass.                SAMUEL BRASHIERS.

P. S. Since writing, I found in my possession a letter in answer to one of mine on the subject of my claim under the treaty of Fort Jackson, dated 28th January, 1828, from Colonel G. W. Owen, then a member to Congress from Alabama, in which i am informed that I have received all the land claimed by me before the Indian agent, being three hundred and twenty acres, under the third section of the act of Congress of 3d March, 1817, and that in his report on my claim he says:

" In this case the only doubt in my mind is, whether Brashiers, who was under age at the commencement of the war, but was nevertheless actively friendly, ought not to have been considered as a warrior, and entitled to a full section under the first section of the act of Congress."

It is true that I did sign a claim for three hundred and twenty acres of land, not that I ever pretended to any claim under the act that granted that amount of land, but because it was the one pointed out to me by the agent, the only one that he would record; and when I consented to put my name to it, I flattered myself that the Government would allow me some future explanation on the subject. As the agent in his report, as quoted above, has been so much deceived in my age, it may be necessary to inform you that I was born in June, 1792. Whatever may have been the real motive of the agent in forcing me to claim as he did, or whatever he and I may have done in it, truth is still the same always, and we cannot alter it by our acts. So I trust that what has been done could not weaken my title, nor prevent the Government, on the receipt of the necessary facts, from the same view it would originally have taken.

My claim to one mile square of land, under the treaty at Fort Jackson, is founded on the following condensed facts:

I was born and principally brought up in the Creek nation, having my descent on the part of my mother from a white man named McGillavary, and a Creek Indian woman.

I was of age at the commencement of the war, and took an active part in favor of the United States. I lived on the land I claimed at the time of the treaty.

From these circumstances I am of opinion that you will readily discover that my right to the balance of this section, one hundred and thirty acres, is undoubted; my claim under the late treaty being three hundred and twenty acres more, making in all four hundred and fifty acres, which, from what can be established, I am bound to believe will be conceded to

Your honor's obedient
And very humble servant,
S. B.

———

COMMISSIONER'S OFFICE,
*Fort Leavenworth, November,* 1833.

Enclosed herewith are the talks with the Kickapoos and the Pottawatamies residing with them. It is only necessary to observe that the last talk was held with all the chiefs. There is an entire satisfaction, if Kishkoo and a few followers are excepted. Kishkoo is not a chief, and possesses little influence in the nation, separate from his band. The chiefs have been deterred from expressing their approbation of the land given by treaty, by threats from the Kishkoo party, who were flattered by some traders residing near the Osage river, that Government would change their location. Hence, while they (chiefs) were unwilling to leave the land assigned them, they proposed that I should, as a kind of arbiter, settle the matter, which I have done. In a private talk with Kishkoo at my office, I admonished him against taking his people on to the Shawnees' land, or the land contiguous to the Osage river. He assured me he would only go out to hunt, but not to fix his camp on these lands. When Kishkoo's followers find he is not able to give them land on the Osage river, most of them, I think, will leave him and join their friends on the Missouri river. Every possible indulgence has been shown to Kishkoo; he has not the least reason to complain; the land secured by treaty is good and abundant; the tribe is well protected by the fort; which also furnishes a ready market. I do not apprehend any further difficulty on the subject; the nation is very happy that the question is settled. Should any individuals of the tribe presume to raise, hereafter, unfounded objections, a decisive negative will alone check their querulous petitions.

Most respectfully,

Yours, &c.,

HENRY L. ELLSWORTH,

*U. S. Commissioner.*

---

On September 2d, Mr. Ellsworth, one of the commissioners, held a council with the Kickapoos at their village, near Fort Leavenworth; the Kickapoos were unwilling to delay longer for the arrival of the other commissioners.

The talk was as follows:

Mr. Ellsworth.—Friends and brothers of the Kickapoo nation: The Great Spirit has permitted us to meet once more in council. When I was here before, I told you that the other commissioners were expected to arrive; I have since learned that they have been taken sick; we have all been equally instructed by your great father: I have little to say now; I wish to know if you have any objections to make against the treaty, by which your great father has given you these lands; I have come to do you good, and wish you to tell me all that is in your hearts. No answer being made, and the Indians being embarrassed, Mr. Ellsworth continued: My brothers and friends, your great father saw that your condition in Missouri was not good, and wished to give you a better place. Your great father held a council with you, in which your nation was consulted, and asked what they wished to do; after a long delay spent in talking, your nation signed a treaty to come here. The chiefs and braves signed the treaty with your great father; the name of Kishkoo and many others occur in it. It was sent to your great father; he read it, to know if it was good for you; your great father wished you also to be satisfied, and sent men to examine this land; they did so, and made alterations that were for your benefit. You will see by the treaty that your great father has been anxious to make you happy; the engagements made have been fulfilled, and you have received the share of money promised you. Your great father promised to build you mills, that you may have flour; he will give you hogs, corn, and cattle, whenever you seem prepared to receive them. Your great father promised to give you a blacksmith, to mend your guns and farming utensils; he has promised to give you the worth of five thousand dollars a year, in goods or money as you might choose, and to furnish you with schools whenever you should want them. Your great father has promised to do all this for you on the land where you now live; and as you have signed this treaty, will any of you rise up and say it shall not stand good? I have been over your land, and say it is good; can any one say it is not good? I am your friend, and have no interest to deceive you; I will now tell you why I think your land is good. You are close to a river; can send up and down what things you may raise: you have nothing to fear from hostile bands, for you are near a fort that can protect you. If you raise corn and chickens, you will always find a good market at the fort. I have not much more to say; I am glad you have so good a place assigned to you. I have visited other Indian tribes, and do not think I noticed any having so good land as that belonging to the Kickapoos. Your great father hopes you are willing to live here; it is his wish that you should all live here as brothers, and cannot approve of the tribe being separated. Where else could you go? There is no other land for you; the Shawnee Indians will not permit you to remain on their land. Look over your lands and find a place for a settlement, and your great father will make good all his promises to you. The Great Spirit knows what has been said is true.

Muscahtewishah.—All you have said is truth; but there has arisen among us many parties: we cannot agree. I will briefly tell the reason. I will let you know all that is in our minds. I call the Great Spirit to witness. He that sent us into the world to live well also wanted every thing done right. We know that you are our friend, and are employed to see us righted in all our concerns. We will call you father. It is hard we cannot get our minds settled in the proper way. We know that the Great Spirit sent us into the world to live as brothers; that he hears me this day. All that we want is that our young men and women may be pleased as well as ourselves. I am not trying to deceive you; the Great Man who rules the earth knows this. I only want to tell you our ideas. Our great father should not think hard of his warriors. My own wish is that all should be done in order. My father, we wish you to listen attentively to our request. We know that when you would hold a treaty with red skins, you wish that the land got from us shall satisfy you. We believe you have come to settle with us in a just and equitable manner, that all may be pleased and satisfied. I would not hide from you what our young men have in their minds. The Great Spirit hears what we say. We do not wish to dispute and quarrel; but to settle all things in peace. Hear what the young men have told me. They will not be satisfied but with that land where a mission is placed on the Osage river. Our party of the Osage river are now telling you what is their wish. It is the desire of our party to get the land if it can be got; it is also the wish of our chiefs. It lies in the fork of the Osage. We know that the land belongs to no one. It is but a little place. I wish to let you know that our young men and the chiefs do not agree, as they did some time ago; some wish one thing, some another. Some would go to the Prairie, where there is game. We are like fish in the water, we jump at whatever is thrown to us. I cannot get settled in my own mind. We know, as you said, that it is the wish of our great father that this land should be settled. You are our friend, and will listen to us. We are afraid on this account: we are afraid of the wicked water brought us by our white friends. We wish to get out of its reach by land or water. I hope that if we could get that piece of land that we should live there better than here, on account of that dreadful water. I ask you as a favor to pardon me if I have said any thing wrong.

Mr. Ellsworth.—I have listened to what you have said. I am glad you consider me your friend. I have come a great distance to see you, and my other red friends. I come to ask nothing of you but to do you good. Let me now talk to you about those things which your great father intended for you. I know what your great father thinks. He wishes all the tribe to live together. Your great father considers the Kickapoos a brave nation, and wishes all the warriors together. In no instance has he consented that a tribe should divide. You ask for the land lying on the Marias de Cygne. That land has been given to others. Your great father has asked all the red men on the other side of the Mississippi river to come over this side and live, and some will be settled on that land. The Creeks and other red men are coming over, so that it is impossible to give you that land, as three or four different parties are on their way now to look at it. You have made two objections to your present situation. The scarcity of game, and the introduction of the wicked water. In regard to the first, it is obvious that the game will soon be gone, when all the other Indians shall come over. Your great father is going to help you in another way, by supplying you with cattle and farming utensils. The wicked water of which you speak has been carried two hundred miles farther in the country. Your great father was very sorry when the wicked water was brought into the country, but he will stop it, and will punish the wicked men who brought it in by judges sent to try them. Your great father will not divide the annuity. The mills must be built here, and every other provision of the treaty fulfilled here on this ground. I advise you as a friend what to do. I advise you to come and settle on this land, where your great father will endeavor to make you happy. I will come and see you again, and tell your great father all your wishes. Still he knows that many of the tribes are well satisfied with their lands.

An Indian.—The place we mean is not yet taken up by the Menomonies.

Mr. Ellsworth.—Many other tribes must be supplied, the Pottawatamies and others; had you gone to that land you would have been among strange tribes, and could not be happy among a nation of another language.

An Indian.—The tribe of whom you speak has got other lands

Mr. Ellsworth.—Every piece of vacant land is required to satisfy the many Indian tribes now on their way from the other side of Mississippi river, and I hope when I write your great father I shall be able to tell him you are all satisfied.

Principal Chief (to the tribe).—I recollect what has been agreed upon by council and treaty last year. I was the first to come and settle on these lands after the others had signed the treaty; I then thought that the minds of all had been settled. The land is good, and I like it.

Mr. Ellsworth.—It is now proper that you should come to an agreement among yourselves; matters should be settled one way or another; I hope you are all now of one mind.

Kishkoo —You have heard what is our own wishes about the lands on the Osage river; without that we cannot be satisfied. I do not say it merely expressing my own wish, but that of our young men and women.

Mr. Ellsworth.—Your great father will be angry should you go to the Osage river; he wishes to save you from trouble; to suffer you to go on that land would only be deceiving you. The speakers in the opposition here have all signed the treaty; should you now advise your young men against it, your great father will hold you responsible for the consequences. If any are opposed to the treaty, let them say so: I will give their names to their great father.

Mr. Ellsworth.—Some one remarks that a chief who is absent is opposed to it. I ask if there are any present who oppose it?

Kishkoo.—I am opposed to it. I am afraid my women and children will freeze in the winter here. Many of our young men and chiefs have opposed it in my hearing. I heard last fall after the treaty, we must come over here. Early in the spring I started to see General Clark; I told him I was not satisfied, nor had been; that I had nothing to do with what had been done; that I wished that piece of land on the Osage river. Governor Clark told us you would give an answer.

Mr. Ellsworth.—We have power to settle the affairs of the Indians, but it is impossible to give you any lands below, they have all been settled otherwise. In my opinion, and as your friend, I tell you this is the best place for you. Is there any thing more?

Kishkoo.—Nothing further, except that I am afraid of the cholera, and on that account desire to go out and hunt on the prairie.

Mr. Ellsworth.—If you intend to go to the prairie only to hunt, and will come back and settle on your lands, on this understanding you have my consent to go.

Kishkoo.—We have thirty camps here now, and only a few have come over; the rest are on the other side of the Kanzas river, on the Shawnee lands, occupied I think in drinking and rioting.

Mr. Ellsworth —I hope the chiefs will lend their influence to bring them all over here.

Kishkoo.—I suppose what has been said will be sent to our great father; we will wait for his answer.

Mr. Ellsworth.—You must come over on your lands; I speak the sentiments of your great father.

E. A. ELLSWORTH,

*Secretary pro tem.*

*September 2d.*

---

*A second talk with the Kickapoos and Pottawatamies at Fort Leavenworth, November 13th instant, A. D.* 1833.

Mr. Ellsworth —Brothers: Your chiefs are all now assembled, and I wish to say a few words to you. I understand you are anxious to have the stipulations contained in the treaty fulfilled; but you know the reason why this has not been done; you have expressed dissatisfaction at your location, and your great father wished this matter first settled. When I talked to you some time ago all the chiefs seemed satisfied. One of your braves, with his band, did not give his consent, but wished to go to the Osage river. You recollect I told you this was impossible, for there was no land for him, and your great father will not divide the tribe. I wish to know what the determination of the Kickapoos and Pottawatamies is. Are they satisfied with the land given them by treaty? If they are so, then the stipulations contained in the treaty will be fulfilled.

Head Chief.—The President has sent you here to arrange for us. You are the man to do it, and we now leave it to you. The Government has placed us here, and I suppose you will help us

Prophet.—You have been on our land and seen it. We leave it to you to say.

Mr. Ellsworth —If you wish my advice and opinion, I have been on the land and crossed it in several directions; I could not select for you a better place. The land is good, and you are on a river, and near a fort, and have a good market. I therefore give my opinion in favor of the land secured you by treaty.

First Chief —We are then willing to accept the land, and say no more about it. What I am now agoing to tell you is not to hurt your feelings; and if I say any thing disrespectful, I wish you to correct and forgive me, for I speak for the nation, not for myself.  We have had the promise of a teacher.  There have been persons offering to teach us at their own expense. I would like to have those for teachers whose principles are good, and who fear God.  I wish our great father to know of our wish, that is the reason I speak.

Mr. Ellsworth.—Who do you wish for a teacher?

Prophet.—Mr. Johnson.

Mr. Ellsworth.—Your great father wishes you to be happy, and in this respect will gratify you.

Chief.—We wish an agent to reside with us.  Our present agent lives at a great distance.  We would like one who lives on our own lands.

Mr. Ellsworth.—Mr. Cummings, your agent, is a good man, and your great father has sent another, Mr. Miller, to help him.  They will attend to all your wants, and come when you call for them.  You can send to them from the fort almost every day, and it is only one day's easy ride from their house to your village.  Your tribe is small, and every tribe cannot have a separate agent; but all your wants shall be attended to.

Chief.—We want our mill now, and to know where it is to be built.

Mr. Ellsworth.—The selection of a site shall be made as soon as possible after the lines can be run.  Mr Cummings has just-built a mill for himself, and one for the Delawares, and is a very good hand to advise you.

Chief.—We wish an interpreter to be appointed by Government.  The one we employ now is a very good one.

Mr. Ellsworth.—I will consider what you say on this subject, and am glad that the objections and difficulties about the land are entirely removed.

A true copy from the record:

E. A. ELLSWORTH,
*Secretary pro tem.*

---

ROSSVILLE, GEORGIA, *November* 4, 1833.

SIR: The enclosed paper, marked A, will exhibit the power intended to be conferred by the late Cherokee council on the delegates appointed to attend the next Congress.

At the close of the session, Ross presented a power of attorney, requesting its signature by all the members of the committee and council, capable of various constructions, and which was accordingly signed by all except John Ridge and Richard Fields; who withheld theirs for the reason, as they alleged, that it was intended to mislead the executive officers of the Government into a belief that the delegation were clothed with full powers to treat, which was not the fact.  Mr. Ross and Mr. Taylor, both members of the delegation, acknowledged this to be their object, but said in justification of the intended deception, that without such a showing they could not elicit the views of the Executive in relation to their affairs, after what had passed.

Would it not be well to put the question, upon presenting their credentials, whether the committee and council intended to give them such powers as they contemplate the President and Secretary of War will infer from the face of that power of attorney?

By the enclosed letter, B, it will be seen with what venom Ross attacks the open advocates of a treaty.  It was no doubt dictated by him, and is acknowledged to have been circulated and signed by the common Indians at the solicitation of his brother-in-law, Elijah Hicks; and may safely be regarded as a true specimen of his (Ross's) feelings.

There appears to be no other alternative than to prosecute with energy the enrolling business.

Great dissensions exist among the intelligent part of the nation. In this state of things I would ask the privilege of employing the aid of such members of their tribe, with a promise of pay according to their services rendered, so as not to exceed four dollars per day.

The annuity placed at the disposal of the agent would afford us great facilities, whilst the necessitous condition of many poor and needy families would seem to require it immediately on their enrolment.

About five hundred have enrolled, and the prospect for rapid increase brightens every day.

Allow me to notify those who enrolled under Governor McMinn that they must be off this winter, or be removed as intruders, where they have received a part or full pay for their interest in this country; and we will have from three to four thousand removed by the latter part of the next spring.

A certain proportion of money must, however, be paid on improvements, say from one fourth to a half, in order to enable them to pay their debts before their departure. It is therefore desirable, and even important, that an early appropriation should be had from the next Congress for this purpose.

Should the fate of the reservees be decided in time, and the above measure adopted at an early period, a commissioner of claims may be needed, who should be entrusted with funds to pay *bona fide* claims against emigrants, not exceeding a certain amount on the valuation of improvements. But should the removals of the present season be limited, the Indian agent can discharge this duty very readily.

I would thank you to submit this communication for the inspection of the President and the Secretary of War as early after its arrival as possible.

I have the honor to be,

Most respectfully,

Your obedient servant,

BENJ. F. CURREY.

ELBERT HERRING,
*Commissioner of Indian Affairs, Washington City.*

---

### A.

*Resolved,* By the committee and council, in general council convened, that a delegation be, and is hereby appointed to represent this nation before the next Congress of the United States, which shall consist of two members, whose duty it shall be to memorialize the Executive and Congress of the United States, in behalf of this nation, and by all the means in their power to induce it to protect the Cherokee nation east of the Mississippi from the encroachments of the States upon her soil and jurisdiction, and upon all other subjects of grievances of this nation.

*Be it further resolved,* That the compensation of the said delegation shall be to each two dollars per day, and who shall be required, and it is hereby made their duty to keep a record of their expenses, and report the same to the treasurer of the nation.

*Be it resolved,* That John Ross, the principal chief of this nation, be requested, and he is hereby requested to accompany the said delegation.

*Be it further resolved,* That the sum of fifteen hundred dollars be, and is hereby appropriated out of the funds of the nation not otherwise appropriated, to defray the expenses of the said delegation

RICHARD TAYLOR,
*President Committee.*

RED CLAY, *October* 25, 1833.

WILLIAM ROGERS,
    *Clerk N Committee.*

The council cannot concur with this resolution, inasmuch as the number of delegates is far less than the affairs of the nation imperiously demands, under the present difficult situation of our affairs.

GOING SNAKE, his x mark,
*Speaker Council.*

A. McCoy, *Clerk N. Council.*

The number was filled at five, including the principal chief.

----

### B.

At a meeting of the undersigned citizens of Coosoowatee District, convened at Rabbit Trap, to consider the expediency of changing the representation from this district to the National Committee, the undersigned have unanimously adopted the following considerations and resolutions:

Whereas, it appearing that the honorable John Ridge is at present a member of committee, and from Coosoowatee District, and having been elected a representative of said citizens at the last election holden under our constitution, and viewing said constitution to be yet in force where it is not changed by the competent authority, and claiming a right to change our members whenever their political opinion and acts become exceptionable; and whereas the said representative having ceased to maintain the great principles on which he was elected, viz , patriotism and firmness to our cause, and our views of it remaining unchanged; and having a right as a free people to confer our suffrages on some person else whose views are more in accordance with ours, our interests, and present struggles with the United States: Therefore

*Resolved,* That this meeting request the honorable John Ridge, as a member of the committee from this district, to resign and vacate his seat as our counsellor; and that the relations of constituent and representative may be dissolved for the present.

*Resolved,* That a copy of these proceedings be furnished Mr. Ridge, and one to the president of the committee, for the information of that body, in order to enable the proper department to fill the vacancy, should this incumbent acquiesce in the expressed sense of this meeting.

SUBSCRIBERS.

| | |
|---|---|
| Elijah Hicks, | Oosahnahlee, |
| Katihee, | Chelahketeekee, |
| Kulconookaskee, | Sutteyan, |
| Bear Meat, | Toowayahlo, |
| Thos. Woodard, | Oohahlookeeskee, |

Skontakee,                    Atohee Katigiskee,
Moses McDonald,               Skaquah Wahkichah,
Cold Weather,                 Chunahstrodi,
Soloowoyah,                   George Hicks.
Climahwee,

---

CHEROKEE AGENCY, *November* 4, 1833.

SIR: I have just received the enclosed resolution of the Cherokee council, with a note from John Ross, requesting that it be forwarded to you without delay. He also states that the delegation expects to meet at this agency on the 20th December, on their way to Washington.

I suppose the reason why he requests it to be forwarded without delay is, that your decision upon the subject of the $3,500 may be known before the delegates set out, as they know that I have no annuity money on hand, and that if I had, my instructions from the department would not permit me to pay it to Mr. Taylor.

Very respectfully,
Your obedient servant,
H. MONTGOMERY.

ELBERT HERRING, Esq.,
*Commissioner of Indian Affairs, Washington City.*

---

FORT LEAVENWORTH, *November* 4, 1833.

SIR: I have drawn on the War Department a draft (a copy of which is enclosed) in favor of Dr. W. S. May, for his professional services during our trip to the Pawnees. When he was employed, there was much cholera here among the troops. The commander here employed another physician to aid the surgeon at the post in his duties.

Twenty-five rangers were detailed, and ready to start with me before I hired Dr. May. The rangers were suddenly ordered to Jefferson barracks. I took, therefore, a few soldiers only, but could not dispense with a physician He was much needed, for all were sick more or less during the tour.

The compensation is one hundred dollars a month for medical services, and an allowance of seven dollars is made for medicines furnished by Dr. May.

I hope the draft will be paid, if possible. I am under the necessity of incurring some expense before an appropriation is made by Congress, or stop short in the midst of apparently useful exertions.

I have the honor to be,
With the highest respect,
Yours obediently,
HENRY L. ELLSWORTH.

To the Honorable LEWIS CASS,
*Secretary at War.*

EXECUTIVE OFFICE,

*Tallahassee, Florida, November 5, 1833.*

SIR: I have this day drawn a bill upon the War Department for ten thousand dollars, in favor of General Wiley Thompson, Indian agent, in conformity to the instructions of the department of the 9th of August last.

I am exceedingly gratified in being able to inform the department that I am perfectly satisfied, from an interview I had with Blunt and Davy a few days since, in company with General Thompson, that they intend to emigrate, have completed principally their preparations, and are ready to go off the moment Blunt's son arrives from Kentucky (and he is daily expected) with the whole or nearly the whole of their party. Those of the Indians who have been dissatisfied, I am now of opinion, can be got off without any great difficulty.

To insure success, however, General Thompson and myself hold a final talk with them at their towns on Saturday next.

The draft is drawn at this time, as it is deemed advisable, *perhaps*, on that occasion, to advance for the Indians one or two thousand on account of the treaty, to enable them to purchase provisions necessary to be accumulated before they embark; and with regard to which, otherwise, they would have difficulty. If the *least doubt* should be created of their fidelity, nothing will be paid them, nor under any circumstances, without taking efficient security to prevent any possible loss to the Government on such contingency. It is considered, however, that under present circumstances the exercise of such discretion is absolutely necessary; without it Blunt could not get the provisions, or charter the vessel that will accompany his small boat and canoes. General Thompson has drawn the whole amount of ten thousand dollars from the Central Bank of Florida, which cashed the draft for him, and has placed to his credit as Indian agent on deposite in the bank. Eight thousand dollars thereof will remain there till it is called for to pay Blunt and Davy after they have embarked; and if he pays them nothing, as above stated the balance will be returned and placed on deposite as aforesaid also. The negotiation by the bank, of this draft, paying *specie* for it, &c., has saved the Government considerable expense, and afforded great facility to us. Its credit and safety are unquestionable; and I have no hesitancy in assuming, as an officer and also as an individual, all responsibility on its account. I trust, therefore, that no difficulty will occur in the acceptance and payment of this draft, even if the department should consider the precise terms of the instructions in regard to being satisfied that the Indians had *fully completed* their arrangements, and commenced the removal of their whole party, were not adhered to strictly.

I am, sir,
    Very respectfully,
      Your most obedient servant,
        JAMES D. WESTCOTT, Jr.,
        *Secretary and Acting Governor of Florida.*

Honorable LEWIS CASS,
    *Secretary of War, Washington.*

COLUMBUS, GEORGIA, *November* 5, 1833.

SIR: I have the honor of reporting that I arrived at this place on the 1st instant.

I would have written previously, but that I wished first to ascertain the feelings in this quarter, in relation to the object of my present mission.

I have been to the agency, and have seen several persons from the interior of the Creek country. It gives me pleasure to say that all with whom I have conversed appear to acquiesce with the greatest cheerfulness in the principles laid down for the future operations of the marshal, namely, that his action will be limited to the reserves upon which the Indians will be located. From these, I have assured all who have inquired, in the most unequivocal language, that intruders would be removed, agreeably to the obligations of the treaty. The justice and propriety of this course appear to be generally admitted; and also that the Executive cannot do less, and at the same time respect the provisions of the treaty. On these accounts, as well as from the assurances of those well acquainted with the affairs of the Creeks, no further difficulties need be apprehended; and the most confident expectations may be entertained, that all those who fall under the character of intruders will remove upon a simple application, whenever the boundaries of the reservations are designated. The intruders generally, although of that class of fearless and enterprising men who usually form such settlements, are nevertheless, many of them, well informed and courteous gentlemen, and do not pretend that they can for a moment hold possession of these reservations against the provisions of the treaty, and the action of the Executive. I have no doubt, therefore, that they will generally remove, and the few who may remain will be evidently and too grossly in the wrong to excite either the support or the compassion of their fellow citizens. Nor am I of the opinion that the excitement, about which so much has been said, has been either really as violent or as general as has been represented; or that the Executive, armed with a power sufficient to prove both its determination and ability to fulfil the treaty, would have encountered any forcible resistance. But, after the countenance which these intruders have received from the Executive of their own State, had the United States again appeared upon these lands with a feeble military array, there are settlements in which it would have met a positive resistance with arms.

This evil may be considered as having been generated by the lenity of the United States. Had the first orders for the removal of the intruders been rigidly and vigilantly enforced, the ideas which now prevail with many on this subject would not have had an existence, nor the numbers which now give so much character to the evil have ever been accumulated. But the humane forbearance of the General Government has been by many misconstrued into either an inability or an unwillingness to enforce the provisions of the treaty, and consequenty as holding out an indirect encouragement to settlers. The injunctions of the President on this subject shall be by me carefully promulgated, and will I hope remove those erroneous impressions, which, united with the sentiments which appear now to exist, will, I feel satisfied, relieve us from further difficulties, similar to those which have transpired.

Mr. Bright has not yet arrived. I shall, however, in a few days, visit all the towns of the nation, with the view, in conjunction with the chiefs of each town, of fixing upon the great outlines which are to determine the boundaries of the reservations for each town. Also, at the same time, my efforts will be extended towards acquiring information which may enable us to correct any errors of the census, and which may also enable us to locate the individual sections in a manner to give the most general satisfaction.

Your instructions do not vest us with any discretionary power, in those cases "in which it may be proper, in our opinions, to suspend the removal of persons from any part of the country;" but we are directed to report our views of such cases for the consideration of the President. Now, it is probable that we may not be able timely to apprise you of our views on those cases, or to have all the portions of the country designated, in which the individual locations are to be made, before the time will arrive at which the marshal will have again to operate. Under these suppositions, allow me respectfully to suggest the propriety of so far modifying the orders to the marshal, that he may feel authorized to suspend his operations at our request, or to limit them to such districts as we shall designate.

From the questions which have been put to me by many persons in this quarter, I foresee a source of new difficulties with the reservations, in case the Government should be adverse to the contemplated course. It involves this simple question: will or will not an occupant, by consent or lease from the Indian, be considered an intruder under the treaty?

The land of the Indian being defined by the metes and bounds of the survey, he being placed in the possession, and having the right under the treaty of selling the same or of living upon it, these rights, it seems to me, carry with them also those of renting and leasing. In fact, these latter rights have already been exercised by the Indians, and there are many white men now residing under them in the Creek nation, and who do not appear to have been considered by the marshal as intruders.

The system will insure to those who have speculated many of their purchases, as they can take leases for the five years; and then, as the Indian will receive his patent, he can convey a good title to a purchaser. But it is doubtful in my mind if the Government can look into such a consequence, and still more doubtful that any good would result from it, if it were so to look.

I have thought it proper, however, to bring the subject to your notice, for, if the Government is disposed to oppose such a system, the sooner its determination is known the better.

Many of the Indians, whose names are on the census roll, have died since it was taken. I presume, in such cases, the location will have to be made in the name of the heirs.

I doubt much if General Parsons succeeds in realizing the expectations raised by his letter to the President, in reference to obtaining a delegation of the Creek chiefs empowered to treat for these reservations. Since my arrival in this quarter, I have understood, from very good authority, that the principal chiefs of the nation have come under very heavy bonds not to treat without a full guarantee of the rights of the speculators; and also they have come under bonds to compel the common Indian, by the exercise of all their influence over him, to fulfil his bargain for the sale of his reservation. These bonds may be considered illegal, and such as a court of justice would declare void. But the evil of them is nevertheless insurmountable, from the impressions they create, and their consequences. These, in my mind, put any hope of a treaty out of the question.

Believe me to be, sir,

Very respectfully,

Your obedient servant,

JOHN JAMES ABERT,

*Lieut. Col.*

Hon. Lewis Cass,

*Secretary of War.*

---

SUPERINTENDENCY OF INDIAN AFFAIRS,

*St. Louis, November 6, 1833.*

SIR: I have the honor to enclose to you herewith a report from General Street, under date of 1st October, of an examination of the country ceded to the Winnebagoes west of the Mississippi, and its delivery by him to a portion of said tribe who have emigrated. Also two other reports of 24th October; the one of a selection of a site for the school buildings, the other of an offer made by Colonel Taylor, commanding at Prairie du Chien, to transfer to him the saw mill on the west of the Mississippi for public use. The lists referred to by General Street as marked A and B were not forwarded by him.

The site selected I would consider greatly preferable to one on the east of the Mississippi. The offer of the mill I view as a fortunate circumstance, as it will greatly facilitate the erection of the necessary buildings.

I have the honor to be,

Very respectfully,

Your obedient servant,

WILLIAM CLARK.

Hon. ELBERT HERRING,

*Commissioner of Indian Affairs, Washington City.*

---

UNITED STATES INDIAN AGENCY AT PRAIRIE DU CHIEN,

*October 1, 1833.*

SIR: The surveyor, Captain Craig, being about to run the southeastern and southern lines of the tract of country ceded to the Winnebagoes west of the Mississippi, I availed myself of the opportunity to go along and explore the country. I passed out through the country, and joined the surveyors near the Red Cedar river. Went to the extreme western boundary of the cession at Red Cedar, and examined the country on that river, the Wa-pee-sa-pee-nee-can, and Turkey river, and its two principal branches, and Yellow and Gerrard rivers. Taking a ride through the country south of Gerrard's river, between the Mississippi and Turkey rivers, I was out seventeen days, during which time I saw a part of the purchase from the Sioux, and passed through the purchase from the Sacs and Foxes in numerous directions. The distance on a direct line from Prairie du Chien to where the line crosses Red Cedar is about seventy miles. This is a beautiful stream, about eighty-five or ninety yards wide, clear, bold, and of sufficient depth for Mackinaw boats. The adjoining lands rolling and rich prairie, and large bodies of timber on the river and the streams putting into it. The Wa-pee-sa-pee-nee-can is about fifteen or twenty yards wide, of tolerable depth, muddy shores, and milky colored water—land and timber inferior to that on Red Cedar. Turkey river is from forty to forty-five yards wide, and very much resembles Red Cedar, except in size and the character of its shores, those on Turkey river being three times the height of those on Red Cedar, and very much resemble the bluffs of the Mississippi.

On Turkey river, and the whole distance to within a mile of the Mississippi, is a fine agricultural country, and the prairies not very large. There are considerable bodies of valuable timber on Turkey, Yellow, and Gerrard rivers, and the shores of the Mississippi.

I had never rode through a country so full of game. The hunter who accompanied me, though living most of his time in the woods, expressed his astonishment at the abundance of all kinds of game except buffalo; and the surveyors saw and killed many about thirty or forty miles west of Red Cedar, on the same purchase. Elk and deer are abundant in the prairies, and bear in the woodlands. The sign of fur animals, particularly rats and otters, is considerable on all the streams and ponds, and very abundant on Wa-pee-sa-pee-nee-can and Turkey river; and on the former I saw, for the first time, a beaver dam in progress, on which there had been two new logs put during the night previous to our visit, and every appearance that the ingenious animals had been at work until disturbed by our approach.

It is a beautiful and fertile country, and, with a little attention to agriculture, is capable of sustaining the whole Winnebago nation; and if the proper measures are pursued, and inducements held out to the Indians, in a few years many hundreds will be settled in that country, producing 1,000 bushels of grain and potatoes, and the *cry of distress* no longer assail the ears of the Government.

The country abounds with fine mill streams, and situations for mills with abundance of rock are frequent. If a mill was built, and the Indians learnt to raise wheat, they would in a few years grow a sufficiency in this country for the sustenance of the whole nation, and live in great plenty.

After exploring, I delivered the country to the Indians agreeably to your directions in your letter of the 24th of May last; and the following Winnebago Indians (see list A) immediately established themselves at an old Sac village on Turkey river, near the southern line of the cession, and about twenty-five or thirty miles from Prairie du Chien. These with their women and children number sixty-eight souls. A party of about two hundred and eighty, or three hundred, remain to secure the crop, and then follow to the same village. Add to these the Indians contained in list B, who are along the west shore of the Mississippi on the purchase from the Sacs, who with their families passed from the Wisconsin to this country some time since, and you have all that I know of on the lower section of the cession. On the upper half, purchased of the Sioux, a trader (of the American Fur Company, Mr. Bailey,) says the Sioux told him there were eighty lodges of the Winnebagoes, and complained that they hunted over the line. I saw Wabashaw, the Sioux chief, but he did not complain to me, but a few days before. I have not been able to visit the upper part of the tract this season, but mean to do so as early as possible in the ensuing.

From these statements you will perceive that many Winnebagoes have gone over to the west of the Mississippi, and I have strong reasons to believe, from the assurances of the Indians, that numbers will go over this winter to *hunt* and *remain*, and make their villages, and cultivate the soil, if any encouragement is extended to them, and corn and potatoes given them to plant in the spring.

All of which is most respectfully submitted.

I am, sir,

Your most obedient servant,

JOS. M. STREET,

*U. S. Indian Agent.*

Gen. WILLIAM CLARK,
*Superintendent of Indian Affairs, St. Louis.*

---

SAINT LOUIS, *October* 24, 1833.

SIR: I regret that circumstances not within my control have prevented an earlier answer to your letter of the 28th August, covering copies from the department in relation to the location of the Winnebago school. Anxious to ascertain whether a proper site for the school could not be found on the west of the Mississippi, upon the lands ceded by the United States to the Winnebagoes, and desirous personally to examine the whole cession, that I might speak of the resources from personal supervision, I crossed the Mississippi on the fifth, and did not get back to the agency until the 22d September. During this absence your letter arrived. Intending immediately after the 30th September to descend to St. Louis to pay over the $3,500 as directed in your letter of the 7th September, I have delayed my answer until the present moment.

In my tour of observation west of the Mississippi, I accompanied the surveyor who was running the southeastern and southern lines of the cession. The southeastern line commencing about nine miles above Fort Crawford, on the Mississippi, passes within five or six miles of Prairie du Chien, back of the Bluffs, on the west bank of the Mississippi.

In examining the country nearly opposite Fort Crawford, west of *this line,* and between Yellow river and Gerrard river, I find a most desirable country, and free from the objections contained in the letters from the Department. I therefore beg leave, in compliance with your letter of the 28th August last, to name to you as an eligible site for the Winnebago school, a place situated about nine or ten miles from Fort Crawford, on the west of the Mississippi, and within the limits of the country ceded to the Winnebagoes, on the dividing ridge between Yellow river and Gerrard's river, and about four miles from the United States saw mill on the former river. At this point there is a small rich prairie, and a spring rising in the adjoining timber near the summit of the ridge. The surrounding country generally woodland, with spots of rich prairie, and abounding in fine streams of water. The particular site selected for the school is near the summit of the dividing ridge, where a fine spring of water bursts out in the edge of the timber. To the west of this situation the ridge expands into a large open fertile prairie, forming the dividing ridge between Turkey river and the Mississippi, beautifully spotted with small islands of timber.

From a thorough examination, I am convinced that no situation free from the important objections of the department can be obtained east of the Mississippi, ror does the country present so many advantages.

All of which is most respectfully submitted.

I have the honor to be,

Sir, your most obedient servant,

JOS. M. STREET,

*United States Indian Agent.*

General WILLIAM CLARK,

*Superintendent Indian Affairs at St. Louis.*

---

FORT LEAVENWORTH, *November* 6, 1833.

SIR: I have the honor to inform the department that the hostile tribes are fast assembling here to make peace. The Pawnees, some with proper feelings, although one of their villages containing 2,500 inhabitants, has been burnt last summer by the Delawares, who at the same time destroyed the corn and other vegetables; in addition to this, two Pawnees have been killed by the Delawares the last three months. The Delawares claim to be the grand fathers of all the tribes around here; a brave of the Delawares has been slain by the Pawnees, and it has hitherto been impossible to assuage the grief of the friends of the deceased. The Delawares demanded of me, in private council, $1,000 for each scalp taken from their nation before a treaty could be made.

I have tried to show them the impropriety of the demand; the great sufferings of one village of the Pawnees; the cession of the Pawnees of the land in dispute; and, also, the provision for a large common hunting ground south of the Platte river. I now believe that by to-morrow noon the Pawnees and Delawares will shake hands.

The Kickapoos rejoice to hear of the Otoe treaty, which secures to them their land. The Otoes, as I remarked in a former communication, seemed to have a good claim to part of the lands embraced in the Kickapoo grant.

I shall make a special report on the Kickapoo difficulty—a dissatisfaction with the land; a difficulty, however, nearly adjusted.

I hope by next mail I shall be able to inform you peace is made. Several more parties await the issue of the council; and be assured no efforts of mine, either day or night, will be spared to stay the scalping knife and the arrows.

In haste, I am yours sincerely,

H. L. ELLSWORTH.

Hon. E. HERRING,

*Indian Commissioner.*

---

FORT LEAVENWORTH, *November* 6, 1833.

SIR: This is to inform you of my having drawn two more small drafts o the War Department, viz., *one of two hundred and fifty dollars* to Zadoc$^{n}$

k

Martin, dated 4th November, 1833. This is for two yoke of cattle which I bought for the Pawnee tribe; thirty-two days' labor, with a team, a man, two cows, and the hire of a servant, all amounting to the sum.

One for $440, dated November 6, 1833, in favor of Alexander G. Morgan, being in part payment of his account against the commissioners for goods furnished. Mr. Morgan is the sutler at this post, and the person of whom we have bought our goods. I hope the draft will be paid.

Yours, most respectfully,<br>
HENRY L. ELLSWORTH,<br>
U. S. Commissioner.

Hon. E. HERRING,
    Indian Commissioner.

TUSCALOOSA, November 6, 1833.

SIR: I received, a few days ago, your last communication, enclosing me a copy of your letter to Col. Abert. I am glad to say that the course there indicated in reference to the leases and the approval of the contracts to be made with the Indians, as also to the measures to be adopted towards the settlers, are very generally approved here.

I have made them known to all the leading members of the Legislature with whom I have had an opportunity of conversing, and they have expressed a very decided satisfaction. I not only explained the contents of the letter to the Governor, but gave it to him to read. He seems not only willing that the instructions there stated should be pursued, but that every thing should be done here that may be thought necessary, both by himself and by the Legislature, to give effect to them, and to prevent any obstruction from the operation of the State laws, or through the State officers in the Creek countries.

I was introduced to day to a gentleman in the Legislature, who resides on the Indian lands in Talladega, and stated particularly to him the measures intended to be pursued towards the settlers. He says the people in Talladega will gladly acquiesce in such a course, and readily remove from the Indian reservations, where they do not purchase them with the full sanction of the certifying agent. The determination about the leases, he says, will be universally approved.

The same explanation was received a few days ago by four or five of the settlers in that country with evident gratification. They said that if any of the settlers in the Creek nation objected to such a course, the people of Talladega would help to drive them out of the nation. Every thing that I have seen and heard convinces me of a great difference between the characters of the settlers in Russel and those in Talladega, and probably in the other counties.

I believe the speculators will make a great effort to produce an excitement about the leases. Their object was to sustain them by force of the State laws. The company in Columbus, I understand, have bought up between three and four thousand Indian reserves, advancing in each case about ten dollars. If they have to purchase and pay, it will take a large sum of money. By leasing they would have had five years to pay it, and that by keeping accounts against the Indians for whiskey, &c., till they chose to think they had given them enough for their titles.

It will be necessary for the Legislature here to take measures to prevent these contracts from being enforced by the State laws, and to save the Indians from being exposed to vexatious and harassing proceedings from the State courts and justices. Their dread of being sued and taken to jail will make them submit to every oppression. The Governor and many of the members of the Legislature express a desire to do whatever may be necessary for their protection.

I have thought it best to wait here for the district attorney. I have had several letters from him, and expect him here in the course of next week. I saw Mr. King, the Senator from this State, at Montgomery, and have received letters from him to several of his friends in the Legislature, who are active in promoting your views in relation to this business. I have also been much assisted by Col. John Crowell, who is still here; and, from his very general acquaintance with the influential members of the State Government, has been enabled to render essential service in promoting the objects I have had in view.

The Governor tells me he is about to communicate to the Legislature on this subject, and that he shall express his satisfaction with the course intended to be pursued on the part of the United States, and that he has no apprehension that any further difficulties will arise.

I shall confer with the district attorney, on his arrival here, as to the measures proper to be taken for the further protection of the Indians, and for the relief of the parties charged in the indictments. He will remain here during the session of the Legislature.

I am, sir, &c.,<br>F. S. KEY.

To the SECRETARY OF WAR.

P. S. A further return of the census has been recently received from Barbour county. Its white population amounts to 3,571, making in all the counties (except Coosa and Macon, the returns from which are not yet received) 11,525. In these two counties, which are small, the number, I am told, will not exceed 1,500.

I will add, that it seems generally considered here (and such is my own opinion) that the only certain way of effectually protecting the Indians is by the Government buying (say at the minimum price at which they sell the public lands, or at a higher price where the quality of the reservation justifies it) all the reserves that may not be sold by them to individuals, paying them a part of the price here, and the balance after their removal; and taking, at the same time, measures for immediately removing them. The Indians, I have no doubt, will be generally ready when the locations are made both to sell and remove.

———

CHEROKEE AGENCY, Nov. 7, 1833.

SIR: Sometime in the early part of last spring the Young Wolf intruded upon me, and took in possession some part of my land that I was improving;

made use of many of my rails, &c. I instituted suit against him in the circuit court of this district; the suit was taken up to the Supreme Court and there decided, as you will see from the order of said court to remove said Wolf; but some short time previous to the final decision of said suit, Wolf enrolled and gave in his place to be valued. I now call upon you to stop the agents from valuing and taking into possession my place. You will therefore please instruct our agent, Colonel Montgomery, to that effect.

I can furnish you with any evidence you may wish, should you not be fully satisfied after seeing a copy of the order.

Very respectfully,<br>Yours, &c.,<br>ELIZABETH WALKER.

Mr. Elbert Herring.

---

Amohee District, *Cherokee Nation:*

*To the Marshal of said nation, or any legal officer.*

You are hereby commanded to measure one fourth of a mile, from a new improvement made by Mrs. E. Walker, and so much of the farm and improvement of Young Wolf you will put in possession of said E. Walker, which was decided in the Supreme Court on the 28th day of October in favor of E. Walker, as will appear of record: herein fail not. Given under my hand and seal at Red Clay, this 2d day of November, 1833.

CHARLES H. VANN,<br>*Clerk Supreme Court, Per Dan. McCoy.*

A true copy of the original, as is placed in the officer's hands.

---

Ireokee, Creek Nation, *Nov.* 7, 1833.

Friend and Brother: Sir, We are again under the necessity of addressing you on the various troubles with which we find ourselves infested, since the extension of jurisdiction of the State of Alabama over our territory. We hope you will in an affectionate manner represent to our father, the President, the following case. In one of the new counties in this territory there was five of our red men indicted for an alleged murder of another red man; the parties had the good fortune to be released, but the lawyers that defended them has, as we think, made large and exorbitant charges, for which we refer you to the honorable Samuel W. Mardis, a member of Congress from the State of Alabama. By this reference we avoid many statements, believing that he will be able to give you a more full, competent, and satisfactory account of the whole case, the whole matter having transpired in his vicinity, better than it would be possible for us to write. At the time we made the treaty in March, 1832, it is our understanding that the President told us that if any thing of the nature of which we now complain should happen to us, that if we would make it known to him he would relieve us, for and during the term of five years, at which time we might expect to be left to the entire control of the authority of the State of Alabama. On this subject we feel much solicitude; hope and request that our great father, the President, will now stretch out his arm and afford us the aid we require; the persons that were arraigned at the bar are poor, and have nothing to pay with; it is requested that the Government will have it settled for them; and let us hear from you.

We remain your affectionate red brothers, &c.,

|                          |              |
|--------------------------|--------------|
| TUS-KE-NEHAW,            | his x mark.  |
| LITTLE DOCTOR,           | his x mark.  |
| HOPACTH-LE-YOHOLO,       | his x mark.  |
| MAD BLUE,                | his x mark.  |
| YOHOLO MICCO,            | his x mark.  |
| WILLIAM McGILVRAY,       | his x mark.  |
| MARION WAY,              | his x mark.  |
| TUS-HOCHEE FIXICO,       |              |
| TUCKEBACHEE MICCO,       |              |
| TALLYSEE FIXECO,         |              |
| TUS-COME-HAJO,           |              |
| SPOKE OAK HARGO,         |              |
| MOCK-LUTIS-A-HARGO,      |              |
| MOTOWA-HARJO,            |              |
| YOHOLO MICCO, of KYELIJA.|              |
| PAS-BO-RE-MALLAW.        |              |

The Hon. LEWIS CASS,
    *Secretary of War.*

----

[EXTRACT.]

CHOCCHUMA LAND OFFICE, *Nov.* 8, 1833.

DEAR SIR: The agent for locating Indian claims is now at Columbus, attending to his duties before the land sales come on at that place. He has completed all those in this district, but will not, as he informed me, make a report for some time, as he believed that he had made reservations that were not contemplated by the treaty, and that he might have further time to examine and do justice to the claimants as well as the United States he reserved the land from sale, but will at a future period examine the claims more minutely, and make a final decision. This course was deemed best, as it gave every opportunity to the Indian to make up his case.

I would suggest to you the propriety of not acting on any claim until you have first heard from Colonel Martin, the locating agent, and I would also suggest the propriety of ordering Colonel Martin to Washington during the next session, as there is no doubt but what an attempt will be made to have allowances made to Indians for pretended claims.

I am, very respectfully,
    Your obedient servant,
        SAMUEL GWIN.

Hon. LEWIS CASS,
    *Secretary of War.*

FORT LEAVENWORTH, *November* 8, 1833.

SIR: Peace will be concluded at this council between the hostile Indians upon terms highly satisfactory; the wampum has been exchanged, but the speeches not finished; it is a happy day for the Indians here

By a mountain trapper, on his way down the Missouri, I have learnt the use of the still noticed in a former communication as having been sent up the river by the American Fur Company.

That company have a fort at the mouth of Yellow Stone river. There a distillery of whiskey is established, and in the most successful operation. Mr. Sublitz, of St. Louis, just from there, says he tasted the whiskey made there and found it of an excellent quality. Report says the M ndan village supplied them this year with 2,000 bushels of corn. I think this exaggerated. The company, however, have transported corn in steamboats, and engaged a considerable quantity more to be taken next spring. Mr. Sublitz says the justification offered for a supposed breach of the law is, that the law does not forbid *making* whiskey, it only precludes its introduction. I make no comment.

It will be gratifying to the department to learn that the Kickapoo dissatisfaction with their land is removed. I have held two councils with the chiefs and warriors, and examined *personally* the whole tract.

The location is a most favorable one, the land is good, and water communication most easy. *The chiefs have accepted the land*, and are now anxious to have the things promised in the treaty. It will be expedient to run the lines as soon as practicable.

While the chiefs of the Kickapoos were together, I talked with them about their agent, for I understood they had applied for a separate agent. The fact is, they do not need a separate agent any more than the Delawares and Shawnees. The tribe is a small one, and after the rations are issued I do not know what an agent could do.

The head chief told me he was *tricked* in signing a paper for a new agent; he liked the old one, but some men got him to sign a paper before they told him what was written on it. They are anxious to have a mill erected soon, and Mr. Cummings, their agent, has some experience in this business, having just finished a mill for the Delawares, and also one for himself.

The petitions of Indians unexplained are entitled to little consideration.

Excuse the freedom of my communication, and believe me.

Yours, respectfully and obediently,
HENRY L. ELLSWORTH.

Hon. E. HERRING,
*Indian Commissioner, Washington.*

---

COLUMBUS, *November* 8, 1833.

SIR: I arrived here this morning at 8 o'clock, having left Chocchuma on Tuesday night, 5th instant, having closed the business in that district at present; having, as I believe, located all claims justly entitled under the treaty (when found on the registers furnished me as my guide, &c.) ex c e perhaps some floating claims which possibly may be held up by owner. I am happy to have it in my power to say that I believe I shall have the same success here, from the great number of claims already located in this district.

I left Chocchuma on Tuesday, in the second week of the sale of the public lands. As I am extremely pressed with business at this moment; I shall write to the department again in a short time more fully, and after progressing further with matters here. I am happy to say to you I am in possession of the registers sent me from Washington. I received them on the 18th October, by an express from this place. Your esteemed favor of the 27th September came to hand on the 18th October, with regard to all of which I will write you more fully in a few days.

I have the honor to be, very respectfully,
GEO. W. MARTIN.

Hon. Lewis Cass.

P. S. The registers I received from Washington are deficient as regards the citizens or five years' claims, as I find no such claims alluded to in any part of the said registers; these claims are under the 14th article of the treaty. If there is any such register I should like to know it; there are many complaints of the defects of the one furnished by Colonel Ward.

Respectfully,

G. W. M.

———

Choctaw Agency, *November* 8, 1833.

Sir: I will now proceed to show what will be the situation of some of the Choctaw families on this river in a short time, unless assisted.

The twelve months' rations will terminate in December and January, and in February almost all the last year's emigrants will be thrown on their own means for subsistance.

Corn in this quarter can scarcely be had at any price, even with those having the means to purchase, and but few if any of the Indians are able to buy. Many of them must therefore suffer, unless I am correct in the following opinion, or the Government extend the hand of charity to them.

I am clearly of the opinion, that upon a fair construction in the spirit of the treaty, they have a just claim upon the Government for corn until it is raised by them, unless, by their own negligence, they fail to make corn during the first season. The object of feeding them twelve months, as expressed, was to allow time to grow corn. The last *June freshet destroyed* their crops, and there has been no neglect on their part; the hand of Providence has left them in this situation, and as I humbly conceive, fairly upon our Government, until they can, by human industry, raise a crop. I therefore think that their farms should be examined, and all those who have lost their crops should be allowed to draw the corn part of their ration until their corn is fit for use next fall. There can be no frauds; the high water mark will be plain here for years to come, and it is known where each family lived at the time of the freshet. Unless something is done these people will suffer. If I am sustained in the opinion given, and it is within the control of the department, there is still time for relief; but if the action of Congress is necessary, I fear even with a disposition to relieve them, that before the necessary legislation can take place, they will suffer.

The situation of these people requires that something should be speedily done for them.

I have not let this application be known to any one, because they are a people who will build their hopes upon small grounds, and when disappointed, make no allowance, but charge it all to the treaty, as they are constantly taught to do by designing men.

I have the honor to be
Your obedient servant,
F. W. ARMSTRONG, C. A.

Elbert Herring, Esq.,
*Commissioner Indian Affairs.*

---

*November* 9, 1833.

Sir: I am daily the more impressed with the conviction that so soon as we shall have made the location of these reserves, a great mass of them will be occupied by lessees.

The moment a section or half section is located, and the Indian put in the possession of the same, it to my judgment ceases to be national domain, and becomes individual property, the owner acquiring all the rights under the law which appertain to individual property. These rights must be those common to all private property, unless the law under which this particular property is held contains exceptions. On looking into that law, we find the Indian restrained in some of these usual rights. These restraints are, 1st. That if he sells, the manner of conveyance must be such as the President may direct. 2dly. That the contract of sale shall not be valid till approved by the President. And, 3dly. If he does not sell, he cannot demand a deed or patent till after five years shall have expired. Beyond these exceptions, it appears to me that the Indian possesses all the rights of ownership to the particular tract which shall be assigned to him.

Now, then, if my views are correct, the Indian may rent or lease his particular tract, and the individual to whom he so rents or leases may occupy the same, and cannot under such an occupation be considered an intruder and liable to the forcible ejectment provided for by the treaty and laws. As another consequence, you will readily perceive how easily under the form of leases possession of these reservations may be held by the whites until the five years have expired, when the fee simple title must issue to the Indian, and he then have it in his power to convey that title to whom he pleases, for what he pleases, and without the approbation of any one. Any embarrassment, therefore, to the title by the disapprobation of the President to contracts of sales, can last no longer than five years; and in the meantime, the purchaser can hold possession in the form of a lease.

It becomes, then, a question for consideration, whether efforts in behalf of the Indian, in relation to leases, can under the treaty produce any other results than a temporary embarrassment of the title, and a consequent injury to the State, which such an embarrassment will throw in the way of the settlement of these lands.

The great hope of safety to the Indian will, in my opinion, be found to depend mainly upon the competition of purchasers. This will, I think, generally insure a fair rate of sale. The approbation of the contract afterwards will rather, I think, prove to be matter of form, as, if withheld, the effect may be so easily evaded.

I have generally said, not as from authority, however, that the contracts already made for sales could not be considered or acted upon by the certifying agent, as they were prior to that condition of things which gave the Indian a power to sell. But it appears that he possesses this power after the locations are made, as these must be considered the result of his selections. The competition of purchasers may take place, then, immediately after the individual locations, and will, I am disposed to think, generally, insure a fair equivalent.

The Indians are usually good judges of land, and their settlements will be found to embrace many valuable tracts.

There is an ordinance at the end of the constitution of Alabama, passed by the convention, which declares, among other things, that "they for ever disclaim all right and title to the waste or unappropriated land lying within this State, and that the same shall be and remain at the sole and entire disposition of the United States."

This declaration, together with the power vested by the constitution in the United States over Indian affairs, and the law of 1807, are, I think, conclusive against the State of Alabama in relation to this Indian question. The constitution of Alabama does not date before 1819, and of course this ordinance. It must, therefore, be taken for granted, that the State had a knowledge of the "constitution and laws of the United States" when it was admitted, and that the ordinance was made under that knowledge. You do not notice the ordinance in your correspondence with the Governor. It probably escaped your observation.

Your replies to the Governor have had a powerful effect upon the community in this quarter, in convincing those who would be convinced both of the moderation and right of the United States; but it appears to me that our labors will materially change this question, and will oblige you hereafter to draw largely upon this ordinance in justification of any forcible expulsion of intruders from the reservations.

I think it may be urged with some plausibility that the constitution of the United States, the laws in relation to Indian affairs, and the ordinance above alluded to, had in contemplation only that condition of things in which the Indian lands were still held in common; or were, in other words, a national domain. From such, the right of the United States to expel intruders by an armed force has undoubtedly the sanction of law and precedent; but where these lands cease to be a national domain, become a dismembered and individual property within the jurisdiction of a State, it appears to me that in this condition they constitute cases not in the contemplation of the constitution or the laws of the United States, or at least cases which may occasion some doubts of the right of ejectment by a military force. The character of the possessions becomes essentially altered by the acts of locating the same, and of assigning them as private property to individuals, and I think the jurisdiction alters with the character, from direct national protection to the more indirect redress of individual suits in courts of law.

Now it appears to me, that the moment we make the locations of the lands, and assign to each individual his particular lot, that moment they become under the treaty individual or private property, lose their national and acquire individual rights, and are removed from the protecting power of the United States in relation to intruders, as contemplated by its laws. So that if my reasoning be correct, the parts of the country which will be exempt from the action of the marshal, are the parts over which this action could be exercised with the greatest legal propriety, as they yet constitute a national domain; and the parts which will not be exempt from his action, the reserves, are those over which it can be exercised with the least, as they will constitute individual or private property.

I am fully aware that the treaty contemplated and promised the expulsion of intruders from the individual reservations, as from public lands. The doubts with me are, if this change in the character of the property were considered at the time of making the treaty, and if under this change, the process devised by the United States laws for the removal of intruders from a national domain can be applied.

I do not presume to argue a topic of this kind with one as well versed in national law as yourself, but merely to expose the reflections which a calm view of events in this quarter give rise to.

There is no doubt but you will be called upon, in the course of time, to remove intruders from these reservations; it may therefore not be an idle moment which may be devoted to some of the difficulties of the case.

I say to every one that from these reservations intruders will be removed, and the general plans among the whites of avoiding such a consequence is by purchase or lease from the Indian.

If by a purchase which is approved, the question is at once settled, and the land passes to the whites. If by a lease, the course may not be approved. It may be considered an evasion of the treaty, and the lessee be looked upon as an intruder. But nevertheless, a lease is a title so well known to our laws that I doubt if a forcible ejectment of a lessee can be accomplished without violent excitement.

Those who endeavor to hold by neither purchase or lease will be but few, and generally of a class which will meet with little sympathy at any course pursued in ousting them. The lessees will be your most troublesome cases, as they will constitute a class both respectable and numerous. Should they be considered intruders under the treaty, and their forcible expulsion be contemplated, I must repeat a former remark, that when attempted it should be by a force that will prove your ability as well as earnestness, or you will meet with resistance and probably with defeat.

The spirit of emigration is said to be rapidly extending itself, and all those who have sold are ready to move west as soon as the sales are approved, and the balances due to them paid. The difficulties to which they have been exposed by intruders, and by the laws of Alabama, have had no small share in promoting this spirit. They linger, however, about their homes with great fondness, and arrest any disposition to move on the slightest evidence of adequate protection where they are. A deputation had been nominated to visit the Arkansas, and select a place for those disposed to emigrate. It was not sent, however, as the marshal appeared to move off intruders at the time it was ready to depart, which was considered and acted upon as evidence that they might remain unmolested where they were. So it is, that the very execution of this treaty foils the policy of the Executive. On this account, therefore, it becomes advisable that the class under the definition of intruders, who can be forced off of the reservations, should be as limited as possible. Coercion to emigrate is prohibited by the treaty, but this can mean only a coercion by physical force. An indirect coercion, by increasing their embarrassments where they are, will tend much to promote a desire to emigrate, and probably, in the end, to effect this object, so desirable to the United States, and so advantageous to the Indian; in fact, so intimately connected with his preservation, it may be found necessary to declare that after a certain period the annuities will be paid entirely, and to those only who are west of the Mississippi.

This last measure would completely relieve the Government from the many obstacles thrown in the way of emigration by those traders who find it to their interest to keep the Indians here.

I have not yet entered upon the actual execution of the duty of defining the circumscribing bounds of these reservations, because 1st, it has taken till now to gather from the census book all the necessary facts, and to obtain other requisite information; 2d, I wished the principles upon which I mean to operate, as laid down in your instructions in relation to the future action of the marshal, to go before me, as they had been generally so well received; and 3dly, I am waiting for the arrival of Mr. Bright.

The delay, however, is working to our advantage, and will much facilitate the execution of the duty.

With great respect, &c.,<br>
JOHN J. ABERT,<br>
Lieut. Col. Top. Eng.

Hon. Lewis Class,
    Secretary of War.

---

Fort Mitchell, Nov. 11, 1833.

Sir: I arrived here this morning, having been delayed last night by the breaking down of the stage.

I find that nothing further has been done by the civil authorities of the State for the purpose of arresting the persons indicted for the murder of Owen, or of enforcing the process of attachment issued against Major McIntosh. I presume, from what I hear, and from what I see stated in a late Alabama paper, (which I shall try to get permission to enclose to you,) that they mean to wait until they hear the result of the application to the President.

I found your letter here, but Major McIntosh has not yet received his. I showed him the copy you gave me.

I have had the papers shown me by Major McIntosh, in explanation of the occurrence between him and the civil authority, copied, and enclose them herewith. No process has ever been issued, or if issued, attempted to be served on the soldiers charged with the murder. The sheriff came with subpœnas for several of the soldiers, (I presume to go before the grand jury,) and was allowed by Major McIntosh to go into the garrison to serve them. He went in, but could not find the men. The solicitor's letter the major was certainly not bound to comply with. The attachment, a copy of which I enclose, he refused to obey. I do not consider him very wrong there, as I think the process should state (according to the bill of rights and constitution of Alabama) in what the contempt of court consisted. There is besides a gross mistake in the name; and certainly his refusal to deliver up a detachment of men, or to name the persons guilty, and the witnesses to prove the offence, were most unfounded pretences for charging him with a contempt of court. He is confident that if these men had been delivered up they would have been convicted and executed, or perhaps sacrificed to the fury of the intruders without a trial. The excitement among this body of men has been great, and still continues. There is, however, no truth in the rumors we have heard of their being assembled in arms, or of the sheriff's having collected or called for a posse, and I am satisfied that nothing will be done until we can have time to make our arrangements. The sheriff was a well disposed union man, but he has been forced to resign. A coroner has been appointed to discharge the duties of sheriff till a new one is elected, and he fortunately happens to be a man that　*　*　* and Major McIntosh thinks very favorably of.

I have sent for and obtained a copy of the laws of Alabama, and find that a justice of the peace, as also a coroner and sheriff, may take bail in such cases. It may be desirable to adopt this course, and give bail for their appearance at the next term, and then take measures for the removal of the cases.

I shall send off early in the morning to the clerk of Russel county for copies of the indictments, and of all the proceedings of the court, both against Major McIntosh and the men. I have also sent this evening to Columbus, to Colonel Abert, and expect to see him early in the morning. It seems to be generally thought, even by some of the nullifiers, that if the reservations can be located, and the removal of settlers enforced for the present only against those who may be found within those locations, that there will be no further difficulty. * * * thinks that with vigorous efforts this may be accomplished before the 15th. I shall be better able to judge of this when I see Colonel Abert.

My object now is to collect all the information I can here, and go on to Mobile with the certified copies of papers I may get from the clerk, and confer with the district attorney.

　　*　　　　　*　　　　　*　　　　　*　　　　　*

The condition of the Indians is most deplorable. They are already almost starving; very few of them have made any corn; almost all of them have sold their land two or three times over, for any trifle that has been offered them. I met crowds of them going to Columbus, with bundles of fodder on their heads to sell, and saw numbers of them in the streets there, where they exchange every thing they carry for whiskey.

　　*　　　　　*　　　　　*　　　　　*　　　　　*

* * * believes, however, that they cannot be got to agree to authorize the chiefs to go to Washington and sell out for them, because they doubt whether they will be fairly dealt with by the chiefs. Perhaps, if they could be assured that this should be done by commissioners to be appointed by the President, it might obviate the objection. He thinks that if Congress would authorize the opening of an office, and buying their lands here, upon fair and liberal terms, they would all sell and remove. I have

84‡

sent for one of the chiefs mentioned by the President; the others I find are a great way off. If I see it likely that I shall stay here long enough, I will send an Indian for them; if not I will endeavor to see them as I return. I may perhaps also be able to communicate with them through Colonel Abert, who will be in their neighborhood. General Parsons' letter I shall be able to deliver in Mobile, as I understand he is there.

Your obedient servant,<br>F. S. KEY.

Hon. Lewis Cass.

P. S. Lieutenant Manning and three of the soldiers are indicted.

---

Columbus, November 11, 1833.

Sir: I returned last night from a short excursion into the nation, and have to repeat an opinion expressed in my first letter from this place, that I do not believe any farther difficulties are to be apprehended in this quarter, and that the principles laid down in your instructions as a guide for the operations of the marshal hereafter, appear to be received with general satisfaction.

Mr. Key passed through this place on his way south last night. I did not see him. Report couples his journey with the late disturbances in Alabama, and thereby gives an appearance of success to the game which has been played by this presumptive evidence of alarm at Washington. After the momentary excitement got up on the death of Owen had died away, characters and events were generally too well appreciated here to leave either lasting or favorable impressions; and the power and right of the General Government is too well known to leave any just apprehensions that forcible resistance would be offered to its action, should circumstances make it necessary for it again to appear in the field, provided its attitude was such as to awe the desperate.

The presentment of the grand jury, and the refusal of the commanding officer at Fort Mitchell to yield up the men applied for by the sheriff, or rather, perhaps, I should say his not aiding to seek them out and deliver them up, are circumstances which tell badly in a well organized community, but in this quarter they are not, I think, viewed so heinously. Less than the first could not I think have been expected from an intruder jury, one of whom was on the marshal's list for expulsion; and in relation to the second, it is a very general impression that it would have been merely a yielding up of the men to lawless violence. It would have been too precious an opportunity to have been lost of teaching the troops of the United States the effect of obeying the orders of their own Government in such cases.

The venue could have been changed, but of this the officer was probably not aware; and he viewed the surrender of his men as a sacrifice of those who had merely done their duty by obeying the orders of the Government, or exercised the right of self-defence in defending their own lives.

It is an unfortunate case, and the worst which has occurred here, as one cannot defend it without taking for granted that neither judge, jury, nor advocate were to be trusted—a case in which I think the governor might have taken strong ground with more plausibility than in reference to the removal of the intruders by a military force. But I perceive (by the papers) that he has contented himself in merely laying the facts before you. Mr. Key will probably put this affair in a train for legal adjustment, and where an impartial trial can be had.

The point now of the greatest public interest in all this business is the course which the governor may pursue in his message to the legislature, which meets during the latter part of this month. I have reason to believe that it will not be inflammatory, from expressions that are repeated as coming from him; and Mr. Key's visit, which I cannot help coupling with these events, will probably create such a determination, if it has not been already formed.

The entire amount of the late Creek lands is about 15,000,000 acres, and the amount of the reservations about 2,150,000. The portion of good land may be stated at one-fifth of the whole, so that the reservations call for about twice as much good land as there is in the entire Creek country. And as their settlements are generally on good land, the probability is that the reservations will cover nearly all of the most desirable land in the nine counties, into which this part of the State is divided. This may account to you for the great avidity which is shown for these reservations.

The Creeks, although always spoken of as composed of separate towns, are generally scattered up and down the water courses, and not in compact settlements. One of these towns lies in a length of forty miles in the valley of a creek; and those in the upper parts, where it is mountainous, entirely occupy the valleys. This much increases the difficulty of establishing, in the first instance, certain outlines for the towns, and will render the individual locations, in many cases, a necessary first step. They are generally scattered about in families in every direction, and the distinction of towns, in whatever it may have at first originated, is now and has been for some time, as far as settlements are concerned, more nominal than real. I am preparing therefore the necessary details from the census book (which requires no little time) to locate in the first instance either generally or individually, as the case may seem to require.

I make these remarks, not with a view of eliciting any further instructions (those we have are sufficiently ample), but merely to account for my letters being still dated from this place.

Believe me to be, &c.,
J. J. ABERT,
*Lieut. Col. Top. Eng.*

Hon. LEWIS CASS,
*Secretary of War.*

P. S. A note received since dark from Mr. Key, informs me of his a at Fort Mitchell, and his desire to see me there. I shall be with him in the morning.

---

FORT MITCHELL, *November* 12, 1833.

SIR: Mr. Key leaves this to-morrow for Tuscaloosa.

I took the opportunity while in conversation with him of explaining to him the substance of my letters to you since my arrival, and was particular to bring to his notice the views which suggested themselves to me in reference to the character of the Indian lands after the individual locations were made, and the probability of numerous leases which might be used in order to evade the provisions of the treaty. He considered that notice to the chiefs that these locations were only provisionary, and not final till after receiving the approbation of the President, would still keep them exempt from the character of private property.

The rule which appears to have been pursued by the marshal is, that settlers by consent of the Indians were not of that class of intruders which were to be removed.

Being now prepared, I shall commence to locate as rapidly as possible, generally or individually, as either course may be the more convenient, and as fast as I can find suitable assistants.

As Mr. Key will himself write to you upon other matters in this quarter, it is unnecessary that I should.

Allow me to correct an erroneous opinion in my last, in which I said that probably the officer (commanding at Fort Mitchell) was not aware the venue could have been changed had he or his men have submitted to the court which issued the process against them. It is his opinion, and that of every one with whom I have conversed, that under the circumstances existing here the judge would not have changed the venue.

Respectfully, &c.,

J. J. ABERT,
*Lieut. Col. Top. Eng.*

Hon. Lewis Cass,
*Secretary of War.*

---

Treaty Ground, Forks of the Wabash,
*November 12, 1833:*

Dear Sir: When I had the pleasure of meeting you at Buffalo, N. Y., in August last, and ascertaining that there was to be a council of the *Six Nations*, in that vicinity, on the 1st of September, you deemed it important, in case they should refuse to go to Green Bay, that I should be present to communicate to them what I knew of the Indian country west of the Mississippi, the condition of the emigrant Indians, and the benevolent views of the Government in their removal. After I had ascertained that we would not meet the Miamies in council until October, I immediately returned from the Wabash, in compliance with your advice and suggestions.

On my arrival at Buffalo the last of August, I was informed that the Oneidas and Onondagas had sent word that they could not meet in council until the middle of September, and that the council had been postponed accordingly. This I regretted, because my previous engagements to be at Chicago, to aid in the Pottawatamie treaty, would not for it permit me to delay. I had, however, an interview with the chiefs and principal men of the Seneca tribe, who expressed to me their determination not to remove to Green Bay. They observed, "we know that country, for some of us have seen it; it is too far north for us, and we do not like the title to the land. If we remove, we want a permanent home, and therefore we prefer the country west of the Mississippi." I endeavored to persuade them to send some of their best men to visit the Senecas west of the Mississippi, and informed them that they had requested me to see their brothers in New

York, and request them all to come and live with them, that the *Six Nations* might again be united and become a powerful people. Although I could not attend this council, I sent them a talk by their agent, James Stryker, esq., which I have heard was well received.

Permit me, sir, to state a few things in reference to the New York Indians, for the consideration of the department. When they first contemplated removing to Green Bay, the policy of the Government, with regard to the removal of the Indians from the east to the west of the Mississippi, was not settled. Even as late as 1826, the then Secretary of War, the Hon. James Barbour, contemplated reserving all the country west of the Mississippi, and not included in the State of Missouri and Territory of Arkansas, and east of the Mississippi, the country west of Lakes Huron and Michigan, as the exclusive abode of the Indians. Since that time the Indian title has been extinguished. That part of this country situated south of the Ouisconsin and Fox rivers and Green Bay; and that south of Grand river and Saganaw Bay, M. T., lived the once powerful nations of Chippeways, Ottaways, Pottawatamies, Sauks and Foxes, who resided here, have been provided with a permanent home west of the Mississippi; and all of them, except about 3,000 of the Chippeways and Ottoways in the northern part of the peninsula, under treaty stipulations to remove. The Winnebagoes, by their treaty in 1832, have been obliged to remove north of the Ouisconsin. But all that are acquainted with this country, and the condition of the Indians, agree in opinion, that they cannot live there, and that they will sooner perish by the sword than to do it. They will no doubt move upon their lands west of the Mississippi, as soon as they can do it with safety from their old enemies, the Sioux. There will then be no Indians left west of Lake Michigan, and below N. Lat. 46°, except the Menomonies, who number only 2143 souls, and the few New York Indians that may have removed to Green Bay.

It is also to be remarked, that the Ouisconsin and Fox rivers, and Green Bay, is one of the great natural channels of communication between the lakes and the Upper Mississippi; and from the enterprise of our citizens, there is no doubt the southern bank of this great thoroughfare will soon be settled by our people. With these facts before us, I ask what rational probability is there, should the New York Indians consent to move here, that they will long enjoy the undisturbed possession of this country? If it is an eligible one for settlement (and I believe it is), and our citizens occupy the south bank of the river, they will not rest until they own the north bank also; and even if this should not be the case, does our past experience teach us, that Indians thus situated, with a border population pressing upon them, and mingling with them, is favorable to their improvement and civilization? We all know it is not. And should they remove there now, the force of circumstances, which even the Government could not control, would render another removal necessary, and that very soon. The general policy of the Government, therefore, economy, and the best interests of the Indians, all point out the west as the only land of rest and hope for them. I maintain it would be most economical to remove them west at once: for the land in the Indian territory they cannot and will not sell; but the 500,000 acres the United States would get by the exchange at Green Bay, would more than refund to the Government the whole expense of their removal and settlement west.

From a letter I have recently received from a young Seneca by the name of *Pierce*, I am informed they will send on a delegation to Washington; and from what I know of the state of feeling among the Senecas, they will remove west if the President advises to it. Can they not be advised and permitted to explore this country? If so, they ought to be at Pittsburg, and take a steamboat about the first of April. They would arrive at Fort Gibson in about 15 or 20 days, and this is within 100 miles of the Seneca settlements. If they were accompanied with a discreet and judicious man, the expense need not exceed $300 to each person of the delegation. I have communicated my views frankly and fully, and I cheerfully leave the whole matter to the superior wisdom of the department.

With great respect,
Your obedient servant,
J. F. SCHERMERHORN,
*Commissioner West.*

Hon. ELBERT HERRING, *Commissioner.*

---

EXECUTIVE OFFICE,
*Tallahassee, November* 12, 1833.

SIR: I am happy to inform the department that I have just returned with General Thompson, the agent, from the visit to the Appalachicola towns, which I stated in my last I had appointed to make, and that we ascertained satisfactorily that Blunt and Davy would go off *this fall*, as soon as the Indian boys arrive from Kentucky. They have made full preparation, except the purchase of provisions, for which we advanced them fifteen hundred dollars, and took a voucher, of which the enclosed is a copy. *I assure the department no apprehensions need be entertained of any difficulty as soon as the boys arrive.* By the next mail I will communicate fully all the particulars to the department.

I am, very respectfully,
Your obedient servant,
JAMES D. WESTCOTT, Jr.,
*Secretary and Acting Governor.*

The Hon. SECRETARY OF WAR.

---

These may certify that General Wiley Thompson, Indian agent, has this day paid to the undersigned, John Blunt and Davy Elliott, the sum of fifteen hundred dollars. This payment is made pursuant to the instructions from Acting Governor Westcott to General Thompson, and is on account of the treaty of Blunt and Davy with the United States, ratified February, 1833. It is to be expended in completing the final preparation of themselves and people who accompany them to the west; and they are to hold themselves all in readiness to go off as soon as Blunt's son arrives from Kentucky.

Blunt and Davy agree to become responsible for this amount, and Stephen Richards guarantees their responsibility and its expenditure as aforesaid, and its return, if any thing should occur requiring it, when demanded.

> JOHN BLUNT,   his x mark.
> DAVY ELLIOTT, his x mark.
> STEPHEN RICHARDS.

Witness:
Wm S. Pope, *Sub Agent.*
H. V. Snell.
J. D. Westcott, Jr., *Acting Governor.*
*November* 10, 1833.

I have no hesitancy in stating that I have not the least doubt of Blunt and Davy's going off, and of the expediency, propriety, and, indeed, necessity of the within advance.

> WM. S. POPE, *Sub Agent.*

We agree to the above.

> ISAAC BROWN,
> H. V. SNELL.

I certify the within and foregoing to be a true copy.

> WILEY THOMPSON,
> *Agent Florida Indians.*

---

EXECUTIVE OFFICE,
*Tallahassee, Florida, November* 13, 1833.

Sir: On yesterday I advised the department of my return from the Appalachicola towns, which I had visited with the agent, General Thompson, to attend to the execution of the treaty with Blunt and Davy, and I promised to communicate by this mail the particulars to the department.

Blunt and Davy, with Stephen Richards, the interpreter, visited me at this place on the 27th October, and had a full conversation with the agent and myself. They still complained greatly of the last treaties concluded by Col. Gadsden with the upper towns. Blunt and Davy again stated to me that their people were leaving them, and going to the upper towns and to the Creek nation, and among the Seminoles; and that my instructions to the sub-agent, and my orders sent to the other chiefs to send their Indians home were even disregarded. They complain that good faith had not been observed towards them, inasmuch as they were assured when they made their treaty that all proper efforts should be used to get the other towns to go *with them.* Blunt also complained that he had not received remuneration for the robberies by the whites of his property since the treaty.

A memorandum of the conversation will be enclosed to the department by General Thompson by this mail.

The last difficulty was, as will be seen by the memorandum, easily obviated. I assured him if the Government should allow him any thing, it should be sent to him to the nearest United States fort or post to his residence. I refer the department particularly to this memorandum of our conversation on this subject, as it may be important hereafter.

To remedy the first complaint, I appointed the 9th instant to visit the towns, and hold a talk with the Indians, and see that matters were all set right and my orders obeyed.

When I got there I found that the sub-agent had just come home, after an absence of nearly three months in Louisiana. I knew of his visit, but not of his protracted absence, and could not account for not having heard from him.

General Thompson, the agent, being introduced to the Indians in council, gave them the talk, of which a copy will also be enclosed by him to the department. Their reply will also be enclosed by him at the same time.

To remedy the complaint of Blunt, in regard to good faith not having been observed towards him as aforesaid, I consented to address a letter for Yellow Hair to the President, which is enclosed in another communication by the same mail with this.

General Thompson, by my instructions, paid Blunt and Davy fifteen hundred dollars, as I advised the department by last mail. I am confident our course in this respect will be approved.

The Creek agent, and Colonels Abert and Bright, have been written to respecting our runaways to the Creek nation, and furnished with a list of their names, &c. Those in the Seminole nation have been ordered up home, and those in the upper towns have been sent out.

Nothing now exists to delay the departure of Blunt and Davy with the *principal* portion of their people but the absence at the Indian School in Kentucky of the boys belonging to their towns. They will not stir a step, however, till the boys arrive; but are prepared to go off immediately on their arrival.

I have written "to Col. R. M. Johnson, or the superintendent of the Indian school at Great Crossings, Kentucky," on that subject, a copy of which I enclose.

I beg the department will renew the instructions given on that subject some time since. All the boys from the Appalachicola towns should be sent home as speedily as possible. Blunt and his party are incurring heavy expenses daily, and if the return of the boys is delayed beyond the middle of January, I am afraid of continued delay in the embarkation. While at Appalachicola I procured a list of the boys now at the school in Kentucky, which is enclosed, annexed to the copy of the letter to Col. Johnson. I would suggest that the best route home is by Nashville, Tennessee, Huntsville, Alabama, to Columbus, Georgia, and thence to Mount Vernon, Florida, by steamboat, when they are but a few miles from home.

It will be necessary for the department to decide what amount will be due Blunt and Davy for the advance of annuity, and to transmit the funds, or authority to draw therefor, to the Executive of Florida by the time the boys arrive.

Should Yellow Hair's proposition be acceded to, funds must also be transmitted to pay his party at the same time. I respectfully suggest that the rule I have proposed in a statement of population, &c., forwarded to Mr. Herring, be adopted for the ascertainment of the amount of annuity to be paid to the emigrants, deducting for those who remain behind; and that the same proportion also of the ten thousand dollars, to be paid to Blunt and Davy, be deducted. I have notified him he would not be paid for those who did not go.

Blunt has requested me, as his friend, to write to New Orleans to know what rifles can be got for; and he intends to have one hundred sent down to the Balize for his party, with also considerable goods. As this will not be done till he is about starting, Yellow Hair's can be purchased at the same time, if his proposition is agreed to, and if the Executive here is advised so to do by the department.

I would suggest the authority to the Governor here to appoint an agent to go along with Blunt and Davy to the mouth of the Sabine, to protect them and their party from the depredations of scoundrels who may meet them along the coast, and rob them or force them to violence. He can select a trustworthy man for two hundred and fifty dollars the trip.

I trust the department will be satisfied I have done my duty in this business. I know I have left nothing undone in my power to perform; but I am gratified that the arrival of Governor Duval, which is hourly expected, will afford the Government the benefit of his better judgment and riper experience.

I have the honor to be, sir,
Your most obedient humble servant,
JAMES D. WESTCOTT, Jr.
Hon. Lewis Cass, *Secretary of War, Washington.*

---

Executive Office,
*Tallahassee, Florida, Nov.* 12, 1833.

Sir: No obstacle exists to the execution of the treaty concluded last fall with the Appalachicola Indians but the absence of the boys at your school from these towns.

I advised the War Department last spring, and renewed the information twice during the summer and this fall, that these boys must be sent home. Col. Gadsden, the commissioner who concluded the treaty, also stated to the department the necessity of their return. The department have informed me that advice of this necessity was communicated to the superintendent of the school; and in a recent communication to me stated also that it has been repeated. Gov. Duval, while in Kentucky last summer, was written to by me on the subject; and I learn also wrote to the head of the school.

Notwithstanding these circumstances, no information of the boys has been received here. A report is in circulation that some of them have died of the cholera; and it and their absence occasion considerable anxiety and uneasiness among their relations. They refuse to stir a step under the treaty till these boys get home, and till they are satisfied who of them are living. I beg to be advised on this subject by you on return of mail, and that all the boys may be sent home as soon *as possible.*

Upwards of two hundred and fifty Indians are now living at heavy expenses awaiting their arrival. They had better come home via Nashville, Tennessee, Huntsville, Alabama, and Columbus, Georgia, and from thence to Mount Vernon, Florida, by steamboat; they are then within five miles of their homes. A list of the boys is annexed. Gen. W. Thompson has also written to you on this subject this day.

I am, very respectfully,
Your obedient servant,
JAMES D. WESTCOTT, Jr.

Col. Johnson, or the
   Sup't at the Indian School, *Ky.*

85‡

1. Jack-vacca-pechasse, or Cowdriver, belonging to Old Cowdriver, or Mulatto King's town, and his son.

2. Arsler, same family and town.

3. Tommy and Town. The town is called Choconicla.

4. Aaron, from *Spanawacka*, or Cochrane's, or Davy's town. This is the town lowest down the river.

5. Billy, Col. Blunt's son. Blunt's town is called Jola.

6. Sampson, from Cochrane's or Davy's town.

7. Washington, old Hogan's son. And

8. Ned. These are both from Choconicla. The first belongs properly to Attapulgas.

---

EXECUTIVE OFFICE,
*Tallahassee, November* 13, 1833.

SIR: Enclosed are five statements or lists showing the population of each one of the Indian towns on the Appalachicola, designating the number of women, children, &c., and all those ready to emigrate, and those who refuse to go; the deaths since the treaty with Blunt in 1832, portion of annuity paid to each town in 1833, and other information which it has been deemed useful for me to procure for the use of the department and of the Executive of this Territory, and also a general statement compiled from the foregoing. Not having access to the old pay rolls, (they being in possession of Major Phagan,) and being without data of every kind to aid or correct my labors, and having to rely solely upon the answers of the Indians and the interpreter to my verbal inquiries, it cannot be expected that my statements are wholly without error. I believe, however, they are substantially correct; and I flatter myself the department will find them useful. A note to the general statement compiled from the particular lists, contains a rule for the apportionment and distribution of the annuity, which I consider just, and which will save great difficulty hereafter, if observed.

I am, respectfully,
Your most obedient servant,
JAMES D. WESTCOTT, Jr.,
*Acting Governor, &c.*

Hon. E. HERRING,
Com. of Indian Affairs, Washington City, D C.

## Census of Spane Watka, or Davy's, or Cochrane's Town, May, 1833, with also notes made November 9, 1833.

| | Names of Indians. | Age. | Rank. | No. of wives. | No. of children living in family. | No. of slaves. | Total. | Quota of annuity. | Remarks and notes. |
|---|---|---|---|---|---|---|---|---|---|
| 1 | Davy | 46 | Hd. chief | 1 | - | - | 2 | $35 00 | Ready to emigrate; got a canoe, &c., November 9, 1833. |
| 2 | Oathla Hajo | 30 | Sd. chief | - | 1 | - | 2 | 7 00 | Do. |
| 3 | Cotcheliceico b | - | | 1 | 1 | - | 3 | 7 00 | Is dead, and also his child; none but his wife to go; she is ready: November 9. |
| 4 | Conchattee | 35 | | 1 | 3 | - | 5 | 7 00 | Ready to emigrate; got a canoe, &c.: November 9, 1833. |
| 5 | Talladig Hajo c | 30 | | 2 | 5 | - | 8 | | These are the second chiefs entitled to $7 each; they have, however, gone to the Creek nation; gone to a town called Tewethlee, in the upper nation. Jim Bryor or 'Tustanuchre Emathla, a Creek, induced them to go, and said he would pay their expenses: November 9, still absent. |
| 6 | Coathlocco c | 35 | | 1 | - | - | 2 | | |
| 7 | Charly Emathla c | 25 | | 2 | 2 | - | 5 | | |
| 8 | Foosu Hajo | 30 | Warrior | 1 | 1 | - | 1 | 3 25 | Ready to emigrate; got a canoe, &c.: November 9, 1833. |
| 9 | Nocoosa Hajo b | 35 | | - | - | - | 3 | 3 25 | Dead, and also his child; his wife is ready and willing to go off; got a canoe. |
| 10 | Miccopoilga | 35 | | 1 | - | - | 1 | 3 25 | Ready to go off; got a canoe, &c. |
| 11 | Oso Hajo | 35 | a | - | 2 | - | 4 | 3 25 | Refuses to go; has gone to the Seminole nation, and took his wife and children with him: November 9. |
| 12 | Noceosa Emathla | 30 | a | 2 | 3 | - | 6 | 3 25 | Do. |
| 13 | Chenasti Hajo | 40 | a | - | - | - | 1 | 3 25 | Do. |
| 14 | Timmocca b | 20 | | - | - | - | 1 | 3 25 | |
| 15 | Semojathchu | 18 | | 1 | - | - | 2 | 3 25 | Dead since May, 1833. |
| 16 | Cochus Hajo e | 40 | | 1 | - | - | 2 | - | Going; got a canoe, &c., November 9. |
| 17 | Holathlu Halthla c | 40 | | 1 | 1 | - | 3 | - | With Coathlosso and others in Creek nation; went off before May, 1833. |
| 18 | Tallahassee Hajo c | 30 | | 1 | - | - | 2 | - | Do. |
| 19 | Alithka c | 30 | | - | - | 12 | 1 | - | Do. |

## Census of Spane Watka, or Davy's, or Cochranes' Town, May, 1833—Continued.

| | Names of Indians | Age. | Rank. | No. of wives. | No. of children living in family. | No. of slaves. | Total. | Quota of annuity. | Remarks and notes. |
|---|---|---|---|---|---|---|---|---|---|
| 20 | Foosche Mathla ♂ | 35 | - | 1 | 3 | - | 5 | $3 25 | Wife dead since May; ready to go; got a canoe, &c. |
| 21 | Scona | 13 | - | - | - | - | 1 | 3 25 | Ready to go; got a canoe, &c. |
| 22 | Simsumca | 22 | a | - | - | - | 1 | 3 25 | Do. |
| 23 | Sitochu | 24 | a | - | - | - | 1 | 3 25 | Gone to Seminole nation since annuity. |
| 24 | Sofotiga | 15 | a | - | - | - | 1 | 3 25 | Do. |
| | | | | 17 | 22 | | 63 | $98 25 | |
| | Add the quota due absentees had they been present, not paid | | | | | | | 37 75 | |
| | | | | | | | | $136 00 | |

The first three were entitled, had they been present, to $7 each, and the three last to $5 25 each—$37 75; being absent, they were not paid, and the amount was distributed among the other Indians; these Indians are the immediate descendants and relations of old Cochrane, who is mentioned at the treaty of Camp Moultrie, and dissatisfied with the treaty made by Davy, &c., although Coathlocso signed it. See treaty in annuity of 1832 3.

d Memorandum of those who died previous to May, 1833, and since the treaty for emigration.

1. Ock Jonalatta.
2. Octa Hajce Hajo.
3. Polea.
4. Coxus Hajo.
5. Tuki Fmathla.
6. Forehatchee Micco.
7. Corehadjo.
8. John Boy.

Some of these I understand were women and some children, but I can not distinguish them.

### RECAPITULATION.

| | |
|---|---|
| Head chiefs, warriors, &c. | 24 |
| Wives | 17 |
| Children | 22 |
| Total number of town in May, 1833 | 63 |

d 8  Dead previous to May, and since treaty.
Add 63  Population in May, 1833, as above stated.
———
71  Number of souls in town at the time of the treaty in 1832, and making the number 256, with Blunt's Indians as specified in treaty.
c Deduct 23  Gone to Creek nation.
———
48
a Deduct 13  Gone to Seminoles.
———
35
Deduct 6  Dead since annuity.
———
29
d Deduct 8  Died since treaty, and previous to payment of annuity.
———
Leaving 21  Souls ready to go off.

c 7  Warriors gone to Creek nation.
8  Wives.
8  Children.
———
23

a 5  Warriors gone to Seminole nation.
3  Wives.
5  Children.
———
13  Number of souls gone to Seminole nation.

Mem.—Those gone to the Seminole nation are connexions of Octa Micco, and are near the Withlabuchy.
Their portion of the annuity as above is $16 25.
b Memorandum of deaths since May, 1833:—6 Men, women, and children, as above stated in notes.

*Census of Choconicla, (the Indian town formerly ruled by Yellow Hair, formerly ruled by Vaccapichassie, or Cowdriver, alias Mulatto King,) taken in May, 1833, at payment of annuity, with notes and remarks, made November 9th, 1833.*

| No. | Name of male heads of families. | Age. | Rank. | No. of wives. | No. of children living in family. | No. of slaves. | Total. | Quota of annuity. | Remarks.—All these except in regard to payment made November 9, 1833. |
|---|---|---|---|---|---|---|---|---|---|
| 1 | John Yellow Hair, or Nocose Ahola - - | 20 | Head chief | 1 | - | - | 2 | $30 00 | Wishes to go with Blunt, and is prepared. |
| 2 | Yohola Heyo - - | 30 | 2d chief | 1 | - | - | 2 | 7 00 | Wishes to go with Yellow Hair and Blunt, and is prepared: his wife will stay. |
| 3 | Comipehola - - | 20 | do | 1 | 4 | - | 6 | 7 00 | |
| 4 | Tallassee Mathla - - | 20 | do | 1 | 1 | - | 3 | 7 00 | |

Census of Choconicla, taken in May, 1833—Continued.

| No. | Name of male heads of families. | Age. | Rank. | No. of wives. | No. of children living in family. | No. of slaves. | Total. | Quota of annuity. | Remarks. |
|---|---|---|---|---|---|---|---|---|---|
| 5 | Lathla Hola - | 30 | 2d chief | 1 | 3 | - | 5 | 7 00 | Remarks.—All these except in regard to payment made November 9, 1833. |
| 6 | King, or Vaccupachassie, or Cowdriver, the mulatto - | 70 | do | 1 | 1 | 1 | 4 | 7 00 | Slave called Tom. |
| 7 | Cotcha Hajochee - | 30 | do | 1 | 2 | - | 4 | 7 00 | |
| 8 | Coosa Hajo - | 27 | do | 1 | - | - | 2 | 7 00 | Wishes to go with Yellow Hair, and is prepared. |
| 9 | Conip Hajo - | 25 | do | 1 | 1 | - | 3 | 7 00 | |
| 10 | Tustenuky Cochochinickee - | 30 | do | 1 | 1 | - | 3 | 7 00 | |
| 11 | Yaholatehee, or Factor - | 50 | Warrior | 1 | 1 | - | 3 | 3 25 | |
| 12 | Citchosee - | 30 | do | 1 | - | - | 2 | 3 25 | |
| 13 | Nocosa Chopca - | 35 | do | 1 | 1 | - | 3 | 3 25 | Wishes to go with Yellow Hair, and is prepared. |
| 14 | Nocosa Hajo - | 35 | do | 1 | - | - | 2 | 3 25 | Wishes to go with Yellow Hair, and is prepared. |
| 15 | Hichita Mathla - | 35 | do | - | - | - | 1 | 3 25 | Reported sick: paid to Yellow Hair. November 9, stated to have died since payment of annuity in May. |
| 16 | Nocoshoochie - | 35 | do | - | - | - | 1 | 3 25 | Wishes to go with Yellow Hair, and is prepared. |
| 17 | Chowastia - | 50 | do | 1 | - | - | 2 | 3 25 | |
| 18 | Yahaja - | 25 | do | 1 | - | - | 2 | 3 25 | |
| 19 | Charley - | 20 | do | 1 | 2 | - | 4 | 3 25 | |
| 20 | Fushajo - | 30 | do | - | - | - | 1 | 3 25 | |
| 21 | Chatto Hajo - | 26 | do | 1 | 2 | - | 4 | 3 25 | |
| 22 | Isaac - | 15 | do | - | - | - | 1 | 3 25 | Wishes to go with John Yellow Hair, and is prepared. |
| 23 | Inspa - | 35 | do | 1 | - | - | 2 | 3 25 | |
| 24 | Inspa Hajo - | 25 | do | 1 | - | - | 2 | 3 25 | November 9, stated to have died since payment of annuity in May. |
| 25 | John Attaway - | 25 | do | - | - | - | 1 | 3 25 | Reported sick: paid to Insapa Hajo. Wishes to go with Yellow Hair, and is prepared. |
| 26 | Micoochee - | 45 | do | - | 2 | - | 3 | 3 25 | November 9, stated to have died since payment of annuity in May. |

| No. | Name | | Age | Class | | | | | Amount | Remarks |
|---|---|---|---|---|---|---|---|---|---|---|
| 27 | Assahe | — | 20 | do | — | — | 0 | 1 | 3 25 | Reported sick: paid to Yellow Hair. Wishes to go with Yellow Hair, and is prepared. |
| 28 | Sampson | — | 50 | do | 1 | 4 | 0 | 6 | 3 25 | |
| 29 | Lewis | — | 14 | do | — | — | — | 1 | 3 23 | Do. |
| 30 | Jacob his son | — | 14 | do | — | — | — | 1 | 3 25 | Do. November 9, stated to have died since payment of annuity in May. |
| 51 | Untilla | — | 50 | do | — | — | — | 1 | 3 25 | |
| 32 | Amattaha | — | 45 | do | 1 | 2 | — | 4 | 3 25 | N. B.—Four women are stated to have died this summer since payment of annuity, and also six children: in all, with said warriors, making fourteen souls. |
| 33 | Siaboska | — | 25 | do | 1 | — | — | 2 | 3 25 | |
| 34 | Tony | — | 25 | do | 1 | — | — | 2 | 3 25 | |
| 35 | Hietska | — | 13 | Y'ng warrior | — | — | — | 1 | 3 25 | |
| 36 | Tommy | — | 14 | do | — | — | — | 1 | 3 25 | |
| 37 | Clemmy | — | 12 | do | — | — | — | 1 | 3 25 | Do. |
| 38 | Charley | — | 13 | do | — | — | ? | 1 | 3 25 | |
| 39 | Tepiga, Tigertail's nephew | — | 12 | do | — | — | — | 1 | 3 25 | |
| 40 | Sucky | — | 13 | do | — | — | — | 1 | 3 25 | |
| 41 | Parney | — | 14 | do | — | — | — | 1 | 3 25 | In addition to those named above, there are some unmarried women and eight children ready to go with Yellow Hair, and most probably eight or ten more men, and see Attapulgee's, or Emathlocee's town, from which some also wish to go. |
| 42 | Murkay, orphan | — | 13 | do | — | — | — | 1 | 3 25 | |
| 43 | Mahoneesehay | — | 13 | do | — | — | — | 1 | 3 25 | |
| 44 | Aischaschy, Walker's son | — | 10 | do | — | — | — | 1 | 3 25 | |
| 45 | Davy | — | 13 | do | — | — | — | 1 | 3 25 | |
| 46 | Poty | — | 11 | do | — | — | — | 1 | 3 25 | |
| | Folotiga, widow of Heatuga, late head chief | | — | — | — | — | — | — | 7 00 | Paid to his father. |
| | Wisey, Attun, Tustalle, Sunday, Josiah, Weeky, Tohole, Conappee, Ben; nine boys, were paid one dollar each, by direction of head chief Yellow Hair | | — | — | — | — | — | — | 9 00 | Paid to Yellow Hair. |
| | | | | | 23 | 26 | 1 | 96 | $236 00 | |

## Census of Choconicla, taken in May, 1833—Continued.

### RECAPITULATION.

| | |
|---|---|
| Head Chief, Second Chiefs, Warriors and Boys - | 46 |
| Nine Boys receiving $1 each - | 9 |
| Totoliga, Hiauga's widow - | 1 |
| Wives - | 23 |
| Children - | 26 |
| Slaves - | 1 |
| Five old widows and four free negroes, not included in said list | 9 |
| | 115 souls. |

N. B.—Four have died in this town since payment of annuity in May, 1833; also, four women and six children. See remarks made November 9th, 1833.

### Census of Totointha, the upper town on the Appalachicola, at payment of annuity in May, 1833.

| No. | Names of male heads of families. | Age. | Rank. | No. of wives. | No. of children living in family. | No. of slaves. | Total. | Quota of annuity. | |
|---|---|---|---|---|---|---|---|---|---|
| 1 | Conchaltimico | 60 | Hd. chief | 2 | | 24 | 27 | $30 00 | The head chief's son sick; paid to his father. |
| 2 | Coosa Hatchee | 40 | Tustanugge | 1 | 2 | | 4 | 7 00 | |
| 3 | Hepia Tustenugge | 40 | Secd. chief. | 1 | 2 | | 4 | 7 00 | |
| 4 | Okillas Neha | 40 | do | | | | 4 | 7 00 | |
| 5 | Capixta Tustenugge | 40 | do | 1 | 2 | | 4 | 7 00 | |
| 6 | Fulma Hajo (Billy) | 35 | do | 1 | 2 | | 4 | 7 00 | |
| 7 | Lathlapixciao or Joe Miller | 23 | do | 1 | 1 | | 3 | 7 00 | Joe Miller is also interpreter. |

| No. | Name | | Warrior | Amount | | | | | Rate | Remarks |
|---|---|---|---|---|---|---|---|---|---|---|
| 8 | Tommyaholo | - | Warrior | 50 | - | 1 | - | 4 | 3 25 | |
| 9 | Luppe Mico | - | do | 40 | - | - | - | 1 | 3 25 | |
| 10 | Occoskee | - | do | 35 | - | 1 | 2 | 4 | 3 25 | |
| 11 | Conippenathla | - | do | 45 | - | 1 | 3 | 5 | 3 25 | |
| 12 | Noccooselee | - | do | 30 | - | 1 | 1 | 3 | 3 25 | |
| 13 | Charlee Hajo | - | do | 30 | - | 1 | 1 | 3 | 3 25 | |
| 14 | Tustenukyjule | - | do | 40 | - | - | - | 1 | 3 25 | |
| 15 | Wacceholata | - | do | 30 | - | - | - | 1 | 3 25 | Paid to Joe Miller; reported sick. |
| 16 | Efenathla | - | do | 50 | - | 1 | 3 | 4 | 3 25 | |
| 17 | Tallaficcico | - | do | 40 | - | 1 | 3 | 5 | 3 25 | Paid to head chief, reported sick. |
| 18 | Emithlichee | - | do | 30 | - | 1 | 2 | 4 | 3 25 | |
| 19 | Opithleyola | - | do | 30 | - | 1 | 2 | 4 | 3 25 | Do. |
| 20 | Coosa | - | do | 20 | - | 1 | 1 | 3 | 3 25 | |
| 21 | Chemastee | - | do | 25 | - | 1 | 1 | 3 | 3 25 | |
| 22 | Nealocochee | - | do | 30 | - | 1 | 2 | 4 | 3 25 | Paid to Joe Miller; reported sick. |
| 23 | Shogan | - | do | 30 | - | - | - | 2 | 3 25 | Do. |
| 24 | Talmasee | - | do | 25 | - | 1 | - | 1 | 3 25 | Said to be in Afaller or Refarter town in the Creek nation, November 9, 1833. |
| 25 | Oakmulgee | - | do | 30 | - | 1 | - | 2 | 3 25 | |
| 26 | Oakmulgee 2 | - | do | 40 | - | - | 1 | 3 | 3 25 | |
| 27 | Neaficcico | - | do | 25 | - | 1 | - | 1 | 3 25 | |
| 28 | George | - | do | 30 | - | 1 | - | 2 | 3 25 | |
| 29 | Tommy Tustenuggo | - | do | 40 | - | 1 | 2 | 4 | 3 25 | |
| 30 | Ohowa | - | do | 25 | - | - | - | 1 | 3 25 | |
| 31 | Melowee | - | do | 30 | - | 1 | - | 2 | 3 25 | |
| 32 | Huckelusty | - | do | 35 | - | 1 | - | 2 | 3 25 | Paid to Compmathla; reported sick. |
| 33 | Micco Poilga | - | do | 30 | - | 1 | - | 1 | 3 25 | Paid to Joe Miller; reported sick. |
| 34 | Ohoyathla | - | do | 25 | - | - | 2 | 4 | 3 25 | Do. |
| 35 | Cotcheficcico | - | do | 35 | - | 1 | - | 2 | 3 25 | Do. |
| 36 | Ochusee Hajo | - | do | 35 | - | 1 | - | 1 | 3 25 | |
| 37 | Emathla | - | do | 35 | - | - | 2 | 4 | 3 25 | |
| 38 | Allatichee | - | do | 30 | - | - | - | 4 | 3 25 | |
| 39 | Ficcico | - | do | 35 | - | 1 | 1 | 2 | 3 25 | |
| 40 | Chonchattee | - | do | 40 | - | - | 1 | 1 | 3 25 | Do. |
| 41 | Metahakee | - | do | 18 | - | - | - | 1 | 3 25 | Do. |
| 42 | Nomithliga | - | do | 23 | - | 1 | - | 1 | 3 25 | |
| 43 | Foos Hajo | - | do | 25 | - | - | 1 | 3 | 3 25 | |
| 44 | Possac Hajo | - | do | 50 | - | 1 | - | 1 | 3 25 | |
| 45 | Succaluthchee | - | do | 25 | - | - | - | 1 | 3 25 | |

## Census of Totintha, May, 1833—Continued.

| No. | Names of male heads of families. | Age. | Rank. | No. of wives. | No. of children living in family. | No. of slaves. | Total. | Quota of annuity. | Remarks. |
|---|---|---|---|---|---|---|---|---|---|
| 46 | Sopinee | 25 | do | 1 | | | 2 | 3 25 | Paid to head chief; reported sick. |
| 47 | Sampea | 20 | do | | | | 1 | 3 25 | |
| 48 | Jno. Blue or Gen. Jno. Silly | 15 | Y'ng warrior | | | | 1 | 3 25 | |
| 49 | Johnny | 13 | do | | | | 1 | 3 25 | |
| 50 | Samhootchee | 14 | do | | 1 | | 2 | 3 25 | |
| 51 | Pimpooitchee | 35 | Warrior | | 1 | | 2 | 3 25 | |
| 52 | Tomochee | 24 | do | | 1 | | 2 | 3 25 | |
| 53 | Maichee | 14 | Y'ng warrior | | | | 1 | 3 25 | |
| 54 | Chalkoo | 13 | do | | | | 1 | 3 25 | |
| 55 | Laboola | 15 | Warrior | | 1 | | 2 | 3 25 | |
| 56 | Holomagachee | 20 | do | | 1 | | 2 | 3 25 | |
| 57 | Scarholochee | 12 | Boys | | | | 1 | | These five are boys, and were absent at the payment of the annuity, and I refused to pay them, not being satisfied they should draw if they really existed. The head chief promised to produce them, but did not. |
| 58 | Harry | 13 | do | | | | 1 | | |
| 59 | Sanny | 10 | do | | | | 1 | | |
| 60 | Chattochee | 11 | do | | | | 1 | | |
| 61 | Senatchee | 12 | do | | | | 1 | | |
| | | | | 30 | 46 | 24 | 160 | $231 25 | |

### RECAPITULATION.

| | | |
|---|---|---|
| Head chief, second chief, warriors, and young warriors, and boys | - | 61 |
| Wives | - | 30 |
| Children, (not including young warriors or boys) | - | 46 |
| Negroes, (slaves) | - | 24 |
| Total | - | 161 |

| | |
|---|---|
| Total brought forward | 161 |
| Add also five old women not included in list | 5 |
| Add also six free negroes not included and not allowed annuity | 6 |
| Total population of Totointha | 172 souls |
| Amount of quota of annuity to this town | $231 25 |

## Census of Altapulgus, or Emathlee Town, May, 1833.

| | Names of Indians. | Age. | Rank. | No. of wives. | No. of children living in family. | No. of slaves. | Total. | Quota of annuity. | Remarks. |
|---|---|---|---|---|---|---|---|---|---|
| 1 | Tustenuggo Hajo | 35 | Head chief | 2 | 2 | - | 5 | $30 00 | |
| 2 | Paos Tustenuggy | 50 | 2d chief | 1 | 1 | - | 1 | 7 00 | |
| 3 | Yatta Hajo | 30 | do | 1 | 1 | - | 3 | 7 00 | |
| 4 | Contalamathla | 35 | do | - | - | - | 2 | 7 00 | |
| 5 | Echo Emalatcha | 40 | do | 1 | 1 | - | 3 | 7 00 | November 9: says he wishes to go with Blunt and Yellow Hair, and is prepared to go. |
| 6 | Tuseki Hajo | 30 | Warrior | 1 | 1 | - | 2 | 7 00 | |
| 7 | Cotchaluthu | 50 | Warrior | 1 | 1 | - | 3 | 3 25 | Has a son in Kentucky, at school. |
| 8 | Pocheese, (B.) | 15 | Y'ng warrior | 1 | - | - | 1 | 3 25 | |
| 9 | Lemalitchu Tustanuggee, Hajo's son | 15 | do | 1 | - | - | 1 | 3 25 | |
| 10 | Peivathla | 30 | Warrior | 1 | 1 | - | 3 | 3 25 | |
| 11 | Leochee | 15 | Y'ng warrior | - | - | - | 1 | 3 25 | |
| 12 | Lioffeca | 18 | do | - | - | - | 1 | 3 25 | |
| 13 | Loafchinca, (B.) | 14 | do | - | - | - | 1 | 3 25 | Wish to go with Yellow Hair to Texas, and are prepared to go. November 4, 1833. |
| 14 | Halatca, (B.) | 14 | do | - | - | - | 1 | 3 25 | |
| 15 | Chebana, (B.) | 14 | do | - | - | - | 1 | 3 25 | |
| 16 | Toney | 25 | Warrior | 1 | 1 | - | 2 | 3 25 | |
| 17 | Natta | 20 | do | - | - | - | 1 | 3 25 | |
| 18 | Wilsey | 14 | Y'ng warrior | - | - | - | 1 | 3 25 | |
| 19 | Chepanee, paid to Tachen, (P.P.) | 14 | Warrior | - | - | - | 1 | 3 25 | |
| 20 | Tommy | 20 | do | 1 | 1 | - | 2 | 3 25 | |
| 21 | Tinca | 30 | do | 1 | 1 | - | 2 | 3 25 | |
| 22 | Op Relago | - | - | - | - | - | - | - | Upon inquiry, after their names were given in, I ascertained they were Creek Indians, and had claimed land under Governor Cass's treaty in the Creek nation. |
| 23 | Allegee | - | - | - | - | - | - | - | |
| 24 | Philip | - | - | - | - | - | - | - | |
| 25 | Lepothka | - | - | - | 2 | - | 2 | - | |
| 26 | Osika | 25 | do | 1 | 1 | - | 3 | 3 25 | |

## Census of *Attapulgus*, May, 1833—Continued.

| | Names of Indians. | Age. | Rank. | No. of wives. | No. of children living in family. | No. of slaves. | Total. | Quota of annuity. | Remarks. |
|---|---|---|---|---|---|---|---|---|---|
| 27 | Punaka - | - | - | 1 | - | - | - | $3 25 | This is also a Creek Indian similarly situated. |
| 28 | Aunocha - | 21 | do | 1 | - | - | 2 | 3 25 | |
| 29 | Nocoscechokinechee | 30 | do | 1 | 1 | - | 3 | 3 25 | Wishes to, and is prepared to go with Yellow Hair to Texas. November 9, 1833. |
| 30 | Sammy - | 14 | Y'ng warrior | - | - | - | 1 | 3 25 | Improperly given in by Paos Tustanuggee; a small child, not paid, included in statement. |
| 31 | Punta - | - | - | - | - | - | - | - | Same as Punta. |
| 32 | Muttathlega | 87 | Warrior | - | 1 | - | 1 | - | |
| 33 | Istochee - | 35 | do | 1 | - | - | 4 | 3 25 | |
| 34 | Chefuiar Hajo - | - | - | - | 2 | - | 4 | 3 25 | Same as Punta. |
| 35 | Occathla - | - | do | 1 | - | - | 1 | - | |
| 36 | Stimmut Lathlagee | 18 | do | - | - | - | 1 | 3 25 | |
| 37 | Oawithlaga, (B.) | 15 | do | - | - | - | 1 | 3 25 | |
| 38 | Cotchetia - | 25 | do | - | - | - | 1 | 3 25 | |
| 39 | Jayaka - | 25 | - | - | 1 | - | 1 | 3 25 | |
| 40 | Semissa - | 25 | - | 1 | - | - | 3 | 3 25 | |
| 41 | Nittia, Boy | 10 | - | - | - | - | 1 | 3 25 | ⎱ Orphans. |
| 42 | Jimessa, Boy | 8 | - | - | - | - | 1 | 3 25 | ⎰ |
| 43 | Infotata - | 20 | Warrior | 1 | 1 | - | 2 | 3 25 | |
| 44 | Tachifea - | 16 | do | 1 | - | - | 1 | 3 25 | |
| 45 | Wakiga - | 30 | do | 1 | - | - | 2 | 3 25 | |
| 46 | Emathlachee | 35 | do | - | 1 | - | 3 | 3 25 | |
| 47 | Toby - | 22 | do | - | - | - | 1 | 3 25 | |
| 48 | Johung - | 30 | do | 1 | 2 | - | 4 | 3 25 | |
| 49 | Simkanie - | 35 | do | 1 | - | - | 2 | 3 25 | |
| 50 | Sammy - | 30 | do | 1 | 1 | - | 2 | 3 25 | |
| 51 | Yatta Hajo - | 35 | do | 1 | - | - | 2 | 3 25 | |

| | | | | | |
|---|---|---|---|---|---|
| 52 | Totcheleg | - | - | - | - |
| 53 | Chefranee | - | - | - | - |
| 54 | Hathee - | - | - | - | - |
| | | 22 | 15 | - | 80 | $185 25 |

{ These are small boys whom I declined paying, considering too small to draw, having parents, and being included in statement.

54
11
———
43

## RECAPITULATION.

| | | | |
|---|---|---|---|
| Head Chiefs, Warriors, and Young Warriors | - | - | 43 |
| Wives | - | - | 22 |
| Children | - | - | 15 |
| | | | 80 |
| Add seven old women not included in list | - | - | 7 |
| Total population of Attapulgus | - | - | 87 souls. |

Amount of annuity paid in 1833, $185 25. The number who have died since the annuity not given.

Memorandum of those who wish to emigrate from this town:

5 warriors
3 wives
2 children and others
———
10 souls.

N. B.—Portion of annuity of those Indians of this town who wish to go with Blunt and Yellow Hair:

| | | |
|---|---|---|
| Emathtochee | - | $7 00 |
| Lochee | - | 3 25 |
| Lioffeca | - | 3 25 |
| Nocosechocinca | - | 3 25 |
| Lofechinca | - | 3 25 |
| | | $20 00 |

Vide letter and list, &c.

Two or three women will go with them besides, &c.

*Census of Iola or Blunt's town, taken May, 1833; with also notes made November 9, 1833, stating what Indians are ready to emigrate, &c.; what have died, &c.; with also a statement of those who died before annuity, and since the treaty in 1832.*

| No. | Indian Names. | Age. | Rank. | No. of wives. | No. of children living in family. | No. of slaves. | Total. | Quota of annuity. | Remarks and notes. |
|---|---|---|---|---|---|---|---|---|---|
| 1 | John Blunt | 60 | Hd. chief of all the towns | 1 | 4 | 8 | 14 | $40 00 | Ready to go; got a canoe, &c.; his wife is old Vaca's daughter; he says she shan't go, &c. |
| a 2 | Tuskina Haw | 40 | Sec'd chief | 1 | 2 | — | 4 | 7 00 | Dead since annuity; wife and child going. |
| 3 | Hopia Hajo | 35 | — | 1 | 1 | — | 3 | 7 00 | Ready to go; got a canoe, &c. |
| a 4 | Tuskennehee Hajo | 40 | — | 1 | 2 | — | 4 | 7 00 | One child dead; not going; got a canoe, &c.; child died since annuity. |
| 5 | Lathla Hajo | 40 | — | 1 | 4 | — | 6 | 7 00 | Going; got canoe, &c. |
| 6 | Cotcha Holo | 30 | — | 1 | 2 | — | 2 | 7 00 | Do. |
| 7 | Hoaspa | 43 | — | 1 | — | — | 4 | 7 00 | Do. |
| 8 | Echo Hajo | 30 | — | 1 | 2 | — | 4 | 7 00 | Do. |
| a 9 | Cotcha Tustenuggee | 30 | — | 1 | — | — | 1 | 7 00 | Paid to Hosper; one child dead; going; got a canoe, &c. |
| 10 | Conip Hajo | 30 | — | 1 | 1 | — | 3 | 3 25 | Do. |
| 11 | Tommy Aholo | 35 | — | 1 | 1 | — | 3 | 3 25 | Do. |
| 12 | Eholahaja | 25 | — | 1 | 1 | — | 3 | 3 25 | Do. |
| 13 | Emathlahaja | 25 | — | 1 | 1 | — | 3 | 3 25 | Do. |
| a 14 | Temothliga | 25 | — | 2 | 2 | — | 5 | 3 25 | Both wives have died since annuity; children and self going; got a canoe, &c. |
| 15 | Eoyothpe | 20 | — | — | — | — | 1 | 3 25 | Going; got a canoe, &c. |
| 16 | Maseeoyee | 25 | — | — | — | — | 1 | 3 25 | Do. |
| 17 | Pocca Hajo | 20 | — | — | — | — | 1 | 3 25 | he is married since annuity to Davy's sister. |
| 18 | Sitchee | 16 | — | — | — | — | 1 | 3 25 | Paid to his father; going; got a canoe, &c. |
| 19 | Poaka | 15 | — | 1 | — | — | 1 | 3 25 | Paid to Blunt. |
| 20 | Tithlaga | 18 | — | 1 | — | — | 1 | 3 25 | Do. |
| 21 | Cealata | 14 | — | 1 | — | — | 1 | 3 25 | Do. |
| 22 | Paos Hajo | 25 | — | 1 | 2 | — | 4 | 3 25 | Do. |

| No. | | Name | | | | | | | | | Remarks |
|---|---|---|---|---|---|---|---|---|---|---|---|
| 23 | | Sathabothka | 25 | - | 3 | 25 | 1 | - | - | - | Do. This is the carpenter or boat-maker of a town. |
| 24 | | Miccohalye | 35 | - | 3 | 25 | 4 | - | 2 | 1 | Do. |
| 25 | | Ahlathaholya or Jno. Mealy | 30 | - | 3 | 25 | 4 | - | 2 | 1 | Do. |
| 26 | | Tommy Hajo or Jack Mealy | 25 | - | 3 | 25 | 8 | 1 | 4 | 2 | Do. one wife and two children dead since annuity. |
| 27 | | Ceatto | 12 | - | 3 | 25 | 1 | - | - | - | Do. |
| 28 | b | Teithka | 25 | - | 3 | 25 | 4 | - | - | 1 | Runaway to the Ofallee or Refarlee towns in the nation since May. |
| 29 | | Sialithkee | 18 | - | 3 | 25 | 1 | - | 2 | - | Paid to Cotchka Hajo; going to emigrate; got a canoe, &c. |
| 30 | | Sosa or Capt. Westcott | 12 | - | 3 | 25 | 1 | - | - | - | Do. |
| 31 | b | Waccihajo | 30 | - | 3 | 25 | 4 | - | 2 | 1 | Runaway to Ofallee or Refarlee since May. |
| 32 | b | Nocpostaga | 25 | - | 3 | 25 | 1 | - | - | - | Paid to Wacci Hajo; do. |
| 33 | | Sulletiga | 12 | - | 3 | 25 | 1 | - | - | - | Going; got a canoe, &c. |
| 34 | | Sockelosa | 30 | - | 3 | 25 | 1 | - | - | - | Paid to Chefotka; do. |
| 35 | | Cheewannee | 12 | - | 3 | 25 | 1 | - | - | - | do. |
| 36 | | Cotchee | 12 | - | 3 | 25 | 1 | - | - | - | Paid to Col. Blunt; do. |
| 37 | b | Johnny | 25 | - | 3 | 25 | 4 | - | 2 | 1 | Paid to Hoaspa; runaway to Ofallee since May; this is a half-breed rascal. |
| 38 | | Sammy | 30 | - | 3 | 25 | 5 | - | 3 | 1 | Ready to emigrate; got a canoe, &c. |
| 39 | | Chefixico Hajo | 30 | - | 3 | 25 | 3 | - | 1 | 1 | Do. |
| 40 | b | Socha Toathka | 18 | - | 3 | 25 | 1 | - | - | - | Runaway to Afallee since May. |
| 41 | b | Sintithchee | 15 | - | 3 | 25 | 1 | - | - | 1 | Do. |
| 42 | | Coleha Hajo | 25 | - | 3 | 25 | 3 | - | 1 | 1 | Ready to emigrate; got a canoe, &c. |
| 43 | | Tewisthka | 20 | - | 3 | 25 | 1 | - | 1 | 1 | Do. |
| 44 | | Totehiaka | 15 | - | 3 | 25 | 3 | - | - | 1 | Do. |
| 45 | | Emathachee | 24 | - | 3 | 25 | 1 | - | 2 | - | Do. |
| 46 | b | Pallapoosa | 23 | - | 3 | 25 | 3 | - | - | 1 | Paid to Hoaspa; do. |
| 47 | | Pairhosamthee | 35 | - | 3 | 25 | 2 | - | 2 | 1 | Runaway to Afarlee since May. |
| 48 | | Sinichee | 12 | - | 3 | 25 | 4 | - | - | - | Ready to emigrate; got a canoe, &c. |
| 49 | | Polo | 12 | - | 3 | 25 | 1 | - | - | 1 | Paid to Tommy Hajo; do. |
| 50 | b | Ocoska or Daniel | 30 | - | 3 | 25 | 2 | - | 1 | 1 | Runaway to Afarlee since May. |
| 51 | | Ellessa | 11 | - | 3 | 25 | 3 | - | - | - | Living with Vacca, and also his wife; called Asaha; going to Texas, |
| 52 | | Abothka | 11 | - | 3 | 25 | 1 | - | - | - | Ready to emigrate; got a canoe, &c. |
| 53 | | Smithka | 13 | - | 3 | 25 | 1 | - | - | - | Paid to Ma Hajo; do. |
| 54 | | Bathhajo | 11 | - | 3 | 25 | 1 | - | - | - | do. |
| 55 | | Inloathee, half negro | 65 | - | 3 | 25 | 1 | - | - | - | Runaway to Refarlee since May. |
| 56 | | Cotchaficcico | 30 | - | 3 | 25 | 5 | - | 3 | 1 | Ready to emigrate; got a canoe, &c.: |
| 57 | a | Ceoyanee | 15 | - | 3 | 25 | 1 | - | - | - | Paid to Hospa; sick; dead since May. |
| 58 | | Echeehola | 25 | - | 3 | 25 | 3 | - | 1 | 1 | Ready to emigrate; got a canoe, &c. |

## Census of Iola or Blunt's town, taken May, 1833—Continued.

| No. | Indian names. | Age. | Rank. | No. of wives. | No. of children living in family. | No. of slaves. | Total. | Quota of annuity. | Remarks and notes. |
|---|---|---|---|---|---|---|---|---|---|
| a 59 | Yatta Heyo | 25 | | 2 | 3 | | 6 | 3 25 | Ready to emigrate; wife and child died since May. |
| 60 | Ochifee | 15 | | | | | 1 | 3 25 | Ready to emigrate; got a canoe, &c. |
| 61 | Mingo | 25 | | | | | 1 | 3 25 | Do. |
| 62 | Saffo Buchee | 12 | | | | | 1 | 3 25 | Do. |
| 63 | Talmassa | 50 | | | | | 1 | 3 25 | Do. |
| b 64 | Timalatchee | 28 | | | 3 | | 4 | 3 25 | Runaway to Ofallee since May, 1833, and took his family. |
| b 65 | Kingithga | 13 | | | | | 1 | 3 25 | Do.          being his brother, |
| a 66 | Holochee | 12 | | | | | 1 | 3 25 | Dead since May. |
| a 67 | Tommy | 12 | | | | | 1 | 3 25 | Do. |
| Paid to Col. J. Blunt for five orphan boys at $1 each | | | | | | | 5 | 5 00 | |
| | | | | 34 | 58 | 9 | 173 | $289 50 | |

## RECAPITULATION.

| Warriors | - | - | - | - | - | 67 |
|---|---|---|---|---|---|---|
| Wives | - | - | - | - | - | 34 |
| Children | - | - | - | - | - | 58 |
| Negro slaves | - | - | - | - | - | 9 |
| Five orphan boys | - | - | - | - | - | 5 |
| | | | | | | 173 As above stated, |

Total number of souls at payment of annuity in May, 1833

N. B. Several children born since May; four or five should be added to this.

*Census of Iola or Blunt's town, taken May,* 1833—Continued.

(B.) Memorandum of deaths in Blunt's town since the treaty and peace to May, 1833.

| | |
|---|---|
| 1. Otalke Ahdo. | 11. Hotchofee. |
| 2. Old John Mealy. | 12. Ehakolo Chopka. |
| 3. Cumathlachee. | 13. Otalkejachee. |
| 4. Micco Hajo. | 14. Ischeeya. |
| 5. Alligator. | 15. Alluta Tustanuckee. |
| 6. Locko Emathla. | 16. Nimihometta Tustanukee. |
| 7. Elecologee. | 17. Eno Mattee. |
| 8. Ochofee Eckofee. | 18. Emafitchee. |
| 9. Stonuuggee. | 19. Mechackee. |
| 10. Soffickikee. | 20. Stalktanofkee.                      20 |

Total number of souls in Iola when treaty was formed   -   -   -   193
Some of these are women, some children, but I cannot distinguish them with certainty.

Memorandum of Blunt's negroes.

| | |
|---|---|
| 1. Joe aged 60 years. | 6. Herson 18 months old. |
| 2. Bob aged 45 years. | 7. Hamiah 12 years. |
| 3. Mundy aged 35 years. | 8. Cuffee 50 years. |
| 4. Cudjo aged 30 years. | Grace has stolen one negro. |
| 5. Melly aged 20 years. | Mealy owns one other negro woman. |

There are four or five free negroes in Iola, viz.

1. Old Adam aged 120 years. Blunt don't want to take him away, and is not willing to go.
2. Alumnee aged 60; living, and will go with Blunt.
3. Sampson 30; executed October 29, by Indians for rape and murder.
4. And one or two more who will go off with the party.

Deduct deaths in Iola since May, 1833, as above.

Warriors   -   -   -   .   -   -   -   -   4
Women   -   -   -   -   -   -   -   -   4
Children   -   -   -   -   -   -   -   -   5
                                                        —— souls 13.

Total of present population not including four or five small children born since May, 160 souls.

*b* Memorandum of runaways to Creek nation, as above.

$37 75 is the amount of annuity due those runaways, as above.
Warriors   -   -   -   -   11
Wives   -   -   -   -   5
Children   -   -   -   -   11

                                                    27 souls—deduct 27

Number ready to emigrate   -   -   -   137 souls
Add five young children born this summer   -   -   5
Number who will go off certainly   -   -   -   142 souls
289 50
35 75

$153 75 is due the emigrants according to the above apportionment of the annuity

*General statement respecting Indian towns on the Appalachicola, taken Indians in council, at*

| Name of town. | Name of chief. | Amount of annuity paid in May, 1833, to town. | Population belonging to these towns in May, 1833. | | | | | | | |
|---|---|---|---|---|---|---|---|---|---|---|
| | | | Chiefs and warriors. | Wives. | Children. | Slaves. | Free negroes. | Old women, widows, &c. | Others not heretofore included. | Total in May, 1833. |
| Totoivithla - | Econ Chatti Micco | $231 25 | 61 | 30 | 46 | 24 | 6 | 5 | - | 172 |
| Choconicla - | John Yellow Hair* | 226 00 | 46 | 23 | 26 | 1 | 4 | 5 { Totiga 1 9 boys 9 | | 115 |
| Attapulgus - | Tustanugge Hajo | 185 25 | 43 | 22 | 15 | - | - | 7 | - | 87 |
| | | $642 50 | 150 | 75 | 87 | 25 | 10 | 17 | 10 | 374 |

*The following towns are included in the treaty of* 1832,

| | | | | | | | | | | |
|---|---|---|---|---|---|---|---|---|---|---|
| Iola - - | Colonel Blunt - | $289 50 | 67 | 34 | 58 | 9 | †4 | - | 5 boys 5 | 168 |
| Spanewatka - | Davy Elliot - | 98 25 | 24 | 17 | 22 | - | - | - | - | 63 |
| | | $387 75 | 91 | 51 | 80 | 9 | †4 | - | 5 | 231 |
| Brought down from other towns - | | 642 50 | 150 | 75 | 87 | 25 | 10 | 17 | 10 | 374 |
| Total of all the towns - - | | $1,030 25 | 241 | 126 | 167 | 34 | 14 | 17 | 15 | 605 |

* See Yellow Hair's letter and list on the same, and copies of pay rolls, &c.
† These four are not included in the total.
‡ This sum of $37 75 is not included in the sum of $98 25, paid this town in May, 1833, to increase the general fund, and was distributed among all the towns. The sum of $16 25, away since the payment, &c. Blunt's Indians, who have gone to the Creek nation, have all The difference in the population (264) at time of treaty, and the aggregate of the number ad interim, &c.: 256 is the number stipulated in the treaty; but I presume it was not enough,

| | | | |
|---|---|---|---|
| Ready to emigrate | - | - | - | - |
| Gone to Creeks | - | - | - | - |
| Gone to Seminoles | - | - | - | - |
| Dead since treaty | - | - | - | - |

Present population, including deaths since the

*from the pay rolls and census of May, 1833, and from report of talk November 9, 1833.*

| Number of deaths since treaty in 1832, and prior to May, 1833. | Number of deaths since payment of annuity in May, 1833, as reported November 9, 1833. | Number gone to Creek nation, & their quota of annuity, according to pay roll of 1833. | | Number gone to Seminoles, and their quota of annuity, according to pay roll of May, 1833. | | No. willing & ready to emigrate, & am't of their annuity, according to pay roll of May, 1831. | | Population at treaty of 1832. |
|---|---|---|---|---|---|---|---|---|
| | | No. of souls. | Annuity. | No. of souls. | Annuity. | No. of souls. | Annuity. | No. of souls. |
| Not given - | Not given - | 3 | $3 25 | | | | | |
| Not given - | 14 | - | - | - | - | 16 | $64 50 | |
| Not given - | Not given - | - | - | - | - | 10 | 20 00 | |
| - | 14 | 3 | $3 25 | - | - | 26 | $84 50 | |

*concluded with Colonel Gadsden, by Blunt and Davy, &c.*

| | | | | | | | | |
|---|---|---|---|---|---|---|---|---|
| 20 | 13 | 27 | $35 75 | - | - | 142 | $153 74 | 193 |
| 8 | 6 | 23 | $37 75 | 13 | $16 25 | 21 | 72 00 | 71 |
| 28 | 19 | 50 | $73 50 | 13 | $16 25 | 163 | $225 74 | 264 |
| - | 14 | 3 | 3 25 | - | - | 26 | 84 50 | |
| 28 | 33 | 53 | $76 75 | 13 | $16 25 | 189 | $310 24 | 264 |

the absentees having ran away previously; although, since the treaty, their portionment went due those gone to the Seminole nation, is included in the $98 25, those Indians having gone gone since the annuity; and their portion is, therefore, included in the amount paid his town. new ready to go away, dead since treaty, ran away, &c., is owing to the birth of children or the difference is occasioned the same way, &c., or both.

| | | | | | | |
|---|---|---|---|---|---|---|
| - | - | - | - | - | - | 163 |
| - | - | - | - | - | - | 50 |
| - | - | - | - | - | - | 13 |
| - | - | - | - | - | - | 47 |

treaty, and runaways     -     -     -     273 souls.

## *General statement respecting Indian towns*—Continued.

The portion due the Appalachicola towns of the $5,000 annuity given by the treaty of Camp Moultrie, has generally been about $1,000. I had no data to govern me in paying the annuity, Major Phagan having all the old pay rolls; and, as the Indians told me lies, (as that they had always got $3 25, small boys and all,) I paid them $30 25 more than $1,000; and had those who were in the Creek nation from Davy's town been at home, and received their share, I should have overpaid the towns, in all, $68; $30 25 added to $37 75, their portion, being $68.

I think the following is a fair distribution of the annuity, considering the situation of the towns, advantages of each, &c. &c., as well as population; and, indeed, every thing which should be considered:

Allow Blunt $40, each second chief in his town $7, and each warrior $3, allowing eight second chiefs and excluding small boys, the portion to his town would not exceed    -    -    -    -    -    -    -    -    - **$270**

Allow Davy $35, each second chief in his town $7, and each warrior $3, allowing six second chiefs and excluding small boys, the portion to his town would not exceed    -    -    -    -    -    -    -    -    -    - **120**

*Allow Yellow Hair $30, each second chief in his town $7, and each warrior $3, allowing nine second chiefs and excluding small boys, the portion to his town would not exceed    -    -    -    -    -    -    - 

*Allow old Vaccapichassic $30, each second chief in his town $7, and each warrior $3, allowing nine second chiefs and excluding small boys, the portion to his town would not exceed    -    -    -    -    -    -    - **210**

Allow Tustanugge Hajo $30, each second chief in his town $7, and each warrior $3, allowing five second chiefs and excluding small boys, the portion to his town would not exceed    -    -    .-    -    -    -    -    - **170**

Allow Econ Chitte Micco $30, each second chief in his town $7, and each warrior $3, allowing six second chiefs and excluding small boys, the portion to his town would not exceed    -    -    -    -    -    -    -    - **230**

**$1,000**

If this rule of calculation is adopted, there cannot be any great difficulty in making the estimates of the amounts to be paid to the emigrating Indians. Under that rule the Executive, when Blunt embarks, by reference to the list from which the foregoing is taken, may ascertain the sum due him in a moment; and also in regard to Davy; and deduction can be made for those who do not go with him, and cannot be compelled to go.

Under this rule Yellow Hair's party will receive, altogether, $84, calculating Weeky, a boy, $3; of which $19 must be deducted from Attapulgus, and $65 from Choconicla.

In truth this rule—and leaving it in some measure to the discretion of the Executive to decide who are entitled and who not—is the only way to avoid confusion, embarrassment, error and difficulty. There will be no trouble in getting the Indians to agree to it.

---

* If Yellow Hair goes away, old Vacca will be head chief; and I would therefore allow this.

DISTRICT ATTORNEY'S OFFICE,
*Mobile, Alabama, November* 13, 1833.

SIR: I had the honor to receive, some days ago, your letter of the 17th ultimo, stating that the marshal of the southern district of Alabama had informed the War Department that suits would probably be instituted against him for removing intruders from the ceded lands, agreeably to the instructions of the Government; that the President had directed that when suits might be brought in the State courts, that I should cause them to be removed into the district court of Alabama, and there defended; and should there be suits which could not thus be removed, then I was further requested to conduct the defence of the marshal before the State courts, and when I could not attend, authorizing me to employ some competent person to perform that duty; and yesterday's mail brought me your letter of the 29th ultimo, containing further instructions in reference to the same subject. Your letter of the 17th of last month requires from me no further answer than to state, that I will strictly conform to the spirit of your instructions, attending in person to the defence of those who may be proceeded against civiliter for acts done in the performance of duty, and of their instructions, whenever I can do so without great professional sacrifice; and when prevented from attending, I will embrace the authority you have been pleased to delegate to me; and will, under your instructions, depute some competent person to perform the duty. As yet, I have heard of no suit against the marshal of the character anticipated. Your letter of the 29th ultimo enlarges the instructions contained in the letter which preceded it, and acquaints me that the President, under the circumstances alluded to, felt it an act of justice to the person exposed to the prosecutions referred to, to have every measure taken for their defence at the expense of the United States, and that as the prosecutions already instituted were of a serious character, I was further directed to repair to the scene of these proceedings, *unless* the duties expected of me could as well be performed without such personal examination, and to enter upon the defence of the persons who are or may be prosecuted for any act properly done in this matter, &c. &c., in addition to which, you have been pleased to favor me with your opinion of the construction, purview, and meaning of the 7th section of the act Congress passed March 2, 1833, entitled "An act further to provide for the collection of duties on imports;" a copy of which is furnished with your letter, with instructions to apply under it to the district judge of Alabama for writs of habeas corpus, &c.; and stating that the President had it in contemplation to despatch a gentleman of eminent legal attainments to aid me in this business, &c. In answer thereto, I have the honor to state that with every disposition to carry into effect, to the utmost of my humble ability, the just and benevolent views of the President in regard to those who have been unfortunately subjected to the prosecutions alluded to, I have to express my deep regret that your instructions have reached me at a period at which it is placed out of my power to repair to the scene of the proceedings adverted to without great professional injury. On the 25th instant our circuit court will commence its session, followed by the federal court, on the 2d Monday of December, and our supreme court on the first Monday of January next. Largely engaged as I am in those courts, it is not, I presume, expected that I should leave here, to the great injury if not ruin of clients, but a few days before their session, for a remote country, there probably to remain until after their close. As, however, the circuit court of Russell county, in the ceded territory, in which the indictments alluded to were found, closed its *semi-annual* session a few days ago, and will not again sit for six months, I am of opinion that the duties expected of me, at least for the present, can be nearly as well performed without my repairing to the ceded country as if I were to go there. If, however, any thing should occur hereafter which shall render it necessary for me under my instructions to repair to the territory in question, I will most cheerfully do so after the adjournment of the courts, and sooner if practicable. Suffer me to add in conclusion, that I will take great pleasure in co-operating with any gentleman of legal attainments that the Government may be pleased to despatch upon the business; and that I will contribute my best and most zealous exertions to accomplish the just views of the President in regard thereto, as expressed in your letters.

I have the honor to be,<br>
Very respectfully,<br>
Your most obedient servant,<br>
JNO. ELLIOTT.

Hon. Lewis Cass,
    *Secretary of War.*

---

Fort Mitchell,<br>
*November* 13, 1833.

Sir: During the investigation of Indian claims last winter, I advanced the cash for the claim of Susannah McIntosh and Jane Hawkins; their claim was for emigrating themselves and families at their own expense, for which they were entitled by the treaty to fifteen dollars a head.

They had supposed the money would be here to pay them at that time, and gave Benjamin Hawkins powers of attorney to collect for them, which was transferred to me by Hawkins, for which I advanced the cash.

If you are not satisfied, and will direct Col. Abert to investigate the matter while here, it will save me perhaps some trouble. I have laid out of the use of the money since last winter, and should be glad to receive my pay. I have no doubt but that I can furnish such evidence as will be satisfactory.

Your early compliance will much oblige me.

Respectfully, your obedient servant,<br>
THS. CROWELL.

Elbert Herring, Esq.

---

Executive Office, Tallahassee,<br>
*November* 13, 1833.

Sir: Enclosed is a letter from Nocose Aholo, or John Yellow Hair, head chief of Choconicla, who wishes to emigrate with a portion of his town at the same time with Blunt and Davy, and to the same place. It is proper that I should state to the department the following circumstances in explanation of his views and motives, and which show the feelings which influence him.

Yellow Hair is the son of old Yellow Hair, a chief, who has been dead some years. Originally the five towns composing the Appalachicola band, (although each town was ruled by a separate chief,) were all under the control of a head chief or king. Cochrane, when living, ruled the lowest town, called Span-e-wat-ka; Blunt ruled Iola; Emath-lockee-mia, dead, ruled Attapulgus; Old Yellow Hair, Choconicla and Econchattemico, commanded To-to-mithla. Yellow Hair was also head chief or king of all the towns. Blunt, Cochrane, and himself were friendly to the Americans; and their friendly conduct and valuable services, while the other chiefs were inimical to us, is, I doubt not, remembered by the President. Yellow Hair was an intrepid and talented Indian, and was greatly confided in by the American officers during the British and Seminole wars. He had received orders from the officer commanding on the Georgia and Florida frontier (Col. Arbuckle) to overhaul all boats passing his town on the Appalachicola. This order he executed zealously, and was of essential service. A canoe of Indians having refused, however, to come to his landing place, after being hailed, he fired into it, and it appearing that they were not hostile Indians, as supposed, but friendly, he was ignominiously broke by the aforesaid officer from his rank as head chief, and also as chief of Choconicla.

There are many gentlemen now living in Florida well acquainted with the circumstances, and all join in condemning the course pursued toward him as unjust, and an ill requital for his valuable and friendly services to us. He became dispirited in consequence, and soon after died. Blunt succeeded to the station of head chief of the towns, and Mulatto King, or Vacapichassee, the cowdriver, was made head chief of Choconicla, by *Colonel Arbuckle*. Mulatto is a half negro and Indian, was always a bitter enemy of the Americans, is bad tempered, insubordinate and mischievous, and would be more so but that he is totally without courage. This was the state of affairs at the treaty of Camp Moultrie in 1825, (see 7 vol. L. U. S. p. .) In the conclusion of that treaty the influence of Blunt and Cochrane in favor of our Government, I have learned from all the commissioners, was of great advantage; and it was in a great measure in consideration of their aid in making the treaty, and also their and Yellow Hair's past services, that the five towns on the Appalachicola river, and also Eiremathla town, were permitted to remain as stipulated in the additional article to said treaty. Since the making of the treaty Mulatto King has been continually endeavoring to break down Blunt's authority as head chief, and has succeeded in rendering it merely nominal. This is one reason why Blunt has been so ready to emigrate. Young Yellow Hair has always lived in what is called Mulatto King's reserve, upon the same settlement where his father formerly resided. This settlement is particularly specified in the aforesaid additional article of the treaty, and although in the same reserve is somewhat *separate* and distinct from Mulatto King's settlement. Young Yellow Hair has always been surrounded by his relations, who are hostile to Mulatto King. Some two years ago Mulatto King, upon a quarrel with Blunt, was broken by him, and *Hiatiga*, then second chief of the town, was made chief in his place, and *young Yellow Hair* second chief. The Governor considered Blunt had the authority to do so, and as Mulatto King had been guilty of divers acts of misconduct, had disobeyed orders, was impudent and troublesome, and behaved altogether quite badly, he did not disapprove Blunt's course. Hiatiga was an intelligent and smart Indian, and exceedingly well disposed, consulting the true interests of the town; he was in favor of going with Blunt to Texas. Blunt invited him and young Yellow Hair to go with his exploration party to Texas, and paid their expenses out of his own funds. Last spring Hiatiga, while on a visit to Gov. Duval on business, *died.* Yellow Hair, as second chief, succeeded of right to his station as head chief. In May last I visited the towns to pay the annuity; I found that no head chief had been formally recognized, Blunt delaying from motives of policy. He had been endeavoring for some time to *conciliate* Mulatto King, and had taken one of his daughters as a wife with that object in view. He thought perhaps by reinstating him as chief, he might be induced to become more friendly. He consulted me about it, and I agreed with him in opinion. Yellow Hair magnanimously said he would relinquish all his claim, if by such course old Mulatto could be induced to conduct the interests of the town. Such propositions were accordingly made to Mulatto King, and he *apparently* agreed to them, but the same *night* he was discovered by Blunt and his friends using his restored power mischievously, and he would not consent, as he had agreed to do, to abide by the wishes of a majority of the people of his town on the question of emigration, that majority, *at that time,* being *considerably* in favor of going with Blunt. Blunt and his friends (the said majority) in consequence, *the next morning before the payment of the annuity,* designated Yellow Hair as chief, and I recognized him as such; paid him as such; and he and his friends addressed a letter to Col. Gadsden, requesting him to come over and conclude a treaty accordingly. Mulatto King has a good farm, on the best land in the reserve, in cultivation. It is rented chiefly to white men, who till it for him for a portion I understand of the crop. The other Indians have but little, and are obliged to work for him and his white lessees, and they are kept miserably poor and half starved. Hence Mulatto King and the other Indians have entirely different interests and different feelings and views in regard to emigrating.

Mulatto King, assisted by his white friends interested to keep him here, commenced on Yellow Hair, promoted their united efforts to destroy his influence. He was enabled by the assistance of some whites to get a considerable quantity of goods shortly afterwards, which he distributed among the Indians to gain them over to his side, and by such aid and means, and by the propagation of false reports prejudicial to the country to which Blunt proposed to go, &c., he created considerable disaffection.

I regret being compelled to state that the temporary sub-agent, Mr. Pope, did not *in my opinion* use proper exertions to prevent such results, and on the contrary *I fear* rather sided with Mulatto King. Mulatto King, to effect his object, pretended now to be willing to emigrate, but pointed to Arkansas as the best country, &c. He declared, however, the other day to me, that he never had the least idea of going away, even if all his Indians left him, either to Arkansas or elsewhere. At his instance, however, Col. Gadsden was requested again to attend at his town, and did so.

To ascertain who was the chief, I understand he consulted the Indians then present, a majority of whom designated Mulatto King, who was also stated to be the chief by the sub-agent. I had regarded Yellow Hair as the head chief of the town, and think he should have been so considered.

Colonel Gadsden succeeded in concluding the last treaties, not yet ratified, and one of which is signed by Mulatto King, Tast Amigga Hago, who has succeeded Emathlochee, and also by Yellow Hair. Yellow Hair's letter *enclosed,* shows what was his belief of its provisions with regard to himself, and also those of the other chiefs; and the interpreters, Joe Miller and Black Jim, say they also thought it reserved Yellow Hair some land. If it had done so, Yellow Hair intended to have sold it forthwith to the Government, and have gone away with Blunt, and he made this proposition to me before he understood the treaty correctly. The sub-agent informs me, and I have no doubt, that the treaty was endeavored to be fully explained to the Indians by Colonel Gadsden; but the misunderstanding has I presume arisen in consequence of the employment of the interpreters above named, instead of Stephen Richards, the Government interpreter, to whom, however, I understand Mulatto King objected. If the Government will accede to Yellow Hair's proposition contained in his letter, and will make him a *present,* (if it must be considered so,) of such sum as will enable him to get off with his party and sustain them a few months, (and *what should be paid him* he is willing to leave to the department,) he will go away with Blunt. He refers all to the department, and will be satisfied with such allowance as may be made to him. If he could be allowed, in case he takes 26 souls, (as he proposes *at least* to do,) $1,000, and equipments, expenses, advance of annuity, &c., I think it would be about right. His removal will have a beneficial effect in regard to the rest.

Blunt considers the Government should aid Yellow Hair, in justice to him. He says, and correctly too, that when he made his treaty, although he requested, from motives of policy, (under a belief that the object could by such course be more easily effected,) that the towns should be treated with *separately, yet that it was promised him that every proper effort should be used to induce the other towns to go* WITH HIM. He is fearful that his small party may meet with difficulty, which would not occur was he reinforced by Yellow Hair and his warriors, in whom he places great confidence.

Yellow Hair's situation will be a most unfortunate one if the Government do not accede to his proposition. His friends and Mulatto King's cannot ever agree; and as the latter in the recent treaty has reserved only *his own* plantation, Yellow Hair must remain upon it, or become houseless and landless. Under these circumstances, when the friendship and services and ill usage of his father is considered, and the President was once acquainted with, and cannot have forgotten them; when his own correct deportment is taken into view, it does appear to me a case is presented which should not be overlooked by the Government.

I regretted the disagreement in opinion which occurred (as the department has been advised) between Col. Gadsden and myself, in regard to the recognition of Yellow Hair, and the more as I believed, and still believe that had he been looked to as the chief, there would have been but very little difficulty in getting three fourths of all the *towns* to have gone off with Blunt before this; and as the conclusion of the last treaty, according to the views of Mulatto King, and the misunderstanding in regard to it, has created serious obstacles to the execution of that with Blunt and Davy, as the department has been heretofore informed. When I solicited the designation of Colonel Gadsden to execute the treaty, it was because I believed there would difficulties arise which the person who made the treaty could best obviate, and that if he had undertaken that duty, *having both objects in view,* the whole course of policy observed towards all the towns would

88‡

have been *harmonious.* Colonel Gadsden, I am confident, considered he was pursuing the best course in regard to Mulatto King, but I am still convinced it was calculated not only to destroy the proper authority of the Executive over the Indians, to create embarrassments with Blunt and Davy, but was not either so consonant with justice and right as that I had adopted. I am happy, however, that the Government is afforded an opportunity, by acceding to Yellow Hair's proposition, to pevent all further dispute or difficulty among the chiefs and Indians, or between them and us on the subject.

I am, sir,<br>
Very respectfully,<br>
Your obedient servant,<br>
JAMES D. WESTCOTT, Jr.,<br>
*Acting Governor.*

Hon. E. Herring,<br>
  Commissioner *of Indian Affairs, Washington City.*

---

SUPERINTENDENCY OF INDIAN AFFAIRS,<br>
*St. Louis, November* 13, 1833.

SIR: I have the honor to forward to you herewith, by the hands of Col. George Croghan, (Inspector General,) the plats and field notes of the surveys of the Sac and Fox half-breed reservations, between the Mississippi and Demoine rivers, which have been lately returned to this office.

The duplicate plats of those surveys, together with a copy of the notes, are retained in this office, and will be delivered to the surveyor of the lands of the United States, for the States of Illinois and Missouri, should they hereafter be required in that office.

I have the honor to be,<br>
With high respect,<br>
Your obedient servant,<br>
WM. CLARK.

Hon. E. Herring,<br>
  Commissioner *of Indian Affairs.*

---

COLUMBUS, GEORGIA, *November* 14, 1833.

SIR: The counties in which any difficulties have ever existed in this quarter, or are likely again to occur, are those of Coosa, Talapoosa, Chambers, Macon, and Russell, all adjoining each other, and embracing the great mass of Indian settlements.

Coosa contains about 1,600 disposable half sections, after deducting section number 16 of every township, it being reserved to the State by the act of March 2d, 1819. The number of heads of families residing in this county is about 1,030, which will require all the land of the county but about 570 half sections.

Talapoosa county includes about 1,750 disposable half sections. The number of heads of families in this county is about 860, which will require all the land of the county but about 890 half sections.

Chambers county includes about 1,350 disposable half sections, and contains about 600 heads of families, who will require all the land of this county except 750 half sections.

Macon county includes about 1,750 disposable half sections, and contains about 1,500 heads of families, who will require all the land of this county except about 250 half sections.

Russell county includes about 1,600 disposable half sections, and contains about 1,230 heads of families, who will require all the land of this county but about 370 half sections.

Except in Talapoosa and Chambers there is probably not a township in all the extent of country embraced by these counties in which there are not, at this time, Indian settlements, and where there were not at the time the treaty was made. Some of the tribes are extremely diffused in their settlements; the Hillabees, for instance, of Talapoosa, and the Uchees of Russell.

The latter are not properly Creeks, but are a people long since conquered by them, and held in a state of servitude until the time of Colonel Hawkins, who got them manumitted, and settled them in the neighborhood where they now are. From that time they rated as Creeks, are covered by such in the treaty, and are entered upon the census roll.

From these facts you will perceive the extreme difficulty, if not impracticability of determining upon any general boundaries for these Indians exclusive of those in Chambers, except the boundaries of the county lines. I am therefore ready for the marshal now, in reference to all that part of the Creek country in which intruders may be troublesome, by giving for his guide the county lines, except in Chambers and in a few townships of Talapoosa. I can imagine no other safe guide short of the individual locations.

It may also be well to state that within these counties, Chambers excepted, the Indian rights will cover much more than all of the desirable land, and many of them, I fear, will have to be located upon barren sand hills and uninhabitable swamps. The white man, therefore, if he comes among them, must come upon their better reserves; there is no where else where he can live; and get there he will, I have no doubt, nolens volens, on the side of the Government.

Great numbers of the Indians are anxious to sell, and will do so, I have no doubt, so soon as located; and these are all ready to emigrate, and will go, I have no doubt, whenever the sales are approved and they receive the stipulated equivalent, if an agent were on the ground and ready to conduct them.

My efforts in locating will be immediately given to the counties I have named in this letter. Those above I mean to commit to the care of Judge Tarrant, with authority to employ as many assistants as may be necessary to insure a rapid execution of the work, contemplating, however, to visit him before he gets through.

With great respect, &c.,

J. J. ABERT,
*Lieutenant Colonel Topographical Engineers.*

Hon. Lewis Cass,
*Secretary of War.*

P. S. The information of this letter, in relation to the position of the Indians, is derived principally from those who surveyed the land.

LITTLE ROCK, A. T., *November* 14, 1833.

SIR: I arrived at this place on the 9th with the delegation of Chickasaws who are going west in search of a new home for their people; and on the evening after my arrival at this place, I was violently attacked with the pleurisy, but have so far recovered as to be able to sit up.  At this point we had some horses to shoe and some clothing to procure, also provision to last us to Fort Towson, which duty has been performed by the young men who accompany me.  And on yesterday the delegation moved out ten miles to a better range for their horses.  On their setting out, the old chiefs waited on me at my room, and positively said they would not leave me while there was hope of my being able to travel, if they had to wait on me for weeks.  I mention this circumstance to apprise you how hopeless I think it is to depend upon those people to procure a home for themselves, unless aided by every means in the power of Government.

The party consists of the old chiefs and captains, and some of the most intelligent in the nation, and seem to be sensible of the condition of their people and the necessity of procuring a new home for them; they seem to be in good cheer and fine spirits, but from what I can learn are lacking in concert or any fixed principle of operation; but I hope to be able to remedy those deficiencies before we enter the frontier.  I am requested by the head chiefs of the nation, as well those with me as those left behind, to say to you that a large portion of the nation has become dissatisfied with the late treaty, and wish it so amended as to embrace the amendment proposed by Generals Coffee and Eaton to the delegation last winter at Washington City.

I am directed to say that is all the alteration wished for, and that it is not their wish to interfere with great principles of the treaty; and I am requested to ask permission of the department to permit me to bring on a delegation to Washington, to consist of eight or ten persons, immediately on our return, to effect the amendment proposed, in order that it may be laid before the Senate at the next Congress for their sanction; or they would respectfully leave it to the department to send a commission to the nation for the above purposes.

They request me to say to you, that could the amendment asked for be made during the ensuing spring, that it would quiet the nation, and that all parties would unite in removing their people to a new home.

I should be happy to receive your instructions upon this subject on my return to the agency, (of which you shall be advised in due time), in order that I might apprise the chiefs of it, as they will be anxious to know the result.

The disease under which I have labored for the last five days is so far removed that I flatter myself that I will be able to proceed on our journey to-morrow, and continue it without further interruption.

At the request of the chiefs, Mr. William S. Henderson, of Memphis, has been added to the two gentlemen appointed to accompany me; and it gives me pleasure to say that all is disposed to make the journey as comfortable as possible, and with all the means in their power to promote its objects.

I am, with great respect,
Your obedient servant,
BENJ. REYNOLDS,
*Indian Agent.*

Hon. ELBERT HERRING,
*Commissioner of Indian Affairs.*

FORT MITCHELL, *November* 14, 1833.

SIR: Since my last I have made another effort to obtain from the clerk of Russell county copies of the indictment, and other proceedings of the circuit court for that county, against the officers and men of this garrison.

The clerk was not at home, but I was informed by a young man that orders had been given by the solicitor that the records and proceedings of the court should not be seen, nor any copies of them given. He told me, however, that a Tuscaloosa paper contained copies of the judge's letter to the governor, and of all the papers except the indictments. This paper I have obtained, and find that the governor has sent, with his late communication to you, copies of them.

I presume when he receives your answer he will take his measures; and if he determines these prosecutions shall be enforced, he will order out the militia.

In such a state of things he will, perhaps, before he issues such an order, appoint a new sheriff here, and have process issued on the indictments against Lieutenant Manning and the men, and possibly have the attachment renewed against Major McIntosh.

By the laws of Alabama bail is allowed in all criminal cases, "except in capital cases where the proof is evident or the presumption great." I am well informed that, both here and at Montgomery, the general sentiment is declared that they cannot be bailed. Here in this county there is but one justice of the peace. He is an intruder, who has a fine plantation between here and Columbus. He was here yesterday, and declared publicly at the tavern, that the killing of Owen was a base and inhuman murder. If bail should be refused they must go to jail, and the jail to which they would be sent is in Montgomery.

If the civil process of Alabama can be thus used, it is obvious that the military force here cannot be employed by the Government of the United States for the purpose for which they intend it, and the Government may as well withdraw the troops and abandon its purpose. If the commander of the post, and his officers and men, can be thus disposed of, what is to prevent this justice of the peace from issuing warrants, and committing all the officers and men of the post for trespasses or assaults upon the intruders, or any other offences with which they may be charged. The intruders also may harass them with civil process, and require surety of the peace, &c., and the justice may allow or refuse bail as he pleases. I am sensible, however, that we must submit to some wrong, indeed to every thing that has any appearance of legality. But if the process of Alabama is grossly abused, and applied to defeat a lawful object, and a plain duty of the General Government, and to take from them the only power by which they can act efficiently in accomplishing such object and fulfilling such duty, why shall not the officers of Government assert the right of the Government on its own soil—the right of removing intruders who use those or any means of obstructing the Government in its lawful purpose? If the sheriff of Russell county has a right, because Alabama has jurisdiction here, to execute the process of her courts, the marshal of the United States has a right, if this sheriff is an intruder upon her lands, to remove him. If these two rights are in conflict, as they evidently will be, is the Government of the United States to yield?

I have made these suggestions for your consideration, in order that you may determine whether, if such a state of things occurs as a palpable abuse on the part of the State authorities of her legal process, for the purpose of defeating the Government's measures, your officers may not be instructed to meet this process, *even though legal as to its forms*, with the assertion of the Government's right to remove the persons coming with such process, as intruders, from the public lands. These people are all residing here by the indulgence of the Government; shall it not withdraw that indulgence when it is thus abused?

In the present state of things, however, we are to consider all legal process as not to be opposed or evaded by the assertion of this right to remove intruders, or in any other way.

I have therefore advised the officer, Lieutenant Manning, and the men who are indicted, to submit to the process that may issue on the indictment, and to offer bail; and if the bail is refused, to submit to the commitment.

If the attachment against Major McIntosh should be renewed by the clerk, or by the order of the solicitor, or by the judge out of court, I consider it not legal process, and have so advised him.

I have thought it best to request the district attorney and the marshal to meet me at Tuscaloosa, for which place I am to set out in the stage to night. I have not much apprehension that any process will be served until I can arrange with the district attorney as to our course of proceeding, and return. But I have told the gentlemen here if such a thing could occur, and they should feel any difficulty as to how they should act, to endeavor to prevail on the officers to hold up the process till I return, by giving him security that they will then appear before him. The present coroner, if such process comes to him, they have no doubt, will grant this indulgence.

I hope the Legislature of the State will see the necessity of preventing the conflicts that must occur from the present state of things; at all events I shall be able there to learn whether there is any prospect of the State's persisting in opposing the Government in the course which it is now taking to fulfil the stipulations of the treaty. I shall require the marshal to send a deputy to this vicinity forthwith. There is now no means of redressing whatever outrages may be committed upon the Indians; nor of letting it be seen that the measures of the Government now in operation here must not be frustrated.

Colonel Abert is preparing to commence his surveys, and hopes to be ready in time. I will write again from Tuscaloosa.

I am, sir, with great respect,

Your obedient servant,

F. S. KEY.

Hon. Lewis Cass,
    *Secretary of War.*

The three men named in the newspaper as indicted are still in the garrison; all the others composing the detachment, except one, and among them the man who shot Owen, have deserted.

---

Fort Leavenworth, *November* 14, 1833.

Sir: I have the honor to inform you that every thing goes well in our council of peace; all the neighboring tribes have made peace and returned home, except the Kansas and Ioways. It was too expensive to detain them; those who yet come in and sign the articles are equally parties.

The Kansas have just arrived, well prepared for council. I apprehend no difficulty with them. The Ioways and Omahaws have more dissatisfaction. The Ioways are expected tomorrow.

A limited delegation of Pawnees, Ottoes, and Omahaws accompany me to Fort Gibson, to make peace with the Osages, Creeks, Cherokees, &c.

The operations here must benefit the Indians who have emigrated, and induce many others to come.

The speeches of the Indians breathe a good spirit. My hopes now are upon Congress, and I would gladly labor with you a few months to digest and introduce some of the improvements suggested in my former letters; but my services, I suppose, will be required at Fort Gibson to close the remaining business of the commission, and I work cheerfully anywhere.

Yours, respectfully,<br>HENRY L. ELLSWORTH.

Honorable E. Herring,
   *Indian Commissioner, Washington.*

---

Fort Mitchell, *November* 15, 1833.

Sir: I was unable to leave this place last night, as I had intended, the stage being full. If I am disappointed again tonight, I shall endeavor to make some other arrangement.

I have obtained all the information I can in this neighborhood as to the number of the intruders upon the Creek lands. There has never been a census in the new counties, but there is an assessment of the inhabitants now making, which will be completed in a week or two, by which their numbers will be ascertained. Their votes have been taken on several occasions, and the numbers taken in all the counties may be had at Tuscaloosa.

There can be no doubt of the numbers being greatly overrated by the Governor. In Talladega county, which is very fertile and much cultivated by whites, they polled upwards of eight hundred votes; and in Chambers county, between three and four hundred. I have met with nobody who does not say that there are more whites in those two counties than in all the others in the nation. These votes were taken at a contested sheriff's election; and as many of the settlers are men without families, it is generally thought that the whole white population of those counties would not exceed more than treble the number of voters. This would make the whole number of whites in the nation about seven thousand. The Indians are numbered at twenty-three thousand; and several intelligent persons who have been much through the nation assure me that the whites cannot amount to more than one third of the number of Indians.

In this county (Russel) there are but two company beats, as they are called, and not more than sixty voters. There is to be an election here on the 23d for a justice of the peace; and they seem, from the brigade order of General Scott, to be organizing and appointing officers in all the counties.

As to the character of these intruders, there are some I hear of in this neighborhood who are peaceable and well disposed; most of them are violent and clamorous. The universal opinion seems to be, that if the officer and men could have been taken, they would certainly have been executed. I have heard of several such declarations having been made, recently by men who were on the grand jury, and they put it upon the ground that resistance to the military is lawful; that they have no right to use force; and if they do, and death ensues, that it is murder. They avow their expectation to carry their point by bringing the laws of the State to bear both upon the military and the deputy marshal, and the Indians. I leave you to judge what can be done, with such means in the hands of such men, for the protection of the Indians. They will set up their pretended contracts, and send them to jail by scores.

Whether these poor creatures foresee these dangers, or are sufficiently pressed by their present miseries, they are brought to the determination to leave the country. I am well assured that an emigrating agent here could now take off nine tenths of them.

I have endeavored to ascertain whether they could, under such circumstances, be prevailed on to send a deputation of their chiefs to Washington. The universal opinion here is, that it would be impossible  The speculators and their agents have them completely in their power. Ben Marshall thought that some of the chiefs who had been heretofore adverse to selling would perhaps agree to go to Washington, to see what bargain they could make with the Government for their own reservations; and that if they returned, and found that they could get a fair price put upon their lands, which the Indians might take if they could not sell on better terms here, it would induce the others to sell out; and that if an agent was then appointed to come here and certify as to their contracts according to the provisions of the treaty, and authorized to buy for the Government, all the reservations might be disposed of, and the Indians removed. We mentioned one or two chiefs as likely to agree to this. Colonel Abert has proposed it to one of them, and also to another not mentioned by Marshall, but they declined it. I think it, however, almost certain, that if Congress would authorize the sending out an agent with such powers, the lands would nearly all be sold immediately, and the Indians removed.

You may judge of the character of the intruders in Talladega from the resolutions passed at their meeting. I am told that the great majority of them are well disposed, and treat the Indians with kindness. There has been a meeting also at Chambers county, called by the factious and violent, and a lawyer from Columbus attended, and attempted to excite them by a speech. He was replied to and put down by an old gentleman, (one of the intruders,) who exhorted them to trust to the indulgence of the Government, and submit to whatever was required of them. He succeeded in confounding the agitators, and no resolutions were passed.

I suppose the Legislature will see the necessity of bringing this matter to an issue, and either deny or assert the right of the United States to keep possession of their lands. If they admit the right, they will of course control their Governor and their courts, and oblige them to protect and respect the Government officers and agents, and aid them, instead of obstructing them, in the discharge of their duties. The danger is that they will not like to take the responsibility, but leave the matter as it is to the Governor and the civil authority. If they pursue this course, they might as well deny the right of the Government, and call on their Governor to resist it. It must produce the same result, and can be met only in the same way. I hope to be able to form some opinion of their views.

   *   *   *   *   *   *   *   *

I shall endeavor to make some arrangement with the district attorney for the safety of the persons now under prosecution, and to guard as far as practicable against further efforts of the same kind against the persons in the public employment. The distance of the United States judge from the place of these prosecutions, and the contempt with which I am sure his authority would be treated by the officers of the State here, will, I fear, render this very difficult to accomplish.

I am, sir, &c.,<br>F. S. KEY.

Honorable LEWIS CASS.

---

TALLADEGA COUNTY, ALABAMA,<br>Mardisville, November 15, 1833.

SIR: Your letter of the 17th ultimo has been received I am pleased with the appointment of Col. Abert to assist in locating the Indian reservations. It will be an arduous task, and require men of intelligence, firmness, and of incorruptible integrity, to do it right.

Col. Abert and Mr. Bright have not yet arrived; as soon as I am notified of their arrival I will immediately attend them, and proceed to business.

It is much to be regretted that the Indians have heretofore refused to sell their reservations to the General Government, and I have thought that a plan might be adopted which would succeed, but have been fearful to mention it to the department, not knowing the views of the Government on the subject and the means necessary to effect it.

Very respectfully,<br>I am, &c.,<br>LEONARD TARRANT.

To ELBERT HERRING, Esq.,
 Commissioner Indian Affairs.

---

TALLAHASSEE, FLORIDA, November 16, 1833.

SIR: In pursuance of instructions from the acting Governor of this Territory, I have the honor to transmit you the enclosed; and am,

With great respect,<br>Your obedient servant,<br>WILEY THOMPSON,<br>Agent for Florida Indians.

Hon. E. HERRING,
 Commissioner Indian Affairs.

---

Memorandum of conversation with Col. Blunt and Davy Elliott, by Mr. Westcott, October 28, 1833. S. Richards interpreter. Present, General Thompson, agent, and several other gentlemen.

Mr. Westcott stated to him he had sent for him and Davy, to know why they had not got ready.

Col. Blunt said he had intended to have gone off in July, and had got nearly ready, but that in consequence of Col. Gadsden's treaty with the other

89‡

towns in June, his people became dissatisfied and would not go, and many ran away; that Col. Gadsden told him also he had better wait till fall. He said he would have had no difficulty in getting off in July but for the last treaties, and the inducements held out for his Indians to go to those towns. He complained a good deal, that good faith had not been observed towards him; that he had always been a friend to the whites, that Mulatto King had been their enemy; and Col. Gadsden now befriended Mulatto. He said he would have gone off in July without his son, relying on the promises of Col. Gadsden and Mr. Westcott that he should be sent; but said their promises to endeavor to induce the other Indians had been broken, and he would not now rely upon them any longer; and would not go until he saw his son with his own eyes.

Mr. Westcott told him his son would be here as soon as possible, and that he had been written for several times; and he showed him the letter. After considerable conversation on this point, Blunt was somewhat better satisfied, but declared he would not stir a step till he saw his son, and did not care for the consequences. He said he knew all the power the white people had over him, and that he could live in Florida a citizen if he chose, although the Governor should forbid him; and that the Government could not drive him away. After being reasoned with some time, and the dishonor of breaking the treaty enforced upon him, he said he never had the slightest idea of breaking the treaty; he was always anxious to go; he now wanted to go; he would not stay if the whites wanted him to. He had been getting ready since the treaty; but he said he had been deceived, and trifled with, and imposed upon. All the whites knew he was their friend in the Seminole war, and in the British war. General Jackson knows it; Col. Gadsden knows it; Gov. Duvall knows it. Old Mulatto King was their enemy; he was always mine for that reason. When I was General Jackson's guide, he was skulking in the swamps, and in the negro fort with the hostile Indians and Spaniards, and Indians and negroes. I have been, since Yellow Hair's death, head chief of these towns; Governor Duvall knows it. I had a right to break old Walker, and I did so; his Indians wished it: I made Hiatiga chief; Governor Duvall said I was right. Hiatiga died, and I made Yellow Hair chief; you said I did right. But now Col. Gadsden and Judge Pope side with Walker, and make a treaty with him. They have broke me as head chief; Walker says so. If they had made the treaty with Yellow Hair, almost all the people of Attapulgus and Choconiela would have gone with me to Texas. Yellow Hair still wants to go, but Walker says Col. Gadsden made him chief, and he will not let his people go; and my people run away to his town, and he harbors them. He says Arkansas is the best place, and that they can stay three years, and then go or not as they please. I have heard Col. Gadsden say the reserve was granted by the treaty of Camp Moultrie to Mulatto King; Col Gadsden knows it was granted, as he then told me, and as the Governor told me also, in reward for Cochrane and old Yellow Hair, and my services and friendship. Old Yellow Hair had always been friendly, and a good warrior for the whites, and they knew it; and although he had been broke, they included his place in consequence of his being a good Indian; if you look at the treaty you will see it is so. Cochrane is dead; Yellow Hair is dead; and Col. Gadsden has forgotten his friendly talks to me. John Yellow Hair wants to go with me now, and has got ready; but he has no money.

Relying in what Col. Gadsden told me he would do, I paid Hiatiga and Yellow Hair's expenses to Texas with my exploring party, and now they can't go.

Mr. Westcott told him that Yellow Hair might go in the place of the people who had run away; he also told him that some white people, and among others Col. Gadsden, thought he was willing his people should go away, and then he would go away with all the money; and he told him if this was his notion, he would be deceived, as he would not be paid only in proportion for those he took.

Blunt said the white people who said this were fools. Did they suppose he would go to Texas without warriors, unable to protect himself? It was not true. Every Indian in his town, and every white man there knew it was not true, and knew the trouble he had put himself to to get his people to go with him; and that but for Walker's treaty there would have been no difficulty; since then they run away like turkeys, some to Tampa, some to the Creek nation, some to the upper towns, and some he did not know where. Col. Gadsden had broke him by that treaty, and he had now no power. He said Col. Gadsden had done what caused his Indians to run away, and he ought to be blamed for it, and not him. The President or governor should tell Col. Gadsden to hunt them up and bring them back, and make them go. He said it was very unjust that he should suffer, and his money be kept back when he was not to blame.

Mr. Westcott told him he made inconsistent excuses, and asked him why he did not tell Col. Gadsden this when he saw him in September; and that Col. Gadsden had told him (since) that at the time he (Blunt) was satisfied, and made no trouble.

Blunt says: I did not talk to him much. I had nothing to do with him. He had promised me a boat; and I asked him for it, and he said he would get it. I did not want much talk with him. He is mistaken.

Mr. Westcott told him Col. Gadsden said he told him that he would pay for his robberies; and that Blunt told Col. Gadsden that he, Mr. W , had promised he should be paid for them. Blunt said, in answer, that Col. Gadsden did not understand him. I told him that you said you would try to get it for me, but I did not say you had promised it. You wrote, in your letter to me, that you could not say whether the Government would allow me or not. I asked him to help me: he is wrong. I did not want much talk with him, for he had not used me well.

Mr. Westcott told Blunt that he must go away this winter. The President had the power to drive him off, and he would do it if he violated his treaty. He was mistaken in his right to stay, &c , &c. Considerable conversation occurred on this point, and Blunt stated again he was ready to go as soon as he got his money and his son arrived; but, as he had made no crop, he must have an advance of $1,500 or $2,000 now, to aid him in getting provisions, or he could not get and keep his Indians together, &c. He said he wanted the governor to go over and see the other town, and give them a talk, and make them send his Indians back, and tell them they had not Col. Gadsden's authority for their course, as they said they had; make them behave themselves, &c., &c.

Mr. Westcott told him he would go over on the 9th of November, and hold a talk at Walkerstown, and see all was set right, &c.

Blunt asked what the treaty with Walker was. He said, after it was read to him, that he had heard the Indians say it was different; and he requested Mr. Westcott to fetch it over and explain it to the Indians. He said Yellow Hair told him to tell Mr. Westcott he wanted to go off with their party, and would take twenty or thirty Indians with him, but he wanted some money. He said he wanted to know how, if he went away, his pay for the robbery of Stafford, and that of Grace, and Phagan's debt, would be paid him. *Mr. Westcott told him he had written to Washington about it, and, if the Government agreed to pay him, they would send it to any place near Texas he might wish. He then said there was a United States fort on the road from Natchitoches to Gains's ferry, about twenty-five miles this side of the Sabine, where he could get it, and Mr. Westcott assured him it should be sent to him.*

Mr. Westcott explained to him what was necessary to be done in regard to evidence of his claim, and advised him to employ an agent to collect the proof, and Blunt stated he would employ Mr. Snell. Mr. Westcott told him he would advise with Mr. Snell, and aid him; and when he went over on the 9th of November, would inform him more particularly about what was necessary. After a good deal of other conversation, Blunt and Davy agreed to go off in ten days after. Blunt arrived, but they begged for an advance on account of their payment, to purchase provisions, without which they could not keep the Indians of their towns together

Mr. Westcott said he would decide as to this on the 9th.

*Talk with the Indians at Appalachicola, in Council, on the 19th of November, 1833.*

Friends and brothers: Listen to my talk. Your great father, the President of the United States, is anxious to secure your present and future welfare, prosperity, and happiness. He has always complied with his promises and treaties made to and with you. He will continue to watch over your interests, and will faithfully comply with all his promises to you. While he is thus anxious for your welfare, and prompt in a faithful compliance with all his promises to you, he expects and requires on your part an honest and faithful compliance with all your treaties and promises. There was a treaty made at Camp Moultrie: do you remember it? According to the stipulations in the additional article to that treaty, by which you possessed the reserves where you are now located, if you commit any outrage, or should be guilty of any misconduct, the President will have a right to drive you off the reserves, and send you to the Seminole country: this I hope you have not forgotten. John Blunt and Davy Elliott made a treaty some time ago with Colonel Gadsden: their towns are bound by that treaty, and all their people must go with them. It is said that the chief of the other towns encourage the people of Blunt's and Davy's towns to run off, and that some are harbored in the other towns. All who belonged to Blunt's and Davy's towns, at the formation of Blunt's treaties, are bound by that treaty. The chiefs of the other towns must not permit Blunt's or Davy's people to stay among them; they must drive them off. The governor, who is present, has a list of the Indians of the different towns: he will presently inquire to know where they are. It is said some are in the Creek nation; they must be brought back, and not suffered to go out of the reserves. Remember the consequences which, according to your treaty at Camp Moultrie, will follow misconduct. Those of Blunt's and Davy's town who have gone off will not receive any annuities unless they return to their own towns. They wont get their expenses paid hereafter; the governor will take down their names; they must be given up to Blunt, and go with him; they will not be suffered to stay. Since the formation of Blunt's and Davy's treaty many of their people have died; some have left their towns; two hundred and fifty-six then belonged to Blunt's and Davy's towns; there are not so many now. John Yellow Hair, with his people, desire to go with Blunt; others in the other towns wish to go; they must not be interrupted. You remember that you promised Colonel Gadsden that all who wished to go might do so; you must not depart from your promise; if you do, it will be misconduct, for which your great father may send you off the reserve. All who wish to go with Blunt and Davy from the other towns can give their names to the acting governor, and he will write about them to the War Department. Blunt has a right to take away with him all his family and all who wish to go with him. No person shall be suffered to interfere with him. No one who wishes to go must be disturbed. Remember your promise to Colonel Gadsden, and remember the consequence of misconduct. I will be displeased if you interfere with any of Blunt's people, or persuade them or any others not to go; all who are in Blunt's and Davy's towns are bound to go, and all in the other towns who wish to go have a right to do so; and any attempt to prevent any one going would be a fraud upon the United States, and would displease your great father, the President. Blunt and his people go off shortly, so as to be able to make a crop in their new abode the ensuing year. He has delayed too long already, and the time has expired in which he was to go.

Friends and brothers: You are bound by treaties and promises to stay within your reserves; you must comply with your promises. Bad white men bordering upon your boundary sometimes disturb you. When they do so, you must not attempt to take power into your own hands; your great father, the President, has promised to protect you; he will protect you. He has told the governor; he has sent me as agent, and Judge Pope as sub-agent, to protect your rights. Where differences arise between yourselves, or between you and the whites, make it known to the governor, myself, or Judge Pope, you shall be protected.

Friends and brothers: Your great father, the President, has sent a law to you, forbidding the use of whiskey; he has seen the bad effects of its use among his white children; he has marked its destruction of the health, the character, the purse, and the peace of families and neighborhoods among the whites; and he knows that it produces the same effects among his red children. He knows that it will make you quarrelsome, and poor, and wretched, and miserable; that your young men, instead of becoming good and honorable braves and warriors, will, by the use of whiskey, be made sickly, and lazy, and poor, and mean. He, therefore, desirous of your prosperity and happiness, says you must neither use it nor suffer it to be brought within your reserves. He has seen the good effects of the same law in the army and navy of the United States, and he knows that the use of whiskey will injure alike his white and his red children; and therefore not only requires your obedience to his law, but wishes to know how you approve of it. I wish all the chiefs and sub-chiefs to answer. You will be expected to obey and enforce it. You must not suffer any to be brought after this into the reserves, either in bottles, jugs, or casks. You must break the bottles and jugs, knock the heads out of the casks, and throw the contents on the ground.  Before I leave you, I wish to impress on your minds again that you must not in any way molest any person who wishes to go with Blunt or his warriors; but, on the contrary, persuade all to go who desire to go.  By thus complying with your treaties and promises, you will insure the friendship and protection of your great father, the President. If you do not listen to my talk, if you violate your treaties and promises, he will be displeased.  Remember the consequences of misconduct.

Conipeahola, on behalf of the upper towns, said they had listened to the talk; it was good and should be remembered.  The treaty of Camp Moultrie is remembered by all the chiefs and Indians.  All the stray Indians shall be sent back to their towns; no one shall be stopped.  The wives of the Indians of the lower towns who were taken from the others by the Indian laws can be taken by their relations.  By the Indian laws Vaca had a right to take back his daughter, Blunt's wife.  The Indians should observe their own laws; the whites have no right to alter them while we do not break their laws; but we will mind your talk.

All the chiefs said the law prohibiting whiskey was a good one, and they were glad of it.

John Yellow Hair said he wanted to go off with Blunt, and was ready, with twenty-five others, to go off, if the Government would pay him for his land and expenses; and he wished the acting governor to write a letter for him to that effect.  The acting governor informed him he had no land reserved to him by the last treaty with Colonel Gadsden, except his interest as one of the town in the section and half reserved to Mulatto King for the use of the town; and he explained to him the treaty.  Yellow Hair stated he thought the treaty reserved him a section when he signed it, and was so told by the interpreters, Joe Miller and Black Jim, or he would not have signed it.  The interpreters being present, and being called upon, said he told the truth, and they so understood the treaty; and all the other chiefs present said they so understood it when it was made.  Joe Miller made several protestations of having been mistaken, and appeared to be much frightened, and considerable excitement was created by the discovery of the misunderstanding of the treaty.  Yellow Hair, after consultation with his friends and the other chiefs, requested the acting governor to write a letter setting forth the facts to the President, and asking for an allowance in his favor; which was done, and signed by himself and other chiefs, after being read to them and corrected.  After adjustment of several other matters of business respecting claims for negro slaves, the council broke up.

WILEY THOMPSON,
*Agent for Florida Indians.*

---

DISTRICT ATTORNEY's OFFICE,
*Mobile, Alabama, November* 16, 1833.

Sir: I received by this morning's mail your letter, dated "Fort Mitchell, the 12th November," instant, requesting me to meet you at Tuscaloosa as early as possible, for the purpose of conferring in reference to the important and interesting matters embraced in your letter, in pursuance of instructions to that effect from the War Department.  In reply thereto, permit me to state that no one can be more solicitous than myself to discharge the obligations I have contracted towards the General Government, or feel a more earnest desire to promote the great ends it has in view by your mission. But, sir, situated as I am, the sessions of the circuit court of this county and the district court of the United States for this district both approaching, the former to commence on the 25th instant, the latter on the 2d Monday of December next, I cannot absent myself from this city before their adjournment without violating the obligations I have contracted towards my clients, and entailing upon myself professional injury, if not ruin. I flatter myself with the hope, however, that you may have it in your power to settle the unpleasant controversy now existing between the General and State Governments without my presence; and upon this subject I would respectfully recommend to you to confer with the following senators, Hogan, Lyon, Chapman; and with the following representatives, Hopkins, Ormond, Jackson, Creegh, Rains, Hallett, Chamberlain, and the delegation generally from the northern part of the State. In regard to the persons unfortunately subjected to criminal prosecutions, referred to in your letter, more perhaps can be done for their protection here than at Tuscaloosa, as the judge of the district court of the United States for this district will be here by the second Monday of December next, if indeed they should shortly be in custody.

I am, sir, very respectfully,

Your most obedient servant,

JNO. ELLIOTT.

Francis S. Key, Esq.

---

District Attorney's Office, Mobile, Ala.,

*November* 17, 1833.

Sir: I have the honor to acknowledge by the mail of yesterday the receipt of your letter of the 31st October last, transmitting a copy of the instructions addressed by you on the day last mentioned to Francis S. Key, esq., and requested my co-operation with him in carrying them into effect.

By the same mail I also received a letter from Mr. Key, dated "Fort Mitchell," the 12th November instant, advising me of his arrival there; that he intended to leave in a few days for Tuscaloosa, as it might be desirable to make some application to the legislature (now in session) or to the governor, requesting me to meet him at Tuscaloosa by the time of his arrival there; and if I could not reach Tuscaloosa by the time he named, then to forward a letter stating when he might expect me, in order that he might have my aid and co-operation in a mission the success of which is so greatly to be desired. In reply to which, and by the mail of yesterday, I addressed to him a letter, a copy of which is herewith enclosed. Convinced, as I am, that the positions assumed by the President and yourself in regard to the imperative obligations imposed upon the Federal Executive by the Creek treaty are incontrovertible, I regret very deeply that the circumstances detailed in my letters, and over which I can exercise *no control*, prevent me, *for the moment*, from affording that *immediate* active agency and co-operation to the Government which it has been pleased to ask from me. Animated, notwithstanding, by a deep and earnest solicitude, as far as may be in my power, for the success of the contemplated action of the

Government in this respect, and for the removal of the unpleasant controversy between the General and State Governments, I will leave here the moment I can do so without violating the sacred and imperative obligations of professional duty, which I trust will be during the second week of the session of our courts. More than this, in my peculiar position, and as the Government is so ably represented by Mr. Key, I trust will not be required by the spirit of my instructions.

I have the honor to be,

Very respectfully, sir,

Your most obedient servant,

JNO. ELLIOTT.

Hon. LEWIS CASS,
     *Secretary of War.*

----

STATE OF GEORGIA, HARRIS Co., *November* 18, 1833.

DEAR SIR: If it is not assuming too much for an humble citizen, as I am, to address one of your grade and rank in this great republic, on a local matter, and that without the pleasure of a personal acquaintance, I would fain make some inquiries respecting the territory now in the possession of the Creek Indians.

I have just finished reading your communication to the Governor of Alabama, and am somewhat at a loss to know whether an individual would be justifiable to purchase, at a *bona fide* consideration, Indian reservations. I am aware that those purchases, to make them valid, must be recognized by the President; and his express approbation must be given before any title can vest in the purchaser. The Indians have nearly all of them sold their reservations to companies of individuals, and now the locating agent is busily employed in locating of the Indians. Now, my inquiries run to this point—would I be ejected from my possession, if I should purchase some one or two of them, and settle a farm on them the ensuing year? The Indians are determined to sell their reservations, and, with a few exceptions, have done so. In that section of country there is some very desirable spots of farming land; and at this time I could buy, of either the Indians or of those whites above alluded to, at a fair price; but that will not be the case long, for if the point is once determined that they will hold the land they have thus bought, land will be so high in that country that I could not buy. The country is spotted, and the Indians will get by far the most desirable part of it.

If I mistake not, you place other settlers, or those who settle on the residue of the territory, as mere tenants at the will of the Executive; so I would not be justifiable in settling any of that land.

I may have taken a wrong view of the subject, and therefore for myself, as well as hundreds of others, I have thus written to you, in as respectful a manner as I knew how, desiring correct information on this all-important subject: therefore, an answer is earnestly and respectfully solicited.

I am, dear sir, with considerations of respect,

Your very obedient servant, &c.,

JOHN J. SLATTER.

**N. B.** If you shall be disposed to confer the favor that I ask at your hands, be kind enough to write me at Mulberry Grove, Harris Co., Georgia, *(speedily.)*

Yours, &c.,

J. J. S.

To the Hon. LEWIS CASS,
 *Secretary of War.*

---

BUFFALO, *November* 18, 1833.

DEAR SIR: I am aware that I owe an explanation, by way of apology, for my long silence; but relying on the confidence you have in me, and which I have done nothing that I am conscious of to diminish, I can only say, just now, that my time has been incessantly occupied, leaving me not one moment to devote to any thing but what immediately pressed.

The delegation to Green Bay has returned. The man who acted for the Senecas had gone some time before. He is a brother of Dr. Jamison, deceased, who you know belonged to the navy, and was an Indian of the Seneca tribe. He has furnished the facts for the communication enclosed, marked No. 3. The remainder of the delegation will send their report by me during the winter. The enclosed communications, marked numbers 1 and 2, are from the Seneca chiefs, on the subject of a delegation to Washington. The first is from the recusants; and I beg you to have copies of them made and preserved before they leave your office, if they do so at all, for in my hurry I have preserved none.

The Indians on all the reservations are anxious to unite in the deputation to Washington. When the arrangements are made I will write further.

You will please say to Mr. Kurtz that I have received the order from Ingersoll, in my favor, for $2,100, that I have paid the Indians all their annuities this year and the last, and they owe me $2,000. I have waited for an account from Oneida, and one from this place, (the individual being absent,) before I could make out *complete* returns. They will be furnished by 1st January.

In haste,

Most truly and respectfully,

JAMES STRYKER.

Judge HERRING.

---

No. 1.

BUFFALO CREEK, *Oct.* 3, 1833.

SIR: The undersigned, chiefs of the Seneca, Onondago, and Oneida nation of New York Indians, beg leave to present to you their wishes in relation to matters which have recently engaged their attention very much. A proposition was made to them some time ago by the Government agent to send a delegation to Green Bay for the purpose of settling off land for themselves there, with a view to future emigration, and they have also had intimations conveyed to them that the Government is desirous to have them go either to Green Bay or west of the Mississippi. On this subject they

90‡

have been very much divided, and in consequence of the difference of opinion among them great difficulties have arisen; the chiefs have separated from each other that formerly acted together, and one party has taken steps to depose the other from authority. Hence, some embarrassment has arisen in the management of our affairs, but for the existence of which we neither blame the Government nor our agent. The latter has acted towards us to our satisfaction. We wish, however, to see the President and the Secretary of War in person; and for this purpose we ask the consent of the President for our agent to conduct to Washington, the ensuing winter, a delegation from our tribes, to consist of such number as may be deemed proper, and when they come to Washington they will be authorized on the part of their people to speak and act for them; and they will be made acquainted from the President and Secretary themselves what is best for their nations to do; what course they should pursue under present circumstances, in order that all their difficulties may be settled, and they may be fully apprised of the policy of the Government in relation to all their affairs; and when so advised they will report to their people all they have heard and seen.

|  |  |
|---|---|
| LITTLE JOHNSON, | his x mark. |
| WHITE SENECA, | x |
| BIG KETTLE, | x |
| CAPTAIN COLE, | x |
| ONONDAGA PETER, | x |
| GREEN BLANKET, | x |
| TALL PETER, | x |
| GEORGE KANFRETADIE, | x |
| TOMMY JEMMY, | x |

MARIS B. PIERCE, *Interpreter*

Signed by the chiefs in our presence:
JAMES YOUNG.
THOS. B. STODDARD.
JAMES STRYKER, *Agent.*

To the Hon. LEWIS CASS,
    *Secretary of War.*

---

No. 2.

BUFFALO, *October* 3, 1833.

SIR: We, the undersigned, principal chiefs of the Seneca nation, residing in the State of New York, having been long impressed with the importance of some permanent provision for our people, listened favorably to the proposal of the Government to send a delegation to Green Bay, and we have also felt disposed to have a delegation go to the country west of the Mississippi, for the purpose of looking at western lands, with a view to the future emigration of our people. In consequence of such disposition on our part, some of our chiefs have become opposed to us, and have been urged on by some white people to make trouble among us. They have made trouble, and by the help of a few designing and violent young men, who did not understand the views of the Government, they attempted to depose some of us from office. But they have only effected a division among our people. The whole matter was presented before a recent council of the six nations, but o definite result was arrived at.

We are therefore anxious that a delegation of our numbers should go to Washington accompanied by our agent, that we may have an opportunity of submitting all our concerns to the President. Those of our people who are opposed to sending delegations west do not understand our true interests. They have requested to send a delegation on their own account to Washington. We want one on ours; and we know much good will be done to us and our people by having an opportunity to meet in person with the Secretary, and state our separate views and be directed a right. We wish to submit ourselves and our people to the advice and direction of the Government.

| | |
|---|---|
| YOUNG KING, | his x mark. |
| POLLARD, | x |
| CAPT. BILLY, | x |
| SENECA WHITE, | x |
| CAPT. STRONG, | x |
| DESTROY TOWN, | x |
| HENRY TWO GUNS, | x |
| JOHN SNOW, | x |
| STEVENSON, | x |
| JOB PIERCE, | x |

Signed by the chiefs in our presence:
NATHANIEL T. STRONG, *Interpreter.*
H. P. WILLCOX.
JAMES STRYKER, *Agent.*

To the Hon. LEWIS CASS,
　　*Secretary of War.*

---

## No. 3.

BUFFALO RESERVATION, *Nov.* 16, 1833.

George Jamison, a native of the Seneca nation, has the honor respectfully to report as follows:

That with a view to explore the country lately proposed by the Government upon certain conditions as a permanent future home for the Six Nations, he left the Buffalo reservation on or about the 5th September, 1832, and arrived on Fox river, in the Green Bay country, in season to join the survey, in the progress of which, and in capacity of axe-man, he enjoyed the most favorable opportunities for examining the outline and general features of the tract in question.

That taking the five hundred thousand acres as a body, it very much resembles the State of New York, west of the Genessee river, equalling its best sections in fertility, and perhaps offering a great variety of soil; that having spent the past winter upon one of the branches of Fox river, he is able to speak no less favorably of the climate of the country; and judging from experience, he is prepared to say that, if there be any preference, it is in favor of the Green Bay over his native air for temperature and salubrity.

The country, as far as he explored it, in quest of a favorable location for himself, appeared to be finely watered by living springs, by small lakes abounding in fish, and by streams traversing the country in various directions, affording water power adequate to all the milling and manufacturing purposes of a dense population. In particular was he pleased with the facilities for marketing the pine and other valuable timber, which abounds upon the ridges that skirt the borders of these mill-streams.

The proportion of woodland and prairie, interspersed as they are over the face of the country, struck him as peculiarly favorable to the partial advancement attained by people in agriculture; and that after spending much time and means for the purposes above mentioned, and having fairly tested the soil and climate by actual experiment, he has given the best evidence of his satisfaction with both by removing his family to the country, and has prolonged a visit amongst his people at this time in the hope of inducing them to follow his example; but is at length compelled to admit that his testimony in favor of his new abode, and the substance of this report, has hitherto failed to awaken the earnest attention which the importance of the subject so justly merits.

The reasons for our indifference to the paternal scheme of Government, familiarly known as the Green Bay measure, are numerous and conflicting, as might be expected of a community made up of hunters, scholars, and farmers, into which three classes we may at this day properly be ranked.

The first class is composed of hunters, old men principally, who have outlived the age for enterprise, whose inborn love of woods and the chase is nearly equipoised by a superstitious faith in the dying words of Red Jacket, well known to have been hostile to this scheme.

The second class is inconsiderable in numbers, but yet numbering in it our educated men, chiefly young men more given to theory than action. These pretend to see nothing attractive in the Green Bay plan, foretell the period (should we adopt it) when we should once more be invited to "make room," and regarding our race as foredoomed to insignificance within the borders of a territory no less than where we now are, qualify themselves for civilized employments rather than for the task of civilizing us.

The third class comprehends the bulk of the nation, not easily aroused by benefits purely prospective, or by considerations of thrift to result from their own future labors upon new land; the love of gain is not yet sufficiently developed to overcome the native love of ease, characteristic of all classes. Large portions of our present possessions are suffered to lie waste.

The superiority of title which is offered us over that which we inherited to our homes here has very little in it to interest a people not yet speculative enough to appreciate the distinction so recently expounded to our southern brothers.

From a happy and united people we have become so broken and divided that there remains scarcely a common sentiment amongst us to be appealed to; a desire to perpetuate the Seneca name and nation, is perhaps the only and abiding one.

Having briefly adverted to some of the impediments in the way of all projects for our improvements, I turn in despair from the Green Bay to the Mississippi measure, with something like faith in its ultimate accomplishment; many of all parties admit that this scheme may contain all the good which an enlightened guardianship and wise forecast could suggest in our behalf; as far as we understand it, it seems capable of adaptation to our threefold character, and awakens curiosity to understand it more in detail.

As far as it has been developed, it lays hold on the Indian mind. The Pagan party foresee in it a possible relief from the incomprehensible strife of opinions which is so constantly subdividing us. The educated or declamatory portion of that class ask, where so likely as on the frontier of Missouri. can we hope to illustrate our schemes of Indian civilization?

When can we better hope to stipulate with Government for some future limitation to the doctrine of eternal, pupilage so humiliating to individuals, and which protracts indefinitely our national emancipation?

In a word, each of the three classes see or fancy something in this latter plan to advance its favorite theory of happiness. But it is equally true, that something more express is required to produce a concerted action upon it. Wherefore the plan (if any be digested) should be more specifically explained; for example, the country proposed is understood to lie beyond the bounds of any State or Territory, to border upon lands colonized by Cherokees, Choctaws, and various other nations like ourselves in a partial state of civilization, also upon territory hereafter to be inhabited by the whites, also fetching us in contact with our wild brothers of the forest.

Therefore to the facilities for understanding the subject which our agent here promptly supplies, there might be added maps of the Indian territory, showing our future relative position. To these topographical particulars a variety of other topics might be enlarged upon very much to the advancement of the Government policy, and which it would be impertinence in me to dictate.

The hope of perpetuating the Seneca name is, however, the only feeling by which we can, as a nation, be wrought upon; and in view of this could the foes and opposers amongst us be compelled to look at what attracts their general curiosity through the blank stipulations of such a treaty as could safely be indicted, one party would be armed with the means and facts wherewith to overcome the selfishness of the few and the wilful blindness of the many to fix the general mind; something like chapter and verse is wanting, to overcome the artfully cherished horror with which the majority regard any treaty touching a final title to their homes.

In conclusion, the vastness of the Government bounty, and the air of vague munificence with which it is propounded, produce a corresponding sentiment or sensation, if it please you, but no definite purpose.

Our agent has a great work before him, and should this communication contribute to second his earnest and unwearied exertions, it will compensate me for the time I have bestowed on the question of emigration; and trusting that this liberty will be excused, I take leave to subscribe,

Very respectfully,

GEO. JAMISON. his x mark.

Witness: TH. B. STODDARD.

To the Hon. ELBERT HERRING, Esq.
Commissioner of Indian Affairs, &c. &c.

---

EXECUTIVE DEPARTMENT, GEORGIA,
Milledgeville, Nov. 18, 1833.

SIR: Since the date of my last, various considerations and circumstances have induced me to forbear troubling you on the subject of our Indian affairs, which, at this time, it would be unnecessary for me to give you in detail; suffice it to say, I have not hitherto been able to perceive that you could render us any additional aid in the great object of furthering Cherokee emigration more than you have already done.

Indeed the duty now devolves principally upon the authorities of Georgia to manage this novel and perplexing subject with prudence to a successful issue. The Legislature of Georgia is now in session, and if my views can be sustained by appropriate legislation, I entertain but little doubt of successful results.

With Major Currey I continue to have free correspondence and cordial co-operation.

Before the reception of this you will, doubtlessly, have received the results of the late Cherokee council held at *Red Hill,* Tennessee; from which you will readily perceive that Ross and his party are still disposed to throw every obstacle they probably can in the way of a final and satisfactory adjustment of the existing difficulties.

Permit me to suggest that the intended Cherokee delegation to Washington are wholly undeserving the courtesy and marked attention of the official authorities at Washington. Moreover, as I stand informed at present, I incline to the opinion that they have not the most distant idea of an immediate treaty; and that therefore it would be inexpedient to press upon them further and extraordinary inducements to enter into a treaty. If a treaty can be effected at all, I consider it necessary and proper that the leading friends of emigration amongst the Cherokees should have a due share in any and all arrangements which should be proposed. Their interest and views are surely entitled to more weight and consideration than that of their opponents.

Amongst those who have recently enrolled will be found the names of William Hicks, John McIntosh, John Miller, and Young Wolf, who deserve special regard as worthy men, who act candidly with their people, and favor the emigration plan. I am authorized to add the names of William Coody, John Ridge, Old Ridge, Boudenot and his father, *Waity.* None can desire more than myself a treaty arrangement which shall finally settle and put to rest this whole matter, with all its attendant heartburnings and disquietudes.

But it appears to me that the argument has been completely exhausted; we must now do our duty, and teach Ross and his disorganizing supporters their weakness and folly.

In haste, I am,

Very respectfully,

Your obedient servant,

WILSON LUMPKIN.

Hon. LEWIS CASS,
   *Secretary of War.*

---

FORT LEAVENWORTH, November 19, 1833.

SIR: I have the honor to enclose to the Government a copy of an agreement between the Otoes, Omahaws, and Ioways, antecedent to the treaty of peace. I am sensible I trouble you with the perusal of many documents, and therefore will study conciseness.

There are now two Omahaws in confinement at this garrison; eight Ioways and three Otoes lately escaped; all charged with killing individuals belonging to the Ioway or Omahaw nation. There is also one Ioway not yet taken, making nine criminals from that tribe. What the United States can do with them under existing laws, I do not perceive. It is certain that the criminals deserve (in a moral point of view) some punishment; and it is important, for the dignity and influence of the Government, that those who have escaped should be *retaken*.

The origin and progress of the quarrel is simply this: a vagrant or roving Ioway (residing sometimes with the Ioways, at others with the Omahaws or Otoes) killed an Omahaw; a small party of Omahaws (among whom were the two now in confinement) killed an Ioway. The chief of the Omahaws made peace with the Ioways, and agreed to pay a certain sum by a given day. The stipend was on the way, but would not have arrived in time. A party of nine Ioways with three Otoes, without the knowledge of the chiefs, went up to the Omahaw nation and killed six or seven Omahaws. These are the criminals.

By a treaty of peace, made at Prairie du Chien before any of these murders, I understand (for I could not find a copy of the articles) the parties agreed to deliver up the murderers for punishment to the United States. I have, therefore, done nothing to compromit the Government, nor permitted the future disposition of the criminals to interfere with a general peace.

Permit me respectfully to suggest, that as those two now in confinement have shown more obedience to the laws of the United States, a less period of confinement for them (if this shall be the punishment) will, I think, strike the Indians as just.

Most respectfully, yours, &c.,<br>HENRY L. ELLSWORTH,<br>*U. S. Commissioner.*

Hon. E. Herring,
*Indian Commissioner, Washington.*

P.S. I intended to have sent this from Fort Leavenworth, but could not. I send by way of express to Fort Gibson.

H. L. E.

---

*Articles of Agreement entered into between the Otoes, Ioways, and Omahaws, tribes of Indians, antecedent to the treaty of peace made at Fort Leavenworth, in November,* 1833.

Whereas the Otoes, Ioways, and Omahaws, with other tribes, have been convened at Fort Leavenworth to make peace; and whereas certain individuals belonging to the Omahaw and Ioway nation have been killed; and whereas three Otoes and nine Ioways were confined with two Omahaws at the garrison of Fort Leavenworth, charged with said offence; and whereas the three Otoes and the nine Ioways escaped from their confinement, and have been again demanded by the United States.

It is hereby agreed by the undersigned chiefs and warriors, in behalf of their respective tribes, that the peace now made at Fort Leavenworth shall be obligatory on said tribes, but shall not affect the right of the United States to demand and punish the offenders so far as the President may think proper.

It is further agreed by the undersigned, that the Otoe and Ioway tribes shall respectively deliver to the commanding officer at Fort Leavenworth the individuals of their tribes charged with said offences on or before the

1st day of June, 1833, then, with the two Omahaws still confined, to be dealt with as the President may direct.

In witness whereof, the undersigned have hereunto set their hands and seals this 18th day of November, 1833, at Fort Leavenworth.

*Otoes.*

his mark.

SHA MON NE RA SAY, or Tolan,                                x  [L. s.]
ACHE RA SACH RAY, or He that strikes the Osage,  x  [L. s.]
CHA HAH GAH HE GAH, or Buffalo Chief,              x  [L. s.]

*Omahaw.*

WAH CON RAY,                                                        x  [L. s.]

*Ioways.*

MAHOS RAH, or White Cloud,                              x  [L. s.]
TARRON HAN, or Keeper of Deer,                        x  [L  s.]
MY NO GUS HONNA, or He that fears nothing,   x  [L. s.]
WAS CO MONEY, or Fast Walker,                         x  [L. s.]

*Socs.*

AMOY, He that eats,                                              x  [L. s.]
AS REN HE QUA, The Bottle,                               x  [L. s.]
MOHCUA, The Horrible Man,                               x  [L. s.]

In presence of
H. L. ELLSWORTH, *U. S. Commissioner.*
E. A. ELLSWORTH, *Sec'y pro tem.*
JOHN DOUGHERTY, *Indian Agent.*
ANDREW S. HUGHES, *U. S. Agent to the Ioways.*
JOHN DUNLAP,
WILLIAM DUNCAN,
B. W. HUGHES,
JEFFREY DORWAY, his x mark.

----

[EXTRACT.]

COLUMBUS, *November* 19, 1833.

SIR: I am as yet uninstructed in what manner the department will direct that clause of the treaty in which there is nine hundred and sixty acres of land allowed to Delilah and her five children, and also to Peggy Trahern and her children, and to the widow of Pucksunubbee, &c.

I say I am uninstructed how these claims shall be located; that is, shall they be located on lands selected by me, or by themselves; shall they be located in quarter sections or in one entire tract?

I am desirous to hear from the department, and know in what manner I am to run these claims.

I have the honor to be,
GEORGE W. MARTIN.

----

RAYMOND, MISS., *November* 19, 1833.

SIR: Pursuant to your letter of *instructions* respecting intruders on th Chickasaw territory, I have, by my deputy, caused the notices, warning them to leave said territory, to be posted up throughout the nation in this State, and herewith enclose an account of the expenses consequent thereon. The per diem allowance is as low as I possibly could have procured a competent person to have performed said services for.

The trip was quite a disagreeable one, as well as expensive. My deputy had to leave a horse on the road and procure another for the trip. I mention these circumstances to avoid the imputation of extravagance in the charge, and I hope the department will put a due estimate on the services.

You will please arrange, by check on the United States Branch Bank at Natchez, for amount of account.

Respectfully,<br>Your obedient servant,<br>SAMUEL W. DICKSON

To the Hon. LEWIS CASS,
        Secretary of War.

---

WESTERN CREEK AGENCY,<br>November 20, 1833.

SIR: I herewith transmit to you a roll of the strength of the Creek nation on the Arkansas, and I am sorry to say that they have greatly diminished in number within the last three years, in consequence of the country being more unhealthy than usual, though they are progressing in improvements and industry; and with proper encouragement will, I think, in a very few years, place them in a happy and comfortable situation. Ardent spirits have in a great measure disappeared from this nation.

I have the honor to be, sir,<br>Very respectfully, your obedient servant,<br>JOHN CAMPBELL.

ELBERT HERRING, Esq.,
        Commissioner of Indian Affairs.

*A Roll of the Census of the Creek Nation west of the Mississippi river,* the 30th September, 1833.

| Towns, &c. | Creek Indians. | | | | White people | | Chero-kee Indians. | | Free blacks. | | Slaves. | | Total. |
|---|---|---|---|---|---|---|---|---|---|---|---|---|---|
| | Males over 15 years old. | Females over 16 years old. | Males under 16 years old. | Females under 16 years old. | Males. | Females. | Males. | Females. | Males. | Females. | Males. | Females. | |
| Coweta　Town | 62 | 79 | 48 | 47 | 2 | 2 | 1 | - | 3 | 2 | 90 | 87 | 423 |
| Broken Arrow " | 65 | 73 | 55 | 34 | 9 | - | - | - | - | - | 50 | 40 | 326 |
| Talladega " | 76 | 54 | 41 | 28 | - | - | - | - | - | - | 28 | 24 | 251 |
| Ufaula " | 43 | 45 | 23 | 18 | - | - | - | - | - | - | 1 | 1 | 131 |
| Chow-wockolee " | 32 | 34 | 13 | 14 | - | - | 1 | - | - | - | 1 | - | 95 |
| New York " | 12 | 15 | 10 | 13 | . | - | - | - | - | - | - | - | 50 |
| Wockokoy " | 19 | 16 | 7 | 6 | 1 | - | - | - | 3 | - | 35 | 30 | 117 |
| Sandtown " | 26 | 26 | 15 | 10 | - | - | - | - | - | - | - | - | 77 |
| Cosada " | 35 | 38 | 14 | 13 | - | - | - | - | - | - | - | - | 100 |
| Hitcheta " | 44 | 34 | 29 | 25 | 1 | - | - | - | - | - | 20 | 13 | 166 |
| Coiga " | 36 | 37 | 16 | 12 | - | - | - | - | - | - | 10 | 9 | 120 |
| Big Spring " | 82 | 80 | 52 | 37 | 12 | - | - | - | 3 | 2 | 20 | 12 | 300 |
| Oakelta Ockney " | 71 | 56 | 36 | 19 | 1 | - | - | - | - | - | 12 | 11 | 206 |
| Lowocolo " | 27 | 21 | 10 | 3 | - | - | - | - | - | - | 3 | 1 | 70 |
| Hatchee Chub-bee " | 12 | 7 | 5 | 3 | - | - | - | - | - | - | - | - | 27 |
| Total　- | 642 | 615 | 374 | 287 | 26 | 2 | 2 | - | 9 | 4 | 270 | 228 | 2,459 |

This part of the Creek nation numbered near three thousand three years ago; and they are on the decline ever since their arrival here, from the prevailing diseases of the country. There are not more than a fourth of the Indian children that were born in this country now living. There is a great want of medical assistance here for the first two or three years after the emigrants reach this country, that they might receive all the necessary medical aid, until their constitutions became formed and assimilated to the climate.

JOHN CAMPBELL,
*Agent for Creeks.*

WESTERN CREEK AGENCY.

Montgomery, Alabama,
*November 22, 1833.*

Dear Sir: I have been waiting here since Saturday, with the expectation of seeing the district attorney and marshal, and have just received a letter from the former acquainting me with his engagements at the courts in Mobile, and the impossibility of his leaving that place before the 15th or 20th of next month. He has suggested my proceeding now to Mobile, and going thence with him to Tuscaloosa, after the periods he mentions.

I have thought it best to proceed to Tuscaloosa to-morrow, and after remaining there as long as I may find it expedient, to see him at Mobile afterwards, if necessary. I have been induced to adopt this course from several considerations; but principally from a letter I have received to-night from Tuscaloosa, from which I think I see already that the Governor is well disposed, and will not press us with these prosecutions.

I have sought every opportunity of ascertaining the probable disposition of the Indians towards a treaty with the Government for their reservations. I have had the means, since I wrote last, of learning the opinions of several gentlemen well acquainted with the Indians, and some of them of considerable influence among them. They think a treaty may be made, provided it is stipulated that each Indian is to receive severally the price of his reservation. They say the Indians would not consent to this now; but that when they find the choice pieces of land on which they have settled and built (under the instruction of the whites who mean to buy or have bought them) since the treaty, will not be located for them, but that they will be made to go to the improvements they held at the time of the treaty, or else hold a floating right with those who have no improvement, to be located in a body, containing some good and some bad land, they will become dissatisfied, and willing to treat with the Government.

These views I think very reasonable, and it is highly probable that when Colonel Albert and Mr. Bright have got on pretty well with the locations in this way, the Indians will consent to send on a delegation of chiefs, or make a treaty here.

The gentlemen here who hold these opinions are Judge Benson, Colonel Benjamin Fitzpatrick, and Captain John Martin. The two latter gentlemen are well acquainted with the Indians, and much respected by the most important chiefs. Colonel Fitzpatrick speaks their language well.

If you think it desirable, they would, I believe, accept a commission to undertake the business. Captain Martin has told me he would, if Fitzpatrick would act with him. Judge Benson has mentioned it to Fitzpatrick, and he says he seems rather unwilling to undertake it, but he believes, if the President wished him to act, and it did not occupy him too long, he would consent to it.

From all I can learn of these gentlemen, I should think them more likely to succeed than any others that could be got. Colonel King, of the Senate, can inform you of their qualifications. Captain Martin is the person who has surveyed lately the road through the Creek nation, from this place to Columbus. Colonel Fitzpatrick, I understand, is known to the President, and ardently attached to him. You will find on the files of your department a long letter from him to Major Eaton on the subject of the Indians. I expect to see General Parsons in Tuscaloosa, and shall deliver him the President's letter, and confer with him on the subject. He is there as a candidate for a judgeship, and would not be disposed, I understand, to make another attempt with the Indians, and would be unable to succeed if he did.

I fully believe, from all I have heard, that nothing can save the Creeks from impositions and oppression of all kinds, and defeat the aims of the speculators upon their lands, and quiet all future troubles here so effectually as their bargaining in some way with the Government. If you approve of engaging these gentlemen, or any others in the way I have suggested, it may be important they should receive their authority and instructions as soon as they can be sent. Mr. Bright and Mr. Tarrant have both, as I hear to-day, arrived at Fort Mitchell, and will, no doubt, begin immediately; so that by the time these gentlemen would hear from you, the Indians would be in a proper state to be approached on the subject.

I am, sir, &c.

F. S. KEY.

Hon. Lewis Cass, *Secretary of War.*

---

LAFAYETTE, INDIANA, *November 23, 1833.*

DEAR SIR: I have the pleasure to transmit to you by Mr. M. C. Dougherty, a treaty concluded with the Quapaws, the talks at the council, and a report of the whole. I trust they will prove satisfactory, and meet the approbation of the department. It was my intention to have met with my fellow commissioners west before this, and have submitted the treaty to them for their approbation and signature. The season is now so far advanced that I know not where we shall meet. I have, therefore, deemed it necessary to transmit those papers to the department by a special messenger, Mr. Dougherty, whom I have assured shall be paid the usual allowances in such cases. I presume it is necessary to have these documents to lay before Congress as early in the session as possible.

I leave here this morning for St. Louis, where I hope to arrive in ten days. The Miami treaty has failed. It was a public treaty, and not a private negotiation as I recommended, and as was contemplated in the private instructions to Governor Porter. You will soon receive the report of the commissioners.

With great respect, &c.,

J. F. SCHERMERHORN,
*Commissioner West.*

Hon. Elbert Herring,
*Commissioner.*

---

*Minutes of a council held with the Quapaw Indians, at New Gascony, A. T., May* 10th *and* 13th, *inclusive,* 1833.—Present, J. F. Schermerhorn, commissioner, &c. west, on the part of the United States, and the following chiefs: Hickatton, Sarassin, Tonnonjinka, and Hakeketteda, and the warriors of said tribe.

The commissioner on the part of the United States delivered to them the following talk:

Brothers of the Quapaw nation: We thank the Great Spirit that he has permitted us to meet to day in council, to take into consideration your peculiar situation, and to make known to you the views and wishes of your **great** father, the President of the United States. He knows all the difficulties that have attended your removal to Red river, and the peculiar trials through which you have passed. He has heard of your return to your old homes, and the troubles that attend you here. He wants you to take counsel from him, and remove to the lands set apart by the Congress of the United States as the permanent home of the Indians, west of the State of Missouri and Arkansas territory. You know the country is a good one. He will there take care of you, and protect you from all harm from the white men or his red children. He will give you as much land as is necessary for your comfortable subsistence. He will furnish you with agricultural implements, ploughs, axes, hoes, cattle, and a farmer to teach you how to farm and cultivate your fields. He will also send men to assist you in building houses, and give your women wheels and looms, and learn them to spin and weave, and make cloth to clothe you and your children. You will have here a permanent home. Your father will never ask you to remove again. Open your ears to the counsel of your great father, and you will find him ever your friend and protector.

The following reply was made by the principal chief, Hickatton:

My father: We have heard what you have said to us. When we started to Red river, we had provisions enough for part of the way only. We suffered for want of it before we got there.

My father: You say we shall be provided with good land; we are afraid to go there. It is a cold country; we are afraid our cattle will die in the winter.

My father: There are many red men that have spilt the blood of white men. The Quapaws have never done it. We pray, therefore, for our great father to take pity on us. We want to remain here on the land which was formerly ours, and our bones to be buried by the side of our ancestors. If we are permitted to stay here, we shall not trouble our white brothers.

My father: We are afraid to leave here again and go among other nations more powerful than we, where we cannot defend ourselves. The Caddos, when we were on Red river, killed four of our men, and we were too weak to resent the injury. We want to continue here, anywhere, even in the swamps where the whites will never settle. If our great father will grant our request, he may keep our money, we will give it all up to him.

To which the commissioner answered:

Brothers: Your great father cannot grant your request. His great council have set apart a country for all his red children; and it is best they should live by themselves, where the bad white men shall not be permitted to disturb and trouble them. The people of Arkansas will not consent to have you stay here, and you had better remove to a land where you will rest in peace. Think of this matter well, and let me know your answer on Monday. To-morrow is the Lord's day, on which we worship the Great Spirit. We cannot counsel to-morrow.

Council, Monday, May 13, 1833. Hickatton addressed the commissioner as follows:

Father: The place to which we went on Red river was not good. A great many of our people died there; our crops of corn were destroyed by the high water. We suffered very much with sickness and hunger. We are glad our great father will now give us good land. I know I have to die; it matters not where it is, here or on Red river, or at the new home promised us. In the direction where we are now to be sent we used to hunt, and we have been robbed of our furs. It may be so again. If the white people trouble us in the country to which we are to remove, we hope our great father will send them from us.

Sarassin, the second chief, said:

Father: What the head chief has said I also say. I have always listened to the advice of my white brethren, and will do so again. Our old chiefs always told us to listen to our white brethren; we have done so.

Hickatton asked when they should go and view the country. They were told, in the fall.

My father: Now we have taken hold of the counsel of our great father, we want you to furnish us with one hundred bushels of corn in the course of the summer, for the poor of our nation. We wish you to give us one hundred blankets before we move. We want our four chiefs each to have fifty dollars a year out of our annuity; they have all the business of the nation to attend unto; we want also some guns and powder, and all our just debts paid. We wish Mr. Barraque and our agent to remove us, and an interpreter to accompany us on our removal, and to continue with us so long as our great father may think proper to let him stay. We want Bernard Boon for an interpreter. We are now ready to take hold of the pen.

The commissioner replied:

Brothers: It will rejoice the heart of your great father to hear that you have hearkened to his counsel and advice. I will say further, you ask for a great deal from your great father. He wishes to do all he can for you, and he is willing to comply with all you ask. If you see fit to exchange your permanent annuity for one of twenty years, he will agree to give you $1,000 dollars a year to establish a school in your nation, so that your children may learn to read and write, and work like white men.

To which the chief repled: We are all agreed to do what our great father thinks is best for us to do.

---

INDEPENDENCE, MISSOURI, *November 23, 1833.*

SIR: I have the honor to enclose you a copy of a treaty of peace and friendship made by the different tribes; and also to inform you of my progress thus far towards Fort Gibson.

The Government is not a party to the treaty, and therefore uncommitted by my acts. I know the Government at present do not feel bound to interfere in the claims of one tribe against another; but permit me to say unless the Government will lend its aid (at the request of the tribes) the small tribes will be destroyed. They ask me, with great anxiety, *will not our great father protect us in our new homes?*

To relieve the Government from the charge of violating good faith by extending jurisdiction, I have obtained the request of the tribes that an umpire should be appointed *between* them.

I regret that it was not possible to send our joint report before the meeting of Congress. The absence of Mr. Schermerhorn, the sickness of Governor Stokes, and my detention among the northwestern tribes will, I trust, be deemed a sufficient apology.

I have, during a few months, collected much authentic information relative to the course of trade, and the price of goods among the Indians, and hope soon for time to communicate the facts in my possession.

Yours, most respectfully,

HENRY L. ELLSWORTH.

Hon. E. HERRING, *Indian Commissioner.*

**P. S.** When the Osages and others have signed the articles of peace, the board will forward a copy. I have hastened off this to inform you on what principles the treaty is made.

---

Whereas the United States are now endeavoring to advance the welfare of the red men by assigning them all a permanent home in the west; and whereas the number and contiguity of the tribes will render necessary some regulations to protect life and property; and whereas our great father has, through his commissioner, our friend H. L. Ellsworth, convened many tribes together by delegations, to make a treaty of peace and friendship: Now in order to show our willingness to listen to the advice of our great father, and believing it good for our people to live in amity with those who the Great Spirit has marked as brothers, the undersigned tribes or nations, viz., Delawares, Pawnees, Shawnees, Kanzas, Ioways, Otoes, Omahaws, Kickapoos, Weas, Peorias, Piankeshaws, Kaskaskias, Ottoways, Pottawatamies, do hereby mutually covenant with each other, and bind ourselves on the following articles of agreement:

Article 1. All hostile acts shall immediately cease, and each tribe mutually agrees with the other to maintain peace, to respect the rights of persons and property, and do all in their power to perpetuate the friendships hereby declared and established.

Article 2. No private revenge shall be sought, and all damages sustained by either tribe in any war party is hereby cancelled, settled, and forgiven. But any individual shall have the right to prefer his claim against any individual of another tribe for horses lost or stolen, or any other property wrongfully taken or detained to the adjustment of the umpire hereafter mentioned.

Article 3. To preserve peace and good will, the parties hereto hereby agree not to seek personal revenge for injuries hereafter committed, or to make these injuries the cause of war; but to refer the matter of difficulty through their respective agents to such umpire as the President shall appoint to adjust and decide upon the same; and said tribes hereby agree to abide the decision of said umpire; and also to deliver up the offender against any article herein mentioned, to be punished by the laws of the United States now in force, or such as may be adopted hereafter.

Article 4. Believing an annual assembly of the red men will be conducive of much benefit, we hereby request our great father to designate the time and place of meeting, together with the number of representatives from each tribe by them to be appointed, and provide adequate means to defray the expense of the same.

Article 5. It is agreed that the flag of the United States shall be our protection and token of friendship whenever and wherever we meet.

Article 6. As all the tribes called together have not yet arrived, it is agreed that those who shall hereafter arrive, and shall become parties to this agreement by subscribing the same, shall be entitled to all the privileges, and bound by the same obligations as fully as if now present.

Article 7. Whereas it is proposed by said commissioner that the Osages,

Cherokees, Creeks, Choctaws, Seminoles, and any other tribes residing north of the Red river may become parties to this agreement; we hereby declare our entire willingness that all such shall become parties to the same, by subscribing these articles and giving due notice thereof; and these articles shall be binding on those who subscribe the same.

In witness whereof, we have set our hands and seals at Fort Leavenworth this 12th day of November, 1833.

## DELAWARES:

| Indian. | Translation. | Signature. |
| --- | --- | --- |
| Meh-shay-quo-wha, | Patterson, | his x mark. |
| Nah-ko-min, | | his x mark. |
| Tah-whe-la-lin, | Captain Ketchum, | his x mark. |
| Nonon-do-gnomon, | | his x mark. |
| Shaw-wak-nock, | The white man, | his x mark. |
| Sha-con-di-ah-hing, | Long house, | his x mark. |
| On-loo-ho-tah-nah, | John Gray, | his x mark. |
| Nah-kah-pash, | Moses, | his x mark. |
| To-le-tah-say, | | his x mark. |
| Kah-ke-toh-wah, | Big man, | his x mark. |

In presence of

HENRY L. ELLSWORTH, *United States Commissioner.*
EDWARD A. ELLSWORTH, *Secretary pro tem.*
B. RILEY, *Major Commanding.*
JNO. DOUGHERTY, *Indian Agent.*

## SHAWNEES:

| Indian. | Translation. | Signature. |
| --- | --- | --- |
| Lah-to-wah, | John Berry, | his x mark. |
| Pew-sah-tah, | William Perry, | his x mark. |
| Wy-lah-lah-piah, | | his x mark. |
| Wah she-kah-konsay, | Cornstalk, | his x mark. |
| Kah-kous-kah, | McNair, | his x mark. |
| Chah-kas-kah, | Spy Buck, | his x mark. |
| Chah-wah, | | his x mark. |
| Lee-sah, | Lewis, | his x mark. |

In presence of

RICHD. W. CUMMINS, *Indian Agent.*
ANDREW S. HUGHES, *Sub-Indian Agent.*
J. L. BEAN, *U. S. Sub-Indian Agent for U. Mo.*
F. W. MILLER, *U. S. Sub-Agent.*
A. G. MORGAN, *Sutler U. S. Army.*

## KICKAPOOS:

| Indian. | Translation. | Signature. |
| --- | --- | --- |
| Pat-sa-che-haw, | | his x mark. |
| Kan-ne-kuh-kah, | Prophet, | his x mark. |

In presence of

WM. N. WICKLIFFE, *Captain 6th Infantry.*
ASA RICHARDSON, *1st Lieut. 6th Infantry.*

## POTAWATOMIES:

| Indian. | Translation. | Signature. |
|---|---|---|
| Quah-quah tah, | | his x mark. |
| Noh-sha-com, | | his x mark. |

In presence of
 JOHN NICHOLAS, 1st Lieut. 6th Infantry.

## OTTAWAS:

| Indian. | Translation. | Signature. |
|---|---|---|
| Oh-kah-no-quah-seh, | | his x mark. |
| Chi-cah, | Pole Cat, | his x mark. |

In presence of
 R. SEVIER, Lieut. 6th Infantry.

## PEORIAS AND KASKASKIAS.

| Indian. | Translation. | Signature. |
|---|---|---|
| Wah-pi-shah pah-noh, | White Shield, | his x mark. |
| Pah-nee-kah-wah-tah, | Big Harry, | his x mark. |
| Ke-moh rah niat, | Jim Peorias, | his x mark. |
| Geh-mah-sheh, | Le Coigne, | his x mark. |

In presence of
 J. CONRAD, Lieut. 6th Infantry.
 J. DUNLAP.

## WEAS:

| Indian. | Translation. | Signature. |
|---|---|---|
| Quih-wah, | Negro leg, | his x mark. |
| Wah-pon-iniah, | Swan, | his x mark. |
| Joh-tah kah-puah, | One who stands by himself, | his x mark. |
| She-kohn-lah, | Charley, | his x mark. |
| Ke-she-wah, | Bull, | his x mark. |

In presence of
 JOHN T. IRVING, Jr.
 A. SHANE, Interpreter for Shawnees.
 JAMES CONNOR, Interpreter for Delawares.

## OTOES:

| Indian. | Translation. | Signature. |
|---|---|---|
| She-moh ne kah say, | Iotan, | his x mark. |
| Ah-che-kah-sucker, | He that strikes the Osages, | his x mark. |
| Keh-gah-ne-gah rah, | He that judges for himself, | his x mark. |
| Chak-wong-guh-he-gah, | Buffalo chief, | his x mark. |

In presence of
 BABTISTE PEORIA, his x mark,
  *Inter. for Peorias, Kaskaskias and Weas.*

## OMAHAS:

| Indian. | Translation. | Signature. |
|---|---|---|
| Wah-con-ray, | | his x mark. |

In presence of
PETER CADUE, his x mark,
    *Inter. for Kickapoos, Ottawas and Pottawatomies.*

## GRAND PAWNEES:

| Indian. | Translation. | Signature. |
|---|---|---|
| Shah-re-tah-rich, | Ill natured man, | his x mark. |
| Lah-pah-con-rah-coble-sha, | The mouth chief, | his x mark. |
| Ah-sah-ron-kah-re, | Wild stud horse, | his x mark. |
| Tay-loo-kah, | Buffalo bull, | his x mark. |

In presence of
    LOUIS LA CHAPPELLE, his x mark,
        *Interpreter for all the Pawnees.*

## TAPPAGO PAWNEES.

| Indian. | Translation. | Signature. |
|---|---|---|
| Ska-lah-lay-shah-rho, | The only chief, | his x mark. |
| Ta-rah-she-tap-potch, | The continual mo-ver, | his x mark. |
| Kish-kay, | He that strikes the bones, | his x mark. |
| Te-le-la-loo-li-ah-rho | He that makes himself chief, | his x mark. |

## REPUBLICAN PAWNEES:

| Indian. | Translation. | Signature. |
|---|---|---|
| Ah-shah-lay-koh-she, | The dead horse, | his x mark. |
| To-lah-le-rah, | The medicine buffalo, | his x mark. |
| Kah-tah-rah-te-koo-tush | Big axe, | his x mark. |
| Tah-kish-ne-rah koo, | The man that kills many, | his x mark. |
| Tah-lak-kah-wah-ko, | The name of a chief, | his x mark. |

## PAWNEE LOUPS:

| Indian. | Translation. | Signature. |
|---|---|---|
| Pah-kah-le-koo, | Big voice, | his x mark. |
| Pah-shoo-she, | The brave, | his x mark. |
| Kah-kah-la-le-shah, | The carrion crow, | his x mark. |

## KANZAS:

| Indian. | Translation. | Signature. |
|---------|--------------|------------|
| Nom-pa wa-rah, | White plume, | his x mark. |
| Ky-he-ga-wat-inga, | The foolish chief, | his x mark. |
| Ky-he ga-war-cheke, | The hard chief, | his x mark. |
| Me-cho-shin-gtch, | The little white bear, | his x mark. |
| Pah-hus-kah-gah-rah, | The white hair striker, | his x mark. |
| Jook-tah-lah-say, | Grey eyes, | his x mark. |
| Wah-ho-bah-ke-gah-ra, | The carrier of the war god, | his x mark. |
| Tah-ga-sug hah, | The man chaser. | his x mark. |
| Nah-he-ta pie, | | his x mark. |
| Chah-ga-shin-gah, | The little old man, | his x mark. |
| Wah-la-gah, | | his x mark. |

Witnesses to the Kanzas, 16th November, 1833 :

HENRY L. ELLSWORTH, *United States Commissioner.*
EDWARD A. ELLSWORTH, *Secretary pro. tem.*
B. RILEY, *Major United States Army, C.*
M. G. CLARK, *Indian Agent of Kanzas.*
JNO. DOUGHERTY, *Indian Agent.*
AND. S. HUGHES, *Sub-Indian Agent for Ioways, &c.*
JON. L. BEAN, *U. S. Sub-Agent for U. Mo.*
A. RICHARDSON, *Lieut. U. S. Army.*
JOHN DUNLAP.
JOHN T. IRVING, Jr.
CLEMENT LESSERT, *Interpreter for the Kanzas.*
LOUIS LA CHAPPELLE, his x mark, *Inter. for all the Pawnees.*

## IOWAYS.

| Indian. | Translation. | Signature. |
|---------|--------------|------------|
| Ma-hos-kah, | White Cloud, | his x mark. |
| Tar-ro-haw, | Keeper of deer, | his x mark. |
| Wy-nogues-konna, | He that fears nothing, | his x mark. |
| Was-co-money, | Fast walker, | his x mark. |

In presence of
ASA RICHARDSON, *Lieut. United States Army.*
JOHN DUNLAP.
JOHN T. IRVING, Jr.
CLEMENT LESSERT, *Interpreter for the Kanzas.*

## SACS:

| Indian. | Translation. | Signature. |
|---------|--------------|------------|
| Amoy, | He that eats, | his x mark. |
| Wath-we, | | his x mark. |
| Ashe se gua, | The battle, | his x mark. |
| Alea-ke-wa, | Terrible man, | his x mark. |

In presence of
LOUIS LA CHAPPELLE, his x mark, *Inter. for all the Pawnees.*

## PIANKESHAWS:

| *Indian.* | *Translation.* | *Signature.* |
|---|---|---|
| Mon son-shak, | Jim, | his x mark. |
| Larharsh, | The axe, | his x mark. |
| Nah-hah son-wah, | | his x mark. |

Witness to Piankeshaws:
 H. L. ELLSWORTH, *U. S Commissioner.*
 JNO. DOUGHERTY, *Indian Agent.*
 RICHD. W. CUMMINS, *Indian Agent.*
 P. L. CHOUTEAU, *Interpreter*, his x mark.
 F. W. MILLER, *U. S. Sub-Indian Agent.*
 LOUIS LA CHAPPELLE, *Interpreter*, his x mark.
 BAPTISTE PEORIA, *Interpreter*, his x mark.
 JOHN DUNLAP.
*Shawnee Agency, November* 21, 1833.

---

CHEROKEE NATION, *November* 23, 1833.

DEAR SIR: I am a native Cherokee, living in this nation, and married to a Mary Ann Battes, owned and acknowledged by the Creek chiefs to be a descendant of their tribe.

Acting for her, under the provisions of the late treaty with the Creeks, my name was registered for a reservation last winter. The location is now in operation, and the agent is of the impression my wife's name ought to have been registered instead of mine; this I insisted upon at the time my name was reg.stered, but was told by the agent it made no difference.

I now ask, is it necessary for me to take my wife, with a very young family, through the inclemency of the weather, a distance of something like two hundred miles to be located? Will not myself answer every purpose, as I never expect to live on it? I had rather dispose of the reservation to the Government than to an individual. So soon as I am located I shall dispose of it to the best advantage.

I have the honor to be, &c.,

ROBERT ROGERS.

LEWIS CASS, Esq.

---

INDIAN AGENCY,
*Chicago, November* 23, 1833.

SIR: Permit me to call your attention to my letter of the 19th of August last, in which was enclosed a deed from Francis Burbonnois, junior, to Erastus Bowen, for one section of land reserved to the former by treaty of Prairie du Chien of 29th July, 1829.

Mr. Bowen has been anxiously awaiting the decision of the President in this matter, so that if favorable he might commence his improvements; and if against, that he might withdraw the money deposited in my hands, and apply it to some other purchase. Mr. Bowen is a very respectable citizen of this county, and requests the favor of as early an answer to this letter as may be convenient.

I have the honor to be,

Very respectfully, sir,

Your most obedient servant,

TH. J. V. OWEN.

ELBERT HERRING, Esq.,
*Indian Commissioner, Washington City.*

---

INDEPENDENCE, Mo., *November* 24, 1833.

SIR: I have drawn two drafts on the War Department, one in favor of A. G. Morgan, sutler at Fort Leavenworth, for $1,083 $\frac{76}{100}$, and one in favor of T. and R. Aull, of Independence, for $400, dated 24th November, 1833. The former is for sundries for the Pawnee and other Indians, and the latter for sundries at Independence, for the outfit to Fort Gibson.

All expenditures are made by myself, and nothing will be found in the account but necessaries.

Most respectfully,

H. L. ELLSWORTH,
*Ind. Com. West.*

Hon. LEWIS CASS.

---

COLUMBUS, GEORGIA, *Nov.* 24, 1833

SIR: From the best views which I am able to take of affairs in this quarter, I am forced to the conclusion that all delays in the execution of the treaty will serve only to give decided advantages to the class of speculators upon these Indian lands. Of this all parties seem aware; and those persons anxious to purchase, but who have hitherto desisted, now say that they must either enter the field with their antagonists or abandon all expectations of obtaining any of the reservations. They say, also, the check upon unfair purchases being in the certifying agent and the after approbation of the President, no evil can ensue to the Indian by purchasing from him so soon as the locations are made. On these accounts I am urged by them to bring to your notice the propriety of at once prescribing the form of the contract.

Allow me to beg of you to take this subject into your immediate consideration. Purchases will be made, and to a great extent, so soon as the locations are made; and these had better be done regularly than irregularly, as the latter will only serve to increase existing embarrassments.

It appears to me that the most early and the most rapid execution of all the provisions of the treaty is not only the best course, but is now expected by all parties here, and would do every thing to tranquillize the feelings which have been excited. The simple indication of the form of the contract would of itself do wonders. It has to be made known, and, believe me, sir, the sooner the better, both in relation to individuals and to future Government action in this quarter.

Very respectfully, &c.,

J. J. ABERT,
*Lt. Col. Top. Engineers.*

Hon. LEWIS CASS,
*Secretary of War.*

*Extract of a letter from John J. Abert to Commissioner of Indian Af
fairs, dated November 24, 1833.*

"I was upon the eve of sending an express to Judge Tarrant, with the
necessary papers and directions for him to locate in the upper counties,
when he arrived here with Mr. Bright. So I gave the papers to Mr.
Bright, with those for two more counties; and he has gone to locate, and
will employ Judge Tarrant under him. We divided the work as equitably
as we could, and before many days I shall have my net spread over all the
counties under my charge. I shall push the work with all the activity in
my power, increasing the locators as fast as I can find profitable work for
them, myself riding around every where, and superintending the whole,
that is of those counties under me. Nor have I a doubt that Mr. Bright will
also infuse great activity in his operations. I take him to be a very worthy and capable man.

"The preparing of the papers for the locators has been a more serious
job than I had at first anticipated. This writing of Indian names cannot be
done very rapidly, and the sheets had to be ruled with proper columns for
the purpose of furnishing the facts which would identify the location, and
also enable the patents to issue. This will be rather a worrying job, but
patience and perseverance will get it through. It might have been much
simplified when the survey was in hand by proper anticipations.

"As to the census, I believe it to be much more correct than we have
heretofore supposed, and doubt if it were done over again that it would be
done better. It was an extremely difficult task, and if to be improved at
all can be only by those who are and have been for some time intimately
acquainted with the Indians. We shall lop off those who, from their
age, are evidently not heads of families; or where the same man has given
in twice or more under different names; that is when we can ferret this out.

"Have you any evidence of the action of the Creeks upon the 29th section of article 6 of the treaty? We are in want of something of this kind.
You need send no drawings to us; they are useless. A table of the fractions
would be valuable, but for this we have written to Florence."

---

FORT GIBSON, *November 26, 1833.*

SIR: I have just received a letter from Mr. Ellsworth, dated at Fort
Leavenworth, and I suppose he has written to you also.

His trip to the west, as I predicted, has been of little importance towards
forwarding the views and advancing the interests of the Government. He
has brought in and is conducting to this place a party of the Pawnees of
the river Platte. I can see no advantage, and foresee great expense, in
bringing these Indians here at this time.

They are at peace with the United States, and not at war with any of the
nations about here. When I was in the Senate of the United States in
1818–1819, we ratified treaties with the Grand Pawnees and three of their
subordinate tribes; since which, I believe, there is no complaint of their
conduct towards the citizens of the United States.

There is an existing difference between the Omaha tribe, concerning the
murder of an Omaha boy at Cahonnis trading house, and the subsequent
murder of the son of Crane, an Ioway chief. But this has nothing to do

with the Indians in this quarter. And even now, while Mr. Ellsworth is conducting the Pawnees of the Platte to this place, the Clermont band of Osages has been driven from the great Western Prairie by the Pawnees and Camanches, who have killed the brother of Clermont, and a near relation of the Black Dog, two warriors of the Clermont band. I mention these circumstances to satisfy you that the party under the conduct of Mr. Ellsworth are not the formidable rovers of the great prairie.

The Government has required of us (if possible) to bring these Pawnees and Camanches to a treaty, so as to secure peace to the nations around us, the Choctaws, the Creeks, the Cherokees, the Osages, the Kanzas, the Shawanees, and the Delawares, with the other smaller tribes, and also to secure safety to the traders on the Santa Fe road.

But, as I said in a former despatch, these Pawnees and Camanches, Arabs of the prairie, are not to be successfully approached without considerable presents, and proper management. And the commissioners not having the means of furnishing presents, an advantageous interview with them is not to be expected.

The Government has recommended the exhibition of an imposing military force on their hunting ground; but this will have no effect. The experiment was tried last spring. These wild Indians are very numerous, and they are all well mounted on good horses. They came fearlessly into the vicinity of our camp, and actually made prisoner one of the mounted rangers in sight of our party. They then retreated, and our troops pursued for four days without success, having no prospect of overtaking the enemy.

The commissioners have been amused with various schemes and promises of the traders to bring these Indians to a friendly conference, and have always been disappointed. Their promises and plans are nonsense. There is, in my opinion, but one method of accomplishing this object. There are among the Osages seven or eight Pawnee and Camanche prisoners. If the Government would purchase these prisoners and restore them to their friends, and add a few presents suitable to their wants, and furnish a sufficient escort of dragoons for the safe conduct to and return from this place, the Indians might be persuaded to come; and being assured of protection, and convinced of the friendship of the whites, they would have confidence in the Government, and be induced to be at peace.

There is no other way of approaching them with any prospect of success. They stand in no fear from the military force of the Government. It cannot be brought to bear upon itinerant hordes of mounted savages on a prairie of a thousand miles square, abounding in game of the kind they require for subsistence, and with the Rocky Mountains in their rear.

I have deemed it proper to make these observations, in order that the Government may not be misled or misinformed in regard to one of the objects mentioned in the instructions to the Commissioners of Indian Affairs, and to which their attention has been particularly directed.

You will perceive, sir, that all my communications relative to the improvement of the condition of the Indians, have been predicated upon the supposition that a military garrison was to be continued at this place. It is the most proper place for the operations of Government, as regards the safety of the citizens of the United States, and the control of all the nations south of the Missouri river.

A few days ago I observed that a memorial to Congress has been passed by the Legislature of Arkansas, for the purpose of removing the troops to the boundary line between that Territory and the Indians. I do not know what this memorial contains, and perhaps I am travelling out of the line of my assigned duties to notice it. But this I do know, that a removal of the garrison from this place, at present, would be productive of the most disastrous consequences, as regards the peace and tranquillity of the surrounding nations. They would be at war in six months. This spot, at the head of steamboat navigation, and at the junction of three large rivers, is the most commanding position in this country, not only for the protection of the whites, but also for subjugating the refractory tribes. No doubt it would be gratifying to some of the officers of the garrison to be stationed in a more civilized neighborhood. And it might suit the views of the people of Arkansas to furnish the corn and beef consumed at this post, which are now furnished by the Creeks and Cherokees. I observe that the legislature have hedged in their representative to Congress, by sending a deputation from both houses to enforce the objects of the memorial. But as regards the convenience and utility in the operations of Government, and the preservation of peace and order among the Indians, the removal of the garrison would be most unfortunate.

If the memorial expresses any fear of an attack from a combination of the Indians of the west, these fears are groundless. They have as much reason to fear an attack from Tennessee or Kentucky, or an invasion of the Turks or Chinese.

The Indians understand their interests and the advantages of their situation too well to hazard so fatal an experiment.

I have the honor to be,

With very great respect,

Your obedient servant,

M. STOKES.

Hon. LEWIS CASS, *Secretary of War.*

---

SUPERINTENDENCY OF INDIAN AFFAIRS,

*St. Louis, November* 29, 1833.

SIR: I have the honor to transmit to you herewith the plats and field notes of the survey of the Delaware lands, and the subdivision of those assigned to the Weas and Piankeshaws, Kaskaskias, and Peorias, as executed by the Rev. Isaac McCoy, and lately returned by him to this office, in which they have been recorded.

By a letter lately received from Commissioner Ellsworth, I learn that he has settled the difficulty which existed with the Kickapoos in relation to the lands which have been assigned to them. I have therefore instructed Mr. McCoy to survey them, agreeably to the stipulations of the treaty.

I have the honor to be,

With great respect,

Your most obt. servt.,

WM. CLARK.

Hon. E. HERRING, *Com. Ind. Affairs.*

P. S. The map returned by Mr. McCoy does not show the scale upon which it is constructed, nor have either of the sketches (Nos. 2 and 3) a scale or meridian line laid down.

---

EXECUTIVE OFFICE, TALLAHASSEE, *Nov.* 29, 1833.

SIR: The communication from the department of the 31st ult. has been received. Having been present at the treaty made with Blunt and Davy

I recollect that the sum of $3,000 was stipulated to be paid to them, and I believe the commissioners did pay the amount, for the purpose of bearing the expense of an exploring party in the fall of 1832, or winter of 1833, who undertook to find some other country, out of the limits of the United States, as the future residence for the Indians belonging to the towns of Blunt and Davy on the Appalachicola river. Since my return here, I have been made acquainted, by Mr. Wescott, the acting Governor, with the course he pursued in executing the treaty referred to. It appears that Blunt, in May last, agreed to leave the United States by the 20th July following; but before the time fixed for his departure arrived, he gave notice to the acting Governor that he could not get off as he had promised, and set up a number of excuses. He alleged his son, and the other Indian boys at the school in Kentucky, could not be left behind; that his Indians had run away and refused to go with him, &c. &c. The department, as I am informed, have been fully advised of all the particulars. Since then Mr. Wescott has been constant in his efforts to get them off, and I am happy to learn, finally succeeded in getting them again to agree to remove from the country in ten days after the arrival of the boys from Kentucky; and I hope that the department will direct *that all the boys* shall immediately be sent to Appalachicola, Blunt's town.

Exercising that discretion which was confided to him, Mr. Wescott, to promote the emigration of the Indians, after consulting with the agent, Gen. Thompson, and the sub-agent, Mr. Pope, made a further allowance to Blunt and Davy of $1,500. I am not aware of any thing that can be done, nor can I at present suggest any course different from that pursued by the acting Governor, and which he submitted to the department, as being better calculated to effect the speedy execution of the treaty.

The legislature of the Territory commences its session the first Monday in January next. The executive will not have it in his power to leave the seat of Government for some time. The agent, Gen. Thompson, who is now at his post, has received orders to return to this place by the first of January next, to attend the execution of the treaty, and to enforce such orders or instructions as the department shall give to the superintendent. The most prompt attention will be paid to any instructions given by the department, and every thing which the superintendent can do to meet the views of the Government will most cheerfully be done.

I believe every particular in the instructions of the 31st ultimo had been performed by Mr. Wescott before its receipt; but they will again be repeated, if necessary. In regard to the robbery of Blunt, he, by the advice of Mr. Wescott, had previously appointed a Mr. Wall as his attorney to collect his evidence, &c., which, in addition to that previously transmitted by Mr. Wescott, will, I understand, be forwarded to the department in time for the action of Congress.

I am satisfied, from what Mr. Wescott says, no delay will take place on this ground. I trust the arrival of the Indian boys will not be delayed.

I am, respectfully,
Your obedient servant,
WM. P. DUVAL.

Elbert Herring, Esq., *Com. Ind. Affairs.*

I have the honor to enclose a copy of my instructions to the agent, Gen. Thompson, of the 23d instant.

93‡

TALLAHASSEE, INDIAN OFFICE,
*November 23, 1833.*

SIR: You will proceed from this place to the agency immediately, and take possession of the same, and all the books and papers in relation to Indian affairs.

It would be proper to impress on the chiefs the necessity of preparing on their part to execute the treaty lately made.

The Indians belonging to Blunt's and Davy's towns, who have gone down in the Seminole nation, must be ordered back to their respective towns to emigrate with their chiefs.

It will be important that you should attend to the emigration of the Indians residing on the Appalachicola river; and after you have done what the situation of the business at the agency demands, you will report yourself here to the superintendent by the 1st of January next, when you will receive further instructions.

When ordered from your agency your expenses will be paid, but not to exceed three dollars per day while in actual employment.

I am, respectfully,
Your obedient servant,
WM. P. DUVAL.

Gen. WILEY THOMPSON,
*Agent for the Florida Indians.*

———

COLUMBUS, GEORGIA, *November 30, 1833.*

SIR: I returned from the upper part of Russell county, where I had been locating, last night; and having shown to the principal assistant for Russell how I wished him to proceed, I mean, in the course of this day, to go by Fort Mitchell into Macon county, and set an assistant at work there.

We shall leave the fractional reservations until we receive the table of fractions, for which we have written to Florence. But all others will be located, and from the result of the experiments in locating, to which I attended personally, I should not be surprised if the whole of the counties under my charge were finished by the last of January.

My plan is to have a principal assistant for each county, with as many subordinates under each as can be profitably employed—the whole continually superintended by myself.

Mr. Bright has under his care the following counties: Talapoosa, Coosa, Talladega, Randolph, and Benton. I take Russell, Macon, Barbour and Chambers; the greater number of heads of families to my share being considered fully compensated by the rougher country under Mr. Bright. Mr. B. has Judge Tarrant as one of his principal assistants. I have Major Brodnax. And after all that you may have heard of the last gentleman, I must say, as the result of my experience, that I do not believe any one could easily understand Creek matters, particularly in the counties under me, without the aid of his knowledge of them. Nor have I yet found him to be otherwise than correct and honorable.

I have to acknowledge the receipt of your letter of the 16th. I fear much that if all settlers, lessees, rentees, and others, are to be considered in the class of intruders, subject to forcible ejectment by the marshal, he will find his duty extremely troublesome, and will need a greater power than has yet been employed. I have become acquainted with several cases in which, during his last round, he admitted whites complained of to compromise, pay the Indian for the damages done, and then to remain tenants by consent. This would rather indicate the course which his judgment of circumstances made necessary.

I have been endeavoring to ascertain the white population of these counties, but find it very difficult to get at correctly. I am however assured, from pretty good authority, that Talladega can furnish about 800 voters, Chambers about 400. This of course means grown males. There are probably about 25,000 whites of all ages and sexes in the nine counties, with a greater proportion than usual in the old States of grown males.

Complaints will be made against intruders by the Indians, at the instigation of purchasers, with the sole object of putting the latter in possession without trouble to them, and before the President will have time to act upon the contracts.

Believe me to be,
Very respectfully, sir,
Your obedient servant,
JOHN J. ABERT,
*Lieutenant Colonel United States Top. Engs.*

Hon. Lewis Cass,
    *Secretary of War.*

Are we at liberty to give to these Indians any paper or certificate of their locations?

---

Shawanoe, Jackson County, Miss.,
*November 30, 1833.*

Sir: The Hon. H. L. Ellsworth, commissioner, &c., has informed me that the board of Indian commissioners had recommended the surveying, as soon as practicable, of the lands of the Seneca and Shawanoe Indians, according to treaty with those tribes held on Cowskin river, December 29th, 1832.

I beg leave to say that I should be happy to be allowed to make the surveys. Under instructions from General Clark I shall complete the survey of the Kickapoo lands in the course of a few weeks. The Seneca lands, I believe, are not within his superintendency, and on that account I trouble you with this.

Allow me to say further, that I should be pleased to be instructed to survey the reservation for half breeds, on the southwest side of Mississippi river, which was set apart by treaty of Prairie du Chien, July 15th, 1830.

Most respectfully, sir,
Your obedient servant,
ISAAC McCOY.

Honorable Lewis Cass,
    *Secretary of War.*

---

New York, *November 30, 1833.*

Sir: In compliance with your order of 20th instant, we have shipped to Baltimore eight bales of Mackinac blankets, as per invoice enclosed. In lieu of the 3¼ points you ordered we have sent 3 points, of equal size to the former 3½ points. Woollen goods of every description are much higher this year than last; we have, however, charged these blankets at our very lowest prices. It is impossible to effect insurance beyond Baltimore, neither could we make arrangements to pay the transportation beyond that place. We have directed our agents to have them forwarded with the greatest despatch. You have herewith invoice, bill of lading, and policy of insurance.

The amount of invoice please remit in the usual way by draft on New York, and oblige

Your most obedient servants,<br>SUYDAM, JACKSON & CO.

Elbert Herring, Esq.

We have advised Colonel Montgomery of the shipment of the blankets, and sent him a memorandum of the quantity.

----

Fort Mitchell, November 30, 1833.

Sir: Your letter of the 21st inst., on the subject of my claim for the amount to which Susannah McIntosh and Jane Hawkins would be entitled for removing themselves and families to the west of the Mississippi, has just come to hand.

You say that immediately on the receipt of the papers from the commissioners, copies of them were sent to the Creek agent west, with directions to procure such information from the parties there as would enable the department to decide on the case. I have no doubt but the information when received will be satisfactory, but I am sorry it should be so long delayed, which keeps me out of the money I am justly entitled to. Let the information be what it may, I think I have in my possession evidence sufficient to prove that they gave the powers of attorney upon which I paid the money. Before I would pay it I carried the holder of them before the commmissioners, and received their advice. They promised me to recommend in their report the money to be sent here.

The powers of attorney are witnessed by persons living in Arkansas. I can also prove that Susannah McIntosh has written to this country stating that such powers were given, and, perhaps, authorizing the payment of some debts that she owed in this country. The transaction was open and fair, done, as I before stated, in the presence of the commissioners, and upon their advice that there would be no difficulty. It was a moneyed transaction; I paid not a cent else but money for the claim. I think there has been sufficient time for the agent west to have given the information required, and I do hope that some measures will be taken to get the necessary information, if what I can give is not satisfactory, in order that I may receive my pay, which I am in need of.

Yours respectfully,<br>THOMAS CROWELL.

Elbert Herring, Esq.,
       Washington City.

TUSCALOOSA, *November* 30, 1833.

DEAR SIR: I should have written to you by the last mail but had nothing decisive to communicate. Now, I hope I am enabled to say that our difficulties here are in a fair way of being terminated.

I presented your letter to the governor, who expressed a strong disposition to accede, as far as he possibly could, to the wishes of the Government. He wished to know whether the locations of the Indian reservations were in progress; when they would be completed; and whether, in case of any difficulty with settlers, who might be situated on those reservations, he could have an opportunity of applying the power of the State for their removal, so as to make it unnecessary for the United States to interfere.

I told him, (as I was enabled to do, by letter from Col. Abert, and from the information I had obtained at Montgomery, of the arrival of Messrs. Bright and Tarrant, at Fort Mitchell,) that there was every reason to believe that the reservations would be located by the 15th of January; and I explained to him how it was contemplated to locate them, as far as possible, in large tracts, comprehending as many of the Indians' rights as could be brought together, so as to expedite the work. I informed him that Col. Abert had seen many of the settlers, and stated to them the order of the Government under which he was acting, and the manner in which the orders for the removal of intruders would cease to operate on all the lands except the reservations; and that I had been assured by Col. Abert that all the persons he had seen expressed their satisfaction with the course he intended to pursue; that I therefore apprehended no difficulty with the settlers who might be so situated, who could have no motive to desire to remain on the reservations which were so soon to be sold by the Indians, and from which, (unless they purchased the Indian titles with the approbation of the President, according to the provisions of the treaty,) they would necessarily have to remove; that if any such settlers, however, should refuse to remove, the Government would make known its orders in relation to them; that these orders I had no doubt would be to enforce in such cases (if they should occur) the removal of the parties; that if the power of the State should be applied so as to produce their removal before the United States officers could act in the execution of their orders, there would of course be no case for their action. I endeavored, however, to convince him that the power of the State, if he meant the power of Russell county, would be entirely inefficient to accomplish such a purpose.

I then applied to him to know the situation of the prosecutions against the officers and soldiers, and deputy marshal, as to which, from the refusal of the clerk to give me copies, or to let me see his records, I was entirely uninformed, and stated that I hoped it would not be considered necessary to press the prosecutions. Just then I received a letter from Major McIntosh, informing me that the sheriff had been to the fort—had served the capias on Lieutenant Manning, and taken his bond, by way of bail, for $500, for his appearance at the next term of Russell circuit court (which by the laws of Alabama) he had no right to do; so that the bond is void; and had asked leave to go into the garrison and arrest the soldiers; and went in, and returned saying he could not find them. I told the governor this, and he seems well satisfied, and I apprehend nothing more will be done about the prosecutions. He has manifested, throughout, a disposition to remove all grounds of difference now existing, and to prevent the recurrence of any others. He means, in a day or two, to make a further communication to the legislature on the subject, stating your reply to his last communication, and showing that he considers the controversy settled.

You will wonder, when you hear this at his inaugural speech delivered the day before yesterday, and it is not easy to account for it. But from the speech, notwithstanding, I am satisfied he means to pursue a pacific course.

I have examined the census of the new counties here. Returns have come in from all, except three of the least populous; the total of white inhabitants of those returned, is 7,954, of which Russell contains 272; the remaining three, from the best information I can obtain, will not add more than 2000 to this number.

I have had letters from Mobile, from the marshal, who is sick, and from the district attorney. The process against Mr. Austill, the deputy, is in the sheriff's hands at that place, but not yet served. I think it best to stay here a day or two longer, and have not yet determined whether it will be necessary for me to go to Mobile. I shall write again before I leave this, if I do not go by the next mail.

I am, sir, &c.,

F. S. KEY.

Hon. Lewis Cass,
  Secretary of War.

CHEROKEE AGENCY, December 3, 1833.

SIR: Your communication of the 7th ultimo was received yesterday, on my return from a tour through the lower parts of the Cherokee Agency, and the enclosed letter to Ridge and Vann despatched this morning to its address.

The appraisers have been in service for some two or three weeks. The natives were generally disposed to take the advantage anticipated by your letter of instructions under date of the 16th September. But, through the vigilance of these officers, it is to be hoped the Government will be protected against impositions to any considerable extent. So far, however, as I have been informed, they appear to have given general satisfaction.

In order that they may be able to prosecute the business already before them, as well as that which will probably arise hereafter, in time for all to get off before the season for removal is too far spent, it has been considered advisable for them occasionally to take different routes, accompanied each by one enrolling agent, who being sworn can act as assistant assessors, and at the same time prosecute the duties of his own office, the better subserving the public interest without additional expense.

In your communication of the 16th September last, you say the sum will be inserted in the estimates submitted to Congress to meet the claims for abandoned improvements, and request me to make as correct an estimate as possible of the probable number of improvements which will be left, the quantity of acres, and value of each, and the persons to whom they belong.

I have deferred making answer to that part of your letter, hoping that it would be in my power by this time to more fully satisfy the call than it was at the date of its receipt, but find it impracticable, even after having passed through a greater portion of their settlements, to say who all will go this season; for in a day's time the most stubborn opposers are sometimes suddenly converted, while, on the other hand, those who appeared most inclined to favor the wishes of the Government, by some unhappy calculation in their chances of fortune, are found lending their whole influence to defeat purposes insuring the prosperity and happiness of their people.

The following, however, is a statement of the names of those whose places have been valued, the number of improvements, and their valuation, with the respective numbers in family; which may be taken as an average applicable to the whole tribe.

| | | No. in family. | | No. of improvements. | | Valuation. |
|---|---|---|---|---|---|---|
| 1. | Thomas Wilson | - 7 | - | 3* | - | $1,600 00 |
| 2. | John Duncan | - 16 | - | 2 | - | 1,233 00 |
| 3. | James Wiekel | - 6 | - | 1 | - | 415 00 |
| 4. | Samuel Nelms | - 6 | - | 1 | - | 124 00 |
| 5. | Martin Downing | - 9 | - | 1 | - | 96 00 |
| 6. | Young Wolf | - 8 | - | 2 | - | 837 62½ |
| 7. | James McDaniel | - 16 | - | 3 | - | 2,300 00 |
| 8. | Bears Track | - 7 | - | 1 | - | 134 00 |
| 9. | Colakuska or John McIntosh | 16 | - | 1 | - | 740 00 |
| 10. | John McDaniel | - 1 | - | 2 | - | 447 75 |
| | | 90 | | 17 | | $7,927 37½ |

\* Two improvements not valued.

The average appears from the foregoing improvements to be $8,000 to ninety persons. Eight hundred and fifty stand subject to removal, enrolled, and under my superintendence. According to the above, carrying out the proportional amount, it would be seventy odd thousand dollars.

Should the business go on as prosperously as has been anticipated, the number will be increased threefold, or perhaps even more; which would make the appropriation necessary equal to two hundred and fifty thousand dollars, at least, for the present season.

Double this amount, however, and if there should be a demand for it the same will be at your command, and if not required it can very readily be converted to other public purposes. There are at least ten thousand Cherokees. Nine hundred thousand dollars, according to the foregoing estimate, would be eventually required to satisfy this description of claims.

For the average number of acres of cleared land, allow me to refer you to the appraisers' rolls, recently sent to your office.

Should this communication not prove satisfactory on the subject, it will be in my power by the time I can be informed of the same, perhaps, to answer more fully.

Do, if you please, urge a speedy appropriation; for there are many families now awaiting anxiously a rise in the waters to set out, that they may prepare in the west for the next year's crops; and it will be impossible for them to get off without a proportion of their dues for improvements beforehand. They are accountable here for their contracts since the extension of the Tennessee laws, and most of them are much in debt; consequently, cannot get off without pecuniary aid from Government.

I have the honor to be,
Most respectfully,
Your very obedient servant,
BENJ. F. CURREY.

ELBERT HERRING, Esq.,
*Commissioner of Indian Affairs.*

FORT MITCHELL, ALA., *December* 3, 1833.

SIR: Soon after the Creek treaty of 1832, I requested you would inform me if contracts made for Indian reservations, by taking Indian bonds, would be considered valid by the department previous to the locations being sanctioned by the President; and, in reply, Mr. Herring informed me they would not, inasmuch as the Indian had no title until his location had been sanctioned. Upon this information I made myself contented, while large speculating companies have been formed and purchased up nearly all the land by taking the Indian bonds; and they state that they have it from you that the titles will be good. This I don't believe: I have too much confidence in the present Administration to believe, for one moment, that such claims would be considered valid. It would be worse than useless for me to attempt to give you any information in relation to the manner in which these speculators have conducted the business, as the facts have long since been made known to you; but, in conclusion, permit me to remark, that while the *friends* of the *Union* have been lending their small influence in behalf of the Government measures, these sets of nullifying speculators have been making their purchases and setting every thing at defiance. Several persons, as well as myself, wish to purchase a farm, but if those villainous contracts should in any manner be considered good, no other persons will have any chance to get land.

Will you please inform me if contracts made previous to the location will be good; or will they be considered good only after the Indian has been located, and that location sactioned by the President; or will any kind of obligation from the Indian be good, if another purchaser goes before the certifying agent and makes a better bargain for the Indian, and such bargain meets the approbation of said agent? You will much oblige a friend by giving this information as soon as possible.

I beg you will pardon me for troubling you on a subject which must be daily ringing in your ears from all quarters.

I am, very respectfully,
Your obedient servant,
S. C. BENTON.

Hon. LEWIS CASS,
*Secretary of War, Washington City.*

---

OSAGE AGENCY, *December* 3, 1833.

SIR: I have the honor to inform you of my safe arrival at this place with the Indian delegation of Pawnees and Otoes. Many of the Osages are absent on their hunts; several of the principal chiefs are here, and others will be called in, and peace, I doubt not, concluded between these long contending tribes. Clermont's band will be visited by the delegation on their return from Fort Gibson, and another opportunity afforded to smoke and eat with the Osages in fuller council. I write now more particularly to apologise in behalf of Mr. Dougherty, for his omission to transmit his annual returns.

The cholera confined him a considerable time in the early part of the fall, and he entered into my service as soon as he was able to ride. I cannot omit to assure the department of the great importance of his services on my excursion. Understanding the languages of several tribes, and possessing

their confidence, he enabled me to progress more rapidly and more economically. I rely yet much on his aid in completing the general peace. It is due also to him to say, that he seems ardently bent on the civilization of the tribes under his charge, and will co-operate fully in the views of Government to accomplish the object.

Mr. Dougherty proposes returning by the way of St. Louis to visit his family; should any purchases be made at St. Louis for the Indians under his charge, I would recommend that the purchases be made by him in preference to others, as I find by a comparison of prices, and quality of goods, that his purchases are better than those made through the agency of others. I trust, however, some better arrangement will be made in the purchase of Indian goods, than receiving them with one or two profits, charged upon them by the respective dealers through whose hands they now pass.

I have the honor to be, respectfully,
Yours obediently,
HENRY L. ELLSWORTH.

Hon. E. HERRING,
*Indian Commissioner, Washington.*

---

SUPERINTENDENCY OF INDIAN AFFAIRS,
*St. Louis, December* 4, 1833.

SIR: I take the liberty of enclosing to you herewith, a report of Captain Gordon, provisional sub-agent, who has lately returned from paying the annuities due the Senecas, in which he states his apprehensions of difficulties between the white settlers and the bands of Shawanees, formerly of Cape Girardeau, and who have latterly moved from White river in Arkansas, and encamped within this State on Cowskin river, and near the Senecas.

The chiefs and head men of this band visited me in September, and informed me that they were unwilling to join the Shawanees of Ohio, on the land assigned them on Kanzas river; that their band stopped on Cowskin river on lands they believed was outside of the State, and would go no further; and requested that a small piece of land might be given to them on the said Cowskin river, (or Six Bulls,) near the tract assigned to the Shawanees and Senecas from Lewistown, in exchange for a part of the lands which were assigned to this band by the treaty of 1825.

I have communicated my views on this subject to the commissioners west, who have been furnished with copies of the various talks of those Indians, and the views of the department in regard to their petitions; and have expressed an opinion favorable to their assigning to this unfortunate band of Shawanees a small piece of land where they wish to settle, for a part of their claim adjoining the Kanzas reservation.

In the latter part of Mr. Gordon's report, he states certain information which he had received of the American Fur Company having established a distillery at Fort Union, (Yellow Stone river,) and of their making and vending whiskey in quantity, &c.

As this is a new case, I must beg leave to ask the instructions of the department therein. If proof can be obtained of the facts charged, shall I revoke the license of the American Fur Company, and sue their bond? How is a revocation of a license at those distant trading posts to be enforced?

This license may be revoked, but before information thereof reaches so distant a post, (being eighteen hundred miles,) a sale of the whole of the stock may be effected, and the proceeds taken off.

The law of the 6th of May, 1822, gives the superintendent of Indian Affairs power to grant license; but neither that law, nor the act of the 9th of July, 1832, prohibiting the introduction of ardent spirits into the Indian country, gives power to the superintendent or Indian agents to revoke a license without the special authority of the President.

I have the honor to be,
With great respect,
Your most obedient servant,
WILLIAM CLARK.

The Hon. ELBERT HERRING,
 *Commissioner Indian Affairs, Washington City.*

---

SAINT LOUIS, *November* 5, 1833.

DEAR SIR: In accordance with your instructions of the 14th August, I proceeded to the Senecas from Sandusky, and Senecas and Shawanees, from Louistown, near the southwest corner of the State of Missouri, and paid them their annuities respectively, for the year 1833, and in the manner prescribed by the department. I also delivered for their use the blacksmith's tools, iron, steel, &c. Those for the Senecas of Sandusky I delivered into the hands of James Pool, United States blacksmith. The other set, intended for the benefit of the Senecas and Shawanees from Lewistown, I delivered to Lieutenant Van Horne, acting sub-agent, there being as yet no blacksmith for them employed. The money for the support of blacksmith shop, pay of miller, &c., for the Senecas from Sandusky, and for the support of blacksmith shop for the Senecas and Shawanees, I delivered over to Lieutenant Van Horne, and have the honor herewith to submit abstracts and vouchers of the transactions.

I examined the different water courses on the lands of the Senecas for a mill site, and am of opinion that there is no good one; being, however, a very imperfect judge of such matters, and conscious of it, I attach very little importance to my own opinion in this matter.

During my stay in that quarter I made a visit to the camp of the Shawanees from Cape Girardeau, for the purpose of delivering to them the message you had charged me with in regard to their removal on to their lands near the Kanzas river. None of their chiefs were at home, and consequently nothing could be effected. I learned from those at their camp that they were determined not to move until driven by force. They have located themselves on a river called Cowskin, in the heart of the white settlement, and the greatest anxiety prevailed on the part of the whites for their immediate removal. Some complaints were made of their stealing hogs, &c. I observed that the worst possible state of feeling subsisted between the whites and themselves, and am clearly of opinion that unless they remove or are removed in a short time, that acts of hostility will inevitably be the result.

On my return from the Senecas' sub-agency, I fell in with some gentlemen from the mountains who had made some stay at the mouth of the Yellow Stone river. They informed me that the American Fur Company have established a distillery at Fort Union, and are making and vending whiskey in quantity, having purchased, as my informants stated, a large quantity of corn from the Indians for that purpose. This news has been confirmed to me by other and different persons who have subsequently arrived from that country. Believing that the communication of this piece of information is a duty which I owe to you, to the department, and to myself, I accordingly make it, without comment on the facts, and most respectfully submit it, with that which precedes it, to your consideration.

I have the honor to be, sir,

Your most obedient servant and friend,

WILLIAM GORDON,
*Provisional Sub Indian Agent.*

General WILLIAM CLARK,
*Superintendent Indian Affairs.*

---

CREEK AGENCY, *December 6, 1833.*

SIR: Our locating goes on with great spirit, and I see no reason yet for doubting that the whole of the counties under me will be completed in January, as stated to you in my last letter. The system which I have adopted works much to my satisfaction; nor do I hear of any discontent with it from any one.

I have seen many, and heard from many of the intruders, and still am of the opinion they will remove from the reserves as soon as they are located; that is, those who have been heretofore considered as intruders, and subject to ejectment by a military force. How your rule will operate which places in that class tenants at will and lessees, I cannot yet say.

But, although your opinion that the fee simple of these lands does not pass from the United States until the patent is issued, is unquestionably correct, yet it does appear to me that by the treaty and the locations, a title less than fee simple passes, and which courts of law will sustain. These titles may be transferred, and the transferee will then possess the rights of the transferer. Now then, sir, pardon the question, but is it advisable to disturb by a military power a possession or title which a court of law will sustain?

I feel very sensibly the position in which my letters from this quarter place me. But I have acted upon the principle of occasionally giving the reverse of the medal, then merely to echo back sentiments which I know to be already entertained. The latter course would make my letters of little value, and leave you unapprised of views which you may have to meet.

The Indians in this neighborhood are extremely anxious to sell; in fact, they are selling as fast as we locate, and generally at fair, and frequently, to my judgment of the land, at high prices. The avidity to procure their land has had its effect in raising the prices, and they say that by withholding the patent they can always coerce the fulfilment of the contract.

The collisions in bargaining between the whites has really improved many of the Indians in the knowledge of their possessions, and in the

means of protecting themselves. They ask higher prices, and do not renew their sales since the locations without additional stipulations.

Very respectfully, &c.,

JOHN J. ABERT,

Lieut. Col. Top. Eng.

Hon. Lewis Cass,
    Secretary of War.

Columbus, December 6, 1833.

Sir : The land sales are just brought to a close in this district for the
present.

I have succeeded in registering and reserving such claims as have been
presented and are entitled to be located, taking the register made by Major
F. W. Armstrong, and the treaty, and also the citizen register, which I
found in the possession of Colonel W. Ward, the former agent, for my
guide.

If you recollect, I said to you in a former letter that I should in all cases
require of the reservee (applicant) to make *a true* representation of the
facts on filing his application; that on his failing so to do, and claiming
lands to which he or they were not justly entitled under the treaty, he
might hazard, and in all probability would lose the land to which he was
entitled; that if I found there had been any such fraudulent attempts by
making a wrong location, designed to cover better land with the reserve, I
should, on discovering the fraud, raise the reserve thus improperly located,
and have the land sold. Under this rule I raised a reserve which had been
made and designated on the map, for a section of land, on the first week of
the sales. The particulars of the case are these: an individual representing
Captain James Shields, one of the reservees, did, through a fraudulent
design, procure a location of a section of land, which section did not
include the residence, &c. of said reservee, as required by the 19th art. of
the treaty; but knowingly and with fraudulent designs, presented his
claim as laying on a section of much better quality, saying, I was informed
and believe, that before the mistake could be discovered and remedied he
would be able to buy the land, should the fraud ever be discovered. In
this, however, he was mistaken, as one of the deputy surveyors who surveyed the land and knew on what section the house and improvement of
Captain Shields's property belonged, came forward and certified to the fact,
that the location that was marked on the maps as a reserve did not embrace
the house and improvement of said Shields, leaving no shadow of doubt as to
the fraud; in consequence of which I felt myself bound from the position I
had first taken, and the more fully to protect the interests of the Government, by putting a stop to the mighty scheme of fraud which I believed in
all probability was in contemplation to the prejudice of the interest of
Government; consequently, I directed Major Dowsing, the register, to
erase the marks designating the reserve on the map, likewise to offer the
land for sale as other public lands, which was done; and by this act I feel
confident I have put a stop to that mode of fraud more finally than by any
other course that possibly could have been adopted. However, there was a
similar fraud attempted on the lands on which the mission house Mayhew
is established, which also proved abortive, (this was the most glaring

attempt at fraud I ever knew,) and those lands, &c. brought the Government a good price. The checking of these frauds has caused me some frowns, and perhaps threats, of the designing ones, but I value them not a pin. I have undertaken this important trust, and, although at a great sacrifice, I will do my endeavors to bring it to a close in a proper manner, as far as my feeble abilities will permit.

I have been and yet am much embarrassed in the progress of this business, for the want of the necessary maps. I have never been furnished, as seemed contemplated by the War Department, with the first map; consequently I had to ride like a postboy from Chocchuma to this place, say four times, in the last two or three months, at least one thousand miles, through a wilderness; having, in part, to pack my provisions, and sometimes compelled to sleep in the woods. I wrote the surveyor general on receipt of your favor of July last, and sent him an extract of the letter from the department, but he did not seem to me to understand that he was to furnish me with any maps, nor has he ever done so. I have located the claims which lay in that section of the nation which he has offered for sale, (which, by the by, is but a small part,) and there are no maps, as yet, furnished of the balance, or any part thereof. What am I to do? It will be an endless job for me to wait and attend the sales of lands as they may hereafter be offered for sale. Would it not be better that I should be furnished with copies of maps in all cases as soon as they can be made out after the survey is done? by which means the locating of the claims might be brought to a more speedy close.

Mr. Hayward, in his reply to the War Department calling on the surveyor for maps for my use, said, in answer, that the locating agent, under former treaties, had had reference to the maps in the district land offices. There would be no objection to this mode as regards any treaty made prior to the treaty at Dancing Rabbit, as there never has been, as I believe, one hundredth part of the claims to locate; and that, too, at a round of some seven to nine hundred miles, to include the four offices in this State, and God only knows how far it is, *or may be*, to include the one in Alabama, as I am uninformed at what place the Indian lands in that State will likely be sold. There are a great many reserves in that part of the Choctaw nation. These lands have been surveyed some time since, and it would be but trifling for the surveyor general to furnish me with the maps, that I might locate these claims then belonging to the Indians under the treaty, as well also the surveyor general of this State. It would be a much more speedy and convenient mode of transacting this business to be furnished with the maps, which would enable me to close the business and bring it to a termination as shortly after the surveys are completed as practicable, otherwise it will be utterly out of my power to continue in the office. I have a large family, and but just settled in a new country; my lands yet to improve and put in a state for cultivation, requiring much labor and attention; all of which require my personal and strict attention. I have thirty-five to forty in family, and a disproportion of laborers, consequently creating a responsibility on me and my time paramount to all other considerations.

It may be proper here to state, that the department may be fully advised of all things touching my official acts, as well as touching my office, as far as practicable, there having been many spurious efforts to pass false claims through my office, hoping thereby to procure lands to which they from the treaty and the register seemed not to be entitled. I have ever met such pretence with promptness and decision, of course to the discomfiture of the designing; and I am sorry to say, that many of these groundless claims were presented at my office with much address, and urged on me with great earnestness, by a *gentleman* (much honored by the citizens of this State), and who even took occasion to admonish me, that should *his claims* be rejected by me, they should be presented to a higher tribunal; leaving me to infer he would bring all such before Congress, or perhaps first the War Department; should they fail at the department, thence to Congress, &c. Should this effort at fraud be persevered in, it is possible it may be effectual at Washington, procuring there what could not be allowed here. Should it be so, I have one consolation—my skirts are clear.

I have the honor to be, &c.,

GEO. W. MARTIN.

Hon. Lewis Cass.

P. S. Should you wish to confer with any one who has been present during the sales at Chocchuma, I cite you to Judge Black, senator from this State; Mr. Jno. Bell and Mr. Dickinson, from Tennessee.

---

General Land Office, *December* 7, 1833.

Sir: I have had the honor to receive from the office of Indian affairs a copy of a letter dated the 13th ultimo, from General Clark of St. Louis, stating that he had forwarded therewith "the plats and field notes of the surveys of the Sac and Fox half breed reservations between the Mississippi and Desmoine rivers, which have been lately returned to this office." I therefore have to request that certified copies of the plats and field notes above mentioned may be furnished to this office for my information, and such official action in relation thereto as may be necessary.

I am, very respectfully, sir,

Your obedient servant,

ELIJAH HAYWARD.

The Hon. Lewis Cass,
*Secretary of War.*

---

Fort Mitchell, *December* 8, 1833.

Sir: On counting the individual locations made up to this day, I find that we have completed one ninth of the whole of the locations in the counties under my care; and if the weather does not prove extremely inclement and unfavorable, I hope by the 15th of January to furnish the marshal with such a map as will prevent the possibility of his making a mistake between an Indian reservation and a section belonging to the United States.

The system of leasing these lands has not, I think, been pursued as extensively as I was at one time led to suppose; but that of purchasing is followed with all imaginable activity. Willing sellers and buyers will always make a brisk trade. Both exist in this county.

Conversing today with several intelligent gentlemen, they all agreed in the opinion that the Indians who sold would emigrate as soon afterwards as arrangements could be made for conducting them; and that it mattered not how much or how little they received, all would generally be wasted before they emigrated.

It appeared also to be a general opinion among them that, counting upon the results of these sales as a means of support, the Indian had neglected his crops, and was living upon his expectation.

They likewise agreed with me that it would be a great misfortune to these people were they to arrive at their new homes without the means of stocking their farms.

To meet these two contingencies, namely, that of their debts here, and that of stocking their farms in the west, there is but one resource, the results of the sales of the land; but if they receive the whole of these results it will be wasted. There must, therefore, be some plan adopted of saving a part for them.

The plan which met the approbation of these gentlemen, and who had come here to buy, was to pay half of the purchase money to the Indian, and the other half to the certifying agent, that is to the United States, for the Indian's use after his arrival west.

I respectfully suggest the same to your better judgment.

Yours, &c.,

JOHN. J. ABERT.

Hon. Lewis Cass, *Secretary of War.*

---

At Camp, Coosa County, Al., *December* 8, 1833.

Sir: In proceeding to Fort Mitchell agreeably to your instructions of the 14th October, I learned that Col. Abert was at Columbus in Georgia, where I joined him, and entered upon the duty of making the necessary arrangements for locating the Indians, agreeably to the treaty of the 24th March, 1832, in doing which Col. Abert and myself were of opinion that it would facilitate the business to divide the ceded territory, he to superintend the location of one portion and myself the other.

We accordingly divided the territory, he taking the south and southeastern, and myself the northern and western.

After making all the necessary arrangements, I proceeded to the most southwestern part of the district allotted to me, and commenced locating the Indians belonging to the Hickory Ground town, who I found were anxious to be located, and afforded me all the necessary facilities, and who I found well satisfied with the location, with the exception of a few who were rejected on account of their not being entitled agreeably to the terms of the treaty.

I find there must have been great impositions in taking the cen was unfortunate that any were enrolled in the census who were not entitled, because it induced them to believe that it gave them a sort of title that no after act or investigation should deprive them of. I have ever believed that we would find more difficulty and embarrassment in investigating the census list than all the rest of the duties, which I have in some degree already realized.

After completing the location of the Hickory Ground town I proceeded to the next adjacent town, who positively refused to be located, alleging that their principal chief, E Path-le-yo-ho-le, had informed them that I was not locating the Indians agreeably to the treaty; that by the terms of the treaty all the Indians were entitled to land. I remained with them about three days, using all the arguments and inducements that I could invent to induce them to be located, but all to no purpose; they were unwilling to be located until they could hear from their principal chiefs. I have left them, and am now proceeding to another town, where I expect to be met in the same way, as I am informed that E Path-le-yo-ho-le has been endeavoring to infuse the same doctrine into all he could have influence with.

I have thought it my duty to give the department the most early information of the conduct of the Indians on this subject, in order that, if they still persist I may receive some aid and advice from the department; still I am in hopes they will become convinced of their error, and will suffer the location to go on, and will lend their aid; which if they do not, even if they were to remain passive, it would be almost impossible to locate them, especially as it is by and through them alone that we derive all the information with respect to their names, settlement, &c.

By the instructions of the 14th October, Col. Abert and myself were requested to report our views as to the necessity of removing the citizens who have settled in the ceded territory.

On this subject I have taken some pains to ascertain, as far as in my power, whether or not it would be necessary to remove any of the citizens from any part of the territory, but as yet have not been able to obtain any information that in my opinion would render it necessary to remove any of the citizens residing amongst the Indians.

Should any thing occur that in my opinion would render it necessary to remove any of the citizens, I will lose no time in apprising the departure of it.

From the obstinacy and tardiness of the Indians, I can form no idea at present when the location can be completed.

I have the honor to be,
Most respectfully,
Your obedient servant,
J. BRIGHT.

Hon. Lewis Cass,
  *Secretary of War.*

---

Louisville, Barbour Co., Alabama,
*December 9,* 1833.

Sir: I received a letter from Elbert Herring, a letter stating that my letter to you of the 31st ultimo had been referred to that office, and in reply have to state that Col. J. J. Abert and James Bright are appointed to locate the Creek reservations, and that a copy of my letter has been sent to them for their information; and that an additional favor would be conferred by my communicating to these any farther views on the subject, and in reply I will state to you that if those gentlemen want any assistance, and you will instruct them to call on me, I will endeavor to prevent all frauds that can be done, and think, from the acquaintance that I have with the Indians and respectable whites that reside in the nation, that many may be prevented, and I will endeavor to do equal justice to Indians.

Yours respectfully,
F. W. PUGH.

Hon. Lewis Cass.

CREEK AGENCY, *December* 9, 1833.

SIR: I have time only, before the closing of the mail, to acknowledge the receipt of your instructions to us as certifying agents. Of course we cannot act until after making the locations. Mine are pushed with all the activity in my power.

If the suggestion in my letter of yesterday was approved, and a rule containing it added to those we have, we could protect the Indian to the extent of one half of the purchase money, and reject all claims of payments beyond the other half; otherwise, I fear debts will be made to the whole amount, and proof exhibited, which, although erroneous, will in many cases be out of our power to reject.

Depend upon it, debts will be made to the whole amount of money of many of the purchases, as soon as the rules are known. I shall keep them to myself, therefore, for some days, until I can send round and caution the Indians. It is rather to be regretted that we have to make them public so long before we can act under them.

The form of the contract is not prescribed. This might have been made public long since to advantage. For the want of it, I say that all contracts must be in such form as the laws of the State require in such transactions.

Your obedient servant,
J. J. ABERT,
*Lieutenant Col. U. S. Army.*

Hon. LEWIS CASS,
*Secretary of War.*

P. S. Mr. Bright is somewhere in Coosa. Judge Tarrant in Talladega. I do not know Mr. McHenry, nor where he is. We shall have to meet somewhere to divide the labor, which will have to be on a geographical basis; and each having lists of his own heads of families, we cannot conflict.

———

FORT GIBSON, *December* 11, 1833.

SIR: I have the honor to advise you of my safe arrival here with the delegation of northern Indians. The Osages received the Pawnees and Otoes with great kindness, and gave them the wampum of peace.

As some of the Osage warriors were absent, articles of agreement will be signed on the return of the Pawnees in a few days. The Cherokees and Creeks whom I have seen rejoice to meet the northern Indians. A council will be held the 14th.

The establishment of peace among the Indians seems to afford *great joy* and promises much good. But whatever may be the benefit of my individual services since September last, (and allow me to call them arduous,) I should have left all unattempted, had I been apprised of the wishes of Government, as contained in the instructions, which I saw for the first time on my return to Fort Gibson.

In apologising, permit me to say that I should not have drawn any draft, had not the agent of Gen. Clark misapprehended the wishes of Gen. C. relative to some United States goods unappropriated at Fort Leavenworth. Disappointed in part of these goods, I was compelled to buy of the sutler, to whom I gave a draft, with a suggestion that no appropriation was yet made to pay it.

95‡

In July I wrote from St. Louis, advising the Government of the plan of the commissioners to visit the northern tribes.   I left St. Louis when the cholera was raging, with the promise of Governor Stokes to join me on the way in a few days.   Gov. Stokes was taken sick and confined a long time, and so late as September he was dangerously ill, in ascending the Missouri.   He had received a few despatches, but expecting soon to meet me, did not communicate the contents or even write me a line before I started for the Pawnee country.   I had not the least intimation, therefore, that the Government (in consequence of want of funds) wished the commissioners to delay in accomplishing with all possible despatch the objects named in the first instructions.

Among the most important of these were the difficulties between the northern tribes, the Delawares, Pawnees, and others.   Nor from a letter dated at Shawnee Agency, from Gov. Stokes, in September, (very kindly offering to approve of my acts, if reasonable, wishing success, but doubting the possibility of my meeting the Pawnees,) received on my return from the Pawnees, did I mistrust any new instructions.   Let me advert to the situation of the Indians on my arrival at Fort Leavenworth.   I found many war parties out, and many new ones on foot.

The Delawares had just returned from burning a whole Pawnee village, and destroying their corn.   The return trail had been artfully made through the Kickapoo settlement, where emigrants were arriving.   The Kickapoos justly feared an attack, if not destruction.

Gen. Clark, of the Kanzas agency, complained, too, of the constant interruption of war parties going through his tribe against the Pawnees, and declaring by a letter that he would resign unless aid could be given him.

The Delawares said they had complained to Government in vain, and would take revenge against the Pawnees, who, by the way, were defending their own land.

The commissioners had disappointed the northern Indians in not visiting them the last year.

Agents gave assurance that the commissioners would come this year, and thereby arrested many hostile acts.

The Government, I knew, were anxious for the report from the commissioners; this would not be judiciously made, without visiting the country and Indians north of the Osage reservation.

The Kickapoos, and Pottawatamies connected with them, were dissatisfied with their location; the adjustment of this difficulty could not be delayed.   A general peace was also thought antecedent to much progress with civilization.

Under these circumstances, I felt called upon to act alone.   The urgency of the case may be supposed from my starting with eight soldiers, (all I could get,) still laboring under the debility of the cholera myself, and taking my son as secretary from the hospital, unable to ride but a few miles the first day.   A violent attack of the fever and ague would have driven me back after the second day's march, had I not preferred being carried in a wagon, with daily chills, than fail in an attempt to restore peace.

I have incurred but a *trifling expense.*

What I have done is in part communicated.

The expenditures have been made with *strict economy*, as will appear by my vouchers, soon to be transmitted.   I was fearful lest the northern Indians should not be visited during the lifetime of the act under which we were appointed.

I say this because there will be no time previous to July next when the streams, or the return of the Indians from their hunts, would make a journey successful.

I can say also, that information derived from a personal conversation with seven Pawnee Picts and two Camanches, during my journey, will enable the commissioner to obtain a good if not the only intercourse with the Mexican Indians adjoining Red river.

I ought to observe that the Potawatamies were expected at Fort Leavenworth in the fall to explore a country. Colonel Pepper wrote he should reach there by 15th October.

I must confess that I felt more anxiety to explain my conduct, because some *may* have intimated the inutility of bringing the Pawnees here.

It has been supposed, and that too by my colleague, Governor Stokes, that the Pawnees of the Platte and the Pawness of Red river were not at war with the Cherokees, Creeks, and Choctaws.

The fact is, and the talks will show it, that the Pawnees of the Platte are at war *indiscriminately* with all south of the Kanzas river. It is equally true that all the tribes south of said river have considered the Pawnee Picts and the Pawnees of the Platte the same people, connected by language and by blood. How important to show them the difference between the American and Mexican Indians.

Among 10,000 Pawnees of the Platte, only one could be found to understand the language of the Picts.

I must stop. I have made a long letter; I have assumed high responsibility; the necessity is stated.

I yet trust my act will meet your approbation.

I am, sir, with high respect,
Yours obediently,
HENRY L. ELLSWORTH.
Hon. E. Herring,
*Indian Commissioner, Washington.*

---

Columbus, Georgia, *December* 12, 1833.

Sir: The necessity of having a form of contract to be generally followed in these land speculations, and the time which will elapse before the certifying agents can meet for that or any other purpose, has induced me to adopt one without further delay.

I have put it in the hands of a printer for the use of all persons, and have requested a friend during my absence, as I am on my way to Chambers county, to send you a copy as soon as any are struck off. I hope it may meet with your approbation.

Very respectfully, &c ,
JOHN J. ABERT,
*Lieut. Col. Top. Eng.*
Hon. Lewis Cass, *Sec'y of War.*

---

State of Alabama,                      *county:*
Be it known to all men, that I,                      of the Creek nation of Indians in the State of Alabama, do hereby bargain, sell, and convey to                      all my right, title, and interest in a certain tract of

land, being the                         half section of section number         in
township number               and range number                 in the county of
               and in the State aforesaid; being the tract of land located in
my name, in conformity with a treaty made and concluded with the Creek
nation of Indians and the United States, on the twenty-fourth day of March,
one thousand eight hundred and thirty-two, for and in consideration of the
sum of                 dollars, whereof the sum of               dollars has
been paid to me, and is hereby acknowledged to have been received: the
balance of said consideration money, namely, the sum of           dollars,
is to be paid                 on delivery of the patent for the
said tract of land to the said
This contract being subject to the certifying agent and the approbation of
the President of the United States, agreeably to the provisions of the treaty
aforesaid.                                                        [SEAL.]

       Signed, sealed, and delivered in our presence, this       day of
one thousand eight hundred and thirty-

       Personally appeared before me                 a judge of the county
of               of the State of Alabama, the said               being
the purchaser within named; and, being duly sworn, deposeth and saith,
that the amount of                 dollars being the consideration
money for the said tract of land, is correct, as stated in the within contract,
and that the amount of                     dollars, acknowledged
to have been received by the said         was actually paid by him as
stated in the within contract.
       Signed, acknowledged, and sworn to before me, this       day of
one thousand eight hundred and thirty-

       I certify that I have examined the contract between the said
a Creek Indian, and            for the conveyance to the latter of a
tract of land, being the               of section           in township
             and range           in the county of             State
of Alabama: that the said           has appeared before me, and after
the transaction was fully explained to him he approved the same: the sums
stated to have been received by him were

       I consider the price given a full value of the land, and certify the con-
tract, for the consideration of the President of the United States.

       ———

                 SUPERINTENDENCY OF INDIAN AFFAIRS,
                         St. Louis, December 12, 1833.
       SIR: My bill of exchange of this date, in favor of Henry S. Coxe, esq.,
cashier of the Branch Bank of the United States at this place, for four
thousand seven and twenty-nine dollars, is for that sum received of him on
account of expenses of running the lines called for by the 7th article Prairie
du Chien treaty, of 15th July, 1830, and under the appropriation of 2d March,
1831, and which, when paid, will be chargeable to me on that account.
       I have the honor to be,
             With high respect,
                 Your most obedient servant,
                         WILLIAM CLARK.

Hon. LEWIS CASS, Secretary at War.

WASHINGTON, *December* 13, 1833.

SIR: The 3d article of the Creek treaty authorizes the President to direct the mode of surveying the reserves under the treaty, and to approve the contracts for their sale.

A friend of mine is desirous of knowing whether any regulations have been adopted by the President under the article, and if so, what they are.

If you can with propriety furnish the information which he seeks, I will be obliged to you for so doing.

With great respect,

I am, &c. &c.,

J. C. CALHOUN.

Gov. CASS.

---

COMMISSIONER'S OFFICE,

*Fort Gibson, December* 13, *A: D.* 1833.

SIR: The commissioners have the honor to inform the department that the return of Mr. Ellsworth has enabled them to form a board at this place, and the several subjects referred to them will be resumed immediately. The commissioners have to acknowledge the receipt of the following letters: one of the 4th April, 1833, one of the 1st June, 1833, and one of the 3d July, 1833; all directed to Fort Gibson. These were received by Governor Stokes on his return. Also a letter dated 26th July, 1833, received by Governor Stokes while at St. Louis. Also one dated 17th August, 1833, from the honorable Secretary of War, and one from your department of the same date. Also one of June 6th, 1833. These three last were forwarded to Governor Stokes, and reached him at Independence, in Missouri, on his return to Fort Gibson. Mr. Ellsworth had not the pleasure to peruse any of the above until his return to this post. Also one dated September 17th, 1833, and one dated September 18th, 1833. The two last received by Mr. Ellsworth at Fort Leavenworth.

By direction of the board,

E. A. ELLSWORTH,

*Secretary pro tem.*

Hon. E. HERRING,

*Indian Commissioner, Washington.*

---

ST. LOUIS, *December* 14, 1833.

DEAR SIR: I arrived in this city about the 28th ultimo from my surveying expedition. I commenced work at the mouth of the Kanzas river, on the Missouri, and run north one hundred miles, to the northwest corner of the State of Missouri; the first sixty miles of which passes through one of the finest tracts of land on the waters of the Missouri, particularly that part laying west of the line. From the northwest corner of the State we run east nine miles and sixty chains, where we established a corner on the northern boundary of Missouri, on the high grounds in Grand river, as our point of departure for the source of the Boya river; from this corner we run on the high grounds in Grand river to the high grounds separating the waters of the Des Moines on the east, from those falling into the Missouri on the west, and continued up these high grounds one hundred and fifty miles to a small lake forming the source of the Boya river, which, by observation, I found to be in north lat. 42° 20', and the magnetic variation of the needle to be 8° 20' east; this line is principally through a high prairie country with good soil and well watered. From this point I run and corrected a line 47 miles and 62 chains, to the upper forks of the Des Moines river, where Major Boone established his corner last season; on this line the soil is good generally, but the country has many rice ponds and small lakes, and is almost destitute of timber. Passing on to Prairie du Chien, where we procured provision and the escort ordered by the Government, we proceeded to run the southern boundary of the Sac and Fox cession of 1830, from where Major Boone left off last season to the Des Moines river, a distance of 147 miles, through an excellent country, particularly so on the Ioway and Des Moines rivers below or south of the line. A little below where this line strikes the Des Moines, not far from its junction with the cottonwood fork, is a good situation for a fort, if one should be deemed necessary to hold in check the Sioux, Sacs and Foxes, Winnebagoes and Ioway Indians; from this point we meandered the Des Moines to its forks, on a base of 20 miles and 21 chains, and by the meanders 37 miles and 70 chains. In meandering this stream we found an abundance of bituminous coal, and on the margin of the river some specimens of the anthracite, and also slate of good quality. It was now the 18th of October, and cold weather had already set in, and we had to abandon the work. Lead ore abounds from the Mississippi for 40 miles out. The appropriation for running the lines under the treaty of Prairie du Chien of 1830 is nearly exhausted, and this work will have to stop for the present. If the purchase made of the Sacs and Foxes last season is to be surveyed, and you should be kind enough to confer that appointment on me, I should not only feel grateful, but would commence the work immediately, as some parts of it are in a much milder latitude, and is timbered. The compensation allowed me last season was only $5 per day, the same that Major Bean and General Hughes received. I had both the labor and the responsibility of the work to be done, and of the party, while they had little else than mere travelling. If the appropriation for carrying into effect the Sac and Fox treaties of last season is $6,000, (for I have not seen it,) I would undertake the survey for the appropriation; if, however, the surveyor should be required to examine the country as to its mineral productions, and to analyze them, more hands would be necessary. $8 per day is little enough for a competent surveyor, with all the responsibility of the party and the work resting upon him.

If you see proper to give me the appointment, a letter to General Clark, St. Louis, or if to myself, will find me at the Femme Osage post office, St. Charles county, Missouri, until February; after that at Galena, Illinois.

With sentiments of the highest regard,

I remain your sincere friend and well wisher,

JAMES CRAIG.

Hon. Lewis Cass.

———

WASHINGTON, *December* 15, 1833.

SIR: I enclose you another letter from Mr. Dougherty, making additional inquiries as to the sale and purchase of Creek Indian reserves. Will you be kind enough to favor me with an answer to his inquiries as soon as your convenience will permit, and accompany the answer with a copy of the regulations adopted as to the purchases already made of the reservees by citizens of Georgia and Alabama.

Very respectfully,

THOMAS F. FOSTER

Hon. LEWIS CASS.

———

MILLEDGEVILLE, *December* 5, 1833.

DEAR SIR: Please excuse me for again troubling you with a request for some further information in relation to my Indian affairs. Please ascertain from that department having charge of the execution of the late treaty with the Creek Indians, whether a purchase made by one Indian of another will be opposed if fair, and whether a patent will issue to the Indian buying. To make the question plainer, if a portion of the Indians were desirous of selling their reservations to one of their chiefs, for which he was to pay a fair price, would a patent for the reservations sold issue to the Indian chief purchasing? Now some of the Indians are desirous of doing so, for the purpose of greater security against interruption and molestation in the possession of their reserves whilst they think proper to remain on them. They want some of the money for their land to enable them to start to Arkansas, and a white man will not pay them any unless they will consent for him to go into possession, and they are afraid to do that for fear he will turn them out. They have greater confidence in their chiefs, and the chiefs in them, and they can make their contracts with their chiefs in perfect confidence that they will not be turned out of possession until they are ready to emigrate. It is not known whether a contract thus made here will be ratified or approved by the Government. I can see no objection to it myself, and I know it will in many cases be greatly to the interests of the Indian that such contract should receive the countenance of the Government. I have been requested by the friends of a small town of Indians to obtain this information if possible. You will confer a very great favor on me by assisting in obtaining the information desired, if you can do so. Write me at La Grange, as we shall adjourn before your answer can reach.

Very respectfully, your friend,

WM. DOUGHERTY.

Hon. THOMAS F. FOSTER.

———

FORT GIBSON, *December* 17, 1833.

SIR: I make this hasty communication to express to you the great embarrassment of my situation at this time. Mr. Ellsworth has just arrived here at this garrison, bringing with him about fifty Pawnees of the Platte river, and some Otoes. He is also accompanied by a band of Osages, and others of that nation have arrived to the number of one hundred more. He has insisted on summoning the chiefs and head men of the neighboring nations of Creeks, Cherokees and Choctaws, and a deputation from the Senecas. The purpose he says is to shake hands and make peace.

Although I was opposed to this expedition as unnecessary, inasmuch as we have treaties of peace with the Pawnees of the Platte river and the Otoes, and the neighboring nations about here are not at war with them;

yet I have been unwilling to protest against this measure, and thereby produce unkind feelings with my brother commissioner; and as the honor and
credit of the Government requires that these Indians should be well treated
while here, and those from the Platte having followed the commissioner six hundred miles by his invitation, they will not be satisfied with
being sent away naked as they came. Among them are several women,
wives of the chiefs, who are broken down by the fatigue of the journey, and
cannot return home without horses. You know, sir, that we have not the
means of gratifying the reasonable expectations of these Indians; and I
write this letter without being able to foresee how we shall get out of the
present difficulty? I know of no other way than to give them the horses
purchased for this expedition, and hope you will tolerate, if you cannot
approve of the measure.

You have, no doubt, received the two treaties concluded by Mr. Ellsworth.
I have not had time, since his arrival, to examine them and to decide upon
the utility of the provisions which they contain. If they are approved by
the Government, my opinions on the subject are immaterial.

I am, sir, with great respect,
Your obedient servant,
M. STOKES.

The Hon. Lewis Cass,
    Secretary of War.

---

SUPERINTENDENCY OF INDIAN AFFAIRS,
St. Louis, December 17, 1833.

Sir: Enclosed herewith, I have the honor to transmit to you the account,
abstract, and vouchers of the Rev. Isaac McCoy, for expenses of surveying
the lands assigned to the Piankeshaws, Weas, Kaskaskias, and Peorias, and
for extending the survey of the lines of the Shawnee lands, the field notes
and plats of which surveys were forwarded on the 29th November.

I have paid Mr. McCoy's drafts to the amount of one thousand dollars,
and as I am subject to his call for payment of the balance of his account, as
well as the expenses of surveying the Kickapoo lands, which he has been
instructed to commence, I shall have to draw on the department shortly
for funds for those objects. In the mean time I should be glad to know
whether the compensation, as charged by Mr. McCoy in the present accounts, is satisfactory to the department.

I have the honor to be,
With great respect,
Your obedient servant,
WM. CLARK.

The Hon. E. Herring,
    Commissioner Indian Affairs, Washington City.

---

WESTERN CREEK AGENCY, Dec. 18, 1833.

Sir: Your letter of the 4th November reached me by the last mail. I have
forwarded my accounts at the end of each quarter regularly; and immediately after the 30th September last I forwarded my returns for the quarter

and for the last year, and if they have been delayed by the mail and have not reached the department in due time, it is not my fault. I will forward a complete statement of all my bus'ness here in a short time, so that the department may at once see how the business stands. If there is any particular return that has not reached the department, I would be glad to be informed of it.

I have written, in September last, on the subject of provisions to the emigrants that were brought on by Gen. Chilly McIntosh, sixty in number, with two other persons that came on in June last—in all, sixty-two. Gen. McIntosh has been feeding his party since their arrival, the 1st September, with the expectation that the Government would make him the proper allowance. It would be desirable for some person to have charge of this business. Lieut. Van Horn has closed his business with the Senecas, and would no doubt attend to this business with pleasure, if instructed to that effect.

I have the honor to be, sir,
Very respectfully,
Your obedient servant,
JOHN CAMPBELL.

Elbert Herring, Esq.,
Commissioner of Indian Affairs.

---

Tuscaloosa, December 18, 1833.

Sir: The governor has not yet made his communication to the legislature, and the commissioners have not yet reported. As it is quite uncertain when this may be done, and it does not seem to me that my presence is any longer necessary here, I think of returning tomorrow, and trust that a few days after you receive this I may have the pleasure of communicating to you in person the state of things here.

The governor, I presume, will express to the legislature his desire that no obstructions should be presented to the course the agents of the government are instructed to take in fulfilling the stipulations of the treaty; but that, on the contrary, the necessary legislative enactments should be made for the protection of the Indians, and to prevent any contracts being enforced against them except such as are made and approved conformably to the treaty.

I enclose you a copy of the correspondence between us, also of a letter I have written to the marshal, and another to Col. Abert. I have written also to Mr. Elliott, the district attorney, and shall leave the letter here for him, giving him a particular account of what has taken place here, and called his attention to such objects as I thought it desirable should be accomplished. The prosecutions, I am satisfied, will not be pressed. No further effort has been made to serve the process on the soldiers, and Mr. Austill is near the judge, so that a habeas corpus can be obtained for his discharge if the sheriff should think proper to arrest him, which, however, I do not think he will do.

I have no longer any apprehension that the legislature will adopt any course calculated to produce or countenance opposition on the part of the settlers. I believe they will pass a law making it penal for any person to occupy the reservation of an Indian without having his' title conveyed according to the provision of the 3d article of the treaty, and approved by the President.

Still I apprehend it will be impossible entirely to relieve the Indians from being harassed with civil process, and otherwise subjected to great impositions and oppressions; the only effectual remedy for them, as I believe, being the sale of their lands and their removal.

The district attorney will be here in a week, and will remain to the end of the session. I have requested him to communicate whatever may occur to you.

I am, sir,

Very respectfully,

Your obedient servant,

F. S. KEY.

The Hon. Lewis Cass,
*Secretary of War, Washington.*

---

Executive Department, Tuscaloosa,

*December* 16, 1833.

Sir: The Secretary of War, in his letter of the 31st October, which you did me the honor to deliver on your arrival, states that you have been placed fully in possession of the views of the President in relation to the difficulties which have arisen from the orders of the Government for the removal of the settlers from the territory ceded by the Creek Indians in March, 1832.

These I am satisfied you have communicated with frankness and without reserve in the several conversations we have had on the subject. I am anxious to lay before the legislature, which is now in session, all the information I have received and can obtain, and with that view, and to prevent any misunderstanding which might proceed from a want of accuracy in my own recollection, I have to request that you will, in answer to this note, furnish me with the substance of the explanations you have already given, and also with any other intelligence you may think proper to communicate in connexion with the existing controversy. Information has been received through the medium of the public journals of Washington city, that ten companies of United States troops are marching to Fort Mitchell, for the purpose of executing the orders of the Government, for the expulsion of the settlers from the ceded territory. Statements of this kind are not usually relied on, but contracted as this is by the Globe, it has obtained general credence, has already produced much solicitude and some excitement in the counties situated in the Creek country, and will, I apprehend, if true, disappoint in some degree the hopes with which you, as well as myself, have been encouraged, that this unpleasant business would be brought to a speedy and satisfactory termination.

I trust you have it in your power to allay the anxiety which this supposed movement of the troops has produced, and shall be gratified to learn that it has no connexion with the pending controversy.

I have the honor to be,

With great respect,

Your obedient servant,

J. GAYLE.

Francis S. Key, Esq.

TUSCALOOSA, *December* 16, 1833.

SIR: I have just received your note, and will proceed to state the substance of the communications I have had the honor to make to you since my arrival, as to the views of the President in relation to the orders you mention.

I informed you that I had seen Col. Abert in the Creek country, who was engaged in locating the Indian reservations; that he had employed the requisite assistants so as to expedite the discharge of that duty, and believed that it would be completed by the 15th of January. From the manner in which Colonel Abert and Mr. Bright were instructed to proceed, the lands intended for the Indians will be laid off, as far as consistent with the provisions of the treaty, united in large bodies, leaving the subdivisions of the tracts among the individual Indians to be hereafter designated, and thus showing the position of the reservations. By this means all that portion of the ceded territory lying without the reservations will be designated and released from the stipulations of the Creek treaty, and the orders to the marshal will not operate upon the settlers on those lands. Those among the settlers who may be found upon the Indian reservations will have it in their power to purchase the right of the Indians whose lands they occupy, and an agent will be appointed by the President, who may be daily expected, to certify all such contracts according to the provisions of the treaty. So that every settler so situated will have it in his option either to purchase the Indian's title and remain, or leave the land for others to purchase. I expressed to you the solicitude of the President to make arrangements for the purchase, on the part of the Government, of those Indian reservations, and for removing the Indians, and that I had been taking measures here for accomplishing this purpose which I hoped would be successful; that the President was convinced that this measure was necessary for the preservation of the Indians, and on every account advantageous to the people of Alabama; that in reference to this subject, I had satisfactorily ascertained that a large proportion of the Indians were now willing to leave the State, and that I had written to the Secretary of War that I believed the Indians owning the reservations would be disposed to sell and emigrate as soon as agents were sent out with authority for that purpose. I also stated to you that Colonel Abert had informed me that many of the settlers had called upon him since he came to the State, to ascertain the course intended to be pursued by the Government, to whom he had fully stated these views, and that without exception they had expressed their satisfaction; that as far as I could judge, from the conversations I had held with many persons in the State, I believe the same satisfaction very generally prevailed.

I repeat the hope and belief which I expressed to you in our conversations, from these circumstances, that when the reservations for the Indians are thus located, few, if any of the settlers on these portions of the land, will, if left to pursue their own course, be so unreasonable as to refuse either to buy of the Indians or to remove from their lands and let them sell to others.

I showed you in a late interview a copy of the letter I had received from the Secretary of War to Colonel Abert, in answer to inquiries of that officer, which stated the course the President would think proper to pursue in exercising the power given him by the 3d article of the treaty, of directing the manner in which these tracts to be laid off for the Indians may be conveyed by them, and of approving such contracts.

By this it appears that the President will not consider any contract with an Indian for his reservation as made on "a fair consideration" as required by that article, unless the price is equal to the minimum price at which the public land is sold. As it is intended that the reservations shall be laid off so as to give them land at least equal to the average quality of the public land, it is not to be presumed that a less sum would be a fair price. He will also require the certifying agent to take proper measures to have undoubted evidence of the actual payment of the purchase money. The President's views are also fully expressed in that letter as to a species of contract which it is generally said has been resorted to, or is intended to be resorted to, by some of the persons who have been dealing with the Indians for the reservations.

The conveyances which he will approve of must be conveyances of the Indian's whole title, by which he will get a full equivalent for his land, so as to secure to him, as far as possible, the fair payment of the consideration, and the means of obtaining a permanent and beneficial provision. Leases with the Indians for the five years during which the provisions of the treaty for their protection will extend, or for any portion of that time, he will not approve. Such contracts would keep them in a state of abject dependence, subject to impositions, victims to all the miseries which have ever been fatal to their race.

These determinations of the President will, I trust, appear not only humane towards the Indians, and called for by the true spirit and meaning of the treaty, but just and beneficial towards the people of Alabama.

In reference to the last subject mentioned in your note, I can only say that I am entirely without information. No letter that I have received since leaving Washington has mentioned any thing upon the subject of sending troops for any purpose to any part of this State; nor can I believe that the movement of the companies to which you refer justifies any excitement in the Creek counties. However, I should hope that as your excellency is fully advised of the views of the President, and of the course which he feels bound to take in fulfilling the obligations of the Creek treaty, it is not to be supposed, from any circumstances, that any change of that course can be intended. Hoping that nothing will occur to prevent the restoration of mutual confidence and harmony, so sincerely desired by the President,

I am, sir,
With great respect,
Your obedient servant,
F. S. KEY.

To Gov. GAYLE.

P. S. I understand that the orders of the marshal are not to be executed till the 15th of January; and I am assured that the reservations will be then designated so that the orders will then operate only on the reservations.

---

TUSCALOOSA, *December* 18, 1833.

DEAR SIR: I received last night a letter from Mr. Elliott, in which he mentions your wish to know whether the locations of the reservations will be completed in time to enable you, in the execution of the orders of the War Department, to ascertain on the 15th January which public lands are clear of the reservations, and whether it may not be desirable to extend the time for enforcing the orders, if it should appear that the locations will not be completed by that day.

From the instructions given to Colonel Abert and Mr. Bright, and the communications I have received from Colonel Abert since I left him, I have no doubt of the reservations being sufficiently designated to enable you to proceed by that day; and it is very desirable, and I am sure will be practicable, to avoid any postponement. The effect of it would be to encourage the disaffected and the speculators to believe that the orders would not be enforced, and thus make their execution more difficult. The location of each Indian's reservation will probably not be made by that time, as it is expected that a large number of reservations will be located together in a body, but the tracts intended for these united reservations will be designated, so that you can distinguish the portion of land where the reservations will be made.

If it should happen, at the time appointed, that in some part of the ceded territory the work even in this way cannot have been accomplished, yet, without doubt, it will only be a very small portion of it thus undesignated; and while you are executing your duties upon the parts where the reservations are designated, the locating agents will complete the residue.

You will perhaps receive further instructions from the Secretary of War, in reference to your discharge of these duties. If, however, you should not, I would call your attention to that part of the Secretary's letter to you in which you are instructed to "use as much forbearance as is consistent with the execution of your duty before a resort is had to actual force." I have reason to believe that very generally, throughout the Creek counties, the settlers will move from the reservations. I have no doubt this will be the case in Talladega, as I am so assured by respectable persons from that county. If there is difficulty anywhere it will probably be in Russell county; I would suggest to you, therefore, the propriety of beginning in the other counties, and of ascertaining, before you call in the aid of the military, that the settlers will not remove without the application of force.

Many of the settlers upon the reservations are disposed to purchase the Indian titles, according to the provisions of the treaty; and an agent may be expected by the time appointed to certify such contracts, to be presented to the President for his approval, according to the third article of the treaty. Those who may make such contracts, and obtain the agent's certificate, may be allowed to remain until the President's determination upon the contracts shall be made known. Those also who may remove peaceably from the reservations may desire to move their crops and families to other portions of the public lands lying clear of the reservations. I see nothing in your instructions forbidding you to allow this to be done for the present by such persons, until the President may determine whether they shall leave the ceded territory or not; provided that you are satisfied that such persons will not interfere improperly with the Indians.

It has occurred to me that you may not be able, consistently with your other duties, to undertake personally the execution of the orders of the Government, and to continue in these counties while these operations are in progress. If such should be the case, I have thought it would be important to select a deputy for the discharge of this duty, who should add to the other necessary qualifications an acquaintance with the Creek country, the Indians, and the settlers, and who might be known and respected among the persons on whom the orders were to operate. Of Mr. Austill I have the very highest opinion, but it will readily occur, both to you and him, that under present circumstances he might meet with difficulties and opposition that would not be in the way of another. I have thought of

   *     *     *     *     and having made every inquiry into his character and qualifications, am satisfied that he would discharge these duties very faithfully. I take the liberty, therefore, of mentioning him to you, in case you should be unable to attend yourself, or should be unprovided with a deputy to whom you could confide the execution of duties so important, and requiring very peculiar qualifications. I have ascertained from   *   *   that, if called upon, he would be willing to undertake the duty.

I have reason to believe the governor and legislature of the State will adopt measures calculated to give aid to the General Government in fulfilling the stipulations of the treaty: and I trust you will meet with no obstruction in the execution of your orders.

I am, sir, very respectfully,
Your obedient servant,
F. S. KEY.

Robert L. Crawford, Esq.,
 *Marshal Southern District Alabama.*

**P. S.** Tell Mr. Austill he will hear from Mr. Elliott what course is to be taken in reference to the prosecution against him. In the meantime, I presume the sheriff, knowing he can serve the process at any time, will have no disposition to arrest him. I think there is no inclination here that any of the prosecutions should be pressed.

---

Tuscaloosa, December 18, 1833.

Dear Sir: I believe I shall leave this for Washington to-morrow, and as I do not consider it necessary to return by Fort Mitchell, I think of taking my route so as to avail myself of the steamboats of Ohio. I received your last letter, and hope you are making progress with the locations. I have undertaken to answer for you here that they will be done in time.

The district attorney writes to me from Mobile that the marshal has understood that the locations will not be completed by the 15th January, and suggests whether an extension of the time cannot be obtained. I have written to him that this cannot be done. If it is postponed, the settlers will never believe the Government in earnest, and will make their arrangements to remain, and we shall have more trouble than ever. If you should not be able to make the separate locations, you can at least designate the portions intended for reservations, so as show what will be clear of them.

Let Russell be the last done, as it will be important that the marshal should finish his operations in the other counties before he goes there.

I send you a copy of my letter to him. I think the legislature will pass a law here to protect the Indians, making it penal for any person to occupy their reservations without a title made and approved by the President according to the treaty. Other provisions will be introduced to prohibit the speculators from harassing them with the laws of Alabama.

As to the instructions about the leases, and the other points embraced in the Secretary's letter to you, they are approved of by every body here, nor do I think any body but speculators will object to them.

Without them the stipulations of the treaty would have been wholly evaded.

Yours respectfully,

F. S. KEY.

Colonel ABERT,
 *Near Fort Mitchell, Alabama.*

---

TALLADEGA COUNTY, ALABAMA,
*Mardisville, December* 19, 1833.

SIR: Joseph Bruner has applied to me to locate the tract of land allowed him by the treaty of the 24th of March, 1832; and after having advised with Mr. James Bright on the subject, I have selected for him the south half of section twenty-seven, township eighteen, and range 5 east, in the district of Montivallo. It is the one he had selected for himself, and we are of opinion he sold it well, and has not given the purchaser an opportunity of much speculation.

I am, &c.,

LEONARD TARRANT.

ELBERT HERRING, Esq.

---

MARSHAL'S OFFICE,
*Southern District of Ala., Mobile, Dec.* 20, 1833.

SIR: The 15th day of January is close at hand, the time fixed upon for the removal of intruders from the Creek lands.

The intervention of the State authority has created considerable uneasiness with me. Capiases have been issued, and executed upon some of the individuals who are charged with being accessory to the death of Owen, while engaged in the execution of instructions from the Government, and Mr. Austill is now in custody of the sheriff of this county upon the same charge.

It is not known whether the writ of habeas corpus will be sustained by the district judge, and in the removal of these persons it is more than probable that more blood will be shed; should it be so, I shall be placed in the same situation that Mr. Austill and Lieutenant Manning are; and I do not believe it is the wish or intention of the Government to have any of its officers, engaged in the execution of their instructions, implicated in the least as to person or property, or character.

I am daily expecting a letter from Mr. Key. In consequence of the district court being in session, I was unable to see him at Tuscaloosa.

In a letter to him I suggested the propriety of an extension beyond the 15th January. Should the locations be not completed by that time, the planting is some time off, and no great injury could result to any person.

I request to be informed and instructed what shall be done with the property of an intruder that may be left after he is removed; also whether it is required that I, or the person sent by me, shall be with the troops when the removal is made; or whether an order from me to the commanding officer at Fort Mitchell to remove the whole in a body would not answer, and whether persons keeping the United States mail horses and drivers are to be included in the order for removal.   An early answer is requested, directed to this place.

Very respectfully, &c.,<br>
ROBT. L. CRAWFORD,<br>
Marshal South. Dist. Ala.

Hon. Lewis Cass,
    *Secretary of War.*

---

SUPERINTENDENCY OF INDIAN AFFAIRS,<br>
Detroit, December 20, 1833.

Sir: I have the honor to enclose the several accounts of the commissioners who concluded the treaty at Chicago on the 26th and 27th September last. The delay in their transmission has been unavoidable.   By the supplemental articles of the treaty you will observe that a part of the consideration money for the two valuable reservations in Michigan, south of Grand river, viz., $25,000 was to be paid to the bands residing thereon, in goods, provisions, and horses; and, at their request, the commissioners agreed that fifteen thousand dollars of this should be paid to them the present year.   Two thousand dollars of goods were accordingly delivered to Topenebee and his band at Chicago, and the balance of ten thousand dollars' worth of goods and three thousand dollars' worth in horses, were delivered to these particular bands on their reservations in Michigan.   This duty was assigned to me, as will appear by a letter of instructions prepared and signed by all the commissioners previously to my leaving Chicago, which I have transmitted with the treaty to the War Department.

Owing to the public duties which I had to perform on the Wabash and Tippecanoe, it was impossible for me to reach the St. Josephs, and attend to the fulfilment of these stipulations of the Chicago treaty until lately, having come past these two reservations on my way home.   By the treaty you will perceive that the Indians have acknowledged the receipt of all the goods and horses, viz., sixty thousand dollars' worth of goods and five thousand dollars' worth of horses to the Prairie (a large body of) Indians residing west of Lake Michigan; and twelve thousand dollars' worth of goods, and three thousand dollars, worth of horses to the Wood Indians, or those residing on the reservations in Michigan.   Notwithstanding this, regular abstracts of the purchase and issues have been prepared, and are forwarded with the accounts; and to each individual who furnished goods or horses, a draft was given on the Secretary of War for the amount due, payable at the ratification of the treaty, after an appropriation shall have been made by Congress for this purpose.   In the case of goods purchased, the draft is annexed to the bill or invoice of the goods.   The abstracts show the amount payable to the respective individuals.   For goods or horses purchased and delivered to the Indians on the reservations in Michigan, under the authority mentioned above, given to me by the other commissioners, the drafts are necessarily signed by me on behalf of myself and the other commissioners. In the joint report of the commissioners to the Secretary of War, which accompanies the treaty, you will find it stated that the expenses of the treaty exceeded the amount appropriated by Congress, for which I trust the reasons therein given will prove satisfactory. For the excess, being $2,536 53, the commissioners drew two drafts, one for $1,536 53, in favor of Newberry and Dole, and the other for $1,000 in favor of James Kinzie, payable on the ratification of the treaty, after an appropriation shall be made. The sum of $10,000 appropriated by Congress was paid by the Bank of Michigan, and the commissioners drew a draft for this amount in favor of C. C. Trowbridge, esq., cashier.

I am, very respectfully,<br>Sir, your obedient servant,<br>G. B. PORTER.

ELBERT HERRING, Esq.,
            *Commissioner of Indian Affairs.*

CHICAGO, *October* 7, 1833.

Whereas a treaty has been concluded with the united nation of Chippewa, Ottawa, and Pottawatamie Indians, at Chicago aforesaid, on the 26th and 27th days of September, A. D. 1833. And in the supplementary articles thereto, executed by such of the said nation as resided on the reservations in the territory of Michigan, south of Grand river, it is stipulated that there shall be delivered goods, provisions, and horses, to the value of twenty-five thousand dollars, of which it has been agreed that fifteen thousand shall be delivered the present year, and which the chiefs and head men have requested may be delivered to them on their reservations; and, as it is not convenient nor deemed necessary that all the commissioners should attend to the procuring and distribution of the said goods, provisions, and horses, it is agreed that the same shall be attended to by George B. Porter, one of the said commissioners, and that all matters relating thereto, as well the signing of the necessary abstracts and certificates of purchase as making out the accounts for the same, shall be done by him the said George B. Porter.

Given under our hands the day and year first aforesaid.

G. B. PORTER,<br>TH. J. V. OWEN,       } *Commissioners.*<br>WILLIAM WEATHERFORD, }

Witness:
WM. LEE D. EWING,
        *Secretary to the Commissioners.*

HOUSE OF REPRESENTATIVES, *December* 23, 1833.

SIR: I received by yesterday's mail a petition from certain citizens of the counties of Barbour and Macon, in the Creek country of Alabama, praying that the settlers in said counties may not be forcibly removed therefrom, agreeably to the late order of the President of the United States.

In addition to this petition I am convinced, from the almost daily inquiries I receive on the subject, that there is a deep anxiety in the public mind

97‡

in that State as regards the course intended to be pursued by the Government towards the settlers; an anxiety doubtless increased by the late concentration of military force at Fort Mitchell.

Feeling no desire to bring the subject *unnecessarily* before Congress, and thus to provoke what may perhaps be an irritating discussion, I would respectfully inquire of you if it is the intention of the department, in case the reservations in the Creek country are not located by the 15th of January next, to order an instant removal of the settlers by military force; or in any way to employ the military in possessing or dispossessing individuals of these reservations, according to an adjudication of their respective claims, by the marshal or some other officer of the Government. If military force be contemplated, I should be glad to learn against what class of settlers, and under what circumstances.

I am aware that the location of the reservations was undertaken with a view of being completed by the 15th of January next; and it was thought that the necessity of enforcing the order for the removal of the settlers would thereby be obviated, as the treaty was not supposed to render such removal obligatory on the President after the *reservations were located.* I have, however, lately been informed that it is very improbable that the locations can be completed by that time, and I am desirous of knowing if a more distant day than the 15th of January next cannot be set apart, in order to give full time for the *entire locations to be made* before the order of removal may be thought necessary.

In relation to that class of settlers whose improvements may be covered by the reservations, I am informed that the number is comparatively small, and in almost every case the settlement has been made by the consent of the Indian whose reservation was most likely to include it. In some instances contracts have been consummated on the part of the settler, by the entire payment of the amount agreed on. In others, a part has been paid, and the Indian is under obligations to perfect a title upon the payment of the balance as soon as the proper agent of the Government can attest the contract. To treat such persons as *"intruders,"* and to expel them by military force, permit me to say, would be most unjust. To set aside such contracts would lead to endless lawsuits. No other than a judicial tribunal can satisfactorily determine these questions of right in relation to *individual* property. The reservation becomes *private property* as soon as it is located and assigned to a particular Indian, and certainly cannot be reached by the act of 1807, which refers only to *public lands.*

I have delayed making the above inquiries until this time, under the hope of receiving some information which would render them unnecessary. If it be the intention of the department to dispense with the employment of military force against the settlers, I shall be happy to have it in my power to relieve my constituents from such an apprehension. If, however, such is not the intention, it will be my duty to bring the subject before Congress as soon as possible. I should be happy to receive your earliest answer.

I am, very respectfully,
Your obedient servant,
DIXON H. LEWIS.

Hon. Lewis Cass,
*Secretary of War.*

SUPERINTENDENCY OF INDIAN AFFAIRS,

*Detroit, December* 23, 1833.

SIR: Accompanying this you will receive the accounts of the expenses incurred under the direction of Mr. Schermerhorn, General Marshall, and myself, in the negotiation lately held with the Miami Indians for the purchase of their lands in the State of Indiana.

For the amount due to the several individuals, as set forth in the abstract, drafts were drawn on the Secretary of War, "payable after an appropriation shall have been made by Congress for the purpose of defraying the expenses of the negotiation;" conforming in all this, as well as in all other respects, to the instructions contained in the letter from the War Department of the 15th of July last. As some money, however, was absolutely necessary to meet certain expenses, I availed myself of the suggestions contained in the letter referred to, and it has been advanced by the Bank of Michigan, viz., for two vouchers in this abstract, " No. 40, Murdock McLane, $120, and No. 44, General William Marshall, $339 71." Drafts were drawn in the manner above stated, payable to these individuals respectively, and being by them endorsed on receipt of the money, they are now held by the bank.

To the detailed report of our proceedings, which is forwarded to the War Department, I must refer for an explanation of the causes which occasioned the expenditure of more money than might otherwise be thought necessary. Being satisfied, however, that there was " as little expenditure of time and money as was practicable;" that " the provisions and presents were purchased upon the most economical terms;" and that " such rules were adopted for their issuing and distribution as effectually prevented waste or misapplication," I submit these accounts under the confident hope that they will be found just and correct.

In my letter of the 20th, enclosing the accounts of the Chicago treaty, I assigned the reasons for the delay in the transmission of all these documents. I have been busily engaged (I might truly say night and day) since my return home.

I have the honor to be,
Very respectfully,
Your obedient servant,
G. B. PORTER.

To ELBERT HERRING, Esq.,
*Commissioner of Indian Affairs.*

END OF VOLUME IV.